20-95

Butterworths
Police Law

Butterworths
Police Law

Sixth Edition

Jack English OBE QPM MA

Ex-Assistant Chief Constable, Northumbria Police
Ex-Director of the Central Planning, Instructor Training and
Police Promotion Examinations Unit
Ex-Chief Examiner to the Police Promotions Examinations Board

Richard Card LLB LLM FRSA

Professor of Law and Chairman of the School of Law at
De Montfort University, Leicester

Butterworths
London, Edinburgh, Dublin
1999

United Kingdom	Butterworths, a Division of Reed Elsevier (UK) Ltd, Halsbury House, 35 Chancery Lane, LONDON WC2A 1EL and 4 Hill Street, EDINBURGH EH2 3JZ
Australia	Butterworths, a Division of Reed International Books Australia Pty Ltd, CHATSWOOD, New South Wales
Canada	Butterworths Canada Ltd, MARKHAM, Ontario
Hong Kong	Butterworths Asia (Hong Kong), HONG KONG
India	Butterworths Asia, NEW DELHI
Ireland	Butterworth (Ireland) Ltd, DUBLIN
Malaysia	Malayan Law Journal Sdn Bhd, KUALA LUMPUR
New Zealand	Butterworths of New Zealand Ltd, WELLINGTON
Singapore	Butterworths Asia, SINGAPORE
South Africa	Butterworths Publishers (Pty) Ltd, DURBAN
USA	Lexis Law Publishing, CHARLOTTESVILLE, Virginia

© Reed Elsevier (UK) Ltd 1999

A CIP Catalogue record for this book is available from the British Library.

Fifth Edition 1996
Reprinted 2000

ISBN 0 406 98146 9

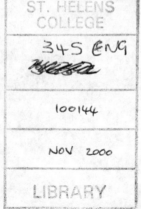
Printed by Butler & Tanner Ltd, Frome and London

Visit us at our website: http://www.butterworths.co.uk

Preface

We originally wrote this book to fill the gap left by the demise of *Moriarty's Police Law*, which for over 50 years had satisfied a particular need by explaining all aspects of the criminal law, together with those procedures which govern the processes of law enforcement, which are of particular concern to the police. Because of its concern with matters which also represented day-to-day problems encountered by members of the public in coming to terms with the criminal law, it provided an explanation of the law in terms which were easily understood by those who had received no legal training.

As in previous editions, we have written *Butterworths Police Law* with these points in mind. The book is not a reference book. It does not reproduce the law without explanation. Nor is the text broken up by constant references to footnotes which set out the effect of court decisions; instead, the effect of such decisions is incorporated in the explanations which are given to each aspect of the law as it is encountered by the reader.

We have prepared the material included in this book in a way which recognises the needs of police officers, of those who wish to study the criminal law, and of members of the public who wish to refer to a legal text which is written in terms which they can understand. However, it remains faithful throughout its pages to its title, *Police Law*, and sets out to cover comprehensively those areas of law and legal procedures with which all police officers are concerned. The syllabus of the qualifying examinations for promotion has been borne in mind throughout preparation of the text, and it is our hope that the availability of this book will ensure the success of those who enter for either of those qualifying examinations. The book was extended when changes were made to the qualifying examinations with the introduction of 'OSPRE'. This edition has been further extended to accommodate recent additions to the OSPRE syllabus.

We have tried to summarise the law as it was on 1 December 1998, although we have been able to insert in proof some changes up to 1 January 1999.

It is reported that new Police (Discipline) Regulations will come into force on 1 April 1999. As copies of the intended regulations are not available at the time of writing, we have been unable to make any comment upon their effect. However, we have included, where necessary, references to changes which will take place when provisions included in the Police Act 1996 replace some existing provisions of the Police and Criminal Evidence Act 1984.

February 1999

Jack English
Richard Card

Contents

CHAPTER 2

Elements of criminal procedure   14

CHAPTER 3

Police powers   31

CHAPTER 4

Police questioning and the rights of suspects   71

CHAPTER 5

Treatment, charging and bail of detained persons   95

CHAPTER 6

Identification methods   121

CHAPTER 7

The law of evidence   140

CHAPTER 8

The police   179

CHAPTER 9

Traffic: general provisions   201

CHAPTER 10

Use of vehicles   253

CHAPTER 11

Control of vehicles   288

CHAPTER 12

Public service vehicles   317

CHAPTER 13

Goods vehicles   336

CHAPTER 14

Lights and vehicles   361

CHAPTER 15

Traffic accidents   377

CHAPTER 16

Driving offences   384

CHAPTER 17

Drinking and driving 401

CHAPTER 18

Children and young persons 430

CHAPTER 19

Intoxicating liquor laws 451

CHAPTER 20

Betting, gaming and lotteries   473

CHAPTER 21

Aliens   489

CHAPTER 22

Animals, birds and plants   494

CHAPTER 29

Disputes   582

CHAPTER 30

Homicide and abortion   591

CHAPTER 31

Public order offences other than those related to sporting events or industrial disputes   604

CHAPTER 32

Public order offences related to sporting events and those connected with industrial disputes   644

CHAPTER 34

Offences relating to prostitution, obscenity and indecent photographs 676

CHAPTER 35

Drugs 689

CHAPTER 36

Theft and related offences, robbery and blackmail   703

CHAPTER 42

Preventive justice   790

Table of statutes

References in this Table to *Statutes* are to Halsbury's Statutes of England (Fourth Edition) showing the volume and page at which the annotated text of an Act may be found. Page references in **bold** type indicate where the section of an Act is set out in part or in full.

CHAPTER 1

General principles

We are concerned in this book with those branches of the law of England and Wales which are of particular relevance to police officers.

The word 'law' can be used in various senses, for example the laws of nature and the laws of cricket. We are concerned in this book with 'law' in the most commonly used sense of that term, viz a binding rule imposed on a person and governing his conduct, which is enforceable in the courts of the land by means of a penalty or sanction.

SOURCES OF ENGLISH LAW

There are two sources of English law: common law and legislation.

Common law

Common law is that part of English law which is not the result of legislation, ie it is the law which originated in the custom of the people and was justified and developed by the decisions and rulings of the judges.

In modern times legislation has played a preponderant part in the branches of the law dealt with in this book. As will be seen, very few offences are now governed and defined by the common law (ie the rulings of the judges). Moreover, the House of Lords, in its capacity as the senior appellate court in this country, has held that the judges do not now have the capacity to extend the criminal law, by creating new offences or widening existing ones. Examples of common law offences are murder, manslaughter and incitement.

Although most offences are now governed by legislation, most of the general principles of criminal liability are derived from the common law. For example, most of the general defences to crime and most of the rules concerning accomplices to crime are to be found in the rulings of the judges, and not in legislation.

The common law has been built up on the basis of the doctrine of precedent, under which the reported decisions of certain courts are more than just authoritative legal statements whose effect is persuasive, since they can be binding (ie must be applied) in subsequent cases. In the context of courts with criminal jurisdiction, it is the decisions of the House of Lords, Court of Appeal (Criminal Division) and Divisional Court of the Queen's Bench Division (each of which has a criminal jurisdiction limited to appeals) which have binding effect. Whether or not such a decision is binding in a particular case depends on the relative standing of the court which made the decision and the court in which that decision is subsequently cited. The reason is that the doctrine of precedent depends on the principle that the courts form a hierarchy which, in the case of courts with criminal jurisdiction, is in the following descending order: House of Lords; Court of Appeal (Criminal Division); Divisional Court of the Queen's Bench Division; Crown Court and magistrates' courts. The basic rule is that a decision by one of the three appellate courts is binding on those courts below that in which it was given and, save in exceptional circumstances, will be followed by a court of equal status. A decision which is not binding under the above rules is nevertheless of persuasive authority, and may be cited to a court in a subsequent case.

Legislation

Statute

The majority of offences are defined and regulated by statutes, ie Acts of Parliament. Sometimes, statute has provided an offence where none previously existed: examples are the offence of incest and the various offences relating to firearms. In other cases, statute has replaced common law offences with statutory offences; an example of this was the enactment of the offence of rape in 1976.

The impact of statute has been limited in relation to the general principles of liability. As we have already said, most of these are still provided by the common law.

Subordinate legislation

A statute may give power to some body, such as the Queen in Council, a minister or a local authority or other public body, to make Orders in Council, regulations and bylaws (respectively) and prescribe for their breach. This method of creating criminal offences is of increasing importance in the present day, although it is not new. A good example is the power of the Secretary of State for Transport under the Road Traffic Act 1988 to make regulations concerning the construction and use of motor vehicles. Acting under this power, he has made a large number of detailed regulations on a variety of matters, such as the efficiency of brakes and the lighting of vehicles. Prosecutions for breach of these regulations are regularly instituted. Subordinate legislation made at central government level is normally required to be made by way of 'statutory instrument' (SI).

Legislation of the European Union

This has little direct impact on our criminal law at present, but an example of a piece of European legislation which is of importance to such law is Regulation 3820/85 (which is concerned with the driving hours of drivers of goods vehicles).

European Convention on Human Rights

Under the Human Rights Act 1998, English and Welsh courts are legally obliged, so far as possible, to read, and give effect to, Acts of Parliament, Orders in Council, and subordinate legislation in general in a way which is compatible with the rights and fundamental freedoms set out in the European Convention on Human Rights and the First Protocol to it ('the Convention rights').

This obligation, however, does not affect the validity or enforcement of any incompatible Act of Parliament or Order in Council made under the royal prerogative, nor of any incompatible Order in Council, regulation, bye-law or the like made under statutory powers if primary legislation prevents removal of the incompatibility.

Where a superior court determines that a provision in an Act of Parliament or Order in Council made under the royal prerogative is incompatible with a Convention right, it may make a declaration of that incompatibility. In addition, if a court determines that a provision of subordinate legislation made under statutory powers is incompatible with a Convention right, and it is satisfied that the primary legislation concerned prevents removal of the incompatibility, it may make a declaration of that incompatibility. The effect of such a declaration will be that a government minister may, by order, amend the legislation, as he thinks appropriate, to remove the incompatibility. Such an amendment will also be possible without a declaration of incompatibility if a government minister or the Queen in Council thinks that a piece of legislation is, in the light of a finding of the European Court of Human Rights, incompatible with the United Kingdom's obligations under the Convention.

GENERAL PRINCIPLES OF CRIMINAL LIABILITY

Criminal liability

Reference to a Latin maxim at this stage seems unavoidable. The maxim, which embodies the cardinal principle of criminal liability, is *actus non facit reus, nisi sit mens rea*—an act does not make a person legally guilty unless the mind is legally blameworthy. As is implied by this maxim there are two elements of criminal liability:

(a) the outward conduct which must always be proved against the accused (which is customarily known as the actus reus); and

(b) the state of mind which, apart from exceptional offences, it must be proved that the accused had at the time of the relevant conduct (customarily known as the mens rea).

Of course, the definition of these two things varies from offence to offence, but if the relevant conduct and state of mind can be proved by the prosecution the accused is guilty unless he can rely successfully on a defence.

Actus reus

It would be wrong to think that proof of the relevant conduct required for an offence is limited to proof of an act on the accused's part. There are two reasons.

First, some offences can be committed (and, indeed, some can only be committed) by a failure to do a particular act on the part of a person who was under a legal duty to do that act; an example of such an offence is that of failing to provide a specimen of breath, without reasonable excuse, when required to do so under the Road Traffic Act 1988, s 6. It should also be noted that there are some offences whose definitions require neither an act nor an omission but simply the existence of a state of affairs on the part of the accused; an example is the offence of being found drunk in a public place, contrary to the Licensing Act 1872, s 12.

The second reason why more than an act on the accused's part must be proved is that rarely, if ever, is a mere act (or omission or state of affairs) sufficient for criminal liability for a substantive offence. The definitions of offences often specify surrounding circumstances, such as time and place, which are essential to render the act etc criminal. Sometimes the definition requires a consequence to result from the act or omission, such as the consequence of the unlawful death of another human being in murder. These specified circumstances and/or consequences are part of the actus reus of an offence.

Mens rea

Despite occasional judicial utterances to the contrary, it is clear from the application of mens rea in the courts that it has nothing necessarily to do with notions of an evil mind or knowledge of the wrongfulness of the act. The accused's ignorance of the criminal law is no defence, nor generally is the fact that the accused did not personally regard his conduct as immoral or know that it was so regarded by the bulk of society.

The expression mens rea refers to the state of mind expressly or impliedly required by the definition of the offence charged. This varies from offence to offence, but typical instances are intention, recklessness and knowledge.

Intention

A number of offences require the accused to have acted with a particular intent: in murder the accused must have acted with intent unlawfully to kill, or cause grievous bodily harm to, another person; in theft the accused must have dishonestly appropriated another's property with intent permanently to deprive him of it. Generally speaking, 'intention' refers to a state of mind in relation to a potential consequence of one's act. In some crimes, that consequence must actually result in order for there to be criminal liability; in others, such as theft, it is not necessary that the intended consequence should occur.

In law, a person 'intends' a consequence of his conduct if he has decided to bring it about, in so far as it lies within his power, no matter whether he desires that consequence or not. A person who has not decided to bring about a particular consequence, but who foresees that it will almost certainly result from his conduct, does not thereby intend that consequence, although if such foresight is proved a jury or magistrates' court may find that he did intend that consequence to result.

Recklessness

In some offences 'recklessness', either as to the consequence required for the actus reus or as to a requisite circumstance of it or as to some other risk, suffices for criminal liability as an alternative to some other mental state such as intention or knowledge.

In law, 'recklessness' bears two different, and mutually exclusive, meanings:

(a) subjective recklessness; and
(b) *Caldwell*-type recklessness (named after the House of Lords' decision of that name in which it was recognised),

which have in common the fact that they are both concerned with the taking of an unjustified risk.

Subjective recklessness means the *conscious* taking of an unjustified risk. A person acts with subjective recklessness as to a consequence of a deliberate act of his if, when he carries out that act, he *actually foresees* that the consequence may possibly result from his act and in all the circumstances it is unreasonable for him to take the risk of it occurring. He acts with subjective recklessness as to a circumstance surrounding his act if, when he carries out that act, he *actually realises* that the circumstance may possibly exist, provided it was unjustifiable for him to take the risk of its existence.

A person is *Caldwell*-type reckless as to a particular risk which surrounds his conduct if that risk would be obvious to an ordinary person who stopped to think and either:

(a) he has recognised that there is some risk involved and has nevertheless persisted in his conduct; or
(b) *he has not given any thought to the possibility of there being any such risk.*

In many offences where recklessness suffices, it is limited to subjective recklessness. Examples are malicious wounding or infliction of grievous bodily harm, common assault, common battery and rape. However, in other offences, such as criminal damage, recklessness means *Caldwell*-type recklessness.

Knowledge

Many offences expressly or impliedly require 'knowledge' as to the circumstances by virtue of which an act, omission or state of affairs is criminal. Generally speaking, where 'knowledge' is required as to a circumstance it suffices that the accused actually knew of the existence of the circumstance or was wilfully blind as to it (ie he realised the risk that it might exist but deliberately refrained from making inquiries).

Proof of a state of mind

In proving whether the accused had a requisite intention, subjective recklessness, knowledge or some similar state of mind, regard must be had to:

(a) the statements of the accused; and
(b) the conduct and circumstances of the accused, and the presence of any motive, since these *may* give rise to the inference that he had the necessary state of mind.

Certain acts are known to be likely to produce certain consequences which are frequently spoken of as the 'natural and probable' consequences of those acts. The Criminal Justice Act 1967, s 8, provides:

'A court or jury in determining whether a person has committed an offence—
(a) shall *not be bound* in law to infer that he intended or foresaw a result of his actions by reason only of its being a natural and probable consequence of those actions, but

(b)   shall decide whether he did intend or foresee that result by reference to all the evidence, drawing such inferences from the evidence *as appears proper* in the circumstances.'

Strict liability

In the case of some offences, the courts have held that a person can be convicted of a particular offence despite the fact that he was blamelessly inadvertent, ie had no type of mens rea, as to a particular element of the actus reus (or sometimes even though he had no type of mens rea as to any element of the actus reus). These offences are known as offences of 'strict liability'. Most strict liability offences are minor in nature, but this is not always so; for example, a person can be convicted of the offence of abducting a girl under 16 despite the fact that he neither knew nor ought to have known that she was under 16.

The overwhelming majority of strict liability offences are statutory offences. Clearly, an offence is not one of strict liability if the statutory definition expressly uses a word such as 'intentionally', 'recklessly' or 'knowingly'. The fact that a statutory definition does not use any word importing the concept of mens rea does not necessarily mean that the offence is one of strict liability; it depends on whether or not the courts are prepared to imply a requirement of mens rea into the definition. The basic rule is that, where a statute is silent on the point, it is presumed that Parliament intended mens rea to be required to be proved (so that the offence is not one of strict liability), unless this is rebutted by clear evidence that Parliament intended the contrary. Such evidence includes the wording of the definition of the offence and of other offences in the statute, the subject matter of the offence, its aim, and the maximum punishment. Thus, if other offences in the statute contain a word like 'knowingly' and/or if the offence in question concerns something which is not 'truly criminal' and only punishable with a fine, the presumption that mens rea is required to be proved is very likely to be rebutted. By way of example, many offences in the Road Traffic Acts have been interpreted as being of strict liability.

Where an offence is one of strict liability as to an element or elements of its actus reus, the prosecution must not seek to prove mens rea as to that element or those elements.

DEFENCES

Infancy

It is irrebuttably presumed that a child under 10 years of age cannot be guilty of an offence.

Until 30 September 1998, children between the ages of 10 and 14 years were presumed to be incapable of committing crime, but this presumption could be rebutted by proof beyond reasonable doubt that when the child did the act charged he knew that it was seriously wrong. This rule was abolished, in relation to anything done on or after 30 September 1998, by the Crime and Disorder Act 1998, s 34.

Insanity

Everyone is presumed sane until the contrary is proved. The mere fact that a person is medically insane is no defence, but a person has a defence if he is proved to be legally insane. The test of insanity for the purposes of legal responsibility is provided by the *M'Naghten Rules*, which were laid down in 1843. These rules comprise three elements, which must be proved by the accused (unless it is the prosecution which alleges insanity). At the time of the conduct in question:

(a) *the accused must have been suffering from a 'disease of the mind'*, ie an impairment of the mental faculties of reason, memory and understanding due to a disease (whether organic or functional, and whether permanent or transient) as opposed to some external factor like a blow on the head;

(b) *the accused must have been suffering a 'defect of reason'* due to disease of the mind, ie a deprivation of reasoning power (as opposed to momentary confusion or absent-mindedness);

(c) *as a result, the accused must not have known the physical nature and quality of his act or, if he did know this, not have known he was doing 'a legal wrong'.* The mere fact that, because of a defect of reason due to a disease of the mind, the accused acted under an irresistible impulse is not enough.

A defence of insanity is only appropriate where mens rea is in issue. It is not available where the offence charged is an offence of strict liability as to every element of the actus reus, ie one where no mens rea is required.

Accused persons are rarely advised to plead insanity when tried in the Crown Court because, if their defence succeeds, they will be found not guilty by reason of insanity and are liable to be ordered to be detained in a secure mental hospital until the Home Secretary is satisfied that this is no longer necessary for the protection of the public.

Automatism

Generally, it is a defence that the accused was in a state of automatism at the time of the act in question. An act is done in a state of automatism if it is done by the muscles without any control of the mind (eg a reflex action, or a spasmodic or convulsive act) or if it is done during a state involving loss of consciousness (eg somnambulism, or concussion, or a hypoglycaemic coma resulting from insulin taken by a diabetic).

It should be noted that, if the alleged cause of automatism in a case in the Crown Court is ruled by the trial judge to be a disease of the mind, he will direct the jury to consider only the defence of insanity, so that an acquittal on the ground of the defence of (non-insane) automatism will not be possible.

In the case of the defence of (non-insane) automatism, as opposed to insanity, the accused does not have to prove his defence. Instead he simply has the burden of adducing sufficient evidence to raise the issue; if he does this he must be acquitted unless the prosecution disproves his alleged automatism. In terms of his burden of adducing evidence, it is up to the accused to indicate the nature of his alleged incapacity and since, generally speaking, the mere statement 'I had a blackout' or 'I can't remember what happened' will be totally insufficient, the accused's evidence will very rarely be sufficient unless it is supported by medical evidence.

Sometimes, non-insane automatism is self-induced in that it results from something done or not done by the accused (as where a diabetic becomes an automaton as a result of taking insulin, or, having taken insulin, failing to eat sufficiently thereafter). In such a case, the accused cannot be convicted of an 'offence of specific intent' (which is defined below). Nor can he be convicted of an offence which does not require a specific intent *unless* either his automatism was caused by his voluntary intoxication *or,* before he became an automaton, he was aware that something he did or failed to do was likely to make him aggressive, unpredictable or uncontrollable with the result that he might endanger others (as opposed simply to becoming unconscious), and he deliberately disregarded the risk.

Intoxication

The rules relating to the effect of intoxication in criminal liability are the same whether the intoxication was caused by drink or drugs. Intoxication is not in itself a defence. It is no excuse that because of intoxication the accused's power to judge between right and wrong, or to exercise self-control, was impaired.

In most cases a person's intoxication is regarded as 'voluntary'. Intoxication is voluntary if it results from knowingly taking alcohol or some other drug. There are two exceptions: intoxication is not voluntary where it is caused by something taken under and in accordance with medical advice, or where it is caused by a non-dangerous drug (ie a sedative or soporific drug) provided that the accused is not aware of the risk of becoming unpredictable or aggressive when he takes it. These cases of involuntary intoxication are dealt with below.

Where the accused was voluntarily intoxicated, ie intoxicated as a result of his knowing consumption of drink or drugs otherwise than under and in accordance with medical advice, he may rely on his intoxication as evidence that he lacked mens rea if, but only if, the offence requires proof of a specific intent. Even if an offence is one of specific intent, an intoxicated, mistaken belief that he is acting in self-defence will not excuse the accused. Where an offence does not require a specific intent, an accused may be convicted of it if he was voluntarily intoxicated at the time of committing its actus reus, even though because of his intoxication he did not have the mens rea normally required for that offence, and even though he was then in a state of automatism.

The following have been held to be offences of specific intent in this context: murder; wounding or causing grievous bodily harm with intent contrary to the Offences Against the Person Act 1861, s 18; criminal damage contrary to the Criminal Damage Act 1971, s 1(2) (provided that it is only alleged that the accused intended to endanger the life of another by destroying or damaging property); theft; robbery; burglary with intent to steal; the common law offences of kidnapping and false imprisonment; and attempt to commit an offence.

Conversely, the following have been held *not* to be offences of specific intent: manslaughter; maliciously wounding or inflicting grievous bodily harm (contrary to the Offences Against the Person Act 1861, s 20); assault occasioning actual bodily harm; assault on a constable in the execution of his duty; indecent assault (at least where the conduct was unequivocally indecent); rape; taking a conveyance without lawful authority; and offences against the Criminal Damage Act 1971, s 1(1) or (2) (with the exception of an offence under s 1(2) where only an intention—as opposed to intention or recklessness, or recklessness to endanger life—is alleged).

The situation is different where a person is involuntarily intoxicated. Intoxication is involuntary in the cases outlined above, and also where it is not self-induced (as where a person's glasses of lemonade have been laced with vodka or where he has been secretly drugged).

Where an accused is involuntarily intoxicated, he can use evidence of his intoxication as evidence that he lacked the mens rea for the offence in question (whether or not it is an offence of specific intent). However, if it can be proved that a defendant had the necessary mens rea when the offence was committed, it is no defence that involuntary intoxication led him to commit an offence which he would not have committed when sober, and this is so even though because of his intoxication he acted under an irresistible impulse.

Duress

The defences of duress by threats and duress of circumstances are restricted to cases where an accused is threatened with death or serious physical injury to himself or another unless he acted as he did to avoid the threatened harm. The defence of duress by threats deals with the case where the threat comes from another person and, expressly or impliedly, is in the form of an order to do a particular, nominated act or suffer the harm; the defence of duress of circumstances deals with the case where the threat of death or serious physical injury is of any other type (as where the threat comes from the surrounding circumstances).

A threat of serious psychological injury or harm to property cannot give rise to either defence. The threat must be such that an ordinary, sober person of reasonable firmness sharing the accused's characteristics would have responded as the accused did. Because this 'ordinary person' is someone of reasonable firmness he is not invested with a characteristic of the accused which did not make the accused less able to resist the threat than an ordinary person of reasonable firmness. In addition, the ordinary person of reasonable firmness is not invested with a characteristic of the accused, such as pliancy, vulnerability to pressure or timidity, since it would be a contradiction in terms to invest an ordinary person with these. On the other hand, if the accused is in a category of persons who might be less able to resist pressure than people outside that category, the characteristic which puts him in that category may be a relevant one. Obvious examples are age (a young person may not be as robust as a mature person); pregnancy (added fear for the unborn child); serious physical disability (may inhibit self-protection), and a recognised mental illness or psychiatric condition (may make the person more susceptible to pressure).

The defences of duress by threats and duress of circumstances are not applicable in respect of conduct committed after a threat has ceased to be operative. Neither defence is available to a person who is charged with murder or attempted murder. Apart from this they are generally available in respect of other offences, including road traffic offences.

The defence of duress by threats is not available to a person who voluntarily and with knowledge as to its nature joined a criminal organisation or entered into a conspiracy, knowing that other members might bring pressure to bear on him, and who was an active member when he was put under such pressure.

Coercion

This is an alternative defence to duress for married women in the circumstances which we now outline. It is a defence on a charge of any offence, other than murder or treason, for a wife to prove that she committed the alleged offence in the presence of, and under the coercion of, her husband. It will be noted that the accused wife has the burden of proving this defence. In contrast, an accused does not have to prove the defence of duress; he merely has to adduce evidence that he is covered by that defence, whereupon it is for the prosecution to prove that he is not (otherwise he must be acquitted). On the other hand, the defence of coercion can apply where the threat is of something less than death or serious bodily harm, although there must be some (as yet undetermined limit) on the type of threat that can suffice.

PARTIES TO A CRIME

There are a number of ways in which people may participate in an offence.

Perpetrators

A perpetrator is otherwise known as the principal. Normally, it is clear who is the perpetrator; he is the person who, with the relevant mens rea, fires the fatal shot in murder, or has intercourse in rape, and so on. Of course, there can be more than one perpetrator, as where a group of men enter a building as trespassers in order to steal therein; in such a case there are said to be joint perpetrators of the offence.

If a person makes use of an innocent agent in order to procure the commission of an offence, he is the perpetrator of the offence, even though he is not present at the scene of the offence and does nothing with his own hands. Thus, a person who kills another by posting a time bomb to him which is delivered by an innocent postman, or who employs a child under ten (the age of criminal responsibility) or a trained dog to remove goods from a shop, may be convicted of murder or theft, as the case may be, if he acts with the appropriate mens rea.

Accomplices

A person who aids, abets, counsels or procures the commission of an offence (an accomplice) is liable to be tried and punished for that offence as a principal offender.

The terms 'aiding' and 'abetting' are often used together, but they refer to different things; 'aid' describes the activity of a person who assists the perpetrator to commit the principal offence, and 'abet' describes the activity of a person who encourages the perpetrator to commit it, whether or not in either case he is present at the time of commission. 'Counsel', which means 'encourage', does not add anything strictly but is used to describe encouragement before the commission of the principal offence. A person 'procures' the commission of an offence where he sets out to see that it is committed and takes appropriate steps to produce its commission.

It can be seen from the above that basically there must be some assistance or encouragement by a person of the commission of an offence by another before he can be convicted as an accomplice to it. That assistance or encouragement must be given before, or at the time of, the commission of the offence. Someone who assists the perpetrator after the commission of an offence is not liable as a party to it, but one who assists the perpetrator to escape detection or arrest may be guilty of the statutory offence of assisting offenders, dealt with later in this chapter.

The assistance or encouragement of the perpetrator which must be proved against an alleged accomplice may take a variety of forms. Examples are: holding a woman down while she is raped; keeping watch; shouting words of encouragement; providing a jemmy to a burglar, and buying paper for use by a forger. A person is not an accomplice to an offence merely because he stands by when it is committed and does nothing to prevent its commission, but if he was deliberately present at the scene of the crime and it can be proved that his presence encouraged the perpetrator, as he intended it should, he can be convicted as an accomplice. Unless the deliberate bystander does something to signify his approval it will normally be difficult to prove these things, although his presence will be prima facie evidence of them.

The mens rea required of an accomplice is, firstly, an intent to assist or encourage the commission of the offence. This is proved by proving that the accused's aim or purpose was to assist, encourage or procure the commission by the perpetrator of the act which constitutes or results in the principal offence. Alternatively, an intent to assist or encourage may be inferred from proof that the accused realised that his conduct does, or will virtually certainly, assist or encourage the perpetrator; this is not possible where the case rests on an allegation only of procuring. Secondly, it must be proved that the accused had knowledge of the facts essential to constitute the offence which is being or is likely to be committed and contemplated as a real possibility that the perpetrator was acting or might act with the mens rea required for the offence (although, of course, the accused need not know that those facts constitute an offence, nor need he know any more details). These requirements apply even though the offence in question is one of strict liability.

Unforeseen consequences of a joint criminal enterprise

Sometimes an accomplice can be liable for the unforeseen consequences of the perpetrator's acts.

If in the course of a joint criminal enterprise, a person accidentally commits the actus reus of an offence of a different type from that intended, neither he nor the accomplice will be guilty if they lack the necessary mens rea required for that offence. It will be different, of course, where the offence concerned is not of a type which requires foresight of the necessary consequence. This could be so in cases of manslaughter and unlawfully wounding or inflicting grievous bodily harm contrary to s 20 of the Offences against the Person Act 1861 for example. A person is guilty of manslaughter if death results from the commission by him of an unlawful act likely to harm another, even though he did not foresee that death or grievous bodily harm was likely to result. If one person encourages another to assault a man with fists, and he unexpectedly dies in consequence of the blows received, they are each guilty of manslaughter.

However, it is different where the perpetrator commits an incidental offence intentionally, which the second party has not assisted or encouraged him to commit. Where a man encourages a second to commit burglary and to use his jemmy to frighten off anyone who may come upon them and the perpetrator, disturbed by the householder in the course of the burglary, strikes him with the jemmy and kills him, both parties are guilty of burglary, but is the accomplice guilty of murder? The House of Lords has held that an accomplice can be convicted of an incidental offence if it is proved that he contemplated as a real possibility that the perpetrator might commit it but still participated in the enterprise. In some cases the accomplice will have agreed to or authorised the commission of the incidental offence but this is not necessary. If it was proved that the accomplice in the circumstances set out above had contemplated as a real possibility that the jemmy might be used intentionally to kill or do grievous bodily harm to someone in such circumstances, the accomplice could be convicted as an accomplice to murder even without proof that he had agreed to its use for that purpose and even though he had forbidden the use of violence.

In the case above, the accomplice contemplated as a real possibility the act carried out by the perpetrator. But what if he did not contemplate the act? The House of Lords has held that even if an accomplice intended or foresaw that the principal would or might act with the mens rea for the principal offence which was committed, he cannot be convicted as a party to that offence if the perpetrator's act is fundamentally different from the act intended or foreseen by the accomplice. On the other hand, if the perpetrator's act, though different, is as dangerous as that foreseen as a 'real possibility' by the accomplice, as where the actual act was stabbing with a knife and that foreseen as a real possibility was shooting to kill, an accomplice cannot escape liability for the offence.

A person who cannot in law perpetrate a particular offence may nevertheless be convicted as an accomplice to it. For example, a woman can be convicted of rape as an accomplice where she has encouraged or assisted a man to rape another woman.

Where an accused is alleged to be an accomplice to an offence, the charge may allege that he aided, abetted, counselled or procured it, and he will be convicted if he is proved to have participated in one or more of these four ways.

Vicarious liability

Vicarious liability means liability for the acts of another person which the accused has not authorised and of which he was ignorant.

Vicarious *criminal* liability is exceptional; it is imposed only on employers and, in some cases, certain other people with a similar status. It arises in three ways:

(a) Where a statute states that it is an offence for a person 'himself, or by his servant or agent', to do something, that person is vicariously liable if the prohibited act is done by his employee or agent in the course of his employment.

(b) Where a statutory strict liability offence uses a word like 'sell', 'expose for sale', or 'use', which connotes an activity which can be performed by an employee on behalf of his employer, an employer (or the like) can be vicariously liable for a prohibited 'selling' etc by his employee (or the like) in the course of his employment.

(c) Certain statutes, like the Licensing Act 1964, impose duties on a licensee and make it an offence for him knowingly to contravene them. If a licensee completely delegates his statutory responsibilities as licensee to someone else such as an employee, and the delegate knowingly contravenes one of these duties, the conduct and the state of mind of the delegate are imputed to the licensee, who is consequently vicariously liable for the offence in question. If this were not so, licensees could easily escape their statutory responsibilities by permanently absenting themselves from the premises, leaving someone else in charge.

Assisting offenders

The Criminal Law Act 1967, s 4 provides that, where a person has committed an arrestable offence, any other person who, knowing or believing him to be guilty of the offence, or of some other arrestable offence, does without lawful authority or reasonable excuse any act with intent to impede his apprehension or prosecution is guilty of an offence. Such a person is not guilty, as an accomplice, of the arrestable offence which has been committed, because his conduct occurs after its commission; the offence under s 4 is a separate offence. By way of example, if A knows that his friend, B, has committed an offence of murder and, with intent to impede the arrest or prosecution of B, disposes of the gun used by B to commit the murder, A is guilty of the offence of assisting offenders contrary to s 4 of the 1967 Act.

Concealing offences

Like the last offence, this offence is not a form of participation in crime but is mentioned here for convenience. It is governed by the Criminal Law Act 1967, s 5, which provides that, where a person has committed an arrestable offence, any other person who, knowing or believing that the offence or some other arrestable offence has been committed, and that he has information which might be of assistance in securing the prosecution or conviction of an offender for it, accepts or agrees to accept for not disclosing it any consideration other than the making good of loss or injury caused by the offence, or the making of reasonable compensation for it, is guilty of an offence.

Prosecutions for offences contrary to ss 4 or 5 of the 1967 Act may only be instituted by or with the consent of the Director of Public Prosecutions.

INCITEMENT, ATTEMPT AND CONSPIRACY

It is a common law offence to incite the commission of an offence, and a statutory offence to attempt to commit an indictable offence or to be a party to a conspiracy to commit an offence. These offences are committed on the making of the incitement, attempt or conspiracy and it is irrelevant that the substantive offence to which they relate is not committed or (except in the case of attempt) even attempted. Indeed, if the substantive offence is committed, no question of attempt normally arises, and where there has been incitement the inciter becomes a party as an accomplice to the substantive offence and is not normally proceeded against for incitement. Conspiracy differs from the other two offences in that, even where the conspirators have committed the substantive offence, there are circumstances in which a charge of conspiracy is appropriate as best representing the overall gravity of what has occurred, although the appellate courts have discouraged the practice.

Quite apart from the statutory offence of conspiracy to commit an offence, there is also the common law offence of conspiracy to defraud.

We describe the elements of the offences of incitement, attempt and conspiracy in ch 38, below.

EXEMPTION FROM CRIMINAL LIABILITY

Ambassadors, Ministers of Foreign States and Commonwealth High Commissioners and members of their families and staff are immune from criminal proceedings whilst in the United Kingdom in that capacity. In the case of members of the service staff immunity is extended to members of staff only in respect of acts in the course of their duties. These immunities are more restricted if the person concerned is a national of the United Kingdom. The Home Office should be contacted in cases where a person who is dealt with for an offence claims diplomatic immunity. The Metropolitan Police maintain an index of persons who are entitled to diplomatic immunity.

In addition, the Consular Relations Act 1968 grants immunity to consular officers and employees who are engaged in consular functions. In addition, *career* consular officers may not be arrested or detained pending trial unless the offence is grave (an arrestable offence as defined in ch 3) and the detention is authorised by a warrant or order of the court. *Honorary* consular officers are not immune from the jurisdiction of our criminal courts nor from arrest or detention. Such persons are generally retained in a part-time capacity and will usually hold office on account of the status which it confers.

The provisions of ss 6–11 of the Road Traffic Act 1988, which are concerned with drink/driving, apply to consular personnel (but not to Ambassadors etc). However, if a positive roadside specimen is provided there can be no arrest and the procedure must end there. Such a person would be liable to penalty if he failed to provide such a specimen.

CHAPTER 2
Elements of criminal procedure

INSTITUTION OF CRIMINAL PROCEEDINGS

Responsibility for prosecutions

Although the police may institute criminal proceedings, the responsibility for the conduct thereafter of such proceedings lies with the Director of Public Prosecutions. The one exception is in the case of various minor traffic offences, and even then only where the 'pleading guilty by post' procedure (described below) is adopted.

The Director of Public Prosecutions is the head of the Crown Prosecution Service. The Director is under the general supervision of the Attorney-General. The Director's functions are discharged on his behalf and under his direction by Crown Prosecutors working in the Crown Prosecution Service.

The Director's principal function is to take over the conduct of criminal proceedings (with the road traffic offences exception mentioned above) instituted on behalf of a police force (whether by a police officer or other person) once they have been instituted. This includes cases where the proceedings have been so instituted at the instigation of a private individual. In addition, the Director may actually institute criminal proceedings where this is appropriate, eg because of the difficulty or importance of the case.

There is generally nothing to prevent a private individual instituting and conducting criminal proceedings, and such private prosecutions are occasionally instituted. In addition, criminal proceedings for various types of minor offences are instituted and conducted by officials of local authorities or other public bodies (in which case the Director is not obliged to take over even if the public officer has brought the accused to the police to be charged), and criminal proceedings for cases of serious or complex fraud may be instituted and conducted by the Director of the Serious Fraud Office. However, the Director of Public Prosecutions may intervene at any time and undertake the conduct of proceedings by a private individual or such an official, even if his purpose is to offer no evidence against the accused in the public interest and thereby to abort those proceedings.

An exception to the general rule that a police officer, private individual or public official may institute criminal proceedings is that there are numerous offences where the leave of the Attorney-General or of the Director of Public Prosecutions is required. For example, proceedings for an offence under the Official Secrets Acts 1911 and 1989 or for one of the offences relating to racial hatred under the Public Order Act 1986 may only be instituted by or with the consent of the Attorney-General, and proceedings for over 50 offences may only be instituted by or with the consent of the Director. In the latter case, the Director's functions can, of course, be exercised by a Crown Prosecutor on his behalf. Where proceedings for an offence may only be instituted by or with the consent of the Attorney-General or of the Director, this is indicated at the appropriate point in this book.

Criminal proceedings are initiated in one of two ways:

(a) by laying an information and then securing the accused's presence before a magistrates' court by an arrest under a warrant or by a summons; or
(b) by an arrest without warrant, followed by a charge.

Laying an information

An essential prerequisite to the issue of a summons or a warrant of arrest is 'laying an information'.

An information may be laid by the prosecutor or by his counsel or solicitor, or by a person authorised on his behalf. An information laid by the police cannot be laid in the name of the police force but must be laid by the chief constable or some other person authorised by him. However, if the informant is not named in the information it is not invalid if the accused knew the informant to be a member of the particular force and his actual identity can easily be established. An information need not be in writing or on oath, unless a warrant of arrest or search warrant is sought. However, as a matter of practice, police informations are always laid in writing.

An information must be laid before a justice of the peace or the clerk to the justices (or an authorised assistant) on behalf of a justice. A *written* information need not be delivered to a justice or justices' clerk personally in order to be so laid, since it is laid when received by a person authorised to receive it on behalf of a justice or the clerk for onward transmission (and it can be presumed that any member of the clerk's staff authorised to handle incoming mail is so authorised). The information must then be transmitted to a justice or the clerk for consideration to be given to the issue of process (ie a warrant or summons).

The information must contain such particulars as are necessary to give the accused reasonable notice of the nature of the charge, including the statutory provision alleged to have been infringed. Not more than one offence may be alleged in one information, although several informations may be set out in one document.

Normally, an information must be laid before a justice (or justices' clerk or authorised assistant) for the area in which the offence was committed. However, if the offence was committed on the boundary between two or more areas (or within 500 yards of such a boundary) the information may be laid in any of those areas. The same is the case if the offence was committed in any arm of the sea or other water lying between such areas or if it was begun in one area and ended in another.

An information relating to an offence triable only summarily cannot generally be tried unless it was laid within six months from the time when the offence was committed. An example of an exception to this general rule is provided by the Vehicles Excise and Registration Act 1994, which permits an information to be laid in respect of offences of using or keeping a vehicle without an excise licence up to three years after the commission of the offence. The general rule does not apply to informations relating to an offence which is triable on indictment. There is no set time limit in the case of such an offence, unless its parent statute expressly provides one.

Summonses

A summons is a written order issued and signed by a justice of the peace or by a justices' clerk (or authorised assistant) on behalf of a justice. It is directed to the person named in the information and requires him to appear before a named magistrates' court for the area at a specified time and date to answer the particular charge(s) set out in it.

For the sake of completeness, it should also be noted that a summons may also be issued as a result of a complaint. A complaint is a written or verbal allegation made before a justice to the effect that a person has committed a breach of the law which is *not a criminal offence*. (If the complaint is proved, that person may be bound over to keep the peace.)

It should also be noted that, where a justice or justices' clerk (or authorised assistant) is satisfied that any person in England or Wales is likely to be able to give material evidence, or to produce any document or thing likely to be material evidence, and that that person will not attend voluntarily at a magistrates' court or will not voluntarily produce that document or thing, the justice may issue a summons directing attendance or production. Unlike other summonses, such a summons may not be served by post. A justice may refuse to issue a witness summons if he is not satisfied that the application was made as soon as reasonably practicable after the accused pleaded not guilty. Crown Courts are also empowered to issue witness summonses in prescribed circumstances.

Service of summonses The Magistrates' Courts Rules 1981 deal with the various methods by which a summons may be served. It may be served by:

(a)   delivering it to the person to whom it is directed; or
(b)   by leaving it for him with some person at his last known or usual place of abode; or
(c)   by sending it by post in a letter addressed to him at his last known or usual place of abode.

It is no longer necessary that, where a person fails to appear after service of a summons either by leaving it for him with some person at his last or usual place of abode, or by sending it by post to him at his last known usual place of abode, it is proved that the summons came to his knowledge.

The Magistrates' Courts Rules provide that, in any instance in which a summons may be sent by post to a person's last known or usual place of abode, the rules shall have effect as if they provided also for the summons to be sent in the manner specified to an address given by that person for that purpose. Lawful service of a summons may therefore be effected and proved by sending the summons for a summary offence, by post, to such a nominated address. The Interpretation Act 1978, s 7 provides that service is deemed to be effected when a pre-paid, properly addressed letter which contains the document which is to be served is posted. Unless the contrary is proved, service is deemed to be effected at the time at which the letter would be delivered in the ordinary course of post.

Service of a summons on a corporation may be effected by delivering it at, or sending it by post to:

(a)   the registered office of the corporation, if that office is in the United Kingdom; or

(b) any place in the United Kingdom where the corporation trades or conducts its business, if there is no registered office in the United Kingdom.

Proof of service is usually by means of a certificate of service signed by the person who effected the service, or who posted the summons. Such a certificate contains details of the place, date and time of posting or of service by delivery.

Postal service of a summons issued in England and Wales is permitted throughout the United Kingdom. The Scots issue a 'citation' instead of a summons and this may be served by post in England and Wales. Northern Irish summonses cannot be served by post in England and Wales.

Warrants of arrest

A justice of the peace (but not the justices' clerk or anyone else) may issue a signed warrant to arrest, instead of a summons, when information is laid before him to the effect that a person has, or is suspected of having, committed an offence. Such a warrant remains in force until it is executed or withdrawn. If the original is lost a justice may issue a replacement. However, an arrest warrant must not be issued in the first instance unless the offence to which it relates is either triable on indictment or punishable with imprisonment, or the accused's address is not sufficiently established for a summons to be served on him. An arrest warrant may be endorsed with a direction that the person to be arrested shall on arrest be released on bail, with or without sureties. This is known as 'backing for bail'.

Other warrants

For the sake of completeness, mention may be made of other warrants which may be issued by a justice or magistrates' court on an information being laid.

Warrants to arrest a witness Such a warrant may be issued by a justice under the Magistrates' Courts Act 1980, s 97 where he is satisfied that a person who could give material evidence etc is unlikely voluntarily to attend court. Such a warrant will only be issued where a summons would be ineffective.

Warrant for distress or commitment The Magistrates' Courts Act 1980, s 76 authorises a magistrates' court to issue a warrant of distress or of commitment where a person is in default of payment of a sum adjudged to be paid by a conviction or order of a magistrates' court.

The purpose of a warrant of distress is clear from its official title, 'a warrant of distress for the purpose of levying the sum which is unpaid'. Such a warrant is usually executed by a bailiff but it may be directed to the constables of a police area. It requires that goods be seized; this is done initially by labelling the goods, after which they are in legal custody. Any electrical plant, line or meter belonging to a public electrical supplier cannot be seized, nor can wearing apparel or bedding, nor tools or implements of the person's trade. It is an offence for any person to remove the goods, or the marks placed on them to signify seizure.

A warrant of commitment orders the defaulter to be arrested and committed to prison. It may be issued *either* where it appears on the return to a warrant of distress that the defaulter's assets are insufficient to satisfy the sum adjudged *or* instead of a warrant of distress. If it considers it expedient, the magistrates' court may fix a term of imprisonment and suspend the issue of the warrant until such time and on such conditions as it thinks fit. A receipt must be obtained for the defaulter when he is handed over to a prison pursuant to a warrant of commitment.

Search warrants We discuss this type of warrant in ch 3, below.

This is not an exhaustive list of warrants which may be issued by a justice or magistrates' court, as will be seen from the contents of the next paragraph but one.

Execution of warrants

A warrant of arrest, or of commitment, or of distress, or a search warrant, may be executed anywhere in England and Wales by a constable acting in his police area. In addition, by the Criminal Justice and Public Order Act 1994, s 136 a warrant issued in England, Wales or Northern Ireland for the arrest or commitment (or a like warrant issued in Scotland) of a person may, without endorsement, be executed by a constable of a police force of the country of origin or of one of the 'home countries', as well as by any other persons within the directions of the warrant.

Certain warrants may be executed by a constable who does not have possession of the warrant at the time:

(a)   warrants to arrest a person in connection with an offence;
(b)   warrants under the Army Act 1955, Air Force Act 1955, Naval Discipline Act 1957 or Reserve Forces Act 1980 (desertion etc); and
(c)   warrants relating to the non-appearance of a defendant, warrants of distress, warrants of commitment, warrants to arrest a witness and warrants to arrest someone for non-compliance with a summons to make a deposition in connection with committal proceedings or 'sending for trial' proceedings (under the Magistrates' Courts Act 1980, ss 55, 76, 93, 97 and 97A and the Crime and Disorder Act 1998, Sch 3).

However, in such cases the warrants must, on the demand of the person concerned, be shown to him as soon as practicable (Magistrates' Courts Act 1980, s 125).

Except in the above cases a warrant may not be executed by a constable who does not have it in his possession at the time. Thus, for example, a constable must be in possession of the warrant when executing a search warrant.

Entry to execute warrants The Police and Criminal Evidence Act 1984, s 17 permits a constable to enter and search premises, including any vehicle, vessel, aircraft or tent, for the purpose of executing a warrant of arrest issued in connection with or arising out of criminal proceedings, or a warrant of commitment issued under the Magistrates' Courts Act 1980, s 76. This power of entry and search is only exercisable where the constable has reasonable grounds for believing that the person whom he is seeking is on the premises. Where the premises consist of two or more separate dwellings, the entry and search is restricted to any common parts of the building and the dwelling in which the constable reasonably believes that the person may be.

This power of search under s 17 is only a power to search to the extent that is reasonably required for the purpose for which the power of entry is exercised.

CLASSIFICATION OF OFFENCES BY METHOD OF TRIAL

Offences can be classified as indictable offences, summary offences and offences triable either way, according to their mode of trial. The Interpretation Act 1978, Sch 1 defines these offences as follows:

(a) 'indictable offence' means an offence which, if committed by an adult, is triable on indictment, whether it is exclusively so triable (eg murder or robbery) or triable either way;

(b) 'summary offence' means an offence which, if committed by an adult, is triable only summarily (eg most driving offences); and

(c) 'offence triable either way' means an offence which, if committed by an adult, is triable either on indictment or summarily (eg theft or unlawful wounding).

COURTS OF CRIMINAL JURISDICTION

The guilt or innocence of persons charged with an offence against the criminal law is a matter to be decided in a court of justice. There are two methods of trying persons accused of criminal offences. One is by judge and jury in the Crown Court after committal, or sending, for trial on an indictment; the other is summarily by a magistrates' court without a jury. With a few exceptions, all criminal proceedings in the Crown Court begin in a magistrates' court since an accused tried in the Crown Court must normally have been committed, or sent, for trial there by a magistrates' court.

Magistrates' courts

A magistrates' court is normally composed of two or three justices of the peace, when exercising the powers referred to in this chapter. Some statutes permit particular offences to be tried by a single justice but such instances are rare. The normal sittings of a magistrates' court take place in a properly appointed court house on appointed days of the week. On other occasions, or in other places, a court may sit as an occasional court but with quite limited powers. A single justice may perform the functions required of examining justices, who sit for the purpose of deciding whether or not there is sufficient evidence against a particular person to merit his committal for trial at the Crown Court (see below). A stipendiary (ie paid) magistrate may always sit alone and has all the powers of two lay justices.

In criminal matters a magistrates' court has jurisdiction in relation to the following matters:

Offences triable summarily only

A magistrates' court for a county, a London commission area or the City of London has jurisdiction to try all summary offences committed within its area. In addition, the justices have jurisdiction to try an offence committed outside their area if it appears to them to be necessary or expedient, with a view to the better administration of justice, that the person charged should be tried jointly with, or in the same place as, some other person who is charged with an offence within that area, and who is in custody or is being proceeded against within their area. An example would be where someone is charged with stealing goods in area 'X' and someone else is charged with handling them in area 'Y'. The jurisdiction of magistrates' courts in relation to offences committed on the boundary between areas in close proximity to those boundaries is set out on p 15.

As indicated earlier in this chapter, persons appearing before a magistrates' court do so either in answer to a summons or under arrest. At the commencement of a summary trial, the accused is asked to plead guilty or not guilty to a written charge called 'the information', which will have been read over to him by the clerk of the court. We have shown above that where the proceedings are initiated by way of a summons or an arrest warrant, that will have resulted from the laying of an information. Where proceedings have been initiated by an arrest without warrant, the information will come into being as a result of the accused being charged (which normally occurs at a police station).

Guilty plea Persons who appear before the court will have the charge read over to them and will be asked if they plead guilty or not guilty. If an accused pleads guilty the court must be satisfied that it is a clear and unequivocal plea. On a plea of guilty being entered, the court may convict without hearing evidence. In practice, however, the facts of the case are outlined by the prosecution and the accused or his legal representative is at liberty to dispute those facts should he wish to do so and may also put before the court any mitigating facts which he feels that the court should consider before passing sentence. The court will also usually hear any evidence by the prosecutor of any previous recorded convictions of the accused and of his general character in order to enable it to decide the appropriate penalty. The accused may also ask the court to take into consideration, when passing sentence, other offences which he has committed.

Pleading guilty by post In the case of many offences triable *summarily only*, the Magistrates' Courts Act 1980 permits pleas of guilty to be entered at a magistrates' court (or where the accused is 16 or 17 when the summons is issued, at a youth court) without the necessity for the accused person to attend the proceedings, or for any witnesses to be called. There are certain conditions which must be fulfilled:

(a) the proceedings must be by way of summons;
(b) the offence must not be one for which the accused can be sentenced to more than three months' imprisonment;
(c) the clerk of the court must have been notified by the prosecutor that the accused, when served with the summons for the offence, was also served with:
  (i) a notice explaining the prescribed procedure;
  (ii) *either* a concise statement of the facts of the case which will be put before the court in the event of him notifying the clerk of his plea of guilty *or* a copy of such written statement or statements complying with the Criminal Justice Act 1967, s 9(2)(a),(2)(b) and (3) (proof by written statement) as will be so placed in those circumstances;
  (iii) if any information relating to the accused will or may, in the circumstances, be placed before the court by or on behalf of the prosecutor, a notice containing or describing the information; and
(d) the accused or his solicitor must have notified the clerk of the court that he wishes to plead guilty. On receipt of this notification, the clerk will inform the prosecutor.

Where the accused does not appear and proof of service of such documents is given, the court may hear and dispose of the case in the absence of the accused and the absence of the prosecutor. The documents are read to a court before a conviction is registered.

Should an accused appear, although the notification referred to in (d) has been received, the court may, with his consent, proceed as just described but the accused may make oral submissions with a view to mitigation of sentence, in place of a written submission which he may have sent to the clerk.

Not guilty plea If an accused pleads not guilty the court must hear the evidence and, at the request of either party, the court will order all witnesses out of court so that evidence may be independently presented. The proceedings will be opened by the prosecutor outlining the facts of the case and calling his witnesses one by one to give evidence to the court. Each witness will either take the oath or affirm and will give his evidence during *'examination-in-chief'*. After the prosecutor has asked questions to introduce and identify his witness, he may not ask *leading questions* in relation to the facts in issue. Leading questions are those which may usually be answered 'yes' or 'no'. For example, a prosecutor may not ask, 'Did you see the defendant standing outside the premises at 2 East Street?' Instead he should ask, 'Where was the defendant when you saw him?'

When a witness has given evidence for the prosecution he may be *cross-examined* by the defence upon any aspect of the evidence which he has given. Leading questions may be asked. The object of a cross-examination is to test the truth or credibility of the evidence or to diminish its value.

At the conclusion of the cross-examination the prosecution has a right to *re-examine* the witness upon *any new facts* which have come to light, or to clear up ambiguities which may have arisen, during cross-examination. Leading questions may not be put, nor may new evidence be introduced.

The accused or his legal representative may then address the court, whether or not he calls witnesses. The Police and Criminal Evidence Act 1984, s 79, which also applies to trials in the Crown Court, requires that, if the defence intends to call two or more witnesses to the facts of the case and those witnesses include the accused, the accused must be called before the other witness or witnesses unless the court in its discretion otherwise directs. Such a direction is likely where, for instance, a witness is to speak of an occurrence before the matters about which the accused is to give evidence.

When a witness for the defence, including the accused, has given his evidence, he may be cross-examined by the prosecution and may then be re-examined by the defence on any new facts or ambiguities which have arisen during the cross-examination.

When the prosecution and defence have finished calling their evidence, each side has a right to address the court (except that the prosecution does not have the right if the accused has not called witnesses and is not legally represented), the prosecution's closing speech coming before that of the defence.

The court may adjourn to consider its verdict and may seek the advice of its clerk by specific request. If it decides to convict, its pronouncement of this verdict will usually be followed by evidence by the prosecutor of any previous recorded convictions of the accused and of his general character in order to enable the court to decide on the appropriate penalty. A plea in mitigation may be made by the accused or his legal representative. The accused may also take the opportunity to ask the court to take into consideration, when passing sentence, other offences which he has committed.

A magistrates' court may, before beginning to try an information, or inquire into an offence as examining justices, or at any time during such proceedings, adjourn the proceedings to a time which they it fixes. It may remand the defendant, either in custody or on bail. If the remand is in custody, the remand will be for a maximum of eight clear days; if the accused is allowed bail, the remand may be for longer with the consent of both parties. Remands may be for longer periods after conviction where the proceedings are adjourned for a medical report or for other enquiries to be undertaken.

Offences triable either way

The Magistrates' Courts Act 1980, Sch 1 lists certain offences, including theft and unlawful wounding, as being triable either way. In addition, certain statutory offences are specified by the statute in question as being triable either way. An offence which is triable either way may be tried either on indictment in the Crown Court or summarily in a magistrates' court.

Where it is tried depends on the following rules.

Where an accused appears or is brought before a magistrates' court charged with an either-way offence, the court must cause the charge to be written down, if this has not already been done, and to be read to the accused. The court must explain to the accused in ordinary language that he may indicate whether (if the offence were to proceed to trial) he would plead guilty or not guilty; and explain in ordinary language that if he indicates that he would plead guilty:

(a) the court must proceed as if the proceedings constituted from the beginning the summary trial of the information, and the court had asked whether he pleaded guilty or not guilty; and

(b) he may be committed for sentence to Crown Court if the court is of the opinion that one of the grounds set out below exists.

The court must then ask the accused whether (if the offence were to proceed to trial) he would plead guilty or not guilty. If he indicates that he would plead guilty the court must proceed as if the proceedings constituted from the beginning the summary trial of the offence and the accused had pleaded guilty. If the court is of the opinion:

(a) that the offence or the combination of the offence and other offences associated with it was so serious that greater punishment should be inflicted for the offence than the court has power to impose; or

(b) in the case of a violent or sexual offence, that a sentence of imprisonment for a term longer than the court has power to impose is necessary to protect the public from serious harm from him,

the court may commit the offender in custody or on bail to the Crown Court for sentence.

If the accused indicates that he would plead not guilty, or fails to indicate how he would plead, the court must afford first the prosecutor and then the accused an opportunity to make representations as to which mode of trial would be more suitable. The court must consider the nature of the case; whether the circumstances make the offence one of a serious character; whether the punishment which a magistrates' court could inflict would be adequate, and any other relevant circumstances.

If, having considered these issues, the magistrates' court decides that trial on indictment is more suitable, it will commence to hold committal proceedings in respect of the offence (see below). On the other hand, if the court decides that summary trial is more suitable it must explain to the accused that the offence appears more suitable for summary trial and that he can either consent to such trial or, if he wishes, be tried on indictment. He must also be warned that, if he is tried summarily and is convicted, he may be committed for sentence by the Crown Court if one of the grounds described above exists. If the accused consents to summary trial, the magistrates' court will proceed to it (in the same way as described above in relation to offences triable summarily only); if he does not so consent, committal proceedings will be held, just as it would if it had decided that trial on indictment was more suitable.

Committal proceedings When conducting committal proceedings, the magistrates' court is said to be sitting in its capacity as examining justices; the court's duty is to conduct a preliminary enquiry into the case. All it has to decide is whether there is evidence on which a reasonable jury properly directed *could* convict.

A magistrates' court has jurisdiction to act as examining justices in respect of any indictable offence wherever it was committed. If it did not enjoy such jurisdiction a person who was arrested for offences committed in various parts of England and Wales would have to be committed for trial in each area in which he committed offences. The law relating to committal proceedings was amended by the Criminal Procedure and Investigation Act 1996.

In committal proceedings oral evidence is not admissible (ie witnesses may not be called), and only the following forms of evidence are admissible -

(i) Written statements A written statement is admissible if it purports to be signed by the person who made it and it contains a declaration by that person to the effect that it is true to the best of his knowledge and belief and that he made the statement knowing that, if it were to be tendered in evidence, he would be liable to prosecution if he wilfully stated in it anything which he knew to be false or did not believe to be true. Before such a statement is tendered in evidence a copy must be given, by or on behalf of the prosecutor, to each of the other parties to the proceedings.

If such a statement is made by a person under 18 years old, it must give his age; if it is made by a person who cannot read it, it must have been read to him before he signs it and it must be accompanied by a declaration by the person who so read the statement to the effect that it was so read; and if it refers to any other document as an exhibit, the copy given to the other parties to the proceedings must be accompanied by a copy of that document or by such information as may be necessary to enable the party to whom it is given to inspect that document or a copy of it.

(ii) Depositions A justice of the peace may issue a summons addressed to a reluctant witness who is likely to be able to make a statement containing material evidence, or produce a document or other exhibit likely to be material to committal proceedings. Such a person may have his evidence taken before a justice as a deposition. Such a deposition and documents and other exhibits to which it refers are admissible in committal proceedings provided that a copy has been given to the other parties and, if there is reference to any other document as an exhibit, it is accompanied by a copy of that document or such information as will enable those parties to inspect it.

(iii) Documents or other exhibits referred to in written statements or depositions of the type referred to above are admissible in committal proceedings.

(iv) Statements made by witnesses who are unlikely to attend trial The Criminal Justice Act 1988, ss 23 and 24 (see pp 154-158) make provision for the admissibility at trial, in certain circumstances, of statements made by persons who are, for various reasons, unlikely to be able to attend the trial of an accused. Similar provisions as to admissibility apply at committal proceedings.

(v) Other documents   The Criminal Procedure and Investigations Act 1996 makes provision for certain documents which are provided for by statute to be admissible in committal proceedings.

A magistrates' court inquiring into an offence as examining justices must on consideration of the evidence:

(a) commit the accused for trial if it is of the opinion that there is sufficient evidence to put him on trial by jury for any indictable offence;
(b) discharge him if it is of the opinion that he is in custody for no other cause than the offence under inquiry.

Where examining justices are satisfied that all the evidence tendered by or on behalf of the prosecutor falls within the provisions relating to written statements and documents (set out above), they may commit the accused for trial without consideration of the contents of any statements etc, unless the accused, or one of the accused, has no legal representative acting for him in the case, or such a legal representative has requested the court to consider a submission that there is insufficient evidence to put the accused on trial by jury for the offence.

Committal to be dealt with   The Criminal Justice Act 1988, s 41 makes provision for a person committed for trial in the Crown Court for an offence triable either way also to be committed to be dealt with for a summary offence if such offence is :

(a) punishable by imprisonment or involves obligatory or discretionary disqualification from driving, and
(b) arises from the same or connected circumstances as the offence triable either way.

Offences triable only on indictment

At the time that this book went to press, magistrates' courts have two alternative functions in respect of these offences.

First, and this has been the traditional function, they conduct committal proceedings in respect of a person charged before them with an indictable-only offence. Of course, there is no question of that person electing trial by a magistrates' court; the magistrates' court will move straight to committal proceedings. The proceedings will be conducted in the same way as described above.

Second, since January 1999, a new process is being substituted across England and Wales following piloting which began in that month. It is not yet known when the new process will become general. The new process, introduced by the Crime and Disorder Act 1998, is the 'sending for trial' procedure.

The 1998 Act provides that, where an adult appears or is brought before a magistrates' court charged with an indictable-only offence, the court *must* send him forthwith to the Crown Court for trial:

(a) for that offence; and
(b) for any either-way or summary offence with which he is charged which fulfils the 'requisite conditions'.

The 'requisite conditions' are that:

(i) the either-way or summary offence appears to the court to be related to the indictable-only offence; and

(ii) in the case of a summary offence, it is punishable with imprisonment or involves obligatory or discretionary disqualification from driving.

Section 51 deals with the situation where an adult who has been sent for trial subsequently appears before or is brought before a magistrates' court charged with an either-way offence or summary offence which fulfils the 'requisite conditions' described above. Section 51 provides that the magistrates' court *may* send the accused forthwith to the Crown Court for trial for the either-way or summary offence.

There are also provisions for an adult co-accused (or, in some cases, a juvenile co-accused) of an adult satisfying the above criteria to be sent for trial with that person, even though that co-accused is not charged with an offence which – in relation to him – must be tried on indictment.

Notice of transfer procedures - offences involving children in sex, violence or cruelty

By the Criminal Justice Act 1991, s 53 where a person has been charged with a sexual offence or an offence of violence or cruelty the Director of Public Prosecutions may serve a 'notice of transfer' on the magistrates' court in whose jurisdiction the offence has been charged. To be valid the notice must be served before the magistrates begin committal proceedings. The effect of a notice of transfer is to transfer the case directly to the Crown Court, without committal proceedings taking place. The Director may only serve such a notice if of the opinion that:

(a) there is sufficient evidence to warrant committal;

(b) a child who is the alleged victim, or who is alleged to have witnessed the commission of the offence, will be called as a witness at the trial; and

(c) that such transfer is necessary to avoid any prejudice to the welfare of the child.

Where such a notice of transfer is served, the proposed place of trial must be a Crown Court centre equipped with live television link facilities. Those so equipped are listed in a Practice Direction issued in 1992.

In areas where the 'sending for trial' procedure operates, the provisions relating to notice of transfer do not apply in respect of an 'indictable only' offence.

Open court

The Magistrates' Courts Act 1980 requires that, subject to the provisions of any enactment to the contrary, the proceedings of a magistrates' court should be in open court, ie open to the general public. Examining justices have the discretion not to sit in open court if they feel that to do so for the whole or part of the committal proceedings would not serve the ends of justice. There are other limited exceptions concerned with the likelihood of serious public disorder or where matters of national safety are being considered. The public have a general right of access to courts but children under 14 may not be permitted to enter unless they are babes in arms.

A magistrates' court inquiring into an offence as examining justices may consider video recordings of testimony from child witnesses in certain cases, notwithstanding that the child witness is not called at the committal proceedings. For these provisions and the definition of 'child' for these purposes see p 142.

Youth courts

A youth court is a summary court and is composed of justices who are specially selected because of their qualifications. No more than three justices may sit and the bench must contain at least one man and one woman. In exceptional cases a court may sit without a representative of one or other of the sexes or it may consist of a single stipendiary magistrate. In the London Metropolitan area there are no limits on a stipendiary magistrate sitting alone in the youth court. The general public do not have a right of access to proceedings in a youth court.

A magistrates' court before which a person under 18 (hereafter described as a 'juvenile') appears charged with an offence which, in the case of an adult, is triable only on indictment or triable either way must deal with it *summarily* unless:

(a)   the charge is one of homicide; or
(b)   the offence is so grave that under specific statutory powers he, if found guilty, may be sentenced to be detained for a long period; or
(c)   he is charged jointly with an adult (ie a person who has attained 18) and the court considers it necessary in the interests of justice to commit the case for trial.

With certain exceptions, no charge against a person under 18 may be heard summarily by a magistrates' court other than a youth court. The exceptions, which allow trial by a magistrates' court, are:

(a)   where the juvenile is charged jointly with an adult;
(b)   where an adult is charged with aiding, abetting, counselling, procuring, allowing or permitting an offence with which a juvenile is charged;
(c)   where the fact that the person is a juvenile is discovered in the course of proceedings in a magistrates' court, the court may hear and determine the proceedings;
(d)   where a juvenile is charged with aiding etc an offence committed by an adult; and
(e)   where the charge against a juvenile arises out of circumstances which are the same as, or are connected with, those which give rise to an offence by an adult (eg a theft by a youth and a handling by an adult).

The Magistrates' Courts Act 1980 recognises the specialist nature of youth courts by requiring a court which finds a juvenile guilty of an offence other than homicide in any of the circumstances set out above to send the case to a youth court to be dealt with as if that juvenile had been found guilty by that court. In effect, they must send the case to the youth court for sentence to be passed. An 'adult' court has the discretion to remit a juvenile, who has been jointly charged with an adult, to a youth court for trial if the adult pleads guilty, is committed for trial or is discharged and the juvenile himself pleads not guilty.

On occasions problems are caused in respect of the hearing of indictable offences where the person charged is a juvenile at the time of the commission of the offence but is an adult when it finally comes to trial. In such circumstances the appropriate date at which to determine whether an accused has turned 18 for the purpose of the above procedures is the date of his appearance before the court when it determines which mode of trial is to be adopted, which is not necessarily his first appearance.

The 'pleading guilty by post' provisions described on pp 20-21 do not generally apply to proceedings in a youth court. The only exception is where the accused is aged 16 or 17 when the summons is issued.

The sentencing powers of courts generally are limited in relation to children and young persons.

Crown Court

The Crown Court may sit in any part of England and Wales. For convenience the locations of the Crown Court are grouped in six circuits. The towns on the list of Crown Court locations are divided into three tiers. In the first, sittings of the High Court are held for civil cases as well as of the Crown Court for criminal cases (and such civil matters as are within its jurisdiction). On the other hand, in second and third tier locations only sittings of the Crown Court are held. The jurisdiction of a Crown Court is exercisable by any judge of the High Court, any circuit judge, any recorder, or, in the case of appeals from magistrates' courts and committals for sentence, a judge of the High Court, circuit judge or recorder sitting with not more than four justices of the peace. It will be appreciated that, particularly when a Crown Court is concerned with appeals, the presence of justices may be of benefit to the proceedings. However, the justices must defer to the judge or recorder on matters of law. High Court judges do not sit at third tier locations.

The Crown Court has jurisdiction over all offences which are triable only on indictment and also over offences triable either way in respect of which the accused has been committed or sent for trial on indictment. Trials on indictment are always heard with a jury. Indictable offences are divided into four classes for the purposes of trial in the Crown Court; these classes depend on the seriousness of the offence. When committing, or sending, a person to a Crown Court, magistrates' courts will commit him to the appropriate tier of the Crown Court according to this classification.

A person who has been convicted by a magistrates' court may appeal to the Crown Court against sentence if he pleaded guilty, or against conviction or sentence if he pleaded not guilty. There is also a right of appeal against the making of certain orders, for example orders 'binding over' a person to be of good behaviour. The Crown Court also deals with people convicted in a magistrates' court who have been committed to it for sentence.

The Central Criminal Court in London is a Crown Court.

Court of Appeal (Criminal Division)

Appeals to this division are normally heard by a court consisting of three of the following: the Lord Chief Justice, Lords Justice of Appeal and judges of the Queen's Bench Division of the High Court. A circuit judge may take up one of these positions in certain specified circumstances.

If convicted of an offence on indictment before the Crown Court, a person may appeal to this court against *conviction* with the leave of the Court of Appeal or trial judge. On an appeal against conviction, the Court of Appeal can dismiss the appeal, allow it and quash the conviction, or substitute a conviction for another offence if it appears that the accused should have been convicted of that offence, rather than the one of which he was actually convicted. If fresh evidence has come to light, the court may order a new trial. It may also do so in any other case where the interests of justice so require.

A person convicted on indictment before the Crown Court may appeal against *sentence* with the leave of the Court of Appeal, and so may a person who has been sentenced by the Crown Court on committal for sentence. On *appeal* against sentence, the Court of Appeal may vary a sentence but cannot increase it. However, the

Attorney-General may (in certain cases) refer a sentence to the Court of Appeal with its leave if it appears to him to be unduly lenient. On such a reference, the court may impose a more severe sentence.

Divisional Court of the Queen's Bench Division

This Court's jurisdiction is normally exercised by two judges, one of whom is usually the Lord Chief Justice or a Lord Justice of Appeal and the other a judge of the Queen's Bench Division. One function of the Court is to hear appeals on points of law from magistrates' courts or from the Crown Court in respect of appeals from magistrates' courts to the Crown Court. Such appeal is known as appeal by case stated, since the magistrates' court or Crown Court is asked to 'state a case', ie set out its reasons for its finding on the basis of its interpretation of the law in relation to the facts found by it. The Divisional Court is not concerned with any form of re-trial.

Another function of the Divisional Court is *judicial review* of the decisions of an inferior court or other body. In such cases the Divisional Court will examine whether there was authority or power by which the decision made could have been properly reached; whether the procedure followed the rules of natural justice; or whether the exercise of discretion on the part of the decision-making body was lawful. Thus the court is not examining the correctness of the decision but whether it was lawfully and reasonably reached.

Following such a review the Queen's Bench Divisional Court may issue certain orders or writs.

Mandamus This is an order of the Court demanding that a person, inferior court or other body carries out a duty. It could be that a magistrates' court might refuse to hear a charge because the members of the court were in sympathy with the actions of the defendants. An order of mandamus could be obtained in such a case to require that court to hear the case and decide it on its facts, disregarding any personal views which might be held.

Prohibition This order requires an inferior court or tribunal not to do something improper.

Certiorari This order is used to quash a decision made by an inferior court or tribunal. Such an order could be made where it is alleged that the justices had an interest or a bias in a particular case.

Habeas corpus This is a writ to secure the release of a person who is unlawfully or unjustifiably detained, whether in a prison or in some private place. It is available in any case in which it is alleged that a person has been deprived of his liberty without authority.

House of Lords

This court is composed of the Lord Chancellor, ex-Lord Chancellors, Lords of Appeal in Ordinary and any other peers who hold or have held high judicial office. It is the highest court in the land and hears criminal appeals from the Court of Appeal or the Divisional Court of the Queen's Bench Division, but only where:

(a) the court has certified that a question of law of general public importance is involved; *and*
(b) the court or the House is satisfied that the point of law is one which ought to be considered by the House; *and*
(c) leave to appeal to the House has been given by the court or the House itself.

European Court

For the sake of completeness mention must be made of the Court of Justice of the European Communities. The impact on our criminal law of the law of the European Communities is limited, although growing, and is confined to matters with a 'European' element, such as controls over firearms, aliens and road transport. If at a trial or on an appeal, a question is raised as to the *interpretation* of a piece of EU law the matter can be referred to the European Court, and if the question is raised on appeal in the House of Lords it must be so referred, for a 'preliminary ruling' on the interpretation of that law. In the event of a referral the English proceedings will be postponed to await the ruling, which must be applied by the English court when it is given.

JURISDICTION OF SERVICE AUTHORITIES TO DEAL WITH CRIMINAL OFFENCES

The Acts relating to service personnel make provisions for concurrent jurisdiction in respect of civil and service courts. The only offences with which a service court cannot deal are treason, murder (including aiding, abetting, counselling or procuring suicide), manslaughter and rape. It is for the chief officer of police to decide. He should, where practicable, consult the serviceman's commanding officer before making his decision. The chief officer may also consult the Director of Public Prosecutions before making a final decision. There are certain factors which should be considered:

(a) Where the person or property of civilians is affected, the offence should normally be dealt with by a civil court; where that is not the case, it should be dealt with by a service court where it has jurisdiction.
(b) It is desirable, where possible, to avoid preventing servicemen who are about to be sent overseas from travelling with their units, especially if there are reasons to believe that the offence was committed with a view to avoiding overseas service. In most circumstances, therefore, unless the offence is serious or the service court does not have jurisdiction, proceedings should be instituted by a service court.
(c) Where the offence, whilst affecting the property of civilians, was committed on duty and amounted to a breach of that duty, or consisted of a minor assault on a civilian or minor offence against his property and was committed on service premises, it should be dealt with by the commanding officer.
(d) Difficulty and expense may be taken into account, as it would be unfair to ask witnesses to travel long distances to a service tribunal. The service court's jurisdiction does not extend beyond service personnel.

In circumstances where a serviceman and a civilian are jointly involved in the commission of an offence, the proceedings against both should take place in a civil court.

Persons who are arrested without warrant *and are charged with an offence* must be brought before a magistrates' court in accordance with the Police and Criminal Evidence Act 1984, s 46 (p 114) and this will equally apply to service personnel who have committed a criminal offence. Where it is considered that it will be desirable to have the case dealt with by a service tribunal, it may be best to apply for an adjournment. If any form of 'discharge' is granted by the civil court it may give grounds for a plea of autrefois acquit (ie be a bar to trial) before a court martial.

Where a serviceman commits a traffic offence whilst driving a service vehicle the appropriate service authority should be informed before the hearing.

CHAPTER 3

Police powers

Throughout this book, but particularly in this and the next five chapters, references are made to the Police and Criminal Evidence Act 1984; in the rest of this chapter we shall refer to it simply as the 1984 Act, and (unless otherwise indicated) reference to section numbers are to sections of the 1984 Act.

Conduct in breach or in excess of a relevant statutory or common law power may cause the police officer concerned to be liable in civil law or in criminal law. It may also render inadmissible evidence obtained as a result.

CODES OF PRACTICE

The 1984 Act required the Home Secretary to issue Codes of Practice, approved by both Houses of Parliament, to provide, within the terms of the Act, strengthened safeguards for the suspect and workable guidelines for the police. Five Codes of Practice have been issued under the 1984 Act. All were amended and re-issued in 1995 and the Search Code has since been further amended.

A police officer is liable to disciplinary proceedings for a failure to comply with any provision in one of the Codes, but such a failure does not of itself render him liable to civil or criminal proceedings (although it is admissible in such proceedings where a case is founded on some other ground). Evidence obtained in a way which involves a breach of a Code is not automatically inadmissible at the trial stage but the magistrates or judge may rule that it is inadmissible on the grounds (in the case of a confession) that it was obtained by oppression or is unreliable or (in the case of any evidence) that it poses a threat to the fairness of the proceedings. This is a matter to which we return on pp 160-161 and 170-171.

Police powers are dealt with in the following order in this chapter:

(a) powers to stop and search;
(b) powers to conduct a road check;
(c) powers to arrest without warrant;
(d) powers of entry and search in relation to an arrest;
(e) powers to search under a search warrant;
(f) general provisions on entry, search, seizure, access and retention.

POWERS TO STOP AND SEARCH

Before the 1984 Act there was no general power (ie one possessed by all constables) to stop and search for stolen goods, articles for use in offences under the Theft Act 1968 and offensive weapons. However, Acts of local application did give (to varying extents) such stop and search powers to constables in the local police force in particular circumstances. These powers were repealed by the 1984 Act, s 1 of which gives *every* constable, subject to certain requirements, a power to stop and search for stolen goods, articles for use in offences under the Theft Act 1968 and offensive weapons. There is only one power to stop and search which is not possessed by every constable; it is provided by s 6 of the Act, which gives a special power to a constable employed by 'statutory undertakers' (ie bodies authorised by statute to carry out any railway, road transport, inland navigation or harbour undertaking). Such a constable may stop, detain and search any vehicle before it leaves a goods area included in the premises of the 'statutory undertakers'. A goods area is any area used wholly or mainly for the storage or handling of goods.

Before the 1984 Act various statutes had given *every* constable the power to stop and search for particular articles, for example, controlled drugs, firearms, and game or poaching equipment. These general powers (which we deal with under the relevant offences) have not been affected by the 1984 Act. In addition, as we show at appropriate points, subsequent statutes have introduced general powers to stop and search for particular articles.

All powers to stop and search, other than the power under s 6, above, or the power under the Aviation Security Act 1982, s 27 (hijacking), are subject in their exercise to the Code of Practice for the Exercise by Police Officers of Statutory Powers of Stop and Search (hereafter referred to as the Stop and Search Code). The Code applies to all stops and searches under powers:

(a) requiring reasonable grounds for suspicion that articles unlawfully obtained or possessed are being carried;
(b) authorised under s 60 of the Criminal Justice and Public Order Act 1994, which we explain on p 35;
(c) authorised under s 13A of the Prevention of Terrorism (Temporary Provisions) Act 1989, which we explain on p 36;
(d) exercised under para 4(2) of Sch 5 to the Prevention of Terrorism (Temporary Provisions) Act 1989 (power of examining officer to stop and search a person on arrival in, or departure from, Great Britain).

The power under s 1 of the 1984 Act to stop and search

Section 1(2) of the Act states that a constable:

(a) may search any person or vehicle ('vehicle' includes vessels, aircraft and hovercraft), *and* anything which is in or on a vehicle, for stolen or prohibited articles or an article to which s 1(8A) applies; and
(b) may detain persons or vehicles for the purpose of such a search.

Section 1(3) provides that a constable only has this power to search if he has *reasonable grounds for suspecting* that he will find stolen or prohibited articles or an article to which s 1(8A) applies; he must of course have such grounds *before* carrying out a search. Reasonable force may be used in the exercise of these powers, but every effort should be made to persuade a person to co-operate and force should only be used as a last resort. A compulsory search may only be made if it is established that the person is unwilling to co-operate.

Where a police officer has reasonable grounds to suspect that a person is in innocent possession of a stolen or prohibited article, the power to stop and search exists notwithstanding that there would be no power of arrest. However, every effort should be made to secure the voluntary production of the article before the power is resorted to.

Stolen or prohibited articles

Section 1 merely empowers a constable to search a person or vehicle for stolen or prohibited articles or an article to which s 1(8A) applies if he has reasonable grounds for suspecting that he will find such articles. A 'prohibited article' is defined as:

(a) an offensive weapon (which by s 1(9) means any article made or adapted for use for causing injury to persons, or intended by the person having it with him for such use by him or by some other person); or

(b) an article made or adapted for use in the course of or in connection with an offence of burglary, theft, taking a conveyance without authority or obtaining property by deception, or intended by the person having it with him for such use by him or by some other person.

An article to which s 1(8A) applies is any article in relation to which a person has committed, or is committing or is going to commit, an offence under s 139 of the Criminal Justice Act 1988, ie an article with a blade or point.

It is interesting at this stage to examine the existing police practice of searching persons on football coaches for offensive weapons before allowing them to proceed to football grounds. Many of the articles which such persons carry will no doubt fit the description of offensive weapons, but the likely possession of those weapons must be viewed objectively. The Code makes it clear that a reasonable suspicion cannot be founded upon a person's belonging to a particular group and, unless there are particular reasons for suspecting an individual of possession of such a weapon, a search would be unlawful and, in addition, the officer would be guilty of a disciplinary offence.

Places in which powers to search can be exercised

Section 1(1) of the 1984 Act states that a constable may exercise any powers under s 1:

(a) in any place to which at the time when he proposes to exercise the power the public or any section of the public has access, on payment or otherwise, as of right or by virtue of express or implied permission; or

(b) in any other place to which people have ready access at the time when he proposes to exercise the power but which is not a dwelling.

Persons have a right to use streets and highways; they have express permission to enter cinemas, theatres or football grounds subject to paying an entry fee and they may remain there until that particular entertainment is over, when permission to be there ceases. There is an implied permission for persons to enter buildings to carry out business transactions with the owners, and even to use a footpath to a dwelling house for the purpose of paying a *lawful call* upon the householder. That implied permission remains until withdrawn by the householder or the owner of the business premises.

'Place to which people have ready access' in (b) is wide in meaning. It extends the power of search to any place (other than a dwelling) to which the public have access in fact, whether lawfully or not; for example, a private field or grounds into which people regularly gain access as trespassers.

Section 1(4) states that, if a person is in a garden or yard occupied with, and used for, the purposes of a dwelling or on other land so occupied and used, a constable may not search him under s 1 unless the constable has reasonable grounds for believing that:

(a)   he does not reside in the dwelling; and
(b)   he is not in the place in question with the express or implied permission of a person who resides in the dwelling.

Similar restrictions apply to the search of a vehicle (or anything in or on it) in such a place. By s 1(5), a constable may not search it unless he has reasonable grounds for believing that:

(a)   the person in charge of the vehicle does not reside in the dwelling; and
(b)   the vehicle is not in the place in question with the express or implied permission of a person who resides in the dwelling.

In effect, the only places in which a constable cannot exercise these powers are dwelling houses, the curtilage of dwelling houses if the person or vehicle is there lawfully, or any other place which is secure and does not permit ready access.

Seizure of articles

Section 1(6) provides that suspected stolen or prohibited articles, or an article suspected to be one to which s 1(8A) applies, found in a search may be seized.

Power under Sporting Events (Control of Alcohol etc) Act 1985 to stop and search

It is convenient at this stage to refer to related powers of search aimed at the prevention of football hooliganism which are provided by the Sporting Events (Control of Alcohol etc) Act 1985. By s 7(3) of the Act, a constable may stop a football coach or minibus containing football fans going to or from a match, and search it, if he has reasonable grounds to suspect that an offence under the Act of causing or permitting alcohol to be on the vehicle, or of possession of alcohol on it, or of drunkenness on it, is being or has been committed. A constable also has the same power under s 7(3) to search (but not to stop) a railway carriage.

The power to search under s 7(3) is limited to searching the vehicle or carriage. However, under s 7(2) a constable has a general power to search a person whom he reasonably suspects is committing or has committed an offence under the Act. This power extends not only to the offences mentioned in the previous paragraph but also to offences under the 1985 Act of possessing alcohol, a firework (or other pyrotechnic device) or a bottle or can at a football match or while entering the ground.

The offences under the 1985 Act are explained in more detail in ch 32, below.

Power to stop and search in anticipation of violence

The Criminal Justice and Public Order Act 1994, s 60 provides further powers to stop and search. It provides that where a police officer of the rank of inspector reasonably believes that:

(a) incidents involving serious violence may take place in any area in his locality, and that it is expedient to give an authorisation under the section to prevent their occurrence; or
(b) that persons are carrying dangerous instruments or offensive weapons in any locality in his police area without good reason,

he may give an authorisation that the powers conferred by the section are to be exercisable at any place within that locality for a specified period not exceeding 24 hours.

Where an inspector gives such an authorisation he must, as soon as it is reasonably practicable to do so, cause an officer of or above the rank of superintendent to be informed.

The authorisation may be extended once only for a further 24 hours on the authority of an officer of or above the rank of superintendent, where expedient, having regard to offences committed, or reasonably suspected to have been committed, in connection with the activity. Thereafter further use of the powers requires a new authorisation.

Such authorisations must be in writing and must specify the grounds on which it is given and the locality and the duration of their validity. If it is not practicable to do this at the time it must be done as soon as possible. It is for the authorising officer to determine the period of time in which he proposes to exercise these powers. It should be the minimum period he considers necessary to deal with the risk of violence.

Police powers

Where an authorisation is in force under s 60 of the 1994 Act a constable in uniform is empowered:

(a) to stop any pedestrian and search him and anything carried by him, for offensive weapons or dangerous instruments;
(b) to stop any vehicle and search the vehicle, its driver and any passenger for offensive weapons or dangerous instruments.

These stops and searches may be carried out *whether or not the constable in question* has any grounds for suspecting that the person or vehicle is carrying weapons or articles of that kind. A constable may seize any dangerous instrument or article which he has reasonable grounds for suspecting to be an offensive weapon. A 'dangerous instrument' is one which has a blade or is sharply pointed; a vehicle includes a 'caravan'; and an 'offensive weapon' is as defined by s 1(9) of the 1984 Act (see p 33). A person carries a dangerous instrument or an offensive weapon if he has it in his possession.

In addition, where an authorisation is in force under s 60 of the 1994 Act, a constable in uniform has power:

(a) to require any person to remove any item (eg a face mask) which the constable reasonably believes that person is wearing wholly or mainly for the purpose of concealing his identity;
(b) to seize any item which the constable reasonably believes any person intends to wear wholly or mainly for that purpose.

A driver of a vehicle which has been stopped is entitled to obtain a written statement to that effect, if he applies within 12 months. The same rights apply to pedestrians or a person in a vehicle.

A person who fails to stop or (as the case may be) to stop his vehicle or to remove an item worn by him when required to do so by a constable exercising these powers commits an offence. Failure to remove an item when required is an arrestable offence.

Factors for consideration

The Crimianl Justice and Public Order Act 1994, s 60 is aimed at the prevention of violence which is reasonably anticipated. Its powers therefore relate to incidents which *may take place* and it is submitted that the incidents with which the section is concerned are incidents of serious personal violence. The section refers to instruments etc which might be used in such incidents, not in incidents directed against property.

'Locality' is not defined and this was intentional, as the extent of a 'locality' will differ in relation to the nature of the incident. An anticipated serious disorder at a pub would be in a small 'locality' whilst one within a housing estate would be in an extensive 'locality'. Provided that thought has been given to defining the locality, and this can be proved, a court is unlikely to rule that the authorisation was invalid. The authorising officer should not set a geographical area which is wider than that he believes necessary for the purpose of preventing anticipated violence.

Whether or not it is expedient to give an authorisation may involve consideration of the effectiveness of other powers, and the resources available to deal with the type of incidents which may arise. Provided that such judgements are made in good faith, a court is unlikely to interfere.

Powers to stop and search for the prevention of terrorism

Sections 13A and 13B of the Prevention of Terrorism (Temporary Provisions) Act 1989 provide police officers with powers in respect of vehicles and their occupants and pedestrians respectively.

Vehicles and their occupants

By s 13A, where it appears to him that it is expedient to do so in order to prevent acts of terrorism, a police officer of or above the rank of assistant chief constable (or commander) may give an authorisation in writing that the powers set out in s 13A to stop and search vehicles and persons shall be exercisable at any place within his area, or a specified locality within his area, for a specified period not exceeding 28 days. Such an officer may, from time to time, authorise the exercise of these powers for a further period of 28 days. The officer should set the minimum period he considers necessary in the circumstances, and a geographical area no wider than is necessary.

The powers set out in s 13A which are exercisable if an authorisation is given under the section are as follows. A constable in uniform may:

(a)   stop any vehicle;

(b) search any vehicle, its driver or passenger for articles of a kind which could be used for a purpose connected with the commission, preparation or instigation of acts of terrorism.

In the exercise of these powers, the constable may stop and carry out searches whether or not he has grounds for suspecting that the particular person or vehicle is carrying such articles.

The driver of a vehicle which has been stopped is entitled to obtain a written statement to that effect if he applies within 12 months.

A constable may not require a person to remove any of his clothes in public other than any headgear, footwear, outer coat, jacket or gloves.

A person who fails to stop his vehicle when required to do so by a constable in the exercise of these powers, or who wilfully obstructs him in the exercise of these powers, commits an offence.

Pedestrians

Section 13B of the 1989 Act authorises an officer of or above the rank of assistant chief constable (or commander), where it appears to him to be expedient to do so in order to prevent acts of terrorism, to give an authorisation that the powers to stop and search persons conferred by the section shall be exercisable at a place specified in that authorisation. Those powers are to stop any pedestrian and to search him, or anything carried by him, for articles of a kind which could be used for a purpose connected with the commission, preparation or instigation of acts of terrorism. The constable does not need to have grounds for suspecting the presence of such articles before exercising his powers. The requirement to remove clothing in public must be limited to headgear, footwear, outer coat, jacket or gloves. An offence is committed by a person who fails to stop for a constable exercising these powers or who wilfully obstructs such a constable.

A person stopped by a constable under this section shall be entitled to obtain a written statement that he was stopped under these powers if he applies for such a statement within 12 months.

Reasonable suspicion

The Stop and Search Code gives the following guidance on what may be 'reasonable suspicion' for the purposes of the 1989 Act s 1 and of other statutory powers of stop and search which require a reasonable suspicion.

Whether reasonable grounds for suspicion exist will depend on the circumstances in each case, but there must be some objective basis for it. An officer will need to consider the nature of the article suspected of being carried in the context of other factors such as the time and the place, and the behaviour of the person concerned or those with him. Reasonable suspicion may exist, for example, where information has been received such as a description of an article being carried or of a suspected offender; where a person is seen acting covertly or warily or attempting to hide something; or where a person is seen carrying a certain type of article at an unusual time or in a place where a number of burglaries or thefts are known to have taken place recently. But the decision to stop and search must be based on all of the facts which bear on the likelihood that an article of a certain kind will be found.

For example, reasonable suspicion may be based upon reliable information or intelligence which indicates that members of a particular group or gang, or their associates, habitually carry knives unlawfully or weapons or controlled drugs.

Subject to what is said below, reasonable suspicion can never be supported on the basis of personal factors alone without supporting intelligence or information. For example, a person's colour, age, hairstyle or manner of dress, or the fact that he is known to have a previous conviction for possession of an unlawful article, cannot be used alone or in combination with each other as the sole basis upon which to search that person. Nor may it be founded on the basis of stereotyped images of certain persons or groups as more likely to be committing offences.

However, where there is reliable information or intelligence that members of a group or gang who habitually carry knives unlawfully or weapons or controlled drugs, and wear a distinctive item of clothing or other means of identification to indicate membership of it, the members may be identified by means of that distinctive item of clothing or other means of identification. Other means of identification might include jewellery, insignias, tattoos or other features which are known to identify members of the particular gang or group.

It is important to ensure that powers of stop and search are used responsibly by those who exercise them or authorise their use. An officer should bear in mind that he may be required to justify the use of the powers to a senior officer and in court, and also that misuse of the powers is likely to be harmful to the police effort in the long term and can lead to mistrust of the police by the community. Regardless of the power exercised all police officers should be careful to ensure that the selection and treatment of those questioned and searched is based upon objective factors and not upon personal prejudice. It is also particularly important to ensure that any person searched is treated courteously and considerately.

The guidance in the Stop and Search Code on what might be 'reasonable suspicion' has been stated fully because of its importance to police officers. The issue of whether or not an officer had reasonable grounds for suspecting possession of stolen or prohibited articles will frequently arise, and, as we have indicated already, failure to observe the provisions of the Code is a disciplinary offence, quite regardless of any other liability which might arise. The important factor is that the issue will be judged objectively in the light of the knowledge which was available to the police officer when he made his decision. This may be a description given to the officer when briefed for duty of a person suspected of offences. However, such a general description of a person would not allow a search by itself; the officer would have to apply his mind to the circumstances surrounding the particular person under observation. The fact that such person appeared to be seeking an opportunity to commit a similar type of crime might reinforce suspicion sufficiently to satisfy the objective test.

Again, although information received from a member of the public may constitute a basis for reasonable suspicion, whether it actually does so depends on the content and nature of the information as well as the credibility of the informant. If the manager of a filling station tells a police officer that a man, of whom he gives a description, stole two cartons of cigarettes from the kiosk before driving off in a green Escort which was damaged on the front offside wing, the issue is fairly clear. If the officer sees an Escort of that description, driven by a man of the description given by the station manager, he may accept that the information which he was given was clear and that it was given by a reliable witness. He may reasonably act upon that information since it provides him with the necessary reasonable suspicion.

The Stop and Search Code does not affect the ability of an officer to speak to or question a person in the ordinary course of his duties (and in the absence of reasonable suspicion) without detaining him or exercising any element of compulsion. It is not the purpose of the Code to prohibit such encounters between the police and the community with the co-operation of the person concerned and neither does it affect the principle that all citizens have a duty to help police officers to prevent crime and discover offenders.

Nothing in the Stop and Search Code affects:

(a) the routine searching of persons entering sports grounds or other premises with their consent or as a condition of entry. The last phrase is concerned with the right of the proprietors of sports grounds etc to make entry to the ground conditional upon a would-be entrant submitting to a search. It is submitted that, if this is done, the search should be carried out by someone other than a police officer, even if the proprietors are paying for the services of the officer. It is no part of a police officer's duty to enforce the rights of proprietors of sports grounds etc;

(b) the ability of an officer to search a person in the street with his consent where no search power exists. In those circumstances, an officer should always make it clear that he is seeking the consent of the person concerned to the search being carried out by telling the person that he need not consent and that without his consent he will not be searched.

If an officer acts in an improper manner this invalidates a voluntary search. Juveniles, persons suffering from a mental handicap or mental disorder and others who appear not to be capable of giving an informed consent should not be subject to a voluntary search.

Factors to be considered before carrying out a search

Section 2(1) of the 1984 Act provides that, if a constable detains a person or vehicle in the exercise of the power under s 1 or any similar power to stop and search, he need not subsequently carry out that search if it appears to him that no search is required or that a search is impracticable. These circumstances will frequently arise: a person will often be detained on valid grounds for the purpose of a search and then satisfy the constable of his bona fides by answering his questions, or because of other circumstances which come to the attention of the officer. In such a case it is unnecessary to search and the detention will not be unlawful merely because the search was not carried out.

The Stop and Search Code additionally points out that there is no power to detain a person against his will in order to find grounds for a search.

Procedure before carrying out a search

The following procedure is provided by s 2(2) to (5) of the 1984 Act and the Stop and Search Code. Before a search of a detained person or attended vehicle takes place the officer must take reasonable steps to give the person to be searched or in charge of the vehicle the following information:

(a) his name and the name of the police station to which he is attached;
(b) the object of the search; and
(c) his grounds or authorisation for making it.

If the inquiries are linked to the investigation of terrorism, the officer must give his warrant number or other identification number and not his name. If the officer is not in uniform he must show his warrant card. In doing so in the course of terrorism inquiries, he need not reveal his name.

Unless it appears to the officer that it will not be practicable to make a record of the search (in a multiple situation perhaps), he must also state that a person who has been searched (or the owner or person in charge of a vehicle that has been searched, as the case may be) is entitled to a copy of the record of the search if he asks for it within one year. If a person wishes to have a copy and is not given one on the spot, he should be advised to apply to the officer's police station.

If the person to be searched, or in charge of a vehicle to be searched, does not understand what is being said, or there is any doubt about his ability to understand English, the officer must take reasonable steps to bring the information required to his attention. If that person is deaf or cannot understand English and has someone with him, the officer must establish whether that person can interpret or otherwise help him to give the required information.

Conduct of search

Every reasonable effort must be made to minimise the embarrassment that a person being searched may experience. By s 2(8) a person may be detained for a search for such time as is reasonably required to permit a search to be carried out either at the place where the person or vehicle was first detained or nearby.

The co-operation of the person to be searched must always be sought, even if he initially objects to being searched. A forcible search may be made only if it has been established that the person is unwilling to co-operate (eg by opening a bag) or resists. Reasonable force may be used as a last resort, but only if this is necessary to detain the person or to search him. The length of time for which a person or vehicle may be detained will depend on the circumstances, but it must be reasonable and not extend beyond the time taken for the search.

The Stop and Search Code advises that, where the exercise of the power requires reasonable suspicion, the extent of the search will be related to the nature of the article sought and the circumstances. If a person is seen to put an offensive weapon into a particular pocket, then, unless there are grounds for suspecting that it has been moved elsewhere, the search must be confined to that pocket; whereas, if the article sought may easily be concealed anywhere on the person, the search may have to be more thorough.

The term 'nearby' in s 2(8) is not defined but it is submitted that it should be interpreted quite narrowly. To move a vehicle from a congested spot into a side street, or a person from the public gaze into an alley, would be a reasonable action to take and would not prevent the search from being 'nearby'.

An officer who is not in uniform may not stop a vehicle for the purpose of a search.

Removal of clothing

A constable is not authorised under s 1 of the 1984 Act, or under any other power of stop and search, to *require* a person to remove any of his clothing in public other than an outer coat, jacket or gloves. However, there is nothing to prevent a constable from asking a person to remove more than outer clothing in public.

The Stop and Search Code restricts searches in public to a 'superficial examination of outer clothing'. If, on reasonable grounds, a more extensive search is considered necessary (eg by requiring a person to take off a T-shirt or headgear) it must be done out of view of the public, for example in a police van or a police station if there is one nearby. Any search involving more than the removal of an outer coat, jacket or gloves, headgear or footwear, may only be made by an officer of the same sex and may not be made in the presence of anyone of the opposite sex unless the person being searched specifically requests it. Every reasonable effort must be made to reduce the embarrassment caused.

A search in a street itself should be regarded as being in public, even though the street is empty at the time the search begins. As a search of a person in public should be a superficial examination of outer clothing, such searches should be completed as soon as possible.

Record of search

A constable who has carried out a search under s 1 of the 1984 Act, or under any other power of stop and search, is required by s 3 to make a record of it in writing, unless it is not practicable to do so (as where a large number of searches are quickly required or where operational reasons, such as public disorder, dictate otherwise). Leaving aside this exception, the record must be made as soon as practicable; on the spot unless circumstances (such as other immediate duties or very bad weather) make this impracticable, and it must be made on the form provided for this purpose (the national search record). Section 3 states that the record must include a note of the person's name, if the constable knows it, but the person must not be detained merely to find out his name. If the constable does not know the name, a description should be included in the record. If a vehicle is searched, the record must include a description of it. A record is required for each person and each vehicle searched, except that, if a person is in a vehicle and both are searched for the same reason, only one record need be made.

It must be stressed that, although the record form has sections which require a name, address and date of birth, there is no obligation upon such a person to provide such information and that he may not be detained whilst such checks are made.

The following information should always be included in the record of a search even if the person does not wish to identify himself or give his date of birth:

(a) the name of the person searched, or (if he withholds it) a description of him;
(b) a note of the person's ethnic origin;
(c) where a vehicle is searched, a description of it, including its registration number;
(d) the object of the search;
(e) the grounds for making it (ie the reason for suspecting the person or the authority for search, depending on the power being used);
(f) the date and time it was made;
(g) the place where it was made;
(h) its results;
(i) a note of any injury or damage to property resulting from it; and
(j) the identity of the officers making it (except in the case of inquiries linked to an investigation into terrorism, when the warrant or other identification number and duty station of the officer(s) should be recorded).

Unattended vehicles

If an unattended vehicle, or anything in or on such a vehicle, is searched the constable is required by s 2(6) of the 1984 Act to leave a notice:

(a)   stating that he has searched it;
(b)   giving the name of the police station to which he is attached;
(c)   stating where any application for compensation should be directed; and
(d)   stating where a copy of the search record may be obtained.

A vehicle which has been searched must, if practicable, be left secure. The notice must be left inside the vehicle if this can be done without damaging the vehicle. The Stop and Search Code allows variations to permit provision of a different address for matters of compensation and receipt of search record.

POWERS TO CONDUCT A ROAD CHECK

Statutory power

Section 4 of the 1984 Act governs the conduct of road checks by police officers for the purpose of ascertaining whether a vehicle is carrying:

(a)   a person who has committed an offence other than a road traffic offence or a vehicle excise offence;
(b)   a person who is a witness to such an offence;
(c)   a person intending to commit such an offence; or
(d)   a person unlawfully at large.

For the purposes of the section, a 'road check' consists of the exercise in a locality of the power conferred by the Road Traffic Act 1988, s 163 (power of a constable to stop a mechanically propelled vehicle or pedal cycle on a road, see Sch 9) in such a way as to stop all vehicles or vehicles selected by any criterion.

The section is mainly concerned with setting up road checks to arrest actual or intending criminals or escaping prisoners. The purpose of the check will be to stop all vehicles or selected vehicles. It may be that the person the officers are seeking to arrest is known to be in a black Ford Escort car and therefore only vehicles similar to that description will be stopped. It does not in any way affect an officer's powers to deal with road traffic matters and he may stop as many vehicles as he thinks necessary for that purpose. As the definition requires the stopping of a multiple of vehicles, an officer who wishes to stop a single vehicle, which he reasonably suspects may be carrying a person who has committed or intends to commit an offence etc, may do so under the powers given by the Road Traffic Act 1988, s 163, which are unaffected in such circumstances.

Authorisation of road checks

A road check must be authorised in writing by an officer of the rank of superintendent or above. Section 4 limits the instances in which authorisation may be given, as follows:

(a)   if the commission of an offence, or the intention to commit an offence is involved, the officer must have reasonable grounds for believing that the offence is a serious arrestable offence (see p 61) and for suspecting that the person is, or is about to be, in the locality of the proposed check;
(b)   if it is to trace a witness to an offence, the officer must have reasonable grounds for believing that the offence is a serious arrestable offence; and

(c) if it is to arrest a person who is unlawfully at large, the officer must have reasonable grounds for suspecting that the person is, or is about to be, in that locality.

Section 4 recognises that there will be emergencies in which it will not be practicable to obtain the authorisation of a superintendent in sufficient time for a road check to be effective. In such circumstances, authorisation may be given by an officer below the rank of superintendent, but the officer who authorises in such circumstances must, as soon as practicable:

(a) make a written record of the time of authorisation; and
(b) cause a superintendent (or above) to be informed.

The superintendent (or above) may then authorise, in writing, the road check to continue. If he decides it should not continue, he must record the fact that it took place, and its purpose (including the relevant serious arrestable offence).

Time limits, records and searches

The maximum period for which a road check may be authorised is seven days, but written authorisation may be given for a further period not exceeding seven days if a superintendent (or above) believes that a road check ought to continue.

The authorisation may be for a road check to be carried out throughout the 24 hours of each day, or may be limited to specified times.

The record (ie written authorisation) which must be kept of a road check will show:

(a) the period during which the road check is authorised to continue;
(b) the name of the officer who authorised it;
(c) the purpose of the road check (including any relevant serious arrestable offence); and
(d) the locality in which vehicles are to be stopped.

The person in charge of a vehicle stopped in a road check is entitled to obtain a written statement of the purpose of the road check if he applies for such a statement within 12 months. It is only the purpose which needs to be stated in such a notice.

The Act does not give direct powers to a constable to search a vehicle stopped in a road check. However, he is empowered to do so:

(a) if he has reasonable grounds for suspecting that it contains stolen or prohibited articles (s 1); or
(b) for the purpose of arresting someone for an arrestable offence if he has reasonable grounds to suspect that the person is there (s 17); or
(c) under powers granted by any other statute, eg the Firearms Act 1968.

Common law powers

The power under s 4 does not affect or replace the existing common law power to set up road checks in relation to apprehended breaches of the peace. This common law power, which depends upon the immediacy of the threatened breach of the peace, was clarified in 1984 by the Divisional Court in a case concerning the stopping of vehicles carrying striking miners to picket lines. One of the judges expressed the relevant law in the following words:

'If the police on reasonable grounds believe that a breach of the peace may be committed, the police officer is not only entitled but under a duty to take reasonable steps to prevent that breach occurring. Provided they honestly and reasonably form the opinion that there is *a real risk of a breach of the peace in the sense that it is in close proximity both in time and place*, then the conditions exist for reasonable preventive action. The possibility of a breach must be real to justify preventive action. The imminence or immediacy of the threat to the peace determines what action is reasonable.'

Having stopped the vehicle under this power, the police may also search it thereunder. Anyone who insists on continuing his journey is liable to arrest under the common law power to arrest for an apprehended breach of the peace (see p 51).

Clearly, where the imminent breach of the peace would involve the commission of a serious arrestable offence a road check can be operated either under s 4 or under the common law power. The procedural safeguards laid down for s 4 road checks do not, of course, apply to those under the common law power.

Prevention of terrorism: police cordons and prohibitions or restrictions of parking

Sections 16C and 16D of the Prevention of Terrorism (Temporary Provisions) Act 1989 provide powers to impose a police cordon and to prohibit or restrict parking. Section 16C permits an officer of at least the rank of superintendent, where he considers it expedient to do so in connection with an investigation into the commission, preparation or instigation of an act of terrorism, to authorise a cordon to be imposed on an area specified by him in that authorisation. (An officer below that rank may do so where there is great urgency.) Schedule 6A to the 1989 Act provides that the area on which a cordon is imposed must, so far as is reasonably practicable, be indicated by means of police tape or in such other manner as appears to the police officer responsible for carrying out the arrangements for applying the cordon to be appropriate. The area concerned will be specified in the authorisation. The period of time initially specified must not exceed 14 days, but may be extended by a superintendent (or above) by one or more written variations but the overall period must not exceed 28 days. Persons (whether in premises or not) must leave the area when ordered to do so by a constable in uniform and drivers or persons in charge of vehicles must move them out of the area (a constable has power to remove such vehicles). A constable in uniform may prohibit or restrict vehicular or pedestrian access to a cordoned area. Offences are committed by those who do not comply with the constable's requirements under the Schedule. The Schedule also gives a superintendent power to issue an authority to search premises wholly or partly within the cordoned area.

Section 16D permits a police officer of or above the rank of assistant chief constable (or commander), where it appears to him to be expedient in order to prevent acts of terrorism, to give an authorisation to any constable to prohibit or restrict the leaving of vehicles, or their remaining at rest, on a specified road or part of a road. This is to be done by the placing of traffic signs. Such an authorisation may remain in force for a period not exceeding 28 days, but this may be extended by further periods not exceeding 28 days.

Persons who fail to move vehicles when ordered to do so by a constable commit offences, as do those who park in contravention of such a prohibition or restriction. The section provides defences for those who prove that they had lawful authority or some other reasonable excuse. Those with current disabled persons' badges are not exempt from these requirements and have no lawful authority or reasonable excuse for failure to comply on those grounds. The powers to impose these restrictions are additional to any other powers available to a constable.

VOLUNTARY ATTENDANCE AT POLICE STATION

Section 29 of the 1984 Act deals with persons 'assisting the police with their inquiries' (or, as it describes them, those in voluntary attendance at a police station for the purpose of assisting with an investigation). It provides that, where, for the purpose of assisting with an investigation, a person attends voluntarily at a police station or at any other place where a constable is present, or accompanies a constable to a police station or any other place without having been arrested, he is entitled to leave at will unless he is placed under arrest. In addition he must be informed at once that he is under arrest if a decision is taken to prevent him leaving at will. The Detention Code goes further, requiring that at any stage at which a person voluntarily attending is cautioned, the officer must tell him that he is not under arrest and is free to leave and must remind him of his right to free legal advice. The police should assist a 'volunteer' who asks how he should go about obtaining such advice.

POWERS TO ARREST WITHOUT WARRANT

An arrest may be authorised by a warrant issued by a justice of the peace. The law relating to the issue and execution of warrants has already been explained.

We are concerned here with the circumstances in which an arrest may lawfully be made without a warrant, and we shall deal with this matter in the following order:

(a)   arrestable offences;
(b)   offences for which there is a specific statutory power of arrest; and
(c)   other offences.

Arrestable offences

Definition

The term 'arrestable offence' is defined in s 24(1) as being:

(a)   an offence for which the sentence is fixed by law (essentially murder); or
(b)   an offence for which a person of 21 years of age or over (not previously convicted) may be sentenced to imprisonment for a term of five years (or might be so sentenced but for the restrictions imposed in relation to minor cases of criminal damage by s 33 of the Magistrates' Courts Act 1980);
(c)   an offence to which s 24(2) applies.

Examples of arrestable offences under (b) above are manslaughter, rape, indecent assaults, offences involving wounding or grievous bodily harm, theft, robbery, burglary, offences under the Theft Acts involving deception, blackmail and handling stolen goods.

Section 24(2) declares that certain offences are arrestable although they do not come within the provisions set out in (a) or (b). The offences to which this subsection applies are:

(a) offences for which a person may be arrested under the Customs and Excise Acts, as defined in the Customs and Excise Management Act 1979, s 1(1) (viz that Act and a series of other 1979 Acts);

(b) offences under the Official Secrets Act 1920 that are not arrestable offences by virtue of the term of imprisonment for which a person may be sentenced in respect to them;

(c) offences under any provisions of the Official Secrets Act 1989, except ss 8(1), (4) or (5);

(d) offences under the Sexual Offences Act 1956, ss 22 (causing prostitution of a woman) or 23 (procuration of girl under 21);

(e) offences under the Theft Act 1968, ss 12(1) (taking motor vehicle or other conveyance without authority etc) or 25(1) (going equipped for stealing etc);

(f) any offence under the Football (Offences) Act 1991;

(g) an offence under the Public Order Act 1986, s 19 (publishing etc material intended or likely to stir up racial hatred);

(h) an offence under the Obscene Publications Act 1959, s 2 (publication, or possession with a view to publication for gain, of obscene articles);

(i) an offence under the Protection of Children Act 1978, s 1 (taking or making etc indecent photographs or pseudo-photographs of children);

(j) an offence under the Criminal Justice and Public Order Act 1994, s 166 or s 167 (football ticket touting and car hire services touting, respectively);

(k) an offence under the Prevention of Crime Act 1953, s 1(1) (prohibiting the carrying of offensive weapons without lawful authority or reasonable excuse);

(l) an offence under the Criminal Justice Act 1988, s 139(1) (offence of having article with blade or point in public place);

(m) an offence under the Criminal Justice Act 1988, s 139A(1) or (2) (offence of having article with blade or point (or offensive weapon) on school premises);

(n) an offence under the Criminal Justice and Public Order Act 1994, s 60(8)(b) (failure to comply with request to remove a face mask);

(o) an offence under the Football Spectators Act 1989, s 16(4) (failure to report in compliance with a restriction order);

(p) an offence under the Protection from Harassment Act 1997, s 2 (harassment);

(q) an offence under the Crime and Disorder Act 1998, s 32(1)(a) (racially-aggravated harassment).

The powers of arrest without warrant conferred in respect of arrestable offences also apply to the offences of:

(a) conspiracy to commit any arrestable offence;

(b) attempting to commit any such offence other than an offence under the Theft Act 1968, s 12 (1) or any other offence in s 24(2) which is only triable summarily;

(c) inciting, aiding, abetting, counselling or procuring any such offence.

These offences are deemed to be arrestable offences for the purposes of the 1984 Act.

Powers to arrest without warrant

Section 24(4) and (5) of the 1984 Act provides that any person may arrest without a warrant:

(a) anyone who is *in the act of committing* an arrestable offence; and

(b) anyone whom he has reasonable grounds for suspecting *to be committing* such an offence;

and that where an arrestable offence *has been committed*, any person may arrest without a warrant:

(a) anyone who is guilty of the offence; and
(b) anyone whom he has reasonable grounds for suspecting to be guilty of it.

It is important to note that an arrest, purportedly on the basis that an arrestable offence has been committed, will not be covered by the latter provision—and will be unlawful—not only if it transpires that no actus reus of such an offence has ever been committed but also if it transpires that, while an actus reus was committed, the actor lacked the required mens rea for the offence.

Section 24(6) and (7) provides further powers to a *constable* to arrest without a warrant as follows:

(a) where a constable has reasonable grounds for suspecting that an arrestable offence has been committed, he may arrest without a warrant anyone whom he has reasonable grounds for suspecting to be guilty of the offence;
(b) a constable may arrest without a warrant anyone who is about to commit an arrestable offence; and
(c) a constable may arrest without a warrant anyone whom he has reasonable grounds for suspecting to be about to commit an arrestable offence.

These provisions are difficult to recall until applied to practical circumstances. It is reasonable that all citizens should be allowed to arrest persons who are actually found committing, or are reasonably suspected to be in the act of committing, an arrestable offence. It would be quite ridiculous to require citizens to ignore such offences which were being committed. In the same way, if a person's house has been burgled and he finds someone hiding in the garden in suspicious circumstances with property concealed nearby, it would be unrealistic to deny him the power to arrest in such circumstances. He knows that an arrestable offence has been committed and has clear grounds for suspecting the particular person to be guilty of it. The situation changes in circumstances in which a person is merely observed to be acting suspiciously when there is no knowledge that a particular arrestable offence has been committed. In such a case, it is sensible to restrict to constables the power to arrest on reasonable suspicion that an arrestable offence has been or is about to be committed, particularly since constables are trained to observe, question and apply their minds to circumstances which might amount to 'reasonable suspicion'.

There may be grounds for arresting a suspect on the sole basis of the word of an informant but any police officer should treat that information with considerable reserve.

The term 'reasonable grounds for suspecting' means honest belief founded on grounds which would lead an ordinary cautious person to the conclusion that the person arrested was guilty. As in the case of most other police powers where phrases like 'reasonable grounds for suspecting' or 'reasonably suspects' are used, it is not enough that such reasonable grounds for suspicion exist; the constable must actually suspect the matter in question. In a recent case, the House of Lords considered the term 'reasonable grounds for suspicion' in relation to terrorist offences, where the arresting officer's suspicion was formed as a result of a briefing which had been given to him by his superior officer. It held that, although an officer could not have a reasonable suspicion simply because he had been instructed to arrest someone, a reasonable suspicion need not be based on the constable's own observations. It could be based on what he had been told, or on information given to him (even anonymously). Thus, a reasonable suspicion could be derived from the information given at the briefing. The answer to the question of whether there was a reasonable suspicion does not require a court to look beyond what was in the constable's mind at the time of the arrest. The issue was not whether he thought his suspicions were reasonable but whether a reasonable person looking at all the circumstances and what was in the constable's mind would think that his suspicions were reasonable.

The purpose of an arrest in these circumstances is to make a person answerable to a charge. Consequently, if a person who has been arrested on reasonable suspicion that he has committed an arrestable offence is able to prove that the arresting officer knew, at the time of the arrest, that there was no possibility of a charge being made, the arrest will be held unlawful because the arresting officer will have acted for an improper purpose. Thus, for example, arrests should not be made to teach a person a lesson where it is known that there is no possibility of a charge. On the other hand, there is no reason why an arrest should not be made for the purpose of interviewing a person reasonably suspected of committing an arrestable offence, in the hope of obtaining a confession, as in such a case the possibility of a charge still exists.

Specific statutory power of arrest

Section 26 of the 1984 Act repealed all previous statutory powers to arrest (including those provided by local Acts) with two exceptions. First, certain powers were specifically retained viz:

(a) the arrest of absentees and deserters from HM Forces and Visiting Forces;
(b) the arrest of persons under emergency powers or terrorism legislation;
(c) the arrest of persons who are absent from places of detention or who have broken bail;
(d) the arrest of trespassers on some military lands;
(e) the arrest of persons reasonably suspected of being guilty of offences relating to entering and remaining on property contrary to the Criminal Law Act 1977, ss 6 to 10;
(f) the arrest of persons reasonably suspected of committing offences of drinking and driving and driving whilst disqualified;
(g) the arrest of persons reasonably suspected of committing offences contrary to the Public Order Act 1936, s 1 (prohibited uniforms); and
(h) the arrest at the direction of the presiding officer at a polling station of persons suspected of personation.

Second, it has been held by the Divisional Court that, because s 26 conflicts with another provision in the 1984 Act in this respect, a constable's power under the Criminal Justice Act 1967, s 91(1) to arrest a person for the offence of being drunk and disorderly in a public place has not been repealed by s 26.

Further statutory powers to arrest persons reasonably suspected of committing one of a number of offences under the Public Order Act 1986 have since been provided by that Act. The 1986 Act also added a similar power to arrest for offences contrary to the Trade Union and Labour Relations (Consolidation) Act 1992, s 241. The Football Spectators Act 1989, s 2(4) empowers a constable to arrest a person on reasonable suspicion of committing the offence of unauthorisedly entering, or remaining at, a designated football match. By the Crime (Sentences) Act 1997, s 18, a constable may arrest without warrant any person whom he reasonably suspects has committed an offence under s 17 of that Act (breach of conditions of release supervision order).

Other offences – power to arrest without warrant

The power to arrest for offences other than arrestable offences, or those specified in the last paragraph, is provided by s 25 of the 1984 Act, which states:

'Where a constable has reasonable grounds for suspecting that any offence which is not an arrestable offence has been committed or attempted or is being committed or attempted, he may arrest the relevant person if it appears to him that service of a summons is impracticable or inappropriate because any of the general arrest conditions is satisfied.'

Section 25 is helpful to those charged with the responsibility for law enforcement. Most police officers in service before the 1984 Act will have experienced situations in which they attempted to deal with a person who had committed an offence for which there was no power to arrest, and who was uncooperative and refused to provide his name and address or gave a name and address which the officer could not accept as being correct. The absence of a power to arrest in such circumstances was a peculiar omission.

The section refers to a constable arresting a 'relevant person' and this means any person whom the constable has reasonable grounds to suspect of having committed or having attempted to commit the offence, or of being in the course of committing or attempting to commit it.

As indicated above, a 'relevant person' may be arrested if it appears to the constable that the service of a summons is impracticable or inappropriate because any of the *general arrest conditions* are satisfied. The general arrest conditions are set out by s 25(3):

(a) that the name of the relevant person is unknown to, and cannot be ascertained by, the constable;
(b) that the constable has reasonable grounds for doubting whether the name furnished by the relevant person as his name is his real name;
(c) that—
   (i) the relevant person has failed to furnish a satisfactory address for service; or
   (ii) the constable has reasonable grounds for doubting whether the address furnished by the relevant person is a satisfactory address for service;
(d) that the constable has reasonable grounds for believing that arrest is necessary to prevent the relevant person—
   (i) causing physical injury to himself or any other person;
   (ii) suffering physical injury;
   (iii) causing loss of or damage to property;
   (iv) committing an offence against public decency; or
   (v) causing an unlawful obstruction of the highway; or
(e) that the constable has reasonable grounds for believing that arrest is necessary to protect a child or other vulnerable person from the relevant person.

These general arrest conditions merely follow a reasonable and common sense process of thought. An arrest may be made without warrant if the person is not known to the constable and his identity cannot readily be ascertained; or if the constable has reasonable grounds for doubting whether a name furnished is the real name; or if a satisfactory address for service of a summons has not been established; or if the constable has reasonable grounds for believing that the arrest is necessary to prevent injury or harm, an offence against public decency, or unlawful obstruction of the highway; or if the constable has reasonable grounds for believing that the arrest is necessary for the protection of children or vulnerable persons. On each of these occasions an arrest is necessary to prevent someone escaping the consequences of his unlawful act or to prevent harm, damage or the like.

Paragraph (c) of the general arrest conditions refers to a 'satisfactory address' for the service of a summons. This need not be the relevant person's own address. Section 25 provides that an address is satisfactory if it appears to the constable that the relevant person will be at it for a sufficiently long period of time for it to be possible to serve him with a summons, or that some other person specified by the relevant person will accept service of the summons for the relevant person at that address. The arrest of the driver of a foreign goods vehicle will not be justified under s 25 if that driver can provide a satisfactory address at which he may subsequently be found (perhaps on his next trip) or if he provides the name and address of some person who will accept service on his behalf.

Section 25(5) also provides that an arrest is not authorised under para (d) on the basis of preventing the relevant person committing an offence against public decency, unless members of the public going about their normal business cannot reasonably be expected to avoid the person arrested.

A police officer must consider carefully the necessity to arrest when deciding whether or not to do so. Not every refusal to provide a name and address at the officer's first request necessitates an arrest. Such a refusal should be followed by an explanation of the consequences of a continued refusal to provide an identity and an address which the officer believes to be true, and only if there is a continued refusal to provide such an identity and address should the arrest be made. However, the Divisional Court has accepted that where a person, whose name was unknown to a constable, was reasonably suspected by the constable of having committed an offence, these requirements are satisfied by the questions, 'What is your name?' and 'What is your address?', followed by a refusal to answer. In the event of refusal to answer, the offender should be told that he is being arrested in relation to the particular offence *and* for refusing to give his name and address. If an arrest is made, s 30 of the Act requires that a person arrested by a constable at a place other than a police station must be released if a constable is satisfied, before the person arrested reaches a police station, that there are no grounds for keeping him under arrest. It follows that, should an arrest be made on the grounds that a satisfactory name and address have not been provided but they are subsequently provided (or the person is identified in some other way), the arrested person must be instantly released. A record of such a release must be made as soon as practicable after the release.

As a result of s 25, the itinerant dealer who commits offences against the Road Traffic Acts may now be arrested and dealt with if he is unable to establish his identity or a satisfactory address at which a summons may be served. A person who is found to be in possession of offensive weapons (other than those in respect of which a specific power of arrest already lies under the Prevention of Crime Act 1953 or the Criminal Justice Act 1988) may be arrested if he is unable to establish his identity or a satisfactory address, or if the constable has reasonable grounds to believe that the arrest is necessary to prevent him causing physical injury to someone or damage to property. Although the constable may exercise his right to seize such an offensive weapon at the time, the conduct or declared intention of the relevant person may be such that the constable may reasonably form the belief that such person is still likely to injure someone unless arrested.

The power to arrest where it is necessary to prevent a person causing an unlawful obstruction to the highway is essential to the peace-keeping process because of the general tendency for protesters to obstruct highways for particular reasons. It must be stressed that this power, together with the other powers set out at (d) and (e) in s 25(3) of the 1984 Act is applicable even though the identity and address of the person concerned are known.

Power to arrest at common law

At common law a police officer or anyone else has power to arrest without warrant in certain circumstances, and this power is not affected by the 1984 Act. The common law power exists:

(a) where a breach of the peace is committed by the person arrested in the presence of the person making the arrest; or

(b) where no breach of the peace has occured in the presence of the person making the arrest, but he reasonably believes that such a breach by the person arrested is about to occur or is imminent; he will not have such a belief if there is no real and present threat to the peace.

We define 'breach of the peace' on p 604.

These common law powers of arrest are important to police officers. They are in no way restricted by the nature of the place in which the breach of the peace occurs or is anticipated. The arrest within the above terms is a preventative measure and should be effected wherever it is necessary to preserve the peace; even on private premises and even if no member of the public is present. If two men are fighting, that is a breach of the peace regardless of all other considerations and an arrest by anyone who sees it occur is justified. It may be that the stage at which a fight actually occurs has not been reached but a constable reasonably believes that it will occur in the immediate future; in such a case he may arrest those in dispute. Likewise, where an actual fight may have been discontinued but a constable reasonably believes that the argument is not at an end and that the fight is likely to be resumed, and a breach of the peace occur, an arrest is justified.

Once a constable reasonably foresees a breach of the peace, he is entitled to remain on premises in which, until that time, he has been a trespasser.

Cross-border powers to arrest

The Criminal Justice and Public Order Act 1994, s 137 provides that, where:

(a) a suspected offence is an arrestable offence; or

(b) in the case of any other offence, it appears to a constable that service of a summons is impracticable or inappropriate for any of the reasons specified in s 138(3) (which are the general arrest conditions set out in the 1984 Act, see p 49),

a constable of an English or Welsh police force who has reasonable grounds for suspecting that such an offence has been committed or attempted in England and Wales and that the suspected person is in Scotland or Northern Ireland, may arrest without warrant the suspected person wherever he is in Scotland or Northern Ireland. Scottish officers and those of the Royal Ulster Constabulary have similar powers within England and Wales.

Where a person is arrested in Scotland or Northern Ireland under this power, he must be taken to the nearest convenient designated police station in England or Wales or to a designated police station in the police area where the offence is being investigated. This must be done as soon as reasonably practicable.

Arrest without warrant for fingerprinting

Section 27 of the 1984 Act permits a constable to arrest without warrant a person who fails to comply with a requirement for fingerprinting made under that section. Section 27 provides that if a person:

(a) has been convicted of a recordable offence, ie an offence conviction for which is recorded in national police records;
(b) has not at any time been in police detention for an offence; and
(c) has not had his fingerprints taken in the course of an investigation of the offence or since the conviction,

any constable may at any time not later than one month after the date of the conviction require him to attend at a police station in order that his fingerprints may be taken. The requirement must give the person a period of at least seven days within which he must attend, and may direct him to attend at a specified time of day or between specified times of day.

A constable may arrest without warrant a person who has failed to comply with such a requirement.

The following offences are recordable:

(a)   any offence punishable with imprisonment;
(b)   loitering or soliciting for the purposes of prostitution (Street Offences Act 1959, s 1)
(c)   improper use of public telecommunications system (Telecommunications Act 1984);
(d)   tampering with a motor vehicle (Road Traffic Act 1988, s 25);
(e)   sending letters etc with intent to cause distress or anxiety (Malicious Communications Act 1988, s 1);
(f)   offences of giving intoxicating liquor to a child under five, exposing children under 12 to risk of burning, failing to provide for safety of children at entertainments (Children and Young Persons Act 1933, ss 5, 11 and 12);
(g)   drunkenness in a public place (Criminal Justice Act 1967, s 91);
(h)   failing to deliver up authority to possess prohibited weapon or ammunition, possession of assembled shotgun by unsupervised person under 15, possession of air weapon or ammunition for air weapon by unsupervised person under 14, possession of air weapon in public place by unsupervised person under 17 (Firearms Act 1968, ss 5(6), 22(3), 22(4) and 22(5));
(i)   trespassing in daytime on land in search of game, refusal by such trespasser to give name and address, five or more found armed in daytime in search of game and using violence or refusing name and address (Game Act 1831, ss 30, 31 and 32);
(j)   being drunk in highway or public place (Licensing Act 1972, s 12);
(k)   obstructing constable or local authority officer inspecting premises for use as registered club, permitting drunkenness on licensed premises, failing to leave licensed premises when requested to do so, allowing prostitutes to assemble on licensed premises, permitting licensed premises to be used as a brothel, allowing

constable to remain on licensed premises when on duty, supplying intoxicants or refreshments to a constable or bribing a constable (Licensing Act 1964, ss 45, 172, 174, 175, 176 and 178);

(l) making false statement in relation to an application for a sex establishment licence (Local Government (Miscellaneous Provisions) Act 1982);

(m) falsely claiming a professional qualification (Nurses, Midwives and Health Visitors Act 1979);

(n) taking or destroying game or rabbits by night (Night Poaching Act 1828, s 1);

(o) wearing police uniform with intent to deceive, unlawful possession of police uniform (Police Act 1996, s 90);

(p) causing harassment, alarm or distress, failing to give notice of public procession, failing to comply with condition imposed on public procession, taking part in prohibited public procession, failing to comply with a condition imposed on a public assembly, taking part in a prohibited assembly, failing to comply with directions (Public Order Act 1986, ss 5,11,12(5),13(8),14(5),14B(2) and 14C(3));

(q) failing to provide a roadside specimen of breath (Road Traffic Act 1988, s 6);

(r) kerb crawling, persistently soliciting women (Sexual Offences Act 1985, ss 1 and 2);

(s) in connection with sporting events, allowing alcohol to be carried on public vehicles, allowing alcohol to be drunk on such vehicles, allowing alcohol to be carried in some other vehicles, trying to enter designated sports ground while drunk, unauthorisedly drinking (or supplying) alcohol at a designated sports ground (Sporting Events (Control of Alcohol Etc) Act 1985, ss 1(2), 1(4), 1A(2), 2(2), 5B(3), 5C(4), 5C(5), and 5D(3)); and

(t) taking or riding a pedal cycle without the owner's consent (Theft Act 1968, s 12(5)).

The provisions of s 27 require careful consideration. In the first instance it must be recognised that if a person has been in police detention for the offence, at any time, a requirement under s 27 for fingerprinting cannot be made. If a person is arrested for burglary, released on bail without his fingerprints having been taken, and is subsequently convicted of that offence, s 27 cannot apply at any future stage. Since the section is only concerned with those who have been convicted of a recordable offence, it has no application during the course of investigation at any stage prior to a person's conviction. In addition, if fingerprints have been taken during the course of the investigation, the section cannot apply even though those fingerprints may have been lost or spoiled.

In most instances involving the commission of recordable offences the person will have been in police detention at some stage; probably he will have been arrested at the time of commission and admitted to bail soon afterwards. Nevertheless, some offenders may be dealt with by way of summons for a recordable offence, there being no necessity to effect an arrest at or after the time of the offence. In such instances fingerprints may be taken after conviction within the provisions of s 27.

Arrest of service personnel – absentees without leave and deserters

The Army Act 1955 and the Air Force Act 1955 generally run in parallel. Section 186(1) of those Acts gives a constable power to arrest without warrant any person whom he has reasonable cause to suspect of being an officer, warrant officer, non-commissioned officer or soldier (or airman) of the regular forces who has deserted or is absent without leave. Warrants authorising such arrests may also be issued by justices of the peace. Persons so arrested must be brought before a magistrates' court as soon as practicable.

The Naval Discipline Act 1957, s 105 makes similar provisions in respect of naval personnel. Whether or not such a person admits being an absentee or deserter he *must* appear before a court. Where a court is satisfied that such a person is a deserter or absentee, it will remand him in custody to await a service escort unless he is also in custody for some other reason.

Immediately such an arrest has been effected, the appropriate service authority must be informed and provided with all particulars of the case, stating whether the identity of the person arrested is disputed and whether his behaviour is refractory. Details of escort arrangements should be noted. Where an escort arrives before the court rises the person concerned can be handed over immediately, thereby avoiding his committal to prison or to other civil custody. Where the escort is likely to arrive quite soon, the court will usually commit such a person to police custody. The court must provide a certificate giving details of the serviceman's arrest (or surrender: see below).

Absentees frequently surrender to the police, having simply overstayed their leave. Such persons need not be taken before a magistrates' court but they may be if this is desirable for any reason. In such a case the court will remand the person in custody to await a service escort, subject to the same rules as just set out. Where an absentee serviceman is not taken before a court, a certificate must be made out by the officer of police who causes the serviceman to be handed over to the escort. Care must be taken in completing this certificate. If it is incorrectly completed or is not signed by the officer in charge of the police station, it is inadmissible in evidence at a subsequent court-martial.

In all such cases of arrest or surrender the appropriate authority to be informed is:

(a)   if a naval rating or Royal Marine, the Commodore, HMS Nelson, Portsmouth PO1 3HH (Metropolitan Police report to Naval Provost Marshal, London);
(b)   if a soldier, the Central Criminal Record and Intelligence Office, Royal Military Police;
(c)   if an airman, the HQ RAF Provost and Security Services (UK).

On occasions the service authorities may issue a warrant to arrest a serviceman. In such a case, the serviceman should be arrested and handed to a service escort. He need not be placed before a court unless he is to be dealt with for some other reason. The appropriate certificate must be handed over to the escort.

PROCEDURAL REQUIREMENTS FOR LAWFUL ARREST

The following provisions apply to all arrests:

The nature of an arrest

An arrest involves a deprivation of liberty to go where one pleases. An arrest is normally effected by the seizing or the touching of a person's body with a view to restraint. Another example would be where a person is deprived of liberty where he is detained by the automatic activation of the door locks inside a car specially designed by the police as a trap. Where unreasonable force is used to effect an arrest the arrest is unlawful. It is possible to effect an arrest merely by words if they bring to the person's notice that he is under restraint and will be compelled to remain, and he submits to that compulsion.

The varied circumstances in which the arrests envisaged by the 1984 Act may occur dictate the likely processes of the arrest itself. If the arrest occurs outside, it is probable that some form of physical restraint will be applied as the constable will be anxious to ensure that his prisoner does not escape. However, if the person arrested is a quiet, elderly person who is not physically capable of such escape, physical restraint would be unnecessary and undesirable. In the same way, persons already in custody who are arrested for other offences do not require a show of restraint, nor would it serve any purpose.

Information to be given on arrest

Section 28 of the 1984 Act provides that where a person is arrested, otherwise than by being informed that he is under arrest, the arrest is not lawful unless the person arrested is informed that he is under arrest as soon as practicable after his arrest. This is so whether or not the fact of his arrest by a constable is obvious. In addition, no arrest is lawful unless the person arrested is informed of the ground for arrest at the time of arrest, or as soon as practicable after. This is a separate requirement to that set out above. Hence, a person must be told two things: that he is under arrest and the ground which exists for the arrest. While it is preferable that the person arrested is informed of the precise offence for which he is being arrested, eg 'I am arresting you for an offence of burglary which I have seen you commit', this is not essential (although the ground given must be a valid one). It suffices if, by the use of commonplace language, he is informed of the type of offence for which he is being arrested, so that he has the opportunity to give information which would avoid the arrest. Thus, where a constable making an arrest reasonably suspected that the offence was theft, handling, or taking a conveyance (a car), her statement that she was arresting the suspect for unlawful possession of a car was held to be sufficient. Section 28 exempts an officer from the necessity to give either item of information if it was not reasonably practicable to do so by reason of the person's escape before the information could be given.

The Code of Practice for the Detention, Treatment and Questioning of Persons by Police Officers (hereafter referred to as the Detention Code) additionally requires that a person must be cautioned upon arrest for an offence unless:

(a) it is impracticable to do so by reason of his condition or behaviour at the time; or
(b) he has already been cautioned immediately prior to arrest and before questions, or further questions, were put to him as a person suspected of an offence.

The above requirements must be carried out on all occasions unless escape prevents this happening or, in the case of the caution only, the person's condition or behaviour makes it impracticable. The caution must be in the following terms:

'You do not have to say anything. But it may harm your defence if you do not mention when questioned something which you later rely on in court. Anything you do say may be given in evidence.'

The Detention Code states that a juvenile should not be arrested at school unless this is unavoidable. In the event of this happening, the head teacher or his nominee must be informed.

Arrest elsewhere than at a police station

Section 30(1) of the 1984 Act requires that, where a person is arrested by a constable for an offence (or is taken into custody by a constable having been arrested for an offence by someone other than a constable) at any place other than a police station, he must be taken to a police station as soon as practicable. However, the inclusion of 'as soon as practicable' allows for the circumstances in which it would be unrealistic to take such a person directly to a police station. This is expressly stated by s 30(10) which provides that a constable may delay taking an arrested person to a police station if that person's presence elsewhere is necessary in order to carry out such investigations as it is reasonable to carry out immediately; in such a case any questions put to the arrested person should be confined to those investigations. It follows from all this that, where a person is arrested for a theft which he was seen to commit but the property was not in his possession when arrested after a chase, a constable carrying out one of the duties of his office, to protect property, could quite properly retrace the route of the chase with his prisoner in order to recover the stolen property as soon as possible. However, in circumstances where the property is not in imminent danger of being lost in consequence of any delay in effecting its recovery, the prisoner should be taken immediately to a police station unless it is essential that he indicates the precise place in which the property has been hidden or the place at which it was disposed of.

If there is any delay in taking an arrested person to a police station, the reason for it must be recorded on first arrival there. With certain exceptions, the police station to which the person arrested must be taken under s 30 must be a 'designated police station'. This term is explained in ch 5, but in essence it refers to a police station approved for the purpose of detention of prisoners. In exceptional circumstances, a person arrested may be taken to any police station. These circumstances are where:

(a) the constable is working in a locality covered by a police station which is not a designated police station; or
(b) he is a constable belonging to a police force maintained by an authority other than a police authority (eg the British Transport Police).

The exception at (a) recognises the situation which exists within many police forces. A 'designated police station' may be many miles from the place at which an arrest is made. If a person is arrested for an offence in respect of which he is likely to be released on bail more or less immediately, it would be unrealistic to require him to be taken to a designated police station many miles from the scene of the arrest. Neither exception applies if it appears to the constable that it may be necessary to keep the arrested person in police detention for more than six hours, in which case the person arrested must be taken to a *designated* police station.

In addition, any constable may take an arrested person to *any* police station if:

(a) the constable has arrested him without the assistance of any other constable and no other constable is available to assist him; or
(b) the constable has taken him into custody from a person other than a constable without the assistance of any other constable and no other constable is available to assist him

and (in either case) it appears to the constable that he will be unable to take the arrested person to a designated police station *without the arrested person injuring himself, the constable or some other person.*

This provision recognises the occasions upon which police officers, acting on their own, experience sufficient difficulty merely removing the prisoner to the nearest police station.

When the person is arrested and taken to a non-designated police station, and there is no officer present at that police station to act as a custody officer, the inspector at that designated police station to which that person would have been taken must be informed. If the first police station to which an arrested person is taken is not a designated police station, he must be taken to a designated police station within six hours unless he is previously released.

A separate custody record must be opened as soon as practicable for each person who is brought to a police station under arrest. We discuss custody records in the next chapter.

Arrest for a further offence

Where a person is under arrest at a police station for an offence and it appears that, if released, he would be liable to arrest for some other offence, s 31 requires that he be arrested for that other offence. The usual procedures to be followed after an arrest must be carried out; the person must be told that he is being arrested for that other offence and what the reasons are for that arrest, and he must be cautioned. This must be done whether or not it is intended to release him at that time.

POWERS OF ENTRY AND SEARCH IN RELATION TO AN ARREST

Search on arrest for an offence

Section 32 of the 1984 Act provides that, where a person has been arrested elsewhere than at a police station, a constable may search him if the constable has reasonable grounds for believing that the arrested person may present a danger to himself or others. The constable may seize and retain anything which he has reasonable grounds for believing that the person searched might use to cause physical injury to himself or another.

Section 32 goes further and also empowers a constable in such a case:

(a) to *search* the arrested person for anything which he might use to assist him to escape from lawful custody or which might be evidence relating to an offence; *and*

(b) to *enter* and *search* any premises in which the arrested person was when arrested or immediately before he was arrested for evidence relating to the offence for which he has been arrested.

The power to search only extends to a search which is reasonably required for the purpose of discovering any such thing or any such evidence. A constable may not search a person under (a) unless he has reasonable grounds for believing that the person may have concealed on him anything for which a search is permitted under (a). Similarly, a constable may not search premises under (b) unless he has reasonable grounds for believing that there is evidence for which a search is permitted under (b) on the premises. A constable searching a person under (a) may seize and retain anything, other than an item subject to legal privilege (see p 62), if he has reasonable grounds for believing that the person might use it to escape from lawful custody or that it is evidence of an offence or has been obtained in consequence of the commission of an offence.

Neither of the powers under s 32 authorises the removal of clothing in a public place other than an outer coat, jacket or gloves.

Section 32 gives statutory authority to 'on the spot' searches at the time of an arrest. That search may be for weapons or dangerous articles, for things which may assist escape, or for things which may be evidence of an offence. Thus, if a man is arrested for burglary and pulls a knife on the constable at the time of arrest, the constable has reason to believe that he is a danger and may search him for other weapons; if the man has shown a will to escape the constable may search him for things which might assist him to do so; if the constable has reason to believe that he may find evidence of an offence, for example property stolen whilst committing the burglary for which the person was arrested and other burglaries which he may have committed prior to his arrest, he may search him for such evidence. The power to search for evidence is particularly important since, if such property is not recovered at the time of such arrest, it is likely to be disposed of by the arrested person if an opportunity presents itself.

Similar considerations will apply to arrests made upon premises. 'Premises' includes any place and, in particular, includes any vehicle, vessel, aircraft or hovercraft, any offshore installation, and any tent or movable structure. If a police officer is seen approaching the premises in which a thief is lodged, it is likely that the thief will conceal the property within those premises. If he leaves and is arrested outside, it is reasonable that the constable should be empowered to examine the premises which he has immediately vacated.

Section 32 deals with the problem of communal occupation (including bedsit premises) by stating that where there are two or more separate dwellings, the search must be limited to the premises in which the arrest took place or in which the arrested person was immediately before his arrest *and* any part of the premises which the occupier of the dwelling uses in common with the other occupiers of other dwellings comprised in the premises. In the case of a bedsit, therefore, the constable would be able to search the room in which the arrested person was found and the common kitchen and lounge area used by all of the residents. It may be that a thief occupying one room may, on seeing the approach of a constable, enter the room of his neighbour and hand over property to him to conceal on his behalf. If the constable knows that the thief was in that room immediately before his arrest he is empowered to search it.

Police officers must recognise that this section does not provide any general powers of search either of persons or premises when an arrest is made. The particular circumstances described in the section must exist. If a man is arrested for an indecent assault and is known to be of a non-violent disposition, there are no grounds for an 'on the spot' search; nor would there be, in most circumstances, reason to search premises unless articles had been used in the commission of the offence.

Entry to premises to effect an arrest etc

The 1984 Act abolishes all the common law rules which gave a constable power to enter premises without a warrant, except that the power still exists at common law to enter premises to deal with a breach of the peace or to prevent it.

Section 17 of the Act provides that, without prejudice to any other enactment, a constable may enter and search any premises for the purpose:

(a) of executing a warrant of arrest issued in connection with or arising out of criminal proceedings, or a warrant of commitment issued under the Magistrates' Courts Act 1980, s 76;

(b) of arresting a person for an arrestable offence;

(c) of arresting a person for an offence under the Public Order Act 1936, s 1 (prohibited uniforms), or an offence under the Public Order Act 1986, s 4 (fear or provocation of violence), or an offence under the Criminal Justice and Public Order Act 1994, s 76 (failure to comply with an interim possession order), or an offence contained in the Criminal Law Act 1977, ss 6 to 8, or 10 (offences of entering and remaining on property)—in this last case the arresting constable must be in uniform;

(d) of arresting, in pursuance of the Children and Young Persons Act 1969, s 32(1A), any child or young person who has been remanded or committed to local authority accommodation under s 23(1) of that Act;

(e) of recapturing any person who is, or is deemed for any purpose to be, unlawfully at large while liable to be detained -
   (i)   in a prison, remand centre, young offender institution or secure training centre, or
   (ii) in pursuance of the Children and Young Persons Act 1933, s 53 (dealing with children and young persons guilty of grave crimes), in any other place;

(f) of recapturing any person who is unlawfully at large and whom he is pursuing (ie chasing); or

(g) of saving life or limb or preventing serious damage to property.

Except in the case of saving life or limb or preventing serious damage, the powers of entry and search under s 17 are only exercisable where a constable has reasonable grounds for believing that the person whom he is seeking is on the premises. With the same exceptions, they are limited in respect of premises consisting of two or more dwellings in the same way as with the powers to search described above. A search under s 17 may only be made to the extent that it is reasonably required for the purpose for which the power of entry is required. The Court of Appeal has ruled that a police officer, when exercising his right of entry by force under s 17, must give any occupant present the reason why he is seeking entry even if that reason is apparent in the circumstances, unless circumstances make it impossible, impracticable or undesirable. If the real reason is to arrest a person inside for an arrestable offence, for instance, it is insufficient to tell the occupants that the officer wishes to 'speak to' that person about the offence.

As in the case of search on arrest, the word 'premises' is given a wide meaning. It includes any place and, in particular, includes any vehicle, vessel, aircraft or hovercraft, any offshore installation, and any tent or movable structure.

Arguments will arise in respect of the power to enter and search for the purposes of arresting someone for an arrestable offence. They are likely to be concerned with whether this applies to an arrestable offence which is known to have been committed or whether reasonable suspicion that the person has committed the offence is sufficient. It is submitted that it would be unreasonable to interpret these powers to enter and search separately from the circumstances in which the Act allows an arrest without warrant for an arrestable offence; if so a reasonable suspicion will suffice.

Entry and search after an arrest

Before the 1984 Act there was no general right to enter a dwelling house without a warrant to search for or to seize evidence after an arrest had been effected. In the absence of the occupier's consent a warrant was necessary. Section 18 of the Act empowers a constable to enter and search any premises occupied or controlled by a person who is under arrest for an arrestable offence, if he has reasonable grounds for suspecting that there is on the premises evidence, other than items subject to legal privilege, which relates to that offence or to some other arrestable offence which is connected with or similar to that offence. 'Premises' bears the same meaning as in the case of search on arrest. A search of any person, who has not been arrested, which is carried out during a search of premises must be carried out in accordance with the Stop and Search Code.

A search under s 18 is only permitted to the extent that it is reasonably required for the purpose of discovering such evidence. Premises in the occupation of a person arrested for burglary may therefore be searched for evidence of that offence, or for evidence of other similar offences (ie the proceeds of other burglaries or large-scale thefts). The arrest of that person would not authorise a search for drugs unless he was also arrested for an arrestable offence of that nature.

A constable may seize and retain anything for which he may search under the above power.

The Searching of Premises Code provides that a search under s 18 may not be made without the written authorisation of an officer of the rank of inspector or above, unless it is carried out before a person is taken to a police station in circumstances where the presence of that person at the place in question is necessary for the effective investigation of the offence. A mere record of an oral authorisation made in an inspector's notebook is normally insufficient to constitute a written authorisation; unless wholly impracticable the authorisation must be given on the Notice of Powers and Rights which should be given or left as explained on pp 67-68. If a search is carried out without prior written authorisation in the situation described above, the constable must inform an officer of the rank of inspector or above that he has made the search as soon as practicable.

The effect of s 18 is that if a man who is a television retailer is arrested in the living quarters above his shop premises on a charge of theft of television sets, the constable would be empowered to search not only his living quarters but also the shop premises after arrest as they are premises 'occupied or controlled' by that person. If the constable searches the shop premises before taking the man to a police station, he must inform an officer of the rank of inspector or above that he has done so as soon as practicable.

Section 18 requires that an officer who authorises a search, or who is informed that a search has been made, must record in writing (in the custody record, if there is one) the grounds for the search and the nature of the evidence which was being sought. If the person in occupation or control of the premises is in police custody at the time that the search is carried out, the record must be made in his custody record.

POWERS TO SEARCH UNDER A SEARCH WARRANT

There are many statutes which provide particular powers to enter and search premises under the authority of a warrant and the 1984 Act does not affect any of these provisions. However, s 8 of the Act does provide justices with a general power to issue warrants to enter and search premises. 'Premises' includes any place, including any vehicle, vessel, aircraft or hovercraft, any offshore installation, and any tent or movable structure.

Section 8(1) provides that if, on an application made by a constable, a justice is satisfied that there are reasonable grounds for believing that:

(a) a serious arrestable offence has been committed; and
(b) there is material on premises specified in the application which is likely to be of substantial value (whether by itself or with other material) to the investigation of the offence; and
(c) the material is likely to be relevant (ie admissible) evidence; and
(d) it does not consist of or include items subject to legal privilege, excluded material or special procedure material (which are described in pp 62-63); and
(e) *any* of the conditions specified in sub-s (3) applies,

he may issue a warrant authorising a constable to enter and search the premises. Subsection (2) authorises a constable to seize and retain anything for which a search has been authorised.

A constable should never apply for a search warrant under s 8 where the material in question may consist of or include items prima facie subject to legal privilege, excluded material or special procedure material. In such a case application should be made to a circuit judge under the provisions of Sch 1 of the 1984 Act described in pp 63-64.

It is vital to remember that the justice must be satisfied that all the points from (a) to (d) above are satisfied. If that is so, then it is necessary for him to be satisfied of the existence of any one of the conditions set out in sub-s (3) referred to in (e) above, namely that:

(a) it is not practicable to communicate with any person entitled to grant entry to the premises;
(b) it is practicable to communicate with a person entitled to grant entry to the premises but it is not practicable to communicate with any person entitled to grant access to the evidence;
(c) entry to the premises will not be granted unless a warrant is produced; or
(d) the purpose of the search may be frustrated or seriously prejudiced unless a constable arriving at the premises can secure immediate entry to them.

These conditions merely follow previously accepted practice: (a) would apply if there was no one occupying the premises at the time; (b) would apply if, for example, there was a caretaker to a block of flats who had master keys and who could therefore allow access but would have no right to grant access to the material; (c) would apply in the usual circumstances in which a warrant is sought, and (d) in circumstances in which the nature of the evidence is such that it could be easily disposed of if the occupier was aware of police interest. There are various terms included in s 8(1) which require explanation.

Serious arrestable offence Schedule 5 to the 1984 Act defines certain offences as always being serious arrestable offences. They are:

(a) treason;
(b) murder;
(c) manslaughter;
(d) rape;
(e) kidnapping;
(f) incest with a girl under 13;
(g) buggery with a boy under 16;
(h) an indecent assault which constitutes an act of gross indecency;
(i) causing an explosion likely to endanger life or property (Explosive Substances Act 1883, s 2);
(j) intercourse with a girl under 13 (Sexual Offences Act 1956, s 5);
(k) possession of a firearm with intent to endanger life or use to resist arrest or carrying a firearm with criminal intent (Firearms Act 1968, ss 16, 17 and 18);
(l) hostage taking (Taking of Hostages Act 1982, s 1);
(m) hijacking (Aviation Security Act 1982, s 1);
(n) torture (Criminal Justice Act 1988, s 134);
(o) causing death by dangerous driving (Road Traffic Act 1988, s 1);
(p) causing death by careless driving when under the influence of drink or drugs (Road Traffic Act 1988, s 3A);

(q) endangering safety at aerodromes, hijacking ships, seizing or exercising control of fixed platforms (Aviation and Marine Security Act 1990, ss 1, 9 and 10);
(r) taking, making etc indecent photographs or pseudo-photographs of children (Protection of Children Act 1978, s 1); and
(s) the publication of obscene matter (Obscene Publications Act 1959, s 2).

Section 118 provides that any offence included in the Drug Trafficking Act 1994, s 1(3)(a)-(f) will also be a serious arrestable offence.

Section 116 states that *any other arrestable offence* is serious only if its commission has led to any of the consequences set out below, or is intended to lead to any of those consequences:

(a) serious harm to the security of the State or to public order;
(b) serious interference with the administration of justice or with the investigation of offences or of a particular offence;
(c) the death of any person;
(d) serious injury to any person;
(e) substantial financial gain to any person; and
(f) serious financial loss to any person.

If the arrestable offence consists of making a threat, it is 'serious' if the consequences of carrying out the threat would be likely to lead to one of the consequences set out above at (a) to (f).

The term 'injury' includes any disease and any impairment of a person's physical or mental condition.

Financial loss is 'serious' for the purpose of the section if, having regard to all the circumstances, it is serious for the person who suffers it. Whether or not a loss, actual or intended, is serious will depend partly on the victim's circumstances. A theft of £1,000 worth of property from a millionaire would perhaps not represent serious financial loss in the minds of some justices, whilst the loss of £100 worth of property by a pensioner could be considered to be serious in those circumstances.

Items subject to legal privilege These are defined as communications between lawyer and client and items enclosed with or referred to in such communications. This only applies if the material is in the possession of a person entitled to possess it. Items held with the intention of furthering a criminal purpose are specifically excluded from being items subject to legal privilege, even though that intention does not exist on the part of the holder (eg a solicitor) but does on the part of another (eg a solicitor's client).

Excluded material This means:

(a) personal records (ie documents relating to the health of an individual or counselling given to him) acquired or created by a person in the course of a trade, business etc or for the purpose of any paid or unpaid office and held in confidence by him;
(b) human tissue or tissue fluid taken for diagnosis or medical treatment and held in confidence; or
(c) journalistic material (ie material acquired or created for the purpose of journalism and held by the person acquiring or creating it for that purpose) consisting of documents or other records and held in confidence.

Special procedure material This is journalistic material, other than excluded material, and material, other than items subject to legal privilege and excluded material, held in confidence and acquired or created in the course of any trade, business etc (eg confidential business material, perhaps details of a motor company's intended new model).

Production orders etc

Although a justice may not issue a search warrant in respect of material of any of the three types set out above, s 9 of the 1984 Act recognises that there may be occasions in which it is necessary to enter premises and search for excluded material or special procedure material by providing that a constable may obtain access to such material by making an application under Sch 1 to the Act. Under Sch 1 a circuit judge may make a 'production order' or, in certain cases, issue a search warrant. Similar provision is made by the Prevention of Terrorism (Temporary Provisions) Act 1989, Sch 7 for production orders in respect of such material for the purposes of a terrorist investigation.

These provisions are intended to protect the confidence of the maker or holder of the record etc, and not that of the suspect. Consequently, it is open to the maker or holder voluntarily to disclose the material. It is only where there is no consent on his part to do so that the special provisions of s 9 and Sch 1 come into play.

An application under Sch 1 must be made by a constable. The person who has custody of the material must be notified of the application for the order (and of the material sought) and allowed to attend the hearing of the application and make representations. Unless he is in custody of the material, there is no need to give notification to a suspected person. In exceptional circumstances, an application may be heard in the absence of notification of the application to the person with custody of the material.

The basic order which a circuit judge may issue under Sch 1 is a 'production order'. This requires the person apparently in possession of the material in question *either* to produce it to the constable for him to take away *or* to give the constable access to it not later (*in either case*) than the end of a period of seven days from the date of the order or the end of such longer period that the order may specify. The making of such an order depends on a set of 'access conditions' being fulfilled. The Divisional Court has held that, before granting the application, the judge must be satisfied that it is substantially the last resort, ie that other practicable methods of obtaining the material have been exhausted without success.

The requirement of notice, together with the seven (or more) days' grace referred to above, gives a person plenty of time in which to dispose of incriminating material. Because of this, Sch 1 provides that a circuit judge may issue a search warrant if satisfied that a set of 'access conditions' is not fulfilled. But he may only do so if he is also satisfied that:

(a) a production order has not been complied with; or
(b) service of a notice of an application for a production order may seriously prejudice the investigation; or
(c) it is not practicable to communicate with anyone entitled to grant entry to the premises or access to the material; or
(d) the material is subject to some requirements of secrecy or is likely to be disclosed in breach of it.

The Divisional Court has emphasised that the issue of a search warrant under the present provisions is a major infringement on individual liberty and that, consequently, it is essential that the reason for authorising this procedure should be made clear.

The Code of Practice for the Searching of Premises by Police Officers (hereafter referred to as the Searching of Premises Code) requires that an inspector or above be present and in charge of a search under a Sch 1 search warrant. The Code also contains further provisions concerning such a search.

Procedure before application is made for a search warrant or a production order

The relevant provisions are contained in the Searching of Premises Code. Where information is received which appears to justify an application for a search warrant or a production order, the officer concerned must take reasonable steps to check that the information is accurate, recent and has not been provided maliciously or irresponsibly. An application is not permitted on the basis of information from an anonymous source where corroboration has not been sought. The nature of the articles and their location must be established as specifically as possible.

The officer must also make reasonable inquiries to establish what, if anything, is known about the likely occupier of the premises and the nature of the premises themselves, and whether they have been previously searched (and, if so, how recently); he must also obtain any other information relevant to the application.

An application for a justice's search warrant may not be made without the authority of an officer of at least the rank of inspector (or, in a case of urgency where no officer of this rank is readily available, the senior officer on duty). In addition the Searching of Premises Code requires that other than in a case of urgency, the community relations officer must be consulted before a search takes place which might have an adverse effect on police/community relations. In urgent cases, the local police community liaison officer should be informed of the search as soon as possible after it has been made.

An application for a 'production order' or a Sch 1 search warrant under the authority of the Police and Criminal Evidence Act 1984 may not be made without the authority of an officer of at least the rank of superintendent.

The making of an application

Between them, s 15 of the 1984 Act and the Searching of Premises Code provide the following rules for all search warrants. An application for a search warrant must be supported by information in writing, stating:

(a) the enactment under which the application is made;
(b) the premises to be searched and the object of the search; and
(c) the grounds on which the application is made (including, where the purpose of the proposed search is to find evidence of an alleged offence, an indication of how the evidence relates to the investigation).

Although the identity of an informant need not be disclosed, the officer must be prepared to deal with questions about the accuracy of previous information provided by that source or other related matters.

All applications must be supported by an information in writing and the constable must answer on oath any question asked by the justice. If an application is refused, no further application may be made for a warrant to search those premises unless supported by additional grounds. A search warrant authorises entry *on one occasion only* and each warrant must have two certified copies.

Execution of a search warrant

An entry on or search of premises under a warrant is unlawful unless the provisions of s 15 of the Act just mentioned and those in s 16 are complied with. Section 16 of the Act sets out the following provisions which apply to all search warrants.

A warrant may be executed by any constable. It may authorise other persons to accompany any constable executing it. Entry and search must be within one month of issue and must be at a reasonable hour unless the purpose of the search may be frustrated by entry at such time.

Where the occupier of the premises is present, the constable must, before the search begins:

(a) identify himself (by warrant or other identification number in the case of terrorism inquiries) and, if not in uniform, show his warrant card (but in so doing in the case of terrorism inquiries, he need not reveal his name);
(b) produce the warrant to him; and
(c) supply him with a copy of it.

The constable must act likewise in relation to a person in charge of the premises in the absence of the owner.

A search under a warrant may only be a search to the extent required for the purpose for which the warrant was issued; the same applies where articles are seized for which the warrant has provided no authority.

Save in exceptional circumstances the media should not be invited to be present when a search warrant (or any other investigative procedure) is being executed, nor should they be invited to police briefings prior to the execution of a search warrant, because reports emanating from such involvement are liable to prejudice a fair trial.

GENERAL PROVISIONS ON ENTRY, SEARCH, SEIZURE, ACCESS AND RETENTION

We have already described a number of specific rules in relation to this. In addition, the Searching of Premises Code lays down a number of rules which apply to searches of premises:

(a) undertaken for the purposes of an investigation into an alleged offence, with the occupier's consent, other than searches made in the following circumstances:
   (i) routine scenes of crime searches;
   (ii) calls to a fire or burglary made by or on behalf of an occupier or searches following the activation of fire or burglar alarms;
   (iii) searches where it is unnecessary to seek consent where in the circumstances this would cause disproportionate inconvenience to the person concerned (see p 67);
   (iv) bomb threat calls;
(b) under powers conferred by ss 17 (entry to arrest/search), 18 (entry and search after arrest) and 32 (search on arrest) of the 1984 Act (see pp 57-60 above); or
(c) undertaken in pursuance of a search warrant issued in accordance with s 15 of the 1984 Act (see p 64) or under Sch 1 to the 1984 Act (special procedure material and excluded material, see pp 63-64) or under s 7 of the Prevention of Terrorism (Temporary Provisions) Act 1989.

On the other hand, the Searching of Premises Code does not apply to the exercise of a statutory power to enter premises or to inspect goods, equipment or procedures if the exercise of that power is not dependent on the existence of grounds for suspecting that an offence may have been committed and the person exercising the power has no reasonable grounds for such suspicion. This exception will exclude from the Code application inspections etc by local authority inspectors under health and safety provisions.

In what follows it must be borne in mind that 'premises' includes any vehicle, vessel or aircraft, and any tent or movable structure.

Entry other than with consent

The officer in charge must first attempt to communicate with the occupier or any other person entitled to grant access to the premises by explaining the authority under which he seeks entry to the premises and ask the occupier to allow him to do so, unless:

(a) the premises to be searched are known to be unoccupied;
(b) the occupier and any other person entitled to grant access are known to be absent; or
(c) there are reasonable grounds to believe that to alert the occupier or any other person entitled to grant access by attempting to communicate with him would frustrate the object of the search or endanger the officers concerned or other persons.

The circumstances at (c) might exist where there are known to be a number of persons on the premises all of whom are suspected of being involved in the offence, any of whom could dispose of the evidence whilst these procedures are being followed; or, in the case of entry to search for an armed criminal, where danger might arise if he was warned of imminent arrest. Although in the circumstances set out in (c), an officer need not comply with the requirements as to identification, production of his warrant card (if not in uniform) and search warrant (if any) before effecting entry, he must do so before conducting the search (except that it is enough if he gives a copy of the search warrant at the first reasonable opportunity if the search is under a search warrant).

If a search warrant includes a schedule of documents to be searched for and the schedule has been detached when a copy of the warrant is given to the occupier of the premises, the search is unlawful and there is no right to retain anything seized. This is so even if an uncertified photocopy of the schedule is attached to the rest of the warrant.

Where the premises are occupied the officer must:

(a) identify himself (by warrant or other identification number in a terrorist investigation) and, if not in uniform, show his warrant card (although he may do so without revealing his name in a terrorist investigation); and
(b) state the purpose of the search and the grounds for undertaking it.

He must do these things before a search begins, unless there are reasonable grounds to believe that to do so would frustrate the object of the search or endanger someone.

Searches with consent

The Searching of Premises Code provides that, if it is proposed to search premises with the consent of a person entitled to grant entry, the consent must, if practicable, be in writing. Before seeking such consent the officer in charge must state the purpose of the proposed search and inform the person concerned that he is not obliged to consent and that anything seized may be produced in evidence. If, at the time, the person is not suspected of an offence the officer must tell him so when stating the purpose of the search. An officer cannot enter and search premises or continue to search premises if consent has been given under duress or is withdrawn before the search is completed.

In the case of a lodging house or other similar accommodation, a search should not be made on the basis solely of the landlord's consent unless the tenant is unavailable and the matter is urgent.

It is unnecessary to seek consent where in the circumstances this would cause disproportionate inconvenience to the person concerned, for example, where it is reasonable to assume that innocent occupiers would agree to, and expect that, police would take the proposed action. Examples are where a suspect has fled from the scene of the crime to evade arrest and it is necessary quickly to check surrounding gardens and readily accessible places to see whether he is hiding; or where police have arrested someone in the night after a pursuit and it is necessary to make a brief check of gardens along the route of the pursuit to see whether stolen or incriminating articles have been found.

Use of force

Where the police are acting under a warrant or under one of the above statutory powers, reasonable force may be used if necessary in the following cases if the officer in charge is satisfied that the premises are those specified in the warrant:

(a) where the occupier or another person entitled to grant access has refused to allow entry;
(b) it is impossible to communicate with such a person;
(c) the premises are known to be unoccupied or the occupier etc is known to be absent; or
(d) there are reasonable grounds to believe that to do so would frustrate the object of the search or endanger someone.

Notice of powers and rights

An officer who conducts a search of premises under a search warrant issued under the 1984 Act or the Prevention of Terrorism (Temporary Provisions) Act 1989, or under a power given by the 1984 Act (see below), or with the occupier's consent, must, unless it is impracticable to do so, provide the occupier with a copy of a notice in a standard format:

(a) specifying whether the search is made under warrant, or with consent, or in the exercise of powers under ss 17, 18 and 32 of the 1984 Act;
(b) summarising the extent of the powers of search and seizure conferred in the Act;
(c) explaining the rights of the occupier and of the owner of property seized;
(d) explaining that compensation may be payable in appropriate cases for damage caused in entering and searching premises, and giving the address to which an application for compensation should be directed; and
(e) stating that a copy of the Stop and Search Code is available to be consulted at any police station.

If the occupier is present, copies of the notice, and of the warrant (if the search is made under warrant), should if practicable be given to the occupier before the search begins, unless the officer in charge of the search reasonably believes that to do so would frustrate the object of the search or endanger the officers concerned or other persons. If the occupier is not present, copies of the notice, and of the warrant where appropriate, should be left in a prominent place on the premises or appropriate part of the premises and should be endorsed with the name of the officer in charge of the search, the name of the police station to which he is attached and the date and time of the search. The officer's warrant number, not his name, should be given in the case of a terrorism investigation. The warrant itself should be endorsed to show that this has been done.

Conduct of searches

Premises may be searched only to the extent required for the purposes for which the warrant was issued. This means that a search cannot be made in places where the articles specified in the warrant could not possibly be found or for longer than necessary to find those articles. This is emphasised by the Searching Code which states that premises may be searched only to the extent necessary to achieve the object of the search, having regard to the size and nature of what is sought. (A warrant to search for television sets would not authorise the examination of the contents of small drawers.) The constable executing the warrant must endorse it, stating whether the articles or persons sought were found, and whether any articles were seized, other than articles which were sought. Executed warrants and those not executed within the permitted time must be returned to the clerk to the justices (or to the appropriate officer of the court if issued by a judge). A warrant which is so returned must be retained for a period of 12 months during which time it may be inspected by the occupier of the premises to which it relates.

A search under warrant may not continue under the authority of the warrant once all of the things specified in it have been found, or the officer in charge is satisfied that they are not on the premises.

The search itself must be conducted with due consideration for the property and privacy of the occupier of the premises searched, and with no more disturbance than necessary. Reasonable force may only be used to conduct the search where it is necessary because the co-operation of the occupier cannot be obtained or is insufficient for the purpose. An occupier must not be discouraged or prevented from securing the services of a friend, neighbour or other person to witness the search, unless the officer in charge has reasonable grounds to believe that this would seriously hinder the investigation or endanger the officers concerned or other people. A search need not be unreasonably delayed for this purpose. If the premises have been entered by force the officer in charge must satisfy himself, before leaving, that they are secured either by arranging for the occupier or his agent to be present or by any other appropriate means.

In determining when to make a search, the officer in charge must always give regard to the time of day at which the occupier is likely to be present, and should not search at a time when the occupier or any other person on the premises is likely to be asleep unless this is unavoidable. If the wrong premises are searched by mistake, everything possible should be done to allay any sense of grievance. In appropriate cases assistance should be given to obtain compensation.

The local police/community consultative group or its equivalent should be informed as soon as practicable after a search where there is reason to believe that it might have had an adverse effect on relations between the police and the community.

Records of searches

The Searching of Premises Code requires that, if premises have been searched, a record of the search must be made.

The record which is made of such a search must be made by or on behalf of the officer in charge of the search, and it must be made on his return to the police station. The record must include:

(a) the address of the premises;
(b) the date, time and duration of the search;
(c) the authority for the search (including a copy of the warrant or written consent where the search was made thereunder);
(d) the names of officers conducting the search (except in the case of inquiries linked to the investigation of terrorism, where the record must state the warrant or other identification number and duty station of each officer);
(e) the names of any persons on the premises (if they are known);
(f) a list of articles seized (or a note of where they are kept) and, if not covered by a warrant, the reason for seizure;
(g) whether force was used and, if so, the reason; and
(h) a list of any damage caused, and the circumstances in which it was caused.

Search registers must be maintained at each sub-divisional police station and the above record must be made, copied or referred to in the register.

Where the premises have been searched under a warrant, the warrant must be endorsed to show:

(a) whether any articles specified in the warrant were found;
(b) whether any other articles were seized;
(c) the date and time at which it was executed;
(d) the names of the officers who executed it (except in the case of enquiries linked to the investigation of terrorism, in which case the warrant or other identification number and duty station of each officer concerned should be given); and
(e) whether a copy, together with a copy of the Notice of Powers and Rights, was handed to the occupier; or whether it was endorsed with the name (warrant number in the case of a terrorism investigation) of the officer in charge, the name of his police station and the date and time of the search and left on the premises (and, if so, where).

General powers of seizure

Section 19 of the 1984 Act gives the police wide powers of seizure in addition to those otherwise provided by the Act or elsewhere. It provides that a constable lawfully on any premises (eg with the occupier's consent) may seize anything on them if he has reasonable grounds for believing that:

(a) it has been obtained in consequence of the commission of an offence; or
(b) it is evidence in relation to an offence which he is investigating or any other offence; *and* (in the case of (a) or (b))
(c) it is necessary to seize it in order to prevent it from being concealed, lost, altered or destroyed.

In the same circumstances (ie (a) to (c)), a constable may require any information contained in a computer and accessible from the premises to be produced in a legible form in which it can be taken away.

Section 19 also provides that no relevant statutory power of seizure authorises the seizure of an item which the constable has reasonable grounds for believing to be subject to legal privilege as defined on p 62.

Record of seizure and access

Section 21 provides that a constable who seizes anything *under any statutory power* must, on request, provide the occupier of the premises or a person who had custody or control of the thing immediately before seizure with a record of what he seized. In such a case, the record must be provided within a reasonable time of the request.

The section also provides for access to a thing which has been seized, and for the photographing or copying of it, by a person who had custody or control of it immediately before seizure.

Retention

Section 22 provides that anything seized or taken away under s 19 may be retained so long as is necessary in all the circumstances. In particular, anything seized under s 19 for the purposes of a criminal investigation may be retained (unless a photograph or copy would suffice) for use as evidence at a trial for an offence, or for forensic examination or investigation in connection with an offence. Moreover, anything may be retained to establish its owner, where there are reasonable grounds for believing that it has been obtained in consequence of the commission of an offence.

Nothing seized on the grounds that it may be used:

(a) to cause physical injury;
(b) to damage property;
(c) to interfere with evidence; or
(d) to assist in escape from police detention or lawful custody,

may be retained after the person from whom it was seized has been freed from detention or custody or has been bailed.

Any person who had custody or control of property prior to its seizure must, if it is retained, be provided within a reasonable time with a list or description of the property, if he asks for one. A person claiming property seized by the police may apply for its possession to a magistrates' court under the Police (Property) Act 1897 and should, where appropriate, be advised of this procedure.

CHAPTER 4

Police questioning and the rights of suspects

In this and the following chapter, we shall make frequent reference to the 'Detention Code' (whose full title is the Code of Practice for the Detention, Treatment and Questioning of Persons by Police Officers). This Code applies to persons in custody at police stations, whether or not they have been arrested, and (except for its provisions as to reviews and extensions of custody) to those who have been removed to a police station as a place of safety under the Mental Health Act 1983, ss 135 and 136. However, persons who are voluntarily at police stations must be treated with no less consideration.

It cannot be pointed out too often that it is essential that police officers follow carefully the procedures set out below. Not only is evidence obtained in breach of them liable to be excluded at the trial judge's discretion in any subsequent court proceedings, but also a failure to comply with the Code is a disciplinary offence.

However, the Code recognises that, whilst a custody officer is required to perform specified functions 'as soon as practicable', there may be unavoidable delays where a large number of suspects is brought to a police station simultaneously to be placed in custody, or interview rooms are all in use, or where there are difficulties in contacting an appropriate adult, solicitor or interpreter.

The Detention Code does not apply to:

(a) persons arrested by police officers from Scotland exercising 'cross-border' powers under the Criminal Justice and Public Order Act 1994;
(b) persons arrested for the purpose of fingerprinting under the Asylum and Immigration Act 1993;
(c) persons served with a notice advising them of their detention under powers contained in the Immigration Act 1971; or
(d) convicted or remanded prisoners held in police cells on behalf of the prison service.

In the rest of this chapter and the next three, there are frequent references to the Police and Criminal Evidence Act 1984, hereafter simply referred to as the 1984 Act.

DOCUMENTATION

Custody records

As we stated in ch 3, above, a separate custody record must be opened as soon as practicable for each person who is brought to a police station under arrest or who is arrested at the police station having attended there voluntarily. All information which is required to be recorded under the Detention Code must be recorded as soon as practicable in the custody record unless otherwise specified. Any audio or visual recording made in the custody area is not part of the custody record.

In the case of any action requiring the authority of an officer of a specified rank, his name and rank must be recorded in the custody record, except where the person is detained under the Prevention of Terrorism (Temporary Provisions) Act 1989 (in which case the record must state the officer's warrant or other identification number and duty station).

All entries in the custody record must be timed and signed by the maker. In the case of a record held on a computer this should be timed and contain the operator's identification. Warrant or other identification numbers should be used rather than names in the case of detention under the 1989 Act just mentioned.

The custody officer is responsible for the accuracy and completeness of the custody record and for ensuring that the record (or a copy) accompanies a detained person if he is transferred to another police station. The record must show the time of, and reason for, a transfer and the time a person is released from detention. As soon as practicable after his arrival at the police station, a solicitor or appropriate adult must be permitted to consult the custody record of a person detained. When a person leaves police detention or is taken before a court, he or his legal representative or his appropriate adult must be supplied on request with a copy of the custody record as soon as practicable. This entitlement lasts for 12 months after his release.

The fact and time of any refusal by a person to sign a custody record when asked to do so in accordance with the Detention Code must itself be recorded.

Interview records

An accurate record must be made of each interview with a person suspected of an offence, whether or not the interview takes place at a police station. The record must state the place of the interview, the time it begins and ends, the time the record is made (if different), any breaks in it, and the names of those present. The requirement to record names of those present does not apply to police officers interviewing a person detained under the Prevention of Terrorism (Temporary Provisions) Act 1989; instead the record must state the warrant or other identification number and duty station of such officers.

An interview record:

(a) enables the prosecutor to make informed decisions;
(b) is capable of being exhibited to an officer's witness statement and used pursuant to the Criminal Justice Act 1967, s 9 (which is described in p 159);
(c) enables the prosecutor to comply with the rules of advance disclosure; and
(d) where the record is accepted by the defence, facilitates the conduct of the case by the prosecution, the defence and the court.

Such a record must, therefore, comprise a balanced account of the interview including points in mitigation and/or defence made by the suspect. Where an admission is made, the question as well as the answer containing the admission must be recorded verbatim in the record. Matters which might be considered to be prejudicial or inadmissible by a court should be brought to the attention of the prosecutor by means of a covering report.

An 'interview' is described in the Detention Code as 'the questioning of a person regarding his involvement or suspected involvement in a criminal offence or offences which, by virtue of the Code, is required to be carried out under caution'. For example, where, after arresting a man for possessing an offensive weapon, police officers asked him in the police car why he had the knife and he told them there had been some trouble and that he had it for his own protection, it was held that this amounted to an interview for the purposes of the Code, so that a record should have been made of it.

On the other hand, the statutory procedure for obtaining roadside specimens and specimens for analysis under the drink/drive legislation does not constitute an 'interview' for present purposes, so the requirements relating to such an interview do not apply to it. Nor does an informal conversation at or near the scene of a crime constitute an 'interview', but it will if it descends into detailed questioning.

In relation to interview records generally, when a suspect agrees to read records of interviews and of other comments and to sign them as correct, he should be asked to endorse the record with words such as 'I agree that this is a correct record of what was said' and add his signature. Where the suspect does not agree with the record, the officer should record the details of any disagreement and then ask the suspect to read these details and then sign them to the effect that they accurately reflect his disagreement. Any refusal to sign when asked to do so must be recorded.

Written interview records must be signed and timed by the maker.

Tape recording

With the exceptions mentioned below an interview at a police station must be tape recorded in accordance with the Code of Practice on Tape Recording if the interview is:

(a) with a person who has been cautioned in accordance with the Detention Code (on grounds of suspicion of his committing an offence) in respect of an indictable offence (including an offence triable either way);
(b) one which takes place as a result of a police officer exceptionally putting further questions to a suspect about an offence described in (a) after he has been charged with, or informed that he may be prosecuted for, that offence; or
(c) one in which a police officer wishes to bring to the notice of a person, after he has been charged with, or informed he may be prosecuted for, an indictable offence (including one triable either way), any written statement made by another person, or the content of an interview with another person, which may be done by playing a tape recording.

However, tape recordings at police stations may be made of interviews with persons cautioned for other offences, at police discretion, provided that the Tape Recording Code is complied with. This also applies to responses after charge in such situations. Any written record must be made during the interview, unless in the investigating officer's view this would not be practicable or would interfere with the conduct of the interview, and must constitute either a verbatim record or, failing this, an account of the interview which adequately and accurately summarises it. If the record is not made during the interview, it must be made as soon as practicable thereafter and the reason must be recorded in the officer's pocket book.

Tape recording is not required in relation to interviews with a person arrested for an offence under the Prevention of Terrorism (Temporary Provisions) Act 1989, other than the offences of displaying in public support for a proscribed organisation, and of withholding information about acts of terrorism, nor in relation to an interview with a person in respect of a terrorism related offence, nor in relation to an interview with a person reasonably suspected of an offence contrary to the Official Secrets Act 1911, s 1.

In addition, the custody officer may authorise the interviewing officer not to tape record the interview in two cases.

(a)   Where it is not reasonably practicable to do so, because of failure of the equipment or the non-availability of a suitable interview room or recorder, and the custody officer considers on reasonable grounds that the interview should not be delayed until the failure has been rectified or a suitable room or recorder becomes available, he may authorise the interviewing officer not to tape record the interview. Priority should be given to tape recording interviews with persons who are suspected of more serious offences.

(b)   Where it is clear from the outset that no prosecution will ensue, the custody officer may authorise the interviewing officer not to tape record the interview.

In these two cases the interview must be recorded in writing and in accordance with the Detention Code. The custody officer must make a note, in specific terms, of the reason for not tape recording.

The tape recording of interviews must be carried out openly but unobtrusively, and it must be made clear to the suspect that there is no opportunity to interfere with the tape recording or tapes. The 'master tape' will be sealed before it leaves the presence of the suspect. A master tape may be either one of two tapes used in a twin deck machine or the only tape used in a single deck machine. A second tape will be used as a working copy and it may be either the other tape in the case of a twin deck machine, or a copy of the master used in a single deck machine. Such a copy must be made in the presence of the suspect and without the master tape leaving his sight.

Checking the record

Unless it is impracticable the person interviewed must be given the opportunity to read the interview record and to sign it as correct or to indicate the respects in which he considers it inaccurate. If the interview is tape recorded the arrangements set out in the Tape Recording Code apply. If the person concerned cannot read or refuses to read the record or to sign it, the senior police officer present must read it over to him and ask him whether he would like to sign it as correct or to indicate the respects in which he considers it inaccurate. The police officer must then certify on the interview record itself what has occurred.

Records of comments outside interview

A written record should also be made of any comments made by a suspected person, indicating unsolicited comments, which are outside the context of an interview but which might be relevant to the offence. Any such record must be timed and signed by the maker. Where practicable the person must be given the opportunity to read that record and to sign it as correct or to indicate the respects in which he considers it inaccurate. Any refusal to sign must be recorded.

The present requirement does not extend to entries made in an officer's notebook and offered to the suspect for authentication. These do not have to be recorded in the custody record.

CAUTIONS

Cautions must be given:

(a) at the stage of reasonable grounds to suspect that a person who has not been arrested has committed an offence (no matter how trivial);
(b) on the arrest of a person (unless it is impracticable or he has already been cautioned); and
(c) after arrest (in the circumstances defined below).

Statements made under caution may be used only for the purposes for which they are provided. To use them for an extraneous purpose, eg to leak to the press whether or not for reward, is legally actionable as a breach of confidence.

Where no arrest has been made

Where a person has not been arrested but there are grounds to suspect him of an offence, he must be cautioned before any questions about it (or further questions, if it is his answers to previous questions that provide grounds for suspicion) are put regarding his involvement or suspected involvement in that offence if his answers or his silence (ie failure to answer a question or to answer satisfactorily) may be given in evidence to a court in a prosecution. The Court of Appeal has held that 'grounds to suspect' means 'reasonable grounds to suspect'.

A person need not be cautioned if questions are put to him for other purposes, for example solely to:

(a) establish his identity or his ownership of any vehicle; or
(b) obtain information in accordance with any relevant statutory requirement or in furtherance of the proper and effective conduct of a search (for example, to determine the need to search in the exercise of powers to stop and search or to seek co-operation while carrying out a search); or
(c) seek verification of a written record.

Assistance is provided by a case where a suspect was being interviewed concerning burglaries and said that he was wanted for 'something bad'. The police officer asked what it was, to which the suspect replied, 'I'm ashamed, I done a rape'. It was held that the officer, at the stage of asking his question, was merely trying to find out what was disturbing the suspect and that there had been no breach of the Detention Code by a failure to caution.

Wherever a person not under arrest is initially cautioned, or is reminded that he is still under caution after a break, he must at the same time be told that he is not under arrest; that he is not obliged to remain at the police station but that if he does he may obtain free and independent legal advice if he wishes. The officer must point out that the right to legal advice includes the right to speak with a solicitor over the telephone. The officer must ask the person whether he wishes to do so.

Since the Detention Code obliges police officers to administer a caution if the answer to a question may be offered in evidence in criminal proceedings, it is necessary to caution motorists when pointing out to them that they have committed an offence as their reply is almost certainly going to be relevant to the proceedings. Indeed, although there is no direct requirement to caution when informing a person that he will be reported for an offence, the admissibility of his reply in evidence may depend upon whether or not he has been cautioned at some stage. Practice may still require that such a reply is included in an officer's report and, if this is so, the offender should be cautioned at some stage before he makes it. The use of a caution when dealing with offenders who commit minor offences is often misunderstood by members of the public who believe that the officer is being officious.

The caution prescribed by the Code is—

'You do not have to say anything. But it may harm your defence if you do not mention when questioned something which you later rely on in court. Anything you do say may be given in evidence.'

Minor deviations do not constitute a breach of this requirement provided that the sense of the caution is preserved.

On arrest

A person must be cautioned on arrest for an offence unless:

(a) it is impracticable to do so by reason of his condition or behaviour at the time; or
(b) he has already been cautioned prior to arrest as described above.

After arrest

Following the arrest of a person, a police officer must caution him (or cause him to be cautioned or remind him that he remains under caution):

(a) before putting to him any questions or further questions for the purpose of obtaining evidence which may be given to a court in a prosecution (unless the questioning immediately follows the arrest);
(b) when arresting him for any further offence in accordance with the Police and Criminal Evidence Act 1984, s 31 (which we dealt with at p 57, above);
(c) when charging him with an offence (or informing him that he may be prosecuted for it); or
(d) when bringing to his notice a written statement or questioning him as permitted by the Detention Code.

Special warnings under the Criminal Justice and Public Order Act 1994 in relation to inferences which may be drawn from silence

When a suspect who is interviewed after arrest fails or refuses to answer certain questions, or to answer them satisfactorily, after due warning, a court or jury may draw such inferences as appear proper under ss 36 and 37 of the Criminal Justice and Public Order Act 1994. This applies when:

(a) a suspect is arrested by a constable and there is found on his person, or in or on his clothing or footwear, or otherwise in his possession, or in the place where he is arrested, any objects, marks or substances, or marks on such objects, and the person fails or refuses to account for the objects, marks or substances found; or
(b) an arrested person was found by a constable at a place at or about the time the offence for which he was arrested is alleged to have been committed, and the person fails or refuses to account for his presence at that place.

For an inference to be drawn from a suspect's failure or refusal to answer a question about one of these matters or to answer it satisfactorily, the interviewing officer must first tell him in ordinary language:

(a) what offence he is investigating;
(b) what fact he is asking the suspect to account for;
(c) that he believes that this fact may be due to the suspect's taking part in the commission of the offence in question;
(d) that a court may draw a proper inference if he fails or refuses to account for the fact about which he is being questioned;
(e) that a record is being made of the interview and that it may be given in evidence if he is brought to trial.

Where, despite the fact that a person has been cautioned, failure to co-operate may have an effect on his immediate treatment, he should be informed of any relevant consequences and that they are not affected by the caution. Examples are when his failure to provide his name and address when charged may render him liable to detention, or when his refusal to provide particulars and information in accordance with a statutory requirement, for example, under the Road Traffic Act 1988, may amount to an offence or make him liable to arrest.

General

Where there is a break in questioning under caution the officer in charge must ensure that the person being questioned is aware that he remains under caution; if there is any doubt the caution should be given again in full when the interview resumes. This is important because the officer may have to satisfy a court that the person understood that he was still under caution when the interview resumed.

If it appears that a person does not understand what the caution means, the officer who has given it should go on to explain it in his own words.

The Detention Code also requires that, if a person is not under arrest when an initial caution is given at a police station (or other premises), the officer must tell him that he is not under arrest and is not obliged to remain with the officer. The officer must also tell him that he is free to leave if he wishes *and remind him that he may obtain free legal advice* if he wishes and that the right to legal advice includes the right to speak to a solicitor on the telephone and ask him if he wishes to do so. This provision imports a significant requirement into the duties of police officers. Not only must an officer tell a person clearly that he is under arrest (and why he is under arrest) when that situation applies, but he must equally tell a person that he is not under arrest (if that is the case) whenever he cautions him if he is at a police station or before formally interviewing him at other premises.

Documentation

A record must be made when a caution is given, either in the officer's pocket notebook or in the interview record as appropriate.

Written statements under caution

All written statements made at police stations after caution must be written on the forms provided for the purpose and be taken in accordance with the rules in Annex D to the Detention Code.

'*(a) Written by a person under caution*
(1)   A person shall always be invited to write down himself what he wants to say.
(2)   Where the person wishes to write it himself, he shall be asked to write out and sign before writing what he wants to say, the following:

"I make this statement of my own free will. I understand that I need not say anything but that it may harm my defence if I do not mention when questioned something which I later rely on in court. This statement may be given in evidence."

(3)   Any person writing his own statement shall be allowed to do so without any prompting except that a police officer may indicate to him which matters are material or question any ambiguity in the statement.

(b) Written by a police officer
(4)   If a person says that he would like someone to write it for him, a police officer shall write the statement, but, before starting, he must ask him to sign, or make his mark, to the following:

"I, . . ., wish to make a statement. I want someone to write down what I say. I understand that I do not have to say anything but that it may harm my defence if I do not mention when questioned something which I later rely on in court. This statement may be given in evidence."

(5)   Where a police officer writes the statement, he must take down the exact words spoken by the person making it and he must not edit or paraphrase it. Any questions that are necessary (eg to make it more intelligible) and the answers given must be recorded contemporaneously on the statement form.
(6)   When the writing of a statement by a police officer is finished the person making it shall be asked to read it and to make any corrections, alterations or additions he wishes. When he has finished reading it he shall be asked to write and sign or make his mark on the following certificate at the end of the statement:

"I have read the above statement, and I have been able to correct, alter or add anything I wish. This statement is true. I have made it of my own free will."

(7) If the person making the statement cannot read, or refuses to read it, or to write the above mentioned certificate at the end of it or to sign it, the senior police officer present shall read it over to him and ask him whether he would like to correct, alter or add anything and put his signature or make his mark at the end. The police officer shall then certify on the statement itself what has occurred.'

Summary

A statement must begin with a declaration to the effect that the person wishes to make a statement. The Code requires that, where police officers write the statement, they must record the exact words said by that person and that they must not edit or paraphrase those words. But for this latter provision, a shortened statement including only the words which a police officer considered to be important could still contain the exact words used, but perhaps not all of them. Provisions are made concerning alterations, corrections and signatures and that (in the event of an inability to read) *the senior officer present* shall read it over and deal with such matters. That officer must then certify on the statement what he has done.

Role of 'the appropriate adult'

The Detention Code also requires that, where the appropriate adult or another third party is present at an interview (see below) and is still in the police station at the time a written record is made, he must be asked to read it (or any written statement taken down by a police officer) and sign it as correct or to indicate the respects in which he considers it to be inaccurate. If he refuses to sign the record as accurate or to indicate the respects in which he considers it to be inaccurate, the senior officer present must record on the record itself, in the presence of the person concerned, what has happened. If the interview is tape recorded the arrangements set out in the Code of Practice for the Tape Recording of Police Interviews apply.

In the case of a *juvenile*, the 'appropriate adult' means:

(a) his parent or guardian (or, if he is in care, the care authority or organisation). The term 'in care' is used in the Code to cover all cases in which a juvenile is 'looked after' by a local authority under the terms of the Children Act 1989; or
(b) a social worker; or
(c) failing either of the above, another responsible adult aged 18 or over who is not a police officer or employed by the police.

A person, including a parent or guardian should not be the appropriate adult if he is suspected of involvement in the offence in question, is the victim, is a witness, is involved in the investigation or has received admissions. In such circumstances it will be desirable for the appropriate adult to be someone else. If the parent or guardian of a juvenile is estranged from the juvenile, he should not be asked to be the appropriate adult if the juvenile expressly and specifically objects to his presence. The fact that a parent participates in questioning a juvenile during the interview does not disqualify the parent from being the appropriate adult. If a child in care admits an offence to a social worker, another social worker should be the appropriate adult.

Although the Code refers to 'the appropriate adult' in the singular, there may be cases where it is appropriate for more than one adult to be present as 'appropriate adults' during the interview of a juvenile, as where both parents are present or where a parent with language difficulties is present and a second adult is present to assist in questions of language.

In the case of a person *who is mentally disordered or mentally handicapped,* the 'appropriate adult' means:

(a) a relative, guardian or other person responsible for his care or custody; or
(b) someone who has experience of dealing with mentally ill or mentally handicapped persons but who is not a police officer or employed by the police (such as an approved social worker as defined by the Mental Health Act 1983 or a specialist social worker); or
(c) failing either of the above, some other responsible adult who is not a police officer or employed by the police.

In the case of people who are mentally disordered or handicapped it may in some cases be more satisfactory if the appropriate adult is someone who has experience or training in their case rather than a relative lacking such qualifications. However, if the person himself prefers a relative to a better qualified stranger his wishes should if practicable be respected.

A solicitor or lay visitor who is present at the police station in a professional capacity may not act as the appropriate adult.

A person should always be given an opportunity, when an appropriate adult is called to a police station, to consult privately with a solicitor in the absence of the appropriate adult if he wishes to do so.

INTERVIEWS

General provisions concerning interviews

As previously stated, the Detention Code defines an interview as 'the questioning of a person regarding his involvement or suspected involvement in a criminal offence or offences which, by virtue of the Code, is required to be carried out under caution. Procedures undertaken under s 7 of the Road Traffic Act 1988 do not constitute interviews for the purposes of the Code'.

The revision of the Detention Code in 1995 removed references to forms of interviews which might occur 'to obtain information or an explanation of facts or, in the ordinary course of the officer's duties', from the definition of 'interview' as a result of problems of interpretation. The Court of Appeal had expressed the opinion that the inclusion of the words 'in the ordinary course of the officer's duties' tended to make a nonsense of previous guidance as it was wide enough to include almost every type of interview.

The guidance is now clear; we are considering an 'interview' which takes place under caution, or which should have taken place under caution. Some decisions of the Court of Appeal continue to be helpful in establishing a divide.

In one case, police officers attended the house of a suspect to arrest him for handling stolen furniture and taking a lorry without consent. The officers put to him that they had seen him some days previously driving the stolen lorry. One of them said, 'What have you got to say about this?' He later said to him, 'But you are not doubting that we saw you last Thursday . . . in the lorry?' It was held by the Court of Appeal that these questions, asked without caution, were for purposes other than establishing identity as the officers already knew the name of the suspect. They were put for the purpose of obtaining evidence and therefore constituted an interview, and should not have been asked until arrival at the police station when the suspect had been informed of his right to legal advice.

In another case, an officer escorting a suspect to the custody office, saw the suspect drop a packet containing four ecstasy tablets. She said to him 'I have just seen you drop this. Things are looking a bit more serious now.' The suspect replied 'Yeah'. The officer asked 'Are these ecstasy tablets?' and the suspect replied 'Yes'. The Court of Appeal held that this was clearly an interview. Even one question regarding a suspect's involvement or suspected involvement in an offence can be sufficient in appropriate circumstances. On the other hand, the Court held, a conversation in which the suspect asks 'What will I get for this?', the officer replied 'What do you mean?', the suspect said 'At court for supplying drugs, what will I get?' and the officer replied 'That's not for me to say', did not amount to an interview. Clearly, the officer's question did not relate to the suspect's involvement in an offence. This conversation was simply an unsolicited comment which had to be recorded etc in accordance with the procedure set out on p 74.

The Court of Appeal has given precise guidance in respect of any notes which might have been made in an interview.

(a) If such a note has, for whatever reason, not been shown to the suspect prior to the arrival of his solicitor, fairness both to the suspect and to the police themselves requires that it be shown in the presence of his solicitor.
(b) If such a note has been shown to the suspect before the arrival of the solicitor, fairness to both sides requires that the solicitor be informed of the facts when he arrives.
(c) Where the court concludes that the police have acted less than fairly the chances that the evidence of the conversation noted will be excluded will be considerably increased.

Before the start of an interview, other than one which is being tape recorded, it is required that each interviewing officer must identify himself and any other officers present by name and rank to the prisoner, except in the case of persons detained under the Prevention of Terrorism (Temporary Provisions) Act 1989 when each officer must identify himself by his warrant or other identification number and rank rather than his name. In all interviews, tape recorded or not, there must be breaks at the recognised meal times and there must also be short breaks for refreshment at intervals of approximately two hours, subject to the interviewing officer's discretion to delay a break if there are reasonable grounds for believing that it would:

(a) involve a risk of harm to persons or serious loss of, or damage to, property; or
(b) delay unnecessarily the person's release from custody; or
(c) otherwise prejudice the investigation.

Meal breaks should normally last at least 45 minutes and shorter breaks after two hours should last at least 15 minutes. If a break is delayed as permitted by the Detention Code and prolongs the interview, a longer break should then be provided. If there is a short interview, and a subsequent short interview is contemplated, the length of the break may be reduced if there are reasonable grounds to believe that this is necessary to avoid any of the consequences set out at (a) to (c) above.

Interviews following arrest

Following a decision to arrest a suspect he must not be interviewed about the relevant offence except at a police station (or other authorised place of detention) unless the consequent delay would be likely:

(a)   to lead to interference with or harm to evidence connected with an offence or interference with or physical harm to other persons; or

(b)   to lead to the alerting of other persons suspected of having committed an offence but not yet arrested for it; or

(c)   to hinder the recovery of property obtained in consequence of the commission of an offence.

Interviewing in any of these circumstances should cease once the relevant risk has been averted or the necessary questions have been put in order to attempt to avert that risk.

Immediately prior to the commencement or re-commencement of any interview at a police station or other authorised place of detention, the interviewing officer must remind the suspect of his entitlement to free legal advice and that the interview can be delayed for him to obtain legal advice (unless one of the exceptions to the right to legal advice applies, which are described on p 90). At the beginning of an interview carried out in a police station, the interviewing officer, after cautioning the suspect, must put to him any significant statement or silence which occurred before his arrival at the police station and must ask him whether he confirms or denies that earlier statement or silence and whether he wishes to add anything. A 'significant statement or silence' is one which appears capable of being used in evidence against the accused. It is the responsibility of the interviewing officer to ensure that all such reminders are noted in the record of the interview.

No police officer may try to obtain answers to questions or to elicit a statement by the use of oppression. Except as provided by the Code, no police officer may indicate, except in answer to a direct question, what action will be taken on the part of the police if the person being interviewed answers questions, makes a statement or refuses to do either. If the person asks the officer directly what action will be taken in the event of his answering questions, making a statement or refusing to do either, the officer may inform the person what action the police propose to take in that event provided that the action is itself proper and warranted.

As soon as a police officer who is making inquiries of any person about an offence believes that a prosecution should be brought against him and that there is sufficient evidence for it to succeed, he should ask the person if he has anything further to say. If the person indicates that he has nothing further to say the officer shall without delay cease to question him about that offence. This should not, however, be taken to prevent officers in revenue cases or acting under the provisions of the Criminal Justice Act 1988 or the Drug Trafficking Offences Act 1986 from inviting suspects to complete a formal question and answer record after the interview is concluded.

Interviews while in detention

The Detention Code provides that if a police officer wishes to interview a detained person, or to conduct inquiries which require the presence of a detained person, it is the custody officer who must decide whether to deliver his prisoner into that officer's custody. In any period of 24 hours a detained person must be allowed a continuous period of at least eight hours' rest, free from questioning, travel or any interruption by police officers in connection with the investigation concerned. This period should normally be at night. The period of rest may not be interrupted or delayed except at the request of the person, his appropriate adult or his legal representative unless there are reasonable grounds for believing that it would:

(a)   involve a risk of harm to people or serious loss of, or damage to, property;

(b) delay unnecessarily the person's release from custody; or
(c) otherwise prejudice the result of the investigation.

These provisions apply also where a person has voluntarily gone to a police station and then been arrested. In such a case the period of 24 hours commences from the time of his arrest and not from his arrival at the police station. Any action which is required to be taken by the Code in accordance with section 8 (visits to drunks etc), or in accordance with medical advice, or at the request of the detained person, his appropriate adult, or legal representative, does not constitute an interruption to the rest period such that a fresh period must be allowed.

As far as practicable, an interview must take place in a properly heated, lit and ventilated interview room. The detained person must not be required to stand.

Tape recorded interviews

When a suspect is brought into the interview room the police officer must without delay, but in sight of the suspect, load the tape recorder with clean tapes and set it to record. The tapes must be unwrapped or otherwise opened in the presence of the suspect. The police officer must then say:

(a) that the interview is being tape recorded;
(b) his name and rank and the name and rank of any other police officer present, except in the case of enquiries linked to the investigation of terrorism where warrant or other identification numbers must be stated rather than names;
(c) the name of the suspect and any other party present (eg a solicitor);
(d) the date, time of commencement and place of the interview; and
(e) that the suspect will be given a notice about what will happen to the tapes.

The police officer must then caution the suspect in the usual way, (see p 76). He must remind the suspect of his right to free and independent legal advice and that he can speak to a solicitor on the telephone in accordance with the provisions of the Detention Code.

The police officer must then put to the suspect any significant statement or silence (ie a failure or refusal to answer a question or to answer it satisfactorily) which occurred before the start of the tape recorded interview, and must ask him whether he confirms or denies that earlier statement or silence or whether he wishes to add anything. A 'significant' statement or silence means one which appears capable of being used in evidence against the suspect, in particular a direct admission of guilt, or failure or refusal to answer a question or to answer it satisfactorily, which might give rise to an inference under ss 34 (p 164), 36 or 37 (p 77) of the Criminal Justice and Public Order Act 1994.

The reader is reminded that a special warning must be given before inferences can be drawn under ss 36 or 37.

If the suspect raises objections to the interview being tape recorded either at the outset, or during the interview, or during a break in the interview, the officer must explain the fact that the interview is being tape recorded and that the provisions of the Tape Recording Code require that the suspect's objections should be recorded on tape. When any objections have been recorded on tape or the suspect has refused to have his objections recorded, the police officer may turn off the recorder. In this eventuality, he must say that he is turning off the recorder and give his reasons for doing so and then turn it off. The police officer must then make a written record of the interview in accordance with the Detention Code. If, however, the police officer reasonably considers that he may proceed to put questions to the suspect with the tape recorder still on, he may do so. He should bear in mind that a decision to continue recording against the wishes of the suspect may be the subject of comment in court.

If a suspect indicates that he wishes to tell a police officer about matters not directly connected with the offence of which he is suspected and that he is unwilling for these matters to be recorded on tape, he must be given the opportunity to tell the police officer about these matters after the conclusion of the formal interview.

Where a tape is coming to an end, the police officer must inform the suspect and round off that part of the interview, remove the tapes and insert new tapes which must be unwrapped or otherwise opened in the suspect's presence. Tapes should be marked with an identification number immediately they are removed from the recorder. A suspect must not be left unattended in the interview room.

Breaks in interview

A break involving the suspect leaving the interview room must be recorded together with the reason for it and the time it was taken. The tapes must then be removed from the machine and dealt with in the same manner as if the interview had been concluded (see below).

A short break, in which both the suspect and the police officer remain in the room, must be recorded on the tape. The recorder may be switched off, but there is no need to remove the tapes. Recommencements must be recorded.

Whenever there has been a break in questioning under caution the interviewing officer must ensure that the person being questioned is aware that he remains under caution. If there is a doubt, the caution must be renewed. The officer must bear in mind that he may have to satisfy a court that the person realised that the caution still applied. He may also have to show that nothing occurred during a break in an interview or between interviews which influenced the suspect's recorded evidence. In view of this, he should consider, at recommencement or at a subsequent interview, summarising on tape the reason for the break and confirming this with the suspect. See p 81 concerning lengths of breaks.

Equipment failure

In the event of a failure of equipment which can be rectified quickly, eg by inserting new tapes, this must be done following the procedures laid down in relation to the changing of tapes. The officer must record the reason and the time the interview recommences. Where the further use of the tape recorder is impossible and no alternative is readily available, the interview may continue without being tape recorded but the authority of the custody officer must first be obtained.

If one of the tapes breaks during an interview it should be sealed as a master tape in the presence of the suspect and the interview should be resumed where it left off. The unbroken tape should be copied and the original sealed in the usual way. If equipment for copying the unbroken tape is not readily available, both tapes must be so sealed and the interview begun again. If a single deck machine is being used and it is one on which a broken tape cannot be copied, the tape should be sealed in the usual way and the interview begun again.

At the end of an interview

At the conclusion of an interview, the suspect must be offered the opportunity to clarify anything he has said and to add anything he wishes. At the conclusion of the interview, including the taking and reading back of any written statement, the time must be recorded and the tape recorder switched off. The 'master' tape must then be sealed with a master tape label and treated as an exhibit. The police officer must sign the label and ask the suspect and any third party to sign it also. If either, or both, refuse to sign the label, an officer of at least the rank of inspector, or if one is not available the custody officer, must be called into the interview room and asked to sign it. In the case of enquiries linked to terrorism, an officer who signs a label must use his warrant or other identification number. The suspect must be given a notice explaining the use which will be made of the tape recording and the arrangements for access to it and explaining that a copy of the tape will be supplied as soon as practicable if the person is charged or informed that he will be prosecuted.

The police officer must make a note in his notebook of the fact that the interview has taken place and has been recorded on tape, its time, duration and date and the identification number of the master tape. Where no proceedings follow in respect of the person whose interview was recorded the tapes must nevertheless be kept securely as required by the Tape Recording Code. Where proceedings follow, the officer must prepare a written record of the interview and sign it. Such a record will be made in accordance with the national guidelines approved by the Secretary of State. Before preparing it the officer may refresh his memory by listening to the working copy of the tape to check its accuracy. The interview record must be exhibited to any written statement prepared by the officer. If the officer's evidence of the interview is accepted by the defence, the evidence must refer to the fact that the interview was tape recorded and may be presented to the court in the form of the interview record. Where the officer's evidence is not accepted by the defence, the officer must refer to the fact that the interview was tape recorded and produce the master tape of the whole interview, as an exhibit, informing the court of any transcription which has been made of which he is aware.

Security of tapes

The security of master tapes is the responsibility of the officer in charge of each police station. A police officer must not break the seal on a master tape required for criminal proceedings, except in the presence of a representative of the Crown Prosecution Service. In such a case, the defendant, or his legal adviser, must be informed and be given a reasonable opportunity to be present. If either is present, he must be invited to reseal and sign the master tape. If not present, or in the event of refusal, this will be done by the representative of the Crown Prosecution Service. If master tapes have been delivered to the Crown Court following committal, application must be made to the Chief Clerk of the Crown Court for the release of the tape for unsealing by the Crown Prosecutor.

Tape recordings as evidence

A tape recording of a police interview with a defendant is primary evidence which, when produced at a trial, becomes an exhibit. If a jury wishes to hear it rather than rely upon a transcript, there is no reason why they should not be allowed to do so. The jury should listen to the full tape recording in open court.

Complaints

If, at any stage, the detained person makes a complaint concerning a matter covered by the Detention Code or the Tape Recording Code it must be recorded in the interview record and the interviewing officer must inform the custody officer who must deal with it in accordance with the Code (see 'Complaints—treatment', p 98).

Where, during the course of an interview which is being tape recorded, a complaint is made about a matter not connected with the Detention Code or the Tape Recording Code, the decision to continue the interview or terminate it is at the discretion of the interviewing officer. If continued, the officer must inform the complainant that the complaint will be brought to the attention of the custody officer at the conclusion of the interview, which must be done as soon as practicable thereafter. Where the interview is being tape recorded, the tape recorder should be left running until the custody officer has entered the room and has spoken to the interviewee. Continuation or termination of the interview should be at the discretion of the interviewing officer pending action by an inspector.

Other points

The custody record must show the times during which the prisoner was not in the custody of the custody officer and the reason why he was removed from his custody; if a request for the delivery of a prisoner out of that custody was refused, the reason for refusal must be recorded. Decisions to defer breaks must be recorded, with grounds, in the interview record. Assuming he is still at the police station when it is made, the person interviewed must be allowed to read the interview record and to sign it as being correct or to indicate what he considers to be inaccurate, but no person may be kept in custody for this sole purpose.

In conclusion, it should be noted that the Codes of Practice do not prevent a police officer from asking questions at the scene of a crime to elicit an explanation which could provide the arrested person with the opportunity to show that he was innocent. The reason is obvious; since the questions are not asked with a view to establishing admissions on which proceedings can be founded, there is technically no interview for the purposes of the Codes. If in the course of asking such questions a suspect makes a confession, it is prima facie admissible (even if the suspect is a juvenile and no adult is present).

In addition, there is no universal rule that, whenever there is a breach of a Code of Practice in a police interview, all subsequent interviews must be tainted and evidence of them excluded. Such a rule would fetter a judge's discretion under s 78 of the 1984 Act, which depends upon the facts of the particular case.

Persons at risk – juveniles and persons affected

If a person is a juvenile, is mentally handicapped or appears to be suffering from mental disorder, the custody officer must, as soon as practicable, inform the appropriate adult of the grounds for his detention and his whereabouts, and ask the adult to come to the police station to see the person.

A juvenile or someone who is mentally disordered or mentally handicapped, whether suspected of crime or not, must not be interviewed in the absence of the appropriate adult unless Annex C (below) applies. Nor may he be asked to give or sign a written statement. An interview is an indivisible process. A failure to involve an appropriate adult in some part of it is a breach of the Code and may render the whole of the interview inadmissible. Annex C is concerned with urgent interviews which are authorised by a superintendent. If a juvenile or mentally disordered or handicapped person is cautioned in the absence of the appropriate adult, the caution must be repeated in the appropriate adult's presence.

If, having been informed of his right to legal advice, the appropriate adult thinks that legal advice should be taken, the provisions of the Code relating to the right to legal advice (p 89) must be followed.

If the appropriate adult is not at the police station when the provisions of the Code dealing with the juvenile's rights are explained, the provisions must be complied with again in the presence of the appropriate adult once that person arrives.

Juveniles may only be interviewed at their places of education in exceptional circumstances and then only when the principal or his nominee agrees and is present. Every effort should be made to contact both the parents, or other person responsible for the juvenile's welfare, and the appropriate adult (if a different person). A reasonable time should be allowed to enable the appropriate adult to attend. Where this would cause undue delay, and unless the offence is against the educational establishment, the principal or his nominee can act as the appropriate adult for the purposes of the interview. It is preferable that a juvenile is not arrested at his place of education unless this is unavoidable. In this case, the principal or his nominee must be informed.

A juvenile or someone who is mentally disordered or mentally handicapped may be particularly open to suggestion. Consequently, special care should always be exercised in questioning such a person, and it is important to obtain corroboration of any facts admitted wherever possible.

If the appropriate adult is present at an interview, he should be informed of the reason for his presence. He should be told that he is not expected to act simply as an observer. He should also be informed that the purposes of his presence are:

(a) to advise the person being interviewed and to observe whether or not the interview is conducted fairly and properly; and
(b) to facilitate communication with the person being interviewed.

The Detention Code directs that if a person appears to be blind or seriously visually handicapped, deaf, unable to read, or unable to speak or has difficulty orally because of a speech impediment, he should be treated as such for the purpose of the Code in the absence of clear evidence to the contrary.

If a person is blind or seriously visually handicapped or is unable to read, the custody officer must ensure that his solicitor, relative, the appropriate adult or some other person likely to take an interest in him (and not involved in the investigation) is available to help in checking any documentation. Where the Code requires consent or signification, then the person who is assisting may be asked to sign instead, if the detained person so wishes.

Interpreters

Foreign languages

The Detention Code provides as follows:

(a) If a person has difficulty in understanding English and the interviewing officer cannot himself speak the person's own language and the person wishes an interpreter to be present, he must not be interviewed in the absence of a person capable of acting as an interpreter, unless the situation is one of urgency or Annex C to that Code (see below) applies.
(b) The interviewing officer must ensure that the interpreter makes a note of the interview at the time in the language of the person being interviewed for use in the event of his being called to give evidence and that he certifies its accuracy.

However, in the case of a tape recorded interview there is no requirement on the interviewing officer to ensure that the interpreter makes a separate note of the interview. The person must be given an opportunity to read it or have it read to him and sign it as correct or to indicate the respects in which he considers it to be inaccurate.

(c) In the case of a person making a statement in a language other than English:

   (i)   the interpreter must take down the statement in the language in which it is made;

   (ii) the person making the statement must be invited to sign the statement; and

   (iii) an official English translation must be made in due course.

These provisions merely follow the rules of common sense, recognising the need for persons who experience difficulty in fully understanding a language to be given every opportunity to compensate for that lack and ensuring that they are not required subsequently to sign a document which they do not understand.

The local Community Relations Council can supply a list of interpreters for people being interviewed by the police who do not understand English.

The deaf and those with a hearing or speech impediment

The Detention Code provides as follows:

(a) If a person appears to be deaf or there is a doubt about his hearing or speaking ability, he must not be interviewed in the absence of an interpreter unless he agrees in writing to be interviewed without one or Annex C (below) applies. Likewise, an interpreter should also be called if a juvenile is interviewed and the parent or guardian present as the appropriate adult appears to be deaf or there is a doubt about his hearing or speaking ability, unless he agrees in writing that the interview should proceed without one or Annex C applies.

(b) The interviewing officer must ensure that the interpreter is given the chance to read the record of the interview and to certify its accuracy in the event of being called to give evidence.

(c) Where an interview is being tape recorded and the suspect is deaf, or there is a doubt about his hearing ability, the police officer must take a contemporaneous note of the interview as well as tape record it.

Most local authority Social Service Departments can supply a list of interpreters for the deaf at police interviews.

General

Interpreters will be provided at public expense and all reasonable attempts should be made to make this fact clear to a detained person. The interpreter may not be a police officer when interpretation is needed for the purpose of obtaining legal advice. In other cases a police officer may interpret if the detained person (or the appropriate adult) agrees in writing.

If a person who has difficulty in understanding English is charged with an offence, and the interviewing officer cannot himself speak the person's language, arrangements must be made for an interpreter to explain as soon as practicable the offence concerned and any other information given by the custody officer.

Where a person in detention cannot communicate with a solicitor, whether because of language, hearing or speech difficulties, an interpreter must be called.

Where a person charged with an offence appears to be deaf or there is doubt about his hearing or speaking ability or ability to understand English, and the custody officer cannot establish effective communication, arrangements must be made for an interpreter to explain as soon as practicable the offence concerned and any other information given by the custody officer.

Documentation and guidance

The action taken to call an interpreter must be recorded, together with any waiver of the right not to be interviewed in the absence of an interpreter. As the interpreter may be needed as a witness at the person's trial, a second interpreter will be needed at that trial.

Vulnerable suspects – urgent interviews at police stations

Annex C of the Detention Code is concerned with urgent interviews at a police station or other authorised place of detention of particularly vulnerable people in particular circumstances. It overrides the safeguards, mentioned above, designed to protect them and to minimise the risk of interviews producing unreliable evidence. Consequently, the provisions of the Annex should only be applied in exceptional cases of need. Annex C provides that if, and only if, an officer of the rank of superintendent (or above) considers that delay will involve an immediate risk of harm to persons or serious loss of or damage to property:

(a) a person heavily under the influence of drink or drugs may be interviewed in that state; or

(b) a juvenile or a person who is mentally disordered or mentally handicapped may be interviewed in the absence of the appropriate adult; or

(c) a person who has difficulty in understanding English or who has a hearing disability may be interviewed in the absence of an interpreter.

Questioning in these circumstances may not continue once sufficient evidence to avert the immediate risk has been obtained. A record must be made of the grounds for any decision to interview a person in the above circumstances.

Legal advice

Access to solicitor

By s 58 of the 1984 Act, a person arrested and held in police custody is entitled, if he so requests, to consult a solicitor privately at any time. The Code provides that the consultation may be in person, in writing or by telephone, and that independent legal advice is available free of charge from the duty solicitor. If a person asks for legal advice, he must be permitted to consult a specific solicitor or another solicitor from that solicitor's firm or the duty solicitor. If advice is not available by these means, or he does not wish to consult the duty solicitor, a person must be given an opportunity to select a solicitor from a list of those willing to provide legal advice. Where a choice is unavailable, two alternatives may be chosen and the custody officer has discretion to allow further attempts. A police officer must not advise the suspect about any particular firm of solicitors. No police officer may at any time do or say anything with the intention of dissuading a person in detention from obtaining legal advice.

Whenever legal advice is requested (and unless Annex B applies, see below), the custody officer must act without delay to secure the provision of such advice. If, on being informed or reminded of the right to legal advice, the person declines to speak to a solicitor in person, the officer must point out that the right to legal advice includes the right to speak to a solicitor on the telephone and ask him if he wishes to do so. If the person continues to waive his right to legal advice the officer must ask him his reasons for doing so. Any reasons shall be recorded on the custody record or the interview record as appropriate. Once it is clear that a person neither wishes to speak to a solicitor in person, nor by telephone, he should cease to be asked his reasons, as he is not obliged to give such reasons.

Where a suspect chooses to speak to a solicitor on the telephone he should be allowed to do so in private unless this is impractical because of the design and layout of the custody area or the location of the telephone.

Delay

The right of access to legal advice may be delayed if, but only if, the person is in police detention for a *serious arrestable offence* (see p 61), has not yet been charged, and an officer of the rank of *superintendent* or above *authorises the delay*. If such authorisation is given orally it must be confirmed in writing as soon as practicable. Delay may only be authorised under this power in three types of case specified in Annex B to the Detention Code.

The first is where the superintendent (or above) has reasonable grounds for believing that access to a solicitor at a time when the detainee wishes to have access:

(a)   will lead to interference with or harm to evidence connected with a serious arrestable offence or interference with or physical injury to other persons; or

(b)   will lead to the alerting of other persons suspected of having committed such an offence but not yet arrested for it; or

(c)   will hinder the recovery of any property obtained as a result of such an offence.

Superintendents should authorise such delays only after careful consideration of these issues. The Court of Appeal has ruled that a superintendent, attempting to justify such a decision, will be unable to do so 'save by reference to specific circumstances, including evidence as to the person detained or the *actual solicitor* sought to be consulted'. Thus, if it is felt that a particular solicitor may by any means bring about one of the consequences at (a)–(c) above, that suspicion would only be relevant to that particular solicitor and would not apply to others selected by the accused. The court stated that a solicitor who deliberately did something, knowing that it would result in consequence (a), (b) or (c), would commit a serious criminal offence. A superintendent must believe that, accident apart, a solicitor would do so.

A solicitor (or appropriate adult) must be permitted to consult the custody record of a person detained as soon as practicable after his arrival at a police station.

The second type of case where delay may be authorised under the above power is that an officer may authorise delay where the serious arrestable offence is a drug trafficking offence and the officer has reasonable grounds for believing that the detained person has benefited from drug trafficking, and that the recovery of the value of that person's proceeds of drug trafficking will be hindered by the exercise of the right to have access to legal advice.

The third type of case where delay may be authorised under the above power is where the offence is one to which Part VI of the Criminal Justice Act 1988 (which concerns confiscation of the proceeds of an offence) applies, viz:

(a) any indictable offence, other than a drug trafficking offence or an offence under Part III of the Prevention of Terrorism (Temporary Provisions) Act 1989; or

(b) certain summary offences related to sex establishments, video recordings and unlicensed cinemas,

and the officer has reasonable grounds for believing that the detained person has benefited from the offence, and that the recovery of the value of any property or benefit obtained from or in connection with the offence will be hindered by the exercise of the right.

Access to a solicitor may not be delayed on the ground that he may advise the person not to answer any questions or that he was initially asked to attend by someone other than the detained person, provided the latter wishes to see him. In the latter case the detained person must be told that the solicitor has come to the police station at another person's request, and must be asked to sign the custody record to signify whether or not he wishes to see the solicitor.

If delay is authorised the detainee must be told the reason and the reason must be noted in his custody record. Once the reason for delay ceases, there may be no further delay in permitting access to a solicitor. *In any case* the detainee must be permitted to consult a solicitor within 36 hours from the 'relevant time' (a term defined in pp 109-110). There are special provisions when a person is detained under the Prevention of Terrorism (Temporary Provisions) Act 1989.

Arrival of solicitor etc at police station

Unless Annex B applies, when a solicitor arrives at a police station to see a particular person, that person must be informed of his arrival whether or not he is being interviewed, and asked if he wishes to see the solicitor. This applies even if the suspect has declined legal advice or having requested it, subsequently agreed to be interviewed without receiving advice. The attendance and the detained person's decision must be recorded. Where a consultation is permitted, a solicitor (or his representative etc) is entitled to be present whilst the detained person is interviewed if the detained person so wishes.

Non-accredited or probationary representatives

If a solicitor wishes to send a non-accredited or probationary representative to provide advice on his behalf, then that person must be admitted to the police station for this purpose unless an officer of the rank of inspector or above considers that such a visit will hinder the investigation of crime and directs otherwise. (Hindering the investigation of crime does not include giving proper legal advice to a detained person. The solicitor's only role in the police station is to protect and advance the legal rights of his client. On occasions this may require the solicitor to give advice which has the effect of avoiding his client giving evidence which strengthens a prosecution case. The solicitor may intervene to seek clarification or to challenge an improper question to his client or the manner in which it is put, or to advise his client not to reply to particular questions, or if he wishes to give his client further legal advice. He may only be required to leave in accordance with the Detention Code if his approach or conduct prevents or unreasonably obstructs proper questions being put to the suspect or his response being recorded, as where a solicitor answers on his client's behalf or provides written replies for his client to quote.)

For the purposes of the codes a 'solicitor' is a person who holds a current practising certificate, a trainee solicitor, a duty solicitor representative or an accredited representative included on the register of representatives maintained by the Legal Aid Board. If a solicitor wishes to send a probationary or non-accredited representative, that person must be admitted unless an inspector (or above) considers that such a visit will hinder the investigation of crime. In exercising his discretion as to admittance to such a person, an inspector must take into account in particular whether the identity or status of the non-accredited or probationary representative has been satisfactorily established; whether he is of suitable character to provide legal advice (a person with a criminal record is unlikely to be suitable unless the conviction was for a minor offence and is not of recent date); and any other matters in any written letters of authorisation provided.

If an inspector refuses access to a non-accredited or probationary representative or a decision is taken that such a person shall not be permitted to remain at an interview, he must forthwith notify the solicitor on whose behalf the non-accredited or probationary representative was to have acted, or was acting, and give him an opportunity of making other arrangements. The detained person must also be informed and the custody record noted. If an inspector (or above) considers that a particular firm of solicitors is persistently sending non-accredited or probationary representatives who are unsuited to provide legal advice, he should inform a superintendent (or above), who may wish to take the matter up with the Law Society.

A breach of the requirement that suspects should generally be allowed access to a solicitor does not necessarily justify exclusion of evidence obtained at the interview. Where a challenge is made, the court must establish whether a request was made and whether it had been refused. If this is so it must then consider whether a delay in compliance with such a request was permissible under s 58. If it was not, the court must then consider whether the evidence obtained at the interview should be excluded under s 78 or by any rule of common law.

Removal of solicitor

A solicitor (or his representative etc) may only be required to leave if his conduct is such that the investigating officer is unable properly to put questions to the suspect. If the investigating officer considers that a solicitor is acting in such a way, he will stop the interview and consult an officer not below the rank of superintendent, if one is readily available, and otherwise an officer not below the rank of inspector who is not concerned with the investigation. After speaking to the solicitor the officer who has been consulted will decide whether or not the interview should continue in the presence of the solicitor. If he decides that it should not, the suspect will be given an opportunity to consult another solicitor before the interview continues and that solicitor will be given an opportunity to be present.

The Detention Code points out that the removal of a solicitor from an interview is a serious step, and if it occurs, the officer of superintendent rank, or above, who took the decision will consider whether the incident should be reported to the Law Society. If the decision was taken by an officer below the rank of superintendent, a superintendent must consider whether to make such a report. A note of guidance in the Code points out that where an officer takes the decision to exclude a solicitor, he must be in a position to satisfy the court that the decision was properly made. In order to do this, he may need to witness what is happening himself.

Other points

A detained person must be permitted to consult a solicitor for a reasonable time before any court hearing.

Any request for legal advice, and the action taken on it, must be recorded in the custody record. If a person has asked for legal advice and an interview has commenced in the absence of his solicitor etc (or the solicitor etc is required to leave) a record must be made in the interview record.

A detained person who asks for legal advice *may not be interviewed or continue to be interviewed* until he has received it unless:

(a) a delay has been authorised in accordance with the provisions in Annex B set out above; or

(b) a superintendent (or above) has reasonable grounds to believe that delay will involve an immediate risk of harm to persons or serious loss of or damage to property, or where a solicitor, including a duty solicitor, has been contacted and has agreed to attend, awaiting his arrival would cause unreasonable delay to the process of investigation; or

(c) the solicitor nominated by the person, or selected by him from a list, cannot be contacted, has previously indicated that he does not wish to be contacted, or having been contacted has declined to attend, and the person has been advised of the Duty Solicitor Scheme but has declined to ask for the duty solicitor, or the duty solicitor is not available; or

(d) the person who wanted legal advice changes his mind.

Where (c) applies, the interview may be started or continued without further delay provided that an inspector (or above) has given agreement for the interview to continue in those circumstances.

Where (d) applies the interview may be started or continued without further delay provided that the person has given an agreement in writing or on tape to being interviewed without receiving legal advice and that an inspector (or above), having enquired into the person's reasons for his change of mind, has given authority for the interview to proceed. Confirmation of the person's agreement, his change of mind, his reasons where given, and the name of the authorising officer, must be recorded in the written or taped interview record at the beginning or re-commencement of the interview. It is permissible for such authorisation to be given over the telephone, if the authorising officer is able to satisfy himself as to the reason for the suspect's change of mind and is satisfied that it is proper to continue the interview in those circumstances.

The name of the authorising officer and the reason for the suspect's change of mind should be recorded and repeated on tape at the beginning or re-commencement of the interview.

In considering whether awaiting the arrival of a solicitor would cause unreasonable delay ((b) above), the superintendent should, where practicable, ask the solicitor for an estimate of the time he is likely to take in coming to the station, and relate this to the time for which detention is permitted, to whether a required period of rest is imminent, and to the requirements of other investigations in progress. If the solicitor says that he is on his way or that he will set off immediately, it will not normally be appropriate to begin an interview before he arrives. If it appears that it will be necessary to begin an interview before the solicitor's arrival he should be given an indication of how long the police could wait so that he has the opportunity to make arrangements for someone else to provide legal advice.

If an interview is begun under (b) above (ie before a person who has asked for legal advice receives it because delay will involve an immediate risk of harm or serious loss or damage), questioning may not continue until the person has received legal advice once sufficient information to avert the risk has been obtained unless some other ground for delay applies.

Where a person who wanted legal advice changes his mind, the interview may be started or continued without further delay provided he has given his agreement in writing or on tape to his being interviewed without receiving legal advice and an inspector (or above) has agreed to the interview proceeding.

CHAPTER 5

Treatment, charging and bail of detained persons

The comments made at the beginning of ch 4 concerning references to Codes of Practice and the Police and Criminal Evidence Act 1984 apply equally to the provisions of this chapter.

TREATMENT OF DETAINED PERSONS

A person detained at a police station as a place of safety under the Mental Health Act 1983 should not be questioned about any alleged offence or asked to make a statement. However, where such a person is, after such detention, reasonably suspected to have driven a motor vehicle with excess alcohol, it is permissible to commence the breath testing procedure where the attendance of those required to carry out a medical examination cannot be expeditiously arranged.

Whenever the Detention Code requires a person to be given certain information he does not have to be given it if he is incapable at the time of understanding what is said to him or if he is violent or in urgent need of medical attention, but he must be given it as soon as practicable.

Where video cameras are installed in the custody area, suspects and other people entering should be informed by prominently placed notices that cameras are in use. Any request by a suspect or other person to have video cameras switched off should be refused.

The Detention Code lays down a large number of rules concerning conditions of detention and medical treatment.

Conditions of detention

(a) So far as practicable, not more than one person shall be detained in each cell.
(b) Cells in use must be adequately heated, cleaned and ventilated. They must be adequately lit, subject to such dimming as is compatible with safety and security to allow people detained overnight to sleep. No additional restraints should be used within a locked cell unless absolutely necessary, and then only suitable

handcuffs. In the case of mentally handicapped or disordered persons, particular care must be taken when deciding whether to use handcuffs.

(c) Blankets, mattresses, pillows and other bedding supplied should be of a reasonable standard and in a clean and sanitary condition.

(d) Access to toilet and washing facilities must be provided.

(e) If it is necessary to remove a person's clothes for the purpose of investigation, for hygiene or health reasons or for cleaning, replacement clothing of a reasonable standard of comfort and cleanliness must be provided. A person must not be interviewed unless adequate clothing has been offered to him.

(f) At least two light meals and one main meal must be offered in any period of 24 hours. Meals should, so far as practicable, be offered at recognised meal times. Whenever necessary, advice must be sought from the police surgeon on medical or dietary matters. As far as practicable, meals provided must meet any special dietary needs or religious beliefs that a person may have; he may also have meals supplied by his family or friends at his or their own expense. Drinks should be provided at meal times and on reasonable request between meal times.

(g) Brief outdoor exercise must be offered daily if practicable.

(h) A juvenile must not be placed in a police cell, unless no other secure accommodation is available and the custody officer considers that it is not practicable to supervise him if he is not placed in a cell or the custody officer considers that a cell provides more comfortable accommodation than other secure accommodation in the police station.

(i) A juvenile must not be placed in a cell with a detained adult.

(j) Reasonable force may be used if necessary for the following purposes—
   (i) to secure compliance with reasonable instructions, including instructions given in pursuance of the provisions of a code of practice; or
   (ii) to prevent escape, injury, damage to property or the destruction of evidence.

(k) A person who is in detention at a hospital may not be questioned without the agreement of the appropriate doctor.

(l) Persons detained must be visited every hour, and those who are drunk at least every half hour. Wherever possible juveniles and other people at risk should be visited more frequently. A person who is drunk must be roused and spoken to on each visit. Visits or rousing of detained persons made in accordance with the Code, or in accordance with medical advice, do not constitute an interruption to a rest period such that a fresh period must be allowed. Should the custody officer feel in any way concerned about the person's condition, for example because he fails to respond adequately when roused, then the officer must arrange for medical treatment.

Documentation

A record must be kept of replacement clothing and meals offered. If a juvenile is placed in a cell, the reason must be recorded.

Medical treatment

(a) If a person brought to a police station or already detained there appears to be suffering from physical illness or mental disorder, or is injured, or fails to respond normally to questions or conversation (other than through drunkenness alone), or otherwise appears to need medical attention, the custody officer must immediately call the police surgeon. In urgent cases, for example, where a person does not show signs of sensibility or awareness the custody officer must send the person to hospital or call the nearest available medical practitioner. This applies even if the person makes no request for medical attention and whether or not he has recently had medical treatment elsewhere (unless brought straight to the police station from hospital). The requirement to call a police surgeon need not apply to minor ailments or injuries not requiring attention, but such ailments or injuries should be recorded in the custody record.

These rules about seeking medical attention are not intended to delay the transfer of a person to a place of safety under the Mental Health Act 1983, s 136, where that is applicable. Where an assessment under that Act is to take place at a police station, the custody officer has discretion not to call the police surgeon so long as he believes that the assessment by a registered medical practitioner can be undertaken without undue delay.

(b) If it appears to the custody officer, or he is told, that a person brought to the police station under arrest may be suffering from an infectious disease of any significance he must take steps to isolate the person and his property until he has obtained medical directions as to where the person should be taken, whether fumigation should take place and what precautions should be taken by officers who have been or will be in contact with him.

(c) If a detained person requests a medical examination the police surgeon must be called as soon as practicable. He may, in addition, be examined by a medical practitioner of his own choice at his own expense. (It is a frequent practice for persons who are arrested for being drunk and disorderly to demand that a doctor be called because they are not prepared to accept that they are drunk. It has often been the practice to refuse such a request because of the public expense involved and the frequency of the request. Bearing in mind that a failure to comply with the Codes is a disciplinary offence, custody officers are advised to treat such requests as requests for a medical examination and to call a doctor on such occasions.)

(d) If a person is required to take or apply any medication in compliance with medical directions, but prescribed before his detention, the custody officer should consult the police surgeon prior to the use of medication. The custody officer is responsible for the safekeeping of any medication and for ensuring that the person is given the opportunity to take or apply medication which the police surgeon has approved. However, no police officer may administer medicines which are also controlled drugs subject to the Misuse of Drugs Act 1971 for this purpose. A person may administer controlled drugs to himself only under the personal supervision of the police surgeon. The requirement for personal supervision will have been satisfied if the custody officer consults the police surgeon (which may be done by telephone) and both the police surgeon and the custody officer are satisfied that, in all the circumstances, self-administration of the controlled drug will not expose the detained person, police officers or anyone to the risk of harm or injury. If so satisfied, the police surgeon may authorise the custody officer to permit the detained person to administer the controlled drug. If the custody officer is in any doubt, the police surgeon should be asked to attend. Such consultation should be noted in the custody record.

These provisions on controlled drugs must always be borne in mind by custody officers as many of the tablets which are issued on prescription are controlled drugs. Although instructions concerning the taking of the tablets may be clearly marked on the bottle, the police surgeon must be consulted.

(e) If a detained person has in his possession, or claims to need, medication relating to a heart condition, diabetes, epilepsy or a condition of comparable potential seriousness then, even though (a), above, may not apply, the advice of the police surgeon must be obtained.

Records must be kept of a request for a medical examination, of the arrangements for any examination made, and of any medical directions given to the police. The custody record must include not only a record of all medication that a detained person has in his possession on arrival at the police station but also a note of any such medication he claims he needs but does not have with him.

It is important to remember that a person who appears to be drunk or behaving abnormally may be suffering from illness or the effects of drugs or may have sustained injury (particularly a head injury) which is not apparent, and that someone addicted to certain drugs may experience harmful effects within a short time of being deprived of their supply. Consequently, police officers should always err on the side of caution when in doubt about calling the police surgeon, and act with all due speed. A medical practitioner need not record his clinical findings in the custody record, but if he does not the record should show where they are recorded.

A detained person may not be supplied with intoxicating liquor except on medical direction. A record must be made of any intoxicating liquor supplied. No person who is unfit through drink or drugs, to the extent that he is unable to appreciate the significance of questions put to him and his answers, may be questioned about an alleged offence whilst in that condition, except in accordance with Annex C to the Detention Code, (p 89 above).

Complaints – treatment

If a complaint is made by or on behalf of a detained person about his treatment since his arrest, or it comes to the notice of any officer that he may have been treated improperly, a report must be made as soon as practicable to an officer of the rank of inspector (or above) who is not connected with the investigation. If the matter concerns a possible assault or the unnecessary or unreasonable use of force, the police surgeon must also be called as soon as practicable; a record must be made of any arrangements made.

A record must be made of any complaint reported under the above provisions, together with any relevant remarks by the custody officer.

RECEPTION OF ARRESTED PERSONS AT POLICE STATIONS

Section 35 of the 1984 Act requires that chief officers of police designate the police stations in their area which are to be used for the purpose of detaining arrested persons; their duty is to designate police stations which appear to them to provide sufficient accommodation for detaining arrested persons. Where a station is designated, s 36 requires that one or more custody officers must be appointed by the Chief Constable or his nominee. They must be of the rank of sergeant (or above) but the section allows another officer of any rank to perform the duties of a custody officer at a designated police station if such an officer is not readily available to perform those duties. Such an officer is only not 'readily available' if he is not actually at the police station and cannot, without much difficulty, be fetched there.

Where an arrested person is taken to a non-designated police station any officer not concerned in the investigation of the offence may, by s 36, assume the responsibilities of a custody officer. If no such officer is available, it may be the arresting officer.

A custody officer's duties are laid down by ss 37 (pp 100-101), 38 (pp 114-115) and 39. Basically, and this is provided by s 39, he is responsible for persons in detention and for ensuring that they and their property are treated in accordance with the Detention Code, and he is responsible for maintaining a chronological and contemporaneous record of every aspect of a person's treatment whilst in detention. These responsibilities cannot be overstated. The provisions in relation to detention are quite complex and the keeping of such a log means that omissions in the keeping of it cannot be corrected. If a duty is carried out but not recorded, the failure to record as required by the Codes is sufficient to raise the issue of disciplinary proceedings. Generally, custody officers must be independent of investigations in respect of detained persons, but may be involved in identification processes or the obtaining of specimens of breath, blood or urine in accordance with the Road Traffic Act 1988, s 7.

Where the Act and its Codes require that certain things are done by a custody officer, the requirement also applies to a police officer other than a custody officer who is performing the functions of a custody officer.

A custody officer is required to perform the functions specified in the Detention Code as soon as is practicable. A custody officer is not in breach of the code in the event of delay provided that the delay is justifiable and that every reasonable step is taken to prevent unnecessary delay. The custody record must indicate where a delay has occurred and the reason why.

Delays may occur in the processing of suspects because, for example, a large number of suspects are brought into the police station simultaneously to be placed in custody, or interview rooms are all being used, or where there are difficulties in contacting an appropriate adult, solicitor or interpreter.

Police detention

A person is stated by s 118 of the 1984 Act to be in police detention for the purposes of the Act if:

(a) he has been taken to a police station after being arrested for an offence, or after being arrested under the Prevention of Terrorism (Temporary Provisions) Act 1989, s 14 or under para 6 of Sch 5 to that Act by an examining officer who is a constable; or

(b) he is arrested at a police station after attending voluntarily at the station or accompanying a constable to it; and -
   (i) is detained there; or
   (ii) is detained elsewhere in the charge of a constable.

In most circumstances, of course, a person's detention begins under (a) on arrival at a police station under arrest. If a person is subsequently removed from a police station, for example, to attend an identification parade or to visit the scene of a crime or on transfer to another station, he is in detention whilst he remains in the charge of a constable. This is important when periods of detention are to be considered by custody officers. By way of an exception, s 118 provides that a person who is at a court after being charged is not in police detention for the purposes of the Act.

As we have already stated, a separate custody record must be opened as soon as practicable for each person detained at a police station.

Limitations on police detention

Section 34 of the 1984 Act provides that no person in police detention may be released except on the authority of a custody officer. It requires that if at any time a custody officer:

(a)   becomes aware, in relation to any person in police detention at that station, that the grounds for the detention of that person have ceased to apply; and
(b)   is not aware of any other grounds on which the continued detention of that person could be justified under the provisions of the Act,

the custody officer must order his immediate release from custody. However, persons who were unlawfully at large when arrested must not be released under these provisions.

A person released in these circumstances must be released without bail, unless it appears to the custody officer that there is a need for further investigation of any matter in connection with which he was detained at any time during the period of his detention, or that proceedings may be taken against him in respect of any such matter, in which case he must be released on bail.

An investigating officer may bring facts to the notice of a custody officer but issues of further detention or release are to be decided by the custody officer. It will be appreciated that custody officers may find themselves in dispute with officers of senior rank in respect of detention issues. If this occurs the superintendent responsible for the police station must be consulted.

Duties of custody officer before charge

Section 37 of the 1984 Act states that the decision whether or not to charge or detain persons arrested without warrant or on a warrant which is not endorsed for bail is that of the custody officer. He should note on the custody record any comment the person may make in relation to the arresting officer's account but should not invite comment. If the custody officer authorises a person's detention he must inform him of the grounds as soon as practicable and in any case before that person is then questioned about any offence. The custody officer must note any comment the person may make in respect of the decision to detain him but must not invite comment, nor may he put specific questions to the person concerning his involvement in any offence, nor in respect of any comments he may make in response to the investigating officer's account or the decision to place him in detention. Such an exchange is likely to constitute an interview and would require the necessary safeguards. If there is insufficient evidence of an offence, the custody officer must release that person either with or without bail, unless he has reasonable grounds for believing that detention is necessary to secure or preserve evidence of the offence or to obtain evidence by questioning him. If the person is detained without charge, the grounds must be recorded as soon as practicable by the custody officer.

If the custody officer determines that he has sufficient evidence to charge the person arrested for the offence for which he was arrested, that person must be charged or released without charge (with or without bail). By way of exception, if the person arrested is not in a fit state to be dealt with in this way (eg because he is under the influence of drink or drugs), he may be kept in police detention until he is in a fit state. If a person is released without charge, and a decision has not yet been taken whether he should be prosecuted, the custody officer must inform him of this.

Information to be given to detained persons

When the custody officer authorises the detention of a person who has not been charged, he is required by s 37 to make, as soon as practicable, a written record on the custody record of the grounds which exist for detention. This must be done in the person's presence and he must be informed of those grounds. (However, if at that time a person is incapable of understanding what is said to him or is violent or is likely to be so, or is in urgent need of medical treatment, the information may be given as soon as practicable, and in any case before he is questioned for the offence.)

At the same time the detained person must be informed clearly of the following rights: his right to have someone informed of his arrest, his right to consult privately with a solicitor and the fact that independent legal advice is available free of charge, and his right to consult the Codes of Practice (which must be available at all police stations). The detained person must also be told that he need not exercise those rights immediately; they may be exercised at any time whilst in detention. He must be given a written notice setting out those rights and informing him of his right to a copy of the custody record at the time of his release. The written notice must also set out the caution in the terms already described and explain the arrangements for obtaining legal advice. The custody officer must also give the detained person an additional notice setting out his entitlements while in custody, which have been described above. The custody officer should obtain the person's signature on the custody record acknowledging receipt of these notices; any refusal to sign must be recorded on the custody record. The person must be asked to signify on the custody record whether or not he wants legal advice at this stage. Where legal advice is requested (and unless delay has been validly authorised, see p 90), the custody officer must act without delay to secure the provision of such advice to the person concerned. A person attending a police station voluntarily who asks about his entitlement to legal advice should also be given such a notice.

The provisions concerning persons with language difficulties, those mentally ill etc and juveniles, which have already been outlined in respect of persons being interviewed, apply equally to persons in custody. If the appropriate adult is already at the police station when information is given to the detained person under the above provisions, the information must be given to the detained person in his presence. If the appropriate adult is not then present, the information must be given to the detained person again in the presence of the appropriate adult once he arrives.

Communication by detained persons with others

A detained person has a right under s 56 to have someone informed at public expense and as soon as practicable of his detention. However, this extends only to one friend, relative or other person who is known to him or is likely to take an interest in his welfare. If the person cannot be contacted, the detained person may choose up to two alternatives. If they cannot be contacted the custody officer may allow further attempts. If a person is moved from one police station to another, the right to have someone informed of his whereabouts arises again.

Section 56, together with Annex B to the Detention Code, provides that a delay in informing someone may only be authorised by a superintendent (or above) where the person has been detained for a serious arrestable offence and has not been charged with it. The authorisation may be given where there are reasonable grounds for believing that telling the person named of the arrest:

(a)   will lead to interference with, or harm to, evidence connected with a serious arrestable offence or interference with or physical harm to other persons; or
(b)   will lead to the alerting of other persons suspected of having committed such an offence but not yet arrested for it; or
(c)   will hinder the recovery of any property obtained as a result of such an offence.

An officer may also authorise delay where the serious arrestable offence is a drug trafficking offence or an offence to which Part VI of the Criminal Justice Act 1988 (confiscation of the proceeds of an offence) applies; and the officer has reasonable grounds for believing that:

(a)   the detained person has benefited from drug trafficking and that the recovery of the value of that person's proceeds of drug trafficking will be hindered by the exercise of the right to have someone notified of the arrest, or (as the case may be)
(b)   the detained person has benefited from the Part VI offence and that the recovery of the value of the benefit will be hindered by the exercise of that right.

If a delay is authorised, then as soon as possible the detained person must be informed of the reason for it and the reason must be noted on his custody record. If given orally, the authorisation must be confirmed in writing as soon as practicable. When the reasons for delay have been removed, for example by the arrest of other persons, the request to communicate must be granted. The right to communicate cannot be delayed for more than 36 hours.

Where an arrest is made under the Prevention of Terrorism (Temporary Provisions) Act 1989 communication to a friend etc may be delayed up to 48 hours.

Visits, letters and phone calls

The Detention Code makes the following additional provisions about what may be called the right not to be held incommunicado.

A person in detention may receive visits at the discretion of the custody officer. Where inquiries by interested persons are received concerning his whereabouts, the information must be given if the prisoner agrees and a superintendent (or above) has not authorised delay in the release of such information. The custody officer must exercise his discretion as to visits in the light of the availability of sufficient manpower to supervise a visit and any possible hindrance to the investigation.

The prisoner must also be supplied on request with writing material. Letters and messages must be sent (at his expense) as soon as practicable, but all letters, other than those to his solicitor, may be read. The prisoner may speak for a reasonable time to one person on the telephone. Whether or not the call can be made at police expense is a matter for the custody officer's discretion. Reasonable calls of a local character will probably be allowed at police expense. Unless the call is to a solicitor, a police officer may listen to the call and may terminate it if it is being abused. A person in detention must be cautioned that what he says in a letter, call or message (other than to his solicitor) may be read or listened to and may be given in evidence. An interpreter may make a call on behalf of a detained person. Where an officer of the rank of inspector or above considers that the sending of a letter or the making of a telephone call may result in Annex B applying, and the person is detained in connection with an arrestable or serious arrestable offence, that officer can deny or delay the exercise of either or both these privileges.

A record must be kept:

(a) of any request made in relation to matters of communication and of the action taken in consequence of that request;

(b) of letters or messages sent, calls made or visits received; and

(c) of any refusal by the prisoner to have information about himself or his whereabouts given to an outside inquirer.

The prisoner must be asked to countersign the record accordingly and any refusal to do so should be recorded.

Children and young persons

Where a child or young person is in police detention, the Children and Young Persons Act 1933, s 34 requires that his parent or guardian must be informed as soon as practicable that he has been arrested; why he was arrested; and where he is being detained. If a supervision order is in force, his supervisor must also be informed. If he is in care, the care authority or voluntary organisation must be informed in place of the parent or guardian. Such steps as are practicable must be taken to identify the person responsible for the juvenile's welfare.

For the purposes of s 34 a young person is a person who has attained the age of 14 years and is under the age of 17 years.

Aliens etc

The Detention Code provides that a citizen of an independent Commonwealth country or a foreign national may communicate at any time with his High Commission, Embassy or Consulate. Such a person must be informed as soon as practicable after being detained of his right to communicate with such agencies, and such agencies must be informed of an arrest. Consular officers may visit to advise such persons and those visits must take place out of the hearing of a police officer.

FURTHER RIGHTS OF PERSONS DETAINED

Access to legal advice

This matter has been dealt with in the previous chapter.

Searching and retention of property

The 1984 Act removes all previous powers to search persons in custody, whether derived from the common or statute law, and substitutes new powers.

Section 54 charges the custody officer with a duty to ascertain the property which a person has with him when he is:

(a) brought to a police station after being arrested elsewhere or after being committed to custody by an order or a sentence of a court; or

(b) arrested at a police station or detained there when answering police bail or is arrested under s 46A (failure to answer police bail (see p 117);

and to record particulars of that property in the person's custody record. To do this a person may be searched to the extent considered to be necessary by the custody officer, but an intimate search may not be carried out under s 54, and a strip search may only be carried out if the necessary requirements set out below are satisfied.

Articles other than those subject to legal privilege (eg letters from solicitors etc) may be seized and retained. However, clothes and personal effects (which do not include cash) may only be seized if the custody officer believes that they may be used by the person:

(a) to cause physical injury to himself or another;
(b) to damage property;
(c) to interfere with evidence;
(d) to assist him to escape;

or if the custody officer has *reasonable grounds* for believing that they may be evidence of an offence.

There will be some difficult decisions to be taken by custody officers who are required to allow a person in custody to retain property of a personal, non-dangerous character. Is a woman's vanity mirror likely to cause harm? It will not do so whilst it remains in its original condition but it will certainly do so if it is broken. This, perhaps, leads to a second question for the custody officer; is the woman in a mental state which might lead her to attempt to take her own life? Whatever decision the officer takes, he should apply his mind carefully to the particular situation which confronts him. If personal articles are retained by the custody officer he must explain why.

In addition, a person who is in custody at a police station or is in police detention otherwise than at a police station may at any time be searched by any constable in order to ascertain whether he has with him any articles which he could use for any of the purposes in (a) to (d) above. A constable may seize and detain anything found in such a search, except that clothes and personal effects may only be seized in the same circumstances as mentioned above.

An examination of the mouth is a non-intimate search which may be undertaken by a constable under s 54(8) of the 1984 Act. A dentist has no power to conduct such examination without consent under these provisions.

Where articles are seized, the person must be told the reason unless he is violent or likely to be violent or is incapable of understanding. Items which are seized on the grounds that they may be used to cause injury, damage, interfere with evidence or assist escape must be returned when the person is released from police detention. The Detention Code states that the custody officer is responsible for the safekeeping of property taken from a person.

Whether property is seized or left with the prisoner, the custody officer must record all property that a person had with him, or had taken from him on arrest. The detained person must be allowed to check and sign the property record. The reasons must be recorded for the retention of each article.

SEARCHES

Strip searches

A strip search is any search involving the removal of more than outer clothing. The Detention Code states that, in order for such a search to take place, the custody officer must believe it to be necessary to remove an article which the detained person would not be allowed to keep and there is reasonable suspicion that the person might have concealed such an article. Strip searches should not be routinely carried out where there is no reason for suspicion that articles have been concealed.

Conduct

The following procedures must be observed when strip searches are conducted:

(a) a police officer carrying out a strip search must be the same sex as the person searched;

(b) the search must take place in an area where the suspect cannot be seen by anyone who does not need to be present, nor by a member of the opposite sex (except an appropriate adult who has specifically been requested by the person being searched);

(c) except in cases of urgency, where there is a risk of serious harm to the person detained or to others, whenever a strip search involves exposure of intimate parts of the body, there must be at least two people present other than the person searched, and if the search is of a juvenile or mentally disordered or mentally handicapped person, one of the people must be the appropriate adult. Except in urgent cases as above, a search of a juvenile may take place in the absence of an appropriate adult only if the juvenile signifies in the presence of the appropriate adult that he prefers the search to be done in his absence and the appropriate adult agrees. A record must be made of the juvenile's decision and signed by the appropriate adult. The presence of more than two people, other than the appropriate adult, may be permitted only in the most exceptional circumstances;

(d) the search must be conducted with proper regard to the sensitivity and vulnerability of the person in these circumstances. Every reasonable effort must be made to secure the person's co-operation and minimise embarrassment. People who are searched should not normally be required to have all their clothes removed at the same time, for example, a man should be allowed to put on his shirt before removing his trousers, and a woman should be allowed to put on her blouse and upper garments before further clothing is removed;

(e) where necessary to assist the search, the suspect may be required to hold his or her arms in the air or to stand with his or her legs apart and to bend forward so that a visual examination may be made of the genital and anal areas provided that no physical contact is made with any body orifice;

(f) if, during a search, articles are found, the person must be asked to hand them over. If articles are found within any body orifice other than the mouth, and the person refuses to hand them over, their removal would constitute an intimate search which must be carried out in accordance with the provisions of the Code set out below;

(g) a strip search should be conducted as quickly as possible, and the suspect allowed to dress as soon as the procedure is complete.

Documentation

A record should be made on the custody record of a strip search. It should include the reason it was considered necessary to undertake it, those present and any result.

Intimate searches

An intimate search is a search which consists of the physical examination of a person's body orifices other than the mouth. 'Body orifices' includes nose, ears, anus and vagina. Intimate searches are governed by s 55 of the 1984 Act.

Authorisation

An intimate search must be authorised by an officer of at least the rank of superintendent. To authorise such a search the officer must have reasonable grounds for believing that:

(a) an article which could cause physical injury to a detained person or others at the police station has been concealed; or
(b) the person has concealed a Class A drug which he intended to supply to another or to export; and
(c) in either case an intimate search is the only practicable means of removing it.

The authorisation of an intimate search may be given orally or in writing, but if orally it must be confirmed in writing as soon as practicable.

Execution

Intimate searches may take place only at:

(a) a police station (but not if it is a drug offence search);
(b) a hospital;
(c) a surgery; or
(d) other medical premises.

Before an intimate search takes place, the reasons why it is considered necessary must be explained to the person to be searched and he must be reminded of his entitlement to have legal advice and the reminder must be noted in the custody record.

An intimate search may only be carried out by a doctor or registered nurse, unless a superintendent (or above) considers that it is not practicable and the search takes place because there are reasonable grounds for believing that an article which could cause physical injury to the detained person or others at the police station has been concealed, in which case it must be carried out by a constable of the same sex and the reason for the impracticability must be recorded. Except in the case of a juvenile, no one of the opposite sex, other than a doctor or nurse, may be present, nor anyone whose presence is unnecessary, but a minimum of two people, other than the person searched, must be present during the search. A search should be conducted with proper regard to the sensitivity and vulnerability of the suspect in the circumstances.

An intimate search at a police station of a juvenile, or person who is mentally disordered or mentally handicapped, must take place in the presence of the appropriate adult of the same sex (unless the person specifically requests the presence of a particular adult of the opposite sex who is readily available). In the case of a juvenile, the search may take place in the absence of the appropriate adult only if the juvenile signifies in the presence of the appropriate adult that he prefers it to be done in his absence and the appropriate adult agrees. A record should be made of the juvenile's decision and signed by the appropriate adult.

See p 136 concerning identification by way of intimate, non-intimate and other samples.

Documentation

After an intimate search has been carried out, a record must be made as soon as practicable on the custody record, stating which parts of the body were searched, who carried out the search, who was present, the reasons for the search and its result. The powers of seizure in respect of articles found are the same as those which apply to other searches.

REVIEWS AND MAXIMUM PERIODS OF POLICE DETENTION

Reviews

Section 40(4) of the 1984 Act requires periodic reviews of the detention of each person in police detention. The review will be carried out:

(a) in the case of a person who has been arrested and charged, by the custody officer; and
(b) in the case of a person who has been arrested but not charged, by an officer of at least the rank of inspector who has not been directly involved in the investigation.

The officer by whom the review is carried out is called the 'review officer'.

There will be some designated police stations at which the custody officer will be an officer of the rank of inspector. Where this is so he could carry out both of the above functions.

Section 40 is precise in relation to when these reviews must be carried out:

(a) the first review must be not later than *six hours* after the detention was first authorised;
(b) the second review must be not later than *nine hours* after the first;
(c) subsequent reviews must be at intervals of *not more than nine hours*.

The purpose of a review

The review officer is responsible under s 40 for determining whether or not a person's detention continues to be necessary.

The case of a person who has been arrested but not charged

Here the review officer must proceed as follows:

(a) Where the person was detained because he was not in a fit state to be charged or released without charge (with or without bail), eg because he was under the influence of drink or drugs, the review officer must consider whether he is now in a fit state to be charged or so released. If he is, one or other of these courses must be adopted. If he is not, further detention may be authorised, but consideration should be given to whether there is sufficient evidence to charge him with an offence.

(b) Where, although there is then insufficient evidence to charge him, the detention of the person has been authorised by the custody officer on the basis that there are reasonable grounds to believe that his detention without charge is necessary to secure or preserve evidence relating to an offence for which he is under arrest or to obtain such evidence, the review officer may authorise further detention if this is necessary on the same basis.

The case of the person who has been charged

The person must be released, either on bail or without bail, unless:

(a) his name and address cannot be ascertained or there are reasonable grounds to doubt the name and address given; or

(b) there are reasonable grounds to believe that detention is necessary for his own protection or to prevent him causing physical injury to any person or loss of or damage to property; or

(c) there are reasonable grounds to believe that the person will fail to answer bail or that his detention is necessary to prevent him interfering with the administration of justice or with police investigations; or

(d) in the case of an arrested juvenile, detention is necessary in his own interests.

General

If, in the light of the above considerations, the review officer authorises the detention of a person (whether charged or not) to continue, the review officer must make a written record of the grounds for the detention as soon as practicable. He must do so in the presence of the detained person *and* inform him of the grounds, unless that person is incapable of understanding, violent or likely to become violent, or in urgent need of medical attention.

The review officer, on all occasions, must give an opportunity for representations by, or on behalf of, the detained person. After hearing any representations, the review officer, or officer determining whether further detention should be authorised, shall note any comment the person may make if the decision is to keep him in detention. The officer must not put specific questions to the suspect regarding his involvement in any offence, nor in respect of any comments he may make in response to the decision to keep him in detention. Such an exchange is likely to constitute an 'interview' and would require the safeguard of the Code's provisions concerning interviews generally. Before conducting a review he must ensure that the detained person is reminded of his entitlement to free legal advice. This reminder must be noted in the custody record. Section 40 requires that the person (unless he is asleep), or any solicitor who is representing him who is available at the time of the review, must be given an opportunity by the review officer to make representations to him concerning the detention. If the detained person is likely to be asleep at the latest time when a review may take place, the review officer should bring it forward so that the detained person may make representations without being woken up. At the discretion of the review officer, persons other than a solicitor, who have an interest in the detained prisoner's welfare, may be allowed to make representations. If the detained person is unfit, by reason of his condition or his behaviour, the review officer may refuse to hear oral representations from him.

The grounds for, and the extent of, any delay in conducting a review must be recorded. Any written representations which are made must be retained. A record must be made as soon as practicable of the outcome of each review and of any application for a warrant of further detention (see p 111) or its extension.

Postponement of review

Section 40 of the 1984 Act allows for the postponement of a review:

(a) if, having regard to all the circumstances prevailing at the latest time for the review in question, it is not practicable to carry out the review at that time;
(b) without prejudice to the generality of (a) above -
   (i) if at that time the person in detention is being questioned by a police officer and the review officer is satisfied that an interruption of the questioning for the purpose of carrying out the review would prejudice the investigation in connection with which he is being questioned; or
   (ii) if at that time no review officer is readily available.

If a review is postponed it must be carried out as soon as practicable after the normal latest time for it. The reason for any postponement must be recorded in the custody record. In the event of a review being postponed, this does not affect the time at which any subsequent review must be carried out. This means that a second review must be carried out nine hours after the latest time at which the first review should have taken place, which time is six hours after the detention was first authorised.

Limits on period of detention without charge

Section 41 of the 1984 Act provides that a person must not be kept in police detention for more than 24 hours without being charged, except that detention beyond that period may be authorised in certain circumstances by an officer of the rank of superintendent (or above) (s 42) or by a magistrates' court (ss 43 and 44).

Calculation of period of detention

Section 41 refers to the 'relevant time', which is the time from which the detention of a particular person is to be calculated. This may be:

(a) in the case where a person, whose arrest is sought in one police area in England and Wales, is arrested in another area, and is not questioned in the area in which he is arrested about the offence for which he has been arrested, *the time at which the person arrives at the first police station in the area in which his arrest is sought, or the time 24 hours after that person's arrest, whichever is the earlier;*
(b) in the case of a person arrested outside England and Wales, *the time at which that person arrives at the first police station to which he is taken in the police area in England and Wales in which the offence for which he is arrested is being investigated, or the time 24 hours after the time of that person's entry into England and Wales, whichever is the earlier;*
(c) in the case of a person who attends voluntarily at a police station, or who accompanies a constable to a police station without having been arrested, and is

arrested at the police station, *the time of his arrest*;

(d)   in any other case, it is the time at which the person arrested arrives at the first police station to which he is taken after arrest, *unless he is in detention in an area* in England and Wales and his arrest for an offence is being sought *in some other police area* in England and Wales and he is taken to that second area for the purpose of investigating that offence, without being questioned in the first area in order to obtain evidence in relation to it. In such a case the 'relevant time' will be 24 hours after he leaves the place where he is detained in the first area or the time at which he arrives at the first police station to which he is taken in the second area, whichever is the earlier.

These provisions appear to be extremely complicated at first sight but they may be summarised for ease of understanding. If we think of the 'relevant time' as the time at which we must start our detention alarm clock we find that the 'relevant time' is *normally the time of arrival at the relevant police station*. However, there are additions and variations which affect the time at which the clock must be started. *It must be started*:

(a)   24 hours after arrest (in the unlikely event of it taking longer than that to get the prisoner to a police station);
(b)   if the person is arrested outside England and Wales, on arrival at the first police station in the area of the offence (or 24 hours after arrival in England and Wales if that is earlier);
(c)   at the time of arrest at a police station (eg in interview room);
(d)   at the time of arrival at the first police station in the area of the offence (when the prisoner is taken to other than a designated police station in the first instance); or
(e)   if the person is in the detention of one force and his arrest is sought by another (and he is not questioned in the area of the first force), the detention clock of the second force will start on arrival at the first police station in the area where the offence was committed (subject to a maximum of 24 hours after leaving his place of detention in the area of arrest).

Section 41 provides a safeguard in relation to a person in police detention who, whilst detained, is arrested for a second offence. The detention clock does not start again with his arrest for the second offence. It also provides for instances in which a person in police detention is removed to a hospital for medical treatment. Normally the period commencing with his journey to hospital and ending with his arrival back in police custody does not count towards his 24 hours in police custody; in effect, the clock may be stopped. However, any period, either during his journey or whilst in hospital, during which he is questioned by a police officer for the purpose of obtaining evidence in relation to an offence, is included in his period of police detention.

Release from detention after 24 hours

If a person has not been charged after 24 hours in police detention he *must* normally be released either on bail or without bail. A person so released must not be re-arrested without a warrant for the same offence unless new evidence justifying a further arrest has come to light since his release but this does not prevent his arrest for failure to surrender to police bail. It is submitted that evidence justifying further arrest would have to be substantial, probably sufficient in itself to justify arrest.

Release after 24 hours is not required if continued detention is authorised or a warrant of further detention is issued under the powers next discussed.

Continued detention

The relevant provisions are set out by s 42 of the 1984 Act. Where an officer of the rank of superintendent (or above) who is responsible for a police station at which a person is detained has reasonable grounds for believing that:

(a) the detention of that person without charge is necessary to secure or preserve evidence relating to an offence for which he is under arrest or to obtain such evidence by-questioning him;
(b) an offence for which he is under arrest is a 'serious arrestable offence' (defined on p 61); and
(c) the investigation is being conducted diligently and expeditiously,

he may authorise the keeping of that person in police detention for a period expiring at or before 36 hours after the relevant time.

This may not be done if the person has been in detention for more than 24 hours from the relevant time when the authorisation of continued detention is sought, nor may such an authorisation be given before the second review of that person's detention, ie the review at 15 hours after detention was first authorised. If the first period of continued detention given does not take the detention time fully to 36 hours (a superintendent will not necessarily authorise an additional 12 hours), a further period may be authorised if the conditions in the previous paragraph are satisfied, up to the maximum of 36 hours. This further period may be authorised at any time during the first extension, and even though more than 24 hours has elapsed from the relevant time.

The person detained must be informed on all occasions of the grounds for his continued detention and the custody record must be endorsed with them. He, or his solicitor, must also be given the opportunity to make representations, either orally or in writing. If when such an extension of detention is authorised the person detained has not yet exercised his right to have some person informed of his detention, or his right of access to legal advice, the custody officer must inform him of his rights, decide whether he shall be permitted to exercise them, and record his decision in the custody record.

A person who has been the subject of continued detention must be released, with or without bail, not later than 36 hours after the relevant time, unless he has been charged, or unless his continued detention is authorised or is otherwise permitted by a warrant of further detention. Such a person may not be re-arrested without warrant for the same offence unless new evidence justifying a further arrest has come to light since his release, but this does not apply to a person who fails to surrender to police bail.

Warrant of further detention

Such a warrant is governed by ss 43 and 44 of the 1984 Act. A magistrates' court may issue a warrant of further detention following an application on oath by a constable which is supported by a written information. The court must be satisfied that there are reasonable grounds for believing that further detention is justified. A person's further detention is only justified for the purpose of ss 43 and 44 if:

(a) his detention without charge is necessary to secure or preserve evidence relating to the offence for which he is under arrest or to obtain such evidence by questioning him;
(b) an offence for which he is under arrest is a serious arrestable offence; and
(c) the investigation is being conducted diligently and expeditiously.

The prisoner must be given a copy of the information and he must be brought before the court. If he is not legally represented, but wishes such representation, the court must adjourn for this to be done and he may be kept in detention during the adjournment.

An application for a warrant of further detention may be made at any time before the expiry of 36 hours after the 'relevant time', or, if it is not practicable for the magistrates' court to sit at that time but it will sit during the six hours following that period, at any time before the expiry of those six hours. It is not sufficient for the police to have the application on the court lists for hearing within the sitting of the court. The application must be brought to the notice of the court before the end of the relevant period.

A warrant of further detention must state the time of issue and the period of detention which it authorises, which must not be longer than 36 hours. It may be extended for a further period, up to 36 hours, but must in no circumstances permit detention beyond 96 hours after the relevant time. A 'magistrates' court' in the present context is a court consisting of two or more justices, sitting otherwise than in open court for the purpose of these provisions.

Where a warrant of further detention is issued, the person must be released from police detention, with or without bail, on or before the expiry of the warrant unless he is charged. He may not be re-arrested for the same offence unless new evidence has come to light since his arrest, but this does not apply to a person who fails to surrender to police bail.

CHARGING DETAINED PERSONS

Procedures

When a police officer considers that there is sufficient evidence to prosecute a detained person, and that there is sufficient evidence for the prosecution to succeed, and that the person has said all that he wishes to say about the offence, he should without delay cease to question him and bring him before the custody officer, except that if the person is detained in respect of more than one offence it is permissible to delay bringing him before the custody officer until the above conditions are satisfied in respect of all the offences. The custody officer is then responsible for considering whether or not the detained person should be charged. If the person is a juvenile or is mentally disordered or mentally handicapped, any resulting action must be done in the presence of the appropriate adult.

A person who is charged or informed that he may be prosecuted for an offence must be cautioned in the terms set out at p 76. He must also be given a written notice showing particulars of the offence charged, which must include the name of the officer in the case (in terrorist cases, the officer's warrant or other identification number instead), the police station and the reference number for the case. The charge must be stated in simple terms but must show the precise offence in law. The notice must begin with the following words:

'You are charged with the offence(s) shown below. You do not have to say anything. But it may harm your defence if you do not mention now something which you later rely on in court. Anything you do say may be given in evidence.'

Where applicable the notice must be given to the appropriate adult.

If, after these procedures have been carried out, a police officer wishes to bring to the notice of a person who has been charged with an offence, or informed that he may be prosecuted for it, any written statement made by another person, or the content of an interview with another person, he must hand that person a true copy of it or draw his attention to the interview record, but he must not say or do anything to invite a reply or comment other than to warn him that he does not have to say anything but that anything he does say may be given in evidence and to remind him of his right to legal advice.

In addition, further questions relating to the offence may not generally be asked of a person after he has been charged with that offence, or informed that he may be prosecuted for it. Exceptions are where they are necessary for the purpose of preventing or minimising harm or loss to some other person or to the public or for clearing up ambiguity in a previous answer or statement, or where it is in the interests of justice that the person should have put to him (and have the opportunity to comment upon) new information concerning the offence, or where he volunteers to make a further statement. This could occur where an accused mentions that property stolen was sold to a second party, or where a reference is made to a day of the week but no date is given, or where the name of a street is given without mention of the town. It could also occur where it would be advantageous to the accused and in the interests of justice for him to have another offence taken into consideration by the court, should he be prepared to admit responsibility. In such cases the accused must be cautioned before further questions are put and the caution must be written at the head of any statement made.

Where a juvenile is charged with an offence and the custody officer authorises his continued detention, the custody officer must try to make arrangements for the juvenile to be taken into the care of the local authority to be detained pending appearance in court. This requirement does not apply if the custody officer certifies that it is impracticable to do so, or, in the case of a juvenile of at least 12 years of age, no secure accommodation is available and there is a risk to the public of serious harm from that juvenile.

Documentation

A record must be made of anything a detained person says when he is charged. Questions put after such a charge and answers given must be contemporaneously recorded in full on the forms provided and the record must be signed by that person or, if he refuses, by the interviewing officer and any third parties present. If the questions are tape-recorded the arrangements set out in the Tape Recording Code apply.

If it is not practicable for a juvenile to be transferred to the custody of a local authority the custody officer must record the reasons and make out a certificate to the effect that it is impracticable, which must be produced before the court together with the juvenile.

Neither a juvenile's behaviour nor the nature of the offence with which he is charged provides grounds for the custody officer to decide that it is impracticable to seek to arrange for his transfer to the care of the local authority. Similarly, the lack of secure local authority accommodation does not make it impracticable for the custody officer to transfer him. The availability of secure accommodation is only one factor in relation to a juvenile aged 12 or over when the local authority accommodation would not be adequate to protect the public from serious harm from the juvenile. The obligation to transfer a juvenile to local authority accommodation applies as much to a juvenile charged during the daytime as it does to a juvenile to be held overnight, subject to a requirement to bring the juvenile before a court under the Police and Criminal Evidence Act 1984, s 46.

DETENTION AFTER CHARGE

Section 46 of the 1984 Act requires that where a person:

(a) is charged with an offence; and
(b) after being charged, is kept in police detention or (in the case of a juvenile) is detained by a local authority,

he must be brought before a magistrates' court as soon as practicable and in any event not later than the first sitting after he is charged (or, if he is to be brought before a magistrates' court in another area, not later than the first sitting of that court after his arrival in that area). If the person is to be brought before a magistrates' court in another area, he must be removed to that area as soon as practicable for the above purpose.

If no magistrates' court is due to sit on the day the person is charged (or on the day he arrives in the other area) or on the next day, the custody officer must inform the clerk to the court that there is a person in the area who has been detained after charge, and the clerk must arrange for a sitting of a magistrates' court not later than the day next following the day on which he is charged (or, if he has been transferred to another area, the day next following the day of his arrival in that area). Christmas Day, Good Friday and any Sunday do not count as 'days next following' for this purpose; thus, for example, the day next following Saturday is Monday.

None of the above provisions requires a person who is in hospital to be brought before a court if he is not well enough.

BAIL

When an investigating officer brings his prisoner before the custody officer, the custody officer may decide that there is insufficient evidence to justify a charge and that there is unlikely to be other evidence obtained; or that there is enough evidence to charge at that stage; or that there is not sufficient evidence available at that stage to charge the prisoner, but that there probably will be when further inquiries have been made. If the first of the decisions is reached the prisoner must be released at once without charge. If the second or third decision is reached, the following actions may be taken if it is decided that there are no further grounds for keeping the person in custody.

Police bail of person charged

Bail here means bail subject to a duty to appear before a magistrates' court.

Adults

Section 38 of the 1984 Act requires that, when a person arrested otherwise than under a warrant endorsed for bail is charged with an offence, the custody officer must, subject to the Criminal Justice and Public Order Act 1994, s 25 (bail for defendant charged or convicted for homicide or rape after previous conviction for such an offence only if there are exceptional circumstances justifying it) order his release from police detention, either on bail or without bail, *unless:*

(a) his name and address cannot be ascertained or the custody officer has reasonable grounds for doubting the truth of a name or address provided by him; or

(b)   the custody officer has reasonable grounds for believing that the person arrested will fail to appear in court to answer bail;

(c)   in the case of a person arrested for an imprisonable offence, the custody officer has reasonable grounds for believing that the detention of the person is necessary to prevent him from committing an offence;

(d)   in the case of a person arrested for an offence which is not an imprisonable offence, the custody officer has reasonable grounds for believing that the detention of the person is necessary to prevent him from causing physical injury to any other person or from causing loss of or damage to property;

(e)   the custody officer has reasonable grounds for believing that the detention of the person arrested is necessary to prevent him from interfering with the administration of justice or with the investigation of offences or of a particular offence; or

(f)   the custody officer has reasonable grounds for believing that the detention of the person arrested is necessary for his own protection.

An 'imprisonable offence' is one punishable by imprisonment.

Juveniles

Section 38 provides that if the person charged is a juvenile the custody officer must order his release from police detention, with or without bail, unless one of the above grounds applies or he has reasonable grounds for believing that the juvenile should be detained in the interests of his welfare.

The section also requires that where a custody officer authorises an arrested juvenile to be kept in police detention, the custody officer must secure that the arrested juvenile is to be taken to local authority accommodation unless the custody officer certifies:

(a)   that by reason of such circumstances as are specified in the certificate, it is impracticable to do so; or

(b)   in the case of a boy aged 15 that no secure accommodation is available and that keeping him in other local authority accommodation would not be adequate to protect the public from serious harm from him.

'Secure accommodation' is that provided for the purposes of restricting liberty. In the case of arrested juveniles who are charged with a violent or sexual offence (as defined by the Act; see below), the reference in (b) to protecting the public from serious harm is to protection from death or serious personal injury, whether physical or psychological, occasioned by further such offences. The term 'sexual offence' in this context means an offence under one of the following Acts:

(a)   the Sexual Offences Act 1956 (other than living on immoral earnings, woman exercising control over a prostitute, or offences connected with brothels);

(b)   the Mental Health Act 1959, s 128 (sexual intercourse with patient);

(c)   the Indecency with Children Act 1960;

(d)   the Theft Act 1968, s 9 (burglary with intent to commit rape);

(e)   the Criminal Law Act 1977, s 54 (inciting incest with girl under 16);

(f)   the Protection of Children Act 1978 (indecent photographs); or

(g)   conspiracy, incitement or attempt to commit any of these offences.

'Violent offence' means an offence which leads, or is intended or likely to lead, to a person's death or to physical injury to a person, and includes an offence which is required to be charged as arson (whether or not it would otherwise fall within this definition).

Except as provided above, neither a juvenile's behaviour nor the nature of the offence with which he is charged provides grounds for the custody officer to retain him in police custody rather than to seek to arrange for the transfer to the care of the local authority on the grounds of impracticability. Similarly, the lack of secure local authority accommodation does not make it impracticable for the custody officer to transfer him. The availability of secure accommodation is only one factor in relation to a juvenile aged 12 or over for whom other local authority accommodation would not be adequate to protect the public from serious harm from the juvenile.

Conditional bail

Section 47 of the 1984 Act states that a release on bail under the detention provisions of the Act shall be a release on bail granted in accordance with the Bail Act 1976, ss 3, 3A, 5 and 5A as they apply to bail granted by a constable as set out below. A custody officer releasing a person on bail under s 38(1) (duties of custody officer after charge) or s 40(10) (which applies s 38(1) to review situations) has power to impose such conditions on bail as appear to him to be necessary:

(a) to secure that the person surrenders to custody;
(b) does not commit an offence whilst on bail; or
(c) does not interfere with witnesses or otherwise obstruct the course of justice whether in relation to himself or any other person.

By s 3A(2) of the Bail Act 1976 however, he does not have power to impose a requirement to reside in a bail hostel. This is obviously because a custody officer will not have sufficient time to make the necessary enquiries before such a condition might properly be imposed.

The combined effects of s 3(4),(5),(6) and (7) of the 1976 Act is to permit the following requirements to be made of a person before he is released on bail:

(a) he may be required to provide a surety or sureties to ensure his surrender to custody;
(b) he may be required to give security for his surrender;
(c) he may be required to comply with conditions which appear necessary to secure that he surrenders to custody, that he does not commit an offence whilst on bail, or that he does not interfere with witnesses or otherwise obstruct the course of justice;
(d) if a parent or guardian of a child or young person consents to be surety for it, the parent or guardian may be required to ensure that the child or young person complies with conditions imposed under (c) above, except that no such condition may be imposed where a young person will be 17 before the time appointed for surrender, and that a parent or guardian may not be required to secure compliance with any requirement to which his consent does not extend and may not, in respect of those requirements to which his consent does extend, be bound in a sum greater than £50.

Where a custody officer has granted bail in criminal proceedings, he or another custody officer serving at the same police station may, at the request of the person to whom it was granted, vary the condition of bail, and in doing so he may impose conditions or more onerous conditions.

Sections 5 and 5A of the Bail Act 1976 provide that, where a custody officer imposes conditions in granting bail or varies any conditions of bail, or imposes conditions, he must give reasons for doing so. This is to enable the person concerned to consider requesting the custody officer to vary those conditions. A note of the custody officer's reasons for imposing conditions must be made in the custody record and a copy must be given to the person concerned.

A person who is bailed enters into a promise to appear as prescribed. That promise cannot be set against a recognisance from him that, it he fails to appear, a specific sum of money shall be forfeit. Instead the 1976 Act provides its own penalties for non-appearance. In serious cases it may be necessary for an accused to find one or more 'sureties', that is persons who *undertake to secure his attendance*. This is done by each surety entering a recognisance to forfeit a specified sum to the Crown in the event of the non-attendance of the accused.

Other points

When bail is granted by a constable a record must be made of the decision in the prescribed manner and the accused must be provided with a copy of that record if he so requests. In practice this copy is given on all occasions.

The Magistrates' Courts Act 1980, s 43 enables a magistrates' court to fix a later time for appearance before it and to enlarge recognisances.

Police bail of person not charged

If the custody officer decides, when the investigating officer brings the person detained before him, that there is insufficient evidence at that stage to charge him, but that there probably will be when further inquiries have been made, he may release the person detained on bail, such bail being conditioned upon his appearance at a police station at a given time, as opposed to appearing at a court. The purpose is to re-assess the evidence then available to make a decision as to whether or not to charge the person detained. Such bail (ie the requirement to attend at a police station) may be cancelled at any time by notice in writing from the custody officer.

Arrest of person for failure to answer to police bail

Section 46A of the 1984 Act provides that a constable may arrest without warrant any person who, having been released on bail subject to a duty to attend at a police station, fails to attend at that police station at the time appointed for him to do so.

Such a person must be taken to that police station as soon as practicable after his arrest.

General

By s 47(3A) of the 1984 Act, inserted by the Crime and Disorder Act 1998 and being piloted in parts of the country at the time of writing, where a custody officer grants bail to a person subject to a duty to appear before a magistrates' court, he must appoint for the appearance:

(a)   a date which is not later than the first sitting of the court after the person is charged with the offence; or

(b)   where he is informed by the clerk to the justices for the relevant petty sessions area that the appearance cannot be accommodated until a later date, that later date.

Section 47(6) of the 1984 Act provides that, where a person who has been granted police bail and either has attended at a police station or has been arrested under s 46A, is detained at a police station, any previous time in custody must be included in any calculation of detention time. In practice, his old custody record will be continued.

Section 47(1) of the 1984 Act provides that nothing in the Bail Act 1976 prevents a re-arrest without warrant of a person released on bail subject to a condition to appear at a police station if new evidence justifying a further arrest has come to light since his release. If such a person is re-arrested the detention provisions of the Act apply as if he has been arrested for the first time but this does not apply to a person arrested for failure to surrender to police bail at a police station, or who has surrendered to that bail and has been arrested for that offence.

Where an offence of absconding whilst on 'police bail' is dealt with by laying an information, the limitation of six months in relation to the laying of an information applies from the time of the failure to surrender. Thus, it is suggested that an information is laid when the failure to surrender occurs. Failure to surrender to police bail cannot be dealt with as a contempt in accordance with this section, as there is no defiance of a court order.

Bail by a court

Section 4 of the Bail Act 1976 states that when a person who is accused of an offence appears before a magistrates' court or a Crown Court in the course of or in connection with the proceedings for the offence, or when he applies to a court for bail or for a variation of the conditions of bail in connection with the proceedings, he must be granted bail if none of the exceptions specified in Sch 1 applies. However, this is subject to the provisions of the Criminal Justice and Public Order Act 1994, s 25 (bail for defendants charged with or convicted of rape or homicide after a previous conviction for such an offence only to be granted if there are exceptional circumstances justifying it).

Schedule 1 provides that bail need not be granted by the court where the offence (or one of them) is *punishable with imprisonment* if the court is satisfied that there are substantial grounds for believing that the accused, if released on bail (whether subject to conditions or not) would:

(a)   fail to surrender to custody; or

(b)   commit an offence whilst on bail; or

(c)   interfere with witnesses or otherwise obstruct the course of justice, whether in relation to himself or any other person; or

(d)   is indictable or triable either way and it appears to the court that he was on bail in criminal proceedings on the date of that offence.

In deciding the above, the court must have regard to the nature and seriousness of the offence; the character, antecedents, associations and community ties of the accused;

the record of the accused in respect of previous grants of bail; and the strength of the evidence available (except where the case is merely being adjourned for inquiries or a report).

Schedule 1 also provides that bail need not be granted by the court where the offence (or one of them) is *punishable with imprisonment*:

(e) if the court is satisfied that the accused should be kept in custody for his own protection or, if a child or young person, for his own welfare; or

(f) if he is in custody under a court order or in pursuance of any authority under the Services Acts; or

(g) if the court is satisfied that there has not been sufficient time to obtain information upon which a decision about bail may be made; or

(h) if the accused has been arrested under the Bail Act 1976, s 7 for absconding or breaking conditions of bail.

Schedule 1 also provides that, where the offence (or all of them) is (or are) not *punishable with imprisonment*, the accused need not be granted bail in the circumstances outlined at (d), (e) or (g), above, or if the court (in the light of the accused's previous failure to do so) believes that the accused, if released on bail, would fail to surrender to custody.

General factors and police powers

The 1984 Act permits the enforcement of bail which is conditioned upon appearance at a police station in the same way as if conditioned for appearance at a magistrates' court.

The Act also allows a person arrested on a warrant endorsed for bail to be released on bail without being taken to a police station, provided that the endorsement for bail does not demand sureties. If sureties are required, the person must be taken to a police station. Police officers will therefore be involved in admitting persons to bail 'on the spot'.

Failure to surrender

By s 6 of the Bail Act 1976, a person who has been bailed commits an offence if he fails without reasonable cause to surrender to custody as required. Moreover, if he had reasonable cause for failing to surrender at the appropriate time, he commits an offence if he fails to surrender to custody at the appointed place as soon after the appointed time as is reasonably practicable.

Arrest for breach of bail

Section 7 of the Bail Act 1976 provides a power to arrest without warrant. A person who has been released on bail in criminal proceedings and is under a duty to surrender into the custody of a court may be arrested without warrant by a constable if:

(a) the constable has reasonable grounds for believing that that person is not likely to surrender to custody, or is likely to break any of the conditions of his bail, or has broken any of those conditions; or

(b) in a case where that person was released on bail with one or more sureties, if a surety notifies a constable in writing that that person is unlikely to surrender to custody, and that for that reason the surety wishes to be relieved of his obligations as a surety.

Unless he was arrested within 24 hours of the time appointed for surrender to custody, the arrested person must be brought before a justice as soon as practicable and in any event within 24 hours. Christmas Day, Good Friday and any Sunday are excluded from the calculation of 24 hours. A person arrested within 24 hours of the surrender-time must be brought before the court at which he was to have surrendered to custody.

Procedure

Where a person has been granted bail by a court and subsequently fails to surrender to custody, that person must be brought before the court at which proceedings in respect of which bail was granted are to be heard. No information should be laid to commence proceedings for such failure. The court in question should initiate proceedings for an offence of failing to surrender to bail on its own motion, following an express invitation by the prosecutor. On the other hand, where a person has been bailed from a police station, to appear either at a magistrates' court or at a police station, proceedings for an offence of failure to surrender to bail should be initiated by way of information or by charging the accused.

Remand to police custody

By the Magistrates' Courts Act 1980, s 128, a magistrates' court has power to remand a person for a period not exceeding three clear days (24 hours if a juvenile) to 'detention at a police station' where there is a need to question him about other offences. Section 128 also requires that such a person must not be kept in detention at a police station unless there is a need for him to be detained for the purpose of inquiries into other offences. If he is kept in such detention he must be brought back to the magistrates' court which committed him as soon as the need for detention ceases. Such a person must be treated as a person in detention for the purposes of the 1984 Act (and this means that he must be treated in accordance with the Detention Code and his detention must be subject to reviews as prescribed by the Act).

CHAPTER 6

Identification methods

The Home Secretary is required by the Police and Criminal Evidence Act 1984, s 66 to issue a Code of Practice in connection with the identification of persons. The relevant Code of Practice (the Code of Practice for the Identification of Persons by Police Officers, hereafter referred to as the Identification Code) is concerned with four methods by which identification can be made; they are: identification by witnesses, identification by fingerprints, identification by photographs, identification by body samples, swabs and impressions.

GENERAL PRINCIPLES

The Identification Code provides certain general principles which apply to all methods by which identification can be made. It provides that:

(a) where a record is made of any action requiring the authority of an officer of a specified rank, the name (except in the case of terrorism inquiries, where the warrant or other identification number should be given) and rank of the officer must be included in the record;

(b) all records must be timed and signed by the maker (or his warrant or other identification number given in the case of terrorism inquiries);

(c) in the case of a detained person records must be made in the custody record unless otherwise specified;

(d) if an officer suspects, or is told in good faith, that a person of any age may be suffering from mental disorder, or mentally handicapped, or mentally incapable of understanding the significance of questions put to him or his replies, that person must be treated as such;

(e) a person who appears to be under 17 must be treated as a juvenile unless there is clear evidence to the contrary;

(f) if a person appears to be blind or seriously visually handicapped, deaf, unable to read, unable to speak or has difficulty orally because of a speech impediment, he should be treated as such for the purposes of the Identification Code in the absence of clear evidence to the contrary;

(g) a record must be made of the description of the suspect as first given by a potential witness. This must be done before the witness takes part in the following forms of identification: an identification parade, a group identification, a video film, a confrontation, or identification by photographs. The record may be made or kept in any form provided that details of the description as first given by the witness can accurately be produced from it in a written form which can be provided to the suspect or his solicitor in accordance with the Code. A copy must be provided to the suspect or his solicitor before any procedures under the Code are carried out.

Where the consent of the suspect to a procedure is required, the consent of a suspect who is mentally disordered or mentally handicapped is only valid if given in the presence of the appropriate adult; and in the case of a juvenile his parent or guardian must consent in addition to the juvenile himself (unless he is under 14, in which case the consent of his parent or guardian suffices in its own right). These provisions follow the general rules of good practice. If there is a suspicion that a suspect is a child or young person or is mentally handicapped etc, the procedure should be followed as a matter of fairness to that individual.

If any information concerning the processes of an identification must be given to or sought from a suspect, it must be given or sought in the presence of the appropriate adult if the suspect is mentally disordered or handicapped, or a juvenile. If the appropriate adult is not present when the information is first given or sought, the procedure must be repeated in his presence when he arrives. If the suspect is deaf or there is doubt about his hearing ability or his ability to understand, the information must be given through an interpreter. Any procedure involving the participation of a person who is mentally disordered, mentally handicapped or a juvenile (whether a suspect or witness) must take place in the presence of the appropriate adult but the adult must not be allowed to prompt any identification of a suspect by a witness.

In the case of a person who is blind or seriously visually handicapped or unable to read, the custody officer must ensure that his solicitor, relative, the appropriate adult or some other person likely to take an interest in him (and not involved in the investigation) is available to help in checking any documentation. Where the Code requires written consent or signification, then the person who is assisting may be asked to sign if the detained person so wishes.

The terms 'appropriate adult' and 'solicitor' have the same meaning as in the Detention Code (see pp 79-80).

IDENTIFICATION BY WITNESSES: WHERE THE SUSPECT IS KNOWN

In a case involving disputed identification evidence, and where the identity of the suspect is known to the police, the methods of identification which may be used are:

(a) an identification parade;
(b) a group identification;
(c) a video film; and
(d) a confrontation by a witness.

A suspect is 'known' for present purposes if there is sufficient information known to the police to justify the arrest of a particular person (the 'suspect') for suspected involvement in the offence. A person is not a 'known suspect' simply because he matches the description of an offender circulated to police officers.

The arrangements for, and conduct of, these four types of identification is the responsibility of an officer *in uniform not below the rank of inspector* who must *not be involved in the investigation;* he is called the 'identification officer'. No officer involved with the investigation may take any part in these procedures.

There will be a breach of this prohibition, not only if an officer investigating an offence participates in the actual identification process but also if he takes the witness to the police station at which an identification is to be attempted. This is understandable since such contact permits the transfer of information concerning the identification.

General rules – identification parade or alternative method

(a) The Identification Code provides that whenever a suspect disputes an identification of him, an identification parade must be held if the suspect consents, except in the circumstances described in (b) or (c) below or where the witness has made an actual and complete identification of the suspect. The significance of this requirement is that, like other breaches of the Codes, a breach of it is liable to render inadmissible evidence obtained thereby. A parade may also be held if the officer in charge of the investigation considers that it would be useful, and the suspect consents. This applies whether or not there is other evidence of identification which appears to be sufficient. In addition, where a witness knows a defendant but does not know him well, an identification parade should be held. If a suspect refuses his consent, a record must be made of the refusal.

(b) A parade need not be held if the identification officer considers that, whether because a suspect is of such singular appearance or for some other reason, it would not be practicable to assemble sufficient people who resembled him to make a parade fair. (It will only be 'not practicable' to hold an identification parade if reasonable steps have been taken to assemble a parade and have produced no result. Clearly, this test is a strict one.) It does not follow from the fact that it is not practicable to hold a parade on one day because of a lack of suitable volunteers that it will be impracticable to hold it at another time. If the identification officer considers that it is not practicable to hold a parade he must tell the suspect why and record the reason. 'Impracticability' means more than mere inconvenience, since it refers to incapability of being carried out. However, an identification officer's judgement that it would be impracticable to hold a parade can only be impugned as being in breach of the Code if it is unreasonable. Where there is no reasonable possibility that a witness will be able to make an identification there is no breach of the Identification Code if one is not held, even though it is requested by the accused.

(c) Where a suspect refuses, or, having agreed, fails to attend a parade, or the holding of a parade is impracticable, arrangements must be made, if practicable, to allow witnesses to see the suspect in a group identification, video identification, or a confrontation. A *group identification* takes place where a suspect is viewed by a witness amongst an informal group of people. The procedure may take place with the consent and co-operation of a suspect or covertly where a suspect has refused to co-operate with an identification parade or group identification or has failed to attend. It may also be arranged if the officer in charge of the investigation considers, whether because of fear on the part of the witness or for some other reason, that it is more satisfactory in the circumstances than a parade.

(d) The identification officer may show a witness a *video-film* of a suspect if he considers, whether because of the suspect's refusal to take part in an identification parade or group identification or because of other reasons, that this would in the circumstances be the most satisfactory course. The suspect should be asked for his consent to video identification. However, if he refuses consent, the identification officer has a discretion to proceed with a video identification, if practicable. A record must be made of the refusal.

(e) If neither a parade nor a group identification nor a video identification procedure is arranged, the suspect may be confronted by the witness. Such a confrontation does not require the suspect's consent, but this procedure must not take place unless none of the above procedures is practicable.

(f) A witness must not be shown photographs or photofit or identikit pictures for identification purposes if there is a suspect already available to be asked to stand on an identification parade.

Under the above provisions, whether the request was made by the suspect or a suggestion was made by an investigating officer, the decisions are made by the 'identification officer', who must arrange and conduct the parade. It will not always be straightforward for him to reach his decision. For example, if the suspect is a hunchback, a parade will be quite impracticable. In such circumstances there will be problems in respect of group identification as, if the only factor which the witness can recall is the deformity, it is unlikely that there will be two persons with similar deformities in any group situation. A confrontation by the witness may have little value and may be extremely unfair to the suspect in such a case as a positive identification may be made for the wrong reasons. In such a case a timed record of the decisions made by the identification officer should be made: if the suspect is in custody, on his custody record, and if not, elsewhere.

Procedure before identification parade, or group or video identification

Before an identification parade takes place or a group identification or video identification is arranged, the identification officer must explain to the suspect:

(a) the purpose of the parade or group identification or video identification;

(b) that he is entitled to free legal advice;

(c) the procedures for holding it (including the suspect's right to have a solicitor or friend present);

(d) where appropriate, the special arrangements for juveniles;

(e) where appropriate, the special arrangements for mentally disordered and mentally handicapped persons;

(f) that he does not have to take part in an identification parade, group identification or video identification and, if it is proposed to hold a group identification or video identification, his entitlement to a parade if this can practicably be arranged;

(g) that, if he does not consent to take part in a parade or group identification or video identification, he may be confronted by a witness and his refusal may be given in evidence in any subsequent trial, and that police may proceed covertly without his consent to make other arrangements to test whether a witness identifies him;

(h) that if he should significantly alter his appearance between the taking of any photograph at the time of his arrest or after charge and any attempt to hold an identification procedure, this may be given in evidence if the case comes to trial; and the officer may then consider other forms of identification;

(i) that a video photograph may be taken of him when he attends for any identification procedure;

(j) whether the witness had been shown photographs, photofit, identikit or similar pictures by the police during the investigation before the identity of the suspect became known;

(k) that if he changes his appearance before a parade it may not be practicable to arrange one on the day in question or subsequently and, because of his change of appearance, the identification officer may then consider alternative methods of identification; and

(l) that he or his solicitor will be provided with details of the description of the suspect as first given by any witnesses who are to attend the parade, group identification, video identification or confrontation.

The identification officer must additionally give to the suspect a written notice (the 'Notice to Suspect') containing this information and give him a reasonable opportunity to read it. The suspect must then be asked to sign a second copy of the notice to indicate whether or not he is willing to participate in the parade or the group identification or co-operate with the making of a video film. The signed copy must be retained by the identification officer.

Nothing in the Identification Code inhibits an investigation officer from showing a video film or photographs of an incident to the public at large through the national or local media, or to police officers, for the purpose of recognition and tracing suspects. However, when such material is shown to potential witnesses (including police officers) for the purpose of obtaining identification evidence, it must be shown on an individual basis so as to avoid any possibility of collusion, and the showing should, as far as possible, follow the principles for video film identification or identification by photographs.

Identification parades

Annex A to the Identification Code directs the form which an identification parade must take.

A suspect must be given a reasonable opportunity to have a solicitor or friend present, and the identification officer must ask him to indicate his wishes in this respect on a second copy of the 'Notice to Suspect'. A parade may take place either in a normal room or in one equipped with a screen permitting witnesses to see members of the parade without being seen. The procedures for the composition and conduct of the parade are the same in both cases (except that a parade involving a screen may take place only when the suspect's solicitor, friend or appropriate adult is present or the parade is video recorded). This exception is an obvious safeguard, if the evidence of the identification is to have any value.

Before the parade takes place the suspect or his solicitor must be provided with the details of the first description of the suspect by any witnesses who are to attend the parade. The suspect or his solicitor should be allowed to view any material released to the media by the police for the purpose of recognising or tracing the suspect, provided it is practicable to do so and would not unreasonably delay the investigation.

Parades involving prison inmates

If a prison inmate is required for identification, and there are no security problems about his leaving the establishment, he may be asked to participate in a parade or video identification. A parade may be conducted in a Prison Department establishment. If it is, it must be conducted as far as practicable under normal parade rules. Members of the public must make up the parade unless there are serious security or control objections to their admission to the establishment. In such cases, or if a video or group identification is arranged within the establishment, other inmates may participate.

If an inmate is the suspect, he should not be required to wear prison uniform for the parade unless the other persons taking part are other inmates in uniform or are members of the public who are prepared to wear prison uniform for the occasion.

The evidential value of a group identification in a prison could be high. Where prison uniform is worn by all, the similarity of dress of all participants will make identification difficult for witnesses who are not certain of the appearance of a suspect.

Conduct of an identification parade

At the earliest opportunity and before the parade takes place the suspect or his solicitor should be provided with details of the first description of the suspect by any witnesses who are to attend the parade.

Immediately before the parade, the identification officer must remind the suspect of the procedure governing its conduct and give him the caution set out on p 76. All unauthorised persons must be excluded from the place where the parade is held.

Once the parade has been formed, everything afterwards in respect of it must take place in the presence and hearing of the suspect and of any interpreter, solicitor, friend or appropriate adult who is present (unless the parade involves a screen, in which case everything said to or by any witness at the place where the parade is held must be said in the hearing and presence of the suspect's solicitor, friend or appropriate adult or be video recorded). No investigating officer should enter the room in which the parade is being held.

The parade must consist of at least eight persons (other than the suspect) who so far as possible resemble the suspect in age, height, general appearance and position in life. One suspect only may be included in a parade unless there are two suspects of roughly similar appearance in which case they may be paraded together with at least 12 other persons. In no circumstances may more than two suspects be included in one parade, and where there are separate parades they must be made up of different persons.

Where police officers in uniform form an identification parade, numerals or other identifying badge must be concealed. It must be remembered that if a complaint concerns a police officer in uniform who was on duty at a particular time, all those on duty at the time who would have had an opportunity to be in the vicinity of any incident, whether in accordance with instructions or not, should be subjected to the identification procedure.

When the suspect is brought into the place where the parade is to be held, he must be asked by the identification officer whether he has any objection to the arrangements for the parade or to any of the other participants in it. The suspect may obtain advice from his solicitor or friend, if present, before the parade proceeds. Where practicable, steps must be taken to remove the grounds for objection. Where it is not practicable to do so, the officer must explain to the suspect why his objections cannot be met.

The suspect may select his own position in the line. Where there is more than one witness, the identification officer must tell the suspect, after each witness has left the room, that he can if he wishes change position in the line. Each position in the line must be clearly numbered, whether by means of a numeral laid on the floor in front of each parade member or by other means.

The identification officer is responsible for ensuring that, before they attend the parade, witnesses are not able to:

(a) communicate with each other or overhear a witness who has already seen the parade;

(b)   see any member of the parade;
(c)   on that occasion see, or be reminded of, any photograph or description of the suspect, nor are given any other indication of his identity; and
(d)   on that occasion see the suspect, either before or after the parade.

The officer conducting a witness to the parade must not discuss with him the composition of the parade, and in particular he must not disclose whether a previous witness has made any identification.

Witnesses must be brought in one at a time. Immediately before a witness inspects the parade, the identification officer must tell him that the person he saw may or may not be on the parade and that if he cannot make a positive identification he should say so but that he should not do so before looking at each member of the parade at least twice. The officer must then ask him to look at each member of the parade at least twice, taking as much care and time as he wishes. When the officer is satisfied that the witness has properly looked at each member of the parade he must ask him whether the person he saw in person on an earlier relevant occasion is on the parade. The witness should make an identification by saying the number of the person concerned. Where this takes place behind a screen it is desirable for the witness to be asked to make a note of the number of the person identified so that he may give direct evidence of that fact. However, if a witness is unable to recall that number at a subsequent trial, evidence from the officer who conducted the parade as to the number called out by the witness is admissible as there is statutory authority for its admission. If the witness makes an identification after the parade has ended, the suspect and, if present, his solicitor, interpreter or friend must be informed. Where this occurs, consideration should be given to allowing the witness a second opportunity to identify the suspect.

If a witness wishes to hear any parade member speak, adopt any specified posture, or see him move, the identification officer must first ask whether he can identify any persons on the parade on the basis of appearance only. When the request is to hear members of the parade speak, the witness must be reminded that the participants in the parade have been chosen on the basis of physical appearance only. Members of the parade may then be asked to comply with the witness's request to hear them speak, to see them move or to adopt any specified posture.

Where video films or photographs have been released to the media by the police for the purpose of recognising or tracing the suspect, the investigating officer must ask each witness after the parade whether he has seen any broadcast or published films or photographs relating to the offence and must record his reply.

When the last witness has left, the suspect must be asked by the identification officer whether he wishes to make any comments on the conduct of the parade. A colour photograph or video film of the parade must be taken. A copy must be supplied on request to the suspect or his solicitor within a reasonable time. Such a record must be destroyed or wiped clean at the conclusion of the proceedings unless the person concerned is convicted or admits the offence and is cautioned. If the identification officer asks any person to leave the parade because he is interfering with its conduct, the circumstances must be recorded.

Group identification

General

The arrangements must as far as practicable satisfy the requirements of an identification parade. A group identification may take place either with the suspect's consent and co-operation or covertly without his consent. The location is a matter for the identification officer although he may take into account representations made by a suspect, appropriate adult, his solicitor or a friend. It should be a place in which other people are passing by, or waiting around informally in groups, so that the suspect is able to join them and is capable of being seen at the same time as others in the group. A group identification should, if practicable, be held in a place other than a police station (for example in an underground station or a shopping centre). Where identification is carried out covertly, it could take place on a route regularly travelled by the suspect, including buses, trains and public places.

While it is appreciated that the general description of people included in a group identification cannot be controlled, the identification officer should consider the general appearance and number of persons likely to be present and must reasonably expect that persons broadly similar to the suspect will appear from time to time during the period of the witness's observation. A group identification need not take place where, because of the unusual appearance of the suspect, none of the locations which it would be practicable to use is likely to make the identification fair.

Immediately after a group identification (whether with or without consent) a colour photograph or a video should be taken of the general scene where this is practicable. Alternatively, the group identification may be video recorded. If it is not practicable to make such a record a the time, such a record must be made later where practicable.

If at the time of the identification, the suspect is on his own, it remains a group identification. The identification officer need not be in uniform. Before the group identification takes place the suspect or his solicitor should be provided with details of the first description and they should be allowed to view any material released to the media for the purpose of recognising or tracing the suspect, provided that it is practicable to do so and it will not unreasonably delay the investigation. Where such releases have been made the identification officer must ask each witness after the procedure whether he has seen them and must record any reply.

Identification with the consent of the suspect

A suspect must be given a reasonable opportunity to have a solicitor or friend present. He must be asked by the identification officer to indicate his wishes on a second copy of the Notice to Suspect. The witnesses, identification officer, suspect's solicitor, appropriate adult, friend and any interpreter for the witness may be concealed from the sight of the persons in the group if this facilitates the identification. The officer conducting a witness to the location must not discuss the forthcoming group identification nor disclose whether a previous witness has made an identification.

Anything said to or by a witness must be said in the hearing of the identification officer and, if present, the suspect's solicitor, appropriate adult, friend or any interpreter for the witness. Witnesses who have not yet attended the identification must not be able to communicate with each other about the case or overhear a witness who has already seen the suspect, nor see the suspect or be reminded of any photograph or description or be given any other indication of his identity. Witnesses must be brought to the place singly and must be told that the person they saw may or may not be in the group and that if they cannot make a positive identification they should say so. The witness must then be asked to observe the group; the manner of doing so will depend upon whether the group is stationary or moving.

Moving group If two or more suspects consent to a group identification, they should each be subject to different identification procedures, which may be conducted consecutively. The identification officer must ask the witness to observe the group and ask him to point out any person he thinks he saw on an earlier relevant occasion. When an identification is made, the identification officer must, where practicable, arrange for the witness to take a closer look and ask if he can make a positive identification. If this is not practicable, the identification officer must ask the witness how sure he is that the person is the relevant person. The duration of the identification process must be such that it is sufficient to allow a proper identification in the circumstances. A suspect must be allowed to take up any position in the group he wishes.

Stationary group Where there are two or more suspects who consent to a group identification, there should generally be two separate procedures. However, if they are of broadly similar appearance, they may appear in the same group. Separate stationary group identifications must consist of different people. The suspect may select his position and may change it between witnesses. The identification officer must ask the witness to pass along or amongst the group and to look at each person at least twice before making an identification. Having done so, he must be asked if the person he saw is in the group and to indicate that person by any means considered appropriate by the identification officer. If not practicable, the witness will be asked to point out that person. He must, where practicable, be asked to take a closer look and confirm his identification. If this is not practicable, he must be asked how sure he is that the person is the one seen on a previous occasion.

Rules common to moving and stationary groups An unreasonable delay by the suspect in joining the group, or a deliberate concealment from the sight of the witness, may be considered as a refusal to co-operate in the identification.

Where a witness identifies someone other than the suspect, that person should be asked if he is prepared to give his name and address. He is not obliged to do so. There is no duty to record persons present in the group or at the place where the procedure is conducted.

At the end of the procedure the suspect must be asked to comment on the conduct of the procedure. If he has not previously been informed the identification officer must tell him of any identifications made by witnesses.

Identifications without suspect's consent

These should, so far as possible, follow the rules set out above. As such an identification will take place without the suspect's knowledge, no solicitor etc will be present. Any number of suspects may be identified at the same time.

Identifications in police stations

These must only take place for reasons of security, safety, or because it is impracticable to hold them elsewhere. The group identification may be in a room equipped with a one-way screen, or elsewhere in the police station. Safeguards applicable to identification parades must be followed where practicable.

Identifications involving prison inmates

These may only take place in a prison or police station and must follow the procedure which is applicable to identifications in a police station. Where an identification takes place in a prison, other inmates may participate. If the suspect is in prison uniform, all persons taking part must be so dressed.

Documentation

Where a photograph or video is taken a copy must be supplied on request to the suspect or his solicitor within a reasonable time. Such records must be destroyed or wiped clean unless the suspect is convicted or admits the offence and is cautioned for it. A record of the conduct of the identification must be made on the forms provided and must include anything said by the witness or suspect about any identification or the conduct of the procedure and any reason why it was not practicable to comply with any of the provisions of the Code.

Video film identification

General

The following rules are laid down by Annex B as to how video identification should be carried out.

Arranging, supervising and directing the making and showing of a video film to be used in a video identification must be the responsibility of an identification officer or officers who have no direct involvement with the relevant case.

The film must include the suspect and at least eight other people who so far as possible resemble the suspect in age, height, general appearance and position in life. Only one suspect shall appear on any film unless there are two suspects of roughly similar appearance in which case they may be shown together with at least 12 other persons.

The suspect and other persons should as far as possible be filmed in the same position or carrying out the same activity and under identical conditions. Provision must be made for each person filmed to be identified by a number. If police officers are filmed, any numerals or other identifying badges must be concealed. If a prison inmate is filmed either as a suspect or not, then either all or none of the persons filmed shall be in prison uniform.

The suspect and his solicitor, friend or appropriate adult must be given a reasonable opportunity to see the complete film before it is shown to witnesses. If he has a reasonable objection to the video film or any of its participants, steps should, if practicable, be taken to remove the grounds for objection. If this is not practicable the identification officer must explain to the suspect and to his representative why his objections cannot be met and record both the objection and the reason on the forms provided.

The identification officer may show a witness a video film of a suspect if the investigating officer considers, whether because of the refusal of the suspect to take part in an identification parade or group identification or other reasons, that this would in the circumstances be the most satisfactory course of action.

The suspect should be asked for his consent to a video identification. However, where such consent is refused the identification officer has the discretion to proceed with a video identification if it is practicable to do so.

Where practicable, the suspect's solicitor, or where one is not instructed the suspect himself, should be given reasonable notification of the time and place that it is intended to conduct the video identification in order that a representative may attend on behalf of the suspect. The suspect himself may not be present when the film is shown to the witness. In the absence of a person representing the suspect the viewing itself shall be recorded on video. No unauthorised person may be present.

Before the video identification takes place the suspect or his solicitor must be provided with the details of the first description of the suspect by any witnesses who are to attend the parade. The suspect or his solicitor must also be allowed to view any material released to the media by the police for the purpose of recognising or tracing the suspect, provided it is practicable to do so and to do so would not unreasonably delay the investigation.

Conduct of video identification

The identification officer is responsible for ensuring that, before they see the film, witnesses are not able to communicate with each other about the case or overhear a witness who has seen the film. He must not discuss with the witness the composition of the film and must not disclose whether a previous witness has made any identification.

Only one witness may see the film at a time. Immediately before the video identification takes place, the identification officer shall tell the witness that the person he saw may or may not be on the video film. The witness should be advised that at any point he may ask to see a particular part of the tape again or to have a particular picture frozen for him to study. Furthermore, it should be pointed out that there is no limit on how many times he can view the whole tape or any part of it. However, he should be asked to refrain from making a positive identification until he has seen the entire film at least twice.

Once the witness has seen the whole film at least twice and has indicated that he does not want to view it or any part of it again, the identification officer must ask the witness to say whether the individual he saw in person on an earlier occasion has been shown on the film and, if so, to identify him by number. The identification officer will then show the film of the person identified again to confirm the identification with the witness.

The identification officer must take care not to direct the witness's attention to any one individual on the video film, or give any other indication of the suspect's identity. Where a witness has previously made an identification by photographs, or a photofit, identikit or similar picture has been made, the witness must not be reminded of such a photograph or picture once a suspect is available for identification by other means in accordance with this Code. Neither must he be reminded of any description of the suspect. Where video films or photographs have been released to the media by the police each witness must be asked after the parade whether he has seen any broadcast or published films or photographs relating to the offence and his reply must be recorded.

Tape security and destruction

It is the responsibility of the identification officer to ensure that all relevant tapes are kept securely and their movements accounted for. In particular, no officer involved in the investigation against the suspect may be permitted to view the video film prior to its being shown to any witness.

Where a video film has been made all copies of it must be destroyed if:

(a) he is prosecuted for the offence and cleared; or
(b) he is not prosecuted (unless he admits the offence and is cautioned for it).

An opportunity of witnessing the destruction must be given to him if he so requests within five days of being cleared or informed that he will not be prosecuted.

Records

A record must be made of all those present at a *parade or group identification* whose names are known to the police. If prison inmates make up a parade the circumstances must be recorded.

A record of the conduct of any parade or group identification or video identification must be made on the forms provided. In the case of a video identification, a record must be made of all those participating in or seeing the video whose names are known to the police.

Confrontation by a witness

If neither a parade, a group identification, nor a video identification procedure is arranged, the suspect may be confronted by the witness. Such a confrontation does not require the suspect's consent, but may only take place if none of the other procedures are practicable.

The rules concerning confrontation, which are set out in Annex C to the Identification Code, are simple. The identification officer is responsible for the conduct of any confrontation of a suspect by a witness. Before the confrontation takes place, the identification officer must tell the witness that the person he saw may or may not be the person he is to confront and that if he cannot make a positive identification he should say so. In addition, before the confrontation, a note must be made of the witness's description of the offender. The note should be made available for examination at trial to act as a safeguard against the risk of auto-suggestion. The suspect must be confronted independently by each witness, who must be asked 'Is this the person?' Confrontation must take place in the presence of the suspect's solicitor, interpreter or friend, where he has one, unless this would cause unreasonable delay. The same rules apply concerning the supply to the suspect or his solicitor of a 'first description' given by witnesses and material released to the media as apply in the other procedures already mentioned.

The confrontation should normally take place in the police station, either in a normal room or one equipped with a screen permitting a witness to see the suspect without being seen. In both cases the procedures are the same, except that a room equipped with a screen may be used only when the suspect's solicitor, friend or appropriate adult is present or the confrontation is recorded on video.

IDENTIFICATION BY WITNESSES: WHERE THE SUSPECT IS NOT KNOWN

Where the identity of a suspect is not known, a police officer may take a witness to a particular neighbourhood or place to see whether he can identify the person whom he said he saw on the relevant occasion. Before doing so, where practicable, a record must be made of any description given by the witness. Care should be taken, however, not to direct the witness's attention to any individual.

The showing of photographs

Annex D of the Identification Code sets out the procedures to be followed if photographs, or photofit, identikit or similar pictures are shown to a witness for identification purposes where the suspect's identity is not known.

An officer of the rank of sergeant or above must be responsible for supervising and directing the showing of photographs, but the actual showing may be done by a constable or a civilian police employee. (This means that most of the responsibility remains with the sergeant etc. The accountability of a constable will be limited to non-observance of the directions given.) The officer must confirm that the first description of the suspect given by the witness has been recorded before the witness is shown the photographs. If he is unable to confirm that the description has been recorded, he must postpone the showing.

Only one witness may be shown photographs at any one time. He must be given as much privacy as practicable and must not be allowed to communicate with any other witness in the case. The witness must be shown not less than 12 photographs at a time, which shall, as far as possible, all be of a similar type.

When the witness is shown photographs, he must be told that the photograph of the person whom he has said that he has previously seen may or may not be among them. He must not be prompted or guided in any way but must be left to make any selection without help. If a witness makes a positive identification from photographs, then, unless the person identified is otherwise eliminated from the inquiries, other witnesses must not be shown photographs. However, both they and the witness who has made the identification must be asked to attend an identification parade or group identification or video identification if practicable unless there is no dispute about the identification of the suspect.

Where the use of a photofit, identikit or similar picture has led to there being a suspect available who can be asked to appear on parade, or participate in a video or group identification, the picture must not be shown to other potential witnesses.

Where a witness attending an identification parade has previously been shown photographs, or photofit, identikit or similar pictures, the suspect and his solicitor must be informed of this fact before the identity parade takes place.

Any photograph used must be retained for production in court if necessary, whether or not an identification is made.

None of the photographs used shall be destroyed, whether or not an identification is made, since they may be required for production in court. The photographs should be numbered and a separate photograph taken of the frame or part of the album from which the witness made an identification as an aid to reconstituting it.

Documentation

Whether or not an identification is made, a record must be kept of the showing of photographs and of any comment made by the witness.

IDENTIFICATION BY FINGERPRINTS

The Police and Criminal Evidence Act 1984, ss 27, 61, 63A and 64 deal with the taking of fingerprints and the circumstances in which fingerprints must be destroyed.

A person's fingerprints may be taken only with his consent (which must be in writing if given at a police station) or in accordance with the provisions of the following paragraph.

Fingerprints may be taken from a person over the age of ten years without consent:

(a) if an officer of at least the rank of superintendent authorises them to be taken (which authority may only be given if the officer has reasonable grounds for suspecting the involvement of the person whose fingerprints are to be taken in a criminal offence and for believing that his fingerprints will tend to confirm or disprove his involvement); or

(b) (i) if the detained person has been charged with a recordable offence (see p 52) or informed that he will be reported for such an offence; and

    (ii) he has not had his fingerprints taken in the course of the investigation by the police; or

(c) if he has been convicted of a recordable offence.

The authorisation given by an officer of at least the rank of superintendent may be given orally or in writing, but if given orally it must be confirmed in writing as soon as practicable. A person must be told the reason before his fingerprints are taken and the reason must be recorded as soon as is practicable. He must be told that his prints may be subject of a speculative search against other fingerprints and a record must be made of this. This means that a check may be made against other fingerprints contained in records held by or on behalf of the police or held in connection with or as a result of an investigation into that offence.

Reasonable force may be used if necessary.

It must be recognised that (a) only applies if a fingerprint will confirm or disprove involvement in an offence. There must, therefore, be a possibility of matching a fingerprint.

In all circumstances (ie whether he consents or not) the person must be informed of the reason before the fingerprints are taken and that they will be destroyed if he is prosecuted for the offence concerned and cleared, or if he is not prosecuted (unless he admits the offence and is cautioned for it). He must also be informed that he may witness the destruction of the fingerprints if he asks to do so within five days of being cleared or informed that he will not be prosecuted. Fingerprints and samples may be retained if they were taken for the purpose of the same investigation of an offence for which a person from whom such a sample was taken has been convicted. This provision was introduced because there were found to be scientific reasons for processing some samples together and it is not technologically possible to separate them afterwards. This could occur where the fingerprints of a number of suspects were all found on a gun and were photographed together. However, the information derived from such a sample must not be used in evidence against that person, or for the purpose of any investigation of an offence.

References to fingerprints in the above provisions refer also to palm prints. When fingerprints are destroyed, access to relevant computer data must be made impossible as soon as it is practicable to do so. A person is entitled to a certificate, to be issued within three months of his application, certifying that this has been done.

The Police and Criminal Evidence Act 1984, s 63A(1), provides that, where a person has been arrested on suspicion of being involved in a recordable offence, or has been charged with a recordable offence, or has been informed that he will be reported for a recordable offence, fingerprints or samples or the information derived from samples taken under any power conferred by the Act from the person may be checked against:

(a) other fingerprints or samples to which the person seeking to check has access and which are held by or on behalf of a police force, or are held in connection with or as a result of an investigation of an offence;

(b) information derived from other samples if the information is contained in records to which the person seeking to check has access and which are held as described in (a).

The Prevention of Terrorism (Temporary Provisions) Act 1989, s 15(10) applies the above provisions about taking fingerprints to the taking of a person's fingerprints by a constable in terrorist cases where the authorising officer is satisfied that it is necessary to do so to help determine whether a person is or has been involved in terrorism, as well as where there are reasonable grounds for suspecting that person's involvement in a particular offence. In such terrorist cases there is no requirement to destroy prints.

Documentation

A record must be made as soon as possible of the reason for taking a person's fingerprints (or palm prints) without consent and of their destruction. If he is detained at a police station when they are taken, the reason must be recorded on his custody record. If force is used a record must be made of the circumstances and those present.

IDENTIFICATION BY PHOTOGRAPHS

The photograph of a person who has been arrested may be taken at a police station only with his *written consent* or, if he does not consent, *in one of the following cases*:

(a) if he is arrested at the same time as other persons, or at a time when it is likely that other persons will be arrested, and a photograph is necessary to establish who was arrested, at what time and at what place; or

(b) if he has been charged with or reported for a recordable offence and has not yet been released or brought before a court; or

(c) if he is convicted of such an offence and his photograph is not already on record as a result of (a) or (b) . There is no power of arrest to take a photograph in pursuance of this provision which applies only where the person is in custody as a result of the exercise of another power (eg an arrest for fingerprinting under the Police and Criminal Evidence Act 1984, s 27, discussed on pp 52-53); or

(d) if a superintendent (or above) authorises it, having reasonable grounds for suspecting the involvement of the person in a criminal offence and where there is identification evidence in relation to that offence.

Case (a), above, will cover situations when multiple arrests are made in public order situations; if used in such a situation it will ease identification of offenders at a later stage. Force may not be used to take a photograph; this is not surprising, as it should always be possible to take a photograph without resorting to force. A suspect must be told that if he should significantly alter his appearance between the taking of the photograph and any attempt to hold an identification procedure this may be given in evidence if the case comes to trial.

The provisions previously described in relation to the destruction of fingerprints apply to photographs, copies and negatives. An opportunity must be given to witness the destruction if the person so wishes. A person whose photograph is taken must be informed of the reason for taking it. He must also be informed that the photograph, negatives and all copies will be destroyed if he is cleared (unless he has a previous conviction for a recordable offence) or is not prosecuted (unless he admits the offence and is cautioned for it or he has a previous conviction for a recordable offence) and that he may witness its destruction if he asks to do so within five days of being cleared or informed that he will not be prosecuted.

All references to photographs include computer images.

Photographs must be kept in a secure manner to ensure that a potential witness in an identification procedure is unable to view them before any such procedure.

Documentation

A record must be made as soon as practicable of the reason for taking a person's photograph under the above provisions without consent and of the destruction of any photograph.

IDENTIFICATION BY BODY SAMPLES, SWABS AND IMPRESSIONS

The Police and Criminal Evidence Act 1984, ss 62 to 64 contains the basic provisions in this area, but (within the terms of these sections) it is the Identification Code which sets out the detailed procedures.

Intimate samples

An intimate sample means a sample of *blood, semen or any other tissue fluid, urine, pubic hair, a dental impression, or a swab taken from a person's body orifice other than the mouth*. Section 62 of the 1984 Act is the relevant provision.

An intimate sample may be taken from a person in police detention only with his written consent. In the case of any procedure requiring a person's consent, the consent of a person who is mentally disordered or mentally handicapped is only valid if given in the presence of an appropriate adult; and in the case of a juvenile the consent of his parent or guardian is required as well as his own (unless he is under 14, in which case the consent of his parent or guardian is sufficient in its own right). An intimate sample may also be taken from a person not in police detention if, in the course of an investigation into an offence, two or more non-intimate samples have been taken which have proved unsuitable or insufficient for a particular form of analysis and such an officer authorises it to be taken and the person concerned (or an appropriate adult) gives his written consent.

In these two cases an intimate sample may only be taken if an officer of at least the rank of superintendent authorises it to be taken because he has reasonable grounds for suspecting the involvement of the person from whom the sample is to be taken in a recordable offence and for believing that the sample will tend to confirm or disprove his involvment.

An intimate sample may also be authorised to be taken in terrorist cases to help determine whether the person in question is or has been involved in terrorism.

Before a person is asked to provide an intimate sample, he must be informed that it may be the subject of a speculative search (a check against other samples or against information derived from other samples) and the fact that this has been done must be recorded as soon as practicable after the sample has been taken. A record must be made of the authorisation by virtue of which the sample was taken; the grounds for giving the authorisation; and the fact that the appropriate consent was given. This must be done as soon as is practicable after the sample is taken. Where such a sample is taken from a person detained at a police station, such records must be made in the custody record.

Where a person refuses, without good cause, to consent to the taking of an intimate sample, in any proceedings for an offence, a court may draw such inferences from the refusal as appear proper.

An intimate sample, other than a sample of urine, may only be taken from a person by a registered medical practitioner and a dental impression may only be taken by a registered dentist.

Before a person is asked to provide one of these samples or swabs he must be warned that a refusal may be treated, in any proceedings against him, as corroborating relevant prosecution evidence. The Code suggests the use of the following words:

'You do not have to provide this sample/allow this swab or impression to be taken, but I must warn you that if you refuse without good cause, your refusal may harm your case if it comes to trial.'

The person must also be reminded of his entitlement to free legal advice and that the sample taken may be the subject of a speculative search against other samples. A record must be made of the giving of this warning and this reminder.

Non-intimate samples

There are separate provisions, contained in s 63 of the 1984 Act, for the taking of a *non-intimate sample*. A non-intimate sample means hair (other than pubic hair) which includes hair plucked by the root; nail clippings or scrapings; swabs taken from parts of the body including the mouth but not any other body orifice; saliva; or a footprint or similar impression (other than an impression of part of a hand). Where hair samples are taken for the purpose of DNA analysis (rather than for other purposes such as making a visual match) the suspect should be permitted a reasonable choice as to which part of the body he wishes the hairs to be taken from. When hairs are plucked they should be plucked individually unless the suspect prefers otherwise and no more should be plucked that the person taking them reasonably considers necessary for a sufficient sample.

Except in the following three cases, a non-intimate sample may be taken from a suspect only with his written consent. The three exceptional cases are:

(a) A non-intimate sample may be taken from a person without the appropriate consent if –
 (i) he is in police detention or is being held in custody by the court or on the authority of a court; and
 (ii) an officer of the rank of superintendent (or above) has authorised it to be taken without his consent.

  Such authorisation may only be given where the superintendent (or above) has reasonable grounds to suspect that the offence in question is a recordable offence and that the sample will tend to confirm or disprove the suspect's involvement in it.

  Where an authorisation is given for the taking of a non-intimate sample, the suspect must be informed, before it is taken, of the grounds on which the authorisation has been given, including the nature of the suspected offence. He must also be told that any sample taken may be the subject of a speculative search.

  Such samples may be taken in terrorist cases to help determine whether a person is or has been involved in terrorism, as well as where there are reasonable grounds for suspecting that person's involvement in a particular offence.

(b) A non-intimate sample may be taken without consent from any person (whether or not he is in custody or detained) if –
   (i) he has been charged with a recordable offence or informed that he will be reported for such an offence; and
   (ii) he has not had a non-intimate sample taken from him in the course of the investigation, or, if he has had a sample taken from him, it has proved unsuitable or insufficient for a particular form of analysis. An *unsuitable sample* is one which, by its nature, is not suitable for a particular form of analysis. An *insufficient sample* is one which is not sufficient either in quantity or quality for the purpose of enabling information to be provided for the purpose of a particular form of analysis such as DNA analysis.

(c) A non-intimate sample may be taken without consent if the person has been *convicted* of a recordable offence. However, this does not apply to any person convicted before 10 April 1995 unless he is a person to whom the Criminal Evidence (Amendment) Act 1997 applies (persons imprisoned or detained by virtue of a pre-existing conviction for a sexual offence or an offence of violence or potential violence, listed in Sch 1 to the Act), and at the relevant time such person is serving a sentence of imprisonment in respect of that offence. Similar provisions are made under the 1997 Act for non-intimate samples to be taken from persons detained following acquittal on the grounds of insanity or a finding of unfitness to plead.

Provision is made by the 1984 Act, s 63A for a constable to require a person convicted of a recordable offence to attend a police station in order that non-intimate samples may be taken. Section 63A of the 1984 Act permits a constable within one month from the date of charge or conviction (as the case may be) or from the date of being informed that a sample is not suitable or is insufficient (as the case may be), to require a person who is neither in police detention, nor held in custody by the police on the authority of a court, to attend a police station in order to have a sample taken. Whilst the section does not require this requirement to be in writing, as arrest may follow refusal, it is submitted that it would be wise to do so.

Reasonable force may be used to take a non-intimate sample without the suspect's consent under the above provisions.

General

A record must be made as soon as practicable of the reasons for taking a sample or impression and the warnings given. If force is used a record shall be made of the circumstances and those present. If written consent is given to the taking of a sample or impression, the fact must be recorded in writing. A record must be made of the giving of a warning that a refusal without reasonable cause to provide an intimate sample may harm the suspect's case if it comes to trial. A record must also be made that the subject has been warned that a sample may be the subject of a speculative search.

Where clothing needs to be removed in circumstances likely to cause embarrassment to the person, no person of the opposite sex who is not a medical practitioner or nurse shall be present (unless, in the case of a juvenile or a mentally disordered or mentally handicapped person, that person specifically requests the presence of a particular adult of the opposite sex who is readily available), nor shall anyone whose presence is unnecessary. However, in the case of a juvenile this is subject to the overriding proviso that such a removal of clothing may take place in the absence of the appropriate adult only if the juvenile signifies in the presence of the appropriate adult that he prefers the search to be done in his absence and the appropriate adult agrees.

A sample or impression must be destroyed as soon as practicable if the suspect is prosecuted and cleared or not prosecuted (unless he admits the offence and is cautioned). Samples need not be destroyed if they were taken for the purpose of an investigation of an offence for which someone has been convicted, and from whom a sample was also taken.

INFORMAL IDENTIFICATION

While formal identification evidence is obtained in the course of procedures carried out under the Identification Code, informal evidence of identification may be admitted provided that the evidence was obtained in good faith and has no adverse effect on the fairness of the proceedings.

Where an accused and a witness are well known to each other, the less is the need for any formal out-of-court identification procedure to be used. However, where the accused asks for a parade, the procedure is governed by the Identification Code and the failure to provide one may result in the exclusion of evidence whether the accused and the witness were previously known to one another or not.

CHAPTER 7

The law of evidence

It is one of the functions of the courts to ensure that the rules of the law of evidence are observed.

It must be noted at the outset that the law of evidence determines two things:

(a) the means by which the facts in issue are proved in a court; and
(b) those facts which may (or may not) be proved in a court.

We shall be concerned with both senses of the term in the rest of this chapter.

In this chapter we are concerned only with the rules of evidence as they apply in criminal cases.

CLASSIFICATION OF EVIDENCE

It is important to explain briefly certain classifications of evidence because certain rules (whether common law or statutory) apply specifically to a particular class of evidence only. Evidence may be classified as follows.

Direct evidence and circumstantial evidence

Direct evidence is evidence which (if believed) directly establishes a particular fact in issue itself. For example, the existence of a firearm alleged to have been possessed by the accused may be proved by its production in court and the fact that he was in possession of it may be proved by a statement from a person who claims to have discovered him in possession.

Circumstantial evidence is evidence of a fact or facts from which a fact in issue may be inferred. Suppose that X is charged with murder. If an eyewitness gives evidence that he saw X fire a gun at the victim, this is direct evidence of a fact in issue. On the other hand, evidence that X was seen in possession of a gun near the scene of the crime shortly before it was committed is circumstantial evidence since it is evidence of a fact from which the fact in issue (that X fired the gun) may be inferred.

Oral evidence, documentary evidence and real evidence

Oral evidence

Most evidence given in a court is oral evidence. This consists of statements made in court by witnesses concerning matters of which they have knowledge, such as something which they have seen, or heard, or felt, or smelt, or touched.

Refreshing memory Witness statements are usually recorded well in advance of trial. Witnesses are permitted to refresh their memory by referring to a document which they made or verified previously, provided that:

(a) it was made or verified at the time, or shortly after the incident, while the circumstances were fresh in the mind of the witness; the document is produced to the court; and

(b) where the witness has no recollection of the events, and is giving evidence as to the accuracy of the contents of the document, it is the original document which is used;

(c) where two witnesses have acted together (and this is common in the case of police officers) they may refresh their memories from notes which they made together.

Hostile witness If, during a trial in a Crown Court, a witness gives evidence which is hostile to the side calling him (it must be 'hostile' as opposed to unfavourable), that evidence may be contradicted by other evidence or, with the leave of the judge, it may be proved that the witness, on another occasion, made a statement which is inconsistent with his previous testimony.

Evidence via live television link By the Criminal Justice Act 1988, s 32, a person other than an accused may, with the leave of the court, give evidence through a live television link at a trial on indictment, in proceedings in a youth court, or on an appeal to the Court of Appeal or to the Crown Court respectively. Section 32 applies to circumstances where:

(a) the witness is outside the United Kingdom; or

(b) the witness is a child under 14, or is to be cross-examined following the admission of a video recording (see below) of his evidence, and the offence charged involves an assault, injury or threat of injury; cruelty; an offence under the Sexual Offences Act 1956, the Indecency with Children Act 1960, the Sexual Offences Act 1967, the Criminal Law Act 1977, s 54 (inciting girl under 16 to have incestuous relationship), or the Protection of Children Act 1978 (taking indecent photographs of a person under 16); or an attempt or conspiracy to commit, or aiding and abetting, such an offence; or

(c) the witness is under 17 or is to be cross-examined following the admission of a video recording of his evidence, and the offence charged is one of the above sexual offences or an offence under the Protection of Children Act 1978.

The offence of arson being reckless as to whether life is endangered is an offence involving the threat of injury to a person for the purposes of (b) above.

Where the court gives leave under s 32 of the 1988 Act for a person to give evidence through a live television link as provided by (b) and (c) above, the person concerned may not give evidence otherwise than through a live television link, unless it appears to the court to be in the interests of justice to give permission to do so. Such permission may be given on the application of a party to the case, or on the court's own motion.

Evidence via video recordings of child witnesses   Special provision is made by the Criminal Justice Act 1988, s 32A for video recordings of testimony from child witnesses to be played at a trial on indictment, in proceedings in youth courts, or in an appeal to the Court of Appeal or the Crown Court respectively. Section 32A does not apply to all such proceedings; it is limited to proceedings in relation to the same range of offences as those in which a child witness may give evidence by a live TV link. It provides that in such proceedings a video recording of an interview conducted between an adult and a child who is not the accused (or one of them) which relates to any matter in issue in the proceedings may, with the leave of the court, be given in evidence in so far as it is not excluded by the court. Subject to the court's power to exclude the whole or part of the video as being otherwise inadmissible evidence, the court must give leave for the video to be given in evidence, unless:

(a) it appears that the child witness will not be available for cross-examination;
(b) rules concerning the disclosure of the circumstances in which the recording was made have not been complied with; or
(c) the court is of the opinion, having regard to all the circumstances of the case, that in the interests of justice the recording ought not to be admitted.

Where the court gives leave, it may direct that part of the recording be excluded in the interests of justice. This power to exclude is intended to be used, for example, where the court considers that a part of the video will prejudice the accused, or one of them, to a degree outweighed by the desirability of showing the whole, or substantially the whole, of the recorded interview.

Where leave has been given, the child witness shall not give relevant evidence (evidence in chief on behalf of the party who tendered the video recording which relates to matters which, in the opinion of the court, is dealt with in the recording and the court has not directed to be excluded) otherwise than by means of a video recording, unless the court gives permission for the witness to give such evidence otherwise than by means of a video recording. The court may give such permission if it appears to the court to be in the interests of justice to give it. Permission may be given on the application of a party to the case or of the court's own motion.

For the purposes of these provisions a 'child' is a person under 14 years of age, or if he was under that age when the video recording was made, is under 15 years of age where the offence concerned is one of assault on, or injury, or threat of injury to a person or cruelty to a person. However, where the offence is one of the sexual offences referred to above or involves taking indecent photographs, 'child' refers to a person under 17 years of age, or if he was under that age when the video recording was made, under 18 years of age.

The Practice Direction (*Crime: Children's video evidence*) requires that, where such a direction is given, the party who made the application to admit the video recording must edit the recording in accordance with the judge's directions and send a copy of the edited recording to the appropriate officer of the Crown Court and to every other party to the proceedings.

Where a video recording is to be adduced during proceedings before a Crown Court, it must be produced and proved by the interviewer, or any other person who was present at the interview with the child, at which the recording was made. The parties may agree to accept a written statement in lieu of the attendance of such a person. The party adducing the video recording must arrange for the operation of the video playing equipment.

Failure to so prepare, which leads to an adjournment for this to be done, may lead to an appropriate award for costs.

Where a video recording is admitted under the above provisions, the child must still be called as a witness, but must not be examined-in-chief on matters dealt with adequately in his recorded testimony. The recording is treated as a direct oral testimony. The court must estimate the weight to be attached to such testimony.

The Criminal Justice Act 1988, s 34A provides that an accused may not himself cross-examine a witness who is to be cross-examined following the admission of a video recording of testimony from him under s 32A

Live television links at preliminary hearings   Section 57 of the Crime and Disorder Act 1998 provides for the use of live television links at preliminary hearings before a court, where an accused is being held in custody. The use of such a link (where it is possible) does not require the consent of the accused, or his legal adviser, but is a matter for the discretion of the court. Section 57 came into force on 30 September 1998 but it has not yet come into general operation. It is to be piloted first. Piloting had not begun when this book went to press.

By s 57(1) of the 1998 Act, in any proceedings for an offence, a court may, after hearing representations from the parties, direct that the accused shall be treated as being present in the court for any particular hearing before the start of the trial, if, during that hearing:

(a)   he is held in custody in a prison or other institution; and
(b)   whether by means of a live television link or otherwise, he is able to see and hear the court and to be seen and heard by it.

The term 'particular hearing' used in s 57(1) refers to any hearing before either a magistrates' court or Crown Court before the start of the trial.

Documentary evidence

Documentary evidence consists of information obtained by the production of a document as evidence of a matter contained in it. A 'document' includes, in addition to a document in writing, a map or drawing; a photograph; a disc, tape or the like; and any film or the like. Where a police officer offers in evidence the confession of an accused which is recorded in a written statement, it is the contents of the statement which are offered in evidence and the evidence is therefore documentary evidence.

Real evidence

Real evidence is the production of an object for the inspection of the court or jury. Where a document (or other object bearing writing) is produced as evidence of the matter contained in it, as opposed to proof of its physical existence, it is, as we have just seen, documentary evidence. The firearm which was produced by a witness in the example quoted above is real evidence. Police officers frequently give evidence of having recovered stolen property; this is oral evidence. When the property is produced for inspection in court, this is real evidence.

Original evidence and hearsay evidence

Original evidence is evidence of a fact by 'first-hand' evidence of it. Hearsay evidence is 'second-hand' evidence, since it consists of evidence of what someone else expressly or impliedly asserted orally, in writing or by conduct (eg a nod of the head) when the object of that evidence is to establish the truth of what was asserted. As an example, a policeman's notebook containing a statement about a stabbing is hearsay evidence of the stabbing. It must be emphasised that not all evidence of what someone else asserted is hearsay. If it is produced merely to prove the fact that it was asserted, as opposed to being produced with the object of establishing the truth of what was asserted, it is original evidence and not hearsay evidence. If the accused says that he acted under a threat to kill him made by Y, evidence of what he said is original evidence because it is produced as evidence that Y uttered a threat, but, if a witness says that X had told him that Y had broken the windows of a greenhouse, this is hearsay evidence since it is produced as evidence of the truth of what X stated, ie that Y had broken the windows.

The distinction between original evidence and hearsay evidence is important, because hearsay evidence is inadmissible in criminal cases unless its admission is exceptionally permitted.

PROOF

The general rule is that the prosecution must prove the existence of any fact on which it relies. There are, however, certain facts which do not need to be proved.

Facts which may be established by means other than proof

Judicial notice

The court may take 'judicial notice' of certain matters which are so notorious or well known that evidence of their existence need not be adduced. One does not have to prove that beer is intoxicating, for example, as this is a matter of general knowledge, whereas it may be necessary to prove that a less well-known drink is intoxicating. When screening devices for the purpose of breath testing were first introduced it was necessary to prove in each case the Home Secretary's approval of the type of device used. With the passage of time, the courts ruled that judicial notice could be taken of the existence of that approval.

Presumptions

Sometimes there is a presumption of law that if a particular fact is proved some other fact must be presumed to exist. There are two kinds of presumption of law: irrebuttable and rebuttable.

When the presumption is irrebuttable, no evidence can be received to contradict the presumed fact. An example of an irrebuttable presumption of law is provided by the rule that a child under 10 is incapable of committing an offence.

Where there is a rebuttable presumption of law, the jury (or magistrates) must find that the presumed fact existed. For example, in relation to the offence of living on the earnings of prostitution, contrary to the Sexual Offences Act 1956, s 30(1), s 30(2) provides that a man who lives with or is habitually in the company of a prostitute is presumed to be knowingly living on the earnings of prostitution, unless he proves the contrary.

Where a fact is presumed by law against the accused, it will be presumed to exist unless he proves the contrary on the balance of probabilities.

Presumptions of law must be distinguished from presumptions of *fact*. When a jury (or magistrates' court) *may* find that a particular fact (the presumed fact) exists on proof of some other fact, the presumption is one of fact. Presumptions of fact play a very important part in the criminal law because they are often the only way by which the accused's state of mind can be proved. A judge may tell the jury that they *may* infer knowledge or intent from the fact that the prohibited act was done by the accused, and if the accused offers no explanation that will normally be drawn. This is a matter of common sense, because people generally are aware of the circumstances in which they act, and they generally do foresee that what does result from their conduct will result from it. Of course, the jury must consider the evidence as a whole, and, if they entertain any reasonable doubt, they must give the benefit of the doubt to the accused because of the general rule that the prosecution has the burden of proof. It must be emphasised that this presumption as to the accused's knowledge or intent is one which the jury (or a magistrates' court) *may* draw; they are never obliged to do so (as is confirmed in relation to intention by the Criminal Justice Act 1967, s 8) and it is for this reason that the presumption is one of fact.

There are, of course, a wide range of other presumptions of fact, which arise because they are suggested by common sense. For example, if X is seen driving a car immediately after an accident, it may be inferred that he was driving at the time of the accident. As a moment's thought shows, presumptions of fact are merely particular and frequently occurring instances of the operation of circumstantial evidence since the nature of circumstantial evidence is that it consists of facts from which other facts may be presumed to exist.

Formal admissions

A confession is a statement wholly or partly adverse to the person who made it, whether made to a person in authority or not and whether made in words or otherwise.

A confession is a *means* of proving the fact admitted. On the other hand, a formal admission *dispenses with the need* for proving that fact since it is conclusive evidence of that fact as against the party admitting it. In criminal cases, provision is made for formal admissions, by or on behalf of either prosecution or defence, by the Criminal Justice Act 1967, s 10. Such a formal admission may be made before or at the proceedings. Unless it is made in court, it must be made in writing. A written, formal admission must be signed by the person making it (or by an officer of the company if made by a company). If a formal admission is made on behalf of an accused who is an individual, it must be made by counsel or solicitor; and if made before trial by an accused who is an individual it must be approved by counsel or solicitor before or at the proceedings. With leave of the court, a formal admission may be withdrawn.

The burden of proof

The general rule is that the prosecution has the burden of proving the accused's guilt beyond reasonable doubt. In more detail, the position is as follows. The prosecution always has the burden of proving beyond reasonable doubt that the accused committed the actus reus of the offence charged with the requisite mens rea. In relation to defences, the accused normally has the burden of adducing sufficient evidence to raise a defence; if he does so it is then for the prosecution to disprove the alleged defence beyond reasonable doubt. Exceptionally, the accused has the burden of proving a defence on the balance of probabilities. These cases can be categorised as follows:

Defence of insanity This was outlined in ch 1, above.

Express statutory provision A statute sometimes provides that it is a defence if the accused proves certain facts. For example, under the Prevention of Crime Act 1953, s 1, it is an offence for a person to have with him an offensive weapon in a public place 'without lawful authority or reasonable excuse, the proof whereof shall lie on him'.

Provisos and exemptions in statutory offences Where a statute governing any offence provides any exception, exemption, proviso, excuse or qualification, as where it prohibits the doing of an act save in specified circumstances (or by persons of specified classes, or with specified qualifications, or with the licence or permission of specified authorities), the onus of proving such an exception, exemption etc is impliedly cast on the accused. This rule is provided in the case of summary proceedings by the Magistrates' Courts Act 1980, s 101, and applies in the case of trial of indictment by virtue of the common law.

Rebuttable presumption of law against the accused We dealt with this on p 144 above.

Corroboration

'Corroboration' is evidence from a source (or sources) independent of the witness whose evidence is to be corroborated, which confirms or supports that evidence in some material particular. Corroboration is not generally required as a matter of law. This means that, generally, although corroboration may aid proof, it is possible for the prosecution to discharge its burden of proof by adducing only one item of evidence.

There are, however, exceptional circumstances in which corroboration is required, either by statute as a matter of law or as a matter of practice.

Corroboration required by statute

In cases under this heading a jury or magistrates' court cannot act, ie the relevant fact is not proved, on uncorroborated evidence given on behalf of the prosecution. These cases are:

(a)   perjury (Perjury Act 1911); and
(b)   speeding (Road Traffic Regulation Act 1984).

Corroboration and the Criminal Justice and Public Order Act 1994, s 32

Prior to the 1994 Act a judge was *required* to give a warning concerning the danger of convicting a person on the uncorroborated evidence of a complainant of a sexual offence or on the uncorroborated testimony of an accomplice. The need for such a warning in these cases has been abolished by s 32 of the 1994 Act. Subsequently, the Court of Appeal has stated that the judge has a *discretion* to give a warning to the jury in respect of a witness in one of these two types of case, just as he can in respect of any witness in any other type of case. It is up to the judge, where some warning is required, to determine what type of warning, if any, needs to be given. Much will depend upon the circumstances of the case, the issues raised and the content and quality of a witness's evidence. For it to be appropriate for a warning to be given, there must be an evidential basis for suggesting that a witness is unreliable; mere suggestions by counsel do not provide such a basis.

Proof of convictions and acquittals

The Police and Criminal Evidence Act 1984, s 73 provides that, where the fact that a person has been convicted or acquitted of an offence otherwise than by a Service Court is admissible in evidence, it may be proved by producing a certificate of conviction or acquittal relating to that offence, and proving that the person named in the certificate is the person whose conviction or acquittal for the offence is to be proved. The certificate must be signed, normally by the clerk of the court where the conviction or acquittal took place. A document purporting to be such a certificate is presumed to be such until the contrary is proved.

Section 73 supplements other previous provisions. The Criminal Procedure Act 1865, s 6 allows convictions and acquittals to be proved by questioning, but if there is a refusal to answer the procedure under s 73 will have to be followed. In addition, the Criminal Justice Act 1948, s 39 allows proof of a previous conviction by a certificate from the Metropolitan Police Commissioner as to that conviction coupled with a showing that the fingerprints of the accused correspond with those on the certificate. Lastly, the Road Traffic Offenders Act 1988, s 31 provides that where a person is convicted of an offence involving obligatory or discretional disqualification, any previous conviction for a driving offence endorsed on a driving licence is prima facie evidence of that conviction.

In any proceedings where evidence is admissible of the fact that the accused has committed an offence, then, in so far as that evidence is relevant to any matter in issue for a reason other than a tendency to show in the accused a disposition to commit the kind of offence with which he is charged, he is rebuttably presumed by s 74 of the 1984 Act to have committed it if he is proved to have been convicted (ie found guilty) of it.

Section 74 also provides that the fact that a person other than the accused has been convicted of an offence is admissible in evidence for the purpose of proving, where to do so is relevant to any issue in the proceedings, that that person committed that offence. If that conviction is proved that person is rebuttably presumed to have committed it. However, where an accused is jointly charged with others who have pleaded guilty, proof of the convictions of those other persons jointly charged, in circumstances in which the jury is encouraged to rely on that evidence in determining the guilt of the accused, is liable to be held inadmissible by reason of its adverse effect upon the fairness of the proceedings in accordance with s 78 of the 1984 Act. We explain the operation of s 78 on pp 170-171.

THE MEANS OF PROOF

Assuming that a relevant and admissible fact is not judicially noticed, presumed in his favour, or formally admitted, a party who has to prove that fact may do so in one or more of three ways: by oral evidence; by documentary evidence; and by real evidence as defined on p 143). The first two types of evidence require further explanation.

Competence and compellability

The general rule is that any person is competent and compellable to give evidence, but there are the following *exceptional cases* where a person is either incompetent (ie not legally able) or not compellable (ie cannot legally be required) to give evidence.

Children It is presumed that a child is competent to give evidence, the court having the power to exclude such evidence where it appears that the witness is incapable of giving intelligible testimony. It is therefore a matter which will be determined by a trial judge in the presence of the jury or by magistrates.

Mentally handicapped persons Such a person is incompetent to give evidence if, at the time, he is incapable of understanding the seriousness of the occasion and of realising that taking the oath involves something more than the duty to tell the truth in ordinary everyday life.

Spouses The rules on competence and compellability cause most problems for police officers when they are dealing with offences involving the spouse of the accused. This issue is now dealt with by the Police and Criminal Evidence Act 1984, s 80.

Section 80 provides that the husband or wife of the accused is *competent:*

(a) to give evidence *for the prosecution* (unless jointly charged with the accused spouse, in which case he or she is only competent if he or she is not, or is no longer, liable to be convicted, either due to pleading guilty or for any other reason); and
(b) to give *evidence on behalf of the accused or any person jointly charged with that person.*

Section 80 also provides that a wife or husband of the accused is *only compellable* to give evidence *for the prosecution or on behalf of a person jointly charged with the accused,* if:

(a) the offence charged involves an assault on, or injury (or a threat of injury) to, the wife or husband of the accused or a person who was at the material time under the age of 16; or
(b) the offence charged is a sexual offence alleged to have been committed in respect of a person who was at the material time under that age; or
(c) the offence charged consists of attempting or conspiring to commit, or of aiding, abetting, counselling or procuring or inciting the commission of, an offence within (a) or (b), above.

For the purposes of (b), a 'sexual offence' is an offence under:

(a) the Sexual Offences Acts 1956 and 1967;
(b) the Indecency with Children Act 1960;
(c) the Criminal Law Act 1977, s 54 (inciting girl under 16 to have incestuous relationship); or
(d) the Protection of Children Act 1978 (taking indecent photographs of person under 16).

A husband or wife of the accused is *compellable* to give evidence *on behalf of the accused.*

There is a limitation on the above rules concerning the compellability of the accused's spouse, since such a spouse is never compellable if he or she is jointly charged with his or her spouse, unless he or she is not, or is no longer, liable to be convicted, either as a result of pleading guilty or for any other reason.

The above rules only apply to people who are married; they do not apply where the marriage is void in law, whether on grounds of bigamy, polygamy or otherwise. People who are divorced are always competent and compellable to give evidence in cases involving their former spouse as accused.

The failure of the spouse of an accused to give evidence must not be the subject of comment by the prosecution.

Co-accused Generally, a co-accused person is not competent to give evidence for the prosecution against the other accused person. However, he is competent if he has pleaded guilty, or if no evidence has been offered against him, or if he is tried separately from the other accused.

Privilege

Self-incrimination A person required to answer questions or produce documents may refuse to do so on the grounds that the evidence may incriminate him. Exceptions to this rule are created by a number of statutes concerned with 'trusts', the care and protection of children; and investigations carried out by the Serious Fraud Office.

Lawyer/client Communications between a lawyer and his client which are concerned with the giving of legal advice and those between a lawyer, his client and a third party which are concerned with litigation are privileged. Privilege is not afforded in respect of communications in the furtherance of crime or fraud. In addition, where such communications are disclosed from other sources (document coming into possession of police) or where privilege is waived by the lawyer's client, such evidence may be given.

Public policy and public interest immunity Evidence may be excluded on the grounds that its disclosure would be harmful to the nation or the proper functioning of the public service (such as the disclosure of the identity of informants or the siting of police observation posts). Where a claim of public interest immunity is successful no adverse inference may be drawn against the witness failing to give evidence. Notice should be given of an intention to claim such privilege. Public interest immunity may apply to many police matters; information relied upon for the issue of search warrants; reports to the DPP; and files relating to the investigation of complaints (although disclosure of working papers and reports prepared by investigating officers may be ordered where the public interest in disclosure outweighs that in preserving confidentiality) and disciplinary matters connected with the police. However, any written complaint made about the conduct of a police officer is not privileged. Privilege cannot be claimed in respect of statements made within a police 'grievance' procedure alleging either racial or sexual discrimination.

Oral evidence: the rule against narrative

Generally, a witness may not be asked whether he made a statement before the hearing to the same effect as his testimony in court and such a statement may not be proved by another witness. This general rule is sometimes called the 'rule against narrative'. An example of the general rule is provided by a case where a person charged with murdering a girl gave evidence that the gun went off accidentally while he was trying to patch up a quarrel with her. The accused's father was not permitted, because of the general rule, to give evidence that two days after the shooting the accused had told him that the defence would be accident.

The following exceptions to the general rule against narrative may be noted; where they apply previous consistent statements of witnesses may be proved:

Statements forming part of the res gestae   If the previous statement was made actually or approximately contemporaneously with the event to which it relates, evidence of it may be admitted to establish the truth of some fact narrated by the witness in court. The statement is said to form part of the res gestae (things which have occurred); it will only be admitted if it is sufficiently proximate to the event in issue. The test is to ask whether the statement was so clearly made in circumstances of spontaneity or involvement in the event that the possibility of distortion or concoction can be disregarded, as opposed to being made by way of narrative of a detached prior event. In the case referred to above, for example, the accused told some friends *shortly after* the gun went off that it had done so accidentally, and the friends' evidence of the accused's statement was admitted as res gestae.

Negativing fabrication   If it is alleged that a witness has fabricated his testimony, a previous oral or written statement of his rebutting this is admissible.

Identification of the accused   In answering a question about his identification of the accused, a witness may refer to a previous statement of his. This statement is admissible whether or not the identification is close enough to the crime in question to be part of the res gestae.

Statements of the accused   It is common for the prosecution to give in evidence statements made by the accused to the police. Where these contain an admission of guilt, they are confessions (discussed later). Where they are favourable to the accused, often called 'self-serving statements', they do not, unless part of a confession, constitute evidence of the facts stated. However, if the accused gives evidence to the same effect, they may be relied on by him as proof of consistency and are admissible as evidence of his reaction to police questions.

Early complaint in sexual offences   Statements made by the victim after an offence has been completed are generally excluded because they are not relevant to the offence itself. However, in sexual cases a *complaint* made by the victim may be admissible if:

(a)   the complaint was freely made and not elicited by leading or intimidating questions; and

(b)   it was made as soon after the act complained of as could reasonably be expected in the circumstances.

This is easily understood. There is a significant difference between a complaint blurted out by a distressed girl and a statement forced from her lips by irate parents. Where the above test is satisfied both the fact that the complaint was made and the actual words used are admissible. They are not admitted as evidence of the facts complained of, but as evidence of the consistency of the victim's conduct with the story told by her (or him) in the witness box, and as tending to negative her (or his) consent. The evidence of the complaint cannot constitute corroboration, since a person cannot corroborate himself.

The fact that the complaint was made in answer to a question does not necessarily affect its admissibility. Parents may say to their daughter, 'Whatever's happened to you?', as a result of which a complaint is made. It is spontaneous and freely given and, if made as soon as could reasonably be expected after the act complained of, is admissible.

Oral evidence: oath and affirmation

As a general rule, oral evidence must be given under oath or affirmation. By way of exception, the Children and Young Persons Act 1933, s 33A provides that the evidence of a child under 14 in criminal proceedings is to be given unsworn. It also provides that a deposition of such a child's unsworn evidence may be taken for the purpose of criminal proceedings as if that evidence had been given on oath.

Where it is not possible to administer the oath in the manner appropriate to a witness's religious belief, or where he objects to being sworn, it is permissible for him to make a solemn affirmation instead.

Unsworn evidence may also be given by a person called simply to produce a document.

Documentary evidence

It is a general rule that the contents of a document may be proved only by production of the original. However, there are now so many exceptions to this general rule that it has lost much of its importance. When one of these exceptions applies, secondary evidence of the contents of the document may be given.

The principal exceptions whereby secondary evidence of the contents of a document may be given are as follows:

(a) Where the original is proved to have been lost or destroyed, secondary evidence of the contents may be given.
(b) The contents of public documents can always be proved by means of secondary evidence, although some statutes providing this exception for a particular type of public document limit the nature of this secondary evidence. A 'public document' is a document made for the purpose of the public making use of it and being able to refer to it. Examples are registers of births, deaths and marriages, the contents of which can be proved by a copy of an entry certified by a person who has lawful custody of the register.

  Judicial notice is taken of Acts of Parliament. A statutory instrument is proved by production of the Queen's Printer's copy.
(c) By the Bankers' Books Evidence Act 1879, ss 3 to 5, an examined copy of any entry in a banker's book kept in the ordinary course of business is admissible as prima facie evidence of such entry.

Under the heading of documentary evidence, mention may be made of certain statutory provisions which specially provide for evidence to be given by the production of a document. Examples of these appear later in this chapter, when we discuss exceptions to the rule against hearsay.

INADMISSIBLE MEANS OF PROOF

It is generally inadmissible to seek to prove facts by evidence of opinion or by hearsay evidence. There are, however, exceptions in both cases.

Opinion

Opinion evidence is generally inadmissible because it is the function of the court or jury, and not of a witness, to draw conclusions from the facts proved. If a witness alleges that a particular driver was at fault and caused an accident, that evidence is inadmissible because that is the issue which the court or jury must decide. A fine line can sometimes exist between 'opinion' and 'fact', and for this reason evidence as to the identification of a person or thing (which must always be an opinion to some extent) is admissible. In addition, by way of exception to the general rule the following opinion evidence of experts is admissible:

(a) opinion evidence of experts on points (outside the knowledge or experience of a jury) of science or art, such as doctors of medicine, forensic scientists, metallurgists or literary experts;
(b) opinion evidence from persons who are experts in handwriting comparison; and
(c) opinion evidence by a lawyer shown to have knowledge of a particular system of foreign law.

The Crown Court (Advance Notice of Expert Evidence) Rules 1987 prescribe procedures to be followed in relation to the mutual disclosure between parties of expert evidence which is to be offered in proceedings in the Crown Court.

Hearsay

As we have already said, hearsay evidence is 'second-hand' evidence since it consists of evidence of what someone else expressly or impliedly asserted orally, in writing or by conduct when the object of that evidence is to establish the truth of what was said or written. Hearsay evidence is generally inadmissible because the law of evidence generally requires a fact to be proved by direct evidence of it. Of course, not all evidence of what someone other than a witness said or wrote is hearsay. If it is produced merely to prove the fact that it was said or written, as opposed to the truth of what was said or written, it is original evidence and not hearsay evidence, and therefore admissible if relevant to the facts in issue. This distinction can be illustrated as follows.

If a witness says that the deceased, while in hospital with injuries from which he unexpectedly died, told him, 'Fred did this to me', this is hearsay evidence since it is produced as evidence of the truth of what the deceased stated, ie that Fred caused the injuries. For the same reason, it would be hearsay evidence for a witness to say (at an indecent assault trial), 'Hales told me that he saw Tate indecently assault Mrs Bird'. The sense of this is obvious: Hales could be called to give that evidence, and it can be argued that since the deceased in the first example cannot be cross-examined the inadmissibility of the evidence about his statement is also sensible.

By way of contrast, it is not necessarily hearsay evidence for evidence to be called to show that the accused said that he had acted under a threat of death made by Jones, or for a witness to say 'Mrs Bird complained to me that Tate had fondled her breasts'. This is original evidence of the fact that a threat had been made, or that an early complaint had been made (which is relevant in sexual offences, as we have seen). The latter statement is, however, hearsay if it is intended to show the fact that the sexual offence has been committed.

In some exceptional cases, evidence which is undoubtedly hearsay is nevertheless admissible. These exceptions can be summarised as follows:

Statements received as part of the res gestae

An oral statement made by a person involved in an unusual, startling or exciting event is admissible as part of the res gestae as evidence of the facts stated, provided it was so clearly made spontaneously that, in the light of the circumstances, the possibility of concoction can be disregarded. If the issue is one of murder it is probable that a statement made by the victim, 'Don't shoot, Sidney', which was made as (or immediately before) the gun was fired would be admissible as part of the res gestae, although it is hearsay, and that likewise the victim's agitated shout immediately afterwards, 'Look what you've done. Get a doctor, quick', would be admissible. Where a man was stabbed and, whilst being given first aid treatment by a constable, named his attackers, this evidence was admitted as a part of the res gestae at the trial of the accused after the declarant had died.

While the length of time before or after the event about which the statement is made is relevant, admissibility is not restricted to circumstances in which statements are made at the time of the actus reus. In one case, an injured man crawled for an hour to reach a house at which he named his attacker. He subsequently named his attacker again when he identified him to a police officer whilst being transported to hospital by ambulance. It was submitted that too great a time had elapsed between the incident and the statements. It was held that the crucial question was whether there had been a real possibility of concoction or distortion. At the time that the deceased made the statements, were his thoughts so dominated by what had happened that they could be regarded as unaffected by ex post facto reasoning or fabrication?

Another example of the operation of the res gestae rule is provided by a case where two police officers saw a man being jostled by two others. The assailants went into a doorway where the victim's wallet was found. The victim lunged at the men and said 'they're the ones: these two mugged me of my wallet'. The victim, although summoned, did not attend the hearing and the issue surrounded whether these statements, which were clearly hearsay when repeated by the police officers, could be admitted as part of the res gestae. It was held that, looking at the nature of the incident as a whole, the statements were relevant and were properly admitted. Whilst the res gestae rule should not be used as a device to avoid calling a witness, there was no reason to believe that the Crown had done so in these circumstances.

Confessions

Although hearsay, a total or partial confession of guilt is generally admissible. We deal with the law relating to confessions separately, below.

Declarations of contemporaneous bodily or mental state

A witness may give evidence of another person's declaration as to his bodily condition at the time of the declaration, but not as to its cause. In addition, a witness may give evidence of another's declaration as to his state of mind (including his opinions, dislikes and fears) at the time of the declaration, provided that state of mind is directly in issue at the trial or of direct or immediate relevance to an issue at the trial.

Dying declarations

A dying declaration is admissible, but only in cases of murder or manslaughter. A 'dying declaration' is an oral or written statement made by a deceased person, in relation to which it can be proved that:

(a) the deceased was in a settled and hopeless expectation of death at the time;
(b) he would have been a competent witness had he lived; and
(c) the circumstances of the death were the subject of the declaration.

This is an obvious exception to the general rule. The potential witness has since died and is unable to give the evidence himself. The fact that he was in imminent danger of dying at the time of making the statement renders it unlikely that his declaration would be untrue. If there is a risk of concoction or distortion by the deceased, a dying declaration will not be admitted. The deceased's statement, in the case referred to above, naming his attackers was not a dying declaration because he did not realise that he had been mortally wounded.

Other statements made by persons since deceased

Although statements made, and records kept, by persons who have subsequently died are normally inadmissible hearsay, the following are admissible:

(a) if the deceased was under a duty to record acts performed by him, written or oral statements made by him contemporaneously in pursuance of that duty are admissible; and
(b) declarations made by the deceased against his own pecuniary or proprietary interests are admissible.

If exception (a) did not exist, matters of official public record, for instance, could not be admitted as evidence if the record-keeper was no longer available to give evidence because he was dead. It is submitted that records made in a police officer's notebook are records made contemporaneously in pursuance of a duty to do so, and are therefore admissible under exception (a) if the officer has since died.

Evidence admissible under the Criminal Justice Act 1988, ss 23 or 24

These two sections render admissible hearsay evidence contained in documents if their requirements are satisfied. A video recording counts as a 'document' for the purpose of these sections.

First-hand hearsay Section 23 of the Criminal Justice Act 1988 allows a statement made in a document to be admissible as evidence of any fact stated therein of which direct oral evidence would be admissible if:

(a) any condition relating to the person who made the statement which is specified below is satisfied, viz -

    (i) that the person who made the statement: is dead or by reason of his bodily or mental condition unfit to attend as a witness; or is outside the United Kingdom and it is not reasonably practicable to secure his attendance; or

    (ii) that all reasonable steps have been taken to find the person who made the statement but he cannot be found; or

(b) the statement was made to a police officer or some other person charged with the duty of investigating offences or charging offenders, and the person who made it does not give oral evidence through fear or because he is kept out of the way.

A statement can be 'made in a document' by a person for the purposes of this section even though he himself did not write it, if his oral statement is contemporaneously recorded by the police officer to whom it was made. Normally the statement must be signed by its maker to be admissible, but if he is physically unable to sign the document it will also be admissible if he has clearly indicated that it is accurate after the document has been read back.

The words 'unfit to attend as a witness' apply not only to a person's physical inability to attend a court but also to his mental capacity when there to give evidence. The Court of Appeal has said that there is nothing to prevent the written evidence of a witness being admitted under this section where he is too ill to give evidence at the time of the trial, even though his evidence is the only evidence against the accused. In the case concerned the landlord of a public house had seen three men burgling the pub and had them under observation in a well-lit room for 5-10 seconds. He recognised two of them who were regular customers. Even though this was the only evidence upon which the prosecution relied, there was nothing in the wording of s 23 which prevented such evidence from being given.

Where it is necessary to consider allowing a witness statement to be read on the grounds that it is not reasonably practicable to secure the witness's attendance, the judge should consider the matter as at the date of the application. It would be difficult to apply s 23 with any certainty if a judge had to consider future possibilities of securing attendance.

In relation to the aspect of 'fear' the issue may involve witnesses who have made statements concerning an offence and who later make a second statement saying that they are too afraid to give evidence. Where such events occur, the second statements concerning their state of mind are not excluded by the hearsay rule when they are put in evidence solely to prove the state of mind of the maker of the statement. Where a man committed an offence of aggravated burglary and made threats of violence towards two persons who later said that they were afraid to give evidence, the statements of those persons concerning the reasons for their fear were admitted as well as the statements which they had made immediately following the offence. Although it is sufficient that the witness is in fear as a consequence of the commission of the material offence or of something said or done (by the accused or anyone else) subsequently in relation to that offence and the possibility of that witness testifying as to it, the fear need not be in that form. It is enough that, for whatever reason, fear is established.

The Divisional Court has ruled that the test of fear does not have to be based on reasonable grounds, so long as the court is sure that the witness is in fear. The fear need not have arisen as a result of something which has happened since the commission of the offence.

In order to satisfy the requirements of s 23, there must be oral evidence of fear on the part of the witness, otherwise the written statement is not admissible, but that evidence may, for example, be given by a police officer.

Business etc documents   Section 24 lays down another rule relating to documentary evidence. It is concerned with documents created or received by a person in the course of a trade, business, profession or other occupation, or as the holder of a paid or unpaid office. It provides that, if the information contained in such a document was supplied by a person who had, or may reasonably be supposed to have had, personal knowledge of the matters dealt with, a statement in the document is admissible as evidence of any fact on which direct oral evidence would be admissible. The purpose of the section is to enable a document to speak for itself. Parliament's intention would be defeated if oral evidence was to be required in every case from a person who was either the creator or keeper of the document, or the supplier of the information contained in the document.

Special rules are laid down for written statements prepared for the purpose of pending or contemplated criminal proceedings or of a criminal investigation. A custody record has been held to be such a statement. Written statements of the present type are admissible in two cases: (a) if the requirements of (a) or (b) of s 23, above, are satisfied and (b) if the person who made the statement cannot reasonably be expected (having regard to the time that has elapsed and all the circumstances) to have any recollections of the matters dealt with in the statement.

Where a police officer has noted down a statement, the statement is made for the purposes of the present rule by the officer and not by the person who addressed it to him. In such a case, therefore, the question is whether the constable cannot reasonably be expected to recollect the matters in the statement, and not whether the person who addressed those matters to him can. Similarly, where a man presented a stolen Switchcard at a supermarket check-out and a supervisor saw him making off in a car, the registered number of which she noted, a record made by a second supervisor, at the dictation of the first, was held to be a document created or received in the course of a business, profession etc for these purposes. Where such a person makes a record, the fact that she can recall other matters which occurred at the time (such as the colour of the offender) did not mean that she could be expected to remember the registered number of the car. The section admits a 'statement in a document' where a document was 'created or received' by a person in the course of a trade, business or profession.

General   A statement admitted under ss 23 or 24 is not capable of corroborating evidence given by the person making it.

A court may accept an authenticated copy of a document, and this includes enlargements of microfilm copies.

A court has a discretionary power to exclude evidence which satisfies the requirements of s 23 or s 24 if it is in the interests of justice to exclude it. This could be exercised, for example, on the ground that the document in question may not be authentic or because the court considers that the probative value of the evidence is outweighed by the prejudicial effect it is likely to have on the accused. The admissibility of a disputed computer record should be decided at a trial within a trial.

In addition, essentially, a statement admissible under ss 23 or 24 may be contested on grounds of credibility in the same way that oral evidence can be contested.

In estimating the weight to be attached to a statement admitted under ss 23 or 24, the court must have regard to all the circumstances from which any inference can reasonably be drawn as to the accuracy or otherwise of the statement.

Where a statement admissible under ss 23 or 24 was prepared for the purpose of pending or contemplated criminal proceedings or of a criminal investigation, it may not be given as evidence without the leave of the court, and the court must not give leave unless it is of the opinion that the statement ought to be admitted in the interests of justice.

Evidence from computer records

If a statement sought to be admitted under the Criminal Justice Act 1988, ss 23 or 24, is produced by a computer, it must also comply with the Police and Criminal Evidence Act 1984, s 69(1).

Section 69(1) provides:

'In any proceedings, a statement in a document produced by a computer shall not be admissible as evidence of *any fact stated therein* unless it is shown:
(a) that there are no reasonable grounds for believing that the statement is inaccurate because of improper use of the computer;
(b) that at all material times the computer was operating properly, or if not, that any respect in which it was not operating properly or was out of operation was not such as to affect the production of the document or the accuracy of its contents; and
(c) that any relevant conditions specified in rules made under the section are satisfied.'

The phrase 'document produced by a computer' is uncertain. The Court of Appeal, however, has indicated that it would be reluctant to accept that a document produced on a word processor, rather than a typescript or by a pen, thereby became a document to which s 69 applied (ie a document produced by a computer) rather than a document produced by the writer. If such documents are within the terms of s 69, almost every business document would be subject to that section, which cannot have been the intention of Parliament. The mere fact that there are defects in the print-out produced by a computer does not bring the case within (b) above. Thus, in the case of an intoximeter device, provided that the part of the Intoximeter device which is a 'computer' is functioning correctly and is calibrated and correct, the malfunctioning of the printer (or of its clock) does not render the evidence produced by it inadmissible.

It must be emphasised that s 69 does not render computer-generated evidence admissible as a matter of course if its conditions are met. Consequently, for example, a document produced by a computer may be shown to be accurate and reliable but be held to be inadmissible as hearsay evidence which does not satisfy s 23 or s 24 of the Criminal Justice Act 1988.

Schedule 3 to the Police and Criminal Evidence Act 1984 provides that, where it is desired to give evidence in accordance with s 69, a certificate:

(a) identifying the print-out containing the statement and describing the manner in which it was produced;
(b) giving such particulars of any device involved in the production of that print-out as may be appropriate for the purpose of showing that the print-out was produced by a computer;
(c) dealing with any of the matters mentioned in s 69(1), above; and

(d) purporting to be signed by a person occupying a responsible position in relation to the operation of the computer;

is evidence of any matter stated in it. It is an offence for a person to make a statement in such a certificate, which is tendered in court, which he knows to be false or does not believe to be true.

In estimating what weight to attach to computer-generated evidence, the court must apply the same considerations as in the case of documentary records.

Oral evidence may be given of anything of which evidence could be given by certificate, and it may be given by a person who does not 'occupy a responsible position in relation to the operation of the computer'. Consequently, the requirement in s 69 of proof by the prosecution that the computer has been operating satisfactorily can be satisfied by the evidence of a person familiar with the operation of the computer, who need not be a computer expert. In a recent case, the House of Lords held that evidence by a store detective that computerised cash tills were working satisfactorily was admissible where it was apparent from the nature of her evidence that she was thoroughly familiar with the operation of the tills and the central computer, even though she did not understand the technical operation of the computer. The House pointed out that the only requirements concerned with such evidence as to the operation of a computer are those related to the provision of a certificate under Sch 3. Lord Griffiths said that he suspected that it would rarely be necessary to call an expert and that in the vast majority of cases it would be possible to discharge the burden by calling a witness *who was familiar with the operation of the computer in the sense of knowing what the computer was required to do, and who could say that it was doing it properly.*

Evidence by certificate

The Criminal Justice Act 1948, s 41(1) permits a certificate signed by a constable, or qualified person, certifying that a plan or drawing exhibited in criminal proceedings is a plan or drawing made by him of the place or object specified in the certificate, and that the plan or drawing is correctly drawn to a scale so specified, to be accepted as evidence of the relative position of things shown on the plan or drawing. The plan etc is admissible to the same extent that oral evidence would be admissible. A 'qualified person' means a registered architect or a chartered engineer of one of certain types.

In order for the certificate to be admissible, a copy of such a plan etc must be served on the accused at least seven days before the hearing. Moreover, if the accused serves the appropriate notice that he requires the attendance of the person who signed the certificate, the certificate will not be admissible.

Evidence by written statements

The admissibility of written statements and depositions in committal proceedings has already been discussed in ch 2, above. Schedule 2 to the Criminal Procedure and Investigations Act 1996 permits such a written statement or deposition admitted in evidence in committal proceedings to be read at the trial in the Crown Court if it purports to be signed by a justice, unless:

(a) it is proved that the statement was not signed by the justice;

(b) the Crown Court at its discretion prohibits the document being read; or

(c) a party to the proceedings objects to its being read (in which case the court can overrule the objection if it considers it to be in the interests of justice to do so).

The Criminal Justice Act 1967, s 9 also makes provision for the admissibility of written statements in proceedings other than committal proceedings. It provides that a written statement signed by the person who made it is admissible as evidence to the like extent as oral evidence given by that person. There are certain conditions which must be satisfied:

(a) the statement must contain a declaration by that person to the effect that it is true to the best of his knowledge or belief and that he has made the statement knowing that, if it were tendered in evidence, he would be liable to prosecution if he wilfully stated in it anything which he knew to be false or did not believe to be true;

(b) before the hearing at which the statement is tendered in evidence, a copy of the statement must be served, by or on behalf of the party proposing to tender it, on each of the other parties to the proceedings; and

(c) none of the other parties or their solicitors must, within seven days from the service of the copy of the statement, have served a notice on the party so proposing objecting to the statement being tendered in evidence under the section.

In practice, statement forms carried by police officers incorporate the declaration at (a) so that the evidence of any witness can be offered in written form if it is accepted by the other side. Although the provisions at (b) and (c) seem to suggest that agreements are reached in advance of the hearing there is nothing to prevent agreement being reached at the trial itself.

A statement made by a person under 18 tendered in evidence under s 9 must state his age; if a statement is made by a person who cannot read, it must be read to him before he signs it and be accompanied by a declaration by the person who so read the statement to the effect that it was so read; and if the statement refers to any other document as an exhibit, the copy served on the other party must be accompanied by a copy of that document or by such information as may be necessary to enable that party to inspect that document or a copy of it. Copies of such written statements may be served in the same way as a summons.

Regardless of this procedure having been carried out, the party whose witness it is may nevertheless call that person to give evidence and the court may require, of its own motion or following an application from any party, that that person attends to give evidence.

Expert reports

An expert report is admissible in evidence in criminal proceedings, whether or not the person making it attends to give oral evidence. However, if it is proposed that the maker of the report shall not give oral evidence, the report is only admissible with the leave of the court. In determining whether to give leave, the court must have regard to the contents of the report; the reasons why it is proposed that oral evidence shall not be given; the likely risk to fairness in relation to the accused; and any other relevant circumstance. An 'expert report' is one written by a person dealing wholly or mainly with matters on which he is (or would if living be) qualified to give expert evidence.

Proof of convictions and acquittals

The provisions relating to how such proof may be made, which we discussed above, afford another exception to the rule against hearsay.

CONFESSIONS

For the purposes of the rules which follow, a 'confession' is defined by the Police and Criminal Evidence Act 1984, s 82 as including 'any statement wholly or partly adverse to the person who made it, whether made to a person in authority or not and whether made in words or otherwise'. Because of the phrase 'in words or otherwise', an accused's confession may simply consist of a gesture of acceptance of a statement adverse to him made by another. Statements made which are intended to vindicate a suspect, for example, where he gives explanations intended to justify his possession of goods, and if taken to be true, would do so, do not amount to a confession, even if they are later shown to be false or inconsistent with the maker's evidence. In such a case, however, a record should be made as soon as possible; the reason for there being no contemporaneous notes should be recorded and the suspect should be given an opportunity to check the record.

A video re-enactment by the accused can constitute a confession. This was held in a case where a video recording made willingly by an accused (who had already made an oral confession and who had been reminded that he was under caution and that he was not obliged to participate) in which he re-enacted his actions when strangling a woman was held to be admissible evidence because the video recording had been made reasonably soon after the oral confession and the accused had been properly warned and made it voluntarily. In such a case the accused should be shown the recording and given an opportunity to make, and have recorded, any comment he wished to make concerning the recording.

Section 76(1) of the 1984 Act allows a confession by an accused person to be given in evidence against him in so far as that confession is relevant to a matter in issue in the proceedings and has not been excluded by the court under s 76(2) on the basis explained below. Thus, if an accused makes a confession to an offence of burglary and mentions involvement in an offence of wounding on another occasion, his confession to burglary will be admissible at his trial for that offence since it is relevant to a matter in issue but, if he has not also been charged with wounding, his confession to wounding is not admissible since it is not relevant to a matter in issue in the proceedings.

Most confessions will be tape recorded in consequence of the requirements of the Code of Practice on Tape Recording (p 73).

Exclusion

Section 76(2) of the 1984 Act provides that confessions by oppression must always be excluded. 'Oppression' includes torture, inhuman or degrading treatment, and the use of threats or violence. Apart from this, 'oppression' bears its ordinary dictionary meaning, viz 'the exercise of power or authority in a burdensome, harsh, or wrongful manner; unjust or cruel treatment'. It will almost inevitably involve some impropriety on the part of the interrogator. The fact that a confession has been obtained in circumstances involving a breach of a Code of Practice does not in itself constitute oppression. However, bullying questioning may exceptionally amount to oppression.

If a confession is induced by anything said or done which falls short of 'oppression' it will only be excluded if the thing said or done was likely, in the circumstances existing at the time, to render unreliable any confession which might be made by the accused in consequence thereof. An example of something which will be held to be likely to render a confession unreliable is the use of hostile and intimidating interview techniques. For such a likelihood of unreliability to be found there is no need for any hint of impropriety. Where a suspect was mentally handicapped and was interviewed without an adult person being present, it was held that once it had been established that there had been a breach of the code of practice, the onus was on the prosecution to satisfy the judge beyond reasonable doubt that the confession was not obtained in breach of s 76(2). 'The circumstances existing at the time' were all important in relation to reliability.

Where it is shown that there has been aggressive and hostile questioning it becomes a matter of degree as to whether the threshold is passed beyond which the behaviour of police officers has made the confession unreliable in all circumstances. However, all of the circumstances must be examined. In the course of an interview concerning drug offences an officer interjected, implying that if the suspect did not tell the truth he would be held in custody. Some sixteen minutes later he confessed to an offence. The trial judge refused to exclude his confession being satisfied that the accused was astute, had experience of being interviewed at a police station, and that his will had not been broken. He had continued to deny other offences. The Court of Appeal endorsed the trial judge's decision.

The question frequently arises whether or not, in relation to the issue of unreliability, the expert evidence of a psychiatrist or psychologist should be admitted as to a person's mental condition at the time when a confession was made. Such expert evidence may be admitted to show that a confession is unreliable because of psychological abnormalities if, but only if, it is to the effect that the accused was suffering from mental handicap, mental illness or a personality disorder so severe as to be categorised as mental disorder. It is not enough to allege that an accused is 'not exceptionally bright and is possibly of dull intelligence and very suggestible'.

It has not yet been decided whether interviewing a drug addict when he is withdrawing falls within the present provision. However, the Court of Appeal has held that, if it is, the question of 'likely to be rendered unreliable' depends on whether or not the addict was fit to be interviewed in the sense that his answers could be relied upon in the circumstances. This, the court held, is a matter for those present at the time. The court held that, where experienced police officers considered a person fit to be interviewed and a doctor who saw him after the interview was of the same opinion, there was no reason to believe that a confession was likely to be unreliable. (The court also refused to exclude the evidence obtained by the confession under its discretionary power to exclude unfair evidence provided by s 78 of the 1984 Act, described on pp 170-171.)

If it is alleged that a confession was or may have been obtained by oppression or in consequence of anything said or done which was likely to render the confession unreliable, the court must not allow the confession to be given in evidence against that person except in so far as the prosecution proves beyond reasonable doubt that the confession (notwithstanding that it may be true) was not obtained by these means.

Section 76(4) provides that, even if a confession, or a part of it, is excluded under the above provisions, this does not affect the admissibility:

(a) of facts discovered as a result of the confession; or
(b) where the confession is relevant as showing that the accused speaks, writes or expresses himself in a particular way, of so much of the confession as is necessary to show that he does so.

The effect of (a) is as follows. If evidence of a fact is discovered as a result of a confession, or part of a confession, and that confession, or a relevant part of it, is excluded under s 76(2), that evidence may nevertheless be adduced by the prosecution. However, no reference should be made to the fact that the discovery was the result of a confession; only the accused, or someone acting on his behalf, may disclose this. Thus, if A is arrested for thefts of motor cars and makes a confession which includes details of the persons to whom he sold the vehicles, and that confession is excluded, the prosecution may give evidence of the recovery of the vehicles from those persons but it may not mention that they were discovered as a result of the excluded confession.

The effect of (b) is that, if there is something in a confession, or part, excluded under s 76, which shows that the accused writes, speaks or expresses himself in a particular manner, and this serves, for example, to identify him with whoever committed the offence, so much of the confession as is necessary to show the characteristic referred to is admissible.

Confessions by the mentally handicapped

Section 77 is concerned with confessions made by mentally handicapped persons. Where the case against such an accused depends wholly or substantially upon his confession and the court is satisfied that he is mentally handicapped and that the confession was not made in the presence of an independent person, the jury must be warned of, or the magistrates' court must heed, the need for special care before convicting the accused in reliance on the confession. A police officer or a person employed for, or engaged on, police purposes is not an independent person in this context. Generally speaking, to question a suspect in such circumstances amounts to a breach of the Detention Code (Code of Practice for the Detention, Treatment and Questioning of Persons by Police Officers).

In establishing whether a defendant is mentally handicapped it is not appropriate to attempt to take figures provided by intelligence tests in one case and then to apply them slavishly to another in order to define some rigid line, the crossing of which would lead automatically to the exclusion of confession evidence. Each case must be looked at on its own facts.

Of course, if a mentally handicapped person's confession is obtained by oppression or by words or conduct likely to make it unreliable (as in a case where the accused confessed at a fifth interview after 36 hours' detention and without having received any legal advice), the confession will be inadmissible.

Procedure – tape-recorded confessions at the Crown Court

The procedure to be followed in preparation for proceedings in the Crown Court in relation to tape recordings of police interviews with suspects are laid down in a Practice Direction by the Court of Appeal. Tapes must be produced and proved by the interviewing officer, or any other officer who was present at the interview; the prosecution must provide a tape machine operator; counsel must indicate the parts of a recording which it may be necessary to play, and the prosecution must be prepared in advance to do so.

ACCUSED'S RIGHT OF SILENCE

The position before the Criminal Justice and Public Order Act 1994

The accused's 'right of silence' had been widely interpreted to cover not only the right not to be compelled to incriminate oneself, but the right to refuse to co-operate in any way with a police investigation. The prosecutor was not permitted to make any reference to such silence or lack of co-operation during questioning. The rule against self-incrimination had been extended to include a refusal to offer any explanation for events. Any failure to mention facts when questioned, or silence at an interview, did not, of itself, show guilt nor did it strengthen or corroborate the evidence of a prosecution witness. A failure to advance at an earlier stage any explanation offered at trial was not something to be taken into account.

The position since the Criminal Justice and Public Order Act 1994

The 1994 Act permits a court to draw such inferences from an accused's failure to mention facts as appear proper. The circumstances generally, in which such inferences may be drawn are:

(a) where an accused has failed, when questioned under caution or on being charged or officially informed that he may be prosecuted, to mention facts later relied upon as part of his defence, and which it is reasonable to expect him to have mentioned (s 34);
(b) where an accused fails, without good cause, to give evidence or answer questions at trial (s 35);
(c) where an arrested person fails or refuses to account for possession of objects, substances or marks when requested to do so (s 36);
(d) where an arrested person fails or refuses to account for his presence at a particular place, when requested to do so (s 37).

In the above cases, an inference may be drawn in relation to:

(a) the determination of applications for dismissal of charges made in relation to serious or complex fraud in respect of which notice of transfer has been given;
(b) the determination of the issue of whether a person accused of an offence (of whatever type) has a case to answer;
(c) the determination of whether a person is guilty of the offence charged.

However, an inference cannot be drawn under ss 34-37 in respect of a failure to disclose facts in an interview or other questioning which is inadmissible in law or excluded by way of discretion.

An adverse inference drawn under ss 34-37 cannot be the sole basis for a finding of a case to answer, issue or dismissal of a notice to transfer, or for a finding of guilt. This is provided by s 38(3) and (4). For this reason the changes will not assist in overcoming the problems demonstrated by the well-publicised prosecution of parents of an abused child, both of whom remained silent as to which one of them perpetrated the injuries, which were not in dispute. Because the prosecution was unable to establish the guilty party, both parents were acquitted. In such a case, the only evidence on the key issue of identity would be the inference, something which would be caught by the terms of s 38(3) and (4).

When evidence is to be offered and admissibility

Subject to any directions given by the court, evidence which tends to establish the particular failure may be given before or after the evidence which tends to establish the fact which the accused is alleged to have failed to mention. Thus, where the interview is concerned with the accused's possession of a stolen watch, evidence of his failure to offer an explanation for his possession of it, may be given before, or after, evidence of it being found in his possession. In most circumstances, the most appropriate time will be after evidence of his possession of the property has been given. These provisions do not prejudice the admissibility of evidence of his silence or other reaction which would be admissible apart from the section (eg reaction to things said in his presence and hearing which relate to his involvement in an offence).

Effect of accused's silence when questioned under caution or on being charged or officially informed that he may be prosecuted

By s 34, where it was reasonable to expect the accused to have mentioned facts on which he later relies in his defence, a court or a jury may draw such inferences as appear proper from a failure to mention any fact which a person could reasonably have been expected to mention when questioned under caution, charged or officially informed that he might be prosecuted.

It should be noted that there are significant areas of overlap between this rule and that which applies under s 36 and s 37 (referred to above). However, unlike s 36 and s 37, s 34 is not confined to the questioning of persons who are under arrest.

In addition, s 36 and s 37 operate irrespective of whether a fact is relied upon as part of the defence, or irrespective of whether any defence is in fact made. By contrast, it is this reliance which is at the heart of s 34. Lastly, under s 36 or s 37, a constable is under duty to explain the effect of the requirement in ordinary language, while the key pre-requisite in s 34 is the formal caution.

The Court of Appeal has held that there are six formal conditions to be met before an inference may be drawn by a jury:

(1) there must be proceedings against a person for an offence;
(2) the alleged failure must occur before the person is charged [or – it is submitted – when charged or officially informed of the risk of prosecution];
(3) the alleged failure must occur during questioning under caution by a constable;
(4) the constable's questioning must be directed towards trying to discover whether or by whom the alleged offence had been committed;
(5) the alleged failure must be to mention any fact relied upon in his defence;
(6) the accused's failure to mention a fact which in the circumstances existing at the time the accused could reasonably have been expected to mention when so questioned. 'Time' refers to the time of questioning and account must be taken of all the relevant circumstances existing at the time. 'In the circumstances' includes such matters as the time of day, the defendant's age, experience, mental capacity,

state of health, sobriety, tiredness, knowledge, personality and legal advice, which might all be relevant. These are matters for the jury.

In this case, the Court of Appeal said that the jury should not be concerned with the correctness of a solicitor's advice, nor with whether it complies with the Law Society guidelines. Advice given is a circumstance which a jury may wish to consider but neither the Law Society by its guidance, nor a solicitor by his advice can preclude consideration by a jury of an issue which Parliament has left to the jury to determine. For the purposes of (5), a fact can be relied on even though the accused does not give evidence at his trial, since an accused can rely on a fact by evidence through a witness on his behalf or through cross-examination of a prosecution witness.

Although a person under 17, or a vulnerable suspect, must not be interviewed in the absence of an appropriate adult, except in the case of an urgent interview under Annex C to the Detention Code (Code of Practice for the Detention, Treatment and Questioning of Persons by Police Officers), s 34 is not confined to questioning that amounts to an 'interview'. However, Note 11B to that Code states that juveniles and vulnerable suspects may be particularly prone to provide information which is unreliable, misleading or self-incriminating. It goes on to state that 'special care should therefore always be exercised'. This must be true with equal force in respect of any failure to state facts. There is also the distinct possibility that such a person will not understand the significance of the caution, or believe that an obligation to answer exists. For these reasons, a court would be slow to draw an inference from a failure of a vulnerable suspect to disclose facts subsequently relied upon, certainly in questioning which occurs in the absence of an appropriate adult.

Because the questioning need not occur at a police station, there is no requirement that the questions must be in the presence of a solicitor or other legal representative. Inferences can be drawn in respect of questioning in the absence of such a person, although whether a court will choose to do so may be a different matter. However, if the questioning occurs in circumstances where a legal adviser should have been present, but was not, because of a breach of the Detention Code by the police, the absence of a legal adviser may be important. In such instances, an argument arises for the exclusion from evidence of the record of that interview, pursuant to s 78 of PACE (described below), which may have the effect of preventing any inference from being drawn.

An inference may be drawn from any failure to mention a fact later relied on as part of the accused's defence, and which occurs at or prior to (but not after) charge for the offence, or being officially informed etc. The fact that an accused was charged with one offence will therefore not prevent an inference being drawn in respect of another offence for which he is subsequently questioned.

An inference may only be drawn from a failure to mention facts which the accused could have been reasonably expected to mention when questioned. This wording requires the court to assess the situation at the time of that questioning, not with the benefit of hindsight as at the date of trial.

Effect of accused's silence at trial

Section 35(1) of the 1994 Act permits an inference to be drawn at the trial of a person who has attained the age of 14 years unless:

(a) the accused's guilt is not in issue, or
(b) it appears to the court that the physical or mental condition of the accused makes it undesirable for him to be called upon to give evidence.

However, this will not apply if, at the conclusion of the evidence for the prosecution, it is established that the accused will give evidence.

An accused's guilt will not be in issue if he has pleaded guilty and the hearing is merely concerned to resolve matters relevant to sentencing. Nor will it be in issue in preliminary hearings or in issues concerning the admissibility of evidence.

Where such an inference may be drawn, the court must, at the conclusion of the evidence for the prosecution, satisfy itself (in the presence of the jury where applicable) that the accused is aware that:

(a) the stage has been reached at which evidence can be given for the defence; and
(b) he can, if he wishes, give evidence; and
(c) if he chooses not to give evidence, or having been sworn, without good cause refuses to answer any question, it will be permissible for the court or jury to draw such inferences as appear proper from such failure or refusal.

It is mandatory to give such a warning. Where a court omits to do so but does not draw any adverse inference from a failure to give evidence, the omission does not render a conviction unsafe.

For the purposes of (c), a refusal will be taken to be without good cause where a person, having been sworn, refuses to answer any question unless:

(a) he is entitled to refuse to answer the question by virtue of any enactment, whenever passed or made, or on the ground of privilege; or
(b) the court in the exercise of its general discretion excuses him from answering it.

The privilege against self-incrimination and the common law doctrine of legal professional privilege will therefore apply. Outside such matters 'good cause' may be limited to relevance and propriety and perhaps where a question may be considered oppressive.

The Court of Appeal has rejected a submission that reasons or excuses for silence might exist which could properly be advanced by defence counsel without the need for evidence. An example had been given of a defendant with previous convictions who had attacked the character of a prosecution witness and did not want to give evidence as he would then be liable to cross-examination concerning his criminal record. The Court of Appeal said that the acceptance of such a submission could lead to bizarre results. A defendant with a record would be in a more privileged position than one with a clean record.

The Court of Appeal ruled that, apart from the exceptions included in s 35(1) it is open to a court to decline to draw an inference from silence where the circumstances of the case justified such a course. However, there must be some evidential basis, or exceptional factors, making that a fair course to take. The inferences permitted by s 35 were only such as 'appear proper'.

The Court highlighted the need for a jury to be told that:

(a) the burden of proof remained on the prosecution;
(b) the defendant was entitled to remain silent;
(c) an inference could not by itself prove guilt;
(d) the jury had to be satisfied that the prosecution had established a case to answer before drawing such an inference (although it would be apparent that the judge must have done so or the question of the defendant giving evidence would not have arisen, but the jury may not have believed witnesses upon whose evidence the judge would have relied in coming to that conclusion); and

(e) if despite any evidence relied upon to explain silence or in the absence of any such evidence, the jury concluded that silence could only sensibly be attributed to the defendant's having no answer, or none that would stand up to cross-examination, they might draw an adverse inference.

Where a man was convicted of eight counts of theft and attempted theft but had only been interviewed by the police in respect of one offence, he could not claim that the police had deprived him of his right to comment while matters were fresh in his mind and that the judge should not therefore, have allowed the jury to draw inferences from his silence at trial. The Court of Appeal said that nothing had prevented him from making a statement to his legal advisers whilst matters were fresh in his mind.

The Court of Appeal said that it was impossible to anticipate all of the circumstances in which a judge might think it right to advise a jury against drawing an adverse inference, nor would it be wise to give examples as each case must turn on its own facts. It said that it would not lightly interfere with a judge's exercise of discretion and warned against advocates giving evidence dressed up as a submission. There must be evidence to support such reasons.

Effect of accused's failure or refusal to account for objects, marks etc

Section 36 of the 1994 Act permits an inference to be drawn where:

(a) a person is arrested by a constable and there is -
   (i) on his person; or
   (ii) in or on his clothing or footwear; or
   (iii) otherwise in his possession; or
   (iv) in any place in which he is at the time of his arrest;
   any object, substance or mark, or there is any mark on any such object, and
(b) that another constable investigating the case reasonably believes that the presence of the object, substance or mark may be attributable to the participation of the person arrested in the commission of an offence specified by the constable; and
(c) the constable informs the person so arrested that he so believes, and requests him to account for the presence of the object, substance or mark; and
(d) the person fails or refuses to do so,

then, if in any proceedings for the offence so specified evidence of these matters is given, the court, judge or jury may draw such inferences from the failure or refusal as appear proper. These provisions apply to the condition of clothing or footwear as they apply to a substance or mark thereon. They do not preclude the drawing of inferences which could properly be drawn apart from the section.

Effect of accused's failure or refusal to account for presence at a particular place

Section 37 of the 1994 Act provides that in certain circumstances, a court may draw such inferences as appear proper from the failure or refusal to account for certain matters. Such inferences are permitted where:

(a) a person arrested by a constable was found by him at a place at or about the time the offence for which he was arrested is alleged to have been committed; and

(b) that or another constable investigating the offence reasonably believes that the presence of the person at that place and at that time may be attributable to his participation in the commission of the offence; and

(c) the constable informs the person that he so believes, and requests him to account for his presence; and

(d) the person fails or refuses to do so.

Once again, the provisions of the section do not prevent the drawing of any other inference which could properly be drawn apart from the section.

EVIDENCE OF DISPOSITION

We are concerned here with evidence of a person's tendency to think or act in a particular way. Such evidence may relate to conduct on other occasions (similar fact evidence), to his character or to any previous convictions. All three types of evidence are generally inadmissible.

Evidence of similar facts

The general rule is that evidence of similar facts related to the accused (ie that he behaved in a similar way on previous occasions) is inadmissible in evidence if it is of no particular relevance apart from its propensity to show a tendency towards wrongdoing in general, or towards the commission of the particular crime charged. In one case, for example, where the accused was charged with obtaining a pony and cart by deceptions concerning the state of his family and of his bank account, it was held that evidence tending to show that he had obtained fodder on two occasions by deceptions concerning his business was inadmissible because it was of no particular relevance apart from showing that the accused was a man of generally fraudulent tendencies.

As implied in the last paragraph, similar fact evidence is admissible if it is of particular relevance apart from its propensity to show a tendency towards wrongdoing in general, or towards the commission of the particular crime charged, but it will only be admissible if it has a positive probative value. A common way in which this requirement may be satisfied is if there are similarities which are either unique, in which event its probative value would approach that of a fingerprint, or striking, when its probative value would vary depending on how striking the similarity was. These strict rules may lead to the exclusion of similar fact evidence in some cases, particularly where the identity of an assailant needs to be proved. However, probative value can arise even in the absence of unique or striking similarity. The repetition of similar, though mundane, allegations can sometimes have probative force if arising in the absence of collusion.

Where, at the trial of a man for rape and incest against two of his daughters, the evidence of each girl had described a long course of conduct in relation to each of them, the House of Lords held that all of the circumstances taken together gave strong probative force to the evidence of each of the girls in relation to the incidents involving the other and that (since that probative value outweighed the prejudicial effect of the evidence) the judge had been right to admit it. However, in a case where there was evidence that the rapist was always 'gentle' that was not enough; the similarity was not unique or striking and thus not sufficient to identify the assailant.

Admissible similar fact evidence has the following uses:

(a) To show that the particular accused committed the particular crime charged. Under this heading, admissible similar fact evidence may be admitted to prove a system, and thereby to prove either the actus reus or the mens rea of the crime charged. If B embarks on activities which involve a series of deceptions of the same type (eg pretending to be collecting for charity), the nature of the deception and the systematic course of conduct are of particular relevance to the issue of dishonesty and evidence concerning them is admissible. Where particular facts, upon which the prosecution relied in relation to charges of indecent assault and rape, bore a striking similarity to previous sexual behaviour which had taken place between the defendant and, with her consent, a former girlfriend, the girlfriend's evidence was held to be admissible under the 'similar fact' rule as this evidence had positive, probative value.

(b) Similar fact evidence may be admitted to support the identification of the accused as the man who committed the particular crime and in appropriate cases to rebut an alibi.

If it is sought to adduce evidence of the commission of one offence by the accused as similar fact evidence to support the identification of the accused as having committed one or more other offences, the jury must be directed to consider first whether, disregarding the similarity of the facts, the other evidence is sufficient to make them sure that the accused committed the first offence. Only if they are so sure is evidence of similarity admissible to prove that the accused committed the second offence. An identification about which the jury are not sure cannot support another identification of which they are also unsure, however similar the facts of the two offences may be. However, the position is different if the evidence shows that the offences are so 'welded together' that they must have been committed by the same person. In such a case, the evidence in relation to each charge may assist in identifying the offender.

(c) Similar fact evidence is admissible to rebut some 'defences' raised by the accused, such as accident, ignorance or mistake, whether or not it amounts to a system. In one case, for example, a couple charged with killing a baby whom they were fostering pleaded that the death had been accidental. Evidence was admitted that the bodies of other babies who had been fostered had been found in the gardens of their present and previous houses; this evidence was held to have been properly admitted to rebut the plea that the baby's death was accidental.

Even if similar fact evidence has a positive probative value, the judge has a discretion to refuse to admit it where it is tendered by the prosecution if the prejudicial effect outweighs its probative value.

Evidence as to the accused's character

An accused person may always give evidence of his own good character.

If he does so, the judge must direct the jury that evidence of good character is relevant to the jury's assessment of the accused's credibility. It is also obligatory for the judge to direct the jury that the previous good character of the accused may be regarded by them as a relevant factor when they are considering whether he was the kind of person who was likely to have behaved in the way alleged by the prosecution.

On the other hand, the prosecution may generally not give evidence of the accused's bad character. There are, however, a number of exceptions to this general rule. First, of course, evidence of the accused's character may be admitted as part of similar fact evidence under one of the exceptional rules whereby such evidence is admissible.

Second, if the accused seeks to establish his own good character during proceedings, either by giving evidence or by cross-examination of a witness, the prosecution may give evidence of his bad character in rebuttal. Third, certain statutes enable evidence to be given of the accused's bad character; the most important is the Criminal Evidence Act 1898 (dealt with below).

Evidence as to previous convictions

The accused's previous convictions may sometimes be proved *irrespective of whether he is a witness*. The leading examples of this are where the evidence of such convictions is admitted as part of similar facts evidence under the exceptional rule whereby such evidence is admissible and where the accused is charged with handling stolen goods (see p 774). In addition, where the accused puts his character in issue by seeking to establish his own good character, the prosecution may be allowed to prove his previous convictions as part of his bad character.

Cross-examination of the accused as to his character and previous convictions is governed by the Criminal Evidence Act 1898, s 1(f) of which provides that a person charged *and called as a witness* shall not be asked, and if asked shall not be required to answer, any question tending to show that he has committed or been convicted of or been charged with any offence, other than that with which he is charged, or is of bad character unless:

(a) the proof that he has committed or been convicted of such other offence is admissible in evidence (as it is on a charge of handling stolen goods, as we have noted above) to show that he is guilty of the offence with which he is charged; or
(b) he has personally or by his advocate asked questions of the witnesses for the prosecution with a view to establishing his own good character, or has given evidence of his good character, or the nature or conduct of the defence is such as to involve imputations on the character of the prosecutor or the witnesses for the prosecution or the deceased victim of the alleged crime; or
(c) he has given evidence against any other person charged with the same offence.

EXCLUSION OF UNFAIR EVIDENCE

The purpose of all the rules concerning the gathering of evidence and the manner of its presentation in court is to ensure absolute fairness to an accused person. The Police and Criminal Evidence Act 1984, s 78 provides that, in any proceedings, a court may refuse to allow evidence (including confessions) on which the prosecution proposes to rely to be given if it appears to the court that, having regard to all the circumstances, including the circumstances in which the evidence was obtained, the admission of the evidence would have *such* an adverse effect on the fairness of the proceedings that the court ought not to admit it. Thus, after all the rules of evidence discussed in this chapter have been applied, a court *may* in the exercise of its discretion nevertheless refuse to admit a piece of evidence which would otherwise be admissible on the grounds that it would be too unfair to do so. Rules of law which *require* a court to exclude evidence are unaffected by s 78.

There is no general requirement for the police to have acted in bad faith before evidence is excluded under s 78. Bad faith on the part of police officers will usually lead to the exclusion of evidence, but evidence may be excluded even though the police acted in good faith.

An example of the operation of s 78 is provided by a case where a person had been convicted on evidence based solely on a confession obtained after police had falsely pretended that his fingerprints had been found at the scene of the crime; the Court of Appeal ruled that such evidence should have been excluded under s 78 on the ground that it posed a threat to the fairness of proceedings. Another example is provided by various cases where evidence obtained after a significant and substantial breach of the provisions described in ch 4 relating to the right to legal advice or to the conduct of an interrogation has been excluded on the ground that in the circumstances of the case it would be unfair to admit it. A man was stabbed with a knife handed to the assailant by the accused. The accused provided a written statement in which he said that he gave the assailant the knife and helped him to drive away. He was then cautioned and arrested for having an offensive weapon and impeding the arrest of the assailant. He was later interviewed in relation to these offences. The first statement which he made was excluded under s 78 on the grounds that it was not made within the limits of the code of practice, but the second interview, which related to his offences, was admitted. The Court of Appeal held that the second interview should have been excluded. The defendant could have felt himself bound to the admission made in the first statement.

For such a second interview to be admitted the accused must have been given a *safe and confident* opportunity of withdrawing admissions. It is advisable in such cases that it be shown that the accused had the opportunity of taking legal advice between the first and second interview. Giving a caution is insufficient.

Section 78 does not affect the common law power of a court to exclude evidence on the basis that its prejudicial effect is likely to be greater than its probative value.

ADVANCE DISCLOSURE OF EVIDENCE

The Criminal Procedure and Investigations Act 1996 contains provisions relating to the advance disclosure of information which apply where:

(a) a person charged with a summary offence pleads not guilty;
(b) a person of 18 or over charged with an either-way offence, in respect of which a court proceeds to summary trial, pleads not guilty;
(c) a person under 18 charged with an indictable offence, in respect of which a court proceeds to summary trial, pleads not guilty.

The provisions also apply where a person is charged with an indictable offence and is committed or sent for trial, or proceedings are transferred for trial, to the Crown Court.

The 1996 Act sets out a procedure which is summarised below:

Primary disclosure by prosecutor The prosecutor must disclose previously undisclosed prosecution material to the accused if the prosecutor considers that the material might undermine the prosecution case. At the same time, he must give the accused a document specifying any non-sensitive prosecution material which has not been disclosed to the accused.

Compulsory disclosure by the accused Where cases are to be tried on indictment, the accused is required to provide the prosecutor with a defence statement containing specified information concerning his defence. This must be provided after the accused has received information about the prosecution case and after primary disclosure by the prosecutor.

Voluntary disclosure by the accused Where the case is to be tried summarily, the accused may give a defence statement to the prosecutor.

Secondary disclosure by the prosecutor The prosecutor has a duty to provide additional prosecution material which might reasonably assist the defence disclosed by the accused.

Application by accused for disclosure Following secondary disclosure by the prosecutor, the accused may apply for the disclosure of material which has not at that time been disclosed and which he reasonably believes may assist his defence.

Continuing duty of prosecutor to disclose The prosecutor must continually keep under review (until the trial is concluded) the question of whether there is a need for further disclosure to the accused because certain evidence undermines the prosecution case, or because it may assist a defence disclosed by the accused.

Protected material Material such as photographs or pseudo-photographs of victims of sexual offences, or reports of medical examinations may only be disclosed to an accused's legal representative who must give an undertaking that the material will not be retained by the accused and will not be shown to unauthorised persons except in connection with the proceedings or for the assessment or treatment of a defendant (whether before or after conviction). Where an accused has no legal representative disclosure must be made to an authorised person such as a prison governor or his nominated representative or the officer in charge of a police station or any other person appearing to the prosecutor to be an appropriate person.

Inferences where there are faults in disclosure by accused Where an accused fails to give a defence statement, gives one out of time, puts forward inconsistent defences, puts forward at his trial a defence which differs from that set out in his defence statement, puts forward an undisclosed alibi, or calls a witness to support an alibi about whom he made no disclosure in his defence statement, the court, or any other party with the leave of the court, may make such comment as appears appropriate. In such circumstances, the court or jury may draw such inferences as appear proper in deciding whether the accused is guilty of the offence concerned. In such matters the court must have regard to the extent of the differences between the actual defence and that disclosed in advance and as to whether there is any justification for it.

A person may not be convicted of an offence solely on such an inference.

The Criminal Procedure and Investigations Act 1996 (Defence Disclosure Time Limits) Regulations 1997 require disclosure by the accused within 14 days after disclosure by the prosecutor. That period may be extended by the court, on the application of the accused, if the court is satisfied that the accused could not reasonably have acted within that period. There is no limit upon such an extension, or further extensions.

Where such a period expires on a bank holiday or at a weekend, it is extended so as to expire on the next day which is not such a day.

The Regulations do not prescribe a particular period of time in relation to disclosure by the prosecution. However, the Criminal Procedure and Investigations Act 1996, s 13 requires such disclosure as soon as is reasonably practicable in the particular circumstances described in the section.

Police procedure

Police procedure is controlled by the 'Disclosure: Criminal Procedure and Investigations Act 1996: Code of Practice under Part II'. In summary:

The officer in charge of the case

The officer in charge of the case is responsible for the recording and retention of materials and this includes negative material resulting from the interview of persons who could give no positive evidence. This officer must make such material available to the disclosure officer.

The disclosure officer

The duties of the disclosure officer may be carried out by the officer in charge of the case. Where this is not done there must be full consultation between both officers. The disclosure officer is the link between the investigators and the Crown Prosecution Service and is responsible for providing the material for 'primary disclosure' and performing any other tasks required by the prosecutor. He must ensure, by liaison with the officer in charge of the case where that is a different person, that all material is made available for examination.

Separate schedules of all non-sensitive material and sensitive material (if there is none this fact should be noted) which may be relative to the investigation should be prepared. The schedule of sensitive material should exclude that which is a part of the prosecution case. In the first instance, such schedules need only be prepared in the case of indictable or either-way offences or where there is likely to be a not guilty plea at summary trial. Where an offence has been witnessed by a police officer, or an either-way or summary offence is admitted, such a schedule is not required unless there is a subsequent not guilty plea. Material which is extremely sensitive may be disclosed to the prosecutor separately.

The disclosure officer must then identify material which might undermine the prosecution case. He must also make available any record of a first description of an alleged offender; any explanation for the offence which may have been given by the accused; material which casts doubt upon the reliability of a confession; and any material casting doubts upon the reliability of a witness. In addition, he must draw the attention of the prosecutor to any other material retained by the investigator or other parties which may fall within the requirements for primary disclosure. This is the material which the defence will wish to inspect at this stage. The prosecutor may request additional information.

When the defence statement has been received, the disclosure officer must review the material and inform the prosecutor of any material which might assist the defence. If this duty is carried out by the prosecutor, the disclosure officer remains responsible for ensuring that it is done. When this has been done, secondary disclosure can be made. Even after this has been done, the disclosure officer is under a continuing duty to review material to identify items which should be disclosed. A disclosure officer may be directly involved in the disclosure of material, which the prosecutor has agreed to disclose, to the defence

The Code requires investigating officers to pursue all reasonable lines of inquiry whether they point towards or away from the suspect. Records should be made of all such inquiries. Such officers are also under a duty to continually review material with a view to disclosure. It is therefore important that they are made aware of the content of any defence statement.

OFFENCES AGAINST ADMINISTRATION OF JUSTICE

Perjury

The Perjury Act 1911, s 1(1) provides that it is an offence for any person, lawfully sworn as a witness or interpreter in a judicial proceeding, to wilfully make a statement material in that proceeding which he knows to be false or does not believe to be true.

A person is 'lawfully sworn' if the court or the person before whom the oath is taken is authorised to administer it, and no objection is made by the person taking it. A person, as an alternative to taking the oath, may affirm or declare that he will tell the truth if he has no religious belief, or his beliefs do not permit him to swear on oath, or it is not reasonably practicable, without inconvenience or delay, to administer an oath in the manner appropriate to his religious belief. A 'judicial proceeding' is a proceeding before any court, tribunal or person having by law power to hear, receive and examine evidence on oath. The presence of the word 'wilfully' means that it must be proved that the person concerned made that statement deliberately. A 'material statement' is one which may affect the decision of the court.

Section 13 of the Act states that a person shall not be convicted of perjury solely on the evidence of one witness as to the falsity of any statement alleged to be false, so that there is a requirement of corroboration in this respect. Section 7 deals with aiding, abetting, counselling, procuring or suborning the commission of perjury. It provides that a person who commits such offences will be tried and punished as if he were a principal offender.

All of these offences are arrestable offences. Someone who incites another to commit an offence of perjury is also guilty of an offence.

Perverting justice

The common law offence of attempting to pervert the course of justice is a substantive common law offence and it is therefore not governed by the Criminal Attempts Act 1981, dealt with in ch 42.

The offence may be concerned with the destruction of evidence, the making of false statements, intimidation of witnesses or attempts to influence members of a jury. Police officers may be prosecuted for these offences if they carry out such acts which are intended to defeat or pervert the due course of justice.

The Criminal Law Act 1967, s 5(2) described on p 196, provides an offence to deal with those who cause police time to be wasted, but the wasting of police time does not necessarily mean that any person was put in jeopardy. Where persons are put at risk of unnecessary arrest or wrongful conviction as a result of things done by another person, it may be more appropriate to charge such person with attempting to pervert the course of justice.

INTIMIDATION OF WITNESSES, JURORS AND OTHERS

The offences generally

Jury nobbling and witness intimidation are becoming significant problems. The Criminal Justice and Public Order Act 1994, s 51 is intended to deal with activities which prevent a prosecution being brought or being properly considered by a jury, and reprisals which are threatened or taken against certain persons after a criminal trial has been concluded.

Intimidation etc before or during a trial

Section 51(1) provides that a person who does to another:

(a) an act which intimidates, and is intended to intimidate, that other person;
(b) knowing or believing that the other person is assisting in the investigation of an offence, or is a witness or potential witness, or a juror or potential juror, in proceedings for an offence; and
(c) intending thereby to cause the investigation or the course of justice to be obstructed, perverted or interfered with,

commits an offence.

Thus, all that is required is the doing of an act to another which intentionally results in that other person being intimidated. An act or threat made directly to a witness or juror will suffice but so will, for example, a threat to the wife of such a person to the effect that, unless her husband changes his evidence (or fails to vote for the acquittal of a defendant) her face will be slashed. The person making such a threat clearly intends the husband to be intimidated, as well as the wife, and has thereby carried out an act to the husband through the medium of his wife. The husband will therefore be the 'other person' for the purposes of the section.

The Divisional Court has held that the terms of s 51(1) embrace conduct by an offender, whether or not he is physically present when the threat is made, for example, where he sends a letter or makes a telephone call. The Court said that to require the presence of the person doing the act at the time it took effect, would deprive the section of much of its utility as such an offender might choose to act with stealth to protect his anonymity.

'Intimidation' includes putting a person in fear by an exhibition of force or violence, whether to persons or property. This interpretation is well established within other parallel legislation. Section 51(1)(a) requires an act which 'intimidates' and thus, the person must have been put in fear by a threat. In Scotland, intimidation has been held to be measured by whether the accused's conduct would induce 'serious apprehension of violence in the mind of a man of ordinary courage'. Threats to 'put your windows in etc' can therefore be effectively dealt with.

The section does not demand that the person who is intimidated is actually assisting in the investigation of an offence at the time, or be a witness or potential witness, or a juror or potential juror, in proceedings for an offence. It is sufficient that the accused believes that the person so intimidated is involved in that way. An 'investigation into an offence' means an investigation by the police or other persons charged with the duty of investigating offences or charging offenders.

There must be an intention to intimidate. An attempt to persuade a person to change his testimony without threats will not be sufficient for these offences. There must be knowledge or belief that a person is assisting an investigation in one of the ways specified. This must be an actual knowledge or belief (ie no substantial doubt) about the matter. The accused must also intend, by the intimidating act done to the other person, to cause the investigation or the course of justice to be perverted, obstructed or interfered with. However, in this respect, s 51(7) provides that if it is proved that such an act was done with the required knowledge of belief, it shall be presumed, unless the contrary is proved, that the accused did the act with the required intention. Thus, the onus is upon the accused to show in such circumstances that he did not have such an intention.

Reprisals against witnesses, jurors and others

Section 51(2) provides that a person who does or threatens to do to another person:

(a)   an act which harms or would harm, and is intended to harm, that other person;
(b)   knowing or believing that the other person, or some other person, has assisted in an investigation into an offence or has given evidence, or particular evidence, in proceedings for an offence, or has acted as a juror or has concurred in a particular verdict in proceedings for an offence; and
(c)   does or threatens to do the act because of what (within para (b) above) he knows or believes,

commits an offence.

It must be shown that the accused did, or threatened to do something to another person, which results in harm (or would result in harm) to that other person. There is no requirement that the other person is actually intimidated thereby. As in the case of a s 51(1) offence, such an act may be carried out through the medium of a third party, with the intention of harming the second party. The remaining points which have to be proved are similar to those already discussed in relation to s 51(1). The act carried out or threatened must be intended to harm that person.

Section 51(4) provides that the harm which may be done or threatened may be financial as well as physical (whether to the person or a person's property), and similarly as respects an intimidatory act which consists of threats. The Court of Appeal has held that 'harm', other than financial harm or damage to property, bears the ordinary meaning of physical harm. As a result, it allowed the appeal against conviction under s 51(2) of a man who had spat in the face of a witness and verbally abused her. There had been no proof that the woman had been harmed.

Proof of knowledge or belief that the other person, or some other person, has assisted in an investigation or has given evidence etc is also required.

However, a third factor is involved which is not involved in the case of subsection (1). It must be proved that the accused did, or threatened to do the act because of what he knows or believes about the assisting in an investigation or the giving of evidence etc. In this respect, s 51(8) provides that if it is proved that the act was done or threatened within the 'relevant period' with such knowledge or belief, the accused shall be presumed, unless the contrary is proved, to have done the act with the motive required by the section. For the purposes of this presumption, the 'relevant period' in relation to:

(a)   a witness or juror begins with the institution of proceedings and ends with the first anniversary of the conclusion of the trial, or of any appeal;
(b)   a person who has assisted in the investigation of an offence (or is believed by the accused to have done so) *but who was not a witness* in proceedings for an offence, is the period of one year beginning with the act (or believed act) which assisted the investigation; and
(c)   a person at (b) above *who was also a witness* in proceedings for an offence, is the period beginning with the act (or believed act) which assisted in the investigation and ending with the first anniversary of the conclusion of the trial, or of any appeal.

However, it must be appreciated that the 'relevant period' is only of significance in relation to the presumption which leads to the burden of proof of motive being switched to the accused. It does not prevent a prosecution outside that time; if there is a prosecution outside such time, the presumption will no longer apply and it will be necessary to prove the requisite motive.

Common factors in relation to both offences

Section 51(5) provides that the intention/motive required (in either case) need not be the only or predominating intention/motive with which the act is done or threatened. This should exclude defences based upon the fact that the primary intention of the perpetrator was to avoid a miscarriage of justice.

Police powers

Both offences are arrestable offences.

These offences are additional to existing common law offences. The common law offence of 'embracery' deals with interference with a juror with an intention to prejudice the administration of justice. Interference with witnesses or jurors is punishable at common law either as a criminal contempt of court or as an attempt to pervert the course of justice. Reprisals against witnesses or jurors when a case has been disposed of, may be punishable as a criminal contempt of court.

All of these offences, however, require positive proof of a specified intent on the part of the accused. It cannot be presumed in certain circumstances, as it can be in an offence under s 51.

CORRUPTION

Common law

Where a person who is in a position of trustee to perform any public duty, accepts a bribe to act in a corrupt manner in the discharge of that duty, he commits an offence of corruption contrary to common law. An offer of a bribe, or an attempt to bribe such a person, is also a common law offence.

Statutory offences

Public Bodies Corrupt Practices Act 1889, s 1

A person commits an offence who, by himself, or in conjunction with another person, corruptly solicits or receives, or agrees to receive for himself or another, any gift, loan, fee, reward, or advantage whatsoever as an inducement to, or reward for, or otherwise on account of any member, officer or servant of a public body, doing or forbearing to do anything in respect of any matter or transaction whatsoever, actual or proposed, in which the public body is concerned. A 'public body' is a council of a county, city or town, municipal borough, board, commissioners and any other body with power to act under legislation relating to local government, public health, poor law, or otherwise to administer money raised by rates.

In addition, every person who by himself, or in conjunction with another person corruptly gives, promises or offers any gift, loan, fee, reward or advantage whatsoever to any person, whether for the benefit of that person or another, as an inducement or reward for, or otherwise on account of any member, officer or servant of any public body, doing or forbearing to do anything in respect of any matter or transaction whatsoever, actual or proposed, in which the public body is concerned, commits an offence.

In relation to these offences, the word 'corruptly' does not mean dishonestly. It is concerned with doing an act which the law forbids as tending to corrupt, deliberately. Where it was claimed by a defendant that he had offered a bribe merely to expose corruption, it was held that 'corruptly' meant with intention to corrupt and that his motive was irrelevant. It is no defence to claim that the person concerned did not in fact act in the manner forbidden.

A prosecution for such an offence may not be instituted without the consent of the Attorney-General.

Prevention of Corruption Act 1906, s 1

The offences created by this Act are similar to those set out above but are committed by 'agents' of a 'principal'. An agent is any person employed by or acting for another. A person serving under the Crown or under any corporation, or any borough, district or county council, or any board of guardians, is an agent. The corrupt act must relate to the principal's affairs or business. The term 'principal' includes an employer.

Offences are committed when corruptly giving or agreeing to give, or offering any gift or consideration to an agent to do, or forbear from doing, any act in relation to his principal's affairs or business, or for showing or forbearing to show favour or disfavour to any person in relation to those affairs. It is similarly an offence for such an agent to corruptly accept or obtain, or agree to accept or attempt to obtain from any person such a gift or consideration for those purposes. Offences are also committed by persons who give to an agent any receipt, account, or other document in respect of which the principal is interested and which contains any statement which is false, or erroneous, or defective in a material particular, and to his knowledge is intended to mislead the principal. Similarly, an offence is committed by an agent who knowingly uses, with intent to deceive his principal, such receipt etc.

CHAPTER 8

The police

ORGANISATION, JURISDICTION AND LIABILITY

Organisation of police forces

The Police Act 1996, ss 1,2,3 and 4, provide that England and Wales are divided into police areas. These police areas are those listed in Sch 1 to the 1996 Act, together with the City of London police area and the Metropolitan Police District. A police force, with a police authority, must be maintained for every area listed in Sch 1. Changes to police areas, including a reduction or increase in the number of them, are a relatively simple matters, requiring no more than an order of the Home Secretary. He does not, however, have the power to alter the City of London police area nor to abolish the Metropolitan Police District. Police authorities must consist of seventeen members, but the Home Secretary may, by order, increase the size to a specified odd number greater than seventeen. The authority must consist of nine members of a relevant council (one wholly within the police area), five independent members appointed by the other members of the authority from a short-list prepared by the Home Secretary, and three magistrates for the area concerned.

Section 6 of the 1996 Act imposes the duty upon every police authority to secure the maintenance of an efficient and effective police force for its area. In discharging its functions, a police authority must have regard to:

(a) objectives determined by the Home Secretary and by itself;
(b) 'performance targets' set by itself at the direction of the Home Secretary (which direction may be general in character and applicable to all police authorities, or may be directed at one or more particular authorities);
(c) codes of practice issued by the Home Secretary; and
(d) direction from the Home Secretary in consequence of a report from an inspector of constabulary to the effect that the force is not efficient or not effective, or that it will become so unless remedial action is taken.

The police authority must also set its local policing objectives after consulting the chief constable and considering the views of the community on policing in the area.

Local policing objectives must be consistent with the Home Secretary's objectives. The police authority must also produce a 'local policing plan' stating its priorities for the year and the resources available and setting out all of these objectives and targets. The draft of such a 'local policing plan' will be prepared by the chief constable for consideration by the police authority. Changes must not be made to it without consultation with the chief constable. In discharging his duties, a chief constable must have regard to the local policing plan.

The Metropolitan and City of London Police Forces are under the direction and control of their respective Commissioner, and the Home Secretary performs a role corresponding with that of a police authority in respect of the Metropolitan Force.

Police forces for the areas listed in Sch 1 to the 1996 Act are under the direction and control of the chief constable appointed under s 11 of the Act. Sections 11 and 12 of the 1996 Act permit a police authority to appoint chief constables and assistant chief constables subject to the approval of the Home Secretary and to call upon any of these officers to retire in the interests of efficiency or effectiveness. A chief constable, in consultation with his police authority, must designate an assistant chief constable to exercise all of the powers and duties of chief constable during any absence, incapacity or suspension from duty of the chief constable, or during any vacancy in the office of chief constable. No more than one person may be so authorised. That person may only act in that capacity for a period exceeding three months with the consent of the Home Secretary.

Each police authority must keep a 'police fund' into which all receipts will be paid and from which all expenditure will be met. The Home Secretary, for each financial year, makes a grant from central funds to police authorities and to the Receiver for the Metropolitan Police District. The remainder of the finance will be met from the council taxes of the local authorities within that police area. Civilian employees within a police force, although employed by a police authority, are under the direction and control of the chief constable.

Appointments and promotions to any rank below that of assistant chief constable are made by the chief constable. Those ranks are superintendent, chief inspector, inspector, sergeant and constable.

National police organisations

The Police Act 1997 makes provision for the setting up of a National Crime Intelligence Service and a National Crime Squad, each of which has its own Service Authority whose duty is to maintain the Service in question.

National Crime Intelligence Service

The functions of the National Criminal Intelligence Service are to:

(a) gather, store and analyse information in order to provide criminal intelligence;
(b) provide criminal intelligence to police forces in Great Britain and Northern Ireland, to the National Crime Squad and other law enforcement agencies; and
(c) act in support of such police forces, the NCS and other law enforcement agencies carrying out their criminal intelligence activities.

The Director General is appointed by the Service Authority. Provision is made for the Director General and police service members to retain their status as constables.

The NCIS is under the direction and control of the Director General who must have regard to the service plan issued by the NCIS Service Authority. The Director General must submit an annual report of the activities of NCIS to the Service Authority. The Director General may obtain the views of chief officers of police, the Director General of the National Crime Squad and the Commissioners of Customs and Excise, as he considers appropriate. Collaboration agreements may be made.

The Home Secretary may determine objectives for the NCIS, set performance targets, and issue codes of practice.

The 1997 Act provides for the making of discipline regulations relating to the conduct of members of NCIS and the maintenance of internal discipline. Discipline regulations have already been made in respect of senior police members of the Service. They generally correspond to the discipline regulations applicable to senior members (ie assistant chief constables and above) of police forces. Likewise regulations have been made in respect of the handling of complaints made from, or on behalf of, members of the public. They generally mirror the regulations relating to complaints against the police, which have been made under the Police and Criminal Evidence Act 1984 (see pp 183-188).

National Crime Squad

The function of the NCS is to prevent and detect serious crime which is of relevance to more than one police area in England and Wales. The NCS may also, at the request of a chief officer of police in England and Wales, act in support of the activities of his force in the prevention and detection of serious crime. It may also act in support of NCIS activities (at the request of the Director General of the NCIS), and co-operate with other police forces in the United Kingdom or other law enforcement agencies in the prevention and detection of serious crime.

There are corresponding provisions about the appointment of the Director General of the Service, about objectives set by the Home Secretary, about control and about the disciplinary and complaints procedures, to those which apply to the NCIS.

Jurisdiction of constables

The Police Act 1996, s 30 deals with this. It provides that every member of a police force has all the powers and privileges of a constable throughout England and Wales and the adjacent United Kingdom waters. A special constable has such powers within his police force area and, where the boundary of that area includes the coast, in the adjacent United Kingdom waters, and in areas contiguous with that area. 'United Kingdom waters' means the sea and other waters within the seaboard limits of the territorial sea. These powers are extended in the case of special constables for the City of London, whose powers extend not only to the Metropolitan Police area, but also to those areas contiguous to the Metropolitan Police area. Where special constables are sent to another police force area as part of a mutual aid scheme, they have all the powers of the special constables of that area.

The Criminal Justice and Public Order Act 1994, s 136 empowers constables of forces in England and Wales to execute arrest warrants issued in England and Wales in Scotland and Northern Ireland, and vice versa (see p 18). Powers of arrest for arrestable offences are similarly extended to officers operating 'cross border' by ss 137-140 of that Act.

Representation

The Association of Chief Police Officers, the Superintendents' Association and the Police Federation represent the interests of the various members of police forces. A member of a police force is not permitted to be a member of a trade union, or of any association having as one of its objects control or influence over pay, pensions or conditions of service of any police force. However, persons who were members of trade unions before joining the police force may retain that membership with the approval of their chief constable. These restrictions also apply to police cadets.

Liability

The Police Act 1996, s 88 states that a chief officer of police is vicariously liable for torts committed by his constables in the performance or purported performance of their duties. This means that civil claims may be pursued against a chief officer, as well as against (or instead of against) the officer alleged to have committed a wrongful act. However, it has been held in the High Court that a chief officer is not necessarily liable for conduct in the purported performance of a constable's duty if the conduct was clearly for a purpose unrelated to the constable's duty—as where he threatens not to report an illegal immigrant in return for sexual favours. Any damages or costs awarded against a chief officer must be paid out of police funds. Those awarded against the constable concerned may be paid or part paid from police funds at the discretion of the police authority, and it has been held that they should be so paid if the constable acted in good faith.

Special provision is made by the Police Act 1996, s 97 in relation to officers seconded to central service (including the NCIS or NCS); it is the Home Secretary (and not their chief constable) who is vicariously liable for their torts.

No action lies against a constable or his chief constable for a negligent failure to identify and arrest a criminal where that failure results in his committing further offences. Nor can an investigating officer conducting disciplinary proceedings (or his chief constable) be liable in tort to the officer under investigation if he negligently conducts the proceedings or acts in breach of his duty under the relevant regulations described on pp 182-183. Nor can a constable carrying out traffic duties (or his chief constable) be liable for injuries to a road user caused by a constable's failure to give warnings of hazards of which the constable was aware but for which he was not responsible.

As a matter of public policy, chief constables are not generally liable to their subordinates who are injured by rioters in the course of controlling serious public disorder. In addition, chief constables are not liable for the negligent handling by a senior officer of a complaint made by one police officer against another, nor is the senior officer.

Although an individual police officer may be liable for a statutory tort under the Race Relations Act 1976 if he discriminates against someone, on the ground of his membership of a racial group, in performing his duties, s 53 of that Act has the effect of preventing the officer's chief constable being vicariously liable.

POLICE COMPLAINTS AND DISCIPLINE

Changes to be effected in relation to police disciplinary procedures

The reasons for change

In 1991 the Police Complaints Authority, in its Triennial Review, voiced concern about the police complaints procedure. One of the concerns was the high standard of proof required to secure the conviction of a police officer for a disciplinary offence. The Authority called for the level of proof required in minor cases to shift from 'beyond reasonable doubt' to 'the balance of probabilities'.

The Police and Magistrates' Courts Act 1994

The foundations of a new system were laid within the 1994 Act but the legislation is now within the Police Act 1996. These 1994 Act provisions experienced a stormy passage through both Houses of Parliament. Nevertheless, enabling provisions which will lead to new disciplinary procedures survived. However, promises were made, particularly in relation to consultation which might lead to consensus. This has delayed the implementation of new procedures. The current Government (which attacked the proposals quite fiercely when in opposition) therefore referred the matter to the Home Affairs Committee.

New regulations are therefore awaited at the time of writing. The Home Secretary has indicated that he intends to reduce the standard of proof in disciplinary cases so that some issues may be decided upon 'the balance of probabilities' rather than beyond reasonable doubt. It will be interesting to see how this is brought about if police disciplinary offences continue to be offences against the law (offences in punitive regulations made under the authority of a parent Act of Parliament). In addition, the 'double jeopardy' rule, which currently prevents a police officer who is acquitted of an offence by a criminal court from being charged with a disciplinary offence which arises from the same circumstances, is to be abolished. While the reasons for that change can be appreciated, it will be interesting to see if unfair advantage is taken of this provision on occasions. The new regulations will provide for:

(a) a 'fast track' dismissal system;
(b) means to prevent early retirement before disciplinary matters have been dealt with;
(c) pension forfeiture where an officer is convicted of a criminal offence; and
(d) giving the Home Secretary power to direct the Police Complaints Authority to carry out an investigation in exceptional cases where there is no complaint.

For the present, however, the 1985 Regulations remain in place. However, this chapter incorporates the provisions contained in the 1996 Act in relation to complaints and discipline, recognising that these changes will be made soon after publication. The various sections of the Police Act 1996 which will replace sections of the 1984 Act currently in force, are included in square brackets.

Complaints

In this section reference is made to various sections of the 1984 Act which will, in due course, be replaced by sections of the 1996 Act which are not yet in force.

[The Police Act 1996, s 66 and Sch 5 deal with constitution of] The Police and Criminal Evidence Act 1984, s 83 set up a body known as 'the Police Complaints Authority' (hereafter 'the Complaints Authority') which consists of a chairman (who is appointed by the Queen) and not less than eight other members (who are appointed by the Home Secretary). These appointments are for a period of three years at a time. The Home Secretary may remove these members from office for various reasons. With the consent of the Home Secretary and the Treasury, the Complaints Authority may set up regional offices in any part of England and Wales.

Section [67 of the 1996 Act] 84 of the 1984 Act requires that, where a complaint is submitted to a chief officer of police, he must take any steps that appear to him to be desirable for the purpose of obtaining or preserving evidence relating to the conduct complained of. A 'complaint' for the purposes of this part of the Act is any complaint about the conduct of a police officer which is submitted by a member of the public, or on behalf of a member of the public and with his written consent. Thus, a complaint which is registered by a representative organisation, on behalf of a complainant, is to be regarded as a complaint from that person if he has consented in writing to his cause being taken up by that body.

Having taken steps to obtain or preserve evidence relating to the conduct complained of, the chief officer must determine whether he is 'the appropriate authority' in relation to the officer against whom the complaint was made. In relation to an officer in the Metropolitan Police, the 'appropriate authority' is the Commissioner. In relation to an officer of any other force, the 'appropriate authority' is the chief officer of police. The only exception is where the complaint is against an assistant chief constable or above, in which case it is the police authority; in such a case the police authority carries out the various functions, described below, which are vested in the chief officer in the case of other ranks. A chief officer may delegate any of his functions relating to police complaints, other than participation in a disciplinary tribunal, to an assistant chief constable (or the equivalent in the case of the Metropolitan or City of London Forces). If the chief officer determines that he is not the appropriate authority, because the complaint relates to an officer in another force or to a senior officer, he must send details of the complaint to the 'appropriate authority' and inform the complainant that this has been done.

If the conduct complained of has already been the subject of criminal or disciplinary proceedings, the provisions of the Act which relate to the recording and investigating of complaints do not apply in respect of that conduct.

Section [69 of the 1996 Act] 85 of the 1984 Act provides that if a chief officer determines that he is the appropriate authority in relation to a complaint, he must record the complaint and consider whether the complaint is suitable for informal resolution, and he may appoint an officer from his force to assist him with that decision. If it is not suitable, he must appoint an officer from his own or another force to investigate it formally. The investigating officer must, *as soon as practicable* (without prejudicing his or any other investigation in the matter), inform the officer who is the subject of the complaint of the nature of that allegation or complaint, in writing. A delay until the conclusion of criminal proceedings against a complainant is a breach of the requirement and may entitle the officer to have the proceedings discontinued. Mere delay which gives rise to prejudice and unfairness may, by itself, amount to an abuse of process.

Informal resolution of complaints

This is governed by s [69 of the 1996 Act] 85 of the 1984 Act. If it appears to a chief officer that a complaint is suitable for informal resolution he must seek to resolve it informally and may appoint an officer from his force so to resolve the complaint. A complaint is not suitable for informal resolution unless the member of the public concerned consents to informal resolution *and* the chief officer is satisfied that, even if proved, the conduct would not involve criminal or disciplinary proceedings against the officer concerned.

The officer appointed to resolve informally such a complaint is required by the Police (Complaints) (Informal Resolution) Regulations 1985, as soon as it is practicable, to seek the views of the complainant and the member concerned about the matter and take such other steps as appear to him appropriate. If it appears to the appointed officer that the complaint had in fact already been satisfactorily dealt with at the time it was brought to his notice he may, subject to any representation made by the complainant, treat it as having been informally resolved.

The appointed officer shall not, for the purpose of informally resolving a complaint, tender any apology to the complainant on behalf of the member concerned unless he has admitted the conduct in question.

A complainant is entitled to a copy of the record of informal resolution within three months.

If, after attempts at informal resolution have been made, it is apparent that it is impossible to resolve the complaint, or if for any other reason it appears that the complaint is unsuitable for informal resolution, an investigating officer must be appointed by the chief officer to investigate it formally. The investigating officer in such circumstances must not be the officer who has attempted informal resolution.

Investigation of complaints

The rules which follow apply whether or not there has been an attempt at informal resolution; they are contained in s [69 of the 1996 Act] 85 of the 1984 Act. Unless the complaint is one which is supervised by the Complaints Authority, the investigating officer must submit his report to the chief officer. If a chief officer requests the chief officer of another force to supply an investigating officer, that officer must be supplied.

Referral of complaints to the Authority

Sections [70 and 71 of the 1996 Act] 87 to 94 of the 1984 Act are the governing sections. Complaints alleging that the conduct complained of resulted in the death of or serious injury to some other person must be referred to the Complaints Authority by the chief officer of police. A 'serious injury' for these purposes means any fracture, damage to an internal organ, impairment of bodily function, a deep cut or deep laceration.

In addition, there must be referred to the Authority complaints of the following types, specified in the Police (Complaints) (Mandatory Referrals etc) Regulations 1985:

(a) assault occasioning actual bodily harm;
(b) corruption (Prevention of Corruption Act 1906, s 1); or
(c) a serious arrestable offence within the meaning of s 116 of the 1984 Act.

Any other complaint *may* be referred to the Authority by the chief officer of police. Alternatively, the Authority may require the submission of any other complaint for its consideration.

In addition, s [71]88 allows reference to the Complaints Authority by the chief officer of any matter which appears to indicate that an officer may have committed a criminal offence or behaved in a manner which would justify disciplinary proceedings and *which is not the subject of a complaint*, if it appears that it ought to be referred by reason of its gravity or of exceptional circumstances.

Supervision of investigations by the Authority

The Complaints Authority must supervise the investigation of any complaints which have been referred to it because they involve death or serious injury or are of a nature specified in the above regulations, and it must supervise any other complaint referred to it under the provisions set out above if it considers that it is desirable and in the public interest that it should do so. The Complaints Authority must either select, or approve the appointment of, an investigating officer in respect of complaints which it supervises. It may impose requirements as to a particular investigation. A member of the Complaints Authority is entitled to be present at the interviews of police officers conducted as part of the investigation. The investigating officer must submit his report to the Complaints Authority, sending a copy to the chief officer of police.

When the Complaints Authority has considered a report, it must submit an 'appropriate statement' to the chief officer and, if it is practicable to do so, must send a copy to the officer whose conduct has been investigated. In addition, if it concerns a complaint, and it is practicable to do so, it must send a copy of the appropriate statement to the person by or on behalf of whom the complaint was made. An 'appropriate statement' is a statement which:

(a) states whether the investigation was or was not conducted to the Authority's satisfaction;
(b) specifies any respect in which it was not so conducted; and
(c) deals with any such other matters as the Home Secretary may by regulations provide.

Separate statements may be issued in respect of the disciplinary and criminal aspects of an investigation (see later with regard to the meaning of 'criminal').

No disciplinary charge may be brought before the appropriate statement is submitted to the chief officer, nor may he or the Director of Public Prosecutions bring criminal proceedings before that time, unless it appears to the Director that there are exceptional circumstances making it undesirable to wait.

Steps to be taken after investigation

We are concerned here with the steps to be taken by a chief officer of police after he has received a report from an investigating officer, if the investigation has not been supervised by the Police Complaints Authority, or after he has received a report contained in an 'appropriate statement' from the Complaints Authority, if the investigation has been supervised. These matters are dealt with by [s 75 of the 1996 Act] s 90 of the 1984 Act. The following provisions concerning 'steps to be taken' are the steps to be taken when s 90 has been replaced.

If, on receiving a report, a chief officer considers that a criminal offence may have been committed by a member of his force, he must send a copy of the report to the Director of Public Prosecutions. After the Director has dealt with the question of criminal proceedings, the chief officer must send the Complaints Authority, in such cases as are prescribed by regulations, a signed memorandum stating whether he has brought (or proposes to bring) disciplinary proceedings in respect of the conduct which was the subject of the investigation, and, if not, giving his reasons.

In certain cases to be specified by regulations, if the chief officer considers that the report does not indicate that a criminal offence may have been committed he must send the Authority a signed memorandum to that effect, stating whether he has brought (or proposes to bring) disciplinary proceedings in respect of the conduct which was the subject of the investigation, and, if not, giving his reasons.

Where an investigation relates to conduct which was the subject of a complaint and it was not supervised by the Complaints Authority then the chief officer may be required by regulations under s [75 of the 1996 Act] 90 of the 1984 Act to send the Authority a memorandum and at the same time send a copy of the complaint, or of the record of the complaint, and a copy of the report of the investigation.

Where such a memorandum states that the chief officer proposes to bring disciplinary proceedings, it is his duty to bring and proceed with them, and if such a memorandum states that he has brought such proceedings, it is his duty to proceed with them.

Directions by the Authority

Where a memorandum states that a chief officer of police has not brought disciplinary proceedings, or does not propose to do so, the Authority may recommend him to bring such proceedings. A chief officer may not discontinue disciplinary proceedings that he has brought in accordance with such a recommendation. If, after the Authority has made such a recommendation and has consulted the chief officer, he is still unwilling to bring disciplinary proceedings the Authority may *direct* him to do so. However, the Authority may withdraw such a direction. A direction must include the Authority's reasons for doing so.

A chief officer must advise the Authority of what action he has taken in response to a recommendation or direction, and must furnish the Authority with such information as it may reasonably require for the purpose of discharging its function.

Review of manner of dealing with complaints

Section [77 of the 1996 Act] 95 of the 1984 Act requires police authorities and inspectors of constabulary to keep themselves informed as to the workings of the above complaints procedures.

The Complaints Authority is obliged by s [79]97 to submit an annual report to the Home Secretary as well as any special reports which he may request. It may also report to him any exceptional matters coming to its notice. Where it has reported to the Home Secretary on its own initiative an exceptional matter, it must send a copy to the police authority and chief officer of any police force concerned. The Home Secretary must lay before Parliament every report from the Authority and it must be published. The Authority is also obliged to send copies of its annual report to every police authority together with any statistical or general observations which it considers should be brought to the attention of that police authority.

Confidentiality

Information received by the Complaints Authority is confidential. It may only be disclosed by a person who is, or has been, a member, officer or servant of the Authority to the Home Secretary, officers of the Authority or to other persons who are concerned with the process; or for the purposes of criminal, civil or disciplinary proceedings; or in the form of a summary or other general statement made by the Authority which does not identify individuals to whom it relates. It is an offence for any member, officer or servant (or ex-member etc) to disclose information in breach of these provisions.

A letter to a complainant from the Complaints Authority setting out the results of its investigation is confidential. It does not have to be sent to the police authority and the authority (or the media) can be restrained from publishing it.

Public interest immunity

It can happen that a complainant, having failed under the complaints procedure, will wish to bring a civil action against the police officer or his chief constable, or that the officer in question will wish to sue the complainant for defamation.

Documents which come into existence in relation to the investigation of a complaint will not be available for the preparation of the case, and for use as evidence, if they are covered by public interest immunity, unless the court orders their disclosure. The law is as follows. Documents relating to the police complaints procedure are not as a class entitled to public interest immunity. However, particular documents may be entitled to public interest immunity on the grounds of their contents, and it is possible for a sub-category of documents relating to police complaints to be immune as a 'class'. An example of such a sub-category is a report prepared by an investigating officer for the Police Complaints Authority. A 'contents claim' to immunity, or a 'class claim' of a recognised sub-category, will not necessarily succeed, because the court will order disclosure where the public interest in the administration of justice outweighs the public interest in preserving the confidentiality of the documents in question. In deciding whether a claim of public interest immunity should be upheld, the court is entitled to inspect the document if it wishes to do so.

Regulations governing complaints

The [1996] 1984 Act authorises regulations to be made:

(a)   requiring chief officers of police to supply copies of complaints, or the record of complaints, to persons by or on behalf of whom the complaint was made and to the officer against whom it was made;

(b)   providing procedures for the informal resolution of complaints and for giving complainants records of outcomes;

(c)   providing procedures to allow police officers to comment orally or in writing upon complaints for informal resolution;

(d)   providing procedures following withdrawal of complaints;

(e)   providing procedures relating to dealings with the Complaints Authority generally; and

(f)   giving chief officers powers to delegate functions, other than those of hearing disciplinary charges.

The Police (Complaints) (Informal Resolutions) Regulations 1985 have been made dealing with some of these matters. Where a complainant consents to informal resolution, the complaint is treated as having been withdrawn for the purposes of the Police (Dispensation from Requirement to Investigate Complaints) Regulations 1989. By these regulations, the Complaints Authority may dispense with complaints which are anonymous, repetitious, incapable of resolution, repetitious following the informal resolution of a previous similar complaint, or vexatious; or where the complainant has delayed making a complaint for more than 12 months and either there was no good reason for the delay or injustice would be likely to be caused.

Discipline regulations

The police officer occupies a unique role within society and it is fitting that the highest possible standards are demanded of a constable, who, in addition to being answerable to the laws of the land in the same way as any other citizen, is also answerable to a disciplinary code. In the case of superintendents and below, the Code is set out in the Police (Discipline) Regulations 1985. The Regulations deal with procedures for cases in which a member of a police force may be dealt with by dismissal, requirement to resign, reduction in rank, reduction in rate of pay, fine, reprimand or caution.

At the time of writing the Police (Discipline) Regulations 1985 are being re-written. The Police and Magistrates' Courts Act 1994 (whose provisions in the present respect have been repealed and restated in the Police Act 1996) made alterations to the police disciplinary procedures, including those established within the Police and Criminal Evidence Act 1984. It is reported that the new disciplinary regulations and procedures seek to shed the cumbersome, legalistic and lengthy nature of such proceedings with a view to assisting formal action to encourage police officers to improve their performance. It is said that the new procedures will free police managers to deal with the failures of officers more flexibly, to encourage officers to improve their performance and behaviour.

The intention at the time of the passage of the 1994 Act through Parliament was to make provisions for an officer who had been acquitted on a criminal charge to be judged by a disciplinary tribunal for a similar, disciplinary offence which would carry a less onerous burden of proof. Lengthy consideration of this proposal, and other matters under consideration as a result of the 1994 Act, have caused some delay in providing new regulations. However, the reader is reminded that the 1985 Regulations, which are discussed below, may soon be revoked. It is understood that one of the proposals currently being discussed is to produce one, all-embracing, disciplinary offence.

Under the 1985 Regulations the basic rule is that disciplinary proceedings against an officer of the rank of superintendent or below are heard by his chief constable. There are two exceptions to this.

First, the regulations provide for a different chief constable to hear disciplinary charges when the officer's own chief constable has an interest in the case, other than in his capacity as that officer's chief constable, or is a material witness in the case.

Second, the regulations allow a chief constable to direct (where he considers it appropriate) that disciplinary charges be heard by an assistant chief constable designated to act in the absence of the chief constable (provided that the decision to take those proceedings has been taken by an assistant chief constable in accordance with the Police (Discipline) Regulations 1985). However, such a designated assistant chief constable will only have power to punish by way of reduction in pay, fine, reprimand or caution. An officer found guilty and punished by an assistant chief constable will have a right to appeal to the chief constable, who will not be permitted to award a greater punishment than that awarded by the assistant chief constable.

Disciplinary proceedings against assistant chief constables and above are dealt with by different regulations which are outside the scope of this book; however, it may be noted that disciplinary proceedings against such officers are dealt with by the police authority and not the chief constable.

The punishments which may be awarded for breaches of discipline have already been mentioned. The offences, which must be proved beyond reasonable doubt, are as follows:

Discreditable conduct This offence is committed by a member of a police force who acts in a disorderly manner or any manner prejudicial to discipline or reasonably likely to bring discredit on the reputation of the force or of the police service. The offence applies to conduct on or off duty and it is always a question of fact and degree in deciding whether the conduct of an officer is discreditable or not. The potential width of this offence is shown by a High Court decision that it covers assisting another officer to cheat in a police examination. Minor altercations which might be viewed lightly if they took place between members of the public are likely to be viewed seriously if police officers are involved in them.

Misconduct towards a member of a police force This offence is committed where the conduct of a member of a police force towards another such member is oppressive or abusive, or where a member of a police force assaults another member.

Disobedience to orders This offence is committed where a member of a police force, without good and sufficient cause:

(a) disobeys, or neglects to carry out, any lawful order, written or otherwise; or
(b) fails to comply with any requirement of a Code of Practice for the time being in force under the Police and Criminal Evidence Act 1984, ss 60 or 66; or
(c) contravenes any provisions of the Police Regulations containing restrictions on the private lives of members of police forces, or requiring him to notify the chief officer of police that he, or a relation included in his family, has a 'business interest' (for the definition of 'business interest', see p 195)

Because of the inclusion of the words 'without good and sufficient cause' a failure to carry out a task because of the pressure caused by other duties is not necessarily an offence. The offence embraces all forms of orders, whether spoken, written or provided by regulations. A chief constable's 'force orders', a formidable document, contains many hundreds of such orders.

Neglect of duty This offence is committed where, without good and sufficient cause, a member of a police force:

(a) neglects or omits to attend to or carry out with due promptitude and diligence anything which it is his duty as a member of a police force to attend to or carry out; or
(b) fails to work his beat in accordance with orders, or leaves the place of duty to which he has been ordered, or having left his place of duty for an authorised purpose fails to return thereto without undue delay; or
(c) is absent without leave from, or is late for, any duty; or
(d) fails properly to account for, or to make a prompt and true return of, any money or property received by him in the course of his duty.

Falsehood or prevarication This offence is committed where a member of a police force:

(a) knowingly, or through neglect, makes any false, misleading or inaccurate oral or written statement or entry in any record or document made, kept or required for police purposes; or
(b) either wilfully and without proper authority, or through lack of due care, destroys or mutilates any record or document made, kept or required for police purposes; or
(c) without good and sufficient cause alters, erases or adds to any entry in such a record or document; or

(d) has knowingly, or through neglect, made any false, misleading or inaccurate statement in connection with his appointment to the police force.

The job of a police officer involves the keeping and maintaining of a multiplicity of records. This regulation is designed to ensure that police records are properly kept and that accurate statements are made by officers.

Improper disclosure of information This offence is committed where a member of a police force:

(a) without proper authority communicates to any person any information which he has in his possession as a member of a police force; or
(b) makes any anonymous communication to any police authority, or any member of a police force; or
(c) without proper authority makes representations to the police authority or the council of any county or district comprised in the police area with regard to any matter concerning the force; or
(d) canvasses any member of that authority or of such council with regard to any such matter.

Police officers have access to much information concerning members of the public and the first part of this regulation is concerned with the preservation of confidentiality.

Corrupt or improper practice This offence is committed where a member of a police force:

(a) in his capacity as such, and without the consent of the chief officer of police or the police authority, directly or indirectly solicits or accepts any gratuity, present or subscription; or
(b) places himself under a pecuniary obligation to any person in such a manner as might affect his properly carrying out his duties as a member of the force; or
(c) improperly uses, or attempts to use, his position as a member of the force for his private advantage; or
(d) in his capacity as a member of the force, and without the consent of the chief officer of police, writes, signs or gives a testimonial of character or other recommendation with the object of obtaining employment for any person or of supporting an application for the grant of a licence of any kind.

Thus, an officer is prohibited from accepting gifts within his job without permission; from incurring debts likely to affect the proper discharge of his duties; or from providing character references in his capacity as a police officer without permission to do so.

Abuse of authority This offence is committed where a member of a police force treats any person with whom he may be brought into contact in the execution of his duty in an oppressive manner and, without prejudice to the foregoing, in particular where he:

(a) without good and sufficient cause conducts a search, or requires a person to submit to any test or procedure, or makes an arrest; or
(b) uses any unnecessary violence towards any prisoner or other person with whom he may be brought into contact in the execution of his duty; or improperly threatens any such person with violence; or
(c) is abusive or uncivil to any member of the public.

Racially discriminatory behaviour This offence is committed (without prejudice to the commission of any other offence) where a member of a police force:

(a) while on duty, on the grounds of another person's colour, race, nationality, or ethnic or national origins, acts towards that other person in a way involving abuse of authority (as defined above); or
(b) in any other way, on any of those grounds, treats improperly a person with whom he may be brought into contact while on duty.

Neglect of health This offence is committed where a member of a police force neglects, without good and sufficient cause, to carry out any instructions of a medical officer appointed by the police authority or, while absent from duty on account of sickness, commits any act or adopts any conduct calculated to retard his return to duty.

Improper dress or untidiness This offence is committed where without good and sufficient cause a member of a police force while on duty, or off duty in uniform in a public place, is improperly dressed or is untidy in his appearance.

Damage to police property This offence is committed where a member of a police force wilfully, or through lack of due care, causes any waste, loss or damage to any police property; or fails to report as soon as reasonably practicable any loss of, or damage to, any such property issued to him, or used by him, or entrusted to his care.

Drunkenness This offence is committed where a member of a police force renders himself unfit through drink for duties which he is, or will be, required to perform, or which he may reasonably foresee having to perform.

Drinking on duty or soliciting drink This offence is committed where a member of a police force, while on duty, without proper authority, drinks, or receives from any other person, any intoxicating liquor; or, while on duty, demands or endeavours to persuade any other person to give him, or to purchase or obtain for him, any intoxicating liquor.

Entering licensed premises This offence is committed where a member of a police force, while on duty, or while off duty but wearing uniform, enters, without good and sufficient cause, any premises in respect of which a licence or permit has been granted in pursuance of the law relating to liquor licensing or betting and gaming or of the law regulating places of public entertainment. As a result, although powers of entry are provided by the relevant statutes in favour of police officers, the discipline regulations ensure that these powers are not abused.

Criminal conduct This offence is committed where a member of a police force has been found guilty by a court of law of a criminal offence. Provided that the police officer has been found guilty of a criminal offence, it is irrelevant that he has simply been absolutely or conditionally discharged or placed on probation.

Being an accessory to a disciplinary offence This offence is committed where a member of a police force incites, connives at, or is knowingly an accessory to, any offence against discipline.

Representation at a disciplinary proceeding

The Police and Criminal Evidence Act 1984, s 102 provides that, on the hearing of a disciplinary charge against a police officer of the rank of superintendent or below, the punishment of dismissal, requirement to resign or reduction in rank may not be awarded unless he has been given an opportunity to elect to be legally represented at the hearing. This representation may be by counsel or solicitor. An officer who could be legally represented under s 102, but is not, may only otherwise be represented at the hearing of a disciplinary charge by another member of a police force.

The above provision for legal representation is something of a compromise. There is no general right of legal representation, as instances which fall outside the possibilities of the above punishments will only allow the officer charged to be represented by another member of a police force. The procedures must be set in motion by chief officers of his force, but it is only the chief officer who will be aware of the likely punishments in the circumstances. Notice must be given to the officer that, because of the punishment which might be awarded for his offence, he is entitled to legal representation at his hearing. This will place on an assistant chief constable who has been concerned with investigating the case the difficult burden of deciding the punishment which the chief officer is likely to award, without any consultation taking place with the chief constable!

If an officer fails without reasonable cause to give notice in accordance with the regulations that he wishes to be legally represented, or gives notice in accordance with the regulations that he does not wish to be represented, the punishment of dismissal, requirement to resign or reduction in rank may be awarded without his being legally represented. Officers should therefore give careful consideration to these issues and might be well advised to take advantage of this right on every occasion in view of the severity of these sentences. The Police Federation will offer advice in such cases and may use Federation funds to defray charges where officers have elected to be so represented.

Disciplinary appeals

Changes in the disciplinary appeals procedure were provided for, in the first instance, in the Police and Magistrates' Courts Act 1994. They are now contained in the Police Act 1996. The information contained in the final three paragraphs under this heading which relates to appeals tribunals is contained in s 85 of the Police Act 1996 which is not in force at the time of writing. The provisions which currently apply, but will soon be replaced, are to be found in the Police Act 1964, s 37. Appeals currently lie to the Home Secretary but will, in the near future, lie to a tribunal. For convenience, we describe the situatiuon under s 85, indicating in square brackets where the law is different at the time of writing.

Section 85 of the Police Act 1996 provides that a member of a police force who is dismissed, required to resign or reduced in rank may appeal to [a police appeals tribunal] against the decision except where he has a right of appeal to some other person (to the chief constable where the charge has been heard by a lesser rank). Section 85 provides that in that case, he may appeal to the police appeals tribunal from any decision of that other person [as a result of which he is dismissed, required to resign or reduced in rank]. Where a police appeals tribunal allows an appeal it may, if it considers it appropriate to do so, make an order dealing with the appellant in a way which appears to be less severe and in which he could have been dealt with by the person who made the decision. Unless an order is made by the tribunal, an appellant shall pay his own costs. [At the time of writing, in the absence of an order by the Home Secretary, the appellant's costs will be paid from police funds.]

A police appeals tribunal must consist of four members:

(a) a chairman chosen from a list of persons with a seven year general qualification within the meaning of the Courts and Legal Services Act 1990 (currently only barristers and solicitors have this) who have been nominated by the Lord Chancellor;

(b) a member from the police authority (or a person nominated by the Home Secretary where he is the police authority);

(c) a member from a list of persons maintained by the Home Secretary who are (or within the past five years have been) chief officers of police, other than those of the authority concerned; and

(d) a retired police officer of appropriate rank.

The chairman carries a casting vote in the event of an equality of votes.

An appeals tribunal may determine a case without a hearing but shall not do so unless both the appellant and the respondent have been afforded an opportunity to make written or, if either so requests, oral representations and any such representations have been considered. At a hearing the appellant will have the right to be represented by a serving member of a police force or by counsel or solicitor. The respondent will have similar rights and may also be represented by the clerk or other officer of the authority.

The decision of an appeals tribunal is final; there is no further avenue of appeal.

Double jeopardy

The Police and Criminal Evidence Act 1984, s 104(1) at the time of writing provides that where a member of a police force has been convicted or acquitted of a criminal offence he shall not be liable to be charged with any offence against discipline which in substance is the same as the offence of which he has been convicted or acquitted. However, the Police Act 1996, Sch 9 provides for the repeal of s 104(1). Thus, the rule against double jeopardy will cease to apply when the revised disciplinary procedures are introduced. It is clear that this is in response to pressure from the Police Complaints Authority. Comment was made in Committee Stage in the House of Commons that 'principles of natural justice which have existed in this country since the 13th century would be contradicted by the proposal'. The arguments advanced in favour of repeal certainly appear to be contrived.

RESTRICTIONS UPON PRIVATE LIVES OF MEMBERS OF POLICE FORCES

General

The Police Regulations 1995 impose a number of general restrictions upon the private lives of police officers. Schedule 2 to the Regulations lists the restrictions:

(a) A member of a police force must at all times abstain from any activity which is likely to interfere with the impartial discharge of his duties, or which is likely to give rise to the impression amongst members of the public that it may so interfere. However, the House of Lords has ruled that service as a school governor is not such an activity even though such service involved interviewing applicants for teaching posts, about whom a constable might have confidential information. The regulations specially provide that a member of a police force must not take any active part in politics.

(b)   A member of a police force must not reside at premises which are not for the time being approved by the chief officer of police.

(c)   A member of a police force must not, without the previous consent of the chief officer of police, receive a lodger in a house or quarters with which he is provided by the police authority or sub-let any part of the house or quarters.

(d)   A member of a police force must not, unless he has previously given notice to the chief officer of police, receive a lodger in a house in which he resides and in respect of which he receives a rent allowance or sub-let any part of the house.

(e)   A member of a police force must not wilfully refuse or neglect to discharge any lawful debt.

Incompatible business interest

The Police Regulations 1995 require that a member of a police force must inform the chief officer in writing of any business interests of himself or of a relative included in his family, unless that interest was disclosed on appointment. The chief officer must then decide if that business interest is compatible with the member's duties as a police officer. There is a right of appeal to the police authority against the decision of the chief officer. If an interest is found to be incompatible, the officer's services may be dispensed with after he has been given the opportunity to make representations.

A 'business interest' includes:

(a)   any office or employment for hire or gain held by the member of the police force, or any business carried on by him;

(b)   a shop kept in the area of the police force by a spouse (not being separated from the member) or a relative living with him; or

(c)   a liquor or betting and gaming licence or permit (or certain similar types of licence) held by the member, his spouse (not separated) or a relative living with him, or a pecuniary interest in such a licence.

PROBATIONARY SERVICE

The Police Regulations 1995 provide that a member of a police force appointed in the rank of constable is always on probation for the first two years of his service. This applies to all members of a police force appointed in the rank of constable other than a member who transfers to the force, from another force, having completed the required period of probation therein. Where, in the opinion of the chief officer of police, the period of probation was seriously interrupted by a period of absence from duty, by reason of injury or illness, probation may be extended for a longer period, not exceeding 12 months, as determined in the particular circumstances. It may also be extended for other reasons. An officer, who transfers from one force to another and has already successfully completed not less than one year of probationary service in that or any other police force, will thereafter be on probation for one year (unless extended as above). However, the chief officer of police may reduce this period, provided that the total probationary service is not less than two years.

This period of probationary service is used to establish whether or not a person is fitted mentally and physically to perform the duties of a constable. A probationer constable may be discharged at any time if his chief officer considers that he is not so fitted. The word 'mentally' is not used to indicate a level of academic acceptability. The demands of the job can be considerable and the pressures can be too much for those who are not equipped to handle certain situations. The chief officer may also dispense with the services of a probationer if he considers that he is not likely to become an efficient or well-conducted police officer.

Where a chief officer is considering dispensing with the services of a probationary constable under these regulations, the probationer constable must be shown any report containing judgements and opinions on him. However, it has been held that where the grounds for dispensing with his services are that in the opinion of medical officers he is too overweight to carry out his duties satisfactorily, there would be no purpose in such action as any further observation could not alter the decision.

The term 'chief officer of police' for the purposes of the regulations relating to probationary service, includes an assistant commissioner of the Metropolitan Police.

WASTEFUL EMPLOYMENT OF POLICE

The Criminal Law Act 1967, s 5(2) states that it is an offence for a person to cause any wasteful employment of the police by knowingly making to any person a false report tending to show that an offence has been committed or that the informant has any information material to any police inquiry, or giving rise to apprehension for the safety of any persons or property.

In the absence of the offence under s 5(2), an informant would commit no offence by making false reports of events which could lead to extensive police activities and inquiries, as where a person falsely reports that he has seen a person drowning at sea and thereby causes expensive and time-consuming activities on the part of the police.

DATA PROTECTION

The Data Protection Act 1984 is concerned with the security of information stored on computers (including police computers) concerning particular persons. Those who record and use personal data must act in accordance with certain principles set out in Sch 1 to the Act:

(a) the information to be contained in personal data must be obtained, and personal data must be processed, fairly and lawfully;
(b) personal data must be held only for one or more specified and lawful purposes;
(c) personal data held for any purpose or purposes must not be used or disclosed in any manner incompatible with that purpose or those purposes;
(d) personal data held for any purpose or purposes must be adequate, relevant and not excessive in relation to that purpose or those purposes;
(e) personal data must be accurate and, where necessary, kept up to date;
(f) personal data held for any purpose or purposes must not be kept for any longer than is necessary for that purpose or those purposes;
(g) an individual is entitled -
    (i) at reasonable intervals and without undue delay or expense:
        (a) to be informed by any data user whether he holds personal data of which that individual is the subject; and
        (b) to access to any data held by a data user; and
    (ii) where appropriate, to have such data corrected or erased;
(h) appropriate security measures must be taken against unauthorised access to, or alteration, disclosure or destruction of, personal data and against accidental loss or destruction of personal data.

The first seven of these principles are concerned with personal data held by computer users. The eighth (and last) is concerned additionally with personal data in respect of which services are provided by persons carrying on computer bureaux.

'Data' means information recorded in a form which can be processed by equipment operating automatically in response to instructions given for that purpose. 'Personal data' means data consisting of information which relates to a living individual who can be identified from that information (or from that and other information in the possession of the data user), including any expression of opinion about the individual but not any indication of the intentions of the data user in respect of that individual. A person carries on a 'computer bureau' if he provides other persons with services in respect of data, and a person provides such services if:

(a) as agent for other persons he causes data held by them to be processed as described above; or
(b) he allows other persons the use of equipment in his possession for the processing as mentioned above of data held by them.

Data users, including chief police officers, who store personal data must register with the Data Protection Registrar unless all the information which they store is exempt from the provisions of the Act. Information which is exempt includes that concerned with national security; the prevention or detection of crime; apprehension or prosecution of offenders; tax collection; some health and social records; payrolls and accounts and matters stored on personal computers for personal use. Thus the manual files retained within command and control systems and within the Police National Computer (PNC) will sit outside the need for registration, but other matters will not. Personal files kept by chief police officers will be subject to the principles in Sch 1 to the Act. However, whilst information so stored which refers to the opinion of supervisory officers as to an individual's suitability for promotion will be classed as 'personal data' as it is concerned with opinion, a statement of the chief officer's intentions in relation to that individual's advancement is excluded from material classified as 'personal data' as it represents an indication of intention and is therefore not subject to the eight principles in Sch 1.

Section 5(1) of the 1984 Act states that a person must not hold personal data without being registered as a data user (or as a data user who also carries on a computer bureau). Section 5(2) prohibits a registered person:

(a) holding personal data not specified in the entry in the register;
(b) holding or using personal data for a purpose not specified in the entry;
(c) obtaining personal data, or information to be contained in it, from a source not described in the entry;
(d) disclosing personal data to a person not described in the entry; or
(e) directly or indirectly transferring personal data to a non-specified country or territory outside the United Kingdom.

Contraventions of s 5(1), or the knowing or reckless contravention of the prohibition in s 5(2), is made an offence by s 5(5).

By s 5(4) of the 1984 Act an employee or agent of a data user in respect of whom there is an entry in the register is subject to the same restrictions on the use, obtaining, disclosure or transfer of data.

Section 21 of the 1984 Act makes provision for disclosure of information held. An individual is entitled to be informed whether data stored by a user includes personal data. He is also entitled to be supplied with a copy of such information, the terms of which should be easily understood.

The Criminal Justice and Public Order Act 1994, s 161 added further subsections to s 5 of the 1984 Act. Subsections (6),(7) and (8) create an offence of procuring the disclosure of personal data held on a computer; or offering to sell such data which has been procured in contravention of the Act. These offences were added to end the activities of agencies which, at that time, offered to sell information concerning persons' bank balances, salaries and credit ratings.

Data protection under the Data Protection Act 1998

The Data Protection Act 1998 will replace the 1984 Act when it is brought into force. The 1998 Act is concerned with the regulation of processing of information relating to individuals, including the obtaining, holding, use or disclosure of such information.

Principles

Unless exempted by the provisions of the Act, a 'data controller' is obliged to comply with certain 'data protection principles' in relation to all 'personal data' in relation to which he is data controller. A 'data controller' is a person who (alone or jointly or in common with others) determines the purposes for which and the way in which any personal data are, or are to be, processed. It follows that each chief constable is a data controller.

The 'data protection principles' are:

1. Personal data shall be processed fairly and lawfully and, in particular, shall not be processed unless:
    (a) the data subject has given his consent, or the processing is required by law, or is necessary in the interests of the administration of justice, or in certain other cases; and
    (b) in the case of 'sensitive personal data' (eg an individual's racial origin, his political or religious belief, his health or his commission (or alleged commission) of an offence), the data subject has given his explicit consent or the processing is necessary for the data controller to exercise or perform any right or duty imposed by law on the controller in connection with employment, or the processing is necessary in the interests of justice, or in certain other cases.
    This principle does not usually apply to the processing of personal data for the purpose of preventing or detecting crime.
2. Personal data shall be obtained only for one or more specified and lawful purposes, and shall not be further processed in any manner incompatible with that purpose or those purposes.
3. Personal data shall be adequate, relevant and not excessive in relation to the purpose or purposes for which they are processed.
4. Personal data shall be accurate and, where necessary, kept up to date.
5. Personal data processed for any purpose or purposes shall not be kept longer than is necessary for that purpose or those purposes.
6. Personal data shall be processed in accordance with the rights of data subjects under the Data Protection Act 1998.
7. Appropriate technical and organisational measures shall be taken against unauthorised or unlawful processing of personal data and against accidental loss or destruction of, or damage to, personal data.

8.   Personal data shall not be transferred to a country or territory outside the European Economic Area unless that country or territory ensures an adequate level of protection for the rights and freedoms of data subjects in relation to the processing of personal data.

'Data' means information which:

(a)   is being processed by means of equipment operating automatically in response to instructions given for that purpose;
(b)   is recorded with the intention that it should be processed by means of such equipment;
(c)   is recorded as part of a relevant filing system or with the intention that it should form part of a relevant filing system; or
(d)   does not fall within paragraphs (a), (b) or (c) but forms part of an educational, health or public record of a prescribed type.

'Personal data' means data which relate to a living individual who can be identified:

(a)   from those data, or
(b)   from those data and other information which is in the possession of, or is likely to come into the possession of, the data controller,

and includes any expression of opinion about the individual and any indication of the intentions of the data controller or any other person in respect of the individual.

Registration

'Data controllers' must register with the Data Protection Commissioner in order for personal data to be processed if the data falls within types (a) or (b) above, but not (normally) in the case of the other types of data. Thus, the manual files retained within command and control systems do not require registration, but data stored on the PNC do.

By s 21(1) of the 1998 Act, it is an offence to process personal data unless an entry in respect of that data controller has been registered.

Unlawful obtaining etc of personal data

Section 55(1) of the 1998 Act provides that a person must not knowingly or recklessly, without the consent of the data controller:

(a)   obtain or disclose personal data or the information contained in personal data, or
(b)   procure the disclosure to another person of the information contained in personal data.

Breach of s 55(1) is an offence.
Section 55(1) does not apply to a person who shows:

(a)   that the obtaining, disclosing or procuring –
     (i)   was necessary for the purpose of preventing or detecting crime, or

(ii)   was required or authorised by or under any enactment, by any rule of law or by the order of a court;

(b)   that he acted in the reasonable belief that he had in law the right to obtain or disclose the data or information or, as the case may be, to procure the disclosure of the information to the other person;

(c)   that he acted in the reasonable belief that he would have had the consent of the data controller if the data controller had known of the obtaining, disclosing or procuring and the circumstances of it; or

(d)   that in the particular circumstances the obtaining, disclosing or procuring was justified as being in the public interest.

By s 55(3), a person who sells personal data is guilty of an offence if he has obtained the data in contravention of s 55(1). Section 55(4) provides that a person who offers to sell personal data commits an offence if he has obtained it in contravention of s 55(1) or if he subsequently does so.

Prohibition of requirement as to production of certain records

Section 56(1) of the 1998 Act provides that a person must not, in connection with:

(a)   the recruitment of another person as an employee;

(b)   the continued employment of another person; or

(c)   any contract for the provision of services to him by another person,

require that other person or a third party to supply him with a relevant record or to produce a relevant record to him.

Likewise, s 56(2) provides that a person concerned with the provision (for payment or not) of goods, facilities or services to the public or a section of the public must not, as a condition of providing or offering to provide any goods, facilities or services to another person, require that other person or a third party to supply him with a relevant record or to produce a relevant record to him.

Breach of either of these provisions is an offence.

A 'relevant record' in these provisions includes any record of a conviction or caution obtained by a data subject from a data controller who is a chief officer of police or the Director General of the NCIS or NCS.

Section 56(1) and (2) do not apply to a person who shows that:

(a)   the imposition of the requirement was required or authorised by or under any enactment, by any rule of law or by the order of a court; or

(b)   in the particular circumstances the imposition of the requirement was justified as being in the public interest (which it will not be if the alleged justification is that it would assist in the prevention or detection of crime; in such a case a certificate of criminal record will be available from the Criminal Records Agency – when it is established).

CHAPTER 9

Traffic: general provisions

TERMINOLOGY

Throughout the chapters which deal with traffic law, the terms 'mechanically propelled vehicle', 'motor vehicle' and 'road' will appear. These terms will have the meanings set out below, unless specifically defined in another manner within the particular context.

Mechanically propelled vehicle This may be petrol driven, oil or steam driven or propelled by electricity. Whether or not a vehicle is mechanically propelled is a question of fact. Motor cars which are broken down on a road remain mechanically propelled vehicles. The fact that they may not be driven at that particular time is irrelevant. Before a vehicle can cease to be a mechanically propelled vehicle it must be in such a condition or in such circumstances that there is no reasonable prospect of it ever being driven again. The extent to which a vehicle has been immobilised will be the critical factor when considering whether or not it remains a motor vehicle. A motor car in a scrap yard, which has been stripped of all of its mechanical means of propulsion without there being any reasonable prospect of the restoration of motive power, will obviously not be a mechanically propelled vehicle. However, a motor car which is similarly stripped down in a garage for the purpose of effecting repairs remains a motor vehicle as there is a reasonable prospect of it being restored to its former mobility.

Motor vehicle This is defined by the Road Traffic Act 1988, s 185 as being a mechanically propelled vehicle intended or adapted for use on a road. 'Electrically assisted pedal cycles' are not motor vehicles nor are mechanically propelled invalid carriages of a prescribed type.

The words '*intended or adapted for use on a road*' are important. Some motor vehicles are quite obviously 'mechanically propelled' but they are not 'intended or adapted for use on a road'. An obvious example is a go-kart. Whether or not some motor vehicles are intended or adapted for use on a road will depend upon the evidence as to their construction. The test is whether a reasonable person looking at the vehicle, would say that its general use encompassed possible general road use, and the particular use to which a particular person put a vehicle is irrelevant. A mechanically propelled vehicle originally manufactured for use on a road may cease to be a 'motor vehicle' for the purposes of s 185 if it is subsequently altered, but only if such alterations are very substantial. In one case, a dumper truck, which was used on a site for the transport of material around that site and was occasionally driven on adjoining roads for short distances, was held not to be a motor vehicle because there was no proof of general use on roads as opposed to occasional use. On the other hand, in another case, a Euclid earth scraper, which was primarily used to dig up earth on a building site and carry that earth under its own power to other places, was held to be intended for use on a road when evidence of its general use on roads and of its capability of reaching a speed of 45 mph was given. Evidence was also offered to prove that the earth scraper was too large to be transportable and generally travelled from site to site by road.

Road This is defined by the Road Traffic Act 1988, s 192 as meaning any highway and any other road to which the public has access and including bridges over which a road passes. The same definition is provided in relation to the Road Traffic Act 1960.

A highway allows members of the public a right of way on foot, riding, accompanied by a beast of burden or with vehicles and cattle. The term is therefore wide enough to embrace public footpaths, public bridleways and public carriageways, which we define on p 245. It is reasonable to assume that the highway is the area of right of way as defined by its fences. Consequently, grass verges are generally a part of the highway, but this depends upon who erected the fences. If it was the highway authority, the fences will clearly mark the limits of the highway. If the fences were erected by an adjoining landowner, this will not necessarily be so.

Apart from a highway, 'road' in the road traffic legislation means any road to which the public has access. A road is a definable way for passage between two points and the essential factor is whether or not, as a question of fact, the public have access to it. A private road leading to a farmhouse, which was maintained by the farmer, has been held to be a 'road' on evidence being offered that there was no gate and that it was regularly used by persons who had no business at the farm. It is necessary to prove two things if it is alleged that a road is public for the purpose of the road traffic legislation. The first is to prove that it is a road (as described above) and the second that it is used by the public. It has been decided that any road may be regarded as a road to which the public have access, if members of the public are to be found on it who have not obtained access either by overcoming a physical obstruction or in defiance of a prohibition, express or implied. A pavement which is partly publicly owned and partly privately owned is a road if the public have access to the whole of it. It is essential to show that the public in general have access. Access which is restricted to certain classes of persons is not usually sufficient to make a road 'public'.

Save in exceptional circumstances, a car park is not a 'road', although it may be a 'public place' (a term used in other contexts in road traffic legislation).

REGISTRATION

For a variety of reasons, all mechanically propelled vehicles used or kept on roads in Great Britain must be registered with the Secretary of State. All records relating to mechanically propelled vehicles are retained by the Driver and Vehicle Licensing Agency, formerly DVLC, at Swansea. One of the purposes of central registration is to ensure the payment of vehicle excise duty; another is separately to identify all mechanically propelled vehicles used or kept on roads by allocating to each a registration mark which is different from any mark assigned to any other vehicle.

The Vehicle Excise and Registration Act 1994, s 21 provides that it is the duty of the Secretary of State to register a vehicle on the first issue by him of a vehicle licence or a nil licence (ie a licence for a vehicle exempt from excise duty), or where particulars in respect of the vehicle are received by the Secretary of State from a motor dealer, before the first licence is issued. The provisions in respect of motor dealers allow the Secretary of State to issue 'blocks' of registration numbers to suitable motor dealers who are then in a position to allocate particular numbers to vehicles purchased by customers, supply the necessary registration plates and send the details of each vehicle and its owner to the DVLA when the transaction is completed. This speeds up the process and allows the immediate issue of a vehicle excise licence. The registration mark assigned to a vehicle must be fitted in the prescribed manner. Since it is the responsibility of the Secretary of State to register vehicles, the use of an unregistered mechanically propelled vehicle on a road simply constitutes the offence of use without a vehicle excise licence. If it has been registered, but registration plate have not been fixed on it, an offence is committed by the driver or, if the vehicle is not being driven, by the person keeping the vehicle.

In addition to the assignment of a registration number on initial registration, the Secretary of State has power to assign new registration numbers to a vehicle in place of its existing ones. He also has power to assign to a vehicle (whether on first registration or not) registration numbers previously assigned to another vehicle. It is these powers which give effect to the practice of trading in personalised number plates. The Secretary of State may also grant to a person the right to retain a registration number by transferring it from one vehicle registered in that person's name to another such vehicle. This is of particular relevance where someone wishes to transfer a number to a new car from one which he is disposing of.

MOTOR VEHICLES: REGISTRATION MARKS AND DOCUMENTS

Registration document

When the Secretary of State registers a mechanically propelled vehicle he issues a registration document and, unless a registration mark has already been assigned by a motor dealer who has received a 'block' of numbers, assigns a registration mark to that vehicle. Even if a vehicle is exempt from the requirement to be licensed (see p 202), it must still be registered. A registration document contains the registered particulars of the vehicle and the name and address of the person shown in the register as the owner or keeper of the vehicle. The Road Vehicles (Registration and Licensing) Regulations 1971, reg 6 provides that where a registration document is lost, stolen, destroyed, mutilated or accidentally defaced, or where the figures and particulars on it have become illegible, the Secretary of State will issue a duplicate replacement. A police officer can require the owner to produce a registration document and he must produce it for inspection if he is at any reasonable time required to do so. There are no provisions for later production as there are in the case of licences or insurance certificates.

The registered owner of a mechanically propelled vehicle is not necessarily its legal owner, and possession of a registration document is not in itself proof of ownership.

Notification of change of ownership

Where registration book issued before 24 March 1997

The Road Vehicles (Registration and Licensing) Regulations 1971, reg 12 deals with the procedures to be followed when there is a change in the ownership of a mechanically propelled vehicle in respect of which the current vehicle registration book was issued in respect of the vehicle before 24 March 1997. The previous owner of the vehicle must deliver the registration document to the new owner (and may leave the licence on the vehicle) and must forthwith notify the Secretary of State of the change of ownership, stating the registration mark of the vehicle, its class and make and the name and address of the new owner.

The registration document carries a tear-off slip which may be completed to the above effect by the previous owner. The new owner of the vehicle, if he intends to use or keep the vehicle upon public roads otherwise than under a trade licence (see below), must forthwith enter his name and address in the space provided in the document and send it to the Secretary of State. If the new owner does not intend to use or keep the vehicle on public roads, he must forthwith notify the Secretary of State in writing that he is the owner of the vehicle, giving the registration mark of the vehicle, its make and class, the name and address of the previous owner and the fact that he does not intend to use or keep it on public roads. If the new owner intends to use the vehicle on public roads solely under a trade licence, he must give written notice to the Secretary of State of his name and address and those of the previous owner after three months from acquisition or when there is a further change of ownership, whichever is the sooner.

Where registration book issued on or after 24 March 1997

Regulation 12A is concerned with changes of ownership affecting vehicles in respect of which the registration document was issued on or after 24 March 1997. The regulation recognises the change in the form of the registration document issued for such vehicles. In effect, where there is a 'private' sale or transfer of a vehicle, that is to a person other than a motor vehicle trader, the registered keeper must forthwith send to the Secretary of State:

(a)   that part of the registration document which relates to a change of keeper showing the name and address of new keeper;
(b)   the date of transfer;
(c)   a signed declaration that this information is correct to the best of his knowledge; and
(d)   a signed declaration made by the new keeper to the effect that this information is correct.

The part of the registration document which gives particulars of the new keeper must be given forthwith to that new keeper.

Where the new keeper is a motor trader, but the registered keeper is not, the registered keeper must send to the Secretary of State, on the part of the registration document which relates to a transfer to a motor vehicle trader:

(a)   the name and address of the trader;
(b)   the date of transfer;
(c)   a signed declaration to the effect that he transferred the vehicle to the motor trader on the date specified; and
(d)   a signed declaration from the motor trader that the vehicle was transferred to him on the date specified.

Regulation 12A(4) makes special provision for transfers of vehicles, for a limited period, within the motor trade. For a period of three months from the time when the vehicle was last owned by a person who is not a motor vehicle trader, the vehicle may be transferred within the motor vehicle trade without notification to the Secretary of State of changes of ownership, provided that the vehicle is used on public roads only under a trade licence.

Failure to notify the Secretary of State is not a continuing offence and therefore the time limitation upon proceedings runs from the day of the transfer of the vehicle. If, therefore, a period of six months has passed since the transfer of a vehicle no proceedings may be taken against either of the parties to the transaction if they have failed to comply with the requirement to notify the Secretary of State forthwith.

Notification of other changes

An owner of a registered vehicle who changes his address is required by the Road Vehicles (Registration and Licensing) Regulations 1971, reg 13 forthwith to enter his new address in the space provided in the registration document and send the document to the Secretary of State.

In the event of a vehicle being broken up, destroyed or sent permanently out of Great Britain, reg 14 requires notification of that fact and the surrender of the registration document.

Regulation 10 is concerned with procedures which must follow any alteration to the vehicle which renders the particulars in the registration document incorrect. Such alterations must be notified to the Secretary of State forthwith in writing by the owner and the registration document surrendered for amendment. This would apply, for example, if a motor car was re-sprayed or fitted with a new engine, since the details of colour and engine numbers are contained in the document. Should the alteration necessitate changes to the vehicle excise licence, it must also be surrendered by the owner for amendment.

Registration marks

The registration mark assigned to a vehicle is a means of identifying that particular vehicle. The Road Vehicles (Registration and Licensing) Regulations 1971, reg 18 requires that registration marks must be displayed in particular ways. In the case of a motor bicycle, with or without a sidecar, the registration mark must be displayed on the rear of the vehicle; there is no requirement for a front number plate to be fitted to a motor bicycle. In all other cases the registration mark must be fixed on both the front and back of the vehicle, so that in normal daylight the figures and letters are easily legible from a distance of 75 feet from either the front or rear. In the case of a motorcycle the distance is 60 feet. (An invalid carriage (not being a motor bicycle) and a pedestrian controlled vehicle may use front plates which face sideways in each direction.)

Schedule 2 to the 1971 Regulations requires all vehicles first registered on or after 1 January 1973 to be equipped with reflex reflective registration plates. These plates are yellow with black letters (at the rear) and white with black letters (at the front). There are exemptions from this requirement for vehicles exceeding 3 tons unladen weight fitted with reflective 'long vehicle' boards; stage carriages; works trucks; and agricultural machines.

Vehicles registered prior to 1 January 1973 required plates with white, silver or light grey letters on a black surface. However, there is nothing to prevent such vehicles from having reflex plates fitted and it is submitted that it is not unlawful for such vehicles to have one plate of the 'old' type and one reflex plate.

Trailers may have either type of plate fitted.

Offences

It is an offence for a person to drive or, if the vehicle is not being driven, keep on a public road a mechanically propelled vehicle which is required to have a registration mark fixed to it, whilst no mark is fixed or exhibited. There is a defence available if the accused proves that there has been no reasonable opportunity to register the vehicle and that the vehicle was being driven on a public road for the purpose of being registered. If the registration mark is in any way obscured, or rendered or allowed to become not easily distinguishable, the person driving the vehicle or, if it is not being driven, keeping it commits an offence. However, it is a defence to prove that all reasonable steps were taken to prevent the driving or the like occurring. The offence includes instances in which tow bars are fitted to vehicles in such a way that the rear registration mark is obscured.

Trailers

It is important to recognise that the above offences can only be committed by drivers or keepers of mechanically propelled vehicles. However, reg 22 requires that an owner must ensure that there is displayed on a trailer, or the rearmost trailer, the registration mark of the towing vehicle. However, trailers attached to vehicles used on public roads only in passing from one part of a person's land to another part of his land may display the plate of any mechanically propelled vehicle which is similarly restricted and owned by that person, provided the vehicle's total distance of travel on a public road is less than six miles a week. If a trailer plate is obscured, the only appropriate charge would be one which alleged that it was not displayed.

Forgery, fraud or falsity

The Vehicle Excise and Registration Act 1994, s 44 makes it an offence to forge, alter, fraudulently use on a public road, fraudulently lend, or fraudulently allow another to use on a public road a registration mark to be fixed to a mechanically propelled vehicle. These offences also apply to trade plates (see below), licences and registration documents. Where a person is charged with forging a licence it is not essential to prove an intention to avoid paying duty, it is sufficient to prove an intention to induce a person exercising a public duty to accept it as genuine, and by reason of so accepting it, to act or refrain from acting in a way which he would otherwise not have done to his own or another's prejudice. Thus, the alteration of a licence to avoid attracting attention whilst an application for an excise licence was pending, is a forgery for the purpose of the section.

By s 45, a person who is required by the Act to furnish particulars of the vehicle as its keeper (eg on a change of ownership) commits an offence if he furnishes particulars which to his knowledge are false or in any material particular misleading.

LICENSING

The Vehicle Excise and Registration Act 1994, s 29 provides that if any person uses or keeps on a public road any mechanically propelled vehicle for which a licence is not in force, not being a vehicle exempted from duty under the Act, he is guilty of an offence. Whilst the actual section refers to 'vehicle' as opposed to 'mechanically propelled vehicle', s 62(1) of the Act defines the term 'vehicle' as meaning a mechanically propelled vehicle.

The section contains a number of terms which require definition.

Uses This term is described in ch 10, below. An employer is liable for use by his employee even though blamelessly unaware of what the employee is doing. It is not good practice to proceed against the employee in normal circumstances.

Keeps Section 62(2) of the Act states that a person keeps a mechanically propelled vehicle on a public road if he causes it to be on such a road for any period no matter how short, when it is not in use there. If the description 'use' cannot be applied to the vehicle's presence on the road at any particular time, it is 'kept' on that road by any person who causes it to be there. It is a question of fact in each case who that person is. It may be a driver who has parked it there whilst the vehicle still remains under his control. It may be the owner who allows it to remain in a back street unlicensed, or it may be some person in temporary possession. If an unlicensed vehicle is repaired at a garage and placed outside on the road by the proprietor when the repairs have been effected, the garage proprietor is keeping the vehicle on a road without there being an excise licence in force.

Public road A public road is one which is repairable at public expense. Whether or not a road is repairable at public expense can be established by the local authority who will be able to say whether it has been 'adopted' in the sense that a highway authority is responsible for its maintenance under the Highways Act 1980 or under another enactment. In most instances, particular reference to authorities is unnecessary as the road concerned is commonly known to be a public road and justices are entitled to apply their knowledge to such matters. It is advisable that inquiries are made when use on roads within new housing estates is alleged, as it is possible that the roads are still the responsibility of the builder if development work is still continuing or has recently finished.

Mechanically propelled vehicle Whether or not a vehicle is 'mechanically propelled' has already been discussed. As we have seen, it is not necessary to prove that the vehicle was intended or adapted for use on roads. Any mechanically propelled vehicle, including a go-kart, which is actually used or kept on a public road requires a vehicle excise licence regardless of whether or not it was intended or adapted for use on road.

Licence is in force The prosecutor invariably offers evidence of the lack of a vehicle excise licence but this does not strictly need to be proven. Once use or keeping of a mechanically propelled vehicle on a public road has been established, the accused must prove that it was licensed. A 'licence' in this context includes a trade licence (discussed below). Where a licence is obtained by means of a cheque which is dishonoured the licence is void from the time of issue; consequently the use or keeping of a vehicle thereafter in such a case is a using or keeping of an unlicensed vehicle.

Not being exempted Exemptions are listed in the Vehicle Excise and Registration Act 1994, Sch 2. The most significant exemptions from the necessity to be licensed under the Act are police and fire brigade vehicles, ambulances and health service vehicles, veterinary ambulances, invalid carriages not exceeding 10 cwt, vehicles for export, vehicles imported by members of foreign armed forces and vehicles which are used only for purposes related to agriculture, horticulture or forestry and are on public roads only in passing between different areas of land occupied by the same person and the distance so travelled on public roads in doing so does not exceed 1.5 kilometres. An electrically assisted pedal cycle is also an exempt vehicle.

When used for particular purposes, a vehicle may also be exempt for that purpose only. One case is where the vehicle is used only for the purpose of submitting it by prior arrangement for examination or re-examination for a test certificate (or a vehicle weight test) or of taking it from such an examination or re-examination. This exemption also applies to a charge of 'keeping'. Thus, if a driver parks whilst on his way to the testing station simply for the purpose of buying something in a shop, such 'keeping' of the vehicle on a public road is exempt because it is still possible to say that the vehicle was on the road *solely* for the purpose of going to the testing station. Another case is where it is used in the course of that examination; another is where, having been refused a test certificate, a vehicle is taken by prior arrangement for repair etc.

Vehicles used by or for persons with particular disabilities may, in certain circumstances, be exempt.

Foreign vehicles are exempt if brought temporarily into the country for a period of one year. The term 'foreign' includes vehicles from the Isle of Man or the Channel Islands. Visitors from abroad may purchase a vehicle in this country with the intention of exporting it and then use it here without licensing it before taking it out of Great Britain. Northern Ireland licences are treated as licences issued here. The Road Vehicles (Exemption from Duty) Regulations 1986 exempt vehicles imported by members of visiting forces, members of a headquarters or other organisation, or a dependant of such a person. This exemption lasts for a period of 12 months only.

Duration and issue of licence

Excise licences may be issued for a period of 12 months or for six months for vehicles in respect of which the annual rate of duty exceeds £50. In addition, where an application is made for a 12-or six-month licence, the Secretary of State may issue (and subsequently renew) a temporary licence for 14 days. Other than temporary licences, licences are valid from the first day of the month on which they are taken out. An application may be made out by any person who must make a declaration and furnish particulars which are prescribed. The licence is issued to the vehicle, not the person who makes the application, and it does not authorise that person to use or keep any other vehicle. On the sale of a vehicle the licence must either be returned to DVLA with an application for a rebate of duty, or be transferred with the vehicle. It cannot be transferred to a new vehicle.

It has been the practice for many years to allow 14 days' grace for the renewal of vehicle excise licences. The period of grace only applies where an application for a licence was made before the previous one expired and it is limited to a period of 14 days which immediately follows the expiration of the previous licence. It would not therefore apply to a new vehicle or to one which had been laid up for the winter and then brought back into use. If a licence is not obtained within the period of 14 days, then proceedings will probably be taken for unlicensed use whenever it occurred during that period, even though a licence was obtained in the currency of the rest of the month in question. Although the idea of this period of grace is to allow for postal delays in respect of licences which were applied for within the currency of the previous licence, proceedings are not usually taken in respect of use within the following period of 14 days if a licence is applied for (and obtained) within that period. It cannot apply to the circumstances set out in the next paragraph.

The Road Vehicles (Statutory Off-Road Notification) Regulations 1997 require that, where a vehicle licence expires on or after 31 January 1998, the keeper must make a 'required declaration' not later than the day upon which the licence ceases to be in force (three months after such expiry in the case of motor traders). The declaration is to the effect that the vehicle will not be used or kept on a public road and that a licence will be taken out before any such use. It is an offence to fail to make such a declaration.

Rates of duty

Licences cost differing amounts depending upon the nature of the vehicle and its particular use. For example, motorcycles and tricycles attract lower rates of duty than private saloon cars. The Vehicle Excise and Registration Act 1994, Sch 1, sets out the rates of duty applicable to all mechanically propelled vehicles. It sets the basic rate (which applies where no other rate is set by the schedule) and this is the rate which applies to private cars. Buses are charged according to their seating capacity and goods vehicles are charged according to their 'revenue weight'. This is, in most circumstances, the plated gross or plated train weight of the vehicle (see p 343) but where a vehicle does not have such a plated weight there will be a 'design weight certificate' in force in respect of the vehicle and the weight shown on that certificate is the revenue weight for the purposes of the 1994 Act.

Some vehicles, which would otherwise have fallen within the goods vehicle rates of duty, are declared by Sch 1 to be either 'special' or 'special concessionary vehicles'. The basic rate of goods vehicle duty is payable in respect of *special vehicles* regardless of their revenue weight. Such vehicles have a revenue weight exceeding 3,500 kg and are digging machines, mobile cranes, works trucks or road rollers. 'Digging machines' are machines designed for use for trench digging, excavating or shovelling which are used on public roads for such a purpose or for getting to or from the place where they will so operate, and 'mobile cranes' are cranes designed for use on site which are used on public roads only in connection with work in the immediate vicinity of that road or in travelling to or from that place.

A 'works truck' is a goods vehicle (other than a straddle carrier) designed for use on private premises and used on public roads only for carrying goods between such premises and a vehicle on a road in the immediate vicinity, or in passing from one part of any such premises to another or to other private premises in the immediate vicinity, or in connection with road works while at or in the immediate vicinity of the site of such works. A drive of one and a half miles through congested roads is not from one set of premises to another which is in the immediate vicinity, nor is a journey of six-tenths of a mile. The test to be applied is concerned with the journey on a road, not with the distance the premises are apart. While 'vicinity' connotes a degree of closeness, 'immediate vicinity' connotes a very considerable degree of closeness. Thus, the use of dumper trucks licensed at a special vehicle rate for the purposes of local shopping on behalf of persons working at a 'road works' site or for a journey to the homes of employees is not authorised.

Special concessionary vehicles attract duty at 25 per cent of the general rate. They include agricultural tractors (used solely on public roads for purposes of agriculture, horticulture or forestry or for hedge or verge cutting alongside public roads); 'light agricultural vehicles' (basically one-seater three, or four wheeled agricultural motorcycles of a revenue weight not exceeding 1,000 kg); electrically propelled vehicles; and snow clearance vehicles.

A recovery vehicle is a vehicle which is constructed or permanently adapted primarily for the purpose of lifting, towing and transporting a disabled vehicle or for any one or more of those purposes. For a vehicle to be classified as a recovery vehicle for the purpose of attracting a lower rate of duty, it must be being used for:

(a)   the recovery of a disabled vehicle;

(b)   the removal of a disabled vehicle from the place where it became disabled to premises at which it is to be repaired or scrapped;

(c)   the removal of a disabled vehicle from premises to which it was taken for repair, to other premises at which it is to be repaired or scrapped;

(d)   carrying fuel and other liquids required for its propulsion and tools and other articles required for the operation of or in connection with integral or permanently mounted apparatus designed to lift, tow or transport a disabled vehicle;

(e)   repairing a disabled vehicle at the place where it became disabled or to which it had been moved in the interests of safety after becoming disabled; or

(f)   drawing or carrying one trailer if the trailer was, immediately before a vehicle became disabled, being drawn or carried by the disabled vehicle.

The rate of duty applicable to a recovery vehicle is the basic goods vehicle rate where the revenue weight exceeds 3,500 kg but does not exceed 12,000 kg; three times that rate from 12,000 to 25,000 kg; and five times that rate if the revenue weight exceeds 25,000 kg.

When recovering or removing a disabled vehicle from the place where it became disabled, a recovery vehicle may carry the driver, passenger and any load which was in or on the vehicle immediately before it became disabled and persons and their personal effects from the place where the vehicle is to be repaired to their destinations. Such a vehicle may also be used to remove vehicles at the request of a constable or local authority, and whilst proceeding to and from permitted assignments. If a recovery vehicle is used outside these purposes, it is no longer a recovery vehicle for the purposes of this Act. Nor is it a recovery vehicle if it is used to recover more than two vehicles at any time.

Use for purpose attracting higher rate of duty

An excise licence carried by a vehicle will indicate that a certain rate of duty has been paid. If that vehicle is a private motor car it will have attracted the rate applicable to such a vehicle. An agricultural tractor is a special concessionary vehicle and whilst used as such attracts only 25 per cent of the general rate of duty. However, if used outside the purposes of agriculture, horticulture or forestry, or for the cutting of verges, it is no longer a special concessionary vehicle and the appropriate full rate of duty as set out in the Vehicle Excise and Registration Act 1994, Sch 1, will be payable. For example, the haulage of bricks for use on the farm (eg building a pig sty) has been held to be an authorised use, but use to haul bricks to a worker's cottage has been held not to be an authorised use. The distinction is clear; the first was for use on a part of the working farm; the second for use to repair an ancillary dwelling.

Exhibition of licences

An excise licence must be fixed to a vehicle in a holder sufficient to protect the licence from the effects of the weather to which it would otherwise be exposed. Consequently, an externally displayed licence must be completely enclosed in a waterproof container. An excise licence must be exhibited on the vehicle so that the particulars are clearly visible in daylight from the nearside of the road, as follows:

(a)   on an invalid carriage, tricycle or bicycle, on the nearside in front of the driving seat;

(b) on a bicycle with sidecar, on the nearside of the handlebars or the nearside of the sidecar;

(c) on a vehicle with a windscreen extending across the vehicle, on the nearside of the windscreen; or

(d) on any other vehicle, on the nearside window of the driver's cab (if it has one), or on the nearside of the vehicle in front of the driver's seat, or towards the front of the vehicle in the case of a pedestrian controlled vehicle.

Immobilisation of unlicensed vehicles

The Vehicle Excise Duty (Immobilisation, Removal and Disposal of Vehicles) Regulations 1997 authorise the immobilisation and removal of stationary unlicensed mechanically propelled vehicles on public roads in circumstances in which an 'authorised person' (a person, such as a police officer or local authority employee, authorised by the Secretary of State) has reason to believe that an offence is being committed under the Vehicle Excise and Registration Act 1994, s 29(1), below, (unlicensed vehicle used or kept on public road) where such a vehicle is stationary on a public road. The Regulations apply throughout England and Wales.

The vehicle may be wheelclamped where it stands, or moved to another place on the same or another public road and wheelclamped there. This may be done by the authorised person or a person acting under his direction. Where this has been done an immobilisation notice must be fixed to the vehicle indicating that the device has been fitted and warning that no attempt should be made to move the vehicle until it has been released from the device and providing other information, including the charge for release, removal and disposal. Before an authorised person can release such a vehicle a valid excise licence must be produced or a 'surety payment' must be made. A voucher will be issued to a person who makes such a payment. Where a licence cannot be obtained immediately the 'surety payment' permits the vehicle to be used unlicensed for a period of 24 hours. The payment will be returned upon production of a valid vehicle excise licence. The Regulations authorise the immediate removal of such a vehicle to the possession of an authorised 'custodian'. In addition, where a vehicle has been clamped for a period of 24 hours without release, it may be removed to the custody of such a person. Where this has been done, a removal fee will be charged additionally, together with charges for storage.

The 1997 Regulations create the following offences:

(a) unauthorised removal of or interference with an immobilisation notice: reg 7(1) and (2);

(b) removal, or attempted removal, of an immobilisation device: reg 7(3);

(c) false declaration to secure release of vehicle from an immobilisation device: reg 8(2);

(d) false declaration to secure possession of impounded vehicle: reg 13(1);

(e) false declaration in obtaining voucher or a refund relating to a surety payment: reg 16(1) and (3); and

(f) forgery, fraudulent alteration, fraudulent use, or the fraudulent lending of a voucher relating to surety payment: reg 16(2) and (3).

Offences related to licences

The most common offences committed contrary to the Vehicle Excise and Registration Act 1994 are as follows:

(a) using or keeping a mechanically propelled vehicle on a public road without having in force an excise licence: s 29 (described above);

(b) using or keeping a mechanically propelled vehicle on a public road without the requisite licence being fixed to and exhibited on the vehicle in the way outlined on pp 210-211: s 33;

(c) forging, fraudulently altering, fraudulently using, fraudulently lending or allowing to be used by any other person, an excise licence: s 44 (described above);

(d) making, in connection with an application for the issue of a licence, a declaration which to the accused's knowledge is false or in a material respect misleading: s 45;

(e) supplying false information or producing false documents in relation to the design weight of a vehicle (for the purposes of establishing the revenue weight): s 45;

(f) forgery, alteration or use of a certificate (design weight certificate), or knowingly lending or allowing such a certificate to be used, or without reasonable excuse making or having in possession such a certificate: s 45;

(g) altering, defacing, mutilating, or adding anything to an excise licence, or exhibiting on any vehicle such a licence: s 59 and the Road Vehicles (Registration and Licensing) Regulations 1971, reg 7; and

(h) exhibiting anything which is intended to be, or could be, mistaken for a licence: s 59 and the Road Vehicles (Registration and Licensing) Regulations 1971, reg 7.

Proceedings for offences and admissibility of evidence

Section 47 of the 1994 Act provides that proceedings for offences of using etc without a licence, of using a trade licence outside permitted uses (see later), and of using a licensed vehicle for a purpose which attracts a higher rate of duty than that paid, can only be instituted by the Secretary of State or a constable; such a person is known as the authorised prosecutor. Moreover, no prosecution may be instituted by a constable for these offences without the approval of the Secretary of State; proof that such approval has been given is required at the outset of proceedings in court.

Proceedings instituted by an authorised prosecutor for one of the above offences or for an offence under s 44 or 45 of the Act (forgery or false statements etc) may be instituted within six months from the date on which sufficient evidence came to the prosecutor's knowledge to warrant proceedings, subject to a maximum limit of three years from the commission of the offence. This means that, if the Secretary of State institutes proceedings as the authorised prosecutor, the six-month time limit runs from the time when the required evidence came to his knowledge. The six-month limit replaces the normal rule requiring that proceedings for summary offences be taken within six months from the commission of the offence. Section 47 of the Act allows proof of the date upon which evidence came to the knowledge of the authorised prosecutor, or proof that the Secretary of State has approved the institution of a prosecution by a constable, to be given by means of a certificate signed by or on behalf of the authorised prosecutor or, as the case may be, the Secretary of State. Such a certificate is conclusive evidence of the facts stated, and is deemed to be properly signed unless the contrary is proved.

Section 52 allows certified extracts from DVLA records to be admissible to the same extent as oral evidence. Evidence may therefore be offered of the last date upon which a mechanically propelled vehicle was licensed by means of such a certified extract.

Section 46 of the Act requires that, where one of the offences mentioned above (except forgery) is alleged to have been committed in relation to a particular mechanically propelled vehicle, the person keeping the vehicle must give such information as he may be required by or on behalf of a chief officer of police or the Secretary of State to give as to the identity of the person or persons concerned in the offence. Failure to do so is an offence, unless the accused keeper satisfies the court that he did not know and could not with reasonable diligence have ascertained the identity of the person or persons concerned. The requirement is also extended to any other person (besides a 'keeper') who may have such knowledge, and (in cases of unlicensed use) to the person alleged to have been using the vehicle. Both types of person commit an offence if they fail to give such information as to identity as it is in their power to give. A request under s 46 is, in practice, made by serving on a person a form requiring the specified information. A reply to such a request must be made in writing.

TRADE LICENCES

Without modification, the requirement that all mechanically propelled vehicles used or kept on a road should be individually licensed under the Vehicle Excise and Registration Act 1994 would cause considerable problems for motor traders, through whose hands many vehicles pass, most of which are retained for a short period of time. The purpose of trade licences is to permit traders temporarily to use vehicles on public roads for restricted purposes without the necessity for licensing in the manner described above. Trade licences are inexpensive and in consequence their permitted uses are carefully defined.

Who may apply for a trade licence?

By s 11 of the 1994 Act, a motor trader may apply to the Secretary of State for a licence to cover all mechanically propelled vehicles which are from time to time temporarily in his possession in the course of his business as a motor trader. Any motor trader who is a manufacturer may also be granted a licence for the purpose of allowing him to carry out research and development work in the course of his business as a manufacturer, and for all other vehicles which are from time to time submitted to him by other manufacturers for testing on roads in the course of that business.

The term 'motor trader' means a manufacturer or repairer of, or dealer in, mechanically propelled vehicles. A person is treated as a dealer in such vehicles if he carries on a business consisting wholly or mainly of collecting and delivering mechanically propelled vehicles.

A person whose business is that of modifying vehicles (by fitting accessories or otherwise) or of 'valeting' vehicles (which means the thorough cleaning of a vehicle prior to first registration or in order to prepare it for sale, and includes removing wax and grease from the exterior, engine and interior) is also a 'motor trader'.

A vehicle tester may also apply for trade licences to cover his use of vehicles submitted to him for testing in the course of his business. A vehicle tester is a person, other than a motor trader, who regularly in the course of his business engages in the testing on roads of mechanically propelled vehicles belonging to other persons.

Persons who satisfy the Secretary of State that they intend to commence business as motor traders or vehicle testers may also take out licences.

Trade licences may be taken out for a period of 12 months. Shorter term licences are also available but are seldom used. The holder of a trade licence is issued with two plates (which are generally referred to as 'trade plates') in respect of each licence held. These plates consist of red letters on a white background and show the registration mark assigned to the holder of the licence. One of the plates contains a means by which the licence may be fixed to the plate; it must be displayed at the front of the vehicle so as to be clearly visible at all times during daylight. The licence is therefore available for inspection by police officers and the registration mark itself is traceable to the motor trader who holds that licence. If the trader satisfies the Secretary of State that the vehicles which he will use in the course of his business will include motor bicycles as well as other vehicles, he may be issued with a second plate for the motor bicycles only. The licence duty is currently about half of that payable by the keeper of a private motor car. Trade licences for motor bicycles only are much cheaper. The plates remain the property of the Secretary of State and must be returned when the trader ceases to be the holder of the licence.

Non-permitted uses of trade licences

Section 12 provides that the holder of a trade licence is not entitled by virtue of *that licence:*

(a) to use more than one mechanically propelled vehicle at any one time; or
(b) to use any vehicle for any purpose other than a permitted one (see below); or
(c) to keep any vehicle on a road if it is not being used thereon.

However, there is nothing to prevent a motor trader from holding more than one licence to permit use of more than one vehicle at any one time.

It is an offence, contrary to s 34(1), for the holder of a trade licence to use on a public road a greater number of vehicles than permitted by his licence (or licences), or to use a vehicle for a non-permitted purpose. The subsection also punishes the keeping on a public road of a vehicle using a trade licence, if it is not being used at that time.

Restrictions on use of trade licences

The Road Vehicles (Registration and Licensing) Regulations 1971, reg 34 states that no person who is not the holder of a trade licence shall use a vehicle on which is displayed trade plates or a trade licence. However, this does not prevent a person driving a vehicle on a road with the consent of the licence holder, when the vehicle is being used for the licence holder's business. Thus, an employee may drive vehicles in the course of his employer's (the licence holder's) business.

Permitted purposes

The use of mechanically propelled vehicles by a *motor trader* under a trade licence is controlled by regs 33 to 37 of the Road Vehicles (Registration and Licensing) Regulations 1971.

Regulation 35 provides that no person, being a motor trader and holder of a trade licence, shall use any mechanically propelled vehicle on a public road by virtue of that licence unless it is a vehicle which is temporarily in his possession in the course of his business. In addition, the regulation requires that no person, being a motor trader and holder of a trade licence, shall use a mechanically propelled vehicle on a public road by virtue of its trade licence for a purpose other than a 'business purpose' and other than one of the purposes specified:

(a) for the test or trial of the vehicle, or its equipment or accessories in the ordinary course of construction, modification or repair, or after completion in either case;

(b) for proceeding to or from a public weighbridge to ascertain its unladen weight, or to or from any place for its registration or inspection by someone acting on the Secretary of State's behalf;

(c) for its test or trial for the benefit of a prospective purchaser, including going either to or from a place of such test or trial at the instance of the prospective purchaser;

(d) for its test or trial for the benefit of a person interested in promoting publicity in regard to the vehicle, including going either to or from a place of such test or trial at the instance of such a person;

(e) for delivering it to a purchaser;

(f) for demonstrating the operation of the vehicle or its accessories or equipment when handed over to a purchaser;

(g) for delivering it between parts of the motor trader's own premises or to the premises of another manufacturer, dealer or repairer, or bringing it back from there directly to his own premises;

(h) for proceeding to or from a workshop where a body, or a special type of equipment or accessories, is to be or has been fitted to it or where it is to be or has been painted, valeted or repaired;

(i) for proceeding from the premises of a manufacturer, repairer or dealer to a railway station, airfield or shipping dock for the purpose of transportation, or for proceeding to such premises from a railway station etc to which it has been transported;

(j) for proceeding to or from any garage, auction room or storage place where vehicles are usually stored or offered for sale and at which the vehicle is to be or has been stored or offered for sale as the case may be;

(k) for proceeding to or from a place of testing or to a place to be broken up or otherwise dismantled.

The use of a vehicle with a trailer is regarded as the use of a single vehicle under the licence.

A 'business purpose' is a purpose connected with the motor trader's business as a manufacturer or repairer of, or dealer in, mechanically propelled vehicles, or a purpose connected with such a business in relation to trailers provided that business is carried on in conjunction with his business as a motor trader, or a purpose connected with the modifying of vehicles (whether by the fitting of accessories or otherwise).

Regulations 36 and 37 deal respectively with manufacturers' research vehicles and use by vehicle testers. The first restricts use to manufacturers for research and development purposes and the second restricts testing to vehicles and trailers drawn thereby, or any accessory or equipment on the vehicle or trailer, in the course of a business as a vehicle tester.

The above purposes are the only purposes for which mechanically propelled vehicles may be used under a trade licence, and even then only in the course of the business of the holder. If an employee used the trade plates and licence to remove his own private car to a paint shop for spraying, not in the course of his employer's business, the use would be unlawful. If the holder of the licence used under trade plates a vehicle which was in his possession in the course of his business to visit a cinema in the evening, that use of the motor vehicle would be unlawful as it would not be in the course of his business as a motor trader.

Carriage of goods or burden

Regulation 38 prohibits the use of a vehicle under trade plates for the conveyance of goods or burden of any description except:

(a) a load which is carried by a vehicle being used for the purpose of testing or demonstrating the vehicle, or its accessories or equipment, within the terms of (a), (c), (d) or (f), above, and is carried solely for that purpose, and which is returned to the place of loading without having been removed from the vehicle (except in the case of an accident or for demonstrating its operation to a purchaser when handed over to him, or when the load consists of water, fertiliser or refuse);

(b) in the case of a vehicle which is being delivered or collected and is being used for a relevant purpose (as described in (e) to (j) above), a load consisting of another vehicle used or to be used for travel to or from the place of delivery or collection;

(c) any load built in as a permanent part of the vehicle or permanently attached to it;

(d) a load consisting of parts, accessories or equipment designed to be fitted to the vehicle and tools for so fitting them, when the vehicle is being moved between premises in the course of manufacture or transhipment; or

(e) a load consisting of a trailer, the vehicle carrying the trailer being used to deliver the trailer to a purchaser, or to move it between premises in the course of manufacture, or to take it to a place of transhipment.

Although these provisions appear to be complex at first, their effect is simply to prohibit the carriage of goods on vehicles being used under a trade licence in all but the narrowest of circumstances. It may be that a 'test and trial' will necessarily involve the use of a vehicle with a load. If so, provisions limit the carriage of the load to the duration of that trial. In most circumstances in which a goods vehicle is observed being used under a trade licence whilst carrying a load, an offence will be committed. Some vehicles have what might be described as built in loads, such as essential engineering equipment, and vehicles which are on their way to have accessories etc fitted may carry these accessories etc with them for that purpose. None of these loads is being carried for a commercial purpose connected with the use of the vehicle in the accepted sense of the word 'commercial'. The regulation makes similar restrictions in respect of use by vehicle researchers and vehicle testers.

Carriage of passengers

Limitations are imposed upon the carriage of passengers in motor vehicles which are being used under a trade licence. Regulation 40 requires that the holder of a trade licence shall not use a mechanically propelled vehicle on a public road by virtue of that licence for carrying any person on the vehicle, or on any trailer drawn by it, except a person carried in connection with a purpose for which the holder of a trade licence may use the vehicle on a public road by virtue of that licence.

Trade plate and trade licence offences

We have already dealt with the offence under s 34(1) of the 1994 Act relating to non-permitted use of trade licences. Breach of the regulations relating to loads or passengers is also an offence.

Regulation 32 of the 1971 Regulations provides offences of alteration, defacement, mutilation of, or addition to, trade plates, or the exhibition of plates which have been so treated. Section 44 of the 1994 Act provides that the offences thereunder of forgery, fraudulent alteration or use, or fraudulent lending or allowing to be used by any other person, of excise licences and registration marks also apply to trade licences and trade plates.

DRIVING LICENCES, PENALTY POINTS AND DISQUALIFICATION

Driving licences

The licensing of drivers of motor vehicles is dealt with by Part III of the Road Traffic Act 1988 and the Motor Vehicles (Driving Licences) Regulations 1996.

Section 87(1) of the Road Traffic Act 1988 states that it is an offence for any person to drive on a road a motor vehicle of any class otherwise than in accordance with a licence authorising him to drive a motor vehicle of that class. The onus is upon a person found driving a motor vehicle on a road to prove that he is licensed to drive as this is a fact peculiarly within his own knowledge. It is *desirable* that there should be, where possible, a statutory demand for production.

The activities which may be described as 'driving' in relation to a motor vehicle are discussed in ch 16, below and it is sufficient to bear in mind that the essence of 'driving' is the use of the driver's controls (or, at least, one of them) in order to control the movements of the vehicle, however that movement is produced, provided that what occurs can in any sense be described as driving.

It is an offence, under s 87(2), for a person to cause or permit another person to drive on a road a motor vehicle of any class otherwise than in accordance with a licence authorising that other person to drive a motor vehicle of that class. For the meaning of 'permit' and 'cause' see ch 10, below.

For driving licence purposes, motor vehicles are divided by the 1996 Regulations into various categories and it is essential that licences are checked not only to establish the identity of the driver, but also to ascertain that he is authorised to drive the particular vehicle in which he is found. The classes are:

Category	Class of vehicle included	Additional categories covered
A	Motor bicycles but excluding any motor vehicle in category K	B1, K and P
A1	A sub-category of category A comprising learner motor bicycles but excluding any motor vehicle in category P.	P
B	Any motor vehicle, other than a vehicle included in category A, F, K or P, having a maximum authorised mass exceeding 3.5 tonnes and having not more than 8 seats in addition to the driver's seat, including - (i) a combination of such a vehicle and a trailer where the trailer has a maximum authorised mass not exceeding 750 kg, and (ii) a combination of such a vehicle and a trailer where the maximum authorised mass of the combination does not exceed 3.5 tonnes and the maximum authorised mass of the trailer does not exceed the unladen weight of the tractor vehicle.	F, K and P
B1	A sub-category of category B comprising motor vehicles having three or four wheels and an unladen weight not exceeding 550 kg,	K and P

Category	Class of vehicle included	Additional categories covered
B1 (inv carrs)	A sub-category of category B comprising motor vehicles which are invalid carriages.	
B+E	Combination of a motor vehicle and trailer where the tractor vehicle is in category B but the combination does not fall within that category.	
C	Any motor vehicle having an authorised mass exceeding 3.5 tonnes, other than a vehicle falling within category D,F,G or H, including such a vehicle drawing a trailer having a maximum authorised mass not exceeding 750 kg.	
C1	A sub-category of category C comprising motor vehicles having a maximum authorised mass exceeding 3.5 tonnes but not exceeding 7.5 tonnes including such a vehicle drawing a trailer having a maximum authorised mass not exceeding 750 kg.	
D	Any motor vehicle constructed or adapted for the carriage of passengers having more than eight seats in addition to the driver's seat, including such a vehicle drawing a trailer having a maximum authorised mass not exceeding 750 kg.	
D1	A sub-category of category D comprising motor vehicles having more than eight seats but not more than 16 seats in addition to the driver's seat and including such a vehicle drawing a trailer with a maximum authorised mass not exceeding 750 kg.	
C+E	Combination of a motor vehicle and trailer where the tractor vehicle is in category C but the combination does not fall within that category.	B+E
C1+E	A sub-category of category C + E comprising any combination of a motor vehicle and trailer where - (a) the tractor is in sub-category C1, (b) the maximum authorised mass of the trailer exceeds 750 kg but not the unladen weight of the tractor vehicle, and (c) the maximum authorised mass of the combination does not exceed 12 tonnes.	B+E
D+E	Combination of a motor vehicle and trailer where the tractor vehicle is in category D but the combination does not fall into that category.	B+E
D1+E	A sub-category of category D + E comprising any combination of a motor vehicle and trailer where - (a) the tractor vehicle is in sub-category D1, (b) the maximum authorised mass of the trailer exceeds 750 kg but not the unladen weight of the tractor vehicle,	B+E

Category	Class of vehicle included	Additional categories covered
	(c) the maximum authorised mass of the combination does not exceed 12 tonnes, and	
	(d) the trailer is not used for the carriage of passengers.	
F	Agricultural or forestry tractor, but excluding any vehicle included in category H.	K
G	Road roller.	
H	Track-laying vehicle steered by its tracks.	
K	Mowing machine or vehicle controlled by a pedestrian.	
P	Moped.	

Part 2

Category	Class of vehicle included
C1+E (8.25 tonnes)	A sub-category of category C + E comprising any combination of a motor vehicle and trailer in sub-category C1 + E the maximum authorised mass of which does not exceed 8.25 tonnes.
D1 (not hire or rew)	A sub-category of category D comprising motor vehicles in sub-category D1 driven otherwise than for hire or reward.
D1+E (not hire or rew)	A sub-category of D + E comprising motor vehicles in sub-category D1 + E driven otherwise than for hire or reward.
L	Vehicle propelled by electrical power.

The term 'maximum authorised mass' has the same meaning:

(a) in relation to goods vehicles as 'permissible maximum weight' in the Road Traffic Act 1988, s 108(1) (p 337), and

(b) in relation to any other vehicle or trailer as 'maximum gross weight' in the Road Vehicles (Construction and Use) Regulations 1986, reg 3(2) viz the weight which the vehicle is designed or adapted not to exceed when on a road.

Regulation 40 of the 1996 Regulations provides that where a person passes a test prescribed in respect of any category for a licence which authorises the driving of motor vehicles included in that category or in a sub-category of that category, the licensing authority must grant him a licence which will authorise him to drive vehicles of all classes included in that category or sub-category unless his licence is restricted to such vehicles fitted with automatic transmission, or vehicles specially adapted for the disabled, in which cases his entitlement will be restricted to similar vehicles within that class. Such holders are also authorised to drive those vehicles shown in column 3 above as additional categories or sub-categories with the same limitations as set out above, should the test have been taken on those types of vehicles. However, where the additional category is F, K or P the limitation in respect of 'automatics' will not apply.

The 1996 Regulations parallel new categories of vehicles with the old categories which were described by the replaced 1987 Regulations. They provide that licences (whether full or provisional) granted before 1 January 1997 are valid in respect of the new categories of vehicle, as set out in the table to the regulations.

Full driving licences issued to those who have passed the appropriate test are granted until the holder achieves the age of 70 years. After that age, the licence can be renewed for periods of three years. When the time for renewal arrives, it is the duty of the licence holder to make application for renewal: there is no requirement for reminders, nor are there any days of grace in respect of renewal. Those licences which authorise the holder to drive prescribed goods or passenger-carrying vehicles will be renewable on the holder's 45th birthday, or after five years, whichever is the *longer*, or where the licence is issued to a person between 45 and 65 for the period ending on his 66th birthday or after five years, whichever is the *shorter*. A licence granted after the age of 65 will remain in force for one year only.

When there is a prosecution for an offence under s 87, the issue is whether the accused was driving the vehicle otherwise than in accordance with the licence at the material time, and a licence taken out later in the day does not excuse unlicensed driving earlier in that day. However, the Road Traffic Act 1988, s 88 provides that it is lawful for a person to drive provided that an application for renewal of a licence under Part III of the Act has been received; or the driver holds a Community licence, a Northern Ireland licence, a British external licence, a British Forces licence or an exchangeable licence. In the case of an application for a licence it must relate to a date which covers the driving in question; if the application is for a provisional licence, the conditions of such a licence must be being complied with.

The Road Traffic Act 1988, s 97(1) requires the Secretary of State to issue a licence to a person who applies in the prescribed manner, pays the appropriate fee, and supplies necessary evidence to support his application. Section 98 requires the licence to be in the form of a photocard of a description specified by the Secretary of State, or in such other form as he may specify. Photocard licences were introduced in 1998, but pre-existing licences remain in force until they expire or the holder's details expire. Where a licence is issued in the form of a photocard an applicant must supply the licensing authority with a photograph which is a current likeness of him and with a specimen signature which can be electronically recorded and reproduced on the licence. If any other form of licence is granted, the holder must forthwith sign the licence in ink. Defaced or lost licences may be replaced by the licensing authority. If a lost licence is subsequently found it must be returned to the authority.

Disqualification of persons under age

A person may also be disqualified from driving a particular class of vehicle by reason of age. A person is disqualified from holding or obtaining a licence to drive a motor vehicle of a particular class if he is under the age applicable to that class of vehicle. The minimum ages at which persons may drive particular classes of vehicles are listed by s 101 of the 1988 Act, which provides that a person below the minimum age to drive a particular class of vehicle is disqualified from holding a licence to drive that class of vehicle. The requirements of s 101 are amplified by the Motor Vehicles (Driving Licences) Regulations 1996, reg 7. The minimum ages are as follows:

(a) 16 years:
    (i)   Invalid carriage.
    (ii) Moped. This means a motor vehicle which has fewer than four wheels and -
        (a) in the case of a vehicle the first use of which occurred before 1 August 1977, has a cylinder capacity not exceeding 50 cc and is equipped with pedals by means of which the vehicle is capable of being propelled, and
        (b) in any other case, has a maximum design speed not exceeding 50 kph and, if propelled by an internal combustion engine, has a cylinder capacity not exceeding 50 cc.

(iii) Agricultural or forestry tractor, provided it is a wheeled vehicle not exceeding 2.45 metres in width and driven without a trailer (other than a two-wheeled or close coupled four-wheeled trailer not exceeding 2.45 metres in width). The person must have passed a test for category F or be proceeding to or from such a test.

(iv) Disability living allowance. Sixteen-year-olds in receipt of a higher rate disability living allowance under the Social Security Contributions and Benefits Act 1992 may drive a small vehicle (see below) if it is driven without a trailer.

(b) 17 years:

(i) Motorcycle, other than a moped or a large motor bicycle.

(ii) Small vehicle. This means a motor vehicle (other than an invalid carriage, moped or motor bicycle) which -

(a) is not constructed or adapted to carry more than nine persons inclusive of the driver, and

(b) has a maximum gross weight not exceeding 3.5 tonnes, and includes a combination of such a vehicle and a trailer.

(iii) Incomplete large vehicle not exceeding 3.5 tonnes.

(iv) Road roller which is not steam-propelled, whose unladen weight does not exceed 11.69 tonnes, which has no pneumatic, soft or elastic tyres, which is not constructed or adapted to carry a load other than equipment of the vehicle.

(c) 18 years:

(i) Medium-sized goods vehicle. This means a motor vehicle constructed or adapted to carry or haul goods and not adapted to carry more than nine persons inclusive of the driver, with a permissible maximum weight exceeding 3.5 tonnes but not 7.5 tonnes and includes a combination of such a vehicle and a trailer where the relevant maximum weight of the trailer does not exceed 750 kg. However, the age of 21 applies if such a vehicle is drawing a trailer and the maximum authorised mass of the combination exceeds 7.25 tonnes.

(ii) Vehicle of a class included in sub-category D1 which is an ambulance and which is owned or operated by a health service body or a National Health Service Trust.

(iii) A motor vehicle and trailer combination of sub-category C1 + E the maximum authorised mass of which does not exceed 7.5 tonnes.

(iv) Other motor vehicles in special circumstances. A person of 18 may drive a large goods vehicle of a category to which a training agreement applies, and which is owned by his employer or a registered heavy goods vehicle training establishment, provided that he is employed by a registered employer in accordance with the Training Scheme and that he is a registered employee. In addition, a person of 18 may drive a large passenger vehicle where:

(a) the driver of the vehicle holds a provisional licence authorising the driving of the vehicle and is not engaged in the carriage of passengers, or

(b) the driver holds a full passenger-carrying vehicle driver's licence and -

(i) is engaged in the carriage of passengers on a regular service over a route which does not exceed 50 km, or

(ii) where he is not so engaged, is driving a vehicle of a class included in sub-category D1,

and the vehicle is operated under a PSV operator's licence, a permit under the Transport Act 1985 (educational and other purposes), or a community bus permit.

(v) Incomplete large vehicle exceeding 3.5 tonnes but not exceeding 7.5 tonnes.

(d) 21 years:

(i)   Large passenger vehicle, ie passenger vehicle with more than nine seats inclusive of the driver.

(ii)   Large goods vehicle, ie exceeding 7.5 tonnes.

(iii) Large motor bicycles unless the person concerned passed a test on or after 1 January 1997 for a motor cycle in category A (other than sub-category A1) and the standard access period (two years before the date in question excluding any period of disqualification or during which the licence was not in force) has elapsed, or unless the vehicle is an armed forces vehicle or is being driven by someone subject to the orders of a member of such a force, or unless it is being driven by someone who (before 1 January 1997) passed a test authorising him to drive a large motor vehicle. A 'large motor bicycle' is, in the case of a motor bicycle without a sidecar one whose engine output exceeds 25 kilowatts or has a power to weight ratio exceeding 0.16kw/kg, or in the case of a sidecar combination, a combination having a power to weight ratio exceeding 0.16kw/kg.

(iv)   All other motor vehicles. This residual category covers generally those motor vehicles which do not normally carry passengers or carry or haul a load, eg a mobile crane.

The regulations permit members of the armed services, aged 17 or over, to drive large motorcycles, and medium and large goods vehicles which are owned by the Secretary of State for Defence and are being used subject to his orders. Clearly this exemption is not a general one and the nature of the use of the vehicle at the time must be taken into account.

Although these provisions appear to be complex at first sight, the vehicles with which police officers are generally concerned are motor cycles, private saloon cars, goods vehicles and public service vehicles. Mopeds may be ridden at 16, motorcycles (unless they are large bicycles) and private cars at 17 and public service vehicles and large goods vehicles generally at 21. Goods vehicles carry plates which show their permissible weights and those under 3.5 tonnes may be driven at 17, those between 3.5 and 7.5 tonnes at 18 and those in excess of 7.5 tonnes at 21 (18 when under an approved heavy goods vehicle training scheme) in most circumstances. Small passenger vehicles, which are generally private cars (as the seating of such a vehicle must not exceed nine), may be driven at 17. Passenger vehicles with more than nine seats may, with the exceptions outlined, only be driven by a person of 21 years; most vehicles of the 'transit' type fall within this category.

Grant of licences

A person may apply for a driving licence at any time within two months of the date from which the licence will take effect. Where the application is for a large goods or passenger-carrying vehicle driver's licence, it must be made three months in advance of such date.

Full licences

Where the application is for a full licence, an applicant must satisfy the licensing authority that he has passed a test at the time of his application. In support of his application he must produce a certificate as prescribed by the Regulations certifying that he has passed the appropriate practical driving test. This is, in effect, proof that he has passed the theory test also, as the practical test cannot be taken without evidence being offered of success in the theory test.

The Motor Vehicles (Driving Licences) Regulations 1996, Part III deals with the constituent parts of driving tests, and the certificates to be issued to those who take tests. The Regulations require that tests be conducted in two parts, a theory test and a practical or unitary test. Schedule 7 to the Regulations sets out the matters to be dealt with within a theory test and Sch 8 similarly deals with matters to be included in a practical or unitary test. The 1996 Regulations introduced a requirement that, where a person produces to an examiner an appropriate licence which does not include a photograph, he must satisfy the person conducting the test as to his identity by producing a document to establish his identity as prescribed by Sch 6 (all of which have a photograph) or a document of a like nature. However, if the person's identity is clearly apparent from the facts known to, or other evidence in the possession of, the person conducting the test, this will be satisfactory.

Provisional driving licences

Full licences may only be granted to those who have passed the relevant test of competence to drive that class of vehicle. Provisional licences are issued to those who wish to learn to drive motor vehicles and are issued subject to conditions set out in the Motor Vehicles (Driving Licences) Regulations 1996, reg 15. These conditions are concerned with the need for supervision, distinguishing marks, the drawing of trailers and the carriage of passengers. However, these conditions do not apply where a provisional licence holder has passed a test by virtue of which he is entitled to be granted a licence authorising him to drive a vehicle of the class then being driven.

Supervision With the exceptions listed below, a provisional licence holder must not drive or ride a motor vehicle otherwise than under the supervision of a qualified driver who is present with him in or on the vehicle. 'Qualified driver' means:

(a) in the case of the supervision of the driver of a motor vehicle of a class included in category B (other than sub-category B1) by a person whose licence is limited by virtue of a notice served under s 92(5)(b) of the Road Traffic Act 1988 to vehicles of a particular class, a person who holds a full licence authorising him to drive a vehicle of a class included in category B (other than sub-category B1) and who would in an emergency be able to take control of the braking and steering functions of that vehicle. Notices served under s 95(2)(b) specify that the Secretary of State is satisfied that a person who took a test and was suffering from a disability would be a danger to the public unless driving is restricted to a particular class of vehicle;

(b) in any other case, a person who is a relevant licence holder and either -
   (i) is a member of the armed forces of the Crown acting in the course of his duties for naval, military or air force purposes, or
   (ii) is at least 21 years of age and has been a relevant licence holder for an aggregate period of three years or more.

A 'relevant licence holder' means a person who holds a full licence other than an LGV trainee driver's licence, a Northern Ireland licence or a Community licence.

In the case of the supervision of the driver of a large goods or passenger-carrying vehicle of any class, there is no requirement that such a person should have been a relevant licence holder for an aggregate period of three years or more.

The supervisor's duty is to make up for any deficiencies in the skill of the learner; as part of his duty he must participate in the driving to such extent as could reasonably be expected to prevent danger to other persons or property. Because he has a right of control over the learner driver, a supervisor can be convicted as an accomplice to a driving offence committed by the learner driver if he deliberately fails to prevent it when he could reasonably have done so. For example, if a learner drives with an excess alcohol level, his supervisor can be convicted as an accomplice, if he is aware that the learner has been drinking and may be 'over the limit', and deliberately refrains from stopping the learner driving.

A provisional licence holder is not required to be supervised while undergoing a test. Although an examiner will be with him, the examiner is there for the purpose of assessing his competence, not for the purpose of supervision (and therefore not for the purpose of interference when a lack of skill is evident). The examiner is not, therefore, similarly exposed to charges of aiding and abetting offences by the learner.

A provisional licence holder is not required to be supervised if he:

(a) is driving a motor vehicle of a class included in sub-category B1 or B1 (Invalid carriages) or in category F, G, H or K which is constructed to carry only one person and not adapted to carry more than one person;
(b) is riding a moped or motor bicycle with or without a sidecar; or
(c) is driving a motor vehicle, other than a vehicle of a class in category C, C+E, D or D+E, on a road in an exempted island (a term which covers small islands like Lundy and the islands in the Isles of Scilly, other than St Mary's).

Category B1 vehicles may have three or four wheels and an unladen weight not exceeding 550 kgs. It follows, for example, that a small three- or four-wheeler with two seats requires a supervisor in order to be driven by a provisional licence holder, whereas if it is constructed with only one seat it does not (unless it has since been adapted to carry more than one person). The removal of a seat from a two seater does not alter the position since it will have been constructed with two. It must be emphasised that there is a total exemption for two-wheeled motor bicycles, whether fitted with a sidecar or not.

Other licence conditions Motor vehicles which are driven or ridden by persons holding a provisional driving licence must display on the front and on the back of the vehicle the letter 'L' (or 'D' in Wales) in such a manner that it is clearly visible from a reasonable distance to other persons using the road. It is an offence for the holder of a provisional licence to drive a vehicle which is not so marked.

The drawing of trailers by a motor vehicle driven by the holder of a provisional licence is prohibited, with the exception of the holder of a provisional licence authorising the driving of a vehicle of a class included in category B + E, C + E, D + E or F, (combination vehicles where the tractor falls in category B, ie not exceeding 3.5 tonnes or nine seats or agricultural or forestry tractors) in relation to motor vehicles of that class.

Holders of provisional licences authorising the driving of mopeds or motor bicycles with or without a sidecar must not drive such a vehicle while carrying on it another person.

Regulation 15(7) requires that the holder of a provisional licence authorising the driving of a motorcycle other than a learner motorcycle must drive under the supervision of a 'direct access instructor' who is accompanying him on another motor bicycle; is able to communicate with him by radio other than a hand-held radio; who is supervising only that person or, at the most, one additional provisional licence holder; and is carrying a valid certificate issued by the licensing authority. The requirement concerning communication by radio does not apply to a person who has impaired hearing provided that a suitable means of communication with the instructor is arranged in advance. Direct access instructors hold additional qualifications in respect of larger motorcycles.

Offences

We have already said that a person who drives a motor vehicle on a road otherwise than in accordance with a licence authorising him to drive the class of vehicle in question commits the offence of unlicensed driving, contrary to s 87(1) of the 1988 Act.

It should be noted that, when a police officer discovers an offence of driving without a driving licence in circumstances in which the offender's driving would not have been in accordance with any licence that could have been granted to him, the police officer should include in the report reference to whether or not the conditions applicable to that licence were being complied with. The reason is that this is important to the court in relation to the penalty points awarded for the offence.

Motor bicycles: some special rules

The Road Traffic Act 1988, s 97(3) provides that a provisional licence shall not authorise a person under the age of 21 years, before he has passed a test of competence to drive:

(a) a motor bicycle without a sidecar unless it is a 'learner motorcycle' or its first use occurred before 1 January 1982 and the cylinder capacity of the engine does not exceed 125 cc, or

(b) a motor bicycle with a sidecar unless its power to weight ratio is less than or equal to 0.16kw/kg.

A 'learner motor bicycle' is one which is either propelled by electrical power or has the following characteristics:

(a) the cylinder capacity does not exceed 125 cc,
(b) the 'maximum net power output' of its engine does not exceed 11kw.

The power to weight ratio is assessed on the basis of the relationship of the maximum power output to the actual weight of the machine with a full tank and normal equipment. 'Maximum net power output' means the maximum net power output measured under full engine load. Provisional licence holders who ride motor bicycles in excess of the power specified commit the offence of riding otherwise than in accordance with the conditions of their licences. The reason is that the provisional licence which they hold does not authorise the riding of that particular class of vehicle.

The Secretary of State may refuse to grant a provisional licence for motor bicycles or mopeds to the holder of a previous provisional licence. A provisional licence for motor bicycles (or mopeds) may be held for a maximum period of two years in the first instance. If a test allowing the issue of a full licence is not passed by him during this period a person may be prohibited from holding a provisional licence for a period of 12 months. This is to prevent motorcyclists from riding indefinitely under the authority of a provisional licence. The two-year period allows sufficient time for motorcyclists and moped riders to undertake the two-part practical training which is applicable to them, within an approved training course for motorcyclists and moped riders. The first part is concerned with the basic handling and control of machines. The training for the first part of the test can be undertaken without the necessity to ride on a road. The second part of the test is the normal 'on the road' training to drive which takes place under the supervision of instructors.

A provisional licence does not authorise a person, before he has passed a test of competence to drive, to drive on a road a motor bicycle or moped, except where he has successfully completed an approved training course for motorcyclists or is undergoing training on such a course and is driving a motorcycle or moped on a road as part of the training. Certificates will be issued to those who have successfully completed such courses. Certificates issued to successful candidates may not be submitted in support of an application for the grant of a full licence if they are three or more years old.

The requirement that a person is not authorised to drive a motor bicycle on a road unless he has passed a test of competence to drive, without having successfully completed an approved training course, does not apply to a person who is a provisional entitlement holder by virtue of having passed a test in respect of category P (mopeds) on or after 1 December 1990, unless that person has subsequently been disqualified from driving until such time as he passes a test. Nor shall such a person be required to produce such a certificate on applying for a test of competence to drive a motor bicycle. Similar exemptions exist in favour of persons resident on exempted islands.

Regulation 41 of the 1996 Regulations provides that where a person passes a test for a licence authorising the driving of motor bicycles of any class (category A), such a test being passed on or after 1 January 1997, the licensing authority shall grant:

(a) where the test was passed on a motor bicycle, with or without a sidecar, the engine of which has a maximum net power output of not less than 35 kilowatts, a licence authorising the driving of all classes of motor bicycles included in category A;

(b) where the test was passed on any other motor bicycle without a sidecar, a licence authorising him to drive a standard motor bicycle (a motor bicycle which is not a large motor bicycle) but a licence granted under this provision shall authorise the driving of all classes of motor bicycles in category A upon the expiration of the 'standard access period' (see below);

(c) where the test was passed on a motor bicycle and sidecar combination the power to weight ratio of which does not exceed 0.16 kw/kg, a licence authorising the driving of standard motor bicycles but such a licence will authorise such a person to drive all classes of motor bicycles and combinations after the expiration of the standard access period.

The 'standard access period' is the period of two years commencing on the date upon which a person passes a test for a licence authorising the driving of standard motor bicycles of any class other than a class included in sub-category A1 (which covers learner motor cycles except mopeds) but disregarding any period of disqualification or other period during which the licence has ceased to be in force.

At 17 years or over, a person will be able to seek a licence to drive motor bicycles. If he is tested on a motor bicycle without a sidecar of 75 cc, but not more than 120 cc, success will bring a category A1 licence. Success in a test involving the use of a motor bicycle of 121 cc which is capable of a speed of 100 kph will bring a full standard licence (which, of course, includes A1 entitlement). Before being permitted to drive a 'large motorcycle' a candidate must be at least 21 and must pass a test on a motor bicycle with a maximum net engine power output of 35kw. However, a person of less than 21 may take a test for a 'large motorcycle' entitlement if he has held a full standard category A licence for a period of two years. Someone over 21 is permitted, after holding a full standard category A licence for a period of two years, to drive large motorcycles without undergoing a further test.

Full licence as provisional licence

The Road Traffic Act 1988, s 98(2) provides that a full licence, other than one restricted to a specially adapted vehicle for a person with a physical disability, may act as a provisional licence for any other classes of vehicle, unless the holder is below the minimum age at which the other class of vehicle may be driven.

Section 98(2) does not apply to a licence in so far as it allows the holder to drive vehicles of a class included in category B + E, C + E, D + E, or K or in sub-category B1 (invalid carriages), C1 or D1 (not for hire or reward). Holders of full licences restricted to vehicles with automatic transmissions, may use those licences as provisional licences to drive manually-controlled vehicles of a category or sub-category as specified in the Table to reg 17. These provisions apply equally to holders of Community licences.

In the case of licences authorising the driving of motor bicycles of sub-category A1 or standard motorcycles (those which are not large motor bicycles), such licences do not authorise the driving of large motorcycles (exceeding 25kw maximum net power output or power to weight ratio exceeding 0.16 kw/kg) by a person under the age of 21.

Physical fitness of drivers

Section 92 of the 1988 Act provides that an applicant for a driving licence must declare his physical fitness to drive, stating whether or not he is suffering, or has in the past suffered from any relevant or prospective disability. (The term 'disability' for the purposes of the section includes disease and the persistent use of drugs or alcohol, whether or not such misuse amounts to dependency):

(a) a relevant disability means any prescribed disability and any other disability likely to cause the driving of a vehicle by him to be a source of danger to the public; and
(b) prospective disability means any other disability which, by virtue of its intermittent or progressive nature, may become a disability of the type specified in (a) in course of time.

The disabilities prescribed for the purposes of (a) are :

(a) epilepsy;
(b) severe mental handicap;
(c) liability to sudden attacks of disabling giddiness or fainting;
(d) liability to sudden attacks of giddiness or fainting due to a heart condition for which a 'pace-maker' has been fitted; or
(e) the inability to read in good daylight (even with the aid of glasses, if worn) a vehicle registration mark containing letters and figures 79.4 mm high at a distance of 20.5 metres. In the case of mowing machines and pedestrian controlled vehicles the distance is 12.3 metres.

The Secretary of State must refuse an applicant a licence if satisfied that the applicant is suffering from one of these disabilities. This does not apply to those who have had a previous licence and whose disability is one of absence, deformity or loss of use of a limb provided that the condition has not become more acute, nor does it apply if the application is for a provisional licence. Epileptics may be granted licences if free from attacks for one year, or if for the past three years attacks have been restricted to times while asleep provided that the driving of the vehicle in accordance with the licence is not likely to be a danger to the public. Those fitted with 'pace-makers' may satisfy the Secretary of State that their driving will not be a source of danger.

Existing licences (including Community licences of persons normally resident in Great Britain) may be revoked totally if such a disability as described above actually arises, or may be revoked and replaced with shorter term licences if a prospective disability (as described above) arises. Licences may be issued which allow the driving of vehicles of a special construction; for example, a vehicle fitted with hand controls for a person who has lost both legs) or they may allow driving subject to certain specified conditions. Persons holding driving licences who suffer an actual or prescribed disability must notify the Secretary of State forthwith. Failure without reasonable excuse to do so is an offence.

A person who holds a licence and drives a motor vehicle of the class authorised on a road commits an offence if he knowingly made a false declaration in relation to a relevant disability to obtain the licence. A similar offence is committed where he fails, without reasonable excuse, so to notify specified disabilities during the currency of the licence. A person who drives a motor vehicle on a road, otherwise than in accordance with a licence, commits an additional offence if a licence has earlier been refused on account of such a disability. These offences may also be committed by holders of Community licences normally resident in Great Britain.

The Road Traffic Act 1988, s 96(1) creates the offence of driving a motor vehicle on a road with uncorrected defective eyesight. The offence lies in driving while the eyesight is such that the requirement to read registration marks at the specified distances given above cannot be complied with. The defect in eyesight may be one which cannot be corrected or one which is not for the time being sufficiently corrected to enable the driver to satisfy the above requirement. Thus, a registered blind person necessarily commits the above offence if he drives on a road, while a person with impaired vision does not if his vision is sufficiently corrected by wearing spectacles (provided, of course, that he wears them).

A constable may require a person driving a motor vehicle to submit to an eyesight test; it is an offence to refuse to submit to such a test.

Foreigners and driving licences

Persons temporarily present

The Motor Vehicles (International Circulation) Order 1975, art 2 states that it is lawful for *a person resident outside the United Kingdom who is temporarily in Great Britain* to drive for a period of 12 months from the date of his last entry into the United Kingdom if he holds a Convention driving permit, a domestic driving permit of a country outside the United Kingdom, or a British Forces (BFG) driving licence, authorising him to drive the vehicle in question, provided he is not disqualified (eg by age) from holding a British licence.

What has just been said is subject to qualification in respect of large passenger-carrying vehicles and large goods vehicles. A holder of either type of permit may drive such a vehicle if he is resident in an EEA (European Economic Area) state, but only if it has been temporarily brought into Great Britain if he is not so resident. In the case of a holder of a BFG, he may drive a large passenger-carrying vehicle (but not a large goods vehicle) if he is resident in an EEA state, but only if it has been temporarily brought into Great Britain if he is not so resident. In the cases set out in this paragraph no other licence is required.

Generally, any person may cause or permit holders of such Convention or domestic driving permits to drive vehicles which they are authorised by their permit to drive. In the phrase 'temporarily in Great Britain', 'temporarily' is an element other than simply a time element. It involves a presence for casual purposes, eg a holiday, as contrasted with regular habits. For example, an overseas student studying here is not 'temporarily' resident here.

A Convention driving permit is usually referred to as an 'international driving licence'. In Britain it is issued by the AA or RAC. The term 'domestic driving permit' refers to the licence issued by the driver's own country and it is therefore lawful for a visitor to Great Britain to drive for a period of one year on the authority of his own, local driving licence. A British Forces (BFG) driving licence is issued in Germany to servicemen, their dependants and civilians attached to British Service Units. This regulation merely recognises that persons visiting from abroad would experience difficulty in undertaking a test in Great Britain while they are temporarily in this country. These documents are treated as driving licences in every respect and a constable's powers to demand production of a licence and to demand the holder's date of birth apply equally to them.

Resident foreigners

The Motor Vehicles (Driving Licences) Regulations 1996, reg 74 makes the same provision for a person from abroad who becomes resident in Great Britain, the 12-month period in this case running from when he became a resident. Someone from abroad who is in this country but who falls outside the term 'temporarily in Great Britain', eg an overseas student, will be resident in Great Britain.

General

A person who becomes resident in Great Britain who is the holder of a relevant permit and is not disqualified for holding or obtaining a licence in Great Britain is, during the period of one year after he becomes so resident, treated as the holder of a licence authorising him to drive all classes of small vehicles (generally vehicles not constructed or adapted to carry more than nine persons inclusive of the driver and vehicles not exceeding 3.5 tonnes, including a combination of such a vehicle and a trailer), motorcycles or mopeds which he is authorised to drive by that permit. A 'relevant permit' is a 'domestic driving permit', a 'Convention driving permit', or a British Forces (BFG) driving licence. Where a question arises as to whether a person is normally resident in Great Britain or the United Kingdom, a person is deemed to be normally resident if he shows that he will have lived there for not less than 185 days preceding a test appointment.

Holders of driving licences issued by states within the EEA (Community licences) who become resident in Great Britain are authorised to drive here without the need to exchange their licences for British licences within a year of becoming resident. Such persons do, however, have a right to exchange their licences. Where matters of validity, standards of health and fitness, and disqualification are concerned, the exchange of licences is mandatory. Resident Community licence holders are subject to the same medical requirements as holders of British licences. Community licence holders resident in Great Britain who wish to drive medium-sized or large goods vehicles and passenger-carrying vehicles of any class must, after a period of 12 months residence, deliver their licences to the Secretary of State and provide details prescribed by the Road Traffic Act 1988, s 99B. They will be issued with counterparts. The right to the issue of British driving licences is restricted to persons normally resident in the United Kingdom. Community licence holders are also entitled to be licensed to drive a taxi or private hire vehicle or to drive small buses for charitable or similar purposes provided that their Community licence authorises them to drive cars.

Persons who become resident in Great Britain and who hold British external licences granted in the Isle of Man or Jersey authorising the driving of large goods vehicles or passenger-carrying vehicles, and who are not disqualified from holding or obtaining a licence in Great Britain, may drive such vehicles under the authority of those licences for a period of one year from the date upon which they became resident.

People permitted to drive in this country under a domestic driving permit etc who take out a provisional licence during the 12-month period in order to take a driving test need not comply with the normal conditions applicable to a learner driver if they are still driving under the authority of their domestic permit etc at the time (ie within the 12-month period).

The Road Traffic Act 1988, s 108(2) empowers the Secretary of State to designate non-EEA countries for the purpose 'exchangeable licences' where he is satisfied that tests are satisfactory. He may, however, restrict approval to the grant of exchange licences to particular circumstances, impose conditions to which they are subject, and limit the exchanged licence to particular classes of vehicles.

Production of driving licences

By virtue of the Road Traffic Act 1988, s 164(1) a constable or vehicle examiner may demand the production of a driving licence and its counterpart by the following people:

(a) a person driving a motor vehicle on a road; or
(b) a person whom a constable or vehicle examiner has reasonable cause to believe has been the driver of a vehicle at the time when an accident occurred owing to its presence on a road; or
(c) a person whom a constable or vehicle examiner has reasonable cause to believe has committed an offence in relation to the use of a motor vehicle on a road; or
(d) a person who is supervising the holder of a provisional licence while the holder is driving a motor vehicle on a road; or
(e) a person whom a constable or vehicle examiner has reasonable cause to believe was supervising the holder of such a licence when an accident occurred owing to the presence of the vehicle on a road or when an offence is suspected of having been committed by the holder in relation to the use of a vehicle on a road.

When a licence is produced to a constable or vehicle examiner pursuant to a request under s 164(1), he is entitled to ascertain the name and address of the holder of the licence, its date of issue and the authority by which it was issued. Section 164(2) also provides a power whereby a constable may require a person in circumstances prescribed by the Motor Vehicles (Driving Licence) Regulations 1996 to state his date of birth. These circumstances are:

(a) where that person fails to produce forthwith for examination his driving licence on being required to do so by a constable; or
(b) where, on being so required, that person produces a licence which the police constable has reason to suspect:
    (i)   was not granted to that person, or
    (ii) was granted to him in error, or
    (iii) contains an alteration in its particulars made with intent to deceive; or

(c) where, on being so required, that person produces a licence in which the driver number has been altered, erased or defaced; or
(d) where that person is a person supervising the holder of a provisional licence while the holder is driving a motor vehicle on a road, or is someone whom the constable reasonably suspects to have been supervising such a person when an accident occurred or an offence was committed, and the constable has reasonable cause to suspect that he is under 21 years of age.

It is an offence to fail to state a date of birth when so required.

Section 164(4A) provides that, where a constable to whom a provisional licence has been produced by a person driving a motor bicycle has reasonable cause to believe that the holder was not driving it as a part of the training being provided on a training course for motorcyclists, the constable may require him to produce the prescribed certificate of completion of such a course.

A traffic warden is empowered to demand the production of a driving licence where he has reasonable cause to believe that an offence has been committed in contravention of the pedestrian crossing regulations or by leaving a vehicle in a dangerous position.

The term 'licence' means a licence under the Road Traffic Act 1988, Pt III or a Community licence.

Failure to produce licence

Section 164(3) and (5) of the Road Traffic Act 1988 provides that:

(a) where a licence has been revoked by the Secretary of State but the holder has not surrendered it and its counterpart; or
(b) where the holder has failed to produce his licence and its counterpart to a court when lawfully required to do so; or
(c) where the Secretary of State has served notice on a Community licence holder in pursuance of s 99C (relevant disability) or s 115A (conduct of holder of LGV or PCV Community licence) requiring delivery of the licence to him,

a constable or vehicle examiner may require the holder to produce them and on production may seize them. Section 164(4) empowers a constable to require the holder of a licence to produce it and its counterpart where he has reasonable cause to believe that a false statement was knowingly made to obtain it.

A person who fails to produce his licence and its counterpart, or a certificate of completion of a training course for motorcyclists, when required to do so under any of the provisions of s 164 commits an offence. However, an offence of failing to produce a licence is not committed if the person produces a current receipt for the surrender of the licence issued under the fixed penalty procedure (p 306) and, if required, produces the licence in person immediately on its return at a police station specified at the time of the request, or if within seven days of the request he produces the receipt in person at that police station and, if requested, produces the licence there in person immediately on its return. In addition in proceedings against any person for an offence of failing to produce a licence it is a defence for him to show that:

(a) within seven days after the production of his licence and its counterpart was required he produced them *in person* at such police station as may have been specified by him at the time its production was required; or
(b) he produced them *in person* there as soon as was reasonably practicable; or

(c)   it was not reasonably practicable for him to produce them there before the day on which proceedings commenced (ie laying of information).

If a licence is not produced at the time its production was required, it is the usual practice of the police to make out a form HO/RT1 which will be produced at the police station nominated, together with the driving licence. This is merely a practice followed by the police and there is no statutory requirement that this be done.

Disqualification by a court and penalty points

Obligatory disqualification

The Road Traffic Offenders Act 1988, s 34(1) deals with disqualification from driving following a conviction for an offence involving obligatory disqualification. On conviction for such an offence, a court must order disqualification for at least a specified minimum period, unless the court for special reasons thinks fit to order a shorter period of disqualification or not to order disqualification at all. These offences, which are all offences under the 1988 Act unless otherwise indicated, are:

(a)   manslaughter (common law offence, see RTOA 1988, Sch 2) ;
(b)   causing death by dangerous driving (s 1);
(c)   dangerous driving (s 2);
(d)   causing death by careless driving when under the influence of drink or drugs (s 3A);
(e)   driving or attempting to drive whilst unfit through drink or drugs (s 4(1));
(f)   driving or attempting to drive with excess alcohol in breath, blood or urine (s 5(1)(a));
(g)   failure to provide specimen for analysis (where specimen required to assess ability or alcohol level at time offender driving or attempting to drive) (s 7(6));
(h)   motor racing and speed trials on a public highway (s 12); or
(i)   aggravated vehicle-taking (Theft Act 1968, s 12A).

In the case of most of these offences, the specified minimum period of disqualification is 12 months. However, in the case of the offences of causing death by dangerous driving, manslaughter, or causing death by careless driving while under the influence of drink or drugs, it is two years. The same minimum period applies in relation to a person on whom more than one disqualification for a fixed period of 56 days or more has been imposed within the three years immediately preceding the commission of the offence. However, a disqualification imposed as a result of an offence committed by using vehicles in the course of crime or in respect of a conviction for stealing or attempting to steal a motor vehicle, joy-riding or going equipped to steal etc a motor vehicle, or attempting to commit any such offence, is disregarded for this purpose, as is an interim disqualification on committal for sentence.

If the conviction is for any of the above offences which are connected with the drink-driving laws, that is an offence under ss 3A, 4(1), 5(1)(a), or 7(6) of the 1988 Act referred to above, and there has been a previous conviction for such an offence within the preceding ten years, a court *must* order disqualification for a period of not less than three years, unless there are special reasons for not doing so.

'*Special reasons*' are reasons special to the circumstances of the offence, as opposed to special to the offender. It is of no consequence that the loss of a driving licence will lose the offender his job, that he is a man of previous good character and/or that he has driven for many years without having been convicted of any motoring offence. The courts' approach is strict in this respect. They have refused to accept as special reasons the hardship to a country doctor and his patients or the problems caused for a disabled man. An example of a case where there would be reasons special to the offence is where a man, who thinks that he is drinking non-alcoholic drinks, has his drink 'laced' without his knowledge. In such a case, it is open to the court in its discretion to mitigate the period of disqualification, or not to disqualify at all, because of special reasons. Special reasons might have been found in the case of the country doctor if the country doctor had been called out to a man suffering a heart attack in circumstances in which no other doctor could reasonably have been summoned to attend.

Discretionary disqualification

The Road Traffic Offenders Act 1988, s 34(2) deals with discretionary disqualification. Where a person is convicted of an offence which is shown in Sch 2 to the Act to be one which carries discretionary disqualification and either:

(a) the penalty points to be taken into account on that occasion number fewer than 12, or
(b) the offence is not one involving obligatory endorsement,

the court may disqualify for any period which it thinks fit. Disqualification may not be for an indefinite period, since the court must state the period of disqualification (although it may be for life). Particulars of any disqualification must be endorsed on the licence or its counterpart. Offences which carry discretionary disqualification usually carry obligatory endorsement. However, the Road Traffic Act 1991 removed the requirement for obligatory endorsement for the offences of stealing etc motor vehicles.

Endorsement and penalty points

The Road Traffic Offenders Act 1988, ss 28 and 44 provide that, where a person is convicted of an offence involving obligatory endorsement and the court orders particulars of the conviction to be endorsed on his licence, the endorsement must include:

(a) particulars of the offence, including the date when it was committed; and
(b) the number of penalty points to be attributed as shown in respect of the offence in Sch 2 to the Road Traffic Offenders Act 1988 (or, where a range of numbers is so shown, a number falling within the range).

However, where an offender is convicted and the court imposes disqualification under s 34 of the Road Traffic Offenders Act 1988 no penalty points are to be attributed for that offence. This provision removes the possibility of 'double disqualification'.

Where a person is convicted of two or more offences included in Sch 2, all of which are committed on the same occasion, the number of points awarded is generally the highest single figure applicable to one of those offences.

Schedule 2 lists the offences which carry penalty points. Where a person is convicted for aiding and abetting offences involving obligatory disqualification the number of penalty points to be attributed to the offence is 10. The offences of dangerous driving, causing death by careless driving when under the influence of drink or drugs, driving or attempting to drive vehicles when under the influence of drink or drugs or with excess alcohol in breath, blood or urine, failing to provide a specimen for analysis, all carry obligatory endorsement of 3–11 penalty points, in addition to obligatory disqualification (unless there are special reasons). However, as indicated above, if disqualification is ordered the licence will not be endorsed with penalty points.

The offence of failing to stop after an accident carries 5–10 points, as does that of failing to report an accident. Insurance offences carry 6–8, careless driving 3–9 and failing to provide a specimen for a screening breath test 4. Any contravention of the construction and use regulations which constitutes an endorsable offence carries 3 points, as does a failure to comply with traffic directions, with the directions of school crossing patrols or with pedestrian crossing regulations. All offences of exceeding a speed limit carry 3–6 penalty points or 3 (fixed penalty). Offences concerned with driving licences carry 3–6 penalty points, except driving whilst disqualified by a court order which carries 6 points.

Unless there are special reasons for not doing so a court *must* endorse a person's licence if he is convicted of an offence shown in Sch 2 to the Road Traffic Offenders Act 1988 to be one in respect of which endorsement is obligatory.

Obligatory disqualification for repeated offences

The Road Traffic Offenders Act 1988, s 35 requires that, on conviction for an offence involving discretionary disqualification and obligatory endorsement or an offence involving obligatory disqualification in respect of which no order is made under s 34, where the award of the penalty points for the offence, together with those already endorsed on the licence, brings the total to 12, the offender must be disqualified for a minimum period of six months if the points have been accumulated within three years of the commission of the offence for which penalty points are then awarded. If the total is in excess of 12 this may be recognised by disqualification for a longer period. Once the disqualification has been imposed the driving licence is in effect wiped clean. However, 'wiping clean' is restricted to disqualification under s 35 for repeated offences. Where a disqualification is imposed under s 34 for a specific offence, the penalty points previously accumulated remain effective at the end of the period of disqualification until the expiry of three years from the date of the offence for which they were imposed. It is important to note that disqualification as a result of this 'totting-up' procedure is in respect of convictions within the three years immediately preceding the commission of the offence in question (not a conviction for that offence).

It is also important to remember that, where the 'totting-up' rules are satisfied, a court must impose a disqualification for six months or more, unless it is satisfied, having regard to all the circumstances, that there are grounds for mitigating the normal consequences of the conviction and therefore thinks fit to disqualify for a lesser period or not at all. The Road Traffic Offenders Act 1988, s 35(4) states that no account is to be taken, as a ground for mitigating the normal consequences, of any circumstances which are alleged to make the offence or any of the offences not a serious one; nor of any hardship other than exceptional hardship; nor of any circumstances which, within the preceding three years, have already been taken into account in ordering the offender to be disqualified for a shorter period or not to be ordered to be disqualified at all. Exceptional hardship which would be caused to a person other than the offender (for example a dependent, invalid wife) may be taken into account.

A person who is already the holder of a driving licence authorising him to drive a vehicle of a particular class is disqualified by s 102 of the Road Traffic Act 1988 from holding another licence for that class of vehicle. This is to prevent a person from holding more than one licence. If he was able to do so he could share out his penalty points by holding two licences indicating different addresses.

Use of vehicle in commission of crime: discretion to disqualify

The Powers of Criminal Courts Act 1973, s 44 provides that if the Crown Court is satisfied that a motor vehicle was used (by the person convicted or anyone else) for the purpose of committing or facilitating the commission of an offence, it may disqualify the person convicted for such a period as it thinks fit from holding or obtaining a licence to drive. 'Facilitation' will include use after the offence for disposal of property or avoiding apprehension or detection. This power may only be exercised by the Crown Court on convicting an offender of an offence punishable on indictment with imprisonment for a term of two years or more, or when sentencing such a person after his conviction before a magistrates' court.

Disqualification: offenders in general

The Crime (Sentences) Act 1997, s 39 empowers a court on conviction of any offence to order the offender to be disqualified from holding or obtaining a driving licence. A court may only make an order under s 39 if the Secretary of State has notified it that it may exercise the power to do so. The same restriction applies under s 40 of the 1997 Act to the power of a magistrates' court to order disqualification in a case of default in paying a fine.

Effect of order of disqualification

The Road Traffic Offenders Act 1988, s 37 provides that, where a licence holder is disqualified by order of a court, the licence shall be treated as revoked with effect from the beginning of the period of disqualification. However, where the disqualification is for a fixed period shorter than 56 days in respect of an offence involving obligatory endorsement or the order is made under s 26 (interim disqualification), this will not prevent the licence from again having effect at the end of the period of disqualification.

Removal of disqualification

The Road Traffic Offenders Act 1988, s 42 provides that a person who has been disqualified by a court may apply to have the disqualification removed as follows:

(a) if the disqualification is for less than four years, after two years;
(b) if it is for less than 10 but more than four years, when half the disqualification has expired; or
(c) in any other case (life or 10 or more years), when five years have passed.

Disqualification until passing of driving test

The Road Traffic Offenders Act 1988, s 36 provides that, where a person is disqualified under s 34 (obligatory disqualification) on conviction for manslaughter by the driver of a motor vehicle, or for causing death by dangerous driving, or for dangerous driving, or is disqualified under ss 34 or 35 (repeated offences) in such circumstances or for such period as the Secretary of State may prescribe, or is convicted of an offence involving obligatory endorsement which may be prescribed by the Secretary of State, the court must order him to be disqualified until he has passed the appropriate driving test.

Where a person is disqualified under s 34 on conviction for any other offence carrying obligatory endorsement, the court may order him to be disqualified until he has passed the appropriate driving test.

The term 'appropriate driving test' means an extended driving test where a person is convicted of an offence involving obligatory disqualification or is disqualified under s 35, and the ordinary driving test in any other circumstances.

A person disqualified until he has passed a driving test under s 36 is permitted by s 37(3) to take out a provisional licence, once any fixed period of disqualification has expired, in which case he may drive under the conditions applicable to such a licence. Such an order of disqualification ends when a certificate of competence is produced to the Secretary of State. A person who drives under a provisional licence granted for these purposes, but who does not comply with the conditions attached to such a licence, commits an offence contrary to the Road Traffic Act 1988, s 103, of driving while disqualified.

Disqualification - holders of Community licences

The Driving Licences (Community Driving Licences) Regulations 1996 added s 91A to the Road Traffic Offenders Act 1988. The section provides that within those sections of the 1988 Act concerned with the production of a licence to a court in the event of conviction for an offence involving obligatory or discretionary disqualification, the term 'licence' includes references to a Community licence. Section 91A(4) requires a court to notify the Secretary of State of any endorsement made to a counterpart of a Community licence and s 91A(5) requires a court to send a Community licence and its counterpart (if any) in the event of a convicted person being disqualified from driving. The Secretary of State will notify the EEA state concerned of the disqualification.

Revocation of licence of 'new driver'

Under the provisions of the Road Traffic (New Drivers) Act 1995, where a qualified driver commits an offence involving obligatory endorsement during his 'probationary period' (two years from becoming a qualified driver) and the penalty points to be taken into account on that occasion number six or more, the court must send the Secretary of State a notice containing the particulars to be endorsed on the counterpart of the person's licence together with the licence (and counterpart). A similar requirement is made of a fixed penalty clerk, where a fixed penalty offence is involved. The Secretary of State must, by notice, revoke that licence. Such a licence may not be restored until the person concerned has passed a relevant driving test within the relevant period (not more than two years).

The prescribed probationary period will come to an end:

(a) where an order is made under the RTOA 1988, s 36 (disqualified until a test is passed);

(b) after revocation of the licence by the Secretary of State (as described in the preceding paragraph) where the licence is restored, after passing a test; or

(c) where the driver has been driving on a provisional licence plus test certificate which have been revoked, where a full licence is granted after passing a test.

Obtaining licence, or driving, while disqualified

The Road Traffic Act 1988, s 103 creates two offences which can be committed by a person disqualified from holding or obtaining a licence: obtaining a licence whilst so disqualified, and driving a motor vehicle on a road while so disqualified. The section deals with those disqualified by a court (including those disqualified until they pass a test); these offences do not apply where the disqualification is by reason of age. We explain in ch 16 what constitutes 'driving' for the purposes of the commission of an offence under the 1988 Act.

The prosecution must prove, not only the order of disqualification (by means of certificate of conviction or entry in a court register), but that the person before the court is the person so disqualified. It is not enough to prove that the person charged has the same name and date of birth and lived at the address shown at the time of the conviction. However, although the Divisional Court has stated that proof of identity may be given by:

(a) admission under the Criminal Justice Act 1967, s 10;
(b) fingerprints under the Criminal Justice Act 1948, s 39, or
(c) evidence of a person who was present in court when the disqualification was imposed.

This cannot mean that an admission other than a formal one under s 10 is irrelevant, or that evidence linking the defendant with 'driving' when the offence for which he was disqualified was imposed is insufficient. Similarly, a statement made under the Criminal Justice Act 1967, s 9 which refers to a person whom the deponent knew and stating that the deponent knew him under a particular name may entitle justices to find sufficient evidence of identification.

By s 103(3) of the 1988 Act, a constable in uniform may arrest without warrant any person driving or attempting to drive a motor vehicle on a road if he has reasonable cause to suspect that person of being disqualified. This power of arrest does not apply in relation to persons disqualified by reason of age. It is important to remember that this power is restricted to circumstances where a disqualified person is 'driving' or attempting to drive. It does not extend to someone who has been driving, although for the purposes of the power of arrest a person will still be driving after he has stopped the vehicle, switched off the engine and got out of the driver's seat if his reason for ceasing to drive is sufficiently connected with the actual driving of the vehicle. This test will not often be satisfied.

Offender escaping consequences of endorsable offence by deception

The Road Traffic Offenders Act 1988, s 49 provides that where, in dealing with a person convicted of an endorsable offence (ie one involving obligatory or discretionary endorsement), a court was deceived regarding any circumstances that were or might have been taken into account in deciding whether, or for how long, to disqualify him and the deception constituted or was due to an offence committed by that person, then, if he is convicted of that offence (the one then before the court), the court has the same powers of disqualification as had the court which was deceived. However, the court must take account of the order made by the first court on his conviction for the endorsable offence.

If a person produces a licence which he has obtained free of endorsement by failing to provide particulars of those endorsements, he may escape disqualification on the 'totting-up' provisions of the penalty points system. This section allows a court, when convicting that person of an offence of obtaining such a licence without giving particulars of current endorsements, to disqualify him even though the offence then being dealt with is not one which carries penalty points.

Effect of disqualification upon holders of large goods vehicle or passenger-carrying vehicle drivers' licences

The Road Traffic Act 1988, s 115(1)(a) requires that a large goods vehicle or passenger-carrying vehicle driver's licence must be revoked if, in relation to its holder, prescribed circumstances occur, or his conduct is such as to make him unfit to hold such a licence. Section 115A(1) of the 1988 Act makes similar provision in respect of the holder of a LGV Community licence or a PCV Community licence.

The 'prescribed circumstances' referred to in s 115A are set out in respect of a large goods vehicle driver's licence or a LGV Community licence by the Motor Vehicles (Driving Licences) Regulations 1996, reg 52. They are that, in the case of the holder of such a licence who is under the age of 21, he has been convicted or is by virtue of the Road Traffic Offenders Act 1988, s 58 (*effect of endorsement without hearing*), to be treated as if he had been convicted, of an offence as a result of which more than three penalty points are to be taken into account. Where such large goods vehicle licences are revoked, the cases in which such persons must be disqualified indefinitely or for a fixed period must be determined by the licensing authority. Where it determines that the disqualification shall be for a fixed period, such a person must be disqualified until he reaches the age of 21 or for such longer period as the licensing authority may determine. No corresponding provisions have been made in respect of large passenger-carrying vehicle licences.

Regulation 53 applies to circumstances in which large goods vehicle or passenger-carrying vehicle drivers' licences are treated as revoked by the Road Traffic Offenders Act 1988, s 37 (effect of disqualification by order of court). The Road Traffic Act 1988, s 117 is modified by reg 53 to provide that, where the licence to be treated as revoked is a large goods vehicle driver's licence held by a person under the age of 21, the licensing authority must order that person to be disqualified either indefinitely or for a fixed period, and where it determines that it shall be for a fixed period, he must be disqualified until he reaches the age of 21 or for such longer period as the licensing authority determines. Where the licence revoked is held by any other person, or is a large passenger-carrying vehicle driver's licence:

(a) the licensing authority may order that person to be disqualified either indefinitely or for a fixed period, or

(b) except where the licence is a provisional licence, if it appears to the licensing authority that, owing to that person's conduct, it is expedient to require him to comply with the prescribed conditions applicable to provisional licences until he passes a test, the licensing authority may order him to be disqualified from holding or obtaining a full licence until he passes the test.

Where a licensing authority orders disqualification until a test is passed, the test must be a test for a licence authorising the driving of any class of vehicle in Category C (other than C1), C+E, D or D+E which, prior to his disqualification by order of the court, the offender was authorised to drive by his revoked licence.

MOTOR VEHICLE INSURANCE

The Road Traffic Act 1988, s 143(1) states that a person must not use, or cause or permit any other person to use, a motor vehicle on a road unless there is in force in relation to the use of that vehicle by that person or that other person, as the case may be, such a policy of insurance or such security in respect of third-party risks as complies with the requirements of Part VI of the Road Traffic Act 1988. Section 143(4) states that Part VI of the Act does not apply to invalid carriages not exceeding 254 kg unladen weight. The few vehicles of this type which are still in use are covered by the Department of Health. Since electrically assisted pedal cycles are not motor vehicles (unless they fall outside the relevant regulations), the provisions dealing with insurance do not apply to them.

As in the case of driving licences, the onus is upon a person found using a motor vehicle on a road, to prove the existence of insurance as this is a fact peculiarly within his knowledge. However, the Divisional Court has said that it is *desirable* that there should be, where possible, a statutory demand for its production

The terms 'use', 'cause' and 'permit' are discussed in ch 10, below. Basically, a person who drives a vehicle 'uses' it, but 'using' is not limited to driving. 'Use' means 'have the use of', with the result that, for example, if someone parks a motor vehicle on a road he can be said to be using it while it is parked, and it has been held that this is so even though the vehicle has been totally immobilised. Where an employee drives a motor vehicle owned by his employer in the course of his employment, his employer is regarded in law as also using it. A person 'causes' a vehicle to be used when, being in a position to do so, he expressly orders or authorises the vehicle to be used; and he 'permits' a vehicle to be used when he allows another person to use it. In each case, of course, the use must be on a road without there being in force in relation to the use of the person using the vehicle a requisite third-party policy of insurance or security.

The prohibition against using, or causing or permitting the use of, an uninsured vehicle is absolute in the sense that it is no defence that the accused reasonably believed that he, or the person allowed etc to drive, was covered by an insurance policy etc. There is one exception: under s 143(3) of the 1988 Act it is a defence for a person charged with using an uninsured motor vehicle to prove that it did not belong to him and was not in his possession under a contract of hiring or loan, and that he was using it in the course of his employment and neither knew nor had reason to believe that it was not properly insured etc. This is reasonable: an employee will usually have no knowledge of the administrative affairs of his employer.

Can a person be said to permit his vehicle to be used on a road without insurance when he has lent it out on the express condition that it should only be used if its use is covered by insurance and its subsequent use is not so covered? The law provides a rather odd answer. If the condition is directly communicated to the person who uses the vehicle without insurance, the person imposing the condition does not permit his vehicle to be used without insurance. This seems sensible. How can you permit something which you have expressly forbidden? Thus, it is somewhat surprising that the Divisional Court has held that, if the condition as to use being covered by insurance has not been directly communicated to the user but has been communicated to someone else, eg to someone who borrows the vehicle, with a view to it being driven by the user, and it is used in breach of that condition, the person imposing the condition does in law permit uninsured use.

A person cannot permit another's use if he was not in a position to forbid it. Thus A, who supervises B, a learner driver, in B's own car cannot be convicted of permitting its uninsured use.

Third-party insurance policies

Certificate of insurance

The requirement made by s 143 of the 1988 Act is that there must be a policy of insurance (or a security, see later) in respect of third-party risks in accordance with Part VI (ie ss 143 to 162) of that Act in relation to the use of the vehicle by the person using it. By s 147, no policy of insurance has effect unless the insurer has delivered to the person insured a certificate of insurance in the prescribed form. Therefore 'telephone insurance' is not valid; no certificate has been delivered at that time giving evidence of a contract between insurer and insured. Police officers frequently exercise discretion in circumstances in which a company has clearly accepted liability for third-party risks but some technicality has delayed delivery of a certificate. A cover note is a certificate.

What must be covered

Section 145 provides that, in order to comply with the requirements of Part VI of the Act, a policy must be issued by an 'authorised insurer' and must insure such person, persons or classes of persons as may be specified in it in respect of any liability which may be incurred by him or them in respect of the death of or bodily injury to any person (other than the driver) or damage to property up to a maximum value of £250,000 caused by, or arising out of, the use of the vehicle on a road in Great Britain. The policy must also cover him or them:

(a)   in respect of any liability for the emergency treatment of persons injured;
(b)   in the case of a vehicle normally based in Great Britain, in respect of any liability which may be incurred as a result of its use within the territory of any member of the EU, according to the law on compulsory insurance against civil liability in that state or, if it would give higher cover, the law which would be applicable if the vehicle was used in Great Britain; and
(c)   in the case of a vehicle normally based in another EU state, in respect of any liability which may be incurred as a result of the use of the vehicle in Great Britain if, under the law of that other state, he or they would be required to be insured in respect of a liability which would arise under it had the event occurred in that state, and the cover required by that law is higher than that required as indicated in the previous paragraph.

Extent of cover

The nature of the policy held will be specified in the certificate. A policy covering use for social, domestic and pleasure purposes does not cover business use. However, to give a lift to a friend who is on business at the time is not a business use of the vehicle. To help move household goods for a friend without payment is not a business use, but it might be if payment was made. It is usual for non-business policies to exclude use for hire or reward, but s 150 of the Act makes specific provisions for 'car-sharing' schemes. Provided that arrangements are made before the journey, that payment is in respect of running costs and depreciation only, and that the vehicle used is not adapted to carry more than eight passengers, the use is not for hire or reward.

Some policies allow persons to drive with the permission of the insured person if such a person 'holds or has held a driving licence' and is not disqualified. If that person has at any time held a licence, whether full or provisional, it is sufficient in law to satisfy such a requirement. The terms of the policy will have to be examined in circumstances in which the class of vehicle which the person is licensed to drive is different to the class of vehicle which is being driven. If the policy demands that such a person holds or has held a licence to cover the same class of vehicle as is covered by the policy, then use by a person who does not hold (and has not held) such a licence will amount to uninsured use, unless the licence which he holds may act as a provisional one to cover use of the vehicle in question. Similarly, where a person has borrowed a vehicle subject to an implied limitation, of which he was aware, concerning the purpose for which the vehicle was to be driven, he does not have the consent of the owner for a purpose outside that limitation. Where therefore, insurance cover was dependent upon the driver having 'the consent of the owner thereof', use outside that limitation was uninsured use.

The use of trailers in Great Britain does not expressly need to be covered in respect of third-party risks, whereas this is essential in other EU countries. However, the use of trailers in Great Britain is generally covered in all policies of insurance and would seem to be within the use of the motor vehicle in any case. Injury caused to a person by a trailer is certainly caused due to the use of the motor vehicle on a road.

If the terms in which a policy is drawn up do not cover the particular use of the vehicle, an offence is committed regardless of the insurer's willingness to meet liabilities.

Validity

When a policy has been taken out it remains in force until it expires or is validly set aside. If a disqualified driver obtains insurance by failing to disclose his disqualification, then, although such insurance is obtained by means of a false declaration, it remains valid until the company takes steps to set aside the policy. If the company does set it aside, this only invalidates the policy for the future.

It is the practice of some insurance companies to insert restrictive clauses in their policies which can affect their validity in particular circumstances. However, s 148 states that the third-party requirement of s 143 must be covered by companies regardless of restrictions which might be inserted covering the age, mental or physical condition of a driver; the condition of the vehicle; the number of persons carried; the load; the times or areas of use; the horse power cylinder capacity or value of the vehicle; the carrying of any special apparatus or the carrying on the vehicle of special identification marks. Where companies impose such restrictions, which might be, for example, to maintain the vehicle in good condition, not to exceed recommended loads, or to fit a crook lock or alarm system or 'identicar' markings, they are still liable for third-party risks because of s 148.

When a person is apprehended for taking motor vehicles without consent, it is good practice to check any certificate of insurance held by him in respect of motor vehicles. It is the terms of the policy which are important, not the moral implications. If his policy covers the use by him of another vehicle not owned by him or hired to him by a hire-purchase agreement, that policy will cover such use even though the vehicle has been illegally taken. It would be different if the use covered was similar but 'with the consent of the owner of such vehicle'.

Securities and other exemptions from insurance requirements

Securities

A security, rather than a policy of insurance, can satisfy the provisions of Part VI of the Act if it satisfies certain conditions set out in s 146. The security must consist of an undertaking by the giver of the security (who must be an authorised insurer or some body of persons in the business of giving securities which has deposited with the Accountant General of the Supreme Court the sum of £500,000 in respect of that business). The undertaking must be to make good, subject to any conditions specified therein, any failure by the person covered by the security duly to discharge any third-party liability for which insurance would otherwise be required under Part VI of the Act. Use of securities is frequently made by large undertakings, such as bus companies, which would experience unnecessary difficulties in negotiating separate insurance in respect of a large fleet of vehicles. A security is of no effect for the purposes of Part VI unless there is a 'certificate of security' in force in relation to the vehicles.

Exemptions

The offences relating to use without third party insurance or security, which are provided by s 143, are subject to exemptions provided by s 144.

Section 144 also exempts from the requirement for third-party insurance or security vehicles:

(a)   owned by a local authority or a National Parks Authority, at times when they are driven under the owner's control;

(b)   owned by a police authority or the Receiver of the Metropolitan Police, when driven under the owner's control;

(c)   being driven by a person for police purposes by or under the direction of a police constable, or by a person employed by a police authority or the Receiver of the Metropolitan Police. A police officer on duty using his own car for police purposes falls within this exemption;

(d)   owned by the Service Authority for the NCIS or the NCS (when being driven under the owner's control) or when being driven for the purposes of such an Authority by or under the direction of a constable (or by an employee of such an Authority);

(e)   being driven for salvage purposes pursuant to Part IX of the Merchant Shipping Act 1995;

(f)   being used for the purpose of its being furnished under a direction under the Army Act 1955 or the Air Force Act 1955;

(g)   owned by a health service body or NHS trust, at a time when the vehicle is being driven under the owner's control; or

(h)   made available by the Secretary of State to any person, body or local authority under the National Health Service Act 1977 when used within the prescribed terms.

The reasoning behind these exemptions is clear: the vehicles are either owned by or being used by undertakings which are in a position to meet liabilities which might be incurred. Crown vehicles appear to be similarly exempt as s 183, which deals with the application of the provisions of the Act to the Crown, does not mention s 143.

Other requirements in respect of motor vehicle insurance

The Road Traffic Act 1988, s 147(4) requires that where a policy or security to which a certificate of insurance or security relates becomes cancelled, either by mutual consent or by virtue of the provisions of the policy or security, the certificate must be returned to the person who issued the policy within seven days. If a certificate has been lost or destroyed, a statutory declaration to that effect must be made within that period. An offence is committed by a person who fails to comply with these provisions.

Section 154 requires any person against whom a claim is made in respect of any such liability as is required to be insured against by s 145 (eg third-party risks involving death or bodily injury, damage to property or the cost of hospital treatment) to provide particulars of his insurance cover in respect of that liability. It is an offence to fail to comply with such a requirement without reasonable excuse, or wilfully to make a false statement in reply to such a demand. These provisions allow the administrative officers of hospitals etc to recover the cost of emergency treatment from vehicle insurers.

Fraud, forgery etc

By s 174(5) of the Act it is an offence to make a false statement, or to withhold any material information, for the purpose of obtaining the issue of a certificate of insurance or security, or any other document which may be produced in lieu of a certificate of insurance or security. Any person who issues such a document, which to his knowledge is false in any material particular, commits an offence against s 175.

The alternative documents to which s 174(5) refers are specified by the Motor Vehicles (Third-Party Risks) Regulations 1972, reg 7 as follows:

(a)   duplicates of certificates of security;
(b)   certificates of deposit;
(c)   a certificate signed by a police authority etc; or
(d)   in the case of a vehicle normally based in another EU country, or what was Czechoslovakia, Finland, Hungary, Norway or Switzerland, a document issued by the insurer in the prescribed form.

The making of false statements to obtain insurance is not uncommon. The disclosure of previous convictions for motoring offences, particularly those involving endorsement, can lead to high premiums which can be avoided by non-disclosure. In this context, the Rehabilitation of Offenders Act 1974 is important. The Act provides for convictions to become 'spent'. It also provides that where a question seeking information with respect to a person's previous convictions is put to him, otherwise than in proceedings before a judicial authority, the question must be treated as not relating to spent convictions and answers may be made accordingly. Most road traffic offences will have resulted in a fine and as a result will become spent after a period of five years.

The offence of making a false statement contrary to s 174(5) is an absolute offence and it is not necessary to prove that the person who made the statement was aware of its falsity (or even of the risk that it might be false). It is submitted, however, that it would be essential to prove a deliberate act of 'withholding'.

Section 173 makes it an offence for a person, with intent to deceive, to forge, alter, use, lend for use, or allow to be used, a certificate of insurance or a document which may be used in lieu thereof. The section also provides an offence of making, or having in possession with intent to deceive, any document or other thing so closely resembling a document or other thing of the above types as to be calculated (ie likely) to deceive. Uncompleted insurance forms can be documents for this purpose. Thus, where a man was found to be in possession of bogus blank insurance certificates sequentially numbered, the Court of Appeal ruled that since the uncompleted forms were likely to deceive persons seeking insurance cover they could constitute documents so closely resembling genuine insurance certificates as to be calculated to deceive. An expired certificate, if used with intent to deceive, may be such a document.

Persons temporarily in Great Britain

The Motor Vehicles (International Motor Insurance Card) Regulations 1971, reg 5 authorises a visitor to Great Britain to use his motor vehicle under the internationally recognised 'green card' insurance provision. 'Green cards' are referred to in the regulations as 'valid insurance cards'. A peculiarity of this provision is that a green card remains valid after the expiry date shown. This is to prevent the complications which would otherwise arise if holiday visitors decided to extend their stay. A constable's powers in respect of insurance certificates etc apply to 'green cards'.

Certificates of insurance or security issued in Northern Ireland are, of course, valid in Great Britain.

Police powers in relation to motor vehicle insurance

Section 165 of the Act states that:

(a)   a person driving a motor vehicle, other than an invalid carriage, on a road;
(b)   a person whom a constable or vehicle examiner reasonably believes to have been the driver when an accident occurred etc; or
(c)   a person whom a constable or vehicle examiner reasonably believes to have committed an offence in relation to the use of such a motor vehicle on a road,

shall, on being required by a constable or vehicle examiner, give his name and address and the name and address of the owner of the vehicle, and produce for examination the relevant certificate of insurance etc. Failure to do any of these things is an offence. The usual provisions concerning production of documents apply, allowing seven days for production; or production as soon as reasonably practicable; or proof that production was not reasonably practicable before the day on which proceedings were instituted. The documents (unlike a driving licence) need not be produced in person.

The provisions of s 165 which require a person to give his name and address and the name and address of the owner of the vehicle also apply to a supervisor of a provisional licence holder in each of the three circumstances set out above.

LAW RELATING TO HIGHWAYS

Highways

The meaning of the term 'highway' for the purposes of the Highways Act 1980 is given in s 328 of that Act. The section states that the term includes the whole or part of a highway other than a ferry or waterway. Where a highway passes over a bridge or through a tunnel, the bridge or tunnel is, for the purposes of the Act, a part of the highway. Section 328 does not define 'highway'; instead, that term is defined by common law. Basically, *a highway is a way over which all members of the public have the right to pass and repass* by foot, on horseback, or accompanied by a beast of burden or with vehicles or cattle. It follows that the term embraces carriageways, bridleways, and footpaths. In general terms these can be defined as follows.

A carriageway is a way constructed or comprised in a highway, being a way (other than a cycle track) over which the public has a right of way on foot, on horseback, or with vehicles and cattle.

A bridleway is a highway over which the public has a right of way while on foot, on horseback or leading a horse. By the Countryside Act 1968, s 30, the public also has a right to ride a pedal bicycle on a bridleway (provided that the cyclist gives way to pedestrians and persons on horseback). The right to ride a pedal cycle on a bridleway may be controlled by a local authority order. There may be a right on some bridleways to drive animals and such bridleways may be referred to locally as 'droves' or 'driftways'.

A footpath is a highway over which the public has a right of way on foot alone.

The above definition of 'highway' can be contrasted with the definition of 'road' for the purposes of the Road Traffic Acts which is 'any highway *and any other road to which the public has access'* (see p 202 above).

Obstruction of highway

The Highways Act 1980, s 137 states that it is an offence for a person, without lawful authority or excuse, in any way wilfully to obstruct the free passage along the highway of whatever type.

Whether or not there was an *obstruction* is a question of degree for a court to decide; a complete blockage of the highway is not required. Whether or not a use of the highway amounts to an obstruction depends upon whether or not it was unreasonable having regard to all the circumstances of the case, including where it occurs, its duration, its nature, its extent and its purpose, and whether there is an actual as opposed to a potential obstruction. Where a supermarket left trolleys in a pedestrian precinct for the convenience of shoppers there was an obstruction even though no complaint had been made by a member of the public. In another case there was held to be an obstruction where for 15 years a bridleway had been completely blocked by farm gates, tied by twine to hedges and held closed by a loop of twine, which could be opened easily. Simply to cause fear to users of a highway cannot amount to an obstruction. This was held by the Divisional Court in a case where the accused allowed his rotweiler dogs to act in a menacing way behind a fence separating his land from a path constituting a highway. Pedestrians on the path were put in fear but, said the court, the highway was not obstructed.

The term *'wilfully'* in this context means that the particular obstruction was occasioned by some deliberate act which was freely carried out by the defendant; consequently, a motorist who stops at a traffic light showing red does not wilfully obstruct the highway. In one case, a man who addressed a crowd, whose assembly interfered with traffic although traffic movement was not completely stopped, was held to have caused a wilful obstruction because, by the exercise of free will, he caused that obstruction to take place. On the other hand, if a queue forms outside a shop because many customers are attracted to it, it cannot be said that the shopkeeper has committed a deliberate and wilful act which caused the obstruction, as he is trading in a normal way. It would be different if the obstruction was caused because he was trading in an unusual way, for example through the window, as that unusual act would be wilful and would lead to an obstruction.

The question of whether or not a person has *'lawful authority or excuse'* will always be a question for the court to decide. The Police and Criminal Evidence Act 1984 authorises police officers to set up road blocks in certain circumstances (see p 42). Clearly, a road block established in accordance with the provisions of the Act would be set up with lawful authority. Street traders or collectors for charity who are licensed for that purpose have lawful authority. 'Lawful excuse' embraces activities lawful in themselves which are a reasonable use of the highway or incidental to the right of passage. On the other hand, the right to protest does not give a right to obstruct the highway; consequently there is no lawful authority or excuse for such obstruction.

Section 25 of the Police and Criminal Evidence Act 1984 gives a constable the power to arrest where the service of a summons is impracticable or inappropriate because one of the general arrest conditions is satisfied. One of those conditions is that arrest is necessary to prevent the person causing an unlawful obstruction of the highway.

Dangerous parking

The Road Traffic Act 1988, s 22 makes it an offence for a person to cause or permit a vehicle or trailer drawn by a motor vehicle to remain at rest on a road in such a position, or in such condition or in such circumstances, as to involve danger of injury to other persons. The danger may be caused by the manner of the parking, the condition of the bodywork etc which may come into contact with persons, or other circumstances. It has been held that, where a vehicle has been parked without the brake being properly set and the vehicle moves and injures a pedestrian, the offence is committed. See below for other offences of causing danger on or near roads.

Causing danger to road users

The Road Traffic Act 1988, s 22A provides that a person is guilty of an offence if he intentionally and without lawful authority or reasonable cause:

(a)   causes anything to be on or over a road, or
(b)   interferes with a motor vehicle, trailer or cycle, or
(c)   interferes (directly or indirectly) with traffic equipment,

in such circumstances that it would be obvious to a reasonable person that to do so would be dangerous. If the danger would have been obvious to a *reasonable* person, it is irrelevant that the accused was unaware of it.

'*Danger*' refers to danger either of injury to any person while on or near a road, or of serious damage to property on or near a road. In determining what would be 'obvious' to a reasonable person in a particular case, regard must be had not only to the circumstances of which he could be expected to be aware but also to any circumstances shown to have been within the knowledge of the accused.

Where persons are seen on a bridge over a motorway in possession of large pieces of concrete, and then are seen to *balance* these objects on the parapet, they certainly cause those objects to be over a road and it is submitted that the circumstances are such that it would be obvious to a reasonable person that what they were doing was dangerous. The danger lies in the strong possibility that these pieces of concrete will fall. If pieces are dropped they are then caused to be 'on' a road and danger is caused, whether or not the road is being used by traffic at that particular time. Whilst they remain there, they are a source of danger. Protesters who erect a barrier across a road will not normally be guilty of an offence under s 22A if the barrier is solid and easily seen. Although their actions are otherwise unlawful, the essential element of 'danger' is normally missing in such circumstances. However, the stretching of a thin rope or wire across a road would cause the type of danger which the section seeks to outlaw.

A person who deflates a car tyre to a low pressure or interferes with its brakes or steering clearly interferes with it for the purposes of (b), above, in such circumstances that it would be obvious to a reasonable person that to do so would be dangerous.

For the purposes of (c) above, 'traffic equipment' means:

(a) anything lawfully placed on or near a road by a highway authority;
(b) a traffic sign lawfully placed on or near a road by a person other than a highway authority;
(c) any fence, barrier or light lawfully placed on or near a road, to protect street works or undertakings, or items placed by a constable or person acting on the instructions (whether general or specific) of a chief officer of police.

Any such thing placed on or near a road is, unless the contrary is proved, deemed to have been lawfully placed.

Thus, all official road signs, those indicating temporary works or obstructions, road accidents or diversions are covered by the section. The intentional interference with any such sign must be shown to have created the danger envisaged by the section. It is not sufficient merely to show that a sign has been interfered with. A person who removes a hazard warning sign will commit an offence provided that the hazard still exists. If the sign indicates the existence of a hazard associated with road works and those works have been completed (so that no danger then exists), there will be no offence under this section. Where a sign is removed which merely indicates the direction of a town, nuisance has certainly been caused but there is no danger associated with such removal in normal circumstances. If road surfacing operations are marked at night by a series of lamps, the removal of one lamp may or may not cause the type of danger which the section seeks to prevent. If lamps are set at intervals of inches, it may be that the removal of one lamp is insignificant. If there are few lamps and a gap is left completely unmarked, the situation changes.

The offences under s 22A are arrestable offences.

Danger or annoyance on highway

The Highways Act 1980, s 161 prohibits any person, without lawful authority or excuse:

(a) from depositing anything on a highway in consequence of which a user is injured or endangered; or
(b) from lighting any fire on or over a highway which consists of or comprises a carriageway; or
(c) from discharging any firearm or firework within 50 feet of the centre of such a highway in consequence of which a user of the highway is injured, interrupted, or endangered.

Section 161A (1) prohibits a person from lighting a fire on any land not forming part of a highway which consists of or comprises a carriageway, or from directing or permitting such a fire to be lit, when in consequence a user of any highway which consists of or comprises a carriageway is injured, interrupted or endangered by, or by smoke from, that fire or any other fire caused by that fire. However, s 161A(2) provides a defence to a charge under s 161A(1) if it can be proved that at the time the fire was lit the person was satisfied on reasonable grounds that it was unlikely that users of any such highway would be injured, interrupted or endangered by the fire or by smoke from it, or from others caused by it, and either that before or after the fire was lit he did all that he reasonably could to prevent the consequences or that he had reasonable excuse for not doing so. Section 161A is aimed at preventing smoke clouds, caused by straw burning in surrounding fields, blowing over motorways and main roads.

Section 161 also punishes those who allow filth, lime or dirt or other offensive matter or thing to run on to a highway from any adjoining premises. It also prohibits the playing of football or any other game on a highway to the annoyance of a user of the highway. This offence creates many problems for police officers. Usually a complaint is received by telephone from a householder who wishes to complain that he is being annoyed by children playing football in the street. The offence is only committed when the game is 'to the annoyance of a user of the highway'; a person sitting in his house is not a 'user' in the sense intended by the section. Police officers frequently find themselves between the complainant and irate parents and it is helpful to appreciate the essentials of this factor when there is pressure to take action. A person who was not using the highway when annoyed cannot be subsequently annoyed by walking into the street unless the game continues to his annoyance when on the highway.

It is an offence contrary to s 162 to place, for any purpose, a rope, wire or other apparatus across a highway in such a manner as to be likely to cause danger to persons using the highway, unless the accused can prove that he had taken necessary means to give adequate warning. A washing line in a back street with white sheets suspended from it certainly involves the stretching of a rope across the highway, but in the circumstances it can easily be proved that adequate warning was given. However, if the washing is taken in and only the rope is left, there is an offence unless it can be proved that the necessary steps were taken to give adequate warning.

Builders' skips

The Highways Act 1980, s 139 provides that a builder's skip must not be deposited on the highway without the permission of the highway authority; otherwise an offence is committed. Such permission must be in writing; it is granted to a named person and the highway where the skip is to be located is specified. Each skip must be authorised on each occasion; a general permission to place skips is not possible. The authority may impose conditions upon its permission. These may refer to the siting of the skip, its dimensions, the painting of the skip to make it visible, the care and disposal of its contents, the manner in which it is to be lighted or guarded and its removal at the end of the authorised period. Skips must be fitted with two oblong plates of diagonal red and yellow fluorescent or reflective material, similar to those fitted to heavy goods vehicles.

Section 139 also provides that, whatever the conditions imposed, an owner must secure that the skip is properly lighted during the hours of darkness, that it is clearly and indelibly marked with the owner's name and with his telephone number or address, that it is removed as soon as possible after it has been filled, and that all conditions of the permission are complied with. Failure to do so is an offence on the part of the owner. The term 'owner' in relation to a skip which is hired for a month or more, or one which is the subject of a hire-purchase agreement, means the person in possession of the skip under the hiring agreement. Where the commission by any person of an offence under s 139 is due to the act or default of some other person, that other person is also guilty and may be convicted whether or not proceedings are taken against the first-mentioned person.

It is a defence to a charge under s 139 for the accused to prove that the commission of the offence was due to the act or default of another and that the defendant took all reasonable precautions and exercised all due diligence to avoid the commission of the offence by himself or any other person under his control.

The Highways Act 1980, s 140 provides that, regardless of whether or not permission has been obtained, the highway authority or a constable in uniform may require the owner of a skip to remove it, or reposition it, or cause it to be removed or repositioned. To fail to do so as soon as possible is an offence. A request by a constable must be made in person; a request by telephone, for example, is not sufficient.

Use of loudspeakers

The Control of Pollution Act 1974, s 62 bans the operation of loudspeakers in a street between 9 pm and 8 am the following morning for any purpose. It also bans their use at any other time for the purpose of advertising any entertainment, trade or business. The term 'street' means any highway and any other road, footway, square or court which is for the time being open to the public. The ban is therefore effective both in built-up areas and in the country, provided, in either case, the loudspeaker is operated in a 'street'.

The exemptions to these provisions are predictable. They are: use for police, fire or ambulance purposes, or by the Environment Agency or a water undertaking in the exercise of its functions or by a local authority; 'in vehicle' entertainments or announcements; telephones; use by showmen at a pleasure fair; and use in an emergency provided that the loudspeaker is operated so as not to give reasonable cause for annoyance to persons in the vicinity.

The most common exception to the general rule against the use of loudspeakers for advertising is in favour of those who have a loudspeaker fixed to a vehicle which is used for the conveyance of a perishable commodity for human consumption and is used solely for the purpose of informing the public, by means other than words, that the commodity is on sale from the vehicle. Such a loudspeaker must be operated so as not to give reasonable cause for annoyance to persons in the vicinity and it may only be used between noon and 7 pm of the same day. Thus 'ice-cream chimes' can be used between these times, but at no other.

NUISANCES

Generally

It is a common law offence to cause a public nuisance. To offend against the common law the act concerned must obstruct or cause inconvenience or damage to the public in the exercise of their rights. The essence of the offence is that the act is a nuisance to the public in general and not to an individual, or a restricted group of people. An act which is specifically authorised by law, cannot be a public nuisance if carried out as prescribed. This common law offence is little used as most 'nuisances' are covered by statutes.

Nuisances related to noise

Because of difficulties experienced by local authorities and police officers in dealing with 'noise' nuisances, the Noise Act 1996 provided powers for local authorities to serve warning notices upon households from which excessive noise was emanating, such noise being heard during the night. For the purposes of the Act, 'night' is the period between 11pm and 7am. Local authorities are equipped with approved measuring devices which establish noise levels. Where such a notice has been served in respect of the premises, it is an offence for any person to emit from a dwelling-house, within a period specified in the notice, noise which exceeds the permitted level, as measured from within that dwelling.

The Act provides a defence of 'reasonable excuse', the onus of proving which is on the accused. The Act permits local authorities to introduce fixed penalty offences in relation to such nuisances. Local authority officers have a power of entry to a dwelling in respect of which a warning notice has been issued. It is a summary offence to obstruct such an officer and the Act provides powers of seizure and disposal of equipment causing such a noise nuisance.

Depositing litter

There are several provisions dealing with forms of defacement which might generally be described as 'litter'. The Environmental Protection Act 1990, s 87 states that a person commits an offence if he *throws down, drops or otherwise deposits*, in, into or from any place specified in that section, *and leaves*, anything in such circumstances as to cause, or contribute to, or tend to lead to, the defacement by litter of any such place. However, the offence is not committed if the depositing and leaving was authorised by law or was done with the consent of the owner, occupier or other persons or authority having control of the place in or into which that thing was deposited. Section 87 applies to a 'public open place' and to certain other places. A 'public open place' means a place in the open air to which the public are entitled or permitted to have access without payment. Any covered place open to the air on at least one side and available for public use, such as a bus shelter, is treated as a public open place. On the other hand, a telephone kiosk which is so designed that it is enclosed on all four sides with the exception of a six inch gap at the bottom is not a public open place within the terms of the section. In so far as the place is not a public open place, s 87 also applies to a highway or relevant road and any trunk road which is a special road, land of a principal litter authority or within a litter control area of a local authority, Crown land, and land of statutory undertakers or a designated educational authority.

Most offences of depositing litter are quite clear. A person throws down a cigarette packet, fish wrapper or newspaper and leaves it on the pavement. He was in a public open place when he threw down the material and he threw it on to a pavement which is a public open place, thereby causing defacement by litter. The same will apply to a person who drives into the country and deposits litter in a lay-by at the side of the road. The act of depositing is both from and into a public open place. However, if such a person threw the litter over the hedge and into a field he would not, unless the field was a place particularly specified by the section, eg Crown land, commit an offence contrary to s 87. The defacement would not, in these circumstances, be of a place specified in the section. Such a person, would however, commit an offence against the Refuse Disposal (Amenity) Act 1978, s 2, which is examined below.

Where litter offences are dealt with by local authority 'litter wardens' (who must be authorised in writing so to act), s 88 of the 1990 Act permits the use of a fixed penalty procedure. Where such an authorised officer finds a person who he has reason to believe has on that occasion committed an offence under s 87 in the area of that authority, he may give that person a fixed penalty notice. Where this has been done, no proceedings shall be instituted for the offence before the expiration of 14 days following the date of the notice. Such a person may not be convicted of that offence if he pays the fixed penalty within that period.

It must be emphasised that an offence under s 87 is *not* committed by a person on private land who deposits something on private land, as where a person throws his garden waste over his fence into his neighbour's garden or where he enters private land as a trespasser and dumps rubbish there.

The word 'leave' in s 87 has been given a wide interpretation. In one case, a man and his family were living in a tent set up in a country lane. His lorry was parked nearby against which was a pile of scrap metal. The man was sorting through it when seen by police officers. He was convicted of depositing and leaving litter as it was judged that he intended to remove only that metal which was of value. The Divisional Court held that 'leave' for the purposes of the Act does not mean abandon. The metal had been deposited and permitted to remain beside the road for such a time and in circumstances that it could be said to have been left there. The court also held that an article deposited with no intention to remove it could be 'left' after only a short period of time. This is an important judgment. A man who throws down fish wrappers, and refuses to pick them up immediately, commits the offence of depositing and leaving litter. He has no intention of removing the wrappers and this is evidenced by his refusal.

Refuse Disposal (Amenity) Act 1978

The Refuse Disposal (Amenity) Act 1978 extends litter offences to private places in the open air. Section 2(1) provides the offence of abandoning, without lawful authority, on any land in the open air, or on any other land forming part of a highway, anything which has been brought to the land for the purpose of being abandoned there. The section is meant to deal with instances in which a motorist takes refuse quite deliberately into the countryside and abandons it there. Such a person may leave an old mattress at the side of the road or throw it over the fence into a field; in either event he commits an offence. There is no necessity to prove that the refuse was deposited from any particular place; it is sufficient that it is left there. Often such waste is identifiable as it includes marked articles traceable to the person who abandoned it.

Abandoned motor vehicles

The Refuse Disposal (Amenity) Act 1978, s 2(1) also deals with the abandonment of motor vehicles in similar circumstances. The difference is that it is not necessary to prove that a motor vehicle was brought to the land for the purpose of abandonment. The offence is committed by a person who, without lawful authority, abandons on any land in the open air, or on any other land forming part of a highway, a motor vehicle or anything which formed part of a motor vehicle and was removed from it in the course of dismantling the vehicle on the land.

General

In terms of proof, s 2(2) contains a provision which is important in relation to both offences under s 2(1) mentioned in the last two paragraphs. Section 2(2) deals with a person who leaves anything on land in such circumstances or for such a period that he may reasonably be assumed to have abandoned it or, as the case may be, to have brought it to the land for the purpose of abandoning it there. It provides that such a person is deemed to have abandoned it there or, as the case may be, to have brought it to the land for that purpose, unless the contrary is shown. The onus is therefore placed upon the accused to satisfy the court that the vehicle etc was not abandoned once it is proved to have been there in circumstances which suggest abandonment.

It follows from our description of the offences just mentioned that a person who abandons a motor vehicle at the roadside commits an offence against s 2(1) of the 1978 Act. It can also be seen that the caravan traveller who dismantles vehicles either on the highway or adjoining land commits offences against the Environmental Protection Act 1990 if he deposits and leaves pieces of metal, only some of which he intends to take away. When he moves on, abandoning stripped vehicle shells or pieces removed from vehicles, he commits an offence of abandonment under the 1978 Act.

Off-road driving

The Road Traffic Act 1988, s 34 prohibits a person from driving a motor vehicle, without lawful authority, on to or upon any common land, moorland or land of any other description which is not a part of the road, or on any road which is a footpath or bridleway. However, the section permits the driving of a vehicle within 15 yards of a road upon which a motor vehicle may be driven but only for the purpose of parking. The section provides a further defence if the vehicle is so driven for saving life, or extinguishing fire, or for dealing with any other similar emergency.

Nuisance on educational premises

Although not directly concerned with highways this offence is most conveniently examined here. The Local Government (Miscellaneous Provisions) Act 1982, s 40(1) creates an offence which may be committed by a person who is present on educational premises, without lawful authority, who causes or permits nuisance or disturbance to the annoyance of persons who lawfully use those premises (whether or not any such persons are present at the time). The term 'premises' includes playgrounds, playing fields and other premises for outdoor recreation of any school or further or higher education establishment maintained by a local education authority. A constable or an authorised local authority officer may remove such a person from the premises if he has reasonable cause to suspect that he is committing or has committed such an offence. The offence is worded to embrace many possibilities from disturbances caused by irate parents, to nuisances caused by exercising dogs on playing fields. Many educational authorities do not appear to discourage the use of their facilities out of hours, even by those who are not students at those establishments. However, such use, in an orderly fashion, would not offend against the section even where permission had not been directly given to a person to be on those premises.

CHAPTER 10

Use of vehicles

TERMINOLOGY

In various parts of this chapter we shall refer to 'motor cars', 'heavy motor cars', 'bus', 'large bus', 'coach', 'motor tractors' and 'locomotives'. These terms are defined by the Road Traffic Act 1988 or Road Vehicles (Construction and Use) Regulations themselves. All the terms are concerned, of course, with motor vehicles, and hereafter 'vehicle' must be understood in this sense. For the purposes of the present part of this chapter, a 'motor car' is a vehicle constructed or adapted for use for the conveyance of any goods or passengers and whose unladen weight does not exceed 3,050 kg (3 tons), if it is constructed solely for the carriage of passengers and adapted to carry no more than seven of them as well as the driver, or if it is constructed for the conveyance of goods, or 2,540 kg (2.5 tons) in any other case. For the same purposes a 'heavy motor car' is a vehicle (not being a motor car) constructed to carry a load, whether goods or passengers, and whose unladen weight exceeds 2,540 kg (2.5 tons). Although this definition covers buses and coaches, there are some requirements of the regulations which are specific to them. For this reason 'bus', 'large bus' and 'coach' are separately defined. A 'bus' is a vehicle constructed or adapted to carry more than eight seated passengers in addition to the driver, and 'large bus' is a vehicle constructed or adapted to carry more than 16 such passengers. A 'coach' is a large bus with a maximum gross weight of more than 7.5 tonnes and a maximum speed exceeding 60 mph.

A 'motor tractor' is defined as a vehicle which is not constructed itself to carry a load (other than one concerned with its own propulsion or maintenance) and the unladen weight of which does not exceed 7,370 kg (7.25 tons). A 'locomotive' is a similar vehicle, the unladen weight of which exceeds 7,370 kg (7.25 tons).

ROAD VEHICLES (CONSTRUCTION AND USE) REGULATIONS 1986

The Road Vehicles (Construction and Use) Regulations 1986 are made under the Road Traffic Act 1988, s 41. They are divided into two main parts: one dealing with the construction, maintenance and equipment of motor vehicles and trailers; the other with the various uses of motor vehicles and trailers on roads. The 'construction' elements of the regulations are aimed at manufacturers in the main, as they amount to specifications for vehicle production. Many of these provisions are being replaced in relation to most modern vehicles by requirements of an international nature relating to 'type approved' vehicles, and arrangements for the transition to type approval are set out in reg 6 of the Regulations. The date of manufacture or first registration of vehicles will normally be the conclusive factor in deciding whether the 'construction' elements of these regulations apply, or those directed towards type approval. A vehicle which complies with the relevant type approval and has the relevant certificate of type approval or manufacturer's certificate of conformity to the type approval is exempt from certain parts of Part II of the Regulations, concerned with the construction of motor vehicles. Police officers are much more frequently concerned with offences relating to the use of vehicles in contravention of the Regulations.

Certain special types of vehicles are authorised under the Motor Vehicles (Authorisation of Special Types) General Order 1979 and do not have to comply with all of the requirements of the Road Vehicles (Construction and Use) Regulations 1986. The clue to the nature of such vehicles lies within the term 'special'. The vehicles concerned are likely to be track-laying vehicles; those used for special engineering and maintenance purposes; military vehicles; and vehicles used for life-saving operations.

Type approval

As we have already stated most modern vehicles, because they comply with certain international requirements, are exempt from those Construction and Use Regulations which are concerned with the *construction* of motor vehicles. These requirements are commonly referred to as 'Type Approval'.

Compulsory British type approval

Certain motor vehicles and their component parts, but *not trailers*, manufactured in Great Britain on or after 1 October 1977 must be wholly constructed to British Type Approval Standard. These vehicles are:

(a) passenger vehicles with four or more wheels adapted to carry not more than nine persons including the driver; and
(b) passenger vehicles with three wheels, not being a motor bicycle with sidecar attached.

There are various exemptions, examples of which are prototype vehicles, some vehicles which are manufactured for export, motor caravans and special ambulances.

Goods vehicles manufactured in Great Britain on or after 1 October 1982 and first used on or after 1 April 1983 are also subject to compulsory British type approval.

Again, there are various exemptions, for example prototype vehicles, fire engines, pedestrian-controlled vehicles and motor tractors.

The compulsory British type approval schemes are backed up by two offences:

(a) it is generally an offence to sell, supply, offer to sell or supply, or expose for sale a vehicle which does not have a Secretary of State's type approval certificate or a manufacturer's certificate of conformity to the type approval;
(b) using, or causing or permitting to be used, on a road, a vehicle subject in whole or part to compulsory British type approval is an offence, unless it appears from a

certificate of the type referred to in (a) that the vehicle (or its parts) complies with the type approval.

Compulsory EU type approval

The optional system of EU type approval introduced by the Motor Vehicles (Type Approval) Regulations 1980 in respect of certain motor vehicles, trailers and their component parts now applies only to type approval of tachographs. With this exception, the 1980 Regulations have been superseded by the Motor Vehicles (EC Type Approval) Regulations 1992. The 1992 Regulations implement an EC Council Directive requiring member states to set up a system for granting EC type approval for *'light passenger vehicles'*. A light passenger vehicle is defined by the regulations as a motor vehicle which:

(a) has at least four wheels;
(b) has an internal combustion engine;
(c) is constructed or adapted for the carriage of passengers, and is not a goods vehicle;
(d) has no more than eight seats in addition to the driver's; and
(e) has a maximum design speed exceeding 25 kph.

To the extent that they overlap in their application, the EC system under the 1992 Regulations will prevail over the British type approval system.

The 1992 Regulations provide that, subject to specified exceptions, the Secretary of State must not as *from 1 January 1996* issue a first licence to or register a light passenger vehicle unless it either has an EC certificate of conformity or has a Minister's approval certificate issued under the Road Traffic Act 1988, s 58(1). An EC certificate of conformity is issued in respect of an individual vehicle covered by an EC type approval by the holder of that approval (normally the manufacturer). In a few cases, the operative date is 1 January 1998, or 1 January 2000, and not 1 January 1996.

Between 1993 and the relevant operative date, a vehicle with an EC certificate of conformity is deemed to comply with all type approval requirements, with the result that its use or sale will not constitute an offence under the British type approval regulations.

After the operative date, the use on a road of an unregistered light passenger vehicle which is not covered by an EC certificate of conformity or a Minister's approval certificate will be an offence, as will be the sale of a light passenger vehicle without one or other of these certificates.

CONSTRUCTION AND USE OFFENCES: GENERAL

The Road Traffic Act 1988, ss 40A, 41A, 41B and 42 provide various offences which may be committed in relation to the use of a vehicle in a dangerous condition and/or in contravention of the Regulations.

Section 40A makes it an offence for a person to use, cause or permit another to use a motor vehicle or a trailer on a road when:

(a) the condition of the motor vehicle or trailer, or of its accessories or equipment, or
(b) the purpose for which it is used, or
(c) the number of passengers carried by it, or the manner in which they are carried, or
(d) the weight, position or distribution of its load, or the manner in which it is secured,

is such that the use of the motor vehicle or trailer involves danger of injury to any person.

Section 41A makes it an offence for a person to:

(a) contravene or fail to comply with a construction and use requirement as to brakes, steering gear or tyres, or

(b) use on a road a motor vehicle or trailer which does not comply with such a requirement, or cause or permit a motor vehicle or trailer to be so used.

Offences against ss 40A and 41A carry discretionary disqualification; the endorsement of 3 penalty points is obligatory.

Section 41B punishes offences in relation to 'weight'. A person who:

(a) contravenes or fails to comply with a construction and use requirement as to any description of weight applicable to—

    (i)   a goods vehicle, or

    (ii)   a motor vehicle or trailer adapted to carry more than eight passengers, or

(b) uses on a road a vehicle which does not comply with such a requirement, or causes or permits a vehicle to be so used,

commits an offence against the section. Section 41B(2) provides a defence where the alleged contravention relates to any description of weight applicable to a goods vehicle. It provides that in such a case it is a defence to prove either that the vehicle was going to or coming from a weighbridge, or, where the relevant weight limit is not exceeded by more than 5 per cent, that that weight was not exceeded at the time of loading and that load had not been added to.

Section 42 is concerned with contraventions of a construction and use requirement other than those relating to brakes, steering gear or tyres, or those relating to weight, which are dealt with by ss 41A to 41B. It provides that a person who:

(a) contravenes or fails to comply with such a requirement; or

(b) uses on a road a motor vehicle or trailer which does not comply with such a requirement, or causes or permits a motor vehicle or trailer to be so used,

commits an offence.

Those who contravene ss 41B or 42 are not liable to disqualification or to obligatory endorsement under these sections.

An offence of using on a road a trailer which does not comply with regulations is an offence distinct from that of using a defective motor vehicle.

Since the relevant provisions are concerned with persons who use, cause or permit the use of motor vehicles or trailers in contravention of the Regulations, it is important that police officers understand the meaning of these terms.

Use

This term should be given its ordinary meaning. A person uses a vehicle if he controls, manages, operates or otherwise has the use of it as a vehicle.

In law, a person can 'use' a vehicle, even though he does not do so personally. This is because, if a driver of a vehicle is about his employer's business, the employer is also using the vehicle (and can therefore be held vicariously liable), and the words 'causing' or 'permitting' should not be considered. The offence of 'using' covers most eventualities where there is a employer/employee relationship.

Sections 40A, 41A and 42 of the 1988 Act impose a strict liability upon those who use motor vehicles in contravention of the Regulations; consequently, it is irrelevant that the accused did not know of the defect etc, nor ought to have known of it. In one case, a driver was convicted of using a vehicle on a road with a load which had not been properly secured, even though he had taken no part in the loading, and loading was not a part of his responsibility.

It is quite possible that the owner of a motor vehicle may be totally unaware that an offence of using in breach of the Regulations is being committed in relation to his vehicle which is being driven by an employee of his many miles away from his operating centre. Nevertheless, if the vehicle is on the road, upon his business, the employer is using it in addition to his employee driver, and both he and his employee can be convicted of the offence. In one case, where an owner had directed an employee driver to take the vehicle to a garage whenever it required maintenance, it was held that there had been a use with defective brakes by the employer as the vehicle was being used on his business; it was irrelevant that such a general direction as to maintenance had been given.

In general, where defects are 'discovered' which amount to contraventions of the Regulations, charges of 'using' should be considered in respect of the driver and of his employer if the vehicle is used upon his business. There must be clear evidence of an employee/employer relationship, and the employee must be acting in the course of his employment. Thus, where a driver used a stock car on a road he was properly convicted of using the vehicle with defective parts, but the owner, not being the employer of the driver in relation to the business of stock car racing, was held not to have been 'using' the vehicle. He was, however, held to have been permitting the offence because he had knowingly allowed the driver to drive the car in its defective condition, (see below). Because it would not be in the course of his employment, a cleaner who made use of his employer's defective lorry would not render his employer guilty of using it.

In one case, a driver who was self-employed was paid on a daily basis. He paid his own tax and national insurance contributions, and did not work exclusively for the company. When he did work for the company, he wore its uniform, drove its vehicle and collected and delivered loads from and to specified locations. The Divisional Court held that the company was not 'using' the vehicle. It said that *a person is a user only if he is the driver or the owner of the vehicle, but an owner only uses his vehicle if the driver is employed by him under a contract of service and at the material time he is driving on his employer's business,* which the driver in the case was not. The Divisional Court has remarked upon the illogicality and artificiality caused by its insistence upon the need for a strict employer/employee relationship. The Court on one occasion said that it found it difficult to accept that, if a man can 'use' his vehicle through the hands of his servant, he cannot be said to use it at the hands of someone else who, at his specific request, drives it on a journey at the express orders and with the full knowledge of the owner. Illogical or not, the Court has persistently refused to extend the meaning of 'use' on the grounds that a line must be drawn somewhere. Where such a strict employer/employee relationship cannot be established, a charge of 'causing' or 'permitting' must be considered.

Where a vehicle is hired out with a driver for use by another firm, the driver will usually remain the employee of the owner of the vehicle so that a 'using' by the driver will be a 'using' by the owner. Thus, where BRS hired a vehicle together with its driver to another firm for a period of five years, and that other firm was operating the vehicle under its own livery, BRS was held to be using that vehicle when it was found to be overloaded. BRS had been in the business of hiring out vehicles with drivers who remained their employees and the vehicles were being used in the course of that business. Similarly, where the driver of a vehicle who was employed by A was ordered by telephone to pick up a return load on behalf of another company B, that company being responsible for loading the vehicle, its documentation and the selection of route, the Divisional Court held that company A was guilty of using the vehicle when it was found to be overloaded. The Court said that, whilst it might be correct to argue that company B was using the vehicle, this did not mean that company A was not. It was their vehicle and their driver and that driver was employed under a contract of service. However, the owner will not be liable for using the vehicle as it is not being used on his business. Where a company hires another company to transport its goods, the first company is not 'using' the vehicle at the time at which it sheds its load. This is so even where the first company supplies the means of securing the load. The first company is not 'operating' the vehicle at the time in question; it would be different if they had hired the vehicle and operated it themselves.

A man who lends his private motor car to his friend is not liable for 'using' that vehicle if the Regulations are contravened by the friend. However, in certain circumstances, he could be guilty of permitting its use in contravention of the Regulations.

Where a trailer is towed by another vehicle and the offence concerned relates to the trailer, as, for example, where there is a defective part on the trailer, or it carries an insecure load, the information should specify that it was the trailer which was defective or improperly used. This is essential where the tractor unit and the trailer are owned by different persons or companies.

Cause the use

This term, together with 'permitting the use', covers circumstances in which charges of aiding and abetting would otherwise normally be appropriate. To be guilty of causing the use of a vehicle in contravention of the Regulations, an accused must actually have known of, or been wilfully blind as to, the contravention in question. The offence can only be committed by persons who exercise some control over the driver who is using the vehicle. To 'cause' involves some express or positive command or direction from the person 'causing' to the person 'using'. If the foreman of a haulage depot, knowing that a vehicle has a defective tyre, orders an employee to drive the vehicle, the foreman 'causes' the driver to commit the offence. He is in a position to give orders to the employee in relation to the use of the vehicle and does so, and he has knowledge of the defect. In such a case the firm would also be guilty of using the vehicle as it was used on their business and knowledge is not an essential ingredient of that offence. Where a manager was responsible for five vehicle depots at each of which there was a vehicle superintendent, it was held that he could not be guilty of causing the vehicle to be used in a defective condition as he was not in a position to exercise control and could not have guilty knowledge in any case. In that case, for the superintendent to be guilty of causing the vehicle to be used, there would have to be evidence of a requirement to use it and knowledge of the circumstances.

A person who tows another vehicle is causing it to be used on a road.

Permit the use

Like 'causing the use' of a vehicle, a person accused of 'permitting' a vehicle to be used in contravention of the Regulations is not guilty unless it is proved that he actually knew of, or was wilfully blind as to, the contravention in question. However, the meaning of 'permitting' is much wider than the meaning of 'causing'. There does not need to be any express or positive mandate to use a motor vehicle and a general or particular permission to use a vehicle will be sufficient. For the offence of 'causing to be used' described above, there must always be a requirement by someone in authority, directed to someone who is required to obey. In contrast, for a person to be guilty of 'permitting' he must be in a position to forbid another person to use the vehicle, and the term 'permitting' is concerned with a general permission rather than a direct order. If the person who is given control of the vehicle is granted total discretion in relation to its use, he has certainly been given permission to use the vehicle, but he has not been directed to do so in any particular way. Many employees of companies are given general permission to use a firm's vehicle in any way they choose. However, having been given such a general permission by an employer, it is unlikely that such an employer will be liable for contraventions of the Construction and Use Regulations in respect of that vehicle, but in some circumstances he may. There is a distinction between knowledge that the vehicle is being used and knowledge that it is being used unlawfully. A sales representative may be given total use of a motor car. As a driver he will be responsible for its use in contravention of these Regulations but his employers will not normally be liable for permitting, as they are unlikely to have knowledge of the particular unlawful use. However, if the vehicle is being used on company business, a charge of using may be appropriate. If such a person is using the vehicle privately at the time, the company will have no liability unless it can be shown that it knew of the defect but nevertheless gave permission for the vehicle's continued use. If such permission has been directly given, then a charge of permitting will lie.

In a case where a vehicle belonging to a company left its premises in good condition but, while out of the control of responsible officers of the company, employees coupled up a trailer in such a manner that the brakes were defective, it was held that the company officers could not be said to have permitted the offence as no formal permission to do the act was given. In such circumstances, however, the company 'used' the vehicle as it was on its business at the time. In the same way, where the defendant was the owner of a lorry driven on a road by his employee while the brakes were defective, it was held that for a charge of permitting to succeed there must be proof of actual knowledge or wilful blindness on the part of the owner. It was pointed out however, that the owner would have had no defence to a charge of 'using'.

A man who lends his car to his friend allows him to use it with his permission. That permission does not extend to unlawful use of a warning instrument as no permission has been given in that respect. If the tyres were defective, it would be a question of fact as to whether the owner of the vehicle knew of the defect when permission was given to use it.

PARTICULAR REGULATIONS UNDER THE ROAD VEHICLES (CONSTRUCTION AND USE) REGULATIONS 1986

Brakes

The differing braking systems with which differing types of vehicles must be fitted are dealt with in regs 15 and 16 and Sch 3. These provisions include exemptions from the provisions of the Road Vehicles (Construction and Use) Regulations if type approval has been given. However, the fitting of various systems is not a matter of prime concern to police officers. On the other hand, the maintenance of brakes is. Regulation 18 deals with the maintenance of brakes and applies quite generally to braking systems (where fitted under these, or other, regulations).

The purpose of foot braking systems is to be able to stop the vehicle within a reasonable distance under the most adverse conditions. This is a fairly general description of the efficiency of a foot braking system but guidance is given in the Highway Code. The stopping distances given in the Code are related to good cars on dry roads with good brakes and alert drivers, and represent the shortest stopping distances. The Code gives the overall stopping distances for vehicles travelling at 20, 30, 40, 50, 60 and 70 mph as 40, 75, 120, 175, 240 and 315 feet respectively. The provisions of the Code may be relied upon in a prosecution to show that the accused failed to comply with a standard contained in it and, therefore, as tending to establish negligence, but the table cannot be offered in evidence as evidence of overall stopping distances as it is hearsay in that respect.

Braking systems to which reg 15 applies

Regulation 15(1) of the Regulations requires that with certain exceptions (generally embracing specialist types of vehicles) all wheeled vehicles specified in the table set out within the regulation, which were first used on or after 1 April 1983, must comply with the construction, fitting and performance requirements of Community Directive 79/489. The vehicles specified include most vehicles on our roads today. The table indicates the vehicle category set out in the Community Directive, specifying the construction, fitting and performance requirement of each type of vehicle. Other similar vehicles used before that date may comply with these requirements as an alternative to regs 16 and 17.

Regulations 15(1A), 15(1B) and 15(1C) require that, with certain exceptions, the braking systems of most vehicles first used on or after 1 April 1989 must comply with the requirements of Community Directive 85/647. Motor cars, buses of a gross weight not exceeding 5000 kg, and dual purpose vehicles, must comply if first used on or after 1 April 1990. Other motor vehicles (with certain exceptions) first used on or after 1 April 1992, and trailers manufactured on or after 1 October 1991, must comply with Community Directive 88/194. Regulation 15(1D) requires that all such vehicles as specified above first used on or after 1 April 1995 and trailers manufactured after that date must comply with Community Directive 91/422. Once again, other such vehicles may comply as an alternative to the other Directives specified above.

Braking systems to which reg 15 does not apply

Most of the remainder of vehicles, that is those first used before 1 April 1983 and those specifically excluded from reg 15, are covered by the provisions of reg 16. However, all such vehicles *may* comply with the requirements of reg 15 as an alternative to the provisions of reg 16. Certain 'specialist' vehicles are not covered by reg 16. It contains a table which specifies the requirements of Sch 3 to the Regulations which apply to particular vehicles.

Heavy motor cars and motor cars first used on or after 1 January 1968 to which reg 16 applies must be equipped with one efficient braking system having two means of operation; or one efficient split braking system having one means of operation; or two efficient braking systems each having a separate means of operation. No account is to be taken of a multi-pull means of operation unless, at first application, it operates a hydraulic, electric or pneumatic device which causes the application of the brakes with a total braking efficiency of not less than 25 per cent. The braking system must be so designed that, in the event of failure of any part (other than a fixed member or brake shoe anchor pin) through or by means of which the force necessary to apply the brakes is transmitted, there is still available for application by the driver brakes sufficient under the most adverse conditions to bring the vehicle to rest within a reasonable distance. The brakes so available must be applied to at least one wheel if the vehicle is a three-wheeler and otherwise to at least half of the wheels. Braking systems must not affect or operate the pedals or hand lever of any other braking system, nor may they be rendered ineffective by the non-rotation of the engine. At least one means of operation must be capable of causing brakes to be applied directly, and not through the transmission, to at least half of the wheels of the vehicle. The parking brake must be so designed and constructed that it is independent and its braking force, when the vehicle is not being driven or is unattended, must be such that it can be maintained so as to hold the vehicle stationary on a gradient of at least 16 per cent without the assistance of stored energy.

The provisions set out in the paragraph above also apply to heavy motor cars and motor cars first used *before* 1 January 1968 with the exception of those related to the parking brake. In the case of these vehicles the parking brake must be so designed and constructed that:

(a) its means of operation is independent of the means of operation of any split braking system;

(b) it is capable of being applied by direct mechanical action without the intervention of any hydraulic, electric or pneumatic device, or the brakes apply to all wheels; and

(c) it can at all times when the vehicle is not being driven, or is left unattended, be set so as to prevent the rotation of one wheel in the case of a three-wheeled vehicle, and of at least two wheels in the case of a vehicle with more than three wheels.

Two-wheeled motorcycles must be equipped with one efficient braking system having two means of operation; or two efficient braking systems each having a separate means of operation. The application of any means of operation of a braking system must not affect or operate the pedal or hand lever of any other means of operation.

Trailers, other than agricultural trailers, manufactured on or after 1 January 1968 and having a maximum gross weight exceeding 750 kg, must be equipped with an efficient braking system. The system must be such that in the event of failure etc the brakes available are applied to at least one wheel if the trailer has two wheels, and otherwise to at least two wheels. The braking power must be sufficient under the most adverse conditions to bring the vehicle to rest within a reasonable distance. Brakes may be of an overrun type. The brakes of these trailers must apply to all wheels. They must have a parking brake which can be applied and released by a person standing on the ground, by a means of operation fitted to the trailer.

Trailers manufactured before 1 January 1968 (and all agricultural trailers regardless of date of manufacture) require an efficient braking system if they have a maximum gross weight exceeding 750 kg. They may be of the overrun type. The brakes of the vehicle must apply to at least two wheels if the vehicle has no more than four wheels, and to at least half of the wheels if it has more than four wheels. The parking brake must be capable of being set so as to effectively prevent two at least of the wheels from revolving when the trailer is not being drawn.

Whilst the provisions of reg 16 do not apply to trailers which have a maximum total design axle weight not exceeding 750 kg, such trailers manufactured on or after 1 January 1997 are required:

(a) to have a braking device such that the trailer will stop automatically if the coupling separates while the trailer is in motion, or

(b)   be provided with a secondary coupling (eg a chain or cable) which, in the event of separation of the main coupling, can stop the draw bar from touching the ground and provide some residual steering of the trailer.

Such trailers manufactured on or after that date must carry a plate which carries their year of manufacture.

Maintenance and efficiency

Regulation 18(1) requires that every braking system and the means of operation thereof fitted to a vehicle must be maintained in good and efficient working order, and be properly adjusted. This applies to any vehicle to which a braking system is fitted, including a trailer which is not required to have a braking system fitted.

By reg 18(3) braking systems must be so maintained that service braking systems and secondary braking systems have prescribed braking efficiencies:

	Service	Secondary
(a) vehicles to which reg 15 applies, or whose construction etc complies with Community Directive 79/489, 85/647, 88/194 or 91/422:		
(i) not drawing a trailer	50%	25%
(ii) drawing a trailer	45%	25%
(b) vehicles first used on or after 1 January 1968 and complying with reg 16:		
(i) when not drawing a trailer or drawing trailer manufactured after 1 January 1968		
	50%	25%
(ii) drawing trailer manufactured before 1 January 1968	40%	15%
(c) goods vehicles and buses first used before 1 January 1968 having an unladen weight exceeding 1,525 kg being rigid vehicles with two axles (not artics):		
(i) when not drawing trailer	45%	20%
(ii) when drawing trailer	40%	15%
(d) vehicles not shown at (a) to (c) having at least one means of operation applying to at least four wheels (not a bus or artic):	50%	25%
(e) vehicles not shown at (a) to (c) having three wheels and at least one means of operation applying to all three wheels (not a motorcycle and sidecar) when not drawing a trailer, or when drawing a trailer if three-wheeler is classed as a motorcycle:		
	40%	25%
(f) other vehicles not shown at (a) to (c) when not drawing a trailer or, in the case of a motorcycle, when drawing a trailer:	30%	25%

In certain circumstances where a defect arises in an ABS braking systems during the course of a journey, it is permissible for the vehicle to complete its journey, or to be driven to a place where the ABS is to be repaired, without there being a breach of the requirement that every part of a braking system must be maintained in good and efficient working order. However, the affected braking system must still meet the braking efficiencies specified in reg 18(3).

The maintenance of brakes is further dealt with by reg 18(6) which is concerned with the efficiency of parking brakes. It requires that every vehicle or combination of vehicles specified in an item in column 2 of Table II of the regulation, shall be so maintained that the brakes are capable, without the assistance of stored energy, of holding it stationary on a gradient of at least the percentages specified in column 3 of that table. This means:

(i)   those vehicles specified at (a) above:
      (A) when not drawing a trailer   16%
      (B) when drawing a trailer   12%
(ii) those vehicles specified at (b) above   16%
(iii) vehicles other than in (a) above drawing a trailer manufactured on or after 1 January
      1968 and required by regs 15 or 16 to be fitted with brakes   16%

Seat belts

Regulations 46 and 47 deal with anchorage points and seat belts.

Anchorage points

Subject to the exemptions set out below, every wheeled motor car first used on or after
1 January 1965; every three wheeled motorcycle the unladen weight of which exceeds
255 kg and which was first used on or after 1 September 1970; and every heavy motor
car first used on or after 1 October 1988 must be fitted with anchorage points and seat
belts as specified.

Exemptions This requirement does not apply to goods vehicles (other than
dual-purpose vehicles) which were first used:

(a)   before 1 April 1967; or
(b)   on or after 1 April 1980 and before 1 October 1988 which have a maximum gross
      weight exceeding 3,500 kg; or
(c)   before 1 April 1980 or, if the vehicle is a model manufactured before 1 October
      1979, was first used before 1 April 1982 and, in either case, has an unladen weight
      exceeding 1,525 kg.

There are the following exemptions in favour of buses. Minibuses first used before
1 October 1988, which are constructed or adapted to carry more than 12 passengers are
exempt (subject to the special provisions relating to organised trips for children referred
to on p 265 below). So, with the same proviso, are minibuses first used on or after 1
October 1988 which have a maximum gross weight exceeding 3,500 kg, and so are large
buses – other than coaches first used on or after 1 October 1988.

There are also specific exemptions in favour of agricultural motor vehicles, motor
tractors, works trucks, electrically-propelled goods vehicles first used before 1 October
1988, pedestrian-controlled vehicles, imported used vehicles whilst travelling to be fitted
etc, vehicles having a maximum speed not exceeding 16 mph and locomotives.

Where points to be fitted Vehicles first used before 1 April 1982 must be equipped
with anchorage points for seat belts in respect of the driver's seat and the specified
passenger's seat. 'A specified passenger's seat' is a forward-facing front seat. Where
there is more than one forward-facing front seat, the term is applied to the one farthest
from the driver's seat. Passenger and dual-purpose vehicles first used on or after 1
April 1982 must have anchorage points for every forward-facing seat constructed or
adapted to accommodate one adult. Minibuses, motor ambulances and motor caravans
first used before 1 October 1988 must have anchorage points for the driver's and
specified passenger's seats. Vehicles first used on or after 1 October 1988 must have
anchorage points for the driver's seat and all forward-facing front seats. In every other

case vehicles first used on or after 1 April 1982 must have anchorage points for every forward-facing front seat and every non-protected seat. A non-protected seat is one where the area immediately in front and to the sides of the seated passenger is not 'protected'. To be protected the seat must be such that the passenger could not be projected towards a windscreen etc through any aperture ahead of the passenger. The limit of any aperture ahead of such passenger is 165 mm.

The requirements set out in the preceding paragraph do not apply to goods vehicles first used on or after 1 October 1988 which have a maximum gross weight exceeding 3,500 kg, but every such vehicle must be equipped with two belt anchorages for lap belts, for the driver's seat and each forward-facing front seat. Nor do the requirements apply to coaches equipped with anchorage points for all exposed forward-facing seats, provided that they comply with Community Directives or ECE requirements or, in a case where the anchorage point forms part of the seat, do not when a horizontal force is applied to them become detached from the seat of which they form a part, before that seat becomes detached from the vehicle.

Seat belts

Regulation 47, which deals with seat belts, applies to all vehicles covered by the requirements of reg 46 in relation to anchorage points. Such vehicles first used before 1 April 1981 must have seat belts for the driver's seat and the specified passenger's seat. They must be of an approved type and, in respect of these vehicles, 'diagonal belts' are approved. Those first used on or after 1 April 1981 must be provided with three-point seat belts for both the driver's seat and the specified passenger's seat.

Every passenger vehicle, dual-purpose vehicle and all other vehicles fitted with anchorage points as required by reg 46 (other than minibuses, motor ambulances and motor caravans) which are first used on or after 1 April 1987 must additionally be fitted with a three-point belt, lap or disabled person's belt for every forward-facing front seat which is not a specified passenger's seat. Thus, the 'Transit' type of vehicle will be required to have seat belts for all three front seats. Such vehicles must also be fitted with rear seat belts for passengers sitting in the rear of the vehicle who are using a forward-facing seat. Rear seat belts must be provided as follows:

(a) vehicles with not more than two forward-facing seats behind the driver's seat must have *either* an inertia reel belt for *at least one* of those seats, *or* a three-point, lap, disabled person's, or child restraint belt for each of those seats;

(b) vehicles having more than two forward-facing seats behind the driver's seat must have either -
  (i) an inertia reel belt for one of those seats being an outboard seat, and a three-point, lap, disabled person's, or child restraint belt, for *at least one other* of those seats; or
  (ii) a three-point belt for one of those seats and either a child restraint or disabled person's belt for *at least one other* of those seats; or
  (iii) a three-point, lap, disabled person's, or child restraint belt for each of those seats.

The rear seat belt provisions become a little easier to understand if one imagines, in terms of providing an opportunity for all rear seat passengers to 'belt up', that an inertia reel will count as two in the case of a vehicle with only two rear seats, and that an inertia reel belt will count as two in the case of a vehicle with more than two rear seats.

With effect from 10 February 1997, the use of a coach or minibus for the purpose of carrying a group of three or more children in connection with an organised trip is prohibited by reg 48A unless the vehicle has at least as many forward-facing passenger seats as there are children, and each seat is fitted with seat belts. A disabled child in a wheelchair is disregarded for this purpose. For these purposes a child is a person who is three years or more but is under the age of 16.

Without prejudice to the generality of these requirements, a group of such children will be regarded as being on an organised trip if they are being carried to or from their school or from one part of their school premises to another.

Minibuses, motor ambulances and motor caravans first used on or after 1 October 1988 must have three-point belts for the driver's and specified passenger's seats and a three-point or lap belt for any other forward-facing front seat. Coaches equipped with anchorage points as required by reg 46 must have three-point, lap or disabled person's belts for every forward-facing front seat and every non-protected seat.

Where lap belts are fitted to a forward-facing seat of a minibus, motor ambulance or motor caravan or to an exposed forward-facing seat of a coach (other than the driver's seat) either the requirements of Annex 4 to ECE reg 21 must be met, or padding to a depth of not less than 50 mm must be provided on that part of the surface or edge of any bar or the top or edge of any screen or partition which would be likely to be struck by the head of a passenger wearing the lap belt in the event of an accident. Padding need not be provided on any surface more than one metre from the centre of the line of intersection of the seat cushion and the back rest, nor on the instrument panel of a minibus. The revised provisions concerning padding apply to vehicles registered from 7 September 1989 to after 7 September 1990. Such padding must extend for not less than 150 mm on either side of the central point of the seat. Thus, persons who may be thrown forward, and thereby come into contact with obstructions in front of them, are less likely to be seriously injured.

The requirements concerning the fitting of seat belts generally do not apply to vehicles being used under a trade licence or new vehicles in the course of delivery.

Maintenance of seat belts

It is an offence to fail to maintain seat belts and their anchorage points. Buckles must be maintained so that they can be readily fastened and unfastened, and they must be kept free of any obstruction which would prevent them from becoming readily accessible to a person using the seat. Each end of a seat belt must be securely fastened to its anchorage point and the webbing must be free of cuts and other visible faults likely to affect its performance under stress. Within 30 cm of a seat belt anchorage point, the load bearing members or panelling of the vehicle structure must be maintained in sound condition.

Wearing of seat belts

The circumstances in which seat belts must be worn by passengers in motor vehicles are now prescribed in the Motor Vehicles (Wearing of Seat Belts) Regulations 1993 and the Motor Vehicles (Wearing of Seat Belts by Children in Front Seats) Regulations 1993, and not by the Road Vehicles (Construction and Use) Regulations. The 1993 Regulations implement, inter alia, the requirements of Council Directive 91/671/EEC which only applies to vehicles of less than 3.5 tonnes with four or more wheels and a design speed of more than 25 kph. The Directive does not apply to passenger vehicles with more than eight passenger seats if they are designed to carry standing passengers. Vehicles within the scope of the Directive which have not more than eight seats in addition to the driver's seat are referred to in the Regulations as 'passenger cars'.

The offences committed by breaches of the Regulations are punishable under the Road Traffic Act 1988, ss 14 and 15, and not by the Road Traffic Act 1988, s 42 (unlike the other breaches in this part). The requirements created by the 1993 Regulations are not always confined to the description of vehicles set out in the Directive.

Front seat adult passengers Regulation 5 of the Motor Vehicles (Wearing of Seat Belts) Regulations 1993 requires that every person driving or riding in a front seat of a motor vehicle (other than a two-wheeled motorcycle with or without a sidecar) must wear an adult seat belt. The regulation does not apply to a person under the age of 14 years. Nor does it apply if no seat belt is provided for a driver, or is available for a front seat passenger. Failure to comply with reg 5 is an offence under the Road Traffic Act 1988, s 14(3).

Regulation 6 provides the following exemptions from the requirement to wear a seat belt made by reg 5:

(a) a person holding a medical certificate (including that of a EU member state to the effect that it is inadvisable for him to wear a seat belt);
(b) a person using a vehicle constructed or adapted for the delivery of goods or mail to consumers or addresses, while engaged in making local rounds of deliveries or collections;
(c) a person performing a manoeuvre which includes reversing;
(d) a qualified driver supervising a learner carrying out such a manoeuvre;
(e) a person undergoing a driving test where wearing a seat belt would endanger himself or another person;
(f) a person driving or riding in a vehicle being used for fire brigade or police purposes or for carrying a person in lawful custody (this includes the prisoner);
(g) the driver of a licensed taxi whilst being used to seek hire or answer a call, or when carrying a passenger for hire, or a private hire car whilst it is being used to carry a passenger for hire;
(h) a person in a vehicle being used under a trade licence for investigating or remedying a fault;
(j) a disabled person who is wearing a disabled person's belt; or
(k) a person riding in a vehicle whilst in a Crown procession.

In addition to (k), a person who is riding in a vehicle which is taking part in a procession which is held to mark or commemorate an event if either the procession is one commonly or customarily held in a police area or areas, or notice in respect of the procession has been given in accordance with the Public Order Act 1986, s 11 (see pp 623-624).

Rear seat adult passengers Regulation 5 of the Motor Vehicles (Wearing of Seat Belts) Regulations 1993 also prohibits an adult person (ie someone aged 14 or over) from riding in the rear seat of a motor car, or of a passenger car which is not a motor car, if he is not wearing an adult seat belt provided in the vehicle. Persons who fail to comply with the regulation offend against the Road Traffic Act 1988, s 14(3).

Front seat child passengers It is an offence contrary to the Road Traffic Act 1988, s 15(1) and (2) for a person, without reasonable excuse, to drive a motor vehicle on a road in which a child under 14 is in the front of that vehicle unless the child is wearing a seat belt in conformity with the Motor Vehicles (Wearing of Seat Belts by Children in Front Seats) Regulations 1993. Generally, it is irrelevant that a seat belt is not provided or available for the seat. The Regulations set out the rules with which a driver must conform. A 'front seat' is one which is wholly or partially in the front of the vehicle. The Regulations do not apply to two-wheeled motorcycles, with or without sidecars.

The description of the seat belts which satisfy the requirements of the Regulations is prescribed in reg 5:

(a)   in the case of a 'small child' travelling in a passenger car, light goods vehicle (not exceeding 3.5 tonnes), or a small bus (more than eight passenger seats but not exceeding 3.5 tonnes), the seat belt must be a child restraint with a marking required under the Road Vehicles (Construction and Use) Regulations 1986, reg 47(7) or a child restraint approved by another member state;

(b)   in the case of a 'small child' in any other vehicle, the seat belt must be a child restraint approved under reg 47(7);

(c)   in the case of a 'large child', the seat belt must be a child restraint approved under reg 47(7) or an adult belt.

A 'small child' is a child who is under 12 and under 150 cm in height, and a 'large child' is a child under 14 who is not a 'small child'.

Regulation 7 exempts from these provisions:

(a)   a 'small child' aged three or more if a prescribed seat belt is not available for him in the front or rear of the vehicle and he is wearing an adult belt;

(b)   a child for whom there is a medical certificate (including one issued in a EU member state that it is inadvisable for him to wear a seat belt);

(c)   a child under the age of one in a carry cot, provided that it is restrained by straps;

(d)   a disabled child who is wearing a disabled person's belt; or

(e)   a child riding in a motor car first used before 1 January 1965 if -
   (i)   the vehicle has no rear seat; and
   (ii)   apart from the driver's seat, no seat in the vehicle is provided with a seat belt which is appropriate for that child.

In addition, the prohibition created by s 15 does not apply in relation to a child riding in a vehicle which is being used to provide a local service within the meaning of the Transport Act 1985 (see p 325) and is neither a motor car nor a passenger car. The prohibition does not apply in relation to a 'large child' if no appropriate seat belt is available for him in the front of the vehicle.

Rear seat child passengers The Road Traffic Act 1988, s 15(3) and (3A) makes it an offence for a person, without reasonable excuse, to drive a motor vehicle on a road if there is a child of under 14 in the rear of it who is not wearing a seat belt fitted there or, in the case of a 'small child', if there is no rear seat belt and there is an unoccupied seat in the front which is fitted with an appropriate seat belt. Exemption from these requirements is provided by the Motor Vehicles (Wearing of Seat Belts) Regulation 1993, reg 10. An offence is not committed where the motor vehicle is neither a motor car not a passenger car or where the vehicle is a licensed taxi or licensed hire car in which (in each case) the rear seats are separated from the driver by a fixed partition. Further exemptions are provided by reg 10:

(a)   where a seat belt of a description prescribed by reg 8 (ie, an approved child restraint) is not available to a 'small child' aged three or more in the front or rear of the vehicle and he is wearing an adult seat belt;

(b) where the child holds a medical certificate (including that of a EU member state to the effect that it is inadvisable for him to wear a seat belt);

(c) where a child under the age of one is being carried in a carry cot, provided that it is restrained by straps; and

(d) where a disabled child is wearing a disabled person's belt.

The prohibition against the carriage of a child in the rear of a vehicle who is not wearing a seat belt does not apply in relation to a 'small child' in a passenger car if no appropriate seat belt is available to him in the front or rear of the vehicle. Nor does it apply to such a child in the rear of a vehicle other than a passenger car in such circumstances. There is also an exemption in favour of a 'large child' where, in any vehicle, no appropriate seat belt is available to him.

'Availability' of seat belts Schedule 2 to the 1993 Regulations describes the circumstances in which a seat belt will be regarded as not being available. They are where:

(a) another person is wearing the relevant belt;

(b) a child is occupying the relevant seat and wearing a child restraint which is an appropriate child restraint for that child and this renders use of the seat belt impracticable;

(c) a person holding a medical certificate is occupying the relevant seat;

(d) a disabled person (not being the person in question) is occupying the relevant seat and wearing a disabled person's belt and this renders use of the seat belt impracticable;

(e) by reason of his disability, it would not be practicable for the person in question to wear the relevant belt;

(f) the seat is occupied by a carry cot containing a child under one and that cot is secured by straps and it would not be practicable to carry the cot, suitably restrained, elsewhere;

(g) the person in question is prevented from occupying the relevant seat by the presence of a child restraint which could not readily be removed without the aid of tools; or

(h) the relevant seat is so designed that it can be adjusted to increase the space available for goods and effects and when it is so adjusted the seat cannot be used.

Speedometer

The Construction and Use Regulations, reg 35 provides that every motor vehicle must be fitted with a speedometer. It is unlikely that a revolution counter would be accepted by a court as a form of speedometer as it does not readily indicate speed since the needle reading needs to be converted into miles per hour, and the gear in which the vehicle is being driven affects that conversion. Regulation 35 also provides that speedometers fitted to vehicles first used after 1 April 1984 must indicate speed in both miles per hour and kilometres per hour; otherwise the indication given by a speedometer may be either in miles per hour or kilometres per hour. Instead of complying with reg 35, a vehicle may comply with the relevant Community directive or ECE regulations.

The provisions of reg 35 do not apply to a vehicle marked with a marking designated as a type approval mark. There are two types of approval marks in respect of speedometers, one for the traditional type of speedometer and one for speed recording equipment in tachographs. The importance of this is that failure to maintain a tachograph speedometer is an offence against the Transport Act 1968, s 97 if it is compulsorily fitted under the provisions of the Act. However, this will not usually be of concern to police officers since tachograph speedometers will be in addition to the ordinary instrument as they are unlikely readily to indicate speed to the driver.

Other vehicles exempt from the need to have speedometers fitted are:

(a) invalid carriages, motorcycles not exceeding 100 cc, and works trucks (provided in each case they were first used before 1 April 1984);
(b) agricultural vehicles which are not driven at more than 20 mph;
(c) vehicles which legally or physically cannot exceed 25 mph; and
(d) those which have an alternative type approved instrument.

Vehicles first used before 1 October 1937 are also exempt.

Regulation 36 requires that a speedometer must be kept free from any obstruction which might prevent its being easily read and must at all times be maintained in good working order. On a charge involving a breach of this requirement, it is a defence to prove that the defect occurred in the course of the journey being then undertaken or that steps had already been taken to have repairs or replacements effected as soon as possible. These defences cover so many possibilities, and if alleged are so hard to disprove, that enforcement is almost limited to admitted long standing defects in respect of which no repairs have been arranged or when the instrument registers incorrectly.

Speed limiters on motor vehicles

The Road Vehicles (Construction and Use) Regulations 1986, regs 36A, 36B and 70A set out those vehicles which are required to be fitted with speed limiters and deal with the requirement to fix plates on such vehicles showing the speed at which the limiter has been set.

Regulation 36A (coaches and buses)

(a) Every coach first used on or after 1 April 1974 and before 1 January 1988, which would, without the fitting of speed limiter, be capable of exceeding 112.65 kp/h, must be fitted with a speed limiter calibrated to a set speed not exceeding 112.65 kp/h.
(b) Every bus first used on or after 1 January 1988, which has a maximum gross weight exceeding 7.5 tonnes and which would, without the fitting of a speed limiter, be capable of exceeding 100 kp/h, must be fitted with a speed limiter calibrated to a set speed not exceeding 100 kp/h. (Until 1 July 1999, in relation to vehicles used exclusively for transport operations in the United Kingdom and first used before 1 July 1998, the references to 100 km/h have effect as if they were references to 105 kp/h).

Speed limiters which are fitted to such vehicles must be sealed by an authorised sealer in such a manner as to protect the limiter against any improper interference or adjustment and against any interference of its power supply and must be maintained in good and efficient working order. In the case of limiters fitted before 1 August 1992 to vehicles first used before that date and those sealed outside the United Kingdom, the requirement that this must be done by an authorised sealer does not apply. Limiters fitted to coaches described at (a) above and fitted to buses described at (b) above before 1 October 1994 must comply with Part I of the British Standard or the Annexes to Community Directive 92/24. Those fitted after that date to such vehicles must comply with Community Directive 92/24. However, these requirements do not apply to limiters fitted before 1 January 1988, nor where there is compliance with an equivalent standard.

The provisions of the regulation do not apply to vehicles being taken to a place where a speed limiter is to be installed, calibrated, replaced or repaired, or where the vehicle is completing a journey in the course of which the speed limiter has accidentally ceased to function.

Regulation 36B (goods vehicles)

(a)   Good vehicles of a maximum gross weight exceeding 7,500 kg but not exceeding 12,000 kg and first used on or after 1 August 1992, which would, without the fitting of a speed limiter, be capable of exceeding a maximum speed of 60 mph, must be fitted with a speed limiter calibrated to a set speed not exceeding 60 mph.
(b)   Goods vehicles of a maximum gross weight exceeding 12,000 kg, which are first used on or after 1 January 1988 and which would, without the fitting of a speed limiter, be capable of a maximum speed exceeding 56 mph, must be fitted with a speed limiter set at a speed not exceeding 85 kph and the stabilised speed of the vehicle must not exceed 90 kph. (Where the construction of the vehicle and its equipment has resulted in a stabilised speed of 90 kph while the limiter is set at this level, this is permissible).

The provisions of reg 36B do not apply to a vehicle which:

(a)   is being taken to a place where a speed limiter is to be installed, calibrated, repaired or replaced;
(b)   is completing a journey in the course of which the speed limiter has accidentally ceased to function;
(c)   is owned by the Secretary of State for Defence and used for such purposes or is so used by a person for the time being subject to the orders of a member of the armed forces of the Crown;
(d)   is used for fire brigade, ambulance or police purposes; or
(e)   when it is being used on a public road during any calendar week, is being used only in passing from land in a person's occupation to other land in his occupation, and it has not been used on a public road for distances exceeding an aggregate of six miles in that calendar week.

Regulation 70A (plates)

Regulation 70A provides the plating requirements in respect of all such vehicles. All vehicles to which reg 36A or 36B apply must be equipped with a plate which is in a conspicuous position in the driving compartment of the vehicle and is clearly and indelibly marked with the speed at which the speed limiter has been set.

Mirrors

With certain exceptions, every passenger vehicle, goods vehicle or dual-purpose vehicle first used on or after 1 June 1978 must be equipped with an interior rear view mirror and at least one exterior rear view mirror fitted to the offside of the vehicle. If for any reason the interior rear view mirror does not provide an adequate view to the rear, the vehicle must also have an exterior rear view mirror fitted to the nearside of the vehicle. In effect, this means that, when the internal mirror is obscured, the driver commits no offence if there are external mirrors on each side.

Two-wheeled motorcycles remain 'excepted vehicles' from the regulations relating to mirrors and therefore do not require any rear view mirrors. However, if mirrors are fitted to motorcycles first used on or after 1 October 1978, they must comply with the standards set out in the regulations. There are other types of 'excepted vehicles'. These include motor vehicles which are drawing trailers upon which there is some person who can communicate to the driver the intentions of other vehicles to the rear, works trucks with a clear view to the rear, pedestrian-controlled vehicles, and chassis being driven to a body plant.

Locomotives or motor tractors first used on or after 1 June 1978, agricultural motor vehicles not exceeding 7,370 kg unladen weight, agricultural motor vehicles first used after 1 June 1986 which are not driven at more than 20 mph, and some works trucks require only one mirror which must be fitted on the offside.

Vehicles first used before 1 June 1978 are subject to different requirements, as follows. Passenger vehicles adapted to carry more than eight seated passengers exclusive of the driver, goods vehicles and dual-purpose vehicles (except locomotives and motor tractors) must be fitted with at least two mirrors; one externally fitted on the offside, and the other internally or on the nearside externally. The remainder of vehicles (and this includes saloon cars) require only one mirror fitted either internally or externally in such a way that the driver can become aware of traffic to the rear.

In the case of vehicles first used on or after 1 June 1978, mirrors must be fitted in such a way that they remain steady under normal driving conditions; each exterior mirror must be visible to the driver from his driving position, either through a side window or through the area of the windscreen swept by a wiper blade. Interior mirrors and those fitted to the offside must be capable of adjustment by the driver from his driving position (except where the exterior mirror is a 'spring back' type). However, this does not prevent an exterior mirror being locked in position from the outside of the vehicle. In cases where the bottom edge of an exterior mirror is less than 2 m from the road surface when the vehicle is laden, the projection must not exceed 20 cm. If the vehicle is drawing a trailer which is wider than the towing vehicle, the projection of a mirror must not exceed the trailer width by more than 20 cm.

Instead of complying with the above requirements, a vehicle may comply with the relevant Community directive.

Windscreen wipers and washers

By reg 34(1), all vehicles which are fitted with windscreens must be fitted with one or more efficient automatic windscreen wipers, unless the driver can obtain an adequate view to the front without looking through the windscreen, for example by opening the windscreen or looking over it (as is the case with 'wind open' screens and those which fold downwards, which are features of many cars produced before the 1950s).

The wipers fitted must be capable of clearing the windscreen so that the driver has an adequate view of the road in front of both sides of the vehicle and to the front of the vehicle.

Regulation 34(6), which deals with maintenance, demands that every windscreen wiper required by the Regulations to be fitted must, at all times while the vehicle is used on a road, be maintained in good and efficient working order and be properly adjusted. As we have stated, reg 34 demands one or more wipers. If the driver's wiper provides the view ahead and to both sides required by that regulation, any other wiper is not subject to the maintenance requirement.

By reg 34(2), a windscreen washer must be fitted to any vehicle which requires one or more automatic wipers, except an agricultural motor vehicle (other than one first used on or after 1 June 1986 and driven at more than 20 mph), a track-laying vehicle, a vehicle incapable of exceeding 20 mph, or vehicles being used to provide a local bus service. The washer must be such that, in conjunction with the wipers, it is capable of cleaning the area of the windscreen swept by the blades of mud or similar deposits.

In the alternative to the above requirement, a vehicle may comply with the relevant Community directive.

Audible warning instrument

The following provisions are made by reg 37. All motor vehicles, which have a maximum speed of more than 20 mph, must be fitted with a horn but, in the case of an agricultural motor vehicle, only if it is being driven at more than 20 mph. In the case of motor vehicles first used on or after 1 August 1973 the sound emitted by any horn must be continuous and uniform and not strident. This is to ensure that the horns of such vehicles give a sound which is not offensive to the ear. With the exception of emergency vehicles, no motor vehicle may be fitted with a bell, gong, siren or two-tone horn, with the result that horns which play snatches of tunes, such as 'Colonel Bogey' are prohibited. However, vehicles may be fitted with an instrument or apparatus (not being a two-toned horn) to give a sound informing the public that goods are for sale from the vehicle; consequently, ice-cream chimes etc are not prohibited.

The rule against fitting gongs etc does not apply to an anti-theft device nor to an alarm to summon help to a public service vehicle. An anti-theft device must be fitted with a cut-out limiting its use to five minutes.

Where a horn can operate as an anti-theft device, a cut-out must be fitted if the motor vehicle was first used on or after 1 October 1982.

Regulation 37 permits the fitting of 'reversing alarms' to vehicles. These are devices to warn persons that the vehicle is reversing or about to reverse. Such a device is exempted from the requirement that the sound of a warning instrument shall be continuous and uniform but they must not be strident. Such alarms may be fitted to goods vehicles with a maximum gross weight not less than 2,000 kg, buses, engineering plant, refuse vehicles and works trucks. The sound emitted must be such that it is not likely to be confused with the sound emitted from a pedestrian crossing. A reversing alarm may only be used on a stationary vehicle if the vehicle's engine is running and it is about to move backwards or the vehicle is in danger from another moving vehicle.

Horns and other audible warning instruments must be maintained in good and efficient working order at all times.

Instead of complying with the provisions mentioned above concerning the nature and maintenance of audible warning instruments, a vehicle may comply with the relevant Community directive or ECE regulation.

Regulation 99 provides that no person shall sound, or cause or permit to be sounded, the horn or other audible warning device of a motor vehicle when it is stationary on a road at any time. The only exception is when there is danger due to another moving vehicle on or near the road. In addition, it provides that no person shall sound, or cause or permit to be sounded, in a vehicle in motion on a restricted road, a horn etc, between 23.30 hours and 07.00 hours on the following day. This does not, of course, apply to anti-theft alarms or reversing devices. Instruments to advise the public of goods for sale from a vehicle must only be used for that purpose and must not be used between 19.00 hours and 12.00 hours on the following day.

Silencers

Regulation 54 requires that every vehicle propelled by an internal combustion engine must be fitted with an exhaust system including a silencer and that the exhaust gases from the engine must not escape into the atmosphere without first passing through its silencer. Specified noise levels are prescribed but they are directed at the manufacturers. Police officers detect faulty silencers by the nature of the sound emitted which indicates that the exhaust gases are escaping into the atmosphere without first passing through a silencer. This will occur where there is a break or large hole in the pipe. Instead of complying with the above provisions, a vehicle may comply with the relevant Community directive.

Alterations or replacements to exhaust systems are not permitted if they have the effect of increasing the noise.

Although not directly concerned with silencers, regs 97 and 98 also deal with noise. The first provision prohibits the use etc of a motor vehicle in a manner so as to cause excessive noise which could reasonably have been avoided by the driver. The second requires the driver of a stationary vehicle to stop the action of machinery attached to it, or forming part of the vehicle, so far as may be necessary for the prevention of noise or of exhaust emissions.

Wings

Regulation 63 requires that the following motor vehicles be fitted with wings or the like:

(a)   invalid carriages;
(b)   heavy motor cars, motor cars and motorcycles, not being agricultural motor vehicles or pedestrian-controlled vehicles;
(c)   agricultural motor vehicles driven at more than 20 mph; and
(d)   trailers.

Works trucks, unfinished vehicles, living vans, and some agricultural trailed appliances are exempt from the need to be fitted with wings as are the rear wheels of the motor vehicle part of an articulated vehicle whose trailer is used only in connection with the carriage of round timber. Otherwise motor vehicles must be equipped with wings or similar fittings to catch, as far as practicable, mud or water thrown up by the wheels. The provisions in relation to trailers are restricted to the rear wheels, if the trailer has more than two wheels. Instead of complying with these provisions, a vehicle may comply with the relevant Community directive.

Dangerous vehicles

Regulation 100(1) requires that a motor vehicle, every trailer and all parts and accessories of such vehicle or trailer must at all times be in such a condition that no danger is caused or is likely to be caused to any person in or on the vehicle or trailer or on a road. The provision is concerned with danger, and a distant possibility of such danger is not enough. For example, in a case where the radiator grille was missing, the court would not accept that sufficient danger existed of persons coming into contact with the revolving fan blades, because the engine was transverse. It might have been different had the fan blades been at the front of the engine. The provision applies to a vehicle which in its manufactured condition is inherently likely to cause danger to other road users, as well as to vehicles which have become dangerous through lack of maintenance. In relation to the requirement that all parts and accessories must be in such condition that no danger is caused, it is immaterial that parts may be in reasonable condition if they are dangerous because they are not in working order. In a case where a tow bar was in good condition, but the trailer was incorrectly coupled, the user of the vehicle was guilty of using it in a dangerous condition. Separate and distinct offences are involved in using a defective motor vehicle and a defective trailer on a road. This equally applies to articulated vehicles.

Regulation 100(1) also requires that the number of passengers carried, or the manner of their carriage, is such that no danger is caused or is likely to be caused to any person in or on the vehicle or trailer or on a road. Regulation 100(1) also requires that the weight, packing, distribution and adjustment of a load is such that no such danger is caused, or likely to be caused.

As can be seen, by reg 100(1), there are three quite separate and distinct prohibitions contained within the paragraph. The second prohibition is concerned with too many passengers. In one case, where a small four-seater car had been carrying eight passengers, it was found that this caused danger, in that it caused the vehicle to steer badly at all but low speeds. The third prohibition is really aimed at a badly loaded vehicle; insecure loads are dealt with by reg 100(2).

Regulation 100(2) requires that the load carried by a motor vehicle or trailer must at all times be so secured, if necessary by physical restraint other than its own weight, and be in such a position, that neither danger nor nuisance is likely to be caused to any person or property by reason of the load or any part of it falling or being blown from the vehicle or by reason of any other movement of the load or a part of it. In effect, this paragraph deals with insecure loads which for any reason cause danger or nuisance. It is necessary to specify which of these alternatives resulted from the insecurity of the load. Where a substantial part of a solid load falls on to a busy road there is little doubt that danger is caused. In circumstances where a goods vehicle loaded with gravel sheds part of its load steadily into the path of following traffic, there is no doubt that there is a breach of the requirements so to secure the load that no nuisance to persons or property is likely.

In considering whether a load has been adequately secured so that neither danger nor nuisance is likely to be caused one has to consider four things:

(a) the nature of the journey,
(b) the way in which the load was secured,
(c) the way in which the load was positioned, and
(d) the journey to be taken.

What might be secure for one journey in fine weather and on good roads might not be secure for another journey in poor weather and on less good roads. In applying the above test consideration must be given to the route taken. Thus, if the load is a high one, and too high to go under a bridge on the route, so that it is inevitable that the load will be knocked off, the load will not have been so secured that neither danger nor nuisance was likely.

Regulation 100(3) prohibits the use of a motor vehicle or trailer for any purpose for which it is so unsuitable as to cause danger or nuisance to any person on the vehicle, trailer, or on a road. The crucial question is whether the vehicle or trailer was unsuitable. If it is not properly loaded and it is the load which causes the danger or nuisance, this does not affect the suitability of the vehicle itself. In a case where an excavator which was loaded on to a trailer struck a bridge, it was held that the trailer did not become unsuitable when it was so loaded. It was the manner of the loading which was at fault.

Reference has already been made on pp 256-257 to the offences under the Road Traffic Act 1988, s 40A of using, causing or permitting the use of a motor vehicle or trailer which is in a dangerous condition because of the condition of the vehicle's accessories or equipment, the purpose of its use, the number of passengers carried or the manner of their carriage and the weight, or the distribution and security of the load etc. It is submitted that most offences involving dangerous vehicles will now be charged under the Road Traffic Act 1988, s 40A and not under s 42, since a conviction of an offence under s 40A involves the risk of discretionary disqualification and requires the obligatory endorsement of 3 penalty points. Where there is a conviction under s 42 of the 1988 Act for a breach of reg 100 there can be no disqualification or endorsement of the offender's driving licence.

It may be that reg 100(1) will subsequently be revoked. Some aspects of reg 100(2) and (3) have also been overtaken by the arrival of s 40A as they also deal with elements related to danger being caused to persons in consequence of the user of the motor vehicle, or trailer in the manner prohibited by s 40A. It may be, therefore, that reg 100(2) and (3) will be amended to restrict the prohibition created to those acts which result in nuisance only. This can be achieved by removing the word 'danger' from both of these paragraphs. At the time of writing, no such amendments have been made.

Maintenance of glass

All glass or other transparent material fitted to motor vehicles is required, by reg 30, to be maintained in such condition that it does not obscure the vision of the driver while the vehicle is being driven on a road. This regulation is not limited to the windscreen but applies to all glass affecting the driver's vision, such as the rear window and side windows through which he needs to look.

Maintenance of petrol tank

By reg 39, a petrol tank on a motor vehicle first used on or after 1 July 1973 must be reasonably secure from damage, and leakage from it must be adequately prevented (except that this does not prevent a tank being fitted with a pressure release valve). Instead of complying with these requirements, a vehicle may comply with the corresponding requirements contained in EC directives and regulations.

Maintenance of tyres

Regulation 27 prohibits the use, on a road of any motor vehicle or trailer, a wheel of which is fitted with a pneumatic tyre, if:

(a) the tyre is unsuitable for the use to which the vehicle or trailer is being put or to the type of tyres fitted to its other wheels;

(b) it is wrongly inflated for such use;
(c) it has a cut in excess of 25 mm or 10% of the section width of the tyre, whichever is the greater, measured in any direction on the outside of the tyre and deep enough to reach the ply or cords;
(d) it has a lump, bulge or tear caused by separation or partial failure of its structure;
(e) it has a portion of the ply or cord exposed;
(f) the tyre is not maintained in such condition as to be fit for the use to which the vehicle or trailer is being put or has a defect which might in any way cause damage to the surface of the road or damage to persons on or in the vehicle or to other persons using the road.

Also prohibited is the use on a road of:

(a) a passenger vehicle, other than a motorcycle, constructed or adapted to carry no more than eight seated passengers in addition to the driver;
(b) a goods vehicle with a maximum gross weight which does not exceed 3,500 kg; and
(c) a light trailer not falling within (b);

where a pneumatic tyre on a wheel does not have in grooves of the tread pattern a depth of at least 1.6 mm throughout a continuous band comprising the central three-quarters of the breadth of the tyre and round the entire circumference of the tyre. There are special provisions for tyres on a vehicle first used before 3 January 1933.

In relation to large goods vehicles, motorcycles and other vehicles not included above, their use on a road is prohibited if a wheel is fitted with a pneumatic tyre and:

(a) the base of any groove which showed in the original tread pattern of the tyre is not clearly visible; or
(b) either it does not have a depth of 1 mm in the grooves of the tread pattern throughout a continuous band measuring at least three-quarters of the breadth of the tyre and round its entire circumference; or, if the grooves of the original tread pattern of the tyre did not extend beyond three-quarters of the breadth of the tread, any groove which showed in the original tread pattern does not have a depth of at least 1 mm.

As can be seen, all forms of damage to tyres which may result in danger are covered by this regulation. Potential danger is, of course, the reason for the requirement that the contact area of a tyre must have visible tread which must be at least 1.6 mm or (as the case may be) 1 mm deep for three quarters of that contact area (subject to special provisions which apply to special tyres with narrow contact areas).

Regulation 27(2) makes special provision to allow for the use of tyres designed to be used safely when deflated. There are general exemptions in favour of agricultural trailed appliances, agricultural motor vehicles not driven at more than 20 mph and broken-down vehicles being towed at a speed not exceeding 20 mph. The tread pattern and minimum depth of tread provisions do not apply to three-wheelers not exceeding 102 kg with a maximum possible speed of 12 mph or less, nor to pedestrian-controlled works trucks. In addition, the minimum depth of tread provisions do not apply to motorcycles under 50 cc.

Regulation 27(5) prohibits a person using, or causing or permitting to be used, a motor vehicle on a road with a recut pneumatic tyre if its ply or cord has been cut or exposed in the process of recutting. Heavy duty tyres fitted to goods vehicles can usually be recut without causing danger, but tyres fitted to saloon cars do not usually have sufficient thickness of rubber to accept the process.

Special provision is made by reg 27(3) to allow passenger vehicles (not buses) to fit a temporary-use spare tyre, provided the vehicle does not exceed 50 mph.

Mixture of tyres

Regulation 26(1) provides that pneumatic tyres of different types of construction must not be fitted to the same axle of a vehicle. The regulation mentions three types of tyres:

(a) diagonal-ply tyres, which are commonly known as cross-ply tyres;
(b) bias-belted tyres, which are as above but have a reinforcing band around the outer circumference of the tyre under the tread, but on top of the cords; or
(c) radial-ply tyres.

Regulation 26(2) also provides that a motor vehicle, having only two axles must not be fitted with the following combinations of tyres:

(a) cross-plys or bias-belted tyres on the rear axle and radials on the front; or
(b) cross-ply on the rear axle and bias-belted on the front.

This regulation is designed to prevent a gripping tyre from being fitted to the 'steering' wheels, whilst a tyre which is not so stable is fitted to the rear.

Not to emit smoke etc

Regulation 61 provides that no person shall use, or cause or permit to be used, on a road a motor vehicle from which is emitted any smoke, visible vapour, grit, sparks or oily substance which causes, or is likely to cause, damage to property or injury or danger to any person who is, or who may reasonably be expected to be, on the road. This could occur where oil spillage made the road unsafe or fumes badly affected visibility.

This regulation also provides that a vehicle must be maintained so as not to emit any avoidable smoke or avoidable visible vapour.

DUTIES OF DRIVERS AND OTHERS

Position to retain proper view and control

Regulation 104 provides that a driver must at all times be in such a position that he retains full control and has a full view of the road and traffic ahead. A man who drove with a sheepdog on his lap has been held to be in breach of this provision.

Reversing

By reg 106, no person shall drive, or cause or permit to be driven, a motor vehicle backwards on a road further than may be requisite for the safety or reasonable convenience of the occupants of the vehicle or other traffic.

Unnecessary obstruction

Regulation 103 provides that a person in charge of a motor vehicle or trailer must not cause or permit it to stand on a road so as to cause any unnecessary obstruction. The various exemptions within local no-waiting orders in favour of goods vehicles which are loading or unloading has led to a belief by some van drivers that they may double park and even completely block roads for these purposes. This is not so. Any unreasonable use of the road which leads to the obstruction of other road users is an offence against this regulation. An obstruction can be caused by taking up so much of the road that normal two-way traffic is reduced to a one-way flow. In considering whether a particular use was reasonable or unreasonable, a court will apply its mind to the facts, including the duration of the obstruction, the nature of the place where it occurred, the purpose for which the vehicle was there and the *actual* (as opposed to potential) obstruction caused.

Parking facing the wrong way at night

Regulation 101 provides that, except with the permission of a uniformed police officer, a person must not cause or permit a motor vehicle to stand on a road between sunset and sunrise otherwise than with the left or nearside of the vehicle as close as may be to the edge of the carriageway.

The exemptions from this prohibition are predictable: vehicles being used for fire, police or ambulance purposes; taxi stands and bus stops; one-way streets; emergency operations etc. This regulation is not concerned in any respect with lighting requirements: it prohibits vehicles facing the wrong way at night because of the confusion which can be caused by the lights of other vehicles picking out reflective glass in circumstances which might cause the driver to fear that another vehicle is coming towards him on his side of the road. If lights are not displayed in a place where parking lights are required to be shown, then two offences are committed.

Stopping engine and setting parking brake

Regulation 107 provides that no person shall leave, or cause or permit to be left, on a road any motor vehicle which is not attended by a person duly licensed to drive it, unless the engine has been stopped and the parking brake effectively set. The exceptions include a vehicle being used for fire brigade, police or ambulance purposes and special vehicles which use their engines for particular operations other than the driving of the vehicle. Although there is a requirement to do two things, that is stop the engine and set the handbrake, the failure to carry out either of these operations completes the offence under the Road Traffic Act 1988, s 42.

Opening of doors

Regulation 105 provides that no person shall open, or cause or permit to be opened, the door of a motor vehicle on a road so as to cause injury or danger to any person. Breach of this regulation can be committed by anyone – a driver, a passenger or any other person who opens the door of a vehicle. It is not necessary to prove negligence: if the action causes injury or danger that is sufficient.

Trailers

Regulation 86 provides that, where a motor vehicle is drawing a trailer by means of a rope or chain, the length of the rope or chain must not exceed 4.5 m, and must not exceed 1.5 m unless the rope or chain is made clearly visible to other road users within a reasonable distance from either side.

Regulation 86A provides that trailers to which reg 15 (p 260 above) applies, which are not fitted with an automatic stopping device operative in the event of separation, must not be used on a road unless a secondary coupling is attached to the drawing vehicle and its trailer in such a way that, in the event of separation, the drawbar of the trailer would be prevented from touching the ground and there would be some residual steering of the trailer.

Trailers to which reg 15 applies which are fitted with a device which is designed to stop the trailer automatically in the event of separation must not be used on a road unless the secondary coupling is properly attached to the drawing vehicle and trailer.

Trailers which are living vans and have less than four wheels (or have two close-coupled wheels on each side) are prohibited by reg 90 from being used for the carriage of passengers. The only exception is in favour of testing, when a repairer etc may be carried in the van for that purpose.

Regulation 83 limits the number of trailers which may be drawn by a motor vehicle on a road. It limits locomotives to a maximum of three trailers, motor tractors to one laden trailer or two unladen trailers, and heavy motor cars and motor cars to one trailer. For the purposes of reg 83, a vehicle drawn by a steam powered vehicle and which is used solely to carry water for the purpose of the drawing vehicle is not a trailer. For the definition of 'locomotive', 'motor tractor', 'heavy motor car' and 'motor car', see p 253.

Miscellaneous

Regulation 53 provides that mascots, emblems, or other ornamental objects fitted to vehicles first used on or after 1 October 1937 must not be in such a position that they are likely to strike persons with whom the vehicle may collide unless the nature of the mascot is such that injury is not liable to be caused. Regulation 109 provides that no person shall drive, or cause or permit to be driven, a motor vehicle on a road if the driver is in such a position as to be able to see, whether directly or by reflection, a television receiving apparatus or other cinematographic apparatus used to display anything other than information concerning the vehicle or its journey.

CYCLES

Use of motorcycles

The Road Traffic Act 1988, s 23 restricts the carriage of passengers on a motor bicycle to one person who must be carried sitting astride the cycle on a proper seat securely fixed to the vehicle behind the driver's seat. Interestingly, a pillion passenger need not be carried facing the front. The driver commits an offence if a passenger is carried in contravention of this section. The Road Vehicle (Construction and Use) Regulations 1986, reg 102 prohibits the carriage of a passenger on a motor bicycle (whether it has a sidecar attached to it or not) on which there are not available suitable supports or rests for the feet for him.

The Road Traffic Act 1988, s 16 empowers the Secretary of State to make regulations requiring persons driving or riding on a specified type of motorcycle (other than in a sidecar) which is on a road to wear protective headgear. The type of headgear is prescribed by the Motorcycle (Protective Helmets) Regulations 1998. For the purpose of these Regulations, 'motorcycle' means a motor bicycle, including one with a sidecar, and motor tricycles where the paired wheels are less than 460 mm apart. The Regulations do not apply to mowing machines, motorcycles being propelled by a person on foot, or followers of the Sikh religion while wearing a turban. Helmets must comply with various British Standard or EEA specifications. Breach of the Regulations is an offence contrary to s 17 of the Road Traffic Act 1988. However, there is no offence of aiding and abetting the failure to wear a crash helmet, unless the other party is under 16 years of age.

By virtue of the Road Traffic Act 1988, s 18 it is an offence to drive or ride on a motorcycle without wearing eye protectors of the type prescribed by the Motor cycles (Eye Protectors) Regulations 1985. For the purposes of s 18, the Regulations define 'motorcycle' in the same way as in relation to protective helmets. The present requirement does not apply to a person driving or riding on a mowing machine, motorcycles being propelled on foot and a motorcycle temporarily brought into Great Britain by a foreign resident, which has been here for less than one year.

Use of pedal cycles

By the Road Traffic Act 1988, s 24, the carriage of more than one person on a road on a bicycle not propelled by mechanical power is an offence by each of the persons carried, unless it is *constructed* or *adapted* for the carriage of more than one person. A tandem is a cycle *constructed* for the carriage of more than one person, and cycles which have a seat fitted to permit the carriage of a child have been *adapted* for the carriage of more than one person. Whether an attachment to a cycle amounts to an adaptation can be resolved by the question, 'If the vehicle had been originally produced in this form, would it have been produced for the carriage of two persons?'

The wilful riding of a pedal cycle on a footpath or causeway by the side of any road made or set apart for the use or accommodation of foot passengers remains an offence contrary to the Highway Act 1835, s 72. A person rides a cycle, even if he merely sits astride it and propels himself with his feet.

Races or speed trials

The Road Traffic Act 1988, s 31 provides that a person who promotes or takes part in a race or speed trial for pedal cycles on a highway commits an offence, unless that race or speed trial is authorised under, and conducted in accordance with, the Cycle Racing on Highways Regulations 1960. Time trials and bicycle races are dealt with separately by the Regulations.

For a time trial or bicycle race to be authorised, a promoter must in either case give 28 days' written notice to the police, giving times, dates, routes, start, finish, maximum number taking part, arrangements for marshalling and supervision, and the rules of the competition.

Regulation 2 defines 'time trials' as a cycle race or trial of speed involving either single competitors or groups of not more than four competitors, starting at intervals of not less than one minute. In the case of groups they must not compete against one another. The result must depend upon the time taken by a competitor, or if a group any member of it, to reach a finishing point; or on the distance covered in a fixed time.

A 'bicycle race' is defined by reg 2 as a race or trial of speed which is not a time trial. In order for it to be authorised, the following additional requirements must be satisfied. The numbers taking part are restricted to, in not more than two races a year selected by the British Cycling Federation, 100 competitors, and, in any other approved race, 80. Races must not take place during the hours of darkness. If they follow a circuitous route, they must travel at least 10 miles before passing the same point on a highway twice (in whichever direction). No continuous part of the race may be on more than one and a half miles of any road subject to a speed limit of 40 mph or less, and no further continuous part in a 40 mph restricted section may be within three miles of the previous one. A chief officer of police is empowered to make directions as to traffic movement and routes, including the closure of sections of roadway on such occasions.

The Road Traffic (Special Events) Act 1994 permits traffic authorities to make temporary orders restricting/prohibiting traffic in connection with special events or entertainments on a road.

Electrically assisted pedal cycles

An 'electrically assisted pedal cycle' is not a motor vehicle for the purpose of the Road Traffic Acts; such a cycle is a pedal cycle which has a kerbside weight not exceeding 40 kg, or if a tandem 60 kg, is fitted with pedals, has an electric motor of rated output not exceeding 0.2 kilowatts (0.25 kw in the case of a tandem), and is incapable of propelling the vehicle when it is travelling at more than 15 mph. In other words, it is basically a pedal cycle with an auxiliary electric motor which cuts out when the vehicle is travelling in excess of 15 mph.

The Pedal Cycles (Construction and Use) Regulations 1983 require such pedal cycles to have a plate showing, inter alia, the continuous rated output of the motor. The battery must not leak so as to be a source of danger and the cycle must be fitted with a device, biased to the off position, which switches on the motor.

Electrically assisted pedal cycles (of which the best known example is the Sinclair C5) may be driven by anyone aged 14 or over. Unlike motor vehicles, their use does not require an excise licence or insurance. Nor do the requirements of testing, driving licences and protective headgear apply.

Brakes on cycles

The Pedal Cycles (Construction and Use) Regulations 1983, which are made under the Road Traffic Act 1988, s 81, deal with the fitting and maintenance of brakes on pedal cycles and with matters affecting electrically assisted pedal cycles generally. The regulations also refer to fixed wheel and free wheel cycles, and these are defined as follows. Fixed wheel cycles are those so constructed that one or more of the wheels is incapable of rotating independently of the pedals. Free wheel cycles are those which are not so constructed.

Regulation 4 provides that no person shall ride, or cause or permit to be ridden, on a road an electrically assisted pedal cycle unless it is fitted with braking systems which comply with cl 6 of the 1981 British Standard. Regulation 5 prohibits a person from riding, or causing or permitting to be ridden, on a road such a cycle when the brakes have not been maintained in efficient working order.

The braking systems of pedal cycles which are not electrically assisted are also governed by these Regulations. Regulation 6 provides that no person shall ride, or cause or permit to be ridden, a pedal cycle which does not comply with the braking-system requirements in regs 7 or 8. Regulation 7 requires that at least one braking system is fitted to all pedal cycles with the exception of those on which the pedals act directly on the wheel rather than through a gearing system (eg a penny farthing) and those temporarily in Great Britain when ridden by a visitor, such a cycle having a braking system or system complying with provisions of the International Convention on Road Traffic.

Pedal cycles manufactured on or after 1 August 1984 are subjected to additional braking requirements if the saddle height (fully raised and tyre fully inflated) is 635 mm (about 25 inches). Saddle height replaces wheel diameter as the yardstick in the case of cycles manufactured on or after 1 August 1984 because of the production of cycles with small wheels and high saddles which, because of their small wheels, were only required to have one braking system. The additional requirements are that fixed wheel cycles shall have a braking system acting on the front wheel or on at least two front wheels if there are more than one. Free wheel cycles must have two independent systems, one acting upon the front wheel, or at least two front wheels if more than one are fitted, and the other acting upon the rear wheel, or at least two rear wheels if more than one are fitted. In the case of pedal cycles manufactured before 1 August 1984, these additional requirements apply to pedal cycles any wheel of which exceeds 460 mm (approx 18 inches) in diameter including the fully inflated tyre except that the braking system acting upon the rear need only act upon one rear wheel even if there is more than one rear wheel fitted. Non-goods tricycles may have two independent systems both acting upon the single wheel.

Regulation 10 prohibits riding, or causing or permitting to be ridden, on a road a pedal cycle the braking system of which, fitted in accordance with these Regulations, is not in efficient working order. This is the offence most frequently dealt with by police officers but it is not uncommon to find that one of two systems has been removed from a cycle.

Breach of regs 4, 5, 6 or 10 is an offence contrary to the Road Traffic Offenders Act 1988, s 91. A constable in uniform is empowered by reg 11 to test and inspect a pedal cycle for the purpose of ascertaining that the braking requirements are satisfied. This may be done on a road, or on any premises where the cycle is if the cycle has been involved in an accident and that test and inspection is carried out within 48 hours of the accident with the consent of the owner of the premises.

TESTING AND INSPECTION

Powers to test and inspect vehicles are included in the Road Traffic Act 1988 and in the Road Vehicles (Construction and Use) Regulations. In effect, they permit authorised constables to test and inspect motor vehicles on roads, and all constables in uniform to test and inspect motor vehicles on premises, subject to certain conditions. It is helpful to consider both powers together.

Testing vehicles on roads: Road Traffic Act 1988, s 67

Authorised examiners may test a motor vehicle on a road for the purpose of ascertaining whether the requirements relating to its construction and use are being complied with, and also whether there is compliance with the requirement that the condition of the vehicle is not such that its use on a road would involve danger of injury to any person.

There are two types of authorised examiners. First, certain police officers are specially authorised by their chief constables for this purpose. Second, vehicle examiners appointed under s 66A of the Road Traffic Act 1988 by the Secretary of State are similarly authorised to carry out such tests. For the purpose of testing a vehicle an examiner may require the driver to comply with his reasonable instructions and may drive the vehicle. All authorised examiners must produce their authority if required to do so.

The provisions of the section do not mean that the requirement of the Act and the Construction and Use Regulations may only be enforced on a road by authorised constables. Particular offences may still be reported. In addition, a constable who is not an authorised examiner may test a vehicle with the driver's consent. This is borne out by a case where a constable who was not an authorised examiner tested the efficiency of a handbrake with the driver's consent; evidence of his findings were admitted even though he was not an authorised examiner. It is submitted that there is a difference between a power to make a general examination of a vehicle and the examination of a particular part of it because of the suspicion of an offence. If the wall of a tyre is badly split and the fabric exposed, this is observable by any police officer and the examination of the whole vehicle is unnecessary in order to deal with the particular infringement. It does not take a vehicle examiner to notice that the entire exhaust system of a motor vehicle is hanging off.

Where an examination of the vehicle under s 67 is required by an authorised examiner, the driver may elect that the test shall be deferred to a time and place to be arranged. If the driver is the owner, he may choose a period of seven days, within the next 30 days, when the examination may be carried out on premises specified by him. If the driver is not the owner, he must give the owner's name and address and the examiner must make his arrangement with the owner. Once the period has been so specified, the police must give at least two days' notice of the day, within that seven-day period, when the test will be carried out. If no period is specified, seven days' notice must be given of the intention to test.

The right to defer does not apply when it appears to a constable that, following an accident on a road, the test must be taken forthwith. If this is so and the constable is not an authorised examiner, he may require that the vehicle is not taken away until the test has been carried out. The same powers are given when the vehicle appears to be so defective that it ought not to be allowed to proceed.

Testing vehicles off roads: Road Vehicles (Construction and Use) Regulations

Regulation 74 empowers any police constable in uniform or vehicle examiner to test and inspect the brakes, silencers, steering gear and tyres, of any motor vehicle or trailer on any premises where that motor vehicle or trailer is, subject to the consent of the owner of the premises. This represents the basic difference between these powers and those set out above. The regulations are concerned with powers with respect to vehicles 'on premises', and s 67 of the Act with powers with respect to vehicles 'on a road'.

The powers provided by the Regulations are always subject to the consent of the *owner of the premises*. This means that there is no power of entry onto premises for the purpose of inspection. In addition, the test and inspection cannot be carried out without the consent of the *owner of the vehicle*, unless notice of it has been served personally upon him at least 48 hours before the test, or 72 hours before it if service is effected by recorded delivery. The consent of the *owner of the vehicle* is not required if it has been involved in an accident within the preceding 48 hours.

If an owner/driver is seen driving a motor vehicle in a defective condition but the police officer is not in a position to stop the vehicle, and the owner/driver garages his vehicle on return to his home, there is no means by which his vehicle can be examined without his consent as the owner of the premises. If, however, he took the vehicle to a garage proprietor, examination could take place on the garage proprietor's premises with his consent and the absence of consent of the owner of the vehicle could be overcome by notice.

Prohibition of unfit vehicles

The Road Traffic Act 1988, s 69 empowers an authorised constable to issue an immediate prohibition notice if, on an inspection under ss 41, 45, 49, 61, 67, 68 or 77, it appears to him that, owing to any defects in the vehicle, driving it (or driving it for any particular purpose or purposes or for any except one or more particular purposes) would involve a danger of injury to any person. These sections referred to deal with powers in relation to construction and use; test certificates generally; inspections related to plated weights of goods vehicles, public service vehicles and vehicles adapted to carry more than eight passengers which are not public service vehicles; and the testing of the condition of used vehicles at sale rooms etc. A notice under s 69 may prohibit use absolutely, or for one or more specified purposes, or except for one or more specified purposes.

Vehicle examiners appointed under s 66A have a similar power.

The Road Vehicles (Prohibition) Regulations 1992 make provision for a vehicle which is subject to a prohibition issued by an authorised constable, or vehicle examiner, to be driven on a road solely for the purpose of submitting it, by prior arrangement, for test with a view to removal of that prohibition, or for it to be driven in the course of any test for the purpose of the removal of the prohibition, or (within three miles from where it is being, or has been, repaired) to be driven solely for the purpose of its test or trial with a view to the removal of the prohibition.

Inspection of public passenger vehicles and goods vehicles

Special powers of inspection are provided by the Road Traffic Act 1988, s 68 in respect of goods vehicles, public service vehicles and vehicles adapted to carry more than eight passengers which are not public service vehicles. A vehicle examiner or any constable in uniform may require any person in charge of a stationary goods vehicle on a road to take the vehicle to any place within five miles, for the purpose of an inspection by a Ministry examiner, not by the police.

TEST CERTIFICATES

The Road Traffic Act 1988, ss 45 to 47 are concerned with tests of the satisfactory condition of motor vehicles, other than goods vehicles to which s 49 applies. The relevant provisions with regard to such goods vehicles are discussed in the chapter concerning goods vehicles. The Secretary of State is authorised by s 45 to make regulations for the examination of all vehicles to which ss 45 to 47 apply and he has made the Motor Vehicles (Tests) Regulations 1981.

By the Road Traffic Act 1988, s 47(1), a person commits an offence if he uses, or causes or permits to be used, at any time on a road a motor vehicle to which the section applies, and in respect of which no test certificate has been issued within the appropriate period before the said time. In relation to 'use', 'cause' or permit, the reader is referred to pp 256-259.

Which vehicles must be tested?

The answer to this question depends on two things, the type of vehicle and its age.

The following must be examined and receive a test certificate annually, after the period of three years defined in the next paragraph:

(a) passenger vehicles with not more than eight seats, excluding the driver's seat;
(b) rigid goods motor cars, the unladen weight of which does not exceed 1,525 kg;
(c) dual-purpose vehicles;
(d) motorcycles (including three-wheelers and mopeds); and
(e) motor caravans.

Section 47 applies to those motor vehicles of the types just specified which were first registered not less than three years before the time in question (ie the time of the alleged use without a test certificate). If, for any reason, a vehicle is used on a road in Great Britain or elsewhere before being registered, a test certificate must be obtained three years from the date of manufacture. Thus, a serviceman returning from duty abroad who brings into this country a vehicle which is more than three years old must have it tested immediately.

The 1988 Act requires annual tests for the following motor vehicles after one year from first registration:

(a) motor vehicles used for the carriage of passengers and with more than eight seats, exclusive of the driver's (mainly public service vehicles);
(b) taxis licensed to ply for hire; and
(c) ambulances.

Exemptions

The 1981 Regulations exempt:

(a) articulated vehicles other than articulated buses;
(b) invalid carriages not exceeding 306 kg unladen weight (or not exceeding 510 kg if supplied by the Department of Health);
(c) vehicles temporarily in Great Britain for a period of 12 months;
(d) police vehicles maintained in police workshops;
(e) electrically propelled goods vehicles not exceeding 1,525 kg;
(f) some licensed hackney carriages and private hire cars;
(g) a vehicle at a time when it is being used on a public road during any calendar week if it is being used only in passing from land in the occupation of its keeper to other land in his occupation, and it has not been used on public roads for more than an aggregate of six miles in that calendar week; and
(h) vehicles which have a Northern Ireland test certificate.

The Regulations also permit use without a test certificate when a vehicle is being taken to a testing station by previous arrangement for a test, or when it is being brought away from such a test, or while it is being so tested by an authorised person or under his direction. In circumstances in which a test certificate is refused, the vehicle may be moved without a test certificate for the purpose of work being done (once again, by previous arrangement), or for the purpose of delivering it, by towing, to a place where it is to be broken up. Imported vehicles which need to be tested may be driven on arrival in this country to the place of residence of the owner of the motor vehicle.

The test

The Motor Vehicles (Tests) Regulations 1981 require that specified parts of vehicles in Classes I to V, that is all vehicles except those falling within Classes I to III (motorcycles and light vehicles), or Classes V or VI (large passenger-carrying vehicles for more than 12 passengers, public service vehicles etc) or Class VII (goods vehicles of design gross weight exceeding 3,000 kg but not exceeding 3,500 kg) are tested. The specified parts include wheels and tyres, steering, audible warning instruments, front position lamps, rear retro reflectors, stop lamps, direction indicators, rear registration plate lamps, rear fog lamps, hazard warning signal devices, braking, glass and field of vision, mirrors, windscreen cleaning, fuel tanks and pipes, seat belts and anchorages, exhaust (general condition), exhaust (emissions), vehicle identification number, structure and suspension (body, chassis, subframe, mounting or suspension which prejudices steering, braking or seat belt mountings or may otherwise cause danger), seats, doors and other openings to the extent that their condition may cause danger, and registration marks.

The tests are even more extensive for vehicles which fall within Classes V and VI; they require speedometers, speed limiters and speed limiter plates *also* to be examined, and the examination of many interior fittings. Class VII vehicles are inspected in a similar but extended fashion to those in Class IV, the test including such items as tyre loads and speed ratings.

The test for vehicles in Classes III to VII has been extended to include an annual check on the condition of seat belts and anchorages which are fitted to such vehicles, those seat belts not being required to be fitted by the Road Vehicles (Construction and Use) Regulations 1986.

A vehicle may be tested in the one-month period (two months in the case of a public service vehicle) before the expiration of the current certificate, or the time when it must first be tested. This is to permit tests to be taken in sufficient time to have defects remedied prior to the expiry of an existing certificate. Section 48(2) of the Road Traffic Act 1988 permits test certificates which are renewed during the last month of the validity of the previous certificate to be issued to expire 12 months after the expiry of the last certificate, rather than 12 months from the date of the examination. Section 48(1A) makes similar provision in relation to a certificate issued in respect of a first test.

Refusal of test certificate

When a test certificate is refused, a notice of refusal must be issued and the grounds for refusal must be listed on a check list, except that in the case of a motorcycle the notice must state the grounds for refusal and a check list need not be given. All test certificates currently in use must be embossed by the stamp of the examiner or council on whose behalf it is issued. There is a right of appeal, against refusal, to the Secretary of State.

Contents of test certificate

The contents of a test certificate are not prescribed. A certificate must be in a form supplied by the Secretary of State. A certificate usually has a serial number, contains a statement to the effect that the vehicle complied with the requirements on the date of the examination, shows the registration mark of the vehicle, the vehicle testing station number, the date of issue of the certificate, the date of expiry and the signature of the person issuing the certificate. A signature may be a facsimile of the signature of the examiner or of a person so authorised by the Secretary of State. If the previous certificate had expired at the time of the examination, the serial number of the previous certificate may also be shown. Tests can only be conducted at testing stations authorised by the Secretary of State.

Requirement to produce test certificate

The Road Traffic Act 1988, s 165 empowers a constable or vehicle examiner to require a person driving, or reasonably believed by him to have been driving, when an accident occurred or when an offence was committed to give his name and address and the name and address of the owner of the vehicle and to produce certain documents, including a test certificate (if one is required for the vehicle). As with other types of document, there is a proviso which permits production within seven days at a specified police station; or production as soon as reasonably practicable; or proof that production was not reasonably practicable before the day on which proceedings were commenced. Production in person is not required.

CHAPTER 11

Control of vehicles

TRAFFIC SIGNS

These are governed by the Road Traffic Regulation Act 1984 and regulations thereunder.

The term 'traffic sign' for the purposes of the 1984 Act is defined by s 64 of that Act as any object or device (whether fixed or portable) for conveying, to traffic on roads or any specified class of traffic, warnings, information, requirements, restrictions or prohibitions of any description:

(a) specified by regulations made by the relevant Ministers acting jointly; or
(b) authorised by the Secretary of State,

and any line or mark on a road for so conveying such warnings, information, requirements, restrictions or prohibitions.

The section authorises the making of regulations in respect of the size, colour and type of traffic signs. The current regulations are the Traffic Sign Regulations and General Directions 1994. Equipment which is used in connection with traffic signs must be of a type approved in accordance with the Directions.

Section 65 of the 1984 Act empowers highway authorities to cause or permit traffic signs to be placed on or near any road in their area.

Section 66 empowers a constable, or a person acting under the instructions (whether general or specific) of the chief officer of police, to place on a highway such authorised traffic signs indicating prohibitions, restrictions or requirements relating to vehicular traffic as may be required to prevent an obstruction on public occasions or near public buildings or at an authorised cycle race. This section permits police officers to place emergency signs on the road at special events such as air displays. A second power is given by s 67 to a police officer, or a person under the instructions (general or specific) of the chief officer of police, to place on a highway authorised traffic signs indicating prohibitions, restrictions or requirements to prevent or mitigate congestion or obstruction of traffic, or danger to or from traffic in consequence of extraordinary circumstances. Among other things, this section empowers the police to place emergency signs on the road at the scene of an accident. Such signs may be maintained for a maximum period of seven days. The time starts when the signs are placed, so that a sign placed at 2pm must be removed by 2pm seven days after placement. The important feature of the section is that the authorisation is in respect of extraordinary circumstances and the section does not, therefore, authorise the regular placement of signs at locations selected by the police. If the need is a permanent one,the matter must be dealt with by the highway authority.

Failure to comply with a sign placed under the provisions of ss 65, 66 and 67 is an offence contrary to the Road Traffic Act 1988, s 36.

Quite apart from the above, the Traffic Signs (Temporary Obstructions) Regulations 1997 authorise persons not otherwise authorised to do so to place specified traffic signs on roads in connection with temporary obstructions, other than roadworks. The indications given by the signs are specified in regs 4 to 7 and the form which the signs take is prescribed by regs 8 to 14.

Regulation 15 permits a 'keep right' sign to be placed by the crew of an emergency or breakdown vehicle which is causing a temporary obstruction. It is an offence against the RTA 1988, s 36 to fail to comply with such a sign.

In addition, regulation 15 authorises any person to place a 'road vehicle sign' on a vehicle, and to place on any road:

(a) a minimum of four 'flat traffic delineators', 'traffic cones', or 'traffic pyramids'; or
(b) a 'traffic triangle' (at least 45 metres from the obstruction) or 'warning lamp' (used in conjunction with one of any of these signs, including the 'road vehicle sign'),

for the purpose of warning traffic of a temporary obstruction, other than roadworks. It is not in itself an offence to fail to comply with any of these signs.

A 'road vehicle sign' consists of a flexible sheet on which there is a triangle the outer edges of which are red, the inner part being either reflectorised white or fluorescent yellow. It is designed to be fixed to a stationary vehicle, facing approaching traffic. A 'traffic delineator', 'traffic cone' and 'traffic pyramid' is of the 'lane marker' type of device frequently used by emergency services and a 'traffic triangle' or 'warning lamp' (flashing amber signal) is the type of device frequently used by individual motorists.

The placing of traffic signs is, therefore, carefully controlled. The placing of signs otherwise than as prescribed is of no legal effect. Persons do not have a right to paint 'No Parking' on the roadway, or on a sign, outside their premises.

Failure to comply with a traffic sign

The Road Traffic Act 1988, s 35 deals with circumstances in which a constable is for the time being engaged in the regulation of traffic in a road, and s 36 with that in which authorised traffic signs have been placed on or near a road. Section 35 provides that, where a constable is for the time being engaged in the regulation of traffic in a road, a person driving or propelling a vehicle who neglects or refuses:

(a) to stop the vehicle, or
(b) to make it proceed in, or keep to, a particular line of traffic, when directed to do so by a constable in the execution of his duty,

is guilty of an offence.

Section 36 states that an offence is committed by a person driving or propelling a vehicle who fails to comply with the indication given by an authorised traffic sign.

The word 'neglect' simply means 'fail'. The Functions of Traffic Wardens Order 1970 extends the offence of failure to comply with a constable's directions to failure to comply with the directions of a traffic warden employed in the control and regulation of traffic under the authority of that Order. Disqualification or endorsement cannot be ordered if the failure is to comply with the directions of a traffic warden. For an offence to be committed under s 36, the constable or warden must be acting in the execution of his duty, which in this context means his duty to ensure the public safety. It is no defence for a driver to allege that he did not see a traffic sign.

Signs to which s 36 applies

Section 36 applies to any traffic sign which indicates a statutory prohibition, restriction or requirement, *or* to any other traffic sign where it is expressly provided by or under the Road Traffic Act 1988 or the Road Traffic Regulation Act 1984 that s 36 shall apply to the sign; such express provision has been made by the Traffic Signs Regulations 1994, reg 10. Examples of signs to which s 36 applies are described in the next three paragraphs, which deal in turn with signs indicating a prohibition, a restriction and a requirement.

Examples of signs which indicate a *prohibition* are 'No entry', 'No right turn', 'No U turn', 'Lorries prohibited' and 'No overtaking' etc signs. These signs frequently involve the use of symbols only. Except in the case of a 'No Entry' sign, these consist of a red circle with the enclosed symbol in black on a white background. Thus a sign prohibiting entry to lorries would carry the symbol of a lorry with a red circle around it.

Signs dealing with *restrictions* include those dealing with waiting restrictions. These signs have a red outer circle with a blue background and a red band cutting across the face from the top left to bottom right of the sign as seen by approaching drivers. Information concerning the nature of the restrictions in force is provided on a plate, usually attached to the post supporting the sign. A yellow plate with the words 'at any time' in black indicates a total ban on parking, whilst the words '8.00am–6.00pm' would indicate a restriction upon waiting between those hours. Where waiting is limited rather than prohibited, the sign will be of white lettering on a blue background. Restrictions on waiting may be additionally indicated by signs placed on the roadway but such a sign is only effective to create the prohibition or restriction if used in conjunction with a restriction sign or plate of the type referred to above. A single continuous yellow line running parallel with the kerb restricts waiting (other than for loading or unloading) for a period of at least eight hours between 7am and 7pm on a minimum of four days a week. A double continuous yellow line indicates that, additionally, the restrictions may extend on occasions beyond those hours. Broken yellow lines indicate other waiting restrictions, usually unilateral parking schemes, restricting waiting on particular sides of the road on particular days of the week.

Those signs which deal with *requirements* under the section are those which require a driver etc to do something. 'Stop', 'Give Way', 'Keep Right', 'Keep Left', 'Traffic Lights' are all signs which indicate a requirement. The driver must stop his vehicle, turn it in a particular direction or give way to other traffic. These signs vary in appearance. The modern 'Stop' sign is octagonal and coloured red with 'Stop' in white capitals on it, although variations still exist. Other statutory requirements relating to stopping are red traffic lights and manually operated 'Stop' signs at road works. 'Give way' signs consist of a red inverted triangle on a white, circular background with the words 'give way' inside the triangle. White arrows on a blue background indicate the route which a driver must follow. Another example of a sign making a requirement is one requiring certain drivers to telephone for permission to cross automatic level crossings.

For the purposes of s 36, traffic signs placed on or near a road are deemed to be of the prescribed size, colour and type, and to have been lawfully placed, unless the contrary is proved. Consequently, the prosecution do not normally have to offer evidence of the nature of the sign beyond that which satisfies the court of the nature of the restriction, prohibition or requirement in question. However, if the sign is proved not to be of the prescribed size etc, or not to have been lawfully placed, it will not be a valid sign and no offence can be committed in relation to it, unless the breach of the requirement is trivial. There is a presumption that automatic traffic lights are in working order, unless the contrary is proved.

Signs to which s 36 does not apply

Where the provisions of s 36 do not apply to a sign but it is governed by regulations concerning traffic control made by the Secretary of State, the Road Traffic Offenders Act 1988, s 91 states that contravention or failure to comply is an offence under that section.

Particular signs

Certain signs indicate particular requirements. A 'Stop' sign requires that:

(a) every vehicle must, before entering the major road, stop at the transverse lines at the junction, or, if the lines are not visible, at the major road; and

(b) no vehicle may proceed past the transverse line painted nearest to the major road, or, if the lines are not visible, may not enter the major road, in such a manner or at such a time as is likely to cause danger to the driver of any other vehicle on the major road, or as to necessitate the driver of any such other vehicle to change its speed or course in order to avoid an accident.

The latter provision (ie (b)) also applies to 'Give Way' signs. Thus, it is not sufficient to stop, or give way, and then to proceed, if the results of so proceeding are as described. There should be no interference with traffic on the major road. To emerge in such circumstances also indicates an element of carelessness which may amount to careless driving.

The Traffic Signs Regulations and General Directions 1981, reg 23 deals with double white lines, which consist of either two continuous white lines or one continuous white line together with a broken white line painted along the middle of the carriageway itself. Any white unbroken line must be immediately preceded by a white warning arrow painted on the road; otherwise the line is not valid as a sign. If there are two continuous white lines vehicles travelling in both directions are required to keep to the nearside of the nearest continuous white line. A broken line with a continuous line requires vehicles to keep to the nearside of the continuous white line when that line is the nearer of the two to the vehicle. Where there are two continuous white lines, therefore, vehicles travelling in both directions may not cross the nearest line to them. Where there is a broken line nearest, both lines may be crossed if it is seen by the driver that it is safe to do so. It is an offence to stop on either side of the road where there is a double white line marking of either description unless it is done:

(a)   to pick up or set down passengers, to load or unload, or for building operations;
(b)   in connection with road or public utility works;
(c)   by a vehicle used for police, fire or ambulance purposes;
(d)   by a pedal cycle without a sidecar (auto-assisted or not);
(e)   to avoid an accident or because it is impossible to proceed;
(f)   with the permission of a constable in uniform, or when directed by a traffic warden.

The reasons for these exemptions can easily be appreciated. For example, there may be a bus stop or a warehouse along the section of roadway covered by double white lines. Again vehicles may have to stop there because of a traffic jam, and in an emergency situation a driver must stop to prevent an accident.

Records produced as evidence

The Road Traffic Offenders Act 1988, s 20 provides that a record produced by prescribed devices is evidence of a fact related to an offence involving a driver's failure to comply with a traffic sign, contrary to the Road Traffic Act 1988, s 36(1). (Such a record is also admissible in respect of an offence relating to the abuse of a bus lane.) However, the record is only evidence if (in the same or another document) there is a certificate as to the circumstances in which it was produced, signed by a constable, or by a person authorised by (or on behalf of) the chief police officer for the area. The device must be of a type approved by the Secretary of State and must be used in accordance with conditions subject to which the approval was given. The Secretary of State has approved a device designed, or adapted for recording, by means of photographic or other image recording means, the position of vehicles in relation to light signals.

For a document of the type referred to above to be admissible, a copy of it must be served on the person charged with the offence not less than seven days before the hearing or trial. If the person charged, not less than three days before the hearing or trial, requires the attendance of the person who signed the document, the evidence of the circumstances in which the record was produced will not be admissible, although the record produced by the device will.

Traffic surveys

Before an offence can be committed under the provisions of s 35 in relation to a neglect or refusal to comply with a constable's direction, he must be at the time engaged in the execution of his duty. At common law in the context of traffic control, that was limited to the duty to ensure public safety. As a result a constable who was stopping vehicles for the purpose of a traffic survey or census was not acting in the execution of his duty. However, s 35(2) of the 1988 Act amends the common law position by providing that any directions given by a constable in this respect shall be treated as given in the execution of his duty. The constable's direction may be to stop or to proceed to a particular point, but no requirement to give information may be made and no unreasonable delay must be caused to a person who does not wish to provide information. Section 36(4) also provides that signs such as 'Stop at Census Point' and 'Census Point—Stop if required' are traffic signs to which s 36 applies.

Other police powers to stop drivers and pedestrians

Quite apart from the powers given to the police by s 35 of the 1988 Act in relation to the regulation of mechanically propelled vehicles, s 163 of that Act requires that a person driving a mechanically propelled vehicle or riding a cycle on a road shall stop his vehicle on being required to do so by a constable in uniform. Failure to do so is an offence.

In addition, by s 37 of that Act, a person on foot who fails to comply with the signals of a uniformed constable on traffic control commits an offence. Failure to give a name and address in such circumstances is a further offence.

Lastly the Fire Services Act 1947 allows the senior police officer present at any fire to close off streets, or stop or regulate traffic in any street, whenever in his opinion it is necessary or desirable to do so for fire fighting purposes. In the absence of a police officer, the senior fire officer may so act.

PEDESTRIAN CROSSINGS

The Road Traffic Regulation Act 1984, ss 23 and 24 gives powers to local authorities to provide pedestrian crossings on all roads other than trunk roads, and to the Secretary of State to do so in respect of trunk roads. Local authorities, before establishing, altering or removing a crossing, must consult the chief officer of police, give public notice, and inform the Secretary of State in writing. Section 25 authorises the Secretary of State to make regulations in respect of the precedence of vehicles and pedestrians, and generally in respect of the movement of vehicles in the vicinity of crossings. Regulations have been made governing 'Zebra', 'Pelican' and 'Puffin' crossings. Zebra crossings are uncontrolled; Pelican and Puffin crossings are light-controlled. By s 25 of the 1984 Act, a person who contravenes the regulations is guilty of an offence.

'Zebra' crossings

The 'Zebra', 'Pelican' and 'Puffin' Pedestrian Crossing Regulations 1997 prescribe the nature of uncontrolled crossings and the rules governing them. The *limits* of the crossing itself (the walking area for the pedestrians) are indicated by lines of studs between which is an area marked by alternate black and white stripes. Flashing yellow globes indicate the presence of such a crossing to approaching drivers. The globes are mounted on poles which are also marked by black and white stripes. There must be a globe at either side of the crossing; if there is a central reservation or street refuge on the crossing, one or more globes may be placed there. The failure of the lamps does not prevent the crossing being a valid 'Zebra' crossing, so that the provisions of the regulations must still be complied with.

The approach to the crossing from each direction is marked out as a 'controlled area'. It is in effect a defensive area and drivers are made aware that they are entering such an area by white lines situated at each kerb and in the crown of the road on the approaching driver's side. This is known as the 'terminal line' and from it three zig-zag lines stretch to a distance of one metre from the crossing itself where they join a broken white line which is the 'give way' line.

These regulations are concerned with 'Zebra' crossings at which traffic is not for the time being controlled by a police constable in uniform or a traffic warden. Immediately such an officer takes control of traffic movements at such a crossing, the crossing ceases to be an uncontrolled one and the provisions of the regulations cease to apply until that control ceases.

Precedence at a zebra crossing

Regulation 25 states that every pedestrian on the carriageway within the limits of an uncontrolled crossing shall have precedence within these limits over any vehicle. That precedence must be afforded by a driver before any part of his vehicle enters the pedestrian limits of the crossing itself. Where there is a central refuge, each side of it is treated as a separate crossing. It must be emphasised that a pedestrian only has precedence when he or she is within the limits of the crossing before the vehicle enters the limits of the crossing. A pedestrian waiting at the kerbside is awaiting the courtesy of drivers who care to stop; such a person is not entitled to any precedence until he steps on to the crossing.

The driver of a vehicle must always approach an uncontrolled crossing in such a manner that he will be able to stop before reaching it unless he can see that there is no one in the vicinity. Evidence of negligence or a failure to take reasonable care is not necessary; there is a strict duty to accord precedence and the discharge of that duty requires an approach to such crossings that will allow precedence to be given in any circumstances. The only exceptions are in instances where there is a sudden defect in the vehicle or it is pushed on to the crossing by the vehicle behind; in such circumstances a driver is clearly unable through no fault of his to discharge his duty to accord precedence. It is important to recognise that the issue of precedence does not arise until there is the question of who goes first. Clear evidence should be offered that the passage of a pedestrian was interfered with by the passage of a motor vehicle over the limits of the crossing. Taken to extremes, where a crossing spans a very wide street, a vehicle might pass over the limits while a pedestrian was on the crossing without the progress of that pedestrian being in any way interfered with. Alternatively, where a vehicle is stopped at a crossing and the pedestrians have passed the point at which it is waiting, the driver is then at liberty to proceed as precedence has been afforded. If another pedestrian then steps on the crossing as the vehicle moves off, it is submitted that the driver commits no offence (provided no issue of 'who goes first' is raised).

'Pelican' and 'Puffin' crossings

A driver who ignores a red light at a pelican or puffin crossing commits an offence against reg 23 by 'proceeding beyond the stop line' or, if that line is not visible, the post on which the light signal is mounted. At a puffin crossing, a red with amber signal denotes an impending change to green, but it conveys the same prohibition as a red signal. At either type of crossing a steady amber signal when shown alone conveys the same prohibition as a red signal (with the usual proviso applicable to traffic lights), and there may be a green arrow showing, which signals that traffic may cross the stop line to proceed in a particular direction. It is an offence to fail to accord precedence when there is a flashing amber light at a pelican crossing. We explain below what is meant by 'according precedence'.

Both pelican and puffin crossings will have 'controlled areas' on each side of the crossing (or on one side in the case of one-way traffic), this controlled area being indicated by two or more zig-zag lines stretching from the terminal line to the stop line, a line which is met before the limits of the crossing itself are reached. The primary signals shown to both drivers and pedestrians are by synchronised light signals. Whilst a steady green light is shown to drivers, a steady red light is shown to pedestrians. The light signals to pedestrians are, in the case of pelican crossings, steady red, steady green and flashing green figures reinforced by the illumination of a sign which reads 'WAIT'. Those at puffin crossings are by means of red and green figures and the green figure must only be capable of showing when a red light is indicated to drivers.

Audible signals may be used at pelican crossings to indicate to pedestrians when it is safe to cross.

Precedence at a pelican or puffin crossing

The issue of precedence at these crossings is determined to a major extent by the light signals which are showing at the time. There are specific offences within the Regulations dealing with failure to comply with such signals.

However, at pelican crossings a driver may encounter a flashing amber signal which indicates that pedestrians who are on the carriageway or a central reservation within the limits of the crossing before any part of the vehicle has entered those limits, must be accorded precedence. It is an offence for a driver to fail to accord such precedence. The flashing amber signal is peculiar to pelican crossings alone and is not one of the signals shown at a puffin crossing.

Prohibition of waiting

Regulation 18 prohibits a driver from stopping his vehicle in the *limits* of any of the three types of crossing itself unless he is prevented from proceeding by circumstances beyond his control or it is necessary to avoid an accident. Moreover, reg 20 prohibits the driver of a vehicle from causing the vehicle or any part of it to stop in a *'controlled area'* (the zig-zag area). However, this regulation does not apply to pedal cycles without sidecars, whether mechanically assisted or not. Regulations 21 and 22 exempt from reg 20 vehicles:

(a) whose drivers have stopped to comply with requirements of the Regulations,
(b) whose drivers have been prevented from proceeding by circumstances beyond their control,
(c) whose drivers have stopped to avoid an accident;
(d) stopped for fire, ambulance, police or defence purposes, or
(e) in connection with building works, road works or repairs to public utilities.

Vehicles may also halt to make right or left turns. Public service vehicles may stop to pick up or set down passengers but only on the far side of the crossing itself, not on its approach.

In conclusion, it should be noted that reg 19 prohibits a pedestrian remaining within the limits of a crossing longer than necessary for the purposes of crossing with reasonable despatch.

Prohibition on overtaking

Regulation 24 provides that a driver *within a 'controlled area'* of any of the three types of crossing must not overtake on the approach side to a crossing a moving motor vehicle or a stationary motor vehicle according precedence to a pedestrian on the crossing. Once the crossing has been passed it is not an offence to overtake within the controlled area on the other side. For the purpose of this regulation, a vehicle overtakes another if any part of the vehicle passes ahead of the foremost part of another vehicle. The purpose of this regulation is to prevent pedestrians from being struck by overtaking vehicles. It is not surprising, therefore, that the regulation limits the prohibition on overtaking to cases where the vehicle overtaken is the only other vehicle in the controlled area, or is the foremost vehicle. If this was not so, where there were two lines of traffic approaching a crossing, it would not be possible for the traffic on the offside to close up. In relation to the prohibition on overtaking a vehicle which has stopped to accord precedence, such a vehicle includes one which has stopped for this purpose even though a pedestrian intending to cross has not yet stepped on to the crossing.

Because of the drafting of the provision, the ban on overtaking does not apply where the overtaking vehicle was actually on the crossing when it passed ahead of the foremost part of the overtaken vehicle.

School crossing patrols

The Road Traffic Regulation Act 1984, s 26 authorises an 'appropriate authority' to make arrangements for the patrolling, during a specified period, of places where children cross roads on their way to or from school (or from one part of the school to another). The specified period is between the hours of eight in the morning and half past five in the afternoon. Persons may be appointed for this purpose by the 'appropriate authority' which (outside the Metropolis) is the county council.

The stopping of vehicles at school crossings is dealt with by s 28 of the Act. There are various essential points to consider when dealing with an offence under this section. They are related to what a driver must do when required to stop by a school crossing patrol. When, *during the specified period*, a person driving or propelling a vehicle on a road is required by a school crossing patrol in the approved uniform and exhibiting a prescribed 'lollipop' sign to stop so as to allow *children* to cross the road to or from school (or from one part of the school to another):

(a) he must cause the vehicle to stop before reaching the place where the children are crossing or seeking to cross and so as not to stop or impede their crossing; and
(b) the vehicle must not be put in motion again so as to reach the place in question so long as the sign continues to be exhibited.

It is an offence for a person to fail to comply with (a) or for him to cause a vehicle to be put in motion contrary to (b). These are separate offences.

The following should be noted about s 28. First, if a school crossing patrol attempted to stop traffic for children going to an evening class at the school at 7pm, a driver would not commit an offence against this section by failing to stop, because s 28 is limited to the specified period of 8am to 5.30pm. Second, it must be proved that children on their way to or from school were crossing or seeking to cross. The practice of crossing patrols to stop traffic for the parents of children who are coming to collect them has no statutory backing, and no offence would be committed under the section if a driver failed to stop. Third, the duty to stop only exists if the patrol was wearing a uniform approved by the Secretary of State, and any uniform is deemed to be so approved unless the contrary is proved. Home Office Circular 119/1954 approves caps for men, or a beret for a woman, together with a white dust coat or mackintosh. Circular 108/1966 authorises fluorescent jerkins or sleeves to be worn over the approved uniform. Fourth, the stopping of traffic may only be effected by exhibiting a prescribed sign. That sign will display the words 'Stop—Children' in black letters with a black bar on a yellow fluorescent background surrounded by a red fluorescent border. The section states that where the sign is displayed by a school crossing patrol it will be presumed that it is a prescribed sign, and that where it is proved that the sign was exhibited at a place where children were crossing or seeking to cross it will be presumed that they were on their way to or from school, unless (in either case) the contrary is proved.

As long as a prescribed sign has been properly exhibited, a driver must stop even if the children have cleared the road and there are no others seeking to cross. In one case, where a party of children and adults were crossing while the sign was displayed and had cleared the crown of a road, a driver coming out of a side street drove past the exhibited sign, passing narrowly behind the last of the party. The justices dismissed a charge of failing to stop on the grounds that the driver had not impeded their crossing. The Divisional Court gave a direction to convict on the grounds that the words 'so as not to stop or impede their crossing' in (a), above, merely described the manner in which a driver should stop (ie he must not halt across the path which those children would take) and were not meant to indicate that drivers could ignore a properly displayed sign if, in doing so, they would not directly impede pedestrians. Drivers must, therefore, stop and remain stopped while the sign is properly displayed. The duty to stop is absolute. A properly exhibited sign is one on which an approaching driver can see the words on the sign but it need not be proved that it was full face to oncoming traffic.

REMOVAL OF VEHICLES

The police have powers to require the removal of vehicles and to remove them themselves. Local authorities are legally obliged to remove abandoned vehicles.

Powers of police

The Removal and Disposal of Vehicles Regulations 1986, reg 3 allows a constable to require the owner, driver or other person in charge or control of a vehicle which:

(a) has broken down, or been permitted to remain at rest, on a road in such a position, condition or circumstances as to cause obstruction to other persons using the road, or as to be likely to cause danger to such other persons; or

(b) has been permitted to remain at rest or has broken down and remained at rest on a road in contravention of a prohibition or restriction in or under any enactment mentioned in Sch 1 to the Regulations,

to move or cause it to be moved.

The statutory prohibitions or restrictions included in Sch 1, referred to in (b), are concerned with parking in 'no waiting' areas, in the controlled areas of pedestrian crossings or in contravention of traffic signs—including police 'no waiting' signs. The constable's requirement may include a requirement to move the vehicle to some other place which may not be on a road, or a requirement that it shall not be moved to a particular road or to a particular position.

It is an offence against the Road Traffic Offenders Act 1988, s 91 to fail to move or cause a vehicle to be moved as soon as practicable when required under the provisions of reg 3.

Regulation 4 of the 1986 Regulations allows a constable to remove or arrange for the removal of a vehicle which is on a road in the circumstances outlined in (a) or (b), above. He may also do so if the vehicle, having broken down on a road or on any land in the open air, appears to have been abandoned without lawful authority, or if the vehicle has been permitted to remain at rest on a road or any land in the open air in such a position or circumstances as to appear to have been abandoned without lawful authority.

In determining, for the purposes of (a), the question of 'obstruction', a different interpretation is given to that term from that accorded to it in the Highways Act 1980, s 137 and the Road Vehicles (Construction and Use) Regulations 1986, s 103 (see pp 245 and 278, above). This has been stated by the Court of Appeal which held that 'obstruction' in (a) meant more than simply impeding the free access of members of the public to every part of the highway, since what was required was obstructing their passage by hindering or preventing them getting past. That 'obstruction', said the Court, need not be an actual one; it included obstructing people who might be expected to be using the highway. On the other hand, the mere fact that the use of a highway was unreasonable did not make it an obstruction.

The power to remove vehicles from land occupied by any person is subject to giving notice as prescribed by the Road Traffic Regulation Act 1984, s 99 and the Removal and Disposal of Vehicles Regulations 1986, reg 8. The power under reg 4 is very useful when the driver, person in charge or owner of a vehicle cannot be found or that person refuses to move the vehicle.

Regulation 4A empowers a traffic warden to remove a vehicle parked or broken down on a road in circumstances where it is causing an obstruction, where it is likely to cause danger to road users, or where an offence is being committed in relation to a statutory prohibition or restriction included in Sch 1 to the Regulations, referred to above.

Duties of local authorities

The Refuse Disposal (Amenity) Act 1978, s 3(1) obliges local authorities to remove motor vehicles abandoned without lawful authority on any land in the open air or on any other land forming part of the highway within their area. Before removing vehicles the local authority must follow a prescribed procedure in respect of notices which must be affixed to vehicles and served upon the owner of any land in the open air which is involved. It is an offence contrary to s 2 of the Act so to abandon a vehicle. We discuss this offence in ch 9, above, in relation to the law of litter.

DRIVING INSTRUCTION

The Road Traffic Act 1988, s 123 prohibits the giving of driving instruction for money or money's worth unless the person giving the instruction is a registered approved instructor or the holder of a licence authorising him to give such instruction. There must be fixed to, and exhibited on the motor car, the current licence or certificate of registration, in a similar position to that occupied by the vehicle excise licence. Free instruction given as a perk when buying a car from a motor trader is deemed to be given for payment. The section only applies to motor cars and has no application to motorcycles or large goods vehicles. It does not apply to police instructors. Disabled drivers may become registered or licensed instructors.

Registered approved instructor

To be registered a person must satisfy the Registrar that he:

(a) has passed the official driving instructors' examination;
(b) holds an appropriate full licence issued in Great Britain or Northern Ireland;
(c) has held that licence or a current foreign licence for at least four of the preceding six years;
(d) has not been disqualified from driving during any part of the previous period of four years; and
(e) is a fit and proper person to have his name registered.

Licensed instructor

To enable persons to gain experience with a view to undergoing the practical test of ability and fitness to instruct, which is part of the official driving instructor's examination, the Road Traffic Act 1988, s 129 allows the Registrar to grant a licence to give instruction in the driving of a motor car. If a previous licence has been granted, an application may be refused on that ground. An applicant must have passed the written part of the official driving instructors' examination and the practical test of driving ability and fitness to drive, which is also part of the examination. Licence holders may only give instruction from premises named in the licence. If the premises are a driving school the licence holder may only give instruction if properly employed in accordance with rules that there can be no more than one licence holder to each registered instructor. For the first three months of any licence (other than the second of two consecutive ones) the holder either must be under the direct personal supervision of a registered instructor for at least one-fifth of that time and keep a log to that effect, or must undertake a minimum of 20 hours supplementary training. In the case of the latter alternative he must undertake five further hours of training in a second consecutive period.

Offences

A person giving the instruction in breach of s 123 commits an offence, as does his employer if he is employed for that purpose. It is a defence for a defendant to prove that he did not know and had no reasonable cause to believe that his name, or that of his employee, was not in the register.

A person to whom a licence or a certificate of registration has been granted must produce it to a constable or authorised person on being required to do so. Failure to do so is an offence. However, it is a defence to prove in any proceedings for non-production:

(a) that the licence was produced within seven days at a police station specified by a constable or at a place specified by an authorised person (as the case may be); or

(b) that the document was produced at that police station or place (as the case may be) as soon as reasonably practicable; or

(c) that it was not reasonably practicable for it to be so produced at that police station or place before the day on which proceedings commenced.

The Road Traffic Act 1988, s 135(2) states that it is an offence for any unregistered person to wear or display a badge or certificate or to use any name, title or description which implies that he is registered. It also prohibits a person carrying on a driving instruction business from using any such title or description in respect of an unregistered employee, or from issuing any advertisement etc which is misleading in that respect. It is a defence for a person charged with this offence to prove that he did not know, and had no reasonable cause to believe, that his name, or that of his employee, was not in the register at the material time.

The Road Traffic (Driving Instruction by Disabled Persons) Act 1993 amended the Road Traffic Acts to permit the registration of disabled persons as driving instructors. Such persons may only be registered if they hold a current disabled person's limited driving licence and a current emergency control certificate. Such a certificate is only granted after assessment of the person's ability to take control of a motor car of a class covered by his disabled person's driving licence (with or without modifications). If an applicant for registration fails, without reasonable excuse, to disclose a relevant or prospective disability, he commits an offence. So does a registered disabled instructor or a disabled licensed instructor who gives paid instruction without holding an emergency control certificate or in an unauthorised motor car. A person who has employed the instructor to give that instruction will also be liable if one of these two offences is committed.

NOTICE OF INTENDED PROSECUTION

In the case of a number of moving traffic offences, the driver, if not stopped and interviewed by the police at the time, may experience considerable difficulty in recalling the circumstances some weeks after the event. For this reason, the Road Traffic Offenders Act 1988, s 1 states that, in relation to certain named offences, a person shall not be convicted unless:

(a) he was warned at the time of the possibility of prosecution for the offence; or
(b) he was served with a summons for the offence within 14 days of its commission; or
(c) a notice of intended prosecution specifying the nature of the alleged offence and the time and place where it is alleged to have been committed was served within 14 days on him or the person, if any, registered as the keeper of the vehicle at the time of the commission of the offence. (In the case of dangerous or careless cycling the notice must be served on the rider.)

The requirements of s 1 are deemed to have been complied with unless and until the contrary is proved.

The following offences require notice of intended prosecution in one of these forms:

(a) Road Traffic Act 1988
   Section 2   Dangerous driving
   Section 3   Careless, and inconsiderate driving
   Section 22   Leaving a vehicle in a dangerous position
   Section 28   Dangerous cycling
   Section 29   Careless, and inconsiderate cycling
   Section 35   Failing to conform with the indication given by a constable engaged in the regulation of traffic
   Section 36   Failing to comply with the indication given by a traffic sign
(b) Road Traffic Regulation Act 1984
   Section 16   Exceeding temporary speed restrictions imposed under s 14
   Section 17(4)   Exceeding speed restriction on special road
   Section 88(7)   Exceeding temporary speed limit imposed by order
   Section 89(1)   Speeding offences generally
(c) Aiding and abetting any of the above offences.

However, such notice need not be given in relation to an offence in respect of which a full or provisional fixed penalty notice has been given or fixed under the provisions of the Road Traffic Offenders Act 1988.

Warning at the time of the offence

The words 'at the time of the offence' mean at the *time of the incident and not the moment of the offence*. In one case, a warning, given by a police officer at the scene of an incident 35 minutes after its occurrence and while it was still being dealt with, was held to have been given 'at the time'. In other circumstances, where the police immediately traced the driver but the process took two and a half hours, the notice was held to have been given 'at the time'. However, there is obviously a limit, and the matter should be judged in the context of the warning being given as a part of the continuous process of initial investigation. Whether or not warning was given at the time is a question of fact and degree and the best course of action, if there has been any delay at the scene, is to send a written notice.

The warning must be heard and understood by the person concerned, and it must be to the effect that the question of prosecuting him for one or other of the above offences will be taken into consideration. Police officers are advised to warn that the offender will be reported for consideration of the question of prosecuting him for whichever of the above offences is applicable. There is no prescribed form of words and any clear statement to the above effect will do. It is appreciated that it is not always possible to decide whether the prosecution may be for dangerous or merely careless driving but a warning that it may be for either will suffice as the evidence upon which the charge will be based will be similar.

Service of summons or notice of intended prosecution

In circumstances in which an oral notice is not given at the time, then either a summons or a written notice of intended prosecution must be served within 14 days. In reckoning a period of 14 days, the day on which the offence was committed is ignored. A notice sent by post must be despatched so that in the normal time of postal delivery it will arrive within 14 days. If it is so posted, but is held up in the post and is delivered outside the 14-day period, it will be deemed to have been served in the 14-day period; consequently, the driver can still be convicted. It has been held that service of a notice on the wife of the defendant by a constable handing the notice to her was a valid service, since she was a person authorised to accept and deal with her husband's mail. It would be different if the notice was left with a hall porter, as he would not be so authorised. It is better to restrict service by hand to the offender. In the absence of personal service on the offender, it is advisable to serve a notice by sending it by registered post or recorded delivery since in such a case he is deemed to have been served if the notice was addressed to him at his last known address, notwithstanding that the notice is returned as undelivered or is for some other reason not received by him.

Circumstances where non-compliance is no bar to conviction

The Road Traffic Offenders Act 1988, s 2(3) states that a failure to comply with the above requirements is no bar to conviction if the court is satisfied that the name and address of the accused or of the vehicle's registered keeper could not with reasonable diligence have been ascertained in time for service of a summons or notice or that the accused by his own conduct contributed to the failure. These matters must always be resolved by the court but the difference can be appreciated between circumstances in which, on the one hand, the number of the vehicle was known to the police at the time and their enquiries were so slow that notice was served out of time, and, on the other, where the number was not known and extensive inquiries had to be undertaken to establish the identity of the driver.

The Road Traffic Offenders Act 1988, s 2 waives the requirements of s 1 in relation to any offence if, at the time of the offence or immediately thereafter, an accident occurs owing to the presence on a road of the vehicle in respect of which the offence was committed. This exemption exists because in such circumstances the offender will normally be aware of the circumstances surrounding the offence. It does not apply, therefore, if the accident was so trivial that the driver was unaware that the accident had occurred. Here, the requirements of s 1 apply. On the other hand, the waiver of the requirements of s 1 does apply if the driver was unaware of the circumstances of an accident owing to the severity of his injuries, because subsequently the driver will be only too aware that the accident has occurred.

TRAFFIC WARDENS

Every police authority in England and Wales is authorised by the Road Traffic Regulation Act 1984, s 95 to appoint traffic wardens to aid the police to discharge certain functions. Traffic wardens may only be used to discharge duties prescribed by the Secretary of State. Although appointed by the police authority, wardens act under the direction of the chief officer of police. Traffic wardens must wear the uniform prescribed by the Secretary of State; they must not act as traffic wardens when not in uniform.

The Road Traffic Regulation Act 1984, s 95(4) authorises the use of wardens for school crossing patrols and as parking attendants at street parking places provided by the Secretary of State or a local authority. In addition, s 95(5) of the Act authorises the Secretary of State to make an order concerning the functions which traffic wardens may undertake. He has made the Functions of Traffic Wardens Order 1970, the Schedule to which provides that traffic wardens may be employed to enforce the law with respect to:

(a) offences of parking without obligatory lights or reflectors during the hours of darkness;
(b) offences of obstruction of a road by vehicles, or of vehicles waiting, or being left or parked, or being loaded or unloaded, on a road or other public place;
(c) offences against the Vehicles Excise and Registration Act 1994 (eg no vehicle excise licence);
(d) offences related to parking places on highways where charges are made (eg by meters or machines); and
(e) offences committed by causing a vehicle, or any part of it, to stop in contravention of the pedestrian crossing regulations.

The Order also permits traffic wardens to be used in connection with obtaining information from the keeper of the vehicle or relevant person as to the identity of a driver alleged to be guilty of a road traffic offence. They are also permitted to perform duties connected with the interim disposal of vehicles removed in consequence of being illegally, obstructively or dangerously parked; the immobilisation of illegally parked vehicles; and the custody of vehicles removed under statutory powers. Lastly, they are permitted to perform duties in the regulation and control of traffic. Traffic wardens are not permitted to exercise any of their functions when in a moving vehicle.

To enable traffic wardens to carry out their various functions, art 3 of the Order provides that:

(a) drivers and pedestrians must comply with their traffic directions;
(b) traffic wardens have power to obtain the names and addresses of persons reasonably believed to have committed one of the following offences: parking without lights; obstruction; waiting or loading etc; failing to conform to a valid

indication given for the regulation of traffic, or a traffic sign; a vehicle excise offence; or an offence in respect of charges for parking on the highway;

(c) traffic wardens also have power to obtain the names and addresses of pedestrians who fail to comply with traffic directions; and

(d) traffic wardens may require the production of driving licences where they have reasonable cause to believe that an offence has been committed by causing a vehicle, or any part of it, to stop in contravention of the pedestrian crossing regulations or by leaving the vehicle in a dangerous position, or where they are employed to perform functions in connection with the impounding of vehicles and have reasonable cause to believe that an offence of obstruction, waiting etc has been committed.

PARKING GENERALLY

The Road Traffic Regulation Act 1984, ss 5 and 8 permit local authorities to make traffic regulation orders. Most of such orders will be 'no waiting' orders. There is no prescribed form which such orders must follow but they must be properly made in accordance with regulations. Such orders contain exemptions in favour of particular persons or particular types of vehicles. The offences which are committed when the provisions of such orders are contravened are contained in these sections of the Road Traffic Regulation Act 1984.

In addition, the RTRA 1984, s 32 empowers a local authority to provide off-street parking places and to authorise the use as a parking place of any part of a road within their area not being a road within Greater London. Section 35 of the 1984 Act permits local authorities to make parking place orders in respect of places so provided. Sections 45 and 46 permit local authorities to designate parking places on highways within their areas and permit the imposition of charges in respect of such parking. It is an offence against s 47 to fail to comply with the requirements of any order so made.

The Road Traffic Act 1991, Part II makes provision for the decriminalisation of certain parking offences. These offences lead to penalties being required to be paid by the appropriate authority without the offender appearing before a court. There is a system of appeal to parking adjudicators. Once again the particular orders will be made by local authorities which are empowered to employ parking attendants to enforce their provisions.

FIXED PENALTY OFFENCES

The application of the law on fixed penalties for road traffic offences requires police officers to be aware not only of the list of offences which can be dealt with by the fixed penalty procedure but also to be aware of those offences which carry obligatory endorsement of penalty points. Schedule 3 to the Road Traffic Offenders Act 1988 lists the offences which are 'fixed penalty offences'. Schedule 2 indicates the offences which carry obligatory endorsement. To assist the memory of police officers in this respect, aides memoire have been prepared listing the various offences which are non-endorsable fixed penalty offences and those which are endorsable. The aide memoire in relation to endorsable fixed penalty offences also indicates the number of penalty points which apply, and gives a code number for each offence. That for non-endorsable fixed penalty offences includes advice concerning enforcement policies existing within a police force, particularly where a vehicle rectification scheme is in operation.

In general, the non-endorsable fixed penalty offences are concerned with those involving minor defects in the vehicle or its parts; vehicle registration and vehicle excise offences; failure to display goods vehicle plates; stopping on the verge or hard shoulder of a motorway; contravention of certain traffic directions (eg 'give way', 'no entry', 'no U turn', 'one-way' signs and temporary traffic signs); neglect of pedestrian rights; obstruction; waiting and parking offences; lighting and noise offences; offences relating to loads (other than dangerous loads); trailer offences; offences peculiar to motorcycles, and other miscellaneous motoring offences (eg failing to wear a seat belt).

The endorsable fixed penalty offences include those of the Road Vehicles (Construction and Use) Regulations which are concerned with danger (parts, loads, tyres etc); failure to comply with 'Stop' signs, double white lines, traffic lights, directions of a constable; stopping offences in relation to pedestrian crossings and offences of failing to accord precedence under the 'Zebra', 'Pelican' and 'Puffin' regulations; speeding; stopping or reversing on the carriageway of a motorway; driving on a hard shoulder or central reservation; driving on a motorway by a provisional licence holder; use of offside lane of three-lane motorway by a large goods vehicle or passenger-carrying vehicle; breaches of conditions of provisional licences; offences relating to motorcycle passengers; offences relating to the failure to wear a seat belt; leaving a vehicle in a dangerous position, and using a vehicle in a designated play street.

The provisions discussed in this section dealing with fixed penalty offences are contained in the Road Traffic Offenders Act 1988, unless otherwise indicated.

The issue of a fixed penalty notice for a non-endorsable offence

Section 54 of the 1988 Act states that a fixed penalty notice for a non-endorsable offence may be issued where a constable in uniform in England and Wales *finds a person* on any occasion and has reason to believe that on that occasion *he is committing or has committed* a fixed penalty offence. A fixed penalty notice for these offences must be issued at the time or immediately after an offence is committed. It cannot be issued where inquiries are necessary to trace the driver of a vehicle. For example, a driver seen to commit an offence by failing to give way at a junction controlled by a 'give way' sign may at the time or immediately afterwards be given a fixed penalty notice for that offence. If it is not possible to stop him at the time, and he is seen at home after a 'trace' through the police national computer, such a notice may not be issued to him under s 54 since he is not found on *that occasion* to be committing etc an offence. In such a case the conditional offer of a fixed penalty procedure (p 311) will have to be used or a prosecution will have to be instituted.

Section 62 of the 1988 Act provides that where on any occasion a constable has reason to believe that a fixed penalty offence is being or has been committed in respect of a stationary vehicle, he may affix a fixed penalty notice in respect of the offence to that vehicle unless the offence appears to him to involve obligatory endorsement.

Only one fixed penalty notice may be issued on any one occasion. If more than one offence is committed on a particular occasion a constable should either issue a fixed penalty notice for one offence and administer a verbal warning in respect of all other offences, or report the offender in the normal way for all offences committed. However, this will not apply when offences are subsequently detected, as would occur when documents which were subsequently produced were found to be defective in some respect. These offences, subsequently detected, will be dealt with by the officer reporting the offender with a view to proceedings by way of a summons even though a fixed penalty notice has been issued for the original offence.

The issue of fixed penalty notices for non-endorsable offences by *traffic wardens* is restricted to those offences described in the Functions of Traffic Wardens Order 1970 as amended. The Schedule to the order provides that traffic wardens may be employed to enforce the law with respect to:

(a) offences of parking without obligatory lights or reflectors during the hours of darkness;
(b) offences of vehicles obstructing a road, or waiting or being left or parked, or being loaded or unloaded, on a road or public place;
(c) offences against the Vehicles Excise and Registration Act 1994 (eg no vehicle excise licence);
(d) offences relating to parking places on highways where charges are made (eg by meters or machines); or
(e) offences committed by causing a vehicle, or any part of it, to stop in contravention of the pedestrian crossing regulations.

The Road Traffic Offenders Act 1988, s 86 was amended by the Road Traffic Act 1991 to permit the Secretary of State, by order, to permit the use of traffic wardens to deal with fixed penalty offences which involve obligatory endorsement where the vehicle concerned is stationary. At the time of writing, an order has been made adding the offences of vehicle obstruction and leaving a vehicle in a dangerous position.

Fixed penalty notices should not be given to juveniles as there are other recommended procedures for dealing with juveniles which recognise all the circumstances of each case.

The issue of a fixed penalty notice for an endorsable offence

Section 54 states that, *subject to the provisions described below*, a fixed penalty notice for an endorsable offence may be issued where a constable in England and Wales finds a person on any occasion and has reason to believe that on that occasion *he is committing or has committed* a fixed penalty offence. As with a fixed penalty notice in respect of a non-endorsable offence, the notice under s 54 must be issued at the time of, or immediately after, the offence. If it is not so issued the conditional offer of a fixed penalty procedure (p 311) will have to be instituted.

Where it appears to a constable that the fixed penalty offence involves obligatory endorsement, he may only give the offender a fixed penalty notice in respect of the offence if:

(a) the offender produces his driving licence for inspection by the constable;
(b) the constable is satisfied on inspecting the licence that the offender would not be liable to be disqualified because the total number of penalty points would number 12 or more if he was convicted of the fixed penalty offence; and
(c) the offender surrenders his driving licence to the constable to be retained and dealt with in accordance with the Act.

In determining for such purposes whether a person convicted of an offence would be liable to disqualification it must be assumed, where the offence carries a range of penalty points, that the points to be attributed to the offence would be the lowest in the range.

The issue of a fixed penalty notice for an endorsable offence (or a non-endorsable offence) is a matter for the police officer's discretion so far as this is permitted by force policy. Within the limits of such policy, a constable may decide to give a verbal warning for the offence; issue a fixed penalty notice provided that existing penalty points permit such a course of action; or report the offender with a view to proceedings by way of summons.

When considering whether to deal with the offence by way of fixed penalty, and before he asks to see the offender's driving licence, the officer must ensure that the offender is aware of the implications of such a procedure and it is suggested that he uses a form of words which convey the following message:

> 'I am considering the issue to you of a fixed penalty notice for the offence of ...
> It will be necessary for me to examine your driving licence and any penalty points which may be endorsed on it. If after examination I find that it is appropriate to issue you with a fixed penalty notice it will be necessary to surrender your licence to me.'

It is essential that, whatever form of words is used, the offender is not given the impression that he must permit the examination of penalty points endorsed on his licence or that he must surrender it. The Act does not extend the powers of a constable in relation to matters which may be examined in a driving licence, nor does it provide a power to seize a driving licence.

When licence produced at time

If the driver is able to produce his licence, and does so, and provided that the number of penalty points is not such that the driver will be liable to disqualification if points for the fixed penalty offence are added, the constable may issue a full fixed penalty notice. When the constable has examined the driving licence and is satisfied that he is able to issue a fixed penalty notice, because the addition of penalty points for the offence will not combine to a total of 12 or more, he should invite the driver to surrender his driving licence. Again, care must be taken in the choice of words. An officer might say:

> 'Your licence indicates that you may have this offence dealt with by fixed penalty notice. Are you willing to surrender your licence to me? You will be given a receipt.'

Part 3 of the fixed penalty notice gives advice on the procedure to be followed if the offender wishes to request a court hearing. If a driver contests the issue of a fixed penalty notice, his attention should be drawn to this part of the notice. Police officers completing fixed penalty notices should, wherever possible, obtain the full post code as well as the address of the offender, as this assists the clerk to the justices in relation to the registration of subsequent penalties with the offender's home court.

Section 56 of the 1988 Act requires a constable or authorised person to give a receipt for a driving licence so surrendered. The receipt which is given by the officer is incorporated in the fixed penalty notice. Such a receipt is valid for two months from the date of issue (or such longer period as may be prescribed). However, a fixed penalty clerk may issue a new receipt on the application of the licence holder which will expire on such date as may be specified in the new receipt. In any event, a receipt ceases to have effect on the return of the licence to the holder. The section allows the receipt to be produced in place of a licence, subject to the same conditions concerning later production, on a request being made by a constable under s 164 of the Road Traffic Act 1988, provided that, *if required to do so*, the licence holder subsequently produces his driving licence at the specified police station immediately it is returned.

When licence not produced at time

The procedure to be followed when an offender does not produce his driving licence at the time of the offence is dealt with by s 54(4) of the 1988 Act. In any case where:

(a) the offence appears to the constable to be an offence involving obligatory endorsement; and

(b) the person concerned does not produce his licence for inspection by the constable,

the constable may give him a notice stating that if, within seven days after the notice is given, he produces the notice together with his driving licence in person to a constable or authorised person at the police station specified in the notice (being a police station chosen by the person concerned) and the requirements of s 54(5) (set out below) are met he will then be given a fixed penalty notice in respect of the offence. An 'authorised person' is a person at a police station authorised for this purpose by a chief officer of police.

These provisions allow a constable to issue a 'provisional fixed penalty notice' in circumstances in which a driver does not produce his licence at the time of the offence. It would be unfair if there was not a procedure within which drivers who were not in possession of their driving licence at the time of the offence could not take advantage of an opportunity to pay a fixed penalty in preference to court proceedings.

Section 54(5) of the 1988 Act allows a person to whom a provisional fixed penalty notice has been given to produce the notice together with his driving licence *in person* to a police constable or authorised person at the police station specified in the notice within seven days. If he does so and the constable or authorised person is satisfied concerning the issue of accumulated penalty points and such person surrenders his driving licence to be retained and dealt with in accordance with the Act, the constable or authorised person *must* give him a fixed penalty notice in respect of the offence. Only a constable or authorised person may substantiate a provisional fixed penalty notice.

The section specifically excludes offences committed in Scotland and declares that a provisional fixed penalty notice *must not* specify a police station in Scotland.

It must be stressed that these provisions are concerned with extending the fixed penalty provisions to those drivers who are not in possession of their licence at the time of their offence. No offence is committed if the offender fails to produce his driving licence as a result of an offer made under s 54(4). If the constable dealing with such an offender decides that he wishes to examine his driving licence for some reason other than substantiation of a provisional fixed penalty notice, or assessing penalty points on the spot, he must make a requirement under the Road Traffic Act 1988, s 164 and should make it clear that there is a quite separate demand for production to permit examination of those matters prescribed by s 164(1) of that Act, matters which are unconcerned with the issue of penalty points. If, in such a case, an offender fails to produce his licence under the provisions of the Road Traffic Offenders Act 1988, or on production it is found that his penalty points are such that the issue of disqualification arises, he will be prosecuted for the offence in the normal way and the provisional fixed penalty notice is of no further effect.

The form HO/RT 2 has been amended to deal with the production of driving licences consequent upon the issue of provisional fixed penalty notices and the production of driving licence receipts. When HO/RT 2 forms are made out specifically in connection with a provisional fixed penalty notice, the number of the notice should be included on the HO/RT 2.

Endorsements of licences without hearing

Section 57 of the 1988 Act authorises the endorsement by the fixed penalty clerk (without any order of a court) of a driving licence surrendered by a person when he was given a fixed penalty notice under s 54 of the Act. A licence may not be endorsed if a request for a hearing has been received before the end of the suspended enforcement period.

Licences so surrendered will be endorsed either at the time at which the fixed penalty is paid, if this occurs before the end of the suspended enforcement period, or if it does not when the fixed penalty plus one half of that penalty has been registered for enforcement as a fine.

Section 83 deals with the case where a fixed penalty clerk is deceived into endorsing a licence in circumstances in which the licence holder should have been disqualified under the totting-up procedure and the deception constituted, or was due to, an offence committed by the licence holder. It provides that if the licence holder is convicted of that offence, the court before which he is convicted will have the same powers to disqualify as it would have had if it was convicting him of the endorsable offence.

Provisions related to fixed penalty offences generally

No proceedings may be brought for an offence to which a fixed penalty notice relates until 21 days following the day of the notice (or such longer period as may be specified in the notice). This period of time is referred to as the suspended enforcement period.

Where a fixed penalty notice has been given to an offender, no proceedings shall be brought unless that person has given notice requesting a hearing before the end of the suspended enforcement period. If no such notice has been received and the fixed penalty has not been paid before the end of the suspended enforcement period, a sum equal to the fixed penalty plus one half of that amount may be registered against that person as a fine.

In cases in which a fixed penalty notice is affixed to a vehicle and the fixed penalty has not been paid within the suspended enforcement period, *a notice to owner* may be served by or on behalf of the chief officer of police on *any person who appears to him* to be the owner of the vehicle (or a person authorised to act on such person's behalf). Such a notice must give particulars of the offence in question, of the fixed penalty concerned and of the period allowed for response to the notice. It must also indicate that, if the fixed penalty is not paid before the end of that period, the person on whom the notice is served must furnish, before the end of that period, a statutory statement of ownership. The period allowed for response to such a notice is defined by s 63(5) as 21 days from the service of the notice. However, a notice need not be served when a request for a hearing has been made with an admission by the person making the request that he was the driver of the vehicle on that occasion. If a person on whom a notice has been served by or on behalf of a chief officer of police was not the owner of the vehicle at the relevant time and he furnishes in time a statutory statement to the effect that he was not the owner, he is not liable for the offence in question. Otherwise, where a notice is served within six months of the commission of that offence and the fixed penalty has not been paid within the period allowed, a sum equal to the fixed penalty, plus one half of that penalty, may be registered against the person on whom the notice to owner was served as a fine.

Where person receiving was not the driver

The 1988 Act recognises that there will be occasions upon which the person who receives a notice to owner, in his capacity as such, will not have been the driver at the relevant time. Section 63 therefore requires that the notice must indicate that the person on whom it is served may, before the end of the period permitted for response, either request a hearing or, if the person driving at the time wishes to give notice requesting a hearing, furnish, together with a statutory statement of ownership, a statutory statement of facts which has the effect of the actual driver requesting a hearing. (If such a driver is prepared to accept responsibility for the fixed penalty it is implied that he will do so by paying the penalty on behalf of the person to whom the notice is addressed.) Once a statutory statement of facts has been supplied, the person named in the notice to owner is relieved of further responsibility and any sums due by way of fixed penalty may not be registered for enforcement. Once a fixed penalty has been registered for enforcement as a fine against a person on whom a notice to owner has been served, however, no proceedings can be brought against any other person in respect of that offence.

Special provisions are applied to hire vehicles by s 66 of the 1988 Act. For these purposes a hire vehicle is one which is hired for temporary use, as opposed to a vehicle on hire purchase. In such cases, provided a form of agreement has been drawn up between the hire firm and the hirer under the Road Traffic (Owner Liability) Regulations and provided the hire firm produces a copy of this to the police (together with a statement of hirer liability signed by the hirer under that hiring agreement), liability is removed from the hire firm; and the hirer of the vehicle becomes its owner for the purpose of the fixed penalty provisions.

Payment of penalties

Fixed penalties must be paid to justices' clerks in a manner specified within the notice and the money must be dealt with as if it was a fine imposed on summary conviction. Payment may be made by way of a properly addressed, pre-paid letter. The payment is regarded as having been made at the time that the letter would be delivered in the course of normal post. In any proceedings a certificate from a fixed penalty clerk is admissible to prove that a fixed penalty was or was not received by a date specified in the certificate, or that a letter was marked as posted on a date so specified. If a fixed penalty is paid before the end of the suspended enforcement period, no further proceedings may be brought.

The fixed penalty to be paid in respect of an offence is such amount as the Secretary of State may by order prescribe, or one half of the maximum amount of the fine to which the person committing the offence would be liable on summary conviction, whichever is the less. The amounts prescribed by the Secretary of State are currently contained in the Fixed Penalty Order 1992. Under that Order the penalty for offences involving obligatory endorsement is fixed at £40. Where the offence is a non-endorsable offence the penalty is normally £20. However, where the non-endorsable offence consists of a fixed penalty parking offence committed in London the penalty is £40 if it is committed on a red route, or £30 if it is committed otherwise than on a red route.

The term *fixed penalty parking offence* means:

(a) an offence under the Road Traffic Regulation Act 1984 which does not involve obligatory endorsement and is committed in respect of a stationary vehicle; and
(b) road obstruction offences under a variety of statutory provisions.

A 'red route' means a length of road on which there are traffic signs bearing the words 'red route' or red lines or marks.

Penalty registered against person who has no knowledge of the offence

Within such procedures it is obvious that there will be occasions when a penalty is registered against a person who, for some reason, has no knowledge of the offence. This may occur when fixed penalty notices are affixed to vehicles which have changed ownership without DVLA records being amended, or where a driver of someone else's vehicle does not inform the owner of the notice. Section 72 of the 1988 Act therefore provides a procedure whereby registration may be declared void. If registration has followed non-receipt of a request for a hearing and the fixed penalty has not been paid, a statutory declaration may be made to the effect that the declarant was not the person to whom the fixed penalty notice was given or that he had requested a hearing before the end of the suspended enforcement period. Where the registration has followed service of 'notice to owner' on the owner of the vehicle in question, and the penalty has not been paid, the statutory declaration must state either that:

(a) the declarant did not know of the penalty, or fixed penalty notice, or notice to owner, until he received notice of the registration; or

(b) he was not the owner at the time of the offence alleged and that he has reasonable excuse for failing to comply with the notice to owner; or

(c) he requested a hearing as permitted by the notice to owner.

A declaration must be served on the clerk of the relevant court, within 21 days of the receipt of the notification of registration. The effect of the declaration is that the relevant notice, registration or endorsement (as the case may be) is void.

Miscellaneous points

Section 30 requires that, if a person is convicted of an offence involving endorsement and the court is satisfied that he is liable to have penalty points endorsed upon his licence within the fixed penalty procedure for an offence committed on the same occasion as those for which he is convicted, the court must reduce the number of penalty points endorsed on the licence by the number which will be attached in consequence of the fixed penalty offence.

It is an offence contrary to s 62(2) of the 1988 Act to remove or interfere with a notice affixed to a vehicle under s 62(1) unless it is done by or under the authority of the driver or person in charge of the vehicle or the person liable for the offence in question.

It is an offence by s 67 of the 1988 Act recklessly to furnish a statement which is false in a material particular, in response to a notice to owner issued under s 63 of the Act, or to furnish such a statement knowing it to be false in that particular.

Evidence in court proceedings in fixed penalty notice cases

Section 79 of the 1988 Act permits the service of a constable's statement of evidence together with a fixed penalty notice or notice to owner. Such a statement will be deemed to have been served for the purposes of the Criminal Justice Act 1967, s 9 (which we referred to on p 159).

The 1988 Act permits 'statutory statements of ownership or of facts' to be used in evidence. A statutory statement of ownership under the Act is one in which the declarant states whether or not he was the owner of the vehicle at the relevant time. If he was not it will state whether he was ever the owner and, if so, when. A statutory statement of facts is one in which the declarant states that he was not the driver of the vehicle at the relevant time and states the name and address of the person who was.

Conditional offer of fixed penalty

In England and Wales where a constable has reason to believe that a fixed penalty offence has been committed and no fixed penalty notice was given at the time or fixed to the vehicle concerned, a notice of 'conditional offer' may be sent to the alleged offender by, or on behalf of, the chief officer of police. A conditional offer must give particulars of the circumstances and give reasonable information about the alleged offence, and state that proceedings cannot be commenced for the offence until the end of 28 days following the date of issue (or such longer period specified). Such a notice must indicate that if, within that period, the alleged offender pays the fixed penalty to the fixed penalty clerk and, where the offence concerned involves obligatory endorsement and the licence (and its counterpart) is delivered to the clerk at the same time and the clerk is satisfied that the alleged offender, if convicted, would not be liable to disqualification under the Road Traffic Offenders Act 1988, s 35 (disqualification for repeated offences), liability to conviction will be discharged. In assessing liability to such disqualification, it is assumed (where penalty points awardable for the offence are within a range) that the number to be attributed for the offence would be the lowest in the range.

A person issuing a conditional offer must notify the fixed penalty clerk. If payment is made in accordance with the offer and the licence is delivered, no proceedings will be taken for the offence to which the conditional offer relates. The fixed penalty clerk must endorse the counterpart of the licence in appropriate cases and return it to the holder. Where the payment of a fixed penalty is made by means of a cheque which is subsequently dishonoured, the endorsement remains valid, even though the licence holder is then liable to prosecution for the offence. In such circumstances the fixed penalty clerk must, on the expiry of the period specified in the conditional offer, or (if that period has expired) forthwith, notify the person by whom the conditional offer was made that no payment has been made. Where proceedings are brought against a licence holder after he has been notified that a cheque tendered in payment has been dishonoured, the court must order the removal of the fixed penalty endorsement from the licence (or counterpart) and may make any competent order of endorsement or disqualification, in addition to sentence.

The fixed penalty clerk must notify the Secretary of State of any endorsement made on the licence in accordance with these procedures.

Special provisions for dealing with offences by way of fixed penalty

The Road Traffic (Vehicle Emissions)(Fixed Penalty) Regulations 1997 makse provision for specified local authorities to authorise persons to issue fixed penalty notices to users of vehicles within their areas who contravene, or fail to comply with, the Road Vehicles (Construction and Use) Regulations 1986, regs 61 (emission of oil, smoke, vapour, gases, oily substances etc) and reg 98 (stopping of engine when vehicle stationary).

PARKING BY DISABLED DRIVERS

The Chronically Sick and Disabled Persons Act 1970, s 21 requires that a badge of the prescribed form be issued by local authorities for motor vehicles driven by, or used for the carriage of, disabled persons resident within their areas. A badge so issued may be displayed on a vehicle either inside or outside the area of the issuing authority, and exemptions afforded to such persons apply anywhere. Badges may also be issued to institutions concerned with the care of the disabled.

A 'disabled person's vehicle' means a vehicle which is lawfully displaying a disabled person's badge and which, immediately before or after a period of waiting allowed by virtue of any provision in an order which makes special concessions for parking by disabled persons, has been or is to be driven by a disabled person, or (as the case may be) has been or is to be used for carrying disabled person(s) as passenger(s). The circumstances in which a vehicle may lawfully display a disabled person's badge are set out below.

The Local Authorities Traffic Orders (Exemptions for Disabled Persons) (England and Wales) Regulations 1986, as amended, contain a requirement that all no waiting orders etc made by local authorities must contain exemptions in favour of disabled persons' vehicles. However, the requirement to include an exemption does not apply to orders which prohibit the waiting of vehicles of all other classes.

Badges currently in use may be of two different designs but both will be 'orange badges'. Those issued before 2 March 1992 continue to be valid and will show a figure in a wheelchair, the name, validity, name of issuing council and serial number. Those issued on or after that date, if issued to an individual, will carry a photograph of the holder. Badges issued to institutions will carry the seal or stamp of the organisation holding the badge. The new badges are very comprehensive and carry information concerning the situations in which a holder may, or may not, park his vehicle and the time limitations which may apply.

Badges must be displayed in the 'relevant position'. Badges issued before 2 March 1992 may be displayed on the nearside behind the front windscreen or, where there is no windscreen, in a conspicuous position on the vehicle. Those issued on or after that date must, where the vehicle is fitted with a dashboard or facia panel, be displayed thereon, in such a position that Part I (which contains details of the issuing authority) is legible from outside the vehicle. If there is no dashboard or facia panel, the badge must be displayed in a conspicuous position and be legible from outside the vehicle. Similar provisions are made for the display of parking discs, so that the quarter-hour period during which the period of waiting begins is legible from outside the vehicle.

The Disabled Persons (Badges for Motor Vehicles) Regulations 1982, specify the circumstances in which a disabled persons's badge may lawfully be displayed on a motor vehicle. The Chronically Sick and Disabled Persons Act 1970, s 21, makes it an offence for a person to drive a motor vehicle which is displaying such a badge otherwise than in a manner or in circumstances prescribed by the Regulations. It also creates the offence of displaying a badge which is not issued by a local authority. A badge, other than an institutional badge, may be displayed on a moving vehicle if it is being driven by the holder or when he is being carried in the vehicle. The only other circumstance is where the vehicle is being driven in a place subject to restricted access by vehicles but the order concerned provides for access where a disabled person's concession is available to a vehicle lawfully displaying a disabled person's badge, and it would not otherwise be practicable for the vehicle to be driven there to pick up such a person. In the same way, moving vehicles may display such badges whilst leaving the vicinity of the place of disembarkation in these circumstances. When parked, a badge may be displayed if the vehicle has been driven to that place by the holder or has been used to carry him there, or is to be driven from, or he is to be carried from, the place where the vehicle is parked. The same rules apply to the use of institutional badges where the vehicle is being used by the holder (the institution) for the benefit of a disabled person or persons.

The exemptions which apply in favour of disabled persons' vehicles are in respect of prohibiting vehicles waiting beyond a specified period of time, of no waiting orders for vehicles generally (whether in relation to some types or all vehicles), of orders prohibiting waiting for more than a specified period in a street parking place, and of charges and time limit restrictions at parking meters. The only restriction which may apply to disabled persons' vehicles is where there is a prohibition on waiting for a period more than three hours. In such a case a disabled persons's vehicle is exempt for a maximum of three hours (but then must not return for an hour to that place), provided that a badge is displayed showing the time of arrival (disc parking scheme).

The orange badge scheme does not permit parking:

(a) during the time a ban on loading or unloading is in force (indicated by one, two or three yellow marks on a kerb, at a time shown on a post-mounted plate);
(b) where there is a double white line in the centre of the road even if one of the lines is broken;
(c) in a bus or cycle lane when it is in use;
(d) on Zebra or Pelican crossings or on the zig-zag markings before or after these crossings;
(e) in parking places reserved for specific users, eg loading bays, residents, taxis or cycles; and
(f) in suspended meter bays or when the use of the meter is prohibited.

The Road Traffic Regulation Act 1984, s 117 deals with the wrongful use of a disabled person's badge. It provides that a person is guilty of an offence if, when he commits some other offence under the Act (eg contravention of an order relating to parking made under it), the following conditions are satisfied:

(a) a disabled person's badge was displayed on the motor vehicle;
(b) he was using the vehicle in circumstances where a disabled person's concession would be available to a disabled person's vehicle; and
(c) the vehicle was not being used either by the person to whom the badge was issued or for institutional use.

RESTRICTIONS ON THE USE OF MOTORWAYS

The Motorways Traffic (England and Wales) Regulations 1982 impose various restrictions upon the drivers of motor vehicles on motorways. Contravention of the Regulations is an offence. The Regulations limit the classes of vehicles which are permitted to use motorways.

Vehicles which may use motorways

Under the Regulations, Class I and Class II vehicles are, in normal circumstances, permitted to use motorways. Class I includes heavy and light locomotives, motor tractors, heavy motor cars, motor cars and motorcycles of not less than 50 cc and trailers drawn by such vehicles. (These terms are defined in ch 10.) Track-laying vehicles are not within Class I. To be in Class I vehicles must be fitted with pneumatic tyres, must not be agricultural motor vehicles or machines and must not be pedestrian- controlled. All such vehicles must be capable of attaining a speed of 25 mph when unladen.

Class II vehicles are those specially made to transport abnormal, indivisible loads, and large vehicles (eg tank transporters) used by the armed services. In addition, earth movers and similar engineering plant are Class II vehicles if they are capable of attaining 25 mph when unladen.

Direction of driving

Regulation 6 requires the observance of 'no entry' and 'no left or right turn' signs. It also requires that vehicles always have the central reservation on their right or offside, and that, if there is no central reservation, they continue to travel in the direction which was permitted on entry to the motorway and that they are not driven or moved so as to cause them to turn and proceed in, or face, the opposite direction.

Stopping

Regulation 7 requires that no vehicle shall stop or remain at rest on a carriageway of a motorway. When a stop becomes necessary due to breakdown, mechanical defect, lack of fuel, accident, illness or other emergency, or to permit a person carried in the vehicle to recover or move an object which has fallen on to the motorway, or to permit a person to give help to another in any of those circumstances, the vehicle must, as soon and in so far as is reasonably practicable, be driven or moved off the carriageway on to a contiguous hard shoulder where it may stop and remain at rest. Such a vehicle must remain at rest in such a position that, as far as reasonably practicable, no part of it or its load obstructs or causes danger to vehicles using the carriageway. It must not remain for longer than necessary for such purpose.

The regulation makes the obvious exception in favour of drivers prevented from proceeding by 'traffic jams'.

Reversing

The driving or moving of a vehicle backwards is prohibited by reg 8, unless it is necessary to do so to allow it to move forward or be connected to another vehicle.

General usage

Regulations 9 and 10 prohibit driving, stopping or remaining at rest on a hard shoulder (in circumstances other than those permitted) or on a central reservation. Regulation 11 prohibits the driving of motor vehicles on motorways by persons who are authorised to drive the vehicle which they are driving only by virtue of being the holder of a provisional licence. The regulation applies to:

(a) a motor vehicle in category A or B or sub-category C1 + E (8.25 tonnes), D1 (not for hire or reward) or P, and

(b) a motor vehicle in category B + E or sub-category C1 if the provisional licence authorising the driving of such a motor vehicle was in force at a time before 1 January 1997.

The Motor Vehicles (Driving Licences) Regulations 1996 introduced separate driving tests for motor cars with trailers (category B + E), trucks and vans of between 3.5 tonnes and 7.5 tonnes maximum authorised mass (sub-categories C1 and C1 + E) and for buses having more than eight but not more than 16 passenger seats in addition to the driver's seat whether or not they carry passengers for hire or reward (sub-categories D1 and D1 + E). Provisional licences to drive such vehicles may only be issued to persons holding at least a full licence to drive motor cars (category B). Such holders of provisional licences are authorised to drive on motorways while holding provisional licences (as they are full licence holders in respect of category B).

It is an offence, contrary to the Road Traffic Regulation Act 1984, s 17(4), to walk on a motorway except when it is necessary to do so as a result of an accident or emergency, or as a result of a motor vehicle being at rest on a motorway in such circumstances or as a result of illness, or to assist in an emergency.

Regulation 14 provides that the person in charge of an animal shall, so far as is practicable, ensure that it is not removed from or permitted to leave the vehicle while on a motorway. If it escapes or it is necessary for it to be removed from or permitted to leave the vehicle, it must not go on or remain on any part of a motorway other than a hard shoulder, where it must be held on a lead or otherwise kept under proper control.

Use of right or offside lane

Regulation 12 prohibits the following vehicles from using the offside lane of a three-lane motorway at any place where all three lanes are open to traffic:

(a) a goods vehicle which has a maximum laden weight exceeding 7.5 tonnes;
(b) a passenger vehicle which is constructed or adapted to carry more than eight seated passengers in addition to the driver the maximum laden weight of which exceeds 7.5 tonnes;
(c) a motor vehicle drawing a trailer; and
(d) a motor vehicle which is a motor tractor or a locomotive.

The only occasions upon which such vehicles may enter the offside lane of a three-lane motorway, when all lanes are open, is when this is necessary to overtake a wide load.

However, where the number of lanes in a carriageway increases from two to three or more, for example where motorways merge, a vehicle which is travelling in the outer lane may remain there until it is safe to move into the middle lane, or until such time as a change can be made without causing inconvenience to other traffic.

Exceptions and relaxations of effect of regulations

Regulation 15 provides for vehicles other than those within Classes I and II to be permitted to use motorways in emergencies and certain other cases. There are occasions upon which vehicles which would normally be banned must be present to carry out maintenance work or repairs etc. This is permitted by reg 15. In addition, the Secretary of State may authorise limited use to allow excluded traffic access on occasions or in an emergency or to enable it to cross a motorway to gain access to premises abutting on or adjacent to a motorway. Lastly, a chief officer of police (or a superintendent acting on his behalf) may authorise usage by excluded traffic for a period of time during which the use of an alternative road is rendered impossible or unsuitable.

Regulation 16 permits the use of a motorway otherwise than in accordance with the Regulations, upon the direction of a constable in uniform or in compliance with a traffic sign; with the permission of a constable for the purpose of the investigation of an accident; where necessary to prevent an accident or give help as a result of an accident or emergency; where the act is done in exercise of the duty of a constable, firefighter or member of the ambulance service; or where necessary in connection with motorway maintenance or the removal of vehicles.

Regulations 15 and 16 therefore provide the essential exceptions to the rules to permit maintenance, life saving and action by the emergency services.

CHAPTER 12

Public service vehicles

The Public Passenger Vehicles Act 1981 (hereafter referred to in this chapter as 'the 1981 Act') consolidated the provisions of all previous Acts dealing with public service vehicles. Regulations have been made under the Act and regulations made under the previous legislation continue in force. It is essential that persons who offer bus or coach services to the general public maintain high standards and therefore provision for the licensing and control of the vehicles used is made by the Act and the regulations. Such vehicles must be correctly constructed, equipped and maintained to ensure the safety of the travelling public. Those who use the vehicles—drivers, conductors and passengers—must also comply with prescribed standards.

The Road Traffic Act 1988, s 193A makes special provisions in relation to tramcars which are not subject to the general provisions in respect of public service vehicles. Local regulations will be in force where tramcars are used within specific areas.

The Transport Act 1985 made quite extensive changes to the Public Passenger Vehicles Act 1981 by making provisions which would allow 'controlled competition' between bus companies. It, inter alia, removed the requirement for services to be operated under a road service licence and replaced this requirement with a system of registration of local bus services.

DEFINITION: PUBLIC SERVICE VEHICLE

Section 1(1) of the 1981 Act defines a public service vehicle as a motor vehicle (other than a tramcar) which:

(a) if adapted to carry more than eight passengers, is used for carrying passengers for hire or reward; or
(b) if not so adapted, is used for carrying passengers for hire or reward at separate fares in the course of a business of carrying passengers.

There are, therefore, two types of public service vehicles. However, the definitions of both types contain a number of common elements, and we shall deal with these before giving separate consideration to the two types.

Section 1(1) states that, to be a public service vehicle, a vehicle must be a *'motor vehicle (other than a tramcar)'*. The term 'motor vehicle' has already been fully discussed in ch 9, above, but the reader is reminded that it is defined as 'a mechanically propelled vehicle intended or adapted for use on roads'. Horse-drawn passenger carriages are therefore completely excluded from the legislation relating to public service vehicles.

The definitions of both types of public service vehicle require that the vehicle *'is used for carrying passengers for hire or reward'*. These words require further explanation.

Used

The meaning of this term has already been fully considered in ch 10, above, but s 1(2) of the 1981 Act adds that for the purpose of s 1(1) a vehicle is being used for a purpose mentioned in s 1(1)(a) or (b) if it is *being so* used *or if it has been so used and that use has not been permanently discontinued*. This extends 'use' to circumstances in which the motor vehicle is no longer being used at that moment as a public service vehicle, but it is the owner's intention to use it again. Consequently, a public service vehicle does not cease to be so classified merely because its journey is over; it remains such until permanently used for some other purpose. Persons who convey stock racing cars and dragsters to tracks frequently use modified buses or coaches for this purpose. These vehicles are no longer public service vehicles as their use for the carriage of passengers has been permanently discontinued. On the other hand, a bus or coach which, between service runs, is used by an employee to return to his home on an errand remains a public service vehicle as its use as such has not been permanently discontinued.

Hire or reward

Even though a vehicle may be able to carry 50 or more passengers it is not a public service vehicle unless it is used to carry passengers for hire or reward. Once it is so used, it will become a public service vehicle provided the requirements of one or other of the types of public service vehicle are satisfied. If a person owns a minibus and takes out his family, it is not a public service vehicle as it is not carrying passengers for hire or reward. If he owns a 40-seater coach which he only uses to take out his family and friends, then, provided that he never charges them a fare or the like, there is no carriage for hire or reward and therefore the coach is not a public service vehicle.

The term 'hire or reward' in a general sense means a monetary reward legally due under a contract. (However, as we show on the next page, there are some cases of carriage for hire or reward, even though no contract exists.) Money paid or promised under a purely social arrangement (such as a car-sharing scheme) does not make the carriage for hire or reward. A contract to carry a passenger for hire or reward may be made before a passenger boards the vehicle (as in the case of a coach trip) or it may be made aboard the vehicle (as in the case of a bus journey).

The meaning of 'hire or reward' has been extended by s 1(5) of the 1981 Act as follows:

(a)   a vehicle is to be treated as carrying passengers for hire or reward if payment is made for, or for matters which include, the carrying of passengers, irrespective of the person to whom the payment is made and, in the case of a transaction effected by or on behalf of a member of any association of persons (whether incorporated or not) on the one hand and the association or another member thereof on the other hand, notwithstanding any rule of law as to such transactions;

(b) a payment made for the carrying of a passenger is to be treated as a fare notwithstanding that it is made in consideration of other matters in addition to the journey and irrespective of the person by or to whom it is made;

(c) a payment is to be treated as made for the carrying of a passenger if made in consideration of a person being given a right to be carried, whether for one or more journeys and whether or not the right is exercised.

These provisions cover a number of possibilities. (a) is concerned with circumstances which might arise in relation to a club or association. The club etc may own a coach and make it available to members for outings on payment by them. It could be argued that, as club members, they all own the coach and cannot, therefore, be using it for hire or reward. Because of (a), this argument will not succeed because (a) clearly states that the vehicle is to be treated as carrying passengers for hire or reward. (b) will cover the circumstances of the 'all-in' holiday, where one payment is made to an agent for transport, accommodation, meals and courier service. This includes payment for carriage and such payment is deemed by (b) to be a fare, even though it is made in respect of other matters as well. Finally, (c) states that a payment is to be treated as made for the carriage of a person if it is made in consideration of a person being given a right to be carried, eg the purchase of a ticket, whether that ticket allows one or more journeys and even if the journey is never made.

These provisions are not an exclusive definition of the circumstances in which a vehicle is used for carrying passengers for hire or reward. For example, it has been held that, where there is a systematic carrying of passengers for hire or reward which goes beyond what might be described as 'social kindness', there is a carriage for hire or reward. There is no need to prove a legally binding contract. Thus, it has been held that, where school children are regularly carried to school in a private vehicle on the basis of 'petrol money' being paid, the vehicle is used for carriage for reward because there is a systematic carriage for hire or reward going beyond the bounds of social kindness and amounting to a business activity, whether or not direct demands have been made for payment. Likewise, it has been held that, where hotels regularly operate 'courtesy coaches' to be used free of charge by residents and visitors, there is a carriage for hire or reward as the service relates to the business activities of the hotel and the charges made for a room, or for a meal, can be taken to include such amenities.

The extended meaning of 'hire or reward' in s 1(5) is restricted in one special circumstance by s 1(6), which provides that, where a fare is paid in respect of a journey by air and, due to mechanical failure, bad weather or other circumstances outside the operator's control, part of the journey has to be made by road, no part of the fare is to be treated for the purposes of s 1(5) as paid in consideration of the carriage of passengers by road. Thus, the occasional use of coaches to facilitate air travel in emergencies can be made without those coaches becoming classified as public service vehicles.

We now turn to the separate requirements of the definition of the two types of public service vehicle.

A motor vehicle (other than a tramcar) adapted to carry more than eight passengers and used for carrying passengers for hire or reward

Such a vehicle may range from a minibus to a large luxury coach.

Whether or not a vehicle is 'adapted to carry more than eight passengers' is a question of fact to be decided in the particular circumstances. In the case where four of 11 seats in a minibus had been rendered unusable by being turned upside down and blocked off, the Divisional Court upheld a decision by magistrates that the vehicle in that state was not adapted to carry more than eight passengers. The term is not concerned with permanence, it is concerned with the situation existing at a particular moment. The words 'more than eight passengers' indicate that it must be adapted for at least nine. The issue of whether or not the driver is included in the nine is not clear. Previous legislation referred to passengers 'other than the driver' but the 1981 Act makes no separate mention of the driver. Common sense suggests that a driver is not a passenger as he is not a traveller in the true sense. Additionally, the term 'driver' and 'passenger' are separately considered in the Act and in regulations made under its authority. It is noteworthy that parallel EU legislation refers to 'carrying not more than nine persons including the driver'. Until this issue is decided it is better to regard the definition as requiring adaptation to allow the carriage of a minimum of eight passengers plus a driver.

A motor vehicle (other than a tramcar) not adapted to carry more than eight passengers, which is used for carrying passengers for hire or reward at separate fares in the course of a business of carrying passengers

The obvious distinction between a public service vehicle of this type and one of the type just described is that the present type of motor vehicle is one which:

(a) is not adapted to carry *'more than eight passengers'* (a phrase discussed above); but

(b) is used to carry passengers *at separate fares in the course of a business of carrying passengers.*

Two examples of a vehicle not adapted to carry more than eight passengers, which automatically spring to mind, are a family saloon car and a London type taxi. However, such vehicles will not be classed as public service vehicles unless they are used for carrying passengers for hire or reward at separate fares. Normally, of course, the family saloon car is not used to carry passengers at separate fares and even if separate payments are made by passengers this will not normally make the car a public service vehicle. One reason is that, if the payments are made under a social arrangement (eg a car-sharing scheme), the passengers are not carried for hire or reward. The use of taxis in circumstances which would otherwise cause them to be classified as public service vehicles is specially provided for by the Transport Act 1985 (see below).

The term 'separate fares' includes circumstances in which a man hires a vehicle and driver to take a party on a particular outing and then charges each person a separate fare for the journey. If an eight-seater vehicle is hired by one man, who then takes colleagues on the journey with him on payment of separate fares to him, that vehicle becomes a public service vehicle for the purpose of s 1 if the circumstances are outside those permitted by s 1(3) of the 1981 Act, which is examined below.

In order for it to be a public service vehicle, the use of the vehicle must be not only to carry passengers for hire or reward at separate fares, but also be *'in the course of a business of carrying passengers'*. This phrase makes doubly certain that the *normal* type of 'car-sharing scheme' does not make the car in question a public service vehicle since such use of the car would not be in the course of a *business* of carrying passengers. This is made clear by s 1(4) of the 1981 Act, which provides that a journey made by a vehicle in the course of which one or more passengers are carried at separate fares is not to be treated as made 'in the course of a business of carrying passengers' if:

(a) the fare or aggregate of the fares paid in respect of the journey *does not exceed the running costs* of the vehicle for the journey; and

(b) the arrangements for the payment of the fares by the passenger or passengers so carried were *made before* the journey began;

and for the purposes of (a) the running costs of the vehicle for a journey are taken to include an appropriate amount in respect of depreciation and wear and tear.

Therefore, the use of a vehicle for a car-sharing scheme does not make it a public service vehicle, provided the payments made cover no more than the sharing of the travel and the depreciation and wear and tear of the vehicle and that arrangements for payment of them were made before the journey began. If payments made within such a scheme were considered to go beyond these guidelines, it would be for a court to decide whether the elements of hire or reward and of business usage were present; see pp 318-319 above.

Use of taxis at separate fares

Sections 10–16 of the Transport Act 1985 make provision for the use of taxis for the carriage of passengers at separate fares in three types of case.

Under conditions prescribed in a scheme

Section 10 provides that a licensed taxi may be hired for use for the carriage of passengers for hire or reward at separate fares without thereby becoming a public passenger vehicle if:

(a) the taxi is hired in an area where a scheme made under s 10 of the 1985 Act is in operation;

(b) the taxi is licensed by the licensing authority for that area; and

(c) the hiring falls within the terms of the scheme.

The licensing authority in London is the Secretary of State (or his nominee) and in other areas of England and Wales it is the authority responsible for licensing taxis. The 1985 Act extends the provisions of the Town Police Clauses Act 1847, in respect of the licensing of taxis, to all areas.

The licensing authority is empowered to make a scheme for its area and must make such a scheme if the holders of at least 10 per cent of the current taxi licences require the authority to do so. Such schemes *must* be concerned with the designation of places in the area from which taxis may be hired (authorised places), and should specify the requirements to be met in relation to the hiring at separate fares and other factors from time to time prescribed. They *may* deal with fares, display of documents, plates, marks or signs for indicating an 'authorised place', the manner in which arrangements are to be made for the carriage of passengers or the hiring, and the conditions to be applied to the hiring. For the purposes of s 10, the hiring of a taxi only falls within the terms of a scheme if it is hired from an authorised place and the hiring must meet the licensing authority's requirements. A taxi is hired from an authorised place if it is standing at that place when it is hired and the persons hiring it are all present there.

The Criminal Justice and Public Order Act 1994, s 167 created an offence which is committed by those who solicit persons, in a public place, to hire vehicles, whether licensed taxis or otherwise, to carry them as passengers in circumstances other than those described above in which a taxi would be operating lawfully. Taxi touting is an arrestable offence (having been added to the list in s 24(2) of the Police and Criminal Evidence Act 1984). It is a defence for an accused to show that he was soliciting for passengers for public service vehicles on behalf of the holder of a public service vehicle operator's licence.

The soliciting need not refer to any particular vehicle. The mere display of a sign is not soliciting.

Shared taxis by arrangement

Section 11 of the 1985 Act provides the second type of case. It states that a licensed taxi *or licensed hire car* may be used for the carriage of passengers for hire or reward at separate fares without these vehicles becoming a public service vehicle provided that the following conditions are satisfied. These are that all the passengers carried on the occasion in question booked their journey in advance and each of them consented, when booking his journey, to sharing the use of the vehicle on that occasion with others, on the basis that a separate fare would be payable by each passenger for his own journey on that occasion.

Taxis with restricted public service vehicle operator's licences

Section 12 of the 1985 Act permits the holder of a taxi licence to apply for a restricted public service vehicle operator's licence. If the holder of the taxi licence states in his application that he proposes to use one or more licensed taxis to provide a local service, the traffic commissioner must grant the application. However, the commissioner *must* attach conditions to the effect that all vehicles used under the restricted licence must have taxi licences and that they shall not be used under the restricted licence otherwise than for providing a local service, although of course it may still be used as a taxi under its separate licence. The term 'local service' does not include an excursion or tour. Such vehicles are not treated as passenger service vehicles in every case. For example, they need not carry operator's discs and the drivers do not require public service vehicle driver's licences. These restricted licences are referred to as 'special licences'. Vehicles operating under such licences must display a notice 'Bus' at the front plus the destination or route or nature of service, and must carry a fare table.

Circumstances affecting classification as public service vehicles

Section 1(3) of the 1981 Act provides that a vehicle carrying passengers at separate fares in the course of a business of carrying passengers, but doing so in circumstances in which one of the following conditions is fulfilled, is to be treated as not being a public service vehicle *unless* it is adapted to carry *more* than eight passengers. The conditions are as follows:

(a) Where the making of the agreement for separate fares was not initiated by the driver or owner of the vehicle, or by any person who receives any remuneration in respect of the arrangements for the journey, *and* the journey is made without previous, public advertisement of facilities for its being made by passengers to be carried at separate fares (except in the case of journeys, approved by a local authority, made to meet social and welfare needs).

(b) Where the arrangements for bringing together all the passengers were made otherwise than by or on behalf of the holder of the operator's licence under which the vehicle is to be used, or (if there is no such licence) the driver or owner of the vehicle, and otherwise than by any person who receives any remuneration in respect of the arrangements, and the journey is made without previous, public advertisement, and all the passengers are carried for the major part of the journey (allowing for different pick-up and set-down points), and the fares are the same regardless of the distance carried. Thus, a vehicle adapted to carry eight passengers or less is not a public service vehicle in these circumstances, which are exemplified by a group or club outing.

PUBLIC SERVICE VEHICLE OPERATOR'S LICENCE

Section 12(1) of the 1981 Act provides that a public service vehicle must not be used on a road for carrying passengers for hire or reward except under a public service vehicle operator's licence. Such a licence is granted by a traffic commissioner. It is granted to a person, rather than a vehicle. The country is divided into traffic areas, each with its own traffic commissioner, and if a person operating public service vehicles has an operating centre in more than one such area he must obtain separate operator's licences from the commissioner for each area. A public service vehicle licence authorises the holder to use vehicles anywhere in Great Britain. A person who uses a vehicle on a road as a public service vehicle without an applicable public service vehicle operator's licence is guilty of an offence, unless he proves that he took all reasonable care and exercised all due diligence to avoid the commission of that offence.

The Public Passenger Vehicles Act 1981, s 65 provides that it is an offence for a person, with intent to deceive, to forge, alter or use or lend, or to allow to be used by any other person, such an operator's licence, or to make or to have in his possession a document or other thing so closely resembling such a document or other thing as to be calculated to deceive. These offences also apply to licences, certificates of fitness or conformity, or certificates relating to the repute of an applicant, his financial standing or professional competence.

Operator's disc

Where a vehicle is used in circumstances requiring a public service vehicle operator's licence, an operator's disc must be fixed and exhibited on the vehicle adjacent to the vehicle excise licence so that it does not interfere unduly with the driver's view and can easily be read in daylight from outside the vehicle. The disc shows particulars of the operator and of his operator's licence under which the vehicle is being used. When a person is granted an operator's licence, the traffic commissioner will issue him with a number of such discs equal to the number of vehicles which he may use under the licence. There are various detailed provisions as to the form, custody and production of operator's discs, and as to their replacement if they are lost, destroyed or defaced. If a vehicle is used without the requisite operator's disc in the prescribed form exhibited in the prescribed way, its operator is guilty of an offence unless he proves that he took all reasonable care and exercised all due diligence to avoid the commission of that offence.

Production of licence or disc

If he is required by a police officer or certain other officials to produce a public service vehicle operator's licence or disc for inspection, the holder must do so within 14 days.

It is enough, however, if he produces it at his operating centre, head office or principal place of business within the traffic area to which it relates.

Types of licence

A public service vehicle operator's licence may be either a standard licence or a restricted licence.

A standard licence authorises the use of any description of public service vehicle and may authorise use either:

(a) on both national and international operations; or
(b) on national operations only.

A restricted licence authorises the use (whether on national or international operations) of:

(a) public service vehicles *not adapted to carry more than eight passengers*; and
(b) public service vehicles *not adapted to carry more than 16 passengers* (ie basically, minibuses) when used -
    (i) *otherwise than in the course of a business of carrying passengers*; or
    (ii) *by a person whose main occupation is not the operation of public service vehicles adapted to carry more than eight passengers.*

For the purposes of the above definitions, 'national operations' means transport operations wholly within this country. If an operator who requires a standard licence runs trips abroad as part of his operations, he will require a standard licence for both national and international operations.

If the holder of an operator's licence (eg a restricted one) uses a vehicle for a purpose not authorised by it (eg where a standard national licence would be required) he is guilty of an offence, unless he proves that he took all reasonable care and exercised all due diligence to avoid the commission of that offence.

Conditions attached to PSV operator's licence

The Transport Act 1985 provides that where it appears to a traffic commissioner, in relation to an operator to whom he has granted or is proposing to grant a public service vehicle operator's licence, that:

(a) the operator has failed to operate a local service registered under s 6 of the 1985 Act (see below); or
(b) the operator has operated a local service in contravention of that section; or
(c) the arrangements for maintaining the vehicles used under the licence in a fit and serviceable condition are not adequate for the use of those vehicles in providing the local service or services in question; or
(d) that the operator, or an employee or agent of his, has -
    (i) intentionally interfered with the operation of a local service provided by another operator;
    (ii) operated a local service in a manner dangerous to the public; or
    (iii) been guilty of any other serious misconduct (whether or not constituting a criminal offence) in relation to the operation of a local service; or

(e) a condition attached under s 8 of the 1985 Act (traffic regulation condition) to the operator's licence has been contravened;

he may attach to the licence either a condition prohibiting the operator from using vehicles under it to provide any local service of a description specified in the condition or one prohibiting him from so using vehicles to provide local services of any description. In the circumstances set out at (a) and (b), above, the imposition of a condition is only possible if the operator did not have a reasonable excuse, or if the condition is appropriate in view of the danger involved to the public in the operator's conduct, or of the frequency of it.

Conditions may be imposed either when a licence is granted or thereafter.

If the traffic commissioner is required to do so by the holder of the operator's licence or the applicant for it, he must hold an inquiry before attaching a condition, except that he may attach a condition at once in an emergency. However, if he does attach a condition in any emergency before holding an inquiry, this must be followed by an inquiry as soon as reasonably practicable, if an inquiry is requested.

Revocation of PSV operator's licence

In circumstances in which a traffic commissioner revokes an operator's licence, he may order the holder to be disqualified indefinitely or for such period as he thinks fit. Such a disqualification may be limited to just one area.

Plying for hire by large PSVs

Section 30 of the 1985 Act prohibits operators from using on a road in plying for hire public service vehicles which are adapted to carry more than eight passengers. This provision therefore prevents the use of larger vehicles, by public service vehicle operators, in the manner of hire cars.

OTHER PUBLIC SERVICE VEHICLE DOCUMENTS AND RESTRICTIONS

Registration of local services

The Transport Act 1985 abolished the previous requirement for road service licences which were required in respect of services operated over prescribed routes. The provisions of the 1981 Act which dealt with road service licences are replaced by ss 6–9 of the 1985 Act, which are concerned with the registration of local services.

By s 2 of the 1985 Act, a 'local service' is a service, using one or more public service vehicles, for the carriage of passengers by road at separate fares other than:

(a) a journey organised privately by persons acting independently of the vehicle operators etc (see (b) on p 322); or
(b) a service within which every vehicle used is operated under a permit granted under s 19 of the 1985 Act (minibuses and buses operated by educational, religious, social, recreational and other beneficial bodies); or
(c) a service in relation to which (except in an emergency) *either* the place where each passenger is set down is 15 miles or more, measured in a straight line, from the

place where he was taken up *or* some point on the route between those places is 15 miles or more from that place or both (limited stop vehicles).

The responsibility for the registration of local services is vested in the traffic commissioner for each traffic area.

By s 6 of the 1985 Act, no local service shall be provided in any traffic area in which there is a stopping place for that service unless the prescribed particulars of the service have been registered with the traffic commissioner for that area by the operator of that service. These particulars are prescribed by the Public Service Vehicles (Registration of Local Services) Regulations 1986, as amended. Applications to operate a local service may only be accepted from the holders of unconditional public service vehicle operator's licences, or holders of permits under s 22 of the 1985 Act (operators of community bus services), or from persons who are using or proposing to use a school bus belonging to that person for fare paying passengers in accordance with s 46(1) of the 1981 Act. The term 'unconditional' in this respect, means that there is no condition attached to the licence prohibiting etc the provision of the particular service applied for. An application for registration of a service having stopping places in more than one traffic area must be made to the traffic commissioner for the area in which the service will start; there is no need to apply to each commissioner with whom the service will be registered.

The provisions of the 1985 Act relating to the registration of local services do not apply to a London local service (ie a local stopping service with one or more stopping places in London). Local London services are governed by Part III of the 1985 Act. Except in the case of a service provided by London Regional Transport and of certain other services, a local London service must be licensed by the traffic commissioner for the Metropolitan Traffic Area.

Traffic regulation conditions

A traffic authority (county council) may ask the traffic commissioner for any area to determine traffic regulation conditions which must be met in the provision of services in the area to which the conditions are applied. If a trunk road is affected, the authority must have the consent of the Secretary of State to making the application. Before a traffic commissioner *determines* traffic regulation conditions, he must be satisfied that they are necessary to prevent danger to road users, or to reduce severe traffic congestion. In considering what conditions to apply he *must have regard* to the interests of those registered in respect of local services, users of those services and the elderly and disabled. He may then determine the routes of services, their stopping places, when vehicles may stop and for how long, and any other matters prescribed. Such conditions may affect different periods of the year, different days of the week, or different times during any period of 24 hours. In addition, he may impose conditions regulating the roads to be used and the manoeuvres to be performed when turning a vehicle, and limiting the number of vehicles which may be used (or the frequency at which vehicles may be operated) in the provision of a service along all or part of its route whether generally or during particular periods or at particular times.

Once made, these traffic regulation conditions apply generally to *all* services operated in the area or to such *class* of service as may be specified. There is one exception. Where the traffic commissioner is satisfied that the traffic regulation conditions which apply generally would be inappropriate in achieving the particular regulation of traffic which he considers necessary, he may determine conditions which apply only to a *particular* service or services.

Before determining any traffic regulation condition, a traffic commissioner must hold an inquiry if he has received an application from an affected traffic authority or a person who has registered a service. In an emergency he may make a condition without delay but this must be followed by an inquiry as soon as reasonably practicable if a request is received from any such party.

The above conditions do not, of course, apply to a London local service, but if he grants a licence to such a service the traffic commissioner may insert into it conditions similar to those just mentioned.

Certificates of initial fitness

By s 6(1) of the 1981 Act, a public service vehicle adapted to carry more than eight passengers must not be used on a road unless:

(a) an examiner appointed under the Road Traffic Act 1988, s 66A has issued a certificate of initial fitness, stating that the prescribed conditions of fitness are fulfilled in relation to the vehicle; or

(b) a type vehicle or type approval certificate has been issued in respect of the vehicle.

Such public service vehicles must, therefore, have some form of certificate of initial fitness (or equivalent) for use as a public service vehicle. Such vehicles are subjected to stability tests and tests related to suspension, guard rails, brakes, steering gear, fuel tanks, exhausts, lighting, bodywork, windscreens and windows, and other pieces of miscellaneous equipment. These conditions are prescribed in the Public Service Vehicle (Conditions of Fitness, Equipment, Use and Certification) Regulations 1981 or, in relevant cases, EU approval mark regulations.

Applications for fitness certification in respect of single vehicles, or those adapted locally, are likely to be made to the traffic commissioner of the area, who will issue a certificate of initial fitness in respect of that particular vehicle.

It will be appreciated that this procedure would be somewhat tedious in relation to mass produced vehicles of a particular pattern. In such cases the Department of Transport will have caused the vehicle model to be subjected to inspection and will have approved that particular design by a certificate. Provided that there has been such a type approval and there is a certificate that the *particular* vehicle conforms with that type, s 6(1) is satisfied.

Certificates which were in force immediately before the coming into operation of the 1981 Act and which were issued under the authority of the Road Traffic Act 1960 remain valid.

If a vehicle is used in contravention of s 6(1), the operator of the vehicle is guilty of an offence unless he proves that he took all reasonable precautions and exercised all due diligence to avoid the contravention.

Test certificates

Test certificates issued under the Road Traffic Act 1988, s 47(1) must be obtained in respect of public service vehicles one year after their original registration etc. There are provisions which allow the issue of a certificate of temporary exemption in certain circumstances, but the validity of such a certificate must not extend beyond three months.

The provisions of the Road Traffic Act 1988, s 67, which deal with the testing of vehicles on roads for the purpose of ascertaining whether the requirements concerning a vehicle's construction and use and its general condition are satisfactory, apply equally to public services vehicles: see p 000.

LICENCE TO DRIVE

The Road Traffic Act 1988, Part IV is concerned with the licensing of drivers of large passenger-carrying vehicles. Section 110 of the 1988 Act states that licences to drive classes of vehicles which include large passenger-carrying vehicles, shall be granted by the Secretary of State in accordance with Part IV of the Act. Thus, licences to drive large passenger-carrying vehicles are subject to the provisions of both Parts III and IV of the 1988 Act.

Section 111 of that Act requires the traffic commissioner of an area to exercise the functions conferred by Part IV of the Act relating to the conduct of:

(a) applicants for and holders of large passenger-carrying vehicle drivers' licences, and
(b) holders of PCV Community licences.

The offence of driving a large passenger-carrying vehicle otherwise than in accordance with a licence arises under the Road Traffic Act 1988, s 87 but the offence requires additional consideration within this chapter as there are variations, consequent upon the need to comply additionally with Part IV of the Act. In addition, there are requirements made by the Motor Vehicles (Driving Licences) Regulations 1996 ('the 1996 Regulations') which apply only to large passenger-carrying vehicles.

A vehicle is a large passenger-carrying vehicle if it is constructed or adapted to carry more than 16 passengers, whether or not they are being carried for hire or reward. Schedule 2 to the 1996 Regulations provides a multiplicity of categories and sub-categories of vehicles. The various forms of passenger-carrying vehicles are included in variations of category D types of vehicles.

Large passenger-carrying vehicle driving tests

The drivers of large passenger-carrying vehicles generally will be in possession of driving licences issued under Part III of the RTA 1988 for differing categories of vehicles. In order to obtain those licences, they will have been tested on different types of vehicles. The table set out below shows the various categories of passenger-carrying vehicles and gives details of the 'minimum test vehicle' which could be used within that test.

Category or sub-category		Specification
D1	8-16 seats in addition to the driver's seat	D1 vehicles capable of 80 kph
D1+E	Combination vehicle not exceeding 12 tonnes	D1 + trailer having maximum authorised mass of 1,250 kg and capable of 80 kph
D	More than eight seats in addition to driver's seat	D having length of 9 m and capable of 80 kph

Category or sub-category		*Specification*
D+E	D tractor but the combination falls outside that category	D + trailer having maximum authorised mass of 1250 kg and capable of 80 kph

Other persons who may drive large passenger-carrying vehicles

The Road Traffic Act 1988, Part III as amended by the Driving Licences (Community Driving Licences) Regulations 1996 permits holders of Community licences authorising them to drive large passenger-carrying vehicles to drive those categories of vehicles in the United Kingdom. Those who become resident in the United Kingdom may exchange their licences for British ones, but are in any case required to submit to the Secretary of State details of their driving entitlement and other information which is prescribed within a year of becoming resident. Resident Community licence holders who hold licences entitling them to drive passenger-carrying vehicles are made subject to the code of conduct relating to such drivers. Such licences are referred to in the 1988 Act as 'PCV Community licences'. Holders of Convention or domestic driving permits who are resident in the Isle of Man or Jersey may drive a large goods vehicle which they are authorised to drive by that permit during a period of 12 months from the date of their last entry into the United Kingdom. Holders of such permits who are not residents of an EEA state, or the Isle of Man or Jersey, may only drive a large passenger-carrying vehicle brought temporarily into Great Britain. A holder of a BFG (British Forces Germany) public service vehicle driver's licence, who is resident outside the United Kingdom, but is temporarily in Great Britain, may drive any public service vehicle covered by his licence for a period of 12 months if he is resident in the Isle of Man or Jersey. (If he is resident in an EEA state, his licence is valid under other provisions.) Other persons holding such licences may only drive a passenger-carrying vehicle brought temporarily into Great Britain.

Provisional licences

Persons who hold provisional licences to drive large passenger-carrying vehicles are subject to the general conditions under which persons, who are learner drivers, may drive particular classes of vehicles. These are the conditions prescribed by reg 15 of the 1996 Regulations: the need for supervision, the display of learner plates, and the prohibition upon the drawing of a trailer.

However, the prohibition upon the drawing of a trailer does not apply to the holder of a provisional licence authorising the driving of a vehicle of a class included in category D + E (combination of passenger-carrying vehicle with more than eight seats in addition to the driver's seat where the tractor itself fits into category D but the combination does not) while driving such a vehicle.

Regulation 15(8) of the 1996 Regulations prohibits provisional licence holders from driving a passenger-carrying vehicle while carrying passengers. However, exceptions exist in favour of supervisors and holders of passenger-carrying vehicle drivers' licences who are receiving or giving instruction, have given or received it, or are to give or receive it.

Regulation 17 of the 1996 Regulations sets out details of certain full licences which do not carry provisional entitlement to drive other categories of vehicles. Most significant to issues surrounding passenger-carrying vehicle drivers' licences is the provision that a category D1 licence carries provisional entitlement to drive vehicles of category D1 + E and that a category D licence carries provisional entitlement to drive vehicles of categories D1 + E and D + E.

Regulation 7(9) of the 1996 Regulations permit a person of 18 to drive a passenger-carrying vehicle where:

(a) he holds a provisional licence authorising the driving of the vehicle and is not engaged in the carriage of passengers; or
(b) he holds a full passenger-carrying vehicle driver's licence and -
    (i) is engaged in the carriage of passengers on a regular service over a route which does not exceed 50 kilometres, or
    (ii) where he is not so engaged, is driving a class of vehicle included in sub-category D1 (more than eight but less than 16 seats in addition to the driver's seat)

and the vehicle is operated under a PSV operator's licence granted under the Public Passenger Vehicles Act 1981, s 12 or a permit granted under the Transport Act 1985, s 19 (vehicles used by educational and other bodies) or a community bus permit issued under s 22 of the 1985 Act.

Regulation 6(9) of the 1996 Regulations provides that a category B licence holder (but not B1) who has held that licence for at least two years, is over 21 and receives no consideration other than out-of-pocket expenses may drive, on behalf of a non-commercial body, for social purposes but not for hire or reward, a vehicle of a class in sub-category D1 (more than eight but not more than 16 seats in addition to the driver's seat) which is not drawing a trailer and has a maximum authorised mass not exceeding 3.5 tonnes excluding weight attributable to special equipment for carrying disabled passengers, and 4.25 tonnes otherwise. The usual proviso applies in relation to 'automatics'. Where such a driver is aged 70 or over, he must not be suffering from a relevant disability in respect of which the licensing authority would be bound to refuse him a Group 2 licence (within the meaning of reg 65 - higher medical standards for large vehicles). Regulation 70 of the 1996 Regulations provides that a person who held a licence authorising, on 31 December 1996, the driving of vehicles in category D otherwise than for hire or reward, may drive the classes of vehicles included in category D which are driven under a permit granted under the Transport Act 1985, s 19. The amended Minibus and Other Section 19 Permit Buses Regulations 1987 provide that, where such a licence was granted before 1 January 1997, such a person must be the holder of a full driver's licence for category B and sub-category D1 (not for hire or reward).

Validity of large passenger-carrying vehicle drivers' licences

A licence authorising its holder to drive large passenger-carrying vehicles remains in force, unless previously revoked, suspended or surrendered but becomes renewable on the holder's 45th birthday, or after five years, whichever is the *longer*, or where the licence is issued to a person between 45 and 65 for the period ending on his 66th birthday or after five years, whichever is the *shorter*. A licence granted after the age of 65 will remain in force for one year only.

The Road Traffic Act 1988, s 115 provides that a large passenger-carrying vehicle driver's licence must be revoked if there comes into existence in relation to the holder, prescribed circumstances relating to his conduct, and must be revoked or suspended if his conduct is such as to make him unfit to hold such a licence.

Historic buses and those driven by a constable in an emergency

Regulation 47(1) of the 1996 Regulations provides that the provisions of Part IV of the RTA 1988 and the provisions of regs 51-54 of the Regulations shall not apply to:

(a) a passenger-carrying vehicle manufactured more than 30 years before the date upon which it is driven and not used for hire or reward or for the carriage of more than eight passengers;

(b) a passenger-carrying vehicle driven by a constable for the purpose of removing or avoiding obstruction to other road users or to other members of the public, for the purpose of protecting life or property (including the passenger-carrying vehicle and its passengers) or for other similar purposes.

Hours of driving

The number of hours during which a driver may be employed in the driving of a public service vehicle is strictly controlled. To avoid repetition, this matter is discussed in the next chapter.

BUSES OPERATED BY PARTICULAR ORGANISATIONS AND COMMUNITY BUSES

The Transport Act 1985 contains provisions whereby, if certain conditions are observed, such vehicles are permitted to operate outside most, or all, of the general provisions of the Acts relating to public service vehicles. Section 18 of the 1985 Act states that the provisions of s 12(1) of the 1981 Act (need to have a public service vehicle operator's licence) shall not apply to the use of a vehicle under a permit granted under ss 19 or 22 of the 1985 Act.

Section 18 also provides that where a person is the holder of a licence under the Road Traffic Act 1988, Pt III, which was first granted before 1 January 1977, he may drive a 'small bus' at a time when it is being used under such permits, notwithstanding that his licence does not authorise him to drive a small bus when it is being so used.

For these purposes, a 'small bus' is a vehicle which is adapted to carry more than eight but not more than 16 passengers.

Where a Part III licence was granted on or after 1 January 1997, or a Community licence holder is authorised by s 99A(1) of the 1988 Act to drive in Great Britain a motor vehicle of any class, the licence holder may drive a 'small bus' notwithstanding that he is not authorised by his licence to drive such a bus.

For these purposes a 'small bus' is one which, when laden with the heaviest load which it is constructed to carry, weighs:

(a) not more than 3.5 tonnes, excluding any part of that weight which is attributable to specialised equipment intended for the carriage of disabled passengers, and

(b) not more than 4.25 tonnes otherwise.

Buses operated by particular organisations

Sections 19, 20 and 21 of the 1985 Act authorise the use of buses of particular types under permits granted to a body which assists and co-ordinates the activities of bodies within an area which appear to be concerned with education, religion, social welfare, recreation or other activities of benefit to the community. Permits may be granted in respect of small buses (adapted to carry 8–16 passengers) or large buses (adapted to carry more than 16 passengers). A permit for a small bus may be granted by a traffic commissioner or by a body designated by the Secretary of State, either to itself or to any other body to whom, in accordance with the order, it is entitled to grant a permit. A permit in respect of a large bus can only be granted by a traffic commissioner. It may be granted to any of the bodies mentioned above, with the exception of those concerned with recreational activity. Before granting a permit for a large bus, a traffic commissioner must be satisfied that there will be adequate facilities or arrangements for maintaining any bus used under the permit in a fit and serviceable condition. The Section 19 Minibus (Designated Bodies) Order 1987, as amended, lists those bodies approved by the Secretary of State for these purposes.

Section 19(2) of the 1985 Act makes it clear that certain requirements must be met in relation to the use of a bus under a permit before the use of such a vehicle without a public service vehicle operator's licence will be exempt. The vehicle must be being used by the body to whom the permit has been granted; it must not be being used for carriage of members of the general public nor with a view to profit either directly or incidentally; it must be being used within the conditions of the permit and in compliance with any regulations made under s 21 of the 1985 Act. If any of these factors is not being observed, the exemptions under s 18 do not apply, and the operator may be convicted of the offence of operating the vehicle without a public service vehicle operator's licence.

Permits must specify the body to whom they are granted, although they may be granted to named individuals on behalf of the body. Conditions may be attached as required by the 1985 Act or as appear appropriate, in particular conditions limiting the passengers who can be carried to particular classes. The Minibus and Other Section 19 Permit Buses Regulations 1987 govern drivers, conditions of fitness and the forms of permits, documents, marks, plates etc. The conditions applicable to drivers are the same as those set out below in relation to 'community buses'.

Section 46(1) of the 1981 Act states that, even if fares are paid on a school bus (perhaps teachers carried on the transport), the requirements relating to a certificate of initial fitness and to a public service vehicle operator's licence do not apply.

Discs carried by minibuses and other s 19 permit buses

Discs displayed on these vehicles will show the name of the body or person holding the permit, the number, the date upon which it was granted, the name of the issuing body and the words 'Transport Act 1985, section 19 permit vehicle'. The disc will also carry a code letter. The various code letters mean that the use is authorised for:

A — members of the body holding the permit

B — persons whom the body exists to benefit

C — mentally or physically handicapped persons or the seriously ill, and persons assisting them

D — pupils or students at any school, college, university or other educational establishment and staff or other helpers accompanying them

E — other class specified in the permit.

Community bus services

As stated above, s 18 of the 1985 Act states that the provisions in the 1981 Act relating to the licensing of public service vehicle operators do not apply to the use of any vehicle under a permit granted under s 22 of the 1985 Act (a community bus permit). By s 22, a 'community bus service' is a local service provided by a body concerned for the social and welfare needs of one or more communities, without a view to profit, either on the part of that body or anyone else, and by means of a vehicle adapted to carry more than eight but not more than 16 passengers. A 'community bus permit' may be granted by the relevant traffic commissioner for a public service vehicle which is providing a community bus service, or which is, in providing a community bus service, carrying passengers for hire or reward where the carriage of those passengers will directly assist the provision of the community bus service by providing financial support for it. If passengers are carried for hire or reward the vehicle must not be used in the course of a local service. The commissioner must be satisfied with the arrangements for the maintenance etc of the vehicle. A 'Community Bus' disc is issued with each permit.

The Community Bus Regulations 1986 permit a person who is not the holder of a passenger-carrying vehicle driver's licence to drive a vehicle in respect of which a community bus permit exists, provided that he complies with requirements relating to hand-held microphones, a driver's duty to ensure the safety of passengers, and giving his name, that of his employer, and particulars of his licence, to a constable or other person having reasonable cause. In addition, he must:

(a) hold a full licence authorising him to drive vehicles in category B other than vehicles in sub-category B1, and have held it for not less than two years in aggregate and be 21 or over; or

(b) where his full licence was granted under Part III of the Road Traffic Act 1988 before 1 January 1997 hold a full licence authorising driving of vehicles in category B, other than vehicles included in sub-category B1 and sub-category D1 (not for hire and reward) and be 21 or over; and

(c) if 70 or over, must not be suffering from a relevant disability in respect of which the licensing authority would be bound to refuse to grant him a licence to drive a category D1 vehicle (within the meaning of reg 65 - higher medical standards for large vehicles).

A category D1 vehicle is one having more than eight but not more than 16 seats in addition to the driver's seat.

The holder of a community bus permit commits an offence contrary to s 23(5) of the 1985 Act if a condition attached to a permit is contravened. The Community Bus Regulations 1986 set out the obligations of drivers and prescribe conditions of fitness.

These provisions recognise the difficulties in providing adequate bus services in rural areas. Where it is not economically sound to provide local services in some areas, community bus permits allow the use of 'Transit type vehicles'. These public service vehicles may be provided either free of charge, by a local authority or by some other body concerned for the social or welfare needs of communities, or for hire or reward where this will directly assist the provision of the community bus service by providing finance.

CONDUCT OF DRIVERS, CONDUCTORS AND PASSENGERS

The Public Service Vehicles (Conduct of Drivers, Inspectors, Conductors and Passengers) Regulations 1990 regulate behaviour on public service vehicles.

Contravention of any of the following regulations is an offence. Each of the different forms of conduct specified gives rise to a separate offence.

A driver must not:

(a)   while the vehicle is in motion, *hold* a microphone or any attachment thereto unless it is necessary for him, either in an emergency or on the grounds of safety, to speak into that microphone;

(b)   speak to any person either directly or by means of a microphone, whilst the vehicle is in motion, except that he may do so in an emergency or on the grounds of safety, or when speaking to a relevant person in relation to the operation of the vehicle. By way of exception the driver of a vehicle being used other than for an excursion tour, or sightseeing, may use a microphone to make short statements from time to time which are limited to indicating the location of the vehicle or operational matters, provided that he can do so without being distracted from his driving;

(c)   fail to stop as close as is reasonably practicable to the left or nearside of the road when picking up or setting down passengers.

A driver or conductor must:

(a)   take all reasonable precautions to ensure the safety of passengers who are on, or who are entering or leaving, a public service vehicle;

(b)   if requested by a constable or other person having reasonable cause, give his name and that of his employer; in addition a driver must give particulars of the licence by virtue of which he drives the vehicle;

(c)   not smoke, except where the vehicle is not available for the carriage of passengers and it takes place in a 'smoking' area, or where the vehicle is hired as a whole and he has the permission of the operator and the hirer.

A conductor must not, while the vehicle is in motion, distract the driver's attention or obstruct his vision without reasonable cause.

An inspector must, if requested by a constable or other person having reasonable cause, give his name and that of his employer.

A passengers must not:

(a)   put at risk or unreasonably impede or cause discomfort to any person travelling on or entering or leaving the vehicle, or to the driver, inspector, conductor, or employee of the operator, when doing his work on that vehicle;

(b)   smoke or carry lighted tobacco or light a match or cigarette lighter in or on any part of the vehicle where passengers are by a notice informed that smoking is prohibited, unless the vehicle has been hired as a whole and both the operator and the hirer have given their permission to the contrary;

(c)   speak to the driver whilst the vehicle is in motion except in an emergency or for reasons of safety, or to give directions as to the stopping of the vehicle;

(d)   without reasonable cause, distract the driver's attention or obstruct his vision, or give a signal which might reasonably be interpreted by the driver as a signal to stop the vehicle in an emergency or as a signal to start the vehicle;

(e)   remain on the vehicle when directed to leave by the driver, an inspector or conductor on the ground that his remaining on the vehicle would result in the number of passengers exceeding the maximum seating capacity marked on the vehicle in accordance with the Public Service Vehicles (Carrying Capacity) Regulations 1984, or that he has been causing a nuisance, or that his condition is such as would be likely to cause offence to a reasonable passenger, or that the condition of his clothing is such that his remaining on the vehicle would be reasonably expected to soil the fittings of the vehicle or the clothing of other passengers;

(f) play or operate a musical instrument or sound reproducing equipment to the annoyance of any person on the vehicle, or in a manner which is likely to cause such annoyance;

(g) fail to place an article, substance or animal where directed by the driver, inspector or conductor, or fail to remove an article etc from the vehicle on such a direction being given. (This refers to bulky or cumbersome articles and those likely to cause annoyance, risk of injury or damage. There are certain exceptions in favour of guide dogs.)

Certain other offences may be committed by passengers on a vehicle being used for the carriage of passengers at separate fares:

(a) using a ticket which has been altered or defaced or which has been issued to another person and is not transferable;

(b) failing to declare the journey to be taken when requested to do so;

(c) failing to pay the driver or insert the fare in a machine on one-man buses;

(d) failing to pay the appropriate fare to the conductor immediately upon his request;

(e) failing to accept or retain a ticket for the remainder of the journey;

(f) failing to produce a ticket to a driver, inspector or conductor during the currency of a journey; and

(g) failing to leave the vehicle or pay an excess fare at the end of the journey paid for.

Any passenger contravening these regulations may be removed from the vehicle by the driver or conductor or an inspector (or by a constable on the request of one of these people). A passenger who is reasonably suspected by the driver or conductor or inspector of such contravention shall give his name and address on demand.

Conduct which does not give rise to such an offence under the Regulations will sometimes constitute another offence. Staff or passengers who are rude or disorderly may be guilty of offences under the Public Order Act 1986 in serious cases. Passengers who spit upon, soil or deface any part of a public service vehicle may be guilty of an offence under the Criminal Damage Act 1971.

INSTITUTION OF PROCEEDINGS

Proceedings for any of the offences mentioned in this chapter (other than those committed by a passenger) may only be instituted by or on behalf of the Director of Public Prosecutions, or by a person authorised by a traffic commissioner, a chief officer of police or a local authority. For practical purposes, this means that a police officer cannot institute such proceedings unless authorised by his chief constable.

CHAPTER 13

Goods vehicles

DEFINITION

For the purposes of road traffic legislation, a 'goods vehicle' is a motor vehicle or trailer constructed or adapted for the carriage of goods; for this purpose the carriage of goods includes the haulage of goods. 'Adapted' means 'altered physically so as to make fit for the purpose'. If the seating is stripped from a public service vehicle and the vehicle is then fitted out as a mobile shop, it is thereby adapted to carry goods and becomes a goods vehicle. Of course, the opposite can apply. For example, where a goods van was adapted for the carriage of passengers and its only use for the carriage of goods was when it carried samples to the owner's place of business, it was held not to be a goods vehicle. When a vehicle is originally constructed as a goods vehicle, any alterations made to it must be *substantial and dramatic* if its initial classification is to be changed. The fitting of winches and support bars and ancillary equipment is insufficient to convert a goods vehicle into engineering plant for use in the drilling of wells. The test to be applied in cases in which a passenger vehicle has been converted to permit the carriage of goods is to examine its existing form and to ask whether, if it had been constructed in that form originally, it would have been classed as a passenger vehicle or as a goods vehicle. The mere removal of seats from an estate car to permit it to be used for the carriage of goods does not amount to an adaption for these purposes. The seats can be replaced at any time.

In this chapter we shall be concerned with:

(a) the minimum age for driving a goods vehicle;
(b) large goods vehicles drivers' licences;
(c) plating and testing;
(d) operators' licences; and
(e) drivers' hours and records.

MINIMUM AGE FOR DRIVING A GOODS VEHICLE

This depends on whether the vehicle in question is a small, medium or large goods vehicle. The Road Traffic Act 1988, ss 101 and 108 provide as follows:

(a) A '*small vehicle*' is a motor vehicle (other than an invalid carriage, moped or motor bicycle) which -

(i)   is not constructed to carry more than nine persons inclusive of the driver, and

(ii) has a maximum gross weight not exceeding 3.5 tonnes,

and includes a combination of such a motor vehicle and trailer.

Persons of 17 or over (16 if in receipt of a mobility allowance) may drive small vehicles. The term 'permissible maximum weight' is explained below. It should be noted that unladen weights are of little significance in relation to the legislation concerning goods vehicles.

(b) A *'medium-sized goods vehicle'* is a motor vehicle which is constructed or adapted to carry or to haul goods, and which is not adapted to carry more than nine persons inclusive of the driver, and the permissible maximum weight of which exceeds 3.5 but does not exceed 7.5 tonnes and includes a combination of such a motor vehicle and a trailer where the relevant maximum weight of the trailer does not exceed 750 kg.

Persons of 18 or over may drive medium-sized goods vehicles.

(c) A *'large goods vehicle'* (although this term does not appear in the 1988 Act, it is used in the Road Traffic (Driver Licensing and Information Systems) Act 1989 is for convenience used here to describe goods vehicles which exceed 7.5 tonnes permissible maximum weight or which have more than nine seats inclusive of the driver's.

Persons of 21 or over may drive large goods vehicles.

The references to carriage of passengers occasionally cause confusion to those concerned with the problems related to goods vehicles. The limitation to nine persons in (a) and (b) means that a Transit-type of vehicle will be classified as a goods vehicle if it is constructed or adapted to carry or haul a load, even though it retains some seating. This is important because, for example, Transit-types of vehicles are frequently used by employers to carry goods (or to tow a trailer containing goods) in addition to carrying workers who are being transported to their place of work. If such a van seats nine or less it will be a small or medium-sized goods vehicle, depending on its permissible maximum weight; if such a van seats more than nine it will be a large goods vehicle.

Permissible maximum weight

As can be seen from the above definitions, in relation to the ages of persons by whom they may be driven, goods vehicles are divided into three classes which are basically separated by their 'permissible maximum weights'. The permissible maximum weights of goods vehicles are prescribed by the Road Traffic Act 1988, as follows:

Rigid goods vehicle	— its relevant maximum weight
Rigid goods vehicle drawing a drawbar trailer	— the sum of the relevant maximum weights of the motor vehicle and the trailer
Articulated goods vehicle combination	— its relevant maximum train weight
Articulated tractive unit without a semi-trailer	— its relevant maximum weight

An 'articulated goods vehicle' is a motor vehicle which is so constructed that a goods trailer may by partial superimposition be attached in such a manner as to cause a substantial part of the weight of the trailer to be borne by the motor vehicle. An 'articulated goods vehicle combination' is an articulated goods vehicle with the trailer (called a semi-trailer) attached.

The 'relevant maximum weight' of a goods vehicle is the maximum gross weight which is shown on the relevant plate of the vehicle. The relevant plate is always the Ministry of Transport plate if the vehicle has then been fitted with one. If it has not, then the relevant maximum weight will be shown on the manufacturer's plate.

This means that in the case of vehicles which are fitted with both plates, the maximum weight shown on the Ministry plate is always the 'relevant' maximum weight. In the unlikely case of a vehicle having neither type of plate, the relevant maximum weight can be calculated by multiplying the unladen weight by a multiplier listed in the Goods Vehicles (Ascertainment of Maximum Gross Weight) Regulations 1976, Sch 2. This is unlikely to be of any operational significance to police officers.

The 'relevant maximum train weight' of an articulated goods vehicle combination is the gross weight of the unladen motor vehicle and its unladen trailer plus the maximum weight which the combination is permitted to carry. This is shown under the column marked 'gross train weight' on the plate attached to the vehicle.

It should be noted that a person of a certain age may be permitted to drive a certain type of goods vehicle if it is used without a trailer as its permissible maximum weight is within the range which he would be allowed to drive, but that if a trailer is attached it is possible that the sum of the relevant maximum weights of the vehicle and the trailer will prohibit that person from driving it. For example, a person aged 17 may drive a goods vehicle of 3 tonnes maximum relevant weight since, as its maximum relevant weight does not exceed 3.5 tonnes, it is a small goods vehicle. However, if a trailer is attached with a relevant maximum weight of 1 tonne, the sum of the weights is now 4 tonnes and the vehicle has become 'medium-sized' and may no longer be driven by him but only by someone aged 18 or more. The situation is interesting when related to articulated vehicles. The tractive units of many articulated vehicles are quite small and will frequently have a relevant maximum weight under 3.5 tonnes. They may therefore be driven by 17-year-olds. However, when a semi-trailer is attached to the tractive unit the relevant maximum train weight is the deciding factor and this will almost invariably bring the vehicle into the 'medium' or 'large' category. If, for example, the tractive unit is of 3 tonnes and a semi-trailer is attached, and the maximum train weight is 6 tonnes, the vehicle becomes 'medium'. If it exceeds 7.5 tonnes, it would become 'large'.

Exception to normal minimum ages

There are certain exceptions to these general rules in relation to minimum permitted ages for the purpose of driving. Medium and large goods vehicles owned and used by naval, military or air force authorities may be driven by persons aged 17. In addition, there is a heavy goods vehicle training scheme; if a person is registered and employed by an employer who is also registered in the heavy goods vehicle training scheme, he may at 18 drive a large goods vehicle, provided that it is of a class approved by his training agreement or that it is used by a registered heavy goods vehicle training establishment.

LARGE GOODS VEHICLES DRIVERS' LICENCES

Large goods vehicles

For the purposes of the requirements relating to large goods vehicle drivers' licences, a large goods vehicle is a motor vehicle (not being a medium-sized goods vehicle within the meaning of Part III of this Act which is constructed or adapted to carry or to haul goods and the permissible maximum weight of which exceeds 7.5 tonnes.

The licensing requirement

General

The Road Traffic Act 1988, Part IV is concerned with the licensing of drivers of large goods vehicles. Section 110 of the Act states that driver licences under Part III of the Act shall be granted by the Secretary of State in accordance with Part IV of the Act. Such licences, are, therefore subject to both Parts III and IV of the Act. Section 111 of the 1988 Act requires the traffic commissioner for an area to exercise the functions conferred by Part IV of the Act relating to the conduct of:

(a) applicants for and holders of large goods vehicle drivers' licences; and

(b) LGV Community licence holders.

Section 112 provides that the Secretary of State shall not grant a large goods vehicle driver's licence unless he is satisfied, having regard to his conduct, that he is a fit person to hold the licence applied for.

The offence of driving a large goods vehicle otherwise than in accordance with a licence amounts to an offence under Part III (s 87). The offences committed by learner drivers who breach conditions attached to their driving are, in most instances, the same as those committed by learner drivers of other vehicles. There are additional restrictions placed upon learner drivers of large goods vehicles who are under the age of 21.

The provisions of the 1988 Act in relation to the licensing of drivers of large goods vehicles are extended by the Motor Vehicles (Driving Licences) Regulations 1996. Schedule 2 to the Regulations provides a multiplicity of categories and sub-categories of vehicles. The various forms of goods vehicles are included in variations of category C types of vehicles. However, reg 47(1) of the 1996 Regulations provides that Part IV of the Act shall not apply to vehicles of sub-category C1 + E (8.25 tonnes). Sub-category C1 + E is a sub-category of C + E. It comprises a combination of motor vehicles and trailer where the former is in sub-category C1, the maximum authorised mass of the trailer exceeds 750kg but not the unladen weight of the tractor, and the maximum authorised mass of the combination does not exceed 12 tonnes.

For the purposes of the Regulations the term 'maximum authorised mass' has the same meaning, in relation to goods vehicles, as 'permissible maximum weight' as defined in the Road Traffic Act 1988, s 108(1). In relation to other vehicles or trailers, it has the same meaning as 'maximum gross weight' as defined by the Road Vehicles (Construction and Use) Regulations 1986, reg 3(2).

The provisions of Part IV of the 1988 Act which are concerned with driver licensing, and the provisions of the 1996 Regulations, regs 51-54 (large goods vehicle drivers' licences issued to persons under 21; revocation of large goods vehicle drivers' licences and removal of disqualification) do not apply to large goods vehicles of a class included in categories F, G or H (some tractors, road rollers and track-laying vehicles) or sub-category C1 + E (8.25 tonnes), or 'exempted' vehicles (including military vehicles). The list of other 'exempted' vehicles is extensive, covering a variety of vehicles used in public works, industry, agriculture, articulated vehicles the unladen weight of which does not exceed 3.5 tonnes, forces vehicles and emergency vehicles.

The driving test

Goods vehicle drivers will be in possession of driving licences issued under Part III of the 1988 Act for differing categories of vehicles as described in Sch 2 to the 1996 Regulations. In order to obtain those licences they will have been tested on different types of vehicles. The table below sets out the various categories of goods vehicles and gives details of the 'minimum test vehicle' which would have been used in the relevant test.

Category or sub-category		*Specification*
C1	3.5 tonnes but n.e. 7.5 tonnes + trailer n.e. 750 kg	C1 vehicle of 4,000 kg capable of 80 kph
C1+E	C1 tractor, trailer n.e. 750 kgs and mass n.e. 12 tonnes	C1 vehicle + trailer having maximum authorised mass of 2,000 kg, overall length of 8 m and capable of 80 kph
C	exceeding 3.5 tonnes + trailer n.e. 750 kg tonnes	C vehicle, other than articulated vehicle, having maximum authorised mass of 10,000 kg and a length of 7 m and capable of 80 kph
C+E	tractor category C but combination does not fall within that category	Either an articulated combination having a maximum authorised mass of 18,000 kgs and a length of 12 m and capable of 80 kph OR C + trailer of 4 m and maximum authorised mass of 4 tonnes, in aggregate being of 18,000 kg, an overall length of 12 m and capable of 80 kph

Age of drivers in relation to licensing

While the general requirement is that a person who drives a large goods vehicle must be at least 21 years of age, the Motor Vehicles (Driving Licences) Regulations 1996, reg 7, authorises persons of the age of 18 years to drive large goods vehicles of a category to which their training agreement applies, provided that they are employed by a registered employer and that they are registered employees of that employer. The vehicles which they are driving must be owned or operated by their employer or by a registered large goods vehicle driver training establishment. The Motor Vehicles (Driving Licences) Regulations 1996, reg 51 permits such persons to be issued with a large goods vehicle trainee driver's licence. It prescribes additional conditions to which that licence will be subject, some of which are those set out above which relate to the employer/employee relationship.

Provisional licences

These may be of two types. To permit those of 18 years of more to be taught to drive within a training agreement, provisional trainee drivers' licences may be issued. Other learner drivers will be issued with a standard provisional driving licence.

Conditions applicable to provisional licences

Provisional licences of both types are subject to the general conditions prescribed by reg 15 relating to supervision, learner plates and the general restrictions placed upon vehicles being used to draw a trailer. In addition, reg 51(2) provides that where a person holds a LGV trainee driver's full licence, that person will still be subject to the condition that he must drive, as a registered employee of a registered employer, vehicles to which his training agreement applies, which are owned or operated by that employer; and that he must not drive such a vehicle otherwise than under the supervision of a full licence holder for that class of vehicle if the vehicle is being used to draw a trailer.

The requirement, that a vehicle being driven by the holder of a provisional licence must not draw a trailer, does not apply to such a person driving a vehicle of a class included in category C + E.

Full standard licences used as provisional licences

Regulation 17 sets out details of certain full licences which do not carry provisional entitlement to drive other categories of vehicles. The table included within this regulation sets out details of categories of full licences together with the provisional entitlement which is included within that licence. Most significant to issues surrounding large goods vehicles is the provision that a category C licence carries provisional entitlement to drive vehicles of categories C1 + E and C + E.

Regulation 51(3) provides that the holder of a LGV trainee driver's full licence authorising the driving of a vehicle of category C may not drive a vehicle in category C + E (other than vehicles included in sub-category C1 + E the maximum authorised mass of which does not exceed 7.5 tonnes), as if he were authorised by a provisional licence to do so, before the expiration of two years commencing on the date on which he passed a test for category C. Thus, a trainee driver could pass a test for category C vehicles (exceeding 3.5 tonnes + trailer not exceeding 750 kg) but would be unable to use his full licence for category C vehicles as a provisional licence in respect of category C + E vehicles (combinations of motor vehicles and trailers which fall outside category C) until he has held that full licence for a period of two years. This has the effect of preventing young trainee drivers from progressing to the driving of very heavy lorries whilst well below the age of 21.

Drivers from abroad

The Road Traffic Act 1988, Part III as amended by the Driving Licences (Community Driving Licences) Regulations 1996 permits holders of Community licences authorising them to drive large goods vehicles to drive large goods vehicles in the United Kingdom. Those who become resident in the United Kingdom *may* exchange those licences for British ones, but are in any case required to submit to the Secretary of State details of driving entitlement and other information which is prescribed within a year of becoming resident. Such licences are referred to in the 1988 Act as LGV Community licences.

Holders of convention or domestic driving permits who are resident in the Isle of Man or Jersey may drive any large goods vehicle which they are authorised to drive by that permit during a period of 12 months from the date of their last entry into the United Kingdom. Holders who are not residents of an EEA State, or the Isle of Man or Jersey, may only drive a large goods vehicle brought temporarily into Great Britain.

PLATING AND TESTING

There is a system of 'Ministry plating and testing' of goods vehicles. Its purpose is to ensure that the provisions concerning their construction and use are complied with.

Examinations for this purpose are carried out by, or under the direction of, vehicle examiners who may drive the vehicle for this purpose. The driver must remain with the vehicle throughout such an examination and must drive or operate the controls as required.

Before dealing with the system of Ministry plating and testing, we must say something about the rules relating to manufacturers' plates.

Manufacturer's plate

The Road Vehicles (Construction and Use) Regulations require the following vehicles to be fitted with a manufacturer's plate:

(a) every heavy motor car and motor car first used on or after 1 January 1968, which is not a passenger vehicle;
(b) every bus (whether or not it is an articulated bus) first used on or after 1 April 1982;
(c) every locomotive and motor tractor first used on or after 1 April 1973;
(d) every trailer manufactured on or after 1 January 1968 which exceeds 1,020 kg unladen weight (although living vans not exceeding 2,040 kg are exempted if fitted with pneumatic tyres); and
(e) every trailer which is a converter dolly manufactured on or after 1 January 1979.

The usual exceptions apply in respect of land, works, pedestrian-controlled and plant etc vehicles.

The various terms used in the above list are defined by the Road Traffic Act 1988 or by the Regulations themselves. For the purposes of the present part of this chapter, a 'motor car' is a mechanically propelled vehicle constructed or adapted for use for the conveyance of any goods or burden and whose unladen weight does not exceed 3,050 kg (3 tons) (or 3,500 kg (3.5 tons) if the vehicle carries a container or containers to permit its propulsion by gas). For the same purpose, a 'heavy motor car' is a mechanically propelled vehicle (not being a motor car) constructed to carry a load, and whose unladen weight exceeds 2,540 kg (2.5 tons). Although the full definition of these two types of 'car' also covers passenger vehicles, such vehicles are excluded from the present requirements, except that a 'bus' is separately specified. A 'bus' is a mechanically propelled vehicle constructed or adapted to carry more than eight seated passengers in addition to the driver.

A 'motor tractor' is defined as a mechanically propelled vehicle which is not constructed itself to carry a load (other than one concerned with its own propulsion or maintenance), and the unladen weight of which does not exceed 7,370 kg (7.25 tonnes). A 'light locomotive' is a similar vehicle, the unladen weight of which does not exceed 11,690 kg (11.5 tonnes) but does exceed 7,370 kg (7.25 tonnes). A 'heavy locomotive' is a similar vehicle, the unladen weight of which exceeds 11,690 kg (11.5 tonnes).

The Regulations extend the plating requirements to trailers of the 'converter dolly' type. These are trailers with two or more wheels enabling a semi-trailer to move without any part of its weight being directly superimposed on the drawing vehicle. A semi-trailer is the type hitched to an articulated tractive unit and it therefore has no wheels at the front as this part usually rests on the drawing vehicle. A converter dolly amounts to no more than a wheeled platform which provides the semi-trailer with front wheels.

The plate

The plate must be fitted to the vehicle in a conspicuous and readily accessible position. It must contain particulars set out in Sch 2 to the Regulations, including the maximum axle, gross and train weights for the vehicle.

In certain circumstances the only plate a goods vehicle will carry for the first year of its life is its manufacturer's plate, but those vehicles to which the Motor Vehicles (Type Approval for Goods Vehicles) (Great Britain) Regulations 1982 apply will be certified and fitted with a Ministry plate (see below) within 14 days. So far as police officers are concerned, all such vehicles will be fitted with a plate which will give the necessary information concerning weights.

Plated weights are shown as 'gross weights'. The maximum gross weight is the unladen weight of a vehicle plus its maximum permitted load. It therefore represents the total weight of the vehicle as transmitted to the road surface. A vehicle of 5 tonnes unladen weight which is permitted to carry 4 tonnes of cargo would have a maximum gross weight of 9 tonnes. The term 'permissible maximum weight', which is used to establish whether goods vehicles are small, medium or large for the purpose of determining the minimum age for driving a goods vehicle, is the vehicle's 'relevant maximum weight'. In turn the relevant permissible maximum weight is the maximum gross weight shown on the plate. The weight shown on the plate is therefore the 'permissible maximum weight' for the above purpose.

Ministry plate

The Goods Vehicles (Plating and Testing) Regulations 1988 make most heavy goods vehicles and trailers subject to provisions for annual testing. The first examination is for the purpose of plating as well as testing. Goods vehicles subject to type approval will be fitted with a Ministry plate within 14 days and the requirement to have a first examination no longer applies to a motor vehicle where a certificate of conformity or a Minister's approval certificate has been issued. The plating examination includes assessment of the vehicle's axle and gross weights, as well as a test of roadworthiness. These weights are recorded on a 'Ministry plate'.

Every motor vehicle which meets the following requirements, namely:

(a) a plating certificate is in force for the vehicle; and
(b) that plating certificate is a certificate of conformity or a Minister's approval certificate that is treated as a plating certificate by virtue of s 59(4) of the RTA 1988,

shall be submitted for a goods vehicle test on or before the appropriate day. Other motor vehicles, and every trailer, shall be submitted for both a plating examination and a goods vehicle test on or before the appropriate day. The term 'appropriate day' means:

(a) in relation to a vehicle which is a motor vehicle, the last day of the calendar month in which falls the anniversary of the date on which it was registered; and
(b) in relation to a vehicle which is a trailer, the last day of the calendar month in which falls the anniversary of the date on which it was first sold or supplied by retail.

However, the prescription of such dates does not prevent the Secretary of State authorising the submission of a vehicle after the appropriate day.

A number of vehicles do not require a Ministry plate. For example, dual-purpose vehicles not constructed or adapted to form part of an articulated vehicle are exempt (although they are subject to the MOT test). So are breakdown, fire fighting or snow clearance vehicles, living vans whose gross design weight does not exceed 3,500 kg, police vehicles and vehicles temporarily in Great Britain (provided they do not remain for more than 12 months).

The requirements set out above under the heading 'Manufacturer's plate' are in respect of certain vehicles *at the time of manufacture*. On the other hand, the Ministry plating requirements are concerned with a subsequent examination, which on the first occasion includes a 'Ministry plating'. As a result there are differences in respect of the list of vehicles affected. Vehicles still exist which were not the subject of manufacturer's plating at the time of their manufacture, but will nevertheless be subject to Ministry plating and annual testing.

When the plated weight has been determined, a plating certificate is issued showing the date of issue, plated weights and tyre sizes. Those vehicles which were subject to the Motor Vehicles (Type Approval for Goods Vehicles) (Great Britain) Regulations 1982 will already have a certificate of conformity or approval and this, or a substitute issued by the Secretary of State for it, must be produced. The reason is that the certificate is treated as a plating certificate for the purposes of the Regulations and the examiner merely checks to see that no notifiable alterations have been made to the vehicle. If they have not, the certificate of conformity or type approval certificate is deemed to have been issued under the Plating and Testing Regulations.

The plate and plating certificate

The manufacturer's plate is a metal plate which is fixed to the vehicle. It is only significant until Ministry plating takes place, as the particulars on the Ministry plate are deemed to be correct after that examination is carried out. After a plating examination, a Ministry plate and a plating certificate will be issued in respect of the vehicle. They show the maximum gross weights for the vehicle; these may be the same as those shown on the manufacturer's plate but this will not necessarily be so as they may be lower if the Ministry does not accept the weights specified by the manufacturers. The Ministry will not set weights higher than those set by the manufacturer unless the vehicle has been altered to permit it to carry more weight. The Ministry plate is in fact a paper plate; it must be fixed in a conspicuous and readily accessible position in the cab of the vehicle, or (in the case of a trailer) in some such position.

Plates will be attached to both parts of an articulated vehicle, ie to the tractive unit and the semi-trailer. The 'plating certificate' is in most respects a copy of the plate attached to the vehicle but includes, additionally, details of the types of tyres fitted to the vehicle at the time of inspection. Plates issued since 24 March 1994 may contain a space for 'maximum train weight' where a vehicle is used for combined transport operations (the transport of loading units partly by rail in Great Britain and partly by road).

Offences

It is an offence for any person to use, or to cause or permit to be used, on a road a goods vehicle of a class required by the 1988 Regulations to have been submitted for examination for plating if there is no plating certificate in force for the vehicle. The plating *certificate* will normally be held at the office of the company. The circumstances in which a constable may demand its production are the same as those applying to other vehicle documents. The same conditions apply, in relation to a defence being available to those who subsequently produce their certificate, as apply in the case of certificates of insurance (see p 244).

If a goods vehicle is to be permitted to draw a trailer, its plating certificate will specify its maximum laden weight together with its trailer. If, after the relevant date for Ministry plating, it is used to draw a trailer when no such weight is specified, any person using or causing or permitting such use is guilty of an offence.

Any structural alterations made to vehicles after plating must be notified to the Ministry. It is an offence to fail to do so. However, alterations to plated particulars may be made without the necessity for a further examination where a plating certificate is in force for the vehicle and the alterations applied for would not affect the safety of the vehicle on a road.

Temporary exemption

The Ministry is empowered to issue certificates of temporary exemption if, due to exceptional circumstances, an examination cannot be carried out. An example of such a circumstance would be the destruction by fire of the testing station at which the examination was to be carried out.

Goods vehicle testing

Where a vehicle must be submitted for a Ministry plate, it must also be submitted (according to the same provisions as to time) for the first of its annual goods vehicle tests. Goods vehicles submitted for a first examination during the two months preceding the appropriate day may be issued with a certificate which expires on the next but one appropriate day.

Although vehicles which require plating are exempt from the normal MOT test applied to passenger motor cars, they are subject to a more stringent annual test by the Ministry at one of its testing stations. It is an offence to use on a road at any time after the relevant date any goods vehicle required to be tested by the Regulations, when there is no goods vehicle test certificate in force for it. It is also an offence to cause or permit this to be done. In the case of trailers, there will be a disc fitted to the trailer which will give the date on which its test certificate expires. The same exceptions to liability apply as in the case of MOT tests, eg where a vehicle is going by previous appointment to (and from) a test, or while it is undergoing a test, or where a vehicle refused a certificate is going to or from a place of repair, or where it is being towed to the breakers. In addition a certificate of temporary exemption may be issued on the same ground and in the same way as in the case of the Ministry plating requirement.

A goods vehicle test certificate must be produced to a constable in the same cases as a certificate of insurance. The usual time for production applies. It is an offence to fail so to produce it.

OPERATORS' LICENCES

Purpose of licensing

It is essential that strict control is kept over the operation of goods vehicles, partly to protect the environment, partly to promote safety on the roads, and partly to prevent damage to roads. The traffic commissioner for each area is the licensing authority for goods vehicles. He monitors the standard of maintenance of vehicles, checks that drivers do not exceed the maximum permitted periods of driving and working, and ensures that the recommended weight limits for vehicles are not exceeded.

Need for operators' licences

The Goods Vehicles (Licensing of Operators) Act 1995, s 2(1) states that, with the exceptions listed in s 2(2) (see pp 349-350) no person shall use a goods vehicle on a road for the carriage of goods for hire or reward, or for or in connection with any trade or business carried on by him, except under the authority of an operators' licence. By s 2(5), a person who uses a vehicle in contravention of s 2(1) commits an offence.

If a person who is driving a vehicle owns it, or it is in his possession under an agreement for hire, hire purchase or loan, he is deemed to be the user for licensing purposes. In any other case, the user will be the person whom the driver is serving or whose agent he is at the time (s 58(2)). The offence of using a goods vehicle etc without the authority of an operators' licence is therefore one which is committed by the owner or hirer (or the like) of a vehicle. If Brown drives his own vehicle on a road for the carriage of goods for hire or reward without an operator's licence he commits this offence. If Green is driving Brown's vehicle in these circumstances, Brown, the owner, commits the offence, and Green does not.

It is essential to prove that the goods vehicle was carrying goods at the time of the alleged offence. It must also be proved that the goods vehicle was being used *for hire or reward or for or in connection with any trade or business carried out by the user*.

Hire or reward

Generally speaking, a person uses a goods vehicle for hire or reward if he hires out the use of the vehicle, together with its driver, to another person. For example, a furniture remover who uses his employees and his vehicles to assist a customer to move his household effects, a fixed, agreed fee being paid by the customer, uses the vehicle for the carriage of goods for hire or reward. In one case, for instance, where a goods vehicle was hired out to empty a septic tank and dump effluent on to land some distance away, it was held that it had been used for the carriage of goods (the effluent) for hire or reward. In another case, a goods vehicle which was used to remove earth from a site for a fixed fee was held to be used for the carriage of goods for hire or reward.

For or in connection with any trade or business carried on by him

A large number of goods vehicles are used by firms solely for, or in connection with, their own trade or business, as opposed to hauling goods for hire or reward. Supermarket chains operate fleets of vehicles solely for the purpose of effecting deliveries to their retail outlets, with the result that the vehicles are used for or in connection with their own trade or business, and require operators' licences. Likewise, the builder who uses his goods vehicle to carry building materials to the sites where his building operations are being carried out uses the vehicle in connection with his own business and requires an operators' licence. On the other hand, it has been held that a person whose hobby was stock car racing and who transported the stock cars in a converted motor coach did not use that coach for or in connection with any trade or business, even though he competed for prize money and received sponsorship money.

The Goods Vehicles (Licensing of Operators) Act 1995, s 2(4) states that, for the purpose of operators' licensing, a local or public authority is deemed to be carrying on a business. Such an authority must therefore have operators' licences in respect of its vehicles.

Types of operators' licences

There are two types of operators' licences: standard operators' licences and restricted operators' licences.

Standard operators' licences

Standard operators' licences are all embracing in that they authorise the holder to carry goods for hire or reward or in connection with the holder's trade or business. On occasions a licence may be held by a company as opposed to an individual. Where a licence is held by a holding company, any business carried on by a subsidiary company is regarded as being carried on by the licence holder. This provision prevents the formation of subsidiary companies in an effort to avoid the responsibilities of the holder of a licence. However, a company which carries the goods of a second company which is its subsidiary or holding company may, in certain circumstances, hold a restricted licence instead of a standard licence.

Standard licences may authorise transport operations both nationally and internationally, or may be in respect of national operations only. A national transport operation is a transport operation involving the use of goods vehicles for the carriage of goods for hire or reward in the United Kingdom only. Therefore, if an operator wishes to transport goods to various centres in Europe for hire or reward he will require a standard licence which authorises international transport operations. If he does not hold such a licence he will only be able to deliver the goods to a port for despatch abroad, the goods to be picked up by another operator when unloaded at a European port.

Restricted operators' licences

A restricted operators' licence authorises the use of goods vehicles solely for, or in connection with, a trade or business carried on by the holder of the licence, other than that of carrying goods for hire or reward.

General

An operators' licence will normally authorise an operator to use several vehicles. It is issued to the operator and is generally kept at the offices of his company, usually his operating centre. The licence will specify the registration numbers of the vehicles which are authorised to be used. It will also specify, by type, the maximum number of trailers which may be used under the licence and also the maximum number of subsequently acquired motor vehicles which may be so used.

Identity discs

So that vehicles specified on an operators' licence may bear evidence of the fact that they are being used under the authority of a licence, an identity disc is issued in respect of each vehicle which is specified. The disc must be fixed to that vehicle in a waterproof container adjacent to the vehicle excise licence. On occasions an operators' licence will authorise the use of more vehicles than are currently held by the operator and are therefore specified in his licence. If this is the case the operator may use vehicles on a temporary basis for a maximum period of one month. In such instances an 'excess' vehicle will not carry an identity disc. However, after use for a period of one month, the vehicle must be specified in the licence if it is to continue in use.

The information which is given on an identity disc is sufficient to identify its authorised usage. It will show whether the licence is standard or restricted, and if standard whether it is valid in respect of international and national operations, or only of national ones.

The holder of the licence must cause the identity disc to be displayed at all times when the vehicle is specified in his licence, regardless of whether or not the vehicle is being used at the time for a purpose for which a licence is required. The person in control of the vehicle must keep the disc readily legible.

Production of licences etc for examination

The holder of an operators' licence must produce his licence if required to do so by a police constable, vehicle examiner, or by any person authorised by the licensing authority. He may elect whether to produce it at his operating centre, head office or principal place of business within the traffic area of the licensing authority by whom the licence was granted. It will be noted that there is no power to demand production of this document at a police station.

A requirement to produce must be complied with within 14 days.

The Goods Vehicles (Licensing of Operators) Act 1995, Sch 5 provides that no goods shall be carried on a large goods vehicle unless a consignment note is carried by the driver. The provisions do not apply if the goods could be carried without an operator's licence or the vehicle is exempted by regulations. These powers may be exercised by a vehicle examiner, authorised person or a police constable. These provisions are not yet in force at the time of writing.

Forgery etc of documents and powers of seizure

The Goods Vehicles (Licensing of Operators) Act 1995, s 38 provides that a person is guilty of an offence if, with intent to deceive, he forges, alters, uses, lends, or allows to be used, a document or other thing to which the section applies. Section 38 also provides that a person is guilty of an offence if, with intent to deceive, he makes or has in his possession a document or other thing so closely resembling a document or other thing to which the section applies as to be calculated to deceive. Section 38 applies to operators' licences and documents and other things (eg plates) ancillary to them.

Section 39 provides that a person is guilty of an offence if he knowingly makes a false statement in order to obtain the issue of an operator's licence or its variation, or in order to prevent its issue or variation, or in order to procure the imposition of a condition or limitation in relation to such a licence, or in order to obtain a certificate or diploma under the Act.

A vehicle examiner, a person authorised for these purposes by the traffic commissioner, or a police constable, may at any reasonable time enter any premises of an applicant for an operators' licence, or the holder of such a licence, and inspect the facilities for maintaining vehicles. It is an offence to obstruct such a person. Where such a person has reason to believe that a document or article carried on or by a driver, or a document produced to him under the Act, is a document or article in relation to which an offence under s 38 or s 39 has been committed, he may seize it.

When licences are not required

By way of exception to the general rule, that operators must hold licences in respect of all goods vehicles used by them for the carriage of goods for hire or reward, or for or in connection with their own trade or business, the Goods Vehicles (Licensing of Operators) Act 1995, s 2(2) states that this requirement does not apply to:

(a) the use of a small goods vehicle (as defined by Sch 1, see below);
(b) the use of a goods vehicle for international carriage by a haulier established in a member State of the EU (other than UK) and not established in the UK;
(c) the use of a goods vehicle by a haulier established in Northern Ireland (and not in Great Britain) for international carriage; or
(d) to the use of any vehicle of any class specified in regulations (see below).

Small goods vehicle

A 'small goods vehicle' is a goods vehicle:

(a) which does not form part of a vehicle combination and has a relevant plated weight not exceeding 3.5 tonnes or (not having a relevant plated weight) has an unladen weight not exceeding 1,525 kg; or
(b) which forms part of a vehicle combination (not being an articulated combination) which is such that the total plated weight of the combination (except any small trailer) does not exceed 3.5 tonnes (or, if one or more of the vehicles in the combination, other than a small trailer, is not plated, if the total unladen weight of those vehicles, excluding such a trailer does not exceed 1,525 kg); or
(c) which forms part of an articulated combination which is such that the total of the unladen weight of the tractive unit and the plated weight of the trailer does not exceed 3.5 tonnes (or if the trailer does not have a plated weight, the total of their unladen weights does not exceed 1,525 kg).

The description of a 'small goods vehicle' appears to be quite complex until it is realised that the figures of 3.5 tonnes and 1,525 kg are all that it is essential to remember: 1,525 kg represents 30 cwt. Let us examine the type of vehicles which are small goods vehicles by virtue of Sch 1.

Rigid goods vehicles A single goods vehicle without a trailer, which is plated and whose relevant plated weight is 3.5 tonnes or less is a small goods vehicle and does not need to be operated under a licence. The same is the case where the unladen weight of an unplated goods vehicle (and there are not many such vehicles) is 1,525 kg or less.

Rigid goods vehicles plus trailers The first point to note is that all draw-bar trailers with an unladen weight not exceeding 1525 kg are classed as 'small trailers' and must be ignored in the following calculations. If both the goods vehicle and the trailer are plated, and the two relevant weights total 3.5 tonnes or less, the combination is a 'small' goods vehicle and does not need to be operated under a licence. If one or both parts of the combination are unplated, the relevant weight is 1,525 kg or less.

Articulated goods vehicle combinations If the total of the unladen weight of the tractive unit and the plated weight of the semi-trailer is 3.5 tonnes or less, the combination is a 'small' goods vehicle and does not need to be operated under a licence; if the semi-trailer is unplated the relevant weight is 1,525 kg or less.

Vehicles exempt by regulations

Those vehicles which are exempted by regulations are set out in the Goods Vehicles (Licensing of Operators) Regulations 1995, Sch 3. The list is extensive but, for ease of understanding, it is more practical to think in terms of categories of vehicles. Generally, the vehicles exempted are those used by public services. Thus, defence force, police, fire fighting, rescue and ambulance vehicles are exempt; so are vehicles used for purposes such as snow clearance, gritting and refuse disposal. Also exempted are vehicles used as agricultural tractors or machines, dual-purpose vehicles, showmen's goods vehicles, recovery vehicles, cement mixer lorries and vehicles used for funerals. Motor vehicles constructed or adapted primarily to carry passengers or their effects, together with any trailer, are exempt whilst being so used. Of course, the operation of public service vehicles must be licensed under other provisions described in the previous chapter.

Vehicles temporarily in Great Britain

The Goods Vehicles (Community Authorisations) Regulations 1992 established a Community-wide authorisation allowing goods vehicles access to the market in the carriage of goods by road between member states. The Goods Vehicles (Licensing of Operators) Act 1995 and the regulations bring into effect the provisions of Council Regulation No 881/92 which requires that each member state must issue a Community authorisation to any haulier established in that state who is entitled to carry out international carriage of goods by road for hire or reward. Holders of such authorisations do not require operators' licences in other Community countries. The Council Regulation provides for the appointment of 'authorised inspecting officers' who are empowered to demand the production of a certified copy of the authorisation which must be carried on each vehicle operating under its authority. The 1992 Regulations appoint police constables and examiners appointed under the Road Traffic Acts as authorised inspecting officers.

The Goods Vehicles (Licensing of Operators)(Temporary Use in Great Britain) Regulations 1996, in consequence, define a 'foreign goods vehicle' as one:

(a) which is operated by a person who is not established in the United Kingdom and has been brought temporarily into Great Britain;
(b) which is not being used for international carriage by a haulier who is established in a member state other than the United Kingdom;
(c) which is engaged in carrying goods by road on a journey some part of which has taken place, or will take place outside the United Kingdom; and

(d) which, except in the case of use under a Community cabotage authorisation, is not used at any time during the said journey for the carriage of goods loaded at one place in the United Kingdom and delivered at another place in the United Kingdom.

The Regulations exempt the operator of a foreign goods vehicle with a Community *cabotage authorisation* from the requirement to obtain a goods vehicle operator's licence for the carriage of goods in Great Britain on an international journey. EU Regulations lay down the conditions under which non-resident carriers may operate national road haulage services within a member State.

The 1996 Regulations, in addition, provide specific exemptions in favour of goods vehicles of named countries, in specified circumstances.

A 'cabotage authorisation' lays down specific conditions under which non-resident carriers may operate national road haulage services within a member State.

Evidence by certificate

The Goods Vehicles (Licensing of Operators) Act 1995, s 43 makes provisions for evidence to be given by certificate of the facts stated in it. The certificate must be signed by or on behalf of a traffic commissioner. It may certify that a person was the holder of an operator's licence on a particular date; the dates of validity of an operator's licence; the terms and conditions attached to such a licence; that a person is disqualified from holding or obtaining an operator's licence; or that a licence was suspended.

A certificate which purports to be signed by or on behalf of a traffic commissioner must be taken to be so signed unless the contrary is proved.

DRIVERS' HOURS AND RECORDS

The provisions set out below apply whether the driver is the driver of a goods vehicle or of a *passenger vehicle*.

There are two sets of provisions which apply: (a) the so called European rules, and (b) the rules provided by Part VI of the Transport Act 1968 (which are of relatively limited application).

European rules

These rules, provided by the Community Drivers' Hours Regulations (and certain other Regulations) made by the Council of the EU, create common standards for the whole of the Community. Separate sets of regulations relate to drivers' hours and drivers' records. The rules apply to journeys on 'roads open to the public' by a goods or passenger vehicle (as specified below), whether it is laden or not, and whether it is registered in this country, in another EU member state, or in any other country. There is no distinction between journeys made for hire or reward and those made on an operator's own account.

It is to be noted that the rules are concerned with journeys on 'roads open to the public', a phrase otherwise unknown in our law. Where journeys are made entirely within an area which is privately owned, on roads which are privately maintained, the important question is not concerned with ownership of such roads, but with access to them and their use. The fact that they may only be used by persons with business in the privately owned area, eg an airport, is irrelevant. The question is whether the roads are open to the public.

The rules apply to carriage by:

(a) all goods vehicles which exceed 3.5 tonnes permissible maximum weight; and
(b) all passenger vehicles which in construction and equipment are suitable for carrying more than nine persons including the driver.

The meaning of 'permissible maximum weight' in (a) has already been given; essentially, it is the maximum gross weight shown on the relevant plate. Where a trailer is being drawn, the term refers to the aggregate of the maximum gross weight marked on the towing vehicle and the maximum gross weight marked on the trailer in actual use at the time; not to the total weight of the vehicle and the trailer which it might be capable of towing.

Exemptions

Quite apart from the vehicles to which the European rules do not apply because they are outside these general classifications, the European rules expressly do not apply to carriage by the following vehicles which would otherwise fall within them:

(a) vehicles used for the carriage of passengers on regular services where the route covered by the service in question does not exceed 50 km (approx 30 miles);
(b) vehicles with a maximum authorised speed not exceeding 30 kph (approx 20 mph);
(c) vehicles used by or under the control of the armed services, civil defence, fire services and forces responsible for maintaining public order;
(d) vehicles used in connection with sewerage, flood protection, gas, water or electricity services, highway maintenance and control, refuse collection and disposal, telegraph and telephone services, carriage of postal articles, radio and television broadcasting and the detection of radio or television transmitters or receivers;
(e) vehicles used in emergencies or rescue operations;
(f) specialised vehicles used for medical purposes;
(g) vehicles transporting circus or fun-fair equipment;
(h) specialised breakdown vehicles (regardless of the use to which they are being put at the time);
(i) vehicles undergoing road tests for technical development, repair or maintenance purposes, and new or rebuilt vehicles which have not yet been put into service;
(j) vehicles used for non-commercial carriage of goods for personal use;
(k) vehicles used for milk collection from farms and the return to farms of milk containers or milk products intended for animal feed.

In summary, these exemptions refer to vehicles used for the conveyance of passengers for short distances, vehicles of public services and public utilities, ambulances etc, many tractors, showmen's goods vehicles and some breakdown vehicles. As the purpose of keeping records is to exercise control over working hours, the reason for the exemptions can be appreciated. Such vehicles are not generally being used in the competitive business world in which there might be a temptation to use drivers for long periods of driving. In addition, most of the vehicles are controlled by public authorities or public utilities.

The exemptions are interpreted strictly. For example, in relation to exemption (a), buses used under contract by tour operators which are used for single journeys from airports to hotels, where the precise route to be taken is not predetermined, cannot be considered to be a 'regular service' within the terms of exemption granted in favour of regular services where the route covered does not exceed 50 kilometres. This is so whether or not there are occasional stops at tourist attractions. By way of further example, a vehicle used to transport gas appliances is not used 'in connection with gas services' under (d) above, since that phrase is limited to use in connection with the production, transport or distribution of gas, or the maintenance of installations for that purpose. Thus, a British Gas vehicle used to transport gas cookers and the like is subject to the European rules. Similarly, a vehicle used by a private company to collect builders' skips is not an exempted vehicle by reason of its use 'in connection with refuse disposal and collection' as that exemption has been held to be limited to a 'general service performed in the public interest', and not to extend to a commercial service to customers. A vehicle used to transport machinery used in connection with road works is not exempt; it has been held not to be a vehicle used in connection with highway maintenance and control. The reason given was that such a vehicle is being used for the carriage of goods and its connection with highway maintenance and control is too remote.

Further exemptions

Further modifications are provided by the Community Drivers' Hours and Recording Equipment (Exemptions and Supplementary Provisions) Regulations 1986. These regulations exempt from the provisions of the European rules the following vehicles:

(a) vehicles used for the carriage of passengers constructed or equipped to carry not more than 17 persons including the driver;

(b) vehicles which on or after 1 January 1990 are being used by a public authority to provide public services otherwise than in competition with professional road hauliers (such as ambulances and medical vehicles, social services' vehicles for elderly and mentally and physically handicapped persons, those used by coastguard, lighthouse, harbour, airports, railways and waterway authorities);

(c) vehicles used by agricultural, horticultural, forestry or fishery undertakings to carry goods within a 50 km radius of base (in the case of use by fishery undertakings only if used for the carriage of live fish or conveyance of a 'catch of fish');

(d) vehicles used for animal waste or carcases not for human consumption;

(e) vehicles used for the carriage of live animals between farm and market or slaughterhouse;

(f) vehicles used as a shop, at a local market, for door to door selling, or for mobile banking etc;

(g) vehicles used for worship, library services or cultural events, which are specially fitted for such use;

(h) goods vehicles not exceeding 7.5 tonnes permissible maximum weight which are carrying equipment etc for the driver's use in the course of his work within a 50 km radius of his base provided that driving the vehicle is not his main activity;

(i) vehicles which operate exclusively on offshore islands not linked to the rest of Great Britain;

(j) gas or electrically propelled goods vehicles not exceeding 7.5 tonnes maximum permissible weight;

(k) vehicles used for driving instruction with a view to gaining a licence provided there is no trailer used for goods purposes;

(l) any tractor used on or after 1 January 1990 for agricultural or forestry work;

(m) any vehicle which is being used by the RNLI for the purpose of hauling lifeboats;

(n) any vehicle manufactured before 1 January 1947; and

(o) any vehicle which is propelled by steam.

Vehicles used for the collection of sea coal are exempt from the provisions of the European rules on drivers' records only.

European rules on driving periods, rest breaks and rest periods

The rules are set out in the Community Drivers' Hours Regulations. For the purposes of the Regulations a 'driver' is any person who drives a vehicle, even for a short period, or who is in the vehicle in order to be available for driving if necessary; the term 'week' means the period between 00.00 hours on Monday and 24.00 hours on Sunday; and 'rest' means any uninterrupted period of at least one hour during which the driver may freely dispose of his time (which he will not be if he is engaged in doing some other type of work under the direction of his employer).

Continuous driving period	4 ½ hours generally.
Rest breaks	Period of at least 45 minutes, unless the driver is beginning a daily or weekly rest period. This break may be replaced by breaks of at least 15 minutes each distributed within the continuous driving period, or immediately after it, provided that they total 45 minutes.
(Permissive under Regulation 3820/85)	(On regular national passenger services breaks of a minimum time of 30 minutes after a driving period not exceeding 4 hours may be permitted by British regulations, and have been in certain areas (Camden, Kensington and Chelsea, Islington, Westminster and specified parts of Birmingham, Bristol, Leeds, Leicester, Nottingham and Oxford), but only if longer breaks could hamper the flow of urban traffic and it is not possible to take a 15-minute break within a 4-hour period followed by a 30-minute break.)
	Rest breaks must not be taken as a part of a daily rest period.
Daily driving period	9 hours normally but may be 10 hours not more than twice a week.
Longer driving periods: weekly/fortnightly	Drivers must, after no more than 6 daily driving periods, take a weekly rest period. (In the case of national or international carriage of passengers other than on regular services (ie coach tours), it is 12 daily driving periods.) The weekly rest period may be postponed until the end of the 6th day (or 12th day in the case of national or international coach tours) if the total driving time over the 6 (or 12) days does not exceed the maximum corresponding to 6 (or 12) daily driving periods.
	A 'day' in this context does not mean successive periods from midnight to midnight. Instead, it means successive periods of 24 hours beginning with the resumption of driving after the last weekly rest period.
	The total period of driving in any one fortnight shall not exceed 90 hours.

Daily rest period

In each period of 24 hours, the driver must have a daily rest period of at least 11 consecutive hours. This may be reduced to 9 consecutive hours not more than three times a week, provided that an equivalent period is granted as compensation before the end of the following week.

When not reduced, daily rest may be taken in two or three separate periods during a 24-hour period, but one of these must be at least 8 consecutive hours. If this is done, the minimum length of rest for that day must be increased to 12 hours.

Daily rest periods may be taken in a vehicle as long as it is fitted with a bunk and is stationary.

Within extended periods

During each period of 30 hours, when a vehicle is manned by at least two drivers, each shall have a rest period of not less than 8 consecutive hours.

Weekly rest periods

In the course of each week, one of the rest periods shall be extended by way of weekly rest, to a total of 45 consecutive hours. This may be reduced to 36 if it is taken at vehicle base or driver base or to a minimum of 24 if taken elsewhere, but if this is done there shall be compensation by an equivalent rest taken en bloc before the end of the third week following the week in question.

A weekly rest period which begins in one week and continues into the following week may be attached to either of these weeks. In the case of international or national carriage of passengers (coach tours), the weekly rest period may be postponed until the week following that in respect of which the rest is due and added on to that second week's weekly rest.

Rest taken as compensation must be attached to another rest of at least 8 hours and shall be granted, at the request of the person concerned, at the vehicle's parking place or driver's base.

During breaks from driving a driver may not carry out any other work. The term 'other work' does not include waiting time spent on a moving vehicle by a driver who is not driving, or on a ferry or train. Where a driver accompanies a vehicle which is transported by ferry or train, the daily rest period may be interrupted (not more than once), provided that the period includes rest on land before or after the journey and the interruption is as short as possible and does not exceed one hour (including all embarkation, disembarkation and customs formalities etc) and during both portions of the rest period the driver must be able to have access to a bunk or couchette.

If a daily rest period is interrupted in this way, it must be increased by two hours. Thus, a driver may spend ten hours at rest in a bunk on land before embarkation on to a ferry for a journey. If at that stage his lorry has to be taken aboard the ferry by him, he may continue with a rest period, provided the break in his rest does not exceed one hour. If the journey takes four hours he will have had 14 hours of rest. The normal daily rest period is 11 hours (extended by two in these circumstances), so the requirements are met. (If he had not already reduced three daily rest periods to nine hours in the course of the week, he would have complied with these requirements before he began the process of embarkation.) However, such interruptions to a daily rest period cannot occur at both sides of the Channel as the Regulation specifies that such interruptions can occur 'not more than once'.

Provided that road safety is not thereby jeopardised, the Regulation permits departure from the provisions to enable a driver to reach a suitable stopping place, but only to the extent necessary to ensure the safety of persons or of the vehicle or its load. In these circumstances the driver must indicate the nature of and the reason for his departure from these provisions on the record sheet of the recording equipment or in his daily roster. Such a deviation from the requirements of the Regulation may only be made by a driver at the time he is faced with an unexpected situation. It may not be pre-planned by an employer for reasons known before the journey commences.

Offences

A driver of a motor vehicle, who contravenes the above European rules concerning driving periods, rest breaks and rest periods whilst in Great Britain, commits an offence contrary to the Transport Act 1968, s 96(11A). An employer, or a person to whose orders the offender was subject, who causes or permits such a contravention also commits an offence. However, it is a defence to prove that the contravention was due to unavoidable delay in the completion of a journey arising out of circumstances which the person charged could not reasonably have foreseen. In the case of an employer etc, he also has a defence if he proves that the contravention was due to the fact that the driver had for a particular period or periods driven otherwise than in his employment, and that he (the employer etc) could not reasonably have become aware of that fact.

'Cause' and 'permit' bear the same meaning as described on pp 258-259. However, because art 15 of the Community Drivers' Hours Regulations requires periodic checks of tachograph records, it has been held by the Divisional Court that an employer who fails to check a driver's records can be said to permit a contravention of the European rules, if such a check would have revealed the contravention, even though the employer neither knew nor was wilfully blind as to the contravention. The same seems to be true of a charge of 'causing'.

European rules on drivers' records

EC Regulation 3821/85 requires that a tachograph be installed and used in vehicles which are registered in a member state of the EU and are used for the carriage of goods or passengers by road. The Passenger and Goods Vehicles (Recording Equipment) Regulations 1996 apply the provisions of Community Regulation No 2479/95 to the definition of 'the Recording Equipment Regulation' as applied to the Road Traffic Acts. They require that tachographs must be capable of detecting interruptions in the power supply, of recording driving time automatically, and of allowing the removal and refitting of seals by an approved centre to enable speed limiters to be fitted. They also require the protection of cables connected to the transmitter by a steel sheath.

The Transport Act 1968, s 97 makes it an offence for any person to use, or cause or permit to be used, a vehicle to which the Regulation applies if that vehicle is not fitted with an approved tachograph which is in working order and is in operation. Where an approved tachograph was not in working order, it is a defence to prove that it had not been reasonably practicable to repair it and that alternative records were being kept. It is also an offence to use, cause or permit to be used, a vehicle in which there is recording equipment which has been repaired (whether before or after installation) otherwise than in accordance with the Community Recording Equipment Regulation.

The above offences are ones of strict liability, but it is a defence for an accused to prove that he neither knew or ought to have known that the recording equipment had not been installed or repaired, as the case may be.

Tachographs may only be fitted and repaired by fitters or workshops approved by a member state. The tachograph is then sealed and marked. The employer and the driver are responsible for ensuring that the tachograph functions correctly and that the seals on it are unbroken. It is an offence contrary to s 97AA of the 1968 Act to forge, alter or use any seal, with intent to deceive. A seal is 'forged' if it is made in order that it may be used as genuine.

The employer must issue sufficient tachograph record sheets to each driver. These are circular discs upon which the tachograph records certain information. Each driver is responsible for operating switches which separately cause records to be made of driving time, other work or attendance duties, breaks and rest periods. An employer must retain completed discs for a period of at least a year and produce them to an authorised inspector on request. The term 'authorised inspector' includes a constable who, if in uniform, is not required to produce a form of authority.

Each driver must enter on his tachograph record sheet:

(a) his full name;
(b) the date and place where the use of the sheet starts and ends;
(c) the registration number of the vehicle and of any other vehicle to which he changes during his duties;
(d) the odometer reading at the start of the first, and at the end of the last, journey recorded on the sheet and, if there is a change of vehicle, the same reading for the other vehicle or vehicles; and
(e) the time any change of vehicle takes place.

Drivers must not use dirty or damaged tachograph sheets. Damaged sheets must be attached to the sheet which replaces them so that an up-to-date record is always available. Drivers must ensure that tachographs are kept running continuously while they are responsible for the vehicle. Where there is more than one driver, they must change the record sheets to ensure that distance, speed and driving time are recorded in relation to each person's driving.

In respect of the requirement that the tachograph must be in operation, it must be in operation throughout the daily working period. If a lorry driver drives home having finished work for the day this driving comes within the daily working period. He will commit an offence if he has switched off the lorry's tachograph. It would be different, of course, if he drives home in his car, since that vehicle is not required to have a tachograph.

Tachographs must be designed so that an inspecting officer can read the recordings relating to the preceding nine hours without damaging the sheet, if necessary by opening the instrument. Drivers must be able to produce record sheets for the current week, and the last day of the previous week on which they drove. Tachographs must be capable of recording, automatically or semi-automatically, the distance travelled and speed of the vehicle, driving time, other periods of work, breaks from work and daily rest periods, and the opening of the part of the equipment which contains the record sheet. The tachograph fitted to vehicles with more than one driver must be capable of recording simultaneously, but distinctly and on separate sheets, the activities of the two members. Employed drivers must return completed record sheets to their employer within 21 days. It is an offence to fail to do so without reasonable cause, and it is also an offence for an employer to fail to secure that this is done.

Records made by tachographs are evidence of the matters appearing in them, and entries made on record sheets by drivers are evidence of the matters appearing therefrom. If a police officer requires a driver to remove the disc from his tachograph, he should indicate that the tachograph was opened at his request, as the disc will have been marked showing that it has been opened.

Section 99 of the 1968 Act makes various provisions as to the inspection of records and other documents. A constable may require a person to produce, and permit him to inspect and copy, any record sheet. He may also require an owner to produce, and permit him to inspect and copy, any other document, book, register etc kept within the requirements of the European rules. Failure to comply with such a requirement is an offence. A constable has power to detain, enter or inspect a vehicle and its equipment for the purpose of copying records etc and he may enter premises at reasonable times to copy records etc which are required by the rules to be kept. It is an offence to obstruct him in the exercise of the above powers. The existence of the various powers under s 99 does not preclude a police officer making use instead of some other available procedure. This was held in a case where a police officer had previously used the powers under s 99 but not all of the relevant documents had been produced. Suspecting serious irregularities in the conduct of the company's business, including falsification of documents for financial gain, he obtained a search warrant under the Police and Criminal Evidence Act 1984, s 8, under which he seized some relevant documents. The Divisional Court held that the search warrant had been properly granted. The officer had had the choice between proceeding via s 99 or via a search warrant, since the suspected offence was one of forgery, a serious arrestable offence, and it was irrelevant that a charge of forgery had not followed.

The Transport Act 1968, s 99(5) creates offences of making, or causing to be made, record sheet entries which are known to be false and of causing records to be altered with intent to deceive. A record sheet may be seized if there is reason to believe that an offence under s 99(5) has been committed.

Part VI of the Transport Act 1968

The legal requirements as to drivers' hours and records set out in Part VI of the Transport Act 1968, as amended, apply to the drivers of certain goods and passenger vehicles which are not subject to the European rules. The exclusion of those vehicles from those provisions does not necessarily mean that there are no rules about hours or records, since that exclusion only exempts them from the provisions of the European rules. Nevertheless, the provisions of Part VI are now limited to such a small range of vehicles that they are no longer particularly significant to police officers.

If a vehicle is one which is not subject to the European rules and:

(a) it is a passenger vehicle (ie a public service vehicle, or any other motor vehicle constructed or adapted to carry more than 12 passengers); or

(b) it is a goods vehicle which is a locomotive, motor tractor or articulated drawing unit; or

(c) it is constructed or adapted to carry goods other than the effects of passengers; or

(d) it does not fall within any of these classifications but is a vehicle within the meaning of art 1 of the Community Drivers' Hours Regulations other than those specified within art 4 of the Regulations (motor vehicles, tractors, trailers and semi-trailers, other than goods vehicles not exceeding 3.5 tonnes and passenger vehicles suitable

for carrying no more than nine persons including the driver and various types of emergency and specialised vehicles),
it may be subject to these restrictions. However:

(a) light vans (not exceeding 3.5 tonnes plated weight or 30 cwt unplated);
(b) dual-purpose vehicles used for professional purposes by doctors, dentists, midwives, nurses or vets, or for services of maintenance, repair, installation or fitting, or by commercial travellers, or by the AA or RAC; or
(c) vehicles used for making motion pictures, radio or television broadcasting,

are exempted from all provisions except the requirement not to drive for more than 10 hours a day. A day for these purposes is from midnight to midnight.

The plated weight referred to at (a) is the 'permissible maximum weight'. Where a trailer is towed, this term refers to the aggregate of the maximum gross weight on the motor vehicle and the maximum gross weight marked on the trailer in actual use at the time, not to the total weight of the vehicle and any trailer which it might be capable of drawing.

Part VI rules on driving periods, rest breaks and rest periods

For the purposes of the legislation, a driver may be either an employee-driver or an owner-driver. An employee-driver is on duty when he is on duty (whether for the purpose of driving or for other purposes) in the employment by virtue of which he is an employee-driver, or in any other employment of that employer. An owner-driver is on duty when driving the vehicle in connection with his trade or business or doing other work in connection with the vehicle or its load. A driver must not drive a Part VI vehicle for periods amounting in the aggregate to more than 10 hours within a working day. A 'working day' is the aggregate of duty and breaks etc until an 11-hour or, where permitted, a 92-hour rest period is taken.

The Drivers' Hours (Goods Vehicles) (Modifications) Order 1986 restricts the application of the permitted hours provisions in Part VI in relation to goods vehicles, to requirements that the aggregate periods of driving on any working day must not exceed 10 hours; the working day of a driver must not exceed 11 hours; and no restrictions must apply where the vehicle is not driven for periods amounting in the aggregate to more than 4 hours, in each of the working days which make up a particular week. These regulations define 'working day' as any working period (duty period) which can be combined with any other working period which falls within a period of 24 hours.

In the case of passenger-carrying vehicles operating under Part VI of the Act, the provisions of s 96 apply in full and there are therefore additional requirements. Where, in a working day, a driver's hours on duty amount to 5½ hours without at least a 30-minute break for rest or refreshment, the driver then must take such a break, unless that is the end of his work for the day. The working day may exceed 11 hours if during the day he has 'off-duty periods' at least equivalent to the amount of time by which that limit is exceeded, but not beyond 12½ hours. Moreover, if all the working day is spent driving limited stop or tour buses and he has a break of at least 4 hours for rest and refreshment, the working day may extend to 14 hours. There must also be an 11-hour rest period between two successive working days but this may be reduced to 9½ hours once in a working week. A working week for these purposes begins at midnight between Sunday and Monday, unless altered by the licensing authority. A driver must not be on duty for more than 60 hours in a working week and during each working week a driver must be off duty for a period of at least 24 hours. That period of 24 hours may begin in one week and end in another, but may only be taken into account once.

Offences

If a driver contravenes any of the above provisions, he commits an offence; so does his employer or a person under whose supervision he was if he caused or permitted the contravention. It is a defence to prove that the contravention was due to unavoidable delay in completing the journey because of circumstances which were not reasonably foreseeable. An employer or supervisor also has a defence if he proves that the contravention was due to the fact that the driver had for a particular period or periods driven otherwise than in the employment of that employer or as the case may be otherwise than in the employment to which the supervision relates, and that he (the employer etc) could not reasonably have become aware of this.

Part VI rules about drivers' records

The form of the records kept by drivers to whom Part VI applies are prescribed by the Drivers' Hours (Goods Vehicles) (Keeping of Records) Regulations 1987. They consist of drivers' record books which include weekly record sheets divided up into boxes for entry of information relating to each day of the week. However, tachographs may be fitted and, if they are, they replace the need for record books.

Breach of any of the various requirements as to records is an offence.

CHAPTER 14

Lights and vehicles

The lighting requirements for vehicles are now set out in the Road Vehicles Lighting
Regulations 1989, which were made by the Secretary of State under powers conferred
by the Road Traffic Act 1988.

The Regulations define certain terms which are used throughout:

Daytime hours This means the time between half an hour before sunrise and half an
hour after sunset.

Hours of darkness This means the time between half an hour after sunset and half an
hour before sunrise.

Obligatory In relation to a lamp, reflector, rear marking or device, 'obligatory' means
a lamp, reflector, rear marking or device with which a vehicle, its load or equipment, is
required by the Regulations to be fitted.

Optional In relation to a lamp, reflector, rear marking or device, 'optional' means a
lamp, reflector, rear marking or device with which a vehicle, its load or equipment, is not
required by the Regulations to be fitted.

OBLIGATORY LIGHTS

Regulation 18 provides that a person must not use a vehicle on a road, or cause or
permit it to be so used, unless it is equipped with obligatory lamps, reflectors, rear
markings or devices as specified within the Regulations. Schedule 1 to the Regulations
sets out the specific obligatory lighting requirements for different classes of vehicles.
The tables included in Sch 1 deal with the obligatory lighting requirements of vehicles
generally; in Part I with vehicles having three or more wheels; in Part II with solo motor
bicycles and motor bicycle combinations; in Part III with pedal cycles; in Part IV with
pedestrian-controlled, horse-drawn and track-laying vehicles; in Part V with vehicles
drawn or propelled by hand; in Part VI with trailers drawn by motor vehicles, and in
Part VII with trailers drawn by pedal cycles. Column 1 of Sch 1 lists the type of lamp,

reflector, rear marking or device required; column 2 the installation and performance requirement (by reference to other Schedules), and column 3 any exceptions to the general rule.

In general, the Regulations specify the requirements for different classes of vehicles in relation to front position lamps, dim-dip devices or running lamps, dipped beam headlamps, main beam headlamps, direction indicators, hazard signal warning devices, side marker lamps, rear position lamps, rear fog lamps, stop lamps, end-outline marker lamps, rear registration plate light, side retro reflectors, rear retro reflectors and rear markings. These terms are defined by the Regulations as follows:

Front position lamp This is a lamp used to indicate the presence and width of a vehicle when viewed from the front. (This type of lamp was previously referred to as a 'side lamp'.)

Dim-dip lighting device This is a device which is capable of causing a dipped beam headlamp to operate at reduced intensity.

Running lamp A lamp (not being a front position lamp, an end-outline marker lamp, headlamp or front fog lamp) used to make the presence of a moving motor vehicle readily visible from the front. (An alternative to a dim-dip device; in effect, a higher intensity front position lamp.)

Dipped beam headlamp 'Dipped beam' means a beam of light emitted by a lamp which illuminates the road ahead of a vehicle without causing undue dazzle or discomfort to oncoming drivers or other road users.

Main beam headlamp 'Main beam' means a beam of light emitted by a lamp which illuminates the road over a long distance ahead of the vehicle.

Direction indicator This means a lamp on a vehicle used to indicate to other road users that the driver intends to change direction to the right or to the left.

Hazard warning signal device This means a device which is capable of causing all the direction indicators with which a vehicle, or a combination of vehicles, is fitted to operate simultaneously.

Side marker lamp A lamp fitted to the side of a vehicle or its load and used to render the vehicle more visible to other road users.

Rear position lamp This means a lamp used to indicate the presence and width of a vehicle when viewed from the rear.

Rear fog lamp This means a lamp used to render a vehicle more readily visible from the rear in conditions of seriously reduced visibility.

Stop lamp This means a lamp used to indicate to road users that the brakes of a vehicle or combination of vehicles are being applied.

End-outline marker lamp This means a lamp fitted near the edge of a vehicle in addition to the front and rear position lamps to indicate the presence of a wide vehicle.

Rear registration plate light This means a lamp used to illuminate the rear registration plate.

Side retro reflector This means a reflector fitted to the side of a vehicle or its load and used to render the vehicle more visible from the side.

Rear retro reflector This means a reflector used to indicate the presence and width of a vehicle when viewed from the rear.

Rear marking This means a marking as indicated in Sch 19, Part I, to the 1989 Regulations, ie a 'long vehicle' marking.

Each of these lamps, reflectors and devices is obligatory for motor vehicles (with exceptions mentioned later) and some of them are obligatory for trailers drawn by motor vehicles and for other vehicles. Such lamps etc must be fitted in the manner described by the Regulations.

As the requirements have increased over the years, the position of vehicles manufactured before new requirements were made has had to be safeguarded. The various regulations therefore specify the date of application by applying the requirements to vehicles first used on or after a given date. However, reg 4 provides that, even if a vehicle is first used on or after that date, it will be exempt from the requirements of the particular regulation if manufactured more than six months in advance of that date. In some instances this provision is expressly repeated in a particular regulation but generally it must be implied into a particular regulation from reg 4. For example, a vehicle first used on or after 1 April 1980 is required to have a rear fog lamp fitted, but (by virtue of reg 4) such a vehicle is exempt from the requirement if it was manufactured before 1 October 1979.

The 1989 Regulations require that obligatory lamps, reflectors, rear markings and devices are fitted and performing satisfactorily at all times. However, there are certain logical exceptions to this rule, such as incomplete vehicles proceeding to a works for completion, pedal cycles, pedestrian-controlled vehicles, horse-drawn vehicles or combat vehicles. To that list is added a vehicle which is not fitted with any front or rear position lamps, so that if a person is building a motor car from parts and has not yet installed such lights he will not commit an offence by using the vehicle on a road during daylight hours. In addition, the requirements of the Regulations relating to fitting do not apply to a vehicle based outside Great Britain which is on a journey in this country, provided that it has not been here for more than 12 months and that it complies with international requirements. Vehicles going to a port for export are similarly exempt. Hand-propelled vehicles, provided that their overall width does not exceed 800 mm, do not require lamps or reflectors if they are pushed close to the nearside of the carriageway.

For the purpose of the Regulations, a lamp is not treated as being a lamp if it is so painted over or masked that it is not capable of being immediately used or readily put to use, or if it is an electric lamp which is not provided with any system of wiring by means of which that lamp is (or can readily be) connected with a source of electricity.

If it is remembered that, apart from regulating the use of lamps on vehicles during the hours of darkness (and in some cases during daytime hours), the purpose of the Regulations is to ensure that lamps etc which are fitted are correctly fitted and comply with the Regulations, these exceptions are self-evident. A driver who finds that his wiring loom has burned out may lawfully drive that vehicle on a road during daylight hours, as the electric lights could not be connected without the provision of a new wiring system. An enthusiast who is building his own motor car may fit his headlamps and then be unable to secure professional assistance in setting the beams to comply with anti-dazzle requirements. Provided that he paints over or masks those lights, he may use the vehicle during daylight hours.

Front lights

(a) Front position lights

Vehicles with three or more wheels (other than invalid carriages and pedal tricycles) require two front position lamps. The maximum distance at which they may be placed from the side of the vehicle is 510 mm if the vehicle was first used before 1 April 1986 or was manufactured before 1 October 1985. Such lamps on motor vehicles first used or manufactured on or after those dates must be no more than 400 mm from the side of the vehicle (or 150 mm in the case of trailers manufactured on or after 1 October 1985).

Pedal cycles, solo motor bicycles, hand-propelled vehicles whose width (with load) does not exceed 1,250 mm, and invalid carriages require only one front position lamp, which must be fitted on the centre line or offside of the vehicle. Motorcycle combinations with a headlamp on the motor bicycle require a front position lamp on the centre line of the sidecar, or on the side of the sidecar furthest from the motor bicycle. A solo motor bicycle fitted with a headlamp need not be fitted with a front position lamp.

The maximum permitted height above the ground for vehicles first used before 1 April 1986 and trailers manufactured before 1 October 1985 is 2,300 mm. The maximum height restrictions do not apply to large passenger-carrying vehicles or road clearance vehicles. Vehicles and trailers used or manufactured after these dates must be fitted with front position lamps at a maximum height of 1,500 mm or, if the structure of the vehicle makes this impracticable, 2,100 mm. The height limit of 2,100 mm also applies to vehicles first used on or after 1 April 1986 with a maximum speed not exceeding 25 mph.

All front position lamps should be white in colour, unless they are incorporated in a yellow headlamp, in which case they may be yellow. They must be visible from a reasonable distance.

(b) Dipped beam headlamps

Two dipped beam headlamps are required by motor vehicles with three or more wheels in most circumstances. The maximum permitted distance from the side of the vehicle is 400 mm (except in the cases of a vehicle first used before 1 January 1972, or of an agricultural vehicle, engineering plant or an industrial tractor, when there is no specific requirement). There is no minimum distance by which the two lamps must be separated. Solo motor bicycles or combinations, and three-wheelers first used before 1 January 1972 or with an unladen weight of not more than 400 kg and an overall width of not more than 1,300 mm, require only one headlamp on the centre line of the motor vehicle itself. A bus first used before 1 October 1969 need only have one dipped beam headlamp and there are no fitting requirements.

Dipped beam headlamps should generally be not more than 1,200 mm, and not less than 500 mm, from the ground. However, there are no minimum requirements in respect of vehicles first used before 1 January 1956, and no maximum for vehicles first used before 1 January 1952 or, regardless of the date of first use, for agricultural vehicles, road clearance vehicles, aerodrome fire tenders, aerodrome runway sweepers, industrial tractors, engineering plant or home forces vehicles.

The light emitted by a dipped beam headlamp must be white or yellow. The lamp itself must be so constructed that the direction of the beam of light can be adjusted whilst the vehicle is stationary. Where two dipped beam headlamps are required to be fitted, they must form a matched pair and be capable of being switched on and off simultaneously and not otherwise.

(c) Main beam headlamps

The provisions concerning the number of obligatory headlamps to be fitted are the same as those relating to dipped beam headlamps with the exception that large passenger-carrying vehicles are required to have two main beam headlamps, even if first used before 1 October 1969. (This means that such vehicles must have two headlamps, although only one of them needs to be capable of being dipped.) The outer edges of the illuminated areas must not be outside those of the dipped beam headlamps and there is no maximum distance which should separate a pair of such lamps.

Main beam headlamps must emit a white or yellow light and must be constructed so that they can be deflected at the will of the driver to become a dipped beam, or so that they can be extinguished by the operation of a device which at the same time switches on a dipped beam or causes another lamp to emit a dipped beam. Thus headlamps of the 'long range' type are invariably wired so that as they are extinguished a dipped beam is emitted from the normal headlamps. Main beam headlamps must also be constructed so that the direction of the beam can be adjusted whilst the vehicle is stationary.

(d) Dim-dip devices

The regulations require that dim-dip devices must be provided on motor vehicles with three or more wheels first used on or after 1 April 1987. Vehicles having a maximum speed of 40 mph or less and home forces vehicles are exempt, as are vehicles which comply with Community Directive 76/756/EEC as last amended by Directive 89/278/EEC or Directive 91/663/EEC. A running lamp may be fitted as an alternative.

Rear lights

(a) Rear position lamps

Most vehicles with three or more wheels require two rear position lamps. The following vehicles, some of which have three or more wheels, require only one rear position lamp: buses first used before 1 April 1955; solo motor bicycles; pedal cycles with less than four wheels; trailers drawn by pedal cycles; trailers (the overall width of which does not exceed 800 mm) drawn by solo or motor cycle combinations; invalid carriages having a maximum speed not exceeding 4 mph; and vehicles propelled by hand. (See general exemption on p 363 for hand-propelled vehicles not exceeding 800 mm in width.) Some motor vehicles of maximum speed not exceeding 25 mph, and their trailers, require four rear position lamps; the details are set out in Sch 10 to the 1989 Regulations.

Where two rear position lamps are required to be fitted, motor vehicles first used before 1 April 1986 and any other vehicle manufactured before 1 October 1985 must have those lamps so fitted that they are not more than 800 mm from the side of the vehicle. Motor vehicles and other vehicles first used or manufactured on or after those dates must carry rear position lamps which are no more than 400 mm from the side of the vehicle.

There is no minimum distance by which the lamps need to be separated in the case of vehicles used before 1 April 1986 or manufactured before 1 October 1985. In the case of a vehicle first used or manufactured on or after the relevant date, the lamps must be at least 500 mm apart but this may be reduced to 400 mm if the overall width of the vehicle is less than 1,400 mm or to 300 mm if less than 800 mm.

In cases in which only one rear position lamp is required it must be fitted on the centre line of the vehicle or on its offside.

The rear position lamps should be at a maximum height of 2,100 mm, in the case of motor vehicles first used before 1 April 1986 other than buses, or trailers manufactured before 1 October 1985, or agricultural or horse-drawn vehicles, industrial tractors and engineering plant, but no maximum is specified for buses first used before 1 April 1986. There are no minimum height requirements in the case of these motor vehicles. In the case of a vehicle first used or manufactured on or after the relevant date, the maximum height will be 1,500 mm unless the structure of the vehicle makes this impracticable; in that case lights up to a height of 2,100 mm will be permitted. The rear position lamps of such vehicles are subject to a minimum height requirement of 350 mm.

All rear position lamps must be red.

(b) Rear fog lamps

The 1989 Regulations require that, if it was manufactured on or after 1 October 1979 and first used on or after 1 April 1980, any motor vehicle having three or more wheels, and any trailer drawn by a motor vehicle, must, unless specifically dealt with elsewhere in the Regulations, have at least one rear fog lamp fitted, at or near the rear, on the centre line or offside of the vehicle. If two lamps are fitted there is no requirement concerning the distance these lights are placed from the sides of the vehicle. The minimum height which they may be above the ground is 250 mm. The maximum height is 1,000 mm except that agricultural vehicles, engineering plant and motor tractors may have lamps up to a maximum height of 2,100 mm. Rear fog lamps must be separated from stop lamps by a minimum distance of 100 mm. No more than two lamps may be fitted.

A rear fog lamp must show a red light. It must not be fitted so that it can be illuminated by the application of any braking system of the vehicle. A tell-tale must be fitted to show that the lights are in operation. If two lamps are fitted to a motor vehicle first used on or after 1 April 1986, or on a trailer manufactured on or after 1 October 1985, they must form a matched pair. If two rear fog lamps are fitted, the conditions set out above in relation to an obligatory fog lamp apply to both of them.

Vehicles first used before 1 April 1980 (and this therefore embraces vehicles which were manufactured before 1 October 1979 regardless of date of first use) do not need to be fitted with rear fog lamps. Nor do motor vehicles whose maximum speed is 25 mph or less, nor do motor vehicles or trailers which are no more than 1,300 mm in width, nor do agricultural vehicles or works trucks first used before 1 April 1986. If one of these exempt vehicles is fitted with such lamps there are no restrictions in relation to the number of lamps which may be fitted, but any which are fitted must be separated from stop lamps by a minimum distance of 100 mm and must not be capable of illumination by a braking system.

(c) Stop lamps

Stop lamps must show a red light. Motor vehicles having three or more wheels, and trailers drawn by a motor vehicle, must, unless otherwise stated, be fitted with two stop lamps. Solo motor bicycles, combinations, invalid carriages and trailers drawn by motor cycles, together with motor vehicles or trailers first used before 1 January 1971, need only be fitted with one stop lamp. Motor bicycles of less than 50 cc first used before 1 April 1986 do not require any stop lamp, nor does any type of motor vehicle first used before 1 January 1936 or a motor vehicle whose maximum speed is 25 mph or less or an agricultural vehicle or works truck first used before 1 April 1986.

Schedule 12 to the 1989 Regulations lays down the following rules. If two stop lamps are fitted they should be on each side of the longitudinal axis of the vehicle. If only one is fitted it should be on the centre line or offside. The minimum separating distance of two stop lamps is 400 mm. The maximum permitted height from the ground is 1,500 mm or, if the structure of the vehicle makes this impracticable, 2,100 mm. The minimum permitted height is 350 mm. There are no maximum or minimum height specifications for motor vehicles first used before 1 January 1971 or for trailers manufactured before that date. There are detailed provisions about the angles of visibility.

The lamps must be operated by the application of the service braking system of the motor vehicle, and this also applies to the stop lamps of any trailer attached to that vehicle. In cases where two stop lamps are required to be fitted, they must form a pair.

It is common practice for enthusiasts to fit additional stop lamps and there is no restriction upon the number of lamps which may be fitted under the Regulations. If additional lamps are fitted, they must comply with the requirements of Sch 12 to the Regulations in all respects other than number, position and angles of visibility. Motor vehicles, other than motor bicycles, first used on or after 1 April 1991 are subject to control in relation to the intensity of such a light projected through the rear windows.

(d) Rear registration plate lamp

All vehicles which are required to be fitted with a rear registration plate must have lighting which is capable of adequately illuminating the rear registration plate.

Other obligatory lights

(a) Direction indicators

The requirements for direction indicators are as follows:

(i) Motor vehicles first used before 1 April 1936 and trailers manufactured before that date *may* have any arrangement of indicators so as to make the intention of the driver clear to other road users but they are not required to have any direction indicators at all.

(ii) Motor vehicles first used on or after that date and before 1 April 1986, and trailers manufactured between 1 January 1936 and 1 October 1985, *must* be provided with any arrangement of indicators so as to satisfy the requirements for angles of visibility.

(iii) Motor vehicles first used on or after 1 April 1986, and trailers manufactured on or after 1 October 1985, are subject to detailed restrictions, set out in Sch 7 to the 1989 Regulations. Motor vehicles with three or more wheels, other than motorcycle combinations, must have a single front indicator, one side repeater indicator and one rear indicator on each side. One additional optional rear indicator may be fitted and any number of side repeater indicators may be added. If fitted, they are subject to most of the restrictions imposed by Sch 7. Trailers manufactured after the specified date must have a rear indicator on each side. Additional optional indicators may be fitted as above. Motor bicycles and combinations must have a single front and a single rear indicator on each side of the vehicle. Paragraph 3 of the Schedule prescribes angles of visibility of direction indicators fitted to the vehicles within this category. Generally, the paragraph demands an outward angle of visibility of at least 80 degrees and this will control the placing of the indicator to allow such an outward angle to occur.

The colour of the light shown by direction indicators is amber in most instances. Motor vehicles first used before 1 September 1965, and the trailer of such a vehicle, may show white or amber to the front or red or amber to the rear. However, if such an indicator is visible from both the front and the back it must show an amber light regardless of the date of first use. All indicators on any side of a vehicle or its trailer must be operated by one switch. There must be a tell-tale to show that the indicators are in operation. Flashing indicators must flash constantly at a rate of not less than 60 and not more than 120 times per minute.

Vehicles whose maximum speed does not exceed 15 mph or invalid carriages having a maximum speed not exceeding 4 mph are not required to have direction indicators fitted, nor are vehicles first used before 1 August 1986 which are agricultural vehicles, industrial tractors or works vehicles.

Agricultural vehicles having an unladen weight not exceeding 255 kg do not require direction indicators.

(b) End-outline marker lamps

These are required on motor vehicles first used on or after 1 April 1991, except those with a maximum speed not exceeding 25 mph; those having an overall width not exceeding 2,100 mm; and incomplete vehicles proceeding to works etc. Their purpose is to indicate the presence of a wide vehicle.

There must be two white lights fitted to the front and two red lights to the rear, not more than 400 mm from the side of the vehicle. Each set must be a matched pair. Any number may be fitted.

(c) Hazard warning signals

These signals are obligatory on motor vehicles having three or more wheels and first used on or after 1 April 1986, with the exception of vehicles which are not required to be fitted with direction indicators. Hazard warning signals which are optionally fitted to other vehicles must comply with the same provisions. Each device must be operated by one switch which causes all direction indicators with which the vehicle or combination of vehicles is equipped to flash in phase. There must be a tell-tale, and the device must be capable of operation without the ignition being switched on.

(d) Side marker lamps

Some motor vehicles, with three or more wheels, and trailers drawn by motor vehicles are required to have side marker lamps. Most are not, since motor vehicles first used before 1 April 1991 and trailers, the overall length of which does not exceed 6 m (or 9.15m if manufactured before 1 October 1990), are not required to have side marker lamps, and nor are the following first used on or after that date:

(i)   motor vehicles whose maximum speed does not exceed 25 mph;
(ii) passenger vehicles;

(iii)   incomplete motor vehicles;
(iv)   those not exceeding 6 m in length;
(v)   those first used before 1 April 1996 complying with Community Directive 76/756/ EEC as amended by Directive 89/278/EEC and Directive 91/663/EEC (and trailers manufactured before 1 October 1985 which comply with these Directives);
(vi)   trailers, the overall length of which, excluding any drawbar and any fittings for its attachment, exceeds 6 m (9.15 m if manufactured before 1 October 1990);
(vii)   agricultural and works trailers;
(viii)   caravans and boat trailers; and
(ix)   trailers complying with the Community Directive.

A side marker lamp is a lamp which will show an amber light, if fitted to a vehicle first used on or after 1 October 1990, unless it is placed within 1 m of the rear of the vehicle, when it may be red. Trailers manufactured before that date may have lamps which show a white light to the front and a red light to the rear.

The obligatory requirements are to have, on each side, two and as many more as are sufficient to ensure that the maximum distance from the front of the vehicle (including any drawbar) to the first lamp is 4 m and the maximum distance from the rear in respect of the rearmost side marker lamp is 1 m. The maximum separation distance of adjacent obligatory lamps on the same side of the vehicle is 3 m or, if this is not practicable, 4 m.

A vehicle, or a combination of vehicles the overall length of which (including any load) exceeds 18.3 m must have additional side marker lamps, one lamp being no more than 9.5 m from the foremost part of the vehicle or vehicles and one lamp no more than 3.05 m from the rear (including loads in both circumstances). Other lamps must be placed to ensure that no more than 3.05 m separates the lamps. Where the length exceeds 12.2m but not 18.3 m and the load is supported by any two vehicles, there shall be lamps placed behind the rearmost part of the drawing vehicle, but not more than 1,530 mm to the rear of that point. If the supported load extends more than 9.15 m to the rear of the drawing vehicle, the lamp shall not be forward of, or more than 1,530 mm to the rear of, the centre of the length of the load. These last provisions do not apply to articulated vehicles.

Side marker lamps must be fitted on each side of a vehicle or trailer as required. They must not be higher than 2,300 mm from the ground. There is no minimum height restriction.

Obligatory reflectors

(a) Rear retro reflectors

The general requirement is for all vehicles to be equipped with two rear retro reflectors. By way of exception, the following vehicles only require one retro reflector: solo motor bicycles; pedal cycles with less than four wheels (with or without a sidecar); trailers drawn by pedal cycles; trailers not exceeding 800 mm drawn by solo motorcycles or combinations; invalid carriages having a maximum speed not exceeding 4 mph, and hand-propelled vehicles. Some restricted vehicles (maximum speed 25 mph) require four reflectors.

Reflectors must be fitted at or near the rear of the vehicle. Motor vehicles first used before 1 April 1986, and trailers manufactured before 1 October 1985, must have reflectors fitted no more than 610 mm from the side. In the case of vehicles first used or manufactured on or after those dates the distance is reduced to 400 mm. (There are certain exceptions to the general rules in respect of buses first used before 1 October

1954, some horse-drawn vehicles and vehicles for round timber; these are specified in Sch 18 to the 1989 Regulations.) Where there is only one reflector it must be on the centre line or offside of the vehicle.

Where reflectors are required to be fitted, the maximum permitted height above the ground is 1,525 mm if the vehicle is a motor vehicle first used before 1 April 1986 (or, if it is a trailer, manufactured before 1 October 1985). For a vehicle first used or manufactured on or after the relevant date, the maximum is 900 mm, unless the structure of the vehicle makes that height impracticable (in which case the maximum is raised to 1,200 mm). The colour of all rear reflectors must be red.

(b) Side retro reflectors

The provision of side reflectors is obligatory on certain motor vehicles with three or more wheels and their trailers. The relevant requirements do not apply to a passenger vehicle (including private cars), nor to an incomplete vehicle travelling to a works for completion etc, mobile cranes, plant and certain earth removal vehicles, nor to a vehicle having a maximum speed not exceeding 25 mph. Nor do they apply to a goods vehicle:

(i)   whose overall length does not exceed 6 m (if first used on or after 1 April 1986); or
(ii) whose overall length does not exceed 8 m (if first used before that date).

The requirements therefore are restricted to long goods vehicles. In the case of such vehicles, first used before 1 April 1986, and trailers manufactured before 1 October 1985, there must be two side retro reflectors on each side of the vehicle. In the case of those first used or manufactured on or after the relevant date, there must be two on each side of the vehicle and as many more as are required by Sch 17 to the Regulations. Side retro reflectors must be amber or, within 1 m of the rear of the vehicle, they may be red. They must not be triangular in shape.

(c) Rear markings

The provisions relating to rear markings relate to 'long vehicle' markings, and therefore most vehicles are exempted from them. In the case of those motor vehicles first used before 1 April 1996 which are not exempted, those which do not exceed 13 m in length need only carry the marker boards with diagonal lines, whereas those which exceed 13m must carry marker boards with the words 'long vehicle' in black on a yellow background surrounded by a red border or, as an alternative, boards of yellow retro reflective material surrounded by a red fluorescent border. Those used on or after 1 April 1996, which are not exempted must carry boards of red and yellow diagonal stripes if they do not exceed 13 m in length; if they exceed 13 m, they must carry boards of yellow retro reflective material surrounded by a red fluorescent border. The same markings are required on certain trailers forming part of a combination of vehicles: if, in the case of a trailer manufactured before 1 October 1995, the overall length does not exceed 11 m, the marking must be of the diagonal line variety; if between 11 m and 13 m the marking may be of any approved variety; and if it exceeds 13 m it must be the 'long vehicle' type, or a board of yellow reflective material surrounded by a red fluorescent border. In the case of a trailer manufactured on or after 1 October 1995 which does not, in combination, exceed 11 m, it must carry a board of red and yellow diagonal stripes; if it exceeds 11 m but not 13 m it may carry boards of such red and yellow stripes or of yellow surrounded by red; and if it exceeds 13 m, the boards must be of yellow surrounded by red.

(d) Pedal retro reflectors

These provisions do not apply to pedal cycles manufactured before 1 October 1985. Pedal cycles manufactured on or after that date must be provided with two amber reflectors on each pedal.

General

The legal requirements so far outlined are in respect of obligatory lights and equipment to be fitted to the various vehicles described. However, in most instances the Regulations do not prevent the fitting of additional lighting etc. The position is:

(a) Any number of optional front position lights may be fitted. If additional ones are fitted they must be white or, if incorporated in a yellow headlamp, yellow.
(b) Dim-dip devices in addition to running lamps and vice versa may be fitted optionally to vehicles.
(c) Any number of optional dipped beam headlamps may be fitted. If additional ones are fitted they must be white or yellow, comply with maximum and minimum height requirements, and be capable of adjustment while the vehicle is stationary.
(d) Any number of optional main beam headlamps may be fitted. They must be white or yellow, electrically connected so that they deflect or extinguish by the dip switch, and be capable of adjustment while the vehicle is stationary.
(e) Any number of rear position lamps may be fitted. They must be red. There are no other restrictions.
(f) The number of rear fog lamps is controlled in the case of vehicles first used on or after 1 April 1980 (or, in the case of trailers, manufactured on or after 1 October 1979). No more than two such lamps are permitted in such a case.
(g) Any number of stop lamps can be fitted. If additional lamps are fitted they must comply with the provisions set out above, except those relating to position and angles of visibility. Rear fog lamps and stop lamps must be red.
(h) Any number of side reflex reflectors may be fitted but all must be amber and none must be triangular in shape.
(i) Any number of rear reflex reflectors may be fitted. Additional ones must be red.

OPTIONAL LIGHTS

Regulation 20 of the 1989 Regulations provides that every optional lamp, reflector, rear marking or device fitted to a vehicle must comply with provisions set out in the respective Schedules to the Regulations. A table included in the Regulations describes the types of optional lamps etc and demands compliance with certain parts of the directions given in the relevant Schedule. These provisions have already been considered in a general sense, since those factors set out above from (a) to (i) are concerned with additional lamps etc which may be fitted (and are therefore optional lamps). However, reg 20 also deals with other optional lamps and devices which are not additional in that sense; there is no absolute requirement to have lamps of that type, but if they are fitted they must comply with certain provisions as follows:

(a) Front fog lamps

These must be white or yellow lights. Where a pair of front fog lamps is used in conditions of seriously reduced visibility in place of the obligatory dipped beam headlamps, they must not be more than 400 mm from the side of the vehicle. There is no minimum height requirement but the maximum permitted height is 1,200 mm, except in the case of agricultural, road clearance and aerodrome vehicles, industrial tractors, plant vehicles and home forces vehicles.

Motor vehicles (other than motor bicycles) first used on or after 1 April 1991 may not have more than two front fog lamps.

(b) Reversing lamps

Not more than two may be fitted; such a lamp must show a white light.

(c) Warning beacons

Warning beacons on vehicles must be mounted so that the centre of the lamp is not less than 1,200 mm from the ground. The lights of such warning beacons must flash between 60 and 240 times per minute at constant intervals. They may be blue, amber, green or yellow as prescribed by reg 11:

(i)   Blue – a blue and white chequered light is permitted from a chequered domed lamp fitted to a police control vehicle and intended for use at the scene of an emergency; a blue light is permitted from a warning beacon or rear special warning lamp on an emergency vehicle.

(ii) Amber – permitted on road clearance, refuse, breakdown vehicles, those with an overall width exceeding 2.9 m, road service vehicles, special vehicles carrying abnormal loads (and escorts when not exceeding 25 mph) and vehicles of HM Customs and Excise (fuel testing vehicles). Regulation 17 requires motor vehicles with four or more wheels, other than those first used before 1 January 1947, which have a maximum speed which does not exceed 25 mph, or any trailer which they are drawing, to be fitted with, and display, at least one amber warning beacon when being driven on an unrestricted dual carriageway road. The Regulations do not apply to such vehicles when merely crossing such a road in the quickest possible manner.

(iii) Green – permitted to be used by registered medical practitioners.

(iv) Yellow – permitted to be used by airport vehicles.

Only permitted vehicles may be fitted with a warning beacon of the appropriate type. However, where a permitted vehicle which is fitted with a warning lamp is used for a purpose other than that to which the permission relates, as where an ambulance is used to take children to school, there is no requirement that the lamp should be covered or removed.

USE OF LAMPS, REFLECTORS ETC

The lamps, reflectors and devices which must, or may be, fitted to vehicles have been considered. We now turn to the various provisions relating to their use.

Red lights to the front

Regulation 11(1) provides that no vehicle may be fitted with a lamp which is capable of showing a red light or retro reflective material to the front. The important word is 'capable': the provision is not confined to the hours of darkness, nor is it necessary that the light is actually shown. The exceptions to the provision are obvious; they include red emergency lights on fire service vehicles, and reflex materials fitted to pedal cycles, motorcycles and invalid carriages (whether to the vehicle or its wheels or tyres) or to traffic signs attached to vehicles (such as motorway maintenance vehicles).

Red lights to the rear

Regulation 11(2) provides that no vehicle may be fitted with a lamp which is capable of showing a light or retro reflective material to the rear other than a red light. The same comments apply to 'capable' as made above. The exceptions are plentiful and include direction indicators, reversing lamps, work lamps, interior illumination, rear number plates, taxi meters, public service vehicle route indicators and the various emergency lights which have already been described.

Maintenance of lamps, reflectors, rear markings and devices

Regulation 23(1) prohibits a person using, or causing or permitting to be used, on a road any vehicle unless every front position lamp, rear position lamp, headlamp, rear registration plate lamp, side marker lamp, end-outline marker lamp, rear fog lamp, retro reflector and rear marking with which it is required to be fitted is in good working order and, in the case of a lamp, clean.

Regulation 23, therefore, requires correct maintenance of all of the lamps, reflectors, markings and devices with which a vehicle is *required* to be fitted. Moreover, in the case of stop lamps and direction indicators reg 23 goes on to require that all stop lamps, running lamps, dim-dip devices, headlamp levelling device, hazard warning signalling devices, and direction indicators, even if they are in excess of those required by law, must be maintained at all times. However, the provisions of reg 23 do not apply to rear fog lamps on a vehicle which is a part of a combination of vehicles, if any part of the combination is not required to have a rear fog lamp. Nor do these provisions apply to a rear fog lamp on a vehicle drawing a trailer; nor to any defective lamp reflector, dim-dip device or headlamp levelling device where the defect arose in the course of the journey on a vehicle in use in the daytime (ie between sunrise and sunset), or if arrangements have been made to remedy the defect with all reasonable expedition; nor, during the daytime, to a lamp, reflector or rear marking fitted to a combat vehicle. (Combat vehicles are military vehicles used for the carriage of guns, tanks etc.)

Driving or parking without lights

Regulation 24 prohibits a person using, or causing or permitting to be used, a vehicle on a road between sunset and sunrise or (while the vehicle is in motion) during daytime hours in seriously reduced visibility unless every front position lamp, rear position lamp, rear registration plate lamp, side marker lamp and end-outline marker lamp required by the Regulations to be fitted is kept lit and unobscured. Subject to reg 24(5) to (9), it also prohibits allowing (or causing or permitting to be allowed) a vehicle to remain at rest (ie parked) in similar circumstances between sunset and sunrise. There are variations to these provisions in respect of motorcycles and trailers not required to be fitted with front position lamps, since the prohibitions are not breached if there are fitted to these vehicles 'ad hoc' front position lamps.

Regulation 24 is concerned with circumstances in which vehicles of certain classes may lawfully park between sunset and sunrise on roads subject to speed limits of 30 mph or less, without showing such lights. These classes of vehicles are goods vehicles not exceeding 1,525 kg, passenger vehicles other than buses, invalid carriages, and motorcycles or pedal cycles (in either case with or without a sidecar). The exemption will not apply to such a vehicle if it has a trailer attached or is carrying a load which requires lamps.

Regulation 24 only permits such a vehicle to park without lights in particular places. These are:

(a) designated parking places on roads; or
(b) a lay-by which is clearly shown to be such; or
(c) elsewhere, provided, if the vehicle is parked on a one-way road, it is facing in the correct direction on either side of the road as close as possible to the kerb, or, if it is parked on an ordinary road, it is properly parked and facing the correct way, and in either case no part of the vehicle is less than 10 m from a junction with the road upon which it is parked, whether the junction is on the same side of the road or not. For the purpose of measuring the distance from a junction, where a curving kerb exists there, the junction is regarded as beginning where the kerb begins to curve.

The specified vehicles may therefore park without lights on a restricted road provided they do so in a street car park, in a lay-by, or *elsewhere* on one-way streets or ordinary roads provided that they are not within 10 m of a junction on either side of the road.

The Regulations exempt solo motorcycles and pedal cycles, which are being pushed close to the nearside kerb, from the need to show front position lights. They also exempt altogether a pedal cycle which is halted and waiting to proceed (for example at traffic lights) if it is kept to the nearside, as well as a vehicle which is parked and properly outlined by lamps or traffic signs (eg a broken-down vehicle).

Use of headlamps

Regulation 25 provides that a person must not use, or cause or permit to be used, on a road a vehicle which is fitted with obligatory dipped beam headlamps unless every such lamp is kept lit:

(a) during the hours of darkness, except on a road which is a restricted one by virtue of a system of street lighting, when those lights are lit; and
(b) during daylight hours in seriously reduced visibility.

There are certain permitted variations; for example, motor vehicles with one obligatory dipped beam headlamp are exempt from the above requirement if a main beam or fog lamp is kept lit. Vehicles which are being towed, those which are parked, and those propelling snow ploughs are exempt from the above requirement. In addition, in the case of a motor vehicle other than a motor tricycle or motor bicycle combination, a pair of main beam lamps may be used as an alternative or, in seriously reduced visibility, a pair of front fog lamps may be used, provided that they are not more than 400 mm from the outer edges of the vehicle.

Regulation 25 appears to be clumsy at first sight but merely requires the use of obligatory dipped beam headlamps at night or during the day when visibility is seriously reduced. Roads in built-up areas with illuminated street lights set not more than 200 yards apart are the only ones in which a vehicle may be used without at least dipped beam headlamps during the hours of darkness. Any light from a headlamp operating a dim-dip device will not be sufficient to satisfy the requirement for minimum use of dipped-beam light in the circumstances described above.

Prohibition of particular usage of lamps or devices

Regulation 27 provides that a person must not use, or cause or permit to be used, on a road any vehicle on which any lamp, hazard signal warning device or warning beacon of a specified type is used in the manner listed below.

Headlamps may not be used so as to cause undue dazzle or discomfort to other persons using the road and shall not be lit when a vehicle is parked. These prohibitions also apply to front fog lamps, with the addition of a prohibition upon use at any time other than in conditions of seriously reduced visibility.

The use of rear fog lamps is similarly restricted but the reference to undue dazzle or discomfort is predictably restricted to following drivers. They must also not be used when a vehicle, other than an emergency vehicle, is parked. Although their use generally is restricted to conditions of seriously reduced visibility, this appears not to be appreciated by some drivers, who switch them on as soon as they join a motorway.

Reversing lamps must not be used for any purpose other than that of reversing. Similarly the use of hazard warning signal devices is restricted to warning road users of a temporary obstruction (or the presence of a school bus which is stationary and loading or unloading school children under 16) when the vehicle is at rest, or, on a motorway or unrestricted dual carriageway, to warn of a temporary obstruction ahead, or, in the case of a bus, to summon assistance for the driver or conductor or an inspector who is on the vehicle.

Blue lamps and special warning lamps may only be used at the scene of an emergency, or to indicate the urgency of the journey or the presence of a hazard on the road. The use of amber lights is similarly restricted but they may also be used in connection with breakdowns or slow moving vehicles on dual carriageways. Green lights may only be used whilst the vehicle is occupied by a registered medical practitioner and used in an emergency. Yellow light beacons may not be lit on a road. Work lamps must not dazzle etc and must not be used other than for illuminating a working area, accident, breakdown or works in the vicinity of the vehicle. No other lamp which is fitted to a vehicle may ever be used so as to cause undue dazzle or discomfort to other persons using the road.

Movement of lamps or reflectors and nature of light

Regulation 12 provides that no person shall use, or cause or permit to be used, on a road a vehicle fitted with a lamp or reflector capable of being moved (by swivelling, deflecting or otherwise) while the vehicle is in motion. However, this does not prevent the fitting of rear lights, reflectors or indicators to a boot lid or other movable part of a vehicle. Nor does it refer to dipping headlights, lamps which may be adjusted to compensate for loads, those moved by the front wheels, retracting headlamps etc, direction indicators, work lamps, warning beacons, pedal reflectors, or reflex material on pedal cycles, motor cycles or invalid carriages. In effect, reg 12 prohibits the movement of lamps statutorily fitted in a prescribed way, other than those lights which are exempted for predictable reasons.

The light shown by lamps covered by the Regulations must be a steady light, in that flashing lights are not permitted (other than warning beacons prescribed for emergency vehicles etc).

Overhanging or projecting loads

Regulation 21 prohibits a person using, or causing or permitting to be used, on a road:

(a) any trailer which projects laterally beyond the preceding vehicle in the combination; or
(b) any vehicle or combination of vehicles which carries a load or equipment,

which (in either case) does not comply with the specifications set out in the regulation. These specifications are as follows:

(a) a trailer, which (or whose load) projects laterally more than 400 mm from the outermost part of the obligatory front position light on that side of the vehicle in front of it, must have white lights to the front which are not more than 400 mm from the outermost projection of the trailer (or, as the case may be, of the load);
(b) a vehicle whose load projects laterally more than 400 mm must have lights at the front and rear not more than 400 mm from the outermost projection of the load;
(c) a vehicle whose load projects more than 1 m to the front or to the rear must have a front or rear lamp not more than 1 m from the foremost or rearmost projection of the load (except that that distance is 2 m in the case of an agricultural vehicle or a vehicle carrying a fire escape); or
(d) a vehicle carrying a load which obscures any obligatory lamps, reflector or rear markings must show a lamp etc in the prescribed position.

These requirements only apply when the vehicle/trailer is being used between sunset and sunrise or in circumstances of reduced visibility, except that in relation to stop lights and direction indicators in (d) the requirement applies in all circumstances.

TESTING AND INSPECTION OF LIGHTING EQUIPMENT ETC

Regulation 28 applies the provisions of the Road Vehicles (Construction and Use) Regulations 1986, reg 74 to lighting equipment and reflectors with which a vehicle is *required* by the Regulations to be fitted. Regulation 74 empowers a constable in uniform to test and inspect lighting equipment on motor vehicles and trailers on any premises, subject to the consent of the owner of the premises.

OFFENCES

Contravention of any regulation contained in the Road Vehicles Lighting Regulations 1989 is an offence contrary to the Road Traffic Act 1988, s 42, except that a breach which relates to a pedal cycle is an offence contrary to the Road Traffic Offenders Act 1988, s 91.

It is also an offence under the Road Traffic Act 1988, s 42, for a person to use on a road a motor vehicle or trailer which does not comply with these Regulations or to cause or permit a vehicle to be so used.

CHAPTER 15

Traffic accidents

The legal obligations which arise in the event of a traffic accident are basically those of stopping and of providing certain information or subsequently reporting the accident to the police. In addition to these general obligations, there is also an obligation to produce proof of insurance at the time or subsequently at a police station if personal injury has been caused.

DUTY TO STOP ETC

The Road Traffic Act 1988, s 170(1) applies where, owing to the presence of a mechanically propelled vehicle on a road, an accident occurs by which personal injury is caused to a person other than the driver of that mechanically propelled vehicle or damage is caused to a vehicle other than that mechanically propelled vehicle or a trailer drawn by it, or to an animal other than an animal in or on that vehicle or a trailer drawn by it, or to any other property constructed on, fixed to, growing in or otherwise forming part of the land on which the road in question is situated or land adjacent to such land. By s 170(2), in such a case the driver of the mechanically propelled vehicle shall stop and, if required to do so by any person having reasonable grounds for so requiring, give his name and address, and also the name and address of the owner and the identification marks of the vehicle.

Thus, if, owing to the presence of a mechanically propelled vehicle on a road, an accident occurs, and:

(a) a passenger in that vehicle or anyone else (whether or not in another vehicle) is injured;
(b) another vehicle is damaged; or
(c) an animal in another vehicle or running across the street is injured; or a bollard or street lamp (or some other thing fixed to or otherwise forming part of the land on which the road is situated or adjacent land) is damaged,

the driver of that mechanically propelled vehicle must stop etc. Of course, an accident may occur owing to the presence of two or more vehicles on a road. If so, the driver of each vehicle must stop etc if the consequences set out above occur.

By way of contrast to the examples given in the last paragraph, the driver of a mechanically propelled vehicle, owing to the presence of which on a road an accident occurs, is not obliged by s 170 (or any other legal provision) to stop etc if:

(a) no one (besides that driver) is injured; and
(b) no vehicle (besides that vehicle or its trailer) is damaged; and
(c) no animal (other than one in that vehicle or its trailer) is injured; and
(d) no property forming part etc of the road or land adjacent to it is damaged.

Having set out the basic framework of s 170, we shall now proceed to examine the three component parts of the provision.

An accident must have occurred owing to the presence of a motor vehicle on a road

The term *'mechanically propelled vehicle'* has already been discussed in ch 9 above. Such vehicles may be petrol, oil or steam driven, or propelled by electricity. A vehicle is a 'mechanically propelled vehicle' whether or not it is intended or adapted for use on a road. Section 170 places duties only upon the drivers of mechanically propelled vehicles; the rider of a pedal cycle has no obligations under it.

We have also examined the word *'road'* previously and have seen that it means 'any highway and any other road to which the public has access, and includes bridges over which a road passes'.

The requirement that the *accident* must have occurred *owing to the presence* of a mechanically propelled vehicle on a road involves the following additional points. First, if the words 'owing to the presence' were to be given their widest possible meaning they would embrace circumstances in which a person, who had been allowed to cross a road by the courtesy of a driver who had stopped to allow him to do so, tripped over the kerb on turning to acknowledge this courtesy. This would clearly be ridiculous. The rule is, therefore, that there must be a direct causal connection between the presence of the mechanically propelled vehicle and the occurrence of the accident. If the driver of a vehicle brakes sharply on approaching a pedestrian who is crossing the road and the noise of that braking so startles the pedestrian that he falls and is injured, there is a direct causal connection between the vehicle and the accident. Likewise, if a cyclist collides with a motor car waiting at traffic lights, it is reasonable to accept that the accident occurred because the vehicle was on the road. There is a direct causal connection between the presence of the vehicle and the accident in that the cyclist was in contact with it. It would probably be different if, in moving to the crown of the road to avoid the motor car, the cyclist over-steered and fell off. The connection in such circumstances is not sufficiently direct. The cause of the accident was the cyclist's clumsy control, rather than the presence of the vehicle.

The second point is the meaning of the word 'accident'. The Divisional Court has held that that word bears its ordinary popular meaning (as opposed to any technical meaning) and that the question is whether an ordinary person would say that an accident has occurred. It also held that, subject to what has just been said, there can be an accident even though part of the chain of events leading to the injury or damage was a deliberate act on someone's part. For the obligations in s 170 to apply to the driver of a mechanically propelled vehicle, it is not necessary that his vehicle is involved in an accident in the sense that it is in collision. For example, if X, the driver of a motor car, carelessly drives it across a junction with a major road, causing vehicles on the major road to take avoiding action which causes them to collide with each other, X certainly causes that accident although he is not involved in the collision. In such a case, the obligations in s 170 will have to be discharged by X, as well as by the drivers of the other motor vehicles.

The accident must have caused one of the specified consequences

As we have seen, these specified consequences are:

(a) Personal injury to a person other than the driver of the mechanically propelled vehicle owing to whose presence on a road the accident occurred. 'Injury' presumably bears its ordinary meaning and, as such, includes cases of shock. It is irrelevant whether the person injured is a passenger in the driver's vehicle, the driver or a passenger in another vehicle, or someone else (such as a pedestrian).

(b) Damage to a vehicle other than the mechanically propelled vehicle, owing to whose presence on a road the accident occurred, or a trailer drawn by it.

The term 'vehicle' is given a wide meaning and includes mechanically propelled vehicles, pedal cycles and horse-drawn vehicles. The dictionary meaning (ie carriage, cart or other conveyance) should be applied and this will include all types of wheeled vehicles, such as fairy cycles, prams or barrows, but not, it is submitted, skateboards, roller skates and similar toys, since they are not produced for some form of conveyance in a general sense.

The essential factor is that the damage must be caused to a vehicle or trailer other than the driver's vehicle or trailer before the duties imposed by s 170 must be discharged. This is reasonable. A driver who damages his own vehicle or trailer is responsible for that damage. The argument is sometimes advanced that this also applies to injured passengers in a driver's vehicle but this is not so. The injured passenger may be a hitchhiker who is a complete stranger to the driver, and it is therefore reasonable that the law should make different demands in the case of personal injuries.

(c) Damage to any animal other than an animal in or on the motor vehicle, owing to whose presence on a road the accident occurred, or a trailer drawn by it.

The term 'animal' means any horse, cattle, ass, mule, sheep, pig, goat or dog. Poultry are not included, nor are cats (no matter how valuable they may be). The section only applies if the injury is to an animal which is external to the vehicle at the time at which the accident occurs. The section assumes that animals of this description which are carried in the driver's motor vehicle will belong either to the driver or to someone who is known to him, and that therefore he need not stop and provide the specified information since his identity will be known to the owner of the animal.

(d) Damage to any other property constructed on, fixed to, growing in or otherwise forming part of the land on which the road in question is situated or land adjacent thereto.

Examples of such property are buildings, traffic signs, street lamps, fences, hedges and trees, provided they 'form part' of the land on which the road is situated or of land adjacent thereto. By way of example, if a motor car collides with a traffic bollard causing damage to it, it causes damage to property which is either constructed on or fixed to land on which the road is situated or land adjacent thereto. This is so whether the bollard is situated in the middle of the road or at the side of the road. It will be a question of fact to be determined by the justices whether or not property which is damaged forms part of, or is adjacent to, such land. If a car collides with the petrol pumps in a filling station adjacent to the road there is little doubt that a court would consider the petrol pumps to be on land adjacent to land on which a road is situated. Should damage be occasioned to a dwelling house which is immediately at the roadside, that house is undoubtedly constructed on land which is at least adjacent to land on which the road is situated. It is probable that, even if a garden exists at the front of the house, justices would consider that the house was constructed on land adjacent to the road. The same considerations would apply to damage to trees or plants which were growing in that garden. If, because of the presence on the road of a motor car, an accident occurs and the motor car leaves the road and is driven through a fence into a field of corn, the accident certainly causes damage to both the fence and the crops which are on land adjacent to the road. Of course, if the car had been driven, under control, through an open gate into a field of corn, the damage to the corn would not have been caused by an accident but a deliberate act of the driver. In such a case, the driver would be guilty of criminal damage to the corn, but would not be obliged by s 170 to stop or provide any information.

The driver of the motor vehicle must stop and, if required by a person having reasonable grounds for so requiring, must give certain information

The term 'driver' has already been explained in a number of other chapters. However, it must be added that, for the purposes of s 170, a person who takes out a vehicle on a road remains its 'driver' until that particular journey is over. Consequently, if a person who is driving to work sees a friend en route and stops his car (and switches off its engine) in order to talk to the friend, he remains the driver for the purpose of s 170 during that time, and, if the presence of the car on the road causes an accident, the obligations imposed by s 170 apply to him. On the other hand, s 170 would not apply if the accident was caused by the car's presence on the road after he had parked it outside his place of work at the end of his journey.

The obligation to stop arises immediately the accident occurs. Thus, in one case, where a bus driver had injured a passenger by braking sharply and had driven on to a rendezvous with an ambulance which he had arranged by radio, the Divisional Court held that he had failed to stop as required by s 170. Whether or not a driver has stopped 'immediately' may be controversial. Where a driver collided with a parked vehicle and drove on for a distance of about 80 yards before stopping and returning to the scene of the accident, justices convicted him of an offence of failing to stop. The Divisional Court said that it would not interfere with that finding, as it was one which was open to the justices on the facts of the case, but said that it was not sure that it would have reached the same conclusion. Because the duty to stop is an immediate one, a driver who leaves the scene and later returns to it does not 'stop' for the purpose of s 170. The term 'stop' means that the driver should stop and remain where he has stopped for such a period of time as in the prevailing circumstances will provide a sufficient period of time to enable persons who have reasonable grounds for so doing to require of him directly and personally the information which the driver may be required to supply. In determining what that period should be, particular regard should be paid to the character of the road or the place where the accident occurred. The duty is that of the driver and his responsibilities cannot be discharged by some other person whom he leaves at the scene. The driver must remain sufficiently near to the vehicle throughout this period of time to allow any person to make the requests permitted by the section. Common sense must be applied when considering the duty to stop. If a driver collides with a vehicle parked in a deserted country lane, it would be unreasonable to expect him to remain there indefinitely. The reasonable approach would be to consider whether his 'stop' was sufficient to allow any person who was nearby and aware of the accident to make such a request. In the case of a stationary vehicle, its driver cannot stop in the physical sense, but must 'stop at the scene' for sufficient time to permit persons to request information.

Section 170 also requires the driver to provide certain information if required so to do by 'any person having reasonable grounds for so requiring'. Such a person will usually be the driver of any other vehicle involved in the accident, a person injured, or the owner of property or of an animal. However, there are other persons who might quite reasonably demand information from the driver of a mechanically propelled vehicle; for example, a relative or friend of a person who has been injured, or a person who witnessed the accident and who is a friend of the owner of damaged property. It will be a matter for the courts to determine in cases of doubt. They may well look differently upon a demand made by a 'nosey parker' as opposed to one made by some person who quite genuinely had the other party's interests at heart.

Section 170(2), which requires a driver to stop and provide this information, is concerned with one offence which may be committed in two ways, either by failing to stop or if, having stopped, failing to provide the information which is required to be given.

If the requirement is made by such a person with reasonable grounds, s 170 obliges the driver to give:

(a) his name and address;
(b) the name and address of the owner of the vehicle; and
(c) the identification mark of the vehicle.

This obligation is absolute in the sense that, if the requirement is made by a person having reasonable grounds to make it, the driver must supply this information. If he refuses or fails to do so he commits an offence which is not excused by any subsequent report which he might make to the police. However, if this information is supplied at the scene the obligations of the driver cease and there is no need to report the accident to the police. (If injury to some person is occasioned there is also a need to produce evidence of insurance; we deal with this below.)

In conclusion, it should be noted that the duty to stop does not cast on the driver the duty to go and seek persons to whom to give the above information.

DUTY TO REPORT TO THE POLICE

The Road Traffic Act 1988, s 170(3) deals with a driver's obligation to report an accident to the police and its wording is important:

'If for any reason the driver of the mechanically propelled vehicle does not give his *name and address* to a person having reasonable grounds for so requiring, he must report the accident.'

Two points must be made at the outset. First, the obligation to report an accident to the police arises whenever the driver has not given his name and address at the scene of the accident, whether or not he was required to do so by anyone there (and indeed, even though he was known personally to any person with reasonable grounds to require his name and address). Second, the obligation to report is to do so at a police station or to a constable as soon as reasonably practicable and, in any case, within 24 hours of the occurrence of the accident and it can only be fulfilled officially and personally; telling a friend who is a police officer will not do, nor will a telephone message to a police station.

It must be remembered that s 170(3) only specifies 'his name and address'. If, therefore, a driver gives his name and address to a person reasonably requiring information, but refuses to give the name and address of the owner or the identification mark of the vehicle, he will not be obliged to report the accident to the police, although he will commit an offence under s 170 in consequence of his refusal to give the other information. This one factor has caused more confusion for police officers carrying out their duties under s 170 than the remainder of the provisions of that section.

The obligation to report, of a driver who does not give his name and address at the scene of the accident, is subject to the following rules as to time. First he must report the accident at a police station or to a constable 'in any case within 24 hours'. This is the maximum period in which the report may be made, so that if the driver does not report until 24 hours or more have elapsed since the accident he is necessarily in breach of his obligation under s 170. However, second, even if the report is made within 24 hours, the driver will nevertheless be in breach of his obligation if he has not made it 'as soon as reasonably practicable'.

What is 'reasonably practicable' is a matter for the court to decide upon in the particular circumstances of each case. If a driver who is not seeking urgent medical attention drives from the scene of an accident and past a police station, in order to go to his home, and only reports the accident 20 hours later, a court is unlikely to find that he reported the accident as soon as reasonably practicable. On the other hand, in a case where a motorist's car left the road and collided, causing damage, at 11pm and the motorist left his address in his car at the scene and was interviewed by the police at 8.30am the next day (at which point of time he reported the accident), the Divisional Court held that the justices were entitled to conclude that in the circumstances there had been no failure to report as soon as reasonably practicable.

OFFENCES

A person who fails to comply with any requirement of s 170 commits an offence. In fact, if he fails to stop (or to give his name and address etc), contrary to s 170(2), and also fails to report the accident to the police, contrary to s 170(3), he commits two offences.

A person charged with such an offence has a defence if *he proves* that he did not know that an accident had occurred. However, in the case of an offence under s 170(3), if, although unaware of the accident at the time of it, he subsequently becomes aware of it within the 24-hour period and fails to report it to the police, he can be convicted of that offence since he will be obliged to report the accident and his failure at that time will be with knowledge of the accident.

INJURY ACCIDENTS: REQUIREMENT TO PRODUCE INSURANCE

Additional obligations are placed by the Road Traffic Act 1988, s 170(5) on drivers of motor vehicles concerned in accidents involving personal injury to another person. Section 170(5) provides that if in the case of a personal injury accident to which s 170 applies, the driver of the motor vehicle does not at the time of the accident produce such a certificate of insurance or security, or other evidence prescribed by regulations:

(a) to a constable, or
(b) to some person who, having reasonable grounds for so doing, has required him to produce it,

the driver must report the accident and produce such a certificate or other evidence.

As in the case of the duty to report an accident under s 170(3), the driver must report the accident (and produce his insurance certificate etc) to a constable and must do so as soon as reasonably practicable, within 24 hours of the accident. It is an offence to fail to do so. However, the offence is subject to the proviso that a person is not to be convicted of this offence by reason only of a failure to produce a certificate etc if, within seven days after the accident, the certificate etc is produced at the police station specified by him when the accident was reported.

Section 170(5) imposes additional requirements upon a driver who is involved in an accident which involves personal injury to some person other than himself. In addition to providing to any person reasonably requiring such information his name and address, the name and address of the owner and the identification mark of the vehicle, he must also produce his certificate of insurance (or other evidence of insurance) to that person or to a constable. It is important to recognise that there are therefore no circumstances in which a driver must report an accident to the police if his duties are fully discharged at the scene. This is true even in circumstances in which a pedestrian is severely injured; if the driver is requested by the pedestrian, or someone acting reasonably on his behalf, to give the particulars required by s 170 and to produce a certificate of insurance, and he does so, that driver has carried out his legal obligations and need not report the accident to the police. It is, of course, not sufficient to wave a certificate of insurance in front of the eyes of a person requiring such information; it must be produced in the sense that the person is able to satisfy himself that an effective insurance is in force.

CHAPTER 16

Driving offences

When we think of someone being put in fear, injured or killed, we tend to think about this being caused by a person who has embarked on activities which would generally be described as 'criminal'. The mugger, the man in the public house who breaks a bottle to provide himself with a weapon, and the sex attacker, all constitute some form of threat to other persons. However, it must not be forgotten that the driver of a mechanically propelled vehicle is in control of one of the most dangerous weapons of all and there is no limit to the harm which can be caused to persons or property by the irresponsible use of a mechanically propelled vehicle.

The common law offence of manslaughter has always been sufficient to deal with a driver who killed another person by driving which showed a culpable disregard for life. However, juries have been notoriously unwilling to convict a driver of manslaughter. It was for this reason that the offence of causing death by reckless driving was introduced in 1956; this offence was replaced by the offence of causing death by dangerous driving in 1992. Although the offence of 'motor manslaughter' may still be charged, it is now much more likely that proceedings will be taken for the offence of causing death by dangerous driving. In terms of maximum punishment, this is a lesser offence than manslaughter. In the relatively rare situation where 'motor manslaughter' is charged, the case will be governed by the rules set out on p 598. The rules relating to causing death by dangerous driving are described later in the chapter.

In addition to the common law offence of manslaughter, statutory offences were created in the nineteenth century to deal with carriages and the like. Although these provisions were enacted before the days of mechanically propelled vehicles, they can be applied to such vehicles. This is important in relation to the third provision next mentioned. The Highway Act 1835 prohibits certain acts in relation to 'carriages', and the Town Police Clauses Act 1847, s 28 deals with the furious driving of any horse or carriage. The Offences Against the Person Act 1861, s 35 still punishes the causing of bodily harm by wanton or furious driving on a road or otherwise by a person having charge of a carriage or vehicle; this charge can be useful in circumstances in which the negligent driving of a mechanically propelled vehicle did not take place on a road or other public place. However, for all practical purposes, driving offences that are committed in relation to mechanically propelled vehicles are governed by the Road Traffic Act 1988. The most serious offences contained in that Act are the offences of dangerous driving and causing death by dangerous driving.

The offences described in this chapter contain a number of general terms, which it is appropriate to define at the outset.

'Driving'

The essence of 'driving' is the use of the driver's controls (or at least one of them) in order to control the movement of the vehicle, however that movement is produced, provided that what occurs can in any sense be regarded as 'driving'. Thus, a person who releases the handbrake and 'coasts' downhill in a car is 'driving' it (and this is so even though the steering is locked). So is a person in the driving seat of a car which is being towed if he has the ability to control its movements by means of the brakes or steering. This is so even if the vehicle is attached by means of a rigid tow bar which is attached to the towing vehicle by means of a ball hitch, and to the vehicle being drawn by means of a shackle. Such a combination leaves the person holding the steering wheel of the towed vehicle with a substantial potential for directional control because he is able (indeed he is required) to keep the towed vehicle in line with the towing vehicle by means of the steering wheel. In such a case it would be irrelevant that the towed vehicle does not have any brakes; directional control through steering is enough. On the other hand, a person in the driving seat of a vehicle on a fixed tow is not driving it, since he cannot control its movements by the use of any of the driver's controls. Nor is a person who is pushing a car and steering it with his hand through the window driving it because this cannot in any sense be so described. Two people may be driving a vehicle at the same time. For example, if A who is in the driving seat operates the clutch and brakes and gear shift but allows his passenger, B, to steer the vehicle, both A and B are driving.

Section 192 of the 1988 Act provides that, except for the purposes of the offence of causing death by dangerous driving, where a separate person acts as steersman of a motor vehicle he is driving the vehicle (as well as any other person engaged in driving it). This covers the case where one person is primarily concerned with the propulsion of the vehicle and another acts as its steersman. It is relevant only in the case of traction engines and the like.

A limited company cannot be convicted of an offence of driving physically committed by one of its employees; nor can any other employer.

It must be proved that the person alleged to have been driving was driving at the time of the alleged offence. Difficulties in this respect have arisen in cases in which a witness has reported an incident to a police officer and at the same time has provided, from memory, the registration mark of the vehicle. The police officer subsequently cannot say in evidence that he was told that the number of the car involved in the incident was that given by the witness, as this is hearsay. In such cases, it would be good practice for the officer to record the number given to him in his note book and to have the witness endorse the entry as being correct and sign it. Such a record then becomes 'joint' and may be referred to by either. The witness's statement should also include the fact that he gave that particular number to the officer and that it was the number of the vehicle seen on that occasion.

'Mechanically propelled vehicle'

This term has been discussed in ch 9 above. The offences under the Road Traffic Act 1988 involving dangerous or careless driving were extended to include the term 'mechanically propelled vehicle' in place of 'motor vehicle' by the Road Traffic Act 1991. The term 'mechanically propelled vehicle' includes all motor vehicles but also includes vehicles which would not be embraced by that term as they are not intended or adapted for use on a road.

'Motor vehicle'

This term has the normal meaning given to it under the Road Traffic Act 1988, s 185, viz a mechanically propelled vehicle intended or adapted for use on roads. We have discussed this term in ch 9 above.

'Road'

A 'road' is defined by s 192 of the 1988 Act as any length of highway or any other road to which the public has access, including bridges over which a road passes. The question of whether or not a place is a road for the purposes of this offence will depend upon the question of usage. We dealt with these matters in more detail on p 202.

'Public place'

For discussion as to what may or may not be a public place, in particular circumstances, see ch 17 below. However, by the Road Traffic Act 1988, s 13A a person is not guilty of an offence involving dangerous or careless driving by virtue of driving a vehicle in a public place other than a road if he shows that he was driving in accordance with an authorisation for a motoring event given under the Motor Vehicles (Off Road Events) Regulations 1995 (see p 400 below). These Regulations empower prescribed bodies to issue authorisations.

It has been held that the foyer of the departure lounge at a Heathrow Airport terminal is a public place for the purposes of an offence of careless driving. The offender was driving an electric buggy in a congested foyer containing seated passengers and walking passengers. Although this occurred in an area to which access was restricted to passengers who had boarding passes and had passed through passport control, it was held to be a public place in that the persons who were there were members of the public, not a special group of persons subjected to any form of screening process which might have endowed them with some special characteristic. A similar decision was made in relation to a hospital car park.

DANGEROUS DRIVING, CAUSING DEATH BY DANGEROUS DRIVING, AND DANGEROUS CYCLING

Dangerous driving

The Road Traffic Act 1988, s 2 provides that it is an offence for a person to drive a mechanically propelled vehicle dangerously on a road or other public place. This offence replaced the offence of 'reckless driving'.

There are two ways in which driving may be dangerous. First, the Road Traffic Act 1988, s 2A(1) provides that a person is to be regarded as driving dangerously if:

(a) the way that he drives falls far below what would be expected of a competent and careful driver; and

(b) it would be obvious to a competent and careful driver that driving in that way would be dangerous.

Section 2A(3) states that 'dangerous' refers to danger either of injury to any person or of serious damage to property.

This test in s 2A(1) is concerned with the manner of the accused's driving and whether it falls *far* below what would be expected of a careful and competent driver in circumstances where it would be obvious to a competent and careful driver that driving in that way would be dangerous. The presence of the word *'far'* will separate offences of dangerous driving from those which should more appropriately be charged as careless driving.

The standard of driving is defined objectively (ie in terms of a competent and careful driver) and it applies to all drivers regardless of the driving experience which they have gained. It would be no defence that the accused was doing his incompetent best. The objective standards to be applied will vary according to the prevailing conditions and to exceptional circumstances which might have existed. In fog, the competent and careful driver would drive in a manner quite different from that which he would adopt in dry, clear conditions. Whilst driving at a speed of 70 mph in an area restricted to 30 mph might be described as dangerous, it would not often be so on a dual carriageway. If it occurred in the middle of the night when the road was not being used by any other person or vehicle, such driving in a restricted area may not be 'dangerous', whilst driving at that speed on a dual carriageway which is restricted by road works may be.

Once it has been established that the actual driving fell far below standards of a competent and careful driver, it becomes necessary to consider whether or not it would be 'obvious' to a competent and careful driver that such driving would be dangerous. In this context, 'dangerous' refers to danger either of injury to any person or of serious damage to property.

In determining for these purposes what would be expected of, or obvious to, a competent and careful driver in a particular case, regard must be had not only to the circumstances of which he should be expected to be aware but also to any circumstances shown to have been within the accused's knowledge. Thus, some subjectivity is introduced at this stage as the court will have to determine the questions of what would be expected of a 'competent and careful driver', and of what would be obvious to him, by reference not only to the circumstances of which he could be expected to be aware but also to any circumstances within the defendant's *actual* knowledge. On the other hand, regard must not be had to any circumstance which the accused wrongly believed to exist. Consequently, it has been held that, where a police officer pursued a stolen car at speed through traffic lights at red, his mistaken belief that the junction was being controlled by other officers (so that he could cross safely) was irrelevant to the issue of dangerous driving.

The courts will therefore be concerned with that which 'falls far below' accepted driving standards and that 'which would be obvious' in relation to the danger caused.

The second way in which driving may be dangerous is provided by the Road Traffic Act 1988, s 2A(2) which provides that a person is also to be regarded as driving dangerously if it would be obvious to a competent and careful driver that driving the vehicle in its current state would be 'dangerous' (in the sense defined by s 2A(3), outlined above). As with s 2A(1), in determining what would be obvious to a competent and careful driver, regard must be had not only to the circumstances of which he could be expected to be aware but also to any circumstances shown to have been within the accused's knowledge. A danger is 'obvious' in this context only if it could be seen or realised at first glance by a competent and careful driver. It is not enough that such a driver would have taken steps to check out whether the vehicle was in a condition which was not dangerous, and by doing so would have discovered the defect, perhaps by examining the underside of the vehicle. Where a newly-purchased second hand car swerved violently out of control and collided with another vehicle it was alleged that this was due to severe corrosion of the vehicle. A traffic examiner stated that it would be necessary to go beneath the vehicle to discover the corrosion. The Court of Appeal said that where a defect existed in a vehicle, it was necessary to show that it would be obvious to a competent and careful driver that driving the vehicle in that condition would be dangerous. However, as in this case, a defect might be such that even a competent and careful driver would not necessarily discover it. Such a defect was not 'obvious' and the issue of whether or not it would be obviously dangerous to drive the vehicle in that condition did not arise unless it could be shown that that knowledge existed.

Similarly, where a wheel detached itself from a vehicle and killed the driver of another vehicle and it was proved that visual checks upon the security of wheels were carried out daily and that a physical check was made once each week, the Court of Appeal said that 'obvious' meant something which could be seen or realised at first glance. In the case of an employee it is important to consider the nature of the instructions given to him and, generally, it would be wrong to expect him to do more that he had been instructed to do in the absence of evidence that those instructions were inadequate.

The Court of Appeal, when considering an appeal by a man convicted of aiding and abetting an offence of causing death by dangerous driving, examined the elements of dangerous driving involving a defective vehicle. It ruled that proof of guilt depended upon an objective test as to the standard of driving, namely, what would have been obvious to a competent and careful driver. The state of mind of the accused is relevant only if, and to the extent that, it attributes additional knowledge to the notional competent and careful driver. The threshold of proof is high. It must be shown that the defect would have been 'obvious' to the 'competent and careful driver'. It is not enough to show that a driver, had he examined the vehicle by going underneath it, would have seen the defect. Mens rea plays no part in the offence as it is concerned with defective vehicles.

Since the definition of dangerous driving is concerned with the *manner* of the driving or *the state of the vehicle*, it might have been thought that driving in a dangerously defective state through drink or drugs could not be regarded *in itself* as dangerous. However, the Court of Appeal has held that it can be, at least if the driver is aware of his condition, as driving in such a condition is itself a manner of driving. This is difficult to accept, but represents the law. Nevertheless, a charge of drink/driving would be more appropriate.

Dangerous cycling

A person who rides a bicycle or tricycle dangerously on a road commits a separate and less serious offence. A person is to be regarded as riding dangerously if he rides in a *manner* which equates to the manner of driving described above.

Alternative verdicts

The Road Traffic Offenders Act 1988, s 24 provides that, where a person is charged with an offence of dangerous driving or dangerous cycling and is found not guilty of such an offence and the allegations in the information amount to or include an allegation of an offence of careless driving or careless cycling, he may be convicted of that offence.

Causing death by dangerous driving

The Road Traffic Act 1988, s 1 provides that a person who causes the death of another person by driving a mechanically propelled vehicle on a road or other public place dangerously is guilty of an offence, which is an arrestable one.

Proof of the offence requires proof that the accused drove a mechanically propelled vehicle on a road or other public place dangerously (in the sense just explained) and that the dangerous driving caused the death of another person (including someone else in the accused's vehicle). It is not necessary to show that the dangerous driving was the sole cause, since it is sufficient that it is more than a trifling cause. An example is a case where two drivers were engaged in a high speed chase and one of them was killed when she collided with an on-coming car, the other driver was convicted of this offence. His dangerous driving had been a cause of the death of the other driver and that 'cause' had been more than 'slight or trifling'. By way of a further example, if a driver deliberately accelerates towards people who are crossing at a pedestrian crossing and knocks down one of them, who later dies, he can be convicted of causing that death by dangerous driving. It will not assist him to allege that the victim was not seriously injured and would not have died if a heart condition from which he suffered had not been aggravated by the shock. His driving is a cause of that death and it is certainly not a trifling cause in such circumstances.

No mens rea need be proved as to the risk of death resulting from the dangerous driving; it follows that it is irrelevant that that risk was unforeseen or unforeseeable, as would be the case where the only obvious risk was of damage to property.

It is not necessary that the driver should have been driving the vehicle (ie it need not have been in motion) at the time that the fatal injury was caused. It is enough that there has been dangerous driving by the driver and that that driving is more than a trifling cause of death. This is shown by a case where a driver took his lorry on to a motorway after having been warned that his brake air pressure gauges were not working (which constituted dangerous driving), and the hand brake system was activated due to loss of air pressure. The trailer unit blocked the nearside lane of the motorway . Some twelve minutes later a lorry collided with it and the driver of that vehicle was killed. The Court of Appeal held that the consequences of dangerous driving are capable of outlasting the time the driver spends at the wheel. It held that the dangerous driving must have not simply existed in creating the occasion of the fatal accident, but in bringing it about. On the facts the consequences of the dangerous driving were not 'spent' and too remote from the accident, and were more than a trifling cause of the death. As a result the driver's conviction for causing death by dangerous driving was upheld.

Causing death by dangerous driving is a serious offence and it is important that the evidence offered to a court is well presented. Identification of the person fatally injured is of extreme importance. Medical evidence will be given at the Crown Court concerning the cause of death of the person injured in the accident. It is essential that a police officer, who was at the scene of the accident and saw the injured person, identifies that person to the pathologist who carries out the post mortem examination. In the absence of such evidence, there is nothing to connect the person upon whom the post mortem examination was carried out with the person injured in the accident. In addition, a careful note must be made of everything observed at the scene of the accident at the particular time at which it occurred. Whether driving can be described as dangerous will often depend upon the particular circumstances existing at the time, such as the state of street lighting and the nature and volume of traffic at that time of day. All fatal traffic accidents must be handled carefully and the possibility of the need for forensic evidence should be considered. There is little purpose in tracing a damaged vehicle suspected of having been involved in a fatal accident if samples of glass, paint and other vehicle debris were not collected at the scene at the time of the accident.

The ingredients of the offences of manslaughter and of causing death by dangerous driving co-exist and are similar. However, it has been stated by the House of Lords that a person who caused death by reckless driving (the offence which previously existed) should normally be charged with that offence, and that a charge of manslaughter should only be brought in the most grave cases. It is assumed that the same view will be taken in relation to charges of dangerous driving. The House also held that counts of manslaughter and of causing death by reckless driving might not be joined in the same indictment; the prosecution must choose which offence to charge. The same will apply to offences of causing death by dangerous driving.

It is not the purpose of the offence of causing death by dangerous driving to punish the driver of a motor car who causes the death of one of his own family by the dangerous manner of his driving. Unless the circumstances are exceptional, it is probable that the punishment awarded by a court will be insignificant in relation to the punishment which such a driver will already have suffered. If particular circumstances exist which appear to make a prosecution desirable in such a case, the advice of the Director of Public Prosecutions should be obtained before such steps are taken.

CARELESS, AND INCONSIDERATE, DRIVING OR CYCLING

Generally

Section 3 of the 1988 Act creates two separate offences by providing that if a person drives a mechanically propelled vehicle on a road or other public place without due care and attention, or without reasonable consideration for other persons using the road or place, he is guilty of an offence. The level of 'bad' driving which must be proved in a charge of careless or inconsiderate driving is considerably less than that required in cases of dangerous driving.

Driving without due care and attention

Whether or not a person has committed an offence of careless driving is dependent upon whether he was exercising that degree of care and attention that a reasonable and prudent driver would exercise in those circumstances. It has been said that the standard is an objective standard, impersonal and universal, fixed in relation to the safety of the other users of the highway. It is in no way related to the degree of proficiency or degree of experience attained by the individual driver, and it is unaffected by the fact that the driver was driving to an emergency.

Bearing in mind the objective approach to be applied, it is no defence that, as a learner, the driver was doing his best, if that best falls short of the standard which might be expected from a reasonably competent driver. If a learner driver applies the accelerator instead of the foot brake and causes an accident he is guilty of driving without due care and attention. There is only one standard of care and his actions fall short of it. In circumstances where a competent driver wears shoes with smooth leather soles and this causes his foot to slip from the brake pedal, the court will have to consider whether in the circumstances a reasonable and prudent driver would have been aware of the possibility of this happening and would not have driven the car with such shoes. In the same way, it is essential to keep in mind that experienced drivers or specially trained drivers do not in consequence of that experience or training owe some higher standard of care. For example, the driver of a police vehicle owes the ordinary standard of care to other persons on the road.

There is no limit to the forms which this offence may take. If a driver gives false direction signals this amounts to driving without due care and attention since it falls below the standard of care of a reasonable and prudent driver in the circumstances because such a driver, realising the possible risks of deluding other road users as to the intended movements of his vehicle, would ensure that he did not give false signals.

There are numerous circumstances in which this offence is quite clearly committed. The Traffic Signs Regulations and General Directions authorise various road markings which demand a certain standard of care. Road markings at the junctions of roads frequently indicate that no vehicle shall pass the line markings in a side street in circumstances which will impede other traffic on the main road. If a collision occurs because a vehicle emerges from such a side street, having passed over the road markings, this provides clear proof that the driver was not paying sufficient attention.

Failure to observe a provision of the Highway Code does not of itself establish driving without due care and attention, but any such failure may be relied on as evidence of it.

In applying the appropriate test as to whether a defendant has driven without due care and attention, all of the circumstances of the case can be considered including evidence that the defendant had been affected by drink or that he had taken such an amount of drink as would be likely to affect a driver, since such evidence may indicate a lack of due care on the part of the driver in driving as he did.

Whether or not an accused driver has fallen below the objective standard of care is a question of fact in every case, and it must be decided upon the particular facts by the justices. These facts are very much within the knowledge of the local justices, and the Divisional Court will not interfere with one of their decisions unless it is one which no reasonable bench of justices could have reached in the circumstances. It will be appreciated that in most circumstances the local justices will be aware of the character of the road or junction at which the incident occurred, the volume and type of traffic which uses the roads and any particular hazards which exist. They are therefore in a much better position to assess whether or not a certain piece of driving was carried out without due care and attention than judges sitting in the Divisional Court in London who have no such local knowledge. In some cases, however, the facts are such that, unless the accused driver offers some explanation consistent with him having taken due care which is not disproved, the only proper inference is careless driving, in which case the justices must convict him (and if they do not the Divisional Court will order them to do so).

Driving without reasonable consideration

Once again, an objective test should be applied as to whether particular forms of driving are carried out without reasonable consideration for other persons using the road. Thus, the question is whether the accused drove without showing the consideration to other road users which would be shown by a reasonable driver. A driver who deliberately drives through flood water at speed, drenching persons waiting in a bus queue, is certainly driving without reasonable consideration. So, it is submitted, is the driver who occupies the fast lane of a motorway, or even the outside lane of dual carriageway, in circumstances in which there is nothing to prevent him from regaining the nearside lane, because he is unreasonably interfering with the progress of other drivers. The irresponsible use of full beam headlamps may also amount to driving without reasonable consideration. Applying the test of the standard of consideration of a reasonable driver, a reasonable driver certainly does not drive towards opposing traffic in this manner. A person may drive without reasonable consideration for other persons using the road even where his lack of consideration is to his own passenger.

General

Because s 3 creates two offences, an information which alleges both alternatives is bad for duplicity. It is sufficient to allege that a person drove without due care and attention at a particular time or place, or that he drove without reasonable consideration at a time and place, since it is not necessary to specify the nature of his negligence in the information. If, following a fatal accident, it appears that there is sufficient evidence to support a charge of careless driving but not of dangerous driving, no such charge should be preferred until after the inquest has been held.

Causing death by careless driving when under the influence of drink or drugs

The Road Traffic Act 1988, s 3A(1), which was added by the Road Traffic Act 1991, provides that it is an offence for a person to cause the death of another person by driving a mechanically propelled vehicle on a road or other public place without due care and attention, or without reasonable consideration for other persons using the road or place, and:

(a) he is, at the time when he is driving, unfit to drive through drink or drugs, or
(b) has consumed so much alcohol that the proportion of it in his breath, blood or urine at that time exceeds the prescribed limit, or
(c) he is, within 18 hours after that time, required under s 7 to provide a specimen, but without reasonable cause fails to provide it.

In essence, to be guilty of an offence under s 3A(1), the accused must be proved to have committed one or other of the offences of careless driving and thereby killed another and be proved to fall within one of the drink/drive elements in (a) to (c).

The term 'unfit to drive though drink or drugs' is explained in ch 17, as are other references to drink or drugs, prescribed limits etc. Other matters concerned with the evidential linking of the driver to the person who received fatal injuries, are discussed above.

Despite the wording of s 3A(1), the offences at (b) and (c), which are based upon the consumption of alcohol in excess of the prescribed limit and upon failure to provide a specimen under s 7 within 18 hours of driving, apply only to persons driving motor vehicles as opposed to mechanically propelled vehicles.

In the circumstances in which this offence will be committed it would be reasonable to say that an offence of careless driving (such offences are described above) was aggravated either by driving whilst affected by drink, or by refusing to provide a specimen for analysis where there was a suspicion of alcohol. In the case of a charge of causing death by dangerous driving, a fairly high degree of negligence on the part of the driver will have to be proved and evidence of the consumption of alcohol may be admitted where it is relevant to the dangerous nature of the accused's driving. In cases of careless driving, the evidential standard in relation to the driving of the accused is not so high. Momentary inattention may be sufficient. Section 3A provides a more serious offence where incompetent driving may have been caused by the consumption of alcohol or drugs.

Alternative verdicts

The Road Traffic Offenders Act 1988, s 24 provides that, where a person is charged with an offence under the Road Traffic Act 1988, s 3A and is found not guilty and the allegations in the indictment amount to or include an allegation of careless or inconsiderate driving or of a drink-driving offence or of failing to provide a specimen for analysis, he may be convicted of that offence.

Careless cycling

There are separate, and less serious, offences of riding a bicycle or tricycle on a road without due care and attention, or without reasonable consideration for other persons using the road.

DEFENCES TO DANGEROUS OR CARELESS DRIVING

Duress by threats and duress of circumstances

Where a person is compelled to drive dangerously or carelessly in order to avoid the threat of death or serious injury to himself or some other person, as where his car is being hotly pursued by an armed gang or where his car has been hijacked by an armed gang who order him to outdistance a pursuing police car, he may have the defence of duress of circumstances (where the threat emanates from the circumstances) or of duress by threats (if he acts under a threat of death or serious bodily harm to himself or another unless he complies with an order). The requirements of these defences are set out on p 9.

Public emergencies

Unless the defence of duress of circumstances applies, police officers, firefighters and ambulance drivers may *not* use the emergency nature of their mission as a defence to a charge of dangerous or careless driving, as they owe the same duty of care to the public at all times.

Automatism

'Automatism' means the involuntary movement of a person's body or limbs, ie movements which are completely beyond his control. There are various medical conditions which may cause involuntary movements of part of the body or even unconsciousness. Some external factors may also cause such body movements. A driver may suffer an epileptic fit and thus lose control of a motor vehicle. A motor vehicle may be entered by a swarm of bees, with the result that the driver is prevented from exercising any directional control over the vehicle, any movements of his arms and legs being caused solely by the action of the bees. The question to be answered is how relevant these issues may be to dangerous and careless driving charges.

The answer is that *generally,* as in the case of other offences, it is a defence that the accused was an automaton. Consequently, a driver who suffers a totally unexpected epileptic fit, or who is overcome by a swarm of bees in the way just described, cannot be convicted of dangerous or careless driving. (We discussed automatism and the question of proof in ch 1, above, to which the reader is referred for further detail.)

However, by way of *exception,* it must be remembered that automatism does not excuse a person from liability for the crimes discussed in this chapter if his automatism resulted from his voluntary intoxication. Nor will automatism excuse such a person if, before he became an automaton, he appreciated the risk that something which he did or failed to do was likely to make him unpredictable or uncontrollable with the result that he might endanger others (as opposed to simply becoming an automaton) and he deliberately ran the risk or otherwise disregarded it.

Moreover, by way of further *exception*, an accused who, for example, falls asleep at the wheel or goes into a hypoglycaemic coma at the wheel can be convicted of careless driving under the ordinary principles of liability, not in relation to the time when he was an automaton but in relation to the time when he realised or should have realised that he was about to become unconscious and should have stopped driving. The reason is clear: to drive in such a case falls below the standard of a reasonable and prudent driver (since he would have stopped).

Mechanical defect

The fact that the driving complained of was due to the sudden mechanical failure of an essential part of a motor vehicle can provide a defence to charges of dangerous or careless driving, provided that the defect was not known by the accused to exist prior to the occurrence which forms the basis of the charge, and was not such that it should have been discovered by a reasonably prudent driver. Thus, where a driver knew that the brakes of his vehicle pulled to the offside but nevertheless drove it, the defence of mechanical defect was held not to be open to him.

Like the defence of automatism, the essence of this defence is that the dangerous situation was caused by a sudden loss of control which was in no way due to the fault of the driver.

SPEEDING

In considering offences of exceeding speed limits it is essential to separate them into those which are related to restricted roads, to roads subjected to a speed limit order, speed limits on motorways, to speed limits introduced by temporary orders, and to limits which affect particular vehicles in particular places.

All offences which are related to exceeding maximum speed limits are offences in respect of which there is discretionary disqualification; the endorsement of 3–6 or 3 (if fixed penalty) penalty points is obligatory.

Restricted roads

By the Road Traffic Regulation Act 1984, s 81 it is not lawful for a person to drive a motor vehicle on a restricted road at a speed exceeding 30 mph. It is an offence contrary to s 89 to do so.

In the present context, a 'restricted road' is basically defined as one upon which there is provided a system of street lighting furnished by means of lamps placed not more than 200 yards apart. The Divisional Court has held that an error of 12 yards between two lamps in a system of 24 does not prevent the road being restricted.

In addition to this basic definition, s 82 provides that a direction may be given that a specified road with street lighting as described above shall cease to be a restricted road for the purpose of s 81 or that a road which is not provided with such lighting shall be a restricted road for the purpose of s 81. Such directions are made by the Secretary of State in the case of trunk roads and by the local authority in the case of other roads.

A road with street lighting which has been de-restricted by a direction must show the prescribed de-restriction signs (including repeater signs). Likewise, a road without such lighting which has been made a restricted road must be provided with the prescribed restriction signs (including repeater signs). If these are not in place, a driver cannot be convicted of exceeding the 30 mph speed limit. However, if they are, it is no defence to such a charge that the accused did not see the signs. The de-restriction or restriction signs which must be used are prescribed by the Traffic Signs (Speed Limits) Regulations and Directions 1969.

The requirement for restriction signs does not apply to a road which is restricted by virtue of having a system of street lighting with lamps not more than 200 yards apart. Consequently, it is no defence for a driver accused of exceeding 30 mph on such a road that no signs were provided.

Roads subject to speed limit orders

Quite apart from the 'restricted' (ie to 30 mph) roads just discussed, there are many other roads which are subject to speed limits. Section 84 of the Act of 1984 empowers the Secretary of State (trunk roads and certain other roads) or local authority (all other roads) to make an order prohibiting the driving of motor vehicles on a specified road at a speed exceeding that specified in the order (either at any time or during specified periods) or at a speed exceeding that indicated by traffic signs in acordance with the order. By s 89, a person who drives a motor vehicle at a speed in excess of that specified for the particular road is guilty of an offence. If a speed limit order is made under s 84, the specified road must bear the prescribed restriction signs (including repeater signs). If it does not, a person cannot be convicted of driving in excess of the specified limit.

Speed limits on motorways

The Motorways Traffic (Speed Limit) Regulations 1974 impose an overall speed limit of 70 mph on any motor vehicle using a motorway. If a section of motorway is subject to a lesser limit, this is expressly listed and that section must bear the prescribed signs indicating the lower limit (otherwise a driver cannot be convicted of exceeding that limit). Contravention of the Regulations is an offence contrary to the Road Traffic Regulation Act 1984, s 17(4).

Temporary speed limits

The Road Traffic Regulation Act 1984, s 88 permits temporary speed limit orders to be made by the Secretary of State when it is desirable to do so in the interests of safety or for the purpose of facilitating the movement of traffic. Such orders may impose temporary maximum speed limits.

The 70 mph, 60 mph and 50 mph (Temporary Speed Limit) Order 1977, which was made under the predecessor to s 88 and continues in force indefinitely, imposes a maximum limit of 60 mph on single carriageways and of 70 mph on dual carriageways. These are general limits which apply to all roads (other than motorways) unless some other speed limit operates by virtue of the provisions described in this chapter.

The 1977 Order also imposes a limit of 60 mph on certain specified lengths of dual carriageways and of 50 mph on certain specified lengths of single carriageways. Such lengths must be provided with the prescribed restriction signs (including repeaters).

By s 89 of the 1984 Act, it is an offence for a person to drive a motor vehicle on a road in excess of an applicable temporary speed limit imposed under the Order.

Minimum speed limits

Section 88 also permits orders to be made imposing minimum speed limits, subject to such exceptions as may be specified. Signs must be displayed if a minimum speed limit is in force in respect of any road. By s 88(7), breach of such an order is an offence. Neither disqualification nor endorsement can be ordered on a conviction for this offence. Such a minimum speed limit only applies, of course, to motor vehicles.

Temporary maximum limits by highway authorities

Section 14 of the 1984 Act permits highway authorities to impose temporary speed limits because of road works or work which is being undertaken near a road, or because of the likelihood of danger to the public or of serious damage to the highway, or for the purpose of cleaning or clearing litter. Such an order cannot continue in force for more than 18 months unless the Secretary of State consents to its further continuance, or in the case of road works, where the authority has stated in the order that the works will take longer, but in such a case the order must be revoked as soon as the works are completed.

A person who contravenes a speed limit imposed under s 14 commits an offence contrary to s 16 of the 1984 Act.

Speed limits on particular vehicles

Quite apart from the various speed limits which apply to roads, speed limits are also imposed on various types of vehicles. The result is that the driver of such a vehicle must not only observe the *speed limit applying to the road* in question but also the *speed limit applying to his vehicle on that road*. A person who drives a motor vehicle on a road at a speed in excess of a speed limit applicable to that vehicle is, by s 89 of the 1984 Act, guilty of an offence.

Schedule 6 to the Act sets out the speed limits applying to particular classes of vehicles as follows:

	Class of vehicle	*M/ways*	*Dual carr*	*Other roads*
1	Invalid carriage	n/a	20	20
2	Passenger vehicle, motor caravan, car-derived van or dual-purpose vehicle drawing one trailer	60	60	50
3	Vehicle of the type mentioned in 2, drawing more than one trailer	40	20	20
4	Goods vehicle (except car-derived van) up to 7.5 tonnes mlw (maximum laden weight) not drawing a trailer	70	60	50
5	Articulated vehicle up to 7.5 tonnes mlw, and goods vehicle drawing one trailer where the combined mlw does not exceed 7.5 tonnes	60	60	50
6	Articulated vehicle over 7.5 tonnes mlw, goods vehicle over 7.5 tonnes mlw and goods vehicles drawing one trailer where the combined mlw exceeds 7.5 tonnes	60	50	40

Class of vehicle	M/ways	Dual carr	Other roads
7 Goods vehicle, other than a car-derived van, drawing more than one trailer	40	20	20
8 Motor tractor, light locos, heavy locos	20	20	20
9 Motor tractor, light locos, heavy locos with certain requirements as to springs and wings being met	40	30	30
10 Works truck	18	18	18
11 Passenger vehicles exceeding 3.05 tonnes u/w or adapted to carry more than 8 passengers:			
Not exceeding 12 m length	70	60	50
Exceeding 12 m length	60	60	50
12 Agricultural motor vehicle	40	40	40

The term 'car-derived van' means a goods vehicle which is constructed or adapted as a derivative of a passenger vehicle and which has a maximum laden weight not exceeding 2 tonnes. It is treated as if it was a passenger vehicle of the type from which it was derived.

A recovery vehicle equipped with a special boom for lifting vehicles is not a motor tractor. It is constructed to carry a load and is not, therefore, restricted to 40 mph on a motorway.

Exemptions from speed limits

The Road Traffic Regulation Act 1984, s 87 exempts fire brigade, ambulance and police vehicles from the statutory provisions imposing speed limits on motor vehicles, if the observance of any such provision would be likely to hinder the use of the vehicle for the purpose for which it is being used on that occasion. This is not a general exemption; the particular purpose of use on each occasion must be examined. The exemption is clearly essential; otherwise, for example, police vehicles would not be permitted to pursue speeding vehicles and would not be permitted to respond as quickly as possible to emergency situations.

Procuring or inciting speeding: a special provision

Section 89(4) of the 1984 Act provides that, if a person who employs others to drive motor vehicles on roads publishes or issues any timetable or schedule, or gives any directions, under which any journey or part of a journey is required to be completed within a specified time, and it is not practicable for that journey (or part) to be completed in the specified time without the commission of an offence under s 89, that publication or issue, or giving of directions, may be produced as evidence that the employer procured or (as the case may be) incited his employees to commit such an offence.

Proof

Section 89(2) of the 1984 Act states that a person must not be convicted of an offence of speeding contrary to s 89 solely on the evidence of one witness to the effect that, in the opinion of the witness, the person prosecuted was driving the vehicle at a speed exceeding the specified limit. The subsection requires corroborative evidence; it does not require that there must necessarily be more than one witness. Although, technically, there is no reason why an offender should not be convicted on the evidence of two witnesses, where one corroborates the other by stating that in his opinion the vehicle was, for example, exceeding a limit of 30 mph, the courts would generally not be satisfied with two such opinions unless the speed was estimated to be far in excess of the limit imposed. Corroboration is therefore usually provided by some mechanical device, which is read by an operator (normally a police officer) who may then give evidence of its reading. These readings will provide corroboration of the operator's opinion of the speed of the vehicle in question.

Corroboration of speed may be obtained by the use of stop watches to assess speeds over a measured distance, but it is usually provided by a speedometer, radar speed meter or vascar. Where a speedometer is used, it is important to establish that the police vehicle containing the speedometer maintained an even distance from the vehicle being checked as this is relevant to the issue of speed.

A police officer's opinion of a vehicle's speed may also be corroborated from scientific calculations made by him (or another) based, for example, on damage to the vehicle and skid marks where it has crashed.

In instances where two police officers are involved in detecting speeding offences, they may keep one record of the transaction provided that both check and acknowledge the accuracy of that record at the time. This frequently occurs where one officer is engaged in checking the speed of the vehicle, whilst another stops and deals with the offending driver.

Radar meters are extremely accurate devices, and the courts will accept evidence of speed which is based upon meter readings provided that the operator can satisfy the court that he is a trained operator and that there is clear evidence of the identity of the particular motor vehicle alleged to have exceeded the speed limit. The vehicle will have been stopped by another officer and clear proof will be required that the vehicle stopped by the second officer was the one which had exceeded a statutory speed limit. Hand-held radar guns have been criticised in the courts but, in the instances in which the readings obtained by such guns have been rejected, it is operator-error which has been the cause of the difficulties. Hand-held guns are accurate, provided the batteries are fully charged or, if they are operating from another source, provided they are properly connected. However, their accuracy is affected if they are operated within a quarter of a mile of powerful VHF or UHF transmissions or within 100 yards of high voltage cables. Care must also be taken to ensure that the beam is not bounced off metal objects and that it could not have picked up a reading from another moving object.

Vascar devices are also in common use within police forces. They record speeds averaged by a vehicle over a specified distance. Operators must be carefully trained as the device is operated by a series of switches. It is essential that the operator is able to satisfy a court that the switches were operated at the right time to ensure that correct distances are recorded and that the vehicle was properly identified, together with the precise moment when it passes the object which marks the limit of the distance over which it is checked.

Devices are approved by the Secretary of State.

The Road Traffic Offenders Act 1988, s 20 provides that records produced by prescribed devices are evidence of a fact related to any offence of speeding. The record must provide (in the same or another document) a certificate as to the circumstances in which the record was produced, signed by a constable or a person authorised by, or on behalf of, a chief police officer for the area in which the offence is alleged to have been committed. The device must be of a type proved to have been approved by the Secretary of State and must be used in accordance with conditions subject to which the approval was given. The Road Traffic Offenders (Prescribed Devices) Order 1992 gave approval to devices designed or adapted for measuring by radar the speed of motor vehicles. An identically named Order in 1993 approved devices designed or adapted for measuring speed by means of sensors, or cables on, or near the surface of a highway and those activated by means of a light beam or beams.

A copy of evidence obtained by means of an approved device must be served on the person charged with the offence not less than seven days before the hearing or trial. If the person charged, not less than three days before the hearing or trial, requires the attendance of the person who signed the document, the evidence of the circumstances in which the record was produced will not be admissible, although the record produced by the device will; this limitation does not apply where the proceedings in question are committal proceedings. Notices may be sent under the Road Traffic Act 1988, s 172, requiring the owner of the vehicle to identify the driver within 28 days. The Divisional Court supported a finding by justices that an unsigned notice sent by a Central Ticket Office Manager 'For the Chief Constable' which was clearly identified as emanating from the Central Ticket Office of the Thames Valley Police had all the hallmarks of authenticity. The requirement that the notice be sent by or on behalf of the chief officer of police had been satisfied.

The Divisional Court has ruled that a 'GR Speedman' device is a computer and the visual image which it produces is admissible in evidence and that the burden of proving that the computer is working correctly can be discharged by a trained and experienced police officer.

Motor racing and rallies

It is an offence contrary to the Road Traffic Act 1988, s 12 to promote or take part in a race or trial of speed between motor vehicles on a highway. Thus, there is a complete ban on racing motor vehicles on a highway.

Section 13 of the 1988 Act creates the offence of promoting or taking part in a 'competition or trial' (other than a race or trial of speed) which involves the use of motor vehicles on a highway if that event is not authorised. Even if authorised, there is an offence if the event is not conducted in accordance with any conditions imposed. The Motor Vehicles (Competitions and Trials) Regulations 1969 deal with such events. Competitions or trials are authorised without the need for an application if:

(a) there are no more than 12 vehicles involved and the event does not take place within eight days of another similar event promoted by the same person or club;

(b) where no merit is attached to completing the event with the lowest mileage and there are no performance tests and no route, competitors are not timed or required to visit the same places, although they may be required to finish at the same place by a specified time;

(c) the highway factor is solely concerned with good road behaviour and compliance with the Highway Code; or

(d) all competitors are members of the armed forces of the Crown and the event is designed solely for the purpose of service training.

Regulation 6 permits the authorisation of other events by the Royal Automobile Club. Such authorisations may be varied or revoked by that organisation. Applications for such events must be made not less than two months before the event is due to be held. If it is to be held on more than one date (except in the case of a specified event, which is an event which is run not more than once a year, for example the 'Veteran Car

Run' and is specified in the schedule to the Regulations), the application must not be made more than six months before the event.

The Road Traffic Act 1988, s 13A states that a person shall not be guilty of an offence against the 1988 Act under ss 1, 2 or 3 by virtue of driving a vehicle in a public place other than a road if he shows that he was driving in accordance with an authorisation for a motoring event given under regulations. The Motor Vehicles (Off Road Events) Regulations 1995 authorise a number of bodies, including the RAC, to issue such authorisations.

Section 33(1) of the 1988 Act prohibits the promoting or taking part in a trial of any description between motor vehicles on a footpath or bridleway unless the holding of it has been authorised by the local authority.

CHAPTER 17

Drinking and driving

Unless otherwise indicated, all the statutory provisions referred to in this chapter are contained in the Road Traffic Act 1988, and all references to sections hereafter are to sections in that Act.

Sections 4 to 11 of the 1988 Act contain provisions concerning various offences relating to drinking and driving. The principal offences are driving or attempting to drive a motor vehicle with an alcohol concentration in excess of the prescribed limit (s 5), and driving or attempting to drive a mechanically propelled vehicle when unfit to drive through drink or drugs (s 4).

Apart from cases where the accused is unfit through drugs or he is below the prescribed limit or the mechanically propelled vehicle is not a motor vehicle, it is the almost invariable practice to prosecute for an offence under s 5 rather than one under s 4. This is because s 5 lays down an objective test; whereas under s 4 it is necessary for the prosecution to prove that the accused's ability to drive properly was for the time being impaired by drink or drugs, which is a question of fact for the justices.

DRIVING ETC WITH EXCESS ALCOHOL

Under s 5(1) of the 1988 Act it is an offence for a person:

(a) to drive or attempt to drive a motor vehicle on a road or other public place; or
(b) to be in charge of a motor vehicle on a road or other public place,

after consuming so much alcohol that the proportion of it in his breath, blood or urine exceeds the prescribed limit.

The driving, attempted driving or being in charge referred to above must be on a 'road or other public place'. A 'road' is basically defined as any highway and any other road to which the public has access. A private road which leads to a farmhouse or the like is not a 'road' for present purposes because, although tradesmen are allowed to use it to get to the house, the access is limited to particular classes of people (as opposed to extending to the public at large). Where a road within a housing estate has not been adopted by the local authority, the determining factor is not whether the road is repairable at public expense but whether the public have access to it. If members of the public are seen there, and their presence is tolerated, it is a road. The term 'other public place' means a place (other than a 'road') to which the public have access. The term therefore includes car parks which are open to the public at the time, and fields in which public events are taking place (such as galas, shows or race meetings). A distinction must be drawn between the car park of a public house and that of a members' club. The first is open to the public at large during licensing hours and is therefore a public place during those hours, but that of the members' club is restricted to members of that club and their guests and therefore it is never a 'public place'. A place can be a 'public place' even though access to it is only permitted after a person has been screened. If those who are admitted pass through a screening process because of a special characteristic or reason personal to themselves (eg because they are members of the caravan club to whose site they seek access, or because they are workers at a factory to whose car park they seek access), the place in question is not a public place. On the other hand, if anyone can pass through the screening process and gain access simply by paying an entry fee (eg a site fee at a caravan park), or by satisfying conditions imposed by the landowner (eg access only for private vehicles), the place is a public place. For example, National Car Parks and traffic lanes leading to cross-channel ferries have been held by the Divisional Court to be 'public places'.

The car park of a community centre, access to which is restricted to members who have been nominated and screened for membership is not a public place at a time when access is restricted to members. Justices are entitled to rely upon their knowledge in determining whether a car park is a public place. When they do so they should indicate that fact to both the prosecution and the defence to give them an opportunity to comment.

Where a car park is a private one or its use has been allocated to a particular organisation it may nevertheless be a public place; the question is whether, as a matter of fact, the public have used it with regularity, so that it has become de facto a place where the public have access and therefore a public place.

'Driving' in the present context bears its normal meaning in road traffic offences. The essence of 'driving' is the use of the driver's controls (or, at least, one of them) in order to control the movement of the vehicle, however that movement is produced, provided that what occurs can in any sense be regarded as 'driving'. In most instances it is, of course, obvious whether or not a person is driving and this rather involved definition is particularly important in unusual circumstances which may confront a constable from time to time. A person who propels a motor cycle or moped by 'paddling' with the feet without the engine running is driving. In such circumstances the movement of the vehicle is being controlled by the driver's hands and he is 'on' the vehicle. Evidence of driving may be circumstantial. Police officers found a car which had collided with a lamp post and the windscreen had damage consistent with someone having hit the screen with his head. They visited the owner's home and found him hiding under the bed dressed only in trousers. A cut on his forehead was bleeding and he smelt strongly of alcohol. The Divisional Court said that the proximity of the time and place was important and coupled with such other evidence, the justices were entitled to find that he had been driving. Where a man was found at 1.20 am in the driving seat of his car on a road, the keys were in the ignition and he replied 'Yes' when asked by a police officer if he had driven there, the Divisional Court said that a court could properly deduce that he had been driving. It did not have to depend upon his admission; the other circumstances supported that deduction. There is no reason why the oral admission of a driver to the effect that he was driving a car should not be admissible in evidence. The Divisional Court dismissed an appeal based on the grounds that the driver had been too drunk to give a reliable confession and that it was therefore prejudicial to

admit it. Although the driver had been drinking heavily, he asked to see the custody officer and to make this admission to him. The custody officer had found him quite friendly, coherent and easy to deal with.

In relation to *'attempting to drive'*, the reader is referred to the Criminal Attempts Act 1981, which we deal with in ch 42, below, and which regulates what is required for an attempt. It is clear from the 1981 Act that what is required is the doing of an act which is more than merely preparatory to the commission of the full offence, coupled with the intention to commit the full offence. It is therefore essential that some act must have been carried out which was more than a merely preparatory step towards the process of driving, and that the person doing the act had the intention of driving. For example, if a person gets no further than sitting in the driving seat of a motor car and searching his pockets for the ignition keys, it is almost certain that the justices would find that his acts were merely preparatory and that he was not attempting to drive (although he could be convicted of the offence of being in charge with excess alcohol). On the other hand, if he finds the keys and gets as far as placing them in the ignition switch it is almost certain that the justices would find that the act was more than merely preparatory, and that therefore he was attempting to drive.

The 1981 Act also provides that a person may be guilty of an attempt even though the facts are such that the commission of the full offence is not possible. Consequently, a person who is attempting to drive even though it was not possible for him actually to drive the vehicle in those circumstances is guilty of attempting to drive it.

In relation to the offence of *'being in charge'*, as a general rule once a person takes a vehicle out on a road or other public place he remains in charge of it until he has taken it off the road or public place, unless he puts someone else in charge of it (as where he hands the ignition keys to another to prevent himself from being able to drive it) or loses effective control over the vehicle in some other way (as where it is stolen or where he has gone to bed). Persons other than the owner or a person in lawful possession or control of the vehicle may assume charge of it. In such cases consideration must be given to whether and where such a person was in the vehicle or how far from it, what he was doing, whether he was in possession of a suitable ignition key, evidence of intention to take control by driving or otherwise, and the position and circumstances of other persons who were also in the vehicle.

Section 5(2) provides that it is a defence for a person charged with 'being in charge of a motor vehicle' etc to prove that, at the time he is alleged to have committed the offence, the circumstances were such that there was no likelihood of his driving the vehicle while the proportion of alcohol in his breath, blood or urine remained likely to exceed the prescribed limit; but in determining whether there was such a likelihood the court may disregard any injury to him and any damage to the vehicle. Where the accused's car had been wheel clamped and there was no evidence to show that the clamp could have been removed by any other means than paying for release, which the accused had refused to do, it was held that there was no likelihood of his driving. It was held that the fixing of a wheel clamp did not 'damage' the vehicle; there was no intrusion into the integrity of the vehicle. Normally, the accused will only succeed in proving this defence if there is expert evidence as to the rate of alcohol destruction by the body which indicates that his alcohol level would not have been above the limit at the time he intended to drive.

'Consuming' is a wide enough term to include other methods of ingestion than through the mouth. Thus, for example, an alcohol level which may have, in part, resulted from the injection of a substance, comes about through 'consumption'.

The last element of the offence under s 5(1) which needs to be explained concerns the *prescribed limits*. They are defined by s 11 of the 1988 Act, which states that the 'prescribed limit' means, as the case may require:

(a)   35 microgrammes of alcohol in 100 ml of breath;
(b)   80 mg of alcohol in 100 ml of blood; or
(c)   107 mg of alcohol in 100 ml of urine;

or such other proportion as may be prescribed by regulations made by the Secretary of State. So far, the Secretary of State has not prescribed any other proportion.

The 35 microgrammes is roughly equivalent to the 80 and 107 mg of the two other levels.

Having set out the requirements for an offence under s 5, we must now describe the procedures which will normally precede a person being charged with that offence and which are regulated by the 1988 Act. These procedures will usually begin with a police officer on the beat requiring a 'screening' breath test; followed by an arrest (whether as a result of a positive test or of a failure to provide a breath specimen for it) and then be followed by a requirement for a specimen of breath (for an evidential breath test) or, in limited cases, a specimen of blood or urine (for analysis).

The details of the early part of this procedure are as follows.

'SCREENING' BREATH TEST

This is a preliminary test to obtain an indication whether the proportion of alcohol in a person's breath, blood or urine is likely to exceed the prescribed limit and therefore to assist a constable in deciding whether further action should be taken. The power to require a 'screening' breath test arises in the circumstances specified by s 6(1) and 6(2) of the 1988 Act.

Section 6(1)

Section 6(1) provides that:

'where a constable in uniform has reasonable cause to suspect:
(a)   that a person driving or attempting to drive or in charge of a motor vehicle on a road or other public place has alcohol in his body *or* has committed a traffic offence whilst the vehicle was in motion, or
(b)   that a person *has been* driving or attempting to drive or *been* in charge of a motor vehicle on a road or other public place with alcohol in his body and that that person still has alcohol in his body; or
(c)   that a person *has been* driving or attempting to drive or *been* in charge of a motor vehicle on a road or other public place and has committed a traffic offence whilst the vehicle was in motion;
he may, subject to s 9 which deals with hospital procedures, require him to provide a specimen of breath for a breath test.'

A number of points need to be noted and explained concerning s 6(1).

First, the constable who requires a screening breath test under s 6(1) must be in uniform both when his suspicion arises and when he makes the requirement. Whether or not a constable was in uniform is a question of fact in each case. A constable wearing his uniform except for his helmet has been held to be in uniform so long as he is easily identifiable as a constable. A court is entitled to assume that a constable was in uniform unless this point is disproved.

A second point is that the power to require a 'screening' breath test does not depend on the person actually having alcohol in his body or actually having committed a moving traffic offence. Instead, it arises where the constable has reasonable cause to suspect such a thing. More fully, a constable has power under s 6(1) to require any person *driving, attempting to drive, or in charge* on a road or other public place to undergo a 'screening' breath test where he has *reasonable cause to suspect* that that person *has alcohol in his body* or has committed a *(moving) traffic offence*. Alternatively, a constable has power under s 6(1) to require a person to undergo a 'screening' breath test where he has *reasonable cause to suspect* that that person *has been driving, attempting to drive or in charge* on any road or other public place with *alcohol in his body* and that that person still has *alcohol in his body* or has committed a *moving traffic offence*. In the second case, it is clear that the suspicion need not arise while the vehicle is in motion. Moreover, the same is true in the first case. Indeed, a uniformed constable may stop motorists, under his common law or statutory powers to do so, in order to see whether there is a reasonable suspicion that they have consumed alcohol, and if a reasonable suspicion then emerges of such consumption, go on to require a screening breath test. Thus, random stopping of motorists is not prohibited, although random breath tests are.

In the explanation just given, we referred to a *'moving traffic offence'*. This term requires further explanation.

The type of traffic offence which the constable must reasonably suspect to have been committed is defined by s 6(8), which provides that 'traffic offence' in this context means an offence under any provision of Part II of the Public Passenger Vehicles Act 1981, the Road Traffic Regulation Act 1984, the Road Traffic Offenders Act 1988 except Part III, or any provision of the Road Traffic Act 1988 except Part V. This effectively covers the range of road traffic offences which could be described as 'moving traffic offences'. All offences which are set out in regulations made under those Acts are also included within this description; for example, offences contrary to the Road Vehicles (Construction and Use) Regulations 1986 or the Road Vehicles Lighting Regulations 1989.

There are some exceptions to the definition of 'moving traffic offence' in the present context. Generally, they relate to the offence of giving driving instruction for payment without being registered or licensed under the Act, to offences related to fixed penalty procedures, and to some provisions concerning public service vehicles.

Section 6(2)

As we have already said, there is another power, under s 6(2), to require a 'screening' breath test. Section 6(2) provides that, if an accident occurs owing to the presence of a motor vehicle on a road or other public place, a constable may require any person whom he has reasonable cause to believe was driving or attempting to drive or in charge of the vehicle at the time of the accident to provide a specimen of breath for a breath test, subject to s 9 (hospital procedure). As opposed to s 6(1), a constable need not be in uniform in order to require a specimen of breath under s 6(2).

The fact that a constable's power to make a requirement of a person under s 6(2) depends on an accident having occurred owing to the presence of a motor vehicle on a road or other public place raises the question of what is *'an accident'* for the purposes of s 6(2). The answer is that 'accident' bears its ordinary meaning, and it has been held that a crash which is deliberately caused falls within that meaning. The person's vehicle need not have been physically involved but there must have been a direct causal connection between his vehicle being on the road and the accident occurring. Where a sequence of events begins on a road and leads to a vehicle leaving the road and colliding with an object some distance from the road, there is an accident for the purposes of s 6(2).

Of course, the fact that an accident has occurred owing to the presence of a motor vehicle on a road or other public place does not entitle a constable to require a specimen of breath under s 6(2) from anyone; that provision only empowers him to make such a requirement of any person whom he has *reasonable cause to believe was driving or attempting to drive or in charge of* the vehicle at the time of the accident.

The reader will remember that the power to require a breath specimen under s 6(1) is framed in terms of a constable having *reasonable cause to suspect* that a person driving etc, has alcohol in his body or has committed a moving traffic offence or having *reasonable cause to suspect* that a person has been driving etc in those circumstances. However, s 6(2) uses the term *'has reasonable cause to believe'*, which requires more than 'reasonable suspicion' since 'believe' requires more than mere suspicion and refers to having no substantial doubt about the facts. The fact that the constable uses the wrong term in expressing himself is not fatal. In one case, an officer stated in evidence that he had required the breath test because he 'suspected' that the defendant was the driver at the time of an accident. It was held that there was enough evidence to link the defendant with the accident and, whilst acknowledging that the words were different, it was recognised that the words used by the officer were no more than a careless use of language. Such decisions are not so important now that evidence of alcohol levels cannot be excluded merely because of a defect in procedure, but such an issue would still be relevant in cases of a failure to supply a screening breath test (as we explain below).

The test procedure

We now turn to the screening breath test procedure which applies once a requirement has been made. Special provisions apply where the person concerned is a patient at a hospital; we deal with these later.

A person may be required under s 6(1) or (2) to provide a specimen either at or near the place where the requirement is made. Alternatively, if the requirement is made under s 6(2) (ie following an accident) and the constable making the requirement thinks fit, a person may be required to provide the specimen at a police station specified by the constable.

Screening devices used by police officers must be approved by the Home Secretary before they may be used. Currently, the Home Secretary has approved two types of device, one which might be described as the 'blow in the bag' type of device and the other 'electronic'. Approved devices of the 'blow in the bag' type are the Alcotest 80, the Alcotest R80A and the Alcolyser. The containers of such devices show the dates beyond which devices should not be used and it is important that these dates are checked. Four electronic devices have been approved by the Home Secretary. They are the Lion Alcolmeter SL2, the Lion Alcolmeter SL2A, the Draeger Alert and the Draeger Alcotest 7410. The Alcolmeter is a battery operated device of compact size into which a plastic tube is inserted. The suspect breathes into the tube until lights appear which register a result. The instrument has three lights which act in combination. A green light indicates that there is less than 5 mg of alcohol per 100 ml of blood, amber indicates 5–70 mg, amber together with red 71–80 mg, and red alone signifies more than 80 mg. The instrument incorporates a sensor which will respond to alcohol only and it is not affected by other breath contaminants. A person supplying a sample for a screening test must blow until the lights indicate that a sufficient sample has been received. Persons with breathing problems can, on occasions, find this difficult; constables should be aware of this and assist by giving precise directions and recognising on occasions that certain persons are unable to provide such a specimen. The Alert is a detector of the semi-conductor type, the conduction increasing in proportion to the concentration of alcohol in the breath. It is larger than the SL2 but is extremely easy to operate, the lights clearly illustrating whether a sample is positive or negative. Its strength is its simplicity. The Alcotest 7410 is a one-button device of high accuracy which gives both audible and visible indication of a positive test. If an alkaline battery is used, it will provide one thousand tests before charging becomes necessary.

The instructions which accompany all screening devices warn that a breath test should not be given until at least 20 minutes have elapsed since the last intoxicating drink was taken. The reason for this is that it is the alcoholic content of deep-lung air, not mouth alcohol which is to be measured. If a drink has been taken within that period the constable should wait until 20 minutes has elapsed before carrying out the test. If a suspect driver is smoking he should be asked to stop and to take two or three deep breaths to clear the lungs of smoke. The Divisional Court has held that the innocent failure by a police officer to follow these instructions does not render the result of a subsequent analysis of a specimen by an Intoximeter device at a police station, and the arrest, unlawful.

The Detention Code of Practice, referred to in ch 4, excludes the 'specimens for analysis' procedures under the Road Traffic Act 1988, s 7 below from the provisions of the Code which relate to 'interviews'. However, no similar exclusion is made in relation to s 6 procedures. It is therefore advisable that, where there is conversation between an officer and a suspect which relates to his condition, that conversation is recorded and read and signed by the suspect. The Divisional Court refused to interfere with a decision of the justices not to exclude evidence subsequently obtained following an officer's enquiry as to whether a suspect had been drinking, to which the suspect replied, 'Yes, I've had a couple of pints'. It said that the justices, although recognising that there had been a breach of the Detention Code, were entitled to find that that breach had not been sufficiently 'significant and substantial' to merit exclusion of the evidence.

Arrest

Section 6(5) provides that a constable may arrest a person without warrant in two cases:

(a) if, as a result of a breath test, he has reasonable cause to suspect that the proportion of alcohol in that person's breath or blood exceeds the prescribed limit; or
(b) if that person has failed (see below) to provide a specimen of breath for a breath test when required to do so in pursuance of this section and the constable has reasonable cause to suspect that he has alcohol in his body.

However, a person may not be arrested by virtue of s 6(5) when he is at a hospital as a patient.

The power of arrest may therefore be exercised if a positive breath specimen is supplied or if there is a failure to provide a breath specimen. However, a driver must be requested to provide such a specimen before he can be arrested under this section, even if his conduct makes this difficult. Where an officer is assaulted and thus prevented from making a proper request, the driver should be arrested under another appropriate provision. The purpose of this power of arrest is to ensure that those suspected of having excessive alcohol in their bodies are taken to a police station to provide a specimen for analysis. It is therefore realistic to provide a power which allows a constable to arrest those who provide positive specimens and those who fail to provide screening samples.

Section 11(2) of the 1988 Act provides that the word 'fails' includes 'refusal'. If a person is given an opportunity to do something and does not do it, there is a failure to comply with that request. Where a person refuses to reply to such a clear request, there has been a failure and it is no defence to allege that the refusal to reply was consequent upon a previous caution. It is essential that the constable makes it clear to the person concerned that he is required to provide a specimen of breath. In a case where a driver refused to wait until a screening device arrived at the scene, having been properly required to provide a specimen, it was held that he had failed to provide a specimen of breath. A demand that a test be deferred until the arrival of a solicitor amounts to a refusal. There can be no acceptance subject to conditions.

The Road Traffic Act 1988, s 11(3) provides:

'A person does not provide a specimen of breath for a breath test or for analysis unless the specimen is sufficient to enable the test or analysis to be carried out, and is provided in such a way as to enable the objective of the test or analysis to be satisfactorily achieved.'

This simplifies matters for police officers. The various screening devices require breath to be supplied in various ways to allow a sufficient sample to be obtained. If sufficient breath has not been supplied there has been a failure. Where a screening device requires the illumination of two lights before a satisfactory specimen has been obtained, there is a 'failure' where only one of those lights is illuminated and a police officer is not required to 'read' such a specimen.

An important point to note about the power to arrest after a failure to provide a breath specimen is that the constable must have reasonable cause to suspect that the driver has alcohol in his body before effecting an arrest.

Clear words must be used in all cases to indicate the reason for arrest and that the person concerned is being compulsorily taken to a police station in consequence of such a failure.

Normally, a constable will exercise his power of arrest in the above two cases but this is not a pre-condition of further steps in the procedure being adopted and is unnecessary if the person concerned is quite happy to accompany the constable to a police station for the next steps in the procedure.

Entry

With one exception police officers do not have power to enter premises without the express or implied consent of the occupier for the purpose of requiring a screening breath test or making an arrest under s 6. Thus, where officers pursued a driver whom they had cause to suspect of driving with excess alcohol and they followed him into the driveway of his house without permission to carry out a breath test, the evidence of the subsequent analysis of a specimen was excluded under the provisions of the Police and Criminal Evidence Act 1984, s 78 because they had acted quite deliberately outside their powers.

The exceptional case where an officer is authorised to enter without consent to require a screening breath test, or to arrest, is provided by s 6(6), which states:

'A constable may for the purpose of requiring a person to provide a specimen of breath under sub-section (2) [which relates to accidents] in a case where he has reasonable cause to suspect that the accident involved injury to another person or of arresting him in such a case under sub-section (5) [where a person has provided a positive breath test or has failed to do so] enter (if need be by force) any place where that person is or where the constable, with reasonable cause, suspects him to be.'

Clearly, the power to enter to require a breath test is limited to cases where the entry is for the purpose of requiring a person, whom we will call X, to provide a specimen of breath under s 6(2) *in a case where a constable has reasonable cause to suspect that the accident involved injury to someone other than X.* On the other hand, it is open to question whether the power to enter to effect an arrest under s 6(5) is limited to cases where a constable has reasonable cause to suspect that the accident involved injury to someone other than X. The use of the words 'in such a case' in the relevant part of s 6(6) is such that it may mean that the power is so limited. That the power under s 6(6) is so limited is supported by the words of Home Office Circular 35/1983 published in 1983. If this is the correct interpretation, a constable will be empowered by s 6(6) to enter premises to breath test a driver involved in an 'injury to another' accident or to arrest under s 6(5) where there has been an 'injury to another' accident, but he will not be empowered by s 6(6) to enter to conduct a breath test or to arrest under s 6(5) in any other case following a positive breath test or a failure to provide a breath specimen. This can hardly be supported as a logical or practical distinction. However, whatever the original intention of those who drafted the legislation, the words of s 6(6) are at least capable of being interpreted in the wider sense that such an entry may be effected to carry out an arrest which would be authorised by s 6(5).

The issue may prove to be unimportant in *some* cases because s 4(7) provides a power of entry to a constable to enter any place for the purpose of arresting a person whom he has reasonable cause to suspect of committing an offence under s 4 (driving, etc whilst unfit through drink or drugs), if that person is in that place or the constable, with reasonable cause, suspects him to be there. The circumstances may be such that a person who has either provided a positive specimen or has refused to provide one can be arrested under s 4(6) on reasonable suspicion of driving etc when under the influence of drink or drugs (which requires proof of his ability to drive properly being impaired). However, not every case where there is a reasonable suspicion of driving etc with alcohol concentration above the prescribed limit (s 5) gives rise to a reasonable suspicion of driving etc whilst unfit (s 4).

A refusal or deliberate failure to admit a police officer acting in the proper exercise of one of these powers of entry amounts to the offence of wilful obstruction of a constable (pp 573-574).

Offence of failing to provide a breath specimen required under s 6

A person who, without reasonable excuse, fails to provide a specimen of breath when required to do so in pursuance of s 6 of the 1988 Act commits an offence contrary to s 6(4) of that Act.

This offence can be committed notwithstanding that the motorist has not been warned that refusal to supply a specimen will be an offence.

We have already explained what constitutes a 'failure to provide a specimen of breath'. There cannot be a conviction for this offence unless the specimen has been required under s 6, and it will not have been so required if the requirement made is invalid for some reason. For example, if the constable is a trespasser at the time of requiring a screening breath test he will be behaving unlawfully and his requirement will not be valid.

In addition, there cannot be a conviction for failing to provide a specimen if the requisite procedure is not validly administered, as will be the case if the device used is not an approved one, or if it is defective, or if the constable fails to comply with the manufacturer's instructions as to *assembly*. However, if the constable realises the defect or mistake he may validly require another breath test to be taken on another device. Provided the constable acts in good faith and not negligently, non-compliance by him with the manufacturer's instructions as to the use of the device does not invalidate the test unless the non-compliance is prejudicial to the accused.

A person cannot be convicted of failing to provide a specimen of breath for a screening breath test unless his failure was without reasonable excuse. It is not a reasonable excuse that the accused did not think that he had consumed any alcohol, nor that he mistakenly believed that the requirement made was invalid, nor that he had consumed alcohol after driving.

It has been stated in a number of cases that no excuse can be adjudged reasonable unless the accused was physically or mentally unable to provide the specimen or its provision would entail a substantial risk to his health. This covers cases such as where the accused was unable to supply a sufficient specimen of breath because of a medical condition, such as bronchitis or shock, or where he was concussed and unable to appreciate the requirement made to him. However, it has also been held that a foreigner who is unable to understand the purpose of the requirement and the penal consequence of a failure to comply has a reasonable excuse. Not surprisingly, a person who has made himself so drunk as to be unable to understand these matters does not have a reasonable excuse, nor does the fact that the accused does not provide a specimen because he is in a state of self-induced agitation. See also p 426.

DRIVING ETC UNDER INFLUENCE OF DRINK OR DRUGS

Section 4 of the 1988 Act provides that:

'(1) A person who, when driving or attempting to drive a mechanically propelled vehicle on a road or other public place, is unfit to drive through drink or drugs is guilty of an offence.
(2) Without prejudice to subsection (1) above, a person who, when in charge of a mechanically propelled vehicle which is on a road or other public place, is unfit to drive through drink or drugs is guilty of an offence.'

Many of the elements of these offences have been dealt with already in relation to s 5. It is worth noting that s 4(3) provides a similar defence for persons charged with 'being in charge' to that provided by s 5(2) for those charged with the corresponding offence under s 5, viz that it is a defence for the accused to prove that there was no likelihood of his driving the vehicle while he remained unfit through drink or drugs.

It remains to be added that 'drink' means alcoholic drink and 'drug' means any intoxicant other than alcohol, including medicines and glue. However, there must be direct evidence that there was an unfitness to drive which was the direct result of drink or drugs. If a person's condition is due to a hypoglycaemic attack, it may be that the attack was the direct result of an injection of insulin, eg because it was injected in too great a quantity. However, other factors, such as failure to eat, may have been the real, effective cause of the attack, in which case the person will not have been under the influence of the drug.

Unfitness to drive

The element of these offences which does call for further explanation is that of unfitness to drive. Section 4(5) of the 1988 Act provides that a person is to be taken to be unfit to drive if his ability to drive properly is for the time being impaired. The evidence before the court on this point will normally include evidence of the accused's driving before his vehicle was stopped; any evidence of driving apparently outside the pattern of normal driving is relevant in that it may show some impairment of the ability to drive properly. In addition, the evidence of the speech of the accused after he was stopped, together with his general manner and demeanour and any apparent lack of co-ordination or control over bodily movements, may be important. The evidence before the court will also normally include the report of a medical examination by a police surgeon, which is extremely important since the surgeon will have required the accused to carry out a series of tests indicative of his ability (or lack of ability) to drive properly. Lastly, the evidence may include the result of the analysis of a specimen of breath, blood or urine required under s 7 of the Act. The procedure relating to such specimens, and the rules relating to the use of their analysis as evidence, are essentially the same as for the offences of driving etc with excess alcohol; we deal with these matters shortly. It must be remembered that the presence of a drug can be detected by a blood or urine test, but not by a breath test.

If an arrest has been effected under s 4 because of alcohol excess, and a subsequent evidential test shows that the driver is below the limits prescribed by s 5, a conviction under s 4 is unlikely unless there is compelling evidence of impairment. The Home Office Circular suggests that if the arrest is for impairment and the evidential breath testing machine shows that there is less than 35 microgrammes, a doctor should be called if drugs are suspected, but if not and there is evidence of impairment, the person should be charged with the appropriate s 4 offence. In such circumstances it is submitted the evidence of impairment would have to be very strong. In any case, the additional evidence of a doctor as to that degree of impairment would assist the prosecution's case. The lack of it could be fatal to a prosecution.

Arrest

By s 4(6) a constable may arrest a person without warrant if he has reasonable cause to suspect that a person *is* or *has been* committing an offence under s 4. If a screening breath test required under s 6 proves to be negative, a constable may still arrest under s 4(6) if he suspects the person is unfit to drive through drugs, or perhaps a combination of drink or drugs.

The power under s 4(7) to enter premises for the purpose of arresting a person under s 4(6) has already been discussed. As we have seen, s 4(7) permits a constable to enter (by force if necessary) any place where that person is or where, with reasonable cause, the constable suspects him to be.

PROVISION OF SPECIMEN FOR ANALYSIS

Section 7(1) of the 1988 Act provides:

'In the course of an investigation into whether a person has committed an offence under s 3A [causing death by careless driving while under the influence of drink or drugs etc], or ss 4 or 5 of this Act a constable may, subject to the following provisions of this section and s 9 below (hospital procedures), require him:

(a) to provide two specimens of breath for analysis by means of a device of a type approved by the Secretary of State; or

(b) to provide a specimen of blood or urine for a laboratory test.'

The offence under s 3A is dealt with in ch 16.

The fact that a requirement under s 7(1) can be made 'in the course of an investigation' into whether a person has committed an offence under ss 4 or 5 indicates that it is not necessary that a screening breath test should have been required (although in a case under s 5 it will normally have been) and that, if there has been such a test, it is irrelevant that there has been some breach in the procedure relating to it or that the constable has acted unlawfully in some other way. Thus, where a constable, in good faith, had administered a screening breath test in a public house car park which, at the time, was not a public place, the subsequent specimen for analysis was held to have been properly required 'in the course of an investigation'. The procedure under s 7 does not constitute an 'interview' for the purposes of the Detention Code referred to in ch 4. However, a magistrates' court can exclude the evidence obtained from the analysis of a specimen if it appears to the court that, having regard to all the circumstances, including non-compliance with the screening test procedure under s 6, the admission of that evidence would have such an adverse effect on the fairness of the proceedings that the court ought not to admit it. This would be an application of s 78 of the Police and Criminal Evidence Act 1984. Section 78 was so applied in a case where a screening test was improperly required (because the officer did not have one of the requisite reasonable suspicions specified by s 6). The Divisional Court held that, since the defendant had been denied the protection afforded by s 6, the prosecutor had obtained evidence which he would not otherwise have obtained and, as a result, the defendant was significantly prejudiced in resisting the charge. The magistrates, it held, were therefore entitled to exclude the evidence, having directed themselves correctly in law.

In normal circumstances, a person required to provide a specimen for analysis will have been arrested, either under s 6(5) or under s 4(6). However, s 7 also permits the procedure to be followed if a person is at a police station other than under arrest, or if he has been arrested on suspicion of an offence other than one under ss 4 or 5. Thus, if a driver reports an accident at a police station, and it is suspected that he has alcohol in his body, he may be required to provide specimens for analysis. Similarly, a person arrested for some other offence (eg burglary) may be so required if it is discovered that he has been driving a motor vehicle. No matter how a person came to be at a police station, if he is there in the course of an investigation into whether an offence under ss 4 or 5 has been committed by him, a specimen may be required under s 7. In addition, a person who alleges that he was a passenger, not the driver of a car, at the time in question, may be lawfully required to provide a specimen as 'a person under an investigation for an offence under either ss 4 or 5'. It is not necessary to show that he was driving. Although, of course, liability for an offence under ss 4 or 5 will depend on proof that he was driving, attempting to drive or in charge at the material time, he can be convicted under s 7 of failing to provide a specimen even if he was not driving etc.

We now turn to the procedure to be adopted under s 7; it should be noted that where the person in question is a patient at a hospital a special procedure, governed by s 9, must be followed.

The specimen to be required

The important part of the procedure under s 7 is that, normally, it is two specimens of *breath* which must be required and that it is only in exceptional circumstances that alternative samples may be required.

Section 7(2) provides that a requirement to provide specimens of *breath* can only be made at a *police station*.

Section 7(3) provides that a requirement to provide a specimen of *blood* or *urine* can only be made at a *police station* or at a *hospital*; and that it cannot be made at a police station unless:

(a) the constable making the requirement has reasonable cause to believe that for medical reasons a specimen of breath cannot be provided (because of inability) or should not be required (for some other reason, such as the taking of a drug which affects blood/alcohol levels). Intoxication preventing a blood specimen being provided is a medical reason; so is shock and distress if those conditions genuinely prevent the provision of a specimen. Provided that a reasonable cause to believe that there are medical reasons exists, it is irrelevant that the constable himself does not believe that for medical reasons a breath specimen cannot be provided or should not be required;

(b) at the time the requirement is made, an approved device or a reliable approved device is not available at the police station, or it is then for any other reason not practicable to use such a device there;

(bb) an approved device has been used at the police station but the constable who required the specimen of breath has reasonable cause to believe that the device has not produced a reliable indication of the proportion of alcohol in the breath of the person concerned; or

(c) the suspected offence is one under s 4 of the Act and the constable making the requirement has been advised by a medical practitioner that the condition of the person required to provide the specimen might be due to some drug;

but may then be made notwithstanding that the person required to provide the specimen has already provided or been required to provide two specimens of breath.

The fact that, where the alleged offence is one under s 4, the constable has been advised by a medical practitioner that the person's condition may be due to some drug, may be proved by oral evidence from the doctor or by the police officer saying what the doctor said to him. In addition, where unchallenged evidence has been given by the custody officer as to what the medical practitioner said and did and as to his completion of a procedural form recording the signed observations of the doctor, justices are entitled to find that this advice had been given. Whilst the endorsement signed by the doctor is, in its contents, hearsay, the fact that the medical practitioner had signed the endorsement and said things which led the officer to complete the remainder of the form in a particular way, indicating that it was concerned with impairment through drugs after medical advice, has been held to be a matter to which the justices were entitled to have regard.

If a constable requires a specimen of blood or urine under s 7(3), the decision as to whether it should be blood or urine is for the constable and he does not have to invite the motorist to express his own preference before making the decision. However, if the constable intends to require a specimen of blood, under the provisions of s 7(3), there are two mandatory requirements which must be fulfilled:

(a) he must, in accordance with s 7(7), warn the person that a failure to provide a specimen may render him liable to prosecution (if this is not done the evidence of the analysis of the specimen is inadmissible);
(b) he must inform the person of the reason why specimens of breath could not be taken.

There are further factors which the constable should bring to the attention of the person concerned. Whilst these factors have been held not to be mandatory by the House of Lords, the House has said that police officers, in order to seek to ensure that a driver is aware of the role of a doctor, should continue to use a formula recommended by Lord Bridge within a previous judgement given by the House. The additional factors included in the formula are:

(a) that the driver is informed that he is required to provide a specimen of blood or urine but that it is for the constable to decide which;
(b) that his only right to object to giving blood will be for medical reasons to be determined by a doctor;
(c) where a driver makes a representation in answer to a question about whether a specimen of blood should be taken, the constable must consider whether the statement proffered is capable of being a medical reason. It is a question of fact whether the statement raises a potential medical reason. A court is entitled to find on the facts that a police officer was not obliged to investigate the matter further;
(d) if the constable concludes that there is no medical reason, he may require a blood specimen, but if he has doubts about the matter, he should seek the opinion of a medical practitioner.

In relation to these non-mandatory requirements, the House of Lords said that what was necessary is that the driver should be aware, whether or not he was told by a police officer, of the doctor's role *so that he does not suffer prejudice*. If a driver appreciates that a blood specimen would be taken by a doctor and not by a police officer, a charge should not be dismissed merely because a police officer has failed to tell the driver that a specimen would be taken by a doctor. The House said that a court should follow a two-stage process:

(a) It should consider whether all of these matters had been brought to the attention of the driver. If the answer to that question was 'No' it should then consider (b).
(b) In relation to the non-mandatory requirements, the issue is whether the police officer's failure to give the full formula deprived the driver of the opportunity to exercise any option open to him, or caused him to exercise it in a way which he would not have done had everything been said.
   (i) If the answer is 'Yes' the driver should be acquitted.
   (ii) If the answer is 'No' the police officer's failure to use the full formula should not be a reason for an acquittal.

The House of Lords said that it would only be in exceptional circumstances that a court would acquit on the grounds that a driver suffered prejudice without having heard evidence from the driver himself which raised the issue of prejudice. These issues are questions of fact. If the court, having heard the driver's evidence, is not satisfied beyond reasonable doubt that he was not prejudiced, he should be acquitted.

The House of Lords also ruled on this occasion that there is no statutory requirement, nor any considerations of fairness, which requires a police officer to ask a driver if any non-medical reason exists in consequence of which a specimen of blood should not be taken. Any such matter might support 'a reasonable cause for failure to provide a specimen' but that is a matter for a court.

Where a constable said in evidence that she had completed the standard procedure form but could not recall the words which she used an appeal was allowed against conviction, the Divisional Court expressing surprise that the justices accepted a submission that there was no evidence of the giving of the warning, as the standard procedure was well known to them. If they were in doubt they should have asked for an explanation and the production of the forms.

A 'reliable device' referred to in s 7(3)(b) is one which the police officer concerned reasonably believes to be reliable. The police officer must believe that the device *is unreliable, not* that *it might be.* Where a police officer thought that the device might be unreliable because the motorist did not appear to be as badly affected as the device indicated and required an alternative specimen, the conviction was quashed on the grounds that a belief that the device might be unreliable is insufficient. However, where a device fails to produce a print-out of its analysis and calibration, this is a malfunction which justifies the officer in concluding that the device is not reliable. It should also be noted that it is unnecessary for the officer at the time, or for a court, to be *absolutely certain* that a machine has malfunctioned. The officer's genuine and reasonable *belief* that a machine has malfunctioned and is therefore unreliable is sufficient. Where an officer reasonably believes that a device is unreliable and unsuccessfully requests the motorist to supply a blood specimen, the breath specimen is subsequently admissible if the officer then finds that the device had in fact operated satisfactorily and had given a correct reading.

It is 'not practicable to use a device' if there is no officer available at the station who has been trained to use the device.

Where a defendant has provided two specimens of breath on a machine which is then found to be defective, he may be lawfully required to provide two further specimens of breath for analysis by another device instead of being required to provide blood or urine. Where this involves a suspect being taken to another police station, the Divisional Court has said that it might be wise, *as a matter of an abundance of caution,* to repeat, at the second police station, the statutory warning that failure may render him liable to prosecution.

Section 7(3)(bb) was inserted by the Criminal Procedure and Investigations Act 1996. Section 7(3)(b) requires evidence that the device, viewed subjectively in the circumstances, was unreliable. It is therefore necessary for the prosecution to prove that the police officer believed that the *device* was unreliable and that there was material or evidence on which, at the time, he could reasonably have formed that view. While decisions of the High Court made in respect of s 7(3)(b) remain valid, the addition of s 7(3)(bb) makes, in some circumstances, the issue of the reliability of the machine itself irrelevant. An alternative specimen may be required where a breath testing device has been used and the constable who required the specimens has reasonable cause to believe that the device has not produced *a reliable indication* of the proportion of alcohol in the breath of the person concerned. Thus, if a device produces two readings which indicate significant differences in the levels of alcohol, it is open to the constable to require an alternative specimen if he reasonably believes that the device has not produced a reliable indication of alcohol in the breath. The latest evidential breath testing equipment incorporates new software which enables it to identify and flag up automatically where it is suspected an interfering substance may be present, or the alleged offender produces mouth alcohol, or the difference between the readings of two specimens is greater than 15 per cent. In such situations a constable will be able to require blood or urine as an alternative.

Specimen of breath

Section 7 requires that the two specimens of breath which have been required under it be analysed by means of a device approved by the Secretary of State. A motorist who has provided one specimen of breath which exceeded the prescribed limit but has failed to provide a second specimen cannot, on the basis of that specimen, be convicted of driving with excess alcohol. He can, however, be convicted of failing to provide a specimen of breath.

Currently, the latest devices to be approved by the Secretary of State are as follows.

Camic Datamaster The machine measures the amount of ethyl alcohol present in a person's breath. It looks only for ethyl alcohol and rejects any other substance which is present in a specimen of breath. The breath analyser is concerned with infrared absorption as a means of determining the presence of alcohol. The machine is combined with a microprocessor (computer) which calculates the validity of any sample provided. A 'run' button initiates the process of analysis and a 'print' button initiates a print-out of the last test. Accuracy checks are fully automatic. Print-outs from the Datamaster show the standard details from satisfactory specimens and record any circumstances in which a non-valid specimen has been detected. The machine detects and records the presence of 'interfering substances'. The clock can be reset by the operator to run in local time in the same way as setting a clock on the standard type of video recorder.

Lion Intoxilyser 6000 This is a microprocessor controlled, multi-filtering infrared spectrometer. It works on the principle that the greater the concentration of alcohol in the breath, the greater the amount of infrared light which is absorbed. It will detect any interfering substance. The machine indicates its status. When ready for use it indicates 'standby'. It indicates it is fully powered up and is ready for analysis, or has started to analyse a specimen, when it indicates 'analyse'. The print-outs include the standard details where there is a satisfactory specimen and otherwise indicate the defect which has been detected. So far as the clock is concerned, the computer software changes the reading between summer and winter time without intervention from the operator.

Intoximeter EC/IR The machine incorporates two separately-controlled systems dealing with the analytical functions of the machine and the input/output control system which controls all aspects of the user interface and controls test sequences and protocols. The flow of electrons through the fuel cell is measured and this indicates the amount of alcohol consumed by the fuel cell. The infrared analysis system follows the general pattern of analysis and detects the presence of ethanol. Mouth alcohol and other 'interfering substances' are detected. The use of the 'enter' key initiates a test and the 'P' key produces a print-out of the latest test. The machine incorporates an internal clock and calendar.

Analysis of breath by the machines

Instructors are trained by the Home Office to teach the use of the breath testing machines. The devices have been well designed to overcome the problems likely to arise from an evidential viewpoint. At the outset the devices are correctly calibrated but in actual use the devices check themselves for accuracy. They check their correct calibration both before and after each of the two breath samples and a record is made of those calibration checks on the eventual print-out slip. The slip therefore shows two separate readings of alcohol levels sandwiched between records of calibration checks to ensure that the devices are operating correctly. The accused is present throughout the procedure and has the opportunity to see the device at work. The officer carrying out the test is not obliged to explain to the motorist that the second specimen must be provided within three minutes of the first, or the test will abort.

The devices provide a timed and dated print-out which gives evidence of two separate readings of alcohol content in the breath of the accused. The normal procedure thereafter is that the constable who has operated the device certifies all copies of the print-out which shows, in addition to the readings, the particulars of the person from whom the sample is obtained, the signature of the officer, and the signature of the person (or a record that such a signature was refused). The constable's statement declares the lower of the two readings given by the device to be at the specified level and certifies that copies of the statement were signed by him and by the accused, or that the accused refused. Where a print-out is not produced in evidence and no oral evidence is given in relation to correct calibration, it is open to a court to find that calibration was correct where there is evidence that the machine was used by a trained operator.

The three devices are 'computers' for the purposes of the Police and Criminal Evidence Act 1984, s 69 and it is therefore necessary for the constable to certify that the computer had been properly used, was operating properly (and if not the defect was not such as would affect the production of the document) and that operating rules had been observed, see p 157. However, where a procedural form was offered in evidence and the certificate stating that the computer was operating correctly had not been fully completed in the spaces left for the insertion of particulars, the Divisional Court said that the justices were entitled to presume, from other evidence such as:

(a) the presence of a trained operator;
(b) the fact that calibration had been checked and found to be correct; and
(c) that the operator had not indicated, at the place where opportunity was provided, that the machine was not working,

that the computer was working. Similarly, where the sergeant had, when deleting a part of the procedural form which did not apply to the procedure which he was following, inadvertently struck out a part of the completed certificate, the Divisional Court said that the justices had been entitled to find that the certificate was valid. No objection had been made in respect of the forms which had been served on the accused and it was obvious in view of the fact that proceedings had been taken, that the part of the certificate had been deleted in error. The fact that the clock on such a device is registering an incorrect time or date is not such a defect as would affect the production of such a document, where satisfactory evidence is offered to that effect. Nor is the fact that the printer omitted the second half of the first character and the second character in every line and printed some parts in smaller print. Provided that the part of the device which is a 'computer' was operating correctly at the time and that it was calibrated and correct, the malfunctioning of the printer does not affect in any way the manner in which the device processes, stores or retrieves the information which is used to generate the statement offered in evidence. The Divisional Court has also ruled that magistrates were not perverse in finding that a device was operating correctly in the case of a refusal, where the police officer had recorded that the machine aborted after only one minute, as opposed to the three minutes which it allegedly allowed. Expert evidence had been given by an experienced engineer to the effect that he had not encountered, in 20 years, an incident involving such a machine aborting after only one minute. The justices had been entitled to conclude that the officer had made an error in recording the time at which the machine aborted.

The officer also certifies that he handed a copy of the statement to the accused who accepted, or declined to accept it. The mere fact that the copy handed to the accused is not signed by the officer does not affect the validity of the original. However, the Act does not restrict evidence of the test to documentary evidence. Oral evidence may be given of the results of a test should the prosecutor, for some reason, choose not to use the simplified procedure. If this is done, oral evidence of calibration should also be given. It will be advisable, in such cases, to serve a copy of the evidence of the police operator on the defendant in accordance with the Criminal Justice Act 1967, s 9.

Defence solicitors have no right to obtain documents kept in relation to breath testing devices, such as the log, repair reports and memory roll with a view to searching for material which might support a submission that the device was defective. They must rely upon the prosecution to fulfil its duty to disclose material evidence which might be of assistance to the defence. The reliability of an approved device can be challenged either by direct evidence of some malfunctioning or by evidence from which the inference of unreliability can reasonably be drawn.

Section 8 provides that it is only the lower of the two readings given by the machine which may be used as evidence; the other must be disregarded. Where one of the two required readings is not obtained within the same operating cycle of the machine, a second cycle must be commenced. In such a case it is the lower of the first specimen taken and the first of the second cycle which should be offered in evidence. However, where neither of the specimens in the first cycle is valid, a second cycle is undertaken and third and fourth specimens are effectively the first and second specimens recognised by the machine.

Section 11(3) applies to specimens of breath for analysis. It provides that a person does not provide such a specimen unless it is sufficient to enable the test or the analysis to be carried out, and is provided in such a way as to enable the objective of the test or analysis to be satisfactorily achieved. This is an important provision, as it is necessary for the person providing the specimen to continue blowing until the indicator lights signify that sufficient breath has been obtained for analysis. If sufficient is not provided, there has been a 'failure' (see later).

Statutory option to replace specimen of breath with an alternative specimen

The prescribed limit in relation to alcohol in the breath is at present 35 microgrammes of alcohol in 100 ml of breath. In practice, machines are kind to persons suspected of these offences but, nevertheless, s 8 provides that if the specimen with the lower proportion of alcohol contains no more than 50 microgrammes of alcohol in 100 ml of breath the person may claim that it should be replaced by a specimen of blood or urine. This is called the 'statutory option'. It applies even though the motorist admits driving with excess alcohol. The burden is upon the person from whom the specimen is required to exercise that option. However, he must be informed of his right to exercise it, unless he makes this impossible (as where he refuses to listen and walks away). Police officers must take care, when explaining this right, not to say anything which might have the effect of dissuading a person from exercising this right, or of depriving him of the opportunity to exercise the option, or of causing him to exercise it in a different way from that which he would have adopted if everything had been explained. If they do say something which might have one of these effects, any conviction resulting from the original analysis will be quashed. The decision whether a 'replacement specimen' shall be of blood or urine is for the constable. In the light of this it is somewhat surprising that he must inform the motorist that he may claim blood or urine.

On the other hand it is not necessary to invite him to express a preference as to whether the specimen should be of blood or urine (since it suffices that he is told that, if he exercises the right to have a replacement specimen taken it will be for the police officer to decide whether that specimen is to be of blood or urine). The House of Lords has ruled that where a police officer decides to require an alternative specimen of blood he must inform the person that the specimen of breath which he has given which contains the lower proportion of alcohol does not exceed 50 microgrammes in 100 millilitres of breath. See pp 413-415 for non-mandatory procedural requirements in relation to the provision of a specimen of blood. In a s 8(2) case, in addition to telling the driver that a specimen of blood 'will be taken by a doctor unless he considers that there are medical reasons for not taking blood', the constable should ask the driver if there are any medical reasons why a specimen of blood could or should not be taken by a doctor. The motorist should be told of the role of the doctor at the outset of the procedure. Where a police officer has, at the outset, explained the whole procedure to a suspect who then exercises the option, it is not essential that the whole procedure be repeated when the suspect exercises the option. The reason is that the information will still be present and effective in the driver's mind. The Divisional Court has held that it is not *strictly* necessary for a police officer to inform the suspect that the breath specimen which that person has provided exceeds the statutory limit, since the fact that an alternative is being offered makes it obvious that the specimen provided shows an alcohol content in excess of the limit. Similarly, where an officer said that the replacement specimen would be used *for court purposes* the Divisional Court said that while those words served no useful purpose they were not misleading.

A suspect has no right to legal advice before deciding whether or not to exercise this option; the requirements of fairness inherent in the statutory option entitle the suspect to know of his option but do not entitle him to legal advice as to the result of exercising it. If a person having been refused access to legal advice declines to exercise his option, the original specimen is admissible. It would seem that if a suspect does not understand that the option exists, because, eg, of a breakdown in communication, the original specimen could be excluded by the court, although it will not be if the suspect's inability to understand is due wholly or partly to his consumption of alcohol. Where the option has been offered and refused, but the suspect then changes his mind, it is for the justices to decide, in accordance with the evidence, whether the procedure had come to an end at a time when the motorist changed his mind. It is likely that a more or less immediate change of mind will be acceptable as in other similar circumstances such words have been held to be 'relevant words and conduct to be taken into account'. However, once the procedure has moved on to the next stage, justices will have grounds to support a conclusion that the issue of acceptance or refusal had been finalised in which case a claim to exercise the option would be ineffective. Where an accused initially declined to exercise such option, but agreed to do so after legal advice one hour later, a court was held to be entitled to decide that enough time had passed to bring the statutory procedure to an end, and to admit evidence of the proportion of alcohol in his breath.

If the option to provide a blood or urine specimen is taken and a blood or urine specimen is provided, the results of the analysis of that specimen at the laboratory replace the lower of the readings of the breath specimen obtained by the machine for evidential purposes, regardless of whether the reading is higher or lower.

Where a motorist gives a reason for not giving blood, which may amount to a medical reason (eg a medically recognised phobia against needles is such a reason), the police officer should ask him for an explanation of that reason (because this may establish that the alleged reason is unfounded) or, if necessary, call a doctor to establish whether there is a medical reason. If this is not done (for example where the motorist is a diabetic who is used to injections but nevertheless claims that he does not like other people putting needles into him), the prosecution cannot rely on the specimen of breath supplied. On the other hand, where a motorist says that he would prefer to provide urine as he does not like needles but accepts that there was no reason why a specimen of blood could not, or should not, be taken by a doctor, and then refuses to supply blood, the police officer is under no obligation to make further enquiries about the motorist's fear of needles. The motorist's two replies, taken together, did not create sufficient doubt as to a medical reason. Consequently, the prosecution will be entitled to rely upon evidence of the breath specimen.

It is a question of fact whether a driver's statement to the effect that he cannot provide blood raises a potential medical reason for not providing a blood specimen and that a court is entitled to find, on the facts, that a police officer was not obliged to investigate the matter further. The Divisional Court has held that, where a driver replied 'I do take tablets' when asked if there was a medical reason why he could not or should not give blood, this was capable in principle of being a valid reason and the police officer should not have gone on to arrange for a specimen of blood to be taken without making enquiries as to the nature of the medication and seeking medical advice if necessary.

Where a motorist has opted to replace the analysis of a specimen of breath with that of a specimen of blood which he opts to provide, it is not necessary for the prosecution to prove the calibration of the breath testing device. The positive specimen of breath, in such circumstances, is no more than a prerequisite for the supply of a specimen of blood; the analysis of the breath specimen ceases to have any probative value in proving the offence.

In addition, where a driver is unable to understand the offer of the option, since his consumption of alcohol has contributed to his inability to comprehend its nature, he cannot allege that the breath specimen became inadmissible because of his failure to comprehend the procedure.

If a motorist given the statutory option is asked to provide a blood specimen, but the police officer is unable to contact a doctor, the police officer has power to ask the motorist to provide a urine specimen instead. If the motorist is unable to do so (eg because he has visited the lavatory in the meanwhile), the lower of the two breath specimens can be used in evidence since the statutory option procedure only prohibits either specimen of breath being used if a blood or urine specimen is provided under it.

Specimens of blood or urine

The option to provide blood or urine in the event of a reading being no more than 50 microgrammes on an evidential breath testing machine has already been explained. Leaving aside this and the case (dealt with later) where the person concerned is a patient at a hospital, the only other exceptions to the rule that evidence must be obtained by means of such a machine are in the event of medical reasons, unavailability of a machine (or of a reliable machine), unreliability of indication, or where the person's condition might be due to a drug; see above.

If an alternative specimen is to be provided, it is the constable who is making the requirement who decides whether it is to be blood or urine. The only exception to this rule is where a medical practitioner is of the opinion that, on medical grounds, blood cannot or should not be taken, in which case the specimen must be of urine. The constable must ask the driver whether there is any reason why a specimen of blood cannot or should not be taken from him by a doctor. There is no obligation for the officer to ask specifically whether there is any such reason based on medical grounds.

Where a medical reason is given (for example that the motorist is taking tablets) there must be evidence that the police officer took this into account or had considered whether it should be a medical reason. Although medical possibilities might appear to be far fetched, it is impossible to *know* that this is so. There must be evidence that the officer has asked questions. Where a 'medical reason' offered is capable of being valid the officer must refer the matter to a medical practitioner. If he does not, a requirement will not have been made pursuant to the Act and evidence of the resulting analysis will be inadmissible.

Where a constable requires blood as an alternative and the person required to give blood refuses but offers urine as an alternative, there is a 'failure' unless such a medical reason exists.

If a specimen of blood is taken, the Road Traffic Offenders Act 1988, s 15(4) provides that it must be disregarded unless it was taken from the accused with his consent by a medical practitioner. Evidence that it was so taken may be given by a certificate signed by the medical practitioner. Blood specimen kits are provided by the forensic science laboratories and are kept at police stations.

A urine specimen must, by s 7(5), be provided within one hour of the requirement and after the provision of a previous specimen. This means that a specimen must be taken and discarded, and another provided (for analysis) within one hour of the requirement. It is a question of fact for the justices to determine as to whether a period of one hour has passed since the requirement was made. Where justices had found that a requirement had been made at 2.10 am and no specimen had been provided by 3.10 am, the Divisional Court declined to become involved in consideration of the possibility of a few seconds discrepancy. It has been held that a constable was entitled to require a specimen of urine where, the breath-analysis device being inoperable, he had required blood but a doctor was unable to obtain such a specimen when the motorist's vein collapsed. The Divisional Court said that the officer's right to change his mind continued up to the time at which *blood was actually taken*. This change of mind can take place either before or after a compliance with a requirement, or after a refusal to supply blood. The rule, therefore, is that an unproductive request for one specimen does not prevent a subsequent request for another specimen from being valid.

This proposition was supported where, after being asked whether there was any medical or other reason why blood should or could not be taken, the motorist said, 'Yes, there is a reason. Ask the doctor.' He then alleged that this had something to do with a condition from which he had suffered when in the army. The sergeant then asked if he would supply blood and he said 'No comment.' The motorist submitted that he could not be guilty of failing to supply urine as he had already refused to supply blood and at that stage he should have been charged with failure to supply blood and the procedure should have ended. The Divisional Court said that the sergeant, having been thwarted in his attempt to obtain a specimen of blood, was perfectly entitled to ask for a specimen of urine and the motorist's refusal to do so amounted to an offence.

Section 15(5) provides that where, at the time a blood or urine specimen was required of the accused, he asked to be provided with such a specimen, evidence of the proportion of alcohol found in the specimen is not admissible on behalf of the prosecution unless the specimen is one of two parts into which the specimen was divided *at the time* it was provided and one part was given to the accused. 'At the time' does not mean 'then and there' nor 'in the presence of the accused'. It suffices that the division is closely linked in time and part of the same event as the taking of the sample. It is, however, desirable that the division takes place in the presence of the accused. There is no obligation to inform a motorist that he may request part of the specimen. Provided that at his request the specimen has been divided and one part has been given to the accused, but it is handed back to the police for some reason, it is irrelevant that he never collects it; the statutory requirement is satisfied, and evidence of the alcohol level in the part retained by the police is admissible.

When a specimen of blood or urine has been obtained from a person, the labels identifying the samples with that person must be carefully made out and attached securely to the samples. The sample is sent to the forensic science laboratory with completed forms FSL1.

HOSPITAL PATIENTS

Section 9 of the 1988 Act lays down a special procedure which applies while a person is at a hospital as a patient. It is a question of fact, for the justices to decide, whether or not a person is a patient at a hospital at a particular time. Section 9 states that such a person must not be required to provide a specimen of breath for a screening breath test, nor a specimen of blood or urine for analysis, unless the medical practitioner in immediate charge of his case has been notified of the proposal to make the requirement.

If the medical practitioner objects on the ground that the requirement, or the provision of a specimen, or (in the case of a blood or urine specimen) the warning about the consequences of failing to provide it would be prejudicial to the proper care and treatment of the patient, the requirement in question must not be made.

If there is no such objection and the requirement is then made, it must be for the provision of a specimen at the hospital. Evidential breath tests cannot be conducted at a hospital, so that a blood or urine specimen must be required in lieu.

It should be noted that if a screening breath test undergone by a patient proves positive, or he fails to undergo it, he may not be arrested, but this does not prejudice the rest of the procedure being followed.

The procedure in relation to hospital patients is strictly controlled. The steps which a constable should take in a 'hospital case' are as follows:

(a) seek out the medical practitioner in charge of the case;
(b) request his consent to the provision of a screening breath test explaining the method of operating the particular device to be used;
(c) obtain that consent before proceeding further. The doctor will give consent if the process is not prejudicial to care or treatment;
(d) if consent is obtained, require a screening breath test;
(e) if the test is negative, explain that there will be no further action;
(f) if the test is positive or the patient fails to provide it, obtain the medical practitioner's consent to the taking of a specimen for laboratory analysis, after having explained the procedure. It must be of blood or urine in the case of hospital patients; and
(g) if consent is obtained, obtain a specimen of blood with the consent of the person, the sample being taken by a medical practitioner, or obtain a urine specimen followed within one hour by a second urine specimen (the evidential specimen).

Within the terms of s 9 it is not strictly necessary to obtain a screening breath test before requiring a specimen for analysis but the explanatory circular states that it is assumed that this will be done. It is good practice to give a person the opportunity quickly to clear himself of suspicion.

Where a requirement to provide a specimen of blood has been made at a hospital but the patient is discharged before the specimen can be taken, that requirement is not varied or discharged by the mere fact that the person to whom the requirement was made is then taken to a police station. The specimen of blood may be taken there. The only exception is if a police officer abrogates the procedure started at the hospital by asking for breath specimens and thereby setting in train the procedure under s 7.

EVIDENCE IN PROSECUTIONS UNDER ss 4 OR 5

The question of the admissibility and evidential value of documents made out in consequence of the various provisions of these sections of the Road Traffic Act 1988 is answered in the Road Traffic Offenders Act 1988, ss 15 and 16. Evidence of the proportion of alcohol or any drug in a specimen of breath, blood or urine provided by an accused must, in all cases, be taken into account and it *must be assumed* that the proportion of alcohol in the accused's breath, blood or urine at the time of the alleged offence was at least that found in the sample. Evidence of a breath, blood or urine specimen is not the only admissible evidence. The result is that, if the analysis or test reveals a proportion below the prescribed limit, but the magistrates are sure from expert evidence that, given the lapse of time between the alleged offence and the provision of the specimen, the proportion of alcohol at the time of the alleged offence was over the prescribed limit, they may convict the accused of an offence under s 5. On the other hand, since the accused's alcohol level *must be assumed to be not less* than that found in the sample, he is not permitted to adduce evidence that, although above the limit when the specimen was taken, he was below it when actually driving.

Although s 15 says that the proportion of alcohol or any drug in a specimen provided by the accused must in all cases be taken into account, there are exceptions. This is because the Road Traffic Offenders Act 1988, s 15 expressly states that evidence derived from a specimen must be disregarded where, in the case of a blood specimen, it was taken without the accused's consent and/or not by a medical practitioner, or where, in the case of a blood or urine specimen, the accused's request for part of it was not properly complied with. Breaches of the procedure laid down by ss 7 to 9 will render the evidence obtained from the specimen inadmissible, because a specimen obtained in breach of that procedure cannot be said to have been obtained under the Act, as the Road Traffic Offenders Act 1988, s 15(3) requires. Lastly, an accused is entitled to adduce evidence of his alcohol consumption in order to show that the devices used are unreliable but this will not normally be an easy task.

Although evidence of a positive roadside test is not relevant to the issue of the level of alcohol found in a specimen provided for analysis under s 7 of the 1988 Act, such evidence may be offered where a defendant seeks to challenge the reliability of an Intoximeter by asserting that he had only drunk a particular amount of alcohol. The assertion may be rebutted by relevant evidence. Evidence of a roadside test is relevant in such circumstances.

Hip-flask defence

The Road Traffic Offenders Act 1988, s 15(3) allows the accused what is often described as the 'hip-flask' defence. It provides that, in all cases under s 5 and in cases under s 4 involving drink, the assumption as to alcohol level must not be made if the accused proves that:

(a) he consumed alcohol before he provided the specimen and, in relation to an offence under s 3A, after the time of the alleged offence and, otherwise, after he had ceased to drive, attempt to drive or be in charge of a vehicle on a road or other public place; and

(b)   had he not done so the proportion of alcohol in his breath, blood or urine would not have exceeded the prescribed limit and, if the proceedings are for an offence under s 4, would not have been such as to impair his ability to drive.

The Home Office Circular of 1983 describes this as 'post-incident' drinking and this may occur where a driver, having been required to provide a screening breath test, locks the door of his car and drinks from a flask in the hope that he will then be in a position to allege that his alcohol level was so increased. It may also occur where a driver has driven home, following an accident, and has then taken a number of drinks in order to make it almost impossible to establish what the level might have been prior to his 'post-incident' drinking. While s 15(3) does not eliminate such possibilities, it places the burden on the accused of satisfying a court that, had he not done so, he would not have exceeded the prescribed limit in a specimen provided for analysis.

In such cases it will almost invariably be necessary for a defendant to call expert medical or scientific evidence in order to discharge this burden of proof, unless non-expert evidence which is called is such that it will enable the court reliably and confidently to reach a sensible conclusion without expert evidence. If justices have been given clear evidence from an expert as to the amount of alcohol necessary to cause a particular driver to exceed the legal limit and have been given plausible evidence as to the quantity of alcohol consumed after the driving etc in question, it is open to them, in spite of any unexplained discrepancies, to find that the defendant has discharged the burden necessary to establish a defence under s 15(3).

Accused who are able to prove the hip-flask defence may nevertheless be liable for the offence of wilfully obstructing a constable in the execution of his duty. This is because the deliberate consumption of alcohol after the alleged offence in order to frustrate the procedure for taking specimens has been held to amount to that offence. In any event, such deliberate consumption is liable to be self-defeating since the accused will often still be in charge of the vehicle at the time of the additional imbibing. It is therefore good practice, in instances in which a driver drinks from a bottle before submitting to testing procedures, to charge that person with an offence of 'being in charge etc' should tests prove to be positive.

Use of certificates

Evidence of the proportion of alcohol in a specimen of breath may be given by the production of the print-out produced by the breath testing device together with the certificate signed by a constable (normally the operator) (which certification may be made on the print-out). As we have already explained, that certification is to the effect that the print-out relates to a specimen provided by the accused at the date and time shown in it. The print-out and certificate are only admissible in evidence on behalf of the prosecution if a copy of it (or both) has been handed to the accused when the print-out was produced, or has been served on him not later than seven days before the hearing. Moreover, the certificate is not so admissible if the accused, not later than three days before the hearing or within such further time as the court may allow, has served notice on the prosecution requiring the attendance at the hearing of the constable who signed the certificate. Whilst the Act makes specific provisions for print-outs to be offered in evidence, it does not require that this be done. Consequently, a police officer may give oral evidence of the readings obtained on the screen of the device, provided that he is able to testify that the device was working properly and was accurately self-calibrating.

Evidence of the proportion of alcohol or a drug in a specimen of blood or urine may be given by the production of a certificate signed by an authorised analyst as to the proportion of alcohol or any drug found in the specimen identified in the certificate. However, except in the case of committal proceedings in respect of an offence under s 3A of the Road Traffic Act 1988, such a certificate is only admissible in evidence on behalf of the prosecution if a copy of it has been served on the accused not later than seven days before the hearing. In addition, the certificate is not so admissible if, not later than three days before the hearing or within such further time as the court may allow, the accused has served notice on the prosecutor requiring the attendance at the hearing of the analyst who signed the certificate.

Where an accused indicates that he will not accept such documentary evidence because there are defects in those documents and new documents are subsequently served by the prosecutor, he must respond to the new documents. If he does not specify that he requires the attendance of the witnesses concerned (in consequence of the second documents) those documents may be admitted by the court.

ALTERNATIVE VERDICTS

The Road Traffic Offenders Act 1988, s 24, as substituted by the Road Traffic Act 1991, s 24, provides that, where a person is charged under s 4(1) of the Road Traffic Act 1988 with driving, or attempting to drive when unfit to drive through drink or drugs, and is found not guilty of that offence, but the allegations in the information amount to, or include, an allegation of an offence of 'being in charge' in those circumstances, he may be convicted of that offence. The same applies where a person is charged with driving or attempting to drive with excess alcohol in his body under s 5(1)(a) of the 1988 Act; he may be convicted of 'being in charge'.

Where a person is charged with having committed an offence under ss 4(1) or 5(1)(a) by driving a vehicle, he may be convicted of attempting to drive.

OFFENCE OF FAILING TO PROVIDE A SPECIMEN REQUIRED UNDER S 7

Section 7(6) of the 1988 Act makes it an offence for a person, without reasonable excuse, to fail to provide a specimen when required to do so in pursuance of s 7. The subsection creates one offence; that is failing to provide a specimen for analysis. Whether that specimen is one of breath, blood or urine is immaterial, provided that there is a failure to provide a specimen. Where a person is charged with failure to provide a specimen of blood for laboratory analysis in circumstances in which an approved breath testing device was not available, and the validity of the request for a sample of blood is challenged, the non-availability of the device must be proved in accordance with the laws of evidence. However, where a defendant contended that there was no direct evidence to prove that there was no approved device available at the police station as there could have been a second machine there, the Divisional Court ruled that evidence that the machine failed to operate together with evidence that the accused was told that it was not therefore possible to take specimens of breath was sufficient. As in the case of the offence under s 6(4), there cannot be a conviction for this offence if the requirement made for it is invalid for some reason; the fact that the person was brought to the police station after a wrongful arrest or after a trespass by the police does not render the requirement invalid.

As we have already said 'fail' includes 'refuse'. However, where a motorist refused to supply a specimen of breath, but within five seconds said that he wanted to change his mind, there was no refusal. The Divisional Court said that the justices had ignored the motorist's words five seconds after his refusal. Regard must be had to all words and conduct in reaching a conclusion. It is submitted that, in the light of this and other rulings, the right to change one's mind will exist until the constable has moved on to the next stage of the procedure. Where a person declines to provide a specimen of breath, alleging a medical reason which is discounted by the police surgeon, there is a failure to provide a specimen without reasonable excuse. The police officer is not obliged to start the procedure all over again. If it were otherwise, recalcitrant motorists could play the system to gain some delay. Once required to provide a specimen an offence is committed if, without reasonable excuse, it is not provided.

We have already referred to what is meant by a failure to provide a specimen of breath and what constitutes a 'reasonable excuse' for such a failure. We have seen that an excuse cannot be adjudged reasonable unless the accused was physically or mentally unable to provide the specimen, or its provision would entail a substantial risk to his health. We have also seen that a foreigner who is unable to understand the purpose of the requirement and the penal consequences of a failure to comply also has a reasonable excuse. In relation to the failure to provide a specimen of blood or urine, most reasonable excuses which a person may have in relation to a failure to provide a specimen of breath are equally applicable to whichever of the alternative specimens is selected by the constable. In addition, there would be a reasonable excuse for failing to provide a specimen of blood where the accused has an invincible repugnance, amounting to a medically recognised phobia, to blood being taken, or where he has refused to sign a form of consent (to providing a specimen of blood) until he has read it. An arrested person who has not been given the opportunity to see a solicitor, or time to read the Detention Code, does not have a reasonable excuse for not providing a specimen in consequence of that lack of opportunity nor does someone who has been advised by his solicitor not to provide a specimen.

Stress caused by self-precipitated agitation cannot amount to a reasonable excuse for failure to provide breath, nor can mental anguish caused by conduct on the part of a police officer which the driver considered to be oppressive. There would have to be a causal connection between such anguish and the failure. Almost invariably, medical evidence will be required for a defence of reasonable excuse. Exceptionally, however, 'shock' experienced in the post-arrest situation and unsupported by medical evidence has been accepted as a reasonable excuse. In this case, an accused had provided one specimen of breath but began to lose composure, sobbing continuously and experiencing difficulty in breathing. She was unable to provide a second specimen. The Divisional Court ruled that the justices were entitled to conclude that she was physically incapable of providing a specimen, whilst accepting that the case was close to the borderline. The need for medical evidence on such a point could not be accepted in absolute terms.

The fact that a driver was so drunk that he could not understand the procedure which was being followed does not amount to a reasonable excuse because it does not relate to the defendant's *capacity* to supply a specimen. However, where a driver failed to provide two specimens of breath and two police officers gave evidence that he appeared to be too drunk to do so, the Divisional Court refused to overturn a decision of the justices that he had had a reasonable excuse for not providing a specimen due to stress resulting from adverse personal and family circumstances which had led to recent breathlessness, although no medical evidence was offered. The justices had reached their decision on unimpeachable findings of fact and the Divisional Court would not interfere.

While a fear of AIDS is not a reasonable excuse for not providing a specimen of blood, a medically recognised *phobia* in relation to contracting AIDS may be. A genuine fear of AIDS, short of a medically recognised phobia, *may*, however, provide grounds for 'special reasons' for not disqualifying the offender from driving. The wording of the relevant provisions is such that a person who fails to provide a specimen under s 7 on the grounds that he has been unlawfully arrested also does not have a reasonable excuse.

We have already indicated that, on requiring a person to provide a specimen in pursuance of s 7, a constable must warn him that a failure to provide it may render him liable to prosecution. Although an omission to do so is no defence to a charge under ss 4 or 5, nor to a charge of failing to provide a screening breath test, contrary to s 6(4), it is a defence to a charge under s 7(6) that such a warning has not been given or has not been understood by the person from whom the specimen is required.

The offence under s 7(6) is as serious as those under ss 4 or 5, since it is punishable in the same way as the offence in respect of which the specimen was required for evidential purposes.

Section 7(6) does not create two separate offences of failing to provide a specimen for analysis, despite the fact that the maximum penalty is higher when the defendant is alleged to have been driving, or attempting to drive the vehicle at the material time than it is when he is alleged to have been in charge of it. As a result, an information framed in terms of s 7(6) alone, without reference to the circumstances in which the requirement was made, is not bad for duplicity. It would be *good practice* to inform an accused of the circumstances surrounding the charge as soon as they had been established. In most cases, the issue of whether a person was driving, attempting to drive, or was in charge of the vehicle will be known at the time of his arrest. It is therefore preferable that the charge should specify whether the investigation was being carried out under ss 4(1), 4(2), 5(1)(a) or 5(1)(b) of the Act.

DETENTION OF PERSONS AFFECTED BY ALCOHOL

Section 10 of the Road Traffic Act 1988 provides that a person who has been required to provide a specimen of breath, blood or urine may be detained at a police station until it appears to a constable that, if he was released and drove or attempted to drive, he would not be committing an offence against either ss 4 or 5 of the Act. In practice this may often involve detention until a negative screening test.

On any question under s 10 whether a person's ability to drive properly is or might be impaired through drugs, a constable must consult a medical practitioner and must act on his advice.

A person must not, however, be detained under s 10 if it appears to a constable that there is no likelihood of his driving or attempting to drive while his ability to drive properly is impaired or while the proportion of alcohol in his breath, blood or urine exceeds the prescribed limit.

COURSES FOR DRINK-DRIVE OFFENDERS

The Road Traffic Offenders Act 1988, ss 34A and 34B apply in a large number of petty sessional areas designated by the Courses for Drink-Drive Offenders (Designation of Areas) Order 1997 and give courts in drink-driving cases the power to order on disqualification that the period of disqualification imposed upon a person convicted of a drink-drive offence may be reduced if he satisfactorily completes a course approved by the Secretary of State. The provisions apply to persons convicted of offences contrary to ss 3A, 4, 5 or 7 where a court makes an order disqualifying a person for a period of not less than 12 months. The reduction must be of not less than three months and not more than one-quarter of the unreduced period. Consequently, a disqualification for 12 months may be reduced to one of nine months.

Persons nominated as course managers may issue approved certificates of completion of such courses. Where a course manager decides not to give such a certificate he must give written notice of his decision to the offender as soon as possible, and in any event not later than 14 days after the date specified in the Order as the latest date for completion. A notice will be treated as having been given to a person if it is sent by registered post or recorded delivery service addressed to him at his last known address, notwithstanding that it was returned marked as undelivered or was for any other reason not received by him.

OTHER OFFENCES

Cycling while unfit

By s 30 of the Road Traffic Act 1988, it is an offence to ride a bicycle or tricycle on a road or other public place while unfit to ride through drink or drugs. Being in charge of a bicycle or tricycle in such circumstances is not an offence under the 1988 Act, but it is an offence under the Licensing Act 1872, s 12, which is described in the next paragraph.

Drunk in charge of a carriage, horse etc

By the Licensing Act 1872, s 12, it is an offence for a person to be drunk while in charge on any highway or other public place of any carriage, horse, cattle or steam engine. A motor vehicle, trailer, bicycle or tricycle is a 'carriage' for this purpose, but a person liable to be charged with an offence of driving or being in charge of a motor vehicle when unfit to drive through drink or drugs should not be charged with the present offence under the 1872 Act since its maximum punishment is far less severe than that for the appropriate offence under the 1988 Act. We deal with the offence under the 1872 Act in more detail in ch 19, below.

Drinking – guided public transport systems

The Transport and Works Act 1992 applies to transport systems which are used, or are intended to be used, wholly or partly for the carriage of members of the public. Its provisions are restricted to railways, to tramways, and to other *guided transport systems* specified by the Secretary of State. The guided transport systems at Birmingham International Airport; Merry Hill Centre, West Midlands; and Gatwick and Stansted Airports have been so specified. The first two systems are, however, no longer in use.

The Act creates two offences involving drink or drugs on such transport systems which can be committed by the following workers:

(a) drivers, guards, conductors, signalmen and others who control or affect the movement of vehicles operating under one of these systems;
(b) persons who couple or uncouple such vehicles or check that they are working properly;

(c) persons maintaining the permanent way (or other support or guidance structures), signalling systems and power supply used by such vehicles; and

(d) supervisors of, and look-outs for, persons engaged in the functions set out in categories (b) or (c) above.

An offence is committed where:

(1) a person in one of the above categories carries out his duties when unfit to carry out that work through drink or drugs;

(2) a person in one of the above categories carries out his duties after consuming so much alcohol that the proportion of it in the breath, blood or urine exceeds the prescribed limit (which is the same limit as prescribed by the Road Traffic Act 1988).

A constable in uniform is empowered to require a screening breath test where he has reasonable cause to suspect that:

(a) a person working on a transport system has alcohol in his body, or

(b) a person has been working on a transport system with alcohol in his body and still has alcohol in his body.

This power is extended to circumstances in which there has been an *accident or dangerous incident* and a constable in uniform has reasonable cause to suspect that, at the time of that event, the person was working in one of the above capacities and that his act, or omission, whilst so working, may have been the cause of the accident or incident. A 'dangerous incident' means an incident which, in the constable's opinion, involved a danger of death or personal injury.

Similar powers to those under the Road Traffic Act 1988 are provided by the Act in relation to arrest and entry, the provision of specimens for analysis, the option to have a breath specimen replaced if the alcohol content in it does not exceed 50 microgrammes in 100 ml of breath, failure to comply with a request, and hospital patients. The penalties for such offences are the same as those provided by the Road Traffic Act 1988, save, of course, that there is no power of disqualification from driving. However, the consent of the Secretary of State, or the Director of Public Prosecutions, is required before proceedings for such offences may be instituted in England and Wales.

The evidential provisions of the Road Traffic Offenders Act 1988 in relation to such offences are repeated in this Act.

Operators of such systems may be vicariously liable for offences committed by employees.

These provisions are important to all police officers. Following a train crash, it is the first police officer on the scene who will be expected to require a screening breath test if it applies.

CHAPTER 18

Children and young persons

The various statutes dealing with children and young persons are partly concerned with punishing adults, particularly those under a duty to care for a child or young person, whose conduct is physically or mentally harmful to him or otherwise harmful to his proper development. They are also concerned with the responsibilities of local authorities to receive a child or young person into their care, and with the power of family proceedings courts to put a child or young person into care, when this is necessary on specified grounds for his welfare.

MEANING OF TERMS

Various terms are used in the relevant legislation with particular meanings. The most common of these terms are:

Child

For most legal purposes of relevance to a police officer, a child is a person under the age of 14 years. However, there are occasions when the term is used in relation to persons who are 14 or over. For example, the Education Act 1996 defines 'child' for the purposes of the legislation relating to child employment as meaning any person not over compulsory school age. In the legislation referred to below relating to street trading and performances abroad a 'child' means someone under the age of 18, and the same is the case in enactments dealing with the responsibilities of a local authority in relation to the welfare of children under the Children Act 1989.

For the purposes of law, a person attains an age on the relevant anniversary of his birth. Section 99 of the Children and Young Persons Act 1933 states that when a person is brought before a court, other than as a witness, the issue of whether or not he is a child or young person must be decided upon inquiry by the court as to the age of the person. If it is later found that the age was different from that established by the court, any judgment or order will not be invalidated.

Young person

For the purposes of the Children and Young Persons Acts 1933 and 1969, in which the term is frequently used, a 'young person' is a person who has attained the age of 14 years and is under the age of 18 years.

Guardian

This term, for the purposes of the Children and Young Persons Acts, includes any person who, in the opinion of the court having cognizance of any case in relation to the child or young person or in which the child or young person is concerned, has for the time being the care of the child or young person.

The term is therefore wide in application, since it covers any person who, at the relevant time, appears to the court to be in charge or in control of a child or young person.

Generally, the Children and Young Persons Acts are concerned with 'guardians' in the wide sense just described rather than the narrower sense of 'legal guardian'.

To be a 'legal guardian' one must be a person appointed, according to law, to be a guardian by a signed and witnessed document (including a will) or by order of a court of competent jurisdiction.

The appointment of 'legal guardians' is dealt with by the Children Act 1989, s 5. Where an application is made to a court (High Court, county court or a magistrates' court) by an individual, the court may, by order, appoint that individual to be the child's guardian if:

(a) the child has no parent with parental responsibility for him; or
(b) a residence order has been made with respect to the child in favour of a parent or guardian of his who has died whilst the order was in force.

A child in this context means someone under 18. This power may also be exercised in family proceedings, where the court considers that the order should be made even though no application has been made for it.

In addition, a parent who has parental responsibility for a child, or the guardian of a child, may appoint another individual to be the child's guardian in the event of his death, provided that this is done in writing and is signed by the person making the appointment or (in the case of a will) signed at his direction in the presence of two attesting signatories. A guardian of a child may only be appointed in accordance with the provisions of this section. The section makes provisions in relation to the death of persons making such appointments.

Responsibilities of parent or guardian

By s 34A of the Children and Young Persons Act 1933, where a child or young person is charged with an offence or is, for any other reason, brought before a court, the court may in any case, and must in the case of a child or young person who is under 16, require a person who is the parent or guardian to attend court during all stages of the proceedings, unless and to the extent that the court is satisfied that it would be unreasonable to require such attendance. 'Parent or guardian' in this context includes a local authority which has parental responsibility for a child or young person, and which has him in its care, or in accommodation which it provides under the Children Act 1989.

Section 55 of the 1933 Act requires that it shall be the duty of the court, where a child, or young person under 16, is found guilty of an offence, to order that a fine, costs or compensation be paid by the parent or guardian, unless the court is satisfied that such parent or guardian cannot be found, or it would be unreasonable to make an order for payment, having regard to the circumstances of the case. In the case of a person of 16 or more, the court may make such an order. These provisions also apply to circumstances in which such fines result from failure to comply with a supervision order or a community service order. These provisions apply to a local authority which has parental responsibility for a child, or young person and which has him or her in its care, or in accommodation which it provides under the Children Act 1989.

The Criminal Justice Act 1991, s 58 empowers a court, where a child or young person is convicted of an offence, to order a parent or guardian to enter into a recognisance to take proper care of him and to exercise proper control over him. A parent or guardian must consent to the making of such an order. If he refuses and the court considers his refusal unreasonable, it may order him to pay a fine not exceeding £1,000. Where the child or young person is under 16, it is the duty of the court to exercise these powers where it is satisfied, having regard to the circumstances of the case, that it is desirable in the interests of preventing him from committing further offences to do so. Where it does not exercise these powers, it must state in open court that it is not so satisfied and give its reasons for so finding.

Such a recognisance may be in a sum not exceeding £1,000 and be for a period not exceeding three years. The order must not extend beyond the date upon which the person becomes 18.

Where a court has passed a community sentence it may include in such a recognizance a condition that the minor's parent or guardian ensures that the minor complies with the requirements of that sentence.

OFFENCES OF CRUELTY

There is much concern in society today about what has become labelled as 'child abuse'. Responsibilities are placed upon social agencies by various Acts of Parliament and this has had the effect of relieving the police of some of their burdens. The circumstances which are embraced by the abstract term 'child abuse' are dealt with by the offences of cruelty towards children and young persons which are governed by the Children and Young Persons Act 1933, s 1. Section 1 of the 1933 Act provides that a person who has attained the age of 16 years and has the responsibility for any child or young person under that age commits an offence, if he wilfully assaults, ill-treats, neglects, abandons or exposes him, or causes or procures him to be assaulted, ill-treated, neglected, abandoned, or exposed, in a manner likely to cause him unnecessary suffering or injury to health. These offences are arrestable offences.

There is much in s 1 which requires explanation and it is necessary to break it up for this purpose. In the first instance we will extract from the section the reference to 'or causes or procures etc' and bear in mind that each of the particular offences which we discuss below is equally committed by those who have the responsibility for a child or young person if they cause or procure the commission of these offences by someone else.

Responsibility for a child

For a person to be guilty of an offence contrary to s 1, he or she must have attained the age of 16 years and have the responsibility for the child or young person under that age.

In this context a person is presumed to have responsibility for a child or young person if:

(a) he has parental responsibility for him under the Children Act 1989 (which the mother and father will both have if they were married to each other when the child or young person was born, or which only the mother will have if the mother and father were not so married, or which another person (including the father in the instance just given) or a local authority may acquire by operation of law); or
(b) he is otherwise liable to maintain him; or
(c) he has care of him.

The basic elements of the offence

Section 1 specifies several ways in which an offence of cruelty can be committed by a person (of 16 or over) with responsibility for a child or young person. It specifies the following, each of which must occur wilfully:

(a) assaulting;
(b) ill-treating;
(c) neglecting;
(d) abandoning; or
(e) exposing,

a child or young person under 16 years in a manner likely to cause him unnecessary suffering or injury to health (including injury to or loss of sight, or hearing, or limbs or organs of the body, and any mental derangement).

Wilfully

'Wilfully' makes it clear that any offence under s 1 requires mens rea on the part of the accused. For example, on a charge of wilfully neglecting there must be an element of mens rea as to the risk of unnecessary suffering or injury to health resulting from the neglect, and if (to continue the example) that charge involves failure to provide adequate medical aid, the requirement of wilfulness can only be satisfied where the accused was aware that the child's health might be at risk if he was not provided with medical aid or where his non-awareness of this risk was due to his not caring whether the child's health was at risk or not.

Assault

'Assault' for the purpose of s 1 requires more than a mere common assault or battery. An assault or battery may amount to no more than frightening a person or giving him a light slap, but this could hardly be done 'in a manner likely to cause unnecessary suffering or injury to health'. Although consent could be an issue in some minor assaults, it must be remembered that mere submission, particularly in the case of children, to a person in authority does not signify consent.

Ill-treat

The term signifies a continuous course of conduct leading to unnecessary suffering. A series of assaults each of which, if considered on its own, would not amount to an offence against the section, might together form ill-treatment over a period of time. Likewise, persistent frightening or bullying will suffice if it is likely to cause unnecessary suffering. It is a defence that the alleged ill-treatment consisted of reasonable correction by a parent or other person entitled to chastise the child or young person.

Neglect

The term signifies a want of adequate care. The likelihood of causing unnecessary suffering or injury to health can be caused by a deliberate omission to supply medical or surgical aid. Direct proof of such likelihood is not always strictly necessary as this may be inferred from the evidence of neglect and its actual effect. The section provides that a parent or other person legally liable to maintain a child or young person or his legal guardian is deemed to have neglected him in a manner likely to cause injury to health if he has failed to provide adequate food, clothing, medical aid or lodging for him or if, having been unable to provide such food, clothing, medical aid or lodging, he has failed to take steps to procure it to be provided under the enactments applicable in that behalf.

Section 1 also declares that if the death of an infant under three years of age is caused by suffocation (other than by disease or a foreign body in the throat) whilst the infant was in bed with a person over 16 who went to bed under the influence of drink, that person will be deemed to have neglected the infant in a manner likely to cause injury to health.

Abandon or expose

It is helpful to consider these terms together since an abandonment frequently leads to exposure. To abandon a child means leaving it to its fate. If a woman, who is living apart from her husband, takes her child to her husband's home and leaves the child at his door, she abandons that child. From the moment of abandonment the child is exposed and, if that exposure leads to suffering, the child has been abandoned and exposed in a manner likely to cause unnecessary suffering. It is also interesting to consider the position of the husband. If he is aware that the child has been left on his doorstep, then, as he cannot disclaim his custodial responsibilities, he also abandons and exposes the child by allowing it to remain there. This exposure does not cover exposure to risk. A father, who took his son and other boys on to a baulk of timber and floated the timber into deep water in London Docks, was not guilty of an offence under this section, because this was not the type of exposure to which the section refers.

Police action in cruelty cases

It is now standard procedure to refer reports of cruelty to children to officers of the National Society for the Prevention of Cruelty to Children. If the Society's investigations reveal evidence to suggest that criminal proceedings are desirable, the Society is empowered, as are the police, to initiate proceedings. However, the Society does attempt, through a process of encouragement, persuasion and warnings, to remedy the situation without recourse to the law whenever possible. The Society has set out the following advice to its branch secretaries:

(a) It is for the Society to decide whether to institute proceedings in any case in which its officers are involved, subject always to any action which the police may consider it necessary to take.
(b) If the Society is considering action, the issue of whether or not the case is one which should be prosecuted under the Offences Against the Person Act 1861 (ch 28 below) should be considered first. If the Society decides that this might be the case, it should be referred to the police.
(c) If the police then decide not to prosecute for an offence contrary to the Offences Against the Person Act 1861 they will return it to the Society for prosecution under the Children and Young Persons Act 1933, s 1.
(d) The Society, when prosecuting under s 1, should bear in mind the advisability in serious cases of asking the magistrates' court to consider committing for trial in the Crown Court.

In all cases of non-accidental injury to children the police are likely to become involved at the outset when fulfilling their role as one of the emergency services. Local authorities, social services, the NSPCC and the police have the power to initiate any civil proceedings before a family proceedings court when a child appears to be in need of care. The police have power to detain children who appear to be in need of care and to take them to safe places. We deal with these matters later in this chapter. Police officers must never feel that the other social agencies have assumed responsibility for these matters. It is still the duty of the police to take some initial action to ensure the safety of any child in circumstances where a report of child abuse is received. Such cases may, in appropriate circumstances, later be referred to other agencies.

OTHER OFFENCES

There are a number of offences under the Children and Young Persons Act 1933 which require little explanation. These offences are committed in relation to children of a specified age, which varies from offence to offence.

Brothels

By s 3, it is an offence for any person of 16 years or more who has responsibility for a child or young person who has attained the age of four years, but is under 16, to allow that child or young person to reside in or frequent a brothel. What is and what is not a brothel is discussed in ch 34, below. It is important to remember that a woman who is a prostitute and receives men in her own room, but does not allow other women to use her room, is not keeping a brothel. This is the most likely situation to come to the notice of the police. Although an offence is not committed in these circumstances, care proceedings (see later) could perhaps be considered (as they should in the case of a brothel).

Begging

Causing or procuring a child or young person under 16 to be in any street, premises or place for the purpose of begging or receiving alms, or of inducing the giving of alms (whether or not there is any pretence of singing, playing, performing, offering anything for sale or otherwise), is an offence contrary to s 4 of the 1933 Act. There is a similar offence under the Vagrancy Act 1824, s 3.

It is also an offence under s 4 of the 1933 Act for the person having the responsibility for such a child or young person to allow him so to act. Such a person allows a child or young person to beg in the street if he fails to prevent it when he could and should have prevented it.

If it is proved that a child or young person was in a street etc for the purpose of begging etc and that a person with responsibility for him allowed him to be in the street etc, that person is presumed to have allowed him to be there for that purpose, until the contrary is proved.

Intoxicating liquor

It is an offence, contrary to s 5, to give, or cause to be given, intoxicating liquor to a child under the age of five years, otherwise than on the orders of a duly qualified medical practitioner or in a medical emergency. This is an offence for which a prosecution is improbable within modern society.

Tobacco

By s 7, it is an offence to sell tobacco or cigarette papers to any person under the age of 16, whether for his own use or not. 'Tobacco' includes cigarettes and any product containing tobacco intended for oral or nasal use, and smoking mixtures intended as a substitute for tobacco. Selling tobacco to a person under the age of 16 is an offence of strict liability. The proprietor of a shop is guilty even when he has played no part in the transaction and knows nothing about it. However, s 7 provides that it is a defence for an accused to prove that he took all reasonable precautions and exercised all due diligence to avoid the commission of an offence. The fact that all possible precautions have not been taken does not rule out the application of this defence. This was held in a case where justices found that staff had been provided with written instructions setting out a procedure to be followed when in doubt about a customer's age, such procedures being regularly reviewed and supervised. The Divisional Court ruled that the justices were entitled to find that this defence had been made out, even though there were other things which the shop proprietor could have done to try to prevent the commission of the offence.

The general use of cigarette machines has led to a situation in which it is difficult to prevent cigarettes from falling into the hands of young people. If it is proved that a machine is being extensively used by persons under 16, a magistrates' court must order the owner to take precautions to prevent such use or, if necessary, to remove the machine. Failure to comply with such an order is an offence. Section 7 places responsibilities upon constables and uniformed park keepers to seize tobacco or cigarette papers from a person apparently under 16 whom they find smoking in any street or public place. These articles will then be disposed of by the appropriate authorities.

None of the above provisions about sale to a child applies to a child who is an employee of a tobacconist or a uniformed messenger employed by a messenger company.

The Children and Young Persons (Protection from Tobacco) Act 1991 prohibits the sale to anyone of unpacked (ie unpackaged) cigarettes by a person carrying on a retail business. It also requires notices to be placed on retail premises and machines concerning the illegality of tobacco sales to persons under 16.

Risk of burning

If a person of or over 16, having responsibility for a child under 12, allows the child to be in a room containing an open fire grate or any heating appliance liable to cause injury to a person by contact with it and it is not sufficiently guarded against the risk of the child being burnt or scalded and in consequence the child is killed or seriously injured, he commits an offence contrary to s 11.

It will be noted that death or serious injury must result from the unguarded fire or appliance and it is almost certain that civil proceedings for a 'care order' (see later) would result from any incident likely to be charged as an offence under this section, which is punishable only by a fine.

The section does go on to say that any proceedings taken summarily under the section will not affect a person's liability to be proceeded against for any indictable offence. For example, if a child died as a result of his injuries it is probable that proceedings on indictment for manslaughter would follow.

Safety at entertainments

Section 12 provides that, wherever an entertainment is provided in a building for an audience mainly of children, then, if there are more than 100 children attending the entertainment, there must be a sufficient number of adult attendants, properly stationed and instructed in their duties, to prevent more people being admitted than can be properly accommodated and to control the movement of those entering and leaving and general safety. If these provisions are not complied with, the person providing the entertainment is guilty of an offence. A constable may enter any building in which he has reason to believe that such an entertainment is taking place, or is about to take place, to ensure that this is being done. The section does not apply to any entertainment in a dwelling house.

EMPLOYMENT

The Children and Young Persons Act 1933, s 18 restricts the employment of children and young persons in many circumstances. It provides that no child or young person under compulsory school age shall be employed:

(a) under 14 to do any work;
(b) to do any work other than light work;
(c) before the close of school hours on school days;
(d) before 7am or after 7pm on any day;
(e) for more than two hours on a schoolday or a Sunday;

(f) for more than eight hours or, if he is under the age of 15 years, for more than five hours in any day-
    (i) on which he is not required to attend school, and
    (ii) which is not a Sunday;

(g) for more than 35 hours or, if he is under the age of 15 years, for more than 25 hours in any week in which he is not required to attend school;

(h) for more than four hours in any day without a rest break of one hour; or

(i) at any time in a year unless at that time he has had, or could still have, during a period in the year in which he is not required to attend school, at least two consecutive weeks without employment.

Breach of this provision renders the employer guilty of an offence, as well as any other person (other than the child or young person employed) to whose act or default the breach is attributable. However, if the employer is prosecuted, he has a defence if he proves that the contravention was due to the act or default of a third party (who has been brought before the court) and that he (the employer) has used all due diligence to comply with the above provisions. However, where the offence is against the provisions set out at (i) above the proviso does not apply, but it shall be a defence for him to prove that he used all due diligence to secure that the provisions were complied with.

Section 18 also empowers local authorities to make byelaws concerning the employment of children. In particular, such byelaws may authorise:

(a) the employment on an occasional basis of children under 14 by their parents or guardians in light agricultural or horticultural duties;

(b) the employment of children aged 13 years (notwithstanding what is said above) in categories of light work specified in the byelaw, or

(c) the employment of children or young persons for one hour before school on a day on which school is open (which is important in relation to the employment of children on newsrounds).

'Light work' in s 18 is defined as work which, on account of the inherent nature of the tasks which it involves and the particular conditions under which they are performed, is not likely to be harmful to the safety, health or development of children, and is not such as to be harmful to their attendance at school or to their participation in work experience, or their capacity to benefit from the instruction received or, as the case may be, the experience gained.

Street trading

Section 20 provides that no child shall engage in, or be employed in, street trading. If there is a breach of this provision, the same rules apply as apply in the event of a breach of s 18 (see above). By way of exception, byelaws made by a local authority may permit children who have attained the age of 14 years to be employed by their parents in street trading; such parents must be authorised in writing.

Dangerous performances

By s 23, no person under 18 may take part in any performance in which his life or limbs are endangered without a local authority licence. Persons who cause or procure this to be done, or parents or guardians who allow it, are guilty of offences. A chief officer of police must authorise proceedings in such cases. The types of performance referred to are those in respect of which a charge is made, or which take place in licensed premises or registered clubs, or which are live or recorded broadcast performances or performances filmed for public exhibition.

Training for dangerous performances

By s 24, no person under 12 shall be trained to take part in any dangerous performance, and no one between 12 and 18 shall be so trained except in accordance with the terms of a local authority licence. Every person who causes or procures a person, or being his parent or guardian allows him, to be so trained is guilty of an offence.

Performances abroad

Section 25 provides that no person having the responsibility for any child under 18 may allow him, nor may any person cause or procure such a child, to go abroad:

(a) for the purpose of singing, playing, performing or being exhibited for profit;
(b) or for the purpose of taking part in sport, or working as a model, where payment in respect of his doing so, other than defraying expenses, is made to him or to another person,

unless a licence has been granted. Such licences can only be granted by a justice of the peace and can only be granted in respect of children of 14 or more. A person who contravenes these provisions commits an offence.

LOCAL AUTHORITY CARE

The Children Act 1989 makes various provisions for children to be brought into the care of a local authority (ie the council of a county (including a unitary authority) or a metropolitan district or London borough council (in England) or a county or county borough council (in Wales). For the purposes of these provisions, a 'child' is a person under 18, unless otherwise stated. The Act is extremely comprehensive and emphasises that the child's welfare is paramount in all matters particularly those concerned with his upbringing, and that delay in deciding such matters is likely to prejudice the child's welfare. The guiding principle of the Act is that the court should not make an order unless to do so is considered better for the child than making no order. Most of the Act's provisions relate to the functions of local authorities and the social service agencies. Those matters which most directly affect the police are considered below. Section 21 of the Act requires local authorities to make provisions for the reception and accommodation of children, including a child who is in police protection (see below). A child whom a custody officer has authorised to be kept in police detention after arrest must be received by a local authority where that officer so requests.

Care and supervision orders

On the application of a local authority or authorised person (NSPCC or other body authorised by the Secretary of State), a family proceedings court (ie that part of a magistrates' court hearing proceedings under the 1989 Act) may make an order:

(a) placing the child with respect to whom the application is made in the care of a designated local authority; or
(b) putting him under the supervision of a designated local authority or of a probation officer.

A court may only make a care or supervision order if it is satisfied:

(a) that the child concerned is suffering, or is likely to suffer, significant harm; and
(b) that the harm, or likelihood of harm, is attributable to -
    (i) the care given to the child, or likely to be given to him if the order were not made, not being what it would be reasonable to expect a parent to give him; or
    (ii) the child being beyond parental control.

'Harm' means ill-treatment or the impairment of health or development.

Such an order may not be made with respect to a child who has reached the age of 17 (or 16 in the case of a child who is married). On an application for a care order the court may make a supervision order, and vice versa.

As can be seen, where a child has been the victim of offences of cruelty or sexual abuse or neglect, an application may be made by a local authority or an authorised person for either of the above orders to be made. In addition, the provisions at (b)(ii), above, provide a means of obtaining a care order in circumstances in which a child who is below the age of criminal responsibility (10) habitually commits a crime, or where a child who is receiving adequate care from the parents, but is so out of control that he is likely to harm himself.

Child assessment orders

The Children Act 1989, s 43 permits a local authority or authorised person to apply to the High Court, a county court, or a magistrates' court sitting as a family proceedings court for such an order where difficulties are being experienced in making an assessment of the needs of such a child. This may be due to lack of co-operation by those who have parental responsibility for the child. Such an order permits assessment to be made over a period not exceeding seven days and may require any person to produce the child to a person named in the order and to comply with specified instructions. However, a court should not make such an order if it is satisfied that there are grounds for making an emergency protection order and that it ought to do so rather than make a child assessment order.

Emergency protection order

There will be occasions upon which action must be taken immediately to protect a child. Section 44 of the 1989 Act empowers the High Court, a county court or a magistrates' court sitting as a family proceedings court, on the application of any person, to make an emergency order for the protection of a child. It may do so if it is satisfied that:

(a) there is reasonable cause to believe that the child is likely to suffer significant harm if—
    (i) he is not removed to accommodation provided by or on behalf of the applicant, or
    (ii) he does not remain in the place in which he is then being accommodated;

   (b) in the case of an application made by a local authority—
       (i)   inquiries are being made with respect to the child under the authority's duty to investigate where a child is suffering, or is likely to suffer, significant harm, and
      (ii) these inquiries are being frustrated by access to the child being unreasonably refused to a person authorised to seek access and the applicant has reasonable cause to believe that access to the child is required as a matter of urgency; or
   (c) in the case of an application made by an authorised person—
       (i)   the applicant has reasonable cause to suspect that the child is suffering, or is likely to suffer, significant harm;
      (ii) the applicant is making inquiries with respect to the child's welfare; and
     (iii) those inquiries are being frustrated by access to the child being unreasonably refused to a person authorised to seek access and the applicant has reasonable cause to believe that access to the child is required as a matter of urgency.

An emergency protection order directs a person to produce a child and authorises the child's removal to accommodation provided by or on behalf of the applicant or the prevention of the removal of the child from a hospital or other place. It also gives the applicant parental responsibility for the child. An emergency protection order has effect for such period, not exceeding eight days, as is specified by the court, but the court has power (on one occasion only) to extend it for up to a further seven days. An emergency protection order can include an exclusion requirement in specified circumstances. Such a requirement enables the child to stay in its home by excluding someone else, such as a suspected child abuser, from it.

Removal and accommodation of children by police in emergencies

Section 46 of the 1989 Act empowers police officers to take a child into 'police protection' in prescribed circumstances. It also places responsibilities upon 'designated police officers', that is officers designated by chief officers of police to conduct inquiries into such cases.

Where a constable has reasonable cause to believe that a child would otherwise be likely to suffer significant harm, he may:

   (a) remove the child to suitable accommodation and keep him there; or
   (b) take such steps as are reasonable to ensure that the child's removal from any hospital, or other place, in which he is then being accommodated is prevented.

As soon as is reasonably practicable after taking a child into police protection, as above, the constable shall:

   (a) inform the local authority within whose area the child was found of the steps that have been, or are proposed to be, taken with respect to the child and the reasons for taking them;
   (b) give details to the local authority within whose area the child is ordinarily resident ('the appropriate authority') of the place at which the child is being accommodated;
   (c) inform the child (if he appears capable of understanding)—
       (i)   of the steps that have been taken with respect to him and of the reasons for taking them; and
      (ii) of the further steps which may be taken with respect to him under this section;
   (d) take such steps as are reasonably practicable to discover the wishes and feelings of the child;

(e)   secure that the case is inquired into by a designated officer; and
(f)   where the child was taken into police protection by being removed to accommodation which is not provided—
    (i)   by or on behalf of a local authority; or
    (ii) as a refuge (ie a voluntary home or registered children's home certified as a refuge);
    secure that he is moved to accommodation which is so provided.

The constable must also, as soon as reasonably practicable, inform:

(a)   the child's parents;
(b)   every person who is not a parent of his but who has parental responsibility for him; and
(c)   any other person with whom the child was living immediately before being taken into police protection,

of the steps that he has taken under s 46 with respect to the child, the reasons for taking them and the further steps that may be taken with respect to him under the section.

When the case has been inquired into by the designated officer, he must release the child from police protection unless he considers that there is still reasonable cause for believing that the child would be likely to suffer significant harm if released.

No child may be kept in police protection for more than 72 hours. However, at any time whilst the child is in police protection, the designated officer may apply *on behalf of the appropriate authority* for an emergency protection order to be made with respect to the child. Such an application may be made whether or not the authority knows of it or agrees to its being made.

Whilst a child is in police protection, the designated officer must do what is reasonable in all the circumstances of the case for the purpose of safeguarding or promoting the child's welfare (having regard in particular to the length of the period during which the child will be so protected).

The designated officer must allow:

(a)   parents;
(b)   any other person with parental responsibility;
(c)   any person with whom the child was living immediately before he was taken into police protection;
(d)   where there is a 'contact order' (an order permitting contact by named persons), any such named person; and
(e)   any person acting on behalf of any of these persons,

to have such contact (if any) with the child as, in the opinion of the designated officer, is both reasonable and in the child's best interest. However, if a child who has been taken into police protection is in accommodation provided by, or on behalf of, the appropriate authority, these contact responsibilities are those of the authority rather than the designated officer.

Abduction of children in care etc

It is an offence against the Children Act 1989, s 49 for any person, knowingly and without lawful authority or reasonable excuse, to take a child to whom the section applies from the responsible person, or to keep such a child away from the responsible person, or to induce or assist or incite such a child to run away or stay away from the responsible person. The offences apply to a child who is in care, the subject of an emergency protection order, or in police protection. A 'responsible person' means of any person who for the time being has care of him by virtue a care order, emergency protection order, or the provisions of s 46 of the 1989 Act (accommodation of children by police in emergencies).

Where such abduction has occurred, s 50 permits a court to issue a 'recovery order'.

Police powers

An emergency protection order may include a requirement directed to a person to disclose the whereabouts of the child and may authorise an applicant to enter premises specified by the order and search for the child. Such a warrant may authorise a constable to assist an applicant where entry is being, or is likely to be denied. It may also direct that a constable be accompanied by a registered medical practitioner, registered nurse or registered health visitor.

If a child or young person is absent without the consent of the responsible person:

(a) from a place of safety to which he has been taken under the Children and Young Persons Act 1969, s 16(3) (supervised person arrested on warrant and so placed for not more than 72 hours);

(b) from local authority accommodation in which he was required to live as a condition of a supervision order; or

(c) from accommodation to which he had been remanded by a court either awaiting trial for an offence, or having been convicted of such an offence;

the Children and Young Persons Act 1969, s 32 will continue to authorise a constable to arrest such a child or young person without a warrant. When so arrested he must be conducted to a place of safety, local authority accommodation, or such other place as the responsible person may direct.

Arrest of young offenders in breach of remand conditions

The Children and Young Persons Act 1969, s 23A provides that a constable may arrest without warrant a young offender who has been remanded or committed to local authority accommodation in respect of any breach of a condition of that remand or committal if the constable has reasonable grounds for suspecting that the offender has broken any of those conditions.

The arrested person must be brought before a justice as soon as is practicable and in any event within 24 hours of his arrest (unless due to appear before a court within 24 hours of his arrest, for example, where he is on remand). In reckoning any period of 24 hours, no account shall be taken of Christmas Day, Good Friday or any Sunday.

LOCAL CHILD CURFEW SCHEMES

Section 14 of the Crime and Disorder Act 1998 provides powers for local authorities to set up local child curfew schemes for children under 10.

A local child curfew scheme is a scheme made by a local authority which enables the authority to give a notice imposing, for a specified period, a ban on children of specified ages (under 10) being in a public place within a specified area:

(a) during specified hours (between 9pm and 6am);

(b) and otherwise than under the effective control of a parent (of whatever age) or of a responsible person aged 18 or over.

The following local authorities may make a curfew scheme: the council of a district (including a unitary authority), a London borough council, the Common Council of the City of London, the Council of the Isle of Wight or the Council of the Isles of Scilly (in England) or a county or county borough council (in Wales). A 'public place' means 'any highway and any place to which at the material time the public or any section of the public has access, on payment or otherwise, as of right or by virtue of express or implied permission'. Streets, shops, the communal areas of blocks of flats, shopping centres, local authority parks and recreation grounds, and amusement arcades, all fall within this definition.

Before making a scheme, a local authority must consult:

(a) every chief constable (or Commissioner of Police) any part of whose area lies within its area; and
(b) such other persons or bodies as it thinks appropriate, such as social services departments, voluntary agencies and the local community (eg residents groups).

A scheme does not have effect until confirmed by the Home Secretary.

Curfew notice

A local authority may only give a notice imposing a curfew (a curfew notice):

(a) subject to and in accordance with the provisions of the local curfew scheme; and
(b) if, after such consultation as is required by the scheme, the authority considers it necessary for the purpose of maintaining order.

A curfew notice given under a curfew scheme may specify different hours in relation to children of different ages.

A curfew notice is required to be given:

(a) by posting it in some conspicuous place or places within the specified area; and
(b) in such other manner, if any, as appears to the local authority to be desirable for giving publicity to the notice.

The maximum duration of a curfew which may be specified by a curfew notice is 90 days. If the local authority wants an extension beyond the specified period it will have to consult again and go through the rest of the procedure set out above.

Contravention

Section 15 of the 1998 Act provides that, where a police officer has reasonable cause to believe that a child is in a public place, unaccompanied, in contravention of a ban imposed by a curfew notice, the officer may remove the child to the child's place of residence unless he has reasonable cause to believe that the child would, if removed there, be likely to suffer significant harm. The officer is not required to be in uniform. The question of what force, if any, the officer may use to remove a child gives rise to similar issues to those involved in the power to remove truants; they are dealt with on pp 449-450.

It may be noted that there is no requirement to take the child home. The decision whether or not to do so is left to the police officer. In making that decision, the officer must also answer the question whether there is reasonable cause to believe that taking the child home would expose the child to the likelihood of suffering significant harm. This is the same question as has to be asked by a police officer before exercising the power under s 46 of the Children Act 1989 (above) to remove a child to suitable accommodation. The officer will normally have knowledge of the area; he may know the child's family and home circumstances. If, for example, he knows that there is a history of child abuse or neglect, he may well conclude that he should not take the child home because there are reasonable grounds to believe that otherwise the child would suffer significant harm and, the threshold criteria being the same, decide to remove the child to suitable accommodation under s 46 of the 1989 Act.

If the officer does decide to take the child home, he is not required to hand the child over to a responsible person. While it is a bar to the removal of the child in the first instance to its place of residence that there is reasonable cause to believe that the child's removal is likely to cause it significant harm, discovery of the absence there of a responsible person is not in itself a bar to the child being left there. However, it is likely that, if there is no responsible person there to look after the child, or that person is likely to abuse the child, the officer will use his power under s 46 of the Children Act 1989 to remove the child to other suitable accommodation on the ground that otherwise the child would be likely to suffer significant harm.

The suitable accommodation to which a police officer will take a child in a breach-of-curfew situation will be a matter for discussion between the relevant agencies prior to the imposition of a curfew notice, so that appropriate arrangements will be in force during the curfew.

Where a police officer has reasonable cause to believe that a child is in a public place, unaccompanied, in contravention of a curfew notice, the officer must also, as soon as practicable, inform the local authority which made the notice that the child has contravened it, however minor the contravention. The local authority will then send a social worker to the child's family to see why the child was in breach of the curfew and then decide whether further action is necessary to prevent any repetition.

CHILD SAFETY ORDERS

These are governed by the Crime and Disorder Act 1998, ss 11 to 13.

A child safety order is an order which:

(a) places a child, for a period specified in the order, under the supervision of the responsible officer; and
(b) requires the child to comply with such requirements as are so specified.

The permitted maximum period of supervision for the above purposes is three months, unless the court is satisfied that the circumstances of the case are exceptional (in which case it is 12 months).

The requirements that may be specified under (b) are those which the court considers desirable in the interests of:

(a) securing that the child receives appropriate care, protection and support and is subject to proper control; or
(b) preventing any repetition of the kind of behaviour which led to the child safety order being made.

The main responsibility of the responsible officer will be to the child and paramount to that will be the need to supervise the child and to ensure full compliance with the requirements of the order. However, the officer also has an important role to play in relation to the child's family circumstances.

The 'responsible officer' will be one of the following who is specified in the order:

(a) a social worker of a local authority social services department; and
(b) a member of a youth offending team.

The child safety order is directed to the child and requires or prohibits conduct specified in it. Where it is linked with a parenting order (below) that order could make associated requirements of the parent. For example, if the child safety order requires a child to be home by 7pm, the associated parenting order could require the parent to ensure that the child is home by then.

Child safety orders are being piloted for 18 months commencing 30 September 1998. Consequently, a court must not make an order unless it has been notified by the Home Secretary that arrangements for implementing such orders are available in the area in which it appears that the child resides or will reside and the notice has not been withdrawn. Nine areas have been selected for the piloting of child safety orders: Hammersmith and Fulham, Kensington and Chelsea, and Westminster (jointly); Lewisham; Hampshire, Southampton, Portsmouth and the Isle of Wight (jointly); Wolverhampton; Sheffield; Luton and Bedfordshire (jointly); Devon; St Helens; and parts of Sunderland.

Child safety orders will be made by magistrates' courts sitting as family proceedings courts.

A child safety order cannot be made without an application by a local authority, ie a council of a county (including a unitary authority), a metropolitan district or London borough council or the Common Council of the City of London (in England) or a county or county borough council (in Wales).

A family proceedings court can make an order only if it is convinced that, with respect to a child under 10, one or more of the following conditions is satisfied:

(a) that the child has committed an act which, if he had been 10 or over, would have constituted an offence;
(b) that a child safety order is necessary to prevent the child committing such an act;
(c) that the child has contravened a ban imposed by a curfew order; or
(d) that the child has acted in a manner that caused or was likely to cause harassment, alarm or distress to one or more persons not of the same household as himself.

Breach of a child safety order

Proceedings for breach of a child safety order must be brought by the responsible officer. Unlike an application for discharge or variation, an application in respect of a breach of a child safety order need not be heard by the same court as made the order; it can also be heard by another magistrates' court sitting as a family proceedings court for the same petty sessions area.

If on such an application it is proved that the child has failed to comply with any requirement in the order, a magistrates' court sitting as a family proceedings court:

(a) may discharge the order and of its own motion make in respect of the child a care order under s 31 of the Children Act 1989 (above); or

(b) may make an order varying the order in the same way as on a variation after an application for discharge.

Breach of a child safety order may also result in the making of a parenting order; it is one of the triggers of such an order.

PARENTING ORDERS

These are governed by the Crime and Disorder Act 1998, ss 8–10.

A parenting order is a court order requiring 'the parent' of a child (ie someone under 14) or (in some cases) a young person (ie someone of 14 or over but under 18):

(a) to comply, for up to 12 months, with such requirements as are specified in the order; and
(b) to attend, for a concurrent period not exceeding three months, and not more than once in any week, such counselling and guidance sessions as may be specified in directions given by the responsible officer.

A parenting order need not include a counselling and guidance session requirement under (b) if the parent has previously been made subject to such an order, although it may do so. Apart from this, an order must contain such a requirement, although it need not contain any requirements under (a).

The reference in (b) to 'the responsible officer' who is to specify the counselling or guidance sessions to be attended is to one of the following, who is to be specified in the order:

(a) a probation officer;
(b) a social worker of a local authority social services department; and
(c) a member of a youth offending team.

The responsible officer's role is also to ensure that parents attend whatever sessions are specified in his directions and to ensure compliance with the order and any requirements under it.

The requirements which may be specified under (a) above are those which the court considers desirable in the interest of preventing any repetition of the kind of conduct which 'triggers' the making of a parenting order or (as the case may be) the commission of any further offence of the type which is a 'trigger'.

Examples of requirements which can be made under (a) are a requirement to ensure that the child is escorted to school every day by a responsible adult, a requirement to exercise control over him and a requirement to ensure that he is home by a certain time of night.

The provisions relating to parenting orders are being piloted for 18 months commencing 30 September 1998 in certain areas (where voluntary parental training and guidance provision is already available); the areas chosen are the same as those in which child safety orders are being piloted.

A parenting order may be made against various people depending on the context. First, it may be made against one or both 'parents', ie biological parents. It is not necessary that a parent should have parental responsibility. Thus an order can be made against the father of a child or young person, who was not married to the mother when the child was born and who has not acquired parental responsibility under the Children Act 1989.

A parenting order may also be made against a person who is a guardian of a child or young person. Guardians are defined here as any person who in the opinion of the court has for the time being the care of a child or young person. Hereafter, the term 'the parent' is used to cover these other people.

Parenting orders may be made in any court proceedings where:

(a) a child safety order is made in respect of a child;
(b) an anti-social behaviour order or sex offender order is made in respect of a child or young person (ie someone aged under 18);
(c) a child or young person is convicted of an offence; or
(d) a person is convicted of an offence under s 443 (failure to comply with a school attendance order) or s 444 (failure to secure regular attendance at school of registered pupil) of the Education Act 1996.

By the nature of these conditions, an order under (a) will be made by a magistrates' court, sitting as a family proceedings court; an order under (b) or (d) by a magistrates' court; and an order under (c) by a youth court or (where the conviction is in the Crown Court) the Crown Court.

If the court is satisfied that 'the relevant condition' is fulfilled, it may make a parenting order in respect of a person who is the parent or guardian of the child or young person.

The 'relevant condition' is that the parenting order would be desirable in the interests of preventing:

(a) in a case falling within (a) or (b), any repetition of the kind of behaviour which led to the child safety order, anti-social behaviour or sex offender order being made;
(b) in a case falling within (c), the commission of any further offence by the child or young person;
(c) in a case falling within (d), the commission of any further offence under ss 443 or 444 of the Education Act 1996.

'Desirable in the interests of' is an unusual piece of legislative phraseology. It is not clear whether the requirement made by it can be satisfied where the object in question is desirable but it is clear that the parent will have no effect in relation to the child's behaviour.

Where an order must normally be made

A court is not normally obliged to make a parenting order if one of the four conditions is proved; it simply has the power to do so. There is one exception: there is a statutory presumption in favour of making a parenting order where the relevant condition is (c) – conviction of an offence – and the offender is under 16 at the time of conviction.

Breach

As long as a parenting order is in force, it is an offence for a parent to fail without reasonable excuse to comply with any requirement included in a parenting order, or specified in directions given by the responsible officer.

Leaving aside the theoretical possibility of a private prosecution, the process is that the responsible officer will report to the police an alleged breach of a parenting order. The police will investigate the allegation, taking statements etc and proceed from there. This can be contrasted with breach of a probation or community service order where it is the Probation Service which brings proceedings and conducts them.

REMOVAL OF TRUANTS TO SCHOOLS OR DESIGNATED PREMISES

Section 16 of the Crime and Disorder Act 1998 provides that, where a direction has been given under the section, a police officer may remove a juvenile of compulsory school age whom he has reasonable cause to believe to be truanting to designated premises or to the juvenile's school.

In order for a direction to be given under s 16, a local authority, which in this context means the local education authority, must have designated premises to which children and young persons of compulsory school age may be removed under s 16, and notified the chief constable for the police area concerned (or the Metropolitan or City of London Police Commissioner, as the case may be) of the designation. The designated place could be a social services department; it could be a school where there are suitable facilities and staff able to deal with children who may have come from other schools.

Where premises have been designated in a police area under s 16 of the 1998 Act, a police officer of, or above, the rank of superintendent may direct that the powers set out below conferred on a police officer under s 16 are to be exercisable as respects any area falling within the police area, which is specified in the direction. The powers will only be exercisable during the period specified in the direction

A direction will probably be made only after discussions between a school and the police about a perceived truanting problem.

Section 16 of the 1998 Act provides that, where a police officer has reasonable cause to believe that a child or young person found by him in a public place in a specified area during a specified period:

(a) is of compulsory school age; and
(b) is absent from a school without lawful authority,

he may remove the child or young person to designated premises, or to the school from which he is so absent. Surprisingly, the constable does not have to be in uniform. The child must be 'found in a public place' by a police officer. There is no power to enter private premises (eg the child's home) nor to remove a truant found on private premises on which the police officer is already lawfully present. 'Public place' has the same meaning as in s 14 of the 1998 Act. Streets, shopping centres, local authority parks, recreation grounds and swimming pools, and amusement arcades, in many of which truanting children tend to congregate and make a nuisance of themselves are all 'public places' within this definition.

For the purpose of the requirement of a reasonable belief in the juvenile's absence from a school without lawful authority, a child's absence is deemed to be without lawful authority unless it is absent with leave, or because attendance at school is prevented by sickness or any unavoidable cause, or because the absence is on a day exclusively set aside for religious observance by the religious body to which his parent belongs.

Although the power under s 16 is not described as a power of arrest, the power of removal must have inherent in it the power to deprive a juvenile of his liberty, and to use reasonable force to do so, despite the fact that the juvenile has neither committed an offence nor attempted to do so.

If it transpired that the police officer did not have the necessary reasonable belief, or the child was not found in a public place, any force used by the officer would be unlawful and he would not be acting in the execution of his duty.

CHAPTER 19

Intoxicating liquor laws

In this chapter we describe the method of control over the supply of intoxicating liquor, which is principally through a system of licensing, and offences relating thereto. Nearly all the statutory provisions in this area are contained in the Licensing Act 1964, referred to in this chapter simply as the 1964 Act.

We conclude the chapter by describing the various offences involving drunkenness which are provided by statute.

TYPES OF LICENCES AND ORDERS

Justices' licences

A justices' licence is granted to a person in relation to particular premises specified in the licence and allows the retail sale on those premises of intoxicating liquor of the types specified in the licence. The licence, which is renewable every three years, may authorise the sale of liquor of all descriptions, or be restricted to certain types of liquor (for example, beer and cider only). There is a general renewal date every three years. The grant of justices' licences is controlled and such matters are dealt with either at the general annual licensing sessions held in February each year or at transfer sessions. Transfer sessions must be held at least four times a year. Licences are valid throughout the 'licensing period' of three years following that date and, subsequently, triennials of that date. The clerk to the licensing justices may grant unopposed renewals in most circumstances.

A justices' licence may be an 'on-licence' or an 'off-licence'; the words 'on' and 'off' refer to where the liquor is to be drunk. Most justices' on-licences also authorise sales for consumption off the premises. The term 'intoxicating liquor' is defined as spirits, wine, beer, cider and any other fermented, distilled or spirituous liquor of a strength of 0.5 per cent or more. Low alcohol drinks are, therefore, intoxicating liquor.

Apart from the ordinary type of justices' on-licence, the justices may grant restaurant licences, residential licences and residential and restaurant licences (which are all forms of on-licences).

Restaurant licences may be granted for premises which are structurally adapted and bona fide used, or intended to be used, for the purpose of habitually providing the customary main meal at midday, or in the evening, or both, for the accommodation of persons frequenting the premises. Such licences may therefore be granted to restaurants which supply the customary main meals, a term which is not defined but can be taken to mean lunches, high teas and dinner. A restaurant licence permits sale or supply to persons taking table meals on the premises for consumption as an ancillary to the meal and in no other circumstances. Persons who are not eating a table meal there may not drink there.

Residential licences may be granted in respect of genuine private hotels or boarding houses which provide breakfast and at least one of the customary main meals. Sale or supply is restricted to residents or their private friends entertained at their expense. Consequently, such a licence is insufficient for any hotel which offers meals to the general public and wishes to supply drinks with those meals. In such a case the hotel would require a combined residential and restaurant licence, in the absence of a full licence for public drinking.

Protection orders

A person who proposes to apply at the next licensing sessions for the transfer of a justices' licence for any premises may apply to a magistrates' court (as opposed to the licensing justices) for a protection order. In addition, if a justices' licence is forfeited or the licensee is disqualified, the justices may grant a protection order to the owner of the premises or someone authorised by him. A protection order operates as a temporary licence, authorising the person named to sell intoxicating liquor on the premises.

Licences for clubs

Two types of club must be distinguished: members' clubs and proprietary clubs. Most clubs are members' clubs. The property of a *members' club* belongs to the members for the time being jointly in equal shares. Consequently, if liquor is supplied to a member of a members' club at a price, this is not a sale but a release by the other members of their interest in the drink supplied. This being so, members' clubs do not need to be licensed in order to run a bar for their members or to supply them with liquor, although some such clubs are licensed. On the other hand, in the case of a *proprietary club*, ie one owned by a particular person or company and normally conducted for profits, someone must hold a justices' licence in order that a bar may be run for its members or that they may be sold liquor, because, even though transactions are limited to members, the liquor will be sold to them since there will be a sale by or on behalf of the proprietor, who is the owner of the liquor.

Occasional licences

An occasional licence may be granted by an ordinary magistrates' court (as opposed to the licensing justices) to the holder of a justices' on-licence allowing him for a period not exceeding three weeks at any one time to sell the liquors authorised by his licence at premises other than his licensed premises. This allows a licensee to provide a bar at such places as a village hall when a particular function is being held. The hours during which the sales may take place will be specified in the licence; they may be any hours which the justices are prepared to allow on any day of the week. However, they may not be granted in respect of Good Friday, Christmas Day or any other day appointed for public fast or thanksgiving.

Such premises are licensed premises whilst the occasional licence remains in force, and the various offences which can be committed by the holder of a justices' licence may also be committed by the holder of an occasional licence. These are the offences of permitting drunkenness or violence on the licensed premises, of allowing prostitutes to assemble there, of permitting the licensed premises to be a brothel or to be used for unlawful gaming, and of allowing constables to remain on the premises or supplying them with liquor or refreshment.

In addition, the holder of an occasional licence has the power to refuse admission and to expel drunks or quarrelsome persons from the premises. Because they are licensed premises, the provisions of the Act (which are described later) restricting the sale or supply to young persons and the employment of young persons in bars also apply.

The important point for police officers to recognise is that the drinking-up time provisions of the Act which are explained below do not apply to occasional licences because the licence actually expires at a given time and when that occurs the premises are no longer licensed premises. The offence of consumption on licensed premises outside the permitted hours cannot therefore be committed. If sales take place after an occasional licence has expired the offence committed is technically one of selling without a justices' licence.

Occasional permissions

The Licensing (Occasional Permissions) Act 1983 was introduced to remove some of the inconsistencies of the system of occasional licensing. Prior to this Act, it was necessary for an unlicensed members' club to ask a licensee to apply for an occasional licence if it was to hold any function upon its premises at which non-members would be allowed to purchase drinks, since the club could not sell to non-members.

By the 1983 Act, licensing justices may grant to an officer or member of any organisation not carried on for the purpose of private gain, occasional permission to sell intoxicating liquor during any period not exceeding 24 hours, in respect of a function held by that organisation in connection with its activities. The justices must be satisfied that the premises are suitable and that there will be no disturbance or annoyance of residents or any disorderly conduct. If they decide to grant an occasional permission, the justices must give that permission in writing, specifying the place, type of intoxicants to be sold and the hours. A particular organisation may not have more than 12 occasional permissions in any period of 12 months. Separate occasional permissions are required where permission is sought for successive periods even though they total less than 24 hours.

If the profits from sales under the authority of occasional permissions go to the club or organisation this is not classed as private gain. Therefore the Act provides a means by which, if a club holds a social evening on its premises, to which non-members are admitted, the club may operate its own bar.

Section 1 of the 1983 Act permits justices to attach conditions to such written permissions if they consider it proper to do so.

Offences

Section 3 provides for a number of offences, whose details are set out in the Schedule to the Act. A breach of the conditions by the holder of an occasional permission is an offence against para 3 of the Schedule. Paragraph 2 of the Schedule provides an offence of knowingly or recklessly making a materially false statement to obtain such a permission. By analogy with the 1964 Act, other paragraphs in the Schedule impose a ban on sales etc to persons under 18, a ban on the holder permitting drunkenness and a ban on other persons procuring drink for drunken persons; breach of these provisions is an offence.

Exclusion

Paragraph 8 of the Schedule gives the holder power to exclude and expel persons who are drunken or quarrelsome. It also provides that a person commits an offence if he fails to leave when requested to do so on the above grounds by the holder or his agent or a constable, and that a constable must, on the demand of a holder or his agent, help to expel any person liable to be expelled under these provisions.

Entry

By para 9 a constable may enter any authorised premises at any time during the hours specified in the occasional permission for the purpose of preventing or detecting any offence under the provisions of the Schedule. It is an offence for any person, either by himself or by another person acting with his consent, to fail to admit a constable who demands entry under these provisions.

REGISTERED CLUBS

We have already explained that most clubs are members' clubs and that the supply of intoxicating liquor at such a club to a member does not involve a sale of it, with the result that a justices' licence is not required for that transaction. Instead, such clubs are merely required to register with the clerk to the justices who issues a registration certificate, maintains a register of such clubs and informs the police of registrations and applications for registration. It follows that these premises are not licensed premises and that the various powers which are given by the 1964 Act to constables in respect of licensed premises do not apply to registered clubs.

To qualify for registration (or renewal of registration), the rules of a club must not allow admission to membership without at least two days between nomination and acceptance. Before registration of premises can be effected it must be shown that the club is established and conducted in good faith and has at least 25 members, that no individual receives or is to receive any pecuniary benefit from the supply of intoxicating liquor, and that the purchase and supply of intoxicating liquor is under the control of a committee. After registration, default in any of these conditions can lead to cancellation of registration. In addition:

(a) disorderly conduct or habitual use for an unlawful purpose;
(b) habitual breaches of rules concerning admission of non-members;
(c) habitual use of the premises for indecent displays, or as a resort for criminals or prostitutes;
(d) frequent drunkenness on the premises; and
(e) illegal sales within the preceding 12 months,

are all grounds for cancellation of registration.

These provisions relating to the supply of intoxicating liquor on club premises are provided by ss 39–58 of the 1964 Act.

PERMITTED HOURS AND EXTENSIONS TO PERMITTED HOURS

The licensing laws in England and Wales are strict concerning the hours during which licensed premises (or premises in respect of which a club is registered) may be open for the sale of intoxicants. By s 59 of the 1964 Act, it is an offence for a person, himself, or by his servant or agent, to sell or supply intoxicating liquor to any person on licensed premises (or in a registered club) outside permitted hours. This applies whether the drinks are to be consumed on or off the premises. It is also an offence under s 59 for the 'customer' in such circumstances to consume it or take it from the premises. The legal provisions concerning permitted hours do not apply to occasional licences; as we have already explained, each such licence has its own permitted hours. There is an absolute duty placed upon licensees and club committees to ensure that permitted hours are observed. They are vicariously liable for the actions of employees in this respect.

On-licensed premises

On weekdays other than Christmas Day or Good Friday	1100 to 2300
On Sundays, other than Christmas Day, and on Good Friday	1200 to 2230
On Christmas Day	1200 to 1500 and 1900 to 2230

On weekdays the licensing justices for any licensing district, if satisfied that the requirements of the district make it desirable, may by order modify the hours for the district so that the permitted hours begin at a time earlier than 1100 but not earlier than 1000.

The hours applicable under the above provisions are known as the 'general licensing hours'.

Off-licences

On weekdays, other than Christmas Day, permitted hours begin at 0800. The Act therefore allows sales on off-licensed premises from 0800 to 2300. These provisions do not apply to the off-sales department of on-licensed premises, which must close when the licensed premises close.

On Sundays, other than Christmas Day, permitted hours begin at 1000 and end at 2230.

On Christmas Day, permitted hours are the same as for on-licensed premises (ie 1200 to 1500 and 1900 to 2230).

Registered clubs

The permitted hours in respect of the premises of a registered club are:

(a) on days other than Christmas Day, the general licensing hours; and
(b) on Christmas Day, the hours fixed by or under the rules of the club in accordance with the following conditions—
    (i) the hours fixed shall not be longer than six and a half hours and shall not begin earlier than 1200 nor end later than 2230;

(ii)   there shall be a break in the afternoon of not less than two hours which shall include the hours from 1500 to 1700; and

(iii) there shall not be more than three and a half hours after 1700.

Restriction orders

Restriction orders may be made by licensing justices (licensed premises) and by a magistrates' court (clubs). These orders may specify any time between 1430 and 1730 hours on weekdays other than Good Friday and between 1500 and 1900 in the afternoon on Sundays and Good Fridays as being non-permitted hours in any on-licensed premises (or part of such premises), or in any registered club. They may apply to particular days of the week and to particular periods of the year and shall not remain in force for more than 12 months. Application for variation or revocation may be made after a period of six months. Where such an order is in force, a notice must be conspicuously displayed stating the effect of the order.

An application for a restriction order may be made by chief officers of police, persons living in the neighbourhood (or their representative), neighbouring businessmen or their managers, or head teachers. A restriction order may be made on the grounds of avoiding or reducing annoyance or disturbance to local residents or workers, to customers of businessmen in the locality or to people at schools there. It may also be made on the grounds that it is desirable to avoid or reduce the occurrence of disorderly conduct in the premises or part of the premises, or in the vicinity of such premises by persons resorting to the premises.

Exceptions to permitted hours rule

Certain sales outside permitted hours are specifically authorised by s 63 of the 1964 Act, and are therefore not offences contrary to s 59. Some of these general exemptions recognise the fact that some people reside on the licensed premises and should not be limited by the permitted hours in their freedom to drink there or offer hospitality to their friends. Other exemptions concern trade dealings or recognise the absurdity which would arise if liquor were allowed to be sold up to a certain time without time being allowed for it to be drunk thereafter.

Residents etc

Dealing with the first type of exemption, s 63 exempts from the rules concerning permitted hours:

(a)   the sale or supply to, or consumption by, a person of intoxicating liquor in any premises where he is residing (with the result that it is not, for example, illegal for the licensee to have a drink after hours, or for a hotel resident to be sold a drink there after hours);

(b)   the taking of intoxicating liquor from licensed premises by a person residing there;

(c)   the supply of intoxicating liquor for consumption on licensed premises to any 'private friends' of a person residing there who are bona fide entertained by him at his own expense, or the consumption of such liquor by those friends;

(d) the supply of intoxicating liquor for consumption on licensed premises to persons employed there, or the consumption of liquor so supplied, if the liquor is supplied at the expense of their employer or the person in charge of the business on the premises.

References in the above list to a person residing on premises are to be construed as including a person not residing there but carrying on or being in charge of the business on the premises.

It follows from the exemptions just listed that all persons who live on licensed premises of any type may drink at any time as they would in any other home. Visiting friends have the same status as they would have in other circumstances. The term 'private friends' in (c) is not defined but a distinction must be drawn between pretend and real friends. Consideration must be given to the nature of the occasion and evidence of any transaction which could involve, in any way, a form of payment for intoxicants. People cannot suddenly assume the status of friends at the conclusion of permitted hours. The intention of the Act was to allow private drinking in private quarters and, although there is nothing unlawful in such drinking in a bar, it is one circumstance which may indicate that friendships were not long standing.

Trade sales etc

Trade sales are allowed by s 63 to all authorised establishments. The section also permits intoxicating liquor for off-consumption to be ordered outside permitted hours, provided that it is not dispatched by the seller during the same period of non-permitted hours. Consequently, if an order is placed outside permitted hours it cannot be delivered until the next period of permitted hours or at any time after that period has intervened. This provision is of little significance now that most off-licence shops are open all day and liquor can be purchased at any time.

Drinking-up time

Provided that the intoxicating liquor was supplied during permitted hours, consumption of it on the premises after the end of those hours is not an offence under s 59 in the following cases:

(a) Consumption may take place on the premises during the first 20 minutes after the end of any period of permitted hours. (It should be noted that sealed containers of liquor for off-consumption may also be taken away during this period.)
(b) Persons taking meals on licensed premises may consume drinks bought as an ancillary to that meal during the first half hour after the end of a period of permitted hours. This is merely an extended drinking-up time for those drinking with a meal. The nature of the meal which is to be taken to allow such extended drinking-up time is not defined. In particular, the meal is not required to be a table meal. Consequently, the provisions can apply to meals served in the bar of a public house. If a contravention of s 59 is charged, it will be for the justices to decide whether the nature of the food consumed is sufficient to meet the exception. Many bars now have machines for the preparation of toasted sandwiches but it is submitted that the provision concerning extended drinking-up time was not intended by the Act to extend to the eating of such sandwiches.

Permitted hours at sports grounds

The Sporting Events (Control of Alcohol etc) Act 1985 is concerned with measures to combat soccer hooliganism. One of the causes of hooliganism was recognised as the availability of intoxicants at soccer matches.

The Act introduces measures which apply to 'designated sporting events' at 'designated sports grounds'. A 'designated sporting event' is a sporting event or a proposed sporting event for the time being designated, or of a class designated, by order of the Secretary of State. An order may apply to events outside Great Britain in certain circumstances. A 'designated sports ground' is any place used (wholly or partly) for sporting events where accommodation is provided for spectators and is for the time being designated, or of a class designated, by order made by the Secretary of State. Such an order may include a provision for determining, for the purposes of the Act, the outer limits of any designated sports ground. Under these provisions the Secretary of State has made the Sports Grounds and Sporting Events (Designation) Order 1985. Under this Order, the following association football club grounds have been designated: Wembley Stadium (which is not simply a football ground); the home association football grounds of all football clubs which are members of the FA or FA of Wales; any other ground in England and Wales used occasionally or temporarily by such a club; grounds used for international matches and Shielfield Park, Berwick-upon-Tweed (specially mentioned because the club, Berwick Rangers, plays in the Scottish League). Sporting events which are designated are association football matches involving at least one team belonging to the Football League or the Football Association Premier League, internationals, European Champion Clubs Cup matches, European Cup-Winners Cup matches or UEFA Cup matches, Scottish League or FA Cup matches at Shielfield Park, and matches outside Great Britain involving a team representing the FA or Football League or Football Association of Wales (or involving an English or Welsh team in one of the three European competitions described above).

The permitted hours

Section 3(1) of the 1985 Act states that permitted hours on licensed premises or registered clubs in such designated sports grounds shall not include any part of *the period* of a designated sporting event at that ground, nor shall there be any 'off supply' during that period. The Act defines *the period* of a designated sporting event as the period beginning two hours before the start of the event or (if earlier), two hours before the time at which it is advertised to start, and ending one hour after the event. If a match is postponed or cancelled, *the period* includes the period in the day on which it is advertised to take place, beginning two hours before and ending one hour after that time. However, s 3(2) permits a magistrates' court to allow, by order, supply in premises (or part of those premises) during such an event, subject to any conditions which the court may wish to impose. Any such order will not apply to any part of the premises from which the designated sporting event, at that ground, may be directly viewed. There must be a condition requiring a person to be in attendance throughout who is responsible for compliance with the order. Written notice of his name and address must be given to the chief officer of police. A magistrates' court must not make such an order unless satisfied that the arrangements are satisfactory. Orders may be varied or revoked by a magistrates' court and (unless sooner revoked) expire on the coming into operation of a further order, or after 12 months, whichever is the sooner. They also cease to have effect if the premises cease to be licensed or registered, or if a justices' licence is transferred.

The Act also makes provisions in respect of emergency situations in which there is no time to refer to a magistrates' court for a revocation or variation of an order under s 3(2). A police officer, of not less rank than inspector, if of the opinion that such sale or supply is likely to be detrimental to the orderly conduct or safety of spectators at a particular designated sporting event *and* that it is impracticable for an application to be made to a magistrates' court for revocation or variation, may give written notice to the person whose name has been given to the chief officer of police stating that, with effect from the time when the notice is given, the order under the section shall, in respect of the sporting event concerned, either cease to have effect, or have effect subject to such modifications as may be specified in the order. Such a notice may be served by leaving it at the licensed premises or registered club or at the address notified to the chief officer of police.

Section 5A permits a relaxation of the provisions in respect of drinking within the ground. Variations are permitted in the case of private facilities for viewing designated sporting events. The restrictions which apply to the possession of intoxicating liquor (and those which exclude from the permitted hours of licensed premises and registered clubs within the area of a designated ground the period of a designated event) are amended to permit sale, supply and possession in a room from which an event may be viewed, which is not open to the general public, at times other than those within a special 'restricted period'. This special period is the period beginning 15 minutes before the start of the event (or the advertised start of the event if earlier), and ending 15 minutes after the end of the event. The same provisions apply in respect of postponed fixtures. The Secretary of State may by order shorten this restricted period or abolish it. Drinking in the Directors' Box overlooking the pitch is therefore restored to a certain extent and may be fully restored by order.

Sections 5B, C and D prohibit any sale or supply under an occasional licence or by a registered club in the area of a designated sports ground on a special occasion during the period of a designated sporting event at such a ground; this prohibition does not apply to sales on the registered premises of a club. Non-retail sales are also prohibited. These provisions prevent the circumvention of the provisions of the Act aimed at the prevention of public drinking within soccer grounds.

Offences

A person who sells or supplies, or authorises the sale or supply of intoxicating liquor at any time which is excluded from the permitted hours by virtue of s 3, or in contravention of conditions imposed under this section, is not guilty of selling outside permitted hours contrary to the Licensing Act 1964, s 59. Instead, he is guilty of an offence contrary to the Sporting Events (Control of Alcohol etc) Act 1985, s 3(10), if he is the holder of the justices' licence or an officer of the club. Any other person who sells or supplies in these circumstances is guilty of a similar offence *if he knows or has reasonable cause to believe* the sale or supply to be such a contravention.

A person is not guilty of an offence of consumption or taking away during non-permitted hours contrary to the Licensing Act 1964, s 59, in instances in which the permitted hours have been suspended by a written notice from a police officer of a rank not less than inspector, unless he *knows or has reasonable cause to believe* that the time is not within permitted hours.

Police powers

Section 6(1) of the 1985 Act provides that, if at any time during the period of a designated sporting event at any designated sports ground, it appears to a constable in uniform that the sale or supply of intoxicating liquor at any bar within the ground is detrimental to the orderly conduct or safety of spectators at that event, he may require any person having control of the bar to close it and keep it closed until the end of that period. A person commits an offence under s 6(2) if he fails to comply with such a requirement.

Section 7(1) of the 1985 Act permits a constable to enter any part of a designated sports ground during the period of a designated sporting event for the purpose of enforcing the provisions of the Act.

Extension of permitted hours in restaurants etc: supper and lunch hour extensions

If the licensing justices (in respect of licensed premises) and the magistrates' court (in the case of registered clubs) are satisfied that the premises are structurally adapted and bona fide used or intended to be used for the habitual provision of substantial refreshment, to which the sale and supply of intoxicating liquor is ancillary, a 'supper hour extension' may be added by the licensee in respect of such premises. This involves an extension of the permitted hours in the evening by one hour in the part of those premises set apart for the provision of meals. It allows the sale, supply and consumption of intoxicants in that part of the premises if drunk by persons taking table meals as an ancillary to that meal.

The extension applies only to that part of the premises which is specified in the order and all other parts of the premises must observe normal permitted hours. The term 'table meal' should be given its normal, everyday meaning. Section 68 of the 1964 Act, which authorises supper hour extensions, allows an apéritif to be taken before the meal and a brandy or liqueur to be taken afterwards in a room other than that in which the meal is taken, provided that the room is set apart for that purpose. Where such an order is in force, advantage may still be taken of the half-hour of drinking-up time with a meal, so that drinking may continue lawfully until midnight or 0030 hours depending on the day of the week.

Likewise, a lunch hour extension may be applied to the premises by the licensee. Where a lunch hour extension is in force, intoxicants may be served with a meal between the first and second parts of general licensing hours on Christmas Day.

Extended hours in restaurants etc providing entertainment (extended hours order)

Section 70 of the 1964 Act allows an extended hours order to be made whereby certain licensed premises or registered clubs are permitted to remain open until 0100 hours. Such premises, together with those which have special hours certificates (see later), are usually referred to as night clubs.

For an extended hours order to be made, the premises must in the first instance have a supper hour extension. The result is that the justices or the clerk of the court will already be satisfied in respect of the structural adaptation and bona fide use of the premises for the provision of table meals, which is one of the conditions for an extended hours order. In addition, the premises must be structurally suitable and bona fide used or intended to be used habitually to provide musical or other entertainment for those attending. The sale and supply of intoxicants must be ancillary to the provision of meals and entertainment, and the extended hours will be limited to the particular part of the premises so used. The section permits extended hours until 0100 hours but the justices may limit the order to a time earlier than 0100 hours if it appears to them to be reasonable to do so having regard to all the circumstances, particularly in relation to the comfort and convenience of those in nearby premises.

The entertainment provided in such establishments must be live entertainment and the refreshment must be substantial. In addition, entertainment must be provided after and for a substantial period before the end of normal licensing hours.

The effect of the order is to allow the sale or supply of intoxicating liquor up to the time at which the availability of meals, or the provision of such entertainment, ceases, and to allow the consumption of those intoxicants within the terms of the normal half-hour drinking-up time following the end of the permitted hours. Consequently, if no meals or entertainments are provided after 2330 hours, the restaurant or club cannot serve drinks after that time. Sale or supply is not permitted in any circumstances to a person admitted after midnight, or less than half an hour before the entertainment is due to end, unless that sale or supply would have been permitted in any case within the terms of the supper hour order. These provisions eliminate the possibility of an early sale of meals with entertainment and late drinking until 0100 hours. The sale or supply of intoxicating liquor under an extended hours order is always linked to the provision of meals or of entertainment.

Special hours certificates in licensed premises and clubs

Sections 76 to 83 of the 1964 Act deal with various provisions concerning premises in respect of which there is a 'special hours certificate'. Where the licensed premises are casino premises or a music and dancing licence is in force for them, and the premises (or part of those premises) are structurally adapted and bona fide used, or intended to be used, for gaming facilities and substantial refreshment (in the case of casino premises), or for the provision of music and dancing and substantial refreshment (in the case of other premises), to which the sale of intoxicants is merely ancillary, the licensing justices may grant with or without limitations a special hours certificate.

Where a certificate of suitability of club premises for music and dancing is in force for a registered club, and its premises are in whole or part structurally adapted and bona fide used, or intended for use, for the provision of music and dancing and substantial refreshment to which the supply of intoxicants is merely ancillary, a magistrates' court may grant with or without limitations a special hours certificate.

A special hours certificate may restrict the hours to a part of the premises. Many premises to which a special hours certificate may be issued are also referred to loosely as night clubs but, unlike extended hours orders, a special hours certificate does not involve a requirement for live entertainment with meals, although there is a requirement that music and dancing will be available with the meals.

Where premises are to be, or are being, adapted for the purposes of obtaining a special hours certificate, the licensing justices or a magistrates' court (as the case may be) may issue a provisional special hours certificate but this does not operate as a valid certificate until the justices or court declare themselves satisfied with the adaptations.

Where a special hours certificate is in force, the permitted hours on *weekdays* extend until 0200 hours in the next morning (0300 hours in those parts of the metropolis specified in the Licensing (Metropolitan Special Hours Area) Order 1961).

Permitted hours:

(a) must end at midnight on any weekday on which music and dancing, or (in the case of casinos) gaming facilities, are not provided after midnight;

(b) must end when the music and dancing, or the gaming, end on a weekday on which music and dancing, or (in the case of casinos) gaming, end between midnight and 0200.

The justices or the court may limit the effect of the certificate to particular times of the day, days of the week, or periods of the year. There is provision for this to be done at any time on application by a chief officer of police. Unlike a supper or lunch hour extension or an extended hours order, a special hours certificate is not simply a 'bolt-on extra' to permitted hours. Consequently, they are not limited in their operation to a period after the end of permitted hours. It follows that the justices or court can impose a start time in a special hours certificate which is earlier than the end of permitted hours. The importance of this is that on the days when the special licence certificate is in force the sale of liquor during the hours permitted by that certificate must be ancillary to the provision of music and dancing (or gaming facilities) and food, even during those hours which are before the end of permitted hours (ie normal closing time).

As can be seen these provisions restrict late night drinking in such premises to situations in which there are music and dancing (or gaming) and refreshment. If the music and dancing (or gaming) are suspended earlier than 02.00 hours the permitted hours are automatically restricted. It must be emphasised that these provisions do not apply where the day in question is a Sunday.

Where a special hours certificate is in force an hour is not lost on the day that clocks go forward; it is added on to the clock.

Exemption orders

The previous two exemptions have been concerned with 'night clubs' and the like but s 74 of the 1964 Act (to which we now turn) makes provision for the extension of hours in pubs and clubs on particular occasions.

The holder of a justices' on-licence or the secretary of a registered club may be granted a 'general order of exemption' when the premises in question are situated in the immediate neighbourhood of a public market or a place where people follow a particular lawful trade or calling. For example, most market towns have a special market day on which farmers from the surrounding area attend the market throughout the day, creating an unusual demand for refreshment. Registers are kept in police stations in which details of such orders are recorded. Orders may be revoked at any time. The purpose of the order is to allow pubs and clubs to remain open at times when there is a particular and unusual demand for refreshment because of the situation of the premises in the way described above. The order is made in respect of named premises and the hours and the days are specified in the order.

On-licence holders and secretaries of clubs may also apply to a magistrates' court for a 'special order of exemption'. These orders are frequently referred to as 'applications for extensions'. The justices may grant such orders without a hearing if written application is received not less than one month in advance of the application. The particular hours which are to be added to the normal permitted hours will be specified in the order. These orders may only be granted in respect of a 'special occasion or occasions'. That term is not defined, but the Divisional Court has emphasised the word 'special' and held that the more frequent an occasion the less likely it is to be held to be special, with the result that weekly debates at the Oxford Union over an eight-week period were held not to be special occasions. These applications are frequently in respect of dinners, dances, weddings, birthday parties or some other festivity. It is a matter for the justices to grant or reject the applications. Such special orders automatically apply to the whole of the premises and are not restricted to a special room. Consequently, it is the practice of justices on occasions, to require an undertaking that normal licensing hours will be observed in other parts of the premises. However, if the undertaking is subsequently ignored, no offence is committed. Special orders of exemption may be granted for more than one day.

Canteens

Some premises upon which liquor is sold or supplied are 'canteens' in respect of which authority is granted by the Secretary of State for intoxicating liquor to be sold or supplied. Such premises will generally be service messes, including those of visiting forces. Permitted hours do not apply to such premises but, if they are ill-conducted, only the Secretary of State can remove their authority to sell or supply. A 'canteen' of the present type must not be confused with a 'licensed canteen' which is licensed for use by seamen. Police officers have no powers in respect of canteens authorised by the Secretary of State.

Parties organised for gain

Section 84 of the 1964 Act is concerned with drinking outside permitted hours on a commercial basis. In a community which seeks late night drinking parties it would be an easy matter to overcome permitted hours by buying large quantities of intoxicating liquor during licensing hours and taking them to premises at which they could be sold to other persons. If evidence was available of a straight sale, the person organising such a party would be guilty of selling without a justices' licence, but it is possible that without any charge of any kind no evidence of sale would be apparent. Of course, if the liquor was given away there would be *no* offence. However, there are a number of possibilities between these two extremes and it is these with which the section is concerned.

Section 84 states that it shall be unlawful before the beginning or after the end of general licensing hours to supply or consume intoxicating liquor at any party organised for gain which is taking place in premises *kept or habitually used* for the purpose of parties so organised at which intoxicating liquor is consumed.

Section 84 does not apply to parties on licensed premises or on premises with an occasional licence, nor to anything done as part of the activities of a canteen, mess or registered club at the canteen, mess or club.

A party is deemed to have been organised for gain if any pecuniary advantage accrued or was intended to accrue to any person concerned in its organisation. In deciding whether such an advantage so accrued or was intended to accrue, no account is to be taken of any expenditure incurred in connection with the party. If a person habitually organises parties in his house and charges a fixed fee for admission, but makes no charges for drinks, this would be a party organised for gain as a pecuniary advantage accrues. The provision of a buffet meal which made the charge seem more reasonable would make no difference as no account is to be taken of such expenditure.

Offences

Offences are committed by anyone who supplies intoxicating liquor for an unlawful party organised for gain, by the occupier of any premises who permits them to be used for such a party, by anyone concerned in the organisation of such a party who permits any person to supply or consume intoxicating liquor there, or by a licensee who delivers (or permits to be delivered) intoxicating liquor outside the general licensing hours to any premises kept or habitually used for such a party. A person who consumes intoxicating liquor at such a party also commits an offence.

Entry, search and seizure

If a justice is satisfied on oath that there is reasonable ground for believing that any premises are kept or habitually used for the holding of unlawful parties organised for gain, he may issue a search warrant authorising entry by a constable at any time or times within one month, by force if necessary, to search for and seize intoxicating liquor suspected of being on premises for supply or consumption in contravention of the above provisions. Persons found on premises when such seizure takes place must, on request, give their names and addresses to a constable. To refuse to do so, or to give a false name and address, is an offence.

SELLING WITHOUT A LICENCE

By s 160 of the 1964 Act, it is an offence to sell or expose for retail sale any intoxicating liquor without a justices' licence or occasional permission. (The reader is reminded that the supply of liquor to a member in a members' club does not involve a sale, so that none of the above offences can be committed regardless of the absence of a licence.)

Where sale or exposure for sale without a licence is alleged, it is for the accused to prove that he had a licence (and not for the prosecution to prove that he did not). Where a person holds a justices' licence for premises, he cannot be convicted of selling without a licence merely because a sale takes place outside permitted hours, as specified in the licence, since there is a licence in force; the appropriate offence to charge is sale outside permitted hours. On the other hand, when it is an occasional licence which is involved, that licence ceases to exist at the time which is stated in it. Any sale after that time is a sale without a licence.

It is an offence under s 160 for a person who holds such a licence or permission to sell or expose for retail sale intoxicating liquor at a place not covered by the licence or permission.

An employee (or agent) who is selling on behalf of his employer (or principal), who is a licensee, is not guilty of the offence of selling liquor at a place other than the one licensed if he is unaware that a licence is not in force there. The selling which is prohibited is that of the licensee. However, if the employee, or agent, is aware the premises are not licensed, he is guilty of aiding and abetting the offence by his employer (or principal), the licensee.

In instances in which intoxicating liquor is sold without a licence or otherwise than in licensed premises, every occupier of the premises who is in any way concerned with that sale or who consents to it is guilty of an offence.

OFFENCES BY LICENSEES AND EMPLOYEES

General

Licensed premises these days are often staffed not simply by the licensee but also by employees (either of the licensee or of the brewery or the like). This does not necessarily mean that the licensee can escape liability where the physical conduct is carried out by an employee, unknown to him. The reasons are as follows. First, in the case of the offence of supplying a constable, the licensee (as well as the actual employee who did so) can be convicted, because technically the selling or supplying is done by the licensee. Second, a number of licensing offences are framed in terms of the licensee knowingly doing the particular thing. Here, the licensee can be convicted of the offence (and he is the only person who can be convicted as perpetrator), despite the fact that he did not do the prohibited thing personally, provided the person who knowingly did do it was someone to whom he had delegated the management of the premises. In such a case it is possible to convict the employee as an accomplice to the offence. Third, some offences expressly state that a person may be convicted of the offence if it is perpetrated by himself or by his servant or agent (who, again, may be convicted as an accomplice).

Selling in breach of a condition of a licence

By s 161 of the 1964 Act, an offence is committed by the holder of a justices' on-licence who knowingly sells or supplies intoxicating liquor to persons to whom he is not permitted to sell or supply it by the conditions of his licence. The holder of a residential licence, a restaurant licence or a residential and restaurant licence commits an offence under these provisions if he knowingly permits consumption of intoxicating liquor on his premises by people for whose consumption he is not permitted by the conditions of his licence to sell it. The essence of the offence is a breach of particular conditions attached to particular licences. All such conditions in respect of a licence are noted in the register of licensed premises for the district.

Off-licence sales

The off-licence departments with which the law is generally concerned are those selling bottled or canned spirits, wines and beers to the general public. As we have seen, they are licensed for off-sales from 0800 (or 1000 on Sundays and Christmas Day) until the end of permitted hours for the district. On-licensed premises may also be authorised by the justices (and normally are) to sell for off-consumption but generally they are restricted to the permitted hours applicable to their on-licence in respect of those sales. Occasionally, there is a difference. Where there is attached to the public house a separate building dealing with off-sales, there will usually be a separate off-licence in force for those premises, or the licence of the public house will have been endorsed to permit off-sales throughout the day in that separate and divided part of the premises.

Section 164 of the 1964 Act provides three offences relating to off-licences:

(a) Where a person, having purchased intoxicating liquor in an off-licence, drinks the liquor -
   (i)   in the licensed premises; or
   (ii) in premises adjoining or near them, which belong to the licensee or are under his control or used by his permission; or
   (iii) on a highway adjoining or near the licensed premises,
   the licensee is guilty of an offence if he is party to that drinking or it is done with his consent.
(b) If the licensee, with intent to evade the terms of the off-licence, takes or allows any other person to take any intoxicating liquor from the licensed premises for the purpose of being sold on his account or for his benefit or profit, the licensee is

guilty of an offence. If the liquor is taken for consumption in any building or tent belonging to the licensee, or hired, used or occupied by him, he is presumed to have intended to evade the terms of his licence unless he proves the contrary.

(c) If the licensee sells any spirits or wine (but not beer) in an open vessel, he commits an offence.

Deliveries of liquor for off-consumption are controlled. However, the relevant legal provisions appear to be of very little consequence when off-licensed premises are open all day, since their main purpose was to prevent order and delivery within a particular break in licensing hours. Deliveries of intoxicating liquor for off-consumption must be recorded in a day book kept on the licensed premises, and a person who is delivering orders from a vehicle should be in possession of a delivery book or invoices accounting for all of the liquor in the vehicle. Offences of selling in breach of these conditions are committed by a licensee, his employee or agent in relation to both the carrying and the selling of the intoxicants. However, a licensee is not liable for such an offence committed by his employee or agent if he proves that it was committed without his knowledge or consent. A constable may examine the day book on the premises and the contents and records carried on any vehicle or conveyance.

Credit sales

Credit sales on licensed premises are made an offence by s 166 unless the liquor is supplied with a meal and is to be paid for together with the meal, or unless it is supplied to a resident to be paid for together with his bill for accommodation. If a prohibited credit sale occurs, both the seller and the consumer commit offences. Where the sale is by a barman or the like, the licensee is also liable.

Sale etc to persons under 18

By s 169 of the 1964 Act, a licensee or his employee must not sell intoxicating liquor to a person under 18. To do so is an offence. The offence need not be committed knowingly. However, it is a defence for a person charged with personally 'selling' to prove that he exercised all due diligence to avoid the commission of such an offence, or that he had no reason to suspect that the person was under 18. Where a licensee is charged as a consequence of the act of some other person, it is a defence for him to prove that he exercised all due diligence to avoid the commission of that offence.

Section 169 provides that a licensee must not knowingly allow a sale to such a person, and he and his employee must not knowingly allow such a person to consume intoxicating liquor in a bar. Under s 169, in addition, a person under 18 must not buy or attempt to buy intoxicating liquor in licensed premises, nor consume it in a bar. Such a person may often be accompanied by an older person and, for this reason, it is provided by s 169 that a person must not buy or attempt to buy intoxicating liquor for consumption by a person under 18 in a bar. Breach of these prohibitions is also an offence. Section 169 does not prohibit persons who have attained the age of 16 from purchasing and consuming beer, porter or cider to drink with a meal in a dining room; no offence is committed by the seller or buyer in such a case.

Some of the offences under s 169 are committed in the licensed premises as a whole, while others are restricted to a bar. A 'bar' includes any place exclusively or mainly used for the sale or consumption of intoxicating liquor. The term does not therefore apply to rooms which are used exclusively for the provision of meals and in which the supply of intoxicating liquor is restricted to persons taking a meal, as an ancillary to that meal. In all other circumstances, the issue of whether a room is a bar will be decided upon the particular circumstances existing at the time of the alleged offence.

In deciding the offences which have been committed in circumstances involving young persons who are drinking on licensed premises, it is helpful first to consider the question of where the drinking is taking place. If it has taken place in a bar then offences of 'consumption' may be charged. If it has not, the appropriate charges will be of sale and purchase, if these can be proved. When reporting offenders for offences involving consumption, the fact that they took place in a bar must be mentioned.

John, aged 17, is in a bar with his friend, David, who is 18. If John orders a pint of beer and is served by the licensee, the licensee commits an offence if he sells the beer. At this stage the issue of whether or not it takes place in a bar is unimportant as the offence of 'sale', unless specifically permitted in the circumstances, can take place anywhere. In addition to the liability of the licensee, John commits the offence of 'purchasing'.

Once John begins to drink from the glass he is guilty of an offence of 'consumption', provided that this takes place in a bar. At this time the licensee and the barman, if they are aware of the situation, may become guilty of knowingly allowing consumption in a bar. The word 'knowingly' in these circumstances applies to the age of the customer, not to the act of the sale. It can be applied to situations in which a licensee deliberately closes his eyes to the obvious. If David had bought the drink, or had attempted to buy it, for consumption in a bar by John, he would have committed an offence.

If the purchase had been made by David with the intention of taking the drink outside so that John might consume it, he would not have committed an offence as it was not bought for John to drink in a bar. The taking outside of drinks purchased on licensed premises is not uncommon and it is quite lawful.

The provisions which restrict sales to persons under 18 apply equally to intoxicants for off-consumption. A licence holder or his employee must not knowingly deliver intoxicants to a person under 18 for off-consumption. It is also an offence for a person to send anyone under 18 to purchase intoxicants for off-consumption. This applies to all licensees and their employees, whether they are in off-licence shops or off-licence departments of supermarkets.

Presence of persons under 18 in a bar

By s 170 of the 1964 Act, a licensee must not employ persons under a specified age in a bar at a time when it is open for the sale or consumption of intoxicating liquor. The specified age is normally 18, but it is 16 if the employee is employed under an approved training scheme. If he does the licensee (but not the employee) is guilty of an offence. These provisions do not apply to persons who are generally employed elsewhere and merely pass through the bar in the course of their duties, such as hotel messengers and waiters. In the present context a person is deemed to be employed by the person for whom he works notwithstanding that he receives no wages for his work.

Generally it is an offence under s 168 for the licensee to allow a person under 14 to be in a bar during the permitted hours, but no offence is committed in the case of a child of the licensee, a child of a resident who is not an employee, or of a child who is merely passing through the bar. The offence does not apply to railway refreshment rooms. Nor does it apply where the person under 14 is in the company of someone of 18 or over and one or both of them is consuming a meal in the bar, provided that there is in force a 'children's' certificate relating to the bar. Such a certificate is obtainable from the licensing justices, who must be satisfied that the premises are a suitable environment for children to be present and that meals and non-alcoholic drinks will be available. If a non-authorised child is in a bar, the licensee is guilty of an offence unless he proves that he exercised all due diligence to prevent the admission of the child or that the child had apparently reached 14. In addition to the licensee, a person who causes or procures a child under 14 to be in a bar during permitted hours, or attempts to do so, is guilty of an offence. The child itself commits no offence.

Confiscation of alcohol – young persons

Section 1 of the Confiscation of Alcohol (Young Persons) Act 1997 provides that where a constable reasonably suspects that a person in any public place other than licensed premises, or in any place (other than a public place) to which that person has unlawfully gained access, is in possession of alcohol and that either:

(a) he is under 18; or
(b) he intends that any of the liquor should be consumed by a person under 18 in that or another similar place; or
(c) a person under 18 who is, or has recently been, with him has recently consumed intoxicating liquor in that or another similar place,

the constable may require him to surrender anything in his possession which is, or which the constable reasonably believes to be, intoxicating liquor and to state his name and address. A person who, without reasonable excuse, fails to comply with such a requirement commits an offence. A constable who imposes a requirement under s 1 must inform the person concerned of his suspicion and that failing without reasonable excuse to comply with his requirement is an offence.

This is a short but useful Act which sets out to deal with the groups of young persons who assemble in public places drinking intoxicating liquor from cans. The provisions of s 1 of the 1997 Act effectively embrace all persons likely to be in such a group, including those who are over the age of 18 if, as they are almost certain to be, they are associated with drinking by those who are under age. Where a person of 18 or over is with a young person who is or has been drinking in such a place, (c) above requires the surrender of intoxicating liquor in the adult person's possession.

Police powers

A constable is empowered to dispose of anything surrendered to him under s 1 in such manner as he considers appropriate.

A constable may arrest without warrant a person who fails to comply with a requirement to surrender made under the 1997 Act.

Other offences by licensees

Drunks and rowdies

A licensee must not permit drunkenness or any violent, quarrelsome or riotous behaviour on the licensed premises, and he must not sell intoxicating liquor to a drunken person. If he does, he commits an offence contrary to s 172 of the 1964 Act. If a licensee is charged with permitting drunkenness on the licensed premises and it is proved that any person on those premises was drunk, it need not be proved that the licensee actually knew or suspected that a person was drunk there but he has a defence if he proves that he and his employees took all reasonable steps to prevent drunkenness on the premises.

The Licensed Premises (Exclusion of Certain Persons) Act 1980 permits courts to make orders in respect of persons convicted of offences of violence or threats of violence on licensed premises, prohibiting such a person from entering specified licensed premises without the express consent of the licensee, his employee or agent. A person who enters in breach of an order commits an offence. The licensee, his employee or agent may expel a person who has entered, or whom he reasonably suspects of entering, in breach of an order. A constable must, on the demand of a licensee, his employee or agent, help to expel any person whom the constable reasonably suspects of being in breach of an exclusion order.

The licensee, his employee or agent may always require persons who are drunk, violent, quarrelsome or disorderly, or whose presence would subject the licensee to a penalty under the 1964 Act, to leave the premises. A constable is required to assist if requested to do so by the licensee, or his employee or agent; he may use such force as may be required. It is an offence for a person to fail to leave when required to do so by the licensee, his employee or agent, or a constable. There is no power to arrest other than the general power provided by the Police and Criminal Evidence Act 1984.

Prostitutes

The licensee must not knowingly allow his premises to become the habitual resort or meeting place of reputed prostitutes, but this does not prohibit his allowing reputed prostitutes to remain in the premises for the purpose of obtaining reasonable refreshment for such time as is necessary for that purpose. There is a difference between serving a prostitute and allowing the premises to become a meeting place. If a licensee contravenes the above prohibition, he commits an offence under s 175 of the 1964 Act.

Under s 176, it is an offence, more serious than the one just described, for a licensee to permit the licensed premises to be a brothel. We discuss offences relating to brothels in detail in ch 34, below.

Gaming

If a licensee allows any game to be played on the premises which would be an offence under the Gaming Act 1968, or allows a requirement or restriction under s 6 of that Act to be contravened, he commits an offence contrary to s 177 of the 1964 Act. The gaming laws are dealt with in detail in ch 20, below.

Constables

The licensee must not knowingly allow a constable to remain on his premises whilst that constable is on duty, unless he is present in the execution of his duty. This offence, which is provided by s 178 of the 1964 Act, is not associated with drinking; it is merely concerned with presence whilst on duty. A different offence, also under s 178, is committed if a licensee supplies any intoxicating liquor or refreshment, whether by sale or gift, to a constable on duty without the authority of a superior officer of the constable. The officer who, with the licensee's consent, calls in for a moment in the warmth causes the licensee to commit the first of these two offences, and the second offence is committed by the licensee if refreshment is supplied. It is a frequent practice that, when officers are performing special duties away from their police station under the supervision of a superior officer, they will take a refreshment break in a public house. The licensee commits no offence if the officers are authorised to be there by the superior officer.

A licensee also commits a further offence under s 178 if he bribes or attempts to bribe a constable.

'ON' AND 'OFF' LICENSEES AND WHOLESALERS: SALES TO OR BY PERSONS UNDER 18

The holder of a justices' off-licence, or an on-licence holder with an off-sales department, or a wholesaler, shall not allow a person under 18 to make any sale of intoxicating liquor unless the sale has been approved by him or by a person of or over the age of 18 acting on his behalf.

In addition, a wholesaler or his employee must not sell intoxicating liquor to a person under 18, nor shall a person under 18 buy or attempt to buy such liquor. The same defences are available to such a wholesaler, as are available to licensees (see p 468).

POWER TO ENTER LICENSED PREMISES

For the purpose of preventing or detecting the commission of any of the above offences against the Licensing Act 1964, a constable is empowered by s 186 of that Act to enter licensed premises, a licensed canteen, or registered club premises for which (or any part of which) a special hours certificate (or a provisional special hours certificate) is in force:

(a)   in the case of licensed premises or a licensed canteen, during permitted hours and during the first half hour after the end of any period of permitted hours;
(b)   where an occasional licence is in force, during the hours specified in the licence;
(c)   where a special hours certificate (or a provisional one) is in force, during the period between 2300 and half an hour after the end of permitted hours for those premises.

The special mention of entry where there is an occasional licence merely recognises the fact that once an occasional licence has expired, the premises are no longer licensed premises. Some registered clubs have special hours certificates and (c) is concerned with entry into such clubs. Entry is permitted into licensed premises which have a special hours certificate at any such time as falls within (a).

There is an extended right of entry under s 186 in relation to premises in respect of which there is a justices' licence in force and to licensed canteens. An entry can be made at any time outside the specific hours mentioned above when a constable suspects with reasonable cause that an offence against the 1964 Act is being, or is about to be, committed. It would be illogical if this power was not provided as the most likely reason for a constable to require admission outside those hours is that unlawful drinking is taking place.

It is an offence under s 186 for any person to fail to admit a constable who demands entry to premises under either of these powers. The licensee commits an offence if an employee, or any other person acting with his consent, fails to give such admittance. The constable must have demanded admission and must have declared that he is a constable. It is advised that constables notify their supervisory officer of their suspicions that liquor offences are taking place on such licensed premises and that they obtain assistance.

Search warrants

The Licensing Act 1964 includes specific provisions in respect of searches of premises in two particular circumstances.

Section 187 provides that, if a justice is satisfied by information on oath that there is reasonable ground for believing that any intoxicating liquor is sold by retail, or exposed or kept for sale by retail, at any place within his jurisdiction, being a place where that liquor may not lawfully be sold by retail, he may issue a search warrant authorising a constable to enter that place (which must be named in the warrant) at any time within one month from the date of issue of the warrant, by force if necessary, and to search the place for intoxicating liquor and seize and remove any intoxicating liquor which the constable has reasonable grounds for supposing to be there for the purpose of unlawful sale, and the vessels containing the liquor.

Where there has been such a seizure under a warrant, any person found in the place is guilty of an offence unless he proves that he was there for a lawful purpose. Warrants under s 187 are primarily concerned with unlicensed drinking dens.

The second power of search under a warrant is concerned with registered clubs, to which there is no general power of entry available to the police. Section 54 allows a justice of the peace, if satisfied by information on oath that there are reasonable grounds for believing that:

(a) there is ground for cancelling in whole or in part a registration certificate held by a club, and that evidence of it is to be obtained at the club premises, or any of those premises; *or*

(b) that intoxicating liquor is sold or supplied by or on behalf of a club in club premises for which the club does not hold a registration certificate or a justices' licence, or is kept in any club premises for sale or supply in contravention of the relevant provisions of the Act;

to issue a warrant authorising a constable to enter at any time within one month the premises of the club, or any of those premises, by force if necessary, and to search them and seize any documents relating to the business of the club.

In practice, when raids on the premises of a registered club are contemplated on the basis of a suspicion that illegal drinking is taking place, in that liquor is being sold to non-members, warrants are obtained under both sections. The warrant under s 187 permits seizure of liquor if it is found that it is being *sold* without a justices' licence and this would occur, regardless of the fact that the premises were registered, if there were sales to non-members. The s 54 warrant allows seizure of documents which would be essential to identify the officers of the club and the members of the committee for the purpose of instituting a prosecution against them.

OFFENCES OF DRUNKENNESS AND POLICE POWERS

Drunkenness is not in itself an offence but becomes so in certain circumstances, which are described below. Drunkenness in this context is limited to intoxication through drink and does not include intoxication through drugs or through glue-sniffing.

Simple drunkenness

The term 'simple drunkenness' is one of practice and not of law. Police officers have for many years used the term to separate the offence of being found drunk from various offences dealing with aggravated forms of drunkenness. This offence of simple drunkenness is often referred to, although not strictly accurately, as one of being drunk and incapable. The offence is governed by the Licensing Act 1872, s 12, which provides that a person is guilty of an offence if he is found drunk on any highway or other public place, whether a building or not, or on any licensed premises. The general arrest provisions of the Police and Criminal Evidence Act 1984, s 25 will apply to such circumstances. It is particularly worth remembering that that section permits an arrest if it is necessary to prevent the person from suffering serious physical harm. Such harm would be likely if he was left unconscious in the open.

Drunk and disorderly

The Criminal Justice Act 1967, s 91 states that any person who in any public place is guilty, while drunk, of disorderly behaviour commits an offence. Such a person may be arrested without a warrant. Where there is an intercom system and locks on the entrance to a block of flats, so that only those admitted by the occupiers are given access to the area, the landing area outside the flats is not a public place for the purposes of this offence. Nor would it be for the purposes of the offence of simple drunkenness.

Drunk in charge of particular things

Section 12 of the Licensing Act 1872 also makes it an offence for a person to be drunk while in charge on any highway or other public place, of a carriage, horse, cattle, or steam engine, or to be drunk when in possession of a loaded firearm. 'Carriage' includes a motor vehicle, but if a person is drunk in charge of such a vehicle the appropriate offence is that under the Road Traffic Act 1988, s 4 (discussed in ch 17, above) and not the present one, since it is a more serious offence which reflects the gravity of the situation. Although a bicycle is a 'carriage', *riding* a cycle while unfit through drink is also an offence under the Road Traffic Act 1988, s 30, and if a person rides while unfit he should be dealt with under that section. However, a person *in charge*, eg pushing a pedal cycle, in such a condition commits an offence only against s 12 of the 1872 Act. The Act does not define the term 'firearm' for the purposes of the section, but that term bears its everyday meaning and includes an airgun.

Drunk in charge of a child

The Licensing Act 1902, s 2 creates the offence of being found drunk on any highway or other public place, whether a building or not, or on any licensed premises, while having the charge of a child apparently under the age of seven years.

Being drunk at a designated sports ground

This offence is dealt with in ch 32.

CHAPTER 20

Betting, gaming and lotteries

The criminal law takes no exception to persons betting or gaming between themselves in the privacy of their own homes or within their own private organisations (provided betting or gaming is confined to the premises of such organisations). However, there is legislation to control betting and gaming activities which occur in particular places and to control forms of betting and gaming which are substantially unfair to members of the public. Legislation also exists to control lotteries in order to ensure that those taking part are treated honestly and to ensure that lotteries are run for charitable or similar purposes and not for private gain.

BETTING

Betting may be defined as the staking of money or other valuable thing on the event of a doubtful issue. We have all witnessed many forms of betting. Friendly wagers are entered into between colleagues every day. To support the efforts of your favourite soccer team, by offering to wager upon the certainty of their success with a pint of beer staked against those who would doubt you, is an everyday fact of life. It is a bet, but the criminal law does not seek to control it. Betting offices (ie betting shops) are in every town, and many villages, and their presence indicates Parliament's desire to see that betting transactions are conducted fairly. It is not an offence in itself to place a bet, but various activities relating to betting are criminal if the person concerned is not authorised in respect of them or if they occur in certain places.

The relevant provisions are provided by the Betting, Gaming and Lotteries Act 1963, as amended.

Bookmaker's permit

A person who acts as a bookmaker on his own account must have a bookmaker's permit, otherwise he commits an offence. Bookmaker's permits are granted by a committee of justices appointed for this purpose in each petty sessional area. Applicants for a permit must advertise their intentions in a newspaper circulating in the area, and they must send notices to the clerk to the justices and to the chief officer of police. If several people set up a bookmaking business in partnership, each of them is required to have a permit.

A bookmaker's permit is not required for the receiving or negotiating by registered pool promoters of bets by way of pool betting. Basically, a bet is by way of pool betting unless it is at fixed odds: football pools are the best example of pool betting.

The holder of a bookmaker's permit must produce it on being required to do so by a constable. It is an offence to refuse to do so, or to fail to do so without reasonable excuse.

Bookmaker's agents

No person may act as an employee or agent of a bookmaker for the purpose of receiving or negotiating bets unless he is 21 or over and authorised in writing by the holder of a bookmaker's permit or betting agency permit (which is discussed later). If a person contravenes this provision, he and the bookmaker commit an offence.

Agents of registered pool promoters are exempt from this provision, as are agents who themselves hold a bookmaker's or betting agency permit or who operate solely on premises occupied by the holder of such a permit.

The result is this: a bookmaker's agent need not satisfy the requirements as to age and written authorisation if he receives or negotiates bets on premises occupied by the bookmaker; but he must if he does so on other premises (eg a racecourse), unless he is the agent of a registered pools promoter, otherwise he commits an offence. Even if the above requirements are satisfied, an agent who receives or negotiates a bet in a street or public place commits an offence under provisions dealt with below.

Places where betting is or is not permitted

Generally, it is an offence to use any premises for the purpose of betting, or to cause or knowingly to permit them to be so used. It is also an offence for betting to take place in streets or other public places.

Lawful use of premises for betting

There are the following exceptions to the general rule that the use etc of premises for betting is an offence:

Approved horse racecourses Certain racecourses are approved by the Totalisator Board for horse racing. Betting and bookmaking may lawfully take place on those premises on any day when they are used solely for horse racing, other than Good Friday or Christmas Day.

Tracks other than approved horse racecourses A 'track' means premises on which races of any description, athletic sports or other sporting events take place. Horse racecourses are 'tracks' but in relation to them the provisions about to be mentioned are limited to unapproved courses; approved courses are dealt with by the provisions referred to above. Under the provisions relating to tracks other than approved horse racecourses, betting and bookmaking may lawfully take place at the track on any day other than Good Friday or Christmas Day. However, bookmaking may not be carried on at a track unless the occupier of it has a track betting licence or unless bookmaking has not been carried on there on more than seven previous days since the previous 1 July. In this latter case seven days' notice of intention to permit bookmaking on the track on a specified day must have been given by the occupier to the chief officer of police, otherwise it will be an offence.

Private premises The Betting, Gaming and Lotteries Act 1963, s 1 legalises forms of betting which occur between persons who either work or reside on the same premises. The office sweep provides a good example of such betting. A fee is paid to draw a ticket bearing the name of a horse. The fees make up the prize money to be divided between the winners. This is betting but, provided that it is internal in character, by its restriction to persons working in the premises (the office sweep) or those residing on the premises (the hostel sweep), there is no offence committed, provided that the organiser is also a worker or a resident there. These provisions equally apply to members of a household or residents in private hotels. In this context 'premises' is not limited to an individual building; it also includes a site with a number of buildings on it (eg a factory site) which is under sole (and not multiple) occupation.

Licensed betting offices The primary purpose of the provisions of the 1963 Act which refer to betting was to remove betting from the streets. The Act provided an acceptable alternative which recognised a person's right to place a bet, whilst regularising the process, by permitting the establishment of licensed betting offices to which the public could go if they wished to place a bet. Licensed persons, and their employees and agents employed upon premises specified in the licence, may effect betting transactions there. Betting office licences are issued by the same committee of justices as issue bookmaker's permits.

Betting office licences can only be granted to the holder of, or an applicant for, a bookmaker's permit to the Totalisator Board, or to a person who, although not the holder of such a permit, is accredited by the holder of a bookmaker's permit (or by the Totalisator Board) as an agent for the purpose of receiving or negotiating bets by way of business on that bookmaker's behalf *and* who is the holder of, or an applicant for, a betting agency permit issued by the committee of justices.

To illustrate the purpose of these various permits and licences, let us consider the position of the large firms of bookmakers. All of the partners in the firm will hold bookmaker's permits. As holders of those permits they may take out betting office licences, which would make them the licence holders and directly responsible for the conduct of the premises. However, if the partners appoint 'managers', these managers will most probably hold betting agency permits and as holders of such permits will be allowed to take out betting office licences. In this way, the manager becomes the holder of the licence for the betting office and is responsible for its conduct. As the Betting, Gaming and Lotteries Act 1963, s 11 authorises a court which convicts the holder of either of these forms of permit of certain offences against the Act to order that a permit is forfeited or cancelled, it becomes important for those involved in extensive bookmaking businesses to protect themselves by having the betting office licences issued to their employees, as the holders of betting agency permits.

Conduct of licensed betting offices

A licensed betting office must be managed in accordance with certain rules. If the rules are contravened, the licensee, and any employee or agent of the licensee who contravenes the rules, is guilty of an offence. There is a statutory defence available to the licensee: that the offence took place without his consent or connivance and that he exercised all due diligence to prevent it. Thus, the licensee is liable in the beginning for all illegal acts of his servants. To avoid his responsibility it is not sufficient for him to prove that he did not encourage the offence, or even know about it. He must show that he did everything possible to prevent it.

The rules applicable to licensed betting offices include requirements that:

(a) a requirement that they must close daily between midnight and 7am, and between 10 pm and midnight between April and August inclusive, and between 6.30pm and midnight at any other time of the year;

(b) they must be closed on Sundays, Christmas Day and Good Friday;

(c) they must not be used for any purpose other than betting (or the use of up to two gaming machines to which Part III of the Gaming Act 1968, below, applies) or the sale of certain types of lottery tickets (or the payment of winnings thereon), or the delivery of entry forms and stakes in a competition involving a substantial degree of skill (or the payment of winnings in respect of it);

(d) no person apparently under the age of 18 years may be admitted;

(e) the betting office licence must be displayed;

(f) no person should be encouraged to bet whilst on the premises;

(g) no visual or sound apparatus may be used on the premises unless the information is related to a sporting event (including betting on that event); to other related, incidental matters (including advertisements), or to betting transactions and results of events related to betting transactions made on the premises;

(h) no music, dancing or other entertainment may be provided or allowed on the premises, other than that set out at (g) above;

(i) drinks, other than alcoholic drinks, may be sold on the premises and there may also be sold pre-packaged sandwiches and other pre-packaged snacks including confectionery, biscuits and cakes. No other refreshments may be served.

Licensees, their employees and agents may refuse to admit or may expel persons who are drunk, quarrelsome, violent or disorderly, or whose presence might cause a contravention of the rules for the conduct of betting offices. It is an offence to fail to leave after such a request. At the request of the licensee or his employee or agent, a constable may help to expel such persons if he has reasonable cause to believe that these circumstances exist.

A constable has the power to enter any licensed betting office to ensure that the rules for the conduct of betting offices are being complied with. It is an offence for any person to obstruct him in such an entry.

Betting in a street or other public place

It is an offence for any person to frequent or loiter in a street or public place, either on his own behalf or on behalf of someone else, for the purpose of bookmaking, betting, agreeing to bet, or paying, receiving or settling bets. The offence is directed towards the removal of the nuisance caused by street betting. The words 'frequent' and 'loiter' should be given their normal meaning. 'Frequent' means to go there often for long enough to effect one of the above purposes, and 'loiter' to hang about for a particular purpose. Before the introduction of licensed betting offices it was a practice for bookmakers to collect their bets in the street. Each bookmaker tended to have 'runners' who collected bets in the street on the bookmaker's behalf. This led to the offence being applied to those who engaged in street betting on their own behalf, and to the runner who did so on behalf of the bookmaker. To prove the offence it is necessary to observe the activities of a street bookmaker over a period of time, during which several people should be observed to approach and complete some form of transaction. Money and pieces of paper should be seen to exchange hands.

The term 'street' is widely defined, so as to include not only a street itself but also:

(a) any bridge, road, lane, footway, subway, square, court, alley or passage, whether a thoroughfare or not, which is for the time being open to the public; and;
(b) the doorways and entrances of premises abutting upon, and any ground adjoining and open to a street.

It must be emphasised that the present offence is not limited to the prescribed conduct in a 'street', as defined, but also prohibits such conduct in a 'public place'.

The extent of the prohibition upon actions which are essentially a part of a betting transaction should also be noted. Any form of arranging, accepting or settling bets is sufficient in itself to complete the offence.

A constable may seize and detain any books, cards, papers and other articles relating to betting which may be found in possession of the person.

Other points on betting

Young persons

It is an offence for any person to have a betting transaction with a person whom he knows, or ought to know, to be under the age of 18 years. It is similarly an offence to employ a person aged under 18 in the effecting of a betting transaction, or to employ him in a betting office. However, these restrictions on employment do not apply to postal transactions.

Search warrants

A search warrant, authorising any constable to enter, if necessary by force, specified premises within 14 days and to search them, may be issued by a justice who is satisfied, by information on oath, that there is reasonable ground for suspecting that an offence under the Betting, Gaming and Lotteries Act 1963 is being, has been, or is about to be committed on those premises. A constable executing the search warrant may seize and remove things reasonably believed by him to be required as evidence.

GAMING

The Gaming Act 1968, s 52 defines gaming as the playing of a *game of chance* for winnings in money or money's worth, whether any person playing the game is at risk of losing any money or money's worth or not. The term 'game of chance' does not include any athletic game or sport but, with that exception, includes a game of chance and skill combined, and a pretended game of chance or chance and skill combined. This definition produces the following results:

Game of skill It is not gaming if the activity is one of pure skill; otherwise contests of skill for prizes would be unlawful, for example an archery or shooting contest. As we have said athletic games and sports are specifically excluded but they would probably be excluded in any case as matters of skill. Runners who compete against one another for money or prizes are therefore not participating in gaming.

Game of chance and skill combined In many forms of gaming it might be possible to allege that there was an element of skill, and it is therefore declared that the term 'game of chance' includes a game of chance and skill combined. The game of 'pitch and toss', involving the throwing of two pennies into the air with the object of leaving them on the ground with heads uppermost, may involve a small element of skill, but it is beyond doubt that it also involves an element of chance and it is therefore gaming.

The Act declares that in determining whether a game, played otherwise than against one or more players, is a game of chance and skill combined, the possibility of superlative skill eliminating the element of chance shall be disregarded. A popular form of fairground gaming involves rolling a coin on to a board which is marked into sections, each section indicating the odds of the wager. If the coin falls completely within a section offering odds of two to one, without any part of the coin touching a line, this is a successful wager at those odds. Before the passing of the Gaming Act 1968, many fairground operators could demonstrate that this was a game involving considerable skill by placing the coin into a winning position on almost every occasion. However, this was a 'superlative skill' and heavy elements of chance still existed for the public. Such a game is now quite clearly a 'game of chance'.

Pretended game of chance or chance and skill combined The term 'pretended game of chance' is included to cover circumstances in which it appears that persons are being offered a play in a game of chance, whereas in reality there is no opportunity for them to win. The game of 'find the lady' is played by inviting persons to place wagers upon the position of the queen when three playing cards, including a queen, have been shuffled into various positions on a flat board. Frequently, the queen has been 'palmed' by the operator and it is therefore impossible to find the lady. This is a pretended game.

We have considered the terms 'gaming' and 'game of chance'. An understanding of those terms is essential in considering offences contrary to the Gaming Act 1968. However, gaming in itself is not unlawful, but it becomes unlawful in certain circumstances.

Gaming in a public place

It is an offence to take part in gaming in any street, or in any other place to which the public have access, whether on payment or otherwise. The term 'street' has the meaning already described in relation to street betting. The offence is restricted to those forms of gaming governed by Part I of the Act (which is referred to on the next page), but this does not present difficulties in practice as all forms of gaming which might reasonably be conducted in a street or public place are included in Part I.

The wide definition of the word 'street' embraces entrances to buildings abutting upon a street. The persons who play pitch and toss, or poker, in a street or public place are therefore guilty of this offence. If they move off a street into the entrance of premises abutting upon a street, they are equally guilty. A good test is whether or not the manner in which they are gaming is or could be a nuisance to the public.

The use of the term 'place to which the public have access' produces the following interesting comparison. If persons engage in gaming in a public service vehicle which is picking up and setting down passengers, they are gaming in such a place. If they play in a similar vehicle which is taking members of their club on an outing, it is no offence as members of the public are not admitted to the vehicle or 'place'.

Gaming on premises licensed for sale of intoxicants

The Gaming Act 1968, s 6 provides an exception to the rule that gaming is not permitted in places to which the public have access, in relation to public houses or other premises with an 'on-licence' (other than a residential or restaurant licence). Section 6 permits the playing of dominoes and cribbage on such premises, but it is open to the licensing justices of the district to impose conditions restricting the stakes for which these games may be played in any public part of the premises. They may also impose conditions to prevent such gaming from becoming an inducement to persons to attend those premises primarily for the purpose of gaming.

The justices, on the application of a licensee, may authorise some other form of gaming upon particular licensed premises. If they do so they must send a copy of their notice to the chief officer of police.

Gaming on uncontrolled premises

Different rules apply as between uncontrolled and controlled premises. If an allegation is made of unlawful gaming on premises, the first step to be taken by a police officer is to ascertain the nature of the premises. Premises are 'uncontrolled' unless they are licensed or registered under Part II of the Gaming Act 1968. It is Part I of the Act which deals with gaming on uncontrolled premises. It applies to all such gaming, with the following exceptions:

(a) gaming with slot machines; this is dealt with by Part III of the Act, referred to below;

(b) gaming at entertainments not held for private gain, such as bazaars and fetes;

(c) gaming which constitutes the provision of amusements with prizes at functions such as bazaars, fetes and dances, provided the provisions of the Lotteries and Amusements Act 1976, s 15 are complied with (including the requirement that the whole proceeds of the entertainment, after deducting the expenses of it, must be devoted to a purpose other than private gain);

(d) gaming which constitutes the provision of amusements with prizes at certain commercial premises, such as amusement arcades and the grounds of a travelling fair, provided the provisions of the Lotteries and Amusements Act 1976, s 16 are complied with (including the requirements that the amount paid for the chance to win a prize does not exceed 50p and that no money prize exceeds £15).

Nature of unlawful gaming

The principal restriction imposed on gaming on uncontrolled premises by Part I of the 1968 Act is concerned with the nature of the gaming. Section 2 provides that, if any of the conditions set out below is fulfilled, the gaming is unlawful, and every person concerned in the organisation or management of the gaming (but not the players) is guilty of an offence. The conditions are as follows:

A. Gaming which involves playing or staking against a bank. All forms of gaming on uncontrolled premises which involve the playing or staking against a bank are unlawful, whether or not the bank is held by one of the players. A game such as roulette may not therefore be played on uncontrolled premises, regardless of whether or not the 'banker' function is offered to the players. The prohibition is in relation to staking against a bank, and includes, of course, the many card games in which there is a bank.

B. Nature of the game is such that its chances are not equally favourable to all the players There are a number of popular card games, the nature of which is such that the chances are not equally favourable to all players. Pontoon (sometimes called vingt et un) or its variant, blackjack, is not equally favourable to all players. No matter how the game may be organised the dealer always holds an advantage. The object of the game is to hold cards totalling as closely as possible to 21. However, if both a player and the dealer hold cards totalling the same number, the rules of the game declare the dealer to be the winner. He has an advantage.

C. Nature of the game involves chances between a player, or players, and some other person and those chances are not as favourable to the player, or players, as to that other person It is difficult to imagine the purpose of this provision as it appears at first sight to repeat the provisions of A and B, above. However, machines might be produced which would fall outside the definition of gaming machines (ie slot machines), which are governed by Part III of that Act, and, if only prizes were offered, rather than tokens for prizes, such a machine might not be caught by the provisions of A, above, and, if the game was equally fair to all the players, it would not be caught by B, and therefore would otherwise fall outside the provisions of Part I as well.

Perhaps the clearest example might be provided by a supermarket owner who offered a 'free' stake in gaming to those who entered his store in circumstances in which it could not be said that there was any charge for taking part. If such gaming was of a type in which the supermarket owner held a more than equal chance of winning, then it could be unlawful. However, most supermarket competitions are in the nature of give-away competitions in which no advantage attaches to the store owner.

None of the conditions A, B and C relating to gaming on uncontrolled premises applies:

(a)   to gaming on a domestic occasion in a private dwelling; 'domestic occasion' is not defined but is obviously intended to separate the occasional game of cards in a private dwelling from a form of commercial enterprise in a private dwelling; nor

(b)   to gaming in a hostel, hall of residence or similar establishment not carried on as a trade or business, provided the players consist exclusively or mainly of residents. This is simply a recognition of the domestic character of workers' hostels and students' halls of residence.

Charges and levies

Part I of the Act contains the following provisions in relation to gaming to which it applies. No charge by way of money's worth may be made for gaming on any uncontrolled premises, other than the actual stakes hazarded; any admission charge made in respect of entry to such premises (other than a recognised subscription to a recognised club) is deemed to be a charge for gaming unless the contrary is proved. The charging of any compulsory or voluntary levy from those taking part in gaming is also prohibited. If any gaming takes place in breach of one of these prohibitions, every person within the organisation or management of the gaming is guilty of an offence.

Gaming on controlled premises

Part II of the Gaming Act 1968 is concerned with gaming (other than by means of slot machines) on premises licensed or registered under that part of the Act. The Gaming Board for Great Britain keeps under constant review the activities of such establishments.

Licensed premises

For the purposes of the Gaming Act 1968, the term 'licensed premises' refers to a commercially operated gaming club which is run for profit and is licensed under the Act. The grant of a licence involves both the Gaming Board and the local licensing justices. First, the applicant must obtain from the Gaming Board a certificate, consenting to his application. Before issuing such a certificate, the Board will have regard to the character, reputation and financial standing of all concerned and the likely conduct of the premises. The certificate may be confined to suitability for bingo. Second, once such a certificate has been issued the licensing justices will consider the application and decide whether or not to grant a licence.

Registered premises

Registration is made by the local licensing justices. The process follows very much the same path as that followed in relation to the liquor licensing laws. Premises which will be registered for gaming are members' clubs, that is clubs run by the members for their own purposes. However, the Gaming Act 1968 also allows miners' welfare institutes to become registered for gaming. The process of registration is the same as that followed for 'licensing'. The justices must not grant a registration to an organisation which is not a bona fide members' club; and they must not register a club if it appears that the principal purpose for which it is established or conducted is gaming, unless the club is a bridge or whist club (in which case it may be registered although its main purpose may be said to be gaming).

Who may participate in gaming on controlled premises?

The only persons who may participate in gaming on licensed or registered premises are members and their bona fide guests. A member can take part in gaming only if 24 hours have elapsed since his original application was made in person on the premises. This is to prevent on the spot memberships or postal transactions by holidaymakers in advance of their arrival.

In licensed clubs guests may be charged for taking part in gaming and such a charge will not affect their status as bona fide guests. This is not true of a registered club; a non-member is deemed not to be a bona fide guest of such a club if he is charged for taking part in gaming there.

A person participates in gaming if he takes part as a player, or, where the game involves playing or staking against a bank, if he holds the bank or has a share in it. Consequently, by way of general description, everyone who is involved, whether as a banker or a player, participates in gaming. The Gaming Act 1968, s 12(2) prevents the licence holder or his employee from participating in the gaming as a player but sub-s (4) allows the holder or person acting on his behalf to hold a bank or to have a share or interest in it.

If these provisions are contravened the holder of the licence or every officer of the club or institute, as the case may be, is guilty of an offence, unless he proves that the contravention occurred without his knowledge and that he exercised all reasonable care to prevent it.

Restrictions upon games played on controlled premises

The Gaming Act 1968, s 13 restricts gaming on licensed or registered premises by requiring that the conditions applicable to gaming, as already described in relation to uncontrolled premises, generally apply. This often leads to these conditions being considered to be of general application and to some confusion as to whether offences are being committed in licensed or registered clubs in which 'banker' games are played. The true position can only be understood by reference to regulations made under the Act.

The Gaming Act (Registration under Part II) Regulations 1969 permit pontoon and chemin de fer to be played on registered premises, but for the purpose of this exception 'pontoon' does not include its variants, such as blackjack, which do not permit the bank to pass from player to player.

The rule in relation to chances being equally favourable would prevent licensed gaming clubs from retaining some advantage to themselves. Although s 12(4) allows the bank to be held by the licence holder, in the same way that it may be held by anyone else, something additional was required to regularise the position in licensed gaming clubs. Generally players do not want, nor could they afford, to hold the bank. If they did hold it, it is probable that they would not be able to meet their commitments. For this reason, the Gaming Club (Bankers' Games) Regulations 1994, therefore, which authorise roulette, dice, baccarat (including chemin de fer), blackjack casino stud poker and Super Pan 9 to be played in accordance with the conditions prescribed, require the licensee to hold the bank in the case of all these games (other than, in some cases, chemin de fer or Super Pan 9, the rules of which dictate otherwise). The conditions referred to include the odds which may be offered. Without the specific authority given by these Regulations, these particular games could not be played lawfully.

To summarise, police officers inspecting licensed gaming clubs will find that the playing of some games may be authorised by the general provisions of the Gaming Act 1968, but most will be conducted in accordance with the Gaming Clubs (Bankers' Games) Regulations 1994.

No person under 18 years may be present in any room in which gaming is taking place, but this does not apply to bingo played in bingo clubs or on other premises in which bingo is an activity. However, such persons are not permitted to take part in bingo.

No gaming may take place on licensed premises on a weekday between 4am and 2pm.

If there is a contravention of the above provisions, the holder of the licence or every officer of the club or institute, as the case may be, is guilty of an offence, unless he proves that the contravention occurred without his knowledge and that he exercised all reasonable care to prevent it.

Bingo clubs

Licences may be granted in relation to bingo only, but activities which can be described as 'gaming for prizes' under the Gaming Act 1968, s 21 may also take place. The only persons who may participate are members or their guests. If 'linked bingo' is being played (ie a number of premises, in which all participants are playing the same game, are linked together), a player need only be a member or guest in relation to the club in which he is present. The conditions under which the bingo may be played in such clubs are set out in the Gaming Act 1968, s 20 which, generally, requires players to be present, the draw to take place at the time, and a claim to have won to be notified to all players before play continues. Section 20 limits the payout for a game to no more than the total of the receipts and a 'pool' to a specified sum (£50,000) in excess of those receipts. Such a 'pool' must not have been accumulated over a period longer than one week. No gaming may take place in bingo club premises except between 10 am and midnight on a Saturday, 2 pm and 1 pm on a Sunday and 1 am and 1 pm on any other day. These provisions do not apply on New Year's Eve, when the permitted times are 2 pm to midnight (if a Sunday) and 10 am to midnight (if any other day).

If these provisions are contravened, the holder of the licence of the premises in question is guilty of an offence, unless he proves that the contravention occurred without his knowledge and that he exercised reasonable care to prevent it.

By way of extension to 'linked Bingo' the Gaming (Bingo) Act 1985 permits games of 'multiple bingo' to be played jointly on different bingo club premises in certain circumstances. The organisers of such games must hold a certificate issued by the Gaming Board. 'Multiple bingo' means a game of bingo played jointly on different bingo club premises in circumstances where:

(a) the draw is determined by the organiser before the beginning of the game, and is announced on each of the premises while the game is being played there;
(b) the game begins and ends at the same time at all premises;
(c) each player plays for a multiple prize (calculated by reference to the stakes hazarded *at all* the premises) *and* a prize of either or both of the following types:
   (i) a prize calculated by reference to stakes hazarded at *a group* of those premises (including the one in which he is playing), and
   (ii) a prize calculated by reference to the stakes hazarded at *the premises* where he is playing.

The Act also provides that the aggregate of the prizes in respect of the game must not exceed the aggregate of the stakes hazarded by the players at the various premises where there are players in that game and that the amount of a prize (the multiple prize) must not exceed £500,000 or such other sum as specified by the Secretary of State. Regulations of 1986 provide that only three games of multiple bingo may be played in any licensed bingo club on any day. The period of time allowed for the playing of a game is 30 minutes.

General

No person may participate in gaming on licensed or registered premises unless he is present at the time the gaming takes place. Moreover, a person who is present may not participate on behalf of an absentee.

GAMING MACHINES

Part III of the Gaming Act 1968 regulates gaming by means of machines. The Act defines the type of machine to which the provisions of Part III relate as being a machine which:

(a) is constructed or adapted for playing a game of chance, the element of chance being provided by means of the machine,

(b) has a slot or other aperture for the insertion of money's worth in the form of cash or tokens.

Such a machine is hereafter referred to as a 'gaming machine'.

This definition of a machine is interesting. In the first instance we consider whether or not the machine is a 'slot machine'. If this is so, we must then consider whether the chance is controlled by the machine. This is true of all of those in which symbols spin when a button is pressed. However, if we consider 'slot bingo', although the stake is put into a slot and then numbers appear on an illuminated board in front of the players, the drawing of the numbers is done by a bingo caller, and therefore the gaming is not controlled by the machine.

Restrictions on use

These restrictions can be divided into three types, depending on the nature of the machine. If the requisite licence or permit has not been obtained, a person who allowed the machine to be on the premises is guilty of an offence if it is used for gaming, unless he proves that this use occurred without his consent or connivance and that he exercised all due diligence to prevent it.

Machines for gaming

These are machines constructed solely for gaming, for example large jackpot machines. All that a player gets for his stake is the chance of winning money. The playing of the machine involves a pure gamble; there is no element of skill in the play. The use of these machines is restricted to licensed gaming clubs or clubs registered under Part II of the 1968 Act.

Not more than three of these machines may be installed in a club registered for gaming. The maximum is four in the case of bingo premises, and ten in the case of other premises licensed under the 1968 Act. A licensing authority can permit more in premises such as casinos. The maximum stake for one operation of the machine is 50 pence and only coins may be delivered as prizes. These machines must not be used at any time when the public are admitted to the building. If these provisions are contravened the holder of the licence or (as the case may be) every officer of the registered club is guilty of an offence unless he proves that the contravention occured without his knowledge and that he exercised reasonable care to prevent the contravention.

Machines for gaming by way of amusement with prizes

Local authorities may grant permits for the use of machines which may be described as machines for gaming by way of amusement with prizes, which are in widespread use in public houses, amusement arcades, cafes and pleasure parks. Such machines may also, however, be used without a permit at a travelling showman's pleasure fair.

The maximum permitted charge for one operation of the machine is 30 pence and the prize, if a money prize, is limited to £5. Non-monetary prizes may be up to £8 in value. There may be a combination prize of cash and prizes with a total value not exceeding £8. However, the House of Lords has ruled that the holder of a permit may offer the winner of a non-monetary prize or token in any one game the right to accumulate his prizes as a result of playing further games and to exchange them for a non-monetary prize of a value exceeding £8 but not exceeding the aggregate value of the prizes or tokens given up in exchange for it. Contravention of these provisions constitutes an offence by the holder of the permit or (as the case may be) by the person in charge of the machines at the fair, unless he proves that it occurred without his knowledge and he exercised all reasonable care to prevent it.

The above restrictions on the use of gaming machines for amusement with prizes do not apply to their use at non-commercial entertainments, such as bazaars, sales of work, dinners, dances, sporting or athletic events and other similar entertainments. The use of gaming machines, of whatever type, is permitted at such entertainments, provided a number of requirements are satisfied; in particular, the whole proceeds of the machine and all other proceeds from the entertainment after the deduction of legitimate expenses must go to purposes other than private gain. 'Expenses' are restricted to actual expenses in the use of the machine.

Machines for amusement purposes

Permits may also be granted for the use of machines in the area of a local authority which might be described as machines for amusement purposes. Such machines are primarily for amusement. The Lotteries and Amusements Act 1976, s 16 is concerned (amongst other things) with these machines, and provides that the maximum stake is 50 pence and that no money prize may exceed £15.

POWER TO ENTER PREMISES LICENSED FOR GAMING

A constable may at any reasonable time enter any premises in respect of which a licence is in force for gaming, and may inspect the premises and any machine or other equipment, book or document on the premises which he reasonably requires to inspect for the purpose of ascertaining whether an offence against the Gaming Act 1968 or regulations made under the Act is being, or has been, committed. In addition, the constable may take copies of any such book or document or of any entry in it and, if any information reasonably required by him for the above purpose is held on a computer accessible from the premises, require it to be produced in a legible print-out. Failure to allow these things to be done is an offence by the licensee or his employee.

A justice may issue a warrant authorising entry, by force if necessary, within 14 days; a warrant may only be issued if the justice is satisfied, by information on oath, that there are reasonable grounds for suspecting that an offence under the Act is being, has been, or is about to be, committed on the premises in question.

LOTTERIES

To constitute a lottery there must be a distribution of prizes, that distribution must be established by chance, and participants must pay for their chance. If no charge is made for a ticket it is not a lottery, unless one must purchase something in order to obtain a free ticket. Where cigarette packets contained free tickets for a draw, this was held to be a lottery because people had to buy cigarettes to enter. However, where free tickets are sent to people together with an offer to sell books etc but there is no necessity to buy before being entered in the competition, this is not a lottery as one does not need to buy goods before being entered in the competition.

The Lotteries and Amusements Act 1976, s 1 declares that all lotteries which do not constitute gaming are unlawful unless they are of a type authorised by that Act and conducted in accordance with conditions prescribed by it. The reference in s 1 to gaming is to cover circumstances in which the activity which is taking place is legal within the provision referring to gaming. If that is so, it is not a lottery for the purpose of the Act. In deciding whether or not the distribution of prizes is gaming or a lottery, the Gaming Act 1968, s 52(3) states that it will be gaming rather than a lottery if the winners are determined by reference to more than three determining factors. Thus, bingo is quite clearly gaming because winners are selected by reference to at least a line of numbers, certainly more than three.

Where a lottery is promoted or proposed to be promoted, anyone who prints, sells, distributes, offers or advertises tickets for the lottery, or who uses, causes or knowingly permits premises to be used in connection with the lottery, commits an offence, unless he proves that (a) the lottery is one legalised by the Act, and (b) at the time of the alleged offence he reasonably believed that none of the conditions prescribed for its legality had been broken. The printing, sale or possession of tickets or other documents for a lottery is not an offence if the accused proves that he had reasonable grounds for believing that the lottery was not being, and would not be, promoted in Great Britain and that the tickets etc were not being, and would not be, used in Great Britain in connection with that or any other lottery.

The lotteries which, provided prescribed conditions are satisfied, are legalised by the Act are:

(a)   small lotteries;
(b)   private lotteries;
(c)   societies' lotteries;
(d)   local lotteries.

Small lotteries

Small lotteries promoted as part of a bazaar, sale of work, fete, dinner dance, sporting or athletic event or other entertainment of a similar character are lawful subject to certain conditions.

The conditions are:

(a)   the whole proceeds of the entertainment (including the lottery) must, after permitted deductions, go to purposes other than private gain; the permitted deductions are the expenses of the entertainment (including those of the lottery), the printing of the lottery tickets, and the prizes (which must normally not exceed £250 in cost in all);
(b)   no money prizes may be awarded;
(c)   tickets must be sold on the premises only and the result must be declared on the premises whilst the entertainment is in progress; and
(d)   the lottery must not be the only real inducement to attend.

Examples of small lotteries are those typically held at the village sports day, the church garden party or a charity entertainment.

If the above conditions are not observed, every person concerned in the conduct or promotion of the lottery commits an offence, unless he proves that he did not consent to or connive at the contravention and exercised all due diligence to prevent it.

Private lotteries

Provided certain conditions are fulfilled, private lotteries are lawful. A private lottery is a lottery promoted for members of a society or club established for purposes other than betting, gaming or lotteries, or for persons who work on the same premises, or for persons who reside on the same premises, and which satisfies the following requirements. First, the lottery must be promoted by persons each of whom is one of the persons for whom the lottery is promoted and, where it is promoted for the members of the society or club, each of whom is authorised in writing by the society's or club's governing body to promote it. Second, the sale of tickets in the lottery must be confined to those for whom it is promoted or, where the lottery is promoted for members of a society or club, to any other people on the society's premises.

The conditions which must be fulfilled are for a private lottery to be lawful are:

(a) the whole proceeds, less printing expenses, must be devoted to prizes in the case of lotteries between workers and residents on premises, and to prizes and/or the purposes of the club or society, if conducted between members of a club or society;
(b) no written notices of the lottery may be given except on the premises or on tickets;
(c) the price of tickets must be the same and must be stated on the ticket;
(d) every ticket must identify each of the promoters, state the persons to whom sale is restricted and state that prizes will only be given to the person to whom the winning ticket was sold by the promoters; and
(e) the full price must be paid for each ticket and tickets must not be sent through the post.

The law is most frequently disregarded by clubs when they use cloakroom tickets for internal raffles. These do not carry the information which the Lotteries and Amusements Act requires.

If any of these conditions is broken, each promoter and each person breaking a condition is guilty of an offence. However, a promoter has a defence if he proves that the offence was committed without his consent or connivance and that he exercised all due diligence to prevent it.

Societies' lotteries

Provided certain conditions are complied with, societies' lotteries are lawful. Societies' lotteries are lotteries promoted on behalf of a society which is established and conducted wholly or mainly for a charitable, athletic, sporting or cultural purpose or for other purposes which are not commercial or profit-making. We are therefore considering lotteries which are not run for private profit and which are not restricted to members of the promoting society. Since tickets in these lotteries are offered to the public, they are of greater concern to the police.

One condition which is necessary to render a society's lottery lawful is that normally it must be registered with the local district council in whose area the office of the society is situated. However, where the total value of tickets put on sale will exceed £20,000, where the annual aggregate proceeds of a series of lotteries are expected to exceed £250,000, or where lotteries held by the same society in the same year or in the preceding three years exceeded £20,000 for a single lottery or £250,000 in aggregate for the year, it must be registered with the Gaming Board of Great Britain. Another condition is that the lottery must be conducted in accordance with a scheme approved by the society.

The other conditions which apply to societies' lotteries also apply generally to local lotteries and are discussed below.

Local lotteries

Provided certain conditions are complied with, local lotteries are lawful. A local lottery is a lottery promoted by a local authority. Two conditions which must be fulfilled to render it lawful are that it must be conducted in accordance with a scheme approved by the local authority and that that scheme must have been registered with the Gaming Board before any tickets are sold.

The most important of the conditions relating to societies' and local lotteries are:

(a) no prize in a society's lottery or a local lottery may exceed £25,000 or 10 per cent of the tickets or chances sold in the lottery, whichever is the greater;

(b) the total value of the tickets or chances sold in any one such lottery must not exceed £1,000,000;

(c) the total value of the tickets or chances sold in all such lotteries held in any one year and promoted on behalf of the same society or local authority must not exceed £5,000,000; and

(d) no ticket may be sold for more than £1.

The other usual conditions concerning information on tickets etc apply.

If any condition relating to a society's or local lottery is not complied with, the promoter of the lottery and any other party to the contravention is guilty of an offence. 'Any other party' includes those who print, sell or distribute tickets or those who possess them for sale or distribution, and those who are concerned with advertising the lottery or in the use of premises for it. It is a defence for a person charged only by reason of being a promoter to prove that the contravention occurred without his consent or connivance and that he exercised all due diligence to prevent it.

National lottery

The National Lottery etc Act 1993 permits the Secretary of State to make regulations providing for the promotion of lotteries that form part of the National Lottery as he considers necessary or expedient. The National Lotteries Regulations 1994 have been made. The Regulations ban the following types of sales of a national lottery ticket: sale to persons under 16 years of age; sale in a street, in a betting office, approved race track or licensed track; sale in premises used wholly or mainly for providing amusements with prizes or by means of slot machines; or any sale in a bingo or gaming club. Contravention of these prohibitions is an offence.

Offences relating to lotteries: search warrants

A search warrant may be obtained in the usual way, authorising entry, by force if necessary, within 14 days, to seize and remove documents etc and arrest and search persons found on the premises reasonably believed to be committing or to have committed an offence relating to lotteries. The terms for the issue of such a warrant are the same as apply, for example, in the case of betting offences.

CHAPTER 21

Aliens

ILLEGAL ENTRY AND SIMILAR OFFENCES

The Immigration Act 1971, s 24 states that a person who is not a British citizen is guilty of an offence if:

(a) contrary to the Act he knowingly enters the United Kingdom in breach of a deportation order or without leave;

(b) if, having only a limited leave to enter or remain in the United Kingdom, he knowingly either -
   (i) remains beyond the time limited by the leave; or
   (ii) fails to observe a condition of the leave;

(c) if, having lawfully entered the United Kingdom without leave by virtue of s 8 of the Act (crew member of ship or aircraft), he remains without leave beyond the time allowed by that section;

(d) if, without reasonable excuse, he fails to comply with any requirement imposed upon him under Sch 2 to the Act to report to a medical officer of health, or to attend or submit to a test or examination, as required by such an officer;

(e) if, without reasonable excuse, he fails to observe any restriction imposed on him under Sch 2 or 3 to the Act as to residence, as to his employment or occupation or as to reporting to the police or to an immigration officer;

(f) if he disembarks in the United Kingdom from a ship or aircraft after being placed on board under Sch 2 or 3 with a view to his removal from the United Kingdom;

(g) if he embarks in contravention of a restriction imposed by or under an Order in Council under s 3 of the Act (provisions aimed at preventing persons from going to specified places on the grounds of safety).

Section 24 provides that a person who commits an offence under (b) above by remaining beyond the time limited by the leave commits that offence on the day when he first knows that the time limited by his leave has expired and continues to commit it throughout any period during which he is in the United Kingdom thereafter. However, a person may not be prosecuted under (b) more than once in respect of the same limited leave.

A constable or immigration officer may arrest without warrant anyone who has, or whom he, with reasonable cause, suspects to have, committed or attempted to commit an offence under s 24 other than an offence under(d).

Assisting illegal entry and harbouring

Section 25(1) of the 1971 Act provides that a person who is knowingly concerned in making or carrying out arrangements for securing or facilitating the entry into the United Kingdom of anyone whom he knows, or has reasonable cause for believing, to be an illegal entrant commits an offence. This is an arrestable offence. Immigration officers are given statutory power to arrest in these circumstances. Subsection (2) makes it an offence for a person knowingly to harbour any person whom he knows or has reasonable cause for believing to be either an illegal entrant or a person who has committed an 'overstaying' offence under (b) or (c) of s 24.

Prosecutions

Section 28 of the 1971 Act provides that an extended time limit will apply to the prosecution of offences under s 24 or s 25. An information relating to an offence may, in England and Wales, be tried by a magistrates' court if it is laid within six months of the commission of the offence, or if it is laid within three years of the commission of the offence and not more than two months after the date certified by a police officer above the rank of chief superintendent to be the date on which evidence sufficient to justify proceedings came to the notice of an officer of the police force to which he belongs. A person charged with such an offence may be tried where the offence was committed or at any place in which he may be. The importance of this provision is that, but for it, an information for an offence under ss 24 or 25(2) would have to be laid within six months of the commission of the offence.

In proceedings for an offence under s 24 of entering the United Kingdom without leave:

(a) any stamp purporting to have been imprinted on a passport or other travel document by an immigration officer on a particular date for the purpose of giving leave is presumed to have been duly so imprinted, unless the contrary is proved;

(b) proof that a person had leave to enter the United Kingdom lies on the defence if, but only if, he is shown to have entered within six months before the date when the proceedings were commenced.

PERSONS WHO HAVE THE RIGHT OF ABODE IN THE UNITED KINGDOM

Section 2(1) of the 1971 Act provides that a person is entitled to have the right of abode in the United Kingdom if:

(a) he is a British citizen; or
(b) he is a Commonwealth citizen who -
   (i)   immediately before the commencement of the British Nationality Act 1981 was a Commonwealth citizen having the right of abode in the United Kingdom by virtue of s 2(1)(d) or s 2(2) of the 1971 Act as then in force; and
   (ii)   has not ceased to be a Commonwealth citizen in the meanwhile.

Section 2(2) provides that, in relation to Commonwealth citizens who have the right of abode in the United Kingdom by virtue of (b) above, the Act applies as if they were British citizens.

The British Nationality Act 1981 is the principal Act now dealing with citizenship. It deals with three categories of citizen:

(a) those who have British citizenship because of a right which is associated with descent, birth, adoption, naturalisation etc;
(b) persons who are citizens of British Dependent Territories which are set out in Sch 6, for example, Gibraltar, Falkland Islands and Bermuda; and
(c) persons who are British Overseas citizens and became such, having been a citizen of the United Kingdom and Colonies, whilst not becoming a British citizen or a citizen of the British Dependent Territories, at the commencement of the British Nationality Act 1981.

Those within (b) and (c) are categorised as Commonwealth citizens.

There are no restrictions upon the movements of persons who are classed as British citizens who may enter, remain and work in the United Kingdom at any time. Such persons are not liable to deportation.

LEAVE TO ENTER UNITED KINGDOM – PERSONS OTHER THAN BRITISH CITIZENS

In consequence of s 3 of the 1971 Act a person who is not a British citizen:

(a) must not enter the United Kingdom unless given leave to do so in accordance with the Act;
(b) may be given leave to enter the United Kingdom (or, when already there, leave to remain in the United Kingdom) either for a limited or indefinite period;
(c) if he is given a limited leave to enter or remain in the United Kingdom, it may be given subject to conditions restricting his employment or occupation in the United Kingdom, or requiring him to register with the police, or both.

Leave may be varied in relation to its duration or conditions. If the limit on duration is removed, conditions are automatically revoked. A person's leave to enter or remain lapses on his going to an area outside the common travel area (which is defined as the United Kingdom, Channel Islands, Isle of Man, and the Republic of Ireland), whether or not he lands there, unless within the period of his original leave he returns to the United Kingdom in circumstances in which he is not required to obtain leave to enter. If he does so return, his previous leave and any conditions attached to it will continue to apply.

DEPORTATION

By s 3(5) of the 1971 Act a person who is not a British citizen is liable to deportation from the United Kingdom if:

(a) having only a limited leave to enter or remain, he does not observe a condition attached to the leave or remains beyond the time limited by the leave; or
(b) he has obtained leave to remain by deception; or

(c)   the Secretary of State deems his deportation to be conducive to the public good; or

(d)   another person to whose family he belongs is or has been ordered to be deported.

In addition, s 3(6) provides for the deportation of a non-British citizen, who has attained the age of 17 years, if he is convicted of an offence punishable by imprisonment and deportation is recommended by a competent court.

IMMIGRATION GENERALLY

As has been seen above, the 1971 Act provides an element of control in respect of non-British citizens. Leave to enter the country must be obtained from an immigration officer and leave may be limited and may be subject to restrictions. Registration with the police may be one of the conditions which is imposed. On the other hand, unlimited leave to enter may be granted and such leave cannot be subject to conditions. However, the important factor is that leave and conditions will be endorsed on the passport or travel document of the person concerned. EU nationals are admitted on proof of European citizenship. Endorsements which are made on such documents are authenticated by a date stamp which shows the immigration officer's identity number and the port of entry. Where entry is refused, the date stamp is applied to the document by means of a cross.

Police officers are often asked to assist immigration officers with their inquiries (it makes a change from others assisting police officers with their inquiries). Such inquiries are frequently urgent and merit a speedy reply by telephone. Confirmation may be required.

No immigration controls are imposed upon persons entering the United Kingdom from the Republic of Ireland but the Home Secretary may exclude or deport persons in certain circumstances. Conditions which are imposed where a person enters at another place within the 'common travel area' apply elsewhere within it. The Immigration (Control of Entry through the Republic of Ireland) Order 1972 applies special provisions in relation to leave to enter, and, in respect of certain foreign nationals and police registration, in the case of entry via the Republic of Ireland.

REGISTRATION WITH POLICE

The Immigration (Registration with Police) Regulations 1972 deal with the registration of aliens. An 'alien' is a person who is neither a Commonwealth citizen, nor a British protected person, nor a citizen of the Irish Republic. Such persons may be required to register with the chief officer of police for the area in which they reside. They will have been granted limited leave to enter which will be subject to a condition of registration and their passports will have been endorsed accordingly. If, in any circumstances, EU nationals are required to register, the Home Office will notify the appropriate police force. Where this occurs, the residence permit will be endorsed in the space provided and this endorsement fulfils the purpose of a police registration certificate.

In respect of other persons who must register with the police, a police registration certificate will be issued which carries the photograph of the person concerned. Police forces maintain records of aliens living within their areas who are subject to registration requirements. Changes of residence must be reported within seven days and changes in other registered particulars, within eight days. This may be done by post but personal attendance may be required.

An immigration officer or constable may require an alien to whom the Regulations apply either to produce a certificate of registration, or to give to the officer or constable a satisfactory reason for failure to produce it, forthwith. Where alterations are being made in registered particulars, a registration officer may require the alien concerned to produce his certificate of registration so that necessary amendments can be made. Where there is a failure to produce at the time, the officer or constable may require that person to produce a certificate of registration at a police station specified by the officer or constable within the following 48 hours.

A person who fails to register as required or to comply with any registration requirement offends against s 26(1) of the 1971 Act.

CHAPTER 22

Animals, birds and plants

DISEASES OF ANIMALS

The Animal Health Act 1981 sets out the duties of various persons in relation to notification of certain animal diseases and the action which must be taken. The administrative responsibilities lie with the Ministry of Agriculture, Fisheries and Food but local authorities must appoint their own inspectors. Constables are frequently appointed as inspectors under the Act and when this occurs they have additional duties and responsibilities to those which all constables have under the Act.

Animals for the purposes of the Act are cattle, sheep, goats, and all other ruminating animals, swine (ie pigs), horses, asses, mules and jennets (ie small Spanish horses). The Minister of Agriculture has power, by order, to add to this list and, for the purposes of the special provisions relating to rabies mentioned on the next page, dogs and cats have been added to the definition of 'animal'.

The Act and orders thereunder specify the diseases with which it is concerned, the most important of which are foot and mouth disease, swine fever and rabies. Persons having animals affected by a specified disease must so far as possible separate them from unaffected animals and speedily inform a constable. A constable on receipt of such information must forthwith inform a local authority inspector and the Ministry's divisional veterinary inspector.

The action which follows is very much related to the particular disease, but action is always directed towards the prevention of the spread of disease. Foot and mouth disease can spread rapidly and the action taken in such cases provides a good example of the general nature of action to be taken. On receiving notification of the suspicion of the disease, the local authority inspector serves a Form 'A' on the stockholder. This makes his premises an infected place and prohibits movement in or out by unauthorised persons or materials. The divisional veterinary inspector, if he serves Form 'C', creates an infected area of 5 miles radius and this can be extended further if necessary.

Any person who does anything prohibited by the 1981 Act, or by an order of the Minister or a regulation of a local authority, or who omits to do something required of him by the Act or an order or regulation, commits an offence if he does not have lawful authority or excuse. It is also an offence for any person, without lawful authority or excuse, to refuse entry to an inspector or other officer, or to obstruct or impede him in entering, or to obstruct or impede an inspector, constable or other officer in the execution of his duty, or to assist another to do so. In the case of each offence, the accused has the onus of proving lawful authority or excuse.

Duties and powers of a constable

The Animal Health Act 1981, s 60(1) directs that the police force of each police area must execute and enforce the Act and every order of the Minister. Section 60 has given quite wide powers to the police for this purpose. These powers are easy to remember because they follow a logical and progressive sequence of things which should be done to prevent the spread of animal diseases.

A person who is seen or found committing, or who is reasonably suspected of being engaged in committing, an offence against the Act may be stopped and detained by a constable without a warrant. In addition, whether so stopping or detaining a person or not, a constable may stop, detain and examine any animal, vehicle, boat or thing related to an offence or suspected offence against the Act, and (if it has been unlawfully removed) require that it forthwith be taken back to the place from which it has been unlawfully removed. The constable may also execute and enforce that requisition. Anyone who obstructs or impedes a constable in the execution of the above powers may be arrested without warrant.

These powers are easily understood if we bear in mind that their purpose is to prevent the spread of disease. For example, a man leaving farmland with an infected animal (or one reasonably suspected of being infected) can be stopped and detained. The constable has the power to require it to be taken back to the farm and to enforce that requirement. If the animal is being removed in a vehicle or other conveyance, the same powers apply.

In addition, a constable has power to arrest any person without warrant whom he reasonably suspects to be committing or to have committed certain offences related to rabies. The offences to which this power applies are the landing or attempted landing of any animal (including a dog or cat) in contravention of a Rabies Order, or the failure by a person in charge of a vessel or boat to discharge any obligation under such an order, or the unlawful movement of any such animal into, within or out of a rabies infected area. A constable may enter (by force, if necessary) and search any vessel, aircraft, vehicle or the like to effect such an arrest or to seize an animal if he reasonably suspects that the person or animal is there.

PROTECTION OF ANIMALS

The Protection of Animals Act 1911 deals with the various ways in which a person can be cruel to animals. The Act defines the term 'animal' as meaning any 'domestic' or 'captive' animal, and goes on to provide further definitions of 'domestic' and 'captive' animals. Cruelty to an animal not covered by these definitions is not an offence under this Act but may be an offence under the Wild Mammals (Protection) Act 1996, the provisions of which are examined below.

Domestic animal

A 'domestic animal' is defined as a horse, ass, mule, bull, sheep, pig, dog, cat, or fowl, or any other animal of whatsoever kind or species, and whether a quadruped or not, which is tame or which has been or is being sufficiently tamed to serve some purpose for the use of man.

This definition embraces most farmyard animals and the two major household pets. Most of the decisions of the courts in relation to whether or not an animal is a domestic animal are unimportant as the animals concerned would certainly have been held to be captive animals. A fighting cock has been held to be a domestic animal, as have wild birds kept in confinement and trained as decoy birds for bird-catching. The first falls within the description 'fowl', and the second within the term 'tame or being sufficiently tamed to serve some purpose for the use of man'.

Captive animal

A 'captive animal' is defined as any animal (not being a domestic animal) of whatsoever kind or species, and whether a quadruped or not, including any bird, fish, or reptile, which is in captivity or confinement, or which is maimed, pinioned, or subjected to any appliance or contrivance for the purpose of hindering or preventing its escape from captivity or confinement.

The definition of 'captive animal' covers most animals which have become, in some way, captive or confined or hindered or prevented from escaping. The definition clearly includes all zoo animals, including captive fish, birds and reptiles, but it is certainly not limited to them. However, the definition does not cover invertebrates; consequently it is not an offence to be cruel to spiders and similar insects, whether captive or not.

The usual question to resolve in relation to wild animals is whether or not they are captive. Temporarily to trap a wild animal does not make it captive; there must be some control exercised over a period of time. A stag which whilst being pursued becomes cornered, or tangled in undergrowth so that it cannot free itself, is not a captive animal. A wild squirrel which is temporarily trapped in a tree does not thereby become a captive animal. The cruel maiming of a hedgehog, by repeatedly beating it with a stick, does not make that animal a 'captive animal' within the meaning of the Act.

Cruelty to animals

The Protection of Animals Act 1911, s 1 provides the offence of cruelty to animals. It defines such cruelty in wide terms. First, it makes it an offence cruelly to beat, kick, ill-treat, over-ride, over-drive, overload, torture, infuriate or terrify an animal. It is not necessary to prove that ill-treatment was deliberate or wilful. The section then goes on to declare that those who cause or procure, or being an owner permit, such conduct are also guilty of cruelty to animals. An omission to take reasonable care and thereby causing unnecessary suffering also constitutes cruelty, as does a positive act which has that result. The section also provides that the following constitute the offence of cruelty to animals: conveyance in a cruel manner, fighting or baiting animals (those who permit premises to be used for this purpose are also guilty), wilful poisoning without reasonable cause, and subjecting animals to operations conducted without due care and humanity. The tethering of a horse, ass or mule under conditions or in such manner as to cause unnecessary suffering also amounts to cruelty to animals under s 1.

Although the Act specifies so many ways in which the offence can be committed, the offence is essentially concerned with any unnecessary abuse of a domestic or captive animal which causes pain or suffering.

The Act excepts things done in the slaughtering, or preparation for slaughtering, of animals for food, unless done in such a way as to cause unnecessary suffering. The coursing of captive animals is also excepted, unless the animals are liberated in an injured or exhausted condition, or unless they are hunted in a confined area from which there is no escape.

Animal fights

A person who, without reasonable excuse, is present when animals are placed together for the purpose of their fighting each other commits an offence, as does someone who published or caused to be published an advertisement, knowing its nature, of such a fight. These offences are particularly relevant to dog fights.

Abandoning animals

It is an offence for an owner or a person in charge or control of any animal to abandon it without reasonable cause or excuse, whether permanently or not, in circumstances likely to cause it unnecessary suffering. The offence extends to those who cause or procure or, being the owner, permit such abandonment. The offence is set out in the Abandonment of Animals Act 1960, s 1, which declares that such acts render a person guilty of the offence of cruelty to animals under the Protection of Animals Act 1911, s 1 and subject to the provisions of that Act which apply to cruelty.

'Abandonment' in the present context does not require permanent abandonment, although it means something more than merely leaving unattended. For abandonment, it must be proved that the accused had intentionally relinquished, wholly disregarded or given up his duty to care for the animal. Where a person has made or attempted to make arrangements for the animal's welfare during a period where he cannot look after it himself, there is no abandonment. Proof of abandonment is not enough; the abandonment must be in circumstances where unnecessary suffering is likely to be caused by it.

Destruction of injured animals

Where the owner of an animal is convicted of cruelty under the above provisions, and the court is satisfied that it would be cruel to keep the animal alive, the court may order the destruction of the animal. Where such an order is not made, but there is evidence that the animal is likely to be exposed to further cruelty, the court may deprive its owner of his ownership and dispose of the animal as it thinks fit.

Police officers frequently find that animals have been injured in accidents. The Protection of Animals Act 1911, s 11 allows a constable to summon a registered veterinary surgeon to any animal, which he finds so diseased, or so injured, or in such a physical condition, that in his (the constable's) opinion it could not be moved without cruelty. It is the opinion of the constable which is important; if the owner is present and refuses to call a veterinary surgeon the constable may nevertheless do so. If the veterinary surgeon finds that it is cruel to keep the animal alive, and issues a certificate to that effect, the constable may have the animal humanely slaughtered. The expenses incurred are recoverable from the owner as a civil debt.

Dogs and cats are excluded from the definition of 'animal' for the purposes of this section. Nevertheless, it is the duty of the police to take action to prevent such suffering and similar action should be taken, although in such circumstances the Act does not authorise the recovery of the money by civil process. If the owner of the dog or cat is present then it is unlikely that difficulties will arise, but the police officer should direct his mind towards the condition of the animal. If a veterinary surgeon is called to an injured cat or dog, his advice should be followed. It must be remembered that the police do not have a specific power to sanction the destruction of an injured cat or dog, but if a constable has such an animal destroyed on the ground that it would be cruel to keep it alive, there can be no doubt that he would have a defence to a criminal charge.

Pets—sale and boarding

The Pet Animals Act 1951 requires that the keepers of pet shops must be licensed with the local authority. Under other legislation, dog-breeding kennels and boarding kennels for dogs or cats must be similarly licensed.

For the purposes of the 1951 Act, the keeping of a pet shop refers to the carrying on at premises (including a private dwelling) of a business of selling animals or pets, including the keeping of animals on those premises for the purposes of such a business. However, a person who only keeps or sells pedigree animals bred by him does not keep a pet shop.

Dog kennels for breeding purposes include any premises, even a private house, where more than two bitches are kept for breeding purposes.

The local authority ensures that licensees comply with the conditions of their respective licences by authorising its officers or a veterinary surgeon to inspect pet shops and kennels.

It is also an offence to sell a pet to a child under 12 years, or to sell pets in a street or public place (except at a stall or barrow in a market).

BADGERS AND OTHER WILD ANIMALS

Badgers

Badgers are not domestic animals and are therefore not protected by the Protection of Animals Act 1911. However, the Protection of Badgers Act 1992, s 1, gives special protection to badgers by creating offences of wilfully killing, injuring or taking any badger, or attempting to do one of these things in contravention of the Act. Section 1(2) provides that if, in any proceedings for attempting to kill, take or injure a badger, there is evidence from which it could be reasonably concluded that at the material time the accused was doing so, he shall be presumed to have been doing so, unless the contrary is shown. If a person is found in possession of a dead badger, or any part of it, he is guilty of an offence under s 1(3) of the Act, unless he can show that the badger had not been killed in contravention of the provisions of the Act, or that the badger, or part, had been sold (whether to him or another) and, at the time of the purchase, the purchaser had no reason to believe that the badger had been killed in contravention of the Act.

Licences may be granted by the Ministry of Agriculture to permit killing or taking to prevent serious damage to crops. Licences may also be granted by the Ministry to permit killing or taking to prevent the spread of disease, and by the Nature Conservancy Council for England or the Countryside Council for Wales to allow taking for scientific purposes, zoological needs or for ringing or marking. Acts authorised by such a licence are of course exempted from being an offence.

Offences of cruelly ill-treating, using badger tongs, or digging for badgers are dealt with by s 2(1) of the Act. Section 2(2) provides, in relation to the offence of digging for a badger, that if there is clear evidence from which it could be reasonably concluded that the accused was digging for a badger, he must be presumed to have been doing so, unless the contrary is shown. Digging for badgers is quite common in some parts of Britain. When the badger is unearthed, dogs are released to fight it. In addition, s 2(1) provides that the use, for the purpose of killing or taking a badger, of a firearm, other than a smooth bore weapon of not less than 20 bore or a rifle using ammunition having a muzzle energy not less than 160 footpounds and a bullet weighing less than 38 grains, is prohibited.

Section 3 creates offences of interfering with a badger sett by intentionally or recklessly damaging it, destroying it, obstructing access to it, causing a dog to enter it or disturbing a badger when it is occupying it. Exemption is provided by s 8 to permit those hunting foxes with hounds to obstruct entrances subject to certain conditions. Under s 4 it is an offence to sell, offer for sale or have live badgers in one's possession or control.

There are exceptions from liability for an offence under the Act for those who find an injured badger and either take it to tend it or kill it as an act of mercy, and for those who unavoidably kill or injure a badger as an incidental result of lawful action. Farmers and others who consider that the action in question is necessary to prevent serious damage to land, crops, poultry or other property are also exempted from an offence of killing, taking or injuring etc. This exemption is subject to a major qualification; if it was apparent before the time that the action was taken that it would prove necessary to prevent such damage (ie there is not a situation of urgency), a person is not exempted if he had not applied for a licence for this purpose as soon as reasonably practicable after the fact became apparent or if an application for such a licence had been under consideration.

Where a constable has reasonable grounds for suspecting that a person is committing an offence under this Act, or has committed such an offence, and that evidence is to be found on that person, or in any vehicle or article he has with him, the constable may without warrant stop and search that person, vehicle or article. He may seize and detain anything which may be evidence of the commission of such an offence. These powers are wide; persons reasonably suspected of badgering may be stopped and searched. If they have dogs, tongs and spades with them, these may be seized.

Where a dog is used in commission of offences of taking etc, cruelty and interference with setts, a court may order its destruction, or may disqualify the offender from keeping or having the custody of a dog for such period as it thinks fit.

Dangerous wild animals

It is an offence to keep a dangerous wild animal without having a local authority licence. The term 'dangerous wild animal' is defined in the Dangerous Wild Animals Act 1976. The animals described could generally be described as zoo animals.

Cruelty to wild mammals

The Wild Mammals (Protection) Act 1996, s 1 makes it an offence for any person to mutilate, kick, beat, nail or otherwise impale, stab, burn, stone, crush, drown, drag or asphyxiate any wild mammal with intent to inflict unnecessary suffering upon it.

Section 2 of the Act exempts from the provisions of s 1:

(a) attempted mercy killing of a wild mammal which has been so seriously disabled (by an act which is not the act of the person concerned) that there is no chance of recovery;

(b) reasonably swift and humane killing of a wild mammal injured or taken in the course of either lawful shooting, hunting, coursing or pest control;

(c) acts authorised under any enactment;

(d) any act made unlawful by s 1 if it was by means of a snare, trap, dog, or bird lawfully used for the purpose of killing or taking any wild mammal; or

(e) lawful use of a poison or noxious substance.

A 'wild mammal' is any mammal which is not a domestic or captive animal within the meaning of the Protection of Animals Act 1911.

Thus, all mammals which are outside the protection of pre-existing legislation are afforded protection by the 1996 Act. Mercy killings and attempted mercy killings are generally exempted from the provisions of the Act, as are authorised acts under existing legislation, and established methods of pest control such as the snaring of rabbits.

It is submitted that some of the exemptions included in s 2 are unnecessary as s 1 carefully defines the ways in which the offence might be committed. Those who are carrying out a 'mercy' killing are unlikely to adopt any of the methods described in s 1, nor are those who follow what is described as 'country pursuits'. It is also submitted that, in any case, such acts as mercy killings and those authorised by law could not be described as being carried out 'with intent to inflict unnecessary suffering'.

Section 4 of the Act provides that where a constable has reasonable grounds for suspecting that a person has committed an offence under the provisions of the Act and that evidence of the commission of the offence may be found on that person or in or on any vehicle which he may have with him, the constable may:

(a) without warrant, stop and search that person and any vehicle or article he may have with him; and

(b) seize and detain for the purposes of proceedings under any of those provisions anything which may be evidence of the commission of the offence or may be liable to be confiscated under s 6 of the Act (a convicting court may order confiscation of any vehicle or equipment used in commission of the offence).

It is essential that police officers dealing with offences under the Act specify the number of animals which were subjected to such cruelty. Section 5 of the Act provides that the maximum fine which may be imposed shall be determined as if the person had been convicted of a separate offence in respect of each such wild animal.

DOGS AND THE LAW

Dogs worrying livestock

The Dogs (Protection of Livestock) Act 1953 declares that the owner of a dog, and, if it is in the charge of a person other than the owner, that person also, shall be guilty of an offence if the dog worries livestock on any agricultural land. Not surprisingly, exceptions are made in relation to certain dogs at large in a field of sheep; dogs of the occupier of the field or the owner of the sheep are not included, nor are police dogs, guide dogs, trained sheep dogs, working gun dogs or a pack of hounds.

The term 'worry livestock' covers *attacking* livestock, *or chasing* livestock in such a way as may reasonably be expected to cause injury or suffering to it, or, in the case of females, abortion, or loss of or diminution in their produce. It also covers a dog *being at large* (meaning not on a lead or under close control) in a field or enclosure in which there are *sheep*.

'Livestock' means cattle, sheep, goats, swine, horses or poultry. For the purposes of this definition, 'cattle' includes bulls, cows, oxen, heifers or calves; 'horses' includes asses and mules and 'poultry' means domestic fowls, turkeys, geese or ducks. Thus 'livestock' can generally be described as farm animals. 'Agricultural land' means land used as arable, meadow or grazing land or for the purposes of poultry farming, pig farming, market gardens, allotments, nursery grounds or orchards. Generally, the land described is agricultural in the general sense of the word but the inclusion of 'allotments' gives a wider meaning to the term. There are many allotment gardeners who keep poultry on their land in towns. Offences of worrying livestock are most frequently encountered on agricultural land near to towns. The town-dweller is more likely to leave his dog free to roam. The country-dweller is usually careful in this respect.

There are two defences which can be offered in cases of livestock-worrying. The first is that the owner of the dog may prove that at the time in question the dog was in the charge of some other person, whom he reasonably believed to be a fit and proper person to be in charge. This would apply where an owner had left his dog with a reliable friend whilst absent on holiday, or even where some reliable person had taken the dog for a walk. The other defence is related to circumstances in which livestock trespass upon someone else's land. If the dog which attacks the livestock is owned by, or in the charge of, the occupier of that land or a person authorised by him, a defence is open to that person provided that he did not cause the dog to attack the livestock.

Police prosecutions for offences under this Act require the consent of the chief officer of police and it is usual for the process report to be endorsed by the chief officer of police. It is good practice for police officers concerned with the prosecution of such offences to check that this has been done.

A constable is empowered to seize a dog, found anywhere, which he reasonably believes to have been worrying livestock on agricultural land and to retain it until the owner is found and has paid the expenses of its detention. This power cannot be exercised if there is a person present who admits to being the owner of the dog or in charge of it. If, on an application by a constable, a justice is satisfied that there are grounds for believing that:

(a) an offence under the Act has been committed; and
(b) the dog in question is on premises specified in the application,

he may issue a warrant authorising a constable to enter and search the premises in order to identify the dog.

The Animals Act 1971 allows the owner of livestock worried by a dog to claim compensation by way of civil process. This Act also provides that a person who is sued in the civil courts for killing or injuring a dog has a defence if he acted in protection of his livestock and gave notice to the police of what he had done within 48 hours.

Stray dogs

The Environmental Protection Act 1990, s 149 requires every local authority to appoint an officer to deal with stray dogs found in its area. Where the officer has reason to believe that any dog found in a public place or on any other land or premises is a stray dog, he must, where possible, seize it and detain it. Where the place concerned is not a public place, he may only seize and detain the dog with the consent of the owner or occupier of the place. Where the dog wears a collar on which appears a person's name and address, or its owner is known, a notice must be served on that person, stating that the dog will be liable to be disposed of if it is not claimed within seven clear days and the expenses of its detention met. After the dog has been detained for seven clear days (or, where a notice has been served, if it has not been claimed and the expenses paid within seven clear days after service of the notice) the dog may be disposed of by way of sale or destruction. Where a dog is sold under the provisions of this section to a person acting in good faith, the ownership of the dog is vested in the buyer.

The officer must keep a register giving particulars of all dogs so seized and disposed of. The register must be available, at all reasonable times, for inspection by the public without charge. The officer must ensure that dogs are properly fed and looked after while they are detained.

Section 150 of the Act requires the finder of a stray dog to:

(a) return it to its owner; or
(b) take the dog:
    (i) to the appointed officer of the local authority for the area; or
    (ii) to the police station which is nearest to the place where the dog was found;

and to inform the officer of the local authority or the police officer in charge of the station where the dog was found. Failure to comply with these requirements is an offence. Where a dog has been taken to an appointed officer, the finder may keep the dog, if he wishes, on informing the officer of this and his name and address. In such a case the finder must keep the dog for at least a month; he commits an offence if he fails to do so.

The Dogs Act 1906, s 3 makes similar provisions in relation to the seizure, detention and disposal of stray dogs by the police but it is anticipated that, in consequence of the 1990 Act, such dogs will be detained by the local authority officer. Section 4 of the 1906 Act makes similar provision to that in s 150 of the 1990 Act concerning the situation where the finder takes a stray dog to a police station and wishes to keep it. It provides that, on informing the police officer of this and of his name and address, he must be given a certificate which includes a description of the dog and gives details of its finding. The finder is, in consequence, obliged to keep the dog for a period of one month. If he does not he commits an offence. This must be explained to him before he agrees to keep the dog. If the finder does not wish to keep the dog it must be dealt with by the police by sale or destruction in the same way as described above in relation to an appointed local authority officer.

Further offences of 'straying' are discussed below under the heading 'Specific offences in relation to dangerous dogs'.

Control of dogs

Collars

The Control of Dogs Order 1992 requires that every dog while on a highway or in a place of public resort must wear a collar with the owner's name and address inscribed upon it, or on a plate or badge attached to it. There are certain exceptions which refer to working dogs used in the countryside in conditions which might make the wearing of a collar dangerous, or to other similar circumstances in other working environments. The exceptions apply to:

(a) any pack of hounds,
(b) any dog while being used for sporting purposes,
(c) any dog while being used for the capture or destruction of vermin,
(d) any dog while being used for the driving or tending of cattle or sheep,
(e) any dog while being used on official duties by a member of Her Majesty's Armed Forces or Her Majesty's Customs and Excise or by the police force for any area,

(f) any dog while being used in emergency rescue work, or
(g) any dog registered with the Guide Dogs for the Blind Association.

Where a dog is found in a highway or place of public resort without the requisite collar, the owner or the person in charge of the dog who, without lawful authority or excuse, the proof whereof is on him, causes or permits the dog to be there without that collar is guilty of an offence.

Leads and muzzles

The Road Traffic Act 1988, s 27 empowers local authorities to make orders designating certain roads within their areas as roads upon which dogs must at all times be kept on a lead. The chief officer of police must be consulted before such an order is made and the local authority is required to publish it and to place signs on the road affected. When such an order is in force, it is an offence to cause or permit a dog to be on such a road if it is not held on a lead. The section permits exceptions to be made by the order, and it expressly provides that the offence just mentioned does not apply to dogs tending cattle or sheep in the course of a business nor to those being used for sporting purposes.

The Dangerous Dogs Act 1991, s 1 makes it an offence for the owner, or person for the time being in charge, of a dog which is bred for fighting and to which the section applies (any dog of the type known as pit bull terrier, Japanese tosa and any other type of dog designated by order of the Secretary of State, currently the *dogo argentino* and the *fila braziliero*) to allow such a dog to be in a public place without being muzzled and kept on a lead. We deal with what constitutes a 'public place' on p 506. It will be noted that a 'public place' includes the inside of a car which is in the public place. The prohibition in s 1 is a strict one. If a dog of the requisite type is in a public place, it must not be allowed to be unmuzzled and must be kept on a lead. Thus, where an owner removed the muzzle from a pit bull terrier because it developed kennel cough and it was therefore cruel to muzzle it, it was held that neither the Act nor the common law allowed a person in control of such a dog to make a value judgement between the safety of the public or the well-being of the dog, and that there were no circumstances in which the necessity of the situation could overtake the prohibition. The word 'type' is not synonymous with 'breed'. 'Type' has a wider meaning than 'breed'. Determining the limits of a type is a question of fact for determination by the magistrates or Crown Court. They are entitled to look at the American Dog Breeders' Association (ADBA) breed standard as a guide. The fact that a dog does not meet that standard in every respect is not conclusive that it is not one of the specified types. Thus, for example, it has been held that, the fact that a dog is near to, or has a substantial number of, characteristics of a pit bull terrier as set out in the ADBA standard is sufficient for the dog to be found to be of the pit bull terrier type. It is relevant to consider whether the dog exhibited the behavioural characteristics of a pit bull terrier but that evidence would not be conclusive.

By s 5 of the 1991 Act a constable (or authorised local authority officer) may seize any dog which appears to him to be a dog to which s 1 applies and which is in a public place when it is not muzzled or kept on a lead.

Dogs fouling land

By the Dogs (Fouling of Land) Act 1996, where a dog defecates on designated land, the person in charge of the dog at that time commits an offence if he fails to remove the faeces from the land forthwith, unless:

(a) he has reasonable cause for failing to do so; or

(b)   the owner, occupier or other person or authority having control of the land has consented (generally or specifically) to his failing to do so.

A local authority may designate for the purposes of the Act any land in their area which is in the open air and to which the public are entitled or permitted to have access (with or without payment). The 1996 Act does not apply to land comprised in or running alongside a highway which comprises a carriageway unless the driving of motor vehicles on the carriageway is subject, otherwise than temporarily, to a speed limit of 40 mph or less. The Act does not apply to land used for agriculture or woodlands; to land which is predominantly marshland, moorland or heath; or to common land to which the public are entitled or permitted to have access other than by a right to access to urban common land.

For the purposes of the Act, land which is covered, if open to the air on at least one side, is land which is open to the air.

The provisions of the Act do not apply to a registered blind person.

For the purposes of the offence, a person who habitually has a dog in his possession is taken to be in charge of the dog at any time unless some other person is then in charge. Placing faeces in a receptacle which is provided on the land amounts to removal. Being unaware of the defecation (whether by reason of not being in the vicinity or otherwise), or not having a device for, or other suitable means of removing faeces, is not a reasonable excuse for failing to remove the faeces.

An authorised officer of the local authority may issue a fixed penalty ticket to a person whom he has reason to believe has committed this offence. The effect of giving notice is that no proceedings may be instituted before the expiration of 14 days following the giving of the notice. A person who pays the fixed penalty within that period may not be convicted of the offence.

Dangerous dogs

Order to keep under control

Complaints are frequently received by police officers to the effect that a particular dog is dangerous. The Dogs Act 1871 lays down the following powers for a magistrates' court in relation to a dangerous dog.

If it appears to a magistrates' court that a dog is dangerous and not kept under proper control, it may order the owner to keep it under control or may order that it be destroyed. The proceedings must be by way of complaint and if initiated by information they are invalid. Complaints may be preferred by a police officer.

Such an order may be made whether or not the dog is shown to have injured any person. It may specify the measures to be taken for keeping the dog under control, whether by muzzling, keeping on a lead or by excluding it from specified places or otherwise. Such an order may also require the neutering of a male dog.

It is not necessary that the dog is dangerous to mankind; it is enough that it is dangerous to other animals of whatever kind. However, in one case, a dog which killed two pet rabbits was held not to be dangerous as it was within the natural instincts of a dog to chase, wound or kill other small animals. This is a surprising view. If followed generally it would undermine the 1871 Act.

The saying that every dog may have two bites is not necessarily true. This saying has arisen because the court will often order the owner to keep the dog under control on the first occasion that a complaint is made. However, the court has the power to order destruction from the outset. There is an appeal to the Crown Court against an order of destruction, but not against an order to keep the dog under control.

The Dangerous Dogs Act 1989 empowers a magistrates' court, when it makes an order under the 1871 Act directing a dog to be destroyed, to appoint a person to do it and to require the custodian to deliver it up. It may also disqualify the owner from having custody for a specified period. There is an appeal to the Crown Court.

The 1989 Act also creates offences of failing to keep a dog under proper control as ordered under the 1871 Act, and failing to deliver up a dog for destruction as ordered. The offences are punishable by fine and disqualification from having custody of a dog for a specified period.

Specific offences in relation to dangerous dogs

The Dangerous Dogs Act 1991, ss 1 and 3 make further provisions in relation to dangerous dogs.

The most important provision is s 1(3) which makes it an offence for a person to have in his possession or control a dog to which s 1 applies (see p 503 above). However, by the Dangerous Dogs Compensation and Exemption Schemes Order 1991, this offence does not apply to a dog born before 30 November 1991 if the following set of conditions is satisfied:

(a) the person wishing to keep the dog must have notified the police of its address, name, age and gender;
(b) the dog must have been neutered;
(c) there must be third party insurance in respect of bodily harm caused by it;
(d) a certificate of exemption must have been issued; and
(e) the terms of the certificate must be complied with.

Section 1(2) prohibits breeding, selling, exchanging, giving or offering to give, advertising or exposing for sale, exchange or gift, a dog specified above in relation to leads etc. It also makes it an offence for the owner to abandon such a dog, or for the owner or person in charge of it to allow it to stray.

Section 3 creates two offences which apply to all dogs.

First, where a dog is dangerously out of control in a public place, the owner or the person for the time being in charge of it is guilty of an offence under s 3(1). The offence is aggravated if the dog, whilst so out of control, injures any person. Strict liability is imposed by s 3(1) on the owners or handlers of such dogs. The test is objective and the state of mind of the owner is irrelevant. However, an owner has a defence if he can prove that at the time of the offence the dog was in the charge of a person whom he reasonably believed to be a fit and proper person to be in charge of it.

Second, the owner or person in charge of a dog commits an offence against s 3(3) if he allows it to enter a place which is not a public place but where it is not permitted to be and, while it is there, it injures any person, or there are grounds for reasonable apprehension that it will do so. There would be such grounds, for example, if a dog attacks someone without prior warning. The offence can be committed by omission if it results in the dog entering the place in question. Consequently, for example, a person who fails to take adequate precautions to prevent a dog escaping into another place 'allows' it to enter that place. Where a dog was secured by a chain which proved to be inadequate and it escaped from a garden, entered a place where it was not permitted to be, and bit the face of a young child, the owner was held to have 'allowed' the dog to enter that place, even though he thought that the chain was adequate. Like the offence under s 3(1), the present offence is one of strict liability.

An aggravated offence under s 3(1) or s 3(3) is committed if the dog does injure any person in these circumstances.

Destruction and disqualification orders

These are dealt with by s 4 or s 4A of the 1991 Act. Section 4(1) provides that, where a person is convicted of an offence against s 1 or 3, the court may order destruction of the dog concerned. Indeed, it *must* do in the case of an offence under s 1 or an aggravated offence contrary to s 3, unless it is satisfied that the dog would not constitute a danger to public safety and, where the dog was born before 30 November 1991 and is subject to a prohibition on its possession under s 1(3), that there is good reason why the dog has not been exempted from that prohibition.

A court may also order a person convicted of any of these offences to be disqualified from keeping a dog for such a period as it thinks fit. Dogs may not be destroyed during the period allowed for notice of, and determination of, any appeal.

Similar provisions are made in the 1991 Act to those set out above in the 1989 Act in relation to the appointment of a person to undertake the destruction of a dog and requiring it to be delivered up for that purpose.

Offences are committed against s 4(8) where a person has custody of a dog while disqualified, or where he fails to deliver up a dog for destruction as ordered.

Section 4A of the 1991 Act provides that where:

(a)   a person is convicted of an offence under s 1 or an aggravated offence under s 3(1) or (3);
(b)   the court does not order destruction of the dog under s 4; and
(c)   in the case of an offence under s 1, the dog is subject to the prohibition under s 1(3),

the court must order that, unless the dog is exempted from that prohibition within the requisite period, the dog shall be destroyed. The requisite period, currently two months, may be extended by the court.

Section 4A also provides that, where a person is convicted of a simple offence under s 3(1) or (3), the court may order that, unless its owner keeps it under proper control, the dog must be destroyed. Such an order may specify the measures to be taken to keep the dog under control whether by muzzling, keeping on a lead, excluding it from specified places or otherwise, and, if it appears to the court that the dog is a male and would be less dangerous if neutered, may require that the dog be neutered.

Public place

The 1991 Act defines a 'public place' as any street, road or other place (whether or not enclosed) to which the public have or are permitted to have access. A private garden is not a public place in this context and neither is any other type of place which people enter by express or implied invitation. On the other hand, a dog in a private car on a public highway is in a public place.

Police powers

As already mentioned, by s 5(9) of the 1991 Act, a constable (or authorised local authority officer) may seize any dog which appears to him to be a dog to which s 1 applies and which is in a public place when its possession or custody is unlawful by virtue of s 1. Such a person may also seize any dog in a public place which appears to him to be dangerously out of control.

If a justice of the peace is satisfied by information on oath that there are reasonable grounds to believe that one of the above offences has been committed, or that evidence of such an offence is to be found on any premises, he may issue a warrant authorising a constable to enter and search them and to seize any dog or other thing which is evidence of such an offence. This power is given by s 5(2) of the 1991 Act.

Section 4B of the 1991 Act makes provision for an order of destruction which may be made by a justice of the peace in respect of a dog which has been seized under s 5(1) or (2) of the Act where there is no prosecution, or where the dog cannot be released without contravention of s 1(3). A justice is not required to make such an order if he is satisfied concerning the factors mentioned in relation to s 4(1) above.

Dogs owned by young persons

Section 6 of the 1991 Act provides that, where a dog is owned by a person who is less than 16 years old, the term 'owner' in the above provisions includes a reference to the head of the household, if any, of which that person is a member.

Guard dogs

The Guard Dogs Act 1975 sets out to control the use of guard dogs on premises. It is an offence for any person to use or permit the use of a guard dog on any premises unless:

(a) a person ('the handler') who is capable of controlling the dog is present on the premises and the dog is under the direct control of the handler; or
(b) the dog is so secured as to prevent it from being at liberty to go freely about the premises.

However, the Act is concerned with what might be described as the commercial use of guard dogs, rather than the family watchdog. It therefore excludes from the term 'premises' agricultural land and land in the curtilage of a dwelling house, thus exempting farm dogs and those confined within a dwelling house or its yard or garden.

When guard dogs are kept upon 'premises' warning notices must be clearly displayed at all entrances to the premises; failure to display such notices is an offence.

A 'guard dog' is one which is used either to protect the premises or property on them, or to protect a person guarding the premises or property. The handler must keep the dog under his personal control at all times unless he has handed over responsibility to another handler, or he has secured the dog so that it is not at liberty to go freely about the premises; otherwise he commits an offence. If the dog is properly secured it is not necessary for the handler to be on the premises all the time. If secured on a long chain, it is a question of fact, for the justices to determine, whether the dog was at liberty to go freely about the premises.

STRAYING ANIMALS

The Highways Act 1980, s 155 states that if horses, cattle, sheep, goats, or swine are found straying or lying on or at the side of a highway their keeper is guilty of an offence.

A person in whose possession animals are is their keeper, whether or not he derives any personal benefit from them. Highways which pass over common or unenclosed land are exempted from these provisions.

Police officers frequently receive reports of straying animals, usually during the night. They are empowered to return them to the keeper's land or to any other place provided for the safe custody of animals. Such places, or common pounds as they were known, are extremely rare today. It is, therefore, usually left to police officers temporarily to secure such animals. It is inadvisable to place animals in a field in which other animals are already grazing, unless it is known that they escaped from that field. The consequences of mixing non-attested cattle with those which have been attested can be expensive.

WILD BIRDS, ANIMALS AND PLANTS

Wild birds

Killing, destroying, damaging or possessing

The relevant statute is the Wildlife and Countryside Act 1981. Section 1 of the Act creates the offences of intentionally killing, injuring or taking any *wild bird*, of intentionally taking, damaging or destroying the *nest of such a bird*, and of intentionally taking or destroying an *egg of such a bird*. It is equally an offence to possess a wild bird, whether alive or dead (including one which has been stuffed and mounted), or any part of it, or an egg (or part of it) of such a bird. 'Knowledge' that the bird is wild is not required. Consequently, an accused's belief that a wild bird was bred in captivity and was therefore not a 'wild bird' does not afford an excuse.

The purpose of the legislation is to provide complete protection to wild birds against the activities such as those of the falconer at one extreme and those of the youthful 'birds'-nester' at the other. The term 'wild bird' is widely defined to include all wild birds which are resident in, or are visitors to, Great Britain, with the exception of poultry (birds which could not readily be described as wild even if free ranging) or game birds (which are protected by separate legislation discussed in the next chapter). In addition, as already implied, 'wild bird' does not include a wild bird which has been bred in captivity. For a bird to be bred in captivity the parent birds must have been in captivity when the egg was laid. This restriction is to prevent the 'nest robbers' from legally rearing falcons and other rare birds in captivity. Captive birds must be ringed and registered.

It is also an offence to disturb any wild bird mentioned in Sch 1 to the Act whilst it is building a nest, or is in, on or near such a nest containing eggs or young birds, or to disturb dependent young of such a bird. Schedule 1 contains all but the commonest of birds. It includes all birds of prey resident in the United Kingdom with the exception of the kestrel and sparrow hawk. Nest robbers target the nests of peregrine falcons, goshawks and eagles. The peregrine, particularly, is highly valued by falconers. Frequent use is made of the provisions relating to 'disturbance' to combat such nest robbers. Where chicks are found in the possession of persons licensed to keep birds of prey, and the circumstances are suspicious, the parenthood of such chicks can be established by DNA fingerprinting. The RSPB will assist in this respect.

Exceptions

For the purpose of day to day enforcement, it is almost certain that persons found in the act of killing wild birds, or in possession of their eggs, will be guilty of an offence against this Act. However, there are some limitations on the offence of killing, taking or injuring a wild bird. Some birds may be killed or taken outside their close season (generally their nesting season); these include the commoner species of duck and goose, plover, snipe and woodcock, which are listed in Part I of Sch 2 to the Act. There are a number of other exceptions, relating to wild birds in general, where the action taken is officially required or done in relation to a disabled bird and in certain other cases.

Sale etc

It is an offence under s 6 of the 1981 Act to sell, or to expose or offer for sale, live wild birds or their eggs, or to publish, or cause to be published, advertisements to that effect.

Wild animals

The Wildlife and Countryside Act 1981 contains similar offences to protect wild animals. These provisions are not so easy for police officers to enforce as those relating to wild birds. The reason is that the protection afforded to wild animals by the 1981 Act is restricted to animals described in Sch 5 to the Act. This leads to problems of identification, concerning which specialist help will be needed.

By s 9 of the 1981 Act, it is an offence intentionally to kill, injure or take any wild animal listed in Sch 5, or for a person to possess such animal alive or dead (in whole or part), without proper authority. The same provisions as in the case of wild birds apply in relation to sale, offering for sale or publishing advertisements.

The animals listed in Sch 5 include most of the less common butterflies, moths, frogs, lizards and newts, porpoises, dolphins, red (but not grey) squirrels and the common otter.

Wild plants

That part of the Wildlife and Countryside Act 1981 which concerns wild plants is more direct as it begins (in s 13) by providing that it shall be an offence for any person intentionally to *uproot* ANY *wild plant*. The only exception to the general rule that this will always be an offence is where the act is done by an 'authorised person'. This term has the same meaning as defined in relation to the killing of wild birds. If a person is found uprooting wild plants (and this is not uncommon in relation to primroses and some other wild plants), he is committing an offence unless he is the landowner or some other authorised person (who should be able to show his authority).

The uprooting of wild plants is perhaps not so common as the picking of flowers. The intentional picking or destruction of wild plants, other than by uprooting, is only an offence if the plant concerned is one listed in Sch 8 to the Act. However, the list of protected plants is quite extensive including all but the most common of our wild plants.

The offences of selling etc referred to in relation to wild birds, also apply to wild plants.

Licences

The above offences relating to wild birds, animals and plants are not committed by a person acting within the terms of a licence granted by the appropriate authority.

Police powers

If a constable suspects with reasonable cause that any person is committing or has committed any of these offences, he may without warrant stop and search that person and search or examine anything which that person may then be using or have in his possession. In each case, if he with reasonable cause suspects that evidence of the offence is to be found, he may seize and detain for the purpose of proceedings under the Act anything which may be evidence of the commission of the offence or may be liable to be forfeited.

For the purpose of exercising his powers as set out above, or for the purpose of arresting a person under the Police and Criminal Evidence Act 1984, s 25 for any of the offences under the 1981 Act, a constable may enter onto any land other than a dwelling house. A justice may issue a search warrant subject to the usual conditions in respect of the offence disclosed.

OFFENCES RELATED TO DEER

The Deer Act 1991 deals with the protection of deer by provisions relating to close seasons, the times of day when deer may be taken and the methods by which this may be done. It also deals with deer poaching.

Taking or killing of deer: in close season or at night

Schedule 1 to the 1991 Act provides close seasons for red, fallow, roe and sika deer. These vary considerably because of the breeding seasons of the different species. It is an offence to take or intentionally kill a deer during its close season. Deer farmers are permitted to take or kill deer out of season, but their deer must be conspicuously marked. Authorised persons (occupiers of land, persons with shooting rights, and persons authorised by them) may *shoot* deer out of season in protection of crops etc. The 1991 Act also prohibits the taking or intentional killing of *any* deer by night (ie between one hour after sunset and one hour before sunrise). This offence relates to *any part* of the year. Neither offence is committed if the taking or killing is done to prevent suffering by an injured or diseased deer.

Other offences

The Act also prohibits the setting of traps, snares, poisoned baits etc (unless this is done to prevent suffering to an injured or diseased deer) and the use of smooth-bore guns and guns having a calibre of less than .240, air pistols, air rifles and bullets other than those which are soft- or hollow-nosed. It also prohibits the discharge at deer of firearms from mechanically propelled vehicles or the use of such vehicles for the purpose of driving deer, and the use of arrows, spears or similar missiles, or of drugged missiles containing a poisoned or stupefying drug.

Deer poaching

The 1991 Act prohibits entry onto land without the consent of the owner or occupier or other lawful authority in search or pursuit of any deer with the intention of taking, killing or injuring it.

Offences are also committed by persons who:

(a)   intentionally take, kill or injure any deer (or attempt to do so);
(b)   search for or pursue any deer with the intention of taking, killing or injuring it; or
(c)   remove the carcase of any deer.

A person is not guilty of any of these offences if his act is done in the belief that:

(a)   he would have had the consent of the owner or occupier of the land if such person knew of his doing it and the circumstances of it; or
(b)   he has other lawful authority to do it.

Police powers

The Act provides a constable, who suspects with reasonable cause that any person is committing or has committed any offence under the Act, with a power, without warrant, to search or examine persons, vehicles, animals, weapons or other things on whom or on which he reasonably suspects evidence of the offence is to be found, and to seize and detain anything which is evidence of an offence and any deer, vehicle, animal, weapon or other thing liable to be forfeited by a court under the Act. For the purpose of exercising his powers, a constable may enter any land other than a dwelling house.

CHAPTER 23

Game laws

The term 'game laws' refers to the law relating to poaching, trespassing in pursuit of game of all varieties, close seasons and the need for licences.

The various game laws are designed to protect the rights of the owners or occupiers of land to kill and take game on their land. In the first instance the right to take game rests with the landowner. However, if he leases the land, the right to take game on it automatically passes to the tenant, unless the landowner expressly reserves that right. Frequently the person with the right to take game may let the 'shooting rights' to another person or to a syndicate of persons.

POACHING BY DAY AND BY NIGHT

Powers in public place

It is best to begin by considering the most likely exercise of a constable's powers in the course of his routine duties. If a constable in any highway, street or public place has good cause to suspect a person of coming from land where he has been unlawfully in search or pursuit of game, and of having in his possession any game unlawfully obtained, or any gun, ammunition, nets, snares, traps or other devices of a kind used for the killing and taking of game, he may search that person or an accomplice of his. He may also stop and search conveyances. The constable may seize and detain any game, articles or other things connected with poaching which he finds. There is no power to arrest without warrant; a summons must be applied for. The most direct way of remembering these powers is by the symbol letter 'S': on suspicion a constable may search, seize and, if necessary, summons. Dogs and ferrets may not be seized.

The above powers are provided by the Poaching Prevention Act 1862, s 2, which goes on to provide that when the person summoned appears before the justices he will be convicted of an offence if it is proved that:

(a) he has obtained the game by unlawfully going on any land in search or pursuit of game;

(b) he has used any article or thing for unlawfully killing or taking game; or

(c) he has been an accomplice to conduct of the type mentioned in (a) or (b).

For the purpose of the above provisions, 'game' includes hares and rabbits and pheasants, partridges, woodcocks, snipes, grouse, black or moor game and *the eggs of each of these birds.*

Day poaching

The Game Act 1831, s 30 provides an offence of poaching by day. It provides that anyone who trespasses by entering or being upon land in the daytime in search or pursuit of game, woodcocks, snipes or rabbits commits an offence. For the purposes of the Act of 1831 'game' includes hares and pheasants, partridges, grouse, heath or moor game, and black game.

'Daytime' begins one hour before sunrise and ends one hour after sunset.

'Trespass' indicates an entry onto land (or presence there) without authority. If a person enters upon another's land without authority, the occupier of that land may order that person to leave at once and is entitled to use reasonable force to eject him should he refuse to go. It is not a criminal offence, at the moment, merely to trespass but a trespasser is criminally liable for any damage which he may cause whilst trespassing. The present offence is committed when a trespass is aggravated by a search for or pursuit of game. Trespass by people coursing or hunting with hounds or greyhounds is not punishable under the Act.

Parliament considered that it was essential to provide protection for gamekeepers as it was quite common for bands of poachers to become violent. It therefore increased the penalties under s 31 in cases where five or more persons trespass together during the daytime for such purposes. This recognises the threat offered by large numbers. Section 32 of the Act seeks to deal with the individual threatening actions of any of these persons. If any one of the five is armed with a gun and he uses violence, intimidation or menaces to prevent any person from exercising his powers under the Act, he and those with him commit a further offence.

The Game Laws (Amendment) Act 1960, s 4A(1) provides that where a person is convicted of an offence under s 30 of the 1831 Act as one of five or more persons liable under the section and the court is satisfied that any vehicle belonging to him or in his possession or under his control at the relevant time has been used for the purpose of committing or facilitating the commission of the offence, the court may make an order of forfeiture in respect of that vehicle.

'Facilitation' shall be taken to include the taking of any steps after the commission of the offence to avoid apprehension or detection, or removing from the land any person or property connected with the offence. Thus, the use of the vehicle 'after the event' is also included. The court is not required, when exercising its powers under this section, to have regard to the value of the property and to the likely financial and other effects upon the offender of such an order.

Powers

A constable has power to require any trespasser in search or pursuit of game to quit and give his name and address. If a constable has reasonable cause for suspecting that a person is committing the offence of trespassing in pursuit of game in the daytime he may enter land for the purpose of exercising this power.

Night poaching

The Night Poaching Act 1828 is concerned with offences of poaching by night. Night commences one hour after sunset and continues until one hour before sunrise. Section 1 of the 1828 Act creates two general offences:

(a)   by night, unlawfully taking or destroying by night any game or *rabbits* on land, open or enclosed (including a public road, highway or path); and
(b)   by night, unlawfully entering or being on any land, open or enclosed, with any gun, net, engine or other instrument for the purpose of taking or destroying game.

For the purposes of these offences, 'game' means hares, pheasants, partridges, grouse, heath or moor game, black game or bustards; it does not include rabbits. The two offences can be contrasted as follows. First, the man who has taken or destroyed *game or rabbits* by night has committed an offence wherever that killing or taking has occurred, be it in a field, in a street or public place. Second, the man who has not killed or taken game, must have unlawfully entered upon land with an instrument for the taking of *game*; for this purpose, the land may be open or enclosed but a public road, highway or path is not within the offence.

Like the Game Act 1831, the Night Poaching Act 1828 provides increased penalties for more aggravated offences. By s 2, anyone committing an offence under s 1 who assaults or offers violence with a gun or other offensive weapon towards any person authorised to apprehend him is liable to an increased penalty. Section 9 provides that if three or more people together enter or are on land by night to take or destroy game or rabbits, and one of them is armed with a gun or other offensive weapon, all are guilty of an aggravated offence.

Powers

A constable who has reasonable grounds for suspecting that one of these offences is being committed may enter land to deal with the offence.

GAME

Rights to take game

We have mentioned the rights of landowners, their tenants and authorised persons to take game on their land. At the opposite extreme, we have looked at those who trespass to take or destroy game or who actually take or destroy it. There is only one further Act which should be considered in order to complete an understanding of the rights of persons to take game. This is the Ground Game Act 1880 which provides that an occupier of land will always have the right to kill and take ground game (ie hares and rabbits) on the land which he occupies, whether or not the landowner has contracted to some other person game rights generally. The occupier may also give written authorisation to other people to kill and take ground game, but he may only authorise (again in writing) one person, in addition to himself, to kill ground game with firearms. Authorisations of these types may only be given by the occupier to his own resident household, people in his ordinary employment on the land and one other person bona fide employed by him in the taking and destruction of ground game.

Game licences

Quite regardless of the issue of whether or not a person is authorised to kill or take game on land, all persons must have a game licence to kill, pursue or take game, or to use dogs or devices for such purpose. The Game Licences Act 1860 requires that a licence be taken out for game, woodcocks, snipes, rabbits or deer. There are exceptions to the rule which are generally related to coursing or hunting, the authorised killing of deer and the killing of rabbits by landowners. The occupiers of land, and persons authorised, do not need game licences in their taking of hares. The Game Act 1831 requires that a licence be held if a person searches for game, but 'game' for the purpose of that Act does not include rabbits.

Close season for game

The Game Act 1831 prohibits taking or killing game on Sundays or Christmas Days. In addition, it prohibits the taking or killing of particular types of game birds during their close seasons, which are as follows:

(a) partridges — 1 February to 1 September;
(b) pheasants — 1 February to 1 October;
(c) black game — 10 December to 20 August;
(d) grouse — 10 December to 12 August.

OFFENCES IN RELATION TO FISH

As fishing increases in popularity as a sport and more fisheries are created (either by the Environment Agency for the general public or by clubs for their members), the likelihood of police involvement at some stage in the enforcement of the freshwater fishery laws increases. There are certain provisions of the Salmon and Freshwater Fisheries Act 1975 which are quite general in nature and can directly concern the police. The provisions of the Theft Act 1968, Sch 1 are also important.

Salmon and Freshwater Fisheries Act 1975

Licensing

The Act requires the Environment Agency (EA) to regulate fishing for salmon, trout, freshwater fish and eels by means of a system of licensing. The fishing licence granted by a water authority authorises the person to whom it is granted to use the instrument specified (commonly a rod and line) to fish for fish named in specified waters between certain dates. A salmon licence will include trout, and any licence which allows fishing for trout also permits fishing for lesser freshwater fish and eels. The EA licence is usually referred to as a 'rod licence', and it is important to realise that all a person is authorised to do by that licence is to use a rod in the EA area.

It is an offence to fish for, or take, fish of a description other than that authorised by the licence, or by means other than that authorised by the licence. It is also an offence to possess, with intent to use it for fishing, any instrument other than that authorised by the licence.

A water bailiff appointed by the EA, or any constable, may require any person who is fishing, or whom he reasonably suspects of being about to fish (or to have, within the last half-hour, fished), in the area of the EA to produce his licence or other authority to fish and to give his name and address. (This power is also available to the holder of a licence if he produces his own licence at the time of his demand.) The 'other authority' referred to must be some alternative form of authority issued by the EA; it does not refer to a riparian owner's consent to fish. Clearly, a person could reasonably be suspected of being about to fish if he was seen approaching water with a rod and tackle, and he could reasonably be suspected of having fished in the preceding half-hour if he was seen leaving the water with such equipment on the approach of a constable.

Failure without reasonable excuse to comply with such a request is an offence, except that, if within seven days after the requirement the person requested produces his licence or other authority at the office of the EA, he cannot be convicted of failing to produce it.

Illegal methods

Quite regardless of the licensing situation, there are certain methods of fishing which are prohibited by the Salmon and Freshwater Fisheries Act 1975. The use of any firearm, as defined by the Firearms Act 1968, is prohibited, as is the use of otterboards, snares, crosslines, setlines, spears, gaffs, stroke-hauls, snatches or other like instruments, or any light. These are typical poaching devices. The otter board is a floating board to which are attached a number of lines. A crossline is one which is stretched across a river with a number of lines etc attached. A setline is any line which is left unattended. Stroke-hauls and snatches are used for the purpose of dragging for fish which are foul hooked. Gaffs may, at certain times, be lawfully used for landing fish which have been caught by rod and line, but not for catching fish. The use of fish roe is also prohibited. This is important because some poachers prepare fish roe into a sticky substance, often referred to as 'taffy', which is attached to the line to attract fish to the bait. The use of explosives, poison or electrical devices with intent to take fish is always an offence unless carried out with consent of the EA.

Powers

A water bailiff appointed by the EA may examine rods, instruments or baits if he has good cause to suspect that they are illegal. He may also stop and search a boat or vessel used in fishing in a water authority area or any vessel or vehicle which he reasonably suspects to contain fish caught in contravention of the provisions of the Salmon and Freshwater Fisheries Act 1975, and he may seize fish, instruments, vessels or vehicles or other things liable to be forfeited under the Act. It is an offence to refuse to allow, or to resist, the execution of the above powers by a water bailiff. However, the bailiff must produce his appointment before searching. It is important that police officers are aware of the powers of a water bailiff as they are frequently called to their assistance.

Water bailiffs and other officers of the EA have power to impose a fixed penalty notice on those whom they find, and reasonably believe to be committing or to have committed an offence under the 1975 Act, in lieu of court proceedings and conviction. This fixed penalty system has similarities with that operating in relation to road traffic offences.

The point to remember in resolving disputes arising between officials and anglers is that these powers are only given to a water bailiff appointed by the EA. Superintendents of club fisheries are frequently referred to as bailiffs but unless they have been authorised by the EA they are not water bailiffs for the purpose of fishery legislation.

At night (as defined by the Night Poaching Act 1828 described above), a water bailiff may arrest without warrant any person illegally taking or killing salmon, trout, freshwater fish or eels, or whom he finds near water with that intent, or who has in his possession any prohibited instruments. The bailiff must place such persons in police custody as soon as possible. Such arrested persons may therefore be placed in the care of a custody officer.

Close seasons for game fishing

The Salmon and Freshwater Fisheries Act 1975, Sch 1 deals with the annual close seasons for taking game fish. There is no purpose in setting out the details as the Schedule places the responsibility upon the EA to make bye laws fixing for their area, or the respective parts of it, the annual close season for fishing for salmon and trout other than rainbow trout. In doing so, the EA is required to observe minimum closure periods. The Schedule gives guidelines in respect of fishing by rod and line for salmon and trout which are subject to variation by local bye laws:

(a) salmon   — 31 October and the following 1 February;
(b) trout   — 30 September and the following 1 March; and
(c) rainbow trout — close season may be dispensed with altogether.

Theft Act 1968

Fish can be the subject of theft but only if:

(a) they are ordinarily kept in captivity, as where someone has bought a dozen live trout and placed them in his private pond, or as in the case of fish at fish farms; or
(b) they have been reduced into possession by or on behalf of someone other than the accused, or that other person is in the course of reducing them into possession, as where an angler (the other person) has put fish in a keep net or has hooked it and is reeling it in.

The Theft Act 1968, Sch 1 deals with the situation where fish do not fall within the above provisions, so that the taking or destroying of them is not theft (nor criminal damage). It provides that it is an offence for a person unlawfully to take or destroy, or attempt to take or destroy, any fish:

(a) in water which is private property (such as reservoirs and privately owned lakes); or
(b) in water in which there is any private right of fishery.

'Private right of fishery' can be explained as follows. The water in *non-tidal* rivers or parts of rivers is not owned by the landowners through, or between, whose land the river flows. However, these landowners (or, to give them their technical description, riparian owners) have a private right to fish in the waters bounded by their banks (or up to mid-stream if the banks are in separate ownership). The public cannot acquire a right to fish in non-tidal rivers by common usage. The right always remains with the landowner unless he lets the land to a tenant, at which time it passes to the tenant unless expressly reserved by the landowner. Of course the owner of a right to fish can, if he wishes, give general permission to the public to use his fishery. By way of contrast, a private right of fishery cannot exist in tidal waters, including the tidal part of a river, with the result that there is generally a public right to fish in them, although it must be noted that salmon is almost universally reserved by fishery boards, and that local Acts may affect other fisheries.

If an offence contrary to Sch 1 is committed by night it is more severely punishable than if committed by day. 'Night' and 'day' bear the same meaning as they do under the legislation mentioned earlier in this chapter.

Powers

The Theft Act 1968, Sch 1 gives a power of arrest without warrant to any person in certain circumstances. The powers are related to the offences of taking, destroying or attempting to take or destroy fish. Any person may arrest without warrant anyone who is, or whom he, with reasonable cause, suspects to be, committing such an offence at night, and may seize anything which on conviction is liable to be forfeited (ie anything possessed at the time of the offence for the purpose of taking or destroying fish). These powers are not available during the daytime.

CHAPTER 24

Firearms

There is no general right to possess firearms in Britain. The Firearms Act 1968 (hereafter in this chapter described as 'the Act') controls the sale and acquisition of all types of firearms and the possession or carrying of those weapons on particular occasions. Other Acts punish the possession of firearms on particular occasions.

DEFINITIONS

Section 57 of the Act defines the term 'firearm' for the purposes of that Act as a *lethal barrelled weapon* of any description *from which any shot, bullet or other missile can be discharged*. It also provides that the term includes any *prohibited weapon*, whether it is such a lethal weapon as aforesaid or not, and any *component part* of such a lethal or prohibited weapon, and any *accessory* to any such weapon designed or adapted *to diminish the noise or flash caused by firing the weapon*.

Nothing in the Act relating to firearms applies to an antique firearm which is sold, transferred, purchased, acquired or possessed as a curiosity or ornament.

Lethal weapon

It is clear from judicial decisions that a lethal weapon means a weapon which is capable of causing injury from which death might result. It need not be designed or manufactured for the purpose of causing such injury; if it is not, it is enough that it is capable of causing such injury if misused.

Consequently, even though the purpose of its designer and manufacturer was to produce a toy, a spring pistol which can fire pellets through a barrel will be a lethal weapon (and therefore a firearm) if, even though misused, it is capable of causing an injury from which death might result.

By way of further example, a signalling pistol which fired an explosive magnesium and phosphorus flare, and which was capable of killing at short range, has been held to be lethal; the fact that the manufacturer did not produce it for the purpose of killing or injuring being held to be immaterial. Many of the air guns which are manufactured would normally only cause a trivial injury but they may be classed as lethal since they could cause death by a pellet striking an extremely vulnerable part of the body, for example, an eye.

Whether or not a weapon is lethal must be assessed in relation to the particular weapon in question, and not to weapons of its type. If the particular weapon is not in working order and is therefore incapable of causing injury from which death might result it is not a lethal weapon, even though a weapon of its type is so capable when in working order.

Under the *basic* definition of a 'firearm', the 'lethal weapon' must be *barrelled* and capable of *discharging* any shot, bullet or other *missile*. To these matters we now turn.

Barrelled   A barrel, in relation to a gun, is a tube through which a bullet or shot is discharged. Traditionally, that tube has been made of metal. However, in the modern world of newly discovered substances which might act as substitutes for metal, it is unlikely that the nature of the substance would be restricted to metal.

Shot, bullet or other missile   The terms 'shot' and 'bullet' are self-explanatory, and the term 'other missile' should be taken to relate to some similar solid object which can be discharged from some form of 'barrelled weapon'. It is unlikely that much difficulty will be experienced in relation to this term as the only 'guns' which are excluded thereby are those weapons designed or adapted to discharge some form of gas, and these are almost certain to be 'prohibited weapons' (see below), and therefore a firearm, in any case. However, a weapon which simply discharged compressed air would not be a prohibited weapon for the purposes of the Act.

Apart from its basic definition, 'firearm' also includes 'prohibited weapons', component parts of a lethal barrelled weapon from which any missile can be discharged or of a prohibited weapon, and certain accessories to any such weapon.

Prohibited weapons

There are two provisions creating offences relating to prohibited weapons: ss 5(1) and 5(1A) of the 1968 Act. These impose controls over and above the need to have a firearm certificate.

By s 5(1), it is an offence to sell, transfer, manufacture, purchase, acquire or possess a prohibited weapon, except by the authority of the Secretary of State. The same applies to 'prohibited ammunition' to which s 5(1) applies, which we define later.

For the purposes of the offence under s 5(1), a prohibited weapon is:

(a) any firearm which is so designed or adapted that two or more missiles can be successively discharged without repeated pressure on the trigger;
(b) any self-loading or pump-action rifled gun other than one chambered for .22 inch rim-fire cartridges;
(c) any firearm which either has a barrel less than 30 cm in length or is less than 60 cm in length overall, other than an air weapon, a muzzle-loading gun or a firearm designed as signalling apparatus;
(d) any self-loading or pump-action smooth-bore gun which is not an air weapon (as defined on p 525) or chambered for .22 inch rim-fire cartridges and either has a barrel of less than 24 inches in length or is less than 40 inches in length overall;
(e) any smooth-bore revolver gun other than one which is chambered for 9 mm rim-fire cartridges or a muzzle-loading gun;

(f)   any rocket launcher, or any mortar designed for line-throwing or pyrotechnic purposes or as a signalling apparatus; or

(g)   any weapon of whatever description designed or adapted for the discharge of any noxious liquid, gas or other thing. This covers a wide variety of weaponry from a flame thrower or a high voltage electric stunning device, to the small gas pistols frequently used by women for self-protection in America. The fact that a stun-gun designed for an electrical charge is not working due to some unknown fault does not change its character as a prohibited weapon. The words 'designed or adapted' mean that any other type of weapon which is converted in any way for these purposes is a prohibited weapon as it has been 'adapted'. These weapons do not need to be either lethal or barrelled *provided* they are capable of discharging noxious liquid, gas or other thing. If the weapon is capable of discharging such a substance, and was either designed or adapted for that purpose, it is prohibited. A water pistol used to discharge gas would not be a prohibited weapon if it was used in an unaltered state, since it would not have been designed to discharge one of the prohibited substances, nor adapted in any way to allow it to do so. The same applies to a washing-up liquid bottle filled with hydrochloric acid. The container was neither designed nor adapted for the discharge of a noxious liquid. Although the issue has not been tested to date, there appears to be little doubt that the word 'noxious' before 'liquid, gas or other thing' applies to all three things. A substance is noxious if it is harmful, hurtful or injurious. All forms of gas projectors are therefore prohibited, from the tear gas gun to the small gas pistol.

The prohibition set out at (c) above was that introduced by the Firearms (Amendment) Acts 1997 to restrict the use of handguns. For the purposes of (c) and (d) above, any detachable, folding, retractable or other movable butt-stock are disregarded in measuring the length of any firearm.

References to muzzle-loading guns are references to guns which are designed to be loaded at the muzzle end of the barrel or chamber with a loose charge and a separate ball (or other missile).

Slaughtering instruments, humane killers, shot pistols used for killing vermin, starting pistols, trophies of war, firearms of historic interest and weapons used for treating animals are exempted from the prohibitions imposed upon weapons falling within (c) above (or, in the case of weapons used for treating animals, within (c) or (g)) subject to conditions set out in the Firearms Act 1997, ss 2-8.

Section 5(1A) was inserted into the 1968 Act by the Firearms Acts (Amendment) Regulations 1992 to bring into effect the requirements of European Council Directive 91/477/EC. By s 5(1A), it is an offence to sell, transfer, purchase, acquire or possess a prohibited weapon to which s 5(1A) applies, except with the authority of the Secretary of State. The same applies to 'prohibited ammunition' to which s 5(1A) applies, which we define below.

For the purposes of s 5(1A), the following are prohibited weapons:

(a)   any firearm which is disguised as another object;

(b)   any launcher or other projecting apparatus which is not a prohibited weapon under s 5(1) which is designed to be used with any rocket or ammunition which is designed to explode on or immediately before impact and is prohibited ammunition under s 5(1) or s 5(1A).

In relation to s 5(1A) only, there are a number of exemptions in terms of weapons and of ammunition. They relate principally to collectors and to possession, purchase or acquisition for use for certain authorised purposes, viz slaughtering animals, sporting purposes, shooting vermin, estate management purposes, and competition and target shooting purposes.

Changes in type

A weapon which at any time has been classified as a prohibited weapon (or as a s 1 firearm or as a shotgun) remains so classified notwithstanding anything done to convert it into a weapon of another type (eg prohibited weapon into a s 1 firearm) or to render it incapable of discharging a missile.

Component parts and accessories

The fact that any component part of a lethal barrelled or prohibited weapon (as defined above) is stated by s 57 of the Act to be a firearm in itself is important. In cases of doubt concerning whether or not a weapon is 'lethal barrelled' in the general sense, it is helpful to remember that if it consists of component parts, which are essentially parts of a 'firearm', then those parts are included within the term 'firearm' and their possession etc is equally controlled. For example, it has been held that an article such as a starting pistol, incapable of discharging a missile because the barrel is solid, but capable of being adapted to do so by boring the barrel, was a firearm because the other parts of the weapon were component parts of a revolver. Likewise, if replicas of firearms are produced for the public but with soft metalled firing pins which render the weapons unusable, they are still firearms if the other components are those of a firearm.

The only accessories which are included within the term 'firearm' by s 57, and are therefore controlled by the Act, are those designed or adapted to diminish noise or flash, ie silencers and flash eliminators. Any other accessory to a firearm is not included. A telescopic sight is an accessory but it is not one covered by the term 'accessory' for the purposes of this Act.

What is ammunition?

For the purposes of the Act, 'ammunition' is defined by s 57 as meaning ammunition for any firearm; a blank cartridge is ammunition. Section 57 provides that the term also includes grenades, bombs and other missiles, whether capable of use with a firearm or not, and also includes prohibited ammunition. A 'bomb' is any explosive substance in a case, or a case containing poison gas, smoke, or inflammable material which might be dropped from an aircraft, fired from a gun or thrown or placed by hand.

Prohibited ammunition for the purposes of s 5(1) is:

(a) any cartridge with a bullet designed to explode on or immediately before impact (eg a 'dum-dum bullet'),
(b) any ammunition which contains, or is designed or adapted to contain, any noxious liquid, gas or other thing, and
(c) if capable of being used with a firearm of any description, any grenade, bomb (or other like missile), or a rocket or shell designed to explode on or immediately before impact,

other than ammunition used for treating animals.

Therefore containers designed or adapted to contain any noxious gas etc for use as a missile or bomb are prohibited ammunition, whether filled or not. The other types of prohibited ammunition are explosive bullets and (if capable of being used with a firearm) grenades, bombs, rockets and shells.

Prohibited ammunition for the purposes of s 5(1A) is:

(a) any rocket or ammunition which is not prohibited ammunition for the purposes of s 5(1) which consists in or incorporates a missile designed to explode on or immediately before impact and is for military use;

(b) any ammunition for military use which consists in or incorporates a missile designed so that a substance contained in the missile will ignite on or immediately before impact;

(c) any ammunition for military use which consists in or incorporates a missile designed, on account of its having a jacket and hard-core, to penetrate armour plating, armour screening or body armour;

(d) any ammunition which incorporates a missile designed or adapted to expand on impact;

(e) anything which is designed to be projected as a missile from any weapon and is designed to be, or has been incorporated in -
    (i) any ammunition falling within any of the preceding paragraphs; or
    (ii) any ammunition which would fall within any of those paragraphs but for its being specified in s 5(1).

What is an antique firearm?

As we have said, antique firearms are exempt from the provisions of the Act relating to firearms, provided they are sold, transferred, purchased, acquired or possessed as a curiosity or ornament. The term 'antique' is not defined. Basically, it is a question of fact and degree for the court to decide; it is unlikely that a court will consider that anything made this century is an antique.

POSSESSION, PURCHASE OR ACQUISITION OF FIREARMS OR AMMUNITION

Section 1 firearms and ammunition

The Firearms Act 1968, s 1(1) states that, subject to any exemption under the Act, it is an offence for a person:

(a) to have in his possession, or to purchase or acquire, a firearm to which the section applies without holding a firearm certificate in force at the time, or otherwise than as authorised by the certificate; or

(b) to have in his possession, or to purchase or acquire, any ammunition to which the section applies without holding a firearm certificate, or otherwise than as authorised by such a certificate, or in quantities in excess of those so authorised.

The section applies to every firearm except:

(a) a shotgun, that is to say a smooth-bore gun (not being an air gun) which -
    (i) has a barrel not less than 24 inches in length and does not have any barrel with a bore exceeding 2 inches in diameter;

    (ii)   either has no magazine or has a non-detachable magazine incapable of holding more than two cartridges; and

    (iii) is not a revolver gun; and

(b)   an air weapon (that is to say an air rifle, air gun or air pistol not of a type declared by rules made by the Secretary of State under the Act to be specially dangerous).

Section 1(1) applies to ammunition for a firearm except:

(a)   cartridges containing five or more shot, none of which exceeds .36 inch in diameter;

(b)   ammunition for any air gun, air rifle or air pistol; and

(c)   blank cartridges not more than 1 inch in diameter.

Under the Firearms Act 1982, s 1, the provisions of the 1968 Act relating to a firearm to which s 1 of the 1968 Act applies are made to apply (with limited exceptions) to an imitation firearm to which s 1 applies, and which has the appearance of being such a firearm and is so constructed or adapted as to be readily convertible into such a firearm. An 'imitation firearm' is anything which at the material time has the appearance of being a firearm (other than a weapon for the discharge of a noxious liquid, gas or other thing) whether or not it is capable of discharging any shot, bullet or other missile.

A person can be in possession of a firearm or ammunition even though he does not have physical custody of it nor keeps it in his home; it is enough that he has control of it (as where he keeps a firearm at the home of a relative for safe-keeping). Indeed, someone can be in possession of a firearm even though he is not aware that he has a firearm under his control. For example, if a man has custody of a firearm in a holdall for only a matter of minutes without giving thought to the nature of its contents, he is in possession of those contents and if a firearm is proved to be a part of them, then possession of it has been established. The fact that possession was brief, or that he did not know or could not reasonably have been expected to know that it contained a firearm, affords no defence. The nature of the legislation was intended, by Parliament, to be draconian. It does not have to be proved that the accused knew that the article possessed was a firearm or ammunition within the relevant meaning of those terms. As already indicated, the offence is one of strict liability as to the nature of the article possessed; consequently, for example, an honest and reasonable mistaken belief that the article was an antique firearm (and therefore exempt from the Act) is no defence. There is one exception; where the alleged offence involves an imitation firearm which is readily convertible into a firearm to which s 1 applies, it is a defence for the accused to prove that he did not know and had no reason to suspect that it was readily convertible.

An offence contrary to s 1(1) of the Act is an arrestable offence. It is also an arrestable offence for a person to sell or transfer to a person other than a registered firearms dealer or person who has a certificate authorising its purchase or acquisition a firearm or ammunition to which s 1 applies.

Shotguns

For the purposes of the Act, a 'shotgun' is a smooth-bore gun (not being an airgun) which:

(a)   has a barrel not less than 24 inches in length and does not have any barrel with a bore exceeding 2 inches in diameter;

(b)   either has no magazine or has a non-detachable magazine incapable of holding more than two cartridges; and

(c)   is not a revolver gun.

If the barrel of a shotgun is shortened to less than 24 inches it is no longer a shotgun, but becomes a firearm to which s 1 of the Act applies.

Shotguns are excepted from the provisions of s 1 but s 2 of the Act states that, subject to any exemption under the Act, it is an offence for a person to have in his possession, or to purchase or acquire, a shotgun without holding a certificate under the Act authorising him to possess shotguns. The reason for these special provisions in relation to shotguns is that the conditions for obtaining a shotgun certificate are different from those which apply in the case of s 1 firearms.

What we said about possession and an accused's state of mind in relation to s 1 is equally applicable here.

An offence contrary to s 2 is an arrestable offence.

Air weapon

Air weapons essentially operate by the release of compressed air and therefore contain no explosive charge. An air weapon is not a firearm for which a firearm certificate is required for its possession, purchase or acquisition. An 'air weapon' is an air rifle, air gun or air pistol which has not been declared by the Secretary of State to be specially dangerous. The Secretary of State has declared that an air weapon will be specially dangerous (and therefore a firearm to which s 1 applies) if:

(a)   on discharge from the muzzle there is a kinetic energy in excess of 6 ft/lb in the case of an air pistol, or 12 ft/lb in the case of a weapon other than a pistol; or

(b)   it is disguised as another object.

This has had the effect of compelling manufacturers to keep within these limits. If weapons are sold as air weapons, it is reasonable to assume that they have been tested to confirm that they are inside these limits.

The Firearms (Amendment) Act 1997, s 48 provides that any reference in the Firearm Acts of 1968 to 1997 to an air rifle, air pistol or air gun includes a reference to a rifle, pistol or gun powered by compressed carbon dioxide. On the other hand, a gas-fired rifle, gun or pistol is not an air weapon and therefore requires a firearm certificate for its possession etc.

Ammunition for shotguns and air weapons, and blank cartridges

Ammunition for a shotgun is excepted from the definition of ammunition for the purposes of s 1 provided the cartridge contains five or more shot (none of which exceeds .36 inch diameter). Consequently, if a cartridge contains only four shot, or one of five shot exceeds 0.36 inch in diameter, it is not exempt from the provisions of s 1 and a firearm certificate is required for its possession, purchase or acquisition.

(The Firearms (Amendment) Act 1988, s 5 makes special provisions in relation to ammunition to which s 1 of the 1968 Act does not apply and which is capable of being used in a shotgun or in a smooth-bore gun to which s 1 applies. It makes it an offence to sell such ammunition to any person who is neither a registered firearms dealer nor a person who sells ammunition by way of trade or business, unless such person produces a shotgun certificate; or shows entitlement to possess without a certificate; or produces a certificate authorising another person to possess such a gun, together with that person's written authority to purchase ammunition on his behalf.)

Ammunition for an air weapon is also excepted from the definition of ammunition for the purposes of s 1. This exception even applies to ammunition for a weapon which may have been declared to be specially dangerous.

Blank cartridges not more than one inch in diameter are also excepted from the definition of ammunition for the purposes of s 1.

Firearm certificates

Section 1 firearm

A person wishing to possess, purchase or acquire a firearm or ammunition covered by s 1 of the Act must have a firearm certificate, which is a certificate granted by a chief officer of police under the Act in respect of any firearm or ammunition to which the section applies. The term includes certificates granted in Northern Ireland.

To obtain a certificate an applicant must apply to the chief officer of police of the area in which he resides and must state such particulars as may be required by the form. Information concerning previous names, residence and convictions, other than those for minor traffic offences, must be given. The applicant must sign a statement to the effect that the statements are true, rather than believed to be true. It is an offence knowingly or recklessly to make a statement false in a material particular. An applicant must provide up to four photographs and the names and addresses of two persons who have agreed to act as referees. Before considering the application, the chief officer will verify the particulars included in the application and the likeness to the applicant of the photographs provided. The information which the applicant is required to give on the application form must be verified by each of two referees by a signed statement that the information is, to the best of his knowledge and belief, correct. In addition, each referee must provide a reference to the effect that he knows of no reason why the applicant should not possess a firearm.

Section 27 of the Act states that a firearm certificate must be granted by the chief officer of police if he is satisfied that:

(a) the applicant is fit to be entrusted with a firearm to which s 1 of the 1968 Act applies and that he is not a prohibited person;

(b) he has good reason for having in his possession, or for purchasing or acquiring, the firearm or ammunition in respect of which the application is made;

(c) in all the circumstances the applicant can be permitted to have the firearm or ammunition in his possession without danger to the public safety or peace.

A chief officer is empowered to impose conditions subject to which the firearm certificate is held. These conditions may refer to the nature of the storage of the weapons or their use. Conditions can be varied at any time by notice in writing to the holder, who may be required to return his certificate for variation.

A person under 18 who applies for such a certificate is capable of having a good reason for possessing it *only* if he has no intention of using if for a purpose other than an authorised purpose under the European weapons directive. An authorised purpose is a sporting purpose, the shooting of vermin, a purpose related to estate management activities, competition shooting or target shooting.

Police officers are required to carry out inquiries on behalf of the chief officer and, with these provisions in mind, they are required to check upon the intended usage of the weapon. If the applicant wishes to have a .22 rifle to shoot vermin in his garden, which is quite small and is surrounded by other dwellings, it is apparent that he could not use it for the purpose declared without danger to the public. However, if he wishes to keep the firearm at home but to use it at an approved rifle club, that would be a different matter. The officer conducting the inquiry should always check the secure place in which the weapon will be stored.

If a firearm certificate is granted, the holder must on receipt sign it in ink. He must at all times keep the firearm and ammunition in a safe place and must inform the chief officer of the theft or loss of the firearm or a change of address.

Shotgun certificates

The conditions relating to applications for shotgun certificates are not quite so strict. An application must be made in the prescribed form to the chief officer of police and there are similar requirements in respect of the submission of photographs, verification and a reference by one referee, supply of photographs, signature of the certificate, and notification of the loss or theft of the certificate or of a change of address.

Such a certificate must be granted by the chief officer of police if he is satisfied that the applicant can be permitted to possess a shotgun without danger to the public safety or to the peace, unless he has reason to believe that the applicant is prohibited by the Act from possessing a shotgun (see below), or is satisfied that the applicant does not have a good reason for possessing, purchasing or acquiring one. It has been held that a refusal to grant a certificate to the wife of a man with two previous convictions for drug offences was justified, where they both continued to associate with drug users. A sporting or competitive purpose is declared by the Act to be a good reason. A person under 18 who applies for such a certificate is capable of having a good reason for possessing it *only* if he has no intention of using it for a purpose other than an authorised purpose. An 'authorised purpose' has the same meaning as under s 5(1A) of the 1968 Act (see pp 521-522).

A shotgun certificate must specify the description of the shotguns to which it relates including, if known, the identification numbers of the guns.

Transfer of firearms etc between authorised persons

The Firearms (Amendment) Act 1997, s 32 requires that where:

(a) a s 1 firearm is sold, let on hire, lent or given; or
(b) a shotgun is sold, let on hire, given or lent for a period of more than 72 hours, by any person,

to a person who is not a firearms dealer nor exempt from holding a certificate, the following requirements must be complied with:

(a) the transferee must produce to the transferor an appropriate certificate;
(b) the transferor must comply with any instructions contained in the certificate; and
(c) the transferor must hand the firearm to the transferee personally.

It is an offence to fail to comply with these requirements. The provisions of s 32 of the 1997 Act apply to transfers of s 1 ammunition.

Each party to the transfer (as described above) of a s 1 firearm or of a shotgun who is the holder of a firearm or shotgun certificate must give notice of the transfer within seven days to the chief officer of police. It is an offence against s 33 to fail to do so. An offence under ss 32 or 33 is an arrestable offence.

De-activation, destruction or loss of firearms or shotguns

The Firearms (Amendment) Act 1997, s 34 requires that where a firearm to which a firearm certificate or shotgun certificate relates is de-activated, destroyed or lost, the certificate holder must give notice to the chief officer of police within seven days. It is an arrestable offence to fail to do so without reasonable excuse.

Grant, refusal, revocation, etc

Persons aggrieved by the refusal of a chief officer of police to grant or renew a firearm or shotgun certificate may appeal to the Crown Court. There is a corresponding right of appeal against a chief officer of police's refusal to vary a firearm certificate or the refusal to vary such a condition.

A firearm certificate may be revoked if the chief officer of police has reason to believe that:

(a)   the holder is of intemperate habits or unsound mind or is otherwise unfitted to be entrusted with a firearm; or

(b)   the holder can no longer be permitted to have the firearm or ammunition to which the certificate relates without danger to the public safety or peace;

(c)   the holder is prohibited from possessing a s 1 firearm; or

(d)   the holder no longer has a good reason for having, purchasing, or acquiring the firearm or ammunition, which the certificate authorises him to have etc;

(e)   if the holder has failed to comply with a notice requiring him to deliver up his certificate.

In addition, a chief officer may partially revoke a certificate in relation to any particular firearm or ammunition held under its authority.

A shotgun certificate may be revoked only if the holder becomes a 'prohibited person', or cannot be permitted to possess a shotgun without danger to the public safety or to the peace.

It has been held that a chief officer, in deciding whether to revoke a shotgun licence, is entitled to take into account irresponsible conduct by the licence holder which does not involve the use of a shotgun. It is a matter for the chief officer's discretion to what extent he should investigate a particular offence.

Where a certificate is revoked the holder must be notified in writing and required to surrender his certificate. It is an offence to fail to comply with such a notice within 21 days of the date of the notice.

An appeal against the revocation of a certificate lies to the Crown Court.

Persons prohibited from possessing a firearm

Certain restrictions are placed on the possession of any firearm or ammunition by a person who has been convicted of a crime and been sentenced to:

(a) custody for life, or to preventative detention, or imprisonment, or corrective training, or youth custody or detention in a young offender institution for three years or more; such a person is banned for life; or

(b) imprisonment or youth custody or detention in a young offender institution from three months to three years, or has been subject to a secure training order, such a person is banned for five years.

Suspended sentences do not count unless they are actually served at a later date. Air weapons are included in this prohibition.

Lawful possession without a certificate

Persons who hold a permit from the chief officer of police of the area in which they reside may possess a firearm (including a shotgun and ammunition) in accordance with the terms of the permit. Such permits are frequently issued where the holder of a firearm certificate dies and a relative requires some form of authority to possess the firearm pending its sale or disposal. It is unusual for such permits to be valid for more than one month. Firearms dealers (if registered—see below) and their employees may possess such a thing without a certificate.

Sections 9 to 15 and 54 of the 1968 Act are concerned with persons who may lawfully possess firearms and ammunition without holding a certificate. These exemptions are generally concerned with those who possess firearms in the course of their duties, that possession in many cases being of a transitory nature. The principal exemptions provided by ss 9 to 15 of the 1968 Act and s 15 of the Firearms (Amendment) Act 1988 are as follows:

(a) an auctioneer, carrier, warehouseman, or the employee of such a person is frequently required to handle other people's firearms and ammunition in the course of his duties. Sensibly the Act permits this but requires such persons to take reasonable precautions for safe custody and to report loss or theft forthwith to the police ;

(b) a slaughtering instrument and its ammunition may be possessed by a licensed slaughterman;

(c) a person carrying a firearm or ammunition belonging to another person who is the holder of a certificate may possess that firearm or ammunition under instructions from, and for the use of, that other person for sporting purposes only. The person carrying the firearm etc can best be described as a 'gun bearer';

(d) a starter at an athletic meeting may possess a firearm for the purpose of starting races only. The Act does not allow him to possess ammunition, so that he is restricted to blanks not exceeding one inch in diameter (which do not, of course, require a certificate);

(e) a member of an approved cadet corps may possess a firearm and ammunition when engaged as such a member in connection with drill or target shooting;

(f) subject to any exclusion of the club or restriction to specified types of rifle by the Home Secretary, a member of an approved rifle club (including a miniature rifle club) or of an approved muzzle-loading pistol club may possess a firearm and ammunition when engaged as such a member in connection with target shooting; an approval of a club may be limited to specified weapons;

(g) possession at a miniature rifle range (usually a side show at a fair) provided that no weapons are used exceeding .23 inch calibre. It should be noted that the owner of the range, unless only air weapons are used, will have a certificate listing the weapons in use. The exception is in favour of the public briefly using those weapons;

(h) a person who does not hold a shotgun certificate may borrow a shotgun from the occupier of private premises and use it on those premises, provided the occupier is present;

(i) a person may use a shotgun at a time and place approved by the chief officer of police for shooting at artificial targets. This exemption is designed to cover a person who is interested in shooting or wishes to receive instruction, but has not got a shotgun certificate. Commonly approved places at which the exemption permits him to shoot include agricultural shows and permanent shooting grounds run by firearms dealers;

(j) a person taking part in a theatrical performance, rehearsal or film may possess a firearm during the performance. This exception does not extend to ammunition, so that any ammunition used would have to be blanks not more than one inch in diameter;

(k) signalling apparatus may be possessed on board an aircraft or at an aerodrome as a part of its equipment. It may also be transferred at an aerodrome from one aeroplane to another, or from or to an aeroplane at an aerodrome to or from an appointed place of storage there;

(l) firearms and ammunition may be possessed on board a ship as a part of its equipment. However, if it is to be removed from the ship a permit to do so must be obtained from a constable. A similar permit is required if the signalling apparatus described at (k) is to be transferred from one aerodrome to another;

(m) a Northern Ireland shotgun certificate authorises possession of a shotgun in Britain; and

(n) any Crown servant or member of a police force who is in possession of a firearm or ammunition in his capacity as such does not require a certificate.

In addition, the Firearms (Amendment) Act 1988 permits a person of 17 or over, without holding a firearm certificate, to borrow a rifle from the occupier of private premises and use it on the premises in the presence of the occupier or an employee of the occupier, if the person so accompanying him holds a firearm certificate in respect of that rifle and its possession and use complies with any conditions in the certificate.

The 1988 Act also makes provision for 'visitor' permits in relation to both s 1 firearms and shotguns. A firearm permit permits a person to possess a firearm and ammunition and to acquire ammunition for it, and a shotgun permit permits a person to possess or acquire a shotgun (although there are exceptions in the case of a shotgun with a magazine). 'Group' applications may be made for not more than 20 permits. These will cover persons visiting Great Britain to take part in competitions. In addition, the Firearms Acts (Amendment) Regulations 1992 extended the Firearms Acts to permit the use of a European Firearms Pass. Persons holding such passes are entitled to acquire in another EU member State firearms to which the pass relates. Such 'passes' are issued in Great Britain by the chief officer of police to holders of an appropriate firearm certificate.

A European Firearms Pass must be produced on demand by a constable.

Lists of exceptions to any rule are always difficult to remember if one attempts to memorise them without bearing in mind some overall rule to which each exception relates. Each of these exceptions is concerned with occasions when persons will possess firearms in Britain temporarily. Most of them are concerned with a very brief moment in time. Imagine the difficulties if each person using a rifle range at a fair had to obtain a firearm certificate before shooting; if each pilot or ship's captain had to apply for a certificate before setting out on a journey; if each starter at an athletic meeting had to obtain a certificate before he started a race. This approach to the recall of these exceptions makes the task much easier.

Prohibited weapons and ammunition

We have already defined these terms. Because weapons and ammunition of this type can only properly be regarded as suitable for military use, s 5 of the Act provides that a person commits an offence if he has in his possession, or purchases or acquires, any prohibited weapon or ammunition without the written authority of the Secretary of State. The offence is one of strict liability as to the fact that the weapon or ammunition is prohibited, so that it is no defence that the possessor is reasonably unaware of the characteristic which makes the weapon or ammunition prohibited.

Museum licences

By virtue of the Firearms (Amendment) Act 1988, s 19 and Sch 1, specified museums do not need to have a firearm certificate, shotgun certificate or s 5 authority, as the case may be, in relation to exhibits displayed or stored at the museum if they have a museum firearm licence granted under those provisions. Specified museums are those registered with the Museums and Galleries Commission for the purpose of making them eligible for a museum firearm certificate.

POSSESSION BY YOUNG PERSONS

Sections 22 to 24 of the Act deal with the possession of all types of firearms by juveniles. The provisions are difficult to remember because of the differing ages which are associated with various weapons in particular circumstances. However, there are certain general rules which assist the memory.

No one under 14 years may have a *firearm* certificate in any circumstances. Those between 14 and 17 years may have a firearm certificate but they may not buy or hire the firearm which they are authorised to possess. Those over 17 years may have a firearm certificate and may buy or hire the firearm which they possess.

A person of any age may have a *shotgun* certificate but if he is less than 17 years he must have acquired the weapon by way of a gift. The detailed provisions of these sections are set out below. In the case of each type of weapon, we shall start our explanation at the age of 17 years.

Section 1 firearms and ammunition

If a person under 17 wishes to have a s 1 firearm, or ammunition for it, he cannot buy or hire it himself; if he does so he commits an offence (and so does the seller or person letting it on hire). However, provided that he is 14 years or over he may receive it, together with ammunition, by way of a gift or loan. Where an adult wishes to buy a firearm as a gift for such a youth, he must obtain a firearm certificate and so must the youth. The seller may then sell to the adult, who may then transfer the weapon to the youth, both notifying the chief officer of police of the transaction by registered post within 48 hours. Certificates granted to persons under 17 are endorsed to the effect that firearms or ammunition cannot be sold or hired to them until the specified date, which is the date of their seventeenth birthday.

The Firearms Acts (Amendment) Regulations 1992 added to s 22 a requirement that a holder of a firearm certificate who is under the age of 18 may only use that firearm for purposes authorised by the European weapons directive. Such purposes are likely to be specified in the certificate. It is an offence to use the weapon for a purpose other than those so specified. An authorised purpose is a sporting purpose, the shooting of vermin, a purpose related to estate management activities, competition shooting or target shooting.

It is an offence to give or lend a s 1 firearm or ammunition to a person under 14 years of age. It is also an offence for such a person to possess such a thing, with certain exceptions. In recalling these exceptions it is helpful to consider those persons who are permitted to possess s 1 firearms without a certificate and to identify the exceptions which might apply to persons under 14 years. The exceptions are:

(a)   when he is carrying the firearm or ammunition for another for sporting purposes, and that other person is the holder of a firearm certificate; or
(b)   when, as a member of an approved cadet corps, he is engaged in connection with target shooting or drill; or
(c)   when he is using the firearm or ammunition at a miniature rifle range or shooting gallery where the only weapons used do not exceed .23 inch calibre; or
(d)   when, as a member of an approved rifle club, he is engaged in connection with target shooting.

Shotguns

It is an offence for a person under 17 to purchase or hire any shotgun. Likewise, someone who sells or lets on hire a shotgun to such a person commits an offence. It is also an offence to make a gift of a shotgun to a person under 15. (These rules also apply to ammunition for a shotgun.) It is, of course, possible for a person of 15 or 16 lawfully to acquire a shotgun by the same process as that outlined in relation to s 1 firearms.

All young persons in possession of shotguns must have a shotgun certificate. Although the Act does not prescribe a minimum age at which a shotgun certificate may be granted, control is exercised by the chief officer of police who must consider the grant of such a certificate in the context of public safety.

Even if he has a shotgun certificate, it is an offence for a person under 15 to 'have with him' an assembled shotgun, except:

(a)   while under the supervision of a person of 21 years or more; or
(b)   while it is so securely fastened with a gun cover that it cannot be fired.

In addition, a holder of a shotgun certificate who is under 18 may not use the weapon for a purpose which is not authorised by the European weapons directive.

Air weapons

The same general rule applies. It is an offence for a person under 17 years to purchase or hire an air weapon or ammunition. The seller or person who lets on hire in such a case also commits an offence. However, as there is no need to obtain any form of certificate, a person under 17 needs only to enlist the aid of an adult to effect the purchase. There are, however, restrictions in relation to possession and they are predictable. A person under 17 commits an offence if he has with him in a public place an air weapon except when:

(a)   as a member of an approved club, he is engaged in connection with target shooting;
(b)   he is using the weapon or ammunition at a shooting gallery or miniature range where the only firearms used are either air weapons or miniature rifles not exceeding .23 inch calibre; or
(c)   the weapon is an air gun or air rifle and is so covered with a securely fastened gun cover that it cannot be fired.

The first two of these exceptions parallel those in relation to s 1 firearms and it would be surprising if this was not so. The third equates the air rifle with a shotgun, in that they must both be in a gun cover when in the hands of young persons. The provisions at (c) relate only to an air *gun* or air *rifle*; a young person who has an air pistol in his possession in a public place commits an offence, even though the pistol is 'securely covered', unless he falls within exception (a) or (b).

There are additional restrictions in relation to a person under 14. It is an offence for such a person to have with him an air weapon or ammunition *in any place* (except at a shooting gallery or in a rifle club), *unless* under the supervision of a person of 21 years or over. However, if the person under 14 fires any missile beyond the premises (including land) on which he is being supervised he commits an offence despite being supervised, and so does the supervisor if he allows him to use the weapon in this way.

It is an offence for any person to make a gift of an air weapon or ammunition to a person under 14. It is also an offence to part with the possession of an air weapon or ammunition to a person under 14 except where that person is not prohibited from having it with him under the circumstances (member of approved club etc) outlined above.

OTHER FIREARMS OFFENCES

Conversion of firearms

It is an offence to shorten the barrel of a shotgun or any smooth-bore gun to which s 1 of the 1968 Act applies (other than one which has a bore exceeding 2 inches in diameter) to a length of less than 24 inches. It is not an offence in either case for a registered firearms dealer to shorten a barrel for the sole purpose of replacing a defective part so as to produce a barrel not less than 24 inches in length. It is also an offence for anyone other than a registered firearms dealer to convert into a firearm anything which, though having the appearance of a firearm, cannot discharge a missile through its barrel.

Having a firearm in a public place

A person commits an arrestable offence contrary to s 19 of the Act if, without lawful authority or reasonable excuse (the proof whereof lies on him), he has with him in a public place a loaded shotgun or loaded air weapon, or any other firearm (whether loaded or not) together with ammunition suitable for use in that firearm.

This section is intended to deter people having with them firearms in a state of readiness for use. Where the firearm is a shotgun or air weapon, it must actually be loaded in order for the offence to be committed; on the other hand, in the case of any other firearm this is not necessary (although the accused must have with him suitable ammunition for the firearm in question). A shotgun or air weapon which has a loaded magazine is loaded, even though there is no round in the breach. An air weapon is loaded if there is a missile in it available for discharge, even though the necessary compression is not yet present.

Section 19 does not use the term 'possession' but 'having with him'. The latter term is a narrower one. As we have seen, a person can be in possession of a firearm if he has control of it, even though it is not in his physical custody and is not immediately available to him. In contrast, although a person can have a firearm with him, even though he is not carrying it, he must have a close physical link with it and it must have been readily accessible to him. A man who has a gun in his pocket clearly has it with him, and the same is true if it is in a bag which he is carrying or in the glove compartment of the car which he is driving. Provided that the firearm is readily accessible to him, a person may even have with him at the time a firearm which he has left in his car which he has parked down the street. Of course, to be guilty of the present offence he must be in a public place at the material time.

The offence is one of strict liability as to the nature of the item in question. Where a woman was arrested and threw away a handbag which was found to contain a loaded pistol which was wrapped in paper, she claimed that she knew that she had the parcel with her, but did not know that it contained a loaded pistol. The Court of Appeal supported the judge's ruling that her knowledge, or lack of knowledge, that the parcel contained a gun, was irrelevant as a matter of law. Similarly, where a man took possession of a loaded shotgun from a co-accused, who was in the course of a robbery at the time, it was held to be sufficient to prove that he knew he was in possession of the shotgun; it was not necessary to prove that he knew that it was loaded. The fact that it turned out to be loaded made him automatically guilty of the offence.

It is difficult to imagine circumstances in which a man could, with lawful authority or reasonable excuse, have with him a loaded shotgun in a public place. The possession of a shotgun certificate certainly does not authorise this. Depending on the circumstances, a gamekeeper, crossing a public highway in the course of his duties, might be considered to have a reasonable excuse for having a loaded shotgun with him. A man who is going to his rifle club with a .22 rifle in his hand and ammunition in his pocket would doubtless be able to prove a reasonable excuse for having the rifle and ammunition with him, provided that he possessed a firearm certificate. It would be otherwise if he was not going to his rifle club.

Trespassing with a firearm

An offence is committed against s 20(1) of the Act if a person, while he has any firearm or imitation firearm with him, enters or is in any building or part of a building as a trespasser and without reasonable excuse (the proof whereof lies on him). A less serious offence is committed under s 20(2) where the trespass is on land; the other ingredients of this offence are identical to those in s 20(1).

We have just said something about 'has with him'. The term 'enters' requires the bodily presence of the defendant to some degree. For the purposes of s 20(1), 'building' refers to a structure which has a roof and is of a reasonably permanent nature; the term 'part of a building' is included to cover instances in which a person may have a right to be in a building, for example a hotel, but is a trespasser in someone else's room, which would be a part of that building. For the purposes of s 20(2), the expression 'land' includes land covered with water, so that a person with a firearm trespassing in a boat on a lake is guilty of this offence.

Possessing with intent to endanger life

The offence is that contrary to s 16 of the Act of possessing a firearm or ammunition with intent by means thereof to endanger life, or to enable another person by means thereof to endanger life, whether an injury has been caused or not.

The section is intended to dissuade criminals from using firearms. If criminals set out to rob a bank and possess loaded firearms there is some evidence to suggest that they intended to endanger life. If they use the firearms to stage a hold-up that inference is reinforced because this strongly suggests that they are prepared to use the firearms against all who might oppose them.

There are two factors to prove: that the accused was in possession of a firearm; and that at the time of that possession he had an intention by means thereof to endanger life. A person who carries a loaded gun merely to give it to a colleague to use, should he be challenged, is equally guilty because he intends to enable another by means thereof to endanger life. The same would be true of an accomplice who carries ammunition for a gunman for use, if necessary, in a bank raid. However, possession with intent that another person should, by means of the firearm or ammunition, endanger life, means more than merely making those objects available to known criminals who could or might endanger life. Such possession is too remote from any subsequent act on the part of the criminal which might show an intention to endanger life. An intention to endanger the life of a person abroad is sufficient for this section; consequently, it covers possession by terrorist groups who may intend their mischief elsewhere. Possession with intent to commit suicide is not covered by this section; an intent to endanger life must relate to the life of another. The present offence is not committed by a person who intended to endanger life for a lawful purpose, as where a person whose house is besieged by an armed gang threatened them with his firearm in self-defence.

Possession with intent to cause fear of violence

It is an offence by s 16A of the Act for a person to have in his possession any firearm or imitation firearm with intent:

(a) by means thereof to cause; or
(b) to enable any other person by means thereof to cause,

any person to believe that unlawful violence will be used against him or another.

This offence was added to the 1968 Act to cover the use of firearms by bank robbers who use such weapons to terrorise bank staff and customers. See below for explanation of the term 'imitation firearm'.

Use of firearms to resist arrest

It is an offence by s 17(1) of the Act for a person to make, or attempt to make, any use whatsoever of a firearm or imitation firearm with intent to resist or prevent the lawful arrest or detention of himself or another person.

Section 17(2) creates a second offence of possessing a firearm or imitation firearm at the time of committing or being arrested for an offence specified in Sch 1 to the Act, unless that person can show that he possessed it for a lawful object. The offences in Sch 1 include theft, robbery, burglary, blackmail, taking a conveyance, assaulting a constable in the execution of his duty, assaulting a prison custody officer acting in pursuance of prison escort arrangements or performing custodial duties at a contracted-out prison, assaulting a secure training centre custody officer in the execution of his duty, rape, abduction of women and children, criminal damage, malicious wounding, assault occasioning actual bodily harm and assault with intent to resist arrest. Where the case is one of possession *at the time of arrest*, it must be proved that the accused had actually committed an offence specified in Sch 1.

For the purposes of both subsections of s 17, a 'firearm' does not include a component part or accessory.

Both parts of ss 17 and 16A refer to an imitation firearm. For the purposes of the Act, an imitation firearm is anything which has the appearance of being a firearm (other than for the discharge of noxious liquid, gas or other thing) whether or not it is capable of discharging any shot, bullet or other missile. An automatic pistol with the firing pin removed has been held to be an imitation firearm; clearly, it fell within the definition. However, some situations are more problematic. For example, some things may have the appearance of being firearms in particular circumstances on specific occasions, but not in others. A piece of roughly fashioned wood held in the hand in a darkened room may certainly have the appearance of being a firearm. It would be a matter for the jury to decide whether it actually did have that appearance in the circumstances in question. It is unlikely that a hand held in a similarly threatening fashion would be sufficient, as it is probable that the court would take the view that 'anything' in the definition above does not include the body itself.

The first offence is quite straightforward. If a firearm or imitation firearm is used in resisting lawful arrest or detention, whether of the person using the firearm, or some other person, the offence is complete. The important words are 'to make, or attempt to make use of' the firearm and the issue of whose possession the firearm was in before that moment does not arise. A man who grabbed a gun from the person arresting him and made use of it in this way would be guilty.

The second offence is concerned with possession at the time of commission of certain offences, or at the time of arrest for their commission. For example, a person who takes a motor car whilst in possession of an air pistol, or even an imitation firearm, commits this offence. Even if he had not possessed the firearm at the time of taking the conveyance, he would be equally liable if he was in possession of it at the time of his arrest.

Carrying firearms with criminal intent

Section 18 of the Act deals with the offence committed by a person who has with him a firearm or imitation firearm with intent to commit an indictable offence, or to resist arrest or prevent the arrest of another, in either case while he has the firearm or imitation firearm with him.

This is another offence which refers to 'having with him' rather than 'possessing', and we would remind the reader of the narrower meaning of the former term, which we set out above.

The intent required by this section is a particular one. It is not sufficient that the accused intended to commit an indictable offence or to resist etc the arrest. He must also intend to have a firearm or imitation firearm with him at the time of that commission or resistance. On the other hand, he does not have to intend to use or carry the gun in furtherance of the indictable offence. Section 18(2) provides that, for the purposes of the section, proof that the accused had a firearm or imitation firearm with him and intended to commit an offence, or to resist or prevent arrest, is evidence that he intended to have it with him while doing so.

General

Except for the offence contrary to s 20(2) (trespassing on land with a firearm) and s 19 (where the offence involves carrying an air weapon), all the above offences mentioned in this part are arrestable offences.

The multiplicity of offences causes difficulties for those charged with the duty of selecting charges or assessing evidence in instances of firearm possession. It is helpful to approach these problems in a particular way. In the first instance it assists to consider the weapon itself. If it is a real firearm any of the above offences may have been committed, but if possession is in a public place without a particular intention the issue of whether or not the weapon is loaded, and the nature of the weapon itself, is important. If it is an imitation firearm then it is obvious that it cannot endanger life or cause serious damage to property. Equally there can be no blame attached to innocent possession anywhere; otherwise children at play would risk arrest. Second, as a separate issue, it is helpful to consider where the possession is alleged to have been. It is obvious that if that possession is to endanger life etc, to commit indictable offences or to resist arrest, it will not matter where that possession occurs. However, if there is no particular intention apparent, the nature of the possession must be considered. If possession is in a building or on land whilst a trespasser, the possession becomes punishable without proof of any particular intention.

If a robber leaves home with a loaded shotgun, intending to use the gun to threaten those who might oppose him or attempt to arrest him, but having no intent to shoot at anyone in any circumstances, he commits an offence against s 19 as soon as he leaves his house, since he has a loaded shotgun with him in a public place without reasonable excuse. His conduct also contravenes s 18, as he intends to commit an indictable offence (robbery) and to resist arrest if necessary. He is also guilty under s 16A, as he intends to cause fear of violence. At this stage, he cannot be guilty of offences against ss 16 and 17 as he does not intend to endanger life etc, has not made use, or attempted to make use, of the firearm for the prohibited purposes, has not committed a Sch 1 offence whilst in possession of the firearm, and has not been arrested while in possession.

POLICE POWERS

Stop, search and arrest in certain cases

Section 47 of the Act authorises a constable to require any person whom he has reasonable cause to suspect:

(a) of having a firearm, with or without ammunition, with him in a public place; or
(b) to be committing or about to commit, elsewhere than in a public place, an offence of 'having with him' a firearm or imitation firearm with intent to commit an indictable offence or to resist arrest (contrary to s 18, above) or an offence of trespassing with a firearm (contrary to s 20, above),

to hand over the firearm or ammunition for examination. It is an offence for a person so required to fail to do so.

Section 47 also provides that a constable who has reasonable cause to suspect the existence of one of the above circumstances (ie (a) or (b)) may search that person and may detain him for the purpose of doing so. This power extends to the search of vehicles and the constable may require a driver to stop for that purpose. A constable may enter any place to exercise his powers under this section.

Production of certificates

Section 48 of the Act states that a constable may demand, from any person whom he believes to be in possession of a firearm or ammunition to which s 1 applies, or of any shotgun, the production of his firearm certificate or his shotgun certificate. If such a person fails to produce the certificate or to permit the constable to read it, or to show that he is exempt from the requirement to have a certificate, the constable may seize and detain the firearm, ammunition or shotgun and may require the person immediately to declare his name and address. It is an offence to refuse to give a true name and address.

The Firearms Acts (Amendment) Regulations 1992 added s 48(1A). Where a constable has made a demand under s 48 and the person to whom it is made fails:

(a) to produce a firearm certificate or (as the case may be) a shotgun certificate; or
(b) to show that he is a person who is not entitled to be issued with a document identifying that firearm under any provisions which in the other member States of the EU correspond to the provisions for the issue of European Firearms Passes; or
(c) to show that he is in possession of the firearm only in his capacity as a recognised firearms collector of another member State,

the constable can demand from that person the production of the certificate issued to that person in another member State relating to the firearm in question. It is an offence for such a person to fail to comply with such a demand. The powers of seizure etc under s 48 then apply.

Search warrant

By s 46 of the Act, a justice, who is satisfied by information on oath that there is reasonable ground for suspecting that:

(a) an offence relevant for the purposes of the section has been, is being, or is about to be committed; or
(b) in connection with a firearm or ammunition, there is a danger to the public safety or to the peace,

may grant a search warrant. The warrant will authorise a constable or civilian officer:

(a) to enter at any time any premises or place specified, if necessary by force, and to search them or any person found there;
(b) to seize and detain anything which he may find on the premises or place, or on any such person, in respect of which or in connection with which he has reasonable ground for suspecting that:
    (i)   a relevant offence has been, is being or is about to be, committed; or
    (ii) in connection with a firearm, imitation firearm or ammunition there is a danger to the public safety or to the peace.

In relation to the power of seizure and detention, this includes power to require information which is kept by means of a computer and is accessible from the premises or place to be produced in a form which is visible and legible and can be taken away.

A 'relevant offence' is any offence under the 1968 Act except that under s 22(3) (person under 15 having assembled shotgun otherwise than under supervision) or an offence related specifically to air weapons.

It is an offence to intentionally obstruct a constable or civilian officer in the exercise of these powers.

Entry into rifle clubs

A constable duly authorised in writing by a chief officer of police, on producing (if required) his authority, may enter any premises occupied or used by an approved rifle club, miniature rifle club, or pistol club and inspect those premises and anything on them, for the purpose of ascertaining whether the requirements relating to its use and any limitations in the approval are being complied with.

FIREARMS OFFENCES UNDER OTHER ACTS

Drunk in charge

It is an offence contrary to the Licensing Act 1872, s 12 to be drunk when in charge of any loaded firearm (including a loaded air rifle).

Discharge near the highway

Section 161 of the Highways Act 1980 provides that a person is guilty of an offence if, without lawful authority or excuse, he discharges any firearm within 50 feet from the centre of any highway which consists of or comprises a carriageway, *and in consequence thereof* a user of the highway is injured, interrupted or endangered. It is important to remember that the discharge is not prohibited in itself. It must also be proved that there was an injury to someone, or that someone's passage was interrupted or interfered with (for example, by being forced to make a detour) or that someone was endangered, ie put in danger of injury. 'Highway' for the purposes of this section is restricted to a public right of way for the passage of vehicles, consequently it does not include footpaths, cycle tracks, bridleways or cattle tracks.

The offence is not committed if the person discharging the firearm has a lawful authority or excuse for doing so, as where the discharge occurred during a clay pigeon shoot which involved shooting down the field and away from the highway.

Wanton discharge in a street

By the Town Police Clauses Act 1847, s 28, it is an offence wantonly to discharge a firearm in any street to the obstruction, annoyance or danger of residents or passengers.

BUSINESS TRANSACTIONS

A 'firearms dealer' is defined by s 57 of the Firearms Act 1968 as a person who, by way of trade or business, manufactures, sells, transfers, repairs, tests or proves firearms or ammunition to which s 1 of the Act applies or shotguns. It is an offence for a person to do any of these things without being registered under the Act as a firearms dealer. By way of exception, it is not an offence for an auctioneer to sell by auction a firearm or ammunition without being registered as a firearms dealer, provided he holds a police permit for that purpose.

The chief officer of police must keep a register of firearms dealers. An applicant must provide details of every place of business (including storage places) in the area, at which he proposes to carry on business as a firearms dealer, and details of the precise nature of the business which he intends to conduct. A registered firearms dealer or his employee is permitted to keep, purchase or acquire firearms and ammunition in the ordinary course of his business without holding firearms certificates in respect of them, and this is so even though the place where the firearm or ammunition is possessed, purchased or acquired by the dealer or employee is not the dealer's place of business or has not been registered as his place of business.

Except on certain specified grounds, the chief officer of police must enter the applicant's name and place(s) of business in the register and grant him a certificate of registration. The chief officer of police may, however, impose conditions upon registration. These conditions are generally concerned with ensuring the safekeeping of firearms. They usually include the following conditions, that:

(a)   the dealer shall, on being given reasonable notice, allow a police officer authorised in writing by the chief officer to enter and inspect his premises;
(b)   hand-guns must be kept in a locked safe;
(c)   other weapons must be chained together by the trigger guards and locked in a rack;
(d)   ammunition is to be stored separately and locked up;
(e)   rifle bolts must be removed and kept separately;
(f)   the windows of cabinets for storage must be illuminated at night; and
(g)   glass door panels and windows must be barred.

In addition, conditions are usually imposed concerning notification of dealings in various types of weapons.

The Act does not permit registration for particular purposes. A person is either a firearms dealer or he is not; there is no right to restrict dealings to shotguns. There is, of course, no need to be registered to deal in air weapons. All certificates of registration are renewable every three years. A new place of business must be notified to the chief officer and must be registered by him, unless the use of those premises for firearms dealing would endanger the public safety or the peace. A registered dealer may be removed from the register if he ceases to deal in firearms, or to have a business place within the area, or if he cannot be permitted to continue in business without danger to the public safety or the peace. Failure to comply with conditions also provides reason for removal from the register. Particular premises may be removed from the register on safety grounds.

Dealer to keep records

A dealer must keep a register of transactions. He must immediately enter in his register the particulars of persons to whom firearms and ammunition are sold or transferred. In the case of a sale or transfer of a firearm to which s 1 of the Act applies (but not of ammunition) he must generally send a notification of this, by registered post or recorded delivery, to the chief officer of police with whom he is registered within 48 hours. Dealers may only sell and transfer such things to a person who holds the necessary certificate, or to a person who is legally entitled to purchase or acquire the firearm or ammunition without a certificate.

Registered dealers must allow police officers, authorised in writing by the chief officer of police, to enter and inspect all stock in hand and must produce their registers for inspection. It is an offence to fail to do so, or knowingly or recklessly to make any false entry in a register. A police officer who is authorised in writing by his chief officer of police to carry out these duties must produce that written authority if required to do so.

CROSSBOWS

Crossbows are not firearms. The Crossbows Act 1987 creates specific offences in respect of crossbows with a draw weight of at least 1.4 kg.

It is an offence for any person to sell or let on hire a crossbow or part of a crossbow to a person under the age of 17. No offence is committed if the seller or hirer believes the person so acquiring to be 17 years of age or older, provided he has reasonable ground for that belief. Similarly it is an offence for a person under 17:

(a) to purchase or hire such a crossbow or part of a crossbow; or
(b) for him to have with him a crossbow capable of discharging a missile, or parts which together (and without any other parts) can be assembled to form a complete crossbow,

unless in either case he is under the supervision of a person who is 21 years of age or older.

Where a constable suspects with reasonable cause that a person is committing or has committed an offence of having with him a crossbow or parts, he may:

(a) search that person for a crossbow or part of a crossbow; or
(b) search any vehicle, or anything in or on a vehicle, in or on which the constable reasonably suspects there is a crossbow or part of a crossbow connected with the offence.

A person or vehicle may be detained by the constable for the purpose of such searches and evidence may be seized. The constable may enter any land other than a dwelling house to exercise these powers.

CHAPTER 25

Explosives

The law controlling explosive substances is concerned with various aspects of their use. From day to day we are concerned with fireworks and their use in public places. The manufacture and general control of explosives needs to be regulated, their storage needs to be made safe, and the unlawful use of such substances must be punished.

FIREWORKS: EXPLOSIVES ACT 1875

For practical purposes, the significance of the 1875 Act is contained in its provisions relating to the storage and use of fireworks. Shopkeepers who wish to store fireworks must be registered with the local authority. Once premises are registered they are subject to inspection by inspectors appointed under the Health and Safety at Work etc Act 1974. Generally, small shops and businesses can store up to 500 lb of small fireworks which are not likely to explode violently. Up to 100 lb can be kept in the part of the premises to which the public have access and the remaining 400 lb must be kept elsewhere in closed metal containers, each container having no more than 100 lb of fireworks inside it. The 100 lb kept in the public part of the shop must be secure, for example in a glass showcase. The idea is that no one should be able to throw a lighted match into a box of fireworks in the shop.

The Fireworks (Safety) Regulations 1997 prohibit the supply of fireworks of erratic flight and mini-rockets, aerial shells, shells-in-mortar, aerial maroons and maroons-in-mortar. These Regulations also prohibit the supply of bangers, including banger/combination fireworks but not wheels with bangers, and prohibit persons under 18 from purchasing fireworks other than caps, crackers, snaps, novelty matches, party poppers, serpents and throw-downs. There are exceptions in relation to supply to 'professional' organisations providing firework displays.

Retailers must not sell fireworks removed from a primary pack or selection pack.

It is an offence to hawk, sell or expose for sale any gunpowder (including fireworks) in any street or public place and this prevents the sale of fireworks in markets. The sale of fireworks to a child apparently under the age of 16 years is an offence under the 1875 Act.

Throwing fireworks

It is an offence to throw, cast or fire any fireworks in or onto any highway, street, thoroughfare or public place. This offence, provided by the Explosives Act 1875, s 80, is extremely useful. Although there are other offences in relation to the use of fireworks in streets and public places, for example under the Highways Act 1980 and the Town Police Clauses Act 1847, this offence is the most easily proved. Cases covered by it include throwing in a street a firework which fails to explode, or the firing of a firework in any street or public place. There are no exceptions to the offence; even the celebration of 'Guy Fawkes' must be restricted to the use of fireworks otherwise than in streets or public places.

EXPLOSIVE SUBSTANCES ACT 1883

The Explosive Substances Act 1883 deals with many offences which can be committed in relation to 'explosive substances'. It is therefore necessary to establish the meaning of that term.

Explosive substance

The term is defined by the 1883 Act. This Act declares that an explosive substance is deemed to include:

(a) any material for making any explosive substance;
(b) any apparatus, machine, implement, or materials used, or intended to be used, or adapted for causing, or aiding in causing, any explosion in or with any explosive substance;
(c) any part of any such apparatus, machine or implement.

It is interesting to consider the width of this definition when we consider the acts of persons who generally become involved in bomb making. The definition begins by including any material for making any explosive substance and thus covers each of the ingredients which would go into making an explosive. However, the explosive itself is only a part of the tools of bomb making. It has to be encased in something, there must be some sort of triggering device and all such items are embraced within the various descriptions of apparatus. The definition is therefore wide enough to cover all the pieces and the ingredients of bomb making.

The Court of Appeal has assisted by removing any doubts which might otherwise have existed about the adjective 'explosive' in its relationship to the word 'substance'. It has ruled that the word will have the meaning applied by the Explosives Act 1875, s 3, which includes gunpowder, nitro-glycerine, dynamite, gun-cotton, blasting powder, fulminate of mercury or of other metals, coloured fires and every other substance, whether similar to those already mentioned or not, used or manufactured with a view to producing a practical effect by explosion or a pyrotechnic effect, including a petrol bomb. It also ruled that 'explosive substance' includes fog signals, fireworks, fuses, rockets, percussion caps, detonators, cartridges, ammunition of all descriptions, and every adaptation or preparation of an explosive as previously defined. The decision has the effect of widening the nature of the substance described by the 1883 Act to include anything which can cause an explosion, or which will burn rapidly.

The Explosive Substances Act 1883 deals with the likely activities of a bomber quite extensively but police officers should always remember, when considering charges which can be preferred in relation to the activities of terrorist bombers, that the Offences Against the Person Act 1861 and the Criminal Damage Act 1971 also deal with similar offences to those set out in the 1883 Act. (These offences are described in ch 28 and ch 37, below.)

Causing an explosion likely to endanger life

Section 2 of the 1883 Act makes it an offence for any person unlawfully and maliciously to cause by an explosive substance any explosion of a nature likely to endanger life, or to cause serious injury to property, whether such injury or damage is caused or not. This offence is also punishable in United Kingdom courts if such an act is carried out by a British citizen in the Republic of Ireland or if committed in relation to hijacking offences in aircraft. An offence under s 2 is an arrestable offence.

Therefore, if someone, without lawful justification or excuse, intending to cause harm, causes an explosion of such a nature that its probable result will be to endanger life or cause serious damage to property, the fact that the explosion has occurred is all that is necessary for the offence to have been completed. If a man explodes a bomb in a crowded cinema it is probable that life will be endangered. It is equally likely that there will be serious damage to property. The fact that the bomb does not kill, or cause such serious damage as might have been expected, is unimportant. The important point to remember in relation to this offence is that the explosion has occurred.

Attempt to cause explosion; making or keeping explosives with intent

Section 3 of the 1883 Act creates two types of offence. Both offences, which are arrestable, apply even where the relevant conduct occurs outside the United Kingdom or a dependency, provided in such a case that the accused is a British citizen. The first offence is being concerned with acts done with the specified intent to cause an explosion, and the second with making or possessing an explosive substance with the specified intent. The offences relate to consequences intended to result in the United Kingdom or the Republic of Ireland.

In examining circumstances which might lead to the identification of offences contrary to this section we should think in terms of those who have not yet caused an explosion but are doing some act with that intention in mind. The section extends, by its terminology, the normal concept of an 'attempt' by making punishable acts which would normally be considered to be preparatory acts. The offences are unlawfully and maliciously:

(a) to do any act with intent to cause by an explosive substance an explosion of a nature likely to endanger life or cause serious injury to property, or to conspire so to cause; or

(b) to make or have in one's possession or under one's control an explosive substance with intent by means thereof to endanger life or cause serious injury to property, or to enable any other person to do so.

If we consider the legal position of our offender who caused the explosion in the cinema in our earlier example, before he caused the explosion, the situation is as follows. Whilst preparing the bomb upon his premises he is making an explosive substance with the necessary intent. From the moment he has completed the making of the bomb, he is in possession of it with intent to cause the explosion in the cinema. When he begins to plant the bomb in the cinema he certainly does an act with the necessary criminal intent. It is unnecessary for any explosion to take place. If it did, an offence under s 2 would be committed. Unless the prosecution is in a position to prove that some positive act was done, it is probably better to charge possession.

Making or possessing an explosive under suspicious circumstances

It will be appreciated that there will often be practical difficulties associated with proving that explosive substances were made or possessed for the purpose of causing explosions likely to endanger life etc. On occasions, the circumstances of the finding, any admissions, and the nature of the explosive device itself may tend to support a charge under s 3, but on other occasions there may be difficulties in proving a particular intention.

Section 4, as interpreted by the Court of Appeal, provides that any person who knowingly makes or knowingly has in his possession or under his control any explosive substance, under such circumstances as to give rise to a reasonable suspicion that he is not making it or does not have it in his possession or under his control for a lawful object (whether an object to take place in the UK or abroad), commits an arrestable offence. If the accused claims that he made, possessed or controlled it for a lawful object, he must prove that this was so, in which case the offence is not committed.

The serious view which is taken of explosive offences is evident from the heavy term of imprisonment which may follow conviction for making, possessing or controlling explosive substances even when no specific intention to use them can be proved. The discovery of a 'bomb factory' today would at the very least lead to charges under s 4 for all persons concerned.

The offence under s 4 covers many modes of involvement. If several persons are concerned in the making, they are equally guilty of the offence; so are those who 'control' the explosive substances as well as those who actually possess them. Each person in a group, if such group has a common design, is responsible for the conduct of a member of that group within the common design: if that amounts to 'possession', all will be guilty.

Prosecutions

A prosecution for an offence under the 1883 Act may not be instituted without the consent of the Attorney-General.

POLICE POWERS AND DUTIES

By the Explosives Act 1875, s 73, a constable may enter at any time, by force if necessary, any place (including a building, vehicle or vessel) upon reasonable cause for believing that any offence has been or is being committed in that place with respect to an explosive if he is in possession of:

(a) a justices' warrant granted following information on oath; or
(b) a written order from a superintendent or other officer of police of equal or superior rank, which may be issued if the case is one of emergency and delay in obtaining a warrant would be likely to endanger life,

and to search for explosives, and take samples of any explosives and ingredients of an explosive. It is suggested that if information is received that explosives are stored upon any premises in a locality in which people normally reside, the case will be one in which delay would be likely to endanger life.

There are certain duties which must be carried out by the police when thefts of explosives are reported. The Hazardous Substances Division of the Health and Safety Executive should be informed of the exact nature and quantity of explosives stolen, the circumstances of the theft, whether the explosives have been stolen from a store or conveyance, and the use to which the explosives are normally put. The Division also require the identity of the caller and details of place, time and date of the theft, together with details of any explosives left behind by the thieves. Where explosives are found, similar notification should be given to the Division.

HM Explosives Inspectorate require details of all cases of illegal manufacture of explosives, even in the case of trivial experimentation by children. The usual details of the person, time, date etc, of offence are required together with details of police action, court action and details of any forensic report on the substance. HM Inspectorate also like to know where the persons concerned obtained their knowledge of the manufacture of explosives.

BOMB THREATS AND BOMB HOAXES

The offences which generally attract the description of bomb hoaxes are those dealt with by the Criminal Law Act 1977, s 51. They are all arrestable offences.

Placing or despatching an article

Section 51(1) creates two offences. The first is committed by any person who places an article in any place whatsoever with the intention of inducing some other person to believe that it is likely to explode or ignite and thereby cause personal injury or damage to property. The subsection declares that the term 'article' includes any substance. The offence would be committed by the man who produced a parcel in a tube train, or in an arena or elsewhere, to which wires were attached together with something which resembled a timing device. If he then, in view of other passengers, pushed the parcel under the seat or elsewhere and left the train, arena etc, he would quite clearly intend to induce others to believe that it was an explosive device. Even though the article was completely harmless, he would commit this offence as the mischief legislated against is the intention to cause panic.

The second offence is to despatch any article by post, rail or any other means whatever of sending things from one place to another with the intention to induce in some other person a belief that it is likely to explode or ignite and thereby cause personal injury or damage to property. The offence therefore embraces any form of despatch, provided the article in question is intended to have the specified effect upon people. A man may send through a post office sorting office a number of such false devices with the intention of causing fear of an explosion to be aroused in the staff of that office. Although the article is incapable of exploding or igniting, the offence is complete.

It is not necessary for either offence for the accused to have any particular person in mind as the person in whom he intends to induce the relevant belief.

The terms in which the offences are described in sub-s (1) are wide enough to include the placing or despatch of real bombs as the term used is 'any article'. This is merely of academic interest because if an actual device was used the charge preferred would be more serious. The point is, however, worthy of mention in legal examinations.

Where a bomb threat involves use of the postal services, an offence may also be committed under the Post Office Act 1953, s 11, which provides an offence which is concerned with sending, or attempting to send, or procuring to be sent, a postal packet which encloses any explosive, dangerous, noxious or deleterious substance, any filth, any sharp instrument which is not properly protected, any noxious living creature, or any creature, article or thing whatsoever which is likely to injure either other postal packets or a post office employee.

The Post Office Act 1953, s 60 also provides an offence of placing, or attempting to place, in or against a post office letter box, any fire, match, light, explosive or dangerous substance or filth etc and that of committing a nuisance in or against the box, or to attempt to do anything likely to injure the box.

While these non-arrestable offences would be committed by any person who dispatched an explosive substance by post, more serious offences should be preferred.

False messages

Section 51(2) of the Criminal Law Act 1997 is concerned with false messages to the effect that an explosive device has been planted. It states that it is an offence for a person to communicate any information, which he knows or believes to be false, to another person, with the intention of inducing in him or any other person a false belief that a bomb or other thing liable to explode or ignite is present at any place or location whatever. The use of the words 'there is a bomb' by a hoaxer is sufficient to give rise to the offence. It is not a necessary ingredient that the person communicating the false information should identify a location.

This offence is aimed partly at the hoax telephone caller. It must be proved that the accused knew or believed that the information which he passed was false, and the circumstances will normally make this issue quite clear. However, it would be different if a man asked a boy to ring the manager of a cinema to warn him of the presence of a bomb on the premises and the boy, believing the story to be true, made the call. The boy would commit no offence as he did not believe that the story was false. On the other hand, the man would commit the offence because he knowingly communicated false information to the boy, with the intention of inducing him to believe that a bomb was liable to explode at the cinema.

When police officers receive such a call, it is essential to gain as much information as possible from the caller, or from the person who is passing on a message received from such a caller. The details should include sex, estimated age, urgency in voice, emotion and accent, together with details of the time, date, duration of call, whether from a private telephone or a call box, and any background voices. All information given by the caller must be established; where, when and why the bomb is likely to explode, description of the type of bomb and its appearance and as many of the actual words used as can be recalled.

Although the offence is most commonly committed by means of a telephone call, it can equally be committed by word of mouth, a letter, or a form of general advertisement. It is not necessary that the accused had any particular person in mind in whom he intends to induce the relevant belief.

CONVEYANCE OF HAZARDOUS SUBSTANCES

Dangerous goods in general

The Carriage of Dangerous Goods by Road Regulations 1996 are concerned with the conveyance by road of various substances which in the event of an accident, or a leak in a storage tank, would be dangerous to the public and to police or rescue personnel who might become involved in the incident. They require the approval and publication by the Health and Safety Commission of documents entitled 'Approved Carriage List', 'Approved Tank Requirements' and 'Approved Vehicle Requirements' and place duties on the operator of, and other specified persons concerned with, any tank or vehicle used for the carriage of dangerous goods.

No operator of a container, tank or vehicle may cause or permit to be carried thereon any dangerous goods unless he has obtained the consignor's declaration in relation to those goods and has taken all reasonable steps to ensure that the goods are in a fit condition for carriage. No passenger (other than a crew member) may be carried on such a vehicle.

The operator of any container, tank or vehicle used for the carriage of dangerous goods must ensure that information, as specified in the Regulations, is displayed on the container, tank or vehicle in accordance with the regulation.

The driver of any vehicle which is being used for the carriage of dangerous goods must ensure that the Transport Documentation (consignor's information, details of the total mass or volume of dangerous goods to be carried, the emergency action code where appropriate, the prescribed temperature where appropriate and the emergency information) is kept readily available on the vehicle at all times while dangerous goods are being carried. He must produce the Transport Documentation to a police constable or a goods vehicle examiner on request.

Where a trailer which is being used for the carriage of dangerous goods becomes detached from the motor vehicle the driver must give the Transport Documentation to the occupier of the premises on which the trailer is parked. The occupier must ensure that the documentation is kept readily available at those premises, or the driver of the vehicle must attach the Transport Documentation to the trailer in a readily visible position.

Where a vehicle is no longer being used for the carriage of dangerous goods, the driver must ensure that any documentation relating solely to dangerous goods which have been carried is either removed from the vehicle or placed in a securely closed container clearly marked to show that it does not relate to any dangerous goods which are being carried.

The operator of a vehicle which is used for the transportation of dangerous goods must keep a record of the information contained in the Transport Documentation for a period of at least three months.

Explosives

The Carriage of Explosives by Road Regulations 1996 lay down additional provisions in relation to the carriage of explosives. They prohibit the carriage of certain explosives in a vehicle, or the carriage of explosives of any kind in a vehicle being used to carry passengers for hire or reward, otherwise than within specified conditions. The Regulations also deal with the suitability of vehicles and freight containers, and with the quantities of explosives which may be carried.

When explosives are carried, vehicles must carry at the front and rear reflectorised orange plates with a black border. Such vehicles must also carry plates on each side of the vehicle, trailer, semi-trailer or freight container, in which the explosives are actually carried, a diamond-shaped plate, orange in colour with a black border bearing certain black letters according to the type of explosives carried. The letters may be 1.2E (with a symbol of an explosion above); or 1.4 with the letter 'E' below. Occasionally, where the explosives carried have not been classified, the diamond-shaped plate will merely carry the symbol of an explosion.

Driver training—vehicles carrying dangerous goods

The operators of vehicles used for the carriage of dangerous goods are required by the Carriage of Dangerous Goods by Road (Driver Training) Regulations 1996 to ensure that the drivers of such vehicles are properly trained. Drivers must hold 'vocational training certificates' which must be carried in the vehicle and produced to a police constable or goods vehicle examiner on request. A driver may only be issued with a vocational training certificate where he has successfully completed training in the carriage of the dangerous goods concerned and he has passed an examination approved by the Secretary of State.

CHAPTER 26

Railways

There are a number of offences which are specifically concerned with railways. Some of them are provided by two Acts of Parliament, the Offences against the Person Act 1861 and the Malicious Damage Act 1861, which were not generally limited to 'railway matters', while others are provided by 'railway legislation'. The enforcement of much of this legislation frequently falls to police officers other than those of the British Transport Police because they happen to be the first to arrive on the scene.

Basically, the two Acts of Parliament named above are concerned with the throwing of articles at railway trains and interference with the railway system itself. In resolving problems concerned with which offences are committed in particular circumstances, it is helpful to remember that the provisions of the Malicious Damage Act are concerned with damage to property while the Offences against the Person Act deals with injuries to persons. Of course, in many circumstances where obstructions are placed on a railway line there may be evidence of offences contrary to both Acts of Parliament.

ENDANGERING THE SAFETY OF PASSENGERS

Interfering with the railway system with intent

The Offences against the Person Act 1861, s 32 is concerned with persons who unlawfully and maliciously carry out certain acts with intent to endanger the safety of any person travelling or being on a railway. Basically, these acts involve *interference* with the railway system itself. The placing of obstructions on a railway, the displacing of parts of it, the moving of points and similar fittings, the showing of a false signal, the concealment of a real one, or the doing or causing to be done of anything else, are all offences contrary to s 32 provided (in each case) that there is an intent to endanger the safety of any person travelling or being upon such railway.

Throwing things with intent

Section 33 of the Offences against the Person Act 1861 deals with the *throwing* of missiles. It provides that it is an offence for any person unlawfully and maliciously to throw, or cause to fall or strike, any wood, stone or other matter or thing, at, against, into or upon any engine, tender, carriage or truck used upon any railway with intent to injure or endanger the safety of any person on the train. In considering the appropriate charge it must be remembered that s 33, as well as s 32, requires the accused's acts to be unlawful and malicious and in particular to be carried out with the specified intent (which, in the case of s 33, is an intent to injure or endanger the safety of any person on the train). Neither section requires the specified intent to be directed at a particular person. Consequently, if a man throws a brick at a train intending to injure or endanger people in general who are on it, he commits an offence under s 33.

General

In the light of the intent to endanger required for s 32 and of the intent to injure or endanger required for s 33, it is clear that both offences are of a serious nature. They are both arrestable offences.

Endangering passengers

There are, of course, occasions where it may not be possible to prove that the act was carried out with an intention to injure anyone or to endanger anyone's safety. Although mischievous and completely irresponsible, many of the acts which are reported to the police are carried out in circumstances which do not give rise to any clear inference of such an intention. To cover such eventualities, s 34 of the Offences against the Person Act 1861 creates a lesser offence which can be committed by any person who, by any unlawful act, or by any wilful omission or neglect, endangers or causes to be endangered the safety of any person conveyed or being in or upon a railway, or who aids or assists therein. This is not an arrestable offence.

The general nature of s 34 requires examination. If young persons throw stones at railway trains but cannot be shown to have done so with the intention to injure or endanger, as specified in s 33, they may nevertheless be convicted of an offence under s 34 since, by their unlawful acts, they have endangered the safety of railway passengers. The same would be so where someone who placed an obstruction on a railway line cannot be proved to have had the intent to endanger a person on the train, which is required by s 32, provided that the obstruction is of such a nature as (in the view of experts) to endanger passengers. In respect of such conduct, and any other conduct covered by s 34, it is irrelevant whether or not the accused ever considered the consequences of his conduct. Section 34 also punishes wilful omissions or neglect. These offences are likely to be committed by railwaymen. A driver who neglected to keep a lookout for signals would certainly be guilty of this offence.

The selection of appropriate charges in instances of dangerous conduct relating to railways is often difficult. Selection may be aided by reference to the consequences of the act but in some cases the crucial point will not be the actual consequences of an act but the potential danger attached to it. For example, where a man cut three spans of copper wire linking together signal boxes, thereby disrupting the signalling system, it was held that he was properly convicted of an offence under s 32 even though the operation of a hand signalling device by an alert signalman averted danger.

It has been held that an acquittal for an offence against s 32 is not a bar to a subsequent indictment for an offence contrary to s 34.

OBSTRUCTION ETC OF ENGINES AND THE LIKE

In considering the offences committed in circumstances involving obstruction etc by objects being unlawfully placed upon a railway line it is helpful to consider from the outset the parallel offences under the Offences against the Person Act and the Malicious Damage Act. While there is, understandably, no parallel offence to that of throwing missiles with intent, the Malicious Damage Act almost repeats the substance of the other two offences already discussed.

Interfering with the railway system with intent

The Malicious Damage Act 1861, s 35 is almost identical to the Offences against the Person Act 1861, s 32. The only difference is in relation to intent. The intention required by the Malicious Damage Act must be to obstruct, upset, overthrow, injure or destroy an engine, tender, carriage or truck using such railway. It is also an arrestable offence.

Obstruction

The Malicious Damage Act 1861, s 36 parallels the offence previously described in the Offences against the Person Act 1861, s 34. This is not an arrestable offence. There must have been an unlawful act, or a wilful omission or neglect, which led to the obstruction of an engine or carriage using a railway (as opposed to endangering the safety of passengers as required by the Offences against the Person Act). If, therefore, persons unlawfully obstruct a line, they commit an offence of the same gravity, whether they do so in such a way that the safety of passengers is threatened, or merely in such a way that an engine etc was obstructed. A person who causes a train to stop or to slacken speed by altering signals or by making unauthorised signals with the arms is guilty of obstructing a train contrary to the Malicious Damage Act 1861, s 36. The offence is also committed by those who cause an obstruction to take place, or who aid or assist this.

An acquittal for the major offence under s 35 is no bar to a prosecution under s 36.

RAILWAY TRESPASS

The question of trespass upon a railway needs to be carefully considered as there are many occasions upon which persons, particularly intending users, are permitted to be upon railway property. A trespasser is one who goes upon the land of another without a right by law to do so or any express or implied permission of the occupier (or his authorised agent). Consequently, any unauthorised entry upon the land of another is a trespass. There may also be occasions where the original entry onto the premises was authorised, but for a particular purpose; a person who uses the property outside the terms upon which entry was permitted becomes a trespasser. For example, a person who is permitted to enter a railway station to meet a passenger is not thereby permitted to trespass upon the railway lines. A person who is validly requested to leave a railway station becomes a trespasser after the expiry of a reasonable time for him to leave has elapsed from the withdrawal of his permission to remain.

Trespass offence

Trespass on railways is an offence under the British Transport Commission Act 1949, s 55. This offence is committed when any person trespasses upon any of the lines of railway or sidings, or in any tunnel, or upon any railway embankment, cutting or similar work belonging, leased to or worked by Railtrack, *or* trespasses upon *any other lands* of Railtrack in dangerous proximity to any such lines of railway or other works or to any electrical apparatus used for, or in connection with, the working of the railway. However, a person must not be convicted of this offence unless it is proved to the satisfaction of the court that public warning has been given to persons not to trespass upon the railway by a notice clearly exhibited at the station on the railway nearest to the place where the offence is alleged to have been committed. The notice must be renewed as often as it is obliterated or destroyed; if it is not, a person cannot be convicted of the offence. The significance of such a notice at railway stations is difficult to assess as the station is likely to be miles distant from the scene of trespass.

It should be noted that the offence only applies to trespassing on the track, land etc of Railtrack; it does not apply where the trespass is on the track, land etc of one of the various companies running restored steam trains. It is useful to police officers to be aware of the provisions of the 1949 Act, but it is preferable to leave enforcement to the British Transport Police and to officers of Railtrack. However, in the interests of the safety of such trespassers it may be necessary for any police officer to take action in such cases. A refusal by a trespasser to leave railway property on such an occasion will amount to an obstruction of a police officer in the execution of his duty, viz the enforcement of the law and the removal of criminal trespassers, within the meaning of the Police Act 1996, s 89(2).

Offences of refusal to quit

The Railway Regulation Act 1840, s 16 states that it is an offence for any person wilfully to trespass upon the railway or any station or premises connected therewith and to refuse to quit upon request by any officer or agent of Railtrack. This offence of trespass is not restricted to the operational areas of a railway system nor to the property of Railtrack, as is the case under the 1949 Act. It can occur anywhere on railway property but the offence is not complete until there is a refusal to quit at the request of any officer or agent of Railtrack. Police officers, other than officers of the British Transport Police, are not 'officers of the company'. There is no need to prove that notices are displayed in such a case.

TICKET OFFENCES

Generally, all offences related to tickets will be dealt with by a railway employee or by British Transport Police officers, but there may be occasions upon which a police officer from a local force may be called to a dispute centred upon whether or not a person has committed a ticket offence. It is therefore helpful to have some understanding of the legal position of those who may be involved in such a dispute.

Travelling without a ticket

In the first instance, the Regulation of Railways Act 1889, s 5(1) provides that every passenger on a railway, on request by an officer or agent or servant of the railway company, must *either* produce, and if requested deliver up, a ticket showing that his fare is paid, *or* pay his fare from the place where his journey started, *or* give his name and address. In default of doing so, the passenger commits an offence. Put in everyday language, a railway passenger must at the request of a railway employee or British Transport Police officer, show, and if required surrender, his ticket. If he does not for any reason, he must pay the fare for his journey; if he is unable to do this he must give his true name and address so that the fare may be recovered from him by civil process, if necessary.

Travelling with intent to avoid paying fare

On occasions a constable may be called to a dispute centred upon an allegation that some person is travelling, or attempting to travel, without having previously paid his fare and with intent to avoid payment. One of two offences may be involved here. Both are provided by the Regulation of Railways Act 1889, s 5(3).

Section 5(3) of the 1889 Act provides, first, that if any person travels, or attempts to travel, on a railway without having previously paid his fare, and with intent to avoid payment thereof, he commits an offence. The intention to avoid payment may be proved by showing that the passenger has ignored opportunities to pay his fare or has taken measures to avoid a ticket inspector. A person who leaves a train without paying his fare when there has been an opportunity to do so, indicates such an intention. In addition, a person who travels on a ticket issued to another person, which is not transferable, clearly indicates an intention to avoid payment. It is not essential to prove knowledge on the part of the accused that the ticket was not transferable. A person, therefore, who produces a concessionary ticket issued to a young person or a senior citizen to which he is not entitled, clearly shows an intention to avoid payment of his true fare. In this respect the term 'fare' means the correct fare for the particular journey and the class of carriage by which the person travels. A person who travels in a first-class carriage with a standard-class ticket may be convicted of travelling without having previously paid his fare, if an intention to avoid payment of the correct fare is indicated by his refusal to pay the excess. It is usual in such circumstances for a ticket collector, if one is carried, to ask such a person to move if he alleges that he has made a mistake, but if the journey has almost been completed it is probable that the ticket collector will demand the excess fare and a refusal to pay indicates an intention to avoid payment.

Second, it is also an offence under s 5(3) knowingly and wilfully to proceed by train beyond the distance for which a fare has been paid. Opportunities exist on all trains to obtain an additional ticket for the excess journey and if opportunities to do so are ignored on the journey, this *may* be taken to indicate a knowing and wilful act. It would be different if the passenger fell asleep and was accidentally taken beyond the destination for which he has paid as he could not be said to have proceeded knowingly and wilfully beyond that point.

Penalty fares

The Railways (Penalty Fares) Regulations 1994 made under the Railways Act 1993, make provision for the charging of penalty fares for failure to produce, when required to do so, a ticket or other authority authorising a person to travel by train or to be present in a compulsory ticket area at a station. The Regulations apply to all train operators.

By reg 3, subject to the provisions of the regulations, and to any rules made under them:

(a) any person travelling by, present on or leaving a train must, if required by or on behalf of the train operator, produce a ticket or other authority authorising his travelling by or his being present on that train, as the case may be; and

(b) any person present in or leaving a compulsory ticket area must, if so required, produce a ticket or other authority authorising him to be present in or leave that area.

Failure to produce a ticket or other authority when so required renders the person liable to be charged a penalty fare by the train operator or someone acting on its behalf. A person is not liable to pay a penalty fare in a case covered by (a) if, when he boarded the train (or a preceding train on his journey, which was operated by the same operator):

(a) there were no ticket etc facilities available for the journey in question;

(b) there was no notice in a prescribed form indicating the penalty fare scheme;

(c) at the station where and when he commenced his journey, a notice was displayed indicating that it was permissible to travel without having such ticket or authority; or

(d) a person in authority (or apparently in authority) at the originating station gave permission to travel without a ticket etc.

These exemptions do not exempt a person who had the opportunity to obtain a fare ticket while on the train (or one of them used on the journey).

There are similar exemptions from liability to pay a fixed penalty fare in respect of a person in a compulsory ticket area.

A person who fails to pay a penalty fare at once must provide his name and address on being required to do so by an authorised person.

In an action to recover a penalty fare, which is a civil action, a defendant may provide the plaintiff with a 'relevant statement' explaining his failure to produce a ticket etc and including particulars of his journey, which must be submitted within 21 days. Where this has been done it will be for the plaintiff to show that the facts of the case do not fall within the exemptions provided by the Act. In any other case it is for the defendant to show that the facts of the case fall within those exemptions.

If a person has been charged a penalty fare in respect of his failure to produce a ticket or other authority when required and he is then prosecuted under the Railways Act 1889, s 5(3) (see above) or for breach of a railway bye law in respect of the lack of a ticket etc, he ceases to be liable to pay the penalty fare. If he has already paid it, it must be refunded.

CHAPTER 27

Pedlars, vagrancy and dealers

PEDLARS

The Pedlars Act 1871 still exists to provide some element of control over those who engage in some forms of door-to-door trading. Not the least of the reasons for this control is that peddling provides for those who commit crime a convenient cover or excuse to visit houses, where they may take advantage of opportunities to steal.

The definition of 'pedlar'

The term 'pedlar' is defined by the Act as meaning a hawker, pedlar, petty chapman (another name for a pedlar), tinker, caster of metals, mender of chairs, or other person who, without any horse or other beast bearing or drawing burden, travels and trades on foot, and goes from town to town or to other men's houses, carrying to sell, or exposing for sale, any goods, wares or merchandise, or procuring orders for goods etc immediately to be delivered, or selling or offering for sale his skill in handicraft.

An important part of this definition is 'travels and trades on foot', which has been held to require that, to be a pedlar, a person must *go round* selling things; he must *trade as he travels on foot*, although he may stop to conduct a particular sale, rather than simply selling from a stall or pitch. Thus, a door-to-door salesman is a pedlar, but someone who stands in one place with a pitch, soliciting custom, is not. Nor is a person who moves a barrow from place to place, waiting at each place for customers to come to him. Provided the words of the definition are satisfied, it is irrelevant that the trade is carried out on a part-time basis or on the basis that the proceeds of sale will go (in whole or in part) to a charity.

Pedlars' certificates

Under the Pedlars Act 1871, a person who acts as a pedlar without a pedlar's certificate commits an offence, subject to certain exceptions. A pedlar's certificate is obtained from the chief officer of police of the district in which the applicant has resided during the month preceding his application. Before granting a certificate the chief officer must be satisfied that the applicant is over 17, is of good character and in good faith intends to carry on the trade of a pedlar. It is an offence to make a false representation with a view to obtaining a pedlar's certificate.

The certificate is renewable annually and authorises the holder to carry on the trade of a pedlar in any part of the United Kingdom. It also permits the pedlar to sell vegetables and fruits within the limits of a market, but only in the district in which it was granted.

Chief officers of police must maintain a register of certificates. The Act permits a chief officer to delegate his functions under the 1871 Act and, in practice, certificates are usually issued within police divisions and signed by the divisional commander on behalf of the chief officer.

An applicant may appeal to the justices against a refusal to issue a pedlar's certificate; the applicant must give to the chief officer, within one week of the refusal, written notice of his wish to appeal.

Justices may summon a pedlar to appear before them at any time and if he fails to appear or, having done so, fails to satisfy them that he is carrying on the business of a pedlar in good faith, the justices may deprive him of his certificate.

Exemption from need for a certificate

The Pedlars Act 1871 states that it is not necessary for certain persons to obtain pedlar's certificates, and these are:

(a) commercial travellers or other persons selling or seeking orders for goods, wares or merchandise, to or from dealers therein, and who buy to sell again;
(b) those who sell or seek orders for books as agents authorised in writing by the publishers of such books;
(c) sellers of vegetables, fish, fruit or victuals; and
(d) persons selling or exposing for sale goods etc in any public market or fair which is legally established.

These exemptions are easily understood when one recalls that the purpose of the Pedlars Act is to give some form of supervision to door-to-door trading activities which would otherwise be uncontrolled and require control. The commercial traveller who, on foot, visited business premises which were also 'houses', in that the businessmen lived on the premises, would have become a pedlar if he was delivering goods to them; but for the exemption he would have required a certificate in such a case. Parliament did not think that this situation required control and the same is true of the other exceptions. The encyclopedia salesman is already authorised by the publishers to sell their product and his purpose in calling at houses is only to sell books. The sellers of vegetables, fruit etc from door to door are local businessmen who are already well-known to both the public and the police. It is, however, interesting to note that a High Court judge has held that lavender is a vegetable and that those who sell lavender from door to door are exempt from the necessity to obtain a pedlar's certificate. The exemption in relation to markets appears to be unnecessary as market traders do not go to other men's houses in any case.

Offences

It is an offence for a pedlar to refuse on demand to show his pedlar's certificate to a justice or constable or to a person to whom he offers his goods for sale (or upon whose private grounds or premises he is found), or to refuse to allow it to be read.

STREET AND HOUSE-TO-HOUSE COLLECTIONS

Street collections

The Police, Factories &c (Miscellaneous Provisions) Act 1916 permits local authorities to make regulations with respect to the places where and the conditions under which persons may be permitted, in any street or public place within their area, to collect money or sell articles for the benefit of charitable or other purposes. It also provides that a contravention of any regulations so made is an offence.

House-to-house collections

The House to House Collections Act 1939 prohibits house-to-house collections for charitable purposes unless the collection is authorised. Such a collection may be authorised by a *licence* (issued by a district council, Commissioner of the Metropolitan Police, or the Common Council of the City of London), or an *order* of exemption (granted by the Secretary of State where the charitable purpose is to be pursued throughout the whole of England or a substantial part of it), or a *certificate* of exemption (granted by a chief officer of police in respect of a collection which is local in character and likely to be completed within a short period of time).

The House to House Collections Regulations 1947 deal with such matters as badges, certificates of authority, collecting boxes and receipt books and duties of collectors and promoters. They prescribe a minimum age of 16 years in respect of collectors. The 1947 Regulations do not apply to a collection under a certificate of exemption. Breach of the regulations is an offence. Section 5 of the 1939 Act punishes the unauthorised use of prescribed badges or certificates of authority, or a thing so closely resembling those articles as to be calculated to deceive.

Police powers

A constable may require any person whom he believes to be acting as a collector for the purposes of a collection for charitable purposes to declare to him his name and address and to sign his name. Failure to comply with such a requirement is an offence.

The Charities Act 1992

The Charities Act 1992 deals, among other things, with public charitable collections, ie charitable appeals made in any public place or by house-to-house visits.

Section 66 prohibits any public collection from being conducted except in accordance with a permit issued by the district council or with an order of the Charity Commissioners. Breach of this prohibition is an offence on the part of the promoter (ie any organiser or controller) of the charity appeal. Section 73 of the 1992 Act permits regulations to be made along the lines of the 1947 Regulations. Section 74 of the 1992 Act replicates the offence under s 5 of the 1939 Act.

These provisions are not in force at the time of writing. When they are, the 1992 Act will repeal the Police, Factories &c (Miscellaneous Provisions) Act 1916 and the House to House Collections Act 1939.

VAGRANCY OFFENCES

Begging

Section 3 of the Vagrancy Act 1824 punishes persons who wander abroad, or place themselves in any public place, street, highway, court or passage, to beg or gather alms, or who cause, procure or encourage any child to do so. The Divisional Court has decided that workmen on strike who seek assistance by asking for contributions towards their cause are *not* begging for the purposes of this section. It should be remembered that the purpose of the section is to prevent persons from frequenting the streets for the purpose of begging to the annoyance of the general public. It is not really concerned with trivial and occasional incidents. It must be shown that the person concerned had, in a sense, taken up the profession of a beggar in preference to work.

Section 4 of the Act deals with the aggravated forms of begging by the exposure of wounds or deformities in public or by seeking charitable contributions of any kind by false pretences.

Sleeping out etc

It is an offence contrary to the Vagrancy Act 1824, s 4 for any person, wandering abroad and lodging in any barn or outhouse, or in any deserted or unoccupied building, or in the open air, or under a tent, or in any cart or waggon, not to give a good account of himself.

It must be emphasised that the offence is only committed by a person who fails to give a good account of himself. People holidaying at a static caravan site and genuine hikers who, being tired and hungry, rest in a barn or outhouse are not guilty of this offence because they can easily give a good account of themselves by explaining their presence. In contrast, a tramp found sleeping in a barn would find it much more difficult to give a good account of himself, particularly if he has made a temporary home in that building.

Two important limits were imposed on the offence by the Vagrancy Act 1935. First, the Act amended s 4 by providing that the reference to a person lodging under a tent or in a cart or waggon does not include a person lodging under a tent, cart or waggon with or in which he travels. It was thereby made quite clear that the present offence was not concerned with gypsies travelling in their own waggons, nor with persons sleeping out in their own tents.

The 1935 Act also requires that before a person can be guilty of the present offence, it must be proved either that:

(a) on the occasion in question, he had been directed to a reasonably accessible place of free shelter and that he failed to apply for, or refused, accommodation there; or

(b) he is a person who persistently wanders abroad and, notwithstanding that a place of free shelter is reasonably accessible, lodges or attempts to lodge in a way described above; or

(c) by, or in the course of, lodging in a way described above he caused damage to property, infection with vermin, or other offensive consequence, or he so lodged in such circumstances as to appear to be likely to do so.

As a result, the present offence is of little practical significance to police officers. The reason is that there are few places of free shelter to which people may be directed, or which are reasonably accessible to the person who persistently sleeps out. The provision of greatest practical significance is that at (c), which can apply to the roadster who destroys hay or feed in a barn by his presence, or who causes the barn or outbuilding to become verminous by his presence.

Powers

The Vagrancy Act 1824 empowers all persons to arrest without warrant any person who is found offending against the Act. The Act requires the person arresting to take that person before a justice, or to deliver him to any constable.

SCRAP METAL DEALERS

Registration of dealers

The Scrap Metal Dealers Act 1964 requires every district council (hereafter 'the local authority') to maintain a register of persons carrying on business in their area as scrap metal dealers.

It is an offence for a person to carry on a business as a scrap metal dealer in the area of a local authority unless he is registered with that authority. The essential elements to prove for this offence are that a business is being carried on in the area of a particular local authority, that the business is one of being a scrap metal dealer, and that the person carrying on the business is not registered with the local authority.

Carrying on a business

For the purposes of the 1964 Act, a person carrying on business as a scrap metal dealer is treated as carrying on that business in the area of a local authority if, but only if:

(a) a place in that area is occupied by him as a scrap metal store; or
(b) no place is occupied by him as a scrap metal store, whether in that area or elsewhere, but he has his usual place of residence in that area; or
(c) no place is occupied by him as a scrap metal store, whether in that area or elsewhere, but a place in that area is occupied by him wholly or partly for the purposes of that business.

(For the purpose of these provisions, 'place' includes land, whether enclosed or not, and a 'scrap metal store' means a place where scrap metal is received or kept in the course of the business of a scrap metal dealer.)

Therefore, a person who has a scrap metal store in the area of a local authority is clearly carrying on a business in the area of that authority and must be registered with it. Also, a person who does not have a scrap metal store in the area of the X local authority but nevertheless lives in the area of that authority must register with it, as must a person with a business address in the area of the X local authority if that business is one of being a scrap metal dealer.

Business as a scrap metal dealer

A person carries on business as a scrap metal dealer if he carries on a business which consists wholly or partly of buying and selling scrap metal, whether the scrap metal sold is in the form in which it was bought or otherwise, other than a business in the course of which scrap metal is not bought except as materials for the manufacture of other articles and is not sold except as a by-product of such manufacture or as surplus materials bought but not required for such manufacture.

This definition is quite complex and difficult to follow unless it is broken up into pieces. In the first instance, the person must carry on a business which consists wholly or partly of buying and selling scrap metal. Therefore persons who merely buy scrap metal are not dealers, nor are those who merely sell it. If this was not so, a farmer who quite regularly sells scrap metal which gathers about the farm might be considered to be carrying on business as a scrap metal dealer if it could be said that his business was partly that of selling scrap metal. If a person both buys and sells it does not matter that the metal is sold in a different form. Consequently, a person who buys scrap vehicles and crushes them into cubes of metal, which he then sells to some other person, is quite clearly a scrap metal dealer. The position of vehicle dismantlers is not quite so clear, as the Divisional Court has decided that a distinction must be drawn between (a) the dismantler who buys old motor vehicles for their parts which he sells as spare parts (the only scrap metal which he sells being the body shells and pieces which are unusable), and (b) the dismantler who buys scrap vehicles for their metal, but as a sideline sells the better parts to customers. The former is not a scrap metal dealer; the latter is.

Scrap metal

The Act describes scrap metal as including any old metal, and any broken, worn out, defaced or partly manufactured articles made wholly or partly of metal, and any metallic wastes, and also as including old, broken, worn out or defaced tooltips or dies made of any of the materials commonly known as hard metals or of cemented or sintered metallic carbides. References to metals, other than 'hard metals' or 'metallic carbides', are references to aluminium, copper, iron, lead, magnesium, nickel, tin and zinc, or, subject to the next sentence, to brass, bronze, gun metal, steel, white metal or any other alloy of these metals. However, if any alloy has two per cent or more of gold, silver, platinum etc, it is not treated as such an alloy. It follows that a person who deals only in precious metals is not a scrap metal dealer.

Alteration in registered particulars

Dealers must notify to the local authority any change in their registered particulars. If they cease to carry on business as a scrap metal dealer, they must notify the local authority who will cancel the entry.

Records to be kept by scrap metal dealers

A scrap metal dealer must keep a bound record book at each place occupied by him as a scrap metal store. He must make entries concerning:

(a) all scrap metal received at that place; and
(b) all scrap metal either processed at, or despatched from, that place.

He may, if he wishes, keep two separate bound books recording matters at (a) and (b) separately but otherwise may not extend the book-keeping by keeping any other books recording dealing in that store.

Records of metals received

The records must show:

(a) the description and weight of the scrap metal;
(b) the date and time of receipt of the scrap metal;
(c) if the scrap metal is received from another person, his full name and address;
(d) the price, if any, payable, if ascertained at the time of the entry;
(e) if the price has not been ascertained, the dealer's estimate; and
(f) if the scrap metal has been delivered by mechanically propelled vehicle, the registration mark of the vehicle (even if it is the dealer's).

Records—metals processed or despatched

The records must show:

(a) the description and weight of the scrap metal;
(b) the date of processing and the process applied, or, as the case may be, the date of despatch;
(c) if despatched on sale or exchange, the full name and address of the person to whom the scrap is sold or with whom it is exchanged, and the consideration for which it is sold or exchanged; and
(d) if processed or despatched otherwise than on sale or exchange, the value of the scrap before its processing or despatch as estimated by the dealer.

These provisions can be easily remembered if it is kept in mind that the provisions are concerned with the prevention of dealings in stolen metals. With this in mind it is logical that dealers will have to be registered and that meticulous records will have to be kept of metals. The idea is that, from the moment that scrap metal is received by the dealer, the records will provide a continuing history of its origin, including the person from whom it is obtained and his mechanically propelled vehicle, through its processing to its ultimate disposal.

Itinerant collectors

Where a person, who is registered by a local authority as a scrap metal dealer satisfies the authority that he carries on, or proposes to carry on, the business of a scrap metal dealer as part of the business of an 'itinerant collector', and not otherwise, the authority may make an order exempting him from keeping the records set out above, but making him subject to the following requirements:

(a) that, when he sells scrap metal, he obtains a receipt from the purchaser showing its weight and aggregate price; and

(b) that he keeps such receipts for two years in such a way that he can produce them on demand to any authorised person.

Before making an order of the above type, the local authority must consult the chief officer of police for their area. This order, limiting the need to keep records, may be revoked by the local authority at any time. Failure to comply with the requirement to keep records as an itinerant collector is an offence.

An 'itinerant collector' is a person regularly engaged in collecting waste materials, and old, broken, worn out or defaced articles, by means of visits from house to house. Most 'tinker' collectors will fit this description as they are regularly engaged in such activities.

Police powers of entry

Section 6 of the 1964 Act empowers a constable at all reasonable times:

(a) to enter and inspect any place registered as a scrap metal store, or as a place occupied by a scrap metal dealer wholly or partly for the purposes of his business; and

(b) to require production of, and to inspect, any scrap metal kept at that place and any book which the dealer is required to keep at that place, or, as the case may be, any receipt (itinerant dealers), and to take copies of or extracts from any such book or receipt.

The term 'reasonable times' is not defined, and must therefore be given a normal, commonsense meaning. Any time during working hours would be reasonable unless particular circumstances (such as some internal operation within the yard which demanded the dealer's uninterrupted attention) indicated the contrary.

Entry under this power can only be effected by force on the authority of a justice's warrant. Such a warrant may be issued under s 6 if a justice is satisfied by information on oath that admission is reasonably required in order to secure compliance with the provisions of the Act, or to ascertain whether those provisions are being complied with. The warrant authorises those having a right of entry to enter within one month, if need be by force.

It is an offence for any person to obstruct the exercise of a right of entry or inspection under s 6, or to fail to produce books or documents which a person has a right to inspect thereunder.

Power of courts to impose additional requirements

Where a person is convicted of carrying on business as a scrap metal dealer without being registered, or being registered, he is convicted of failing to keep records or of any offence involving dishonesty, the court *may* make an order subjecting him to certain additional requirements in respect of his scrap metal store, viz:

(a) that no scrap metal shall be received between 6pm and 8am;

(b) that all scrap metal received at such place shall be kept in the form in which it is received for a period of not less than 72 hours.

The duration of the order specified by the court must not exceed two years. A dealer commits a further offence if he does not comply with the requirements of an order. If he is convicted of such an offence, a further order may be made against him.

Miscellaneous offences

It is an offence, contrary to s 5(1) of the 1964 Act, for a scrap metal dealer to acquire scrap metal from a person apparently under the age of 16, whether that metal is offered on his own behalf or on behalf of someone else. The accused dealer has a defence if he proves that the person from whom he acquired the scrap metal was in fact of or over the age of 16.

By s 5(2), a person who gives a false name or false address to a scrap metal dealer, on selling him scrap metal, commits an offence.

CHAPTER 28

Non-fatal offences against the person

This chapter is concerned with various non-fatal offences against the person, which are distinguishable in a number of ways, such as the degree of harm caused, the way in which it is inflicted and the status of the victim.

The first two offences to be discussed are the separate offences of assault and battery. Rather confusingly, the word 'assault' is used in some statutes to refer to assault or battery. Even more confusingly, the word 'assault' has sometimes been used in decided cases as meaning a 'battery', which is not altogether surprising since this is the meaning normally given to 'assault' in common parlance. Obviously, an officer must take care to ascertain the relevant meaning of 'assault' when he comes across that term in a particular context.

COMMON ASSAULT AND COMMON BATTERY

Assault

A person is guilty of the separate offence of assault if he intentionally or recklessly causes another person to apprehend the immediate application to himself of unlawful force.

The actus reus which must be proved is some act by the accused which causes the victim to fear the immediate application of unlawful force against him.

Any act, even mere words, can suffice if they have the requisite result. An example would be where, during an argument in a pub, someone holding a beer glass loses his temper and shouts out to his antagonist, 'I'll glass you for that'. Although words alone can constitute an assault, threatening words are more likely to be prosecuted as an offence under the Public Order Act 1986, s 4, 4A or 5.

The requirement that the immediate application of unlawful force must be apprehended means that it is an assault to aim a blow at someone, whether or not that blow hits him, unless he is blind or the blow is aimed from behind him or there is some other circumstance which means that he does not apprehend force. The requirement of 'immediacy' has been given a liberal interpretation by the courts. It has been held to be satisfied where a woman has been put in fear by a 'peeping tom' whom she saw through a window, or by a malicious telephone caller who had repeatedly 'hung up', because the woman would not know what the person was going to do next. In another case, where a woman had been caused psychiatric harm after repeated telephone calls and letters from a stalker, the last two of which contained threats, the Court of Appeal held that the jury were entitled to find that the last letter had caused the woman fear of immediate force. It emphasised that the accused, who was known to the woman, lived near her and she thought that something could happen at any time. In a curious statement, the Court of Appeal, albeit accepting the requirement of the apprehension of immediate force, said that it was enough for the prosecution to prove fear of force 'at some time not excluding the immediate future'. In the light of these decisions, the requirement seems to mean little. Cases involving repeated conduct such as the second case just described are now better dealt with by bringing a prosecution for an offence under the Protection from Harassment Act 1997, described on pp 617-618.

If a person is put in fear of immediate force, it is irrelevant that the accused could not in fact carry out his threat; for example, pointing an unloaded gun or an imitation gun at someone who is unaware of its harmlessness can be an assault.

The mens rea required for an assault is an intention to cause the victim to apprehend the immediate application of unlawful force or subjective recklessness as to whether the victim might so apprehend. Subjective recklessness requires that the accused realised the possibility that his act might cause the victim to apprehend immediate unlawful force but nevertheless persisted in doing that act without any justification.

If a person, indulging in a piece of horseplay and mistakenly believing that the other is doing so as well, playfully throws a punch at the other, meaning to miss, he is not guilty of an assault—even though the other does fear immediate force—because he does not intend the other to fear immediate unlawful force and is not subjectively reckless in this respect. On the other hand, rowdies who throw bottles at passers-by on the opposite pavement clearly indicate an intention to cause them to fear being hit (ie immediate force) if they take deliberate aim; if they lob the bottles in the general direction of the passers-by, this may indicate subjective recklessness as to whether any of the passers-by may be put in fear of immediate force.

Battery

A person is guilty of battery if he intentionally or recklessly applies unlawful force to another person. Most batteries are preceded by an assault, but this is not always so. If a person is clubbed down from behind there is certainly a battery, but, if he was unaware that the blow was coming, there cannot be an assault, because there would have been no apprehension by him of the immediate application of unlawful force.

The actus reus of the offence of battery is some act on the part of the accused which results in unlawful force being applied to another. Technically, the slightest degree of force, even a mere touching, suffices, but a prosecution is most unlikely unless some harm has been caused. The force can be applied directly, as where a person hits another with his fist or an instrument, or indirectly, as where someone puts a tripwire across an alley over which another person trips or puts acid in a hand drier which is blown onto the hands of the next user. The fact that a battery requires an application of force, whether by a fist, an implement, a projectile or a liquid, means that those who cause harm in some other way than by applying force, eg by poisoning, do not commit a battery. Causing someone psychiatric harm by a threat does not involve a battery because it does not involve the application of force.

The mens rea required for a battery is an intention to apply unlawful force to the other or subjective recklessness as to whether unlawful force might be so applied. It follows that, if the horseplay referred to above results in a blow landing on the other, there is no battery if the blow is a light one and the person throwing it believed that the other was engaging in the horseplay and therefore consenting to such a blow (because, as we shall see, he will not have intended, nor been reckless as to, the application of *unlawful* force).

Clearly, it is not a battery to hit or shoot someone accidentally (since there is no intention to apply force to another), unless the accused can be proved to have realised the risk that his act, eg of swinging his arm or pulling the trigger, might possibly result in unlawful force being applied to another and unjustifiably decided to do the act regardless (in which case he would be proved to have been subjectively reckless as to the risk).

Assault and battery: unlawful force

It is an integral part of both offences that the force apprehended by the victim, or applied to him, must be unlawful force. In this context, the essential point is that if the victim has given a valid consent to it, or if the force is threatened or applied in self-defence, prevention of crime or the like, it is lawful force. This point is also important in relation to the other non-fatal offences discussed later in this chapter.

Consent

Generally, a person cannot give a valid consent to harm which was intended to cause and/or actually caused 'actual bodily harm'. 'Actual bodily harm' means any injury calculated to interfere with the health or comfort of the victim. 'Injury' in this context is not limited to physical injury; it includes a hysterical or nervous condition. The result of all this is that if a person intends to cause another and/or actually causes him actual bodily harm, it is generally irrelevant whether or not the latter has consented, since, generally, he cannot give a valid consent in such a case. Thus, assuming the other elements of the offence are proved, there can generally be a conviction for an assault or battery or some other non-fatal offence against the person in such a case, despite the victim's apparent consent. For example, men who agree to fight each other to 'settle a score' commit an assault and a battery (or a more serious non-fatal offence) when they fight each other, since actual bodily harm is clearly intended and/or caused. For the same reason, willing and enthusiastic participants in sado-masochistic acts of violence for the sexual pleasure engendered in the giving and receiving of pain can be convicted of an assault, or of a battery (or of a more serious non-fatal offence).

There are, however, exceptions, based on grounds of public policy, to the general rule just stated. A person can give a valid consent to 'any actual bodily harm' caused by reasonable surgical operations or procedures; if he could not the surgeon would commit a battery or an assault occasioning actual bodily harm (below) or some more serious offence against the person.

Likewise, it has been held that a valid consent can be given to ear-piercing, to being tattooed or, even, to being branded with one's spouse's initials, since the causing of bodily harm of these types is not contrary to public policy.

Similarly, those who agree to take part in a lawful sport consent to the rules of that sport and, if those rules allow forms of physical contact, they validly consent to the risk of actual bodily harm which is likely to result from physical contact which is within the rules or is a minor infringement of them. For example, a blow struck in a boxing match under the Queensberry rules (in which boxers wear approved gloves) is not a battery or any other offence, regardless of the injury caused, unless the blow is struck in circumstances far outside the rules (eg hitting an opponent when he is lying unconscious on the floor, or hitting an opponent with a glove in which is concealed a heavy object). Likewise, in soccer and rugger, the participants consent to the risk of actual bodily harm resulting from something within the rules of the game or not too far removed from them, but not to the risk of such harm resulting from something which is far outside the rules, such as a head-butt or deliberately kicking a player who is on the ground.

Not all sports are lawful. For example, a prize-fight, where gloves are not worn and the fight continues until one of the participants can no longer continue, is an unlawful sport. Thus, the participants cannot give a valid consent to the actual bodily harm intended and/or caused, with the result that the force which they apply to each other is always unlawful.

Other points on consent Sometimes when a person has consented to the application of force, his consent is invalid, even though actual bodily harm is not intended and/or caused. Examples are where he is so young or mentally impaired as not to understand the nature of the act committed, or where his apparent consent has been procured by duress.

Assuming it is valid, a consent need not be express; it can be implied from the circumstances. Everyday living demands a certain amount of physical contact. People are often touched in order to attract their attention, and there are constant collisions in shopping precincts, and the consent of people to such things can normally be implied. It is, of course, different if the person touched has indicated that he does not want to be touched. If A tells B, who has been pestering him, to go away, A clearly does not impliedly consent to B touching him soon after in order to attract his attention. Of course, there is a limit to what a person impliedly consents to. There is certainly no consent to a violent blow, allegedly to attract attention, perhaps as a person walked away after an argument. Similarly, one does not impliedly consent to collisions in a shopping precinct caused by hooligans charging about.

Another way of expressing cases based on implied consent is that they fall within a general exception embracing all physical contact which is generally acceptable in the ordinary conduct of daily life.

Normally, the consent of sports players referred to above is implied from their participation in the game, rather than being expressly given.

Other factors which render force lawful

Disciplinary use of force and corporal punishment Parents and other people in loco parentis are entitled as a disciplinary measure to apply a reasonable degree of force to their children or charges old enough to understand its purpose. This power includes using reasonable force to restrain a child from injuring another person or damaging property or engaging in disorderly behaviour. It also includes using reasonable force as corporal punishment. The law on reasonable chastisement by parents and persons in loco parentis was held in September 1998 by the Europeam Court of Human Rights to contravene art 3 of the European Convention on Human Rights (no one to be subjected to torture or inhuman or degrading treatment or punishment) on the ground that it failed to protect children against such treatment, and is to be amended by Parliament (although corporal punishment will not be outlawed completely).

Teachers are no longer entitled by virtue of their position as such to apply reasonable corporal punishment as a disciplinary measure.

Prevention of crime or effecting arrest   The Criminal Law Act 1967, s 3 provides that it is lawful to use such force as is reasonable in the circumstances in the prevention of crime or in effecting (or assisting in) the lawful arrest of offenders, suspected offenders or persons unlawfully at large. Where the accused acts under a mistake as to the circumstances, this provision is applied to the circumstances as he believed them to be. The effecting of an arrest will almost always involve some form of restraint, even if it is only symbolic, and this would be a battery but for the present defence. It must be emphasised that, if the force used to prevent a crime or to make an arrest is unreasonable in the circumstances, it will be unlawful and the person using it will not have a defence to a charge of battery or of another offence against the person. A person has no defence, even though he uses reasonable force, if he is acting in furtherance of an unlawful arrest.

Self-defence and defence of property or of another   Self-defence and the defence of property or of another are common law defences. However, a person who acts in defence of himself or another or of property is almost invariably acting in the prevention of crime, in which case he also has the defence under the Criminal Law Act 1967, s 3. For practical purposes, the terms of both the common law and the statutory defences are identical in their requirements.

The issue of self-defence as an excuse for a non-fatal offence against the person has been summarised extremely well by the Court of Appeal. The Court said that it was both good law and good sense that a person who is attacked may defend himself but that in doing so, he may only do what is reasonably necessary. The test of whether or not the force is reasonable is an objective one, but it is assessed on the facts as the person concerned believed them to be.

The law on defence of property or of another is essentially the same as in self-defence, the essential question being 'was the force used reasonable in the circumstances'. Defence of property does not entitle the owner of property to use force against persons who trespass upon his land without offering force. In such a case the trespasser must be requested to leave before there is any hostile touching. If the trespasser is 'handled', it must amount to no more than is necessary to remove him from the property. If a trespasser offers force, then it may be met with whatever force is necessary to overcome it and remove him. If the owner of the land is severely attacked, even a serious wounding may be excusable if it was occasioned reasonably in self-defence in the circumstances.

For the avoidance of doubt, it must be stated that the mere fact that a person who has used force against another was provoked to lose self-control (as opposed to acting in self-defence etc) is no excuse. Of course, if a person who has used provocative words or conduct then makes some immediately threatening move towards the person to whom his words or conduct are directed, he has carried out an assault and reasonable resistance to it would amount to self-defence. If no more than provocation is involved, this is only relevant in relation to the penalty which the court may award.

Assault and battery: procedural matters

Assault and battery are separate statutory offences of common assault and common battery and should be so charged, under the Criminal Justice Act 1988, s 39. Where the person has been merely 'put in fear' the person must be charged that he 'did assault' that person. If force has been applied, the charge should allege 'did assault by beating'. Proceedings are frequently instituted by private persons. A common example of the institution of a private prosecution for a common assault or battery is where an argument with a spouse or an acquaintance has got out of hand and led to a threat of harm or to fairly minor harm being done. It quite often happens in such a case that proceedings are discontinued by the private prosecutor after a period of reflection.

Witnesses

When common assaults or batteries are committed against children or young persons the wife or husband of the person charged may be called as a witness without the consent of the person charged. Justices may accept the depositions of children whose attendance they consider likely seriously to endanger their life or health. The evidence of a child of tender years is admissible unless it appears that he is incapable of giving intelligible testimony, although such evidence is not sworn.

Certificate of dismissal

If, on a charge of common assault or battery brought by or on behalf of the victim, the justices find that the charge is not proved, or that the assault was justified or so trifling as not to merit punishment, they must make out a certificate of dismissal which (like a conviction for common assault or battery) has the effect of releasing the person concerned from all further proceedings in relation to that offence, whether criminal or civil (ie for damages). Clearly it is important that the victim realises this before an information is laid by him (or on his behalf).

AGGRAVATED ASSAULTS

There are a number of offences of aggravated assault. Among them are assault with intent to rob, assault with intent to commit buggery and indecent assault, which are discussed elsewhere. Like the aggravated assaults discussed below, they require an assault or battery which is accompanied either by a particular intention or by a special circumstance or consequence.

Assault occasioning actual bodily harm

It is an offence, contrary to the Offences Against the Person Act 1861, s 47, to assault any person, thereby occasioning him actual bodily harm. The offence is an arrestable one. What is required is an assault or battery which has occasioned actual bodily harm. Actual bodily harm is any injury calculated to interfere with health or comfort in a more than trifling way. Psychiatric injury (but not mere emotions such as fear, distress or panic which are not themselves evidence of an identifiable clinical condition) can amount to 'actual bodily harm'. Consequently, to cause someone psychiatric injury by a threat of 'immediate' force can amount to an offence under s 47. Where a victim claims to have suffered psychiatric illness or injury as a result of a non-physical assault, there must be psychiatric evidence as to whether the symptoms alleged by the victim amount to a psychiatric illness or injury.

There must be a direct connection between the 'assault' and the bodily harm occasioned and in most circumstances this will be apparent. If the assailant punches his victim in the face and causes actual bodily harm, eg cuts or bruises, there has been a battery and the harm has been occasioned thereby. It may be, however, that an assailant chases his victim who, fearful of the consequences of being caught attempts to jump over a fence and thereby injures himself. In such circumstances there has been an assault, ie the putting of another in fear of immediate force, and that assault has led to the harm done. It is a question of sufficient connection between the two elements. To attempt to escape in that way is reasonable and there is therefore sufficient connection. Only if the action taken by the person assaulted, which led to the bodily harm, was unreasonable in the circumstances would there be an insufficient connection.

The mens rea required for this offence is the mens rea required for an assault or battery (as the case may be). It is not necessary to establish that the defendant intended to cause some bodily harm or was reckless as to the risk of doing so.

Assault with intent to resist arrest

Although assaults upon police officers are dealt with in detail by the Police Act 1996, s 89, it remains an offence under the Offences Against the Person Act 1861, s 38 for a person to assault (ie by an assault or by a battery) any person with intent to resist or prevent the lawful apprehension or detainer of himself, or any other person, for any offence. The provisions of this section are still extremely useful as it deals with assaults on any person effecting an arrest, and therefore includes members of the public who are making 'citizens' arrests'.

Assault on a constable in the execution of his duty

The Police Act 1996, s 89(1) makes it an offence for a person to assault (by an assault or by a battery) a constable in the execution of his duty. While, of course, the accused must have the necessary mens rea for the assault or battery which he commits, it is irrelevant that he does not know that the victim was a constable acting in the execution of his duty. However, if the accused, ignorant that the victim is a constable, applies force to the constable who is exercising one of his powers, and that force would have been reasonable on the ground of self-defence if the victim had not been a constable, the accused does not commit an offence. He will not have intentionally or recklessly applied unlawful force (the mens rea for a battery) because of his ignorance of his victim's status.

The key point about this offence is that the constable must be acting in the execution of his duty. At first sight the offence seems to be quite straightforward as there is a tendency to assume that police officers are in the execution of their duty at all times while they are carrying out duties in the course of their routine work. This is not so, and it is important to remember that on every occasion upon which it is alleged that this offence has been committed the particular duty which was being executed at the time will be examined by the courts.

To be acting in the execution of his duty, a constable must be acting within the general scope of a duty imposed on him by law (such as his duties to protect life and property, to keep the peace, to prevent and investigate crimes and to prevent obstruction of the highway) and he must not be acting unlawfully at the time. Thus, even if a constable is acting within the general scope of one of his duties, he is not acting in the execution of his duty if he has no power to do the thing in question (and is, therefore, committing a trespass against a person or his property). In one case, a man kicked a constable, used foul language and started to walk away. The constable laid a hand on the man's shoulder, not with the intention of arresting him but to detain him for further conversation. This was held to be an unlawful detention against the man's will and therefore the constable was held not to be acting in the execution of his duty in so acting. It would have been different if he had been exercising his power of arrest, as he was entitled to do. Where police officers arrest a man and it is not practicable to give the reason for that arrest at the time, the arrest will be lawful and an assault upon the police officers will, at that time, be committed while they are in the execution of their duty. This is so even if the arrest is subsequently made unlawful by a failure to give the reason for arrest as soon as it is practicable to do so. In another case, a constable stopped a motor vehicle pursuant to the Road Traffic Act 1988, s 163 and detained it, suspecting it to be stolen. He was acting in the execution of his duty, where his suspicion was justified.

The test of whether a police officer is acting in the execution of his duty is judged objectively. Where an officer wrongly believed that he was completing an arrest made by another officer and took hold of a female suspect's arm, he was not acting in the execution of his duty because he was unlawfully detaining the woman at the time at which she assaulted him.

Police officers are frequently asked to assist with the expulsion of persons from premises, where the owner of the premises considers them to be intruders or for some other reason they are unwelcome. An officer may lawfully assist the owner of property in these circumstances, but he is not bound to do so. Unless there are particular circumstances which demand such expulsion, for example, the removal of violent, quarrelsome, disorderly persons from various premises as required by law, or where a breach of the peace is taking place or apprehended, it is unlikely that he will be considered to have been acting in the execution of his duty. Similarly, a constable who arrested a man who was wanted on a warrant for non-payment of a fine, without having the warrant in his possession, was held not to be acting in the execution of his duty as what he did was unlawful. Police officers who arrest without warrant are not acting in the execution of their duty if a power does not exist in the circumstances. However, a constable does not act outside the execution of his duty if what he does involves no more than a trivial touching; indeed there is probably not an assault or battery in any event. In one case, for example, a constable, who touched a man on the shoulder to attract his attention because he wished to speak to him in relation to an offence, was held to have been acting in the execution of his duty. It would not have been so if he had tried to detain him where there was no power to arrest.

Assaults upon constables frequently occur in police stations and, once again, the nature of the duties being undertaken at the time must be examined before this charge is preferred. A person who has not been arrested is entitled to leave a police station at any time unless he is detained under particular provisions which allow detention. An officer who attempts to prevent him from leaving a police station is not acting in the execution of his duty. In one case, two policewomen, in searching a prisoner in accordance with their interpretation of the chief constable's instructions, removed her brassière and were assaulted by the prisoner. It was held that, regardless of those instructions, they were not acting in their duty if they had not personally considered whether such a search was necessary for a lawful purpose, or whether the removal of that garment was necessary for that particular person's protection. This is an interesting decision which clearly places responsibility for lawful search upon the officer conducting it.

Most assaults upon police officers still occur when they are dealing with disorderly persons in the street. The onerous nature of these duties is very much appreciated, as is the immediate pressure placed upon the officer and the suddenness with which assaults occur. However, the actions of the officer will always be considered in the calm of the courtroom! In one case, a group of noisy youths were told to move on by a constable. They were not sufficiently disorderly to merit arrest. All moved with the exception of one who was lying on a seat. He eventually stood up and the officer took hold of his arm whilst he spoke to him, and refused to release it. It was considered that the constable was not acting in the execution of his duty as he did not apprehend a breach of the peace. However, on another occasion youths were shouting, swearing and causing a disturbance in the early hours of the morning. Constables told them to be quiet and go home. One refused and continued with his conduct and assaulted a constable who warned him that he would be arrested. The officer was held to have been acting in the execution of his duty as he had the power to arrest in this instance for a breach of the peace committed in his presence. In another case, where a constable witnessed an argument between a man and his girlfriend which resulted in the girl running away, it was held that he was entitled, after giving the girl directions to her home, to detain the man to speak to him to ensure that he would not follow the girl as he was acting in the execution of his duty to preserve the peace.

On occasions constables are given the authority to enter premises, and if they enter under such an authority they are acting in the execution of their duty. For example, the common law authorises a constable to enter premises to deal with a breach or apprehended breach of the peace (and it also authorises him to remain for this purpose if he is already on the premises); such a constable is acting in the execution of his duty. If a constable enters to deal with a breach, or apprehended breach, of the peace he is discharging a duty. Response to a burglar alarm gives police an implied authority to enter premises for a reasonable time for the purpose of a search, but there is no legal right to enter premises found insecure at night. Where a constable is invited to enter premises by a member of the family and is later told to leave by the occupier, and he is assaulted by the occupier while he is immediately complying with that request, it is an assault upon him in the execution of his duty. On the other hand, he would no longer be in the execution of his duty if he did not comply with the request within a reasonable time because he would become a trespasser; if he was assaulted after the expiry of such a time an offence under s 89(1) would not be committed. Of course, it would be an offence under s 89(1) if the constable had remained to deal with a breach of the peace, because he would then be acting in the execution of his duty.

Under the Police Act 1996, s 89(1) it is also an offence to assault a person assisting a constable in the execution of his duty.

By s 89(3) of the Police Act 1996, the offence may also be committed against constables of Scottish forces or the Royal Ulster Constabulary who are executing warrants or acting in England and Wales by virtue of any enactment. Similar amendments have been made to the laws of those countries to apply equivalent offences to acts against police officers of England and Wales so acting in those countries.

Obstructing or resisting a constable in the execution of his duty

It is an offence under the Police Act 1996, s 89(2) for a person to resist or wilfully obstruct a constable in the execution of his duty, or a person assisting him. To obstruct is to do any conduct which prevents or makes it more difficult for a constable to carry out his duty, and in this sense those who give warning of police speed checks obstruct the constables in the execution of their duty. A man who deliberately drinks alcohol after an accident to negative the breath testing procedure is also guilty of this offence.

The obstruction must be 'wilful', which in this context means that:

(a) the accused's conduct which has resulted in the obstruction must have been deliberate and intended by him to bring about a state of affairs which, in fact, prevented or made it more difficult for the constable to carry out his duty, whether or not the accused realised that that state of affairs would have that effect; and

(b) the accused must have had no lawful excuse. Police officers often experience difficulty in obtaining names and addresses from offenders but a refusal to give such information will not amount to a wilful obstruction unless that person has a duty to give that information, because otherwise he will have a lawful excuse for his refusal. Nor, for the same reason, is it a wilful obstruction to advise someone not to answer police questions which he is not obliged to answer, even if the advice is given in an abusive way. Where a man told his brother repeatedly and in colourful language to say nothing to police officers who were seeking to question him in the street, it was held that, although he might have committed other offences, he did not thereby obstruct a police officer in the execution of his duty. It was not unlawful to so advise a person. Much of the traffic legislation imposes a duty to give particular types of information, but there is no such requirement in relation to most offences. Just as in the case of a failure to provide information, so in the case of other failures to assist the police (eg by failing to accord entry to a constable), there is only a wilful obstruction if the constable has the right to require the assistance in question, so that the accused is under a legal duty to provide it. An example would be where a constable has a statutory right of entry. A refusal to admit the constable in breach of the duty to admit him would be a wilful obstruction.

It has been held that an accused who reasonably believed that the person obstructed was not a constable could not be convicted of the present offence.

Like obstruction, resistance does not require an assault or battery. Probably, any resistance is also an obstruction, but resistance is a more appropriate word in certain cases (such as where a person arrested by a constable tears himself away).

What we said above about 'acting in the execution of his duty' is equally applicable to the offences of obstruction and resistance. Thus, for example, where a person seeks to prevent an arrest which, in the circumstances, is not a lawful arrest, he is not guilty of a wilful obstruction of a police officer acting in the execution of his duty since the officer will not be acting *in the execution of his duty*.

Assault or obstruction of a constable: arrest

A constable may arrest without warrant any person who *assaults* him in the execution of his duty, as an assault always involves a breach of the peace. A constable may arrest any person without warrant who *obstructs* him in the execution of his duty if that obstruction is such that it causes, or is likely to cause, a breach of the peace. These are common law powers which are still available to a constable.

OFFENCES INVOLVING WOUNDING OR GRIEVOUS BODILY HARM

Malicious wounding or infliction of grievous bodily harm

The Offences against the Person Act 1861, s 20 provides two offences: malicious wounding and malicious infliction of grievous bodily harm. Section 20 provides:

'Whosoever shall unlawfully and maliciously wound or inflict any grievous bodily harm upon any other person, either with or without any weapon or instrument, shall be guilty of an offence.'

The offences are arrestable offences.

Both offences have two elements in common: 'unlawfully' and 'maliciously'. The difference between them relates to their actus reus: 'wounding' and 'infliction of grievous bodily harm', and these terms will be discussed first.

Wounding or infliction of grievous bodily harm The term 'wound' indicates a breaking of the continuity of the skin and means both layers of the skin. It is not possible, therefore, to allege that a wound has been inflicted if there is no breaking of the skin. Consequently, all injuries involving broken bones are excluded unless the bone pierces the skin. However, such injuries will amount to grievous bodily harm.

'Grievous bodily harm' means really serious harm; 'bodily harm' can include psychiatric injury but of course such injury must be serious in order to be grievous. It is not essential that the nature of the harm should be either permanent or dangerous.

A wound can be caused or grievous bodily harm can be 'inflicted' even though it does not result from a battery; it is enough, instead, that it directly results from something done by the accused. An example would be where the accused bangs on the locked door of a third-floor flat, threatening to kick it down and injure its occupant, and the terrified occupant jumps out of a window and breaks a leg when he hits the ground. Another example would be where a stalker behaves in such a way as to cause the woman serious psychiatric injury. In both these situations convictions for unlawfully and maliciously inflicting grievous bodily harm have been upheld on appeal. However, there may be difficulty in proving that a 'stalker' or anyone else who causes serious harm by a threat acted with the necessary malice in that he foresaw the possibility of his conduct causing harm.

Consequently, it will normally be more appropriate to charge an offence under s 4 of the Protection from Harassment Act 1997 in such a case. We deal with this on p 618.

Unlawfully This means 'without lawful justification' and is merely intended to except from the offence, in certain circumstances, acts done with a justification rendering the harm lawful, for example harm lawfully caused in self-defence.

Maliciously The mens rea of an offence under s 20 is that the accused should have wounded or inflicted grievous bodily harm 'maliciously'. This does not mean that he must have acted out of spite or ill-will. Instead, what is required is that the accused must have intended his act to cause some unlawful harm to another, or been subjectively reckless as to whether some unlawful harm might result from his act (and this means that he must have realised the risk that some harm might result but unreasonably persisted in taking that risk). It must be emphasised that it is not necessary that the accused should have intended or foreseen harm of the gravity described in the section, ie a wound or really serious harm; foresight that some harm, albeit of a minor character, might result, is enough.

Wounding or causing grievous bodily harm with intent to do grievous bodily harm or to resist or prevent arrest

The Offences against the Person Act 1861, s 18 provides:

'Whosoever shall unlawfully and maliciously by any means whatsoever wound or cause grievous bodily harm to any person with intent to do grievous bodily harm to any person, or with intent to resist or prevent the lawful apprehension or detainer of any person, shall be guilty of an offence.'

An offence under s 18 is, of course, an arrestable offence. Clearly, an offence under s 18 is a very serious one; the nature of the maximum punishment (life imprisonment) is a factor to bear in mind when deciding which of the various non-fatal offences against the person to charge.

Section 18 provides two offences: wounding with intent to do grievous bodily harm or with intent to resist the lawful apprehension or detainer of any person, and causing grievous bodily harm with one of these intents.

Actus reus

What was said in relation to s 20 of the 1861 Act in relation to the words 'unlawfully', 'wound' and 'grievous bodily harm' is equally applicable to s 18. However, s 18 specifies that grievous bodily harm must be 'caused' (as opposed to 'inflicted'). This difference in terminology between s 18 and s 20 raises the question of whether there is a difference of substance. Grievous bodily harm can be 'caused' by a deliberate and culpable omission; but opinions differ as to whether such harm can be 'inflicted' by a deliberate and culpable omission to act.

Mens rea

If the accused is charged with wounding with intent to do grievous bodily harm, or with causing grievous bodily harm with such intent, the word 'maliciously', the meaning of which was explained above, is redundant. An accused may wound or cause grievous bodily harm to any person with intent to cause grievous bodily harm to any person. It is not essential that the harm is caused to the particular person intended. An accused may be convicted of wounding Smith with intent, even though the accused thought that Smith was someone else or fired at Jones and hit Smith by accident. If a person fires a gun into a group of people without taking particular aim, but intending to harm someone, he may be charged with a s 18 offence against the person whom he hits.

The basic distinction between wounding or causing grievous bodily harm with intent to do grievous bodily harm and attempted murder is that, in the former offences, only an intent unlawfully to do grievous bodily harm is required, while the latter requires an intent unlawfully to kill.

Where the accused is charged with wounding with intent to resist or prevent the lawful apprehension or detainer of any person (whether himself or another), or with causing grievous bodily harm with such intent, 'maliciously' is relevant. It must be proved that the accused intended his conduct to cause *some* unlawful harm to another (or was subjectively reckless as to this occurring), ie that he was 'malicious', *and* that he intended to resist or prevent the lawful apprehension or detainer of himself or another.

Clearly, there is some overlap between the two specified intents. Thus, if an accused strikes a police officer, who is attempting lawfully to arrest him, with an iron bar which causes a serious wound it would be possible to charge him in one of two ways. If it is alleged that the wound was inflicted with the intention of causing grievous bodily harm, then the evidence offered should be to support that intention. It will serve no purpose to offer evidence of intention to resist arrest. However, out of the same circumstances the accused could be charged with wounding the officer with intent to resist his own arrest, and in such a case it would be necessary only to offer evidence of the nature of the wound, that he realised his act of striking the officer might cause some harm and that he struck the officer in order to resist arrest. In the circumstances described, where an iron bar was used to cause the wound, there would probably be little difficulty in proving either charge. If a less formidable weapon was used which nevertheless caused a serious wound, it might be difficult to prove an intention to cause grievous bodily harm. It would be much better to prefer a charge alleging an intention to resist arrest.

Differences between s 18 and s 20

It is interesting to consider the essential differences between offences described in ss 18 and 20. If, during an argument, an accused strikes a person with a stick, causing a cut to his head which requires stitches, there has certainly been a wound which was unlawful, in that it could not legally be excused. Malice was apparent, as the act indicated a decision on the part of the assailant to do some unlawful bodily harm. All the essential points required under s 20 to be proved are therefore capable of proof. If we are to consider whether an offence contrary to s 18 is disclosed, we must ask ourselves if it can be proved that the assailant intended to cause grievous bodily harm when the blow was struck. The surrounding circumstances will help; any words said by the accused at the time, the ferocity of the attack and the nature of the weapon used. If the stick used was light in weight and one blow was struck, this would not support the allegation that the accused intended to cause grievous bodily harm. If the stick was heavy and metal tipped, the blow struck was severe, and it could be shown that the accused shouted an intention to do serious harm to the person injured, then an intention to cause the harm which was actually occasioned could be more easily established.

Finally, an important fact to remember is that 'maliciously' for the purpose of s 20 suggests an awareness, at least, that the act may cause some physical harm to some other person. It is not necessary that an accused should have foreseen physical harm of the gravity described in the section, that is, a wound or serious bodily harm. It is enough that it is foreseen that some harm might result. This would not suffice for s 18; an intention to cause grievous bodily harm must be proved, or an intention to resist etc arrest.

RACIALLY-AGGRAVATED NON-FATAL OFFENCES AGAINST THE PERSON

Section 29 of the Crime and Disorder Act 1998 has introduced the following new offences.

Section 29(1) provides that:

'A person is guilty of an offence under this section if he commits:
(a) an offence under section 20 of the Offences against the Person Act 1861;
(b) an offence under section 47 of that Act;
(c) common assault [or battery];
which is racially aggravated for the purposes of this section.'

Section 29(1) does not create one offence which can be committed in various ways but a number of separate ones.

On a charge of an offence under s 29 of the 1998 Act, the prosecution must prove that the accused has committed one of the relevant specified basic offences and that it (the basic offence) was racially-aggravated.

By s 28(1) of the 1998 Act, any of the specified basic offences is racially-aggravated if:

(a) at the time of committing the offence, or immediately before or after doing so, the offender demonstrates towards the victim of the offence hostility based on the victim's membership (or presumed membership) of a racial group, or

(b) the offence is motivated (wholly or partly) by hostility towards members of a racial group based on their membership of that group.

In s 28(1)(a), 'membership', in relation to a racial group, includes association with members of that group; 'presumed' means presumed by the offender (s 28(2)). 'Racial group' means a group of persons defined by reference to race, colour, nationality (including citizenship) or ethnic or national origins (s 28(4)).

OTHER OFFENCES INVOLVING BODILY INJURY

The Offences against the Person Act 1861 includes other offences which are associated with the causing, or attempted causing, of forms of bodily harm. These offences should be considered when circumstances are presented involving actual or attempted harm to a person. They are concerned with particular ways of inflicting harm.

Attempting to choke etc

This offence, which is provided by s 21, consists of an attempt by the accused, by any means whatsoever, to choke, suffocate or strangle any other person, or an attempt by the accused, by any means calculated to choke, suffocate, or strangle, to render any other person insensible, unconscious or incapable of resistance, with intent in any such case thereby to enable himself or any other person to commit any indictable offence, or with intent to assist another to do so.

The offence is arrestable. The offence differs from those against ss 18 and 20. There needs to be only an attempt to render a person unconscious, or incapable of resistance, with intent to commit any indictable offence. A wound etc is not necessary.

Using chloroform etc to commit an indictable offence

This offence is provided by s 22. There must be an unlawful application or administration to, or causing to be taken by, a person a stupefying or overpowering drug, matter or thing, with intent thereby to enable the accused or another person to commit an indictable offence. This offence is an arrestable offence.

Administering poisons etc so as thereby to endanger life etc or with intent to injure etc

Section 23 provides that a person is guilty of an offence if he unlawfully and maliciously administers to, or causes to be administered to or taken by, any other person any poison, or other destructive or noxious thing, *so as thereby to endanger the life of such person, or so as thereby to inflict upon such person any grievous bodily harm.*

Section 24 provides that a person is guilty of an offence if he unlawfully and maliciously administers to, or causes to be administered to or taken by, any other person any poison, or other destructive or noxious thing, *with intent to injure, aggrieve, or annoy such person.*

Both offences are arrestable.

A 'poison' means a recognised poison, in whatever quantity it may be administered etc; a 'noxious thing' is any other drug or thing which is harmful in the dosage in which it was administered etc. The Court of Appeal has held that the word 'administer' is not limited to the direct physical application of a thing but also covers other ways of bringing a noxious thing into contact with the victim, such as the squirting of ammonia solution at the person. A poison, or other destructive or noxious thing, is caused to be taken if it is left for a person who then drinks it. To leave it for the purpose of it being taken would be to attempt to cause it to be taken. The consent of the person to whom the poison is given is no defence to charges under ss 23 or 24. For example, heroin can be a noxious substance for the purposes of these offences. If a shot of heroin is administered to another with his consent, this will amount to an administration for the purposes of this section.

The distinction between the offences under ss 23 and 24 lies partly in the fact that the offence under s 23 requires the additional element that the administration must be such as thereby to endanger life or to inflict grievous bodily harm, and partly in the fact that the requirement of mens rea is not the same for each offence. The differences between the two offences are shown by the words italicised in the definitions given above.

The mens rea required is as follows. The offence under s 23 requires proof of intention or subjective recklessness in relation to the administration etc of a poison or other destructive or noxious thing and as to the causing of some bodily harm, but not in relation to the second element of the actus reus, the endangering of life or causing grievous bodily harm. In the case of an offence under s 24 not only must an intentional or subjectively reckless administration etc of a poison or other destructive or noxious thing be proved but also an intention to injure, aggrieve or annoy. The intention or subjective recklessness referred to above is what is meant by 'maliciously' in the definitions of the two offences.

Torture

The offence of torture is governed by the Criminal Justice Act 1988, s 134. A public official or person acting in an official capacity, whatever his nationality, commits the offence of torture if in the United Kingdom or elsewhere he intentionally inflicts severe pain or suffering on another in the performance or purported performance of his official duties. A person not acting in such an official capacity commits the offence of torture if he commits such an act at the instigation, or with the consent or acquiescence, of a public official or person acting in that capacity, and the official or other person is performing or purporting to perform his official duties when he instigates the commission of the offence or consents to or acquiesces in it.

It is immaterial whether the pain or suffering is physical or mental and whether it is caused by an act or omission. It is a defence for a person to prove that he had lawful authority, justification or excuse for that conduct.

The consent of the Attorney-General is required for a prosecution in England and Wales for the offence of torture. Police officers will certainly find themselves in situations which expose them to allegations of offences under this section, particularly in view of the inclusion of 'mental' suffering. It is submitted that this offence is not applicable to those situations which might arise in the course of interviews in normal circumstances.

Contamination of goods etc with intent

Section 38(1) of the Public Order Act 1986 provides that it is an offence for a person to contaminate or interfere with goods, or make it appear that goods have been contaminated or interfered with, or to place goods which have been contaminated or interfered with, or which have that appearance, in a place where goods of that description are consumed, used, sold or otherwise supplied, with the intention:

(a) of causing public alarm or anxiety;
(b) of causing injury to members of the public consuming or using the goods;
(c) of causing economic loss to any person by reason of the goods being shunned by members of the public; or
(d) of causing economic loss to any person by reason of steps taken to avoid any such alarm or anxiety, injury or loss.

Section 38(2) makes it an offence for a person to threaten that he or another will do, or claim that he or another has done, any of these acts with such intention as is mentioned in (a), (c) or (d) above. Possession of contaminated goods, apparently contaminated goods, materials with which to contaminate goods or to make it appear that goods have been contaminated, is also an offence.

Thus, the activities of groups, including animal rights groups, calculated to hit at businesses with which they are not in sympathy are made punishable under this section. However, it must be remembered that such activities may also amount to attempts to commit offences (for example, attempted murder, if poisons are placed in foodstuffs with an intention of killing, since the placing of the contaminated goods is more than merely a preparatory act which can amount to an attempt). In addition, if someone actually consumes a contaminated product and suffers harm, there will be liability for the relevant 'full' offence against the person, depending on the degree of harm.

A defence is available to a person who, in good faith, reports or warns that such acts have been, or appear to have been, committed. Thus, the broadcast of a warning received, if carried out in good faith, is excused.

An offence under s 38 is an arrestable offence.

Gunpowder etc offences

The Offences Against the Person Act 1861 creates a number of offences related to the use of explosives.

Section 28 provides that anyone, who unlawfully and maliciously, by the explosion of gunpowder or other explosive substance, *burns, maims, disfigures, disables or does any grievous bodily harm to any person*, is guilty of an offence.

Section 29 provides that anyone, who unlawfully and maliciously causes an explosion, or sends or delivers an explosive substance (or any other dangerous or noxious thing), or places or throws at someone any corrosive fluid or any destructive or explosive substance, *with intent to burn, maim, disfigure, or disable any person, or to do some grievous bodily harm* to any person, is guilty of an offence, whether or not any bodily injury is effected.

Section 30 provides that it is an offence unlawfully and maliciously to place or throw in, into, upon, against or near any building or vessel an explosive substance *with intent to do any bodily injury to any person, whether or not any explosion occurs and whether or not anyone is injured.*

It has been held that a petrol bomb is an explosive substance under s 29, since where a person puts petrol and air into a bottle together with a wick, lights that wick and throws the bottle, an explosion must be caused. This decision is equally applicable to the meaning of 'explosive substance' in ss 28 and 30.

The offences under ss 28, 29, and 30 are arrestable offences.

Clearly, there is a good deal of overlap between the three offences, especially those under ss 28 and 29. The major distinguishing features of each offence is indicated by the words italicised. The basic distinction is that s 28 is concerned with where really serious bodily harm is actually caused by an explosion, while it suffices for s 29 that the accused caused an explosion with intent to cause such harm, whether or not it occurred; in fact, s 29 does not require an explosion to occur since it is also concerned with sending or delivering, or placing or throwing, explosives and certain other substances with such intent. Section 30 does not require anyone to be harmed but it does require the accused to act with the specified intent to do bodily injury (which need not be serious injury).

Section 64 deals with making, manufacturing or knowingly possessing explosive substances or machines, engines, or instruments with intent to commit any offence under the 1861 Act, or to enable others to do so. This is not an arrestable offence.

When circumstances are being considered involving the use of explosives, it must be remembered that offences under the Criminal Damage Act 1971 and the Explosive Substances Act 1883 must also be considered. However, if the bomber etc has the requisite specified intent to cause really serious bodily harm (s 29) or bodily injury (s 30), or actually causes really serious bodily harm (s 28), an offence will always be committed under the 1861 Act.

CHAPTER 29

Disputes

Quite a large part of a police officer's time is spent in advising members of the public of action which they may take in relation to disputes involving them and their spouses, cohabitees, landlords and the like. On occasions it is appropriate to have recourse to the criminal law, but on most occasions the most useful approach may be to put them in touch with one of the various agencies which are equipped to deal with such situations. In many cases civil remedies are available and particularly appropriate. It is important for police officers constantly to be aware that they are what might be described as a front-line agency. Because the police service offers an immediate response throughout 24 hours of the day, police officers will most often be involved in such disputes, or incidents, when they occur or very soon afterwards.

DOMESTIC VIOLENCE

The subject of assaults is considered elsewhere. A woman who has been assaulted by her husband or partner is competent and compellable to give evidence against him in a criminal court in relation to that assault, and may wish to do so. However, it will be appreciated that this is frequently an extremely difficult decision for a wife to make. Many women feel trapped and helpless and, being unable to face up to life on their own, prefer to remain with a husband who treats them badly. In such circumstances they will not wish to give evidence against their husbands because of their fear that this will lead to a final breakdown of the marriage. The social services are experienced in the handling of these situations and will help if the wife will accept such aid.

Where women are being subjected to violence by their husbands or partners, the courts can assist without the necessity for the woman to give evidence against her husband or partner in a criminal court. They can do so by applying for one of the orders under the Family Law Act 1996, described below, which are not limited to proceedings between spouses (or ex-spouses) or cohabitees (or ex-cohabitees).

Non-molestation orders

A non-molestation order is an order containing either or both of the following provisions:

(a) provision prohibiting a person (the respondent) from molesting another person who is associated with the respondent;

(b) provision prohibiting the respondent from molesting a relevant child.

The term 'associated with' is given a wide meaning to include spouses, cohabitees, live-in friends or relatives. A 'relevant child' in relation to such proceedings is any child who is living with or might reasonably be expected to live with either party to the proceedings, or any child in relation to whom an order under the Adoption Act 1976 or the Children Act 1989 is in question in the proceedings, or any other child whose interests the court considers relevant.

Such an order may be made:

(a) on the application (whether in other family proceedings or without any other family proceedings being instituted) of a person who is associated with the respondent; or

(b) during family proceedings to which the respondent is a party, if the court considers that such an order will benefit any other party or a relevant child even though no application has been made.

In deciding whether to make a non-molestation order, the court must consider all the circumstances, including the need to secure the health, safety and well-being of the applicant or person for whose benefit the order would be made and of any relevant child.

A non-molestation order may refer to molestation in general, to particular acts of molestation, or both. It may be made for a specified period, or until a further order is made. An order which is made in other family proceedings ceases to have effect if those proceedings are withdrawn or dismissed.

Ex parte orders

Where it appears to be just and convenient to do so a court may make a non-molestation order even though the party against whom the complaint is made has not been given notice of the proceedings. In such cases, the court must consider:

(a) the risk of significant harm if the order is not made immediately;

(b) whether if such an order is not made the applicant will be deterred or prevented from pursuing the application; and

(c) whether there is reason to believe that the party complained against is aware of the proceedings but is deliberately evading service of the notice and the other applicant, or a relevant child, will be seriously prejudiced by the delay involved in effecting service (or substituted service) of the proceedings.

Where an ex parte order is made, it must afford the person against whom it is made an opportunity to make representations as soon as just and convenient, at a full hearing.

Undertakings

Where a non-molestation order could be made, a court may accept an undertaking from any party to the proceedings. Where such an undertaking is given it is enforceable in the same way as a court order, but no power of arrest may be attached to it. Where a power to arrest appears to be appropriate, an undertaking should not be accepted by a court.

Arrest for breach of non-molestation order

Where it appears that the person against whom a non-molestation order has been made has used or threatened violence against the applicant or a relevant child, the court must attach a power of arrest to one or more provisions of the order unless satisfied that in all the circumstances of the case the applicant or child will be adequately protected without such a power of arrest.

This does not apply where the order is an *ex parte order*, but a court may attach a power of arrest to one or more of the provisions of the order where it appears that violence has been used or threatened *and there is the risk of significant harm to the applicant or to a relevant child, attributable to the conduct of the person complained against, if such power is not attached.* Where such a power is attached, it may be for a shorter period of time than the duration of the order generally, but that shorter period may be extended by the court on one or more occasions upon an application to vary or discharge the order.

The power to arrest may be exercised by a constable. He may arrest without warrant any person whom he has reasonable cause for suspecting to be in breach of the provisions of the order to which the power of arrest is attached. An arrested person must be brought before the relevant judicial authority within the period of 24 hours beginning with the time of his arrest. In reckoning the period of 24 hours, no account is to be taken of Christmas Day, Good Friday or any Sunday. If it is not possible for the judicial authority to deal with that person then it may remand him. If he is remanded on bail, the judicial authority may require him to comply (before release on bail or later) with specified requirements to secure that he does not interfere with witnesses or otherwise obstruct the course of justice.

Breach of non-molestation order where there is no power to arrest

Where breaches occur of the provisions of an order in respect of which no power to arrest has been attached, an applicant may apply for the issue of a warrant to arrest the respondent. Such an application must be on oath and the judicial authority must have reasonable grounds for believing that the respondent has failed to comply with the order.

Rights associated with the matrimonial home

Where domestic disputes occur, regardless of whether or not a non-molestation order has been sought, the issue of occupational rights in relation to the matrimonial home still remains. The Family Law Act 1996 seeks to ensure that all sides to a dispute are protected from eviction.

Where one spouse has no estate, etc

The Family Law Act 1996, s 30 provides that, where one spouse is legally entitled to occupy a dwelling-house and the other spouse has no such legal entitlement, that other spouse has 'matrimonial home rights' which means that:

(a) if that other spouse is in occupation, that spouse has a right not to be evicted or excluded from the dwelling-house or any part of it by the other spouse without the leave of the court under s 33 of the 1996 Act;

(b) if that other spouse is not in occupation, that spouse has a right with the leave of the court under s 33 'to enter and occupy' the dwelling-house.

There is therefore, no lawful way by which one party to a marriage can be removed from the matrimonial home without the circumstances being examined by a court (ie the High Court, a county court or a magistrates' court sitting as a family proceedings court). However, s 59 of the 1996 Act provides that a magistrates' court will not be competent to entertain any application, or make any order, where there is a dispute as to a party's entitlement to occupy property by virtue of beneficial estate, interest or contract or by virtue of any enactment giving him the right to remain in occupation, unless it is unnecessary to determine the question in order to deal with the application or make the order. In any case, a magistrates' court may decline jurisdiction if it considers that the application can more conveniently be dealt with by another court. In addition, a magistrates' court has no power to suspend or rescind orders made under the 1996 Act.

Occupation orders

Section 33 of the 1996 Act provides for the making of an occupation order where the applicant has an estate or interest etc entitling him to occupy a dwelling-house or has matrimonial home rights in it and the dwelling-house is or has been the home of the applicant and of someone else with whom he is associated (or was intended by both such people to be their home). If an occupation order is made it may:

(a) enforce the applicant's occupation rights as against the other person (the respondent);
(b) require the respondent to permit the applicant to enter and remain in that dwelling-house or part of it;
(c) regulate the occupation by both parties;
(d) if the respondent is legally entitled to occupy, prohibit, restrict or suspend the exercise by him of his occupation rights;
(e) if the respondent has matrimonial home rights and the applicant is the other spouse, restrict or terminate those rights;
(f) require the respondent to leave the dwelling-house or part of it; or
(g) exclude the respondent from a defined area in which the dwelling-house is included.

In deciding whether to make an occupation order and (if so) in what manner, the court must have regard to all of the circumstances including the housing needs and housing resources of both parties and any child, the financial resources of both parties, the likely effect of any order (or of a failure to make an order) on the health, safety or well-being of each party and child, and the conduct of the parties in relation to each other and otherwise.

Former spouse, cohabitee and situations in which neither spouse has an entitlement to occupy

The 1996 Act makes similar provisions in relation to former spouses and cohabitees where one of them is legally entitled to occupy a dwelling-house. It also makes provision for circumstances in which neither spouse (or ex-spouse) has a legal entitlement to occupy a dwelling-house which is (or was) the matrimonial home. These provisions are set out in ss 35-38.

Breaches of occupation order

The provisions described above in relation to arrest without warrant also apply to occupation orders where such a power has been attached to the order. 'Undertakings' and 'ex parte orders' may be made in respect of these orders in the same way as in the case of non-molestation orders.

Police action

Arrest for other offences

There are many powers of entry and arrest which are associated with incidents involving domestic violence, bearing in mind that offences of assault occasioning actual bodily harm (an arrestable offence), or more serious offences, may have been committed. The powers which exist at common law in relation to breaches of the peace may also be relevant in the circumstances.

Police action—when contact is first made

When a first contact is made with the police, it should be determined whether immediate response is required or whether there is no immediate danger. Such complaints must be recorded bearing in mind that where a crime is alleged, it should be so recorded. Existing records should be checked to establish whether there is any previous record of incidents involving the complainant. Generally, if the victim claims to have been violently assaulted, reconciliation should not be attempted. A woman police officer should attend such incidents where possible as a woman who has been assaulted may prefer to be dealt with by another woman. Any interview at the time should not take place in the presence of the alleged assailant. However, if a complainant wishes to repeat any allegation in the presence of the alleged assailant, she may do so and any reply made by the assailant should be noted.

If hospital treatment is not required, a victim may be taken to a victim examination suite if one is available. A medical examination by a police surgeon or some other doctor with forensic science training is preferable to examination by her own general practitioner. It is important to ensure that children are adequately cared for throughout this procedure. Other members of the family, or neighbours, may prove to be good witnesses in such cases, particularly where the victim is reluctant to become involved.

In domestic violence cases it is essential that the Crown Prosecution Service is fully informed of the circumstances surrounding the family relationships involved, the domestic circumstances and the likely course of future events including whether there is any likelihood of any lasting reconciliation.

It is important to ensure that victims continue to receive help and guidance in such cases. It may also be necessary to remove the victim to a place of shelter before making long-term arrangements with some other social agency. Some police forces have domestic violence units which specialise in such matters. Where it is necessary for the victim to live elsewhere, the police should assist in taking her to a place of refuge. If she subsequently wishes to visit the home for any reason she should be accompanied by a police officer.

The Secretary of State is currently piloting a scheme within which female victims of domestic violence will be spared court appearances which bring them into contact with their attackers.

Where complainant subsequently withdraws complaint

Where a victim subsequently decides to withdraw her complaint and states that she will be unwilling to give evidence in court she should be asked to make a statement to that effect. This will be taken into account by the Crown Prosecutor who may, but is unlikely in most circumstances, to take steps to compel the complainant to give evidence against her husband.

The Crown Prosecutor will also wish to take into account the views of the officer who recorded that statement concerning the validity of the complainant's reasons and her likely reaction to being compelled to give evidence. Where a victim refuses to give evidence it may be possible to continue the case by offering her statement in evidence in accordance with the Criminal Justice Act 1988, s 23.

EVICTION AND HARASSMENT

It is essential for the law to protect tenants of property. If it were otherwise they would be subject to the risk of instant eviction from the premises at the whim of a landlord, or to the risk of extreme measures to ensure that they left the property, such as shutting off the essential services to the dwelling house.

Police officers frequently become involved in disputes concerning landlords and tenants and, although they are usually called to prevent a breach of the peace, it is essential that the correct advice is given to both parties. Personal sympathies must be set aside and a clear explanation of the legal position must be provided together with advice concerning the agencies which may be approached to assist in resolving the dispute.

The Protection from Eviction Act 1977, s 1 provides two offences whose aim is to protect tenants: the offences of eviction and of harassment. The Act specifically authorises district councils to institute proceedings for these offences. Both offences use the term 'residential occupier' and this must first be explained.

A 'residential occupier', in relation to any premises, means a person occupying the premises as a residence, whether under a contract or by virtue of any enactment or rule of law giving him the right to remain in occupation or restricting the right of any other person to recover possession of the premises. Therefore, a tenant, or even a lodger who is living in a furnished room under an agreement with the owner, is a residential occupier. However, a person who hires a room for a short period of time is not a residential occupier. This is fortunate, because otherwise landladies who offered holiday accommodation would be unable to repossess rooms to meet their obligations towards successive visitors. The issue is best resolved by common sense; could the accommodation in question be properly described as the person's residence?

Eviction

Section 1(2) of the 1977 Act provides:

'If any person unlawfully deprives the residential occupier of any premises of his occupation of the premises or any part thereof, or attempts to do so, he shall be guilty of an offence unless he proves that he believed, and had reasonable cause to believe, that the residential occupier had ceased to reside in the premises.'

The manner in which the residential occupier is unlawfully deprived of his occupation is unimportant as any unlawful method will constitute an offence. It is not necessary that any form of violence or intimidation is used, it would be sufficient if the residential occupier was tricked into leaving so that the owner could regain occupation, or that the owner entered by stealth during the residential occupier's absence. The offence requires something in the nature of an eviction. The deprivation of occupation need not be permanent. Consequently, a person who unlawfully excludes a residential occupier from his premises, intending the exclusion to be permanent, can be convicted under s 1(2) even though he repents almost immediately and lets the occupier back in.

An offence is committed by any person who unlawfully deprives, or attempts to deprive, a residential occupier of his premises. The commission of the offence is not restricted to the owner or any person having an interest in the property; it can be committed by anyone and this is meant to prevent the use of other persons to apply pressure in an attempt to dispossess. The only defence is one of reasonable belief that the residential occupier has ceased to reside in the premises.

Harassment

Section 1(3) of the Act deals with harassment and provides:

'If any person with intent to cause the residential occupier of any premises—
(a) to give up the occupation of the premises or any part thereof; or
(b) to refrain from exercising any right or pursuing any remedy in respect of the premises or part thereof;
does any act calculated to interfere with the peace or comfort of the residential occupier or members of his household, or persistently withdraws or withholds services reasonably required for the occupation of the premises as a residence, he shall be guilty of an offence.'

The subsection is therefore concerned with persons who, with the requisite intent, either do some act likely to interfere with the peace or comfort of the residential occupier etc or persistently withdraw services. The actus reus may, therefore, consist of any act, such as intimidation, threats, or even interference with the building, perhaps by removing window frames or doors on the pretence that they are to be replaced. Alternatively it can consist of a lack of action which results in services reasonably required for the occupation of the premises being persistently withdrawn or withheld. This would be so if the landlord failed to pay for essential services to the building or part of the building occupied by the tenant. The use of the word 'persistently' which is used as an adverb to both 'withdraws' and 'withholds' indicates that this must be done for some period of time before those services could be reasonably described as having been persistently withdrawn or withheld.

The intention must be to cause a *residential occupier* to give up permanently occupation of the premises or to refrain from exercising any right or pursuing any remedy in respect of the premises or part of them. This offence therefore cannot be committed in relation to squatters who are in occupation of premises without agreement or any form of residential status.

Where an act likely to interfere with the peace or comfort of the residential occupier or members of his household is carried out with intent to cause the residential occupier *to give up occupation*, it is irrelevant that the act in question is not wrongful in civil law. This was stated by the House of Lords in a case where it held that a landlord who had disconnected a tenant's doorbell could be convicted of an offence under s 1(3), even though the tenant was not entitled under his tenancy agreement to a front door bell (so that the disconnection was not a civil wrong).

The fact that the offence under s 1(3) requires proof of the requisite intention means that proof of the offence may not always be easy. Consequently, s 1(3A) provides that the landlord of a residential occupier or an agent of the landlord commits an offence if he does acts likely to interfere with the peace or comfort of the residential occupier or members of his family, or if he persistently withdraws or withholds services reasonably required for the occupation of the premises, and (in either case) *he knows or has reasonable cause to believe that that conduct is likely to cause* the residential occupier to give up occupation of the whole or part of the premises or to refrain from exercising any right or pursuing any remedy in respect of the whole or any part of the premises. By s 1(3B), a person is not guilty under s 1(3A) if he proves that he had reasonable grounds for doing the acts or withdrawing or withholding the services in question.

Caravans: eviction and harassment

The Caravan Sites Act 1968 makes similar provisions in relation to residential caravans on 'protected sites'.

It is an offence for any person unlawfully to deprive the occupier of his occupation on a protected site of any caravan which the occupier is entitled by the contract to station and occupy, or to occupy, as his residence on that site, if this deprivation occurs during the subsistence of a residential contract.

Moreover, even after a residential contract has expired or been ended, it is an offence for a person to enforce, otherwise than by court proceedings, a right to exclude the occupier from the protected site or from any such caravan, or to remove or exclude the caravan from the site.

The offences of harassment also apply to caravans on protected sites and the acts forbidden in relation to other tenancies are forbidden in relation to caravans both during or after a residential contract, if they are done with intent to cause the occupier to abandon occupation of the caravan or remove it from the site or to refrain from exercising rights or remedies.

A 'protected site' is:

(a) any land in respect of which a site licence is required under the Caravan Sites and Control of Development Act 1960, Part I; or
(b) any land occupied by a local authority and therefore exempt from the necessity of becoming so licensed.

The term 'protected site' does not extend to those which are for holiday use only or are part-time sites.

The term 'the occupier' for the purposes of the Act includes a person who was the occupier within the terms of a residential contract which has expired or been terminated. In the event of the death of the occupier, the widow or widower of that person (provided they were then residing together) or, in default, any member of the occupier's family (if then residing with the occupier) is 'the occupier'.

There is a defence available to a person if he proves that he believed and had reasonable cause to believe that the occupier of the caravan had ceased to reside on the site. This could occur when an occupier left for an extended period without informing the owner and without paying his rent. It would be reasonable for an owner after a period of time to form the belief that such a person had left without paying and without the intention of returning.

Police action

The primary duty of police officers will always be the prevention of a breach of the peace. When allegations are made concerning a dispute affecting a landlord and tenant a police officer should make all inquiries which are possible at that time at the scene of the dispute. If it appears that there may have been an offence in relation to the provisions outlined above in respect of dwellings or caravans, the officer should explain the provisions to the landlord and should warn him of the possibility of prosecution. However, whether or not such a warning is issued at the time, a comprehensive report of the circumstances should be sent to the local housing authority immediately. In appropriate cases, the police should inform the complainant in writing that the complaint has been referred to the housing authority.

Homelessness

The Housing Act 1985, Part III places obligations upon housing authorities and requires them to give help to homeless people. A housing authority must make appropriate inquiries into an application from a person for assistance with accommodation. If they have reason to believe that such a person is homeless or is threatened with becoming homeless, they must make further inquiries concerning the priority of his need and to establish whether or not his predicament was brought about intentionally (since, if it was, he is not entitled to permanent—as opposed to temporary —accommodation).

The authority have a duty to place such persons in accommodation while they make these inquiries if they believe that such a person has a priority need. Persons who are apparently homeless and seek advice from police officers should therefore be referred to the local housing authority, whether or not the persons concerned have been previously resident in that area. The authority are permitted to make inquiries with the housing authority of an area in which such persons have previously resided, should they wish to do so.

CHAPTER 30

Homicide and abortion

The term 'homicide' means the killing of a human being by a human being and when expressed in this all embracing way does not attempt to differentiate between those which are unlawful and those which are not. Offences of homicide are categorised as follows: murder, manslaughter, infanticide, causing death by careless driving while under the influence of drink or drugs and causing death by dangerous driving. Some acts which are carried out in emergencies to prevent violence, either in the commission of crime or against the person, may be sufficiently excusable to escape the criminal law.

The various offences of homicide are all arrestable offences.

MURDER

Murder continues to be a common law offence. It is defined as follows:

> 'The crime of murder is committed where a person of sound mind and discretion unlawfully kills any reasonable creature in being, and under the Queen's peace, with intent unlawfully to kill or cause grievous bodily harm.'

In three types of exceptional case a person is not guilty of murder, even though the definition of that offence is satisfied. Those exceptions are where the accused has the defence of provocation, where the accused suffered from diminished responsibility, or where the person was acting in pursuance of a suicide pact. If any of these defences is successful, the accused is guilty of voluntary manslaughter rather than murder.

The definition of murder is made up of a number of words or phrases, each of which requires explanation. With the exception of the reference to the accused's intent, the terms of the definition of murder also apply to involuntary manslaughter which is discussed later in this chapter.

Person of sound mind and discretion

This phrase is really redundant. It simply refers to the general rule that a person is not legally liable if he is excused from liability under the rules relating to the liability of those who are insane or who are under 10 (the age of criminal responsibility).

We discussed the defence of insanity in ch 1.

Unlawfully

A killing is unlawful unless it falls within one of the following categories:

Prevention of crime or effecting arrest

The Criminal Law Act 1967, s 3 provides that it is lawful to use such force as is *reasonable* in the circumstances in the prevention of crime or in effecting (or assisting in) the lawful arrest of offenders, suspected offenders or persons lawfully at large. It follows that a police officer who accidentally causes the death of someone whom he is lawfully arresting is not guilty of manslaughter, let alone murder, provided that the force used by him was reasonable in the circumstances as he believed them to be (including the degree of resistance offered by the deceased).

Self-defence and defence of another or of property

Self-defence and defence of another or of property are common law defences, and they render a killing lawful. However, a person who acts in defence of himself, or of another or of property, is invariably acting in the prevention of crime, in which case he also has the defence under the Criminal Law Act 1967, s 3. For practical purposes, the terms of both the common law and the statutory defences are identical in their requirements since the crucial question in the common law defences is also whether the force used was *reasonable* in the circumstances as the accused believed them to be. We have explained this in more detail in ch 28, above. A police officer who shoots an armed terrorist who is shooting at him (or someone else) would clearly be using reasonable force, assuming that there is no other way of preventing the terrorist continuing to fire, and he can successfully plead the statutory defence of prevention of crime or the common law defence of self-defence (or defence of another).

Misadventure

Death is caused by misadventure where the killing is not murder, manslaughter, infanticide or causing death by dangerous driving. As an example, if a patient dies as a result of a lawful operation carried out by a surgeon with proper care, the killing is by misadventure, and so not unlawful, and therefore the surgeon is not guilty of any offence of homicide.

Kills

Generally, some form of action is required which proves to be a substantial cause of death. However, 'substantial' in this context simply means 'more than minimal'. Although generally some 'act' is required, if the accused is under a legally recognised duty to act (as where a parent or similar person has the care of a child or helpless person), and fails to act, that failure being a substantial cause of death, he may be convicted of an offence of homicide. Normally the contribution to the death of an act will be easily proved, for example shooting, stabbing, pushing over a cliff, or violently assaulting, a person with fatal consequences, but the act does not need to be so violent nor so obviously connected with the death. Thieves who lock bank staff in a sealed, air-tight vault to secure their escape without an alarm being raised kill their victims as surely as they would by any direct act. A person who steals the food and water left to sustain an injured man who is lost on the fells, whilst his companion seeks assistance, kills that man if he dies from the lack of sustenance, even though the man is not touched in any direct way. If someone deliberately tells a shocking lie to a person suffering from a serious heart condition, his act may kill that person although there is no hostile touching.

If the original act of the accused was a substantial cause of death it does not matter that some other intervening act or event finally caused the death, provided that that intervening act or event was likely to occur. The clearest example of this is where the accused threatens someone who takes evasive action and is killed in doing so, as where a woman jumps out of a first floor window to avoid rape. Provided that evasive action is likely, the threatened act will be a cause of death if it was a substantial cause (as almost inevitably it will be). Another example is where an assailant causes such serious injuries to his victim that the victim can only be kept alive by a life support machine. If, subsequently, because there is no hope of recovery, doctors switch off that machine, the assailant has still killed that person as his act was a substantial cause of death. Even where negligence in the treatment of a victim was the immediate cause of death, this does not exclude the responsibility of the accused, unless the negligent treatment was so independent of his acts and itself so potent in causing death that the accused's contribution was insignificant. In one case a man in attempting to evade arrest snatched a girl in front of him as he fired at police officers. The officers fired back instinctively, killing the girl. Although the officers' act resulted in the girl's death, it was held that the man's act was in law a cause of the girl's death because the officers' reaction was a likely one and the man's act had been a substantial cause of the death. On the other hand, if two men (A and B) fight in a park and A leaves B unconscious but not seriously hurt and B is later killed by a tree which falls upon him when it is blown down by a gale, the fact that the fall of the tree was unlikely means that A's act is not regarded in law as a cause of B's death.

If an act is committed which leads to death, it is legally immaterial that the person injured refused medical treatment. Where a girl was stabbed by an assailant and refused a blood transfusion and died, the act of her attacker was held to be a cause of the killing. A person who commits violent acts likely to lead to the death of his victim must take his victim as he finds him. If the victim's beliefs prevent him from taking actions which might save his life the accused cannot claim successfully that he was not responsible for the death which results.

Reasonable creature in being

Any human being, however deformed or subnormal, is a 'reasonable creature in being' and therefore protected by the law of homicide, provided that it is 'in being' at the material time.

This raises the question of the point of time at which a foetus becomes a human being and therefore a 'reasonable creature in being'. To be a reasonable creature in being a child must have completely emerged into the world and have a separate existence from its mother. To have had that separate existence it is not essential that the cord has been severed or even that the after birth has been expelled, but it must have breathed.

The wilful destruction of a child capable of being born alive before it is born alive may amount to the offence of child destruction, while the intentional procuring of a miscarriage may constitute the offence of abortion; we discuss these offences later in this chapter. If someone injures a pregnant woman, and as a result of the attack she goes into premature labour and her child, although born alive, subsequently dies owing to its prematurity, the assailant is guilty of manslaughter but cannot be convicted of murder despite the fact that he intended to kill the woman or seriously harm her. It would make no difference that he intended also to destroy the foetus in the womb because such an intent does not suffice for murder.

Under the Queen's peace

For the purposes of murder, all persons are under the Queen's peace whether they are Her Majesty's subjects or not. The only persons who are not under the Queen's peace are alien enemies (and possibly rebel subjects) in the actual heat and exercise of war. However, while it is not murder to kill an alien enemy in battle, it is murder intentionally to kill an alien enemy in other circumstances (as when he is a prisoner of war).

When did death occur in relation to the act which caused it?

An offence of homicide may be committed by a person who carries out an appropriate act with the necessary mens rea regardless of the time which has passed since the injury etc was inflicted. However, where the injury alleged to have caused the death was sustained more than three years before the death occurred, or where the person whom it is intended to prosecute for an offence of homicide has already been convicted of an offence in circumstances alleged to be connected with the death, no prosecution for an offence of homicide may be brought without the consent of the Attorney-General.

With intent unlawfully to kill or cause grievous bodily harm

The mens rea required for murder is an intent unlawfully to kill another human being or unlawfully to cause grievous bodily harm to another human being. This is described as 'malice aforethought'. To apply the term 'malice' strictly to the offence of murder can be misleading. The killing itself need not be such that it would normally attract the description 'malicious'; it may even be compassionate, as when a person kills a close relative, who is suffering considerably in the final stages of an incurable illness, by means of a drug overdose. In addition, the word 'aforethought' is also misleading because it suggests that the killing must have been premeditated, which is certainly not a legal requirement. Provided that the accused's fatal act was done with intent unlawfully to kill or cause grievous bodily harm, it is irrelevant that he acted on the spur of the moment, the intention only being formed a brief second before the killing. A person who intends to kill or cause grievous bodily harm will not intend to do so unlawfully if on the facts, as he believes them, his use of force is reasonable to prevent crime, effect an arrest or in self-defence.

Provided that the accused intended unlawfully to kill or cause grievous bodily harm to another human being he is guilty of murder, even though the person whom he killed was not the intended victim. Thus if A fires at B, intending to kill him, but misses and kills C, A is guilty of murder.

MANSLAUGHTER

Manslaughter is a term which covers a variety of unlawful homicides which do not amount to murder. For ease of understanding of the offences of manslaughter, it is better to divide the offence into two varieties, voluntary and involuntary manslaughter.

VOLUNTARY MANSLAUGHTER

Voluntary manslaughters embody all the characteristics of murder including the necessary malice aforethought. It is the presence of particular circumstances acting upon the mind of the person carrying out the fatal act, which has the effect of reducing the nature of the crime. At common law extreme provocation, acting upon the person at the time, lessened his blameworthiness. Hot blooded killings were less offensive to society than cold blooded killings. The Homicide Act 1957 added two further circumstances in which blame might be lessened; first, where the person was suffering from 'diminished responsibility' at the time of his fatal act or omission, and, second, where a killing occurred in consequence of a suicide pact.

Provocation

Provocation is not a defence to any charge other than murder, not even to attempted murder. It is quite distinct from the defence of self-defence, and is based on a sudden loss of self-control in circumstances where the accused may not entertain any belief that he is in danger.

The common law defence of provocation was extensively amended by the Homicide Act 1957, s 3. The present law can be stated as follows:

Provocation can be by acts or words, or a combination of acts or words, and the defence can apply even though the provocative conduct came from someone other than the person killed. Thus, a person who is provoked by grossly insulting words uttered by A and, having lost self-control, attacks A and his companion, B, killing B but not A, may have the defence of provocation. A person may have the defence of provocation even though the provocative conduct was directed at somebody other than himself. Lastly, a person may have the defence of provocation even though the provocative conduct is a reaction to something which he has done, as where the accused's conduct in blackmailing X leads X to provoke him by taunts about his sexual inclinations.

The test of whether the defence of provocation is entitled to succeed is a dual one. The first test is that the alleged provocative conduct must have actually caused in the accused a sudden and temporary loss of self-control as the result of which he killed the deceased; the loss of self-control must have been to such a degree that the accused was for the moment not master of his mind. It must be emphasised that such a loss of self-control must be sudden (although it need not follow immediately after the provocative conduct); the defence of provocation is not open where a killing contains an element of deliberation or premeditation. Because the loss of self-control need not be immediate, the defence of provocation may be available to a 'battered wife' who undergoes a 'slow-burn' (rather than immediate) reaction to the final incident in a protracted series of violence and kills her husband while deprived of the power of reflection.

The second test is that the provocative conduct must be such as might have caused a reasonable man suddenly and temporarily to lose his self-control and to do as the accused did. In applying this test, the reasonable man is a person with the power of self-control of an ordinary person of the same age and sex as the accused, and with such other characteristics (other than exceptional excitability) as would affect the gravity of the provocation to the accused or would affect his power of self-control. Exceptional excitability, pugnacity or intoxication are not characteristics which can be attributed to the reasonable man. Thus, if a person of Chinese origin who is highly sensitive about being a dwarf and who is also drunk is provoked by a grossly insulting remark about his lack of height, the reasonable man test is applied on the basis of whether a reasonable man of the accused's age who was a dwarf and who was sensitive about this, these characteristics being ones which would affect the gravity of the provocation to the accused, would have been provoked. The reasonable man would not be invested with the characteristic of Chinese origin (since this would not affect the gravity of the provocation on the facts of the case) nor with the accused's drunkenness (since this is not a 'characteristic' which can be attributed). It is not enough simply that a reasonable man would have been provoked, since the test also requires that the reasonable man (as defined) would have been provoked to do as the accused did.

The accused does not have to prove to the jury's satisfaction that both tests are satisfied. The Homicide Act 1957, s 3 provides that if, but only if, there is *evidence* on which the jury can find that the accused was provoked to lose his self-control, the judge must leave the defence to the jury. If the defence is left to the jury, the accused must be acquitted of murder and convicted of manslaughter unless the prosecution proves to the jury that one or other or both of the two tests is not satisfied.

For operational purposes, the question of provocation does not affect the action taken by the police officers as it can only be settled at the trial for murder.

Diminished responsibility

The Homicide Act 1957, s 2 provides that where a person kills, or is party to the killing of another, he shall not be convicted of murder if he was suffering from such abnormality of mind (whether arising from a condition of arrested or retarded development of mind or any inherent causes or induced by disease or injury) as substantially impaired his mental responsibility for his acts and omissions in doing or being party to the killing. These are matters for the defence to prove. If proved they will have the effect of reducing murder to manslaughter on the part of the person so affected, but will not affect the liability of other parties to the crime.

'Abnormality of mind' indicates a state of mind so different from that of the ordinary human being that the ordinary man would describe it as abnormal. For this purpose, a person's 'mind' includes his mental ability to control his physical acts in accordance with his judgments, as well as his ability to make rational judgments. The questions of both judgment and will-power therefore arise. It may be that an accused knew that his acts were wrong but some abnormality of mind prevented him from repressing his urge to kill.

For the defence to succeed, the abnormality of mind must have resulted from one of the specified causes, ie, it must result from a condition of arrested or retarded development of mind or any inherent causes or be induced by disease or injury. Thus, abnormality of mind due to hate, jealousy or intoxication is outside the defence. However, an abnormality of mind would be due to a specified cause (disease or injury), if due to alcoholism of such a degree that *either* the brain had been injured so that there was gross impairment of judgment and emotional response *or*, where the brain had not been damaged to that extent, the drinking was involuntary in that the accused was unable to resist the impulse to take the first drink.

The last requirement for the defence to succeed is that the abnormality of mind must have substantially impaired the accused's mental responsibility for his conduct. This requirement is concerned with the extent to which the accused's mind was answerable for his conduct. Whether there was a substantial impairment in this sense is a question of degree; the impairment need not be total but it must be more than trivial or minimal.

Suicide pacts

The Homicide Act 1957, s 4, as amended by the Suicide Act 1961, declares that it is manslaughter, and not murder, for a person to kill another or be party to someone else killing another, if he was acting in pursuance of a suicide pact between himself and the person killed. This is a matter for the defence to prove on a charge of murder.

A 'suicide pact' is a common agreement between two or more persons, having for its object the death of them all, whether or not each is to take his own life. Nothing done by a person entering into a suicide pact may be treated as in pursuance of such a pact unless it is done while he has the settled intention of dying in pursuance of the pact.

A related offence is that of aiding and abetting another's suicide contrary to the Suicide Act 1961, s 2, which provides that a person who aids, abets, counsels or procures the suicide of another, or an attempt by another to commit suicide, commits an offence.

Although there is little difference between the offence of manslaughter and that of aiding and abetting suicide, it must be remembered that one essential difference is that in the case of manslaughter we are considering the survivor of a suicide pact. There is no mention of this in relation to the offence under the Suicide Act 1961, s 2. The person aiding, abetting, counselling or procuring an offence does not need to be a partner in a pact. The offence is aiding etc another to commit suicide (or to attempt to commit suicide). The fact that this offence can be committed even though the suicide attempt fails marks another distinction between the offences.

In some cases the distinction between the two offences is clear. If X and Y make a suicide pact under which X is to shoot Y and then himself and, having shot Y, X is prevented from shooting himself, his liability is for manslaughter under s 4 of the 1957 Act; there is no question of aiding and abetting suicide. Conversely, if M gives N a lethal poison which N then takes, there being no suicide pact, M's liability is clearly only for the offence of aiding and abetting suicide. The difficulty arises in a case where two or more people have agreed to die, and one, at least, of them survives, and it is not clear exactly who did what. A good example is the case of a couple who try to asphyxiate themselves with fumes in a car. They are both found in the back seat, one is alive and the other dead. The survivor will be guilty of manslaughter under s 4 of the 1957 Act if he took the necessary steps (in whole or part) to kill the deceased but only of aiding and abetting suicide if those steps were taken wholly by the deceased. Proving who did what can be difficult.

INVOLUNTARY MANSLAUGHTER

This category covers cases where the accused, who has unlawfully killed another (ie has committed the actus reus of murder), is not guilty of murder because he lacked malice aforethought (ie an intent unlawfully to kill or cause grievous bodily harm) but acted with some lesser degree of mens rea.

There are three types of involuntary manslaughter:

(a) killing by gross negligence;
(b) killing with subjective recklessness as to death or bodily harm;
(c) killing by an unlawful and dangerous act.

Killing by gross negligence

This type of manslaughter may be committed by an act or by a failure to act (if the accused has failed in breach of a legal obligation to do an act); it is irrelevant whether or not the accused's act or omission would have constituted an offence if death had not resulted.

The requirements of manslaughter by gross negligence are:

(a) the existence of a duty of care, ie not to act in way which puts another in peril (unless there is a legally acceptable excuse for doing so) or, as the case may be, not to fail to do an act which one is under a legally recognised duty to do;
(b) a gross breach of duty. Normally, proof of negligence simply involves proof that, whether or not he realised the risk (of which he should have been aware) the person subject to the duty did something, or failed to do something, in a way which fell below the standard of conduct expected of a reasonable person in all the circumstances (including the defendant's expertise and training, if they are relevant in the context). This is not enough in the case of gross negligence. For there to be gross negligence, the accused's conduct must have involved a risk of death to another and in respect of that risk his conduct must have fallen so far below the standard to be expected of a reasonable person, ie be so bad that it should be judged criminal;
(c) the breach must cause death. This simply repeats the requirement of causation which applies to offences of homicide generally.

Killing with subjective recklessness as to death or bodily harm

A person is subjectively reckless as to a risk if he himself foresees that risk as a possible consequence of his conduct and he takes that risk, and in all circumstances it is unreasonable for him to do so.

The present type of involuntary manslaughter will often overlap with constructive manslaughter (referred to below) and manslaughter by gross negligence, but it will not do so where the fatal act is not otherwise unlawful and there is no risk of death.

Killing by an unlawful and dangerous act

This mode of committing manslaughter is commonly known as 'constructive manslaughter'. It cannot be committed by an omission to act; an unlawful act by the accused is required. Two elements must be proved by the prosecution:

(a) *that the accused has committed the actus reus of an offence (other than homicide) with the mens rea required for that offence*; proof of this is proof of the 'unlawful act'. In most cases the offence will be a battery, but constructive manslaughter is certainly not limited to that offence although dangerous driving or careless driving which results in death can never constitute constructive manslaughter;

(b) *that the unlawful act was dangerous*, in the sense that all sober and reasonable people would inevitably recognise that the unlawful act must subject another person to the risk of some harm, albeit not serious harm.

This test is applied on the basis of the facts known to the accused at the time of his unlawful act or, if the act continues over a period of time, which became known during that period. Suppose that a burglar, being confronted by the householder and becoming aware that the householder is old and physically frail, continues his burglarious trespass. If the householder suffers a heart attack and dies in consequence of that trespass and on the facts which became known to the accused all sober and reasonable people would inevitably recognise that his burglarious trespass must subject the householder to the risk of some harm, the burglar is guilty of manslaughter.

INFANTICIDE

The offence of infanticide arose out of a desire to separate certain acts committed by a disturbed mother, who had recently given birth to a child, from the general rules associated with the common law offence of murder. The Infanticide Act 1938, s 1 states that where a woman by any wilful act or omission causes the death of her child, being a child under the age of 12 months, but at the time of that act or omission the balance of her mind was disturbed by reason of not having fully recovered from the effect of giving birth to the child, or by reason of the effect of lactation consequent on the birth of her child, then the offence, regardless of other circumstances, is infanticide rather than murder. If the Infanticide Act had not dealt with these special circumstances the vast majority of the cases within the Act would constitute manslaughter by reason of diminished responsibility in any case. The basis of the law on infanticide is that depression after childbirth, or the effect of breast feeding a child, are factors which can cause a mother to act out of character by committing some wilful act, or omitting to do something which a caring mother would do, that act or omission leading to the death of a child. The Infanticide Act only refers to children under the age of 12 months and this is not surprising, as Parliament had in mind a nursing mother who, in a fit of depression, killed the child which she was nursing. However, it leads to problems when such a mother kills more than one of her children, the other being over the age of 12 months. A charge of infanticide will lie in respect of the child who is under the age of 12 months and one of murder in respect of the child who is over the age of 12 months. However, the defence of diminished responsibility would normally be available to the mother in respect of the killing of the older child.

While infanticide may be charged as an offence in the first instance, it may alternatively be raised as a defence to a charge of murder.

THREATS TO KILL

By the Offences Against the Person Act 1861, s 16, it is an arrestable offence for any person, without lawful excuse, to make to another person a threat to kill that other or a third person, intending that that other person would fear that it would be carried out. The substance of this offence is therefore quite straightforward. An unborn child is not 'another person' for the purposes of this section.

It is not necessary that the person making the threat intends to kill. If a man writes or telephones to another and says that he is a member of a terrorist group and that the group intends to kill that person or someone else, the offence is complete if the person making the threat intends that the person receiving the message should fear that the threat will be carried out. Whether or not the accused is a member of that organisation is immaterial. However, if a similar telephone call was made by a man to his friend as an intended joke, and he admitted at the end of the call that it was a joke, this would be clear evidence that the accused had not intended that it be taken seriously.

Threats uttered in self-defence can amount to lawful excuse provided that it is reasonable in the circumstances to make such threats. A householder, who, hearing a burglar in his house, arms himself with a gun and is subsequently threatened with a crowbar by the burglar, may reasonably request that burglar to halt by threatening to shoot him if he does not. He makes that threat in self-defence.

SOLICITING ANOTHER TO COMMIT MURDER

It is an arrestable offence contrary to the Offences Against the Person Act 1861, s 4 for a person to solicit, encourage, persuade or endeavour to persuade or propose to any person, to murder any other person. There must be some form of communication and this may be in any form. It is not essential that the person solicited etc was affected by the communication.

CHILD DESTRUCTION

The common law offence of murder requires the killing of a 'reasonable creature in being' and this left a gap in the law where a child was yet unborn. It was therefore necessary to protect unborn children, and this is now done by the statutory offences of child destruction and abortion. The offence of child destruction is associated with those unborn children who are capable of being born alive.

The Infant Life (Preservation) Act 1929 is concerned with persons who, with intent to destroy the life of a child capable of being born alive, by any wilful act, cause a child to die before it has an existence independent of its mother. There is a proviso to the offence, namely that a person is not guilty of it unless it is proved by the prosecution that the accused did not act in good faith for the purpose only of preserving the life of the mother. This proviso has been construed by the judges as including acting to preserve the mother's physical or mental health. In addition, the Abortion Act 1967, s 5(1) provides that no offence under the 1929 Act is committed by a registered medical practitioner who terminates a pregnancy in accordance with the provisions of the 1967 Act, which we explain on p 602.

The offence is concerned with 'wilful acts' and there must be some positive action on the part of the person charged, such as strangling a baby as it emerges from its mother. The wilful act must be done with the intention of destroying the life of a child 'capable of being born alive'. 'Capable of being born alive' means capable of being alive at the time when the act was done. A child is capable of being born alive when it has reached a state of development in the womb in which it is capable, if born then, of living and breathing through its own lungs without any connection with its mother. The Act provides a presumption that a child is capable of being born alive at any time after the 28th week of pregnancy. However, the offence can be committed in relation to a younger child if it is proved that it was capable of being born alive.

Perhaps this offence is best understood by examining extreme circumstances. If a man deliberately shoots his pregnant girlfriend in the stomach, her child having developed beyond seven lunar months and the child is born dead, the man will be guilty of child destruction. The act was wilful, he intended to destroy the life of a child capable of being born alive and the child died without having had a separate existence. However, if the child had been born alive and had died after having an existence independent of its mother, the man would be guilty of murder.

Child destruction is an arrestable offence.

ABORTION

The offence commonly known as abortion is somewhat misleadingly described in this way, because the relevant offence does not require the abortion (miscarriage) of a foetus but merely that one of a number of specified acts should be done with intent to procure a miscarriage (whether or not it occurs). However, for convenience, we shall describe the offence as abortion hereafter.

It may be the pregnant woman who acts to end her pregnancy and the law deals with this situation. The actual acts carried out with the intention to procure an abortion may be carried out by someone else and that is a separate issue. There is also the question of the criminal liability of any person who knowingly supplies the means to bring about an abortion.

The woman herself

The Offences Against the Person Act 1861, s 58 states that it is an offence for a woman, being with child and with intent to procure her own miscarriage, unlawfully to administer to herself any poison or other noxious thing, or unlawfully to use any instrument or other means whatsoever.

There are several points to be proved within this offence. In the first instance the section provides that the woman must be pregnant if she is charged with abortion upon herself, it is not sufficient for her to imagine that she is pregnant. There are a number of means by which the offence can be committed. She may take (or unlawfully administer to herself, as the section describes it) any poison or other noxious thing. 'Poison' has been defined as a recognised poison. If such a thing is taken etc, it is irrelevant that the quantity is too small to cause harm. The term 'noxious thing' means any substance, other than a recognised poison, which is harmful in the dosage in which it was administered even though it might be harmless in smaller quantities. Clearly 'noxious thing' is a wide term; even certain forms of oil used in cooking and some forms of soap can be harmful in a given dosage. If a dosage is insufficient to render a substance a noxious thing, although the accused believes it is, there can be a conviction for an attempt to commit an offence under s 58. The term 'instrument' would cover the range of surgical instruments usually associated with medical operations and also the instruments used by the back street abortionist, such as knitting needles. The term 'other means whatsoever' embraces any other way in which a person may seek to bring about an abortion, such as manual manipulation with the fingers. These comments concerning the nature of substances and instruments are equally valid in relation to this offence when carried out by some other person.

If X urges a woman to take something to procure a miscarriage, X can be convicted of incitement, and this is so even though that thing (unknown to X) was harmless and incapable of causing a miscarriage.

Any other person

Section 58 goes on to provide that anyone (other than the woman herself) who, with intent to procure the miscarriage of any woman, unlawfully administers to her, or causes to be taken by her, any poison or other noxious thing, or who, with the same intent, unlawfully uses any instrument or other means whatsoever commits an offence, *whether or not the woman is pregnant*. The words italicised indicate an important distinction between the offence committed by the woman herself and the offence committed by other persons.

This offence is concerned with the abortionist in the generally accepted sense of the word.

Unlawfully: the effect of the Abortion Act 1967

By the Abortion Act 1967, s 5(2), anything done with intent to procure a woman's miscarriage (or, in the case of a woman carrying more than one foetus, her miscarriage of any foetus) is unlawfully done unless authorised by s 1 of the 1967 Act.

The Act legalises abortions (including abortion operations which are unsuccessful or not completed) carried out by a registered medical practitioner in prescribed circumstances. In order for an abortion to be lawful under the Act two registered medical practitioners must in good faith be of the opinion that:

(a) the pregnancy has not exceeded its twenty-fourth week and that the continuance of the pregnancy would involve risk, greater than if the pregnancy was terminated, of injury to the physical or mental health of the pregnant woman or any existing children of her family (a question in the determination of which account may be taken of the mother's actual or reasonably foreseeable environment); or

(b) the termination is necessary to prevent *grave* permanent injury to the physical or mental health of the pregnant woman (a question in the determination of which account may be taken of the woman's actual or reasonably foreseeable environment); or

(c) the continuance of the pregnancy would involve risk to the life of the pregnant woman, greater than if the pregnancy was terminated; or

(d) there is a substantial risk that if the child were born it would suffer from such physical or mental abnormalities as to be seriously handicapped.

In order to be lawful, such an abortion must be carried out in a NHS hospital, NHS Trust hospital or similar place approved by the Secretary of State.

In an emergency an abortion may be carried out by a registered medical practitioner without complying with the above requirements if it is necessary to do so immediately to save the life of a pregnant woman, or to prevent grave permanent injury to her physical or mental health. This might occur during an operation upon the woman or at the scene of, or immediately following, a serious road accident.

The person supplying the means

Section 59 of the Offences Against the Person Act 1861 punishes those who unlawfully supply or procure any poison or other noxious thing, or any instrument or thing whatsoever, knowing that it is intended to be unlawfully used or employed with intent to procure the miscarriage of any woman, whether she be or be not with child. 'Supply' should be given its ordinary meaning of transferring physical control from one person to another, and 'procure' means to obtain possession of something for some other person. To procure, therefore, indicates going out deliberately to seek something for a particular purpose, whilst something may be supplied to a woman which was already in the possession of the accused.

All these offences relating to abortion are arrestable offences.

CONCEALMENT OF BIRTH

The Offences Against the Person Act 1861, s 60 provides that if any woman is delivered of a child, every person who, by any secret disposition of the dead body of that child, endeavours to conceal its birth is guilty of an offence. It is irrelevant whether the child died before, at or after its birth. However, in the case of a stillborn child, it must have reached a sufficient state of maturity that, but for some accidental circumstance, it might have been born alive.

The secret disposition may be done by anyone or by a number of persons, but typically it is done by the mother following an unattended birth. In such a case, the offence is of importance where it cannot be proved how and/or when a child died, so that the mother cannot be convicted of an offence of homicide or of child destruction.

It is not enough to prove that a woman, who denied giving birth, had in fact given birth and abandoned the child's body. There must be evidence of a secret disposition of the child's body in an endeavour to conceal its birth. By 'concealment' is meant concealment from the world at large, but this is not prevented by the fact that some of the woman's friends or confidants know. Clearly, a secret disposition in an endeavour to conceal the birth from a particular person, eg the woman's father, does not constitute the offence. Apart from what has just been said, it is difficult to be precise. Placing the body in a secluded spot, without covering it, may be sufficient if the particular circumstances permit this to be described as a secret disposition in an endeavour to conceal.

An offence under s 60 is not an arrestable offence.

CHAPTER 31

Public order offences other than those related to sporting events or industrial disputes

THE QUEEN'S PEACE

One of the fundamental duties of a police officer is the preservation of 'the Queen's peace'. This term is used in a different sense here from that which applies in the case of murder (see p 594). It has been described in many ways but is generally descriptive of that public peace and good order which is expected to be preserved to allow Her Majesty's subjects to live their lives without due interference from other citizens. It has been described as 'that normal state of the peace and tranquillity' which should always exist in an ordered society and as a 'normal and ordered' state of society.

At the outset, it is essential to give the legal definition of that well known term, 'breach of the peace'.

BREACH OF THE PEACE

To be a breach of the peace, the conduct in question does not have to be disorderly. There is a breach of the peace whenever and wherever (even on private premises):

(a) harm is *actually done*, or is *likely* to be done, to a person, whether by the conduct of the person against whom a breach of the peace is alleged or by someone whom it provokes; or

(b) harm is *actually* done, or is *likely* to be done, to a person's property in his presence; or

(c) a person is genuinely in fear of harm to himself or to his property in his presence as a result of an assault, affray, riot, or other disturbance.

This definition can be justified on the ground that in the cases covered by it, particularly if they occur in public, there is an actual or likely disturbance of the public peace and good order which it is expected that citizens should be able to enjoy. It is for the justices to decide whether or not there has been a breach of the peace in particular circumstances.

A police officer has power to arrest without a warrant a person who commits a breach of the peace in his presence, or a person who has been guilty of such a breach (provided there is a reasonable belief that a renewal of it is threatened), or a person whom he reasonably believes will commit a breach of the peace in the immediate future (although that person has not yet committed a breach).

BINDING OVER

'Binding over' is a precautionary measure; it is not a conviction or punishment. It should not be ordered for some act that is past and not likely to be repeated.

The powers of a magistrates' court to bind over a person to keep the peace or to be of good behaviour, or both, may be exercised either as a complaint (under the Magistrates' Courts Act 1980, s 115) or on the court's own motion under the Justices of the Peace Act 1361 and common law powers. Other courts can also bind over on their own motion, but we shall limit ourselves to the powers of a magistrates' court.

The importance of the fact that a magistrates' court can bind over of its own motion is that a person can be bound over whether or not he has been convicted of an offence; if he has been so convicted, the binding over may be in addition to any punishment imposed.

Where the magistrates act on complaint under the Magistrates' Courts Act 1980 they can only bind a person over if a breach of the peace as defined above is proved beyond reasonable doubt. If they act of their own motion, they must simply be sure that there is a risk of a breach of the peace in the future.

On occasions where there is a breach of the peace, or the risk of one, the person concerned may be engaged upon a lawful activity, eg a demonstration. On such occasions it must be shown that in all the circumstances it was the defendant who was acting unreasonably rather than the other person.

The process of binding over is effected by requiring the individual to enter into a recognisance, with or without sureties, to keep the peace or, alternatively, to be of good behaviour.

A person enters into a recognisance if he undertakes to pay a sum of money fixed by the court if he fails within the time specified by the court to comply with the terms of the recognisance, and a person becomes a surety if he agrees to pay a sum so specified if that other person so fails to comply.

The power to bind over independently of any conviction is exercisable either after an arrest without warrant for an actual or apprehended breach of the peace or upon complaint. Before a person is bound over, he will be told by the court of its intention to do so, and he, the complainant and their witnesses will be heard by the court. The court cannot impose a binding over if the person does not consent but, in the event of a persistent refusal to be so bound, or to find sureties, the person concerned may be committed to prison for a fixed term not exceeding six months or until he sooner complies with the requirements of the court.

RIOT

Section 1(1) of the Public Order Act 1986 provides that, where 12 or more persons who are present together use or threaten unlawful violence for a common purpose and the conduct of them (taken together) is such as would cause a person of reasonable firmness present at the scene to fear for his personal safety, each of the persons using unlawful violence for the common purpose is guilty of riot. Riot is the most serious offence against public order. It is an arrestable offence.

Basically, what is required is that an accused uses violence in the following circumstances that:

(a)   12 or more persons (including the accused) who are present together use or threaten unlawful violence for a common purpose; and

(b)   the conduct of them (taken together) is such as would cause a person of reasonable firmness present at the scene to fear for his personal safety; and

(c)   the accused's use of unlawful violence was for the common purpose.

Riot may be committed in private as well as in public places. Thus, a riot can take place at factory premises, in a club, in a college, at a tickets-only dance at a dance hall or—even—in someone's home.

Use of unlawful violence

A person does not perpetrate the offence of riot merely by threatening unlawful violence; he must actually use violence in the prescribed circumstances. If 12 or more people simply threaten violence for a common purpose in a frightening way, but none of them uses violence, riot is *not* committed.

On the other hand, provided one of 12 or more people actually uses violence for the common purpose, the offence of riot is perpetrated by him (or by all those who so use violence if more than one does). Those who merely threaten violence for the common purpose can, however, be convicted as accomplices to riot if, with the appropriate mens rea, they aid, abet, counsel or procure the use of violence by another (like anyone else who does so).

'Violence' is defined by s 8 of the 1986 Act as 'violent conduct'. It is not limited to violent conduct towards a person or persons since it includes violent conduct towards property (for example, smashing shop windows or overturning cars). Nor is it limited to conduct causing or intended to cause personal injury or damage to property, since it 'includes any other violent conduct (for example, throwing at or towards a person a missile of a kind capable of causing injury which does not hit or falls short)'. Swinging a knife at someone or firing a gun in his direction is violence under the definition in s 8, even though he is not hit.

The requirement that the violence be unlawful excludes from riot the use of violence which is justified by law (for example, under the common law rules relating to the use of reasonable force in self-defence and the defence of another or of property, or under the statutory provisions relating to the use of such force in the prevention of crime or the effecting of an arrest).

Use or threat of unlawful violence for a common purpose by 12 or more present together

The phrase 'present together' does not mean that the 12 or more people should form a cohesive group. Nor need they be present pursuant to an agreement to come together; consequently, they may be 'present together' by accident.

The same comments apply to 'use' and 'violence' as have been made above. If, during public disorder, the residents of a street use or threaten reasonable violence for the common purpose of defending themselves or their property from attack, their use or threat of violence does not constitute a riot because their violence is not unlawful.

In relation to threats, they may be by gestures alone (eg the brandishing of a weapon) or be by words alone, or be by a combination of both (eg waving a car-jack accompanied by words such as 'I'll get you with this'). Although, in the case of words, they will normally be spoken, there seems no reason why it will not do if the threat is communicated by words on placards or banners if the other conditions for riot are satisfied.

Section 1(2) provides that it is immaterial whether or not the 12 or more use or threaten violence simultaneously. Equally, it is immaterial whether or not *any* of the others used or threatened violence at the time of the use of violence by the accused. Provided that 12 or more persons who use or threaten violence are present *together* throughout, and that the violence is used or threatened by 12 or more for a common purpose, the offence of riot can be committed. Thus, it covers the situation where violence is used or threatened in one part of a crowd, then dies away, only to break out in another part at a later time.

It must be proved that the use or threat of violence by the 12 or more present together was for a purpose common to them (or at least to 12 of them). The question is not whether the 12 or more were present for a common purpose but whether they threatened or used violence for a common purpose. The common purpose need not be violence and it need not be an unlawful purpose (although, no doubt, it will normally be so). The common purpose may be inferred from the conduct of those involved; if a large group advance towards police officers, shouting 'kill the pigs', it may be inferred that they are threatening violence for a common purpose.

Conduct such as would cause fear

The question is not whether the conduct of an individual accused would cause fear but whether the conduct of the '12 or more present together . . .' is such as would, *taken together,* cause fear (ie alarm or apprehension). The conduct of the 12 or more must be such as *would* cause a person (ie a third-party bystander) of reasonable firmness present at the scene to fear for his *personal safety*; it does not matter whether it actually caused fear to a person present at the scene or even *might* have.

No person of reasonable firmness need actually be, or be likely to be, present at the scene; in fact, no one else (besides the 12 or more) need be present or likely to be present at the scene. No doubt the case where there are no bystanders will be exceptional; where it occurs proof of the riot may be particularly difficult.

Mens rea

By s 6(1) of the 1986 Act, a person is guilty of riot only if he intends to use violence or is aware that his conduct may be violent. Section 6(5) of the 1986 Act provides that, for the purposes of the offence of riot, a person whose awareness is impaired by intoxication shall be taken to be aware of that of which he would be aware if not intoxicated, unless he proves either that his intoxication was not self-induced (as where his drink has been 'laced') or that it was caused solely by the taking or administration of a substance in the course of medical treatment. 'Intoxication' here means any intoxication, whether caused by drink, drugs or other means (eg glue), or by a combination of means.

VIOLENT DISORDER

Section 2(1) of the Public Order Act 1986 provides that, where three or more people who are present together use or threaten unlawful violence and their conduct (taken together) is such as would cause a person of reasonable firmness present at the scene to fear for his personal safety, each of the persons using or threatening unlawful violence is guilty of violent disorder. The offence is an arrestable one.

To perpetrate the offence, an individual accused must use or threaten unlawful violence in the following circumstances that:

(a) three or more people (including the accused) together use or threaten unlawful violence (whether towards persons or towards property);
(b) the conduct of them (taken together) is such as would cause a person (ie a third-party bystander) of reasonable firmness present at the scene to fear for his personal safety. No person of reasonable firmness need actually be, or be likely to be, present at the scene.

As in the case of riot, violent disorder may be committed in private as well as in public places.

The prohibited conduct for this offence is substantially the same as that of riot (and the comments made when discussing the identical elements in riot are equally applicable here) with the exceptions that:

(a) an individual accused is guilty if he uses or *threatens* unlawful violence;
(b) only three persons (including the accused) who are present together are required to use or threaten unlawful violence;
(c) neither the accused nor the other participants are required to use or threaten unlawful violence for a common purpose.

The operation of the above can be illustrated as follows. If a racist march or static demonstration takes place in the centre of an immigrant community, accompanied by threats of immediate violence which would make a person of reasonable firmness fear for his personal safety, the offence is committed; but not if the taunts are merely (if that word may be used) of a racist nature highly offensive to local inhabitants, although they may give rise to an offence under ss 4A, 5 or 18 of the 1986 Act or s 31 of the Crime and Disorder Act 1998.

By s 6(3) of the 1986 Act a person is guilty of violent disorder only if he intends to use or threaten violence or is aware that his conduct may be violent or threaten violence.

As in the case of riot, a person whose awareness is impaired by intoxication is to be taken to be aware of that of which he would be aware if not intoxicated, unless he shows either that his intoxication was not self-induced or that it was caused solely by the taking or administration of a substance in the course of medical treatment.

Violent disorder is a useful offence to charge since it is not restricted to incidents which might be described as serious public disorder. If three or more gather outside a dance hall using or threatening violence against others, they can be convicted of violent disorder if they are acting collectively and their conduct (taken together) is sufficiently frightening to be liable to affect a person of reasonable firmness.

Where evidence of the involvement of three or more persons is affected by the dismissal of the charges against all but one or two, the one or two may nevertheless be convicted of violent disorder if it is proved that others not charged were also involved; if it is not so proved, the one or two may be convicted of an offence of affray. However, if there is only evidence of violence towards property, a conviction for an offence of affray will not be possible.

AFFRAY

Section 3(1) of the Public Order Act 1986 provides that a person is guilty of affray if he uses or threatens unlawful violence towards another and his conduct is such as would cause a person of reasonable firmness present at the scene to fear for his personal safety. A constable may arrest without warrant anyone he reasonably suspects is committing an affray.

The prohibited conduct is that:

(a) the accused must use or threaten violence *towards* another; and
(b) his conduct must be such as would cause a person of reasonable firmness present at the scene to fear for his personal safety.

Like riot and violent disorder, affray may be committed in private as well as in public places. One result is that, if a fight breaks out at a party in someone's home or at a private function at a discothèque, those who participate in it can be guilty of affray if the terms of the offence are satisfied. In fact any assault—even a domestic one— wherever committed, accompanied by the use or threat of violence, is an affray if it would cause a person of reasonable firmness present at the scene to fear for his personal safety. *Most* of the elements of the actus reus are common to riot and violent disorder.

Use or threat of unlawful violence towards another

Unlike the position in riot and violent disorder, 'violence' here does not include violent conduct towards property.

Another important difference between affray and riot and violent disorder is that a threat of violence cannot be made by the use of words alone, whether the words are uttered orally or displayed or distributed in writing, and however aggressively they are expressed. Of course, an affray can be committed where a threat of violence is made by a combination of words and gestures (such as shouting out, 'I'll get you for that', while brandishing a weapon or even shaking a fist) as well as by gestures alone.

It has even been held that deliberately releasing an excited dog at someone, and at the same time uttering words of encouragement to it to attack, can suffice since the case is indistinguishable from a threat made by words and gestures. It would be different, of course, if a person merely said 'seize him' to a quiet dog lying at his feet, since the threat would be words alone.

An affray, like riot and violent disorder, can only be committed if the violence is 'unlawful' as defined on p 606. Thus, a person who fights another in self-defence cannot be guilty of an affray, although his assailant can be if his use of violence would make a person of reasonable firmness fear for his personal safety.

Conduct such as would cause a person of reasonable firmness present at the scene to fear for his personal safety

This requirement provides an important limit on the offence, and excludes many fights from it. For example, it is most unlikely that a fight between two people, arising out of a personal quarrel but without any danger of the involvement of others, would constitute an affray. On the other hand, a violent street fight outside a pub at closing time undoubtedly constitutes an affray. If three or more are involved it will also constitute the more serious offence of violent disorder.

The reference to the hypothetical person 'present at the scene' is to an 'innocent member of the public within sight or earshot' of the violence.

Where two or more people use or threaten the unlawful violence, it is the conduct of them taken together that must be considered for the purpose of ascertaining whether the conduct would have the required effect.

As in the case of riot and violent disorder no one besides the participants (ie no bystander) need be present, or be likely to be present, at the scene, and it is expressly provided by s 3(4) that no person of reasonable firmness need actually be, or be likely to be, present at the scene. The offence of affray is, in reality, concerned with *three* persons: a person using or threatening unlawful violence, a person towards whom the violence or threat is directed, and a notional person of reasonable firmness. It is not enough that the victim of the violence or threat is put in fear for his personal safety. The question is whether, if the *notional* person of reasonable firmness had been so present, he would have been caused fear for his personal safety.

Mens rea

By s 6(2) of the 1986 Act, a person is guilty of affray only if he *intends* to use or threaten violence or is *aware* that his conduct may be violent or threaten violence. As in the case of riot, a person whose awareness is impaired by intoxication—whether by drink, drugs or other means (or a combination of these)—must be taken to be aware of what he would have been aware of if not intoxicated, unless he proves that his intoxication was not self-induced or that it was caused solely by the taking or administration of a substance in the course of medical treatment.

FEAR OR PROVOCATION OF VIOLENCE

Section 4(1) of the Public Order Act 1986 provides that a person is guilty of an offence if he:

(a) uses towards another person threatening, abusive or insulting words or behaviour; or
(b) distributes or displays to *another person* any writing, sign or other visible representation which is threatening, abusive or insulting,

with intent to cause that person to believe that immediate unlawful violence will be used against him or another by any person, or to provoke the immediate use of unlawful violence by that person or another, or whereby that person is likely to believe that such violence will be used or it is likely that such violence will be provoked.

A constable may arrest without warrant anyone he reasonably suspects is committing an offence under s 4.

The prohibited conduct specified by s 4 is that the accused:

(a) uses towards another person threatening, abusive or insulting words or behaviour; or
(b) distributes or displays to another person any writing, sign or other visible representation which is threatening, abusive or insulting.

The words 'threatening, abusive or insulting' do not bear an unusual legal meaning. Instead, the magistrates will decide as a question of fact whether the accused's conduct was threatening, abusive or insulting in the ordinary meaning of those terms, and this is to be judged according to the impact which the conduct would have on a reasonable member of the public. Masturbation in a public convenience in the view of a stranger is capable of being insulting behaviour because he might be a heterosexual who would be insulted at being taken for a homosexual. Behaviour is not threatening, abusive or insulting merely because it gives rise to a risk that immediate violence will be feared or provoked, nor simply because it gives rise to anger, disgust or distress. This is shown by a case where the accused's activities in disrupting a tennis match at Wimbledon (by running on to No 2 court and distributing leaflets) caused anger among spectators, some of whom tried to hit him as he was removed. The House of Lords did not disturb the magistrates' finding that, albeit annoying and irritating, the accused's behaviour was not threatening, abusive or insulting.

If conduct is threatening, abusive or insulting, it does not matter whether or not anyone who witnessed it felt himself to be threatened, abused or insulted.

The distribution or display of any writing, sign or other visible representation which is threatening, abusive or insulting covers handing out leaflets (distribution) or holding up a banner or placard (display).

Section 4 requires that threatening, abusive or insulting words or behaviour must be used *towards another person* or that threatening etc written material be distributed or displayed to *another*. In relation to the use of threatening, abusive or insulting words or behaviour, 'towards another' imports a requirement that the words or behaviour in question must be directed towards (ie deliberately aimed at) another particular person or persons; if they are not, one must rely on the offence under s 4A of the 1986 Act or the lesser offence under s 5 of the 1986 Act. Conduct is not used towards another if he is not present, in the sense that he can perceive with his own senses the threatening words or behaviour etc. Thus, a person who makes a threat against a person who is out of earshot and only learns of it through a third party who is not under the control or direction of the maker of the threat cannot be convicted of an offence under this section. However, while the person towards whom the behaviour was aimed must have been present to perceive it, this does not mean that the only means of proving that the victim perceived the behaviour is by hearing evidence from that person. Justices may rely solely on evidence from a bystander and may draw the inference that the victim did perceive what was said and done by an accused.

The insertion of 'to another' after 'distributes or displays' requires that the written material be directed towards another particular person or persons (or brought to his notice), rather than simply being distributed (eg by leaflets being left lying around in a shopping centre) or displayed (eg by pinning a poster to a wall in the middle of the night).

Public or private place

With one exception, an offence under s 4 can be committed in private places, such as factory premises, clubs or college premises, as well as in public places, such as football grounds, dance halls, public car parks and shopping precincts. Thus, an offence can be committed by pickets who threaten working colleagues, whether the pickets are inside or outside factory premises, or by protesters who invade a military base.

The exception is that, in order to exclude domestic disputes, s 4 has the effect of providing that the use of words or behaviour inside a dwelling is only an offence if the addressee (ie another person towards whom the words or behaviour are used or the writing etc is displayed) is not inside that dwelling or any other dwelling. Thus, to use threatening, abusive or insulting words towards someone else in the same house cannot be an offence under s 4, and the same is true if such words are shouted to someone in the house next door or displayed so as to be visible only to him. On the other hand, if such words are shouted in a house at a next-door neighbour who is in his back garden, an offence under s 4 will be committed, provided that the other elements of the offence are satisfied.

For the above purpose, 'dwelling' means any structure or part of a structure occupied as a person's home or as other living accommodation (whether the occupation is separate or shared with others) but does not include any part not so occupied, such as a garage, a shop with accommodation over or the communal parts of a block of flats. Thus, if threatening words are shouted from a flat to a shop below, an offence under s 4 may be committed, and so may it if the words are shouted from the shop to the flat upstairs. 'Structure' here includes a tent, caravan, vehicle, vessel or other temporary or movable structure.

Mens rea

The accused must either intend the words, behaviour or writing etc to be threatening, abusive or insulting or be aware that they or it may be. The result of this requirement is that a person, who uses words which are seemingly innocuous but which are addressed to, or heard by, persons to whom (unknown to him) they are highly insulting, is not guilty of the present offence.

A person whose awareness is impaired by intoxication must be taken to be aware of that of which he would be aware if not intoxicated, unless he proves either that his intoxication was not self-induced or that it was caused solely by the taking or administration of a substance in the course of medical treatment.

Section 4 of the 1986 Act also requires that the accused's use of the words or behaviour towards another (hereafter described as 'an addressee'), or the accused's distribution or display to another ('an addressee') of the writing etc, must be intended by the accused or be likely (whether or not the accused realises this) either:

(a)   to provoke the immediate use of unlawful violence *by an addressee or another*; or
(b)   to cause *an addressee* to believe that immediate unlawful violence will be used against him or another.

It will be noted, under para (a), that it is not necessarily an addressee who must be intended or likely to be provoked to immediate violence. It is sufficient that someone else present, towards whom the threatening etc behaviour etc was not directed, was intended or likely to be provoked. Thus, if X shouts at a coloured person whom he knows cannot speak English, 'Paki bastard, go home', intending that this should provoke immediate violence on the part of a group of skinheads who are in the near vicinity, the present offence is committed. On the other hand, for the purposes of para (b), fear of immediate violence, intended or likely, the fear must be on the part of an addressee (although it need not be fear of violence against himself, nor of violence by the accused).

It is important to note that the offence under s 4, unlike those under ss 1 to 3, is not concerned with the reactions of a hypothetical person of reasonable firmness. It has been held that, since constables are under a common law duty to preserve the peace, they are unlikely to respond to threatening, abusive or insulting conduct by using violence. Nevertheless, such conduct directed towards a constable will constitute an offence under s 4 if it is intended or likely to put him in fear of immediate unlawful violence or is intended to provoke him to such violence. If the conduct is so serious as to amount to a breach of the peace and make it likely that a constable to whom it is addressed will have to use violence in the exercise of his common law power to arrest for a breach of the peace, an offence under s 4 will not be committed because the violence likely to be provoked will not be unlawful.

The fact that the unlawful violence which is intended or likely to cause a person to believe will be used or provoked must be *immediate* must be emphasised. However, that term has been given a liberal interpretation by the Divisional Court. 'Immediate' does not mean 'instantaneous'. Instead violence will be 'immediate' if it is likely to result in a relatively short period of time and without any intervening occurrence.

As with the term 'unlawful violence' in other offences in the 1986 Act, the immediate violence which is intended, or is likely, to be feared to be used, or to be provoked, will not be unlawful if it is reasonable force in self-defence, or in prevention of crime, or is otherwise legally justified.

A speaker must take his audience as he finds it. If he uses insulting words at a meeting, he is guilty of the present offence if they are likely to provoke the immediate use of violence by the particular audience he is addressing, even though he does not intend to provoke this and even though his words would not be likely to cause a reasonable person so to react, provided that he intends his words to be insulting or is aware that they might be.

In the reference to an intention to cause, or the likelihood of causing, the apprehension of immediate unlawful violence or the provocation of it, 'violence' means any violent conduct. It includes fear or provocation of violent conduct towards property as well as violent conduct towards persons, and it is not restricted to conduct causing or intended to cause injury or damage but includes any other violent conduct (such as throwing at or towards a person a missile of a kind capable of causing injury which does not hit or falls short).

HARASSMENT, ALARM OR DISTRESS

Section 4 of the Public Order Act 1986 does not deal with many minor acts of hooliganism or other anti-social behaviour which are prevalent, particularly in inner city areas. Such conduct is a particular cause for concern when it is directed at members of especially vulnerable groups, such as the elderly and members of ethnic minority communities, who may feel unable to act themselves to remove the nuisance or who may be deterred from participating in everyday activities or even from leaving their homes. It is at problems such as these, in particular, that the offences under s 4A and s 5 of the 1986 Act are aimed.

Harassment etc which is likely to be caused

Section 4A provides that a person is guilty of an offence if, with intent to cause a person harassment, alarm or distress, he:

(a) uses threatening, abusive or insulting words or behaviour, or disorderly behaviour; or

(b) displays any writing, sign or other visible representation which is threatening, abusive or insulting,

thereby causing that or another person, harassment, alarm or distress.

Section 5 of the 1986 Act provides that a person is guilty of an offence if he:

(a) uses threatening, abusive or insulting words or behaviour or disorderly behaviour; or

(b) displays any writing, sign or other visible representation which is threatening, abusive or insulting,

within the hearing or sight of a person likely to be caused harassment, alarm or distress thereby.

As these two definitions indicate, there is much common ground between these two offences. We shall deal with this first and then consider the elements which distinguish the two offences.

The common elements are that a person must use threatening, abusive, insulting or disorderly words or behaviour, or display any writing, sign or other visible representation which is threatening, abusive or insulting. The words 'threatening, abusive or insulting' have already been discussed and what is said there is equally applicable here. A similar approach applies to 'disorderly', a term with which magistrates are already familiar via the offence of being drunk and disorderly. Thus, it is a question of fact for the magistrates whether the accused's conduct was disorderly in the ordinary meaning of the term. The Divisional Court, in confirming this, has held that an element of 'violence' is not essential for there to be disorderly behaviour, and that neither is an abusive, threatening or insulting character to the behaviour required nor any feeling of insecurity, in an apprehensive sense, on the part of a member of the public.

'Behaviour' is not limited to overt behaviour. It would be open to a court to find that the conduct of a 'Peeping Tom' constitutes insulting behaviour. Indeed, in one case, where a trader installed a video camera in an area used by ladies to try on swimwear, the Divisional Court held that he had been properly convicted of an offence against s 5. The guilty act was the setting up of the camera and letting it run, which amounted to insulting behaviour. This decision is of importance in relation to an offence under s 5.

In relation to any threatening, abusive or insulting writing, sign or other visible representation, the offence is limited to displaying and cannot (unlike an offence under s 4) also be committed by distribution. One result is that handing out threatening, abusive or insulting leaflets is not caught by s 5, unless the leaflets are so printed, and so held, that their contents can be said to be displayed in the sight of another. An important application of s 5 will be the display of graffiti or slogans likely to cause racial harassment.

Another distinction between these offences and that under s 4 is that the words or behaviour need not be used *towards* another person (nor need writing etc be displayed to another). It follows that words or behaviour need not be directed towards another, nor need written material be deliberately brought to the attention of another. Consequently, wearing a threatening, abusive or insulting badge is far more capable of being an offence under s 4A or 5 than under s 4, and the same is true if a T-shirt is worn bearing a slogan or picture which is threatening, abusive or insulting.

An offence under s 4A or s 5 may be committed in a public or a private place, except that no offence is committed where the words or behaviour are used, or the writing, sign or other visible representation is displayed, by a person inside a dwelling and the other person, within whose sight or hearing it occurs and who is likely to be harassed, alarmed or distressed thereby, is also inside that or another dwelling. Consequently, displaying an abusive poster in the front window of a house adjacent to the street is capable of being an offence under s 4A or s 5, whereas if the poster was displayed in a place where it could only be seen by a person in the house or by a person in the first floor flat of the house next door a s 4A or s 5 offence would not be committed. It will be remembered that there is a corresponding provision in relation to an offence under s 4.

The separate elements: s 4A

While the accused's conduct need not be directed towards another (and written material need not be displayed by him to another), there must be a victim in the sense that someone else is actually caused harassment, alarm or distress. 'Harassment, alarm or distress' are not defined by the 1986 Act, they are somewhat vague terms. It has been held that 'harassment' does not require any apprehension about one's personal safety, nor (probably) does 'distress'.

The fact that there has to be an identifiable victim means that some (possibly many) cases falling within s 4A will not be prosecuted under that section because victims of harassment may well be reluctant to go to court and give evidence for fear of reprisals. The offence is intended to protect the vulnerable, and the vulnerable are most likely to be influenced by the fear of reprisals.

The offence is inadequate to deal with harassment (racial or otherwise) for another reason. In some cases, such as racist graffiti on walls or racist chanting, there is no identifiable individual victim who is harassed, alarmed or distressed but, rather, an offence to a section of the public at large.

The offence can be committed by an isolated piece of conduct; persistence is not required.

The accused must either intend his words or behaviour, or the writing etc, to be threatening, abusive or insulting or be aware that they or it may be threatening, abusive or insulting, or (as the case may be) intend his conduct to be or be aware that it may be disorderly.

The accused must also intend his threatening etc words or behaviour or his display of a threatening etc visible representation to cause a person harassment, alarm or distress; it is irrelevant that the person actually caused the harassment etc was not the intended victim. The need for an intent to harass to be proved by the prosecution is a significant limiting factor on the offence, particularly because its proof may be difficult in practice. However, given that the prohibited conduct can be satisfied if an unduly sensitive person is inadvertently caused distress by disorderly conduct, some sort of subjective state of mind does seem to be essential if the offence is not to be too wide. It would have been better if awareness (subjective recklessness) as to the risk of causing harassment etc had been specified as an alternative to intention.

Section 4(A)(3) of the 1986 Act provides two defences which also apply on a charge under s 5 of that Act.

Section 4A(3)(a) provides a defence for an accused who alleges that he was inside a dwelling at the material time. It states that it is a defence for him to prove that he was inside a dwelling and had no reason to believe that the words or behaviour used, or the writing, sign or other visible representation displayed, would be heard or seen by a person outside that or any other dwelling.

Section 4A(3)(b) provides that it is a defence for an accused to prove that his conduct was reasonable, reasonableness being judged objectively. It would be reasonable, for example, to shout a threat at a pickpocket across the street to deter him. This is an exceptionally vague defence and proving it may often be difficult.

A constable may arrest without warrant anyone he reasonably suspects is committing an offence under s 4A.

The separate elements: s 5

While the accused's conduct need not be directed towards another (and written material need not be displayed by him to another), there must be a victim in the sense that what the accused does must be within the hearing or sight of a person likely to be caused harassment, alarm or distress thereby, although no likelihood of violence being provoked or feared is required. We have already commented upon the vagueness of 'harassment, alarm or distress'.

A police officer is a person capable of being subject to 'harassment, alarm or distress' for the purposes of this offence (and for the purposes of the s 4A offence). It is not necessary that a person who is likely to be alarmed should be alarmed for his own safety; it suffices that he is likely to be alarmed about the safety of someone unconnected with him.

The accused must either intend his words or behaviour, or the writing etc, to be threatening, abusive or insulting or be aware that it may be threatening, abusive or insulting, or (as the case may be) intend his conduct to be or be aware that it may be disorderly. Consequently, a person who gives no thought to the nature of his conduct, or who honestly believes that there is no risk of it being threatening etc, does not commit this offence. The provisions concerning intoxication, discussed above, apply equally to an offence under s 5.

Although the accused's conduct must be in the hearing or sight of a person likely to be caused harassment, alarm or distress thereby, the accused is not required to intend such a consequence or to be aware that it might occur.

An accused need not be proved to have intended or been aware that his conduct should be within the hearing or sight of a person likely to be caused harassment, alarm or distress thereby. On the other hand, s 5(3)(a) provides that it is a defence for the accused to prove that he had no reason to believe that there was any person within hearing or sight who was likely to be caused harassment, alarm or distress. There are two other defences, which correspond with those in s 4A. Section 5(3)(b) provides a related defence to that in s 5(3)(a) for an accused who alleges that he was inside a dwelling at the material time. It states that it is a defence for him to prove that he was inside a dwelling and had no reason to believe that the words or behaviour used, or the writing, sign or other visible representation displayed, would be heard or seen by a person outside that or any other dwelling.

Section 5(3)(c) provides that it is a defence for an accused to prove that his conduct was reasonable. As with the defence in s 4A, 'reasonableness ' is judged objectively. In one case, anti-abortionists were charged with an offence under s 5 because of their abusive and insulting conduct in displaying pictures of a newly aborted foetus to persons entering an abortion clinic. It was held that their conduct, viewed objectively, was not reasonable.

Section 5 provides a unique power of arrest. A constable may arrest without warrant any person if:

(a) he engages in offensive conduct which a constable warns him to stop; and
(b) he engages in further offensive conduct immediately or shortly after the warning.

'Offensive conduct' is conduct the constable reasonably suspects to constitute an offence under s 5. The 'further offensive conduct' need not be the same as the first.

For a constable to be acting in the execution of his duty when effecting such an arrest, the person arrested must have been warned to stop such conduct. Where an officer remonstrated with a person who had made racial remarks and behaved in a threatening manner, and was asked to apologise, it was held that the conversation, taken as a whole, was sufficient to convey to him that he should not engage in further offensive conduct.

This power to arrest is not limited to the officer who has personally administered the warning.

RACIALLY-AGGRAVATED PUBLIC ORDER OFFENCES

A person commits an offence under the Crime and Disorder Act 1998, s 31 if he commits an offence under the Public Order Act 1986, s 4, s 4A or s 5 which is racially aggravated. There are three separate offences under s 31, each based on one of the three basic offences under the 1986 Act. The same provisions relating to arrest apply to these offences as apply to the respective basic offences (see above).

An offence is racially aggravated for the purposes of s 31 if:

(a) at the time of committing it, or immediately before or after doing so, the offender demonstrates towards the victim of the offence (or, in the case of a basic offence under the 1986 Act, s 5, the person likely to be caused harassment, alarm or distress) hostility based on that person's membership (actual or presumed) of a racial group; or

(b) the offence is motivated (wholly or partly) by hostility towards members of a racial group based on their membership of that group.

For this purpose, 'membership of a racial group' includes association with members of that group, and 'presumed' means presumed by the offender. A 'racial group' means a group of persons defined by reference to race, colour, nationality (including citizenship) or ethnic or national origins.

HARASSMENT BY STALKERS ETC

Prohibition of harassment

The Protection from Harassment Act 1997, s 1 prohibits a person from pursuing a course of conduct:

(a) which amounts to harassment of another, and
(b) which he knows or ought to know amounts to harassment of the other.

The section provides that such a person ought to know that his conduct amounts to harassment of another if a reasonable person in possession of the same information would think the course of conduct amounted to harassment of the other.

'Harassment' includes alarming such a person or causing that person distress; a 'course of conduct' must involve conduct on at least two occasions; and the term 'conduct' includes speech. While the Act was fashioned with 'stalkers' in mind, it is worth noting that its terms are wide enough to embrace situations in which harassment is caused to neighbours or to persons living in a particular area in which unruly juveniles tend to congregate.

The prohibition of harassment in s 1 does not apply to a course of conduct for the purpose of preventing or detecting crime; nor to a course of conduct pursued under any enactment or rule of law or to comply with a condition or requirement lawfully imposed; nor where, in the particular circumstances, the pursuit of the course of conduct was reasonable. This last limitation is an important curb on the potential width of s 1. It has been stated in the High Court that the 1997 Act was clearly not intended by Parliament to be used to clamp down on the discussion of matters of public interest or upon the rights of political protest and public demonstration. The Court said that it would resist any wide interpretation of the Act. It would have been better if Parliament's intentions had been more clearly set out in the first instance. Perhaps the reasonable man would view certain of the activities of protest groups as harassment.

Section 2 of the 1997 Act makes it an offence to break the prohibition of harassment. It makes that an arrestable offence under the Police and Criminal Evidence Act 1984, s 24(2).

Civil remedy

Section 3 of the 1997 Act makes provision for an actual or apprehended breach of the prohibition of harassment to be the subject of a civil claim by the victim. Damages may be awarded for (among other things) any anxiety caused by the harassment and any financial loss resulting from the harassment. The High Court or a county court may grant an injunction for the purpose of restraining a defendant from pursuing any course of conduct which amounts to harassment. Breach of such an injunction, without reasoanble excuse, is itself an arrestable offence.

Victims should be made aware of these possibilities.

Putting people in fear of violence

Section 4 of the Act creates the offence of putting people in fear of violence. It is committed where a person whose course of conduct causes another to fear, on at least two occasions, that violence will be used against him, where the perpetrator knows or ought to know that his course of conduct will cause that other person to fear that consequence on each of the occasions in question. 'Course of conduct' bears the same meaning as in s 1. The section provides similar defences with the substitution of 'circumstances in which the pursuit of his course of conduct was reasonable for the protection of himself or another or for the protection of his or another's property', for 'the pursuit of the course of conduct being reasonable in the circumstances'. This offence is an arrestable offence by reason of its penalty.

Where a person is charged before a jury with an offence against s 4 and the jury find him not guilty, they may find him guilty of an offence contrary to s 2.

Breach of restraining order

Section 5 makes provision for the sentencing court in the case of a conviction under s 2 or s 4, in addition to any other sentence imposed, to make an order protecting the victim of the offence, or any other person mentioned in the order, from further conduct which amounts to harassment or will cause a fear of violence. If, without reasonable excuse, a person does anything which is prohibited by the order, he commits an arrestable offence.

RACIALLY-AGGRAVATED HARASSMENT OFFENCES

A person commits an offence under the Crime and Disorder Act 1998, s 32 if he commits an offence under the Protection from Harassment Act 1997 which is racially aggravated. There are two separate offences under s 32, each based on an offence under s 2 or s 4 of the 1997 Act respectively. The same powers of arrest apply to them as apply to the basic offences under the 1997 Act.

An offence is racially aggravated for the purposes of s 32 if:

(a) at the time of committing it, or immediately before or after doing so, the offender demonstrates towards the victim hostility based on that person's membership (actual or presumed) of a racial group; or

(b) the offence is motivated (wholly or partly) by hostility towards members of a racial group based on their membership of that group.

For this purpose, 'membership of a racial group' includes association with members of that group, and 'presumed' means presumed by the offender. A 'racial group' means a group of persons defined by reference to race, colour, nationality (including citizenship) or ethnic or national origins.

Indecent or grossly offensive communications

The Malicious Communications Act 1988 makes it an offence for any person to send to another person:

(a) a letter or other article which conveys:
    (i) a message which is indecent or grossly offensive;
    (ii) a threat; or
    (iii) information which is false and known or believed to be false by the sender; or

(b) any other article which is wholly or partly of an indecent or grossly offensive nature;

if his purpose or one of his purposes in sending it is that the message, threat or information should cause distress or anxiety to the recipient or to any other person to whom he intends that it, or its content or nature, should be communicated.

In relation to the sending of a threat, a defence exists if the threat is to reinforce a demand which the person believed he had reasonable grounds for making and he believed that it was a proper means of reinforcing the demand.

The Telecommunications Act 1984, s 43 provides that a person commits and offence who:

(a) sends by means of any public telecommunications systems a message or other matter which is grossly offensive or of an indecent, obscene or menacing character; or

(b) sends by those means for the purpose of causing annoyance, inconvenience or needless anxiety to another, a message that he knows to be false or persistently makes use for that purpose of a public telecommunications system.

The offence is restricted to the use of 'public' telecommunications systems for the purpose of making nuisance telephone calls. It is not an arrestable offence.

In addition, the Unsolicited Goods and Services Act 1971, s 4 creates the summary offence of sending unsolicited material or advertising material which describes or illustrates human sexual techniques. The consent of the DPP is required before proceedings may be instituted.

RACIAL HATRED

Part III (ss 17 to 29) of the Public Order Act 1986 provides six offences relating to racial hatred.

These offences have a number of common features. One is that they each require an intent that 'racial hatred' be stirred up or that 'racial hatred' be likely to be stirred up. Section 17 of the 1986 Act provides that racial hatred means hatred against a group of persons in Great Britain defined by reference to colour, race, nationality (including citizenship) or ethnic or national origins. Hereafter, such a group is described for convenience as a 'racial group'.

As can be seen, a group of persons defined by reference to religion is not a racial group and therefore falls outside the protection of Part III of the Act. However, an attack on a religion may be open to the interpretation that it is likely also to stir up hatred against a racial group identified with it, eg as Jews are associated with the Jewish religion.

None of the offences under Part III of the 1986 Act requires an intent to provoke a breach of the peace, or the likelihood of such a breach (let alone that public disorder results), nor that it be proved that racial hatred was actually stirred up. Instead, it is 'merely' required that the accused should intend to stir up racial *hatred* by his conduct, or that such *hatred* is likely, having regard to all the circumstances, to be stirred up thereby (whether or not the accused realised this would be likely).

All offences under Part III of the 1986 Act require that the material, words or behaviour in question are 'threatening, abusive or insulting'. These words do not bear an unusual legal meaning. Instead, as with offences under ss 4 and 5, the magistrates or jury must decide as a question of fact whether the material etc was threatening, abusive or insulting in the ordinary meaning of those terms, and this is judged according to the impact which it would have on a reasonable member of the public.

Use of words or behaviour or display of written material

Section 18(1) of the 1986 Act provides that a person who uses threatening, abusive or insulting words or behaviour, or displays any written material which is threatening, abusive or insulting, is guilty of an offence if:

(a)   he intends thereby to stir up racial hatred; or
(b)   having regard to all the circumstances, racial hatred is likely to be stirred up thereby.

'Written material' includes any sign or other visible representation. Section 18 does not apply to words or behaviour used, or written material displayed, solely for the purpose of being included in a television or sound broadcasting or cable service. In such a case, however, an offence may be committed under s 22 when the programme is transmitted.

As in the case of an offence under ss 4 or 5 of the 1986 Act, this offence may be committed in a public place (for example, a football ground) or a private place. There is one limit in relation to private places. As in the case of an offence under ss 4 or 5, an offence is not committed by the use of words or behaviour, or the display of written material, by a person inside a dwelling which are not heard or seen except by other persons in that or another dwelling. Thus, racialist taunts shouted from a house to people in the street or displayed on a poster on a window visible in the street are caught, but not racialist abuse shouted inside a house or flat (and only audible within it or another house or flat) or a racialist poster displayed in an inner room of a house.

It is a defence for the accused to prove that he was inside a dwelling and had no reason to believe that his words or behaviour, or the written material displayed, would be heard or seen by a person outside that or any other dwelling.

As already seen, the prosecution must prove that the accused intended to stir up racial hatred by his words, behaviour or display or that such hatred was likely to be stirred up thereby.

Section 18(5) provides that a person who is not shown to have intended to stir up racial hatred is not guilty of an offence under s 18 if he did not intend his words or behaviour or the written material to be, and was not aware that it might be, threatening, abusive or insulting. Unlike comparable provisions in other offences in Part III of the 1986 Act, the accused does not have the burden of proving this lack of intent or awareness.

Racial abuse or harassment unaccompanied by the mental element just described may, nevertheless, result in liability for an offence under ss 31 or 32 of the Crime and Disorder Act 1998.

A constable may arrest without warrant anyone he reasonably suspects is committing an offence under s 18.

Publishing or distributing

Section 19 of the Public Order Act 1986 provides that a person who publishes or distributes written material which is threatening, abusive or insulting is guilty of an offence if:

(a) he intends thereby to stir up racial hatred; or
(b) having regard to all the circumstances, racial hatred is likely to be stirred up thereby.

There must be a publication or distribution to the public or to a section of the public. 'The public' and 'section of the public' are not defined by the Act. In the only reported case which has referred to the point, the Court of Appeal held that a distribution of racialist pamphlets to members of a family living together in one house was not a distribution to 'the public at large'. There is no minimum number of persons to whom publication or distribution must be made in order for it to be to 'the public'. Ultimately, the question must be solved by common sense, the question being whether the publication or distribution has been on a scale and on a basis such as to be describable as being to 'the public'.

A publication or distribution only to members of a club or association is not a distribution to 'the public' but to a 'section of the public', as will be seen. In the case referred to above, the Court of Appeal held that the family was not a 'section of the public'. This decision was sensible; a family group would not normally be described as a section of the public (and doubtless the same is true of other small, domestic groups). In the case the Lord Chief Justice said that 'section of the public' refers to some identifiable group, 'in other words members of a club or association'. However, it is arguable that the term also covers any identifiable group of people whose connection is *not* a private relationship (ie a familial or domestic one) provided that that group is identifiable by some common interest or characteristic. If this is so, the employees of X Ltd are a section of the public, as are the inhabitants of houses in Y street, Members of Parliament, teachers, a football crowd and persons of West Indian descent.

Although the prosecution must prove that the accused intended to stir up racial hatred by the publication or distribution or that such hatred was likely to be stirred up thereby, it does not have to prove any knowledge on the part of the accused in relation to the content of the written matter which he has published, or distributed, although he will almost inevitably have had such mens rea if he is proved to have intended to stir up racial hatred. However, under s 19 of the 1986 Act, it is a defence for an accused who is not proved to have intended to stir up racial hatred to prove that he was not aware of the content of the matter and neither suspected nor had reason to suspect it of being threatening, abusive or insulting. The defence under s 19 is of obvious importance to innocent publishers or distributors, like newsagents.

Possession of racially inflammatory material

Section 23 of the Public Order Act 1986 provides that a person who has in his possession written material which is threatening, abusive or insulting, with a view to its being displayed, published, distributed, broadcast or included in a cable programme service (whether or not by himself) is guilty of an offence if:

(a) he intends racial hatred to be stirred up thereby; or
(b) having regard to all the circumstances racial hatred is likely to be stirred up thereby.

Section 23 makes similar provision in relation to a person who has in his possession a film or sound or video tape.

For the above purposes, regard must be had to such display, publication, distribution, showing, playing, broadcasting or inclusion in a cable programme service as the accused has, or it may reasonably be inferred that he has, in view.

The Act does not define what is required for 'possession' in this context but reference to other areas of the law suggests that actual custody is not necessary provided that there is control over the written matter. The intended publication or distribution need not be by the person in possession. The result of all this is that, if racially inflammatory pamphlets printed by X are deposited with Y for safekeeping in his warehouse until X wishes to collect and distribute them, the present offence can be committed by X and by Y (as long as the pamphlets are in the warehouse) because, since Y (as well as X) is in control of the pamphlets, Y and X are in possession of them.

As with s 19 of the 1986 Act, the prosecution does not have to prove any mens rea on the part of a person charged with possession contrary to s 23 in relation to the content of the written matter possessed by him. Likewise, it need not necessarily be proved that the accused intended racial hatred to be stirred up by the publication or distribution, since it is enough that, if the matter were published or distributed, racial hatred would be likely (having regard to all the circumstances) to be stirred up as a result of the publication or distribution. However, under s 23(3), it is a defence for an accused who is not proved to have intended to stir up racial hatred to prove that he was not aware of the content of the written material or recording, and neither suspected nor had reason to suspect it of being threatening, abusive or insulting. This is of obvious importance to 'innocent' possessors of racialist material, such as warehousemen.

The person in possession of the written material must have been in possession with a view to its publication or distribution. If there is a dispute about this, the magistrates or jury will have to draw such inferences as seem reasonable from the quantity and nature of the material possessed.

A justice of the peace, if satisfied by information on oath laid by a constable that there are reasonable grounds to suspect that a person has possession of written material or a recording in contravention of s 23, may issue a warrant authorising the entry and search of premises where it is suspected the material or recording is situated. A constable executing such a warrant may use reasonable force if necessary.

Other offences

Sections 20, 21 and 22 of the Public Order Act 1986 respectively provide offences relating to public plays, visual or sound recordings, and programmes in broadcasts or cable services, which are intended or likely to stir up racial hatred. A detailed explanation of these offences is outside the scope of this book.

Offences by corporations

Under s 28 of the Public Order Act 1986, the directors, secretaries and similar officers of bodies corporate are liable for offences under Part III of the Act which have been committed by the body corporate with their consent or connivance.

Parliamentary and court reports

None of the above offences applies to a *fair and accurate* report of:

(a) proceedings in Parliament; or
(b) proceedings publicly heard before a court or tribunal exercising judicial authority.

However, in the case of a report of the proceedings of a court or tribunal, the exemption *only* applies if the report is published *contemporaneously* with those proceedings or, if it is not reasonably practicable or would be unlawful to publish a report of them contemporaneously (because of the law of contempt of court), is published *as soon as publication is reasonably practicable and lawful.*

Not arrestable offences

These offences under Part III of the 1986 Act are not arrestable offences.

Limit on prosecutions

No prosecution for an offence under Part III of the Public Order Act 1986 may be instituted except by or with the consent of the Attorney-General.

PUBLIC PROCESSIONS

Advance notice

The Public Order Act 1986, s 11 requires that, where it applies, written notice specifying the date a procession is intended to be held, the time when it is intended to start, its proposed route, and the name and address of the person (or one of the persons) proposing to organise it, must be given to a police station in the police area in which it is proposed the procession will start. Section 11 applies if the procession is public and it is intended:

(a) to demonstrate support for or opposition to the views or actions of any person or body of persons;
(b) to publicise a cause or campaign; or
(c) to mark or commemorate an event.

If such a procession starts in Scotland, it is the first police area in England along the proposed route which must be given notice. The notice may be given by hand not less than six clear days before the date upon which the procession is intended to be held, or if that is not reasonably practicable, as soon as delivery is reasonably practicable. It will be appreciated that it may be impossible to give six clear days' notice of processions which occur quite spontaneously, following some incident concerning which a group feels inclined to demonstrate.

The section permits delivery of the notice by recorded delivery service, if the notice is delivered not less than six clear days in advance. The provisions of the Interpretation Act 1978 under which a document sent by post is deemed to have been served when posted and to have been delivered in the ordinary course of post do not apply to the service of such notices.

The provisions of the section do not apply to processions commonly or customarily held (for example, a procession connected with an annual gala), or to funeral processions organised by funeral directors, (as opposed to processions which suddenly appear in protest at a death).

Each of the persons organising a public procession is guilty of a summary offence if notice has not been so given, or if the details given in the notice differ from the actuality of the procession. It is a defence for a person to prove that he did not know of, or suspect the failure to give such notice, or that differences in the time, date or route occurred due to circumstances beyond his control, or with the agreement of a police officer, or by his direction.

Conditions

The senior police officer (the chief officer of the area or senior officer present at the procession) may impose conditions in relation to any public procession, having regard to its time, place or circumstances, including its route, if he reasonably believes that:

(a) it may result in serious public disorder, serious damage to property or serious disruption to the life of the community; or
(b) the purpose of the persons organising it is the intimidation of others with a view to compelling them not to do an act they have a right to do, or to do an act they have a right not to do.

These conditions may include any measures which appear necessary to prevent such disorder, damage or disruption or intimidation, including conditions as to the route of the procession or prohibiting it from entering any specified public place.

Summary offences are committed by organisers and participants who knowingly fail to comply with a condition. It is a defence for an accused to prove that the failure arose from circumstances beyond his control. A person who incites another to participate in a procession and to fail to comply with a condition also commits an offence. A constable in uniform may arrest without warrant anyone he reasonably suspects is committing these offences.

Prohibition

A chief officer of police may apply to the council of the district for an order prohibiting for a period, not exceeding three months, the holding of all public processions (or any class of procession specified) within that district. The chief officer must reasonably believe that, because of particular circumstances existing, his power to impose conditions will not be sufficient to prevent serious public disorder. Such an order may be made by the council with the consent of the Home Secretary. The Commissioners of the Metropolitan and City of London Police Forces may themselves make such an order in respect of their police areas with the consent of the Home Secretary.

Persons who organise, or take part in a public procession commit an offence if they know that it has been prohibited. Those who incite others to participate in a prohibited procession are also guilty of an offence. A constable in uniform may arrest without warrant anyone he reasonably suspects is committing such offences.

ENTERING AND REMAINING ON PROPERTY

In an effort to protect premises from unlawful occupation, the Criminal Law Act 1977 provides certain offences relating to entering and remaining on premises. Although these offences are often associated with 'squatters', the relevant provisions extend to situations beyond those involving squatting.

The definitions of the various offences refer to 'premises'. Section 12 of the Act defines 'premises' as any building, any part of a building under separate occupation, any land ancillary to a building, and the site comprising any building or buildings together with any land ancillary thereto. The definition would therefore cover a block of flats, a single flat or even the grounds in which the block has been erected. The section goes on to say that the term 'building' includes any immovable structure, and any movable structure, vehicle or vessel designed or adapted for use for residential purposes. In this way protection is extended to residential caravans, houseboats etc.

Violence for securing entry

By s 6 of the 1977 Act, it is an offence for any person, without lawful authority, to use or threaten violence for the purpose of securing entry into any premises either for himself or for any other person, provided that:

(a) there is someone present on those premises at the time who is opposed to the entry which the violence is intended to secure; and
(b) the person using or threatening the violence knows that that is the case.

A constable in uniform may arrest without warrant anyone who is, or whom he with reasonable cause suspects to be, guilty of an offence under this section. For this purpose the officer may enter (by force if need be) and search any premises where he has reasonable grounds for believing that person to be.

Use or threat of violence

The essence of this offence is the use or threat of violence for the purpose of securing entry into premises on which a person opposed to the entry is present: actual entry is not required. It is immaterial whether the entry which the violence is intended to secure is for the purpose of acquiring possession of the premises or for some other purpose. People who use or threaten violence in order to secure entry to a dance are guilty of the present offence if they know that someone inside is opposed to their entry; so are squatters who, with such knowledge, seek to enter a house by such means, and so are protesters who likewise seek to enter a public building or a factory.

The violence used or threatened may be against a person or property (whether he or it is on or off the premises). It is important to recognise that the offence is to use 'violence', not 'force'. Although the difference may seem to be small, it is considerable in certain circumstances. It would no doubt amount to violence against the property to set fire to it to drive out those inside and thereby gain entry, but the degree of force necessary to insert a key and to secure entry does not amount to violence. It would be different if the lock was burst open by using violence against the door.

Someone on the premises opposed to the entry

Someone must be physically present on the premises who is opposed to the entry to them which the violence is intended to secure. One person will suffice and he might equally be the owner of the premises or a trespasser who is opposed to the owner's re-entry. The section does not demand that this person physically opposes entry; it merely requires that the intended entry is against his will. Clearly, the present offence is not committed where someone breaks into an empty house.

Mens rea

In terms of the mens rea required for the offence, the accused must:

(a) intend to use or threaten violence;
(b) intend that violence or threat to secure him entry to the premises for himself or another; and
(c) know that there is someone on the premises at the time who is opposed to the entry in question.

Without lawful authority

An offence is not committed under s 6 if the person using or threatening violence has lawful authority for acting in the prescribed way. This exemption is essential to protect the violent entries which may have to be made by police officers or bailiffs in executing warrants or orders of courts. However, the only entries so protected will be those where the form of violence used to secure entry is authorised by law.

It might be assumed that the owner of the property would always have lawful authority for re-occupying his property which had been unlawfully occupied by those who would exclude him, but this is not so. Section 6(2) states that the fact that a person has any interest or right to possession or occupation of any premises does not give him lawful authority to use or threaten the use of violence for the purpose of securing his entry into those premises.

This situation is interesting. If the tenant of office accommodation went to enter his premises in the morning and found that the office had been taken over by homeless persons, he would commit the offence under s 6 if he attempted to secure immediate entry by the use or threat of violence, knowing that there was someone on the premises at the time who was opposed to such entry, because he would have no lawful authority for his action. Likewise, if a restaurateur, who has been thrown out of his restaurant by rowdies, uses force to re-enter the premises and evict them he will have no lawful authority for his use of violence and can be convicted under s 6.

This means that landlords and other non-residential occupiers must seek to recover possession of their premises by an action in the civil courts, unless it is possible for them to effect a peaceful re-entry.

Of course, if an occupier does succeed in re-entering his premises, he does not commit any offence by proceeding to eject any trespasser, whatever liability he may incur by virtue of his entry.

Displaced residential occupiers and protected intending occupiers

Special provision is made for people falling within the definition of a 'displaced residential occupier' or 'protected intending occupier' of premises or any access to them.

The term 'displaced residential occupier' is defined by s 12 of the 1977 Act as:

'any person who was occupying any premises as a residence immediately before being excluded from occupation by anyone who entered those premises, or any access to those premises, as a trespasser is a displaced residential occupier of the premises as long as he continues to be excluded from occupation of the premises by the original trespassers or by any subsequent trespasser.'

A person who is regarded as a displaced residential occupier of premises by virtue of this provision is regarded as such an occupier also of any access to those premises.

Section 12 also provides that a person who was himself occupying the premises as a trespasser before being excluded is not a displaced residential occupier.

The obvious example of a displaced residential occupier is the householder who discovers squatters in his house when he returns from work or from holiday.

An involved definition of 'protected intending occupier' is provided by s 12A of the 1977 Act.

The first type is an individual who, at the time of the request to leave:

(a) has in the premises in question a freehold interest or leasehold interest with not less than two years still to run;
(b) requires the premises for his own occupation as a residence;
(c) is excluded from occupation of them by a person who entered them, or any access to them, as a trespasser; and
(d) holds, or a person acting on his behalf holds, a written statement, signed by him and witnessed by a magistrate or commissioner for oaths, which -
  (i) specifies his interest in the premises; and
  (ii) states that he requires the premises for occupation as a residence for himself.

The purpose of the statement is to enable the police to identify the protected intending occupier and thereby prevent abuse of the protection given by the Act.

The second type of protected intending occupier is an individual who, at the time of the request to leave:

(a) has a tenancy of the premises (other than a tenancy falling within the other two definitions) or a licence to occupy them granted by a person with a freehold interest or a leasehold interest with not less than two years still to run in the premises;
(b) requires the premises for his own occupation as a residence;
(c) is excluded from occupation of the premises by a person who entered them, or access to them, as a trespasser; and
(d) holds, or a person acting on his behalf holds, a written statement -
  (i)   which specifies that he has been granted a tenancy of those premises or a licence to occupy them;
  (ii) which specifies the interest in the premises of the person who granted that tenancy or licence to occupy (the landlord);
  (iii) which states that he requires the premises for occupation as a residence for himself; and
  (iv) in respect of which there is a statement signed by the landlord and by the tenant or licensee and witnessed by a magistrate or commissioner for oaths.

The third type of protected intending occupier is an individual who, at the time of the request to leave:

(a) has a tenancy of the premises in question (other than a tenancy falling within the other two definitions) or a licence to occupy them granted by a local authority, the Housing Corporation, or a registered housing association or certain other bodies;
(b) requires the premises for his own occupation as a residence;
(c) is excluded from occupation of them by a person who entered them, or any access to them, as a trespasser; and
(d) has been issued by or on behalf of the authority, Corporation or association with a certificate stating that the authority etc is one to which these provisions apply and that he has been granted a licence or tenancy to occupy the premises as a residence.

Even a displaced residential occupier or protected intending occupier does not have lawful authority to use or threaten violence to secure entry to his home. However, s 6(1A) of the 1977 Act provides that the offence under s 6(1) does not apply to a person who is a displaced residential occupier or a protected intending occupier of the premises in question or who is acting on behalf of such an occupier. This exemption does not have to be proved by the accused. Instead, if he adduces sufficient evidence (ie evidence which raises a reasonable doubt) that he was, or was acting on behalf of, such an occupier he is presumed to be, or to be acting on behalf of, such an occupier unless the contrary is proved by the prosecution. This exemption applies only to a charge under s 6. However, if such an occupier is charged with assault or some other offence he may have the general defence of using reasonable force in the prevention of crime (if he has unsuccessfully asked the trespasser to leave, since the latter's failure to do so will be an offence under s 7 (below)) or in defence of property.

Adverse occupation of residential premises

Section 7 of the 1977 Act creates an offence of 'adverse occupation'. It provides that any person who is on any premises (including any access to them whether or not any such access constitutes premises) as a trespasser, after having entered as such, is guilty of an offence if he fails to leave those premises on being required to do so by or on behalf of a displaced residential occupier, or a person who is a protected intending occupier of the premises.

Section 7 is of great importance because it gives a displaced residential occupier or a protected intending residential occupier of premises who has been excluded from them by trespassers, eg squatters, a swifter remedy for recovering possession of them than the available civil remedy. He may require the trespassers to leave and they commit an offence if they fail to do so. A constable in *uniform* may arrest without warrant anyone who is, or whom he, with reasonable cause, suspects to be guilty of this offence, and for this purpose the constable may enter (by force, if need be) and search any premises where that person is or where he, with reasonable cause, suspects him to be.

The term 'protected intending occupier' is explained above. The effect of s 7 is to protect not only the owners or tenants of houses, but also buyers of houses, private tenants and council tenants who have not taken up residential occupation of the premises before being excluded by trespassers. Protection does not, however, extend to persons who occupy premises for business purposes.

There is no time set upon departure and it is submitted that this indicates that the requirement is immediate.

Three defences are provided by the Act, the burden of proof in each case being on the accused:

(a) It is a defence that the accused believed that the person requiring him to leave was not a displaced residential occupier or a protected intending occupier of the premises, or someone acting on his behalf. This plea will rarely succeed, particularly in the light of the requirement in the case of a protected intending occupier of a written statement or certificate to this effect.

(b) Where he was requested to leave by a person claiming to be (or to act on behalf of) a protected intending occupier, it is a defence for the accused to prove that, although asked to do so by the accused at the time that he was requested to leave, the person requesting him to leave failed at that time to produce a written statement, or certificate, complying with the Act.

(c) It is a defence that the premises in question are or form part of premises used wholly or mainly for non-residential purposes. This means, for instance, that people involved in a factory sit-in do not commit the present offence if they fail to leave when required by a resident caretaker, so long as they are not in his flat or in part of the premises used wholly or mainly for access to, or in connection with, the flat.

Trespassing with weapon of offence

Section 8 of the 1977 Act provides an offence of trespassing with a weapon of offence, which can be committed whether or not the trespassory entry was secured by the use or threat of violence. Where an armed trespasser commits an offence under s 6 or s 7, discussed above, the effect of the present offence is to impose further liability on him because of the element of aggravation of his being armed.

Section 8 states:

'A person who is on any premises as a trespasser, after having entered as such, is guilty of an offence if, without lawful authority or reasonable excuse, he has with him on the premises any weapon of offence.'

A power of arrest without warrant is given to a constable in uniform in respect of anyone who is, or whom he with reasonable cause suspects to be, in the act of committing this offence.

The term 'weapon of offence' means any article made or adapted for use for causing injury to or incapacitating a person, or intended by the person having it with him for such use. We discuss an identical definition on p 745.

INTERIM POSSESSION ORDERS IN RELATION TO PREMISES

Obtaining a final possession order in respect of premises can take rather longer than is desirable. As a result an interim possession order, which can be obtained more speedily, has been introduced by rules of court. Breach of such an order was made an offence by the Criminal Justice and Public Order Act 1994. Section 76(2) of the 1994 Act makes it an offence for a person to be present on premises as a trespasser at any time during the currency of such an order. However, the subsection provides that no offence will be committed if such a person leaves within 24 hours of the time of service of the order and does not return, or if a copy of the order was not affixed to the premises in accordance with the rules of court. A person in occupation at the time of service who leaves the premises, commits an offence if he re-enters the premises as a trespasser or attempts to do so after the expiry of the order but within a period of one year from service of the order.

The term 'premises' has the meaning set out at p 625 above.

Section 75 of the 1994 Act provides that a person commits an offence if, for the purpose of obtaining an interim possession order, he makes a statement which is known to be false or is misleading in a material particular, or recklessly makes such a statement. Likewise a person commits an offence if he knowingly or recklessly makes such a statement to resist the making of an interim possession order.

POWER TO REMOVE TRESPASSERS

Direction to leave

The Criminal Justice and Public Order Act 1994, s 61 provides that if the senior police officer (the most senior in rank of police officers present at the scene) reasonably believes that two or more persons are trespassing on land, that they are present with the common purpose of residing there for any period, that reasonable steps have been taken by or on behalf of the occupier to ask them to leave and that:

(a) any of those persons has caused damage to property on the land or used threatening, abusive or insulting words or behaviour towards the occupier, a member of his family or an employee or agent of his; or

(b) those persons have between them brought six or more vehicles onto the land,

he may direct those persons, or any of them, to leave the land and to remove any vehicles or other property they have with them on the land.

Where the persons in question are reasonably believed by the senior officer present to be persons who were not originally trespassers but have become trespassers on the land, he must reasonably believe that the above conditions are satisfied after those persons became trespassers before he can exercise these powers.

There are a number of factors to consider. The senior officer must reasonably believe that two or more persons are on the land as trespassers for the common purpose of residence, no matter how brief that intended period of residence may be. A person may have a purpose of residing in a place notwithstanding that he has a home elsewhere. While these provisions are adequate to deal with mass trespass by New Age Travellers, they are similarly adequate to deal with trespass by gypsies. The term 'land' does not include buildings other than agricultural buildings, nor does it include scheduled monuments or land forming part of a highway unless it is a footpath, bridleway or byway open to all traffic, or a road used as a public path or cycle track. The term includes 'common land', whether public or privately owned common land. The senior officer must also reasonably believe that the occupier of the land etc has taken reasonable steps to require them to leave. The senior police officer present, reasonably believing these facts, may require such persons to leave without further reason if he reasonably believes they have brought six or more vehicles onto the land. If they have not, he must reasonably believe that any of those persons has caused damage to the land or to property on the land, or has used threatening, abusive or insulting words or behaviour towards the persons specified (the occupier of the land, a member of his family or an employee or agent of his). Thus overnight campers are outside these provisions, provided that they have caused no damage to property on the land, or used such words or behaviour.

The requirement concerning damage is in relation to the land or to property on the land. Damage to growing crops, trees or hedgerows would clearly be within the provisions of the section and by s 61 of the 1994 Act, 'damage' includes the deposit of any substance capable of polluting the land.

For the purposes of this section, the term 'vehicle' includes any vehicle whether or not it is in a fit state for use on roads, and includes any chassis or body, with or without wheels, appearing to have formed part of such a vehicle, and any load carried by, and anything attached to, such a vehicle, and a caravan.

Offences

If a trespasser directed to leave complies with that direction, he commits no offence. On the other hand, he commits an offence under s 61 of the 1994 Act if, knowing that a direction has been given which applies to him:

(a)   he fails to leave the land (with any vehicle or other property he is required to remove), as soon as reasonably practicable; or
(b)   having left, he again enters the land as a trespasser within a three-month period beginning on the day on which the direction is given.

(a) and (b) are separate offences.
It is a defence for the accused to prove that:

(a)   he was not trespassing on the land; or
(b)   he had a reasonable excuse for failing to leave the land as soon as reasonably practicable or, as the case may be, for again entering the land as a trespasser.

The defence of 'not trespassing' refers to not trespassing at the time that the senior police officer forms his reasonable belief, and not the time of the prohibited conduct.

Police powers

The purpose of s 61 of the 1994 Act is to give the occupier of the land a swifter remedy for recovering possession of it than the available (and possibly costly) civil remedy. Consequently, s 61(5) is of crucial importance since it provides that a uniformed constable who reasonably suspects that a person is committing one of the above offences may arrest him without warrant.

Section 62 gives a constable power, where such a direction under s 61 has been given, to seize and remove a vehicle where he reasonably suspects that a person to whom the direction was given has, without reasonable excuse, failed to remove a vehicle which appears to the constable to belong to him or be in his possession or control. The same powers apply where such a person has re-entered the land within a period of three months from the date of the direction.

UNAUTHORISED CAMPING WITH A VEHICLE

The Criminal Justice and Public Order Act 1994, s 77 empowers a county council, district council or London borough council to direct unauthorised vehicular campers to leave any land forming part of a highway; any other unoccupied land in the open air; or any occupied land in the open air where they are camping without the consent of the occupier of the land. Such a direction may be addressed to a particular person or persons or to all of the occupants of vehicles on the land. It is not necessary for the local authority to show that there has been any form of nuisance caused by their presence.

Where such notice of a direction has been served, any person who knows that the direction has been given, and that it applies to him, commits an offence:

(a) if he fails, as soon as practicable, to leave the land or remove from the land any vehicle, or any other property which is subject of the direction; or
(b) if, having removed any such vehicle or property, he again enters the land with a vehicle within a period of three months from the day upon which the direction was given.

The section provides a defence where such failure to leave or remove a vehicle or other property as soon as practicable, or the re-entry with a vehicle was due to illness, mechanical breakdown or other immediate emergency. The onus is upon the accused to prove such a defence.

AGGRAVATED TRESPASS

Offence of aggravated trespass

The Criminal Justice and Public Order Act 1994, s 68 states that a person commits the offence of aggravated trespass if he trespasses on land in the open air and, in relation to any lawful activity which persons are engaged in, or are about to engage in, on that land or adjoining land in the open air, does there anything which is intended by him to have the effect:

(a) of intimidating those persons or any of them so as to deter them or any of them from engaging in that activity;
(b) of obstructing that activity; or
(c) of disrupting that activity.

The provisions are aimed particularly at the activities of hunt saboteurs who often go beyond peaceful protest. However, they would equally apply to the disruption of shooting, angling or even the obstruction of new motorway workings.

Some act is required in addition to trespass and that act must be shown to be intended to have one of the effects set out at (a) to (c). Thus a trespasser who gives drugged meat to hounds commits such an act, as does someone who blows a hunting horn to confuse hounds. Indeed, the Divisional Court has held that a trespasser commits an offence under s 68 if he does an act with intent to commit a further act, which is not committed, and thereby to intimidate, obstruct or disrupt a lawful activity, if the act done is sufficiently closely connected with the intended intimidation etc as to be more than merely preparatory to it. On this basis, the Court upheld the conviction under s 68 of a person who had trespassed on land and run after a hunt with the intention of getting close enough to do something to disrupt it. The act must be committed on land in the open air. It could not be committed, for example, within stables. 'Land' does not include land forming part of a highway unless it is a footpath, bridleway etc. A failure to do something is not enough. Trespassers already at a particular spot who refused on an impulse to move to allow other persons to pass would not commit an offence under s 68; whereas it would be an offence if they deliberately placed themselves there with the intention of disrupting the activity.

The offence is one requiring 'intent' to create one of these specified effects. The trespassing rambler who walks through grouse moors will not commit this offence even though he disrupts the shoot, if that was not his intention. If an animal rights protester does so deliberately, shouting or firing maroons to scare birds, he shows the necessary intention to disrupt. Those who protest at the building of a new road will commit the offence if they deliberately sit down on private land in front of the machines.

A constable in uniform who reasonably suspects that a person is committing an offence under this section may arrest him without a warrant.

Direction to leave

By s 69, where the senior police officer present at the scene reasonably believes that:

(a) a person is committing, has committed or intends to commit the offence of aggravated trespass on land in the open air; or

(b) two or more persons are trespassing on land in the open air and are present there with the common purpose of intimidating persons so as to deter them from engaging in a lawful activity or of obstructing or disrupting a lawful activity,

he may direct that person, or those persons (or any of them) to leave the land. It is not necessary for an offence of aggravated trespass to have been committed before a direction can be given under s 69.

A person who, knowing that such a direction has been given which applies to him, fails to leave the land as soon as practicable or, having left, again enters the land as a trespasser within the period of three months beginning with the day on which the direction was given, commits an offence.

It is a defence to a charge of either of the above offences for the accused to prove that he was not trespassing on the land, or that he had a reasonable excuse for failing to leave the land as soon as practicable or, as the case may be, for again entering the land as a trespasser.

A constable in uniform who reasonably suspects that a person is committing one of these two offences may arrest him without warrant.

PUBLIC ASSEMBLIES

Generally

Section 14 of the 1986 Act authorises the senior police officer, on the basis of the same grounds of reasonable belief as in the case of conditions on public processions, to impose such conditions in relation to the place at which any public assembly may be (or continue to be) held, its maximum duration, or the maximum number of persons who may constitute it, as appear to him to be necessary to prevent serious public disorder, serious damage to property, serious disruption to the life of the community or intimidation. In the case of an assembly intended to be held, the senior police officer is the chief officer of police; otherwise he is the police officer most senior in rank present at the scene. Offences under the section are committed by the same classes of persons as in relation to a breach of a public procession condition, and the same power to arrest without warrant applies.

Trespassory assemblies

These are dealt with by the Public Order Act 1986, ss 14A, 14B and 14C.

Section 14A is concerned with the prohibition of a trespassory assembly before it has taken place. Where a trespassory assembly has already commenced, police involvement is limited to the prohibition of its continuance if an officer believes that this is necessary to prevent a breach of the peace. Section 14A is, inter alia, aimed at assemblies of New Age Travellers at such places as Stonehenge at summer solstice time. However, its provisions are more extensive and will cover an assembly which might cause serious disorder, obstruction of the highway, or noise.

Section 14A of the 1986 Act provides that where a chief officer of police reasonably believes that an assembly of 20 or more people is intended to be held in any district at a place on land in the open air to which the public has no right of access or only a limited right of access and that assembly:

(a)   is likely to be held without the permission of the occupier of the land or to conduct itself in such a way as to exceed the limits of any permission of his or the limits of the public's right of access, and

(b)   may result -
    (i)   in serious disruption to the life of the community, or
    (ii)   where the land, or a building or monument on it, is of historical, architectural or scientific importance, in significant damage to the land, building or monument,

he may apply to the council of the district (or Home Secretary in the case of the Metropolitan and City of London Police Forces) for an order prohibiting for a specified period the holding of all trespassory assemblies in the district, or a part of it as specified. An order may only be made with the Home Secretary's consent. Where such an order is made, it will operate to prohibit the holding of an assembly on land in the open air to which the public has no right of access or only a limited right of access and takes place without the permission of the occupier, or in excess of his permission or the public's right of access. Such an order may not prohibit such an assembly for a period exceeding four days or in an area exceeding a circle with a radius of five miles from a specified centre.

It is irrelevant that the anticipated assembly is open to the public or is a private ceremony, but it must be held on land in the open air. This can be contrasted with the power to impose conditions on a public assembly under s 14 of the 1986 Act; there the assembly may be held wholly or partly in the open air. 'Land' in s 14A includes land forming part of the highway. It follows, for example, that an intended peaceful, non-obstructive assembly of 20 or more on the highway (which is by definition trespassing since the public only have a right to pass and re-pass on it and make reasonable use ancillary to such purpose) can be the trigger for an order under s 14A.

It is important to understand that these powers are restricted to assemblies which are reasonably believed to be trespassory in nature. Assemblies *with permission* are not covered by the legislation unless there is a reasonable belief that they will be conducted in such a way as to exceed that permission.

Offences

A person who organises an assembly which he knows to be prohibited under s 14A commits an offence against s 14B. So does a person who takes part, or who incites another to do so.

Police powers

Section 14B provides that a constable in uniform may arrest without warrant anyone he reasonably suspects to be committing an offence under s 14B.

By s 14C, if a constable in uniform reasonably believes that a person is on his way to an assembly within the area to which such an order applies, which the constable reasonably believes is likely to be an assembly which is prohibited by that order, he may, within the area specified in the order:

(a) stop that person, and
(b) direct him not to proceed in the direction of the assembly.

A person who fails to comply with such a direction which he knows has been given to him commits an offence. A constable in uniform may arrest without warrant anyone he reasonably suspects to be committing an offence under this section.

Where a person fails, without reasonable excuse, to remove a vehicle, or enters the land with a vehicle within a period of three months of the direction, a constable may seize and remove that vehicle. The Police (Retention and Disposal of Vehicles) Regulations 1995 set out a procedure for dealing with vehicles so seized or detained, see below.

Raves

The Criminal Justice and Public Order Act 1994, ss 63-65, provide the police with certain powers to deal with 'raves'. The provisions apply to a gathering on land in the open air of 100 or more persons (whether or not trespassers) at which amplified music is played during the night (with or without intermissions) and is such as, by reason of its loudness and the duration and the time at which it is played, is likely to cause serious distress to the inhabitants of the locality; and for this purpose:

(a) such a gathering continues during intermissions in the music and, where the gathering extends over several days, throughout the period during which amplified music is played at night (with or without intermissions); and
(b) 'music' includes sounds wholly or predominantly characterised by the emission of a succession of repetitive beats.

In the first instance, it must be recognised that ss 63-65 do not apply to a gathering which is licensed by a local authority entertainments licence.

'Raves' do not need to be trespassory; nor do they need to be totally in the open air. 'Land in the open air' includes a place partly open to the air. Thus, both an aircraft hangar without doors, or a Dutch barn, would be such a place. The fixed figure of 100 persons may provide difficulties for the police, but perhaps proof of wide circulation of information concerning the holding of a 'rave' will be sufficient.

Where a police officer of at least the rank of superintendent reasonably believes, in respect of any land in the open air, that:

(a)   two or more persons are making preparations for the holding there of a gathering to which this section applies,
(b)   10 or more persons are waiting for such a gathering to begin there, or
(c)   10 or more persons are attending such a gathering which is then in progress,

he may give a direction that those persons and any other persons who come to prepare or wait for or to attend the gathering are to leave the land and remove any vehicles or other property which they have with them on the land. The direction may be conveyed to the gathering by any constable. If reasonable steps have been taken to convey the direction, it shall be deemed to have been given.

A person who knows that such a direction has been given which applies to him who:

(a)   fails to leave the land as soon as reasonably practicable, or
(b)   having left, again enters the land within a period of seven days beginning with the day on which the direction is given,

commits an offence.

Persons occupying or working on the land and their families are exempt from the direction.

Police powers

A constable in uniform who reasonably suspects that a person is committing an offence under this section may arrest him without a warrant.

Where a superintendent reasonably believes that circumstances exist which would justify giving such a direction, he may authorise a constable to enter the land without warrant to ascertain that these circumstances exist and to exercise powers conferred upon him.

Where such a direction has been given, and a constable reasonably suspects that any person to whom the direction applies has, without reasonable excuse:

(a)   failed to remove any vehicle or sound equipment on the land which appears to the constable to belong to him or to be in his possession or under his control; or
(b)   entered the land as a trespasser with a vehicle or sound equipment within the period of seven days beginning with the day on which the direction was given,

the constable may seize and remove that vehicle or sound equipment.

The Police (Detention and Disposal of Vehicles) Regulations 1995 require the service of a notice on the person from whom the vehicle was seized (or the owner where this is not possible) requiring him to claim the vehicle within 21 days. The Criminal Justice and Public Order Act 1994, s 66 permits a court to order the forfeiture of sound equipment but also allows the owner of the equipment (if he is not the person from whom it was seized) to claim it by applying to the court within six months. The Police (Disposal of Sound Equipment) Regulations 1995 provide for the disposal of the equipment where the court has made no such order.

Where a constable in uniform reasonably believes that a person is on his way to such a gathering in respect of which a direction has been given, he may stop that person and direct him not to go in the direction of the gathering. This power may only be exercised at a place within five miles of the boundary of the site of the gathering. This does not apply to occupiers of the land etc. A person who, knowing that such a direction has been given, fails to comply with such a direction commits an offence. A constable in uniform who reasonably suspects that a person is committing an offence under this section may arrest him without warrant.

Summary

The powers which are given to the police after such a direction has been given are quite precise. The particular powers given to a superintendent are not so clear. If such a number of tickets are issued that the number authorised to attend, together with the number of organisers, totals less than 100 (perhaps 99) the superintendent may encounter problems. It is probable that the figure has been made so high that it will avoid the equally noisy and irritating 'garden parties' which continue into the small hours of the morning.

Will a marquee be a place open to the air? If open at one side it is open to the air, but what if all of the flaps are down, or a small opening is left which is no more than the size of a reasonable 'door'? If it is entirely closed up it is certainly not 'open to the air' nor, it is submitted, would it be if no more than a small entrance was left open, as it would then be no different to a building with the door left open. There is no doubt however, that the manner in which sound penetrates canvas would ensure that the 'rave' would be just as noisy as if it had been conducted entirely in the open air. Perhaps more importantly, the legislation allows 'raves' which occur in empty buildings in built-up areas to escape completely. This does not appear to be a logical distinction.

What is meant by 'during the night'? The Act does not define the term. The Minister said during debate in the Commons that it was not intended to mean lighting-up time and that he was content to leave the provisions vague. This is all very well, but it can be argued that 'night' is quite limited during the summer. More importantly, the law should properly define those acts which are prohibited.

PUBLIC MEETINGS

It is an offence, contrary to the Public Meeting Act 1908, s 1, for any person at a lawful public meeting to act in a disorderly manner for the purpose of preventing the transaction of the business for which the meeting was called together. It is also an offence to incite others to do so.

The term 'public meeting' is used in the sense that the meeting is open to the public and not restricted to members of a particular organisation or club. Meetings which are open to the public but held on private premises are therefore public meetings. In such a case, a police officer who reasonably suspects a breach of the peace may enter the private premises. The fact that a meeting is held on a highway does not render it unlawful merely because it is so held. However, the circumstances in which the meeting is held may make the participants liable for other offences, such as obstructing the highway.

Section 1 of the 1908 Act gives constables the power to require a person at a public meeting immediately to give his name and address. However, a constable may only execute this power if requested to do so by the chairman of the meeting. Even when so requested, he must reasonably suspect the person concerned of being guilty of the offence described above before acting. The constable must therefore decide whether or not the person to whom his attention is directed is merely asking questions and making points which the chairman and platform party do not like, or is acting in a disorderly manner for the purpose of preventing the transaction of the business. Refusal or failure to give a name or address, or the giving of a false name and address, is an offence.

PUBLIC ORDER ACT 1936

This Act governs the wearing of political uniforms and participation in quasi-military organisations. It was passed at a time at which the activities of the British Fascist Movement were attracting much attention.

Political uniforms

It is an offence under s 1 of the 1936 Act for any person to wear uniform, in any public place or at any public meeting, which signifies his association with any political organisation or with the promotion of any political object. By way of exception, a chief officer of police, with the consent of the Home Secretary, may by order permit the wearing of such uniforms at a ceremonial, anniversary or other special occasion. The consent of the Attorney-General is required for the continuation of the prosecution of a person charged with this offence.

A 'public meeting' is a meeting held for the purpose of discussing matters of public interest, and may be in a public place or in a private place if the public are permitted to attend (whether on payment or otherwise). There are many organisations (whose objectives are quite harmless) whose members wear some form of identifying clothing within their organisation. This would be within the scope of the section, but for the fact that it only deals with cases where the uniform signifies association with a political organisation or the promotion of a political object *and* it is worn in a public place or a public meeting. It must be emphasised that even members of a political organisation may wear uniforms in private, even in meetings if these are restricted to their own membership.

The term 'uniform' includes any particular article of clothing which is worn by each member of a group and which is intended to indicate his association with such an organisation or object. The article does not have to cover any major part of the body and it is sufficient to prove that the article has been commonly used by members of a political organisation. The berets, dark glasses and dark pullovers used by the IRA identify its members, in the eyes of the public, with a political organisation. In the same way, the wearing of a swastika arm band will still symbolise, in the eyes of the public, association with the Nazi Party.

Police powers

A constable may arrest without warrant any person he reasonably suspects to be committing an offence under s 1 of the 1936 Act.

Quasi-military organisations

Section 2 is concerned with the preparation of private quasi-military forces of any description. Persons who take part in the control or management of any association, or in its training, commit offences if its members or adherents are:

(a) organised, trained or equipped for the purpose of enabling them to usurp the functions of the police or armed forces; or
(b) organised and trained or organised and equipped either to promote a political object by the use or display of physical force, or to arouse reasonable apprehension of that purpose.

In 1963 the Court of Criminal Appeal, when considering the activities of 'Spearhead', an organisation which appeared to be preparing for the possible use of force to promote a political object, ruled that political prejudice must be excluded from the minds of the jury and that the fact that there was no evidence of actual attacks on opponents, or of plans to attack them, did not necessarily remove grounds for 'reasonable apprehension of that purpose'.

Where a person is charged with taking part in the control or management of such an association, as opposed to training, he has a defence if he proves that he neither consented to nor connived at the organisation, training or equipment in contravention of the section. It will be appreciated that in any political organisation in which such military preparations have taken place there may be officials who were unaware of the activities of some of its members, and this defence is intended to cover such officials.

The provision of a reasonable number of stewards to assist in the preservation of order at a public meeting held on private premises is permitted, as is the provision of badges and insignia for them. The instruction of such persons in their lawful duties is also permitted.

TERRORISM AND PROSCRIBED ORGANISATIONS

The Prevention of Terrorism (Temporary Provisions) Act 1989 contains a number of offences, as well as other provisions relating to matters such as arrest, detention and interrogation, necessitated by the situation in Northern Ireland.

Proscribed organisations

Section 2 of the 1989 Act makes it an offence:

(a) to belong or profess to belong to a proscribed organisation;
(b) to solicit or invite support for a proscribed organisation, other than support with money or other property; or
(c) to arrange or assist in the arrangement or management of, or to address, any meeting of three or more persons (whether or not it is a meeting to which the public are admitted) knowing that the meeting is:
    (i) to support a proscribed organisation;
    (ii) to further the activities of such an organisation; or
    (iii) to be addressed by a person belonging or professing to belong to such an organisation.

As can be seen, s 2 creates a wide range of offences dealing with membership or professed membership of proscribed organisations, with the promotion of them, and meetings in support of them.

For the purposes of the Act, the proscribed organisations are at present the Irish Republican Army (IRA) and the Irish National Liberation Army (INLA). The general description 'Irish Republican Army' covers both the official and the provisional wings of that organisation. The Home Secretary has power to add to the list of proscribed organisations.

Section 2 provides a defence for those who joined a proscribed organisation before it was proscribed. Provided that such a person proves that he has not taken part in the activities of the organisation since it became proscribed, he will not be guilty of the offence of membership of that organisation.

Section 1 of the Criminal Justice (Terrorism and Conspiracy) Act 1998 provides special evidential rules in respect of an offence under s 2 of the 1989 Act of belonging or professing to belong to a proscribed organisation where that organisation is a 'specified organisation' for the purposes of the 1998 Act. Section 1 of the 1998 Act provides that, if a police officer of or above the rank of superintendent states in oral evidence that in his opinion the accused:

(a) belongs to a specified organisation, or
(b) belonged at a particular time to an organisation which was then specified,

then that statement is admissible as evidence of the matter stated, although an accused cannot be committed for trial or convicted solely on the basis of it.

Contributions towards acts of terrorism

Section 9(1) of the 1989 Act provides that a person is guilty of an offence if he:

(a) solicits or invites any other person to give, lend or otherwise make available, whether for consideration or not, any money or other property; or
(b) receives or accepts, whether for consideration or not, any money or other property; or
(c) uses, or has possession of, whether for consideration or not, any money or other property,

intending that it shall be applied or used for the commission of, or in connection with, acts of terrorism connected with Northern Irish affairs or acts of terrorism of any other description triable in the United Kingdom (except acts connected solely with the affairs of the United Kingdom or any part of it other than Northern Ireland) or having reasonable cause to suspect that it may be so applied or used.

Section 9(2) provides that a person is guilty if he:

(a) gives, lends or otherwise makes available, whether for consideration or not, any money or other property; or
(b) enters into or is otherwise concerned in an arrangement whereby money or other property is or is to be made available,

knowing or having reasonable cause to suspect that it will or may be applied or used as mentioned in s 9(1).

Section 9 is concerned with contributions to terrorism of the specified types, regardless of the terrorists involved. Section 10 makes rather more stringent provisions relating to contributions to the resources of proscribed organisations.

Section 10 provides that a person is guilty of an offence if, *for the benefit of a proscribed organisation,* he does any of the things prohibited by s 9(1)(a)(soliciting etc money or other property), s 9(1)(b) (receiving or accepting, or using or having possession of, money or other property), s 9(1)(c) (using or possessing etc), s 9(2)(a) (giving, lending etc) or s 9(2)(b) (entering etc—an arrangement for the availability of money etc). Unlike offences under s 9, the prosecution does not have to prove that an accused under s 10 intended or had reason to suspect that the money etc would be used for terrorist purposes. However, an accused under s 10(1)(b) (giving, lending, receiving or accepting money or property for a proscribed organisation) has a defence if he proves that he did not know and had no reasonable cause to suspect that the money or property was for the benefit of a proscribed organisation, and an accused under s 10(1)(c) (entering or being concerned in an arrangement for money or property to be available) has a defence if he proves that he did not know and had no reasonable cause to suspect that the arrangement related to a proscribed organisation.

Because it is irrelevant that the financial assistance is given for consideration, a person who purchases some article, object or property, knowing or having reason to suspect that the money he hands over will be used for terrorism commits an offence under s 9, and a person who buys an article in circumstances where the money benefits a proscribed organisation commits an offence under s 10 unless he proves that he had no reason to suspect that it would benefit such an organisation.

It is an offence contrary to s 11 for any person to assist in the retention or control of terrorist funds (funds connected with acts of terrorism, or the proceeds of acts of terrorism, or the resources of a proscribed organisation). It is a defence for such a person to prove that he did not know and had no reasonable cause to suspect that the arrangement related to terrorist funds.

Powers of arrest and detention and taking of samples

Section 14 of the 1989 Act provides a power of arrest without warrant and provides for the detention of persons arrested for a period up to 48 hours. This period may be extended by the Home Secretary up to a maximum of five days. A constable may arrest without warrant anywhere in the United Kingdom a person whom he reasonably suspects:

(a) to be guilty of an offence under s 2 (above) or ss 9, 10 or 11 (financial assistance for terrorism concerned with Northern Irish affairs etc or for a proscribed organisation); or

(b) to be or to have been concerned in the commission, preparation or instigation of acts of terrorism connected with the affairs of Northern Ireland, or acts of terrorism of any other description except acts connected solely with the affairs of the United Kingdom or any part of the United Kingdom other than Northern Ireland.

The extensive power conferred by (b) can be summarised as covering all acts of terrorism, except those which are 'domestic' (in the sense that they only involve the affairs of the United Kingdom or any part of the United Kingdom other than Northern Ireland).

The rules under the Police and Criminal Evidence Act 1984 in respect of intimate and non-intimate samples (see pp 136-139) are subject to the following differences where a person is detained under s 14 of the 1989 Act.

An officer may only give an authorisation for the taking of an intimate sample if he is satisfied that it is necessary to do so in order to assist in determining:

(a) whether that person is or has been concerned in the commission, preparation or instigation of acts of terrorism to which s 14 of the 1989 Act applies; or
(b) whether he is subject to an exclusion order under the Act;

or if the officer has reasonable grounds for suspecting that person's involvement in an offence under ss 2, 9, 10 or 11 of the 1989 Act and for believing that an intimate sample will tend to confirm or disprove his involvement.

The rules relating to the taking of non-intimate samples are amended in the case of terrorist suspects, so that a police officer may only give an authorisation if he is satisfied of the matters just set out above in relation to intimate samples.

Similar amendments are made to Sch 5 to the 1989 Act.

The reader is reminded of the extended powers of stop and search for suspected terrorists provided by s 13A and s 13B described in ch 3.

Display of support for a proscribed organisation

It is an offence contrary to s 3 of the 1989 Act for a person in a public place to wear any item of dress or to wear, carry or display any article in such a way or in such circumstances as to arouse reasonable apprehension that he is a member or supporter of a proscribed organisation. The carrying of banners or the wearing of favours indicating support for the IRA and INLA amount to offences against s 3.

Failing to disclose information

Section 18(1) of the 1989 Act makes it an offence for a person to fail, without reasonable excuse, to disclose as soon as reasonably practicable to a constable information which he knows or believes might be of material assistance:

(a) in preventing the commission by any other person of an act of terrorism in any part of the United Kingdom, connected with Northern Irish affairs; or
(b) in securing the apprehension, prosecution or conviction of any other person for an offence involving the commission, preparation or instigation of such an act of terrorism.

This is an arrestable offence.

The provisions of this section are wide enough to embrace the failure of close relatives of terrorists to disclose information in their possession as soon as reasonably practicable. It is recommended that relatives of a terrorist, who are not themselves involved in terrorism, should not be investigated with a view to obtaining evidence of offences by them against this section, unless particular extreme circumstances make this desirable. An example of such circumstances would be where the withholding of information could lead to death, serious injury or the escape of a terrorist offender.

Section 18A provides that a person is guilty of an offence if:

(a)   he knows, or suspects, that another person is providing financial assistance for terrorism;
(b)   the information, or other matter, on which that knowledge or suspicion is based comes to his attention in the course of his trade, profession, business or employment; and
(c)   he does not disclose the information or other matter to a constable as soon as is reasonably practicable after it comes to his attention.

Thus, accountants, financial advisers etc, are required to disclose information concerning contributions made to assist terrorism. However, legal advisers are exempted from this requirement by s 18A(3). Any disclosure so made to a constable will not amount to a breach of any restriction imposed by statute or otherwise. It is a defence to show 'reasonable excuse' for non-disclosure.

Possession of articles for terrorist purposes

Section 16A of the 1989 Act prohibits the possession of articles in circumstances giving rise to a reasonable suspicion that the article is in a person's possession for a purpose connected with the commission, preparation or instigation of acts of terrorism. The offence is an arrestable one. Where it is proved that at the time of the commission of such an alleged offence, the person and the article were both present in any premises, or the article was in the premises of which he was the occupier, or which he habitually used other than as a member of the public, the court may accept the fact proved as sufficient evidence of his possession of that article at the time unless it is further proved that he did not at that time know of its presence in the premises in question, or, if he did know, that he had no control over it.

Unlawful collection, recording or possession of information

Section 16B of the 1989 Act creates offences of a person collecting or recording any information which is of such a nature as is likely to be useful to terrorists in planning or carrying out any act of terrorism and of having in his possession any record or document containing any such information. These offences are arrestable offences.
The recording of information includes recording by means of a photograph.

CHAPTER 32

Public order offences related to sporting events and those connected with industrial disputes

Because of the high incidence of unruly behaviour before, during and after soccer matches, a number of Acts deal specifically with offences committed by persons attending such sporting events and give police officers particular powers to deal with such persons.

Recognising the high level of emotional feeling surrounding industrial disputes, the Trade Union and Labour Relations (Consolidation) Act 1992 seeks to ensure that disruption is kept to a minimum, while at the same time recognising the rights of individuals to protest concerning their working conditions.

PUBLIC ORDER AND SPORTING EVENTS

Alcohol on coaches, trains, etc

Sections 1 and 1A of the Sporting Events (Control of Alcohol etc) Act 1985 provide a number of offences whose aim is to prevent drunken behaviour by football fans en route to or from matches, and to prevent them arriving at grounds drunk. These offences are offences of:

(a) causing or permitting the carriage of alcohol on a specified vehicle;
(b) being in possession of alcohol on such a vehicle; and
(c) being drunk on a specified vehicle.

Vehicles specified

Section 1 of the 1985 Act provides these offences in relation to public service vehicles (ie coaches, buses and the like) and passenger trains. It does not apply to all such vehicles but only to those which are being used for the principal purpose of carrying passengers for the whole or part of a journey to or from a 'designated sporting event'. Thus, it does not apply to a bus or train on a normal scheduled service because it is not being used for the principal purpose of carrying passengers to or from a designated sporting event, even if the majority of the passengers are travelling to or from a match, since the words 'used' and 'principal purpose' must refer to use by, and the principal purpose of, the bus or rail company. However, it does apply to a 'football special' or to a coach or train chartered by the supporters' club, provided that it is travelling to or from a designated sporting event.

Section 1A of the 1985 Act provides substantially identical offences to those in s 1 in relation to a motor vehicle which:

(a) is not a public service vehicle but is adapted to carry more than eight passengers; and

(b) is being used for the principal purpose of carrying *two or more* passengers for the whole or part of a journey to or from a designated sporting event.

It will be noted that the definition is not limited to minibuses. It therefore includes the few types of private car which are adapted to carry more than eight passengers.

Designated sporting event

'Designated sporting event' is defined by s 9(3) of the 1985 Act. It means 'a sporting event or proposed sporting event for the time being designated, or of a class designated, by order made by the Secretary of State'. It also 'includes a designated sporting event within the meaning of Part V of the Criminal Justice (Scotland) Act 1980'. A designation order made by the Secretary of State may apply to events or proposed events outside Great Britain as well as those in England and Wales.

In the Sports Grounds and Sporting Events (Designation) Order 1985 made by the Home Secretary, the following classes of sporting events have been specified:

(a) (i) association football matches in which one or both teams represent a Football League or a Football Association Premier League club;
   (ii) international association football matches (including semi-professional and schoolboy ones);
   (iii) association football matches (other than those already specified) in the European Champion Clubs Cup, European Cup Winners' Cup or UEFA Cup, provided in each case that the match takes place at the ground of an association football club which is a member of the Football Association or the Football Association of Wales or at Wembley Stadium;
(b) association football matches within the jurisdiction of the Scottish Football Association;
(c) association football matches outside Great Britain -
   (i) in which one or both teams represent the Football Association or Football Association of Wales or a Football League club; or
   (ii) in competition for the European Champion Clubs Cup, European Cup Winners' Cup or UEFA Cup and one or both teams represent a club which is a member of the Football Association or the Football Association of Wales.

All matches in the Scottish Football League, all matches in the Highland Football League, all Scottish Football League and Association cup matches, all football matches in the three European cups, and soccer internationals, provided in each case that they take place at a designated ground, have been designated by the Sports Grounds and Sporting Events (Designation) (Scotland) Order 1980. The grounds designated by the Order are Hampden Park and the grounds of members of the Scottish Football League or of the Highland League. In addition, the Order designates rugby internationals at Murrayfield as designated sporting events.

Causing or permitting carriage of alcohol on a vehicle

Section 1(2) provides that a person who knowingly causes or permits intoxicating liquor to be carried on a vehicle to which s 1 applies is guilty of an offence:

(a) if the vehicle is a public service vehicle and he is the operator of the vehicle or the employee or agent of the operator; or

(b) if the vehicle is a hired vehicle (eg a chartered train or a football special) and he is the person to whom it is hired or the employee or agent of that person. Thus, an organiser of the supporters' club (or his agent) can be convicted if he permits intoxicating liquor to be carried on a chartered train, but a train guard who fails to prevent this cannot because, although he permits it, he is not a person to whom the train is hired (nor the employee or agent of such a person).

Section 1A(2) provides that a person who knowingly causes or permits intoxicating liquor to be carried on a motor vehicle to which s 1A applies is guilty of an offence:

(a) if he is its driver; or

(b) if he is not its driver but its keeper, the servant or agent of its keeper, a person to whom it is made available (by hire, loan or otherwise) by its keeper or the keeper's servant or agent, or the servant or agent of a person to whom it is so made available.

The causing or permitting of the carrying of liquor on the vehicle must be done 'knowingly', which means that the accused must actually know or be wilfully blind that he is causing or permitting the carrying of liquor on the vehicle.

Possession of alcohol on vehicle

Section 1(3) makes it an offence for a person to have intoxicating liquor in his possession while on a vehicle to which s 1 applies. There is a corresponding offence under s 1A(3) in relation to motor vehicles to which s 1A applies.

Being drunk on a vehicle

Section 1(4) provides that a person who is drunk on a vehicle to which s 1 applies is guilty of an offence. There is a corresponding offence under s 1A(4) in relation to motor vehicles to which s 1A applies.

Police powers

By s 7(3), a constable may stop a public service vehicle to which s 1 applies or a motor vehicle to which s 1A applies (but not, for obvious reasons, a railway passenger vehicle) and may search such a vehicle or a railway passenger vehicle if he has reasonable grounds to suspect that an offence under s 1 is being or has been committed in respect of that vehicle. The provisions of s 2 of the Police and Criminal Evidence Act 1984 and the Search Code thereunder apply to such a search.

It will be noted that the power to search under s 7(3) is to search the vehicle, and not a person on board it. There is, however, a general power under s 7(2) for a constable to search a person, whom he reasonably suspects is committing or has committed an offence under the Act. This is discussed later.

Alcohol, containers, fireworks, etc at designated sports grounds

Section 2 of the 1985 Act provides two offences relating to alcohol, containers, fireworks and the like, and drunkenness at a designated sports ground. It is aimed at preventing drunkenness at matches and at preventing the use of bottles and cans as missiles.

Designated sports ground

A 'designated sports ground' is defined by s 9(2) of the 1985 Act as any place:

(a) used (wholly or partly) for sporting events where accommodation is provided for spectators; and
(b) for the time being designated, or of a class designated, by order made by the Home Secretary.

In the Sports Grounds and Sporting Events (Designation) Order 1985 made by the Home Secretary, the following grounds—all of them (with one exception) association football grounds—have been designated so far: the home grounds of all football clubs which are members of the Football Association or the Football Association of Wales; any other ground in England and Wales used occasionally or temporarily by such a club, or used for international matches; Wembley Stadium (which is not simply a football ground), and the ground of Berwick Rangers.

Period of a designated sporting event

Offences under s 2 of the 1985 Act can only be committed during 'the period of a designated sporting event'. 'Designated sporting event' is defined on p 645. Normally, the period of such an event is the period beginning two hours before the start of the event or (if earlier, as where the start is delayed) two hours before the time at which it is advertised to start and ending one hour after the end of the event. Where a match is postponed or cancelled, the period ends one hour after the advertised start time. In respect of a room in a designated sports ground from which the designated sporting event may be directly viewed to which the public are not admitted (eg the directors' box), there is a different period in relation only to an offence of possession of alcohol etc. This is a 'restricted period' beginning 15 minutes before the start of the event (or advertised start) and ending 15 minutes after the end of the event or 15 minutes after the advertised start (if the event is postponed or cancelled).

Possession of alcohol etc at designated ground

Section 2(1) of the 1985 Act provides that a person who has intoxicating liquor or an article to which s 2 applies in his possession:

(a) at any time during the period of a designated sporting event when he is in any area of a designated sports ground from which the event may be directly viewed; or

(b)   while entering or trying to enter a designated sports ground at any time during the
      period of a designated sporting event at that ground,

is guilty of an offence.

The reference to an article to which s 2 applies is to various types of drinks containers,
for example bottles or a crushed-up can, which can be used as missiles or weapons.
Because these are not offensive weapons per se (except in the case of a deliberately
broken bottle or the like), a conviction for possessing an offensive weapon is most
unlikely if a container is not actually used to cause injury because the necessary intent
to use it to cause injury would be impossible to prove. Consequently, it was not normally
possible for the police to take preventive action before a container was used offensively.
The present provision is aimed at plugging this gap.

To turn to detail, s 2(3) states that an article to which s 2 applies is any article capable
of causing injury to a person struck by it, being:

(a)   a bottle, can or other portable container (including such an article when crushed
      or broken) which is for holding any drink and is of a kind which, when empty, is
      normally discarded or returned to, or left to be recovered by, the supplier; or
(b)   part of an article falling within (a).

However, the definition expressly does not apply to anything that is for holding any
medicinal product.

The container need not be made specifically to hold alcohol, and it is irrelevant that
it has never contained alcohol or that it is broken. An empty lemonade bottle is caught,
as is a coke tin. On the other hand, a re-usable plastic drinks container, a mug, a thermos
flask, a decanter or hip flask is not (although the latter two are likely to excite suspicion
of possession of alcohol), since it is not the kind of container which is normally discarded
or returned to, or left to be recovered by, the supplier.

Possession of fireworks etc

Section 2A(1) of the 1985 Act, which is essentially aimed at reducing the risk of fire,
makes identical provision in relation to the possession of a firework or of distress flares,
fog signals, canisters of smoke or visible gas and similar articles. Matches and cigarette
lighters are expressly excluded.

It is a defence for a person charged with an offence under s 2A(1) to prove that he
had possession with lawful authority.

Being drunk at a designated sports ground

Section 2(2) of the 1985 Act provides that a person who is drunk in a designated sports
ground at any time during the period of a designated sporting event at that ground, or
who is drunk while entering or trying to enter such a ground at any time during the
period of a designated sporting event at that ground, is guilty of an offence.

Misbehaviour at a designated football match

The Football (Offences) Act 1991 creates a number of offences. They can only be
committed at a 'designated football match'. Such matches are designated by the
Football (Offences) (Designation of Football Matches) Order 1991. The Order designates

any association football match played in England and Wales which is a UEFA match, or which involves a Football League or FA Premier League team or a team representing any country or territory, and which is played at a designated sports ground or one occupied by a team in one of the two Leagues.

References in the Act to things done at a designated football match include anything done there in the period beginning two hours before the start of the match or (if earlier) two hours before the advertised start time and ending one hour after the end of the match. If the match does not take place, the period is two hours before the advertised start time until one hour after that time.

Throwing objects

The Football (Offences) Act 1991, s 2 creates offences of throwing anything at or towards:

(a) the playing area or any area adjacent to the playing area to which spectators are not generally admitted; or

(b) any area in which spectators or other persons are or may be present;

without lawful authority or excuse (which it is for the accused to prove).

Thus, those who throw objects onto the pitch, into the players' tunnel etc, or into spectator areas will commit offences. Those who may prove 'lawful authority or excuse' would include vendors who throw packets of crisps etc into the crowd, or spectators who throw money to such persons.

Chanting

Section 3 of the 1991 Act makes it an offence to take part in 'chanting' of an indecent or racist nature. 'Chanting' means the repeated uttering of words or sounds in concert with one or more others, and 'racist nature' means consisting of or including matter which is threatening, abusive or insulting to a person by reason of his colour, race, nationality (including citizenship) or ethnic or national origin.

Pitch invasion

By s 4, it is an offence for a person to go on to the playing area, or any area adjacent to the playing area to which spectators are not generally admitted, without lawful authority or lawful excuse (which it is for the accused to prove).

It is not easy to obtain a conviction where spectators surge forward on to the pitch. Most will contend that they were carried forward unwillingly by the momentum of the crowd. If this is not disproved, a conviction for an offence under s 4 will not be possible, since a person cannot generally be convicted if his conduct was beyond his control. Those who would have lawful excuse for going on to the pitch include trainers and official first aiders.

Sporting events: general police powers

Under the Sporting Events (Control of Alcohol etc) Act 1985

A constable may, at any time during the period of a designated sporting event at any designated sports ground, enter any part of the ground for the purpose of enforcing the 1985 Act. It will be noted that the constable's power of entry is not limited to the 'public' parts of the ground; if necessary for the purposes of enforcing the Act of 1985, he can enter the directors' suite or the manager's office.

In addition, a constable may search a person he has reasonable grounds to suspect is committing or has committed an offence under the Act of 1985 and may arrest such a person.

The powers to search and to arrest are extensive but it must be remembered that 'reasonable grounds to suspect' is a term which is now carefully defined in Annex B to the Stop and Search Code. There must be a sound basis of fact upon which a police officer forms his reasonable suspicion that such an offence is being committed. Searches of supporters entering grounds cannot be carried out under a general belief that such persons are likely to commit these offences and this is specifically stated in the Code. If a person is seen to be carrying a supermarket bag with the distinctive bulge of a 'four-pack', or the outline of bottles etc can be seen inside coat pockets, then a reasonable suspicion exists. The suspicion is directed towards an individual and there is reason to suspect him. It is appreciated that Note 1D to the Code provides that nothing in the Code affects the routine searching of persons entering sports grounds or other premises, *with their consent or as a condition of entry*. The searches which take place outside soccer grounds do not generally take place with consent (they may be accepted under the belief that the police have a right to do so) and a search as a condition of entry to a sports ground is not a search which should be conducted by a police officer, even if he is paid by the proprietor of the ground to do duty there. If a proprietor makes such a condition, it should be enforced by his own stewards as it is no part of a police officer's duty to enforce the rights of such proprietors.

Under the 1991 Act

All offences against the Football (Offences) Act 1991 are arrestable offences.

Exclusion and restriction orders

Exclusion orders

Part IV of the Public Order Act 1986 empowers a court by or before which a person is convicted of certain offences to make an exclusion order prohibiting him from entering any premises for the purpose of attending any prescribed football match there. The court must be satisfied that the making of such an order in relation to the accused will help prevent violence or disorder at or in connection with prescribed football matches. Thus, an order is unlikely to be made if the vicar is convicted of possessing whisky contained in a hip flask at a designated sporting event! The order must be *additional* to a sentence, probation order, or order of absolute or conditional discharge. A 'prescribed football match' is one involving a Football League or the Football Association Premier League team or one which is an international match or a match in the European Champion Clubs Cup, the European Cup Winners' Cup or the UEFA Cup.

It is an offence for any person to enter premises in breach of an exclusion order. A constable who reasonably suspects that a person has entered premises in breach of an exclusion order may arrest him without warrant.

Exclusion orders simply require their subjects to stay away from prescribed matches. They do not go further and require their subjects to report to the police when matches are taking place, but restriction orders do.

Restriction orders

The Football Spectators Act 1989 empowers a court by or before which a person is convicted of certain offences to make a restriction order against him. The purpose of a restriction order is to prevent the person concerned attending designated football matches outside England and Wales. Exclusion orders are clearly inapplicable to matches abroad and it is for this reason that restriction orders were introduced by the 1989 Act.

No restriction order may be made unless the court is satisfied that making it in relation to the accused would help to prevent violence or disorder at or in connection with designated football matches outside England and Wales. A restriction order may only be made in addition to a sentence or probation order.

Offences for which a conviction enables a court to make a restriction order are listed in Sch 1 to the 1989 Act. They include:

(a) offences contrary to the Sporting Events (Control of Alcohol etc) Act 1985;
(b) offences involving violence or threats of violence, harassment, alarm or distress, or racial hatred committed during a period relevant to a designated match, while at, entering or leaving the ground, or while on a journey to or from the match;
(c) offences involving violence or threats of violence against property committed during such a period, or while on a journey to or from the match;
(d) offences of drunkenness committed while on such a journey;
(e) offences contrary to the Road Traffic Act 1988, ss 4 or 5 (drink and driving etc) committed while the accused was on a journey to or from a designated football match; and
(f) offences contrary to the Football (Offences) Act 1991.

Where it is relevant in the above list that the offence was committed while on a journey to or from a designated football match, a 'designated football match' includes one in this country or one outside England and Wales and a restriction order can only be made if the court declares that the offence related to football matches. Otherwise, references in the above list to a designated football match are to a designated match in England and Wales.

Designation of football matches has been made under the 1989 Act by two Orders. By the Football Spectators (Designation of Football Matches in England and Wales) Order 1993, a football match is designated if it is played either at Wembley Stadium, the National Stadium at Cardiff, or at any sports ground in England and Wales which is registered with the Football League or the Football Association Premier League at the time the match is played. The Football Spectators (Designation of Football Matches Outside England and Wales) Order 1990 designates away international matches involving Football Association national sides; matches outside England and Wales involving full or associate member clubs of the Football League or the Football Association Premier League; or matches involving club sides participating in UEFA competitions outside England and Wales.

There is a second power under the 1989 Act to make a restriction order. By s 22, there is a power by Order in Council to list offences under the law of a country other than England and Wales which correspond to offences specified in Sch 1 to the 1989 Act. Section 22 empowers a magistrates' court to make a restriction order against a person convicted of a listed offence in relation to a designated match outside England and Wales.

Provision is made by s 22 of the 1989 Act for evidence of such a conviction to be proved by way of certificate. So far corresponding offences under Scottish law, and under French, Irish, Italian, Norwegian and Swedish law have been listed.

Restriction orders may be for a period of five years where the person is sentenced to a period of imprisonment to take immediate effect (the requirement commencing upon his release from prison), or two years in any other case. A person may apply to the court by which the order was made for termination after one year.

A person who is made subject to a restriction order must report initially to a police station specified in the order within a period of five days beginning with the date of the making of the order. In addition, subject to any exemptions, he must report on the occasions of designated football matches outside England and Wales, designated by the Football Spectators (Designation of Football Matches Outside England and Wales) Order 1990 when required to do so to any police station in England and Wales at the time, or between the times, specified in the notice by which the requirement is imposed. It is the Football Spectators Restriction Orders Authority (a common police service established by the Home Secretary) who will issue such notices. Exemptions may be granted from so reporting on particular occasions. Generally the grant of an exemption is a matter for the Authority. However, an exemption may be granted by the officer responsible for the police station if the application is made within five days of the designated football match in question but he must not do so without first referring the matter to the Authority, unless it is not reasonably practicable to do so. The Authority must grant an exemption if the applicant shows to its satisfaction that special circumstances justify the exemption and that, because of those circumstances, he would not attend the match so exempted.

A person who, without reasonable excuse, fails to comply with the duty to report imposed by a restriction order commits an offence. This offence was added to the list of arrestable offences under the Police and Criminal Evidence Act 1984, s 24(2), by the Crime and Disorder Act 1998, s 84.

Ticket touts

The Criminal Justice and Public Order Act 1994, s 166 makes it an offence for any unauthorised person to sell, or offer or expose for sale, a ticket for a designated football match, in any public place or place to which the public has access or, in the case of a trade or business, in any other place.

The only persons who are 'authorised' are those authorised in writing by the home club or oganisers of the match. The term 'ticket' includes anything which purports to be a ticket, so that false tickets are included. However, where a false ticket is involved a charge of obtaining property by deception would be more appropriate where knowledge of such falsity can be proved. A 'designated football match' is one falling within the designation under the Football (Offences) Act 1991, s 1(1) (see p 649).

Police powers

The offence is an arrestable one.

The provisions of the Police and Criminal Evidence Act 1984, s 32 (search of an arrested person and his vehicle) are extended to the case where the vehicle is reasonably suspected to have been used for any purpose connected with the offence.

LABOUR LAWS

The police are becoming increasingly and inevitably involved in the enforcement of the law concerning trade disputes. Consequently, it is essential that that law is clearly understood by police officers, who are very much in the public eye when dealing with such disputes. The primary piece of legislation dealing with trade disputes is the Trade Union and Labour Relations (Consolidation) Act 1992.

Acts of 'interference' with workers

Section 241 of the Act is not directly concerned with picketing. Indeed, it is not confined to the context of trade disputes. However, that is its normal application. It deals with acts which may or may not be committed away from the picket line but which nevertheless amount to attempts to prevent a worker from exercising his own freedom of choice.

An offence is committed by any person who, with a view to compelling any other person to abstain from doing or to do any act which that other person has a legal right to do or abstain from doing, wrongfully and without lawful authority does one of the following things:

Uses violence to or intimidates such other person or his wife or children, or injures his property

It is essential to realise that only peaceful picketing can be lawful. No matter what a mob may represent itself to be, if that mob or any particular person uses violence or intimidates another person an offence is committed against s 241. Acts committed against a person's spouse, children or property are also punishable. It is not a form of peaceful persuasion to threaten a worker, his family or his property with violence. Instances have recently occurred in which the cars of workers who refused to join a strike have been damaged. In addition to the offence of criminal damage, the present offence is also committed.

Persistently follows such other person about from place to place

The word 'persistently' is not meant to convey any form of permanence in this activity and it is sufficient if a person, or part of the mob outside a works, follows a man from the works and through the streets, shouting at him or making hostile gestures. The following of an employer in an attempt to compel him to reinstate an employee is also covered by this provision.

Hides any tools, clothes or other property owned or used by such other person or deprives him of or hinders him in the use thereof

An effective way of preventing a skilled workman from carrying out his duties would be to prevent him from working by separating him from specialist tools required to carry out his task. If all the miners' lamps for a particular colliery were hidden, this could effectively prevent individual miners, and perhaps the entire workforce, from working.

Watches or besets the house or other place where such other person resides, or works, or carries on business, or happens to be, or the approach to such a house or place

'Watching or besetting' merely describes certain forms of picketing. It must be remembered that all the various types of conduct covered by s 241 are only criminal if they are done wrongfully. As a result, a person engaged in lawful picketing is not guilty under s 241 by virtue of the present provision. What constitutes 'lawful picketing' is described below. There would be little purpose in restricting the nature of picketing at a works to forms of peaceful picketing if pickets could operate outside the houses of individual workers to prevent them from working. This mode of the offence is designed among other things to prevent the removal of picket lines or single persuaders from the works to a dwelling house or its approaches.

Since, like any other offence under s 241, watching or besetting must be done with a view to compelling someone to abstain from doing something which he has a legal right to do, or vice versa, as opposed to with a view to simply persuading him, there cannot be a conviction on the ground of watching or besetting in the absence of proof that someone was either prevented or was likely to be prevented, or intended to be prevented, from doing something etc. The reason is that, in the absence of such evidence, there is no evidence of the watching or besetting being done with a view to compelling someone not to do something etc.

This was held in a case concerning alleged watching and besetting of an abortion clinic, where the accused sought to persuade women not to enter solely by verbal means, with no threat or actual use of force. The Divisional Court held that, in the absence of evidence that anyone was prevented, or likely to be prevented, or intended to be prevented, from undergoing an abortion, the accused had not acted with a view to compelling women not to do so.

Follows such other person with two or more other persons in a disorderly manner in or through any street or road

Although we have already considered the following of persons by those wishing to compel them not to work, this offence differs in that there is no need to prove any form of persistence. The aggravation by being accompanied by two or more persons and the incidence of disorderly conduct are sufficient. This mode of committing the offence can only be committed in a street or road.

Arrest

Offences under s 241 are not 'arrestable offences', but a constable may arrest without warrant anyone he reasonably suspects is committing an offence under the section.

Peaceful picketing: Trade Union and Labour Relations (Consolidation) Act 1992

It is extremely important to understand the law concerning peaceful picketing because of the necessity for police officers to ensure that the activities of the pickets are directed towards pursuits which are permitted by law and do not amount to intimidation of other workers, whether they are workers belonging to the same trade union or not.

The Trade Union and Labour Relations (Consolidation) Act 1992, s 220(1) states that it shall be lawful for a person in contemplation or furtherance of a trade dispute to attend:

(a) at or near his own place of work; or
(b) if he is an official of a trade union, at or near the place of work of a member of that union whom he is accompanying and whom he represents,

for the purpose only of peacefully obtaining or communicating information, or peacefully persuading any person to work or abstain from working. These words contain key requirements for lawful picketing. They are concerned with *the place* where a person attends in contemplation or furtherance of a trade dispute and with *the purpose* for which he attends.

The place

Section 220(1) provides that it is lawful for a person in contemplation or furtherance of a trade dispute to attend at or near *his own place of work*; it does not, of course, authorise access to private premises without the consent of their owner. Except in the case of a trade union official accompanying a member whom he represents at or near the latter's place of work, picketing at some place other than the picket's own place of work is not declared to be lawful. Thus, picketing by 'flying pickets' or by other people who do not work at the place in question (and may not even be members of the trade union engaged in the dispute) is not declared to be lawful by s 220(1), and renders such a picket guilty from the outset of an offence against s 241 of the Act on the ground of 'watching or besetting', however peaceful the picket may be.

It follows that the meaning of 'his own place of work' for the purposes of s 220(1) is of crucial importance. In this respect, s 220(2) and (3) make special provision. Section 220(2) deals with the case of a worker who does not work at any one particular place (for example, a service engineer or train driver) or whose place of work is so located that it is impracticable for him to attend there to picket. It provides that the place of work of such a person is *any premises* of his employer *from* which he works or *from* which his work is administered.

Whether or not picketing is *at or near* the picket's place of work depends upon a common sense approach. In one recent case the Court of Appeal held that pickets, who stood at the entrance to a trading estate, 1,200 yards away from their employer's premises on that estate and would have been trespassing if they had picketed on the estate, were attending (picketing) near their place of work.

There are occasions when the provisions of s 220 described so far would act unfairly against a worker who, having been dismissed from his employment, would be excluded from the right to protest because he would no longer have a place of work at or near which he could attend. Subsection (3) protects such a worker, by stating that where:

(a) his last employment was terminated in connection with a trade dispute; or
(b) the termination of his employment was one of the circumstances giving rise to the dispute,

his former place of work shall be treated as if it was his place of work.

The purpose

Even if the requirement that the picket must be obtaining or communicating information, or peacefully picketing at or near his own place of work is satisfied, his conduct is *only declared to be lawful by s 220(1) if his attendance is for the purpose only of peacefully persuading any person to work or abstain from working*. A person who attends for some other purpose, eg forcibly to prevent workers or deliveries entering premises, is not protected by s 220(1) and is liable for any criminal offence which he may commit; he may also, of course, be liable to pay damages under the civil law for any harm which he causes by molesting a worker or interfering with his right to work. Thus, pickets who link arms and form a physical barrier to prevent movement in and out of works are criminally liable, even though they work there, for an offence against s 241 of the Act and for any other offence which they may commit, as are members of a picket which by weight of numbers seeks to prevent others exercising their right to work since it cannot be said that they are there *only* for fulfilling one of the specified purposes peacefully: intimidation is not peaceful persuasion.

The physical presence of lawful pickets on a highway must represent some form of obstruction and this is permitted to the extent that it is reasonably necessary for such pickets to carry out their task of speaking to their colleagues. However, this right is restricted to those who are lawful pickets in accordance with the provisions of s 220. It is a question of fact as to whether or not the degree of obstruction has passed beyond that reasonably required. Mass picketing clearly goes beyond what is reasonably required and is therefore illegal. So is the total obstruction of an entrance, and so are other measures which have the same effect. Where pickets kept moving by walking around in a circle outside the main entrance to a factory and were required to stop doing so by a police officer, they were held to have obstructed him in his duty by their refusal, as they were carrying out an illegal act.

The police have a duty to limit the size of lawful pickets to a number which appears to be reasonable in the circumstances and a refusal by the organisers to comply with reasonable requests made by the police may amount to a wilful obstruction contrary to the Police Act 1996, s 89(2). There is no statutory power to arrest for that offence and an arrest could only be effected under the power described on p 574 above, if there was an actual or apprehended breach of the peace.

The role of the police

The police must not be concerned with the merits of any trade dispute. Their role is the preservation of the peace, and they must impartially enforce and uphold the law where such action becomes necessary. They have a general discretion in relation to their handling of disputes and of pickets to ensure that all remains peaceful and orderly. It is no part of a police officer's duty to assist with civil remedies; if an employer wishes to identify persons on picket lines or outside his works with a view to civil process, that is his responsibility and police officers should not attempt to identify such persons on his behalf. Additionally, the enforcement of any orders made in favour of employers is the responsibility of officers of the court and police participation must be restricted to ensuring the maintenance of the peace.

The code of conduct issued for the guidance of pickets (which recommends that the number of pickets at any entrance to a workplace should not exceed six) is not a part of the criminal law. The number of pickets in particular circumstances is a matter for police discretion bearing in mind their primary purpose of maintaining the peace.

CHAPTER 33

Indecent assault, sexual offences, procurement and abduction

INDECENT ASSAULT ON A WOMAN

The Sexual Offences Act 1956, s 14 states that it is an offence for a person to make an indecent assault on a woman. The offence is an arrestable offence. An indecent assault is an assault (in the sense of an assault or battery) which in itself, or taken in conjunction with the surrounding circumstances, is capable of being considered as indecent by right-minded people.

The nature of the assault

The offence will frequently involve an actual battery in that there will be some touching of the woman without her consent. If a man places his hand inside a woman's blouse and upon her breast this is an indecent assault if she does not consent to being touched there. Likewise, a resisted, passionate kiss, accompanied by a suggestion of sexual intercourse, is an indecent assault. However, there need not be a touching; if there are actions which cause a women to fear immediate bodily contact (ie an assault in the strict sense) and they are done in circumstances of indecency, there can be a conviction for indecent assault. Thus, there was held to have been an indecent assault where a man sitting opposite a woman in a railway carriage had moved threateningly towards her, inviting her to have intercourse with him. Clearly, his actions amounted to an assault. On the other hand, where a man who was standing still with his trousers undone made an indecent suggestion to a woman, it was held that this was not an indecent assault as he had done nothing to put the woman in fear of immediate bodily contact, and therefore there was no assault.

Because the woman must actually have been touched by the accused, or put in fear of immediately being touched by him, an invitation to her to touch the accused indecently can never be an indecent assault. Thus, where a man exposed his naked penis to a nine-year-old girl and invited her to touch it, there was no indecent assault as he had made no move towards her. Had the girl refused to touch him and the man had then grabbed hold of her hand, or had moved towards her, this would have added the element of assault.

The section does not limit the commission of the offence to men. Consequently a woman may be guilty of an indecent assault upon a woman provided that there is an assault and that assault can be described as an indecent assault.

The circumstances of indecency

The assault must either be indecent in itself or be accompanied by circumstances of indecency on the part of the accused. Thus, there will be an indecent assault by X if he goes up to a female stranger and caresses her breast, since the assault is indecent in itself. By way of further example, where a man exposes his person and grabs hold of a woman's arm to draw her attention to it, he commits an indecent assault since there is an assault upon her together with circumstances of indecency on his part. The test of indecency is that there must be a contravention of the standards of decent behaviour of right-thinking members of society in regard to sexual modesty or privacy. Where the circumstances of an alleged offence can be given an innocent as well as an indecent interpretation, evidence of the accused's motive is admissible both to support or negative that the assault was an indecent one. Consequently, where a man has spanked a young girl on her bottom for no reason apparent to her, his later admission that he did so because of a 'buttock fetish' is admissible to support that the assault was an indecent one.

Consent

An essential element of any assault is lack of consent. There is no true consent if a consent is obtained by fraud as to the nature of the act or the identity of the actor. A doctor who obtains consent to acts which amount to an indecent assault, by falsely alleging that they are part of a correct medical examination, is therefore guilty of this offence. Nor can there be a valid consent if actual bodily harm is intended and/or caused by the accused. Thus the whipping or beating of a woman, even with her consent, amounts to an indecent assault if circumstances of indecency exist.

The section states that a girl under 16 years cannot give a consent which would prevent an act from being an assault upon her. This causes some confusion as it is therefore easy to assume that, if there is indecency, there will always be an assault upon a girl under 16. However, it must be remembered that there must be an assault and that therefore the girl must have been touched or put in apprehension of immediately being touched.

A belief, however reasonable, that a girl under 16 is 16 or over is no defence to a charge of indecent assault. However, a reasonable belief by the accused that the girl is his wife because they have gone through a ceremony of marriage is a defence.

A woman who is a defective cannot consent to an act so as to prevent it becoming an indecent assault, but an accused will only be guilty if he knew or had reason to suspect the women to be a defective. A 'defective' is a person suffering from a state of arrested or incomplete development of mind which includes severe impairment of intelligence and social functioning.

A husband can commit an indecent assault on his wife. Consequently, a husband may be guilty of an indecent assault if he causes his wife to indulge in forms of activity to which she does not consent on the grounds that they were indecent, repellent and abhorrent.

Evidence

If the person assaulted is a child under 14, his evidence in criminal proceedings must be given unsworn, and a deposition of such a child's unsworn evidence may be taken for the purposes of criminal proceedings as if that evidence had been given on oath. This is provided by the Criminal Justice Act 1988, s 33A. The question of the competence of the child to give evidence is one to be considered by the court. There is no statutory requirement that a jury must be warned about convicting on the uncorroborated evidence of a person against whom a sexual offence is alleged to have been committed. However, the Court of Appeal has ruled that a judge retains a discretion to urge caution in regard to a particular witness.

INDECENT ASSAULT ON A MALE

It is an offence contrary to the Sexual Offences Act 1956, s 15 for a person to make an indecent assault on a man. It is an arrestable offence. The same principles apply to such assaults as apply to the offence under s 14. Among these, a boy under 16 cannot give consent, nor can a defective.

This offence can be committed by a man or a woman. The fact that the assault can be committed by a woman necessitates consideration of occasions upon which a woman induces a boy under 16 to have intercourse with her. It is no offence for her to do so provided that she merely permits the act and does not assault the boy in any way. However, if she handles his penis at any time that is an indecent assault upon him as she touches him in circumstances of indecency and any consent which he may give will not in law prevent that act being an assault upon him.

CAUSING OR ENCOURAGING INDECENT ASSAULTS

It is an offence, contrary to the Sexual Offences Act 1956, s 28 for a person to cause or encourage an indecent assault on a girl under the age of 16 for whom he is responsible. The following are treated as being responsible for a girl in this context: a parent or guardian, any person who has actual possession or control of her, and any other person who has custody, charge or care of her. 'Causing or encouraging' includes doing nothing to prevent an indecent assault taking place. In one case, a man merely laughed at his friend's indecent advances to a girl who was baby-sitting in his house; he was convicted of an offence under s 28 because he had a duty to protect the girl in his house.

The offence is not an arrestable offence.

GROSS INDECENCY WITH CHILDREN

The Indecency with Children Act 1960 provides two offences. It makes it an offence for any person:

(a) to commit an act of gross indecency with or towards a child under the age of 14; or
(b) to incite such an act with himself or another.

The Act was passed in consequence of difficulties which had arisen following the decision of the Divisional Court that, where a man invited a nine-year-old girl to touch his exposed penis, there was no assault as she had not been touched by the accused or put in fear of being touched.

The Act therefore fills this gap and deals with a person, male or female, who commits a grossly indecent act *with or towards* a child under the age of 14 years, or incites a child of this age to commit such an offence with himself or some other person. Gross indecency is limited to activities involving indecent contact with the genitalia, including contact through clothing. A person commits an act of gross indecency with or towards a child if he does something grossly indecent directed towards a child with the intention of deriving sexual satisfaction, or if he co-operates with, in something grossly indecent which is done by the child. Examples are where a man masturbates in the presence of a child with intent to derive satisfaction from the fact that it is watching, whether or not he has deliberately attracted its attention, but not if he thought that it was not observing him because his actions will not be against or directed towards the child. Another example would be where a man passively permits a child to touch his genitalia in circumstances where he can be said to invite the child to continue. A person *incites* a child to an act of gross indecency if he expressly or impliedly invites a child to touch his penis or that of another.

Proof that the accused did not know that the child was under 14 is not required. Indeed, a reasonable mistaken belief that the child is 14 or over is no excuse.

RAPE

The Sexual Offences Act 1956, s 1(1) simply declares:

'It is an offence for a man to rape a woman or another man.'

The offence is an arrestable offence.
Subsection (2) provides:

'A man commits rape if:
(a) he has sexual intercourse with a person (whether vaginal or anal) who at the time of the intercourse does not consent to it; and
(b) at the time he knows that the person does not consent to the intercourse or he is reckless as to whether the person consents to it.'

The offence of rape was extended by the Criminal Justice and Public Order Act 1994 so as to cover cases in which the victim is a man.

There are several terms included in the section which must be considered.

Unlawful sexual intercourse

We must begin by considering the term 'sexual intercourse'. The intercourse must be per vaginam or per anum. By s 44 of the 1956 Act, proof of sexual intercourse does not require proof of the completion of the intercourse by the emission of seed; instead, the intercourse is deemed by the section to be complete upon proof of penetration only. Consequently, the slightest penetration of the woman's vagina will suffice and it is not necessary that the hymen be ruptured.

A husband can be convicted of raping his wife if the elements of the offence can be proved.

Without the person's consent

The absence of the person's consent is an essential feature of rape; it must always be proved by the prosecution.

Because of the requirement of absence of consent, it is rape to have intercourse with a woman who is asleep, or otherwise unconscious, and therefore unable to give or withhold consent. Thus, if a woman has been made unconscious by drink, intercourse with her will be without her consent and will therefore be rape.

In addition, an apparent consent is not a real consent, and rape is committed in the following cases:

Where the apparent consent is obtained by fraud as to the identity of the other person

Section 1(3) of the Sexual Offences Act 1956 provides that a man commits rape if he induces a married woman to have intercourse with him by impersonating her husband, but it has now been established that fraud as to the identity of the accused man will in general vitiate the 'victim's' consent if it induces the victim to mistake the accused's identity.

Where submission is procured by personal violence or threats of immediate personal violence

It is a matter of common sense that, if a man beats a person until he or she agrees to intercourse with him, such a 'consent' is not a real consent. Likewise, a consent obtained by putting the woman or man in fear of immediate bodily harm cannot, on any reckoning, be a real consent. On the other hand, a consent obtained by some other type of threat is not thereby regarded as not being a real one; intercourse procured by such a threat may, however, give rise to liability for another offence, described below.

Where the consent is obtained by fraud as to the nature of the act

Thus, a doctor commits rape if he has intercourse with a patient after obtaining his or her 'consent' by deceiving that person into believing that what he or she is about to submit to is part of a medical procedure. On the other hand, if consent is obtained by fraud as to some matter other than the nature of the act, the patient's consent is a real consent and rape is not committed, although there may be liability for another offence, described below.

Where the female is so mentally deficient or young or drunk that her knowledge or understanding are such that she is not in a position to decide whether to consent or resist

An apparent consent by a person in such a case is not a real consent.

The Court of Appeal has stated that there is a difference between consent and submission, ie that a woman who submits does not necessarily consent. If this is correct, the range of cases in which a woman does not consent for the purposes of rape, despite apparently doing so, would not be limited to those just described. However, pending a further clarification on the matter, it should be assumed that the range of cases is so limited.

Mens rea

In order for the accused to be guilty of rape, it must be proved that he knew that the person did not consent to the intercourse or was reckless as to whether that person consented. Recklessness in this context bears its subjective meaning, described in ch 1, above.

Whether or not a man knew that he did not have consent or was reckless in that respect is a matter for the jury. An honest belief on the part of the man that the woman was consenting will prevent him knowing or being reckless as to the absence of consent, whether or not his belief was reasonable. However, the less reasonable an alleged belief in the woman's consent, the less likely a jury is to believe the allegation. It is worth noting that the Sexual Offences (Amendment) Act 1976, s 1(2) states:

> '. . . if at a trial for a rape offence the jury has to consider whether a man believed that a woman or man was consenting to sexual intercourse, the presence or absence of reasonable grounds for such a belief is a matter to which the jury is to have regard in conjunction with any other relevant matters, in considering whether he so believed.'

Self-induced intoxication is not a 'relevant matter'.

If a young woman permitted a casual acquaintance to take her into the hayloft of a barn on their very first meeting, this might certainly lead the man to believe that she might consent. However, she might tell him immediately that she will not permit intercourse; if so, he would know that she had not consented. A forcible act of intercourse at that stage would be rape. However, if the man allowed that moment to pass and exchanged kisses and passionate embraces with the girl, who then failed to oppose his advances, although (as is subsequently proved) she did not consent to intercourse, the jury would have to apply their own good sense, experience and knowledge of human nature to the circumstances, and take into account the reasonableness or otherwise of the man's alleged belief that the woman was consenting to intercourse with him, in deciding whether or not he knew or was reckless as to the absence of consent.

Evidence in rape cases

Early complaint

Although it would normally be inadmissible as hearsay, the terms of an early complaint by the man or woman who alleges that he or she has been raped are admissible evidence on the part of the person to whom it was made, provided the complaint was made at the first opportunity and was not made in response to an inducement or leading question. Provided these conditions are satisfied, the terms of an early complaint are also admissible in evidence given by that person. Where evidence of an early complaint is admissible, it is admissible to prove consistency of the complainant's conduct with the story told by him or her in court and as something to negative consent when that is in issue.

Corroboration

The Criminal Justice and Public Order Act 1994, s 32(1) abolished the common law duty imposed upon a trial judge to give a corroboration direction to a jury in respect of the evidence of a complainant of a sexual offence. However, in some cases, such as failure to make an early complaint, or a history of the complainant making false allegations, the judge would be justified in warning the jury against relying on the complainant's unsupported evidence.

Evidence of other sexual experiences of a complainant

Section 2 of the 1976 Act prohibits, except with the leave of the trial judge, evidence and questions in cross-examination concerning sexual experiences of the complainant with a person other than the defendant. Such matters must be considered in the absence of the jury. The judge must only give leave if he is satisfied that it would be unfair to the defendant to refuse to allow the evidence to be adduced or the questions to be asked. If the proposed questions merely seek to establish that the complainant has had sexual experiences with other men to whom she was not married, so as to suggest that for that reason she ought not to be believed under oath, the judge will exclude the evidence because this is insufficient for a judge to be satisfied that it would be unfair to refuse to allow the evidence to be adduced, or the question to be asked. On the other hand, if the judge takes the view that it is more likely than not that the particular evidence or questions, if allowed, might reasonably lead the jury to take a different view of the complainant's evidence from that which they might take if the evidence or questions were not allowed, the judge must permit the evidence to be adduced or questions asked.

The operation of the principle can be shown by reference to a case where a man was charged with raping a 14-year-old girl and the question to be resolved was one of consent. The complainant, in a witness statement, alleged that she was a virgin and in evidence said that intercourse had been very painful. The defence established during cross-examination that medical evidence suggested that the girl's physical condition was consistent with having had intercourse on more than one occasion but it was inconclusive. The defence sought to cross-examine the complainant merely to establish that she had had intercourse prior to the allegation, but leave to do so was denied. The Court of Appeal held that the girl's past experience went to the fundamental issue of consent. It said that the girl was 12 years younger than the accused. He was not of the same ethnic group as her and was physically unattractive. It had been submitted by the accused's counsel that, even in this day and age, the jury hearing the sordid circumstances that prevailed would tend to form the view that the girl had not consented. Applying the test set out above, and allowing the accused's appeal, the Court of Appeal found that if the jury had been told that the girl had previously engaged voluntarily in sexual intercourse they might have reached a different conclusion about whether or not the girl had consented. Consequently, the judge should have permitted cross-examination as to the girl's previous sexual experience.

Advice in rape cases

(a) To be fully effective, anonymity for complainants must start from the moment when the allegation of rape is made to the police.
(b) Tactful and sympathetic interrogation of complainants is important. Experience and sympathy in the interviewing officer are more important than his or her sex.
(c) Medical examination in a clinical environment, such as a hospital or surgery, should reduce distress, produce an atmosphere of care and concern, and provide for immediate treatment where desirable. As, however, there may be difficulties in the way of having such examinations away from a police station, adequate and suitable

facilities for medical examination in police stations are needed in case it is necessary for such examinations to take place there.
(d) If possible, and if time permits, the police should ensure that the complainant is referred to the appropriate services, whether medical or social; this is best done before the complainant leaves the police station.

This advice is included in the report of the Advisory Group on the Law of Rape (1976) and it is extremely important. The complainant has just undergone an extremely frightening experience and will require all the assurance which it is possible to give.

PROCURING INTERCOURSE WITH A WOMAN BY THREATS OR FALSE PRETENCES

The Sexual Offences Act 1956, ss 2 and 3 contain offences dealing with such conduct. They provide that it is an offence for a person to procure a woman, by threats or intimidation (s 2) or by false pretences or false representations (s 3), to have sexual intercourse in any part of the world.

Neither offence is an arrestable offence. They may be committed either by a man or by a woman; in the case of a man, the intercourse procured may be either with himself or with another man. Liability for either offence arises only when the intercourse has actually taken place. The intercourse need not occur in this country, but the act of procuring must have taken place within the jurisdiction.

For the purposes of s 2, 'threats or intimidation' are not limited to those which vitiate an apparent consent for the purposes of rape, although trivial threats will not suffice. By way of example, a man who procures intercourse for himself or another with a woman by a threat to expose her infidelities to her husband unless she consents to intercourse does not commit rape, as there is no immediate threat of bodily harm, but he is guilty of the present offence, as is a factory foreman who procures intercourse with a female employee who is heavily dependent on her wages by threatening to find reasons to sack her unless she consents to intercourse. On the other hand, a man who procures sexual intercourse by threatening not to take the woman to the cinema otherwise is not guilty of an offence under s 2; it would be ridiculous if such a trivial threat could convert mere immorality into a criminal offence.

For the purposes of s 3, false pretences or false representations are not limited to fraud which vitiates consent for the purposes of rape. Thus, X is guilty of an offence under s 3 if he has intercourse with a woman by deceiving her into believing that he intends to pay her for it; as we have seen, X's fraud would not prevent the woman giving a real consent for the purposes of the offence of rape and X would not be guilty of rape. Apart from requiring that the 'false pretence or representation' should procure the intercourse, s 3 makes no specification concerning these terms. However, reference to other areas of the law suggests that, if A procures intercourse with B by falsely promising to marry her, he can be convicted under s 3 because he will have falsely represented his present intentions.

ADMINISTRATION OF DRUGS TO FACILITATE INTERCOURSE

By the Sexual Offences Act 1956, s 4, it is an offence for a person to apply or administer to, or cause to be taken by, a woman any drug, matter or thing with intent to stupefy or overpower her so as thereby to enable any man to have unlawful (ie extra-marital) sexual intercourse with her. Once again, the offence can be committed by any person. If a group of young men occupy the attention of girls in a café and one of them, in order to facilitate intercourse with one of the girls, adds a stupefying drug to her tea, he commits the offence when she drinks the tea. It is not necessary that the person who administers the drug (or anyone else) should take any further steps to enable himself or another to have intercourse.

The means of drugging are widely described. 'Apply' suggests some form of chloroform; 'administer' covers injecting a drug or the like; and 'cause to be taken' includes encouragement or urging the girl to take the drug herself or slipping a drug into her drink, provided the taking occurs.

The term 'or thing' as included in the section is wide enough to include intoxicating liquor, but it would be necessary to prove that the liquor was administered, or caused to be taken, with the specified intention. Where a man takes home a young girl who is unused to drinking intoxicating liquor, and encourages her to drink until she loses self-control, he is guilty of this offence if he encouraged her with intent to get her 'blind drunk' and thereby to enable him to have intercourse. On the other hand, a man who merely encourages his girlfriend to have one more in the hope that resistance may be rather less in consequence does not act with the intention of stupefying or overpowering the girl, and therefore he is not guilty of the offence.

This offence is not an arrestable offence.

ANONYMITY OF COMPLAINANTS

The Sexual Offences (Amendment) Act 1976, s 4 provides for the anonymity of complainants (male or female) in rape cases (including incitement, attempt or conspiracy to rape and burglary with intent to rape). The Sexual Offences (Amendment) Act 1992, s 1 makes identical provisions (with a few exceptions) for the anonymity of complainants in respect of the offences of indecent assault (whether committed against a man or a woman); indecency with children; procurement of women by threats, false pretences or the administration of drugs; and attempt, incitement or conspiracy to commit one of these offences.

The common provisions of the two Acts are as follows. Where an allegation of an offence to which one of the Acts applies is made, neither the name nor address, nor a still or moving picture of that person shall, during that person's lifetime, be published in England and Wales in a written publication available to the public, or be included in a programme for reception in England and Wales, if it is likely to lead to the identification of the complainant. Where a person has been accused of an offence to which one of the Acts applies, no matter whatsoever which is likely to lead to the identification of the complainant may be so published. Provision is made for the requirements of each Act to be set aside on application being made to the trial judge where it is considered necessary to induce persons to come forward as witnesses and that the applicant's defence will be substantially prejudiced if the direction is not given. Each Act also gives the judge a 'public interest' discretion to set aside these provisions.

If any matter is published or included in a broadcast or cable programme in breach of the above rules, an offence is committed:

(a) in the case of a newspaper or periodical, by any proprietor, editor or publisher of it;

(b) in the case of any other publication, by its publisher; or

(c) in the case of a programme, by any body corporate engaged in providing the service and by anyone involved in the programme corresponding to an editor of a newspaper.

OFFENCES INVOLVING MALE HOMOSEXUALITY

Buggery

It is an offence contrary to the Sexual Offences Act 1956, s 12(1) for a man to commit buggery with another man otherwise than in the circumstances described in s 12(1A). Buggery between men consists of sexual intercourse (which occurs if there is the slightest degree of penetration by a penis) per anum.

Under s 12(1A) of the 1956 Act buggery is not criminal if committed in private provided that both parties consented and had attained the age of 18 years. Such acts will not be considered to be in private if more than two persons take part or are present, or if they take place in a lavatory to which the public have or are permitted to have access, whether on payment or otherwise.

A man cannot give a valid consent for the purposes of the exemption if he is suffering from a state of arrested or retarded development of mind, which includes severe impairment of intelligence and social functioning, but it is a defence to prove that the accused did not know and had no cause to suspect severe mental impairment. It is no defence to show that an accused believed the other man to be 18 or over.

Where it remains an offence, both the active and the passive parties to the commission of buggery are criminally liable; a person is not, of course, a party if the buggery is committed without his consent. In addition, where there is no consent (as defined for the purposes of rape) there is a rape, and rape should be charged as the more serious offence.

It is an offence, contrary to s 16 of the 1956 Act, to assault with intent to commit buggery.

An offence, or attempted offence of buggery, is an arrestable offence if committed by a person of or over the age of 21, where the other person is under the age of 18, as is any such offence by anyone against a person under 16. An assault with intent to commit buggery is also an arrestable offence. It is best first to consider whether an offence of buggery has been committed or merely attempted, or whether there has been an assault with intent to commit it. If there has been penetration by the penis and the parties consented to the act, there has been buggery by both unless the homosexual act is excused because it is in private and both parties have attained the age of 18 years. Even if this is so, if a third party has procured one of them to commit the act, the procurer still commits an offence even though the homosexual act is lawful in these circumstances. If there has been no penetration, has there been an attempt, some act which goes beyond mere preparation to commit the offence? The proximate nature of this act should be immediate, to separate our thinking from an assault with intent to commit buggery. The latter offence could be committed by a man who rendered another unconscious with intent to commit buggery later. If he had rendered him unconscious and immediately engaged in acts leading to an offence of buggery, this would amount to an attempt to commit rape (as well as an attempt to commit buggery).

Another point to be considered is whether or not the act was committed in private; it cannot be in private in any circumstances in a public lavatory or if there are more than the two participating parties present. It must be remembered, therefore, that, if a procurer is present when the act is committed, then three are present and the act of buggery is no longer committed in private.

Gross indecency

The Sexual Offences Act 1956, s 13 creates another complex series of offences by providing that it is an offence for a man to commit an act of gross indecency with another man whether in public or in private, or to be a party to the commission of such an act, or to procure it. The term 'gross indecency' has never really been defined other than to declare that there is no need for physical contact if two men behave in an indecent manner in concert. The offence usually takes one of three forms; mutual masturbation, bodily intertwining and oral–genital contact. All of these acts are included in the 1967 Act as 'homosexual acts' which are lawful in the circumstances described above in relation to buggery. Thus, if committed in private, by no more than two consenting males who have attained the age of 18 years, such acts are lawful.

If any of these conditions is absent we must consider not only those who are directly committing such acts, but also those who may be party to such acts without physically participating. Such a person may have procured the act by arranging for it to take place. A person who is present when the act is committed and who encourages it will also be a party to its commission. Gross indecency committed by a man of or over the age of 21 with a man under the age of 18 is an arrestable offence. So is an attempt to procure such an offence.

Restriction on prosecution

The Director of Public Prosecutions must consent to the prosecution of a man for buggery or gross indecency with another man where either was under 21 at the time of the offence.

Procuring

Any person who procures an unlawful act of buggery or gross indecency is guilty of an offence of buggery as an accomplice. In addition, the 1967 Act created a new offence of procuring another man to commit an act of buggery or gross indecency with a third man, which by virtue of the Act is not unlawful. It must be emphasised that this offence is only committed if the procurer, or male pimp, procures on behalf of someone else.

BUGGERY WITH FEMALES OR ANIMALS

Buggery with an animal is an offence contrary to s 12(1) of the Sexual Offences Act 1956. It is an arrestable offence. It can be committed by a man per vaginam or per anum, or by a woman who permits an animal to have intercourse with her per vaginam or per anum.

Buggery by a man with a woman (ie intercourse per anum) is lawful between consenting parties in private in the same way as if two men had been involved.

INTERCOURSE WITH DEFECTIVES AND GIRLS UNDER 16

Defective women

It is an offence for a man to have unlawful sexual intercourse with a woman who is a defective, or for any person to procure a woman who is a defective to have unlawful sexual intercourse in any part of the world. A woman is a defective if she is suffering from severe mental impairment. This is a state of arrested or incomplete development of mind which includes severe impairment of intelligence and social functioning. Medical opinion should be obtained. It is a defence to these charges for a man to prove that he did not know and had no reason to suspect that the woman was a defective.

It is an offence for an owner or occupier of premises to induce or knowingly to suffer a woman who is a defective to resort to or be on those premises for the purpose of having unlawful sexual intercourse with men or a particular man. Again, it is a defence to such a charge for the accused to prove that he did not know and had no reason to suspect that the woman was a defective.

It is, additionally, an offence under the Mental Health Act 1959, s 128 for a man who is a manager, an officer on the staff, or is otherwise employed in a hospital or mental nursing home, to have unlawful sexual intercourse with a woman who is receiving treatment for mental disorder, or with an out-patient while she is on the premises of the hospital or home. The offence is also committed where such a woman is subject to the guardianship of a man, or is in his custody or care under the Mental Health Act 1983 or other similar provisions which include care within residential care homes.

The above offences are not arrestable offences.

Girls under 13 and under 16

It is an offence, contrary to the Sexual Offences Act 1956, s 5, for a man to have unlawful sexual intercourse with a girl under the age of 13 years. It is no defence to allege that a mistake was made in relation to the age of the girl. The question of consent does not arise; we are merely concerned with whether or not the intercourse has taken place. If there was no consent it would also be rape. This is an arrestable offence.

The Sexual Offences Act 1956, s 6 is concerned with the man who has unlawful sexual intercourse with a girl under 16. A man who has intercourse with a girl under 13 also commits this offence. This is important when considering all of the charges of which a man may be guilty in particular circumstances. As in s 5, the girl's consent is irrelevant. Offences contrary to s 6 are not arrestable offences. However, since the intercourse will constitute an indecent assault on the girl, the power of arrest for indecent assault is available in these circumstances.

Men charged under s 6 have certain defences open to them which are specifically provided by that section. First, the invalidity of a marriage under the Marriage Act 1949 does not make a husband guilty of this offence if he believes the girl to be his wife and has reasonable cause for that belief. Second, a man under the age of 24, who has not previously been charged with a like offence, and who believes the girl to be of the age of 16 or over and has reasonable cause for the belief, is not guilty of this offence. There are two important points to remember about this second defence:

(a) a man is charged when he first appears before a court which has jurisdiction to determine the matter and not when charged by the police or merely committed for trial; and

(b) whether or not a man believed a girl to be of or over the age of 16, and had reasonable cause for his belief, is a matter for the jury if he is tried in the Crown Court.

It is an offence for an owner or occupier of premises to induce or knowingly to suffer a girl under 16 to resort to or be on those premises for the purpose of having unlawful sexual intercourse with men or a particular man. If the girl is under 13 a more serious offence is committed; unlike the offence relating to girls under 16, this offence is an arrestable offence.

INCEST

Incest consists of sexual intercourse between persons of the closest family relationship. A major aim of the legislation is to prevent the birth of children who may be affected because of blood ties. Therefore, in considering the offence as committed by a man, one must consider those women within his immediate family who may be of child-bearing age, that is his granddaughter, daughter, sister or mother. The logic of this can be easily seen; there would be little purpose in including his grandmother, as it is extremely unlikely that there could be a child of such union.

The offence can be committed by a woman of the age of 16 or over, who *permits* a man whom she knows to be her grandfather, father, brother or son to have unlawful sexual intercourse with her. Once again, it can be seen that the object is to prevent close inter-breeding. Grandfather is therefore included, while a grandson is not. By the time a grandson reaches sexual maturity it is unlikely that his grandmother will be of a child-bearing age.

The terms 'brother' and 'sister' include half-brother and half-sister. The offences are concerned with a blood relationship, and it is immaterial whether or not the blood relationship is seated in wedlock. The offences are only committed if, at the time of the unlawful sexual intercourse, the accused man or woman knew of the prohibited blood relationship. To illustrate this, we must consider the circumstances in which a man has sexual intercourse with his wife's daughter, born to his wife whilst he was living with her, but whom he genuinely believes to be the daughter of another man who had an adulterous relationship with his wife. The prosecution must be in a position to prove knowledge of the blood relationship.

Offences of incest are arrestable offences. Attempts are not, except in the case of attempted incest with a girl who is under 13. The Director of Public Prosecutions must consent to the institution of proceedings.

By the Criminal Law Act 1977, s 54 it is an offence for a man to incite a girl under 16 years whom he knows to be his granddaughter, daughter or sister to have sexual intercourse with him. This is not an arrestable offence.

ANONYMITY OF COMPLAINANTS

The provisions of the Sexual Offences (Amendment) Act 1992 concerning anonymity of complainants in relation to certain sexual offences which are set out at page 665, also apply to the offences of:

(a) buggery;
(b) intercourse and procurement of a defective (ie mentally handicapped) woman;
(c) intercourse with a girl under 13;
(d) intercourse with girl between the ages of 13 and 16;
(e) incest;
(f) incitement by a man to commit an offence of incest; and
(g) incitement, attempt or conspiracy to commit such offences.

The provisions of the Act do not apply to the 'other party' in cases of incest and buggery where that other person is alleged to have committed a similar offence as a part of a joint enterprise; in other words that person can be identified.

ABDUCTION OF WOMEN AND GIRLS

The Sexual Offences Act 1956, ss 17 and 19 to 21 provide for offences concerned with the abduction of women and girls.

By force or for sake of property: any age (s 17)

It is an offence for a person to take away or detain a woman of any age against her will with the intention that she shall marry or have unlawful (ie extra-marital) sexual intercourse with that or any other person, if she is so taken away or detained either by force or for the sake of her property or expectations of property. This section merely requires that the woman is taken away or detained, and there is no reference to her being taken away from anyone such as a parent or guardian. An example of this offence would be where a mature woman, who is the heiress to a fortune, is taken away, against her will, and perhaps later detained, so that she may be married (or persuaded to have sexual intercourse, in the hope that this may lead to marriage) in order to enjoy the benefits of her inheritance.

This offence is an arrestable offence.

Unmarried girl under 18 (s 19)

It is an offence to take an unmarried girl under the age of 18 out of the possession of her parent or guardian against his will, if she is so taken with the intention that she shall have unlawful (ie extra-marital) sexual intercourse with men or with a particular man.

The offence is one which is committed against the will of the parent or guardian and that is the important factor to remember. Unlike the previous offence, the girl's wishes are immaterial. It must be proved that the girl was unmarried, that she was less than 18, that she was taken out of the possession of a parent or guardian against his will, that the accused knew that the girl was in the possession of her parent or guardian, and that he acted with the intention that the girl should have sexual intercourse with a particular man or men. The nature of the offence can be wide-ranging, since it includes the case where a man, having been refused consent to marry a girl under 18, takes the girl to his flat and sets up home with her, living as man and wife. If the taking is against the will of the parent or guardian the offence is complete at that point of time since his intention is to have extra-marital intercourse with her. At the opposite extreme, the offence covers the case where a girl is persuaded to leave her parents against their will and to go away with an acquaintance for a weekend at some lovers' retreat, or to move in for the weekend with a group of young men so that they can all have intercourse with her, provided in either case that someone 'takes' her.

The word 'taking' in this context does not indicate any form of permanent deprivation, but the accused's conduct must amount to a substantial interference with the possessory relationship of parent and child. A girl who is taken away for a few days is taken out of the possession of her parent or guardian as the normal possessory relationship of parent and daughter has been substantially interfered with. A young man who merely takes a girl to the cinema or to a dance without her parents' consent does not commit this offence, even if he intends that she shall have unlawful sexual intercourse with him, since this does not substantially disturb the normal parent/daughter relationship.

It is a defence to a charge under s 19 for the man to prove that he believed the girl to be of the age of 18 or over and had reasonable cause for the belief.

This offence is not an arrestable one.

Unmarried girl under 16 (s 20)

It is an offence for a person, acting without lawful authority or excuse, to take an unmarried girl under the age of 16 out of the possession of her parent or guardian against his will.

As in the previous offence there must be a taking of a girl out of the possession of her parent or guardian against his will, and the girl's wishes are immaterial. However, this offence differs from the previous one in that there does not need to be an intention to have unlawful sexual intercourse. The reference to 'unmarried' is unlikely to have any effect in relation to residents in Great Britain but could be significant in relation to immigrant families or visitors to Great Britain. The only factors to prove are that the girl is unmarried, under 16, was taken out of the possession of the parent or guardian without lawful authority or excuse and against his will, and that the accused knew she was in the possession of her parent or guardian. There would be a lawful authority or excuse for a 'taking' where a girl is removed from parental care by a court order or where she is taken in for shelter at the home of a friend following an offence of cruelty by her parent or guardian.

It is no defence to a charge under s 20 for the accused to allege that he reasonably believed that the girl was 16 or over.

This offence is not arrestable. The same is the case with the offence to which we now turn.

Defective woman (s 21)

A similar offence to that described in relation to girls under 18 exists to protect women who are defectives. The offence consists of taking a defective out of the possession of her parent or guardian for the purpose of unlawful (ie extra-marital) sexual intercourse with men or a particular man. It is a defence, for a person charged with this offence, to prove that he neither knew nor had reason to suspect that the woman was a defective.

Police powers

Where it is made to appear by information on oath that there is reasonable cause to suspect that a woman is detained in his jurisdiction for the purpose of unlawful (ie extra-marital) sexual intercourse, and that *either* the detention is against her will *or* she is under 16 or a defective or under 18 and so detained against the will of her parent or guardian, a justice may issue a warrant. The warrant will authorise a constable to search for and take her to a place of safety until she can be brought before a justice. The constable may be accompanied by the person who has sworn out the warrant. The constable may enter (by force, if necessary) any premises named in the warrant.

CHILD ABDUCTION

Two offences of child abduction are provided by the Child Abduction Act 1984. These offences contain a number of common features; these will be dealt with after the separate offences have been outlined.

Abduction from the United Kingdom by parent etc

By s 1 of the 1984 Act, a person connected with a child under 16 commits an offence if he takes or sends the child *out of the United Kingdom* without the appropriate consent. A person is regarded as 'sending' a child if he causes the child to be sent. A prosecution for this offence may only be instituted by or with the consent of the Director of Public Prosecutions.

For the purposes of the offence, a person is 'connected with' a child if:

(a) he is the child's parent or guardian; or
(b) he has custody of the child; or
(c) in the case of a child, whose parents were not married to each other at the time of his birth, there are reasonable grounds for believing that he is its father; or
(d) he is the person in whose favour a residence order is in force in respect of the child.

Only persons falling within these categories can commit the present offence.

The reference to the 'appropriate consent', in relation to the removal or sending of the child out of the United Kingdom, means:

(a) the consent of *each* of the following:
   (i)   the child's mother;
   (ii) the child's father, if he has parental responsibility for him;
   (iii) any guardian of the child;
   (iv) any person in whose favour a residence order is in force with respect to the child;
   (v) any person who has custody of the child; or
(b) the leave of the court granted under or by virtue of Part II of the Children Act 1989; or
(c) if any person has custody of the child, the leave of the court which granted custody to him.

A person does not commit the present offence by taking or sending a child out of the United Kingdom without the appropriate consent if:

(a) he is the person in whose favour there is a residence order in respect of the child; or
(b) he takes or sends him out of the United Kingdom for less than one month,

unless he is in breach of an order under Part II of the Children Act 1989.

A person does not commit the present offence by doing anything without the consent of another person whose consent is required if:

(a) he does it in the belief that the other person has consented or would consent if he was aware of all the relevant circumstances; or
(b) he has taken all reasonable steps to communicate with the other person but has been unable to communicate with him; or
(c) the other person has unreasonably refused to consent.

However, the last alternative (ie (c)) does not apply where the person who refused consent is a person in whose favour there is a residence order or who has custody of the child or where the taking or sending is in breach of any court direction under certain statutory provisions.

There are special provisions where the child is in the care of a local authority or a voluntary organisation, or is the subject of custodianship proceedings or of proceedings (or an order) for adoption.

Abduction of child by other persons

This offence is governed by s 2 of the 1984 Act. It can be committed by anyone other than:

(a) the father or mother (if they were married when the child was born) or the mother (if they were not); or
(b) the child's guardian; or
(c) a person with a residence order, or custody, in respect of the child.

Another important difference from the offence under s 1 is that the child need not be abducted from the United Kingdom.

Section 2 provides that anyone, other than a person mentioned above, commits an offence if, without lawful authority or reasonable excuse, he takes or detains a child under 16 so as *either* to remove him from the lawful control of anyone having lawful control of him *or* to keep him out of the lawful control of any person entitled to it. Removal from control does not require any removal in a geographical sense; it suffices to deflect the child from what he would be otherwise doing with the consent of those having lawful control of him into some activity induced by the accused, as where the accused finds a child in a park pursuing a particular activity (eg playing football) and induces it to go elsewhere in the park for another activity (eg to look for an alleged lost bicycle).

A person is regarded as detaining a child if he causes him to be detained or induces the child to remain with him or another.

It is a defence for the accused to prove that, at the time of the alleged offence, he believed the child was 16 or over. Alternatively, in the case where the father and mother of 'the child in question' (ie the child taken or detained) were not married to each other at the time of birth, it is a defence for the accused to prove that he is the father of the child taken or detained or that he had reasonable grounds to believe he was that child's father. Lastly, a person is not guilty of an offence under s 2 if he mistakenly believed, reasonably or not, in facts which – if they had been as he believed – would have given him a lawful authority or reasonable excuse. On this basis, a man who takes a child, thinking that it is his child whereas in truth it is another child, will not be guilty if, on the facts as he believes them to be, he would have a lawful authority or reasonable excuse for taking the child.

General

For the purposes of both offences, a person is regarded as taking a child if he causes or induces the child to accompany him or any other person, or causes the child to be taken.

It is irrelevant that the child consents to what occurs.

Both offences are arrestable offences.

KIDNAPPING

The offences which have previously been discussed are concerned with the abduction of particular persons, specially protected either because of their vulnerability to sexual exploitation or because of their age. The common law offence of kidnapping knows no such boundaries and can be committed whenever there is an unlawful taking or carrying away of *any* person against *his* or *her* will.

In 1984 the House of Lords held that the offence involves four requirements:

(a) The taking or carrying away of one person by another

It is irrelevant whether the taking or carrying away is to some other place within the jurisdiction or to some place outside it. Although the person taken or carried away is often secreted thereafter, this is not a requirement of the offence.

(b) The taking or carrying away must be by force or by fraud.

'Force' is not limited to physical force or the threat of it. It encompasses any conduct which, coupled with the taking or carrying away (ingredient (a)), overrides the true consent of the person taken or carried away (ingredient (c)). Thus, the exercise of mental or moral power or influence to compel another to do something against his will can suffice if it overcomes his will.

(c) The taking or carrying away must be without the consent of the person taken or carried away

This requirement must be satisfied whatever the age of that person. However, there can be a kidnapping, even though the person carried away consents at first, if he changes his mind and ceases to consent while still being carried away. In the case of a very young child, it does not have the understanding or intelligence to give consent so that the absence of consent will be a necessary inference from its age. In the case of an older child, it is a question of fact for the jury whether the child had sufficient understanding or intelligence to give consent and, if so, whether absence of consent has been proved. Unlike child abduction, the presence or absence of consent on the part of the person having custody or care and control of a child victim is immaterial (except that such consent may support a defence of lawful excuse). Likewise the presence or absence of consent on the part of other people, such as the spouse of a person who is taken, is immaterial.

It must be proved that a person charged with kidnapping knew or was reckless that he did not have the victim's consent.

(d) The taking or carrying away must be without lawful excuse

Clearly, for example, a parent (or other person) with custody of a child will often have a lawful excuse for taking or carrying away the child. An exception would be where this contravenes a court order in relation to the child.

Kidnapping is an arrestable offence.

The House of Lords has held that the conduct of a parent who snatches his own child in defiance of a court order relating to its custody or care and control (such as one making the child a ward of court) should normally be dealt with as a contempt of court rather than as the subject matter of a prosecution for kidnapping, unless the parent's conduct was particularly bad.

The Child Abduction Act 1984, s 5 provides that the consent of the Director of Public Prosecutions to the institution of a prosecution for kidnapping is required wherever the victim is under 16 or where the prosecution is against a parent or guardian etc.

Hostage taking

The Taking of Hostages Act 1982, s 1 makes it an offence for a person of any nationality to detain in the United Kingdom or elsewhere any other person (a hostage) and, in order to compel any state, international governmental organisation, or person, to do or abstain from doing any act, to threaten to kill, injure or continue to detain the hostage. The consent of the Attorney-General is required before a prosecution may be brought for this offence.

CHAPTER 34

Offences relating to prostitution, obscenity and indecent photographs

PROSTITUTE

The term 'prostitute' has no statutory definition. However, it has for many years been accepted that a *prostitute* is a woman (or a man) who offers her (or his) body commonly for sexual intercourse or acts of a sexual nature, in return for payment, and it has been held recently by the Court of Appeal that it is immaterial that the woman (or man) is dishonest and intends simply to pocket advance payment and not to provide sexual services. The term 'sexual intercourse' requires no further explanation. The reference to other acts of a sexual nature extends the definition of 'prostitute'. Masseuses, for example, who carry out acts of masturbation on request are engaging in such acts. So are women who engage in sado-masochistic sessions for the sexual pleasure of their partner. Since sexual intercourse is not required, even a virgin can be a prostitute.

In respect only of a female prostitute, a number of provisions refer to a *'common'* prostitute. Proof that a woman is a common prostitute requires proof that in return for payment she is prepared to offer to men in general to engage in sexual intercourse or acts of lewdness with them. All these points must be proved. If a girl offers herself for intercourse for payment regularly to one man, perhaps a sugar daddy, she is not a common prostitute as she is not offering herself commonly. If she offers herself to a number of men because she is promiscuous and requires no payment for her services, she is not a common prostitute as she is not receiving payment in return. It is not an offence in itself to be a prostitute, but there are a number of offences which can only be committed by, or in respect of, prostitutes.

LOITERING OR SOLICITING BY A COMMON PROSTITUTE

The only offence which can be committed by a female prostitute herself is that of being a common prostitute, loitering or soliciting in a street or public place for the purposes of prostitution, contrary to the Street Offences Act 1959, s 1. To establish a woman's intention to offer her body for prostitution there must be evidence of the accused's recent behaviour in a street or public place. Evidence of such recent behaviour should include evidence that on at least two previous occasions the woman was seen accosting men in the streets and that she was seen to leave with them. It must be remembered that it is possible for a perfectly respectable woman to approach a number of men when asking for directions. However, if she then walks off with them on a number of occasions it is much more likely that she is soliciting. Loitering by a common prostitute does not need to be for the purpose of her making approaches to men; it is sufficient that she loiters for the purpose of being approached by men. Many streets are noted as the haunts of prostitutes and men go looking for them. The prostitutes are loitering for such a purpose. In the same way a prostitute may loiter in a slowly moving vehicle but it must be shown that her purpose was to solicit men, or to be solicited by them. Soliciting need not be by words and can be carried out by all of the accepted forms of non-verbal communication. Movements of the body, arms, hands as well as facial expressions and gestures can be equally compelling forms of solicitation. A deaf and dumb prostitute solicited by making grunting noises accompanied by a gesture with a folded right arm, being bent and straightened. Her meaning was never in doubt! Tapping on window panes, leaning out of windows with signals to indicate price, signalling the position of the entry door with the fingers are all forms of solicitation. The test to be applied should be, 'Is it clear to the reasonable man that he is being offered sex for money?'

Street or public place

'Street' for the purpose of the 1959 Act includes any bridge, road, lane, footway, subway, square, court, alley or passage, whether a thoroughfare or not, which is for the time being open to the public. In addition, the doorways and entrances to premises abutting on a street and the ground adjoining and open to a street are treated as forming part of the street.

The definition is quite wide; in effect, it prohibits loitering or soliciting by prostitutes in places which are upon private property if they are open to a street, and the courts have interpreted the legislation in this way. For example, prostitutes who solicited men from balconies or from behind windows have been convicted of this offence. The words of Lord Parker describe the essence of this offence perfectly. He said:

'I approach the matter by considering what is the mischief aimed at by this Act. Everybody knows that this was an Act intended to clean up the streets, to enable people to walk along the streets without being molested or solicited by common prostitutes. Viewed this way, it can matter little whether the prostitute is soliciting while in the street or is standing in a doorway or balcony, or at a window, or whether the window is shut or open or half open; in each case her solicitation is projected to and addressed to somebody walking in the street.'

The term 'public place' is not defined but generally the courts have accepted that a public place is one where the public go, no matter whether they have a right to go or not. The question of ownership of the property does not therefore arise and attention should be directed towards usage. A garden which is used for a garden party to which the public are invited is a public place whilst that party is in progress. Immediately the party ceases, the garden reverts to its status of a private place. Although the point has not been tested, it is unlikely that such places as public houses, restaurants, dance halls or similar places will be public places for the purpose of the Act. It is more likely that 'public place' will be interpreted in the light of the fact that it is used in the alternative to 'street' in deciding to what it applies.

Cautions

Before proceedings are taken for an offence under s 1 of the 1959 Act, at least two official cautions should have been given to the woman and particulars of such cautions should have been entered in an official cautions register maintained at the police station. If the woman wishes to dispute that her actions amounted to an act in respect of which a caution should be given, she can apply to a court within 14 days for an order directing that the caution be expunged.

The purpose of the provisions on cautioning was to prevent offences rather than to punish and the procedure to be followed by the police is directed towards giving the woman every opportunity to reform. The procedure is as follows:

(a) On the first occasion that a woman is suspected of this offence, obtain the assistance of a colleague as a witness (joint observation).

(b) Tell her what you have seen and caution her. Obtain name, date of birth, address and description to aid later observations. Check name and address, if possible from documents. There is no power to use or threaten force to detain a woman for these purposes; consequently, the use or threat of force in such circumstances is unlawful.

(c) Ask her if she is willing to be put in touch with a welfare, social or probation service for help, or to attend at a police station to see a policewoman, at her convenience.

(d) If seen on a second occasion, the same procedure should be followed.

(e) All cautions must be officially recorded.

(f) If seen loitering or soliciting after having been officially cautioned twice, she may be arrested and charged. A station officer must satisfy himself that two cautions have been so recorded and that they are sufficiently recent (some forces insist that they must be within the preceding 12 months) before accepting the charge.

(g) A complaint from a woman to the effect that she has been cautioned without cause requires investigation in the same way as any other complaint. If the complaint is justified the caution may be expunged without the need to refer the matter to a court.

(h) When a prosecution for an offence under s 1 of the 1959 Act is in progress in court it is not necessary to mention cautions. However, the conduct which occasioned those cautions will probably have to be given to prove that the woman is a common prostitute.

Police powers

A constable may arrest without warrant anyone he finds in a street or public place and suspects, with reasonable cause, to be committing an offence under the 1959 Act.

SOLICITATION BY MEN

The Sexual Offences Act 1985, s 1 deals with 'kerb crawling' and makes it an offence for a man persistently to solicit a woman, or different women, for the purpose of prostitution, from a motor vehicle while that motor vehicle is in a street or public place, or for a man persistently to solicit a woman, or different women, for the purpose of prostitution, in a street or public place while in the immediate vicinity of a motor vehicle which he has just got out of or off. Reference to the offence under s 32 of the Sexual

Offences Act 1956 indicates that 'persistently' in the 1985 Act requires a degree of repetition by more than one invitation to one woman or invitations to different people. As in the case of soliciting by a prostitute, soliciting can be by words or acts; the man must indicate to a woman or women by words or acts that he requires her or their services as a prostitute. Consequently, although merely driving round a red light district does not constitute soliciting, even if it is done persistently, an offence is committed by a man who persistently addresses requests to a woman, or women, for the purposes of prostitution, from a slow-moving or stationary vehicle, if the vehicle is in a street or public place. If he parks the vehicle, and leaves it, persistently to solicit a woman, or women, for the purpose of prostitution, in the immediate vicinity of the vehicle, he commits an offence. This will be so even if the vehicle is parked in a private car park, provided that the solicitation takes place in a street or public place, in 'the immediate vicinity' of his motor vehicle. That which may be described as 'the immediate vicinity' is likely to form the subject of much legal argument. The critical question must be concerned with whether or not the use of the vehicle was one of a series of acts leading *directly* to the solicitation.

In cases where there is a doubt concerning the proximity of the vehicle in this respect, it will be advisable to consider an offence which is contained in s 2 of the 1985 Act. Section 2 creates the offence of a man persistently soliciting a woman, or different women, in a street or public place for the purpose of prostitution. The use of a motor vehicle is not an essential ingredient of this offence.

Section 1 of the 1985 Act also creates offences which are alternatives to those requiring evidence of 'persistent soliciting'. In either of the circumstances described above in relation to s 1 offences, if the evidence falls short of 'persistent soliciting', an alternative offence under s 1 may be committed if there is soliciting in such a manner or in such circumstances as to be likely to cause annoyance to the woman (or any of the women) solicited, or nuisance to other persons in the neighbourhood. The likelihood of nuisance to other persons can be proved even though there is no evidence that other members of the public were present. Justices are entitled to take into account their local knowledge of the area in which the offence allegedly occurred when considering whether behaviour was likely to have caused a nuisance to other members of the public.

The references throughout the 1985 Act to a man soliciting do not include male prostitutes soliciting a woman for the purposes of prostitution. Such conduct is, however, capable of being dealt with under the Sexual Offences Act 1956, s 32, dealt with below.

PERSISTENT SOLICITING OR IMPORTUNING FOR IMMORAL PURPOSE

It is an offence contrary to the Sexual Offences Act 1956, s 32 for a man persistently to solicit or importune in a public place for immoral purposes. The immoral purposes need not be a criminal offence, nor involve prostitution. However, the 'immoral purpose' solicited or importuned must involve sexual activity whether of a homosexual or heterosexual nature. In determining whether a particular purpose was immoral, the standards of ordinary right-thinking men and women living in England today should be applied, consideration being given to the circumstances and nature of the overtures.

The soliciting or importuning must be 'persistent', which requires a degree of repetition by more than one invitation to one person or invitation to different people. Thus, a conviction under s 32 of a man who masturbated at a urinal, whilst watching other men enter and leave, and who turned his body towards another whilst doing so, was upheld on appeal on the ground that there was evidence capable of amounting to persistent importuning.

OTHER OFFENCES INVOLVING PROSTITUTION

Brothels

By the Sexual Offences Act 1956, s 33, it is an offence for a person to keep a brothel, or to manage it, or to act or assist in its management. Perhaps the first question to which we should address ourselves is 'What is a brothel?' Premises are a brothel if they are used by persons of opposite sexes for illicit intercourse or other indecent behaviour. It is not necessary to show that the women resorting to the premises are prostitutes or that they received payment for their services, but there must be at least two women who use the premises in this way. It does not matter that one of them is the occupier, and it does not matter that only one prostitute at a time ever uses the premises. If separate and self-contained flats are separately let, each to one prostitute, it is likely that the building in its entirety will not be classed as a brothel as there is only one prostitute in each of the flats. However, if single rooms are let to prostitutes in one building, it may be sufficient if the rooms are sufficiently close to constitute what might be described as a nest of prostitutes.

In considering the charges to be preferred when it is established that a building is a brothel, we must look at the offence created by the Sexual Offences Act 1956, s 33. The keeper of the premises, who is most likely to be the residential landlord, a manager, who looks after the maintenance and day-to-day needs of the building and its tenants, the 'madame' of the trade and those who act or assist in the management of the brothel are all guilty of offences. 'Assisting in the management of a brothel' covers any conduct which contributes to the management of the brothel. Assistance in the management of a brothel does not require proof that the person actively exercised some control over the brothel or carried out some specific act of management. A person who takes advertisements to a post office and pays for them assists in the management of the brothel. So does a person who discusses with a potential customer the nature of the sexual activities on offer, or who negotiates the price. On the other hand, it has been held that a cleaner at a brothel does not assist in its management.

Related offences

Sections 34 and 35 of the 1956 Act go further and add offences to cover other possibilities in relation to responsibility for the brothel. First, a lessor or landlord of premises (or his agent) who has knowledge of their intended or actual use as a brothel is guilty of an offence (s 34). In addition, the tenant or occupier, or person in charge, of premises who knowingly permits the whole or part of them to be so used is also guilty of an offence (s 35). It will frequently be found that the same person might fit more than one description. For example, the occupier may frequently be the man whom you would consider to be the keeper of the brothel and it is of advantage to consider all possibilities.

Although one tends to think of brothels as places where women practice the trade of heterosexual prostitution, the above offences relating to brothels (ss 33–35 of the 1956 Act) also apply to premises used as brothels for homosexual purposes, by virtue of the Sexual Offences Act 1967, s 6.

Procuring

Other offences related to prostitution are those of any person procuring a woman to become, in any part of the world, a common prostitute, or procuring her to leave the

United Kingdom with the intention of placing her in a brothel elsewhere, or even procuring a woman to leave her usual residence in the United Kingdom with the intention of placing her in a brothel in any part of the world for the purpose of prostitution. These offences are often referred to as 'white slaving'.

Living on immoral earnings

Section 30 of the Sexual Offences Act 1956 makes it an arrestable offence for a man knowingly to live wholly or in part on the earnings of female prostitution. A 'clipper', ie a woman who offers sexual services, takes money and then reneges on that offer, is engaged in prostitution (as we have seen) and the money received represents 'the earnings of prostitution'. A man who lives with or is habitually in the company of a prostitute, or who exercises control, direction or influence over her movements in a way which shows he is aiding, abetting or compelling her prostitution with others, is presumed knowingly to be living on the earnings of prostitution, unless he proves to the contrary. The man whom we know by many names, including 'pimp', who is the manager or organiser of the activities of one or more prostitutes, is the prime offender described by the section. The collection of sufficient evidence is important. Generally, the evidence of the prostitute alone will be insufficient and it is recommended that plain clothes observations of the man's activities over a period of at least four days should be offered in evidence. There must be proof that the woman is a prostitute, that the man lived with her or was frequently in her company and that he appeared to be directing or controlling her movements. It is also helpful if it can be shown that the man had no other source of income, or, if he did, that he lived well above the standard that his income would have allowed.

By the Sexual Offences Act 1967, s 5, a man or woman who knowingly lives wholly or in part on the earnings of prostitution of a man commits an arrestable offence.

Woman exercising control over prostitute

By s 31 of the Sexual Offences Act 1956, a woman commits an offence if she exercises control over a prostitute for the purposes of gain. It is not necessary to show that she is living wholly, or in part, upon that gain. Nor is it necessary to show that the woman exercised persuasion or compulsion over the prostitute, but it is necessary to prove that she exercised influence of some kind over the prostitute.

OBSCENE LITERATURE, DISPLAYS AND PHOTOGRAPHS

Obscene publications

These are governed in general by the Obscene Publications Act 1959, hereafter 'the Act'.

Under s 2 of the Act an offence is committed by a person who:

(a) publishes an obscene article, whether for gain or not; or
(b) has an obscene article for publication for gain, whether for himself or another.

You may therefore sit at home and write as many obscene articles as you wish without committing an offence against the Act. If you circulate copies of these articles to other people, then you publish them and it does not matter that you have not received money or other reward for them. Having written the articles without any intention to publish, you may subsequently commit an offence if, having them in your possession, you decide that you will publish them for gain. To summarise, it is no offence to write or prepare such articles, but it is an offence to publish them, whether for gain or not, or to have them in one's possession with an intention to publish for gain.

What is an 'obscene article'?

An 'article' for present purposes means any article containing or embodying matter to be read or looked at or both, any sound record, and any film or other record of a picture or pictures (such as a photograph, video cassette or computer disk). 'Article' for the purposes of the Act also includes any matter included in a television or sound broadcast or in a cable programme service; obscene publication via a broadcast or cable service is a rather specialised type of obscene publication, and we shall not deal with it further in the book.

An article is deemed to be obscene if its effect, or the effect of any of its items is, taken as a whole, such as to tend to deprave and corrupt persons who are likely, having regard to all the circumstances, to read, see or hear the matter contained in it.

Though a novel may be considered as a whole, a magazine must be considered item by item and, if any one of the items is obscene, this suffices. 'Deprave and corrupt' are strong words; to lead morally astray is not necessarily to deprave and corrupt. Obscenity is not confined to that which has a tendency to corrupt sexual morals; a book depicting the career of a drug addict has been held to be obscene because of its likely effect. On occasions, articles may be directed at persons who may already be considered to have become depraved and corrupted but this may still amount to an offence if the object is to maintain that state of depravity and corruption and to prevent escape from it. Whether an article is obscene because it is likely to deprave and corrupt is essentially a matter for the jury. A juror is as able as anyone to decide the effect upon people, whilst keeping in mind the current standards of ordinary, decent people.

In deciding whether to initiate action in these cases, police officers should take cognisance of current trends in society in coming to a decision regarding the effect of such articles; the reader, viewer or listener must also be considered. If the article tends to deprave and corrupt a significant proportion of those who receive it, it is obscene for the purposes of the Act. It would probably be insufficient if it was likely to affect only a few who were not representative of the 'ordinary man'.

Publication etc

To 'publish' means to distribute, circulate, sell, let on hire, give or lend, or to offer it for sale or hire. 'Publishing' also includes 'making available', as where X gives Y a key to a library containing obscene articles. Additionally, in the case of a record, a film etc 'publish' includes showing, playing, or projecting it. Where the matter is data stored electronically, a person publishes it if he transmits that data. 'Transmit' includes the case where the recipient downloads the obscene matter from the accused's computer where it is stored. We are, therefore, considering every method of passing the article from one person to another. If we return to our consideration of the obscene article written at home, to distribute the manuscript to only one person will amount to publication, whether for gain or not. However, at this stage, it will be difficult to prove that this one person was likely to be depraved and corrupted, particularly if he is a person with an interest in such obscene articles. As it is circulated to more people, the easier it will become to prove that the article was likely to deprave and corrupt them. We must also consider those who publish in the more generally accepted sense and offer on the market such articles for sale. Today, the article is quite likely to be a video recording, or even an audio tape. Those who distribute, sell etc commit offences but so do those who show, play or project obscene articles. The owner of a photographic studio who develops photographs which are obscene publishes them when he sells them or passes them back for gain to their owner; publication to a third party is not required. In deciding upon appropriate charges, once it is clear that an article is obscene for the purposes of the Act one must consider the role of every person who has in any way transmitted the material to someone else. If a person has actually published, the question of gain does not arise; if he merely possesses it for the purpose of publication he must intend to publish for gain, although not necessarily his own.

Defences

It is a defence for a person to prove he had not examined the article and had no reasonable cause to suspect that it was such that his publication of it, or possession, as the case may be, would make him liable under the 1959 Act. He must prove both points. If he has examined it, it is no defence to allege that he had not realised its nature.

The 1959 Act provides a defence of 'public good'. If it is proved that publication was justified as being for the public good on the grounds that it is in the interests of science, literature, art or learning, or of other objects of general concern, a person must not be convicted of the above offences. Expert evidence may be given to establish or negative such a defence. This defence is only relevant once the jury has established obscenity, and is therefore of little operational significance to police officers.

Police powers

If information on oath is laid before a justice that there are reasonable grounds for suspecting that obscene articles are kept on any premises, stall or vehicle in the justice's area for publication for gain, he may issue a warrant authorising a constable to search for and seize any articles which he has reason to believe to be obscene and to be kept for publication for gain. If the justice considers that any articles seized are obscene he may issue a summons to the occupier of the premises etc to appear before a magistrates' court and show cause why the articles should not be forfeited. If the court is satisfied that the articles seized are obscene and kept for publication for gain, it must order their forfeiture.

A search warrant including the words 'any other material of a sexually explicit nature' is invalid, since what is sexually explicit is not necessarily obscene.

The offences under s 2 of the Act are in the list of arrestable offences in s 24(2) of the Police and Criminal Evidence Act 1984 and in the list of 'serious arrestable offences' in Sch 5 to that Act.

Indecent photographs of children

The Protection of Children Act 1978 is concerned with indecent photographs and pseudo photographs of children. Section 1(1) provides that it is an offence for a person:

(a) to take or permit to be taken, *or to make* any indecent photograph or *pseudo-photograph of a child*;
(b) to distribute or show such indecent photographs or *pseudo-photographs*;
(c) to have in his possession such indecent photographs *or pseudo-photographs* with a view to their being distributed or shown by himself or others; or
(d) to publish or cause to be published any advertisement likely to be understood as conveying that the advertiser distributes or shows such indecent photographs or *pseudo-photographs* or intends to do so.

Section 1(4) of the 1978 Act provides a defence to the charges set out at (b) or (c) if the accused proves that either:

(a) he had a legitimate reason for distributing or showing the photographs or pseudo photographs or (as the case may be) having them in his possession; or
(b) he had not seen the photographs or pseudo-photographs and did not know, nor had any reason to suspect, them to be indecent.

'Showing' includes 'making available', as where a person gives another a key to a cupboard containing indecent photographs. The same would be so where a person makes available a password which enables someone to download a 'photograph' stored on a computer to his own computer.

The Criminal Justice Act 1988, s 160 makes it an offence for a person to have any indecent photograph or pseudo-photograph of a child under the age of 16 in his possession. The same defences apply as in the case of the Protection of Children Act 1978 and in addition it is a defence for the accused to prove that the photograph was sent to him without any prior request made by him or on his behalf and that he did not keep it for an unreasonable time.

For the purposes of an offence under the 1978 Act or under s 160 of the 1988 Act, 'possession' bears the same meaning as in offences of possession of controlled drugs (discussed on p 694). It follows, for example, that an assistant in a sex shop containing indecent photographs of children is, like his employer, in possession of them.

References in the above offences to an indecent photograph include an indecent film, a copy of an indecent photograph or film, and an indecent photograph comprised in a film. References to photographs also include the negative as well as the positive version.

It is now possible for a camera to convert an object into electronic data capable of being converted into a photograph, thereby eliminating the need for a negative. For this reason, references to a 'photograph' include not only the negative as well as the positive version, but also include data stored on a computer disc or by other electronic means which is capable of conversion into a photograph. It is also possible to create 'fake' photographs by digital manipulation of photographs which have been electronically stored either by a camera or by scanning a conventional photograph. This digital manipulation is achieved by using widely available 'paint' and image-processing software to rearrange, colour and otherwise transform the objects in a scene. The same software can combine fragments of different images into one new image. Such indecent 'fake' photographs of children are already in circulation. It is for this reason that 'pseudo-photographs have been included within the 1978 Act.

A 'pseudo-photograph' is an image, whether made by computer graphics or otherwise howsoever, which appear to be a photograph. The term includes:

(a) a copy of an indecent pseudo-photograph; and
(b) data stored on a computer disc or by other electronic means which is capable of conversion into a pseudo-photograph.

The term 'indecent' means offending against recognised standards of propriety. A photograph or pseudo-photograph can be indecent even though it is not obscene. The child's age (or in the case of a pseudo-photograph apparent age) is a relevant factor as to whether or not the photograph or pseudo-photograph is indecent, but the circumstances in which it was taken or made, or the motivation of the photographer (or the maker of a pseudo-photograph), is not.

A photograph must be of a child under the age of 16. It is a matter for a court or jury to decide whether an unknown person depicted in an indecent photograph was under the age of 16. There is no need for expert evidence concerning age, the court or jury is as well placed as an expert to assess any argument concerning the age of the person depicted. Expert evidence would therefore be inadmissible. Since a pseudo-photograph will not be an image of a real person with a real age, the Act provides that, if the impression conveyed by the pseudo-photograph is that the person shown is a child under the age of 16, the pseudo-photograph is to be treated for all purposes of the 1978 Act as showing such a child and so is a pseudo-photograph where the predominant impression conveyed is that the person shown is a child under 16 notwithstanding that some of the physical characteristics shown are those of an adult.

Proceedings for the above offences may only be instituted by or with the consent of the Director of Public Prosecutions.

Police powers

A justice may issue a warrant to authorise entry, search for and seizure of such photographs or pseudo-photographs on information laid on oath by a constable or by or on behalf of the Director of Public Prosecutions.

Offences against s 1 of the 1978 Act are included in the list of arrestable offences in s 24(2) of the Police and Criminal Evidence Act 1984 and in the list of 'serious arrestable offences' set out in Sch 5 to that Act.

Harmful publications—children and young persons

The Children and Young Persons (Harmful Publications) Act 1955 deals with books, magazines or similar works which are likely to fall into the hands of children or young persons. If such a publication consists wholly or mainly of stories *told in pictures* (with or without the addition of written matter), and those stories portray the commission of crimes, acts of violence or cruelty, or incidents of a repulsive or horrible nature, in such a way that the work as a whole would tend to corrupt a child or young person into whose hands it might fall, that publication is covered by the provisions of the 1955 Act. The terms 'child' and 'young person' are as defined by the Children and Young Persons Act 1933. A 'child' is someone under 14 years of age, and a 'young person' someone under 18.

Clearly, the offence is concerned with 'horror comics' and the like. Those who print, publish, sell, let on hire or have in their possession for the purpose of selling or letting on hire such items commit offences. There is a defence to a selling or hiring charge: that the person concerned had not examined the contents of the publication and had no reason to suspect that the Act would apply to it.

Police powers

The power of a justice to issue a search warrant is peculiar in relation to this Act. One reason is that the consent of the Attorney-General is necessary before there may be a prosecution. Another reason is that a justice can only issue a search warrant at the time of, or after, the receipt of an information alleging an offence which leads him to authorise the issue of a summons or a warrant to arrest. In effect, therefore, proceedings for the present type of offence must have commenced in respect of a person allegedly involved in it.

This Act, and others similar to it, tend to cause difficulties for police officers considering charges to be preferred against those involved. Examination candidates share this concern. The correct approach is to examine the evidence at hand (or the information given) and from this to establish everyone who had been involved in the process from the outset. We must consider the responsibility of the printer, publisher, wholesaler, retailer or hirer: in other words, all those who handle the material.

Sending indecent material etc through post

The Post Office Act 1953, s 11 provides an ofence which is concerned with sending, or attempting to send, or procuring to be sent, a postal packet which encloses any indecent or obscene matter, or which has on the packet grossly offensive, indecent or obscene marks or designs.

Indecent displays etc

The Indecent Displays (Control) Act 1981 repealed all previous legislation dealing with indecent displays, advertisements etc. The offence prescribed by the 1981 Act is quite simply one of publicly displaying indecent matter. Any person who does this, or who causes or permits it to be done by another, is guilty of an offence. The normal tests of indecency should be applied and matter is publicly displayed if it is displayed in a public place, or in a manner which makes it visible from a public place. The term 'public place' for the purposes of this Act means any place to which the public have access (whether on payment or otherwise) while that matter is displayed. It does not extend to places to which the public are permitted to have access only on payment which is for, or includes payment for, that display. Nor does it apply to a shop, or any part of a shop, to which public access can only be gained by passing beyond an adequate warning notice. However, both of these exemptions will only apply if persons under 18 years of age are not allowed to enter such exempted premises whilst any such display is actually taking place.

The adequate warning notice described in the Act should read as set out below and this notice should be looked for in premises where it is known that such displays are held:

'WARNING
Persons passing beyond this notice will find material on display which they may consider indecent. No admittance to persons under 18 years of age.'

'Matter', for the purposes of this Act, includes anything capable of being displayed, but does not include the actual human body or a part of it. Thus the Act is not concerned with strippers. This is a useful Act to police officers as it can be applied to everything from the display of obscene graffiti scrawled on a wall to indecent film shows etc which are open to the public. The essential elements of the offence are indecency coupled with display to the general public.

Official TV programmes, art galleries, museums, Crown buildings, local authority buildings, theatres and arenas controlled by other legislation are totally outside the provisions of this Act.

Police powers

A constable may seize articles which he has reasonable grounds for believing to be indecent, or to contain indecent matter, or to have been used in the commission of an offence.

In addition, a justice may grant a search warrant, on information on oath, authorising entry within 14 days and seizure of material suspected to have been used in an offence under the 1981 Act.

RECORDS OF SEX OFFENDERS

The Sex Offenders Act 1997, Pt I requires a person who commits any of a certain type of offence, to notify the police of his name and address and any other name and address which that person uses. Such notification must include that person's date of birth, name on the relevant date and any other name used and home address. The relevant date is the date of conviction, finding or caution. Notification must be made within 14 days of the relevant date and may be made in person at a police station in the area where the person's home is situated, or by written notification to such a police station. After such an original notification, other names which may be used, changes of address or, where there is no main residence, premises which they regularly visit, or the fact that he has resided or stayed, for a qualifying period, at any premises in the United Kingdom the address of which has not been notified, must be notified. The term 'qualifying period' means 14 days or more or a stay on two or more occasions within a period of 12 months which amounts to 14 days.

The persons affected by these provisions are those convicted of an offence under Sch 1 to the Act; those found not guilty of such an offence by reason of insanity; those who committed such an offence while under a disability but have been found to have committed the act; and those who have been cautioned by the police after admitting such an offence.

Schedule 1 offences

Schedule 1 includes the offences of rape; intercourse with a girl under 13; intercourse with a girl between 13 and 16 if the offender was 20 years of age or more; and causing the prostitution of, intercourse with, or indecent assault on a girl under 16. Where the victim is under 18, the offences of incest by a man; buggery if the offender was aged 20 or more; and assault with intent to commit buggery are also applicable. Further offences are included where the victim is under 18 or where the offender was sentenced to at least 30 months' imprisonment or admitted to a hospital under a restriction order. They are indecent assault on a man or a woman; indecent conduct towards a child; inciting a girl under 16 to incest; taking, distributing etc indecent photographs of children; possessing indecent photographs of children; or importing indecent photographs of children.

Attempts, conspiracy to commit, incitement and aiding and abetting such offences are also covered by these provisions.

Duration of notification requirement

Persons who are sentenced to life imprisonment, 30 months' imprisonment or more, or who are admitted to hospital under a restriction order will be required to carry out these duties indefinitely; those sentenced to more than six months but less than 30 months for a period of 10 years; those sentenced to less than six months and those admitted to a hospital without being subject to a restriction order for a period of seven years; and persons of any other description, for a period of five years. However, where the offender is under 18, the periods of 10, 7 and 5 years are halved.

Where young offenders are sentenced to detention under a detention training order provision is made for a court to direct that persons with parental responsibility must carry out these duties and to be liable for any failure.

Offence of failure to comply with notification requirements

It is an offence for a person to fail without reasonable excuse to comply with these requirements. It is also an offence to notify the police, in purported compliance with these requirements, of any information which the person concerned knows to be false.

The offence of failure to notify is a continuing one so that proceedings may be taken at any time after such a failure. It may be dealt with at any place where the offender resides or where he is found.

SEXUAL OFFENCES COMMITTED ABROAD BY A BRITISH CITIZEN

Part II of the Sex Offenders Act 1997 makes provision for some sexual offences which are committed outside the United Kingdom by British citizens or persons resident in the United Kingdom to be treated as if they had been committed in England, Wales or Northern Ireland. These offences are set out in Sch 2 to the 1997 Act:

(a)   intercourse with a girl under 13;
(b)   intercourse with a girl between 13 and 16;
(c)   indecent conduct towards a child;
(d)   the taking and distribution etc of indecent photographs; and
(e)   where the victim is under 16, rape, buggery, indecent assault and assault with intent to commit buggery.

The Sexual Offences (Conspiracy and Incitement) Act 1996 provides that certain offences involving conspiracy and incitement to commit sex offences against children outside the United Kingdom may be tried within England and Wales.

CHAPTER 35

Drugs

Modern society could not operate as it does without drugs, and the ever-increasing prescription of drugs, the continuing search for new forms of drugs and the proportionate increase in the likelihood of drug dependence have created a need for strict forms of control. Arguments continue concerning which drugs are addictive and which are not, as do arguments for and against the permitted use of certain drugs such as cannabis which, though perhaps not addictive in themselves, create a feeling of well-being.

CLASSIFICATION OF DRUGS

The Misuse of Drugs Act 1971 provides a number of offences intended to control the misuse of drugs. Drugs which are subject to the Act are designated as 'controlled drugs'. A 'controlled drug' is any substance or product for the time being specified in Parts I, II or III of Sch 2 to the Act. Part 1 of Sch 2 lists 'Class A drugs'; Part II, 'Class B drugs', and Part III, 'Class C drugs'. Drugs can be added to the lists contained in Sch 2 by Order in Council, or moved from one class to another. One of the points of the classification of controlled drugs is that it affects the punishment of some of the offences under the 1971 Act. As a result of a House of Lords' decision, what may appear to be one offence (eg unlawful supply) is in law divisible into distinct offences depending on the maximum penalty for the drug in question.

Class A drugs can be divided into two groups; first, narcotic drugs, such as cocaine, morphine, opium, pethidine, and heroin, and second, hallucinogenic drugs, such as mescaline, LSD and MDMA (ecstasy), however the MDMA is produced. Narcotic drugs are particularly dangerous because of their addictive qualities and hallucinogenic ones because of the violent conduct which the hallucinated taker may engage in. The largest number of controlled drugs fall within Class A. Class B drugs include amphetamines (which are stimulant drugs), such as mandrax, as well as cannabis and cannabis resin. Class C drugs include benzyphetamine, chlorphentermine, mephentermine, methaqualone, phendimetrazine, pipradrol and temazapan.

Although there are a substantial number of substances listed as Class C drugs, they include only those which might generally be described as 'mild'. There are 100 plus drugs listed in Class C and a similar number are listed in Class A. There are fewer Class B drugs; currently about 20. Only an analysis of the substance will prove its nature, but the forms of drug in popular usage on the street are almost invariably Classes A and B.

Because of its particular significance and the ease with which the plant can be grown, the expressions 'cannabis' and 'cannabis resin' are defined by the Act. 'Cannabis' (except in the expression 'cannabis resin') means any part of the genus Cannabis or any part of any such plant (by whatever name designated) except that it does not include cannabis resin, or any of the following products, after separation from the rest of the plant, namely:

(a)   mature stalk of any such plant;
(b)   fibre produced from mature stalk of any such plant; and;
(c)   seed of any such plant.

'Cannabis resin' means the separated resin, whether crude or purified, obtained from any plant of the genus Cannabis.

As indicated above a 'controlled drug' is a specified substance or *product*. In addition 'controlled drug' includes any 'preparation or other product' containing a specified substance or product. Some growing things, such as certain types of mushrooms, contain a specified substance. In their natural state such things are not a specified substance or product, but if they are picked and subjected to some process to enable them to be used as a drug, they become a 'preparation' containing a specified substance and become a controlled drug. If they are picked, packed and frozen they become a 'product' containing a specified substance and become a controlled drug.

The problem of enforcement which confronts police officers always appears to be a matter of identification of a substance. For example, reasonable suspicion that a person is in possession of a controlled drug will arise from circumstances other than the appearance or known character of the substance possessed. If, for example, persons are found on premises apparently under the influence of drugs, and tablets or other substances are found in their possession, it is not unreasonable to suspect that they are in possession of controlled drugs.

UNLAWFUL IMPORT AND EXPORT

The most effective way in which to limit drug trafficking in any country is to restrict the importation of drugs. Section 3 of the 1971 Act prohibits the importation or exportation of a controlled drug, otherwise than as authorised by regulations made under the Act or by a licence issued by the Home Secretary. Breach of this prohibition is not an offence under the Misuse of Drugs Act but it is an offence under the Customs and Excise Management Act 1979, ss 50 and 68. Fraudulent evasion of such a prohibition is also punishable under s 170 of the 1979 Act. The importation or exportation of controlled drugs of all classes is an arrestable offence.

UNLAWFUL PRODUCTION

Section 4(2) of the Misuse of Drugs Act 1971 states that it is an offence for any person unlawfully to produce a controlled drug or to be concerned in the production of a controlled drug. Such an offence is an arrestable offence.

Unlawful

The production of any controlled drug other than as authorised by regulations is an unlawful production. The regulations authorise production by drug companies, by research establishments for experimental purposes and by chemists in the course of their business.

Produce

The term 'produce' means to produce a controlled drug by manufacture, cultivation or any other means, and 'production' has a corresponding meaning. A substance will pass through a number of processes in its production and a person charged must be clearly shown to have taken some identifiable part in the process of production before he can be convicted of this offence. It has been held that the conversion of cocaine hydrochloride into freebase cocaine, in which form it would vaporise and be capable of being inhaled, by dissolving cocaine hydrochloride in water and either baking powder or household ammonia, amounts to production of a Class A drug 'by other means' since the drug, in these two forms, is chemically different. It does not matter that the cocaine hydrochloride was already a Class A drug before the process began. By way of further example, where cannabis plants have been harvested and the plants are then stripped to take out those parts which could be used for smoking, it has been held that this amounts to production of a Class B drug (cannabis) as a controlled drug is produced by some 'other method' than cultivation or manufacture. However, the offence is to produce a controlled drug and it is therefore essential that a controlled drug is actually produced before the offence can be committed. If the process to produce a substance has not been completed, there can be a conviction for attempting to commit the offence of production. Where a person tries to produce a controlled drug but, because of insufficient knowledge, produces a substance which is not in fact a controlled drug, he may nevertheless be convicted of an attempt to produce a controlled drug.

Concerned in the production

The inclusion of these words is for the purpose of widening the net of criminal liability in relation to the production of controlled drugs. The effect of these words is that criminal liability is not limited to those who actually participated in the production of a controlled drug, since those who arrange for the delivery of ingredients to the place of manufacture of such a drug, knowing the purpose for which they are required, are concerned in its production, as is a person who knowingly allows his premises to be used. Not all types of activities covered by 'being concerned in' can properly be described as aiding, abetting, counselling or procuring the actual production of the drug. Consequently, the phrase 'being concerned' widens the ambit of the law beyond that which it would otherwise have.

UNLAWFUL SUPPLY

The unlawful supply of controlled drugs is another activity which is included in the general description of 'drug trafficking'. If a controlled drug is unlawfully imported or produced it must then have a distribution network. The Misuse of Drugs Act 1971, s 4(3) states:

'It is an offence for a person unlawfully to supply a controlled drug to another or to be concerned in the supplying of such a drug to another, or to offer to supply a controlled drug to another, or to be concerned in the making to another of an offer to supply such a drug.'

All the offences described in s 4(3) are arrestable offences, whether the controlled drug concerned belongs to Class A, B or C.

Unlawful

The circumstances in which a controlled drug may be supplied lawfully are set out in regulations made under the Act. They are not difficult to imagine: doctors may issue drugs direct from their own dispensaries, chemists may supply them upon prescription, nurses may supply patients in hospital, laboratory analysts, inspectors and quality controllers may also handle drugs and pass them from one to another. The inclusion of the term 'unlawfully' ensures that all circumstances in which controlled drugs are supplied to a person outside such exceptions amount to offences under the Act.

To supply to another

The term 'supply' means more than the mere transfer of physical control from one person to another: it means to furnish to another the drug in order to enable the other to use it for his own purposes. At one extreme there is the person who supplies the drug addict. He is the one who is usually described as a 'pusher', forming a rung in the distribution ladder between those who illegally import or produce drugs and those who use them. The person who distributes drugs at a party is supplying the drugs to another and is guilty of an offence under s 4(3). So is someone who returns a drug to a person who already owns it so that he can use it, or who hands a 'reefer' to someone so that he can take a puff. On the other hand, a person who hands a drug to another for safe-keeping does not supply it to him. Nor does a person who injects another with heroin if that drug is already in the other's control.

Although a person who makes a joint purchase of drugs for consumption by himself and another, paying with their joint funds, supplies the other when he hands over the latter's share of the drugs, the Court of Appeal has stated that a charge of supplying the latter is undesirable.

Where police officers occupy a house used by suppliers, they may not give evidence of things said by persons who call at the house to obtain supplies of drugs, as such evidence is hearsay. However, evidence given by police officers of incidents within eight days of observation upon premises, during which a great number of people were seen visiting the address, together with evidence of relevant convictions of eight of those persons for offences of possession or supply of heroin, is admissible as it is relevant to the nature of the transactions and the purpose for which the defendants were letting the visitors into the house.

Before an offence of supplying can be committed the substance supplied must be a controlled drug. It is not sufficient that the supplier believed that the substance was a drug, when in fact it was not, although he could be convicted of an attempt to supply in such a case or, depending on the circumstances, of an offer to supply.

To be concerned in the supply

For the purpose of this offence, the wide meaning given to the term 'concerned' when discussed in its application to offences of production should be applied.

To offer to supply

It is the making of an offer which is the important factor in relation to this offence; the extension of the offence to those who may be concerned in the making of such an offer gives considerable width to its application. Whereas one must supply an actual controlled drug before committing the offence of supplying, this is not necessary in relation to the making of an offer and this will be appreciated if it is borne in mind that the offence lies in the making of the offer. Therefore, if an offer is made to supply a controlled drug, an offence is committed even though the substance is not in fact a controlled drug, and even though the accused knows this. Likewise, the offence of offering to supply a controlled drug is committed even if the offeror does not intend to supply anything. Many persons may be involved in the making of the offer. Those who approach people and seek to induce them to purchase drugs or merely receive them are offering to supply; those who send them out into the streets to canvass sale or distribution are concerned in the offer which is subsequently made.

Supply or offer to supply article

The Drug Trafficking Offences Act 1986 added a s 9A to the Misuse of Drugs Act 1971. The section creates summary offences of supplying or offering to supply an article which may be used or adapted to be used (whether by itself or in combination with another article) in the administration by a person of a controlled drug, or which may be used to prepare a controlled drug for administration, believing it would be so used in circumstances which would be unlawful.

However, it is not an offence under the section to supply a hypodermic syringe.

UNLAWFUL POSSESSION

The offences of unlawful possession of controlled drugs are those with which police officers are most commonly involved. The Misuse of Drugs Act 1971, s 5(2) states that it is an offence for a person unlawfully to have a controlled drug in his possession. The unlawful possession of Class A or Class B controlled drugs are arrestable offences. Possession of Class C drugs is not an arrestable offence.

Unlawful

The Misuse of Drugs Regulations 1985 specify when possession of a controlled drug is lawful. They provide that such possession is lawful if it is under the authority of a licence issued by the Home Secretary or under a doctor's prescription. In addition, a constable who comes into possession of controlled drugs in the course of his duties is in lawful possession of them, and so are carriers, postal workers, despatchers, workers in forensic laboratories who examine drugs on behalf of the police, medical personnel, ship's masters etc, in circumstances properly connected with their duties.

Possession

Physical custody of the drug is not necessary for possession but physical control over it is. It follows that a person who has bought a controlled drug is not in possession of it if it is still hidden in the seller's car or stored at the seller's home. On the other hand, a person who leaves a drug in his car or at home while he is away remains in possession of the drug since he retains physical control over it.

Possession can be joint, for example, if two people share a car which they know contains cannabis, they are both in possession of it if each shares with the other the right to control what is done with it. Moreover, s 37(3) of the Act states that for the purposes of the Act the things which a person has in his possession shall be taken to include anything subject to his control which is in the custody of another. Therefore there may be a number of persons in possession of a particular controlled drug. If a man imports cannabis and hands it to his business manager to store pending distribution, both are in possession as the drug is subject to their control. If the business manager then passes it on to the warehouseman to keep until either he or the importer send for the drug, all three are in possession of it for the purpose of the 1971 Act.

Possession cannot begin until the person with control is aware that the thing is under his control; if a drug is slipped into a person's pocket, unknown to him, he is not in possession of it. (As an exception, a person is in possession of a drug delivered to his home, even if he is unaware that it has arrived, provided it is delivered in response to a request by him.)

Knowledge of a thing's quality is not required. It follows that a mere mistake by the accused as to the quality of the thing under his control is not enough to prevent him being in possession. For example, if the accused knows that he is in control of some tablets which he believes to be aspirin (or, even sweets) but which are, in fact heroin, he is in possession of the heroin tablets. Likewise, the Divisional Court has held that if the accused picks up a cigarette containing cannabis and puts it in his pocket, believing that it only contains tobacco, he is in possession of the cannabis.

In the case of drugs in a parcel, packet or other container in a person's physical control, he is in possession of those drugs if he knows that he is in control of that container and that it contains something, even though he thinks that the thing is something different in kind from a drug and even though he has no right to open the container to check its contents.

Possession, once begun, continues as long as the thing is in the person's control, even though he has forgotten about it or mistakenly believes it has been destroyed or disposed of.

Although it is not necessary to prove that a minimum or usable quantity of a controlled drug was unlawfully in the possession of the person charged he must have been in possession of a quantity of it which was visible, tangible and measurable. Persons who are found under the influence of a drug are not then in possession of it for the purposes of this offence, even though traces of it are found in a blood or urine sample. This is because, once consumed, the thing changes its character and can no longer be considered a controlled drug. However, evidence of the presence of a drug in a blood or urine sample can be given to support an allegation of possession of the drug in its true state at some earlier time, ie before it was taken into the body.

Defence

A person is not criminally liable for the unlawful possession of a controlled drug in the circumstances outlined by s 5(4) of the 1971 Act.

Section 5(4) provides that where, in any proceedings for an offence of unlawful possession contrary to s 5(2), it is proved that the accused had a controlled drug in his possession it is a defence for him to prove that:

(a) knowing or suspecting it to be a controlled drug, he took possession of it for the purpose of preventing another from committing or continuing to commit an offence in connection with that drug and that as soon as possible after taking possession he took all such steps as were reasonably open to him to destroy the drug or to deliver it into the custody of a person lawfully entitled to take custody of it; or

(b) knowing or suspecting it to be a controlled drug, he took possession of it for the purpose of delivering it into the custody of a person lawfully entitled to the custody of it and that as soon as possible after taking possession of it he took all such steps as were reasonably open to him to deliver it into the custody of such a person.

The circumstances outlined at (a) would therefore cover the situation in which a mother found her child in possession of controlled drugs and took them from the child. Provided that she destroyed the drug or handed it over to lawful custody as soon as possible, or took reasonable steps to do so, she would commit no offence. The situation outlined at (b) would cover the circumstances where a person found a bottle of amphetamine tablets in a park and took possession of the bottle to prevent the drug from falling into the wrong hands. Once again, if steps were taken as soon as possible to hand over the drug to lawful custody, the finder's possession would not be unlawful.

POSSESSION WITH INTENT TO SUPPLY

Offences concerned with supplying controlled drugs to another, or offering to supply such drugs, have already been discussed, but it is essential when considering drug offences to consider every stage of the movement of a controlled drug from person to person. Section 5(3) deals with offences of having a controlled drug in one's possession, whether lawfully or not, with intent to supply it unlawfully to another. Such an offence is one which is committed by a 'pusher' immediately prior to his offer to supply the drug, or his actual supply of it. It fills a gap in the process of traffic in drugs. In the beginning, drugs are illegally imported or produced. They will then be possessed by any number of persons if they are stored within an organisation with knowledge on the part of a number of persons who have control over them. All will possess the drugs with intent to supply. Those who go out to peddle the drugs, the 'pushers', possess them with intent to supply them to others. Immediately they supply, or offer to supply, they commit a different offence. The persons who are supplied represent the end of the chain. They possess the drugs unlawfully for their own use.

An offence of possession with intent to supply is an arrestable offence, no matter which class of drug is possessed. It may be committed by persons who are lawfully in possession in the first instance. For example, it can be committed by a doctor who is in possession of drugs lawfully, but has an intention to supply them unlawfully (eg merely for profit, as opposed to bona fide treatment). However, the offence is usually committed by drug pushers and the like.

In terms of proving that possession was with intent unlawfully to supply, evidence of drug-related paraphernalia, evidence of an extravagant life-style and evidence of the possession of large amounts of cash *which can be shown to be likely to be used for the acquisition of stocks of drugs* for present active drug dealing are relevant — but not conclusive — to the issue of *intent to supply* but not normally to the issue of possession. A case where such evidence might be relevant to possession, as well as to intent to supply, is where there is evidence of frequent brief visits by different young men, who then leave carrying small packages, and when the premises (whose occupant is long-term unemployed) are searched large sums of money and some drugs are found. Such evidence may be admitted as evidence that the occupant knew of the drugs and was in control of them (ie in possession) as well as of an intent to supply them. Whilst evidence in the form of documents relating to transactions and cash in the accused's possession is relevant, the relevance of the cash in the accused's possession must be related to evidence of ongoing (and not merely previous) drug transactions in order for it to be admissible. If there is a possibility that such money was in the accused's possession for a reason other than drug dealing, evidence of its possession together with drugs would not be probative of an intent to supply them. For example, where £150 was found in an ornamental kettle it was held that this was not admissible because it proved nothing in relation to a charge of possessing cannabis with intent to supply. On the other hand, where a sum of £16,000 and a gold necklace were found concealed beneath a cooker, it was held that the finding of a large sum of money was capable of being admissible in relation to the issue of intent to supply before the jury.

CULTIVATION OF CANNABIS

The cultivation of cannabis is an arrestable offence. Section 6(2) of the 1971 Act states that it is an offence unlawfully to cultivate any plant of the genus Cannabis. The only lawful cultivation of cannabis is that authorised by a licence issued by the Home Secretary.

Cannabis plants grow quite easily in the British Isles and there are many persons now living in Britain who have the necessary knowledge to ensure successful cultivation of them. The word 'cultivate' indicates some form of attention to the plant during the process of its growth. A person who puts seeds in the ground cultivates, as does he who hoes, waters, prunes or generally cares for a plant during the process of its growth. It is doubtful if a person could be held to have cultivated plants merely because he failed to remove those which were growing wild but this would depend upon the circumstances. If they were deliberately preserved, by caring for the ground in which they were growing, this would amount to the type of care which could be described as cultivation. If any form of cultivation can be proved, then it merely remains for the prosecution to show that the plant was of the genus Cannabis.

SMOKING OF OPIUM

The Misuse of Drugs Act 1971, s 9 prohibits a person from:

(a) smoking or otherwise using prepared opium; or
(b) frequenting a place used for the purpose of opium smoking; or
(c) having in his possession -
    (i) any pipes or other utensils made or adapted for use in connection with the smoking of opium, being pipes or utensils which have been used by him or

with his knowledge and permission in that connection or which he intends to use or permit others to use in that connection; or

(ii) any utensils which have been used by him or with his knowledge or permission in connection with the preparation of opium for smoking.

Offences under s 9 are not common.

'Prepared opium' is opium prepared for smoking and includes dross and any other residue remaining after opium has been smoked.

Most of s 9 is self-explanatory but further explanation must be given to the offence of frequenting.

The term 'frequenting' means to go there often. The more often a person visits a place at which opium is being smoked, the greater the presumption that he is attending that place for that purpose, in the absence of any other reasonable explanation. There is no requirement that a person who frequents a place used for opium smoking must have been shown to have been involved in opium smoking. Significant factors will be the duration and frequency of visits; the nature of the place (if it is a café the possibility of frequent visits being innocent increases); things which actually occurred whilst the accused was there; and his own behaviour when at or near that place. The offence is concerned with events which occur at a 'place'. That place does not need to be a building. Proof that the place is used as an opium den will be necessary.

STATUTORY DEFENCE

Section 28 of the 1971 Act provides a defence in relation to charges contrary to s 4(2) (unlawful production), s 4(3) (unlawful supply), s 5(2) (unlawful possession), s 5(3) (possession with intent to supply), s 6(2) (unlawful cultivation of cannabis) and s 9 (smoking opium, frequenting places used for opium smoking, or possession of utensils used for opium smoking). For convenience, the defence will be explained in relation to the offence of unlawful possession but what is said will be equally applicable (with the appropriate changes of words) to the other offences just mentioned.

Assuming that the prosecution has proved that the accused was in unlawful possession of a controlled drug, he can be convicted of that offence, even though it is not proved that he knew he was in possession of a controlled drug. However, s 28 provides the accused with a defence in the circumstances outlined below. The accused has the burden of proving the defence on the balance of probabilities.

The basic definition of the defence is contained in s 28(2), which states that it is a defence for the accused to prove that *he neither knew of, nor suspected, nor had reason to suspect* the existence of some fact alleged by the prosecution which it is necessary for the prosecution to prove if he is to be convicted of the offence charged. (This does not affect the need for the prosecution to prove the element of knowledge required to establish 'possession'.)

This provision is subject to a qualification, provided by s 28(3), where the accused alleges, and proves, that he did not know, suspect or have reason to suspect that the thing in question was the controlled drug alleged, and proved, by the prosecution to have been involved. In this case, such proof by the accused is not enough to give him a defence. In order to be acquitted he must also prove one of two things:

(a) that he neither believed nor suspected, nor had reason to suspect, that the thing in question was a controlled drug at all; or

(b) that he believed that the thing in question was a controlled drug which he was, in fact, legally entitled to possess (or supply or produce etc as the case may be).

(a) can be illustrated as follows: if A gives B for safekeeping a bottle of tablets which he alleges are aspirin tablets but which are in fact heroin, B will be in possession of the tablets because he is, to his knowledge, in control of the bottle (container) and knows that it contains something but he will have a defence to a charge of unlawful possession if he can prove that he did not believe, suspect or have reason to suspect that the tablets were a controlled drug. Had B been told or had reason to suspect that the bottle contained amphetamines whereas it in fact contained heroin, this would not be a defence as both are controlled drugs.

The following example demonstrates the operation of (b): if an addict is prescribed heroin and is given cocaine by mistake, he is technically in unlawful possession of the cocaine (since it has not been prescribed). Assuming (as seems likely) that he can prove that he neither knew, suspected or had reason to suspect that the thing was cocaine, the addict would have a defence if he also proved that he believed he was in possession of heroin.

In deciding whether a person had 'no reason to suspect' under the above provisions, voluntary intoxication on his part must be ignored.

CONTROLLED DRUGS ON PREMISES

The Misuse of Drugs Act 1971, s 8 is concerned with a person who, being the occupier or concerned in the management of any premises, knowingly permits or suffers any of the following activities to take place on those premises:

(a) unlawfully producing or attempting to produce a controlled drug;
(b) unlawfully supplying or attempting to supply a controlled drug to another, or offering to supply a controlled drug unlawfully to another;
(c) preparing opium for smoking; or
(d) smoking cannabis, cannabis resin or prepared opium.

An offence under s 8 is an arrestable offence.

The occupier

To be 'the occupier' a person does not have to be a tenant or have an estate in the premises. A person is the occupier of premises if he is entitled to exclusive possession of them, in the sense that he has the requisite degree of control over them to exclude from them those who might otherwise carry on one of the forbidden activities there. Thus, a student who had a room in a college hostel was held to be the occupier of it because his contractual licence gave him such exclusivity of possession, whether or not he was entitled to exclude the college authorities. If there is drug-taking in a dwelling house, and it is knowingly permitted by the householder (ie 'the occupier'), he commits an offence under s 8. However, he would not commit that offence, if, in his absence and unknown to him, his teenage son knowingly permits drug-taking on the premises. Nor would the son be guilty of an offence under s 8 on the basis of being 'the occupier' of the premises since he does not have that status. Nevertheless, depending on the circumstances, the son might be guilty of an offence under s 8 on the basis of 'being concerned in the management of the premises', to which phrase we now turn.

Concerned in management

To be 'concerned in the management of premises' a person need not necessarily have any legal interest in them, since the term includes anyone who is concerned in exercising control over the premises or in running or organising them on a day-to-day basis. It is possible that such a person will have some control over who shall be permitted to enter the premises and who shall not, but this is not a prerequisite for a person to be concerned in their management. If drug-taking was generally permitted on the premises of a gaming club, it is possible that only the general manager would have the right to permit entry but other officials of the club might control activities in different rooms. If drug use is generally and knowingly permitted, then all who are concerned in any way in the management of the premises (ie the general manager and other officials) would be guilty of this offence.

Persons who occupy premises as trespassers (and are therefore not 'occupiers' for the purpose of the offence) may nevertheless be concerned in the management of those premises. For example, if drug-taking activities are organised upon premises by squatters, all concerned in that organisation are guilty of the present offence.

Premises

The Act does not define the term 'premises'. The term should be given its normal, everyday meaning, and in this sense 'premises' includes any form of building and the grounds in which a building stands and also land without any building on it. Therefore, the organiser of an open air pop festival who knowingly permitted one of the activities described above would (as a person concerned in the management of the premises) be guilty of the present offence, as would the occupier of the site if he knowingly permitted one of these activities.

Knowingly permits or suffers

'Permit' and 'suffer' are synonymous. In law, a person only permits or suffers something to occur if, physically and legally, he could prevent it but does not do so.

The inclusion of the word 'knowingly' does not mean that actual knowledge that the premises were being used in the particular prohibited way must be proved since 'knowingly' also embraces wilful blindness, ie suspecting what is going on but deliberately refraining from making inquiries. The smoking of cannabis results in a smell which is quite easily identifiable and if, at a party for instance, the occupier of the premises suspects that those assembled there are quite generally smoking cannabis but deliberately looks the other way, it is no defence for him to allege that he was not certain that cannabis was being smoked.

On a charge of permitting the premises to be used for supplying a controlled drug, it is not necessary for the prosecution to prove more than that the accused 'knew' of the supply of a controlled drug; it need not be proved that he knew that it was the particular type of controlled drug supplied. The same is true on a charge of permitting premises to be used for production. Likewise it would seem that on a charge of permitting the smoking of cannabis, an accused could be convicted even if he thought that cannabis resin or opium was being smoked, and so on.

Conclusion

The involvement of those in control of premises adds a further dimension to consideration of the offences which might be committed in particular circumstances. In addition to considering the passage of the controlled drug from person to person, it is necessary to consider the possible liability of the occupier or any person concerned in the management of any premises which may be involved.

POWERS

Search, seize and detain

Section 23 of the 1971 Act provides that, if a constable has reasonable grounds to suspect that any person is in possession of a controlled drug in contravention of the Act or regulations, the constable may:

(a) search that person, and detain him for the purpose of searching him;
(b) search any vehicle or vessel in which the constable suspects that the drug may be found, and for that purpose require the person in control to stop it;
(c) seize and detain, for the purpose of proceedings under the Act, anything found in the course of the search which appears to the constable to be evidence of an offence under the Act.

It must be emphasised that the exercise of these powers to search, seize and detain depends upon there being reasonable grounds to suspect possession of a controlled drug in contravention of the Act or regulations. It is impossible to set out a list of rules which might be applied in determining whether there is a reasonable suspicion that a person is in possession of a controlled drug. There is no general right to search persons who are found by night in areas which drug users are known to frequent. However, such circumstances, accompanied by observation of the passing of substances which have the appearance of being drugs from one person to another, could give rise to such suspicions in the minds of police officers. Reasonable suspicion may exist as a result of information received from another party; this will depend upon the reliability of the person providing the information and upon the likelihood of that information being true in all the circumstances.

The power to search a person must extend to searching things in his immediate possession, for example a suitcase or a holdall. If this was not so the power to search persons would be totally ineffective.

Search warrant

Section 23 of the 1971 Act also authorises a justice to grant a search warrant if, satisfied by information on oath that there is a reasonable ground for suspecting that controlled drugs are, in contravention of the Act or any regulations, in the possession of a person on any premises, or that a document directly or indirectly relating to drug dealing is in the possession of persons on any premises. The warrant will name the particular premises, and it is only those premises (and persons in them) which may be searched on its authority. If necessary, force may be used to enter the premises.

If there is reasonable ground for suspecting that an offence has been committed in relation to any controlled drugs found on the premises or in the possession of anyone there, or that a document so found directly or indirectly relates to drug dealings, the drugs or document may be seized and detained.

Obstruction of a constable

It is an offence intentionally to obstruct a person in the execution of his powers to search under s 23 of the 1971 Act; or to conceal documents, drugs etc from such a person; or to fail without reasonable excuse to produce such documents or books where the production is demanded by a person in the exercise of his powers under s 23. Such an offence is not an arrestable offence.

Evidence—disclosure of site of observation posts

Where the police use hidden observation posts in an area where drug dealing is prevalent, the police officers concerned can refuse to answer questions about the location of those observation posts. There is no essential difference between informers and the providers of observation posts as both provide indispensable assistance in the detection of crime.

DRUG TRAFFICKING

Drug trafficking is being concerned anywhere in producing, supplying, transporting, storing, importing or exporting a controlled drug. The Drug Trafficking Act 1994 provides that, where a person is sentenced at Crown Court for one or more drug trafficking offences, the Crown Court must proceed towards a confiscation order *if the prosecution asks it to do so, or if the Court considers that, although not requested by the prosecution to do so, it is appropriate to do so.* If the Crown Court is asked to proceed towards a confiscation order or decides in its discretion to do so, it must proceed as follows. It must determine on the balance of probabilities whether the drug trafficker has benefited (any payment etc received) from that drug trafficking and, if so, must determine any amount to be recovered and order that amount to be paid. Where a Crown Court considers that it requires further information it may postpone the making of a determination. The Crown Court's powers to make a confiscation order under the 1994 Act do not apply where a defendant is before the Crown Court for sentence with a view to a sentence of detention in a young offender institution or where the Court's powers are limited to dealing with him as a magistrates' court might have done.

The 1994 Act requires the Court to assume that property held by that person since his conviction or within six years preceding the institution of proceedings was payment or reward in connection with drug trafficking. This extends the nature of police inquiries following the arrest of a drug trafficker. Any such 'assumption' made by a court must be based upon prima facie evidence which is sufficient to justify it. The Act sets out a procedure which permits a statement of such dealings to be offered by the prosecutor, which the accused may accept totally or in part. The accused must have been served with a copy.

The 1994 Act also creates an offence of assisting a drug trafficker in relation to his control of proceeds of such drug trafficking, knowing or suspecting that that person is a person who carries on, or has carried on, drug trafficking, or has benefited from it. It is a defence to prove that one did not know these facts or that one intended to disclose these suspicions to a constable and there is a reasonable excuse for not having made that disclosure. The procedures concerned with 'benefits' do not apply to those who are charged with assisting such a person.

The Drug Trafficking Act 1994 also provides offences of:

(a) assisting another to retain the benefit of drug trafficking;
(b) acquisition, possession or use of the proceeds of drug trafficking;
(c) failing to disclose knowledge or suspicion of 'money laundering' of such proceeds; and
(d) 'tipping-off' in relation to police activities into money laundering.

The Criminal Justice (International Co-operation) Act 1990 provides various offences relating to concealing or transferring the proceeds of drug trafficking.

GLUE-SNIFFING

It is an offence, contrary to the Intoxicating Substances (Supply) Act 1985, for a person to supply, or offer to supply, a substance other than a controlled drug:

(a) to a person under 18 whom he knows, or has reasonable cause to believe, to be under that age; or

(b) to a person who is acting on behalf of someone under 18, and whom he knows, or has reasonable cause to believe, to be so acting,

if he knows or has reasonable cause to believe that the substance is, or its fumes are, likely to be inhaled by the person under 18 for the purpose of causing intoxication.

It is a defence for a person who supplies or offers to supply such a substance to show that at the material time he was under 18 and was not acting in the course or furtherance of a business.

CHAPTER 36

Theft and related offences, robbery and blackmail

THEFT

The Theft Act 1968, s 1(1) provides:

> 'A person is guilty of theft if he dishonestly appropriates property belonging to another with the intention of permanently depriving the other of it; and "thief" and "steal" shall be construed accordingly.'

Theft is an arrestable offence. By s 30 of the 1968 Act, the leave of the Director of Public Prosecutions is required for the institution of proceedings for the theft by one spouse of the other's property, unless, by virtue of any judicial decree or order, the spouses were not obliged to cohabit at the material time.

When one considers theft, it is usual to imagine the thief stealing so that he will benefit in some material way but this is not essential. Section 1(2) states that it is immaterial whether the appropriation is made with a view to gain, or is made for the thief's own benefit. Thus, a postman who flushes postal packets down the lavatory to avoid delivering them, or who takes them to give to his son, is as guilty of theft as if he had taken them for his own benefit. The terms of the definition of theft in s 1(1) are defined, in whole or part, by ss 2 to 6 of the 1968 Act.

For the purposes of exposition, it is best to start by noting that to be guilty of theft the accused must be proved:

(a) to have appropriated property belonging to another (the actus reus); and
(b) to have done so dishonestly and with the intention of permanently depriving the other of it (the mens rea).

Appropriation

Section 3(1) of the 1968 Act describes appropriation as:

> 'Any assumption by a person of the rights of an owner amounts to an appropriation, and this includes, where he has come by the property (innocently

or not) without stealing it, any later assumption of a right to it by keeping or dealing with it as owner.'

The essence of this definition is an 'assumption of the rights of an owner'. An owner of property has many rights in relation to it, including the rights to use it, to destroy it, to give it away, to sell it, and so on. The House of Lords has held that, despite the use of the words 'the rights' at the beginning of s 3(1), s 3 as a whole indicates that an appropriation does not require an assumption of all the rights of an owner and that it is enough that there has been an assumption of any of the rights of the owner. This conclusion does violence to the clear words of the section but it must now be regarded as representing the correct interpretation of the words in question. We shall see later on that it is possible to steal from a person who is not the owner but to whom the property 'belongs' for the purposes of theft and that an owner can steal his own property. Presumably, 'the owner' in the House of Lords' formulation must be read as 'the person to whom the property belongs' where the alleged theft is not from the owner.

The House of Lords has ruled that an act amounting to an assumption of a right of the owner done with the authority or consent of the owner can amount to an appropriation of goods for the purposes of the Theft Act 1968. In the case in question, the defendant had been employed as an assistant manager at a shop trading in electrical goods. An acquaintance asked him to supply goods from the shop and accept payment by two stolen building society cheques. The defendant agreed, prepared a list of goods and sought authority from his manager to release the goods. The manager agreed provided that the defendant confirmed with the bank that the cheques were good. He alleged that he had done so. After the goods were released the cheques were returned endorsed, 'Orders not to pay—stolen cheque'. On these facts, the House of Lords held that the assistant manager had properly been convicted of theft.

The House of Lords also stated that it was irrelevant that what had happened might also have constituted an offence of obtaining property by deception. It also endorsed a previous decision of the House which affirmed that, where a taxi driver had dishonestly taken £6 from an Italian visitor's wallet, in addition to the £1 already proffered for a 10s and 6d journey, an appropriation could occur in such circumstances even though the owner had permitted or consented to the property being taken.

A pickpocket who takes someone's wallet clearly appropriates it. An appropriation can occur even though the assumption is only momentary. It has been held, for example, that there was an appropriation where a man wrested a bag from a woman's grasp, even though he then dropped it on the ground and did not make off with it. It remains to be decided whether the mere taking hold of a wallet, handbag or other article by a pickpocket or the like in order to take it constitutes an appropriation; if it is not it is certainly an attempt and could lead to a conviction for attempted theft.

A shopper who removes goods from a shelf in a supermarket and conceals them in his shopping bag thereby appropriates them (because this amounts to an assumption of one of the rights of the owner of the goods), and so does someone who simply puts goods in a supermarket basket without concealing them. In both cases, however, the person concerned would not be guilty of theft if he intended to pay at the checkout because he would not appropriate the goods dishonestly.

A fairly common practice among the dishonest is to switch the price labels on articles in a shop or supermarket, so that a lesser price than the true price is paid at the cash desk. This amounts to an assumption of the rights of the owner, and therefore to an appropriation.

There can be an appropriation by a person even though he never possesses the property concerned, as where, pretending to be the owner, he points to another's car and offers to sell it (because the right to sell is one of the rights of the owner and he has assumed that right).

There may also be an appropriation through an innocent agent. If a person in authority signs a false invoice, intending that innocent people take further steps which result in money being debited and thus appropriated from a bank account, he is guilty of theft.

Appropriation by those already in possession

As already implied, a person can appropriate property even though he is already in possession or control of it. This is made clear by the latter part of s 3(1), which provides that 'appropriation' 'includes, where the accused has come by the property (innocently or not) without stealing it, any later assumption of a right to it by keeping or dealing with it as owner'. It follows that a shop assistant who knowingly sells goods at less than the marked price thereby appropriates them because she has assumed the owner's right to fix the price. Likewise, a watch repairer, who sells a watch left with him for repair, thereby appropriates it because he assumes the owner's right to sell. Another example would be where a person hires a car and later decides to sell it. When he sells or, even, offers to sell, it to another, he thereby appropriates the car because he assumes the right of the owner to sell it.

An important aspect of the latter part of s 3(1) is that it can lead to the conviction of a person who originally came by the property dishonestly without stealing it. Suppose that X helps himself to Y's umbrella in order to go out during a shower but intending to return it. X does not steal the umbrella at that stage because, although he has appropriated it, he did not then intend permanently to deprive Y. However, if X subsequently decides to keep the umbrella or to sell it, and does so, he is then guilty of theft because his later assumption of a right to it by keeping or dealing with it as owner constitutes an appropriation which is accompanied by an intent permanently to deprive Y.

Where property is obtained by deception

While it is clear from the definition of appropriation in s 3(1), as interpreted by the courts, that a person who obtains property by deception may nevertheless steal it, a charge of obtaining property by deception will also be appropriate.

Where a man obtains money from another by telling him that he will invest it on his behalf and in a particular way, when he has no intention of doing so, he will be guilty of obtaining property by deception (see below) as soon as he obtains the money. An appropriation takes place at the same time as he obtains ownership, and an offence of theft also takes place.

An express exception

Section 3(2) excludes a particular type of case, which falls within the definition in s 3(1), from being an appropriation. It provides that 'where property or a right or interest in property is or purports to be *transferred for value* to a person *acting in good faith*, no later assumption by him of rights which he believed himself to be acquiring shall, by reason of any defect in the transferor's title, amount to theft of the property'. The effect of the subsection is that, if A steals goods from B and sells them to C who neither knows nor suspects that they are stolen, a refusal by C to restore the goods (or his actual disposal of them) after his discovery of the theft by A is not theft by him from B.

Property

'Property' is defined by s 4(1) of the 1968 Act as including money and all other property, real or personal, including things in action and other intangible property.

'Real property' means land and things forming part of the land, such as plants and buildings. Although land and things forming part of the land are 'property' for the purposes of theft, there are special provisions restricting the theft of them, which are dealt with later.

'Personal property', in its tangible sense, means movable things which can be owned, such as cars, cheque books and television sets.

A 'thing in action' is intangible property. It is a right to sue, and its inclusion in the definition of 'property' means that someone who dishonestly assumes rights (or a right) of ownership over a thing in action, such as a debt, copyright or trade mark, with the intention of permanently depriving the person entitled to it, is guilty of theft. Thus, if A dishonestly assigns to B a debt owed to A and his partner, C, in order to defeat C's rights, A is guilty of the theft of a thing in action belonging to C. Where a bank account is in credit the bank owes a debt to its customer for the amount of that credit. Consequently, if X dishonestly draws cheques on Y's account and uses the proceeds for his own purposes, he can be convicted of the theft of property belonging to Y because he will have appropriated a thing in action (the debt) owned by Y.

'Other intangible property' covers such things as gas stored in pipes, which is undoubtedly capable of being stolen, and patents.

Despite the wide terms of s 4(1), there are some things which do not, or may not, come within the definition and hence cannot be stolen. A live human body is not property because it can never be owned. The same is true in relation to a human corpse. However, where a body (or part of a body) has undergone a process or other application of human skill (such as embalming or dissecting) for exhibition or teaching purposes it becomes property for the purposes of s 4. In addition, there have been convictions in magistrates' courts for the theft of the products of the human body, such as hair and urine specimens.

It has been held that confidential information, such as a trade secret or the contents of an examination paper, is not property for the purposes of theft, so that the mere abstraction of the information is not theft, and it has also been held that electricity is not property for such purposes and cannot be stolen. There is, however, a separate offence of abstracting electricity, which we deal with later in this chapter.

Land and things forming part of the land

Section 4(2) of the 1968 Act provides that:

'A person cannot steal land, or things forming part of land and severed from it by him or by his directions, except in the following cases, that is to say:

(a) when he is a trustee or personal representative, or is authorised by power of attorney, or as liquidator of a company, or otherwise, to sell or dispose of land belonging to another, and he appropriates the land or anything forming part of it by dealing with it in breach of the confidence reposed in him; or

(b) when he is not in possession of the land and appropriates anything forming part of the land by severing it or causing it to be severed, or after it has been severed; or

(c) when, being in possession of the land under a tenancy, he appropriates the whole or any part of any fixture or structure let to be used with the land.'

Section 4(3) goes on to provide:

'A person who picks mushrooms growing wild on any land, or who picks flowers, fruit or foliage from a plant growing wild on any land, does not (although not in possession of the land) steal what he picks, unless he does it for reward or for sale or other commercial purposes.'

For the purposes of the subsection 'mushroom' includes any fungus and 'plant' includes any shrub or tree.

These complex provisions can be explained as follows:

(a) Land as a whole cannot be stolen except where the appropriator is of a defined class and acts in a defined way. The class of appropriators comprises a trustee or personal representative, or a person authorised by power of attorney, or as a liquidator of a company, or otherwise, to sell or dispose of land belonging to another. The defined mode of appropriation is dealing with the land in breach of the confidence reposed in him. The essence of the offence lies in the dishonest breach of a confidence placed in a person who enjoys a position of trust in relation to the land. As with theft offences generally, this disposition of property does not have to be to the benefit of the trustee etc who causes that disposition. The result of the rule that land as a whole cannot be stolen is that a person cannot steal land as a whole by moving a boundary fence or by occupying it as a squatter, although there could not be stronger examples of assumption of ownership rights. However, it is generally considered that these types of conduct, the former of which is not common today, are better dealt with by civil process.

(b) Things forming part of the land, such as soil, houses, bricks in a wall and fixtures, can only be stolen in the following cases:
   (i) As for land as a whole, by the defined persons in the defined way.
   (ii) Where a person not in possession of the land appropriates the thing by severing it or causing it to be severed. If a trespasser digs up peat, turves or gravel, removes tiles or bricks from a building, digs up flowers or other growing things, picks flowers from a cultivated plant, cuts hay, or cuts down trees or saws off their branches, or causes such severance to be done, he may be convicted of theft (although in many cases it may be more appropriate to charge him with, and convict him of, criminal damage).

   The present provision does not apply to the picking of *wild* mushrooms or fungi nor to picking *from wild* plants and the like. Such conduct is dealt with by s 4(3), as follows. First, the picking of wild mushrooms or other fungi by a person not in possession of the land cannot amount to theft (although clearly there has been a severance) unless it is done for reward or for sale or other commercial purpose. Second, where a person not in possession of the land picks flowers, fruit or foliage from a plant, shrub or tree growing wild, this cannot amount to theft (although, again, there has been a severance) unless the picking is done for reward or for sale or other commercial purpose.

   The practice of wild mushroom gathering is therefore declared to be incapable of amounting to theft if it is done by a person who picks the mushrooms for his own use. It would be different if the mushroom picker arrived with a van and collected mushrooms on a large scale so that they might be sold in the local market. The same considerations apply to flowers, fruit or foliage. The person who picks bluebells or gathers elderberries, blackberries or wild apples, cannot be convicted of stealing them if this is not done for a commercial purpose. At Christmas time, many people pick a few sprigs of holly growing wild in the country. This cannot amount to theft, but it could if done for a commercial purpose (eg to sell it in the market). The term 'pick from' does not include uprooting, which is a clear case of severance covered by s 4(2)(b) and unaffected by s 4(3). In the same way, sawing the top off a Christmas tree is not 'picking from' it and the case is covered by s 4(2)(b) and not s 4(3).

As Christmas approaches, police officers become increasingly involved in the protection of growing things which are a traditional part of Christmas decorations. Vehicles carrying Christmas trees should be accompanied by delivery notes issued by the Forestry Commission or the landowner in question. If they are not, there is reason to suspect that the trees have been stolen.

Before leaving this area, it should be noted that a person who gathers or plucks any part of a 'protected' wild plant without uprooting thereby commits an offence under the Wildlife and Countryside Act 1981, s 13. These matters are discussed in ch 22, above.

(iii) Generally, a person in possession of land under a tenancy cannot steal things forming part of the land. Thus, he cannot be convicted of theft if he digs up a plant on the land, or uproots a plant, or picks blackberries from wild plants on the land in order to sell them. The only exception relates to the whole or part of any structure or fixture let to be used with the land; such is stealable by the tenant. The obvious example of a 'structure' is a building but the term also includes a wall or bridge. A 'fixture' is an article, such as a washbasin or fireplace, which is attached to the land or to a building so as to make a permanent improvement to the land or building; by law it becomes part of the land.

The result of all this is that a tenant may be convicted of theft if he demolishes the garage on the land of which he is a tenant, or if he removes a fireplace there in order to sell it.

For the purposes of the above, a person is in possession under a tenancy regardless of whether the tenancy is a lease for 999 years or a weekly tenancy, and also if he is in possession merely under an agreement for such a tenancy. In addition, he must be treated as being in possession under a tenancy if he remains as a statutory tenant after the end of his tenancy.

Of course, once a thing has been severed from the land it ceases to be part of the land and may thereafter be the subject of theft in the same way as any other piece of personal property, which it has become. In other words, the special provisions of s 4(2) and (3) no longer apply to it.

Wild creatures

Section 4(4) of the 1968 Act states that wild creatures, whether tamed or untamed, are to be regarded as property, but that a person cannot steal a wild creature, not tamed or ordinarily kept in captivity, or the carcase of any such creature, unless either it has been reduced into possession by or on behalf of another person and possession of it has not since been lost or abandoned or another person is in course of reducing it into possession.

This appears to be complex at first but it is more easily understood if it is borne in mind that, while they are alive, wild creatures which are neither tamed nor ordinarily kept in captivity are not owned by anyone, but on being killed or taken they become the property of the owner of the land on which they are killed or taken, or, if he has granted the sporting rights to someone else, the grantee of those rights.

A wild rabbit or pheasant, not tamed nor ordinarily kept in captivity, is not owned by anyone. A captured lion (undoubtedly a wild creature) which is kept in a zoo is in a different position. It is owned by the owner of the zoo. A peregrine falcon flying free is not owned by anyone, but if it has been caught and is kept in captivity, being trained for the purpose of falconry, it now has an owner. Homing pigeons are wild birds but have for years been bred in captivity. They are owned and even when released to fly freely they remain in the possession of the owner if they are trained to return to him. The position is different with bees which can hardly be said to be tamed or ordinarily kept in captivity. Bees kept in a hive are owned and possessed by the hiver but remain so only while they are in his sight and can be followed by him. If they swarm on land to which he has no access, they are no longer in his ownership or possession. These common law rules are based upon common sense; if bees escape and swarm in a person's house, that person may have cause to destroy them and would risk prosecution if they were still owned or possessed by someone else.

The Theft Act 1968 recognises these points, by declaring that wild creatures, tamed or untamed, are property and can therefore be stolen, except that untamed wild creatures which are not ordinarily kept in captivity (or their carcases) can only be stolen in the circumstances outlined at the end of s 4(4).

These are:

(a) where the wild creature has been reduced into possession by or on behalf of another (in which case it remains stealable so long as possession is not subsequently lost or abandoned); or

(b) where another person is in the course of reducing the wild creature into possession.

Thus, it is not theft to poach game on another's land, unless for instance the game is taken from a trap set by another, even another poacher (because another is in the course of reducing into possession), or from a sack into which another has put the product of his own shooting (because there has been a reduction into possession by another).

The term 'reduced into possession by or on behalf of another' in s 4(4) covers the shooting and taking of game by a gamekeeper on his master's behalf. If he shoots and takes the game, it is reduced into his master's possession and therefore the gamekeeper himself can be convicted of theft if he subsequently appropriates it.

If wild creatures are taken and kept alive in some place of confinement, for example in net traps set by poachers, they are temporarily reduced into possession, but if they are released to resume their free state, or escape, that possession ceases. Thus, for example, although it may be theft to shoot and take these creatures whilst in the net it would not be so to shoot them as they ran away after being released by someone else, because possession of them would have been 'lost or abandoned'.

Although s 4(4) means that poachers are not normally thieves, there are other offences, mentioned in ch 23, which they commit.

Belonging to another

The offence of theft requires that the property appropriated should belong to another when appropriated.

The basic rule

Section 5(1) states that property shall be regarded as belonging to any person having possession or control of it, or having in it any proprietary right or interest (not being an equitable interest arising only from an agreement to transfer or grant an interest).

The question of whether the property appropriated belonged to some other person causes no problems in the vast majority of cases. If a wallet is taken from X's pocket it quite clearly belongs to X, since he will almost certainly be its owner (and complete ownership is the clearest example of a proprietary right) and, anyway, it will be in his possession. If goods are taken from a shop they clearly belong to the proprietor of the shop for the same reasons. When there are joint owners of property, one of them will steal from the other if he dishonestly assumes one of the rights of the owner, because the property will also belong to the other co-owner under s 5(1).

A man who takes his radio to a repairer still owns it and therefore it still belongs to him. The repairer now has possession of the radio and if it is then handed to one of his assistants to effect the repair, that assistant has control of it. The radio can now be stolen from either the owner, the repairer or his assistant, and it can be stolen by one of these from the other. For example, if the assistant takes the radio to the pub at lunchtime and sells it, he thereby appropriates property *belonging to another* (to the owner and to the repairer, since the radio is technically still in the repairer's possession). Likewise, if the owner sneaks into the repairer's shop and takes away the radio without paying for the repair he appropriates property belonging to another. A person (A) who lets to another (B) a television set or a motor car thereby parts with possession of it to that other but retains ownership of it. It follows that if B appropriates the thing (eg by unauthorisedly selling it to C) he will have appropriated property *belonging to another*, and so will A if he appropriates it during the hire period (eg by removing it back to his own premises contrary to the hiring agreement).

A person who loses property nevertheless still retains ownership of it, and he also retains possession until the property comes into the possession of another. Thus, 'lost property' is still capable of being stolen. This must be contrasted with the situation where the property has been abandoned. When a person throws away his old bicycle, not caring what happens to it (ie he abandons it), he loses ownership and possession of it. Since the property has no owner or possessor, it cannot thereafter be stolen. It would be different if the owner placed his cycle behind a hedge because the tyre had punctured and travelled the remainder of his journey by bus. In these circumstances the property is not abandoned because the owner cares about what may happen to the bicycle, and it therefore still belongs to him.

Property subject to a trust

Where property is subject to a trust, it is regarded as belonging to the beneficiaries (who have a proprietary interest in it) as well as to the trustees, with the result that trustees who appropriate trust property can be convicted of stealing it from the beneficiaries. There are two exceptions to this.

First, the beneficial interest of a beneficiary under one type of trust, a constructive trust, is not always a sufficient proprietary interest under s 5(1). Consequently, there cannot always be a theft of the trust property, as against him.

Second, charitable trusts and certain other types of trust do not, in law, have beneficiaries, with the result that under s 5(1) the trust property belongs only to the trustees. To prevent trust property being unprotected in such a case against appropriations by the trustees, s 5(2) provides that, where property is subject to a trust, the persons to whom it belongs shall be regarded as including any person having a right to enforce the trust, and that an intention to defeat the trust shall be regarded accordingly as an intention to deprive of the property any person having that right. In the case of a charitable trust, the Attorney-General , although not a beneficiary, has the right to enforce the trust, so that appropriation of a charitable trust fund by the trustees is capable of amounting to theft since the fund belongs to the Attorney-General under s 5(2).

Property received under an obligation to retain and deal with it in a particular way

Section 5(3) provides that, where a person receives property from or on account of another and is under an *obligation* (ie a legal obligation) to the other to *retain* and *deal* with that property, or *its* proceeds, *in a particular way*, the property or proceeds shall be regarded (as against him) as belonging to the other (as against the recipient). Section 5(3) makes it clear that where a person has received property in accordance with its terms, that property or its proceeds (ie things into which it has been converted) is regarded as belonging to another for the purposes of theft, even though ownership, possession and control of the property may have been transferred to the recipient.

The essence of s 5(3) is that property (usually money) or its proceeds is regarded (as against the accused) as belonging to another from or on whose account the accused has received the property if the accused is under a *legal obligation* to that person *to retain and deal* with the property or its proceeds *in a particular way*. Section 5(3) is clearly satisfied where D receives money from P which he is legally obliged to P to use in a particular way (eg to pay it into a Christmas Club which D runs), or where D is legally obliged to P to use in a particular way the proceeds of money received from P (eg to use the money to buy some goods for P). In the latter case, both the money and the goods (its proceeds) will belong to another under s 5(3). Section 5(3) is also satisfied if a shop assistant receives money from a customer for some of his employer's goods, since he has received the money on account of another (the employer) and is under a legal obligation to deal with it in a particular way (to put it in the till). If D or the shop assistant dishonestly appropriates the property in question with intent permanently to deprive, theft is committed. On the other hand, s 5(3) is not satisfied where an employee receives money from a customer for goods which (contrary to his employer's instructions) he is selling on his own account since the money is not received from or on account of another person to whom the employee is legally obliged to retain and deal with it in a particular way.

Property got by another's mistake

Section 5(4) states that:

'where a person gets property by another's mistake, and is under an obligation to make restoration (in whole or in part) of the property or its proceeds or of the value thereof, then to the extent of that obligation the property or proceeds shall be regarded (as against him) as belonging to the person entitled to restoration, and an intention not to make restoration shall be regarded accordingly as an intention to deprive that person of the property or proceeds.'

The important point about this provision is that it only applies where the recipient of property transferred under a mistake is thereby under an immediate legal obligation to restore it (or its proceeds or value). For practical purposes, this provision is only of importance where the transferee has acquired ownership, possession and control of the property to the exclusion of anyone else. If someone else retains one of these things, the property will clearly belong to another under s 5(1). On the other hand, where a person receives exclusive ownership, possession and control of property as a result of another's mistake, s 5(4) neatly avoids the need to go into difficult issues of civil law as to whether the transferor retained a proprietary right or interest in the property. The best example of a case of a legal obligation to make restoration, where a person has received ownership, possession and control of property under a mistake, is where there is a transfer of money under a mistake and the transferor's mistake is one of fact and leads him to believe that the transferee is legally entitled to the money. Thus, if A, by a mistake as to the number of hours of overtime worked, overpays his employee, B, and B, realising the mistake, appropriates the excess amount, B has appropriated money which by s 5(4) belongs to another. The same would be true if the excess payment was made by a cheque (since B would be obliged to make restoration of it to A); if B appropriates the cheque he will appropriate property belonging to another under s 5(4). Likewise, if B cashes the cheque and appropriates the cash received, he will appropriate property belonging to another under s 5(4) because the cash will be the proceeds of the cheque and B would be obliged to make restoration of it to A. On the other hand, if A is induced to give C some money as a gift by a mistaken belief that C is collecting for charity, C cannot be convicted of theft if he appropriates it thereafter because, the requirements of s 5(4) not having been fulfilled, the money will not belong to another (ie other than C) when C appropriates it.

Usually, a mistake on the part of the transferor of property will have been induced by a deception on the part of the transferee. Where this is so, it is much better to charge obtaining property by deception, contrary to s 15 of the 1968 Act, and not theft, thereby avoiding any need to consider the complex wording of s 5(4) and its possible application.

Property of a corporation sole

Section 5 contains one other provision, s 5(5), which can be disposed of briefly. Section 5(5) provides that the property of a 'corporation sole', such as a bishop or the Treasury Solicitor, shall be regarded as belonging to the corporation notwithstanding a vacancy in the corporation. Thus, the property of a bishopric 'belongs to another', and is therefore capable of being stolen, even though the bishop has just died and not yet been replaced by a successor.

Dishonesty

The appropriation of property belonging to another must be committed dishonestly.

The question of dishonesty is one of fact for the jury in the Crown Court and not of law for the judge, subject to the provisions of s 2(1) of the 1968 Act which expressly and as a matter of law exclude appropriations carried out with certain states of mind from being dishonest. Section 2(1) provides:

'A person's appropriation of property belonging to another is *not* to be regarded as dishonest:
(a) if he appropriates the property in the belief that he has in law the right to deprive the other of it, on behalf of himself or a third person; or

(b)　if he appropriates the property in the belief that he would have had the other's consent if the other knew of the appropriation and the circumstances of it; or

(c)　(except where the property came to him as a trustee or personal representative) if he appropriates the property in the belief that the person to whom the property belongs cannot be discovered by taking reasonable steps.'

These provisions are concerned with the accused's belief. It is legally irrelevant that a belief in this context is unreasonable, although, of course, magistrates or a jury are less inclined to accept an alleged belief as truly held if it is an unreasonable one.

Belief in legal right to deprive

By s 2(1)(a), the element of dishonesty is excluded if a person appropriating property belonging to another genuinely believed that he had a right in law to deprive the other of it, whether on behalf of himself or a third person. If his belief is genuine, it is immaterial that there is no legal reason for him to have such a belief or that it is unreasonable, for we are considering what motivated him to do the act, not how other people look upon it. A husband who genuinely believes that he has a legal right to sell his wife's car on the grounds that he considered that her property became his on marriage does not act dishonestly. If a person is owed money and in order to recover that money from his debtor he threatens him with a knife, this will not be theft if he truly believes that he has a legal right to deprive the other of property, even though he recognises that he should not use a knife.

Section 2(1)(a) is limited to cases where the accused believes that 'he has in law the right to deprive'. Where a person acts under a belief in a moral right to deprive, the question of his dishonesty depends on certain tests which are described below.

Belief that the 'owner' would have consented if he had known

The exemption provided by s 2(1)(b) is a sensible one as it is quite possible for friends and neighbours to have the type of relationship which permits free usage of their respective personal possessions. The essence of this exemption is a belief that the person to whom the property belongs would have consented if he had known of the appropriation and its circumstances. A person may believe that his friend would consent to him taking a bottle of wine from his cellar for his own use, but he is less likely to believe the friend would consent if he takes it to sell it because he needs money. The circumstances surrounding the taking are different.

Belief that the 'owner' cannot be discovered by taking reasonable steps

The provisions of s 2(1)(c) are primarily, although not exclusively, concerned with those who find property belonging to another. As with the other provisions in s 2(1), they exempt the accused from dishonesty if he appropriated another's property under a genuine belief (whether reasonable or not) in a particular state of affairs, in this case that the person to whom the property belongs cannot be discovered by taking reasonable steps. The question is not whether the 'owner' could not be found by taking reasonable steps, but whether the accused believed this, but, of course, whether or not the owner could have been so found is of evidential importance in terms of the credibility of an alleged belief that he could not be so found.

If a person finds a £5 note in the street and appropriates it, it will be almost impossible to disprove a claim by him that he believed the owner could not be found by taking reasonable steps (since it would be very rare for the serial number of the note to have been recorded by the person who lost it). It will be different if the note is contained in a purse bearing the owner's name and address (or containing other material identifying the owner): in that case it will be much easier to disprove a claimed belief that the owner could not be found by taking reasonable steps.

The exemption is not restricted to things which are found. Suppose that A's friend, on emigrating, left property under A's care until he should return to this country. If, after many years, during which A has not heard from his friend, A sells the property, honestly believing that he will not return and that he could not be traced by taking reasonable steps, A will not be guilty of theft.

Section 2(1)(c) expressly does not apply to a person who received the property as a trustee of property or a personal representative. This is sensible in view of the special obligations of such a person.

Dishonesty in a general sense

The negative definition of dishonesty in s 2(1) is only a partial definition; consequently, an accused's appropriation may not have been made dishonestly even though the case falls outside s 2(1). Whether or not an accused who appropriated property with some alleged state of mind other than one of the three referred to in s 2(1) did so dishonestly is a question of fact for the jury. This means that, unlike the situation in which a belief of the type referred to in s 2(1) is pleaded (where the judge must tell the jury that in law an appropriation with such a belief is not dishonest), it is not for the judge to tell the jury whether or not an appropriation with the alleged state of mind is dishonest but for the jury to decide this according to the following two-stage test.

The jury must first see whether, given his state of mind, the accused's actions were dishonest according to the ordinary standards of reasonable and honest people. If this actions were not dishonest according to those standards, the matter ends there and the prosecution fails. However, if his actions were dishonest by those standards, the jury must go on to decide whether the accused must have realised that what he was doing would be considered dishonest according to the standards of reasonable and honest people. If he did not realise this, his appropriation will not have been dishonest; if he did it will have been.

Where a theft charge is tried in a magistrates' court the above tests are, of course, applicable and are applied by the justices.

What has been said about dishonesty so far can be brought together as follows. X is charged with the theft of £10 taken from the till of the shop in which he is employed. If, at his trial, X pleads that his employer owed him £10 and he (X) believed that he was legally entitled to deprive the employer of the £10 taken in order to recoup his debt, the trial judge (assuming a Crown Court trial) must tell the jury that—as a matter of law (s 2(1))—X's alleged belief prevents his appropriation being dishonest and that they must acquit X unless the alleged belief is disproved. The same would be the case if X pleaded that he believed the employer would have consented to the taking if he had known of it and its circumstances.

Suppose, on the other hand, that X admits that he knew he had no legal right to the £10 and that he knew the employer would not have consented to his taking it, but claims instead that he took the money to tide him over to pay day, intending to put in £10 from his pay packet, and claims that what he did was a common practice in the shop. Here, X is not pleading one of the beliefs in s 2(1) and the trial judge must tell the jury that, if they do not find that X's claim that he intended to repay has been disproved by the prosecution, they must decide whether or not—given that intention—his appropriation was dishonest and must do so by applying the two-fold test referred to above.

For the sake of completeness, it should be maintained that s 2(2) says what has already been implied, by providing that an appropriation *may* be dishonest notwithstanding that the person concerned intends to pay for what he took. If a collector fails to obtain a valuable antique at an auction, his appropriation would almost certainly be found to be dishonest if he took the antique from the home of the successful bidder and left money in payment, even if that money represented a reasonable purchase price.

Intention permanently to deprive

The appropriation of property belonging to another must be accompanied by an intention permanently to deprive the other of that property. Unless it can be shown that this intention existed at the time of appropriation there can be no theft. The Act does punish the removal of articles from places open to the public, for example paintings from art galleries, without an intention permanently to deprive, and it likewise punishes the taking, without such an intent, of motor vehicles and other conveyances without the consent of the owner, but these two types of conduct are punishable as separate offences and not as theft.

The presence of an intent permanently to deprive will usually be proved by evidence of what the accused did with the property appropriated. If a person takes Y's £5 note and spends it on drink this clearly indicates an intent permanently to deprive Y of the note as he has passed the note into circulation. It is no use the accused alleging that he intended to pay it back. Although this may prevent him being found to have been dishonest, and lead to an acquittal on that ground, he will nevertheless have intended permanently to deprive Y of the thing (the actual £5 note) which he has appropriated. If a car is appropriated and a false registration book is produced, the engine and chassis numbers are altered, and the colour of the car is changed, this is clear evidence of an intent permanently to deprive.

Where the victim of an appropriation only has a limited interest in the property, a person can intend permanently to deprive even though he intends only a purely temporary borrowing. For example, if a housewife hires a carpet cleaner from S for a period of one week to clean all of her carpets, and this is 'unlawfully' borrowed by an associate who is aware of the circumstances and who intends to retain it throughout that period and then to return it to S, the associate intends wholly to deprive the housewife of her special interest in the property, and that intended deprivation is therefore permanent in the circumstances.

In certain limited cases a person can be convicted of theft even though he did not mean permanently to deprive, and even though he positively intended to return the property at some future date (or did actually return it). A conviction in such a case is possible if the case falls within s 6 of the Act, which extends the meaning of 'intention of permanently depriving'.

Section 6(1) provides:

'A person appropriating property belonging to another without meaning the other permanently to lose the thing itself is nevertheless to be regarded as having the intention of permanently depriving the other of it if his *intention is to treat the thing as his own to dispose of regardless of the other's rights;* and a borrowing or lending of it may amount to so treating it if, but only if, the borrowing or lending is for a period and in circumstances making it equivalent to an outright taking or disposal.'

Treating as one's own to dispose of regardless of other's rights

For s 6(1) to operate to 'deem' a person to have intended permanent deprivation it must be shown that there was an intention to treat the thing as his own to dispose of regardless of the other's rights. If a thief takes a valuable painting belonging to B, intending to return it to B only if B pays a ransom for it, he clearly intends to treat the thing as his own to dispose of regardless of the other's rights, because he intends that the other should only get it back by paying for it. A similar solution applies to the long-standing practice, whereby boys take empty bottles from the rear of premises and immediately return them to the owner at the front of the premises to receive the deposit charge on the bottle.

Section 6(1) also catches the rogue who purports to sell property belonging to another in circumstances where it is unlikely that the property will be removed, as where an employee purports to sell a grand piano belonging to his employer which he knows his employer is going to dispose of in a few minutes time. The reason is that the rogue intends to treat the property 'sold' as his own to dispose of regardless of the rights of the other and it is irrelevant that such a disposal is unlikely to occur.

Another type of case falling within s 6(1) is where the accused abandons the property and is indifferent as to whether it is recovered by the person to whom it belongs. If, by the circumstances of the abandonment and/or the nature of the property, it is (to the accused's knowledge) extremely unlikely that the property will be recovered, he can be said to intend to dispose of it regardless of the rights of the other.

If A's car is taken and driven a distance of 200 miles by B and abandoned, the justices or jury are most unlikely to find that there was an intention to treat it as B's own to dispose of regardless of A's rights, as a car is easily identifiable and will certainly be returned to A. Had the property stolen been an overcoat which had been abandoned in a township some distance away this would indicate an intention to treat it as his own etc as B could not have believed that it was likely that the coat would be returned; consequently, he would have intended to treat it as his own to dispose of regardless of the other's right.

In one case, a person, who surreptitiously removed two doors from another property belonging to his council landlord in order to use them to replace doors for which he was responsible at his own council home, was held to have intended to treat the doors as his own to dispose of regardless of the council's rights. In dealing with the doors regardless of those rights, which he consciously did, he showed a clear intention to treat the doors as his own property regardless of the rights of the council.

Borrowing or lending

Section 6(1) provides that a borrowing or lending may amount to treating property as one's own to dispose of regardless of the other's rights, if the borrowing or lending is for a period and in circumstances which make it equivalent to an outright taking or disposal. The Court of Appeal has ruled that this provision is only satisfied by a borrower if his intention is to return the thing only when 'all its goodness or virtue has gone'. This covers the following types of cases:

E takes F's monthly season ticket, intending to return it at the end of the month. E's borrowing is clearly for a period and in circumstances making it equivalent to an outright taking since, when it is returned, the season ticket will be a virtually worthless piece of paper.

G takes an uncrossed cheque from H's wallet, intending to cash it. Before it is cashed it is a valuable security. After this, the cheque, which will have become a virtually worthless piece of paper, will eventually return to H (or be available at his bank). G's borrowing is for a period and in circumstances making it equivalent to an outright taking.

Because their borrowing is equivalent to an outright taking, or disposal, E and G's intention so to act is regarded by s 6(1) as an intent to treat as their own to dispose of regardless of the rights of F and H and, hence, as an intent permanently to deprive.

On the other hand, a cinema projectionist who borrows a film in order to make pirate copies would not intend to treat the film as his own to dispose of regardless of the owner's rights because on its return the film would not have lost all of its goodness or virtue.

An example of a case where a lending would satisfy the present provision would be where J, who has control of his employer, K's, non-refillable can of paint spray, lends it to L, telling L that he can keep it and use it for as long as he likes. J realises that the can may never be returned or may be returned empty. J intends to treat the can as his own to dispose of because, as he knows, the lending is for a period and in circumstances making it equivalent to an outright disposal.

Parting with property subject to a condition

Section 6(2) provides a further explanation of 'treating as one's own to dispose of regardless of the other's rights'. It states that, without prejudice to the generality of s 6(1), where a person having possession or control (lawfully or not) of property belonging to another, parts with the property under a condition as to its return which he may not be able to perform, this (if done for purposes of his own and without the other's authority) amounts to treating the property as his own to dispose of regardless of the other's rights. The sub-section applies to a person who lawfully holds property for another as well as to one who holds it unlawfully, perhaps a thief. If, without the owner's authority, such a person pawns the article under a condition as to its return which he may not be able to perform, he is deemed to intend to treat the property as his own to dispose of regardless of the other's rights. 'A condition as to return which he may not be able to perform' will have to be examined in the circumstances. If the property is pawned with seven days to redeem, and the pawner's pay cheque will arrive within two days and will provide him with more than sufficient money to redeem the property, it can hardly be said that he may not be able to fulfil the condition for the return of the property. On the other hand, if property is pawned for a large sum of money which the pawner has no prospect of receiving within the time allowed, then this is strong evidence that the pawner may not be able to fulfil the condition.

ABSTRACTING ELECTRICITY

As we have already said, it has been held that electricity is not property and therefore cannot be stolen. However, a special offence is provided by s 13 of the 1968 Act, which states:

'A person who dishonestly uses without due authority, or dishonestly causes to be wasted or diverted, any electricity shall be guilty of an offence.'

The offence is an arrestable offence.

For police purposes, the offence will usually be encountered when a person, who has had his electricity supply disconnected, re-connects it and thus uses electricity without authority; or when evidence is found that a consumer has by-passed his meter, since his authority to use electricity supplied by the Board is conditional upon that electricity having passed through the meter before use. No doubt the primary purpose of s 13 was to deal with these matters but the effect of the section is more widespread. If a trespasser enters into property and switches on the lights he undoubtedly uses electricity, and if this use in the circumstances is considered to be dishonest, he will commit this offence. Squatters who occupy premises and dishonestly use lighting, electric fires, refrigerators or appliances, dishonestly use electricity and are guilty of this offence. If, at the same time they use the gas supply, they steal the gas as gas is property for the purposes of theft (and consequently they can also be convicted of burglary).

The section covers wasting or diverting in addition to using. It seems that the person who by-passes his meter could be charged with either dishonest usage or dishonest diversion, as he does not have authority to use in that way and he has certainly caused electricity to be diverted. However, it is possible for one man dishonestly to divert electricity for dishonest usage by another.

There is no restriction within the section to mains electricity. A person who dishonestly uses the power stored in a battery could be guilty of this offence. The section could not be applied to the person who took a motor vehicle without consent, as a modern car re-charges its battery as its power is used.

It is important not to forget that the element of dishonesty must be proved. The provisions of s 2(1) of the 1968 Act are limited to theft, and therefore do not apply to an offence under s 13, but the rest of our explanation of dishonesty for the purposes of theft applies equally to an offence under s 13.

REMOVAL OF ARTICLES FROM PLACES OPEN TO THE PUBLIC

As we have seen an essential element of theft is an intention permanently to deprive the owner of his property. This being so, it is unlikely that a charge of theft would succeed against an art lover who takes a valuable painting from a public gallery, intending to enjoy its presence in his home for a year and thereafter to return it to the gallery. On a charge of theft, the only way of proving an intent permanently to deprive the gallery of its picture would be to have recourse to s 6 of the 1968 Act and to show that the 'borrowing' was for a period and in circumstances making it equivalent to an outright taking or disposal. Proof of this is unlikely, since in the particular circumstances the painting will not have deteriorated in such a way that it could be alleged that it has lost all its goodness or virtue on return and that the taking had therefore amounted to an outright taking. It is for this reason that s 11 of the 1968 Act creates a specific offence to cover cases such as this, whilst taking care not to extend the parameters of the offence beyond them. The section provides:

'Where the public have access to a building in order to view the building or part of it, or a collection or part of a collection housed in it, any person who without lawful authority removes from the building or its grounds the whole or part of any article displayed or kept for display to the public in the building, or that part of it, or in its grounds, shall be guilty of an offence.'

This is an arrestable offence.

There are two key elements to this offence. First the removal of an article must be either from a building to which the public have access in order to view the building or part of it, or a collection or part of a collection housed in it, or from the grounds of such a building. We are therefore concerned with removals of articles from stately homes, national galleries, historic buildings etc, provided they are open to the public in the above sense, or from their grounds. A person who removes the portrait of an Edwardian mayor from the entrance of the town hall does not commit the present offence because, although the public have access to the town hall (or, at least, to the part in question), it is only for the purpose of paying council tax, making inquiries or seeing their councillors; they do not have access in order to view the building, or any collection in it, or any part of the building or collection. If a man removes a painting from a collection in a stately home, access to which is limited to members of the Women's Institute, he does not commit the present offence because the public do not have access to the building in question but only a particular section of the public.

Where an article is removed from a building to which the public have access in order to view a collection or part of a collection housed in it, the offence is not committed if the collection has been made or exhibited for the purposes of effecting sales or other commercial dealings. Thus, removals of paintings from commercial art galleries (which are really shops) are not caught by s 11. Subject to this, it does not matter that the collection in question is one got together for a temporary purpose. The annual art exhibition in the village hall is therefore caught by s 11.

Generally, an offence under s 11 can be committed whether or not the building is open to the public at the time of the removal. There is one exception: if the thing removed is there otherwise than as forming part of, or being on loan for exhibition with, a collection intended for permanent exhibition to the public, it must be removed on a day when the public has access. Thus, if a painting is removed from the collection at the National Gallery it is irrelevant that the Gallery is then closed over the Christmas period, whereas it is not an offence to remove a painting from the annual art exhibition in the village hall on a day when the hall is closed. In this way, the Act recognises a distinction between permanent exhibitions (for example, in museums and galleries) as opposed to temporary or occasional exhibitions (for example, in stately homes). This is understandable as museums and galleries exist to contain treasures which require constant protection from visitors who might 'borrow' them, whereas on days when a stately home or the like is not open to the general public the building resumes its description of a dwelling house and is no different from any other dwelling house.

The second key element in the offence is that it only applies where the thing removed is the whole or part of any article displayed or kept for display to the public in the building, or part of it, to which the public have access or in its grounds. The purpose of this is to separate those things which are there for display and those which are not. If a visitor takes an old vase which forms a part of the display, he commits this offence. If he takes the attendant's coat on the way out he does not, as the coat is not a part of the display.

There must be a removal from the building or its grounds. A visitor who moves the vase from one room to another does not commit the offence, but one who takes it out of the building does. The grounds are protected because many stately homes will have articles in the grounds for display to the public. The value of the article is irrelevant to liability, as opposed to punishment. Section 11 makes it clear that no offence is committed where the person removing an article covered by it has lawful authority for doing so.

There is no need to prove dishonesty in respect of the act of removal but the section does exempt those who believe that they have lawful authority, or that they would have been given authority by the person entitled to give it if he knew of the removal and its circumstances. Therefore, a furniture remover who was removing articles on behalf of their owner would not commit an offence if he took one of the exhibited articles, believing that he had lawful authority to remove it. Likewise, a restorer of oil paintings who carried out work for the owner from time to time would not commit an offence if in the owner's absence he took a painting for its five-yearly restoration, believing that, had the owner been present, he would have consented.

TAKING OR OPENING A MAIL BAG

The Post Office Act 1953, s 53 makes it an offence for any person unlawfully to take away or open a mail bag sent by any ship, vehicle or aircraft employed by or under the Post Office for the transmission of postal packets under contract, or unlawfully to take a postal packet in course of transmission by post out of a mail bag so sent. The section is therefore concerned with two things:

(a) the taking or opening of mail bags in the course of transmission by post; and
(b) the taking of a postal packet from such a mail bag.

These are arrestable offences. The keeping or detaining of mail bags or postal packets is a non-arrestable offence contrary to s 55 of the 1953 Act.

These are not offences of theft as there is no requirement that the specified acts should be committed dishonestly and with intent permanently to deprive a person of his property.

TAKING CONVEYANCES

Section 12(1) of the 1968 Act created specific offences in relation to conveyances, a term which includes almost all 'motor vehicles', which are taken, not for the purposes of permanently depriving the owner of his property, but for the purposes of joy-riding. Section 12(1) provides:

'A person shall be guilty of an offence if, without having the consent of the owner or other lawful authority, he takes any conveyance for his own or another's use, or, knowing that any conveyance has been taken without such authority, drives it or allows himself to be carried in or on it.'

There are two offences under s 12(1), that of taking a conveyance without authority and that of driving or allowing oneself to be carried in or on a conveyance which one knows has been so taken. Both offences are declared to be arrestable offences by the Police and Criminal Evidence Act 1984.

The term 'conveyance' is defined to include any conveyance constructed or adapted for the carriage of a person or persons whether by land, water or air, but it does not include a conveyance constructed or adapted for use only under the control of a person not carried in or on it, and 'drive' is construed accordingly. The term 'conveyance' is therefore wide in meaning and covers almost all motor vehicles, as well as aeroplanes, hovercraft, ships, rowing boats and inflatable dinghies, but it does not cover pedestrian-controlled vehicles, such as some milk floats, electric trolleys which are drawn by hand, and similar conveyances. Nor does it cover pedal cycles. Pedal cycles are covered by a separate offence described on p 723.

Taking without authority

Taking

The mere unauthorised assumption of possession or control is not enough to constitute a 'taking' of a conveyance; *there must be some movement, however small, of it.* The result is that a person who gets into the driving seat of a car and drives it a few feet takes a conveyance, as does a person who climbs into a rowing boat or dinghy and casts it off from the bank. On the other hand people who unlawfully occupy a conveyance, either to shelter or to make love in it, do not take it. Of course, someone who gets into another's car and tries to start it is attempting to take a conveyance, but as the taking would amount to a summary offence, there can be no charge of attempting to take it. In such a case there may be a conviction for the offence of interfering with vehicles, discussed on pp 797-798.

Unauthorised use of a conveyance by a person already in lawful possession or control of a conveyance may amount to a 'taking'. A lorry driver who uses his employer's lorry for his own purposes 'out of hours', or who appropriates it to his own use during the working day in a manner which is inconsistent with the rights of the employer and shows that he has assumed control for his own purposes, thereby 'takes' it. Thus, for example, a lorry driver who makes a serious deviation from his proper route for some private purpose can be convicted of the present offence. A similar principle applies to a person who has borrowed a conveyance if he uses it for a purpose other than that for which he has been given permission or after the time he is permitted to have the conveyance. By so using the conveyance, he takes it.

For the accused's or another's use

Section 12(1) also requires that the taking be for the accused's own or another's use, and this means that either the conveyance must be used as a conveyance or it must be taken for later use as a conveyance. It follows that a person who cuts the mooring rope of a boat and allows it to drift away empty does not commit this offence, whereas he would if he was aboard or if he towed it away for later use as a boat.

Without consent or other authority

The taking must be without the consent of the owner or other lawful authority. An apparent consent to a taking obtained by intimidation (as where A stops a car, grabs the driver by his lapels and successfully demands the loan of the car) is not a true consent, so that the taking will be without consent. On the other hand, a consent which has been obtained by fraud is nevertheless valid and prevents the offence being committed, however fundamental (eg as to the identity of the deceiver) the mistake which is induced.

In relation to a conveyance subject to a hiring or hire-purchase agreement, 'owner' means the person in possession of it under that agreement. It follows that, during the currency of the agreement, such a person cannot commit the present offence in relation to that conveyance since he can hardly be said to take it without the consent of the owner.

The addition of the words 'or other lawful authority' is to excuse acts of removal which amount to taking, such as the removal by an authorised officer of a vehicle which is causing a serious obstruction. Finance companies on occasion reclaim vehicles which are on hire purchase from them when the terms of the agreement have been broken by the hirer, and they will usually have lawful authority to do so under the terms of the agreement.

Not only is the consent of the owner or other lawful authority a defence, but so also is a mistaken belief in the existence of such lawful authority or a mistaken belief that the owner would, if asked, have consented.

Drives or allows self to be driven

In relation to the taking of motor vehicles in particular, but not exclusively, it is frequently the case that, after a vehicle has been taken by one person, it is used to convey a number of persons, each of whom may take a turn at driving. The second offence in s 12(1) deals with this situation, by providing that an offence is committed by anyone who, *knowing* that a conveyance has been taken without the consent of the owner or other lawful authority, drives it or allows himself to be carried in or on it. In circumstances where a vehicle, known to have been 'taken' contrary to s 12(1), is seen to be moving (for it is essential that there is movement in order that a person can be said to be 'carried'), and all the occupants are seen to step out of the vehicle but all deny driving it, the issue of who was driving is unimportant because all have allowed themselves to be 'carried' in the vehicle (since that expression covers a person who was driving).

Where a person takes a vehicle without consent and later picks up friends and takes them for a drive, his friends commit no offence unless they know that the vehicle has been so taken. The same would apply to a person who was given a lift but, should the driver disclose that the vehicle has been unlawfully taken in the course of the journey, the passenger is guilty if he continues to allow himself to be carried.

Aggravated vehicle-taking

The Aggravated Vehicle Taking Act 1992 creates offences of aggravated vehicle-taking by adding s 12A to the Theft Act 1968. An offence is committed where a person has committed an offence under s 12(1) (the basic offence) in any way in relation to a mechanically propelled vehicle and it is proved that, at any time after the vehicle was unlawfully taken (whether by himself or another) and before it was recovered, the vehicle was driven, or injury or damage was caused, in one or more of the following circumstances; that:

(a) the vehicle was driven in a dangerous manner on a road or other public place; the same test of such driving applies as in the offence of dangerous driving (see pp 386-388);

(b) owing to the driving of the vehicle, an accident occurred by which injury was caused to any person;

(c) owing to the driving of the vehicle, an accident occurred by which damage was caused to any property other than the vehicle; or

(d) damage was caused to the vehicle.

The prosecution does not have to prove that the dangerous driving, injury or damage was caused by the accused's driving or by the accused at all. Nor, under (b) or (c), need it be proved that there was any fault in the driving of the vehicle. Once it is proved that the driving, injury or damage was caused during the period between the taking of the vehicle contrary to s 12(1) and its recovery, the accused is fixed with liability for an offence contrary to s 12A, unless he has one of the defences referred to in the next paragraph. A vehicle is 'recovered' when it is returned to its owner or other lawful possession or custody.

The importance of the fact that the aggravating circumstances can occur at any time up to the recovery of the vehicle is shown by a case where a man, who was in the course of taking a vehicle, was 'locked in' the vehicle by an anti-theft device and he then damaged the vehicle in an attempt to escape before the police arrived. An aggravated vehicle-taking offence was committed as damage was caused to the vehicle before it was recovered. It is a defence for an accused to prove that such driving, accident or damage occurred before he committed the basic offence, or that he was neither in, nor on, nor in the immediate vicinity of the vehicle when such driving, accident or damage occurred.

The Act extends the concept of 'joint enterprise' to these offences. Anyone who commits an offence (the basic offence) against the Theft Act 1968, s 12(1), is guilty of aggravated vehicle-taking if the motor vehicle is subsequently involved in one of the sets of circumstances set out at (a) to (d) above. As we have seen, s 12(1) embraces those who drive and those who allow themselves to be carried as well as those who take. Thus, the difficult problem of proving who was actually driving at the time, or who actually took the vehicle in the first instance, is avoided as all offend against s 12(1). That those jointly involved in the enterprise should be similarly treated is reinforced by s 3 of the 1992 Act which amends the Road Traffic Offenders Act 1988, s 34 to provide that the fact that a person who is convicted of an offence under the Theft Act 1968, s 12A, did not drive the vehicle in question at any particular time, or at all, is not to be regarded as a special reason.

Since the maximum penalty is greater where death is caused, s 12A creates two offences: one where death is caused, and the other for other situations. It has been held that there is nothing to prevent charges of both aggravated vehicle-taking (involving an allegation that the vehicle was driven dangerously) and of dangerous driving being preferred.

Pedal cycles

Pedal cycles are not conveyances for the purposes of s 12(1) but are separately dealt with by s 12(5). That sub-section provides that a person commits an offence if, without having the consent of the owner or other lawful authority, he takes a pedal cycle for his own or another's use, or rides a pedal cycle knowing it to have been taken without such authority. What was said above about the various elements of the offence under s 12(1) is equally applicable to the present offence, which is not an arrestable offence.

ROBBERY

The offence of robbery is often described colloquially as 'mugging'.

The 1968 Act provides in s 8(1):

'A person is guilty of robbery if he steals, and immediately before or at the time of doing so, and in order to do so, he uses force on any person, or puts or seeks to put any person in fear of being then and there subjected to force.'

The offence of robbery and the offence of assault with intent to rob are arrestable offences.

No theft; no robbery

Robbery is an aggravated form of theft, the theft being aggravated by the use of force or threat of force. This is the most essential point in understanding the offence. If there is no theft there is no robbery. Where a person uses or threatens force in order to steal but has not achieved the appropriation of any property, and is therefore not guilty of robbery, he can be convicted of assault with intent to rob. There can be no conviction for robbery if it is found that the person who used or threatened force in order to appropriate the property believed that he had a legal right to it, even though he did not believe he was entitled to use force to do so, because the essential ingredient for theft, 'dishonesty', is missing. Similarly, a person who, wishing to cross a river, forcibly dispossesses a man of his boat does not commit robbery if he does not 'intend permanently to deprive' the owner of his property, as that essential ingredient of theft is missing. Of course, in both cases there can be a conviction for some offence of assault (other than assault with intent to rob) and in the latter for taking a conveyance contrary to the Theft Act 1968, s 12.

Use or threat of force immediately before or at time of theft

To constitute robbery, the force must be used or threatened 'immediately before or at the time of' the theft. There can be no robbery if force is only used or threatened after 'the time' of the theft. A person who pushes an old lady to the ground and steals her handbag commits robbery, so does he who approaches her and threatens to punch her in the face unless she hands over her handbag. The first used force in a way which might be considered to be either immediately before or at the time of the theft and the other threatens force immediately before the theft. However, a person, who approaches a lady and steals her handbag without force but, being discovered by her in possession of the bag shortly afterwards, assaults her, cannot be convicted of robbery. This is because the time of the theft will have elapsed when the force is used. Such a man could, of course, be convicted of theft and assault. The 'time' of the theft is not limited to the split second of time during which the initial appropriation with mens rea occurs, since an act of appropriation may be a continuing one, in which case the 'time' of the theft lasts as long as the theft can be said still to be in progress in common sense terms. Thus, there can be a robbery where a person takes property in a shop and, when approached by the owner, uses violence. The act of 'appropriation' would still be continuing at that time.

Whether or not force has been used or threatened immediately before or at the time of stealing is not a difficult question to answer in the vast majority of cases, such as street robberies or house robberies where the accused enters a house, ties up the occupants and then steals property there. However, in a few other cases difficulties can arise. For example, is force used immediately before stealing where A enters the home of a bank manager, ties him up, takes his keys to the bank and drives five miles to the bank where he steals?

Where force is used, it must be used 'on' a person, but it has been held that the force need not be used directly against the person. Consequently, it is enough to use force to obtain possession of property in the physical possession of another. For example, the use of force to snatch a handbag from a woman's grasp is robbery.

In the case of a threat of force, a threat of future force is insufficient; the threat must be 'then and there' to subject another to force. A threat of violence to property will not suffice, nor will the actual use of force against it.

Use or threat of force in order to steal

The force used or threatened must be used in order to steal. If a man during an argument with another, threatens to give him a beating and the man threatened gives money to him not to do so, this cannot be robbery as the threat of force was not made with the intention of stealing. Likewise, a man who knocks a woman to the ground to rape her, but who then changes his mind and instead takes the handbag which she has dropped, is not guilty of robbery or of assault with intent to rob, although he may, of course, be convicted of theft and attempted rape.

Although the force must be used or threatened on a person, it is not essential that the theft is carried out in his presence, provided that it is used or threatened for the purpose of stealing. It is robbery, for example, where a security guard is tied up so that property may be removed from some other part of the warehouse in which he is on duty.

The theft need not be from the person against whom the force is used or threatened. Thus, if A threatens a married couple that he will stab the wife unless the husband hands over his wallet, A can be convicted of robbery.

BLACKMAIL

The offence of blackmail is dealt with by the Theft Act 1968, s 21 which provides that:

> 'A person is guilty of blackmail if, with a view to gain for himself or another or with intent to cause loss to another, he makes any unwarranted demand with menaces; and for this purpose a demand with menaces is unwarranted unless the person making it does so in the belief:
> (a) that he has reasonable grounds for making the demand; and
> (b) that the use of the menaces is a proper means of reinforcing the demand.'

Blackmail is an arrestable offence. The essence of the offence is a demand, so that a person may be guilty of blackmail if the other ingredients of the offence are present, and not merely of an attempt, if he obtains nothing as a result of his demand.

Demand with menaces

For a person to be guilty of blackmail he must have made an unwarranted demand with menaces (with the appropriate mens rea).

The nature of the act or omission demanded is immaterial. An oral demand is made when the words are said; if it is made by letter, it is made when that letter is posted. It is essential that a demand is made. If a person discovers a couple in the act of adultery and demands money for his silence he has made a demand, but not if he merely walks away and the couple follow him and offer to give him money with a plea that he maintains their secret. A demand need not, however, be express, since (taken together with the menaces) it may be implied by a request or suggestion or other conduct.

'Menaces' are not limited to threats of violence, since they include 'threats of action detrimental to or unpleasant to the person addressed'. It is immaterial whether the menaces do or do not relate to action to be taken by the person making the demand. The man who says, 'Pay me £5,000 or my daughter will tell the world that you seduced her', is as guilty of blackmail as the man who reinforces his demand with threats of action by himself.

The judge will not normally need to give the jury a definition of menaces, since it is an ordinary English word. However, in two types of case he will have to tell the jury one or other of the following. First, that if, on the facts known to the accused, his threats might have affected the mind of a person of ordinary stability, they would amount to menaces, even though they did not affect the person to whom they were addressed. Second, that if, although they would not have affected the mind of an ordinary person of normal stability, the threats affected the addressee's mind, they would amount to menaces if the accused was aware of the likely effect of his actions on the victim, eg because he knew of an unusual susceptibility on the victim's part.

With a view to gain or intent to cause loss

The accused must, of course, intend to make a demand with menaces. In addition, he must act either with a view to gain for himself or another, or with an intent to cause loss to another. The terms 'gain' and 'loss' are defined by s 34 of the Act as extending only to gain or loss in money or other property, whether temporary or permanent. Section 34 also provides that:

(a) 'gain' includes a gain by keeping what one has, as well as a gain by getting what one has not; and

(b) 'loss' includes not getting what one might get, as well as a loss by parting with what one has.

The definition of these terms limits blackmail offences to cases with which one would expect a Theft Act to deal, viz those concerned with intended economic advantage or prejudice. If menaces are used with a view to sexual gratification, then (as one would expect) they are dealt with by the Sexual Offences Act 1956.

Unwarranted

As already mentioned, the demand with menaces must be unwarranted; for this purpose s 21 provides that a demand with menaces *is unwarranted unless* the person making it does so in the *belief* that he has reasonable grounds for making the demand *and* that the use of the menaces is a proper means of reinforcing the demand. If a man has sex with a girl after promising payment of £50 and then refuses to pay, a demand by her for the money supported by a threat to inform the man's wife will not be blackmail by the girl if she *believes* that she has reasonable grounds for making such a demand *and* that her threat is a proper means of reinforcing the demand.

An accused does not have to prove these beliefs, but this does not mean that the prosecution must negative the existence of a belief for which there is no evidence since it need only negative the existence of one of the specified beliefs if there is evidence before the court in support of both types of belief; otherwise the jury is obliged to find that the demand with menaces was unwarranted.

Blackmail and robbery

Although it does not require any property to have been appropriated, the offence of blackmail is close in many respects to the more serious offence of robbery by putting in fear and in many incidents where property has been taken by putting someone in fear, it is advantageous to consider both possibilities. In some cases which look like robbery at first glance, blackmail may be a much more appropriate charge. If a person offers violence to a child in a pram unless the mother parts with her money, it can be argued that this is robbery but the issue is not clear. For robbery to be committed the accused must put or seek to put someone in fear of immediate force to *him* or *herself* in order that the accused can steal. It need not be the person from whom the property is stolen who is put in fear, but in the case of the child in the pram it would be necessary to show that the accused put or sought to put the child in fear as it was against the child (and not the mother) that force was threatened. It would not be sufficient that the mother surrendered her money because she was in fear for her child. In such cases it is better to prefer a charge of blackmail in that an unwarranted demand was made of the mother with menaces directed towards the child. If the child was older and was clearly capable of recognising what was happening, there would be little difficulty in proving that the accused had put or sought to put it in fear of immediate force and it would therefore be much easier to prove the offence of robbery.

CHAPTER 37

Criminal damage

The Criminal Damage Act 1971 now deals with most offences which are concerned with damage to property but other legislation still exists which is to some extent parallel with certain aspects of the law contained in the 1971 Act. The Malicious Damage Act 1861 still deals with offences of obstructing railways, or interfering with railway signals, with intent to obstruct or damage a train, and of concealing or removing navigation marks or buoys. Damage related offences are retained under the Explosive Substances Act 1883; for example causing an explosion likely to endanger life or cause serious injury to property. When considering the possible offences committed in particular circumstances it is advisable to examine possibilities under these Acts and, if an intention to injure persons can be shown, the provisions of the Offences against the Person Act 1861 must also be considered (see ch 28).

CRIMINAL DAMAGE

The Criminal Damage Act 1971, s 1(1) provides what is known as the simple offence of criminal damage:

'A person who without lawful excuse destroys or damages any property belonging to another intending to destroy or damage any such property, or being reckless as to whether any such property would be destroyed or damaged, shall be guilty of an offence.'

If the destruction or damage is by fire, the offence is required by s 1(3) to be charged as arson, which carries a higher maximum punishment. As a result there are technically two offences under s 1(1), criminal damage otherwise than by fire, and criminal damage committed by fire.

By the Theft Act 1968, s 30, the leave of the Director of Public Prosecutions is required for the institution of proceedings for criminal damage by one spouse to the other's property, unless, by virtue of any judicial decree or order, the spouses were not obliged to cohabit at the material time.

The terms of the definition of the simple offence in s 1(1) involve more complexity than one might expect. What we have to say about them hereafter is equally applicable to the other offences under the Act, unless the contrary is indicated.

Destroy or damage

Property is damaged if it suffers physical harm which involves permanent or temporary impairment of the property's use or value. If a motor car is scratched when a coin is scraped along its side it is damaged thereby, because its value is impaired; likewise a wall is damaged if slogans are painted on it, as is beer if water is poured into it. If part of a machine is removed, without which it cannot work, the machine is damaged, even though neither it nor the part suffers actual physical injury, because its use is impaired. Consequently, a car is damaged if the rotor arm is removed from its engine.

The test of impairment of use or value does not conclude the matter since if the physical harm is a normal incident of the type of property in question (as in the case of firedoors in the corridors of a public building, which tend to get chipped by trollies and the like) this does not constitute damage. Moreover, if the impairment of use or value is minimal there is no 'damage' for the purposes of the Act. The fact that what is done is rectifiable does not prevent the property being damaged but the amount and cost of rectification are relevant factors in determining whether there has been damage; if they are minimal it may be found that the property has not been damaged. If a man trespasses in a field which is used for the grazing of cattle it will be difficult to prove that he thereby committed damage to the grass. It would be different if he walked through a field of corn, bending and severing the stalks with his feet. In each case the circumstances must be considered, together with the nature of the article alleged to have been damaged, what has happened to it and the above factors.

By the Computer Misuse Act 1990, s 3(6), any alteration, erasure or addition to a program or data held in a computer, which is made by the operation of any function of a computer is not regarded as damaging any computer or computer storage medium (such as a hard or floppy disc) unless the effect on that computer or medium impairs its physical condition.

The destruction of property involves something which goes beyond damage, such as the demolition of a machine, the pulling down of a wall or other structure, or the killing of an animal.

If arson is charged, it must also be proved that the destruction or damage was caused by fire.

Property

Section 10 of the Act defines property as being property of a tangible nature, whether real or personal, including money and:

(a) including wild creatures which have been tamed or are ordinarily kept in captivity, and any other wild creatures or their carcases *if,* but only if, they have been reduced into possession which has not been lost or abandoned or are in the course of being reduced into possession; but

(b) *not* including mushrooms growing wild on any land or flowers, fruit or foliage of a plant growing wild on any land.

The term 'mushroom' includes any fungus and 'plant' includes shrubs and trees.

It can be seen that 'property' is defined by s 10 in a similar way to the definition of that term in the Theft Act 1968 for the purposes of theft. One difference is that land itself, which generally cannot be stolen under the Theft Act definition, is not subjected to any limits on when it can be the subject of criminal damage. A man who moves his fence to capture a little of his neighbour's lawn cannot be convicted of theft of that piece of lawn, but he would be guilty of criminal damage if he damaged it. Another difference is that intangible things, such as copyright, cannot be the subject of criminal damage although they may be stolen.

It must be emphasised that wild mushrooms and wild flowers etc can never be the subject of *criminal* damage. However, as we saw in the last chapter, they can be the subject of theft in certain circumstances, and this is relevant because some cases of damage to such things also involve a theft. In addition, the provisions of the Wildlife and Countryside Act 1981 dealt with in ch 22 now offer protection to some wild creatures and plants in circumstances which would include forms of damage. Therefore damage to the flowers, fruit or foliage of wild plants, although not an offence of criminal damage, is likely to be an offence contrary to the provisions of the Wildlife and Countryside Act.

Belonging to another

The simple offence of criminal damage can only be committed against property belonging to another. If a person wishes to destroy a garden shed or motor car which belongs only to him he is at liberty to do so provided that he does not endanger any other person (see s 1(2), below). The class of persons to whom property is treated as belonging by s 10(2) to (4) of the 1971 Act is by no means limited to the owners of property, but includes a range of other people with a connection with it.

Section 10(2) provides that property is to be treated for the purposes of the Act as belonging to any person:

(a) having the custody or control of it;
(b) having in it any proprietary right or interest (not being an equitable interest arising only from an agreement to transfer or grant an interest); or
(c) having a charge on it.

If a lawn-mower is hired to X he thereby obtains the custody or control of it. If anyone else, including the owner, intentionally or recklessly destroys or damages the lawn-mower without lawful excuse while it is in X's custody or control, that person can be convicted of criminal damage against X.

Co-owners of property each have a proprietary right or interest in the property and if one damages the property he may be convicted of criminal damage since the property 'belongs to another'. The adjective 'proprietary' is included to exclude those with what may be described as a second generation interest, such as insurance companies which, although they have an interest in the property, do not have a proprietary interest.

Finally, persons having a charge on property have a proprietary interest in it. The best example of a charge is where a houseowner buys his house by mortgaging it by way of charge to a building society. As a result of the present provision, the house will belong to the building society, as well as to the houseowner, and if the houseowner intentionally or recklessly damages it without lawful excuse he can be convicted of criminal damage, since the house will 'belong to another'.

Section 10(3) and (4) provides that, as in the case of theft, where property is subject to a trust, the person to whom it belongs shall include any person having the right to enforce the trust; and that property belonging to a corporation sole (such as the Treasury Solicitor or a bishop) in his official capacity is to be treated as belonging to the corporation notwithstanding a vacancy in the corporation.

Mens rea

The mens rea required for an offence under s 1(1) consists of either intention or recklessness as to the destruction of or damage to property belonging to another. To do an act deliberately, eg deliberately throwing a stone, is not enough; the accused must have intended his conduct to result in property belonging to another being destroyed or damaged, or been reckless as to the risk of such destruction or damage resulting from his conduct.

Clearly, if W throws a stone at X's passing car and dents it, as he intended, he has the necessary mens rea, since he intended to damage property belonging to another. Moreover, because of the doctrine of transferred malice, W will still have the necessary mens rea if the stone misses X's car but damages Y's front door. This is not very important in practice because, even if the doctrine of transferred malice did not exist and apply to W's intention, he would undoubtedly be reckless (in the sense explained below) as to the risk of damage to another's property.

A person is reckless as to whether or not any property would be destroyed or damaged if:

(a) he does an act which in fact creates an obvious risk that property will be destroyed or damaged *and*
(b) when he does the act he either has not given any thought to the possibility of there being any such risk or has recognised that there was some risk involved and has none the less gone on to do it.

In relation to the 'obvious risk' referred to in (a), the question is whether the risk would have been obvious to an ordinary, prudent person who stopped to think. If it would have been, it is irrelevant that the risk would not have been obvious to the accused, had he stopped to think, because he was too young or mentally deficient or for some 'other reason would have been incapable of realising the risk'. This is of great importance because of the wording of the first limb of (b).

Recklessness in the present context can be illustrated as follows. Suppose that A fires a highly powered air rifle from his bedroom window at wild birds sitting on the eaves of houses opposite and that A misses the birds but breaks a window in B's house. A cannot be said to have intended to damage another's property; he would never have fired the gun if he had realised that someone else's property might be damaged. Nevertheless, A's act of firing the rifle creates an obvious risk that property belonging to another will be destroyed or damaged and he will be reckless as to that risk if, when he fires, he has not given any thought to the possibility of there being any such risk. On the other hand, he would not be reckless as to the risk, and therefore would not be guilty of criminal damage, if he had thought about the risk and wrongly concluded that there was no risk of destroying or damaging another's property.

Another example would be where a tramp, who has decided to 'doss down' in a barn used for the storage of hay, lights a fire to warm himself and the fire spreads to the hay and burns down the barn. Clearly, the tramp's act of lighting the fire creates an obvious risk that property will be destroyed or damaged and, unless at the time he had thought about the risk and wrongly concluded there was no such risk, he will be guilty under s 1(1) on the basis of recklessness because either he will not have thought about the possibility of there being any such risk or he will have realised that there was a risk involved and none the less gone on to take it.

Without lawful excuse

In order to commit an offence under s 1(1) of the 1971 Act, the accused must destroy or damage another's property 'without lawful excuse'. For the purposes of s 1(1), s 5(2) provides that a person is to be treated as having a lawful excuse if he acted with one of two types of belief:

Belief in consent

Section 5(2)(a) provides that a person has a lawful excuse if, at the time of the act or acts alleged to constitute the offence, he believed that the person or persons whom he believed to be entitled to consent to the destruction of or damage to the property had so consented, or would have so consented if he or they had known of the destruction or damage and its circumstances.

If a business firm was altering its premises and, in the course of doing so, was clearing some old buildings from a yard at the rear, an employee who demolished a valuable building on the site would have a lawful excuse for doing so if he believed that he had been given permission by the foreman when given the general direction, 'Clear that yard at the back'. The test is whether his belief was honest, although the more reasonable the belief was the more likely it is that the justices or jury will find that it was honestly held. If no such direction had been given, but the worker honestly believed that he would have been given permission by the foreman had he asked, this would still amount to lawful excuse.

If an employee overheard his employer say that he would be delighted if the factory burned down so that he would receive money from the insurers and the employee considered that this was in the nature of an instruction to him, this could amount to a lawful excuse if he honestly believed that his employer had consented to the damage. This would be so even though the nature of the act, as a part of some other intended transaction, was in itself criminal.

Defence of property

Section 5(2)(b) provides that a person is to be treated as having a lawful excuse if he destroyed or damaged the property in question in order to protect his own property or that of some other person, or a right or interest (such as a right of way) in property which was or which he believed to be vested in himself or another, *and* at the time of the act he believed that the property, right or interest was in immediate need of protection, and at that time he believed that the means of protection adopted or proposed to be adopted were reasonable having regard to all the circumstances. It is immaterial whether the specified belief was reasonable or not, provided it was honestly held.

Section 5(2)(b) has been interpreted by the courts so that the test in it is partly subjective (ie that it is applied on the basis of what was going on in the accused's mind, including whether he believed the means of protection used are reasonable) and partly objective (in that it is a question for the judge or justices whether, on the facts as the accused believed them to be, the act done was one which protected property or was capable of protecting property). Thus, in one case where an accused claimed that he had a lawful excuse for damaging property (by writing a Biblical quotation with a marker pen on a pillar outside the Houses of Parliament during a demonstration at the time of the Gulf War) because he had done so to protect property in the Gulf States, the Divisional Court held that, even if the accused had believed that he had a lawful excuse under s 5(2)(b), it was necessary for the Court to adopt an objective view of whether, on the facts believed by the accused, what was done by him protected, or was capable of protecting, property. It held that his conduct could not be said to be done to protect property in the Gulf States as such protection was too remote from his conduct. Likewise, where an accused, a squatter who had damaged a door in the house by chiselling off (and replacing) locks, pleaded that he had a lawful excuse under s 5(2)(b) because he had believed that the property was in immediate need of protection and that his actions were reasonable as a means of protection, the Divisional Court dismissed his appeal against conviction. It agreed with the Crown Court that, judged objectively, on the facts as believed by the accused, the damage could not have the effect of protecting the property, and that – anyway – the accused had had no belief in the need for immediate protection of the property.

Not surprisingly, a person is not 'property' within the meaning of s 5(2)(b) of the 1971 Act. Consequently, for example, breaking down a door to recover a child who is being unlawfully detained does not fall within the defence of 'lawful excuse' under s 5(2).

An honest belief in a moral entitlement is not a lawful excuse, nor is an honest belief that the destruction or damage was reasonable in pursuit of some political objective.

The present provision clearly entitles the owner of livestock to kill dogs worrying his sheep if he honestly believes that such immediate action is necessary for their protection.

Lawful excuse in a general sense

Quite apart from the statutory instances of lawful excuse provided by s 5 of the Act, the ordinary, common sense instances of lawful excuse still apply. A police officer, in executing a warrant to search premises, may, if denied entry, break a lock, thereby committing damage. He would certainly not have believed that the owner would have consented, nor have believed that this was necessary in the protection of property, but nevertheless he would have a lawful excuse for his actions because the various statutory powers under which search warrants may be granted authorise entry by force, if necessary. Other examples of lawful excuses besides those provided by s 5 are self-defence and the defence of another.

On the other hand, a belief that in damaging property one is carrying out God's laws or instructions does not amount to a lawful excuse.

Attempt

When no actual destruction results from a deliberate act carried out with the *intention* of destroying or damaging property, a person may be charged with an attempt to commit criminal damage, however low the value of the property intended to be destroyed or of the intended damage. The moment of 'attempt' arrives as soon as something is actually done which is more than merely preparatory to the commission of the offence. Thus, the throwing of a brick at a window, which does not in fact break as it is intended it should, amounts to an attempt to commit criminal damage.

It must be remembered that, since a person is only guilty of an attempt if he intended to commit the crime whose attempt is charged, a person who was merely reckless as to the risk of destruction or damage resulting from his conduct cannot be guilty of an attempt to commit criminal damage.

RACIALLY-AGGRAVATED CRIMINAL DAMAGE

A person commits an offence under the Crime and Disorder Act 1998, s 30 if he commits an offence under the Criminal Damage Act 1971, s 1(1) which is racially aggravated.

An offence of criminal damage is racially aggravated if:

(a)　at the time of committing it, or immediately before or after doing so, the offender demonstrates towards the person to whom the property belongs or is treated as belonging for the purposes of the 1971 Act hostility based on that person's membership (or presumed membership) of a racial group; or

(b)　the offence is motivated (wholly or partly) by hostility towards members of a racial group based on their membership of that group.

For this purpose, 'membership of a racial group' includes association with members of that group, and 'presumed' means presumed by the offender. A 'racial group' means a group of persons defined by reference to race, colour, nationality (including citizenship) or ethnic or national origins.

DESTROYING OR DAMAGING PROPERTY WITH INTENT TO ENDANGER LIFE OR RECKLESSNESS AS TO LIFE BEING ENDANGERED

The Criminal Damage Act 1971, s 1(2) declares that it is an offence for a person without lawful excuse to destroy or damage any property, whether belonging to himself or another:

(a)　intending to destroy or damage any property or being reckless as to whether any property would be destroyed or damaged; *and*

(b)　intending the destruction or damage to endanger the life of another or being reckless as to whether the life of another would be thereby endangered.

This serious offence is often described as aggravated criminal damage. By s 1(3), it must be charged as arson when the destruction or damage is committed by fire. Where an offence under s 1(2) is charged, it is advisable that there should be two counts, one alleging criminal damage with intent to endanger life and the other criminal damage committed recklessly as to whether life might or might not be endangered, so that the jury's verdict can be understood for sentencing purposes (since these two types of mens rea involve very different degrees of fault). This approach is also recommended in relation to a charge under s 1(1).

The offence under s 1(2) can be committed in respect of property which 'belongs' only to the accused, and the reason for this can be easily appreciated. The essence of the offence is the endangering of life and life can as easily be endangered in the accused's own dwelling house as in other property. If a man sets fire to his house which 'belongs' only to him with his wife asleep inside it, it is to be expected that he may be charged with damage with intent to endanger life or recklessness as to life being endangered.

Except for the fact that the property need not belong to another, the provisions of s 1(2) are an extension of the provisions of s 1(1). It is essential to prove the other elements of the offence of criminal damage first, including that the person charged either intended to destroy or damage the property or was reckless in that respect. If the jury are satisfied on these points they may go on to consider whether the accused additionally intended that the destruction or damage would endanger someone's life, or there was a recklessness as to whether human life would be endangered.

'Recklessness' is used in the same sense as in s 1(1) and this is not only in relation to the risk of property being destroyed or damaged but also in relation to the 'risk' that another's life may be thereby endangered. Thus, as far as recklessness is concerned, the question is (a) whether the accused was reckless (in the sense outlined above in relation to s 1(1)) as to whether the property might be destroyed or damaged as a result of his act; and (b) whether the accused's act created an obvious risk that the life of another would be endangered, and when he did the act he either had not given any thought to the possibility of there being any such risk or had recognised that there was some risk involved and had nonetheless gone on to do it. Where a 15 year old boy of low mental capacity set fire to hay upon which other people were asleep and made no attempt to put out the fire or to awaken them, his act created an *obvious* risk. It was held that in this respect, s 1(2) is concerned with that which would have been obvious to a reasonable person of mature years and understanding. The Court of Appeal said that the trial judge was correct in refusing to admit evidence of a psychologist as this did not relate to 'abnormality' but to characteristics of the accused which were within the experience of the jury and the assistance of an 'expert' was not required.

The accused must have intended to endanger life, or been reckless as to whether life would be endangered, *by the destruction or damaging* of property which he intentionally or recklessly caused; it is not enough that he merely intended to endanger life, or was reckless as to whether life would be endangered, by the act which caused the destruction or damage. Consequently, a person who fires a gun from outside a house at a person standing behind a window in it cannot be convicted under s 1(2), even though he intended to endanger that person's life, if he did not intend the damaging of the window to endanger life (and was not reckless as to that damage doing so).

In the event of a charge under s 1(2) being framed so as to charge the accused only with *intending* by the destruction or damage to endanger another's life, evidence of voluntary intoxication can be relevant as evidence that he lacked that intention. However, if the charge includes a reference to the accused being reckless as to whether another's life would be endangered thereby, evidence of voluntary intoxication is irrelevant, just as it is on any charge under s 1(1), since the offence charged is one of basic intent. Self-induced intoxication is irrelevant to the issue of recklessness.

This offence is an interesting one as it is close to the offence of attempted murder in so many respects. The difference lies in the distinction between an intention to kill and an intention to endanger life or recklessness as to whether life is endangered. If terrorists explode a bomb in a building intending to kill a political opponent they commit an offence of attempted murder, as well as the present offence. If it is exploded in a building occupied by supporters of a rival political group it is certainly likely to endanger life but there may not have been an intention to kill. Warnings of intended detonations given by such organisations go some way towards eliminating either of these intentions but, depending upon the circumstances, they may not always eliminate the element of recklessness.

Although the words 'lawful excuse' appear in this offence the excuses provided by s 5(2) do not apply to this offence. 'Lawful excuse' for an offence of this nature will be restricted to those excuses which exist under the general law, such as self-defence and defence of another.

THREATS TO DESTROY OR DAMAGE PROPERTY

Threats to destroy or damage property are dealt with under s 2 of the Act:

> 'A person who without lawful excuse makes to another a threat, intending that that other would fear it would be carried out:
> (a)   to destroy or damage any property belonging to that other or a third person; or
> (b)   to destroy or damage his own property in a way which he knows is likely to endanger the life of that other or a third person,
> shall be guilty of an offence.'

The threat must be to do something which would be an offence against s 1 of the Act. It must be carried out with the intention of inducing a fear in the mind of the recipient that it would be carried out. It does not matter how the threat is received; a letter, a telephone call, a verbal threat or any other means of conveying a message from one to another will suffice. It does not matter that the person who offers the threat does not intend to carry it out, provided that he intends to create the fear that he would do so in the mind of the recipient. Nor does it matter that the recipient is not actually put in fear by the threat.

The threat must be to destroy or damage the property of some other person, or to destroy or damage his (the maker of the threat's) own property in a way which will endanger life. It is interesting to consider this offence in relation to bomb hoaxes (see pp 546–547). Someone who communicates the threat of an explosion to another person, intending that the recipient will fear that the threat will be carried out, commits this offence if the threat is concerned with destruction or damage to property etc. There is often confusion with the offences created by the Criminal Law Act 1977, s 51 in relation to bomb hoaxes. Although that section is largely concerned with persons who place or despatch false articles (which may be harmless) to induce fear of explosion, it also deals with the offence of communicating false information to induce such a fear. That offence is distinguished from the one under s 2 of the 1971 Act by its limitations to false information whereas the offence under s 2 can be committed whether or not the threat involves false information. However, for practical purposes, both are arrestable offences.

The provisions of s 5 relating to 'lawful excuse' apply to threats to destroy or damage another's property but do not apply to threats to destroy or damage the threatener's own property in a way likely to endanger the life of some person.

POSSESSING WITH INTENT

The possession of things to be used for the purpose of causing damage is dealt with by s 3 of the 1971 Act:

> 'A person who has anything in his custody or under his control intending without lawful excuse to use or cause or permit another to use it
> (a)   to destroy or damage any property belonging to some other person; or
> (b)   to destroy or damage his own or the user's property in a way which he knows is likely to endanger the life of some other person,
> shall be guilty of an offence.'

As can be seen, the possession of the 'thing' must be for the purpose of doing something (or causing or permitting something to be done) which would be an offence under s 1. There must be a clear intention to use the thing in such a way or to cause or permit another to do so; and it is not sufficient to prove that the accused realised that it 'might' be so used. Provided that such an intention does exist it is immaterial that there is no immediate intention to use it but only a conditional one. A terrorist group which possesses explosives in a warehouse, intending to use them to destroy or damage property if, and when, the opportunity arises, can therefore be convicted of the present offence.

'Possession' is covered in the section not by the use of the actual word 'possession', but by the use of 'in his custody or under his control'. These precise terms cover the same situations as possession but their use avoids the technicalities of the concept of 'possession'. The explosives contained in a warehouse may be in the custody of the keeper of that warehouse but they may also be under the control of the leaders of the terrorist group, who can order their removal and use at any time.

The offence as described is sufficient to include instances of possession of a terrorist arsenal, the possession of pickaxe handles by protection racketeers, or even the possession of paint or sprays by those who intend to endorse graffiti on the walls of buildings.

Where the offence involves an intent falling within (a), ie to destroy or damage another's property, 'without lawful excuse' is subject to s 5 (with minor modifications), but where the intent falls within (b), ie to destroy or damage property in a way known to be likely to endanger life, it is not.

POWERS

The various offences of criminal damage described in this chapter are arrestable offences.

The Criminal Damage Act 1971, s 6(1) allows a justice, following information given on oath, to grant a search warrant if there is reasonable cause to believe that a person has in his custody or under his control or on his premises anything which there is reasonable cause to believe *has been* used, or is *intended for use*, without lawful excuse to destroy or damage property belonging to another or to destroy or damage property in a way likely to endanger the life of another.

If such a search warrant is granted, a constable may enter (if need be by force) any premises and search for the thing in question. He may seize anything which he believes to have been used or to be intended to be used as aforesaid.

CHAPTER 38

Burglary

Section 9(1) of the 1968 Theft Act defines burglary as follows:

'A person is guilty of burglary if—
(a) he enters any building or part of a building as a trespasser and with intent to commit any such offence as is mentioned in subsection (2) below; or
(b) having entered any building or part of a building as a trespasser he steals or attempts to steal anything in the building or that part of it or inflicts or attempts to inflict upon any person therein any grievous bodily harm.'

It has been held that s 9(1) creates two types of offences, the first being set out by s 9(1)(a) and the second by s 9(1)(b). Because in each type of offence there is a higher maximum penalty if the building entered as a trespasser is a dwelling each of the two types of offence has in it two offences one relating to dwellings and the other to other buildings. If only an offence under s 9(1)(a) is charged and only one under s 9(1)(b) proved, a conviction for the latter cannot be sustained. On the other hand, if a person is tried only for an offence under s 9(1)(b) in the Crown Court and the jury find it not proved, they may return a verdict of guilty of an offence under s 9(1)(a) if they find its requirements satisfied. The definitions of the two offences include many common terms which require explanation. We will give this as we describe the offence under s 9(1)(a) but what is said will be equally applicable to the offence under s 9(1)(b). Both offences are arrestable offences.

BURGLARY CONTRARY TO s 9(1)(a): ENTRY WITH INTENT

The effect of s 9(1)(a) is that a person is guilty of burglary if he enters any building, which term includes an inhabited vehicle or vessel, or part of a building as a trespasser and with intent to commit one of the offences listed in s 9(2), viz to steal anything in the building or part of a building in question, or to inflict on any person therein grievous bodily harm, or to rape any person therein, or to do unlawful damage to the building or anything therein. The following is an explanation of the various terms which are involved.

Enters

In the previous offence of burglary replaced by s 9, the intrusion of part of the body, however small, sufficed for an 'entry'. However, in relation to the modern law of burglary the Court of Appeal has adopted the test of an 'effective entry'. This test excludes minimal intrusions, as where the accused's fingers are inserted through a gap between a window and its frame in order to open the window. However, where a man was found stuck in a downstairs window of a house with his head and right arm inside the window but trapped by the window itself, which rested on his neck, the Court of Appeal held that there had been an entry. The issue of whether he was able, from that position, to steal anything was irrelevant.

Under the old law, an entry could be effected merely by the insertion of an instrument without the intrusion of any part of the body *provided it was inserted to commit a relevant further offence*, but not if it was inserted merely to facilitate access by a person's body. Assuming that this remains the law, a person who, whilst remaining outside a building at all times in a physical sense, inserts his walking stick in an endeavour to remove goods from the building enters the building for the purposes of burglary. So does a person who pokes the barrel of his rifle through the open window of a building in order to shoot at (and therefore seriously harm) someone inside. On the other hand, a person who inserts a jemmy behind a window which has been left ajar, or who pokes the barrel of his rifle through a letter box in order to intimidate the occupant, whom he intends to rape, into opening the front door, does not enter the building because the insertion of the instrument was merely to facilitate access by his body. It is almost certain that the rule which applied under the old law concerning entry by means of an innocent agent still applies. Under this rule a person who uses a child under the age of criminal responsibility to enter a building and steal is regarded as himself entering the building. The same considerations would apply to the use of a trained animal. Dogs are trained to perform a variety of tasks and to sniff out and locate particular articles. It would be possible to train a dog to bring to its master certain valuable articles of property normally found in houses. Entry by a dog in such circumstances would be entry by its handler.

These special rules should not be allowed to obscure the fact that in most circumstances the issue of entry will be quite clear.

As a trespasser

A person enters a building or part of a building as a trespasser if it is in the possession of another and he enters without a right by law or permission to do so; the entry need not involve any force at all.

Rights of entry are granted by statute to certain people, such as the police and public health inspectors, for certain purposes. For instance, a public health inspector entering the premises to check whether there has been a breach of the public health law is not a trespasser, because he has a statutory power to enter for this purpose, but he does enter as a trespasser if he enters premises for the purpose of raping a person inside.

Permission to enter for a particular purpose or purposes may be given only by the occupier or, in the present context, by a person lawfully entitled to be in the building (provided the purpose of entry is not contrary to the interests of the occupier). If a mature girl invites her lover into her parents' house for the purpose of lovemaking, his entry to the building is not as a trespasser, since she is lawfully entitled to be in the building and the purpose of her lover's entry is not contrary to her parents' interests. However, if she invited him on to the premises in order to steal property belonging to her parents, his entry would be as a trespasser as it would be contrary to the parents' interests and therefore the girl could not give a valid permission. These examples represent the extremes of non-trespassory entries and trespassory entries where some form of permission is given.

Permission to enter may be implied, instead of express. For instance, in the case of a shop there is an implied permission for members of the public to enter the public parts of the shop for the purposes of inspecting goods on display or making purchases, and a person who enters for such a purpose is not a trespasser.

This brings us to the next point. A permission to enter will be given for a particular purpose or purposes. A person who enters for a purpose other than one for which he has permission enters as a trespasser. For example, the Court of Appeal has held that a man, who had permission to enter his father's house, entered it as a trespasser when he entered to steal his father's television set because he entered in excess of his permission. Likewise, a person, who enters a shop for the purpose of stealing from the open shelves, enters the building as a trespasser and is technically guilty of burglary, although the practice is only to charge theft.

A permission to enter may not necessarily extend to every part of the building. Thus a person may lawfully enter a building such as a hotel or shop, but trespass in the manager's office or the stockroom; equally, he may be a lawful guest at a meal in a private house but enter a bedroom as a trespasser. In both of these cases the entry as a trespasser will be into a 'part of a building'. On the other hand, if a person enters a building (or part of a building) with a right by law or permission to do so and then stops on after the expiry of his entitlement (as where X, who has entered a shop for a lawful purpose, decides to hide and stay on after the shop closes, and does so, in order to steal) he cannot be convicted of burglary because, although he becomes a trespasser by staying after hours, he has not entered the building (or part) as a trespasser. If, however, he then moves into another part of the building to carry out the theft, he will then commit burglary because he will have entered that part as a trespasser with the requisite intent.

Where a person is given permission to enter a building under a mistake as to his identity, which will normally have been procured by his fraud, the apparent permission is of no effect and he will enter as a trespasser. It is very difficult to prove a mistake of identity, since it must be proved that the mistaken party believed positively that the person in front of him was some other particular person. This is not very important because a person who is given permission under a mistake concerning him is very likely to enter the building as a trespasser, even though the mistake is not as to his identity. For example, if A disguises himself as a meter reader and thereby is permitted to enter X's house, it will only be possible to prove a mistake of identity if X positively thought A was another person, B. Nevertheless, if, as is likely, A disguised himself so as to be able to enter the house for some purpose other than to read the meter, he will enter as a trespasser, as explained previously.

As a final point, it should be noted that the 'owner' of a building may trespass in part of it if that part is in the exclusive possession of someone else. For example, if a householder rents out the rooms in his attic to a student, on terms whereby the student obtains exclusive possession of them, the householder will enter them as a trespasser if he enters without the student's permission.

Building or part of a building

The term 'building' should be given its everyday meaning of a structure of some size with walls and a roof and of a permanent or semi-permanent nature. Although most such structures will be of block, brick or stone construction, this is not essential, and a wooden structure is a building if it satisfies the above test. Dwelling houses, warehouses, shops, office premises and the like are all buildings; so are outhouses and greenhouses (provided they are at least semi-permanent) and substantial portable structures with most of the attributes normally found in buildings, provided that there is an element of permanence in their site. On the other hand, tents, partially-built but unroofed houses, and open-sided barns, are not.

The term 'part of a building' refers to a particular area of a building and has no connection with unfinished buildings. In hotels there are a number of rooms. Guests at the hotel are permitted to use the room which has been allocated to them and those other parts of the hotel which are for general use, such as the bar and dining room, and therefore they do not enter those parts as trespassers. However, they do not have permission to enter the rooms of other guests and to do so is to enter a part of a building as a trespasser. As said on the previous page, a person who conceals himself on shop premises during business hours and emerges when the shop has been vacated and walks into another part of the shop, enters that part of the building as a trespasser because his permission to be on the premises expired with the closing of the shop.

A 'part of a building' does not necessarily mean a separate room; it also includes a physically marked out area in a room, such as the area behind a counter in a shop, from which the accused is plainly excluded, whether expressly or impliedly.

As already indicated, s 9 states that references to a building also apply to an inhabited vehicle or vessel, and this is so whether or not the person having a habitation in it is there at the time. Clearly, a caravan or houseboat which is someone's permanent home is an 'inhabited vehicle or vessel', even though he is not there at the time but, say, abroad on a holiday; so is a caravan or boat which is used as a holiday home, whether mobile or static, in the summer during those weeks or weekends in which it is being so used, but not at other times in the summer and not at all in the rest of the year when it is closed up.

Mens rea

The mens rea required by an offence of burglary contrary to s 9(1)(a) is that, when entering the building or part of a building, the accused must satisfy two requirements.

First, he must know he is entering the building, or part, as a trespasser, or at least be subjectively reckless as to whether he is so entering. In most circumstances the issue will be straightforward and it will be a relatively simple task to prove that the accused knew that he had entered as a trespasser; if, for example, a glass patio-door is smashed to pieces then it is reasonable to assume that the person who entered through the gap realised that he had no permission to enter.

Second, he must enter with intent to commit one of the offences listed in s 9(2):

(a) to 'steal' anything in the building or, as the case may be, the part trespassed in;
(b) to inflict grievous bodily harm on any person in the building or, as the case may be, the part trespassed in;
(c) to rape any person in the building or, as the case may be, the part of the building trespassed in; or
(d) to do unlawful damage to the building or anything therein (whether or not the accused has trespassed in the part in which the damage is intended to occur).

It is, of course, irrelevant that it is impossible for the accused to carry out his intent.

The following is worthy of note in relation to this provision:

Intent to steal

On entering the building, or part, as a trespasser, the accused must have intended dishonestly to appropriate therein property (such as money or valuables) belonging to another with intent permanently to deprive the other of it. In this context, the reader is reminded that obtaining goods by deception can amount to theft, and that it is irrelevant that what has occurred might also constitute an offence of obtaining property by deception, see p 705.

Intent to inflict grievous bodily harm or to rape a person

On entering the building, or part, as a trespasser, the accused must have intended to inflict really serious harm on a person therein or, as the case may be, to have unlawful sexual intercourse with a person therein without her or his consent. Examples falling within these two types of intent are where A enters B's house with intent to break B's arm, having discovered that B is having an affair with his (A's) wife, and where C enters the house of a woman who is a stranger to him, with intent to climb into bed with her while she is asleep in order to have intercourse with her. If C should allege that he entered with intent to steal but saw an opportunity to rape, this would, of course, afford no defence to a charge of burglary contrary to s 9(1)(a).

Intent to do unlawful damage

On entering the building, or part, as a trespasser, the accused must have intended to destroy or damage the building or other property (in the building) belonging to another without lawful excuse (ie to commit an offence contrary to the Criminal Damage Act 1971, s 1(1)). A man who enters the flat of his ex-lover as a trespasser with the intention of breaking up pieces of her furniture, as a punishment for rejecting him, commits burglary. If he enters as a trespasser but only intending to plead with her to take him back, he does not commit burglary if he then loses his temper in consequence of her insistence that the affair is over, and breaks up furniture before leaving.

General point

In most instances, unless there is an admission by the accused, the only way in which one of the requisite intentions will be apparent is if there has been some act almost amounting to an attempt to commit the intended offence.

BURGLARY CONTRARY TO S 9(1)(b): HAVING ENTERED AS A TRESPASSER, STEALING OR INFLICTING GRIEVOUS BODILY HARM, OR ATTEMPTING ONE OF THESE CRIMES

The Theft Act 1968, s 9(1)(b) provides:

'A person is guilty of burglary if having entered a building or part of a building as a trespasser he steals or attempts to steal anything in the building or that part of it or inflicts or attempts to inflict on any person therein any grievous bodily harm.'

What was said above in relation to s 9(1)(a) applies equally to the corresponding terms in this definition.

Section 9(1)(a) distinguished

An important distinction between the offence of burglary under s 9(1)(a) and that under s 9(1)(b) is that the latter requires the accused, having entered a building or part of a building as a trespasser, actually to have committed or attempted to commit in the building or part trespassed in:

(a) the offence of theft (contrary to the Theft Act 1968, s 1);
(b) the offence of unlawfully and maliciously inflicting grievous bodily harm (contrary to the Offences Against the Person Act 1861, s 20); or
(c) the offence of unlawfully and maliciously administering poison so as to inflict grievous bodily harm (contrary to the Offences Against the Person Act 1861, s 23).

Another important distinction is that, unlike the offence under s 9(1)(a), the offence under s 9(1)(b) does not require the accused to have intended to commit one of the above offences when he entered as a trespasser. Consequently if A enters a building as a trespasser, but without one of the intents specified in s 9(2) (so that he is not guilty under s 9(1)(a)) he can only be guilty of burglary (under s 9(1)(b)) if he then steals or inflicts grievous bodily harm or attempts to do either. For example, if a tramp goes into a building to sleep, and not intending to commit any of these offences, he is a trespasser but not a burglar. However, if, being discovered there by a security guard, he then deliberately strikes the guard with a piece of wood lying nearby, he will be guilty of burglary provided that he inflicts grievous bodily harm, whether he intended to or not, since he will have committed the offence of unlawfully and maliciously inflicting grievous bodily harm, contrary to the Offences Against the Person Act 1861, s 20.

Rape and criminal damage have been excluded from the offences whereby burglary can be committed after entry as a trespasser without any of the specified intentions. The exclusion of rape in these circumstances can be explained as follows. If rape is committed after a trespassory entry, that offence is punishable by life imprisonment as opposed to the 14 years, or 10 years if the building was not a dwelling, which might be awarded for burglary. There would, therefore, be little purpose in charging burglary as the full circumstances surrounding the commission of the offence of rape would be taken into account by the court when passing sentence. At the other end of the scale, in the case of theft or grievous bodily harm when the manner in which that offence was carried out amounted only to an offence contrary to the Offences Against the Person Act 1861, s 20, the penalty would be much less than that for burglary. Although the arguments for the inclusion within s 9(1)(b) of criminal damage are stronger than for rape, one can imagine the reluctance of Parliament to allow an offence of burglary where there was a trespass without one of these intents, but the trespasser committed some minor act of damage upon the premises. There was perhaps a need to distinguish between a careless tramp and the man who deliberately entered with the intention of causing damage, such as the mobs who may wish to break up a club following some petty dispute.

Mens rea

Apart, of course, from having the mens rea required for theft, or an offence involving the infliction of grievous bodily harm, or an attempt to commit such, as the case may be, the accused must know or be reckless that he has entered as a trespasser when he commits one of these offences. It is irrelevant whether or not he realised at the time of entry that he was entering as a trespasser. Thus, if a person enters a building, thinking that he has permission, and later realises that he has not and then steals something inside or inflicts grievous bodily harm on someone inside (eg the occupier who is trying to eject him) he is guilty of burglary of the present type.

Examples of s 9(1)(b) offence

The boundaries of burglary contrary to s 9(1)(b) can be illustrated by the following examples. Theft requires the dishonest appropriation of property belonging to another with intent permanently to deprive the other of it. A person who enters an empty house as a trespasser to sleep in it for the night does not commit burglary, nor does he if he switches on the electric fire (because electricity is not property and cannot be stolen). But if he turns on a gas fire, he commits burglary because gas is property and can be stolen.

Fortunately most offences are quite straightforward. There is an unlawful entry and a theft of property, and the buildings usually attacked are dwelling houses, shops, warehouses and offices. However, caravan sites are increasingly visited for the purpose of theft of television sets and it will be necessary in those circumstances to consider the circumstances of the occupation of the caravan in question. As we have seen, if it is not lived in as a full-time residence it is only protected throughout those periods when it is a residence.

Of course, there is some overlap between the two offences of burglary. Where a person enters a building (or part) as a trespasser with intent to steal or to inflict grievous bodily harm therein, and he commits the intended offence or attempts to do so, he can be charged with either offence. In practice, it is normally best to charge burglary contrary to s 9(1)(b) in such a case since it is easier to prove.

AGGRAVATED BURGLARY

The element of aggravation lies in the possession of weapons or explosives at the time of the commission of the offence of burglary. Aggravated burglary is particularly serious because of the aggressive nature of the offence, which could well lead to loss of life for those inside the building. Offences of aggravated burglary are arrestable offences.

Section 10 of the 1968 Act states that a person is guilty of aggravated burglary if he commits any burglary and at the time has with him any firearm or imitation firearm, any weapon of offence, or any explosive. It goes on to define these terms in sub-s (1):

(a) 'firearm' includes an airgun or air pistol and 'imitation firearm' means anything which has the appearance of being a firearm, whether capable of being discharged or not;

(b) 'weapon of offence' means any article made or adapted for use for causing injury to or incapacitating a person, or intended by the person having it with him for such use; and

(c) 'explosive' means any article manufactured for the purpose of producing a practical effect by explosion, or intended by the person having it with him for that purpose.

Firearm, imitation firearm, weapon of offence or explosive

Section 10(1)(a), which states that a 'firearm' includes airguns and air pistols, does not describe the term 'firearm' itself. There is no doubt that this omission is deliberate so that courts may apply the term in a realistic sense and apply it to anything which can be fired and can kill or wound. It is clear that the definition of a firearm given in the Firearms Act 1968 was not included in the Theft Act because it includes component parts. There is very little threat of bodily injury posed by the possession of a magazine case for a rifle.

Things which have the appearance of being a 'firearm' but cannot be fired are covered by the term 'imitation firearm'.

The definition of the term 'weapon of offence' covers not only articles which would be offensive weapons for the purposes of the Prevention of Crime Act 1953, such as coshes, knuckledusters, chains with sharpened links, caps with razor blades in the peak or even pickaxe handles, but also articles made, adapted or intended to be used for incapacitating a person. Articles made for incapacitation, that is, articles having no other real purpose, will include handcuffs, leg irons or a straitjacket: those adapted could include a scarf or a pair of tights knotted at intervals for use for strangulation, and those intended for such use might include drugs to induce sleep or handkerchieves or pads for use with chloroform.

If the article in question is made or adapted for causing injury to, or incapacitating, a person it will be necessary to prove no more than that a burglary was committed by that person and that he was in possession of such a weapon of offence at the time. If it is alleged he was in possession of an article which he intended to use to cause injury or to incapacitate, such as a walking stick or a belt, it would be necessary to prove his intention so to use it. In the absence of an admission, this is only likely to occur where he threatens someone in the building in such a way that he indicates an intention to use that weapon. For the purposes of aggravated burglary, an article not made or adapted to injure or incapacitate can be a weapon of offence, even if the necessary intent is only formed an instant before it is used to injure or incapacitate (which makes an interesting contrast to the different rule which applies to the offence of having an offensive weapon in a public place, described on pp 798-800). Thus, a burglar who uses a screwdriver to enter a house and, when confronted by the occupant, then (and only then) decides to use it offensively in order to steal commits aggravated burglary when he steals, because he will then have with him a weapon of offence. Likewise, a burglar who, when confronted by an occupant in a building, picks up a poker (or some other article which is not offensive in itself) from the fireplace and seriously injures the occupier with it commits aggravated burglary.

As in the case of 'firearm', the definition of 'explosive' indicates Parliament's intention to limit the application of the term to offences where one might allege realistically that the possession of the particular explosive added aggravation to the offence of burglary. This is clear from the fact that the definition requires the article to be manufactured, or intended by the person having it with him, for the purpose of producing a 'practical effect by explosion' and makes no reference to those things which cause a 'pyrotechnic effect' described in the Explosive Substances Act 1883. The section is not aimed at the burglar who buys some sparklers, or other amusing fireworks for his children, immediately prior to committing the offence. It is aimed at the person who enters a building as a trespasser with explosives which are to be used to open a safe or some other secured part of the premises.

In most cases, an offender under the present section intends to use the article to injure or incapacitate someone in the course of a burglary. However, this is not essential; it suffices that he had it with him for such use on another occasion (as, for example, where the burglary is in an empty house and the offender intends to use a cosh to enable him to hijack a get-away car).

Has with him at time of burglary

In order for a burglar to 'have with him' a firearm etc, he must be armed with it; it is not enough that it is readily accessible to him. Thus, if the firearm etc is carried not by the burglar but by an accomplice waiting outside the building, aggravated burglary is not committed. This is a stricter approach than is taken to the phrase 'has with him' in other offences where the term appears. In addition, he must know that he has it with him: a burglar does not have with him a cosh which somebody has slipped into his swag bag, unknown to him, for example.

The person charged with aggravated burglary must be shown to have had with him a relevant article *at the time of committing* the offence of burglary. This is important.

Where the burglary is alleged to have been committed by committing or attempting theft or the infliction of grievous bodily harm after entry as a trespasser, then the possession must be proved at the time at which the theft etc was committed or attempted, because that is the time at which the offence of burglary will have been committed. Where the burglary is alleged to have been committed by an entry with intent to commit one of the offences specified in s 9(1)(a), the accused must be proved to have been in possession at the time of entry, because that is the time at which the offence of burglary will have been committed. Thus, if a thief enters a building as a trespasser intending to steal and he has with him a cosh at the time of entry, he is guilty of aggravated burglary. The time of commission of the burglary is when he entered and a cosh is a weapon of offence per se. If he then only had with him a pocket knife, it would be very difficult to secure a conviction for aggravated burglary *at that point of time*, because—since a pocket knife is not a weapon of offence per se—it would have to be proved that at that point of time he intended to use that knife as a weapon of offence. However, if, confronted by the householder, he pulled out the knife and threatened him, this would be very strong evidence that when he entered he intended to use the knife as a weapon of offence and a conviction for aggravated burglary would be far more likely. Should a man enter a building without a weapon, merely intending to trespass and perhaps to sleep there, he is not guilty of an offence of burglary at that stage. If when confronted by a security guard, he punches him severely and breaks his jaw he is then guilty of burglary because he has inflicted grievous bodily harm on a person in the building after entering as a trespasser. However, had he entered unarmed and then fearing that he might be discovered, armed himself with a lever used for opening crates inside the building, which he subsequently used to strike the guard, causing him grievous bodily harm, he would be guilty of aggravated burglary. This is because he had the lever with him at the time of committing the burglary and the lever was clearly intended for use for causing injury (and was therefore a weapon of offence).

CHAPTER 39

Offences of fraud

In early times judges took an almost light-hearted attitude towards offences which are now described as offences of criminal deception. A judge said in 1704, 'Shall we indict one man for making a fool of another?'. However, attitudes have changed with the passage of time and the emergence of the professional cheat and we now have a multiplicity of offences of criminal deception resulting in the obtaining of property or of a pecuniary advantage or in the evasion of liabilities or the obtaining of services.

OBTAINING PROPERTY BY DECEPTION

The Theft Act 1968, s 15(1) states that any person who by any deception dishonestly obtains property belonging to another, with the intention of permanently depriving the other of it, commits an offence.

Actus reus

Deception

The basic element of the actus reus is a deception by the accused. Section 15(4) states that 'deception' means any deception (whether deliberate or reckless) by words or conduct as to fact or as to law, including a deception as to the present intentions of the person using the deception or any other person. There can be no deception unless a person has been deceived. The wording of s 15(4) requires further explanation.

Words or conduct A deception may be made by words or conduct. Either will allege that something is true, which in fact is untrue. In most circumstances this will be quite clear. An example of deception by words would be where the accused has described bottles of coloured water as whisky and as a result has obtained property, ie money, from the persons deceived. If a man knows that collectors visit certain houses every week to collect pools coupons and money on behalf of pools promoters and shoulders the same type of bag and dresses in similar fashion, it may only be necessary for him to knock on doors in order to be handed the coupons and the money; in such a case the deception is by conduct. If on any occasion the man is asked if he is an authorised collector and he says that he is, he will have added a further deception by words. A person who wears the trappings of a bookmaker at a race meeting and receives bets, intending not to honour successful wagers but to abscond with the money, commits a deception by conduct as to his present intentions.

The use of cheques as a means of deception needs to be examined. If a person steals a cheque book, signs the name of the account holder on a cheque and gives it to someone else, there are various factors to consider outside the possibilities of forgery. There is a deception by conduct in that such a person represents himself to be the account holder and therefore entitled to draw upon that account. If in answer to a question as to his identity he states that he is the person entitled to draw, the case is even stronger because a deception by words is thereby made.

A person who offers his own cheque which subsequently 'bounces' effects a deception by his conduct because the giver of a cheque impliedly represents that the state of facts existing at the date of delivery of the cheque is such that the cheque will be honoured in the ordinary course of events on presentation for payment on or after the date specified in the cheque and, if the cheque bounces, this implied representation, being untrue, constitutes a deception. It may be noted that the deception in such a case is not that the drawer then has sufficient funds in his account to meet the cheque; after all he may have an overdraft facility. Of course, the fact that a person obtains something by means of a 'bouncing' cheque does not necessarily make him guilty of an offence of deception, since he may lack the necessary mens rea discussed later.

Today, most cheques are supported by the use of a banker's card and cheques so supported are guaranteed by the banker provided certain conditions on the back of the cheque card are complied with, whether or not there are funds to meet them. The reason is that if someone (the drawer) offers to pay by cheque supported by a cheque card, and that offer is accepted, and the conditions on the cheque card are complied with, a contract is brought into effect between the payee and the bank whereby the bank is legally obliged to honour the cheque, and it is irrelevant that the drawer's authority to use the cheque card has been withdrawn or that he is exceeding it, or that the drawer was a thief (and not the authorised signatory) and had forged a signature resembling the authorised signatory's. In such a case, there will not be a deception of the type mentioned in the last paragraph. It could therefore be argued that when a person presents a cheque supported by a cheque card, there can never be a deception, since the implied representation that the circumstances are such that the cheque will be honoured is true. However, this is not so. A person who offers a cheque supported by a cheque card thereby represents to the person to whom the cheque is offered that in the circumstances he is actually authorised by the bank to use his card and thereby to oblige the bank to honour the cheque if it is accepted. Therefore, if he is not actually authorised to use the banker's card in those circumstances, either because his authority to use it has been withdrawn or because he is using it in excess of his authorisation or because he has stolen it, he is practising a deception as to that authority upon the person to whom that cheque is offered. A similar analysis applies to the use of credit cards.

The issue of selling goods which are defective is surrounded by a number of problems. A man may sell a motor car which has a defective engine but he may complete that sale without the condition of the engine being debated. The car is there to be examined and test driven by the customer if he wishes to do so. The vendor is not obliged by law to disclose the engine defect. He does not practise a deception by failing to do so. However, if he knows that the engine is defective but nevertheless assures the customer that it is in perfect working order, and thereby induces the customer to buy it, there is a deception by words as a result of which property (ie the purchase price) is obtained.

As to fact or law Most deceptions are in relation to fact. For example, the deceptions referred to above concerning cheques and cheque cards or the condition of a motor car are concerned with facts. Other common examples surround the claims made to social security officers. The woman, who falsely claims that she has lost her purse containing her husband's weekly pay and asks for assistance, obtains money by deception if help is given. Married women who are separated from their husbands may claim benefit for themselves and their children on the basis of there being no income from the husband coming in to the household. If the husband returns and once again contributes to the household budget, there is a deception by conduct each time money is drawn on the assumption that the woman is solely responsible for the family's upkeep. This amounts to a deception in relation to a fact.

Deceptions of law may occur, for example, in relation to wills, where advice is given by an adviser as to the legal meaning of terms within it or as to the validity of the instrument itself. If property is dishonestly obtained by such a deception, an offence is committed.

As to present intentions of the person using the deception or any other person For the purpose of offences of deception, a deception by words or conduct may be as to the present intentions of the person using the deception or any other person. If a man obtains the payment of money as a deposit for the fitting of double glazed windows to houses, which he has no intention of fitting, he obtains that money by deception as to his present intentions. The inclusion of the phrase 'or any other person' covers the situation in which one person (the accused) misrepresents the present intentions of another person. This would be so where a salesman was used to make false promises on the instructions of his employer, who had no intention of honouring such agreements at that time.

Disputes concerning payments for meals in restaurants frequently result in police officers being called. If a customer intended to pay when he ordered the meal, but discovers after he has eaten it that he has left his wallet at home, he cannot be said to have obtained the meal by deception. On the other hand, if he knew that he had no money when he entered the restaurant and had no intention of offering payment in any other way, he will have practised a deception by conduct as to his present intentions by sitting down and ordering from the menu since this conduct implies an intention to pay the price. However, for practical purposes, in the absence of an admission, it is almost impossible to prove that he did not intend to pay at the time of ordering the meal and that factor is always the important one.

Deception by omission The statutory provisions do not say whether or not a person can make a deception by omission, ie by not stating something, but the courts have held that there can be a deception by omission in three situations:

(a) Where a statement is a half-truth because, although it is literally correct, it omits a material matter, it constitutes a deception. For example, it would be a deception to say that one had a clean driving licence if one was awaiting sentence for a driving offence for which endorsement was mandatory.
(b) Where a statement is true when made but, to the knowledge of its maker, becomes untrue before it is acted upon by its recipient, it constitutes a deception. For example, if X, intending to pay, orders a meal in a restaurant but, before it is served, decides not to pay, X's initially true implied representation that he intends to pay will become a deception as to his intentions before the meal is served.

(c) If a person is under a legal duty to state something and his failure to do so deceives someone, this constitutes a deception. For example, a hospital consultant who is required to inform an NHS hospital if one of his patients is a private patient but fails to do so thereby practises a deception as to the status of his patient.

Obtains property belonging to another

In addition to proving deception, the prosecution must prove that it resulted in the accused obtaining property belonging to another. For this purpose, s 15(2) of the Act states that a person is treated as 'obtaining property' if he obtains ownership, possession or control of it, and that 'obtains' includes not only obtaining for oneself but also:

(a) obtaining for another, as where the accused gets money sent to a third party by telling lies; and
(b) enabling another to obtain or retain, as where the accused by deception persuades A to enter into a contract with B under which B receives money from A (enabling another to obtain) or by deception persuades A to allow B to remain in possession of property (enabling another to retain).

'Obtaining property' must hereafter be understood in this wide sense.

The Theft Act 1968, s 34(1) applies the definitions of 'property' and 'belonging to another' in ss 4(1) and 5(1) of the Act (which we have already come across in relation to theft) to the offence of obtaining property by deception. Therefore, 'property' includes money and all other property, real or personal, including things in action and other intangible property. Thus, land may be the subject of this offence, although generally it cannot be stolen.

At the time that ownership, possession or control of the property is obtained by deception the property must 'belong to another' and, by virtue of the application of s 5(1), this means that another person must have possession or control of it, or a proprietary right or interest in it. The effect of this definition can be seen from the following examples:

(a) S gives his watch to T, a jeweller, for repair, thereby transferring to T possession of the watch but retaining ownership of it. If S later recovers the watch by a deception, for example, falsely telling T's assistant that he has already paid for its repair, S obtains by deception property belonging to another because he obtains possession of property which is at that time in the possession of T.
(b) X lends his bicycle to Y, thereby transferring possession but not ownership to Y. If Y later persuades X to make a gift of the bicycle by a deception, Y obtains by deception property belonging to another because he obtains ownership of property of which X is at that time the owner (and therefore in which X has a proprietary right).

It is not enough for the prosecution to prove simply that there has been some sort of misrepresentation on the part of the accused and that he has obtained property belonging to another; it must also prove that the property was obtained as a result of the deception. What is said here about this requirement of a causal link between the deception and the 'obtaining' is equally applicable to the other offences of deception mentioned in this chapter. For the requirement to be satisfied:

Someone must have been deceived As already indicated there cannot be a deception unless someone is deceived. In the light of recent decisions it seems that a person can be deceived even though he is not induced positively to believe a false representation and that it is enough that he is ignorant of the truth and relies on the false representation.

The deception must operate on the mind of the person deceived and be the effective cause of the thing in question being obtained The result is this. If E makes a false representation to F, who sees through it or already knows the truth but transfers property to E (as E intended) *in order to entrap him*, E cannot be convicted of obtaining the property by deception (because someone must have been deceived), although he can be convicted of attempting to commit that offence. On the other hand the Court of Appeal has held that if the deception is the effective cause of the property being obtained, it is irrelevant that at the final moment the victim suspected or even believed that he had been swindled. In the case in question an unlicensed taxi driver picked up foreign passengers at airports, falsely representing by his conduct that he was a taxi driver, that his vehicle was a proper taxi and that the fares would be reasonable. On reaching the destinations he charged grossly inflated fares; ten times the normal fare in one case. By the end of the journey, when the money was handed over, the passengers suspected that the taxi driver was not genuine but felt under a compulsion or obligation to pay the extortionate prices. Dismissing the unlicensed taxi driver's application for leave to appeal against conviction for obtaining the fares by deception, the Court of Appeal stated the principle just set out and held that the jury had been properly directed. The application of the present principle is likely to cause a jury difficult mental gymnastics in a case such as the one referred to. In such a case it may be wise to prefer an additional charge of theft or simply to charge theft.

If the deception occurs after the obtaining, or if the person deceived is indifferent as to the matter to which the deception relates and pays no regard to it in transferring the property, the person making the deception cannot be convicted of obtaining the property by deception (because the deception must operate on the mind of the person deceived), although in the latter case he could be convicted of an attempt. Therefore, where a man obtained petrol at a self-service station, then told the attendant to charge the petrol to the account of his former employer, the offence was not committed as the representation was made subsequent to the obtaining of petrol.

It is obviously important that police officers making inquiries into deception offences ensure that information is included in the statement of the person who has parted with the property etc as to the effect of the accused's words or conduct upon him.

Mens rea

Three elements of mens rea must be proved by the prosecution, that:

(a) the accused made his deception deliberately or recklessly;
(b) the accused obtained the property dishonestly; and
(c) the accused intended permanently to deprive the other (ie a person to whom the property obtained belonged) of it.

In relation to element (c), suffice it to say that what was said about the corresponding element in theft is equally applicable here; in particular the extended meaning of 'intention of permanently depriving' in s 6 applies to the present offence. The other two elements require more discussion.

Deliberate or reckless

The inclusion of both words means that there is no need to prove beyond reasonable doubt that the accused knew that he was making a deception. It is sufficient that he is reckless concerning the truth of his representation. If the deception is deliberate, it is made in the knowledge of the falsity of the statement. A man who sells rings made of base metal, knowingly misrepresenting them to be 9 ct gold, practises a deliberate deception. He tells a deliberate lie, in words, as to an existing fact—the quality of the rings. If he is uncertain as to the nature of the metal and suspects that it may be base, he is reckless if he claims that it is gold and is guilty of this offence. However, it is necessary to distinguish between recklessness and negligence. If an accused believes a statement to be true, even though most men would have easily recognised its falsity, he is not guilty of this offence as at the most he has been negligent. Recklessness in this context involves much more than negligence; it bears its subjective meaning and involves awareness of the possibility of a deception. Therefore, if the rings would have appeared to be of base metal to most men, but were not so recognised by the accused, he is not guilty of a reckless deception as there was no awareness on his part of the possibility that what he was saying was false. The legal position is also interesting when one considers the situation in which a man tells what he believes to be a lie, but which subsequently proves to be true. By doing so he cannot be guilty of the offence as, although he had a guilty state of mind, there was no actus reus because what he said was not a deception. However, such a person could be convicted of an attempt to obtain by deception.

Dishonesty

The partial definition of the term 'dishonesty' provided by the Theft Act 1968, s 2 does not apply to offences contrary to s 15. Instead, the question of dishonesty is always one of fact for the jury or the justices. They must consider whether the obtaining was dishonest according to the current standards of ordinary decent people. If it was not, the accused must be acquitted. If it was, the jury must consider whether the accused must have realised that the obtaining was dishonest by those standards. If they answer this in the negative the accused must be acquitted; only if they find that the accused must have so realised, can they find that the obtaining was dishonest.

OBTAINING A MONEY TRANSFER BY DECEPTION

A person who obtains a bank credit by deception does not commit an offence under s 15 of the Theft Act 1968. The reason is that the credit obtained (a thing in action, a right to sue his bank for the money) has not previously belonged to another. However, he can be convicted of obtaining a money transfer by deception, contrary to the Theft Act 1968, s 15A, inserted by the Theft (Amendment) Act 1996.

Section 15A provides that a person is guilty of an offence if, by any deception, he dishonestly obtains a money transfer for himself or another.

Actus reus

Deception bears the same meaning as in s 15. The deception must result in the consequence that a 'money transfer' is obtained for the accused or another. It is not an offence by deception dishonestly to enable another to obtain a money transfer (whereas it is an offence under s 15 in respect of property belonging to another). The requirements of causation are the same as in respect of an offence under s 15.

By s 15A(2) of the Theft Act 1968, a money transfer occurs when:

(a)   a debit is made to one account,
(b)   a credit is made to another, and
(c)   a credit results from the debit or the debit results from the credit.

For this purpose, an 'account' means an account kept with:

(a)   a bank; or
(b)   a person carrying on a business within s 15B(4) of the Theft Act 1968.

A business falls within s 15B(4) if:

(a)   in the course of the business money received by way of deposit is lent to others;
      or
(b)   any other activity of the business is financed, wholly or to any material extent, out
      of the capital of or the interest on money received by way of deposit.

For the purpose of s 15B(4) 'money' is not limited to sterling; it includes any other currency and the European currency unit (the 'ecu').

The references to 'credit' and 'debit' in s 15A(2) are explained by s 15A(3), which states that they are references to credit or debit of an amount of money. Credits or debits in terms of other choses in action, such as securities, are not caught.

Section 15A(4) provides that it is immaterial whether:

(a)   the amount credited is the same as the amount debited;
(b)   whether the money transfer is effected on presentment of a cheque or by another
      method;
(c)   whether any delay occurs in the process by which the money transfer is effected;
(d)   whether any intermediate credits or debits are made in the course of the money
      transfer;
(e)   whether either of the accounts is overdrawn before or after the money transfer is
      effected.

Thus, without prejudice to other 'defences' being invalid, it is no defence for the accused to raise one of these five points.

The offence under s 15A is primarily aimed at the transfer of funds by telegraphic or electronic means, but it is not limited to this. Where a deception results in the obtaining of a cheque, there is an overlap with an offence under s 15, as explained above, although an offence under s 15A is only committed when the money transfer is effected on presentation of the cheque for payment into an account, ie when the cheque is honoured and an account credited. Where a cheque is cashed an offence is not committed under s 15A because there is not a money transfer under s 15A(2).

Mens rea

The accused must have:

(a)   made his deception deliberately or recklessly (s 15 applies to this offence); and
(b)   obtained for himself or another the money transfer dishonestly.

The comments about these requirements made above in relation to obtaining property by deception are equally applicable here.

OBTAINING A PECUNIARY ADVANTAGE BY DECEPTION

The Theft Act 1968, s 16 states that it is an offence for a person by any deception dishonestly to obtain for himself or another any pecuniary advantage.

Deception in this context has the same meaning as in obtaining property by deception, and it must be a cause of the pecuniary advantage being obtained by the accused (the maker of the deception) or another. The cases in which a pecuniary advantage is to be regarded as obtained for a person are cases where, as described in sub-s (2):

(a)   he is allowed to borrow by way of overdraft, or to take out any policy of insurance or annuity contract, or obtains an improvement of the terms on which he is allowed to do so; or
(b)   he is given the opportunity to earn remuneration or greater remuneration in an office or employment, or to win money by betting.

It is important to recognise that these are the only cases where a pecuniary advantage is regarded as obtained for the purpose of s 16. It is essential that the nature of the pecuniary advantage obtained is specified in the charge and care must therefore be taken to include quite specific details in statements taken from those who have been deceived. It is not necessary that the pecuniary advantage should have been obtained from the person deceived.

Overdrafts, insurance or improved terms

The section is limited to quite specific pecuniary advantages, one of which is being allowed to borrow by way of overdraft. An overdraft exists where a bank account is in debit, and a person borrows by way of overdraft when cheques drawn by him against his bank account are honoured by the bank although that account is in debit. This is the essential difference between a borrowing by overdraft and borrowing by a bank loan, and this section is only concerned with overdrafts. A person who receives a sum of money from a bank as a result of deception obtains property by that deception and should be dealt with under s 15. In comparison, a person who by deception obtains a borrowing by overdraft does not actually receive any money and could not therefore be convicted under s 15. He obtains a 'pecuniary advantage' rather than property.

Although s 16(2) speaks of a person being 'allowed' to borrow by way of overdraft, it is not necessary that there should be any consent on the part of the bank to a borrowing (or increased borrowing) by overdraft. It follows, for example, that, where a bank account is already overdrawn and the holder of the account has been informed that he must not use his cheque card until the overdraft has been cleared, that person obtains a pecuniary advantage by deception if he continues to use that card (since this is a deception of the shopkeeper or the like) because (assuming the conditions on the card are satisfied) the bank will have to honour the cheque, their debit on his bank account will increase and he therefore obtains from the bank the opportunity to borrow further by way of overdraft. Similarly, a person whose bank account is overdrawn and who uses a cheque card to obtain money in excess of the overdraft limit permitted by the bank thereby obtains the opportunity to borrow by way of overdraft. Where this is done dishonestly he is guilty of this offence. If the use of the card in conjunction with a cheque drawn on a British bank occurs abroad, the offence is still triable in England or Wales because that is where the obtaining of the opportunity to borrow by overdraft occurs.

A pecuniary advantage is also regarded as obtained where a person is allowed to take out an insurance policy or annuity contract, or obtains an improvement in the terms on which he is allowed to do so. Insurance companies are particularly vulnerable in cases where favourable terms are obtained due to false statements. Large sums of money may be involved and the essence of the offence is that the terms would have been considerably different had all of the circumstances been known.

Opportunity to earn remuneration or greater remuneration, or to win money by betting

There are two types of pecuniary advantage under this heading. The first is where the person obtains the opportunity to earn remuneration or greater remuneration in an office or employment. 'Employment' is widely defined; a person who obtains work in a self-employed capacity (eg as an auditor or as a builder) is given the opportunity to earn remuneration in an employment for the purposes of s 16. On the other hand a person would not be guilty if he got the tenancy of a pub by deception, since that is not an 'office or employment'.

If a person applies for an advertised job which demands that applicants must be the holders of a particular degree, he commits the offence of obtaining a pecuniary advantage by deception if he dishonestly obtains the job as a result of a deception that he has the degree. He attempts to commit the offence if he is unsuccessful. There are many professions in which increments of salary are available to persons who hold particular qualifications. A person would be guilty of this offence if he dishonestly obtained an increment by falsely alleging that he was in possession of such qualifications.

The second type of pecuniary advantage under the present heading is where a person is given the opportunity to earn money by betting.

The operation of these provisions can be illustrated as follows.

The definition of 'pecuniary advantage' extends protection to bookmakers because most bookmakers extend credit facilities to clients and will accept bets by telephone. The section places the bookmaker in very much the same position as the bank manager. It is not, however, limited to this type of betting transaction. If a bookmaker or betting shop assistant is dishonestly deceived into allowing a person to place a bet, the deceiver has obtained a pecuniary advantage. The pecuniary advantage consists merely of being given the opportunity to win money by betting; it is irrelevant whether the bet is successful.

Mens rea

The mens rea required for an offence under s 16 is that the accused must have made the deception deliberately or recklessly and have obtained the pecuniary advantage dishonestly. Those terms have the same meaning as in the case of obtaining property by deception.

OBTAINING SERVICES BY DECEPTION

We have so far considered the offences related to obtaining property or forms of pecuniary advantage by means of deception. The public are thereby protected from those who would trick them out of their property, and banks, insurance companies, employers and bookmakers are protected against being tricked into conferring a 'pecuniary advantage'.

However, these offences are not sufficient to deal with all the contexts in which deceptions deserving punishment occur. Consequently, the offences of obtaining services by deception and evasion of liability by deception are provided by the Theft Act 1978, ss 1 and 2.

The Theft Act 1978, s 1(1) provides that a person is guilty of an offence if by any deception he dishonestly obtains services from another. 'Deception' in this context has the same meaning as in obtaining property by deception. The deception need not relate to the question of payment. It must be the cause of the services being obtained by the accused (the person making the deception) or another.

Obtaining of services

Section 1(2) defines what constitutes an obtaining of services. It states that it is an obtaining of services where the other is induced to confer a benefit by doing some act, or causing or permitting some act to be done, on the understanding that the benefit has been or will be paid for. This definition requires two conditions to be satisfied:

(a) the accused's deception must induce the other actually to confer a benefit by doing some act, or causing some act to be done by another, or by permitting some act to be done by the accused or another. Examples are where by deception the accused induces the other to repair his car (or X's car) or to give him a taxi ride or a haircut (because he induces the other to confer a benefit by doing an act); where by deception the accused induces the other to tell one of his employees to repair the accused's car or give him (or X) a taxi ride or a haircut (because he induces the other to confer a benefit by causing an act to be done); and where by deception the accused induces the other to let him (or X) enter a football ground without paying (because he induces the other to confer a benefit by permitting some act to be done); and

(b) the benefit conferred in one of the above three ways must be conferred on the basis that it has been or will be paid for. It is not an offence to obtain free services by deception. If A by deception gets B, a taxi driver, to drive him to the station he will obtain services by deception because the benefit conferred is conferred on the understanding that it will be paid for. But if A by deception gets C, his neighbour, to drive him to the station free of charge he will not obtain services by deception because the benefit was not conferred on the understanding that it would be paid for.

It does not matter that the transaction under which the benefit is conferred involves a contract which is illegal or otherwise unenforceable. Thus a man who by deception (eg as to his intention to pay) induces a prostitute to provide him with her professional services may be convicted of the present offence despite the fact that the contract with her is illegal and unenforceable.

Section 1(3) provides that, without prejudice to the generality of sub-s (2), it is an obtaining of services where the other is induced to make a loan, or cause or permit a loan to be made, on the understanding that any payment (whether by way of interest or otherwise) will be or has been made in respect of the loan. This subsection was added by the Theft (Amendment) Act 1996 to overcome a ruling that a mortgage advance could not be described as a service within the provisions of s 1 of the 1978 Act.

Mens rea

The mens rea which the prosecution must prove is that the accused made his deception deliberately or recklessly, and obtained the services dishonestly. What we said about these terms when discussing obtaining property by deception is equally applicable to the present offence.

Overlap with s 15 of 1968 Act

Sometimes a person who obtains a service by deception may also obtain property. Normally it is better to charge under the Theft Act 1978, s 1 in such a case, and not to charge under the Theft Act 1968, s 15 for reasons which are illustrated by the following example.

In circumstances in which a person books into a hotel by deceiving the receptionist into believing that he intends to pay, he obtains a service because he is permitted to stay in the hotel on the understanding that this will be paid for, but he does not thereby obtain property because a stay in a hotel is not 'property' for the purpose of s 15 of the 1968 Act. In the morning such a person will normally be given breakfast and this can be described as property. However, this property has not been obtained by deception since the waiter is not deceived into supplying the breakfast by any words or conduct of the guest, he supplies it because he believes him to be a guest in the hotel and that is true. It would be different if the person had not stayed overnight in the hotel and had gone into the dining room pretending to be a guest.

EVASION OF LIABILITY BY DECEPTION

Section 2(1) of the 1978 Act deals with three offences which are concerned with evading by deception a liability to pay money. The section states that where a person by any deception:

(a) dishonestly secures the remission of the whole or part of any existing liability to make payment, whether his own liability or another's; or
(b) with intent to make permanent default in whole or in part on any existing liability to make payment, or with intent to let another do so, dishonestly induces the creditor or any person claiming payment on behalf of the creditor to wait for payment (whether or not the due date for payment is deferred) or to forgo payment; or
(c) dishonestly obtains any exemption from or abatement of liability to make payment,

he is guilty of an offence.

There are certain common features which emerge from these provisions and it is helpful to bear them in mind as each of these paragraphs is examined. All three offences require a deliberate or reckless deception; the deception must result in one of the specified types of evasion of a liability to make a payment; and there must be dishonesty. Although there are also substantial differences between the offences, it can often happen that the particular circumstances of a case under investigation fit into more than one of these offences.

A 'liability' to make a payment for the purpose of the section is a legally enforceable liability. Therefore the section cannot apply to the 'evasion' of gambling debts or money owed to a prostitute for her services. A liability to pay compensation for an injury is not a liability to make a payment for the purpose of the section if the liability to pay has not been established (in a court) or accepted (by the alleged wrongdoer).

The liability to pay evaded may be the liability of someone other than the accused. What was said in relation to obtaining property by deception is equally relevant here to the elements of 'deliberate or reckless deception' and of 'dishonesty' in s 2. The other elements in s 2 are best dealt with by taking the offences separately.

Remission of liability (s 2(1)(a))

What is required is a dishonest deception by the accused which results in the remission either wholly or in part of an *existing* liability to make payment, whether his own liability or another's. A person secures the remission in whole or in part of a liability to pay if he gets the person to whom the money is payable to agree to extinguish the debt in whole or in part, as where A persuades B, who has lent him money, to agree that the loan need never be repaid (or a lesser sum be repaid), by telling him a false hard-luck story. On the other hand, if C deceives D into believing that a debt has already been paid (or is less than it actually is), C will not have secured the remission of a liability to pay because the creditor cannot be said to agree to extinguish a debt (in whole or part) when he is simply led to believe that it no longer exists (or that it is less than it actually is). The offence of forgoing payment, mentioned below, is the relevant one there.

The offence differs from that provided by s 1 in relation to the advantage gained by the deception. If a man takes his television set to be repaired and deceives the repairer into believing that he will be paid, he obtains a service by deception. In circumstances where the placing of the set for repair is honest, in that there is then an intention to pay, the present offence will be committed if the repairer is subsequently persuaded by means of a deception to remit the whole or part of his repair charge.

Another example of the remission of a debt by means of deception is where a debtor gives a false story to his creditors to the effect that his business is in financial difficulties and that it may therefore be in their interest to accept one-half of what is owed in full settlement of those debts, and the creditors agree to this. In such a case the debt is remitted in part as a result of a deliberate deception and, provided the remission is secured dishonestly, the debtor is guilty of an offence. Even if the debtor hopes that he may be able to pay the part of the debt remitted at some later date, the absence of the words 'with intent to make permanent default' from this offence makes that state of mind irrelevant unless in all the circumstances the justices or jury find that the remission has not been secured dishonestly.

Wait for or forgo payment (s 2(1)(b))

It is probably helpful at this stage to recapitulate upon matters already considered. In s 1 we were concerned with services which were obtained by means of deception and in s 2(1)(a) we considered debts which were cancelled or reduced as a result of deception. Section 2(1)(b) is concerned with deceptions which cause creditors to wait for or forgo payment of an *existing liability to pay*.

Unlike 'remission' in the offence dealt with above, 'forgoing' and 'waiting' do not require that the creditor or person claiming payment on his behalf should agree to forgo or wait for payment.

A person is induced by deception to forgo payment if the deception causes him to give up waiting for payment and (although he does not necessarily agree to extinguish it) to write off the debt, or if he is convinced by the deception that there is no liability to pay.

A person is induced by deception to wait for payment if the deception induces him not to enforce payment for the time being (whether or not the due date for payment is deferred), and in this context s 2(3) of the 1978 Act is of great importance. It provides that a person induced to take a cheque or other security for money by way of conditional satisfaction of an existing liability is to be treated not as being paid but as being induced to wait for payment. It follows that a person, who owes another money and gives him a cheque which (as he knows will happen) is not honoured in due course by his bank, induces the creditor by deception to wait for payment, even though the creditor thinks he is being paid and does not agree to give time to pay.

The mens rea required is more involved than in the other offences under s 2 since it is not enough merely that the accused's deception was deliberate or reckless and that he dishonestly induced the creditor etc to wait for or forgo payment. In addition, the accused must intend to make permanent default, in whole or in part on any existing liability of his to make a payment, or with intent to let another do so.

To consider the position of the man who pays off his debt with a worthless cheque: he knows that the cheque is worthless and his purpose is apparently to satisfy the demands of his creditor. If that is his only intention then, although this causes the creditor to wait for payment by means of a deception, that is the worthless cheque, he knows that he will still have to pay. Unless there is clear evidence that he does not intend to pay in the future, there is no evidence of an intention to make permanent default and no offence is committed. If, having paid with a worthless cheque, the debtor then left his home, leaving no forwarding address, this is some evidence of an intention to make permanent default.

It is interesting at this stage once again to consider the position of those who fail to pay for meals in restaurants. If they enter without the intention of paying and deceive the proprietor or a member of staff, usually by means of their conduct, as to their intentions, they obtain property by means of deception contrary to s 15 of the 1968 Act. In no way can s 16 of the 1968 Act apply as the obtaining of a meal is not the obtaining of a pecuniary advantage. What offence is committed, therefore, by those who enter intending to pay, and therefore do not deceive at the time the meal is supplied? This will depend upon their conduct. If they allege that they were dissatisfied with the meal and provide evidence of their identity so that the proprietor may pursue a civil remedy to obtain his money, they commit no offence. However, should they deceive by alleging that they have already paid the bill, they are practising a deception with intent to make permanent default on payment. The most appropriate charge is s 2(1)(b); that is dishonestly inducing the proprietor to forgo payment. He is deceived into forgoing his charge, that is giving up his claim to a debt which does exist, because he is falsely induced to believe it does not exist. To prove an offence in these circumstances contrary to s 2(1)(a) it would be necessary to show that the proprietor agreed to waive a debt which was known by all parties still to exist.

Exemption or abatement (s 2(1)(c))

Section 2(1)(c) makes it an offence for a person dishonestly to obtain any exemption from or abatement of liability to make a payment. This is in keeping with the general purpose of the 1978 Act which is concerned with deceptions leading to concessions rather than the obtaining of particular property. Unlike the other offences under s 2, s 2(1)(c) is not limited to the 'evasion' of an existing liability to pay since it also covers the 'evasion' by deception of a liability to pay which *does not yet, and never does, exist*. Like 'remission' in s 2(1)(c), 'exemption' and 'abatement' require that the 'creditor' should agree to let someone off the liability to pay (exemption) or reduce the amount which must be paid (abatement). If someone obtains a discount on the price of a package holiday by announcing when he goes to book it that he is an old age pensioner, he commits this offence if that story is false and he acts dishonestly. He does not receive any property as a result of his deception but he does obtain the abatement of a liability to pay. The same can be said about those who submit false claims to an inspector of taxes. If pensioners are permitted to travel at half-price on local buses, use of a pensioner's bus pass by someone else would lead to an abatement of liability by deception. A consultant who had a duty to give information to an NHS hospital concerning patient services received, but who deliberately and dishonestly refrained from giving that information, was held to be guilty of this offence because by his deception by omission he had obtained exemption from patient charges which would otherwise have arisen.

The Act says that in this offence the word 'obtains' includes obtaining for another or enabling another to obtain. This extension of the meaning of 'obtains' covers the circumstances in which false claims are submitted by the accused on behalf of some other person, for example, an accountant on behalf of his client, or an administrative officer of a company who obtains tax exemption for employees who are supplied with company vehicles by alleging that such vehicles are not supplied for private use by those employees.

The mens rea required for the present offence is that the accused must make his deception deliberately or recklessly and dishonestly obtain etc the exemption or abatement. There is no mental requirement corresponding to that of intent to make permanent default in s 2(1)(b).

MAKING OFF WITHOUT PAYMENT

Although not without its problems, s 3 of the 1978 Act is particularly helpful to those charged with the enforcement of the law in situations in which immediate action is essential. The section provides that a person who, knowing that payment on the spot for any goods supplied or service done is required or expected from him, dishonestly makes off without having paid as required or expected and with intent to avoid payment of the amount due is guilty of an offence. The section covers those circumstances generally referred to as 'bilking', for example leaving a restaurant without paying for a meal or leaving a self-service petrol station without paying for petrol received. These provisions are useful in that they cover opportunist offences in which it will often be difficult to prove that any particular intention existed at the time that the goods were supplied or the service was done (so that a deception as to intention cannot be proved). The payment which is required must be one which is legally enforceable. There is no reference to deception in s 3 and the only dishonesty which needs to be shown is that which existed at the time of 'making off'. Dishonesty is a question of fact for the jury or justices and is approached in the same way as in offences of deception. It has been held by the House of Lords that an intention to evade payment *altogether* is part of the mental element to be proved by the prosecution. This is not unreasonable as it is relevant to the issue of 'dishonesty'.

Police officers are frequently called to incidents involving 'making off'. It is common in respect of restaurants where late night revellers eat well and look for opportunities to escape from the restaurant without paying. Restaurants demand payment on the spot from casual customers and this is well known by all. Officers called to such incidents need only be concerned with whether or not the persons concerned made off without paying and with intent to avoid payment. If they ran through the door and into the street that intention is quite obvious. In circumstances in which they discovered that they did not have sufficient money to pay, but gave their correct names and addresses to the proprietor and insisted upon leaving, they will certainly have made off without paying but their conduct does not indicate that they did so dishonestly nor with an intention to avoid payment.

The other common incident involves the self-service petrol station. These stations make it quite clear that payment is demanded on the spot, by posting notices which declare that self-service is in operation and that payment should be made at the kiosk. A motorist who drives out of such a station without paying will experience considerable difficulty in persuading a jury that his actions were not dishonest and not done with intent to avoid payment (although, of course, the onus of proving the offence is on the prosecution). Once again, it would be different if he left his name and address, together with the registration number of his car, with the attendant in the kiosk.

The words 'make off without payment' involve a departure without paying from the place where payment would normally be made. For example, in the case of a taxi, payment may be made while sitting in it or standing at the window and it can therefore be an offence to make off from either place without paying.

The person who is alleged to have made off without payment must be a person who knew that payment on the spot would be demanded from him. If Hales invites three friends to accompany him for a meal and promises to pay the total bill, his three friends do not know that payment will be expected from them. In such circumstances, Hales is the only one to commit this offence if the party leaves without paying.

The section differentiates between transactions which are on the spot cash transactions and those which involve trade credit. If an employee of a garage proprietor goes to his employer's wholesaler, collects spare parts and leaves without signing the invoice, he does not commit an offence. The wholesaler will send an account to the employer; payment was not expected on the spot. However, if such an employee went to an auto discount store at which all transactions were cash transactions and was given goods and then saw the opportunity to leave without paying, he would be guilty of this offence if he left with the intention of avoiding payment.

The term 'knowing that payment on the spot is required or expected' relates to the knowledge an accused must have of when payment must be made. It includes payment at the time of collecting goods on which work has been done or in respect of which a service has been provided. Therefore, a man who collects a radio set which has been repaired and makes off without paying will be guilty of the offence if he knows that payment on the spot is demanded. However, the section does not apply if the payment required or expected is not legally due (eg because the person demanding it is seriously in breach of contract). Nor does the section apply to the supplying of goods or the doing of services which is contrary to the law nor where the service done is such that payment is not enforceable. Consequently, for example, the offence is not committed by the man who makes off without paying a prostitute for services rendered.

Section 3 is not concerned with worthless cheques other than forged ones, because payment by a 'bouncing' cheque (other than a forged one) amounts to payment for present purposes. If a worthless cheque is tendered then offences will be committed contrary to ss 1 or 2 of the 1978 Act or s 15 of the 1968 Act, depending upon what is obtained, as the use of a worthless cheque can amount to a deception.

POLICE POWERS

All the offences of criminal deception contrary to the 1968 to 1978 Acts are arrestable offences, but that of making off without payment is not an arrestable offence.

FALSE ACCOUNTING

The offences of false accounting contrary to the Theft Act 1968, s 17 are not restricted to clerks and other people who are employed in the traditional sense for the purpose of book-keeping. The falsity need not necessarily be with a view to gain since it is sufficient that the falsity is accompanied by an intent to cause loss to another.

Section 17(1) states that:

'Where a person dishonestly, with a view to gain for himself or another or with intent to cause loss to another,
(a) destroys, defaces, conceals or falsifies any account or any record or document made or required for any accounting purpose, or
(b) in furnishing information for any purpose produces or makes use of any account, or any such record or document as aforesaid, which to his knowledge is or may be misleading, false or deceptive in a material particular,'

he is guilty of an offence. Such an offence is an arrestable one.

Section 17(1) creates two quite separate and distinct offences which might be described as the falsification of accounts (s 17(1)(a)) and the use of false or deceptive accounts (s 17(1)(b)). Before examining these offences separately a number of points can be made which apply to both of them.

Mens rea

For the purposes of either type of offence, the accused's conduct must be carried out dishonestly and with a view to gain for himself or another or with intent to cause loss to another. 'Dishonesty' in this context is understood in the same way as in the offences of deception. 'With a view to gain . . . or with intent to cause loss . . .' bears the same meaning as in blackmail.

Account, record or document made or required for any accounting purpose

Another general point is that the acts specified by s 17(1)(a) and (b) must be done in relation to 'any account, record or document made or required for any accounting purpose'. These terms should be given their ordinary meaning. An accounts book, balance sheet or a payroll record is made for an accounting purpose. That is the reason for its existence; it has no other real purpose as it can be used for little other than the keeping of accounts. Documents may be required for an accounting purpose, even though they have other purposes as well as an accounting purpose. For example, a delivery note is for the purpose of allowing the recipient of goods to check that all of the goods ordered have been delivered, but a firm may use that delivery note as an accounting document to be retained in the storeroom to account for stock in excess of that recorded on inventories or stock sheets. Until the additional stock is recorded on an inventory or stock sheet, the delivery note will provide the only account for its presence should an audit take place. It will therefore be used for an accounting purpose at that time. As a further example, a housing benefit claim form which contained the only information used to calculate housing benefit has been held to be a document required for an accounting purpose, despite the fact that it is also used to determine entitlement to benefit.

The forbidden acts relate to accounts, records or documents made or required for an accounting purpose. The terms 'account' or 'record' are wide enough to cover an account or record produced by a mechanical device, such as a taxi meter or the turnstile at a soccer ground which records the number of persons admitted so that the entries may be related to the money collected. The falsification of such an account or record is therefore punishable if done dishonestly and with a view to gain or loss. We now turn to the separate requirements of the two offences.

Falsification of accounts (s 17(1)(a))

What is required here is the destruction, defacement, concealment or falsification of any account etc. If entry to a cinema is recorded by the issue of a ticket by a process which produces a duplicate copy on a roll, the destruction of any part of that record, if carried out with the necessary intent, would be an offence. If some of the duplicate copies were not handed over to the manager so that a false total figure could be shown to cover deficiencies, those copies would be 'concealed' for the purposes of this section. If, to cover deficiencies in the accounts, a corrosive liquid, or other damaging agent, was applied to the duplicate records, this would amount to a defacement. However, the most common offence is always likely to be the falsification of figures in an account, record or document. 'Falsification' covers the preparation of false accounts, as well as the falsification of existing ones.

Section 17(2) states that a person who makes or concurs in making in an account or other document an entry which is or may be misleading, false or deceptive in a material particular, or who omits or concurs in omitting a material particular from an account or other document, is to be treated as falsifying the account or document. However, this is not an exclusive definition of falsification. In one case, it has been held that a turnstile operator, who allowed two people through the turnstile while only recording one of them, falsified the record. It may be that the falsification was within s 17(2) (by omitting a material particular) but if not there was a 'falsification' within the ordinary meaning of that term.

A person can falsify an accounting document by completely failing to fill in a blank form required for an accounting purpose, and even though the particular document so falsified cannot be identified. This surprising ruling was made by the Court of Appeal in a case where it upheld the conviction of an international telephone operator who had failed to log calls on the forms provided for this purpose. The court held that, as soon as a call was made, it was the operator's duty to fill in one of the forms in a pile in front of him and that thereby one of them became a document required for an accounting purpose and the fact that the particular form could not be identified (since the operator might not have chosen to use the first form) did not matter.

Use of false or deceptive account (s 17(1)(b))

Whereas s 17(1)(a) is concerned with those who falsify or destroy etc any account etc, s 17(1)(b) deals with those who, in furnishing information for any purpose, produce or make use of any account or any record or document made or required for any accounting purpose, *knowing* it is or may be misleading, false or deceptive in a material particular.

Of course, a person who has falsified an account contrary to s 17(1)(a) may go on to use it contrary to s 17(1)(b), in which case he will have committed both offences. However, an offence under s 17(1)(b) may also be committed by a person who has not falsified the document in question, for it is not uncommon for persons with a view to gain to use in a dishonest way documents which have been made out erroneously by someone else. If a person, who is entitled to receive payment for money which he has spent on petrol for use in his firm's car, receives a receipt which he knows has been wrongly made out for a higher amount, he commits an offence against s 17(1)(b) if, when making out his claim (furnishing information), he makes use of that receipt since, to his *knowledge*, it is or may be misleading, false or deceptive in a material particular. However, if that employee had not noticed that the receipt was incorrect his actions would not be dishonest, nor would he have the necessary knowledge.

LIABILITY OF COMPANY DIRECTORS FOR OFFENCES OF DECEPTION OR OF FALSE ACCOUNTING

Special provision is made for cases where an offence is committed by a company or other corporate body under ss 15, 16 or 17 of the 1968 Act or under ss 1 or 2 of the 1978 Act through the act and state of mind of one of its 'controlling officers' being attributed to it. That officer will, of course, be liable for the relevant offence under general principles. In addition, it is specially provided that if the offence is committed with the consent or connivance of any director, manager, secretary or other similar officer of the body corporate, or any person purporting to act in any such capacity, he is also guilty of that offence.

COMPUTER MISUSE

The misuse of computer hardware or software may involve one or more of the offences described elsewhere in this book. For example, a person who falsifies the data in an account held on computer by inputting false information can be convicted of falsification of accounts, contrary to the Theft Act 1968, s 17, if he acts with a view to gain or intent to cause loss.

In addition, the misuse of computer hardware or software may involve one or more of three offences under the Computer Misuse Act 1990:

(a)   unauthorised access to computer material;
(b)   unauthorised access with intent to commit or facilitate commission of a further offence;
(c)   unauthorised modification of computer material.

Unauthorised access to computer material

By s 1(1) of the 1990 Act, a person commits an offence if:

(a)   he causes a computer to perform any function with intent to secure access to any program or data held in the computer;
(b)   the access he intends to secure is unauthorised; and
(c)   he knows at the time when he causes the computer to perform the function that that is the case.

The intended access need not relate to any particular program or data or any particular type of program or data, nor to a program or data held in any particular computer. It is immaterial whether the program or data is unauthorisedly accessed directly from the computer containing it or indirectly via another computer.

The scope of this offence is wide, since it covers all forms of computer hacking. Indeed, actual access to any program or data held in a computer is not required, since it is enough that the accused simply causes a computer to perform a function with intent to secure access to a program or data held in it, that intended access being unauthorised to his knowledge.

Access to a program or data is secured by a person if, by causing a computer to perform any function, he:

(a) alters or erases the program or data;
(b) copies or moves it to any storage medium other than that in which it is held or to a different location in the storage medium in which it is held;
(c) uses it; or
(d) has it output from the computer in which it is held (whether by having it displayed or in any other manner).

Intent to secure access to a program or data is to be understood accordingly.

Despite its width the offence does not cover computer eavesdropping; mere surveillance of data displayed on a VDU screen is not enough since the accused must cause the computer to perform a function if he is to be guilty.

In relation to the requirement that the intended access to any program or data held in a computer must be unauthorised, access of any kind by a person is unauthorised if he is not entitled to *control* access of the kind in question to the program or data *and* he does not have consent to such access from any person who is so entitled. Thus all hackers, honest or dishonest, are caught; it does not matter that the accused was seeking access merely out of curiosity or for the challenge and excitement of breaking through a security system designed to restrict access. It is important to stress that access by a person is only authorised where there is appropriate entitlement or consent to access of the kind in question to the program or data. Access by a person entitled to control access of the kind in question is not unauthorised even though he accesses the program or data for an unauthorised purpose.

Unauthorised access with intent

By s 2(1) of the 1990 Act, a person commits an arrestable offence if he commits the unauthorised access offence under s 1 with intent:

(a) to commit an offence to which this section applies; or
(b) to facilitate the commission of such an offence (whether by himself or by any other person).

Section 2 applies to any offence where sentence is fixed by law (eg murder) or for which an offender of 21 or over may be sentenced to imprisonment for five years (eg the various deception offences under the Theft Acts, theft, forgery and criminal damage).

It is immaterial whether the further offence is to be committed on the same occasion as the unauthorised access offence or on any future occasion, and it is also immaterial that the facts are such that the commission of the further offence is impossible.

Unauthorised modification of computer material

By s 3(1) of the 1990 Act, a person is guilty of an arrestable offence if:

(a) he does any act which causes an unauthorised modification of the contents of any computer; and

(b) at the time at which he does the act he has the requisite intent and the requisite knowledge.

A modification of the contents of a computer takes place if, by the operation of any function of the computer concerned or any other computer, any program or data held in the computer is altered or erased, or any program or data is added to its contents. Thus, the offence can be committed in a variety of ways, for example, by the addition or deletion of material contained in a computer or software held in a computer or by interfering with a computer or software by introducing a computer virus by means of an infected disc or some other means. Any act which contributes towards causing a modification is regarded as causing it.

A modification is unauthorised if the person whose act causes it is not entitled to determine whether it should be made and he does not have consent to the modification from anyone who is so entitled.

The 'requisite intent' is an intent to cause a modification of the content of a computer and by so doing to impair its operation, or to prevent or hinder access to any program or data held in it, or to impair the operation of any such program or the reliability of any such data. It need not be directed at any particular computer program or data, or a particular kind of program or data, or at any particular modification or particular kind of modification.

The 'requisite knowledge' is knowledge that any modification which the accused intends to cause is unauthorised.

It is immaterial whether an unauthorised modification or any intended effect of it is, or is intended to be, permanent or merely temporary.

CHAPTER 40

Handling stolen goods and related offences

HANDLING STOLEN GOODS

If goods which had been stolen had no sales outlet then the incidence of theft would undoubtedly diminish significantly. Some thefts occur because the person who appropriates the property wishes to use it himself but others, especially where the appropriator engages in widespread offences of burglary, are committed in the knowledge that there is a ready market for certain types of articles: stereo equipment, television sets and video recorders are all marketable products and seem to be constantly falling from lorries. The law concerning the handling of stolen goods is concerned with punishing not only the ultimate receiver, in the sense that he is the buyer of the property, but all persons who handle that property dishonestly. In considering handling offences the approach to adopt is straightforward. Who knew that the property was stolen and in what way were they concerned in its handling? The Theft Act 1968, s 22(1) states:

> 'A person handles stolen goods if (otherwise than in the course of the stealing) knowing or believing them to be stolen goods he dishonestly receives the goods, or dishonestly undertakes or assists in their retention, removal, disposal or realisation by or for the benefit of another person, or if he arranges to do so.'

The offence is an arrestable offence. In terms of the maximum punishment it is a more serious offence than theft.

In order to establish the nature of the offence it is necessary to consider the meaning of the words 'stolen', 'goods' and 'handling'. It is best to commence with 'goods':

Goods

The term is defined by s 34(2)(b) of the 1968 Act, as follows:

> ' "Goods" includes money and every other description of property except land, and includes things severed from the land by stealing.'

This description is close to that given to 'property' for the purposes of theft. Although s 34(2)(b) does not specifically mention 'things in action', the words 'every other description of property except land' are wide enough to include them, and the Court of Appeal has held that things in action are goods for the purposes of handling. Nevertheless, the handling of 'things in action' is likely to have little significance in the practical aspects of law enforcement.

Stolen

For the offence to be committed, the goods handled must be 'stolen goods' at that point of time. Section 24 of the 1968 Act sets out the meaning of the term 'stolen goods':

(a) goods which have been stolen, contrary to s 1 of the Act;
(b) goods which have been obtained as a result of blackmail, contrary to s 21;
(c) goods which have been obtained by means of deception, contrary to s 15;
(d) goods which have been 'stolen' abroad contrary to the law of that land, provided that had the 'stealing' occurred in England or Wales an offence contrary to the Theft Act 1968, ss 1, 15 or 21 would have been committed.

Hereafter, we use the term 'stolen goods' in this wide sense.

References to stolen goods also include money which is dishonestly withdrawn from an account to which a 'wrongful credit' has been made, but only to the extent that the money derives from the credit. We define 'wrongful credit' below (see p 776).

If a child who is below the age of criminal responsibility appropriates property in circumstances which would amount to theft in a person over that age, a person who dishonestly handles that property is not guilty of this offence as the goods are not 'stolen goods'. However, that person can be convicted of theft, just as a dishonest finder may be convicted of it.

The fact that goods were stolen goods at the time of the handling cannot be proved by evidence of the conviction of the thief, as such evidence is not admissible at the trial of a person charged with dishonest handling. The acquittal of an alleged thief does not prevent the goods being found to be stolen goods. The most usual, and the most effective, way of proving the status of the property is by offering evidence of ownership, the owner identifying the property and describing the circumstances of its loss. It is not necessary to prove that goods were stolen by any particular person; merely that they were stolen by someone and were dishonestly handled by the accused.

When goods cease to be stolen

The issue of proof that the goods were stolen when they were handled raises the issue of when goods which have been stolen cease to be stolen goods. The obvious example of goods ceasing to be stolen is where they are recovered from the thief and returned to the true owner. However, s 24(3) of the Act is helpful in this respect. It provides that no goods shall be regarded as having continued to be stolen goods after they have been restored to the person from whom they were stolen or to other lawful possession or custody. Clearly, this goes further than re-possession by the owner, since it includes cases in which goods have been restored to other lawful possession or custody. When a police officer in the course of his duties takes possession of stolen goods, they are thereby restored to 'other lawful possession or custody' and are no longer stolen;

consequently, it is not an offence to 'handle' them thereafter. If an officer interviews a thief at his home, and the thief admits stealing a watch and hands it over to the officer, it is now in the officer's lawful custody and is no longer stolen goods. If the thief then tells the officer that a man (X) is to call at any moment to examine the watch, which he knows to be stolen, with a view to buying it, there can be no successful charge of dishonest handling against X if the officer returns the watch to the thief in order to allow X to receive it and X does receive it. However, had the thief merely reached the stage at which he had admitted to the officer that he had stolen the watch but had not handed it over, the watch would remain stolen and X could be convicted of handling if he arrived a few minutes later and received the watch.

The issue is in reality whether or not the stolen goods have been taken into possession on the owner's account so that they may be returned to him. Where a security guard marked cartons of stolen cigarettes so that they would more easily be identified in the hands of a handler, they were not restored to the owner as physical possession did not take place. They were not taken out of the possession of the thief. If a police officer sees property inside a parked car which he suspects might be stolen and immobilises the car to ensure that he will have an opportunity of questioning the driver, he does not take possession of the stolen goods unless he immobilises the car with the intention of taking charge of those goods so that they cannot be removed. If he has retained an open mind as to whether he should take possession, and merely immobilises the car to prevent the driver getting away without interrogation, he does not reduce the goods into his possession or custody. It is the state of mind of the officer which is the deciding factor in each case.

Section 24(3) also provides that goods cease to be stolen goods where the person from whom they were stolen and any other person claiming through him have ceased to have rights of restitution in respect of the theft. The right to restitution of property is a matter of civil law.

There are various ways in which the right to restitution may have been lost. An example is where X obtains goods from Y by deception. If Y, on discovering the deception, nevertheless affirms the transaction he thereby ceases to have any right to restitution of the goods, which therefore cease to be stolen goods at that point of time.

In the circumstances in which goods have ceased to be classed as stolen goods for the purposes of this section, the provisions of the Criminal Attempts Act 1981 should be considered. A person may be guilty of an attempt to commit an offence, even though that offence could not be committed. This would be so in relation to handling if the accused handled the goods believing them to be stolen, even though the goods had lost their status as stolen goods.

Goods representing those originally stolen

Section 24(2) provides that references to stolen goods include, in addition to the goods originally stolen and parts of them (whether in their original state or not):

(a) any other goods which directly or indirectly represent or have at any time represented the stolen goods in the hands of the thief as being the proceeds of any disposal or realisation of the whole or part of the goods stolen or of goods so representing the stolen goods; and

(b) any other goods which directly or indirectly represent or have at any time represented the stolen goods in the hands of a handler of the stolen goods or any part of them as being the proceeds of any disposal or realisation of the whole or part of the stolen goods handled by him or of goods so representing them.

'The thief' means the person by whose conduct the goods were originally stolen. 'A handler' means any person who has committed the actus reus of handling with the appropriate mens rea. The Court of Appeal has held that goods are in the hands of the thief or of a handler if they are in his possession or under his control; physical custody is not required.

The 'proceeds rule' provided by s 24(2) is essentially as follows: goods which directly or indirectly represent or have represented the originally stolen goods *in the hands of the thief or a handler as the proceeds* of the disposal or realisation of those stolen goods, or goods so representing those stolen goods, are themselves deemed to be stolen goods. Consequently, once goods have been deemed to be stolen goods by this rule, an offence is committed if they are 'handled' thereafter with the appropriate mens rea.

The rule can be illustrated as follows. A steals a car. He sells it to B for £1,000 and receives that sum in cash. The car and the cash are now both stolen goods, the latter because it directly represents the original goods (the car) in the hands of the thief - as the proceeds of the car's disposal or realisation. Therefore, if A then gives the £1,000 (or part of it) to C, who receives it knowing it has represented the original stolen goods in A's hands and C buys a camera with the £1,000, the camera becomes stolen goods once it is in C's hands because it indirectly represents the original stolen goods in the hands of a handler as the proceeds of the disposal or realisation of goods representing the original stolen goods. Consequently if D receives the camera from C, knowing it has represented the stolen goods in C's hands, D can be convicted of handling stolen goods. However, if E receives the camera from D, unaware that it represents the original stolen goods, and then sells it for cash, the cash which he receives will not become stolen goods because, lacking mens rea, he is not a handler and therefore *that* cash does not *represent the original stolen goods in the hands of a handler* as the proceeds of their disposal or realisation.

Various forms of handling

Handling consists of dishonestly receiving stolen goods, or dishonestly undertaking or assisting in their retention, removal, disposal or realisation by or for the benefit of another person, or dishonestly arranging to do one of these things. The offence of handling therefore covers the passage or handling of the goods through as many pairs of hands as may be dishonestly involved, on their passage to the receiver, and also dealings with them thereafter. Before the Theft Act 1968, the law was primarily concerned with the thief and the receiver but a large grey area existed in respect of those who might handle the goods in some way without actually receiving them. The difficulties have now been eliminated by specifying a number of ways in which a handler may be involved. In resolving the offences which have been committed by all involved in the handling of stolen goods, the manner of the involvement of each must be examined against the options included within the section.

It is essential to remember in the first instance that the section excludes from its provisions those who handle in the course of the original stealing. This is a common sense approach to offences of handling. We are not concerned with thieves who handle stolen goods in the course of their theft as they are punishable in respect of the theft, whatever form that theft may take.

Receiving

To prove this type of handling it must be shown that the accused obtained possession or control of stolen goods from someone else; a finder of goods does not receive them.

The presence of stolen goods on the premises of another does not necessarily mean that they are in the possession or control of the owner of the premises. If a thief calls at the home of a friend and his pockets contain a number of items of stolen property, that stolen property is in the possession of the thief, not the householder. To be a 'receiver' a person need not have contact with the goods in any physical sense, since a person can have control of goods without any physical contact with them. For example, if a thief who is wanted for serious offences enlists the aid of a friend to assist him to escape from the country and, in payment for that assistance, tells his friend that he has hidden a stolen car in a wood and transfers control of that property to him by handing over the car keys, then the friend receives the car when he receives the keys. In the same way, a person may receive property into his possession or control through an employee or agent acting on his orders, in which case the employee or agent is also a receiver.

Often, a receiver is acting solely for his own benefit, but it is unnecessary that a receiver should act to gain any profit or even advantage from his possession of stolen goods. If a person, knowing that goods have been stolen, dishonestly allows the thief to store them in his warehouse so that they may be concealed from the police, he is guilty of handling by receiving whether or not he is offered payment for such use of his warehouse.

Arranging to receive

This requires a concluded agreement between the accused and another (eg the thief) for the receiving of stolen goods by the accused. It is essential that the goods are stolen goods at the time the arrangement to receive is made. Thus, a person (A) does not commit handling where he commissions others to steal a certain type of property which he agrees to receive from them if they succeed in the theft, because at the time of his arrangement to receive there are no stolen goods to which it can relate. (A would, of course, be guilty with the others of a conspiracy to steal and of a conspiracy to handle stolen goods; if the theft was actually committed, A would also be guilty of theft as an accomplice on account of his counselling or procuring.) It would be different if the goods in question had already been stolen and the thieves had approached A and contracted to sell them to him; A would thereby be guilty of arranging to receive stolen goods, and it would be irrelevant whether or not they were subsequently delivered to him.

The other forms of handling set out below differ in a vital respect from receiving, or arranging to receive, in that they must be done 'by or for the benefit of' a person other than the alleged handler.

Undertaking the retention, removal, disposal or realisation of stolen goods for the benefit of another

These four forms of handling cover the case where the accused, either alone or with another, retains, removes, disposes or realises the stolen goods for the benefit of another.

The four activities can be explained as follows: '*Retention*' means 'keeping possession of, not losing, continuing to have'. '*Removal*' refers to the movement of stolen goods from one place to another, eg transporting stolen goods to a hideout for the benefit of the thief or another. '*Disposal*' covers dumping, giving away or destroying stolen goods, eg melting down candlesticks for the thief. '*Realisation*' means the exchange of stolen goods for money or some other property. A person who sells stolen goods as agent for a third party (eg the thief) undertakes their realisation for the benefit of another. However, the House of Lords has held that a person who sells stolen goods on his own behalf does not undertake their realisation for the benefit of another because the buyer benefits from the purchase and not from the realisation (which benefits only the accused).

Of course, a person who undertakes one of these four activities will often be in possession or control of the stolen goods. If he knew or believed they were stolen when he acquired possession or control, he is guilty of handling anyway on the basis of receiving. However, if he lacked such a state of mind at that point of time but realised the goods were stolen when he undertook one of the four activities, he can be convicted of handling on that basis, provided that his 'undertaking' was *for the benefit of another*.

Assisting in the retention, removal, disposal or realisation of stolen goods by another

These four forms of handling are appropriate to cover cases where the accused provides assistance to another person, the thief or another handler, who is going to undertake the retention, removal, disposal or realisation of stolen goods.

For there to be 'assistance', the accused must do something for the purpose of enabling the goods to be retained etc, whether or not he succeeds.

There is some overlap with cases of 'undertaking'. For example, a person who joins with another in removing stolen goods not only undertakes their removal for the benefit of another but also assists in their removal by another.

A person *assists in the retention* of stolen goods by another if he puts the thief in touch with a warehouse keeper, or provides tarpaulins to conceal stolen goods in the possession of the thief or a handler, or tells lies so as to make it more difficult for the police to find or identify stolen goods retained by the thief or a handler. On the other hand, a refusal to answer questions put by the police as to the whereabouts of stolen goods does not amount to handling, although it may well assist in their retention by another. A person, who innocently allows goods to be left on his premises but later discovers that they are stolen, assists in their retention by another if he nevertheless permits them to continue to remain on the premises. Merely to use stolen goods does not suffice, since it does not in itself amount to assistance in their retention.

Turning to the other activities, the following examples can be given.

A person *assists in the removal* of stolen goods by another if he lends a lorry for their removal. He *assists in their disposal* by another if he advises the thief as to how to get rid of the goods. He *assists in their realisation* by another if he puts a 'fence' in touch with the thief.

Arranging to undertake or assist

The effect of the section is further extended by the addition of the words 'or arranging to do so'. Any arrangement to undertake or assist in one of the activities described above can suffice; it is irrelevant that nothing is done pursuant to the arrangement. However, as we mentioned in relation to the offence of 'arranging to receive', it must be proved that the arrangements in respect of these other forms of handling relate to stolen goods; ie the goods in question must be stolen goods at the time of that arrangement. If, at the time that a would-be receiver is arranging to collect and take into his possession crates of stolen whisky, arrangements are made with others (who are aware that the whisky is stolen), for them to help him to load and unload the stolen goods, these other people are guilty of handling in that they arrange to assist in the removal of the goods by another.

By or for the benefit of another person

As we have indicated, in all cases of handling (other than those of receiving and arranging to receive), it must be shown that the acts which were carried out were carried out to assist in retention etc by another or undertaken to retain etc for the benefit of another, and that person should be named in the charge if his identity is known. If it is not, the charge should indicate that the acts were done, as appropriate 'by or for the benefit of' some person unknown and such a charge will have to be supported by strong evidence that that other person existed.

Mens rea

It must be proved that, when he handled the stolen goods, the accused (a) knew or believed that they were stolen, and (b) acted dishonestly.

Knowledge or belief

Wilful blindness, ie deliberately turning a blind eye to the question of whether or not goods are stolen, does not suffice for 'knowledge' or 'belief', but it has been held that if wilful blindness as to the goods being stolen is proved knowledge or belief *may* be inferred from it. This is surprising if the suspicion involved in wilful blindness is not enough for 'knowledge or belief'. Nevertheless, it is important since, in the absence of an admission by the handler, knowledge or belief (at the time of the handling) that the goods were stolen can be difficult to prove, particularly in the common case of sales at bargain prices in public houses, clubs and other places where people assemble, of goods which 'fell off a lorry' and which turn out to have been stolen. Unless the buyer was of below average intelligence or there were other special circumstances, wilful blindness on his part as to the fact that the goods were stolen *may* be capable of proof. If it is, the jury *may* (not must) infer knowledge or belief therefrom. This knowledge or belief that the goods were stolen must exist at the time that the person committed the act of handling in question, and the same is true of the element of dishonesty. Subsequent knowledge or belief is not enough.

It need not be proved that a handler was aware of the precise nature of the goods. If it can be proved that a person received boxes believing them to contain stolen whisky, it is immaterial that the boxes contained stolen wine; he believed that he was receiving stolen goods and therefore he can be convicted of handling.

Frequently, knowledge or belief is proved by reference to the surrounding circumstances. If stolen goods have been carefully concealed on private premises, this suggests not only that the occupier of the premises did not wish to be found in possession of them but also that he knew that the goods were stolen. Likewise, if stolen goods have been altered in form or have had identifying marks removed, this suggests not only that the person who made the alteration or removal did not wish to be found in possession of the goods in their original state but also that he knew that they were stolen. Knowledge or belief that goods were stolen is also very likely to be inferred where the accused denied that stolen goods, subsequently found on his premises, were on the premises or where he claimed that goods contained in containers were of a different description from the stolen goods subsequently found in them.

In general, where a person is found in possession of property which has been recently stolen, a judge may direct a jury that they may infer knowledge or belief if the accused fails to offer an explanation for his possession, or if they are satisfied beyond reasonable doubt that any explanation which is offered is false. This rule is merely an application of the ordinary rules of circumstantial evidence. In addition, the Theft Act 1968, s 27, which applies where the accused is being prosecuted at the trial in question only for handling stolen goods, recognises the difficulties which may exist for the police in proving knowledge in handling offences by allowing special evidence to be offered in certain circumstances. It provides that, if evidence has been given of an act of handling by the accused in relation to the goods in question, the following evidence may be given to assist proof of knowledge or belief that the property was stolen:

(a) evidence that the person charged has had in his possession, or has undertaken or assisted in the retention, removal, disposal or realisation of, stolen goods from any theft taking place not earlier than 12 months before the offence charged; and

(b) provided that seven days' notice in writing has been given to the person charged of the intention to prove the conviction, evidence that he has, within the five years preceding the date of the offence charged, been convicted of theft or of handling stolen goods.

It must be emphasised that these provisions only permit the evidence described in (a) and (b) to be given to prove knowledge or belief that the goods were stolen. It cannot be used for any other purpose, eg to prove dishonesty on the accused's part or an act of handling by him. Thus, if the accused admits such knowledge or belief, evidence described in (a) and (b) is inadmissible.

These provisions are extremely helpful in relation to proof of knowledge. By virtue of (a) the police are able to offer to the court evidence that other stolen goods, that is goods other than those in respect of which the charge lies, have been in the possession of the handler and that those goods were stolen within the preceding 12 months. The handler is therefore shown to have been in possession of other recently stolen property. The more that he can be shown to have possessed, the less likely it becomes that such goods might have been acquired accidentally.

The provisions set out at (b) are exceptional in that proof of previous convictions is almost invariably excluded from the hearing of any charge. However, the nature of the offence of handling is somewhat unique in that the issue of guilt or lack of guilt is seated in the issue of knowledge. It is less likely that a person who has been convicted of theft or handling will have come into innocent possession of stolen goods.

The provisions in (b) must be read with the Police and Criminal Evidence Act 1984, s 73(2), which provides that where evidence of a previous conviction on indictment is admissible by means of a certificate of conviction the certificate must give 'the substance and effect of the indictment and conviction'. Accordingly, where the prosecution wish to adduce evidence under (b), a certificate of a previous conviction for theft or handling which identifies the stolen goods involved is admissible, since the identity of the goods is part of the substance of the conviction. In other words, the certificate is not restricted to stating merely the fact, date and place of the conviction, although the judge has a discretion to exclude a certificate if its prejudicial effect outweighs its probative value. These points were held by the House of Lords in a case where a person was charged with an offence of handling (in relation to the bodyshell of an Escort RS Turbo) and a certificate showed a previous conviction for dishonestly receiving property (a Ford RS Turbo motor car). The House admitted the certificate. Clearly the fact that the goods were similar was highly relevant to the issue of knowledge.

The Court of Appeal has ruled that the provisions set out at (a) do not permit the introduction of details of previous convictions for an offence of handling and this is easily appreciated. The provisions at (a) are concerned with the possession (or retention etc) of goods, other than those in respect of which the charge lies, not with previous convictions.

Dishonestly

This word is provided to excuse legitimate acts of handling. Dishonesty is always a question of fact for the jury or justices, and the same approach is to be taken by them, as it is in relation to the offences of deception. It follows, for example, that if a person knowingly receives stolen goods, but does so in order to restore them to their owner, or to hand them over to the police, his handling is not likely to be found to be dishonest by the jury or justices.

Selecting the correct charge

The various ways, 18 in all, in which an offence can be committed against s 22 can create difficulties for police officers investigating alleged offences. However, it is unnecessary to make exclusive selections of a particular variant of the offence. The section constitutes a single offence of handling stolen goods, which can be committed by receiving or by any of the other ways specified. Consequently, an information or indictment, which simply alleges that there had been a handling of stolen goods, is not bad for duplicity.

Nevertheless, in order to be fair and clear to the accused, the better practice is to particularise the form of handling relied on, and, if there is any uncertainty about the form of handling in question, it is advisable to have more than one information (or more than one count in the indictment). But only two informations (or counts) should generally be used in such a case: one charging receiving, and the other charging the various forms of 'undertaking or assisting in' by or for the benefit of another (or such forms of these as are clearly the only ones relevant).

ADVERTISING REWARDS FOR RETURN OF STOLEN OR LOST GOODS

The Theft Act 1968, s 23 punishes the public advertisement of a reward for the return of any lost or stolen goods which uses any words to the effect that no questions will be asked, or that the person producing the goods will be safe from apprehension or inquiry, or that any money paid for the purchase of the goods or advanced by way of loan on them will be repaid. The printer and publisher of such an advertisement are liable, as well as the advertiser.

SEARCH FOR STOLEN GOODS

The following provision is contained in the Theft Act 1968, s 26.

A justice may grant a warrant, upon information being received on oath that there is reasonable cause to believe that any person has in his custody or possession or on his premises any stolen goods, to search for and seize those goods.

DISHONESTLY RETAINING A WRONGFUL CREDIT

The offence of handling is not committed by someone into whose bank account was received a 'wrongful credit', as defined below, because that credit itself is not stolen goods.

This gap is filled by s 24A of the Theft Act 1968, inserted by s 2 of the Theft (Amendment) Act 1996. Section 24A provides that a person is guilty of an offence if:

(a) a wrongful credit has been made to an account kept by him or in respect of which he has any right or interest;
(b) he knows or believes that the credit is wrongful; and
(c) he dishonestly fails to take such steps as are reasonable in the circumstances to secure that the credit is cancelled.

Actus reus

What is required is the failure to take such steps as are reasonable in the circumstances to secure the cancellation of a wrongful credit made to an account kept by the accused or in respect of which he has any right or interest. Nothing need be done by the accused. The mere omission to take reasonable steps suffices.

A 'credit' refers to a credit of an amount of money. Credit to an account is wrongful:

(a) if it is the credit side of a money transfer obtained contrary to s 15A of the 1968 Act; or
(b) to the extent that it derives from:
  (i)   theft;
  (ii) an offence under s 15A;
  (iii) blackmail;
  (iv) stolen goods.

In determining whether a credit to an account is wrongful, it is immaterial whether the account is overdrawn before or after the credit is made.

Mens rea

The accused must know or believe that the credit is wrongful; he must know or believe the facts which make the credit 'wrongful' in law, although he need not know that they have this effect since ignorance of the criminal law is no defence.

Because failing to take steps is an omission which can continue over a period of time, it suffices that mens rea exists at some point during it; it need not exist from the outset. It follows that those who only become aware of a wrongful credit after it has been made can commit an offence under s 24A.

The accused must dishonestly fail to take such steps which are reasonable in the circumstances to secure that the wrongful credit is cancelled. The approach to this question is the same as in offences of deception and of handling.

Width of offence

Section 24A covers a range of situations. It catches a person who obtains a money transfer by deception, contrary to s 15A of the 1968 Act, if the transfer is made to his bank account and he dishonestly fails to take reasonable steps to secure its cancellation, because the credit which he has failed to cancel is wrongful under s 24A(3).

Section 24A is not, however, aimed at this type of case but at the following. Suppose that X commits a s 15A offence by causing a money transfer to be made to D's account, unknown to D. If D dishonestly fails to take reasonable steps to cancel the credit on discovering the truth, he commits an offence under s 24A because the credit is wrongful under s 24A(3).

Suppose that Y pays money which he has stolen (or obtained by blackmail or by selling stolen goods) into his bank account, and that Y then transfers the credit thereby created to D's bank account. If D dishonestly fails to take reasonable steps to cancel that credit he can be convicted of an offence under s 24A, because the credit will be wrongful under s 24A(4). It would be likewise if the credit had derived from the transfer to D's bank account of a credit wrongfully obtained by Y contrary to s 15A.

CHAPTER 41

Forgery and counterfeiting

The law relating to forgery and counterfeiting is governed by the Forgery and Counterfeiting Act 1981. Part I of the Act is concerned with forgery and related offences, and Part II with counterfeiting and related offences. References to sections in this chapter are to sections of the 1981 Act. Most of the offences described in this chapter refer to the verb 'believe'; in relation to this word, see p 773.

FORGERY

This offence is defined by s 1, which states that a person is guilty of forgery if he makes a false instrument, with the intention that he or another shall use it to induce somebody to accept it as genuine, and by reason of so accepting it to do or not to do some act to his own or any other person's prejudice.

The actus reus of this offence is 'making a false instrument', and by s 9(2) this includes altering an instrument so as to make it false in any respect.

False instrument

'Instrument'

For the purpose of forgery and other offences involving false instruments, s 8 of the Act defines the word 'instrument' as:

(a) any document, whether of a formal or informal character (other than a currency note);
(b) any stamp issued or sold by the Post Office (or a metered postage mark);
(c) any Inland Revenue stamp denoting any duty or fee; and
(d) any disc, tape, sound track or other device on or in which information is *recorded or stored* by mechanical, electronic or other means. To be 'recorded' or 'stored' the information must be preserved for an appreciable time with the object of subsequent retrieval. Examples of items covered are microfilm records and

information on computer tapes or discs, but not electronic impulses in a computer or its 'user segment' (which stores information momentarily while the computer searches its memory, eg to check a password). The result is that computer hacking is not forgery although it is an offence under s 1 of the Computer Misuse Act 1990 (unauthorised access to computer material).

It is important to note that, for present purposes, 'instruments' are limited to the things just listed. The only part of this list which calls for further definition is (a), which tells us that a document, whether formal or informal (other than a currency note), is an instrument. But what is a 'document'? The Court of Appeal has held that a thing is only a document if it conveys two messages: a message about the thing itself (eg that it is a cheque) and a message to be found in the words or other symbols that is to be accepted and acted on (eg the message in a cheque to the banker to pay a specified sum). Thus, cheques, wills, and building society pass books are examples of documents (and are therefore instruments) but paintings (even if falsely signed), false autographs and any writing on manufactured articles or their wrappings indicating the name of the manufacturer or country of origin, are not.

'False'

Section 9(1) defines the adjective *'false'* in relation to 'instrument'. It states that an instrument is false for the purposes of forgery and other offences involving forged instruments:

(a) if it purports to have been *made* in the form in which it is made by *a person who did not in fact make it* in that form; or

(b) if it purports to have been *made* in the form in which it is made *on the authority of a person who did not in fact authorise its making* in that form; or

(c) if it purports to have been *made in the terms* in which it is *made by a person who did not in fact make it in those terms*; or

(d) if it purports to have been *made in the terms* in which it is made *on the authority of a person who did not in fact authorise its making in those terms*; or

(e) if it purports to have been *altered* in any respect *by a person who did not in fact alter it* in that respect; or

(f) if it purports to have been *altered* in any respect *on the authority of a person who did not in fact authorise the alteration* in that respect; or

(g) if it purports to have been *made* or *altered* on a *date* on which, or at a *place* at which, or *otherwise in circumstances* in which, it was *not in fact made or altered*; or

(h) if it purports to have been *made* or *altered* by an *existing person* but he did *not in fact exist*.

This definition of the falsity of an instrument is quite complex and needs to be simplified to assist understanding. The key point is that it is not enough that the document tells a lie (ie contains a false statement); what is required is that it should tell a lie about itself (ie the document itself must pretend to be something which it is not). If a man writes an application for a job as a chemical engineer and falsely alleges that he is studying for a postgraduate degree in that field, that instrument is not a forgery although its contents are untrue. It was made by the applicant, it has not been altered in any way or falsely dated and it is made by an existing person. Should the applicant make out a reference which is allegedly from his former tutor then that would be a false instrument, as it alleges that it was made by a person who did not make it or authorise its making. We must therefore consider an instrument to be false if it lies about itself in relation to the person who made the instrument, or authorised its making, or in respect of an unauthorised alteration, or if it purports to have been made or altered on a date, or in a place, or otherwise in circumstances, in which it was not in fact made or altered, or if it represents itself as having been made or altered by an existing person, who in fact did not exist.

If a person finds a cheque book and makes out a cheque for £100 and signs it in his own name, the cheque is not a false instrument because, even though a person is not the holder of the cheque book, it bears the signature of the person who made out the cheque. However, if he signs the name of the person who holds the account, the cheque is a false instrument as it lies about itself by alleging that it was signed by another who did not make the instrument or authorise its making. On the other hand, a person who opens an account in a false name in order to pay in a stolen cheque, does not make a false instrument when he completes a withdrawal form in that name. The name of the drawer is the same as the depositor's (although false) and the withdrawal form does not purport to be made by a person who did not make it. The term 'authorise its making' is important. Another person may draw up a document on behalf of another (and even sign it on his behalf) without creating a false instrument, providing that he was authorised to do so. A cheque, made out quite properly by the holder of the bank account for the sum of £100 becomes a false instrument when another person alters that cheque to show a sum of £1,000 by adding another zero to the figure shown on the face of the cheque and writing alongside it the initials of the account holder without that person's authority. It would be different if the person making the alteration was authorised to do so.

What we have just said about a false instrument in relation to documents is of course equally applicable to the other types of instrument.

Mens rea

The accused must make the false instrument with the intention that he or another person shall use it to induce somebody to accept it as genuine, and with the intention to induce that person by reason of so accepting it to do or not to do some act to his own or any other person's prejudice. Consequently, it is not enough simply to intend to induce a person to believe that an instrument is genuine. For example, making a false birth certificate solely to induce a belief that one comes from a noble family is not forgery. There is no need for either of the two intended consequences to be achieved. The accused need not intend to induce another human being, it suffices that he intends to induce a machine to respond to the instrument as if it were genuine.

It has been held by the Court of Appeal that a person who makes a false instrument intending to fax it to X and thereby to induce X to accept it (ie the false instrument) as genuine and to act prejudicially intends to use it (ie the false instrument) to induce another to accept it as genuine and to act prejudicially. This is a somewhat strained interpretation since the fax would seem to be a copy and not the false instrument which has been made. A charge of copying a false instrument contrary to s 2 of the 1981 Act (below) would be more appropriate.

The fact or omission intended to be induced must be to the prejudice of the person induced or of someone else. Section 10(1) of the 1981 Act provides that, for the purposes of forgery and related offences, an act or omission intended to be induced is only to a person's prejudice if it is one which, if it occurs:

(a) will result:
   (i)   in his temporary or permanent loss of property (including a loss by not getting what he might get as well as a loss by parting with what he has);
   (ii) in his being deprived of an opportunity to earn remuneration or greater remuneration; or
   (iii) in his being deprived of an opportunity to gain a financial advantage otherwise than by way of remuneration; or
(b) will result in somebody being given an opportunity -
   (i)   to earn remuneration or greater remuneration from him (the person induced); or
   (ii) to gain a financial advantage from him otherwise than by way of remuneration; or
(c) will be the result of his having accepted a false instrument as genuine (or—and this is only relevant to offences under ss 2 and 4 below—a copy of a false instrument as a copy of a genuine one), in connection with his performance of a duty.

This rather complicated provision can be illustrated as follows. If A signs a cheque in B's name, intending to give it to C as payment for a car which C is to hire to A for a day, A has made a false instrument and he intends to use it to induce C to accept it as genuine, and by reason of so accepting it to do some act to his own prejudice, because C's handing over of the car will result in his temporary loss of it (see (a)(i), above). A is therefore guilty of forgery.

If A learns that his rival, C, is about to be promoted and, to prevent this, A writes to C's employer, F, a letter purportedly written by X, a clergyman, which alleges that C is dishonest, A is guilty of forgery because he has made a false instrument with intent to induce F to accept it as genuine, and by reason of so accepting it not to do an act to the prejudice of some other person (C), because F's non-promotion of C will result in C being deprived of an opportunity to earn greater remuneration (see (a)(ii), above).

If, instead, the letter referred to above had said that C was highly efficient, in an effort to secure the promotion for him, A would still be guilty of forgery because he has made a false instrument with intent to induce F to accept it as genuine, and by reason of so accepting it to do an act to his own prejudice, because it will result in C being given greater remuneration (see (b)(i), above).

If A learns that his trading rival, C, is tendering to supply goods to F and, to prevent this, A writes a letter to F which purports to have been written by someone who does not in fact exist and alleges that C produces shoddy goods, A is guilty of forgery. The reason is that he has made a false instrument and intends to use it to induce F to accept it as genuine, and by reason of so accepting it to do some act to the prejudice of some other person (C), because the award of the tender to someone else will result in C being deprived of an opportunity to gain a financial advantage (see (a)(iii), above).

If A makes a false airline ticket in order to get a free flight, A is guilty of forgery because he intends to use the ticket to induce an airline employee to accept it as genuine, and by reason of so accepting it to do some act to the prejudice of the airline by giving a financial advantage (ie the free flight) to A (see (b)(ii), above).

It is clear from (c), above, that the intended prejudice need not be financial in any sense at all, since (c) provides that it is enough that the act or omission intended to be induced will be to a person's prejudice if it will be the result of his having accepted a false instrument as genuine in connection with the performance of any duty, as where a false pass is made to induce a doorkeeper to admit an unauthorised person to premises. The duty referred to here means a legal duty, as opposed simply to a moral one.

In conclusion, it should be noted that by virtue of s 10(2), it is not forgery where the maker of a false instrument intends to induce someone to do something which he is under an enforceable legal duty to do (or to induce someone not to do something he is not legally entitled to do). Thus, if A, who is owed money by C, sends a letter purporting to come from a firm of solicitors and threatening legal action if the debt is not paid, A is not guilty of forgery. The reason is that, even though A intends to induce C to accept the letter as genuine, and by reason of this to pay the money and thereby suffer loss, the act intended to be induced (paying the debt) is something C is legally obliged to do.

An honest and reasonable belief in a legal or moral claim to the action which it is sought to induce does not provide a defence. A worker may genuinely believe that he is entitled to the salary increase which he seeks to gain by use of a false instrument, but such a belief can never amount to a defence to a charge under the Forgery and Counterfeiting Act 1981. If it was otherwise, a person who disagreed with the findings of an examiner appointed for the purpose of conducting driving tests and felt that he was competent to drive, could falsify a certificate of competence to drive. In doing so he would intend to induce an officer, who had a duty to issue full licences only to those who produced a true certificate of competence, to accept the false document as genuine in connection with the performance of his duty and to grant a full licence as a result. It is no defence for such a person to allege that he sincerely believed in his competence to drive.

COPYING A FALSE INSTRUMENT

Section 2 is concerned with the separate offence of copying a false instrument. It provides that it is an offence for a person to make a copy of an instrument which is, and which he knows or believes to be, a false instrument, with the intention that he or another will use it to induce somebody to accept it as a copy of a genuine instrument, and with the intention to induce that person by reason of so accepting it to do some act to the prejudice of himself or some other person.

It is important to remember that s 2 is concerned with what might be described as second generation forgeries. We are considering copies of false instruments from the outset. The essence of the offence lies in the intention to induce a belief that it is a copy of a genuine instrument, whilst in reality it is a copy of a false instrument. The section is meant to close loopholes which might otherwise exist. The essential points to prove are that the original instrument is a false instrument; that the person who made the copy knew or believed this to be so; and that the copy was made to induce someone to act etc. If someone wished to avoid paying his gas bill, he could allege that he had already paid and in support of this he might falsify a receipt for the money made out to appear as if it had been issued by British Gas. Clearly, if he did that he would be guilty of forgery as he would have made a false instrument with the requisite intents. Section 2 ensures that it is equally an offence then to photocopy that false receipt with intent to use that copy in an attempt to avoid payment. The section overcomes the arguments which have surrounded the nature of false instruments. The original false receipt clearly tells a lie about itself as it represents itself to be a true receipt. Arguments have been advanced in the past that a photocopy, or any other copy, does not tell a lie about itself as it merely represents itself to be a copy. These arguments are now academic since s 2 declares the making of such copies to be a separate offence, punishable in the same way as forgery, if done with the necessary intent.

So far we have concentrated on criminal liability for *making* a false instrument with intent that it be used to induce etc (forgery), and for *making* a copy of a false instrument with the like intent (offence of copying a false instrument). What of the user of a false instrument (or copy of such an instrument)? It may be the forger who uses the false instrument (or copy), and if this is so he commits an additional offence. Alternatively, it may be another person who uses it. Sections 3 and 4 deal with offences of use.

USING A FALSE INSTRUMENT

Section 3 makes it an offence for a person to use an instrument which is false, and which he knows or believes to be false, with the intention of inducing somebody to accept it as genuine, and with the intention of inducing that person by reason of so accepting it to do or not to do some act to his own or any other person's prejudice. Section 4 provides an identically worded offence of using a copy of a false instrument. Any use of a false instrument (or, as the case may be, a copy of a false instrument) with the necessary intent suffices. The verb 'use' is wide in meaning and covers, for example, a person who offers, delivers, tenders in payment or exchange, or exposes for sale, a false instrument (or a copy of one).

CUSTODY OR CONTROL OF MONEY ORDERS, SHARE CERTIFICATES, PASSPORTS ETC

Section 5 of the Act provides a number of offences under this heading, which are concerned with the following instruments:

(a) money orders or postal orders;
(b) United Kingdom postage stamps;
(c) Inland Revenue stamps;
(d) share certificates;
(e) passports and documents which can be used instead of passports;
(f) cheques or travellers' cheques;
(g) credit cards; and
(h) birth, adoption, marriage or death certificates or officially certified copies thereof.

Any such instrument is hereafter referred to as a 'specified instrument'.

By s 5(1), it is an offence for a person to have in his custody or under his control a specified instrument which is, and which he knows or believes to be, false, with the intention that he or another shall use it to induce somebody to accept it as genuine, and by reason of so accepting it to do or not to do some act to his own or any other person's prejudice.

This 'possession' offence completes the cycle of offences which are likely to be committed if a false instrument is made for the purposes previously described. If someone makes out a false cheque with intent to induce someone to accept it as genuine, and by reason of so accepting it to do something to his prejudice, he commits forgery contrary to s 1. If he walks through the streets to a bank, with the false cheque, in order to cash it, he commits the present offence under s 5(1). If he then passes the cheque to a bank official in order to induce him to part with money, he commits the offence of 'using' contrary to s 3. Of course, it may be that different people will commit different offences in the cycle, as where the person who makes the false instrument gets other people to engage in the use of such false instruments.

If the intent required for an offence under s 5(1) cannot be proved, one can fall back on s 5(2). This makes it an offence for a person merely to have in his custody or control, without lawful authority or excuse, a specified instrument which is, and which he knows or believes to be, false. 'Lawful authority or excuse' is likely to be limited to such matters as possession by a police officer after seizure of a specified instrument or possession by some other person who is in the course of handing over to the police such an instrument.

Section 5(3) and (4) are aimed at the tools of a forger's trade. Section 5(3) provides that it is an offence for a person to make or to have in his custody or under his control a machine or implement, or paper or any other material, which to his knowledge is or has been specially designed or adapted for the making of a specified instrument, with the intention that he or another shall make a specified instrument which is false and that he or another shall induce somebody to accept it as genuine, and by reason of so accepting it to do or not to do some act to his own or another's prejudice. In this way the Act strikes at a would-be forger even before he starts to make a false instrument. Whether or not the necessary intent for an offence under s 5(3) can be proved will often depend, in part, on the amount of forging equipment etc in the accused's custody or control.

If the intent required under s 5(3) cannot be proved, one can fall back on s 5(4), which makes it an offence for a person to make or to have in his custody or control any such machine, implement, paper or material, without lawful authority or excuse.

We discuss the powers of the police in relation to all the above offences (ie ss 1 to 5) at the end of this chapter.

COUNTERFEITING OFFENCES: GENERAL POINTS

Definition of counterfeit

By the Forgery and Counterfeiting Act 1981, s 28(1) a thing is a counterfeit of a currency note or of a protected coin:

(a) if it is not a currency note or a protected coin, but *resembles a currency note or protected coin* (whether on one side only or on both) *to such an extent that it is reasonably capable of passing for a currency note or protected coin of that description*; or
(b) if it is a currency note or protected coin which has been *so altered that it is reasonably capable of passing for a currency note or protected coin of some other description.*

For the avoidance of any doubt on the matter, s 28(2) goes on to provide that a thing consisting of one side only of a currency note, with or without the addition of other material, is a counterfeit of such a note, and that a thing consisting of parts of two or more currency notes (or of parts of such note(s) and other material) is capable of being a counterfeit of a currency note. Thus, for example, a supposed currency note composed of parts of true currency notes and other materials is a counterfeit, as is a thing which consists of one side only of a currency note as a result of that note being 'split'.

For the purposes of the Act, 'currency note' means:

(a) any note which has been lawfully issued in the United Kingdom, Channel Islands, Isle of Man or Irish Republic; *and is or has been* customarily used as money in the country of issue; and is payable on demand; or
(b) any note which has been lawfully issued in some other country, *and* is customarily used as money in that country.

Thus, a £20 note, a 1,000 lire note and a 100 dinar note are all 'currency notes'; so is an old style £5 note, which is no longer legal tender, but not a French (or other foreign) note which is no longer valid currency in the country where it was issued.

A 'protected coin' is defined as any coin which is customarily used as money in any country, ie any coin which *is still* valid tender at the time.

Passing or tendering

In the offences which we now proceed to discuss, references to 'passing or tendering' a note or coin are not confined to passing or tendering it as legal tender, so that (for example) passing or tendering a note or coin to a coin dealer or as a collector's item is a 'passing or tendering' for the purpose of these offences. A person 'passes' a note or coin to somebody when the latter actually accepts it from him; a person 'tenders' a note or coin when he offers to pass it to somebody. Thus, X tenders a coin to Y if he offers to give it to Y but Y refuses to accept it. On the other hand, simply to produce a bundle of counterfeit notes to impress a lady friend does not constitute a tender of them, since it does not involve any offer to pass them to her or anyone else.

COUNTERFEITING

Section 14(1) states that it is an offence for a person to make a counterfeit of a currency note or protected coin, intending that he or another shall pass or tender it as genuine. Section 14(2) makes it an offence for a person to make a counterfeit of a currency note or protected coin without lawful authority or excuse.

Both offences punish those who make a counterfeit currency note or protected coin; the difference between them is this. If the maker's intention is that he or another shall pass it into circulation, he commits an offence under s 14(1). If he did not so intend, or that intent cannot be proved, he can be convicted of the lesser offence under s 14(2) unless he had a lawful authority or excuse for making the thing.

It is difficult to imagine many instances in which the intention required by s 14(1) will not have existed where a person has made counterfeits; in terms of proof all the circumstances of the discovery of the false notes or coins may be taken into account, together with any explanations offered by the accused. If a particular intention cannot be established, it is difficult to imagine how the counterfeiter could escape the provisions of s 14(2) as there are few circumstances in which one could make counterfeits with lawful authority or excuse. Even the making of such counterfeits as a hobby would be unlikely to be accepted as a lawful excuse for their 'making'.

PASSING COUNTERFEIT CURRENCY

Passing or tendering counterfeit as genuine

By s 15(1)(a) of the Act, it is an offence for a person to pass or tender as genuine anything which is, and which he knows or believes to be, a counterfeit of a currency note or of a protected coin.

We have already explained what is meant by 'pass' and 'tender'. The counterfeit must be passed or tendered as genuine before this offence can be committed. A man who sells to another coins or notes which are false and declares them to be such does not pass or tender them as genuine since he does not hide the fact of their falsity.

Finally, the person who offers the counterfeits as genuine must know or believe them to be false. This protects a person who, without realising their falsity, passes or tenders counterfeits which he has received quite innocently in his change. However, he would commit the offence if, recognising that he had received a false coin or note, he decided to put it back into circulation rather than accept the loss.

Delivering counterfeit to another with intent that it shall be passed or tendered as genuine

Section 15(1)(b) makes it an offence for a person to deliver to another anything which is, and which he knows or believes to be, a counterfeit of a currency note or protected coin, intending that the person to whom it is delivered or another shall pass or tender it as genuine. This subsection therefore deals with the person who knowingly takes counterfeits from the maker and delivers them to a second person who knows they are counterfeit and is to arrange for them to be passed or tendered as genuine.

Delivering counterfeit without lawful authority or excuse

In circumstances in which it cannot be proved that the person who delivered the counterfeit intended that the recipient or another should pass or tender it as genuine, he may be convicted of the offence of delivery without lawful authority or excuse, which is dealt with by s 15(2).

Section 15(2) makes it an offence for a person to deliver to another, without lawful authority or excuse, anything which is, and which he knows or believes to be, a counterfeit of a currency note or protected coin.

CUSTODY OR CONTROL OF COUNTERFEIT CURRENCY AND COUNTERFEITING IMPLEMENTS

The offences of 'possession' of false instruments and of materials and implements for their making dealt with above have their counterparts in ss 16 and 17 in relation to people who have counterfeit currency or counterfeiting materials or implements in their custody or under their control.

Custody or control of counterfeit currency

By s 16(1), it is an offence for a person to have in his custody or control a counterfeit of a currency note or of a protected coin, knowing or believing it to be so and intending either to pass or tender it as genuine or to deliver it to another with the intention that he or another shall pass or tender it as genuine. Section 16(2) makes it an offence for a person to have such custody or control, with such knowledge or belief, without lawful authority or excuse. On a charge under s 16(2) the accused's intention is irrelevant. Whilst a settled intention to hand in counterfeit currency may amount to a lawful excuse, the fact that a person has not yet decided what to do with it cannot amount to such an excuse.

The offences of 'possession' in respect of currency may be committed even though the coin or note is not in a fit state to be passed or tendered or even though its making or counterfeiting has not been finished or perfected. Consequently, these offences may be committed, for example, in relation to the part-finished efforts of a counterfeiter.

Making, custody or control of counterfeiting materials and implements

The distinction between s 16(1) and (2) in terms of the accused's intention is mirrored by the provisions of s 17, which is concerned with the making, custody or control of counterfeiting materials or implements, such as special paper or inks, metal plates and printing or reprographic equipment.

Section 17(1) makes it an offence for a person to make, or to have in his custody or under his control, anything which he intends to use, or to permit any other person to use, for the purpose of making a counterfeit of a currency note or of a protected coin with the intention that it be passed or tendered as genuine. The words 'anything which he intends to use' include *anything used as a part of the process of counterfeiting.* This includes chromolins (printers' proofs used to check the quality of an aluminium plate produced from a film) of a currency note.

Section 17(2) provides that it is an offence for a person without lawful authority or excuse to make or to have in his custody or under his control any thing which, to his knowledge, is or has been specially designed or adapted for the making of a counterfeit of a currency note; no intent that the counterfeit should be put into circulation needs to be proved.

By s 17(3), it is an offence for a person to make or have in his custody or under his control, any implement which, to his knowledge, is capable of imparting to anything a resemblance:

(a) to the whole or part of either side of a protected coin; or
(b) to the whole or part of the reverse of the image on either side of a protected coin.

A person charged with this offence has a defence if he proves that he had the written consent of the Treasury or some other lawful authority or excuse. It is important to note that this is the only offence in the Act where the accused has the burden of proving a lawful authority or excuse.

SUMMARY ON COUNTERFEITING

In conclusion, it is helpful to consider the complete operation and the participation of each person involved when attempting to establish counterfeiting and related offences. If we consider at the outset the discovery of a counterfeiter's den, this discovery will almost certainly involve the finding of materials and implements for counterfeiting. Quite apart from the liability of the person in 'possession' of these things, there may be evidence as to who made them. Thus, a number of offences under s 17 may be revealed at this stage. Any counterfeit currency which is discovered will almost certainly have been made with the intention that someone should pass or tender it as genuine, or at least have been made without lawful authority or excuse. In either event, an offence contrary to s 14 will have been committed.

Where counterfeit currency has been made, there will almost certainly be someone who has it in his custody or control, and if he knows or believes it is counterfeit, he will be guilty of an offence under s 16 if he intends that it should be passed or tendered as genuine, or if he has no lawful authority or excuse for his 'possession'. The first possibility will always embrace the second and this could be commented upon in such circumstances. These offences are complete even if the currency is not in a fit state to be passed or tendered.

If counterfeit currency is discovered at a counterfeiter's den, it is probable that finished currency will already have left the premises. This raises the question of whether it was delivered by some person to another for circulation, or whether it was merely delivered without lawful authority or excuse. Either way, provided the deliverer knew or believed the thing to be counterfeit, an offence under s 15(1)(b) or (2) will have been committed.

Finally the actual introduction of the counterfeit currency into circulation must be considered, and in this context it must be remembered that the lawful authority or excuse exemption does not apply since s 15(1)(a) (which governs this offence) merely requires the passing or tendering as genuine something which the accused knows or believes to be counterfeit.

REPRODUCING BRITISH CURRENCY

This heading can be misleading as it suggests serious offences of counterfeiting. However, the offences covered by this heading are neither serious (since they are punishable only by way of a fine, even if tried on indictment) nor do they require any counterfeiting. The offences in question are governed by ss 18 and 19 of the Act which deal respectively with the reproduction of British currency notes without written consent to do so from the relevant authority, and with the making, sale or distribution of imitation British coins in connection with a scheme intended to promote the sale of any product or service.

These sections are not concerned with counterfeiting in its strict sense (ie notes and coins reasonably capable of passing as currency notes or protected coins), but set out to prevent the use of reproductions in any form, even though the copy reproduced would not fool any reasonable person. If there was no legislation to prevent the production of good quality 'stage money', this could lead to abuse. Colour supplement magazines could print a reproduction of one side of a currency note as a voucher entitling the holder to a reduction on the price of an article in certain stores. This would no doubt be done innocently, but the reproduction might be used falsely by some other person. Many modern copiers can produce good quality copies of colour documents and there is no reason to suppose that machines could not be produced which could reproduce reasonable copies. Section 18, which deals with notes, goes to the extent of prohibiting copies which are not reproduced on the correct scale, in order to prevent 'blow-ups' being produced which may be of assistance to a counterfeiter.

When considering offences of reproduction, one must not ignore the possibility of offences contrary to the previous provisions. If the reproductive processes lead to the production of a copy which is reasonably capable of passing for a currency note, the more serious offences under s 14 of counterfeiting with intent to pass or tender, or of counterfeiting without lawful authority or excuse, should be considered.

PROCEDURE AND POWERS

Search

Sections 7 and 24 of the Act authorise a justice who is satisfied upon information on oath that there is reasonable cause to believe that a person has in his *custody* or under his *control:*

(a)   anything which has been used, or is intended to be used, for the making of a false instrument or copy of a false instrument, contrary to ss 1 or 2;

(b) any false instrument or copy which has been used, or is intended to be used, contrary to ss 3 or 4;

(c) anything which it is unlawful to possess without authority etc, under s 5 (false money orders, stamps etc);

(d) counterfeit currency notes or protected coins, or reproductions; or

(e) anything which has been used, or is intended to be used, for the making of such counterfeit or reproductions,

to issue a warrant authorising a constable to enter premises, search for and seize such objects.

A constable may, at any time after seizure, apply to a magistrates' court for an order for the disposal of objects seized.

Arrest

The *major* offences under Part I of the Act, that is those of forgery, copying a false instrument, using a false instrument, using a copy of a false instrument, custody or control of a false specified instrument with intent, and custody or control of an implement or material for making such an instrument with intent, are arrestable offences. Only the offences of custody or control of a false specified instrument, or of an implement or material for making a false specified instrument, without lawful authority or excuse, are not arrestable offences.

The same type of distinction is applied to counterfeiting offences. Those which are committed with the intention of counterfeits being passed or tendered are arrestable offences. Those involving lack of lawful authority or excuse are not, nor are those concerned with the reproduction of British currency notes and coins.

CHAPTER 42

Preventive justice

There are various offences which are specifically aimed at nipping crime in the bud. Legislation deals with criminal attempts, conspiracies, interference with motor vehicles, the possession of offensive weapons and going equipped to steal. The crime of incitement is still governed by the common law, as are certain types of conspiracy.

ATTEMPT

The Criminal Attempts Act 1981 abolished the common law offences of attempt and of procuring materials with which to commit crime and replaced them by a statutory offence of attempt, which is defined by s 1 of the Act. Section 1(1) provides:

'If, with intent to commit an offence to which this section applies, a person does an act which is more than merely preparatory to the commission of the offence, he is guilty of attempting to commit the offence.'

The offences to which the section applies are described by s 1(4) which provides that the section applies to any offence which, if completed, would be triable in England and Wales as an indictable offence, except:

(a) conspiracy (at common law or under s 1 of the Criminal Law Act 1977 or any other enactment);
(b) aiding, abetting, counselling, procuring or suborning the commission of an offence; and
(c) offences under s 4(1) (assisting offenders) or s 5(1) (accepting or agreeing to accept consideration for not disclosing information about an arrestable offence) of the Criminal Law Act 1967.

It follows that all attempts to commit indictable offences, other than those specified above, are offences contrary to s 1 but attempts to commit summary offences are not. However, it should be noted that a number of statutes providing summary offences also provide specific offences of attempt in relation to them.

Mens rea

The requirement of mens rea plays a particularly important role in the crime of attempt because whether or not a particular act amounts to an attempt may well hinge on the intent with which it is done. For example, to strike a match near a haystack may or may not be attempted arson of a haystack, depending on whether there is an intent to set fire to the haystack or to light a cigarette: the intent colours the act.

The mens rea specified by s 1(1) of the 1981 Act is an 'intent to commit an offence to which this section [ie s 1] applies' and which the accused is alleged to have attempted. This apparently straightforward statement needs further explanation since 'an intent to commit the offence attempted' may involve a number of mental states.

The accused must, of course, intend to commit an act or to continue with a series of acts which, when successfully completed, will amount to or lead to an offence. In addition, if the crime attempted requires some consequence to result from his conduct, the accused must *intend* to cause that consequence. This is so even though some other type of mens rea (eg recklessness) is required or suffices for the full offence. This requirement of mens rea in attempt can be illustrated as follows:

(a) On a charge of attempted murder, it must be proved that the accused intended the unlawful death of another human being. By way of comparison, if the accused had actually killed someone he could be convicted of murder merely because he intended his act unlawfully to cause grievous bodily harm to another person.

(b) On a charge of attempted criminal damage, it must be proved that the accused intended the destruction or damaging of property belonging to another, even though if he had actually destroyed or damaged that property he could have been convicted of criminal damage despite the absence of any realisation on his part that his act might possibly have this effect (provided a reasonable person would have realised this).

Where the actus reus of the crime attempted includes some circumstance, such as the absence of the woman's consent in rape or the fact that the goods handled are stolen in handling stolen goods, the accused will have sufficient mens rea as to that circumstance if he knew or believed that it existed. Moreover, where some lesser mental state as to a circumstance suffices for the full offence or no mental state as to it is required at all, recklessness as to it suffices on a charge of attempt. The reader will recall from ch 1 that there are two types of recklessness, known to the criminal law. If the offence, such as rape, requires the more limited type of recklessness, known as subjective recklessness, as to a circumstance, then that type of recklessness is required on a charge of attempt. In all other cases, the other type of recklessness, *Caldwell* type recklessness, suffices. Thus, in a case of attempted rape it will be sufficient if the offender either knew that the woman did not consent or was subjectively reckless as to whether or not she was consenting. This rule can mean that the requirements on an attempt charge are greater than on a charge for the full offence. For example, on a charge of attempting to commit the offence of unlawful sexual intercourse with a girl under 13, which offence requires no mens rea as to age, it must be proved not only that the accused had decided to have intercourse with the girl but also that he knew or was *Caldwell* type reckless as to the fact that she was under 13, even though if he had succeeded in having intercourse with her he could have been convicted of the full offence despite the absence of any realisation on his part that she might be under 13 and despite the fact that this absence was reasonable on his part.

One last point must be made. The requirement that the accused must intend to commit the offence attempted means that he must have any other mental element, additional to mens rea as to the elements of the actus reus of the crime attempted, required for that crime. Thus, to be convicted of attempted theft an accused must not only have intended to appropriate property belonging to another but have acted dishonestly and with intent permanently to deprive the 'owner' of the property in question. Likewise to be convicted of attempting to commit the offence of damaging or destroying property, intending thereby to endanger the life of another, or being reckless whether another's life would thereby be endangered, the accused must not only have intended to destroy or damage property, but have intended thereby to endanger the life of another or been reckless as to the risk of this occurring.

Actus reus

Section 1(1) of the 1981 Act requires 'an act that is more than merely preparatory to the commission of the offence', ie the full offence which the accused intends to commit. The Act offers no explanation of the rather vague phrase just quoted. Nevertheless, it is obvious that an act is more than merely preparatory to the commission of an offence in a 'last act' case, ie one where the accused has done the last act towards the commission of the full offence which, to his knowledge, it was necessary for him to do in order to commit that offence, even though something more remains to be done by another, innocent person. Two examples of such a case are where X puts poison in another's drink, intending him to drink it and be killed in consequence, and where X posts a parcel bomb to another, intending him to be killed when he opens it; in both cases it is inconceivable that a jury would not find that X had done an act that was more than merely preparatory to the commission of murder.

The 'more than merely preparatory' formula is not limited to 'last act' cases, since it *can* be satisfied where a person still has to take some further step or steps himself before the full offence can be committed by him. In this context it must be emphasised that the question is not whether the accused has done an act which was more than preparatory but whether he has done an act which was more than *merely* preparatory. If it was the former which was the test it would be virtually impossible to get a conviction for attempt, except in a 'last act' case, because every act in furtherance of a criminal intent, other than a 'last act', can be described as preparatory. On the other hand, not every such act can be described as *merely* preparatory. This is because if a person can be said to have got as far as being engaged in the commission of an offence (ie 'on the job'), it will be a major understatement to say that his acts were still *merely* preparatory to the commission of the crime, even though (since some further act was required of him) his acts were still at a preparatory stage.

It is difficult to be more precise than this. Nevertheless, if the approach just advocated is adopted, the solution in most cases where the issue is whether the accused has gone far enough to be guilty of attempt will be fairly easy. Suppose, for example, that X buys matches, paraffin, wellingtons and overalls with the intention of burning down a barn. These acts are clearly all merely preparatory acts and cannot amount to an attempt to commit arson. Suppose that X places all these articles in a car, drives to the scene, takes the articles out of the car and approaches the barn. If X gets no further than this, it is still inconceivable that a jury would find that he has gone beyond the merely preparatory. However, if X gets as far as pouring paraffin over the door of the barn, the jury is likely to find that this act is more than merely preparatory to the arson of it, and that therefore he is guilty of its attempted arson, and it is even more likely so to find if he has gone further and actually struck a match.

Another example can be drawn by reference to the case of a terrorist gunman who lies in wait for his victim before shooting him. Clearly his acts are merely preparatory when he first acquires a rifle for his murderous purpose and when he carries it to the spot where he is to lie in wait. On the other hand, if he gets as far as raising the rifle to his shoulder in order to take aim, a jury is likely to find that he has done an act that is more than merely preparatory and is therefore guilty of attempted murder, and it is even more likely so to find if he has actually taken aim.

Examples of cases where a judge has held that there is or is not sufficient evidence of a more than merely preparatory act are as follows.

In one case, where a man had loaded a gun, disguised himself and had gone to a place where his intended victim could be found, these acts were considered to be merely preparatory. When he later pointed the gun at his intended victim with the intention of killing him and, when foiled, placed a cord around his neck, these acts provided sufficient evidence of attempted murder for consideration by the jury. In another, a man dragged a girl to a secluded spot and threatened her before putting his hand up her skirt in contact with her vaginal area. He then moved his hand to the top of her tights. It was held that there was sufficient evidence of attempted rape upon which a jury could make a decision. Where a mother whose children were in local authority care bought three single ferry tickets for the Republic of Ireland before falsely telling a teacher at the children's school that she had come to take the children to the dentist, it was considered that the acts up to the point of asking the teacher for the children were merely preparatory, but that the jury was entitled to find that asking for the children involved an attempt to abduct them.

However, where a man was seen to approach a post office, ride around the area on a motor cycle and to walk around that area before donning sunglasses and putting his hand into a pocket which appeared to contain something heavy, it was held that this was not sufficient evidence on which a jury could find a more than merely preparatory act in relation to committing robbery at the post office. The fact that the man was later found to be in possession of an imitation gun and a threatening note were matters affecting the issue of 'intent'. His actions were too far removed from an offence of robbery to be considered more than merely preparatory.

In another case, a man was seen in the boys' lavatory block in a school. He was in possession of a rucksack which contained a large kitchen knife, lengths of rope and a roll of masking tape. The Court of Appeal said that there was not much room for doubt about the man's intention and there was clear evidence of preparation, but there was no evidence that he had even put himself in position to commit an offence and he had had no contact or communication with, nor had confronted, any pupil. There was, therefore, no evidence of an act which was more than merely preparatory to an act of wrongful imprisonment. The Court of Appeal also considered the importance of the word 'merely' in circumstances in which men provided themselves with oxyacetylene equipment, drove to a barn, had concealed that equipment in a hedge, approached the barn door and were found examining the padlock to see how best to go about effecting an entry. The Court said that those acts could be considered to be more than *merely* preparatory. The facts were sufficient to allow a jury to find that there had been an attempt. Essentially, the question is one of degree.

Impossibility

Section 1(2) deals with matters which have long been the concern of courts; could one attempt to steal from a pocket if that pocket was empty, or could one attempt to steal from an empty shopping bag? It puts the issue beyond doubt by declaring that a person may be guilty of attempting to commit an offence to which the section applies, even though the facts are such that the commission of the offence is impossible. Therefore, the person who puts his hand into an empty pocket with intent to steal can be convicted of attempting to commit an offence. Likewise, a person who intends to kill another by shooting him in a bed, but who discovers after he has fired the shot that the assumed and intended victim was a pillow, can be convicted of attempted murder.

Section 1(3) purports to reinforce the rule in s 1(2), by declaring that where apart from s 1(3) a person's intention would not be regarded as having amounted to an intent to commit an offence, but if the facts of the case had been as that person believed them to be, his intention would have been so regarded, he is to be regarded as having an intent to commit that offence. The application of s 1(3) is illustrated by a case where the House of Lords held that there was an attempt where the accused had been arrested carrying a package he had brought from India which he believed to contain either heroin or cannabis. Scientific analysis later proved that the package did not contain a controlled drug but snuff or some similar harmless vegetable matter. The House of Lords held that the accused had properly been convicted of attempting to commit the offence of knowingly being concerned in dealing with a drug the importation of which was prohibited. He had had an intent to commit the offence in question, and, with that intent, he had done an act which was more than merely preparatory to the commission of that intended offence (since he had to be judged on the facts as he believed them to be). Likewise, where X handles what he believes to be stolen goods, when they are not in fact stolen, he is nevertheless guilty of an attempt to handle stolen goods.

Other statutory offences of attempt

The Criminal Attempts Act 1981, s 3 applies the provisions of the Act to other existing statutory attempts to commit offences, by stating that the same provisions shall apply to those attempts; that is that a person will be guilty of such an attempt if, with intent to commit the full relevant offence, he does an act which is more than merely preparatory to the commission of that offence. The section therefore ensures a common standard of approach to all offences of attempted crime, even where the specific offence of attempt is created by a particular statute and even where that specific offence relates to a summary offence.

INCITEMENT

It is an offence at common law to incite another person to commit any offence, including a summary one, other than conspiracy. The essence of the crime lies in the incitement; it is therefore irrelevant that the person incited does not in fact carry out the act. Incitement requires an element of persuasion or encouragement or of threats or other pressure. One example is where A offers B a large sum of money if B kills C. A is thereby guilty of incitement to murder, even though his efforts at persuasion or encouragement are totally ineffective and B refuses to have anything to do with the scheme. The element of persuasion or encouragement or of threats or other pressure may be implied as well as express. The incitement in question must, of course, come to the notice of the person intended to act on it. However, if it does not (eg because it is contained in a letter which never arrives), the person making it may be guilty of an attempt to incite.

CONSPIRACY: INTRODUCTION

There are two offences of conspiracy:

(a) it is a *statutory* offence to agree with any other person or persons for the commission of an offence. Statutory conspiracy was introduced, and is governed, by the Criminal Law Act 1977; and

(b) it is a *common law* offence to agree to defraud or, to the extent that the conduct agreed on would not amount to or involve an offence if carried out by a single person, to engage in conduct which tends to corrupt public morals or outrages public decency. Prior to the 1977 Act, an agreement to commit an offence or an agreement to do certain other things was a common law conspiracy but that Act abolished common law conspiracy except to the extent just stated.

Both types of conspiracy require a concluded agreement between two or more people. It is not sufficient for one person to have spoken in the presence of another of his intention to commit a crime, for example; that other person must agree with him that crime be committed. Immediately such an agreement has been reached, the offence of conspiracy is complete; no steps need be taken in furtherance of it, although it will usually be most unlikely that the conspiracy will be discovered or capable of proof if no further steps are taken. A party cannot escape liability for conspiracy by withdrawing from the agreement.

For reasons which are not very convincing, a husband and wife cannot be convicted of conspiracy if they are the *only* parties to the agreement in question.

We now turn to the separate requirements of the two offences of conspiracy.

STATUTORY CONSPIRACY

Section 1(1) of the 1977 Act defines the statutory offence of conspiracy as follows:

'If a person agrees with any other person or persons that a course of conduct shall be pursued which, if the agreement is carried out in accordance with their intentions, either

(a) will necessarily amount to or involve the commission of any offence or offences by one or more of the parties to the agreement, or

(b) would do so but for the existence of facts which render the commission of the offence or any of the offences impossible,

he is guilty of conspiracy to commit the offence or offences in question.'

Thus, a person commits statutory conspiracy if he agrees with any other person or persons *that a course of conduct shall be pursued which, if the agreement is carried out in accordance with their intentions, will necessarily amount to or involve the commission of an offence or offences by one or more of the parties to the agreement.* Special provision is made by s 1(1)(b) for the case where the criminal objective is impossible, and we shall deal with this shortly. First, however, we must make the following points about the words italicised.

The key issue is whether the course of conduct agreed on by the parties would necessarily amount to or involve the commission of an offence by one or more of them if it was carried out in accordance with their intentions. Thus, if A and B agree to have intercourse with a woman without her consent, there is a statutory conspiracy to rape because the course of conduct agreed on—sexual intercourse—would necessarily amount to the commission of rape if it was carried out in accordance with their intentions, viz to have sexual intercourse with a woman without her consent.

The offence which the agreed course of conduct would necessarily amount to or involve may be of any type, including (with one exception) a summary offence. By s 1A of the 1977 Act, s 1(1) applies in certain cases to an agreement to pursue a course of conduct in a foreign country which would amount to an offence under the law of the country concerned.

The exceptional case referred to above is provided by the Trade Union and Labour Relations (Consolidation) Act 1992, s 242. It is that where, in pursuance of any agreement, the acts constituting the offence are to be done in contemplation or furtherance of a trade dispute, that offence is not an 'offence' for the purposes of conspiracy if it is triable only summarily and *not* punishable with imprisonment. This exemption is provided, not to exempt trade union leaders from the criminal law in relation to conspiracies, since conspiracies to commit crimes punishable by imprisonment are still punishable, but to remove the potential danger of conspiracy charges in relation to the many minor offences which might be committed by union members in the course of a dispute, for example, simple obstructions of highways.

There cannot be a statutory conspiracy unless there are at least two parties to an agreement who intend that the agreement be carried out and that the offence they are alleged to have conspired to commit be committed. They can only have the latter intention if they intend or know that the elements of that offence shall or will exist when the conduct constituting that offence is to occur. If these requirements are satisfied, it is no defence to allege ignorance that the course of conduct agreed on was a criminal offence. Surprisingly, because it does violence to the wording of s 1(1), the House of Lords has held that an individual party to an agreement can be convicted of conspiracy, even though he did not intend that it be carried out and the offence intended by the other parties be committed.

Impossibility

Section 1(1)(b) of the 1977 Act deals with agreements which are impossible of fulfilment. It provides that an agreement on a course of conduct which, if the agreement is carried out in accordance with the parties' intentions, would necessarily amount to or involve the commission of an offence or any offences by one or more of the parties *but for the existence of facts which render the commission of the offence or any of the offences impossible* is a statutory conspiracy. This is a sensible provision; the essence of the offence is hatching a plot to commit a crime and this is not made less blameworthy because the actual commission of that crime is rendered impossible because of some fact.

As a result of s 1(1)(b), it is clear, for example, that A and B can be convicted of conspiracy to murder even though their intended victim was already dead when they agreed to kill him.

COMMON LAW CONSPIRACY

As we have already explained, the only types of common law conspiracy which still exist are conspiracy to defraud and, to the extent that the conduct agreed on would not amount to or involve an offence if carried out by a single person, conspiracy to engage in conduct which tends to corrupt public morals or outrages public decency.

Conspiracy to defraud requires further explanation. There can be a conspiracy to defraud without any element of deception since it is sufficient to prove an agreement by dishonesty to deprive a person of something which is his (or to which he is or would be or might be entitled) or an agreement by dishonesty to injure some proprietary right of his. Where the intended victim of an agreement is a person performing public duties, as distinct from a private individual, there can also be a conspiracy to defraud if the agreement is dishonestly to cause such a person to act contrary to his duty (eg in granting a licence or giving information). The causing of economic loss or prejudice, or (as the case may be) the deceiving of a public official into acting contrary to his duty, need not be the purpose of the parties to the agreement, since it suffices if they have dishonestly agreed to bring about a state of affairs which they realised would or might have such a result.

Clearly, the definition of conspiracy to defraud is wide enough to cover cases where the object of the agreement would itself be an offence as well as those where the object would not be criminal. Agreements to steal, or to forge, or to obtain property by deception, and so on, may, of course, be prosecuted as statutory conspiracies to steal etc but, by virtue of the Criminal Justice Act 1987, s 12, they may be charged as common law conspiracies to defraud instead, since they satisfy the definition of conspiracy to defraud.

INTERFERENCE WITH VEHICLES

Section 9 of the Criminal Attempts Act 1981 provides that a person is guilty of the offence of vehicle interference if he interferes with a motor vehicle or trailer or with anything carried in or on a motor vehicle or trailer with the intention that an offence of:

(a) theft of the motor vehicle or trailer or part of it;
(b) theft of anything carried in or on the motor vehicle or trailer; or
(c) an offence under the Theft Act 1968, s 12(1) (taking and driving away without consent),

shall be committed by himself or some other person.

Section 9 states that if an accused person can be proved to have intended that one of these offences should be committed, it is immaterial that it cannot be shown which offence it was.

The section uses the term 'interference' and this interference is linked to the intended theft of vehicles, trailers or their parts, the intended theft of things in or on the vehicles, or the intended taking of the vehicle. The essential point to prove will therefore be interference of a nature which clearly indicates an intention to do one of those things. If a group of rowdy youths rock a vehicle in order to set off its intruder alarm, they certainly interfere with the vehicle but lack the intention to do any of the prohibited acts. On the other hand, if they start to unscrew the aerial or a wing mirror with the intention of stealing it, they commit an offence under the section. The removal of tarpaulins from goods vehicles carrying loads indicates an interference with the intention to steal part of the load, and the use of duplicate keys is a clear indication of intention either to steal the vehicle or to take it without consent.

If a man is seen to try to open the door of one motor vehicle this is certainly an interference with that vehicle if it does not belong to him and he has no permission to do so. However, it is unlikely to satisfy a court that he intends to steal or take the vehicle, or to steal anything contained in it, unless there are further circumstances which point to an intention to commit one of those offences. The intention of the person interfering with vehicles becomes more apparent as attention is paid by him to more than one vehicle, or he is seen to examine the interior of the vehicle through its windows to check its contents, or even to try a number of doors on the same vehicle. The further the interference extends, the more likely it becomes that there is an appropriate criminal intent.

WEAPONS IN PUBLIC PLACES

When one is considering cases of possession of weapons in public places it is helpful to identify possible offences which may have been committed by first considering the nature of the weapon involved. If it is a firearm, it must be borne in mind that a person commits an offence if he has with him in a public place a loaded shotgun or loaded air weapon, or any other firearm (whether loaded or not) together with ammunition for it. This offence is governed by the Firearms Act 1968 and we have dealt with it in more detail in ch 24, above. We now turn to the Prevention of Crime Act 1953, which deals with offensive weapons in public places in general.

Section 1 of the 1953 Act provides that any person who without lawful authority or reasonable excuse, the proof whereof lies on him, has with him in any public place any offensive weapon is guilty of an offence. This is an arrestable offence. The court may make an order as to the disposal of a weapon following conviction.

A person may 'have with him' an offensive weapon even though he is not carrying the article in question, but he must have a close physical link with it and it must have been readily accessible to him. Consequently, 'have with him' is a narrower concept than 'possession', since a person can be in possession of something which is many miles away, as where a thing is left in his parked car in Harrogate while he is in Nottingham. On the other hand, he would still have with him an offensive weapon which he has left in his car while he goes into a nearby public convenience. A person does not 'have with him' something of whose presence he is unaware, such as a cosh which has been slipped into his bag, but once he knows of its presence it is no excuse that, at the material time, he has forgotten about it, as where he puts a cosh in the glove compartment of his car but has forgotten about it, when he is stopped by a patrol car a month later. The accused need not know of the facts which render the article an offensive weapon within the meaning of the statute.

An offensive weapon is any article made or adapted for use for causing injury to the person, or intended by the person having it with him for such use by him. This definition includes two classes of offensive weapons.

Articles made or adapted for causing injury to the person

These weapons are described as offensive per se (ie in themselves). Examples of articles made for causing injury to the person are bayonets, coshes, knuckledusters, swords, flick knives and butterfly knives. Examples of articles adapted for causing injury to the person are a piece of chain whose links have been sharpened and a man's cap in whose peak a razor blade has been inserted with the cutting edge exposed. In the latter type of case, articles which *were* harmless in themselves are made offensive weapons by their deliberate adaptation for use for causing personal injury.

Articles intended to be used for causing injury to the person

This class covers articles which are inoffensive per se (ie in themselves), because they have not been made or adapted for causing personal injury, but which are rendered offensive by the accused's intention to use them for causing injury to the person. Such articles include belts, stiletto-heeled shoes (or any other shoe), walking sticks (or umbrellas) and dog leads, provided it can be shown that there was an *intention* to use the article for causing injury to the person. The difficulty of proving such an intention increases in proportion to the generally non-offensive character of the article in question.

It is not enough that a man, who is in innocent possession of an article, suddenly uses it for an offensive purpose. Where a carpenter took a hammer from his tool bag during a fight and used it, he was not guilty of this offence as he did not have the hammer with him for causing injury to the person. To support a conviction under the 1953 Act, the prosecution must show that an appreciable time before the offensive use the accused had the intention to use it offensively. This is a stricter rule than applies to similar wording in the offence of aggravated burglary (p 745).

Public place

The accused must have with him the offensive weapon in a public place. For the purposes of this offence, the term 'public place' includes any highway, and any other premises or place to which at the material time the public have or are permitted to have access, whether on payment or otherwise. The issue is generally whether the public have access, or are permitted to have it if they wish. Public access is a matter of fact and if access is restricted to certain classes of persons, it must be restricted to some considerable degree before it will be accepted that the public are not admitted. A dance restricted to those under 25 years is a public dance as all classes of those under that age have a right of access. A soccer ground is a public place if paying spectators are admitted; it would be unlikely to be considered so if entry was restricted to elected members, but regard would have to be paid to the nature and restriction of membership. If it was generally available to the public without interview or election by the committee it would probably be different.

The fact that a person is found with an offensive weapon in a private place may lead to a conviction for the present offence. For example, if a visitor to a dwelling house produces an offensive weapon, this gives rise to a strong inference that he brought it with him through the streets and therefore had it with him in a public place.

Lawful authority or reasonable excuse

A person does not commit the offence if he has lawful authority or reasonable excuse for having with him the offensive weapon; the accused has the onus of proving such authority or excuse.

Those who may have offensive weapons with lawful authority include members of the armed services, or police forces, who may carry weapons which are offensive in themselves as part of their duty. On the other hand, it has been held that private security guards do not have lawful authority to carry truncheons or the like. Whether there is reasonable excuse depends on whether a reasonable person would think it excusable in the circumstances to carry the weapon in question, but as a matter of law limitations have been imposed by the courts on what a reasonable man might think in this context. Thus, it has been held that he would not think it reasonable for a person to have with him a weapon for self-defence unless there is an immediate and particular threat to him (as opposed to a constant one), nor would he think it reasonable for a person to have with him a weapon in order to commit suicide with it or for a security guard at a dance hall to carry a truncheon 'as a deterrent' and 'as part of his uniform'. The Court of

Appeal has held that a claim by a person who has been proved to be in possession of a weapon which is offensive per se, that he did not know that the article in question was an offensive weapon, cannot amount to a reasonable excuse. The defence of reasonable excuse could only arise after possession had been proved. It was not possible therefore, for a defendant to argue, having been found to have had an offensive weapon with him, that he did not know that it was an offensive weapon.

ANCILLARY OFFENCES

Having article with blade or point in a public place

The Criminal Justice Act 1988, s 139 provides an ancillary offence to that under the 1953 Act which is useful where a knife or the like cannot be proved to have been made, adapted or intended to cause injury to the person. The section makes it an offence for a person to have with him in a public place an article which is sharply pointed or with a blade, other than a folding pocket knife with a blade not exceeding three inches. This is an arrestable offence. A folding knife which is secured in an open position by a locking device and can only be released from the open position by the pressing of a release button is not a folding pocket knife within the meaning of s 139. An accused has a defence if he proves lawful authority or good reason for having the article with him in a public place, or that he had it with him there for use at work, for a religious reason or as part of any national costume. Whether a person was in possession of such a knife 'for use at work' and whether he had 'a good reason' for possession are matters for the court or jury as the statute uses ordinary, everyday language.

Having article with blade or point (or offensive weapon) on school premises

The Offensive Weapons Act 1996 added a s 139A to the Criminal Justice Act 1988. The section makes it an offence for a person to have any article to which s 139 applies with him on school premises. It creates a similar offence in relation to an offensive weapon to which the Prevention of Crime Act 1953 applies. These are arrestable offences. The term 'school premises' means land used for the purpose of a school excluding any land occupied solely as a dwelling by a person employed at the school. Similar defences exist; a person who proves that he had good reason or lawful authority for having the article or weapon with him on the premises has a defence. So has a person who proves that he had the article or weapon with him for the purposes set out above in relation to s 139. In addition, he may show possession 'for educational purposes'.

Section 139B provides a constable with a power of entry, using reasonable force if necessary, into school premises and the power to search those premises and any person on those premises for articles to which s 139 applies, or to which the Prevention of Crime Act 1953, s 1 applies, if he has reasonable grounds for believing that an offence under s 139A of the 1988 Act is being, or has been, committed. He may seize any articles or weapons discovered in the course of such a search which he reasonably suspects to be such articles or weapons.

General

As we saw in relation to the offence under the Prevention of Crime Act 1953, s 1, a person still has something with him when he has forgotten that he has it with him. This rule applies to the present offences. In addition, it has been held by the Divisional Court that, as in the case of 'reasonable excuse' in the 1953 Act, forgetfulness is not a 'good reason'. In the case in question a man was still in possession of a knife six days after he had used it in connection with his work. He had forgotten that he still had it with him but it was held that that was not a good reason for having it with him at the relevant time. A person charged with an offence under s 139 or under s 139A does not discharge the burden of proving 'good reason' simply by providing an explanation which is not contradicted by prosecution evidence. For example, in the case just referred to, the accused had advanced the excuse that he had the knife in his possession for the purpose of food preparation later in the evening; it was held that the justices were entitled to form the opinion that the alleged 'good reason' was most improbable.

As in the case of 'reasonable excuse' in the 1953 Act, a person has good reason for having one of the above articles with him for self-defence against an immediate threat (as opposed to a constant one).

RESTRICTION OF OFFENSIVE WEAPONS

Manufacture, sale etc of flick knives and gravity knives

The Restriction of Offensive Weapons Act 1959 is concerned with the manufacture and distribution of flick knives and gravity knives. It is an offence for any person to manufacture, sell, hire, offer for sale or hire, or to expose or have in his possession for the purpose of sale or hire, or to lend or give to any person, either of these weapons.

A 'flick knife' is any knife which has a blade which opens automatically by hand pressure applied to a button, spring or other device in or attached to the handle of the knife. A 'gravity knife' is one which has a blade which is released from the handle or sheath thereof by the force of gravity or the application of centrifugal force and which, when released, is locked in place by means of a button, spring, lever, or other device. The flick knife is therefore one with an up-and-over blade and a gravity knife is one which allows the blade to be shaken from the handle. These are weapons which are 'made' for the purpose of causing injury, so that a person who has such a weapon with him in a public place for sale or the like is guilty of the more serious offence under the Prevention of Crime Act 1953, with which we have just dealt.

Manufacture, sale etc of specified weapons

The Criminal Justice Act 1988, s 141 creates a further offence. A person who manufactures, sells or hires or offers for sale or hire, exposes or has in his possession for the purpose of sale or hire, or lends or gives to any other person, any weapon specified by order by the Secretary of State, commits an offence. The importation of such weapons is also prohibited. The Secretary of State has since made the Criminal Justice Act 1988 (Offensive Weapons) Order 1988 listing the knuckleduster, swordstick, handclaw, belt buckle knife, push dagger, hollow kubotan (small truncheon with spikes inside), footclaw, death star, butterfly knife, telescopic truncheon, blow-pipe, kusari gama (sickle and chain), kyoketsu shoge (hooked knife and chain) and maurik kusari or kusari (weights joined by chain). It is a defence to prove that the conduct in question was only for the purpose of making the weapon available to a public museum or gallery.

A justice may issue a warrant authorising entry and search on the application of a constable if he is satisfied that there are reasonable grounds for believing that there are on those premises knives such as are mentioned in the Restriction of Offensive Weapons Act 1959, s 1(1) or weapons to which the Criminal Justice Act 1988, s 141 applies and that an offence under either of these provisions has been or is being committed in relation to them and that one of the essential conditions for a search warrant exists.

Sale of knives etc to persons under 16

In addition, the Offensive Weapons Act 1996 adds a s 141A to the Criminal Justice Act 1988. By that section, it is an offence for any person to sell to a person under the age of 16 years a knife, knife blade or razor blade, any axe, and any other article which has a blade or which is sharply pointed and which is made or adapted for use for causing injury to the person. The section does not apply to articles already controlled by the Restriction of Offensive Weapons Act 1959, or an order made under s 141 of the 1988 Act, or an order made by the Secretary of State under this section. The Secretary of State has made an order in respect of a folding pocket knife with a blade which does not exceed three inches and razor blades permanently enclosed in a cartridge or housing.

The section provides a defence for a person who proves that he took all reasonable precautions and exercised all due diligence to avoid commission of the offence.

Marketing of combat knives

The Knives Act 1997, s 1 represents a further attempt to ban particular types of weapons. It provides that it is an offence to market a knife in a way which:

(a) indicates, or suggests, that it is suitable for combat; or
(b) is otherwise likely to stimulate or encourage violent behaviour involving the use of the knife as a weapon.

The term 'market' includes selling or hiring, offering or exposing for sale or hire, or possession for the purpose of sale or hire. A 'knife' is an instrument which has a blade or is sharply pointed; 'suitable for combat' means suitable for use as a weapon for inflicting injury on a person or causing a person to fear injury; and 'violent behaviour' means an unlawful act inflicting injury on a person or causing a person to fear injury.

Section 1 provides that, for the purposes of the Act, an indication or suggestion that a knife is suitable for combat may, in particular, be given or made by a name or description:

(a) applied to the knife;
(b) on the knife or its packaging; or
(c) in any advertisement which, expressly or by implication, relates to the knife.

Section 2 creates the offence of publishing any written, pictorial or other material in connection with the marketing of any knife , which:

(a) indicates, or suggests, that the knife is 'suitable for combat'; or
(b) is otherwise likely to stimulate or encourage 'violent behaviour' involving the use of the knife as a weapon.

It is difficult to see what this legislation hopes to achieve in relation to public safety as it does not seek to prohibit particular weapons, merely to outlaw certain descriptions being applied to them.

Because of the wide range of the provisions of this Act, it provides some defences. In relation to the offence under s 1, the marketing of a knife for use by the armed forces of any country, or as an antique or curio is exempted. Likewise, in relation to the offence of publishing material under s 2, it is a defence to prove three things: that the material was published in connection with marketing a knife for use by the armed forces of any country or as an antique or curio, that it was reasonable for the knife to be marketed in that way, and that there were no reasonable grounds for suspecting that a person into whose possession the knife might come in consequence of the way in which it was marketed would use it for an unlawful purpose. It is also a defence to a charge under s 1 or s 2 for a person to prove that he did not know or suspect, and had no reasonable grounds for suspecting, that the way the knife was marketed (s 1), or the material (s 2), amounted to an indication or suggestion that the knife was 'suitable for combat', or was likely to stimulate or encourage 'violent behaviour' involving the use of the knife as a weapon. Lastly, it is a defence to either offence for the accused to prove that he took all reasonable precautions and exercised due diligence to avoid committing the offence.

It may be that most police officers will issue a warning rather than attempt the perilous path of proving an offence under this Act!

The Act provides for the issue of search warrants authorising entry, using reasonable force, and search and seizure in respect of knives and publications.

GOING EQUIPPED TO STEAL

The Theft Act 1968, s 25 is concerned with a person, who, when not at his place of abode, has with him any article for use in the course of or in connection with any burglary, theft or cheat. The Police and Criminal Evidence Act 1984 declares that the offence is arrestable.

The mischief aimed at is the carrying of implements which a person intends to use in the course of or in connection with any burglary, theft or cheat. The section does not, therefore, only punish possession in streets or public places; it also catches such persons who are found in possession of implements whilst trespassing upon private property or whilst anywhere else other than at their place of abode. As soon as the accused leaves his place of abode he is guilty of this offence if he has with him articles for one of the specified purposes. It has been decided that, where a person lives in a motor vehicle, it is his place of abode whilst on the site where he intends to abide, but that as soon as the vehicle leaves the site he is no longer at his place of abode.

Although the offence is described in the marginal note to s 25 of the 1968 Act as 'going equipped for stealing etc', and is commonly so described, it is not limited to conduct which could be described as 'going equipped...'. In one case, for example, the Divisional Court held that a person who had 'counterfeit' shirts in a warehouse for use in connection with a cheat had properly been convicted of an offence under s 25; he undoubtedly fell within the words of the offence set out above.

The term 'has with him' has the same meaning as in the Prevention of Crime Act 1953.

The article does not need to be specifically made or adapted for use for one of the specified purposes; any article will do provided that the accused intends to use it for such a purpose.

The specified purposes are that the accused must intend to use the article in the course of or in connection with any burglary, theft or cheat to be committed in the future; it is not necessary to prove that the articles are to be used in connection with any particular burglary etc. Possession to enable someone else to use the articles is sufficient for the purposes of this section. Section 25(5) states that, for the purposes of the present offence, an offence under the Theft Act 1968, s 12, of taking a conveyance, shall be treated as theft, and that 'cheat' means obtaining property by deception contrary to s 15 of that Act.

If a person is found with an article made or adapted for use in committing burglary, theft or cheat, proof of the offence under s 25 is assisted by s 25(3), which states that where there is proof that he had with him such an article that shall be evidence that he had it with him for such use. Of course, this can be rebutted by evidence of a contrary intention. The result of s 25(3) is that, if someone is found trespassing in the grounds of a dwelling house with a bunch of skeleton keys in his pocket, this is evidence that he had those articles with him for use in committing burglary. On the other hand, if he was found merely with the keys to his office and house this would provide no such evidence.

Index